Law School Publications

of

WEST PUBLISHING COMPANY
St. Paul, Minnesota 55102

ADMINISTRATIVE LAW

Davis' Cases, 592 pages, 1959.
Davis Text, 617 pages, 1959.
Davis' Cases, Text and Problems, 2nd
  Ed., 609 pages, 1965.
Merrill's Cases, 720 pages, 1954.

ADMIRALTY

Healy and Currie's Cases and Materials on Admiralty, 872 pages, 1965.

AGENCY

Seavey and Hall's Cases, 431 pages,
  1956.
Seavey's Studies, 451 pages, 1949.
Seavey's Text, 329 pages, 1964.
See Agency-Partnership.

AGENCY PARTNERSHIP

Seavey, Reuschlein & Hall's Cases, 599
  pages, 1962.
Steffen's Cases, 3rd Ed., 733 pages,
  1969.

BANKRUPTCY

MacLachlan's Text, 500 pages, 1956.
See Creditors' Rights.

BILLS AND NOTES

Aigler and Steinheimer's Cases, 670
  pages, 1962.
Britton's Text, 2nd Ed., 794 pages, 1961.
See Commercial Transactions.

COMMERCIAL TRANSACTIONS

Speidel, Summers and White's Teach-
  ing Materials, 1144 pages, 1969.

COMMON LAW PLEADING

Koffler and Reppy on Common Law
  Pleading, 663 pages, 1969.
McBaine's Cases, Introduction to Civil
  Procedure, 399 pages, 1950.
Shipman's Text, 3rd Ed., 644 pages,
  1923.

COMMUNITY PROPERTY

Burby's Cases, 4th Ed., 342 pages, 1955.
Huie's Texas Cases on Marital Property Rights, 681 pages, 1966.
Verrall and Sammis' Cases on California Community Property, 358
  pages, 1966.

CONFLICT OF LAWS

Cramton and Currie's Cases—Com-
  ments—Questions, 915 pages, 1968.
Ehrenzweig's Text, 824 pages, 1962.
Ehrenzweig's Conflicts in a Nutshell,
  2nd Ed., about 330 pages, 1969.
Ehrenzweig and Louisell's Jurisdiction
  in a Nutshell, 2nd Ed., 315 pages,
  1968.
Goodrich's Text, 4th Ed., 483 pages,
  1964.
Scoles and Weintraub's Cases, 956
  pages, 1967.
Selected Readings, 1151 pages, 1956.
Stumberg's Cases, 499 pages, 1956.

CONSTITUTIONAL LAW

Lockhart, Kamisar and Choper's Cases
  — Comments — Questions, 2nd Ed.,
  1497 pages, 1967.
Lockhart, Kamisar and Choper's Cases
  and Materials on The American Con-
  stitution, 2nd Ed., 1062 pages, 1967.
Lockhart, Kamisar and Choper's Sup-
  plement.
Selected Essays, 971 pages, 1963.
See Constitutional Rights and Liberties.

CONSTITUTIONAL RIGHTS & LIBERTIES

Lockhart, Kamisar and Choper's Cases
  and Materials on Constitutional
  Rights and Liberties, 2nd Ed., 1087
  pages, 1967.
Lockhart, Kamisar and Choper's Supplement.

CONTRACTS

Corbin's Cases, 3rd Ed., 1381 pages, 1947. 1953 Supplement, 36 pages.

Corbin's Text, Student Edition, 1224 pages, 1952.

Fuller and Braucher's Cases, 907 pages, 1964.

Simpson's Cases, 592 pages, 1956.

Simpson's Text, 2nd Ed., 510 pages, 1965.

CORPORATIONS

Henn's Text, 735 pages, 1961.

Stevens and Henn's Statutes, Cases and Materials on Corporations and Other Business Enterprises, 1448 pages, 1965.

Stevens and Henn's Practice Projects Supplement, 81 pages, 1965.

CREDIT TRANSACTIONS

Maxwell & Riesenfeld's California Cases on Security Transactions, 371 pages, 1957.

Maxwell & Riesenfeld's Supplement, 68 pages, 1963.

Sturges' Cases, 4th Ed., 599 pages, 1955.

Young's Cases on Consumer Credit, Pamphlet reprint from Dodyk, et al. Law and Poverty, 115 pages, 1969.

CREDITORS' RIGHTS

Riesenfeld's Cases on Creditors' Remedies and Debtors' Protection, 669 pages, 1967.

Riesenfeld's Statutory Supplement.

Young's Cases on Consumer Credit, Pamphlet reprint from Dodyk, et al. Law and Poverty, 115 pages, 1969.

CRIMINAL LAW

Hall & Glueck's Cases, 2d Ed., 699 pages, 1958.

Miller's Text, 649 pages, 1934.

Stumberg's Texas Cases, 505 pages, 1954.

Stumberg and Maloney's Texas Cases Supplement, 117 pages, 1965.

CRIMINAL PROCEDURE

Hall, Kamisar, LaFave and Israel's Materials on Modern Criminal Procedure, 3rd Ed., 1456 pages, 1969.

Hall, Kamisar, LaFave and Israel's Materials on Basic Criminal Procedure, 3rd Ed., 617 pages, 1969.

DAMAGES

Crane's Cases, 3rd Ed., 337 pages, 1955.

McCormick's Text, 811 pages, 1935.

DICTIONARIES

Black's, one volume.

Bouvier's, two volumes.

DOMESTIC RELATIONS

Clark's Cases, 870 pages, 1965.

Clark's Text, 754 pages, 1968.

Madden's Text, 748 pp., 1931.

Paulsen's Cases on Family Law and Poverty Pamphlet, reprint from Dodyk, et al. Law and Poverty, 266 pages, 1969.

DRUGS AND DRUGGISTS

Arthur's Text, 4th Ed., 399 pp., 1955.

ENGINEERING LAW

Simpson & Dillavou's Text, 4th Ed., 506 pages, 1958.

EQUITY

Cook's Cases, 4th Ed., 1192 pp., 1948.

McClintock's Text, 2nd Ed., 643 pages, 1948.

Van Hecke's Cases on Equitable Remedies, 651 pages, 1959.

See Remedies.

EVIDENCE

Cleary and Strong's Cases, 967 pages, 1969.

McCormick's Cases, 3rd Ed., 663 pages, 1956.

McCormick's Text, 774 pages, 1954.

Selected Writings, 1232 pages, 1957.

FEDERAL ANTI-TRUST LAWS

Oppenheim's Cases on Robinson-Patman Act, Pamphlet, 295 pages, 1967.

Oppenheim and Weston's Cases, 3rd Ed., 952 pages, 1968.

FEDERAL ESTATE AND GIFT TAXATION

See Taxation.

FEDERAL INCOME TAXATION

See Taxation.

FEDERAL JURISDICTION AND PROCEDURE

Bunn's U. S. Courts, Text, 5th Ed., 408 pages, 1949.

Currie's Cases on Federal Courts, 823 pages, 1968.

Ehrenzweig and Louisell's Jurisdiction in a Nutshell, 2nd Ed., 315 pages, 1968.

Forrester, Currier and Moye's Cases, 2nd Ed., about 950 pages, 1970.

Wright's Text, 634 pages, 1963.

FUTURE INTERESTS

Gulliver's Cases, 624 pages, 1959.
Powell's Cases, 3rd Ed., 1961.
Simes Text, 2nd Ed., 355 pages, 1966.
See Wills, Intestate Succession, Trusts, Gifts and Future Interests.

GRATUITOUS TRANSFERS

See Wills.

HOUSING AND URBAN DEVELOPMENT

Berger's Cases on Housing, Pamphlet reprint from Dodyk, et al. Law and Poverty, 277 pages, 1969.
Krasnowiecki's Cases, 697 pages, 1969.
Krasnowiecki's Statutory Supplement, 1969.

INSURANCE

Keeton's Basic Insurance Law, 655 pages, 1960.
Keeton's Insurance Law and Torts Supplement (Compensation Systems), 56 pages, 1969.
Vance's Text, 3rd Ed., 1290 pages, 1951.

INTERNATIONAL BUSINESS

Ebb's Cases, 885 pages, 1964.
Ebb's 1968 Supplement.

INTERNATIONAL LAW

Friedmann, Lissitzyn and Pugh's Cases, 1,205 pages, 1969.

INTRODUCTION TO LAW

Fryer and Orentlicher's Cases and Materials on Legal Method and Legal System, 1,043 pages, 1967.
Kimball's Historical Introduction to Legal System, 610 pages, 1966.
Smith's Cases on Development of Legal Institutions, 757 pages, 1965.
See Legal Method.

JURISPRUDENCE

Wu's Cases, 719 pages, 1958.

LABOR LAW

Handler & Hays' Cases, 4th Ed., 916 pages, 1963.
Sovern's Cases on Racial Discrimination in Employment, Pamphlet reprint from Dodyk et al. Law and Poverty, 188 pages, 1969.

LAND USE

Beuscher and Wright's Cases on Land Use, about 683 pages, 1969.

LEGAL BIBLIOGRAPHY

Cohen's Legal Research in a Nutshell, 233 pages, 1968.
How To Find The Law, with Special Chapters on Legal Writing, 6th Ed., 313 pages, 1965.
How To Find The Law Student Problem Book.

LEGAL ETHICS

Pirsig's Cases on Professional Responsibility, 388 pages, 1965.
Selected Readings Legal Profession, 565 pages, 1962.

LEGAL HISTORY

Kimball's Historical Introduction to Legal System, 610 pages, 1966.
Radin's Text, 612 pages, 1936.
Smith's Cases on Development of Legal Institutions, 757 pages, 1965.

LEGAL INTERVIEWING AND COUNSELING

Freeman's Cases, 253 pages, 1964.

LEGAL METHOD—LEGAL SYSTEM

Fryer and Orentlicher's Cases & Materials, 1043 pages, 1966.
See Introduction to Law.

LEGAL WRITING STYLE

Weihofen's Text, 323 pages, 1961.
See Legal Bibliography.

LEGISLATION

Nutting, Elliott and Dickerson's Cases, 4th Ed., 631 pages, 1969.

MASS COMMUNICATION LAW

Gillmor and Barron's Cases and Comment, 853 pages, 1969.

MORTGAGES

Osborne's Cases Secured Transactions, 559 pages, 1967.
Osborne's Cases on Property Security, 2nd Ed., 725 pages, 1954.
Osborne's Text, 1117 pages, 1951.
Sturges' Cases Credit Transactions, 4th Ed., 599 pages, 1955.

MUNICIPAL CORPORATIONS

Michelman and Sandalow's Materials on Government in Urban Areas, about 1,158 pages, 1969.
Stason and Kauper's Cases, 3rd Ed., 692 pages, 1959.

NATURAL RESOURCES

Trelease, Bloomenthal and Geraud's Cases and Materials on Natural Resources, 1131 pages, 1965.

OFFICE PRACTICE

A.B.A. Lawyer's Handbook, 557 pages, 1962.

See Legal Interviewing and Counseling.

OIL AND GAS

Huie, Walker and Woodward's Cases, 848 pages, 1960.

See Natural Resources.

PARTNERSHIP

Crane and Bromberg's Text, 695 pages, 1968.

See Agency-Partnership.

PERSONAL PROPERTY

Aigler, Smith and Tefft's Cases on Property, 2 Vols., 1339 pages, 1960.

Bigelow's Cases, 3rd Ed., 507 pages, 1942.

Fryer's Readings, 3rd Ed., 1184 pages, 1938.

PLEADING AND PROCEDURE

Brown, Karlen, Meisenholder, Stevens, and Vestal's Cases and Materials on Procedure Before Trial, 784 pages, 1968.

Clark's Cases, Modern Pleading, 1042 pages, 1952.

Clark's Text, 2nd Ed., 874 pages, 1947.

Cleary's Cases on Pleading, 2d Ed., 434 pages, 1958.

Cound, Friedenthal and Miller's Cases on Civil Procedure, 1075 pages, 1968.

Cound, Friedenthal and Miller's Cases on Pleading, Discovery and Joinder, 643 pages, 1968.

Cound, Friedenthal and Miller's Civil Procedure Supplement, 1968.

Ehrenzweig and Louisell's Jurisdiction in a Nutshell, 2nd Ed., 315 pages, 1968.

Elliott & Karlen's Cases, 441 pages, 1961.

Hodges, Jones and Elliott's Cases on Texas Trial and Appellate Procedure, 623 pages, 1965.

Hodges, Jones, Elliott and Thode's Texas Judicial Process Prior to Trial, 935 pages, 1966.

Karlen's Cases on Trials and Appeals, 436 pages, 1961.

McBaine's Cases, Introduction to Civil Procedure, 399 pages, 1950.

POVERTY LAW

Dodyk, Sovern, Berger, Young and Paulsen's Cases on Law and Poverty, 1,234 pages, 1969.

Dodyk's Cases on Income Maintenance, Pamphlet reprint from Dodyk, et al. Law and Poverty, 379 pages, 1969.

PRESS, LAW OF

Hale's Text, 3rd Ed., 691 pages, 1948.

QUIZZERS

Ballantine's Problems.

Burby Law Refreshers.

Smith's How to Answer Law Examinations.

Smith Reviews.

REAL PROPERTY

Aigler, Smith & Tefft's Cases on Property, 2 Vols., 1339 pages, 1960.

Berger's Cases on Housing, Pamphlet reprint from Dodyk, et al. Law and Poverty, 277 pages, 1969.

Browder, Cunningham & Julin's Basic Property Law, 1209 pages, 1966.

Burby's Text, 3rd Ed., 490 pages, 1965.

Jacobs' Cases Landlord and Tenant, 2nd Ed., 815 pages, 1941.

Moynihan's Introduction, 254 pages, 1962.

Phipps' Titles in a Nutshell—The Calculus of Interests, 277 pages, 1968.

Smith's Survey, 398 pages, 1956.

See Housing and Urban Development.

REMEDIES

Cribbet's Cases on Judicial Remedies, 762 pages, 1954.

Wright's Cases, 498 pages, 1955.

York and Bauman's Cases, 1271 pages, 1967.

RESTITUTION

Thurston's Cases, 964 pages, 1940.

See Remedies.

SALES

McCurdy's Cases, 480 pages, 1959.

Nordstrom and Lattin's Problems and Materials on Sales and Secured Transactions, 809 pages, 1968.

Vold's Text, 2nd Ed., 611 pages, 1959.

See Commercial Transactions.

SECURED TRANSACTIONS

See Commercial Transactions.

See Sales.

LAW SCHOOL PUBLICATIONS — Continued

SURETYSHIP AND GUARANTY

Osborne's Cases, 221 pages, 1966.
Simpson's Text, 569 pages, 1950.
Simpson's Cases, 538 pages, 1942.
Sturges' Cases Credit Transactions, 4th Ed., 599 pages, 1955.

TAXATION

Chommie's Text on Federal Income Taxation, 742 pages, 1968.
Chommie's Supplement, 1969.
Hellerstein's Cases on State and Local Taxation, 3rd Ed., 741 pages, 1969.
Lowndes & Kramer's Text on Federal Estate and Gift Taxes, 2nd Ed., 951 pages, 1962.
Rice's Problems and Materials in Federal Estate & Gift Taxation, 504 pages, 1966.
Rice's Problems and Materials in Federal Income Taxation, 623 pages, 1967.

TORTS

Green, Pedrick, Rahl, Thode, Hawkins and Smith's Cases, 1311 pages, 1968.
Green, Pedrick, Rahl, Thode, Hawkins and Smith's Cases on Injuries to Relations, 466 pages, 1968.
Hepburn's Cases, 3rd Ed., 540 pages, 1954.
Keeton's Insurance Law and Torts Supplement (Compensation Systems), 56 pages, 1969.
Prosser's Text, 3rd Ed., 1238 pages, 1964.
Seavey, Keeton and Keeton's Cases, 2nd Ed., 1055 pages, 1964.

TRADE REGULATION

See Federal Anti-Trust Laws.
See Unfair Trade Practices.

TRUSTS

Bogert's Text, 4th Ed., 528 pages, 1963.
Powell's Cases, Trusts and Wills, 639 pages, 1960.
Smith's Survey, 167 pages, 1949.
See Wills, Intestate Succession, Trusts, Gifts and Future Interests.

UNFAIR TRADE PRACTICES

Oppenheim's Cases, 783 pages, 1965.
Oppenheim and Weston's Supplement.
Oppenheim's Robinson-Patman Act Pamphlet, 295 pages, 1967.

WATER LAW

Trelease's Cases, 364 pages, 1967.

WILLS

Atkinson's Text, 2nd Ed., 975 pages, 1953.
Turrentine's Cases, 2nd Ed., 483 pages, 1962.
See Wills, Intestate Succession, Trusts, Gifts and Future Interests.

WILLS, INTESTATE SUCCESSION, TRUSTS, GIFTS AND FUTURE INTERESTS

Gulliver, Clark, Lusky and Murphy's Cases and Materials on Gratuitous Transfers: Wills, Intestate Succession, Trusts, Gifts and Future Interests, 1017 pages, 1967.

WORKMEN'S COMPENSATION

Malone and Plant's Cases, 622 pages, 1963.

▼

CRANE AND BROMBERG

ON

PARTNERSHIP

By

ALAN R. BROMBERG

Professor of Law, Southern Methodist University

Successor to the Law of Partnership by
The Late Judson A. Crane,
Professor of Law, University of California,
Hastings College of the Law

HORNBOOK SERIES

ST. PAUL, MINN.
WEST PUBLISHING CO.
1968

To Cookie and Alfred

•

PREFACE

I was flattered when Judson Crane invited me in 1962 to collaborate on a new edition of his Hornbook on Partnership, which I had used and admired through the years. I was distressed when he died in 1964 with little of his share reduced to writing. But, like prudent partners, we had a continuation agreement, and I have carried it out.

What began as a new edition has become a new book. The structure is similar to Crane's 1952 edition, except that I have omitted the chapter on non-profit associations which seemed to me out of place in a volume on profit seeking organizations. The arrangement and numbering of sections is much the same. This will make it easy to use section references to the 1952 work—which were abundant in the cases and law reviews—as a way of finding the same subject matter in this volume.

My special concerns in writing this new Hornbook are these:

(1) I think of partnership mainly as a very flexible form of business organization, but only one of several which may be used. I have given some emphasis to planning, both in choosing among forms and in making agreements to overcome the weaknesses (and to use the strengths) of partnership.

(2) To treat partnership without income taxes misses the point of economic reality. While avoiding the more esoteric aspects of taxation, I have tried to weave in the portions which are basic to understanding what partnerships are good for.

(3) A great believer in legislation, I have stressed the Partnership Acts as positive law, as objects of interpretation, and as candidates for amendment where I think they can be improved.

(4) Regarding the limited partnership as the forgotten man of business organizations, I have paid a good deal more attention to this form which has a number of sophisticated uses.

Much of this book was written with the help of a fellowship grant from SMU Law School and while a Senior Fellow on the Faculty of Yale Law School. I am grateful to both institutions and their Deans, Charles O. Galvin and Louis H. Pollak. Professors Fleming James, Jr. of Yale and Eugene L. Smith of SMU tried to shore up my knowledge of procedure, but should not be held responsible for the outcome. James H. (Hezzy) Miller and Ronald L. Palmer, while students at SMU, did useful research and made valuable suggestions. Mary Nelle Jeffers and Mary Grace Shuey at SMU typed the earlier chapters and Susan Bruce at Yale did the final collating. The library staffs at both schools were exceedingly helpful. To all of them I am greatly indebted.

PREFACE

A less enthusiastic acknowledgment is necessary. Credit the publisher (not me) for many of the citation forms—particularly statutes—in the footnotes. They were drastically altered in editing, and I saw the result only in galley proof. Although the publisher would have changed them, it seemed a waste of everyone's time and money to re-edit and reset them. The reader should try the Table of Statutory Abbreviations when he finds unintelligible material in the footnotes.

ALAN R. BROMBERG

Dallas, Texas
August, 1968

SUMMARY OF CONTENTS

•

TABLE OF CONTENTS

Chapter 1. Introduction

Chapter 2.   Nature and Formation of Partnership

Chapter 3. Special Forms of Partnership and Related Unincorporated Business Associations

Chapter 4. Partnership Property and Interests in Partnership

Chapter 5. Powers of Partners to Act for the Partnership

TABLE OF CONTENTS

Chapter 6. Enforcement of Partnership Rights and Liabilities

Chapter 7. Rights and Duties of Partners Inter Se and Actions for Breach of Duties

Chapter 8. Dissolution and Winding Up of Solvent Partnerships

TABLE OF CONTENTS

Chapter 9. Dissolution and Winding Up of Insolvent Partnerships—Bankruptcy

Appendices

CRANE AND BROMBERG

ON

PARTNERSHIP

CHAPTER 1

INTRODUCTION

Analysis

PARTNERSHIP IN PERSPECTIVE

§ 1. **Partnership is a legal, financial and personal relationship of considerable complexity. It is also a form of business organization, resembling the sole proprietorship in personal liability and ease of creation, but having two or more owners. Partnership differs from corporation principally in lacking limited liability and hierarchical structure. Partnership is an extremely malleable form.**

Partnership is a distinct body of business association law, but contains important elements of contract, property, agency and other basic fields.

In comparison to proprietorships and corporations, partnerships play a small but significant role in the American economy. When corporate taxation is heavy, partnerships flourish.

(a) Comparison with Proprietorship and Corporation

Partnership is a legal, financial and personal relationship.[1] This book is primarily about the legal aspects of the relation, but they are firmly intertwined with the others.

---

[1] Except for marriage, it is hard to think of a voluntary legal relationship that is more intimate or complex, in human terms, than the normal partnership whose members work constantly together. This (along with

Partnership is a form of business organization which can carry on almost any kind of activity.[2] It is particularly suitable for small business, and for combining services of some participants with funds of others on a large or small scale. Partnership can be usefully put in perspective by a brief comparison with the other two principal forms of business organization in the U. S., the sole proprietorship and the corporation.[3]

A man may carry on business as a sole proprietor. No formalities are required. He has total management authority. If he needs the services of others, he may hire them, entering the relation of master and servant, or principal and agent. If he needs funds, he may borrow from others, creating the relation of debtor and creditor. If he needs real estate or equipment, he may rent from others, forming the relation of lessee and lessor, or bailee and bailor. He becomes personally liable to pay all these people for what they furnish him. If there are losses in the business, he must bear them alone, to the extent of his resources. If there are profits, they are all his. This is the simplest form of business enterprise, totally lacking in internal structure.

One or more persons may form a corporation to carry on business. To do so, they must secure from the state a charter or certificate of incorporation pursuant to a statute which authorizes the creation of corporations. They transfer assets to the corporation or perform services for it, and receive in return the evidences of ownership of the corporation, called stock or shares. As stockholders, they periodically elect a board of directors who are charged by statute with managing the business. The directors generally make policy and major decisions but do not individually represent the corporation in dealing with third persons. The latter function is performed by officers selected by the directors, and by persons to whom authority is delegated by the officers or the directors. The same persons may be stockholders, directors and officers; they usually are in small corporations. The officers and directors owe fiduciary duties to the corporation or its stockholders; so, to a lesser extent, do controlling

business difficulties and ease of dissolution) contributes to the high divorce rate in partnership as in marriage. Of partnerships formed in 1959, 60% had disappeared by 1963, based on tax filings. For 1959–63 attrition rates, by year of formation, see U.S. Treasury, Internal Revenue Service, Statistics of Income, U.S. Business Tax Returns 1963, p. 147 (1967). See also id. 137–46 (profit statistics by year of organization and by industry) and id., Partnership Returns 1953, p. 44 (1957) (number of new or successor partnerships filing returns in 1953).

Partnership, by agreement, may be more casual, with some members providing only financing or property, and having no daily contact with one another.

2. There are some restrictions on limited partnerships. See Sec. 26(a) below.

In England, barristers cannot form partnerships. See Abel-Smith & Stevens, Lawyers and Courts, 413, 416–17 (1967).

3. For other forms of business association, see Sec. 24 and Ch. 3 below.

stockholders. The corporation obtains services, funds and property from third persons the same way a sole proprietor does (or by issuing stock to them), and enters the same relations with them. The stockholders, directors, and officers are usually not parties to these relationships in their own right, and have no personal liability in connection with them; they thus enjoy limited liability. If there are losses in the business, the corporation bears them to the extent of its resources; the stockholders indirectly bear them in that the value of their stock declines more or less in proportion to the losses. If there are profits, they are distributed among the stockholders (in proportion to their holdings) or retained in the business, at the discretion of the directors. If distributed, the stockholders enjoy them directly; if retained, the stockholders enjoy them indirectly through some roughly corresponding increase in the value of their stock. The legal existence of the corporation is unaffected by deaths or retirements of officers, directors or stockholders, or by transfers of stock from one person to another.

Partnership lies somewhere between. It requires two or more persons, each of whom is a co-owner of the business. No formality is necessary to create the firm, unless it is to be a limited partnership.[4] The partners have equal right to participate in management, and each has authority to deal with third persons. They owe fiduciary duties to one another or to the firm. The partners usually provide many of the services, funds and property needed for the business. But the firm may also acquire them from third persons, as can a proprietor or corporation. Like a sole proprietor, and unlike a corporate stockholder, each partner is personally liable on debts incurred for these purposes. If there are losses in the business, the partners bear them to the extent of their joint and individual resources. While they may agree among themselves to share losses or pay debts in particular proportions, third persons are not bound by the agreement and may recover in full from any one or more of the partners. If there are profits, they are shared by the partners in the proportions they have agreed upon; they decide whether the profits shall be distributed or retained in the business. The legal existence of the partnership is altered, if not destroyed, by deaths, retirements, or transfers of interests by partners, but this is largely a matter which they can control by agreement.

Partnership is the simplest form of business association of two or more persons. In structure, it is more like the sole proprietorship, except that there are several owners, than like the corporation with its elaborate formal division of roles.

Partnership is very easy to create. No written agreement is necessary, and many firms have no more than an oral understanding that persons will work together and split the profits. Thus, partner-

---

4.   See Sec. 26 below.

ship is the residual form of business association, the one that is created when two or more persons join together to do business but do not take the trouble to adopt any other form.

Though easy to initiate, partnership is not a particularly simple form of organization. Its diverse features fill this volume. Perhaps the most important is malleability: the relations among the partners and the internal structure of the firm can be anything the partners want. Their agreement is determinative, and may produce a highly complex and sophisticated structure.

One cannot sensibly say, in the abstract, that partnership is better or worse than some other form of business organization. One can compare specific characteristics and make judgments about them. One can (and frequently must) decide what is the best form for a particular business. Section 23B below takes a closer look at this process.

(b) The Nature of Partnership Law

A glance at the Table of Contents will reveal the kinds of things with which partnership law deals. There is the question of when a partnership exists; since the relation can arise very informally, disputes often occur over whether the relation has in fact (or in law) been created. Another set of problems centers around the identification and nature of partnership property and partners' interests in the firm, and the relative rights of partners and creditors. The authority of a partner to act for the firm is a matter of some importance. So are the methods by which partners and partnerships sue and are sued. The rights and duties of partners inter se (particularly the financial, managerial and fiduciary) are significant in themselves and because they are so completely subject to alteration by agreement. So, to a great extent, is the effect of change in personnel of the group—for example, by death, retirement or dissension—on the business and the interests in it. Finally, there are questions of failure and bankruptcy.

The laws of contract, property and agency are prominent ingredients of the law of partnership, as they are in the law of corporations. But there are other phases peculiar to the law of partnership. For example, the parties agree that their joint property shall be devoted to their joint enterprise, the partnership business. This results in restrictions on the individual partner's disposition of even such individual rights as he retains in the property. There are limitations on the power of a partner's individual creditors to reach his rights in partnership property, which do not exist in the case of ordinary co-owners. Fiduciary relations are an incident of partnership but not of ordinary contracts. Remedies for breach of partnership relational obligations are not those generally available for breach of contract or for injury to property interests.

Partnership law is best thought of as a distinct body of structural and relational law, parallel to other areas of business association, but importantly intersecting basic areas (like equity and trusts in addition to contract, property, and agency) and statutory preserves (like taxation and bankruptcy).

(c) The Partnership in the United States Economy

There is surprisingly little historical information on the relative role of proprietorships, partnerships and corporations in the American economy. The best figures we have found [5] are derived from income tax returns and thus go back only to the time of World War I. Because of slight differences in the tax and state law definitions of partnerships and corporations, and because of variations over the years in the minimum income necessitating the filing of a return, the figures do not give an exact count of the business population. The net profit figures are measured in tax terms, which change with amendments to the law, and are never likely to coincide with an ideal economic income. Nonetheless, the figures—which are given in Table A—are reasonably comparable among the three forms of organization and from year to year. They thus give the best available picture of the organizations in the business community and their relative profitability over most of the 20th century to date.

Profitability of all forms varies with the business cycle and the economy's general growth and inflation. The net profit of proprietorships has maintained a rather constant ratio to that of partnerships, a little over two to one. Compared to the others, corporate profit has been more volatile,[6] but has ranged between two and three times that of proprietorships. The relative numbers of partnerships and corporations—unfortunately we have no equivalent figures for proprietorships—have varied enormously. Not all the reasons are apparent. Most are probably related to the tax law itself. Undoubtedly the decline in corporations and increase in partnerships in the early 1940's, when partnerships outnumbered corporations,[7] was due to the

---

5. There are also census figures covering some segments of the economy, but not compiled so frequently or over so long a period. They generally separate proprietorships, partnerships, corporations, and sometimes cooperatives, as well as a residual undifferentiated class. For each category, they typically give number and (by kinds of business) sales, payroll and personnel, but no profit figures. Latest references, and the activities covered, are: U.S. Bureau of the Census, Census of Business: 1958 (1961) vol. 1, pp. 5–2ff. (retail trade), vol. 3., pp. 5–2 ff. (wholesale trade), vol. 5, pp. 5–2ff. (selected services); Census of Manufactures: 1958 (1961), vol. 1, pp. 3–2ff. (manufacturing; comparative figures for 1947, 1954); Census of Mineral Industries:

1958 (1961), vol. 1, pp. 3–2ff. (mineral industries; comparative figures for 1954).

6. This should not be taken to mean that partnerships and proprietorships are inherently more stable ways to do business. The statistics must reflect a considerable degree of self-selection: riskier businesses choose to incorporate. See Sec. 23B(e) below. Also, it may be that unincorporated businesses tend to be smaller and somewhat less vulnerable to major swings in the economy, or more flexible in adjusting to them.

7. There is some bias in favor of partnerships; see Notes to Table A regarding numbers.

World War II excess profits tax, which applied only to corporations. A similar but less marked development in the early 1950's coincides with the Korean War excess profits tax.

More detailed figures (see Table B) are published for 1957 onwards and a few prior years. They are also from tax returns, but more directly in that partnership returns were used instead of reconstructing partnership data from individual returns. There is also a count of proprietorships, indicating how dominant these are in number, though not in other respects. The relative positions of the three forms in the latest published year are presented by percentages in Table C. The pre-eminence of the corporation is plain. On the other hand, both proprietorships and partnerships occupy a fairly significant position and appear to enjoy a higher ratio of net profit to business receipts. This is partly because owners' and partners' compensation is not deducted in reaching net profit, although officers' compensation is deducted by corporations. Another factor, probably more potent, is the comparative concentration of proprietorships and partnerships in service occupations with proportionally low overhead, e.g., medicine, law and other professions which, until recently, have been unable to use the corporate form.[8] Relative to other fields, partnerships are most important in agriculture (including forestry and fisheries), services (including the professions), and wholesale and retail trade (particularly retail). In finance, where they were once a very substantial factor, they have declined, probably because stock brokers were permitted by the Stock Exchanges to incorporate from about 1953.

---

8. See Sec. 34A below.

A comparison of proprietorships, partnerships and corporations, by kind of business, and showing number, business receipts and net profit, will be found in U.S. Bureau of the Census, Statistical Abstract of the U.S. 486 (87th ed. 1966).

Table A

Major Forms of Business Organization—Number and Net Profit, 1918–63
[Numbers in thousands; net profits in billions of dollars]

	Sole Proprietorships		Partnerships		Corporations	
	No.	Net Profit	No.	Net Profit	No.	Net Profit
1918		3.1	101	1.2	318	7.7
1919		3.9	176	1.8	320	8.4
1920		3.2	241	1.7	346	5.9
1921		2.4	259	1.3	356	0.5
1922		2.8	288	1.4	383	4.8
1923		4.7	305	1.7	399	6.3
1924		4.8	321	4.8	417	5.3
1925		3.7	309	1.8	430	7.6
1926		3.6	295	1.7	455	7.5
1927		3.3	283	1.8	426	6.5
1928		3.3	272	1.9	444	8.2
1929		3.4	264	1.9	456	8.7
1930		2.7	245	1.1	463	1.6
1931		2.0	230	0.8	460	3.3
1932		1.2	218	0.5	452	5.6
1933		1.2	215	0.5	447	2.5
1934		1.6	222	0.6	470	0.1
1935		1.7	222	0.7	477	1.7
1936		2.2	237	1.0	479	7.3
1937		2.3	261	1.1	478	7.3
1938		2.1	273	1.0	471	3.7
1939		2.5	291	1.2	470	6.7
1940		3.9	373	1.5	473	8.9
1941		6.2	454	2.2	469	16.3
1942		9.0	490	3.5	443	23.1
1943		10.7	491	5.1	421	27.8
1944		11.6	577	5.7	413	26.3
1945		11.9	673	7.1	421	21.1
1946		15.3	885	7.9	491	25.2
1947		15.3	936	7.9	552	31.4
1948		16.8	930	7.7	594	34.4
1949		14.2	929	7.5	615	28.2
1950		15.3	891	8.2	629	42.6
1951		16.5	922	8.4	652	43.5
1952		16.3	1,062	8.4	672	38.5
1953		16.7	983	8.3	698	39.5
1954		17.0	1,036	8.5	723	36.3
1955		18.4	1,028	9.0	807	47.5
1956		21.3	1,120	8.9	885	48.9
1957		20.3	1,047	9.4	940	44.5
1958		20.7	1,007	9.2	990	38.5
1959		21.4	1,016	9.6	1,074	46.8
1960		21.1	1,003	9.0	1,141	43.5
1961		22.6	994	8.9	1,190	45.9
1962		23.9	978	9.3	1,268	49.6
1963		21.1	984	9.3	1,323	54.3

Notes to Table A.

Sole Proprietorships:

Numbers consistent with the other data are not available.

Net profit is that reported on individual income tax returns and is closely comparable with that in Table B. Source: "business profit" and "business loss" items in U. S. Treasury, Internal Revenue Service, Statistics of Income, 1949, Part 1, pp. 209–19 (1954) [1918–49 data]; id., 1958, p. 74 (1960) [1950–58 data]; id., 1963, p. 150 (1966) [1959–63 data]. Source data are summed for the Table. For 1932 and before, data are available only for profitable operations; after 1932, losses are deducted in reaching the net figures shown.

Partnerships:

Numbers. Source: id., 1949, Part 1, p. 71 (1954) [1918–49 data]; Commissioner of Internal Revenue, Annual Reports (1951–64) [1950–63 data]. There is some discrepancy with Table B which lists only active returns while the Commissioner reports all filed. The Commissioner's number is larger by a few per cent in recent years. However, a comparison of his Annual Report figures in the 1940's with those in Table A reveals that his were usually one or two per cent lower, perhaps because they did not include delinquent returns.

Net profit is that reported on individual income tax returns and thus does not include income and loss allocated to corporate partners. However, this does not seem to explain why the Table B figures are typically smaller. Source: "partnership profit" and "partnership loss" items in references listed for Sole Proprietorships, above; the comments there apply here too.

Corporations:

Numbers are active corporations after 1944; before then, no distinction is made between active and inactive. Source: U. S. Treasury Dept., Internal Revenue Service, Statistics of Income, 1949, Part 2, pp. 340–45 (1953) [1918–49 data]; id., 1959–60, p. 230 (1962) [1950–59 data]; id., U. S. Business Tax Returns 1963, p. 181 (1967) [1960–63 data]. These sources also give total receipts of corporations which are generally not available for proprietorships and partnerships except in years covered by Table B.

Net profit is before taxes. Management compensation has been deducted, unlike in proprietorships and partnerships. Source: same as for Number.

Table B

Major Forms of Business Organization—Number Active,
Business Receipts and Net Profit, 1957–63 and Selected
Earlier Years

[Numbers in thousands; business receipts and net profits
in billions of dollars]

	Sole Proprietorships			Partnerships			Corporations		
	No.	Business Receipts	Net Profit	No.	Business Receipts	Net Profit	No.	Business Receipts	Net Profit
1939	1,052	23.5	2.5	291	14.8	1.6	470	132.9	6.7
1945	5,689	79.0	12.1	627	46.6	6.8	421	244.0	21.1
1947	6,624	101.1	15.1	888	59.6	7.7	552	353.8	31.4
1953	7,715	143.8	17.0	959	78.6	8.4	698	534.6	39.5
1957	8,738	162.7	20.2	970	82.0	8.8	940	684.9	44.5
1958	8,800	163.4	20.8	954	77.5	8.6	990	696.6	38.5
1959	9,142	176.2	21.5	949	77.0	8.8	1,074	772.9	46.8
1960	9,090	171.3	21.1	941	72.9	8.4	1,141	802.8	43.5
1961	9,242	171.0	22.7	939	73.4	8.7	1,190	823.9	45.9
1962	9,183	178.4	23.9	932	72.3	8.5	1,268	895.1	49.6
1963	9,136	181.6	23.8	924	71.8	8.7	1,323	948.8	54.3

Notes to Table B.

Numbers are active partnerships and corporations and, presumably, active proprietorships.

Partnership data are based on partnership returns rather than individual returns. See Notes to Table A for other comparisons between the two Tables.

Source: U. S. Treasury Dept., Internal Revenue Service, Statistics of Income, U. S. Business Tax Returns 1963, pp. 84, 157, 181 (1967) [1953–63 data for all forms; 1945, 1947 for partnerships; 1945 for corporations]; id., 1957–58, pp. 62, 65 (1961) [1947 data for proprietorships, corporations]; U. S. Bureau of the Census, Statistical Abstract of the U. S. 486 (87th ed. 1966) [1939 data for all forms, 1945 for proprietorships; tabulates all but the 1947 data, with minor variations in a few instances].

The corporation data include Subchapter S corporations (see Sec. 34C below) as follows:

	No.	Business Receipts	Net Profit
1958	44	11.4	0.1
1959	71	18.9	0.4
1960	90	22.9	0.4
1962	124	29.1	0.7

Source: U. S. Treasury Dept., Internal Revenue Service, Statistics of Income, Corporations 1960–61, p. 303 (1963); id., 1961–62, p. 198 (1964); id., 1962, pp. 180, 279, 330 (1966).

Table C

Major Forms of Business Organization—Number Active,
Business Receipts and Net Profit, 1963, by Percentages

	No.	Business Receipts	Net Profit
Sole Proprietorships	80.3%	15.1%	27.4%
Partnerships	8.1	6.0	10.0
Corporations	11.6	78.9	62.6
Total	100.0	100.0	100.0

Note to Table C. Source: Table B, last line, by computation.

HISTORY AND SOURCE OF PARTNERSHIP LAW

§ 2. Partnership is a very ancient form. Its law contains a fusion of principles from the civil law, the law merchant, the common law, and equity.

The dominant element in current partnership law is the Uniform Partnership Act which codifies much of the earlier decisional law and makes some significant changes. The Uniform Limited Partnership Act (supplemented by the U.P.A.) even more completely dominates the law of limited partnerships, although neither statute answers every question which may arise.

Partnership—using the term in a general way—must be as old as cooperative activity. Indeed, it has obvious origins in family and clan activity of the most ancient and rudimentary sort. As a profit seeking arrangement it has a traceable course from Babylonian share-cropping through classical Greece and Rome to the far-flung trading enterprises of the Renaissance.[9] From the Middle Ages onward in Europe and England, partnership served as an important stimulus to commerce by bringing financier and merchant together in a relation that escaped condemnation as usury.[9A] But our concern in this

---

9. See, e.g., Burns, Partnership, 12 Encyc.Soc.Sci. 3–6 (1934) and references there; Mitchell, Early Forms of Partnership, 3 Select Essays in Anglo-American Legal History 183 (1909) (Middle Ages and Renaissance); Lobingier, The Natural History of the Private Artificial Person, 13 Tul.L.Rev. 41, 56–58 (1938); Origo, The Merchant of Prato 35–161, esp. 101–07 (1957) (Italian trade and finance about 1400, including the details of a number of partnerships); 1 Rowley, Partnership 2–7 (2d ed. 1960); Szlechter, Le contrat de société en Babylonie, en Grèce et à Rome (1947); Stein, Mutual Agency of Partners in Civil Law, 33 Tul.L. Rev. 595 (1959) (Roman law); Scrut-ton, Roman Law Influence in Chancery, Church Courts, Admiralty, and Law Merchant, 1 Select Essays in Anglo-American Legal History, 208, 220–222 (1907) (Roman law compared with English common law, relying heavily on Story, Partnership (7th ed. 1881)).

9A. Mitchell, n. 9 above; Salin, Usury, 15 Encyc.Soc.Sci. 193, 195 (1935). For the theological and philosophical basis of the partnership exemption from usury, as well as the history, see Noonan, The Scholastic Analysis of Usury, esp. 133–53 (1957). For some later uses of partnership to avoid the usury laws, see Sec. 5 n. 43 below, Sec. 14 nn. 9, 40 below.

volume is for partnership in the Anglo-American legal system.[10]

In the early days of the common law, the legal affairs of merchants in England were administered almost exclusively in distinct and varied tribunals such as Courts of Piepoudre, Courts Staple, and Admiralty Courts.[11] Reasons for the special treatment are probably to be found in the methodical slowness and exactness of the common law courts, and the fact that they were not open to all suitors. Trade was carried on largely at fairs or staples, where merchants from many countries gathered to do business. The foreigners had no knowledge of the forms and procedures of the common law courts, and were constantly on the move. It was essential to have, for their benefit as well as for the English merchants who dealt with them, a forum which understood their occupation, accepted their trade usages, and dispensed speedy justice.

These early mercantile courts took cognizance of two forms of partnership well known in continental Europe, the Societas (general partnership) and the Commenda or Societe en Commandite (limited partnership) [12] as well as the related customs, a part of the Law Merchant.[13] This body of custom was the source of the right of account between partners and of the rule of nonsurvivorship in partnership property on a partner's death. Such principles were at variance with the common law, under which neither a joint nor a common tenant who secured possession of the property could be made to account, and survivorship was an incident of joint tenancy.

The mercantile courts were given parliamentary sanction by the Statute of the Staple,[14] which provided that justice was to be done to the foreign trader from day to day, and from hour to hour, according to the law of the staple or the law merchant and not according to common law or local usages. This and later statutes provided for

---

10. For a number of references to other works in Anglo-American and foreign law, see Mersky, The Literature of Partnership Law, 16 Vand.L.Rev. 389 (1963).

11. Scrutton, General Survey of the History of the Law Merchant, 3 Select Essay in Anglo-American Legal History 7 (1909). On the modern meaning of the "law merchant", see Note, 38 Harv.L.Rev. 954, 957 (1925). See also n. 13 below.

12. 8 Holdsworth, History of English Law 192 et seq. (1926); Mitchell, op. cit. supra n. 9.

Cases in the early records indicate frequent use of partnerships for carrying on trade. See those referring to *socii* or general partnerships, The Fair Court of St. Ives (1293) 23 Selden So-

ciety 59; St. Ives (1287) 23 id. 25; St. Ives (1300) 23 id. 77; St. Ives (1317) 23 id. 105; King's Counsel (1273) 46 id. 12; Assize at London (1278) 46 id. 18; King's Counsel (1284) 46 id. 39; Itinerant Justices (1288) 46 id. 45; Court of the Mayor of London on King's Writ (1299) 49 id. 14.

The first Usury Ordinance of the City of London (1363), and a later Ordinance (1391), referred to transactions by partners. Riley, Liber Albus 320, 346. The existence of the *commenda* (the precursor of the limited partnership) was recognized in early cases, St. Ives (1300) 23 Selden Society 77.

13. Burdick, What is the Law Merchant?, 2 Colum.L.Rev. 470 (1902); Scrutton, op. cit. supra n. 11 at 34.

14. 27 Edward III, Statute 2 (1353).

additional merchants' courts. Though the merchant may have had, in the course of time, the right to take his case to common law, he seldom did so; few cases of merchants appear in the law courts before the 17th century.

Mercantile causes came into the regular courts of England by way of the equity side. Equity courts opened their doors to mercantile actions and, in deciding them, took into account mercantile customs. In this stage of development, certain principles were established for partnerships, such as the fiduciary duties of partners inter se, and the right of each to have partnership property applied in equity to partnership purposes. By the time Lord Coke took the bench in 1606, mercantile cases were coming into the common law courts in increasing numbers. For a long while, no legal principles were established; each case was decided on its facts, with the appropriate mercantile custom a fact to be proved to the jury.

When Lord Mansfield became Chief Justice in 1756, the common law began to develop its commercial law. Mansfield was trained in the civil law as well as the common, and had a lively interest in mercantile customs. He set about the task of creating a common law for commercial matters, based largely on the custom of merchants and supplemented by the civil law.[15] He accomplished less for partnership, however, than for other branches of commercial law, such as negotiable instruments, sales, and insurance.[16]

In England and in the United States, the 19th century was a period of considerable use of the partnership form for all kinds of enterprises, and of the development of the common law of partnership. The result was an amalgamation of certain well-established common law institutions (such as joint property and joint obligations) with the more flexible rules of the law merchant as accepted and applied in equity. So much confusion and uncertainty existed, especially as to the incidents of ownership of partnership property and the rights of creditors, that demands for statutory restatement arose. The product in England was the Partnership Act of 1890.[17] In the United States there were instances of codification, such as the

---

15. On Mansfield's use of civil law authorities, see Luke v. Lyle, 2 Burr. 882, 97 Eng.Rep. 614 (1759). On the similarity of civil law and common law of partnership, and the probable influence of the former on the latter, see Scrutton, Roman Law Influence, 1 Select Essays in Anglo-American Legal History 208, 237 (1907); Story, Partnership, especially the Preface (1st ed. 1846).

16. One of Mansfield's important partnership cases was Fox v. Hanbury, 2 Cowp. 495, 97 Eng.Rep. 1179 (1776), dealing with the relative rights of partners and of partnership and separate creditors in partnership property.

17. 53–54 Vict. c. 39 (1890), reprinted in 7 Unif.Laws Ann. 249 (1949). It was basically the work of Sir Frederick Pollock. The Act is annotated in Turner, Pollock on Partnership (14th ed. 1944), reviewed 58 Harv.L.Rev. 470 (1945). A more voluminous treatise on the English law is Lindley, Partnership (12th ed. 1962). See also n. 18 below.

California Civil Code, copied in several other states; it contained a few sections on partnership. A more comprehensive project was that of the Commissioners on Uniform State Laws, then enjoying the first flush of success in their initial commercial codification, the Negotiable Instruments Law.[18] In 1902 they engaged James Barr Ames, Dean of Harvard Law School, to draft a Uniform Partnership Act. On his death, the task was taken over by William Draper Lewis, Dean of the University of Pennsylvania Law School, and completed (with radical change in Ames' approach [19]) in 1914. The U.P.A., and the companion U.L.P.A. (Uniform Limited Partnership Act),[20] completed in 1916, are now law in almost all United States jurisdictions, as indicated by Table D; they are reproduced in Appendices I and II below.

The two Acts are positive law where adopted, and are cited as authority throughout this treatise. Because of its succinct statement, the U.P.A. is also used for headnotes of many Sections. Courts and lawyers are fond of saying that the U.P.A. merely codifies the common law. This easy assertion arose with the Act itself, no doubt to facilitate its passage by legislatures and its acceptance by bench and bar. The assertion is sometimes used as an excuse for ignoring the Act and invoking inconsistent prior precedent. This is an old common law technique [21] for undermining statutes and has little to recommend it. In many respects, depending on a jurisdiction's version of the common law, the Act does merely codify. But in many others, particularly those centering on property and creditors' rights, it makes major changes; these are discussed at various places in this book.

Despite prevalence of the two Uniform Acts, and their exhortations for uniform interpretation,[22] there are variations (A) in the wording of the Acts as passed by the several legislatures,[23] (B) in the way the Acts have been construed by the courts,[24] and (C) between the Acts and the common law or other statutes in jurisdictions which

18. The draftsman of the English Bills of Exchange Act, which inspired the N.I.L., was himself moved by Pollock's Digest of Partnership, which evolved into the English Partnership Act. Britton, Bills and Notes 9 (2d ed. 1961).

19. See Sec. 3(e) below.

For accounts of the drafting of the U.P.A., see Commissioners' Prefatory Note, 7 Unif.Laws Ann. 3 (1949); Lewis, The Uniform Partnership Act, 24 Yale L.J. 617, 638-41 (1915) and references in Sec. 3(e) nn. 76-78 below.

20. The present law of limited partnership is discussed in Secs. 26, 32 and other portions of this treatise.

21. Another is countered by U.P.A. § 4 (1), U.L.P.A. § 28(1): "The rule that statutes in derogation of the common law are to be strictly construed shall have no application to this act."

22. U.P.A. § 4(4); U.L.P.A. § 28(2).

23. Variations are collected in Statutory Notes following each Section in 7 Unif. Laws Ann. (1949) and 8 id. (1922). Many of them are mentioned in this treatise.

24. The U.P.A., with the explanatory notes of the Commissioners on some Sections, and case annotations, is published in 7 Unif.Laws Ann. (1949). The U.L.P.A. is similarly published in 8 Unif.Laws Ann. (1922). Each is supplemented annually.

lack the Uniform Acts.[25] While only the last group of variations is significant in partnership law at large, the differences in all categories are sufficient to make conflict of laws important in particular circumstances.[26]

Even where the U.P.A. is in force, it does not contain all the law of partnership. Matters outside its scope include capacity of persons to be partners, suits by and against partnerships in the firm name, service of process, the effect of the Statute of Frauds on the formation of partnerships and on the rights of partners in partnership realty, fraudulent conveyances and bulk transfers, remedies for the enforcement of obligations (between the firm or partners and third persons, and among the partners) and insolvency administration under the federal Bankruptcy Act.

The U.L.P.A. is a more complete statement of the law of limited partnerships, but is supplemented in many respects by the U.P.A.[27] as well as by matters of the kind just mentioned.

---

25. Iowa probably has the most fully developed common law of partnership in the U.S. Relatively comprehensive statutes differing from the U.P.A. are Ga.Code, §§ 75–101 to 75–315 (1964); LSA–C.C. (La.) arts. 2801–90 (1952) (based on civil law). See also Ala. Code, Tit. 43 (1959).

There are a number of law review articles comparing the U.P.A. with the common law of particular states, usually to propagandize for the Act or to show changes made by its passage. See, e.g., Wright, California Partnership Law and the Uniform Partnership Act, 9 Calif.L.Rev. 206 (1921); Karesh, Partnership Law and the Uniform Partnership Act in South Carolina, 3 S.C.L.Q. 193 (1951); Matthews & Folkerth, Ohio Partnership Law and the Uniform Partnership Act, 9 Ohio St.L.J. 616 (1948); Sher & Bromberg, Texas Partnership Law in the 20th Century—Why Texas Should Adopt the Uniform Partnership Act, 12 Sw. L.J. 263 (1958); Bromberg, The Proposed Texas Uniform Partnership Act, 14 Sw.L.J. 437 (1960); Bromberg, Texas Uniform Partnership Act—The Enacted Version, 15 Sw.L.J. 386 (1961).

26. Conflict of laws problems are not treated in this volume. See Ehrenzweig, Conflict of Laws 423–25 (1962); Annot., Conflict of laws as to partnership matters, 29 A.L.R.2d 295 (1953). The problems are more acute for limited partnerships, since local filing may be a condition of their validity. See Sec. 26 at n. 30 below.

See Spencer Kellogg & Sons, Inc. v. Loban, 204 Tenn. 79, 315 S.W.2d 514 (1958); Note, Partnerships—Conflict of Laws—Legal Entity Concept, 27 Tenn.L.Rev. 304 (1960).

27. U.P.A. § 6(2). Oddly, there is no such provision in the U.L.P.A. where one would ordinarily expect to find it.

Table D

Adoption of Uniform Partnership Act and Uniform Limited Partnership Act as of 1966 (with Year of Enactment)

State	U.P.A.	U.L.P.A.
Alabama	——	——
Alaska	1917	1917
Arizona	1954	1943
Arkansas	1941	1953
California	1929	1929
Colorado	1931	1931
Connecticut	1961	1961
Delaware	1947	——
Florida	——	1943
Georgia	——	1952
Hawaii	——	1943
Idaho	1919	1919
Illinois	1917	1917
Indiana	1949	1949
Iowa	——	1924
Kansas	——	——
Kentucky	1954	——
Louisiana	——	——
Maine	——	——
Maryland	1916	1918
Massachusetts	1922	1923
Michigan	1917	1931
Minnesota	1921	1919
Mississippi	——	1964
Missouri	1949	1947
Montana	1947	1947
Nebraska	1943	1939
Nevada	1931	1931
New Hampshire	——	1937
New Jersey	1919	1919
New Mexico	1947	1947
New York	1919	1922
North Carolina	1941	1941
North Dakota	1959	1959
Ohio	1949	1957
Oklahoma	1955	1951
Oregon	1939	——
Pennsylvania	1915	1917
Rhode Island	1957	1930
South Carolina	1950	1960
South Dakota	1923	1925
Tennessee	1917	1919
Texas	1961	1955
Utah	1921	1921
Vermont	1941	1941
Virginia	1918	1918
Washington	1945	1945
West Virginia	1953	1953
Wisconsin	1915	1919
Wyoming	1917	——

Notes to Table D.

Totals:

U.P.A. is in force in 40 states plus District of Columbia, Guam and Virgin Islands.

U.L.P.A. is in force in 42 states plus District of Columbia and Virgin Islands.

Source: 7 & 8 Unif. Laws Ann. 1966 Pocket Parts at 9. These volumes give the citation for each state, as well as variations in the wording of individual sections. Their California and Washington dates are those of re-enactments while those in the Table are for original adoption. See West's Ann.Cal.Corp.Code, Historical Notes to §§ 15001–43, 15501–30 (1955); RCW (Wash.) Legislative History to §§ 25.04.010–25.04.430 (1961).

A dash indicates not adopted.

PARTNERSHIP AS A LEGAL ENTITY

§ 3. The common law regarded a partnership as an aggregate or collection of individuals. The law merchant took the entity view which was often accepted in equity. Courts continue to vacillate between the theories, using them sometimes to rationalize decisions made on other grounds and sometimes as real bases for decision.

The legislatures can characterize partnerships as entities and have done so for many specific purposes, notably bankruptcy and capacity to sue or be sued in the firm name.

The U.P.A. as finally promulgated did not explicitly adopt the entity theory but the theory predominates in its operative provisions.

(a) Legal Entities

A legal person, or legal entity, is a being or entity recognized by the law (courts or legislatures) as capable of having rights and duties as a distinct unit, e.g., to own and dispose of property, make contracts, commit wrongs, sue and be sued. A legal person, as a prerequisite, must have some factual existence as a distinct unit, and must be regarded by the lawmakers as having property or personal interests worthy of protection. A human being is such an entity; in common law countries and in most of Western society, all human beings are endowed with legal personality, i.e. protected in the enjoyment of their interests through recognition of their rights and capacities.

It is not inherently impossible, and it might be desirable, for a human being to possess multiple legal personalities (e.g., as a family man, business or professional man, agent or trustee, corporate executive) according to his distinct interests, activities and responsibilities. The common law has been reluctant to recognize multiple personality. Some public and ecclesiastical officials have been regarded as corporations sole, apart from themselves as individuals. To some extent a fiduciary (executor, administrator or trustee) has been treated as having a personality distinct from his private capacity.

Often these results are achieved by specific contract with third persons, for example that a trustee shall have no individual liability. But the emphasis has been on the unitary personality of the human being, which he is considered to enjoy as a sort of natural right. Bills of Rights and other constitutional provisions are established to ensure its protection.

A somewhat reverse problem arises with respect to groups of human beings. They may organize for business, social, political, charitable or other purposes. They have a degree of factual unity. Are they entitled to legal personality for recognition of their group interests? Although the end of law in a democratic state is presumably the realization of individual interests, these interests can be promoted by group association and activity. In some situations the law treats the group as a legal person. Normally this will be desirable from the group's viewpoint, enabling it to own property, make transactions and maintain lawsuits. In other instances, the group as an entity is exposed to litigation and effective enforcement of liability against it which it would much prefer to avoid.[28]

Group entities, when recognized by the law, have often been called artificial, fictitious or moral persons. This is because, at least in common law countries in the past, group legal personality seemed exceptional and unnatural, something granted only by special dispensation of the sovereign. Chief Justice Marshall epitomized this view in his classic definition of the corporation: "an artificial being, invisible, intangible, and existing only in contemplation of law." [29] Some commentators still assert that the courts should not recognize the personality of a group entity unless authorized by the legislature, the proper source of lawmaking.[30] Others believe that legal personality is but a useful judicial tool and should be employed when it will accomplish a desired social end.[31]

Business corporations are endowed with legal personality by the statutes under which they are created. They typically have capacity

---

28. For example, joint stock companies with numerous members usually managed to avoid being sued in federal court diversity cases by denying entity status. Unincorporated labor unions have long enjoyed such an advantage. See Sec. 34 at nn. 29–30 below.

Perhaps the most pathetic non-entity cases are those in which unincorporated associations lose property because of inability to take title. See, e.g., State v. Sunbeam Rebekah Lodge, 169 Or. 253, 127 P.2d 726 (1942) (devise to fraternal organization escheated).

29. Trustees of Dartmouth College v. Woodward, 17 U.S. (4 Wheat.) 518, 4 L.Ed. 629 (1819).

30. Warren, Corporate Advantages without Incorporation 12 (1929).

It has been suggested that, in the interests of certainty, only groups registered as corporations by an administrative agency should be treated as such. From this vantage point, the de facto corporation in American law (Sec. 30 below) is an anomaly. Lloyd, Law of Unincorporated Associations 9 (1938).

31. Stevens, Corporations § 2 (1st ed. 1936).

to sue and be sued in the corporate name, to own property, to have perpetual succession, to make contracts and to engage in a wide variety of other transactions.[32]   This has been true for so long, and corporations are such a major part of American business and life, that they are regarded as the archetypal group entities.   For the same reasons, the group entity now seems a much more familiar and less dangerous concept than it did a century or generation ago.

(b) Aggregate and Entity Theories of Partnership

To what extent courts or legislatures have treated or should treat partnerships as legal entities has been a matter of considerable dispute.[33]   It is consistently done in civil law jurisdictions (including Louisiana) by code or by judicial usage.[34]   The common law tradition is otherwise; from an early date the judges insisted on regarding partners as individuals and imposing on them the law of joint or common tenancy in property and the law of joint obligations in contract.   Partnership activities and the rights and duties growing out of them were viewed as those of the partners, and not as those of the partnership as an entity.[35]   This aggregate theory of partnership—

---

32.   Model Business Corp. Act § 4. Statutes are collected, 1 Model Business Corp. Act Ann. 41–183 (1960).

33.   Crane, The Uniform Partnership Act —A Criticism, 28 Harv.L.Rev. 762 (1915); Lewis, The Uniform Partnership Act—A Reply to Mr. Crane's Criticism, 29 Harv.L.Rev. 158, 291 (1916); Crane, The Uniform Partnership Act and Legal Persons, 29 Harv.L.Rev. 838 (1916); Drake, Partnership Entity and Tenancy in Partnership, 15 Mich.L. Rev. 609 (1917); Wright, Opposition of Law to Business Usage, 26 Colum.L. Rev. 917, 927 (1926); Comment, 36 Yale L.J. 254 (1926); Note, 29 Colum. L.Rev. 1134 (1929); Warren, Corporate Advantages without Incorporation 29 et seq. (1929); Jensen, Is a Partnership Under the Uniform Partnership Act an Aggregate or an Entity?, 16 Vand.L.Rev. 377 (1963).

For a summary of many N.Y. cases dealing with this problem, and a discussion of the various theories, see Note, The Partnership as a Legal Entity, 41 Colum.L.Rev. 698 (1941).

By the English Partnership Act § 4(2), a firm in Scotland is a legal person, following a long tradition there. Lindley, Partnership 5–6 (12th ed. 1962). It is otherwise in England. However, under Rules of Court, partners may sue or be sued in the firm name. Turn-er, Pollock on Partnership 20, 123–28 (14th ed. 1944); Lindley, Partnership 301–03, 879–81 (12th ed. 1962).

34.   Crane, The Uniform Partnership Act —A Criticism, 28 Harv.L.Rev. 762, 764 (1915). Trappey v. Lumbermen's Mut. Cas. Co., 229 La. 632, 86 So.2d 515 (1956) and Louisiana references there.

The Puerto Rican Sociedad en Commandita has been treated as an entity. People of Puerto Rico v. Russell & Co., 288 U.S. 476, 53 S.Ct. 447, 77 L.Ed. 903 (1933); see discussion in Mason v. American Express Co., 334 F.2d 392 (2d Cir.1964).

35.   "The tradition of the common law is to treat as legal persons only incorporated groups and to assimilate all others to partnerships . . .. The tradition of the civil law as expressed in the Code of Puerto Rico is otherwise." People of Puerto Rico v. Russell & Co., n. 34 above.

"A corporation is a fictitious person, created by special authority (and by the law of England by the Crown or by Parliament), and endowed by that authority with a capacity to acquire rights and incur obligations, as a means to the end for the attainment of which the corporation is created . . .. With partnerships the case is otherwise; the members of these do

that there is no entity, only individuals—is so closely associated with the common law that it is often called the common law theory of partnership.

Business men, unhampered by legal tradition or metaphysical concern, have inclined toward the entity theory of partnership, which, for this reason, is also known as the mercantile theory. Justice Lindley has described it as follows: "Commercial men and accountants are apt to look upon a firm in the light in which lawyers look upon a corporation, i.e., as a body distinct from the members composing it, and having rights and obligations distinct from those of its members. Hence in keeping partnership accounts, the firm is made debtor to each partner for what he brings into the common stock, and each partner is made debtor to the firm for all that he takes out of that stock. In the mercantile view, partners are never indebted to each other in respect of partnership transactions, but are always either debtors to or creditors of the firm . . .. The partners are the agents and sureties of the firm; its agents for the transaction of its business; its sureties for the liquidation of its liabilities so far as the assets of the firm are insufficient to meet them. The liabilities of the firm are regarded as the liabilities of the partners only in case they cannot be met by the firm and discharged out of its assets." [36]

A two- or three-man firm, informally run by the partners in their own names with little or no help, and with a good deal of casual use of individual assets for firm business (or firm funds for personal affairs) does not look much like an entity in fact. By contrast, no corporation is more entity-like than a large law or accounting firm

---

not form a collective whole, which is regarded as distinct from the individuals composing it; nor are they collectively endowed with any capacity of acquiring rights or incurring obligations. The rights and liabilities of a partnership are the rights and liabilities of the partners, and are enforceable by and against them individually. 1 Lindley, Partnership 4 (4th ed., Ewell Am. ed. 1881).

36. 1 Lindley, Partnership 110 (Ewell 2d Am.Ed.). Lindley's statement is invalid for present U.S. law in two respects. The relation between partner and firm may be debtor-creditor or it may be recipient and maker of a capital contribution. See Secs. 37(a), 65 (a) below. (Even in the latter case, it does not become primarily a relation between partner and co-partner.) Also, in most places, partnership liabilities are regarded as direct liabilities of the partners and may be enforced without prior exhaustion of partnership assets. Secs. 58(e), 60 below.

Equity courts, seeking to carry out partners' intentions, have tended to treat partnerships as entities. Helvering v. Walbridge, 70 F.2d 683 (2d Cir. 1934). A partner contributed to a partnership corporate stock which cost X and was worth more (Y). Held: on partnership sale of the stock for a still higher price (Z), the only taxable gain is Z–Y. In effect, this gives the partnership as an entity a new basis in the stock equal to its value when contributed. Int.Rev.Code of 1954, § 723 (26 U.S.C.A.) changes the result, giving the partnership a basis equal to the partner's cost.

The entity-based dual priorities rule was developed in equity. See Secs. 91A, 91 below. See also below at n. 44. Entity concepts used by the equity courts in bankruptcy matters are discussed by L. Hand, J. in Commissioner v. Lehman, 165 F.2d 383, 385, 7 A.L.R.2d 667 (1948). The partnership as an entity for which the partners are agents is discussed in Sec. 48 n. 8 below.

which has been going for generations, often under the name of someone long since dead, with dozens or hundreds of partners (of whom only a handful, as managing partners or an executive committee, make major decisions), and perhaps as many offices and more employees.[37] These extremes suggest one reason why no consistent theory has evolved: some partnerships are much more like entities than others.

(c) Use of the Theories

The conflict between the common law (aggregate) and mercantile (entity) views of partnership has been apparent in decisions over the centuries and down to the present. A vast number of issues turn on the choice of theory, most importantly the relative rights of partners and creditors in partnership property. Many cases say that a partnership is a legal person,[38] and many others say that it is not.[39]

37. For figures on the year of organization of partnerships filing tax returns in various industries and professions in 1963, see U.S. Treasury, Statistics of Income, U.S. Business Tax Returns 1963, pp. 137–46 (1967).

A distinction, somewhat comparable to that suggested in the text, by size and extent of firm is made in determining whether a partner may claim constitutional protection from self-incrimination by partnership books and records. See Sec. 41 at nn. 74–77 below.

38. Cases of this sort are almost innumerable. Some prior to the U.P.A. are collected in Crane, The Uniform Partnership Act—A Criticism, 28 Harv.L. Rev. 762, 766 n. 37 (1915), in Magruder & Foster, Jurisdiction Over Partnerships, 37 Harv.L.Rev. 793, 795 n. 5 (1924), and in 7 Unif.Laws Ann. 15–16 n. 8 (1949 & Supp.). Some more recent cases include—People v. Zangain, 301 Ill. 299, 133 N.E. 783 (1922); Kuehl v. Means, 206 Iowa 539, 218 N.W. 907, 58 A.L.R. 1359 (1928); Thurston v. Detroit Asphalt & Paving Co., 226 Mich. 505, 198 N.W. 345 (1924); State v. Pielsticker, 118 Neb. 419, 225 N.W. 51 (1929). See also nn. 41–53 below.

Caswell v. Maplewood Garage, 84 N.H. 241, 149 A. 746, 73 A.L.R. 433 (1930): "The logic of the matter, the long existing understanding of the business world whose interests are most vitally affected by the law upon the subject, and not a little of judicial and text-book authority, all declare the theory of legal entity to be the true conception of a partnership. It is not necessary to carry the idea to extremes.

Its limitations will be defined as cases in point arise. It is sufficient for the decision of the case at bar to conclude that in the matter of the agency of a partner there is an entity for which he acts." The state does not have the U.P.A.

39. Cases are collected 7 Unif.Laws Ann. 15–17 nn. 7, 9 (1949 & Supp.) See also nn. 54–58 below.

A Liquid Fuels Tax Act provided that "all taxes collected by a dealer shall be a lien on the franchise or property, both real and personal, of any dealer." Held: the lien for a partnership dealer extended to a partner's separate property. "Since under our law F. Hanson and Company is not a separate entity, it would appear that it was F. Hanson and Frank Morrison who were the dealers and that it was therefore their property which was subject to a lien entered by virtue of the [statute] whether such property was used in the partnership business or individually owned." Morrison's Estate, 343 Pa. 157, 163, 22 A.2d 729, 732 (1942).

"It was not the lease of the firm, because there is no such thing as a firm known to the law." Ex parte Corbett, L.R. 14 Ch.Div. 122, 49 L.J.Bankruptcy 74 (1880).

See also First Nat. Trust & Sav. Bank of San Diego v. Industrial Accident Com'n, 213 Cal. 322, 2 P.2d 347, 78 A. L.R. 1324 (1931); Kent v. National Supply Co., 36 S.W.2d 811 (Tex.Civ. App.1931); Shonnard v. Price, 49 F.2d 794 (S.D.N.Y.1931).

See 8 Holdsworth, History of English Law 198 (1926).

Most cases reached a result which was possible under either view but, since it was more consistent with one than the other, the court reinforced its conclusion by reference to the supportive theory.[40]

In many cases the problem is one of interpreting a written contract to find the intent of the parties. Take, for example, a vehicle liability policy issued to a partnership. In holding that coverage extends to operation of the vehicle in the course of the partnership business, but not in a partner's separate venture, the court may rely on the prevailing businessman's conception of the separateness of the partnership affairs from those of a partner.[41] Decisions of this kind often describe the partnership as an entity, but could equally well rest on the policy's description of the risk insured, without having to characterize the firm.[42] If a borrower at a bank signs a note with a

---

40. The substitution of a partnership for one partner as a plaintiff was an impermissible change of parties. Brooks v. Ulanet, 116 Vt. 49, 68 A.2d 701 (1949). This would seem to be equally true for the addition of the second partner.

Somewhat similar is Zion v. Sentry Safety Control Corp., 258 F.2d 31 (3d Cir. 1958) (Pa. law) (partnership claims against third party were not compulsory counterclaims in third party's suit against one partner).

41. Hartigan v. Casualty Co. of America, 227 N.Y. 175, 124 N.E. 789 (1919). Defendant issued a policy insuring "Hartigan & Dwyer, No. 85–91 Congress St., Troy, Rensselaer County, New York, department store merchant," against liability from "ownership, maintenance or use" of a truck. An accident occurred while the truck was on loan to another firm which consisted in part of the partners in the insured firm. Held: the policy did not cover the accident. "We think that the terms of the policy are unambiguous and limit the liability of the insurer to accidents which happen while the automobile is being used on the business of Hartigan & Dwyer . . . . The policy protects Hartigan & Dwyer from loss by reason of automobile accidents for which their partnership is liable, and to that extent protects them individually as members of such firm; but the Troy partnership as such is not a member of, and is not liable for the torts of the Albany partnership. Furthermore, for the purpose of keeping partnership accounts, merchants constantly resort to the fiction that a partnership is a legal entity, separate and distinct from the partners therein. This rule of convenience is particularly serviceable to keep apart two firms having a common member . . . . The partnerships in this case are not for all purposes to be regarded as legal entities, but, for the purpose of ascertaining the intention of the parties to the policy herein, we are governed by common parlance rather than legal parlance."

See also Kelley v. London Guarantee & Accident Co., Ltd., 97 Mo.App. 623, 71 S.W. 711 (1903).

Cf. Steinfield v. Massachusetts Bonding & Ins. Co., 79 N.H. 422, 111 A. 303 (1920) (partner's individual liability insurance covered his proportionate liability from partnership use of his car).

In Fidelity Phoenix Fire Ins. Co. v. Howard, 182 Miss. 546, 181 So. 846 (1938), noted 25 Va.L.Rev. 104, an auto theft policy excepted acts of insured's employees. Held: the exception covered an employee of another firm with the same members as the insured firm. The court emphasized that the firms had no legal existence apart from their members.

42. See McKinney v. Truck Ins. Exchange, 324 S.W.2d 773 (Mo.App.1959). A workmen's compensation policy was issued in the name of two partners "doing business as Acme Glass Co.," describing their activity as glass making and reciting that they conducted no other business. Thus, by its terms, there was no coverage for an employee castrating a bull on one partner's farm. Nonetheless, the court chose to say

provision that collateral for it applies also to his other obligations, a court may find that the parties intended to exclude his obligations as a member of a partnership indebted to the bank.[43]

The entity theory has been prescribed to uphold the intent of partners that property of the firm be dedicated to carrying out partnership purposes. Examples, primarily from the equity courts, include limitations on the right of a partner to assign his interest in partnership property, or of his individual creditor to levy execution on it.[44]

Some decisions rest unequivocally on the legal entity theory of partnership.[45] A burglary indictment was not defective for describing the premises entered as being owned by a partnership.[46] Admissions by each of the partners, acting outside the scope of the firm business, were not admissions by the firm.[47] A firm composed of minors cannot disaffirm its transactions because of infancy.[48] A statute prohibiting certain loans to bank directors was not violated by a

that a partnership was an entity to this extent, despite the contrary view prevailing in the state on other questions. The farm-owning partner had claimed that the policy was tantamount, by the aggregate theory, to one issued to each partner individually for all his employees.

On the reverse situation, see Parks v. Riverside Ins. Co. of America, 308 F. 2d 175 (10th Cir. 1962) (Okla. law) (liability policy issued to partner for his separate business does not cover partnership business). Compare Steinfield v. Massachusetts Bonding & Ins. Co., n. 41 above.

See also Toenberg v. Harvey, 235 Minn. 61, 49 N.W.2d 578 (1951) (partnership employee covered by partnership's workmen's compensation policy, not by partner's individual policy).

43. Bank of Buffalo v. Thompson, 121 N.Y. 280, 24 N.E. 473 (1890): "We think that among business men a distinction is made between the firm, as an entity, and the members who compose it, and that this language would not be understood as broad enough to cover the indebtedness of a firm of which Thompson was a member and for whose debts, jointly with the other members of the firm, he could be made responsible." Accord, New Bethlehem Trust Co. v. Spindler, 315 Pa. 250, 172 A. 309 (1934).

But see Hallowell v. Blackstone Nat. Bank, 154 Mass. 359, 363, 28 N.E. 281,

13 L.R.A. 315 (1891) (Holmes, J.): "The clause pledging the property for any other claim against the debtor is not inserted with a view to certain specified debts, but as a dragnet to make sure that whatever comes to the creditor's hands shall be held by the latter until its claims are satisfied. Corey on Accounts and Lindley on Partnership have made it popular to refer to a mercantile distinction between the firm and its members. But we have no doubt that our merchants are perfectly aware that claims against their firms are claims against them, and when a merchant gives security for any claim against him, and there is nothing to cut down the literal meaning of the words, he must be taken to include claims against him as a partner." See also In re William Hill & Sons, 186 F. 569 (E.D.Pa.1911).

44. Secs. 42(a), 43(a) below.

45. See also Sec. 70 below. Cf. Sec. 54 (d) below.

46. People v. Zangain, n. 38 above.

47. Caswell v. Maplewood Garage, n. 38 above. See also Note, 17 Va.L.Rev. 295 (1931).

48. Kuehl v. Means, 206 Iowa 539, 218 N.W. 907, 58 A.L.R. 1359 (1928). See also Sec. 7 below.

loan to a partnership composed of bank directors.[49]   A suit against
named individuals as partners is not a suit against the firm.[50]   A statement about a partnership did not libel a partner.[51]   A partner may sue
the firm for damage to his truck used in the business.[52]   A limited
partner can bring a derivative suit in behalf of the firm.[53]

On the other hand, some decisions rest equally firmly on the
aggregate theory.   A tort committed by a partner, followed by his
death and his co-partner's, gives no basis for a remedy against partnership property, since no partnership liability arose.[54]   A sole proprietor's pooling of his merchandise with another's to form a partnership was not a sale requiring him to pay a commission to a broker
with whom he had listed the business.[55]   A conditional sale contract, by which a 2-man partnership bought a truck, was invalid
when filed in the county where one partner lived and the firm
did business, but not in the county where the other partner lived.[56]
Even a limited partnership, which has more pronounced entity characteristics than a general partnership,[57] has been held an aggregate to
the extent that a Canadian corporate limited partner was treated as
having a "permanent establishment" at the limited partnership's
United States office, and thus was ineligible for lower tax rates provided by treaty for foreign corporations without such establish-
ments.[58]

49.   State v. Pielsticker, 118 Neb. 419, 225 N.W. 51 (1929), noted 25 Ill.L.Rev. 101 (1930).   Semble, State v. Haesemeyer, 248 Iowa 154, 79 N.W.2d 755 (1956). The results clearly frustrate the statutory purpose (the statutes referred to loans directly and indirectly) and represent an abuse of the entity theory.

50.   L. C. Jones Trucking Co. v. Superior Oil Co., 68 Wyo. 384, 234 P.2d 802 (1951), noted 6 Wyo.L.J. 217 (1952). The court went on to find that service on one of the partners was sufficient for a judgment binding their joint property.   As a result, a garnishment against a debtor to them was valid, and the garnishee liable for paying them after notice of the garnishment. Aggregate overtones are present along with the dominant entity theme.

51.   Layman v. Readers Digest Ass'n, 412 P.2d 192 (Okl.1966).   The partner failed to show that anyone thought the statement about the partnership referred to him individually.

52.   Smith v. Hensley, 354 S.W.2d 744, 98 A.L.R.2d 340 (Ky.1962).

53.   Riviera Congress Associates v. Yassky, 18 N.Y.2d 540, 277 N.Y.S.2d 386, 223 N.E.2d 876 (1966).

But cf. Grober v. Kahn, 47 N.J. 135, 219 A.2d 601 (1966), discussed Sec. 12 n. 71 below (even if joint venture existed between two persons and family of one, it was not enough of an entity to permit one member to recover counsel fees from other on derivative suit analogy).

54.   Sumner v. Brown, 312 Pa. 124, 167 A. 315 (1933).

55.   McElhinney v. Belsky, 165 Pa.Super. 546, 69 A.2d 178 (1949).

56.   Weingarten v. Universal C.I.T. Credit Corp., 302 F.2d 1 (2d Cir. 1962) (Conn. law).

57.   See Sec. 90B below.

58.   Donroy, Ltd. v. U. S., 301 F.2d 200 (9th Cir. 1962) (Calif. law).   Pressures to protect the tax revenues are strong in a case like this, and may give a better explanation for the result than do the niceties of partnership theory.

It appears that the courts still employ entity or aggregate theories not only as makeweights but also as real bases for decision. Other examples appear throughout this volume.[58A]

Nowhere is the conflict between partnership theories, and with other policies, clearer than in the workmen's compensation and partner's tort cases. In almost all states, a partner is not an employee and is therefore ineligible for workmen's compensation.[59] The reason is that, by the aggregate theory, he is an employer, which precludes his being an employee. As an entrepreneur, he does not belong to the working class for whose benefit compensation acts were passed. A small but growing number of jurisdictions embrace the entity theory by legislation [60] or decision [61] and thereby make a partner eligible for compensation.[62] If the injured worker is not a partner, the courts are often content to apply the entity theory if that will help him overcome an intra-family immunity [63] but are only sometimes willing to aid him with the entity theory by allowing compensation in addition to a tort recovery against a partner whose negligence caused the injury.[64]

58A. See also Spencer Kellogg & Sons, Inc. v. Loban, 204 Tenn. 79, 315 S.W.2d 514 (Tenn.1958); Note, Partnerships—Conflict of Laws—Legal Entity Concept, 27 Tenn.L.Rev. 304 (1960).

59. E.g., In re Ryder's Case, 341 Mass. 661, 171 N.E.2d 475 (1960) (business trust treated as partnership); Herman v. Kandrat Coal Co., 205 Pa.Super. 117, 208 A.2d 51 (1965); Tidwell v. Walden, 205 Tenn. 705, 330 S.W.2d 317 (1959). Cases are collected, Larson, Workmen's Compensation § 54.30 (1966). Even Nebraska (see below at n. 6) so holds. Rasmussen v. Trico Feed Mills, 148 Neb. 855, 29 N.W.2d 641 (1947). See also Sec. 16 nn. 85, 95 below.

60. West's Ann.Cal.Labor Code, § 3359 (partner who receives wages irrespective of profits is employee); M.C.L.A. (Mich.) § 411.7; N.R.S. (Nev.) 616.055 (4) (like Calif.); U.C.A.1966 (Utah) 35–1–43. For applications, see Kramer v. Charlevoix Beach Hotel, 342 Mich. 715, 71 N.W.2d 226 (1955) (partner awarded compensation against insurer); Ayers v. Genter, 367 Mich. 675, 117 N.W.2d 38 (1962) (partner, as employee, barred from negligence action against fellow employee).

61. Trappey v. Lumbermen's Mut. Cas. Co., 229 La. 632, 86 So.2d 515 (1956), noted 7 Hast.L.J. 213 (1956); Rodgers v. Blair, 201 Okl. 249, 204 P.2d 867 (1949). Cf. Superior Ins. Co. v. Kling, 160 Tex. 155, 327 S.W.2d 422 (1959)

(insurer estopped by partner's inclusion in policy and premium payment). Cf. Carle v. Carle Tool & Engineering Co., 36 N.J.Super. 36, 114 A.2d 738 (1955): limited partnership *association* (see Sec. 26A below) is entity whose members are eligible for compensation.

62. When there is no insurance, a partner is still entitled to an award against the firm and his co-partners, subject to their right of contribution from him. De Martini v. Industrial Accident Com'n, 90 Cal.App.2d 139, 202 P. 2d 828 (1949). In effect, this reduces his award by his proportionate share of firm expenses, usually measured by his percentage of profits.

63. Carter v. Carter Logging Co., 83 Idaho 50, 357 P.2d 660 (1960) (partner's son allowed compensation); Keegan v. Keegan, 194 Minn. 261, 260 N.W. 318 (1935) (partner's husband), noted 49 Harv.L.Rev. 155 (1935); Felice v. Felice Office Equipment Co., 34 N.J.Super. 388, 112 A.2d 581 (1955) (partner's wife).

64. Worthington v. Industrial Com'n., 85 Ariz. 310, 338 P.2d 363 (1959) (receipt of settlement in negligence case does not bar compensation), subsequent appeal 88 Ariz. 192, 354 P.2d 47 (1960) (but award reduced by amount received in settlement); Monson v. Arcand, 239 Minn. 336, 58 N.W.2d 753 (1953).

On the other hand, they have generously applied the aggregate theory if that will give the injured worker access to compensation insurance not otherwise available, e.g., where each member of a partnership or joint venture has coverage but the firm does not.[65]

Other policies sometime outweigh the partnership issue, as in the controversy over doctors and other professionals as employees for income tax purposes [66] or in the movement in some states to eliminate intra-family immunities.[67]

(d) Effect of Legislation

There is no doubt of the ability of legislatures to treat partnerships as entities.[68] They have often done so, either by specific mention of partnerships in operative provisions, as in the Bankruptcy Act [69] or in authorizations for suit in the firm name,[69A] or by defining operative words like "person" or "whoever" to include partnerships along with other persons and organizations.[70] Perhaps the broadest of such definitions is in the comprehensive Uniform Commercial Code, by

Contra, Sonberg v. Bergere, 220 Cal.App. 2d 681, 34 Cal.Rptr. 59 (Dist.Ct.App. 1963); Anderson v. Steurer, 391 S.W. 2d 839 (Mo.1965); Mazzuchelli v. Silberberg, 29 N.J. 15, 148 A.2d 8 (1959) citing this text; Fallone v. Misericordia Hospital, 23 A.D.2d 222, 259 N. Y.S.2d 947 (1965), aff'd 17 N.Y.2d 648, 269 N.Y.S.2d 431, 216 N.E.2d 594 (1966) (joint venture).

See Sec. 54(d) n. 30 below.

65. Clawson v. General Ins. Co., 90 Idaho 424, 412 P.2d 597 (1966); W. B. Johnston Grain Co. v. Self, 344 P.2d 653 (Okl.1959).

66. Sec. 34A below. Cf. n. 58 above.

67. The workmen's compensation cases are in n. 63 above. See also Eule v. Eule Motor Sales, 34 N.J. 537, 170 A. 2d 241 (1961), noted 10 Kan.L.Rev. 478 (1962), 14 Stan.L.Rev. 150 (1961), 47 Va.L.Rev. 1450 (1961), (partner's wife may sue firm for his negligent injury to her in scope of business). The N. J. pattern is particularly clear; see Long v. Landy, 35 N.J. 44, 171 A.2d 1 (1961) (wife may sue husband's estate for his negligent injury to her). See also Sec. 54(d) below.

68. United States v. A & P Trucking Co., 358 U.S. 121, 79 S.Ct. 203, 3 L. Ed.2d 165 (1958) (upholding criminal informations against partnership for violation of motor carrier laws and regulations); see n. 70 below. See

also Blau v. Lehman, 368 U.S. 403, 410, 82 S.Ct. 451, 455, 7 L.Ed.2d 403 (1962).

69. Bankruptcy Act § 5, 11 U.S.C.A. § 23, Sec. 91B below.

69A. Secs. 57(b), 59, 60 below.

70. E. g., Unemployment Compensation Law, N.J.S.A. 43:21–19(g) (employing unit includes partnership); Penal Code, 18 Pa.Stat.Ann. § 4103 (1963) ("person" and "whoever" include partnerships).

1 U.S.C.A. § 1 defines "person" in any Act of Congress to include partnership unless the context indicates otherwise. This was used, in United States v. A & P Trucking Co., n. 68 above, to sustain a criminal charge against a partnership under one motor carrier statute. Four dissenters thought the context of this statute excluded a partnership since the other motor carrier statute at issue specifically included partnerships, and since the aggregate theory prevails in the U. S. The majority invoked 1 U.S.C.A. § 1 and the general policy for uniform regulation of motor carriers without regard to their form of organization.

Failure to provide penalties for partnerships as entities does not invalidate a regulatory statute. People v. Schomig, 74 Cal.App. 109, 239 P. 413 (1925); State v. Spears, 57 N.M. 400, 259 P.2d 356, 39 A.L.R.2d 595 (1953); both involving licensing of real estate brokers.

which a person includes an individual or organization, and the latter includes "corporation . . . partnership or association, two or more persons having a joint or common interest, or any other legal or commercial entity." [71]

Partnerships can be taxed as entities.[72] The federal income tax initially did this [73] but has since shifted to an aggregate or conduit, approach for the taxation of income,[74] while retaining entity theory for the ownership of property, filing of returns, making of elections and many other matters.[75]

(e) Effect of U.P.A.

The U.P.A. might have settled the nature of partnership once and for all. Its original chief draftsman, Dean Ames, would have defined a partnership as an entity in the Act; [76] he believed it would give greater clarity and simplicity to partnership law. In addition, he had the approval of his drafting committee on numerous specific provisions based on the entity theory. Dean Lewis, who became the chief draftsman on Ames' death, was unwilling to go so far.[77] He retained most of the specific entity-based provisions since these solved the major problems which motivated the Act. But his version of the definition of partnership is more neutral, and certainly makes no ex-

---

71. U.C.C. §§ 1–201(28), (30). For a more specific acceptance of partnership entity, see id. § 3–105(1) (h) permitting partnerships to issue instruments which are negotiable although payable only from partnership assets, i. e. without personal liability.

72. Tax Review Bd. v. Belmont Laboratories Co., 392 Pa. 473, 141 A.2d 234 (1958). For some of the complications that arise, see Tax Review Bd. of City of Philadelphia v. D. H. Shapiro Co., 409 Pa. 253, 185 A.2d 529 (1962).

See also McKinney's N.Y. Tax Law, § 701 (unincorporated business tax).

73. War Revenue Act of 1917, § 201, 40 Stat. 300, 303 (1917).

74. Sec. 23B(i) below.

75. E. g., Int.Rev.Code of 1954, § 703 (b) (26 U.S.C.A.) (elections by partnership); § 706 (partners and partnerships may have different taxable years, subject to limitations); § 707 (partner may have transactions with partnership in non-partner capacity); § 708 (partnership continues despite transfers of interests unless more than 50% interest in capital and profits is transferred in 12 months); § 741 (sale of interest in partnership results in capital gain or loss, with certain ex-

ceptions); § 6031 (filing of partnership return). Besides the taxation of income to partners rather than to the firm, the main aggregate feature is the exception in id. § 751 to capital gain treatment on the sale of a partnership interest if the firm's assets include more than designated proportions of unrealized receivables or substantially appreciated inventories; see Sec. 40(c) below. For further discussion of aggregate and entity concepts in federal income taxation, see Sec. 65(a) at nn. 19–20 below.

76. The definition in earlier drafts was: "A partnership is a legal person formed by the association of two or more individuals for the purpose of carrying on a business with a view to profit." U.P.A., Second Tentative Draft, § 1(1); Lewis, The Uniform Partnership Act—A Reply to Mr. Crane's Criticism, 29 Harv.L.Rev. 158, 165 (1915). On the Commissioners' change of view, see Helvering v. Smith, 90 F.2d 590 (2d Cir. 1937).

77. His reasons are given in Lewis, op. cit. supra n. 76 at 165–67. See also Williston, The Uniform Partnership Act, 63 U.Pa.L.Rev. 196, 207–09 (1915).

plicit reference to an entity.[78] The Act has both entity and aggregate features;[79] the former are predominant. The only significant aggregate characteristic spelled out in the Act is the joint or joint and several liability of the partners.[80] Even this is phrased as liability for the obligations "of the partnership."[81] Perhaps more indicative of aggregate is the omission of any provision for suits in the firm name (although this has been widely supplied by other legislation[82]). In contrast, entity notions permeate the Act, particularly five critical areas.

(1) *Property.* A partnership can own and convey property (including real estate) in the firm name.[83] Section 24 draws a sharp line between a partner's interest in the partnership and his rights in partnership property. The former is personalty in all cases,[84] is assignable,[85] and may be subjected to a charging order by his individual creditor.[86] In short, the interest in the partnership is the partner's individual property, quite independent of specific partnership property and fairly analogous to a share of stock in a corporation.[87] On the other hand, his rights in specific partnership property, although he is called a co-owner, are wholly subordinated to the rights of the partnership entity as functional owner of the property.[88]

(2) *Creditors' Rights.* Partnership creditors are given priority in partnership assets, and individual creditors in individual assets.[89]

[78] U.P.A. § 6(1): "A partnership is an association of two or more persons to carry on as co-owners a business for profit." It is open to either view of legal personality. The Commissioners' Notes, 7 Unif.Laws Ann. 12 (1949), state: "Ownership involves the power of ultimate control. To state that partners are co-owners of the business is to state that they each have the power of ultimate control." Thus interpreted, the definition is applicable to a corporation, so far as it goes.

Dean Lewis said the Act did not embody the legal person theory. Lewis, op. cit. supra n. 76 at 291. For other comments on this aspect of the Act, see Warren Corporate Advantages without Incorporation 293–301 (1929); Wrightington, Unincorporated Associations and Business Trusts § 36 (2d ed. 1923); Crane, The Uniform Partnership Act—A Criticism, 28 Harv.L. Rev. 762, 769–74 (1915); Jensen, Is a Partnership Under the Uniform Partnership Act an Aggregate or an Entity?, 16 Vand.L.Rev. 377 (1963).

[79] "The language of the Act reminds us of . . . some political platforms. There is some language which will please those who approve the ag-gregate theory. There is other language which will please those who approve the entity theory." Warren, op. cit. supra n. 78 at 300.

[80] U.P.A. § 15. Cf. Sec. 3(f) below.

[81] Accord, U.P.A. § 40(b).

[82] Secs. 57(b), 59, 60 below.

[83] U.P.A. §§ 8, 10, Secs. 38, 50A below.

[84] U.P.A. § 26.

[85] U.P.A. § 27.

[86] U.P.A. § 28. If this happens, he may invoke the exemption laws to the extent relevant.

[87] See Secs. 37(a), 40–45 below.

[88] Thus he may possess the property only for partnership purposes. His individual creditors cannot seize it, nor can he claim homestead or exemption in it against partnership creditors. At death, his rights in it vest in the surviving partners, not in his estate. His right in it is not subject to dower or widow's allowances. U.P.A. § 25, Secs. 40–45 below.

This feature is reinforced by the rules, noted in the preceding paragraph, concerning exemptions and creditors' rights.

(3) *Responsibility.* It is the partnership (not the partners) which the Act holds initially responsible for the acts of the partners as agents [90] as well as for their admissions, knowledge or notice, wrongful acts, and breaches of trust.[91]

(4) *Internal Financial Relations.* In harmony with Lindley's description of the mercantile view quoted in (b) above, the Act contemplates primary financial relations of each partner with the firm, rather than of one partner with all the others. His contributions and advances are made to the firm and are returnable by it; [92] the firm indemnifies him for expenditures in its behalf.[93] Books are kept for the firm [94] and it is the firm to which each partner is accountable as a fiduciary.[95] When an accounting is made, it is for the partnership's affairs.[96]

(5) *Continuity.* The U.P.A. recognizes the continuity of a partnership in many instances when the aggregate theory would not, e.g., despite an accounting [97] or assignment of a partner's interest.[98] Many other events which would probably cause ipso facto dissolution according to an aggregate theory are merely bases for a court to decree dissolution.[99] And, even after dissolution, functional continuity of the business enterprise is accepted in certain cases.[1]

Apart from these specific entity examples, there is the general definition of "person" to include "partnership," [2] and the provision for supplementation of the Act by the law merchant,[3] which is traditionally associated with the entity view.

Courts have generally accepted the entity-based specifics of the U.P.A. And some have recognized in other contexts that the Act tips the balance toward entity theory.[4] Others have ignored this change of atmosphere wrought by the Act. It deserves to be recogniz-

89. U.P.A. §§ 40(h), (i), 36(4), Secs. 90, 91 (b) below.

90. U.P.A. § 9. See also id. §§ 33–35.

91. U.P.A. §§ 9–14.

92. U.P.A. § 18(a), 38(1), Sec. 65(a) below.

93. U.P.A. § 18(b), Sec. 65(b) below.

94. U.P.A. § 19, Sec. 66 below.

95. U.P.A. § 21, Sec. 68 below.

96. U.P.A. § 22, Sec. 72 below.

97. U.P.A. §§ 21–22, Secs. 68, 72 below.

98. U.P.A. § 27, Secs. 42(b), 78(e) below.

99. U.P.A. § 32, Sec. 78 below.

1. E. g., U.P.A. §§ 30, 38(2) (b), 41.

2. U.P.A. § 2.

3. U.P.A. § 5.

4. McElhinney v. Belsky, n. 55 above; X-L Liquors v. Taylor, 17 N.J. 444, 111 A.2d 753 (1955).

Darby v. Philadelphia Transp. Co., 73 F. Supp. 522 (E.D.Pa.1947): "It is submitted that the changing legal concept of a partnership from that which obtained under the common law, to that as the Uniform Partnership Act defines it, and as defined in the Pennsylvania Rules of Civil Procedure, gives warrant in holding that this concept of a partnership as a jural entity for the purpose of venue, is not

ed as a matter of partnership law, especially where it has been reinforced by authority to sue or be sued in the firm name.[5] But it will always allow other kinds of policies, if more important, to achieve an aggregate result.

One state has modified the Act to state that a partnership is an entity,[6] and others have further tipped the balance toward entity by statutory provisions for continuity despite death and certain other events which dissolve by terms of the original U.P.A.[7]

(f) Relation of Entity Theory and Limited Liability

Probably because of the corporate model, limited liability is often considered an attribute or consequence of entity treatment. As a result, the unlimited liability in partnerships has very likely been a stumbling block to their treatment as entities. There is logic in the view; if the group is totally distinct from its members, it follows that the debts are the group's, not the individuals'.[7A] But this is not the only way to look at the matter. A corporation is widely accepted as an entity, but shareholders are often required to become personally liable on its obligations in order to obtain financing.[8] Any obstacle to entity treatment of the partnership in this respect can be overcome by regarding the partners as having agreed to be liable along with the firm, or as having been made liable by statute.

Historically, it appears that the first recognized group entities were colleges, religious bodies and political units (boroughs and villages).[9] Since these were non-commercial, the entity concept seems to have developed independently of any consideration of limited liability.

---

an invasion of the legislative field, but a proper status to afford it in the ever changing economic process." See also In re Finkelstein's Estate, 40 Misc.2d 910, 245 N.Y.S.2d 225 (Surr.1963).

5. See Secs. 57(b), 59, 60 below.

6. R.R.S. (Neb.) § 67–306(1) (1958): "A partnership is an association of persons organized as a separate entity to carry on a business for profit." Read literally, it creates some uncertainty whether the entity is a prerequisite or a consequence of the existence of a partnership. Id. § 67–304(4) confirms that it is a consequence: "This act shall be interpreted and construed in harmony with the 'entity' theory of partnership." The courts have clearly accepted the two sections as embodying the entity theory. See In re Svoboda & Hannah, 180 Neb. 215, 142 N.W.2d 328 (1966). But see Rasmussen v. Trico Feed Mills, n. 59 above.

7. See Sec. 73 esp. at nn. 4, 10, 11 below; Secs. 77(a), 78A below.

7A. Louisiana, with a strong entity tradition from the civil law, almost reaches this result. Individual recovery from a partner is not permitted while the partnership continues, but only after dissolution. See Trappey v. Lumbermen's Mut. Cas. Co., 229 La. 632, 86 So.2d 515, 517 (1956) and references there; Note, Partnerships—Conflict of Laws—Legal Entity Concept, 27 Tenn.L.Rev. 304 (1960).

8. See Sec. 23B(d) below.

9. See Carr, Early Forms of Corporations, 3 Select Essays in Anglo-American Legal History 161 (1909); Goebel, Cases and Materials on the Development of Legal Institutions 328–88 (1946); 3 Holdsworth, History of English Law 469–90 (1927).

CHAPTER 2

NATURE AND FORMATION OF PARTNERSHIP

Analysis

NATURE AND DEFINITION

§ 4. **The main function of definitions of partnership is to decide
when partnership disadvantages are to be imposed on one who denies
he is a partner.**

The prevailing definition is:

**A partnership is an association of two or more persons to carry
on as co-owners a business for profit. U.P.A. § 6(1).**

Aspects of this definition and related presumptions are considered
below:

(a) **The association element (including intent)—Sec. 5.**

(b) **Two or more persons, having legal capacity—Secs. 6–11.**

(c) **The business element—Sec. 12.**

(d) **The profit element—Sec. 13.**

(e) **The co-ownership element (including profit sharing and joint
    control)—Secs. 14–20.**

The critical elements are profit sharing and joint control; in addition, some sort of intent is relatively essential.

No particular form of capitalization or number of partners is required.

(a) Context

What is a partnership?   There are two kinds of answers to this
fundamental question.   One is in terms of the consequences of the relationship if it is determined to exist.   For example, unless otherwise
agreed with respect to internal matters: partners share profits equally,
and losses in proportion to profits; they are personally liable for part-

nership debts; they have very limited rights in partnership property but equal rights in management and broad authority to bind the firm within the scope of its business; they owe each other high-level fiduciary duties; the relation is dissolved by many different events but the business may continue under certain circumstances. Things of this sort are discussed in Chapters 4–9 of this book.

The other kind of answer is in terms of the prerequisites for the existence of the relation, or its essential elements. Most of the present Chapter is devoted to this phase. Far from a metaphysical exercise, it is a dollars and cents matter for a wide variety of business and financial arrangements, and is the most tormented and heavily litigated area of partnership law.[1] In this context, we can reduce the initial question to: When does a partnership exist?

To put the problem is some perspective, consider the ways in which it may arise. If X and Y sign a paper headed "partnership agreement," there is little doubt that they have formed a partnership.[2] The same is true, subject to problems of proof, if they have verbally agreed to be "partners." But many arrangements between X and Y use other words—landlord-tenant, lender-borrower, backer-inventor, buyer-seller, worker-owner, co-investor—with correspondingly different relationships in the minds of the parties. Some relationships use no status-describing words at all.

Most commonly, the nature of the relationship is raised by a creditor who dealt with X and wants to hold Y liable.[3] It is the familiar search for a solvent defendant. If the creditor succeeds in getting X and Y classified as partners,[3A] he can recover from either (assuming the liability arose in the scope of their partnership); contra if they are found to be landlord and tenant, lender and borrower or in some other relation that does not carry vicarious responsibility. Less frequently, the nature of the relationship is raised by a party to it: X sues Y, claiming profits or property held by Y[4] or reimbursement for expenses or losses incurred by X.[5]

---

1. As a rough indicator, the annotations to U.P.A. §§ 6–7, dealing with these problems, fill 19% of the pages of annotations on the whole U.P.A. in 7 Unif.Laws Ann. (1949), covering cases to that date, and 16% of those in the 1966 Supplement covering 1949–66, far more (in each case) than any other single Section or related pair of Sections of the Act.

2. For the rare instances where there is a serious question whether they have done so, see Sec. 5(a) below.

3. E. g., Minute Maid Corp. v. United Foods, Inc., 291 F.2d 577 (5th Cir. 1961), cert. denied 368 U.S. 928, 82 S.Ct. 364, 7 L.Ed.2d 192 (1961).

3A. The creditor gets essentially the same advantage if he can show that X and Y are agent and principal, and that X acted within the scope of his authority.

4. E. g., Newrath v. Schwartz, 110 U.S. App.D.C. 270, 292 F.2d 763 (1961). See Sec. 16 below.

5. E. g., Penrod v. Smith, 9 Ill.App.2d 257, 132 N.E.2d 675 (1956).

The basic question then narrows to: When is partnership imposed on one who denies it? While attempts to define partnership are seldom phrased in such terms, they should be understood primarily [6] as efforts to answer this hard question. Two illustrative cases are discussed at some length in Sec. 14(g) below.

(b) Definitions

Any number of courts, commentators and legislatures have tried their hands at defining partnership,[7] and some have said it is impossi-

[6]. There are, of course, other contexts in which the existence of a partnership is important. See, e. g., Fenton v. State Industrial Accident Comm., 199 Or. 668, 264 P.2d 1037 (1953) (partnership existed and decedent was partner, not employee; hence his family not entitled to workmen's compensation; cf. Sec. 3(c) at n. 59 above); Blumberg v. Palm, 238 Minn. 249, 56 N.W.2d 412 (1953) (P made payments as individual, not as member of partnership, hence entitled to recover because of his minority). But they are comparatively infrequent.

[7]. "Partnership is the relation subsisting between persons carrying on a business in common with a view to profit." Eng. Partnership Act, 1890, 53–54 Vict. c. 39.

"Partnership is a synallagmatic and commutative contract made between two or more persons for the mutual participation in the profits which may accrue from property, credit, skill or industry, furnished in determined proportions by the parties." LSA–C.C. (La.) art. 2801 (1952).

"A partnership is the contract relation subsisting between persons who have combined their property, labor or skill in an enterprise or business as principals for the purpose of joint profit." Bates, Partnership § 1 (1888).

"Partnership . . . is usually defined to be a voluntary contract between two or more competent persons to place their money, effects, labor and skill, or some or all of them, in lawful commerce or business with the understanding that there shall be a communion of the profits thereof between them." Story, Partnership § 2 (3d ed. 1850). Semble, 3 Kent, Commentaries *23.

"Partnership may be tentatively defined as a legal relation, based upon the express or implied agreement of two or more competent persons whereby they unite their property, labor or skill in carrying on some lawful business as principals for their joint benefit." Mechem, Elements of Partnership § 1 (2d ed. 1920).

"The requisites of a partnership are that the parties must have joined together to carry on a trade or adventure for their common benefit, each contributing property or services, and having a community of interest in the profits." Meehan v. Valentine, 145 U.S. 611, 12 S.Ct. 972, 36 L.Ed. 835 (1892). This is probably the most frequently quoted judicial definition. A more elaborate discussion, tied to Meehan v. Valentine, appears in Price v. Middleton & Ravenel, 75 S.C. 105, 55 S.E. 156 (1906), a leading case discussed in Karesh, Partnership Law and the Uniform Partnership Act in South Carolina, 3 S.C.L.Q. 193, 199 ff. (1951).

"A partnership is generally said to be created when persons join together their money, goods, labor or skill for the purpose of carrying on a trade, profession or business, and when there is community of interest in the profits and losses." Commissioner v. Tower, 327 U.S. 280, 286, 66 S.Ct. 532, 535, 90 L.Ed. 670, 164 A.L.R. 1135 (1946).

"A partnership is, in other words, an organization for the production of income to which each partner contributes one or both of the ingredients of income—capital or services." Commissioner v. Culbertson, 337 U.S. 733, 69 S.Ct. 1210, 93 L.Ed. 1659 (1949).

Other judicial definitions are collected 7 Unif.Laws Ann. 22 n. 42 (1949 & Supp.); Words & Phrases, "Partnership" 299–375 (1957).

ble.[8] If their definitional endeavors are not fully convincing, there are several good reasons. One is the tendency (probably inevitable) to use words which in turn require definition. Another is the wide variety of situations which may occur, which have divergent equities and defy tidy classification.[9] Still another is the temptation to describe the familiar partnership relation and impose a test of similarity (however measured) rather than to analyze its essential elements.[10]

The most widely applicable definition and elements are those of U.P.A. §§ 6–7. Section 6(1) is terse: "A partnership is an association of two or more persons to carry on as co-owners a business for profit." The components stated and implied by this language are discussed in succeeding Sections of this Chapter, which also deal with § 7 of the Act creating certain presumptions and non-presumptions, primarily relating to profit sharing. Chapter 3 below considers whether, or to what extent, partnership includes joint venture, limited partnership, business trust, joint stock company and other types of non-corporate organization.

While the U.P.A. definition is positive law in almost all the states,[11] a reader of the cases detects some partiality for the common law versions. It is not extraordinary for a court to ignore the U.P.A. entirely (even when it is in effect) and recite some other definition.[12]

---

8. Malvern Nat. Bank v. Halliday, 195 Iowa 734, 192 N.W. 843 (1923); Blumberg v. Palm, n. 6 above (referring to usual definitions by stating that there is no arbitrary test).

9. "Much learning, both ancient and modern, has gone into the determination of whether those who have pooled their properties and talents in a common endeavor, have thereby constituted themselves 'partners.' Various tests have had their days of primacy, only to be eroded by the scouring action of various unforeseen fact situations. Thus Lord Chief Justice De Grey's famous dictum in Grace v. Smith, 2 W.Bl. 998 (96 Eng.Rep. 587), stressing a sharing of profits as conclusive of the relationship lost its eminence upon consideration of the situation in which profits were shared merely by way of compensation. Other tests have suffered similar compromise. At the present time no test is conclusive, though in modern law the factor of the intent of the parties, gauged by the legal effect of their agreement, bulks large." Barnes v. Barnes, 355 Mich. 458, 94 N.W.2d 829, 831 (1959). See further on Grace v. Smith, Sec. 14(b) below.

10. A comparable difficulty exists in efforts to decide whether an unincorporated organization should be treated as a corporation for certain purposes. See, e. g., Sec. 24 below.

Cf. 1 Lindley, Partnership 1 (Ewell Am. ed. 1881): "To frame a definition of any legal term which shall be both positively and negatively accurate is possible only to those who, having legislative authority, can adapt the law to their own definitions. Other persons have to take the law as they find it; and rarely indeed is it in their power to frame any definition to which exception may not be justly taken. All that they can usefully attempt is to analyze the meanings of the words they use, and to take care not to employ the same word in different senses, where so to do can possibly lead to confusion."

11. Sec. 2, Table D above.

12. E. g., Bard v. Hanson, 159 Neb. 563, 68 N.W.2d 134, 136 (1955): "A partnership is a contract by two or more competent persons to place their money, effects, labor, or skill, or some of them, in a lawful trade or business, and to divide the profit and bear the loss in

Such anachronisms are probably due to inertia and ignorance, of court or counsel, and to research reliance on the legal encyclopedias which are typically oblivious of statutes except as restated in cases. Although the definitions vary both in elements and in emphasis, they are all so general in formulation and application, that one can only speculate whether the results in such cases would have differed if the legally correct definitions had been used.

The following Sections recognize this situation by attempting to correlate the statutory language with some of the common law phraseology still in use.

Two common law elements of partnership seem most important because of their relative objectivity and provability in disputed cases: profit sharing and joint control. Both are implicit in the co-ownership concept of U.P.A. § 6(1).[13] Next most significant would be some sort of intent; this element can be found in the U.P.A. word "association." [14]

The matters treated here are important not only in a law suit over the character of a particular arrangement. They are crucial to the planning of any business or financial relationship—from a lease to an employment contract—if payments are related in any way to profits.

(c) Who Decides?

The role of the judge and jury in determining the existence of a disputed partnership varies according to the type of evidence and the practice of the jurisdiction. In most places, if the only issue is the interpretation of a written agreement,[15] or if the evidence is free from conflict,[16] the matter is one of law and decided by the judge. But this is a comparatively rare case. Usually the terms of the arrangement depend on a partially or wholly unwritten or ambiguous [17] agreement, or on conduct of the parties, and the trier of fact determines what the terms were. Some places the judge decides what is

certain proportions;" citing pre-U.P.A. authority. First Nat. Bank of Brownwood v. Chambers, 398 S.W.2d 313, 316 (Tex.Civ.App.1965) quotes the same definition and cites similar authority, including an encyclopedia.

Rizzo v. Rizzo, 3 Ill.2d 291, 120 N.E.2d 546, 551 (1954) cites U.P.A. § 6 but states a different, pre-U.P.A. version: "The requisites of partnership are that the parties must have joined together to carry on a trade or venture for their common benefit, each contributing property or services, and having a community of interest in the profits." See also Cullingworth v. Pollard, 201 Va. 498, 111 S.E.2d 810, 815 (1960) quoting U.P.A. and proceeding to an encyclopedia definition.

13. Sec. 14(a), (b), (d) below.

14. Sec. 5(a) below.

15. Grosshans & Petersen, Inc. v. Givens, 191 Kan. 650, 383 P.2d 959 (1963).

16. Woodson v. Gilmer, 205 Va. 487, 137 S.E.2d 891 (1964).

17. For an example of an incoherent written agreement, see Fenton v. Industrial Accident Com'n, n. 6 above.

the legal consequence of the terms so found;[18] elsewhere the issue is decided by the trier of fact (with proper instructions from the judge if the jury has this role).[19] The burden of proof is on the person asserting the existence of the partnership.[20] This appears to mean the burden of persuasion. Conceivably it may be affected by statutory presumptions from profit sharing which seem to be directed to the burden of producing evidence.[21] The determination by the fact trier enjoys the usual irreversibility according to the local criterion, such as no evidence to support it, or the evidence is conclusively against it.[22]

(d) Capitalization; Number of Partners

One thing that is significantly not a requirement for partnership is any particular form of capitalization. There is no minimum amount legally necessary to start operations, although business practicalities exert an influence. There is no requirement that the capitalization, if any, be formally stated, as it must be in a corporation.[23] Each part-

---

18. Petition of Williams, 297 F. 696, 702 (1st Cir. 1924); Morgan v. Farrel, 58 Conn. 413, 20 A. 614, 18 Am. St.Rep. 282 (1890); Janney v. Springer, 78 Iowa 617, 43 N.W. 461, 16 Am.St. Rep. 460 (1889); James Bailey Co. v. Darling, 119 Me. 326, 111 A. 410 (1920); Kingsbury v. Tharp, 61 Mich. 216, 28 N.W. 74 (1886); T. R. Foley Co. v. McKinley, 114 Minn. 271, 131 N.W. 316 (1911); Farmers' Ins. Co. v. Ross, 29 Ohio St. 429 (1876); Walker, Mosby & Calvert, Inc., v. Burgess, 153 Va. 779, 151 S.E. 165 (1930).

On the duty of the court to submit a disputed question of the facts of the agreement to the jury with instruction as to what constitutes partnership, see Adamson v. Guild, 177 Mass. 331, 58 N.E. 1081 (1901); T. R. Foley Co. v. McKinley, supra; Mill Factors' Corp. v. Margolies, 210 App.Div. 739, 206 N. Y.S. 434 (1924); and n. 19 below.

19. Berry Refining Co. v. Salemi, 353 F.2d 721 (7th Cir. 1965) (evidence sufficient for jury; directed verdict reversed); Newrath v. Schwartz, 110 U. S.App.D.C. 270, 292 F.2d 763 (1961) (entitled to jury trial on existence and scope of partnership); Mercer v. Vinson, 85 Ariz. 280, 336 P.2d 854 (1959) (sufficient evidence to go to jury); Fyock v. Riales, 251 S.W.2d 102 (Mo. App.1952) (semble; detailed discussion of instructions); First Nat. Bank of Brownwood v. Chambers, 398 S.W. 2d 313 (Tex.Civ.App.1965); Ernst v.

Ernst, 259 Wis. 495, 49 N.W.2d 427 (1951).

On jury instructions, see also Constans v. Ross, 106 Cal.App.2d 381, 235 P.2d 113 (1951) and last par. of n. 18 above.

On the state constitutional right to a jury trial, see Dills v. Delira Corp., 145 Cal.App.2d 124, 302 P.2d 397 (1956) (denied, since partnership actions historically equitable).

20. Anderson v. Evans, 164 Neb. 599, 83 N.W.2d 59 (1957); Zuback v. Bakmaz, 346 Pa. 279, 29 A.2d 473 (1943); Bengston v. Shain, 42 Wash.2d 404, 255 P. 2d 892 (1953); Morris v. Resnick, 268 Wis. 410, 67 N.W.2d 848 (1955).

21. See Sec. 14A(a) below.

22. Nelson v. Seaboard Sur. Co., 269 F. 2d 882 (6th Cir. 1959) (Minn. law); Cyrus v. Cyrus, 242 Minn. 180, 64 N.W. 2d 538, 45 A.L.R.2d 1002 (1954). Cf. Foster v. Till, 6 N.J.Super. 259, 71 A. 2d 146 (1950).

If the standard for reversal is the easier one that the evidence preponderates against the finding, reversal is more common. See Wyatt v. Brown, 39 Tenn.App. 28, 281 S.W.2d 64 (1955); Eder v. Reddick, 46 Wash.2d 41, 278 P.2d 361 (1955).

23. Limited partnerships must, however, list in their certificates the contribution of each limited partner. U. L.P.A. § 2(1) (a) (VI), Sec. 26 below.

ner's capital account is simply credited with the amount of any contribution he makes, or he is shown as a lender (creditor) if that is agreed. There is nothing which must be divided into or expressed as shares other than the agreed shares in profits and losses. One partner may contribute all the capital.[24] This fluidity of capitalization lasts through the life of the firm, so that interests in profits, losses and capital accounts may be freely altered, and assets moved in and out of the firm, by agreement among the partners. In sum, so far as the law is concerned, the partners can start with anything or nothing in the way of capital, and reshuffle at will.

There are no restrictions, either maximum or minimum, on the number of partners. Of course, it takes at least two persons to have a partnership.[25] A limited firm requires at least one general partner and one limited partner.[26] Blue sky laws sometime impose a limit on the maximum number of partners who may join without filing a registration, but no absolute limit. In England, by contrast, partnerships appear to be effectively limited to 20 members (10 if in the business of banking).[27]

(e) Special Definitions

Many jurisdictions formerly recognized the doctrine of "partnership as to third persons" for imposing liability on persons associated with a business, e.g., where the courts were convinced that persons sharing profits ought to share losses even though not co-proprietors.[28] The U.P.A. abolishes the doctrine, save in cases of estoppel from holding out,[29] by providing that "persons who are not partners as to each other are not partners as to third persons."[30] This is an attempt to apply a uniform test, whether the dispute is among the alleged partners or with an outsider. However, the old double standard persists to a degree in the rule of some courts that more evidence is required to establish partnership inter se than is necessary to show partnership as to third persons.[31]

24. See Sec. 12 at n. 55 below.

25. U.P.A. § 6(1).

26. U.L.P.A. § 1.

27. Companies Act, 1948, 11–12 Geo. 6, c. 38, §§ 429, 434(1); Lindley, Partnership 104–05 (12th ed. 1962).

28. See Sec. 14(b) below.

29. U.P.A. § 16, Sec. 36 below.

30. U.P.A. § 7(1).

31. *Pre-U.P.A.* Chisholm v. Cowles, 42 Ala. 179 (1868); Carlson v. Peterson, 130 Neb. 806, 266 N.W. 608 (1936). One claiming to be a partner should be in possession of all relevant evidence, and so may properly be required to prove the allegation more convincingly than a third person. McGregor v. Cleveland, 5 Wend. 475, 477 (N.Y.1836); Robinson v. Green's Adm'r, 5 Har. 115 (Del.1848). It has been said that partnership inter se is commonly held to exist only where actual intent to be partners is present. Rosenblum v. Springfield Produce Brokerage Co., 243 Mass. 111, 116, 137 N.E. 357, 360 (1922).

Under U.P.A. Eder v. Reddick, n. 22 above (stronger evidence necessary inter se); Cyrus v. Cyrus, n. 22 above (different indicium may be important in third person and inter se cases);

A limited partnership [32] is defined as "a partnership formed by two or more persons under the provisions of [U.L.P.A.] Section 2, having as members one or more general partners and one or more limited partners." [33] The reference to Section 2—which requires the filing of a specific certificate—eliminates most controversies about the existence of limited partnerships. But they are recognized in certain cases despite failure to comply with the statutory formalities.[34] Here, however, it is usually the defendant asserting the existence of the limited firm as a bar to personal liability, and the criteria are quite different from those in a controversy about the existence of a general partnership.

The definition of partnership for federal income tax purposes is "a syndicate, group, pool, joint venture or other unincorporated organization through or by means of which any business, financial operation or venture is carried on." [35] It is considerably broader than the U.P.A. concept.[36]

THE ASSOCIATION ELEMENT

§ 5. Partnership is spoken of as a voluntary association based on contract. But the volition or intent need not be specifically to have partnership results; these are imposed if the objective elements discussed later are present. The contract is not a separate requirement but a byproduct of other partnership elements.

The whole arrangement can be extremely informal, and inferred from conduct if not expressed in written or spoken words. A written agreement is, of course, advisable to plan for contingencies and minimize disputes.

Delectus personae exists in partnership.

(a) Volition and Intent

The first element in the U.P.A. definition of partnership is "association." The word connotes two or more persons.[37] It also

---

Mercer v. Vinson, n. 19 above (as to third persons, relation determined from facts rather than from conclusions of parties as to nature of their relation); Raymond S. Roberts, Inc. v. White, 117 Vt. 573, 97 A.2d 245 (1953) (inter se, intent paramount).

32. See generally Sec. 26 below.

33. U.L.P.A. § 1.

34. Sec. 32 below.

35. Int.Rev.Code of 1954, §§ 761(a), 7701 (a)(2) (26 U.S.C.A.).

36. See Sullivan, Conflicts Between State Partnership Laws and the Internal Revenue Code, 15 Tax L.Rev. 105 (1959). See also Sec. 23A below. Some organizations which are partnerships

under local law may be treated as "associations," hence corporations, for tax law; see Sec. 24 and, more generally, Ch. 3 below.

37. See Sec. 6 below. Cf. State v. Ritholtz, 257 Minn. 201, 100 N.W.2d 722 (1960) (foreign partnership, as a result of U.P.A. § 6(1), is subject to service of process on Secretary of State under statute referring to "any union or other groups or associations having . . . members or property without the state"). But cf. In re Grossmayer, 177 U.S. 48, 20 S.Ct. 535, 44 L.Ed. 665 (1900) (foreign partnership not subject to service under provision for associations when adjacent provision dealt with partnerships). See Sec. 13 n. 82 below. As these examples indicate, "association" is used

connotes voluntariness,[38] which in turn implies (or is equivalent to) intent. Persons may become co-owners of property without voluntary act of their own, as by inheritance, but they do not become partners merely by the act of someone else.[39] The courts frequently emphasize that intent is necessary to become a partner.[40] Since the defendant in a partnership-existence case typically testifies that he had no intent of becoming a partner, and probably feels (if he loses) a victim of involuntary servitude, the stress on volition looks contrived.

But the requisite intent need not be focussed on the status of partnership or expressed in its terminology.[41] The question is whether the parties intend a relationship that includes the essential elements of partnership (profit sharing, joint control or whatever they turn out to be). If the parties use partnership language, that is

different ways in different contexts. The U.P.A. sense seems to be no more particularized than a coming together. The word has a very different meaning in federal income tax law. See Secs. 24, 34A below.

38. "In the domain of private law the term association necessarily involves the idea that the association is voluntary." Commissioners' Note to U. P.A. § 6, 7 Unif.Laws Ann. 12 (1949), explaining why voluntariness was not specified in the Act.

39. "It is said there is no such thing as a partnership by implication or operation of law. A partnership can only arise by a voluntary contract of the parties." H. T. Hackney Co. v. Robert E. Lee Hotel, 156 Tenn. 243, 300 S.W. 1 (1927).

Berry v. McCourt, 1 Ohio App.2d 172, 204 N.E.2d 235 (1965): partnership cannot be imposed upon another by donation of property. What the court ignored here in finding the arrangement a trust rather than a partnership, was the acceptance by the donees (sons of the donor) and their operation pursuant to the trust agreement under which he gave.

40. In a tax case dealing with a family partnership, the court saw the crucial question as "whether, considering all the facts—the agreement, the conduct of the parties in execution of its provisions, their statements, the testimony of disinterested persons, the relationship of the parties, their respective abilities and

capital contributions, the actual control of income and the purposes for which it is used, and any other facts throwing light on their true intent— the parties in good faith and acting with a business purpose intended to join together in the present conduct of the enterprise." Commissioner v. Culbertson, 337 U.S. 733, 69 S.Ct. 1210, 93 L.Ed. 1659 (1949). See also London Assur. Corp. v. Drennan, 116 U.S. 461, 6 S.Ct. 442, 29 L.Ed. 688 (1885).

Greene v. Brooks, 235 Cal.App.2d 161, 45 Cal.Rptr. 99 (Dist.Ct.App.1965) (intent ultimate test); Vlamis v. DeWeese, 216 Md. 384, 140 A.2d 665 (1958) (intent revealed by conduct); Zuback v. Bakmaz, 346 Pa. 279, 281, 29 A.2d 473, 474 (1943); Bengston v. Shain, 42 Wash.2d 404, 255 P.2d 892 (1953) (intent ascertained from facts).

"The true, final, satisfactory, conclusive test is . . . What was the real meaning and intention of the parties, as expressed by their contract, whether verbal or written? If they intended to create a partnership, they will be treated as partners inter sese and with respect to third persons; if they did not intend to create that relation, but merely to divide the profits, or to share profits and losses, in a speculation or adventure, they will not be partners inter sese, nor will they be liable as such." Chaffraix v. Lafitte, 30 La. Ann. 631 (1878). See also Sec. 4 n. 9 above.

41. See Raymond S. Roberts, Inc. v. White, 117 Vt. 573, 97 A.2d 245 (1953).

highly persuasive,[42] even though their agreement includes incidents unusual to partnership, such as one associate's assuming all risk of loss [43] or having all management rights.[44] On the other hand, laymen misuse legal terms, and the fact that they call each other partners is not conclusive if the essential elements of partnership are lacking in their relationship.[45] If the elements are present, the

42. See Woodson v. Gilmer, 205 Va. 487, 137 S.E.2d 891 (1964); Kaufman-Brown Potato Co. v. Long, 182 F.2d 594 (9th Cir.1950) (Calif. law).

43. Stafford v. First Nat. Bank, 178 Ark. 997, 13 S.W.2d 21 (1929); Gilpin v. Enderbey, 5 Barn. & Ald. 954, 106 Eng.Rep. 1441 (1822). Such agreements are usually not considered usurious. Gilpin v. Enderbey, supra; Clemens v. Crane, 234 Ill. 215, 84 N.E. 884 (1908); Clift v. Barrow, 108 N.Y. 187, 15 N.E. 327 (1888); Orvis v. Curtiss, 157 N.Y. 657, 52 N.E. 690, 68 Am.St. Rep. 810 (1899). See also Sec. 14(e) n. 40 below.

It is quite common for junior partners in law and other firms to be guaranteed a minimum dollar amount to make up for any shortfall in their percentage share of profits.

44. Commissioner v. Olds, 60 F.2d 252 (6th Cir. 1932), noted 31 Mich.L.Rev. 738, 42 Yale L.J. 265. The sole owner of a business, wishing to train his three daughters in handling money, to divide his property during lifetime, and to reduce taxes, agreed with his daughters to sell each a quarter interest in all he owned, in return for $400,000 notes from each. He was to conduct the business and determine the amount of profits to be distributed. Neither "partnership" nor "partner" appeared in the agreement. The Commissioner attempted to tax the father on the entire income of the business. Held: he was taxable only on one fourth; a partnership had been created.

In re Kennedy's Estate, 321 Pa. 225, 183 A. 798 (1936) grew out of an attempt by decedent's surviving sons, who had been associated with him in business, to impose on his estate the entire burden of losses suffered in the business during several years preceding his death. Their agreement described the relation as partnership. It was peculiar in providing that the title

to the business, the good will and other assets were to be retained by the father, and that the interest of the sons extended only to their share in profits earned during the life of the partnership. Without deciding whether there was a partnership, the court held that the sons, by sharing losses during the life of the arrangement and claiming credit for the losses in their income tax returns, were estopped from obtaining reimbursement from the estate; they voluntarily assumed the losses in the father's lifetime. The court might have found that a partnership existed, despite the unusual feature of complete ownership of capital by one partner.

Greenhouse v. Zempsky, 153 Conn. 501, 218 A.2d 533 (1966).

45. Rosenblum v. Springfield Produce Brokerage Co., 243 Mass. 111, 137 N.E. 357 (1922) ("silent partner" inconclusive; necessary elements, especially community of ownership and control, lacking).

Petition of Williams, 297 F. 696 (1st Cir. 1924) was a bankruptcy proceeding questioning whether a contributor of capital was a partner or merely a creditor. The agreement provided that the other parties should have entire legal and equitable ownership of the property of the firm and all powers of management. The contributor was designated a silent and special partner. *Held*, construing the agreement as a whole, he was not a partner. See also Schumacher v. Davis, 1 F.Supp. 959 (S.D.N.Y.1932); Brotherton v. Gilchrist, 144 Mich. 274, 107 N.W. 890, 115 Am.St.Rep. 397 (1906); Whetstone v. Purdue, 107 Or. 86, 213 P. 1014 (1923); Zuback v. Backmaz, n. 40 above (observing that partner is used to describe companions, fellow workers and friends; alleged partner was foreigner with little knowledge of precise meaning); Morris v. Resnick, 268 Wis. 410, 67 N.W.

parties are partners though they have not so described themselves, or even if they have manifested an intent not to be partners.[46] In

2d 848 (1955) ("partner" may have meant merely business associate when used by an elderly woman).

See also Hamilton v. Boyce, 234 Minn. 290, 48 N.W.2d 172 (1951) (no partnership where evidence showed that written partnership agreement was intended by all parties merely to let one act for others while they were away on a trip).

46. "Assuming some written contract between the parties, the question may arise whether it creates a partnership. If it be complete, if it expresses in good faith the full understanding and obligation of the parties, then it is for the court to say whether a partnership exists. It may, however, be a mere sham to hide the real relationship. Then other results follow. In passing upon it, effect is to be given to each provision. Mere words will not blind us to realities. Statements that no partnership is intended are not conclusive. If as a whole a contract contemplates an association of two or more persons to carry on as co-owners a business for profit, a partnership there is. [citing U.P.A. § 6(1).]" Martin v. Peyton, 246 N.Y. 213, 158 N.E. 77 (1927).

"The parties did intend to create exactly the relationship as shown by the contract, but did not intend that relationship to be called that of partnership. However their intention in this respect is immaterial, . . . and if the contract by its terms establishes a partnership between the parties, even the expressed intent that it should not be so classed would be of no avail. It is the intent to do the things which constitute a partnership that usually determines whether or not that relation exists between the parties." Associated Piping & Engineering Co. v. Jones, 17 Cal.App.2d 107, 61 P.2d 536 (1936). See also Meirelles v. Good, 192 Cal.App.2d 40, 13 Cal. Rptr. 215 (Dist.Ct.App.1951) (one agreement denying partnership, another admitting it); Martyn v. Leslie, 137 Cal. App.2d 41, 290 P.2d 58, 69–70 (1955) (agreement denying partnership).

"The declared intention of the parties in the agreement, as to whether they intend to form a partnership is not controlling, for even if the parties deny an intention by their agreement to form a partnership, if what they have done creates the legal relation or status of a partnership, courts will so interpret the agreement, and declare the rights and liabilities of partners to exist." Southern Can Co. of Baltimore v. Sayler, 152 Md. 303, 136 A. 624 (1927).

"If their contract was for a partnership by necessary legal construction (which we have found that it was), and they intended to make the contract (and this appears from the report) the legal effect of their contract could not be varied by their not supposing it to be what it was." Duryea v. Whitcomb, 31 Vt. 395 (1858).

"If parties intend no partnership the courts should give effect to their intent, unless somebody has been deceived by their acting or assuming to act as partners. . . . It is, nevertheless, possible for parties to intend no partnership and yet to form one. If they agree upon an arrangement which is a partnership in fact, it is of no importance that they call it something else, or that they expressly declare that they are not to be partners. The law must declare what is the legal import of their agreements, and names go for nothing when the substance of the arrangement shows them to be inapplicable. But every doubtful case must be resolved in favor of their intent, otherwise we should carry the doctrine of constructive partnership so far as to render it a trap to the unwary. Kent, C. J., in Post v. Kimberly, 9 Johns. (N.Y.) 470, 504." Beecher v. Bush, 45 Mich. 188, 7 N.W. 785, 40 Am.Rep. 465 (1881).

See also Madison Pictures, Inc. v. Pictorial Films, Inc., 6 Misc.2d 302, 151 N.Y.S.2d 95, 109–10 (Sup.Ct.1956). An agreement for foreign distribution of movies described the parties as buyer and seller, and recited that it expressed "the entire agreement between the parties . . . and there are no oral or implied representations, guarantees or conditions not contained" in it. Nonetheless,

borderline cases, such a negative intent is entitled to consideration and may be effective.[47] It is always worth specifying when setting up arrangements which are not intended to be partnerships but which someone may later assert to be partnerships because there is some form of profit sharing.[48]

(b) Contract

Courts and commentators are prone to describe partnership as proceeding from contract.[49] But this is not the same thing as saying that a contract is an essential element of partnership. It is doubtful that one will ever find a partnership which fails to have at least an informal contract, since the latter is virtually assured by the intent already described as necessary and by the consideration which is inherent in profit sharing (shown below to be essential to partnership [50]) and in the provision of funds and services which are essential as a business matter. In short, contract is a byproduct of the elements essential for partnership, but nothing is gained by postulating it as a separate element.

The courts which mention a contract requirement almost always leave it as a general proposition and spend their energy on the manifestation of intent.

Certainly, apart from the Statute of Frauds,[51] no written contract is necessary, nor is an oral one. The contract (if any is required)

the court held it to be a joint venture and allowed an accounting.

"While the law has always considered the partnership relation one of contract and intention, it makes determination of the status of the parties from their agreement, and draws their intentions from their acts." Runo v. Rothschild, 219 Mich. 560, 189 N.W. 183 (1922).

47. "[W]here the contract under which the business engagement is made contains the express or implied disavowal of an intention to assume the partnership relation, no partnership will be found to exist, unless such declaration is so at variance and so inconsistent with their engagement as to be irreconcilable. If the actual engagements are incompatible with the expression of intention, the latter must yield to the former; but where they can be reconciled the latter must govern." Canton Bridge Co. v. City of Eaton Rapids, 107 Mich. 613, 65 N.W. 761 (1895). See also London Assur. Corp. v. Drennen, 116 U.S. 461, 6 S.Ct. 442, 29 L.Ed. 688 (1885); Phillips v. Phillips, 49 Ill. 437 (1863);

W. F. Bleck & Co. v. Soeffing, 241 Ill.App. 40 (1926); Crawford v. Cotter, 257 N.W. 356 (Iowa 1934); Kingsley Clothing Mfg. Co. v. Jacobs, 344 Pa. 551, 26 A.2d 315 (1942); cases in n. 46 above.

Anderson v. Walker, 256 Iowa 1324, 131 N.W.2d 524 (1964): the parties' written agreement that they are not partners is a significant factor and strong evidence, but not conclusive.

48. Martin v. Peyton, n. 46 above, is the classic demonstration of this.

49. See, e. g., Claude v. Claude, 191 Or. 308, 228 P.2d 776 (1951); Zuback v. Bakmaz, n. 40 above; Eder v. Reddick, 46 Wash.2d 41, 278 P.2d 361 (1955).

50. See, e. g., Sec. 14(b) below. Restatement, Contracts § 19 requires for an informal contract, in addition to manifestation of assent and consideration, capacity (see Secs. 7–11 below) and legality (see Sec. 21 below), which are also necessary in partnership.

51. See Secs. 23, 39 below.

may be inferred, along with intent, from the actions of the persons involved.[52] The U.P.A. draftsmen pointedly omitted contract from § 6 as "unnecessary," although it is not clear whether they thought it was implicit or irrelevant.[53]

A sketchy contract or agreement is obviously an invitation to trouble, not only over the existence of the relationship but over its crucial terms, such as profit and loss shares, scope and duration of business, financing, allocation of rights and responsibilities, and disposition of the business on death, retirement and other events. When a lawyer is called on to prepare a partnership agreement, as all too often he is not, he must explore these and other matters thoroughly with the parties to find their wishes, and help formulate them if necessary. A sample of a comprehensive partnership agreement appears in Appendix V; it will give a better idea of what partnership is like than much abstract discussion of legal principles.

The agreement, whatever its form, is the heart of the partnership. One of the salient characteristics of partnership law is the extent to which partners may write their own ticket. Relations among them are governed by common law and statute, but almost invariably can be overridden by the parties themselves. As one court has long put it, the agreement is the law of the partnership.[54] And most of this law is made and administered outside the legislative and judicial systems. Its importance is enormous, but it can be understood only against a background of what happens in the absence of agreement.

(c) Delectus Personae

The intent necessary to form a partnership, as construed in (a) above, must be that of each of the parties involved. X cannot become Y's partner without Y's so intending any more than he can without intending it himself. This proposition reflects the purposeful and reciprocal character of the relation. It recognizes that partners have significant powers to impose liability on each other as well as to guide their common enterprise. It usually goes by the Latin label *delectus personae* (choice of the person) and has been codified in U.P.A. § 18(g): "No person can become a member of a partnership without the consent of all the partners."

---

52. Cf. Restatement, Second, Agency §§ 1, 15, 26 (principal's manifestation of consent to agency).

53. "To say that the association must be created by contract, is not only unnecessary, but in view of the varied use of the word 'contract' in our law, if the word is used an explanation would have to be made as to whether the contract could be implied, and if so, whether it could be implied in law or only implied as a fact. By merely saying that it is an association these difficulties are avoided." Commissioners' Note to U.P.A. § 6, 7 Unif. Laws Ann. 12 (1949).

54. O'Donnell v. McLoughlin, 386 Pa. 187, 125 A.2d 370 (1956); Slemmer's Appeal, 58 Pa. 168, 176 (1868).

Delectus personae operates mainly to keep out of an existing partnership someone who receives an interest in the firm by assignment [55] or inheritance.[56] However, the necessary consent of other persons may be given or waived by conduct.[57] Or they may give it in advance by their agreement, say by providing for freely transferable interests.[58] Or they may delegate to some of their number (say a managing partner) the authority to consent for all.

Thus *delectus personae,* representing one's right to be particular who his partners are, is an abstract characteristic of the partnership relation which may be watered down in practice. As an analytical tool in deciding whether a given arrangement is a partnership, it only restates the need for appropriate intent by all alleged members.

PERSONS WHO MAY BECOME PARTNERS

§ 6. A partnership is an association of two or more persons, as amplified by U.P.A. § 6.

"Person" includes individuals, partnerships, corporations, and other associations. U.P.A. § 2.

A person must have legal capacity to enter the partnership relation. Incapacity may exist to some extent for—

(a) Minors—Sec. 7.

(b) Married women—Sec. 8.

(c) Trustees—Sec. 8A.

(d) Corporations—Sec. 9.

(e) Insane or incompetent persons—Sec. 10.

(f) Enemy aliens—Sec. 11.

Members of partnerships are usually individual human beings. Some human beings, such as minors, married women, incompetents and enemy aliens, may be subject to certain incapacities which affect their legal ability to contract or become partners. The partnership aspects are considered in the following Sections.

The U.P.A. draftsmen took pains not to limit partners to human beings. They included the phrase "of two or more persons" in the basic definition of partnership in U.P.A. § 6(1) for no other reason than as a cross reference to the broad definition of "person" in § 2 to include partnerships, corporations and other associations as well as individuals.[59] This settles the matter so far as partnership law is con-

---

55. Sec. 42(b) below. An outsider who buys a partner's interest is only an assignee unless the partners consent to admit him.

56. See Sec. 90A(d) below.

57. Polikoff v. Levy, 55 Ill.App.2d 229, 204 N.E.2d 807 (1965), cert. denied 382 U.S. 903, 86 S.Ct. 237, 15 L.Ed.2d 156 (1965).

58. This is characteristic of joint stock companies, Sec. 34 below. So-called mining partnerships, Sec. 27 below, are regarded as having interests freely transferable.

59. Commissioners' Note to U.P.A. § 6, 7 Unif.Laws Ann. 11 (1949).

cerned.[60] But other organizations, notably corporations, may be governed by laws which affect their ability to be partners. See Sec. 9 below.

The Act provides generally for dissolution of partnerships by court order when a partner becomes "incapable" of performing his part of the partnership agreement.[61] Although it is uncertain whether this refers to physical incapacity or legal or both, it gives some basis for arguing that a firm with an incapacitated partner validly exists until dissolved by court decree or, if earlier, by action of the parties.[62]

PERSONS WHO MAY BECOME PARTNERS—MINORS

§ 7. **A minor's contract of partnership, like his other contracts, is voidable by him. He may repudiate personal liabilities to creditors and to co-partners. But his investment in the business is subject to claims of creditors and, in most jurisdictions, to claims of co-partners who have not dealt with him fraudulently.**

A minor's contract of partnership is voidable like his other contracts.[63] He may repudiate personal liability to partnership creditors.[64] Among the partners, the minor's capital contribution is re-

60. A partnership's capacity to be a partner was previously recognized. Riddle v. Whitehill, 135 U.S. 621, 10 S. Ct. 924, 34 L.Ed. 282 (1890); Stem v. Warren, 227 N.Y. 538, 125 N.E. 811 (1920) (joint venture); Houston v. McCrory, 140 Okl. 21, 282 P. 149 (1929); Canfield v. Johnson, 144 Pa. 61, 22 A. 974 (1891); McEvoy v. Grant, 302 Pa. 539, 153 A. 763 (1931) (joint venture); Village of Westby v. Bekkedal, 172 Wis. 114, 178 N.W. 451 (1920).

61. U.P.A. § 32(1) (a), (b), Sec. 78(b) below.

62. But cf. U.P.A. § 31(3), Sec. 76 below (dissolution by event which makes it unlawful for members to carry on business in partnership).

63. Gibbs v. Merrill, 3 Taunt. 307, 128 Eng.Rep. 122 (1810); Kelly v. Halox, 256 Mass. 5, 152 N.E. 236 (1926).

The contract of partnership is not voidable by the adult partner. Until the infant repudiates, he may exercise the usual management powers. Latrobe v. Dietrich, 114 Md. 8, 78 A. 983 (1910); Parker v. Oakley, 57 S.W. 426 (Tenn.Ch.App.1900). See Notes, 11 Colum.L.Rev. 468 (1911), 40 Harv.L. Rev. 472 (1927), 33 Yale L.J. 558 (1924).

See generally Williston, Contracts § 229 (3d ed. 1959); Annot., Law of infant's

contract as applied to contract of or by partnership, 58 A.L.R. 1366 (1929).

64. Todd v. Clapp, 118 Mass. 495 (1875); Folds v. Allardt, 35 Minn. 488, 29 N.W. 201 (1886); Olson v. Veum, 197 Wis. 342, 222 N.W. 233 (1928). A repudiation by the infant of his personal liability is to be distinguished from a repudiation by the partnership. In Kuehl v. Means, 206 Iowa 539, 218 N.W. 907, 58 A.L.R. 1359 (1928) three infants entered into a contract of partnership for the sale of automobiles. An automobile was purchased and partly paid for. Later the partners attempted to disaffirm the sale. A statute provided that: "No contract can be thus disaffirmed in cases where, on account of the minor's own misrepresentations as to his majority, or from his having engaged in business as an adult, the other party had good reason to believe him capable of contracting." When the sale was made, no one dealing with the partnership in the transaction knew of the infancy of the members. The court held that the sale could not be disaffirmed. "The contract of partnership with Friar was valid under the statute until disaffirmed. The Liberty Sales Company therefore was a legal entity on November 29, 1917, and it was competent to enter into the con-

coverable by him, according to some authorities, without deduction for losses incurred in the partnership business; [65] these courts desire to go the full way in protecting him from a disadvantageous transaction. According to others, the partnerships or co-partners are entitled to a lien on his interest for the firm's losses or debts,[66] unless he has been induced by fraud to enter the firm, in which event he is entitled to full restitution from the fraudulent partners.[67] The partnership status, as an executed transaction, is recognized as regards third persons, whose expectations of rights against joint property are a foundation of superior equities; the minor is precluded from getting back his contribution until creditors of the firm are satisfied.[68]

A minor who repudiates is not liable to his co-partner for promised but unpaid capital contributions, although he is accountable for his management of the business and any withdrawals he has made.[69]

Minors are often made partners with their parents for tax savings; see Sec. 23A below. The presence of a minor does not invalidate the partnership in its dealing with third persons; it is regarded as an entity in this respect.[70] Alternatively, third persons are protected

tract with Means. A partnership and its members are not identical. If a partnership has a legal existence, any person may contract with it, even though he be ignorant of its membership. This partnership had a legal existence. Means dealt with it innocently and in good faith. Whereas, under the statute, a minor may disaffirm his own contract, we know of no rule of law or statute which would permit a minor to disaffirm the contract of a legally existing partnership, simply on the ground that he was a member of it."

65. Sparman v. Keim, 83 N.Y. 245 (1880); Thomas v. Banks, 224 Mich. 488, 195 N.W. 94 (1923).

66. Adams v. Beall, 67 Md. 53, 8 A. 664, 1 Am.St.Rep. 379 (1887); Page v. Morse, 128 Mass. 99 (1880); Elm City Lumber Co. v. Haupt, 50 Pa.Super. 489 (1912), semble.

67. Sparman v. Keim, n. 65 above.

An investing partner can have an accounting from infant partners who operate the enterprise, at least where the partnership agreement is found not to be improvident for the infants. Rappaport v. Guidone, 63 N.Y.S.2d 239 (Sup.Ct.1946).

68. Hill v. Bell, 111 Mo. 35, 19 S.W. 959 (1892); Whittemore v. Elliott, 7 Hun 518 (N.Y.1876).

An infant cannot cause a partnership contract with a third person to be rescinded because of his infancy. Latrobe v. Dietrich, n. 63 above.

An infant partner was not allowed to prove in bankruptcy a claim for restoration of his capital contribution. In re W. J. Floyd & Co., 156 F. 206 (D.C.N.C.1907).

An infant who asks for a court-appointed receiver of the firm cannot claim restoration of his capital investment in priority to creditors of the firm. Shirk v. Shultz, 113 Ind. 571, 15 N.E. 12 (1888); Bush v. Linthicum, 59 Md. 344 (1882).

Cf. Blumberg v. Palm, 238 Minn. 249, 56 N.W.2d 412 (1953). The principal issue was whether the payments to third persons were made by a minor individually (the court so found, allowing him to win) or by a partnership to which he belonged (in which case they would not have been repudiatable or recoverable).

69. Sacco v. Schallus, 11 N.J.Super. 197, 78 A.2d 143 (1950), noted 50 Mich.L. Rev. 333 (1951). The adult partner was entitled to dissolution and accounting.

70. See Kuehl v. Means, n. 64 above; Blumberg v. Palm, n. 68 above; Williston, Contracts § 229 (3d ed. 1959).

by regarding the partnership contract as voidable, not void; this leaves the firm intact for transacting business.[71]

PERSONS WHO MAY BECOME PARTNERS—MARRIED WOMEN

§ 8. At common law a married woman had no capacity to become a partner. Her investment in a partnership was, however, subject to the claims of creditors. Modern legislation has in most states given her capacity to be a partner, although in some places she still cannot be a partner of her husband.

At common law, married women, lacking contractual capacity generally, could not become partners.[72] But a married woman having capacity to transfer personal property could contribute capital to a partnership of which she was an ostensible member. The law recognized the entity of the group carrying on the business sufficiently to enforce business obligations against the group assets, including her share in them.[73]

Modern legislation has removed almost entirely the legal incapacities of married women.[74] In most jurisdictions, they may enter partnerships as members,[75] and even become partners with their husbands.[76] In some places, husband-wife partnerships are not sanc-

---

71. Huffman v. Bates, 348 S.W.2d 363 (Mo.App.1961). Cases are collected, Annot., 58 A.L.R. 1366 (1929). See also cases in n. 68 above.

72. De Graum v. Jones, 23 Fla. 83, 6 So. 925 (1887); Bradstreet v. Baer, 41 Md. 19 (1874); Little v. Hazlett, 197 Pa. 591, 47 A. 855 (1901).

73. O'Neil v. Birmingham Brewing Co., 101 Ala. 383, 13 So. 576 (1893); Little v. Hazlett, n. 72 above. See also Nadel v. Weber Bros. Shoe Co., 70 Fla. 218, 70 So. 20, L.R.A.1916D, 1230 (1915).

74. Statutes are collected, 2 Williston, Contracts §§ 269, 269A (3d ed. 1959).

75. Vail v. Winterstein, 94 Mich. 230, 53 N.W. 932, 18 L.R.A. 515, 34 Am.St. Rep. 334 (1892); Brooks v. Merchants' Nat. Bank, 125 Pa. 394, 17 A. 418 (1889).

F.S.A. (Fla.) § 620.011 was added to the local U.L.P.A. and defines "person" to include "persons owning property and doing business together as husband and wife." Presumably it was intended to authorize husband and wife to form a limited partnership, although the approach is puzzling.

76. Fla. and Mich. statutes in n. 75 above, n. 77 below.

Marcrum v. Smith, 206 Ala. 456, 91 So. 259, 20 A.L.R. 1303 (1921); Hulsman v. Ireland, 205 Cal. 345, 270 P. 948 (1928); Heyman v. Heyman, 210 Ill. 524, 71 N.E. 591 (1904); Hoaglin v. C. M. Henderson & Co., 119 Iowa 720, 94 N.W. 247, 61 L.R.A. 756, 97 Am.St. Rep. 335 (1903); Suau v. Caffe, 122 N.Y. 308, 25 N.E. 488, 9 L.R.A. 593 (1890); Main Cloak & Suit Co. v. Rosenbaum, 42 Ohio App. 12, 181 N.E. 556 (1931); Claude v. Claude, 191 Or. 308, 228 P.2d 776 (1951); Italo-French Produce Co. v. Thomas, 31 Pa.Super. 503 (1906); Northampton Brewery Corp. v. Lande, 138 Pa.Super. 235, 10 A.2d 583 (1940), citing this text; Burwell v. South Carolina Tax Comm., 130 S.C. 199, 126 S.E. 29, 38 A.L.R. 1256 (1924); Raymond S. Roberts, Inc. v. White, 117 Vt. 573, 97 A.2d 245 (1953); Sparks v. Kuss, 195 Wis. 378, 216 N.W. 929 (1927). See Notes 12 Minn.L.Rev. 544 (1928), 13 Iowa L.Rev. 352 (1928), 12 Marq.L.Rev. 240 (1928); Annot., Validity of partnership agreement between husband and wife, 157 A.L.R. 652 (1945).

tioned because the possibility of contention and litigation is considered too inconsistent with the family relation.[77]

If disabilities prevail, wives are exempt from partnership liability,[78] and entitled to recover as creditors any capital contributions they have made.[79] In such jurisdictions, the marriage of a female partner dissolves the firm.[80]

Where permitted, a partnership between spouses, like any other partnership, may be the product of formal agreement[81] or informal arrangement,[82] and results in the same joint or joint and several liability.[83] However, when the issue is one spouse's liability to third parties for acts of the other spouse, the courts (and probably juries too) seem more hesitant to find partnership than if the parties were not married.[84] The reverse is likely to be true if partnership helps

77. Voss v. Sylvester, 203 Mass. 233, 89 N.E. 241 (1909); Haggett v. Hurley, 91 Me. 542, 40 A. 561 (1898) (protecting wife from liability to third persons); Farmers' Co-op. Creamery Co. of Saranac v. Huhn, 241 Mich. 23, 216 N.W. 370 (1927); Board of Trade v. Hayden, 4 Wash. 263, 30 P. 87, 32 P. 224, 16 L.R.A. 530, 31 Am.St.Rep. 919 (1892).

De facto firms are sometimes recognized with incidents of partnership. Tomkovich v. Mistevich, 222 Mich. 425, 192 N.W. 639 (1923) (wife-partner can join in action for trespass to partnership property).

It took the Michigan legislature at least two tries to overcome the case law. Mich.Laws 1941, No. 272 amended the state's U.P.A. § 6(1) by inserting "which may include husband and wife" after "persons." Mich.Comp. Laws § 9846 (1945). Socony-Vacuum Oil Co., Inc. v. Texas Co., 113 F.Supp. 514 (E.D.Mich.1953) construed the amendment to permit spouses to be partners with third persons but not to be the sole partners. Mich.Laws 1957, No. 59 changed § 6(1) (now M.C.L.A. § 449.6(1)) to read: "A partnership is an association of 2 or more persons which may consist of husband and wife, to carry on as co-owners a business for profit; any partnership heretofore established consisting of husband and wife only, formed since Jan. 10, 1942 shall constitute a valid partnership." The 1942 date was when the 1941 amendment became effective.

78. Edgerly v. Equitable Life Assur. Soc., 287 Mass. 238, 191 N.E. 415 (1934); Flint v. Culbertson, 159 Tex. 243, 319 S.W.2d 690 (1958), noted 38 Texas L.Rev. 511 (1960) (joint stock company; partnership analogy). Cf. In re Dixon, 18 F.2d 961 (W.D.Mich. 1926) (no bankruptcy adjudication of wife as member of partnership with husband since she is not indebted as a partner).

79. King v. Matney, 259 S.W.2d 606 (Tex.Civ.App.1953). See Teas v. Kimball, 257 F.2d 817 (5th Cir. 1958) (Tex. law). For a fuller discussion and later statutory developments, see Amsler, The Status of Married Women in the Texas Business Association, 43 Texas L.Rev. 669, 674–78 (1965). See above at n. 73 for the priority most states give outside creditors over the wife.

80. Sec. 76 at n. 96 below.

81. Claude v. Claude, 191 Or. 308, 228 P.2d 776 (1951).

82. Stephens v. Stephens, 213 S.C. 525, 50 S.E.2d 577 (1948) (separated wife entitled to accounting); Raymond S. Roberts, Inc. v. White, 117 Vt. 573, 97 A.2d 245 (1953) (farm partnership on lands held by entirety, joint bank account, both spouses gave full time to farm, vehicles registered in wife's name; wife liable to third person for vehicle repairs).

83. Ibid.

84. See Anderson v. Evans, 164 Neb. 599, 83 N.W.2d 59 (1954) (no husband-wife partnership despite joint ownership of lands, joint bank account and

one spouse against a third person.[85]   When the issue is between the spouses, the wife will probably be favored.[86]

Most husband-wife partnerships which were deliberately organized were almost certainly intended to save federal income taxes.[87] Since 1948, income-splitting of spouses has been permitted by statute,[88] so that partnerships are no longer useful or used for this purpose. The less deliberately organized partnerships are usually asserted and denied in divorce cases.[89]

The Spanish- or French-derived system of community property of husband and wife, in force in eight states,[90] has many partnership features and is grounded in partnership principles.[91]

talking over farm matters); U. S. Lumber Co. v. McDonald, 68 Wash.2d 741, 415 P.2d 77 (1966) (semble, not reaching question whether they could legally be partners); Cooper v. Knox, 197 Va. 602, 90 S.E.2d 844 (1956) (wife handled all funds and books for contracting business, once accepted a job for it, instructed workmen and read blueprints).

Cf. M. Lit Inc. v. Berger, 225 Md. 241, 170 A.2d 303 (1961): H and W ran tavern, possessed liquor license in names of both; held: no partnership, so property owned by entireties could not be reached by charging order (see Sec. 43(b) below) of H's individual creditor. Rushing v. Polk, 258 N.C. 256, 128 S.E.2d 675 (1962): H (car owner) not partner of W who was driving at time of accident and received payment or expense contribution from her car pool operation, But see Raymond S. Roberts, Inc. v. White, n. 82 above.

85. See Nickerson v. Ribicoff, 206 F. Supp. 232 (D.Mass.1962): W of electrical contractor took phone orders, transmitted orders to salesmen, located H in emergency, helped with books and bills; held: W is partner, entitled to Social Security old age benefits based on her share of partnership income as self employment income.

Crane & Bromberg Law of Partnership HB—4

86. See Claude v. Claude, n. 81 above; Stephens v. Stephens, n. 82 above. But see Olson v. Olson, 66 Ill.App.2d 227, 213 N.E.2d 95 (1965) (H not partner in farm owned by W and farmed by him, hence not required to assume half of mortgage on divorce). Cf. Akers v. Stamper, 410 S.W.2d 710 (Ky.1967) (H partner, entitled to half interest in motel and other property in W's name).

87. Cf. Farris v. Farris Engineering Corp., 7 N.J. 487, 81 A.2d 731 (1951) in which a husband persuaded the court that there had been no real partnership with his wife (who was then divorcing him and claiming half the business), only a tax-saving device.

88. Revenue Act of 1948, §§ 103, 301, 62 Stat. 111, 114 (1948); current provision; Int.Rev.Code of 1954, § 2(a) (26 U.S.C.A.) See Sec. 23A below.

89. See Peck v. Peck, 16 Ill.2d 268, 157 N.E.2d 249, 73 A.L.R.2d 723 (1959); Claude v. Claude, n. 81 above; Stephens v. Stephens, n. 82, above.

90. See Sec. 45(c) below.

91. DeFuniak, Principles of Community Property § 95 (1943).

PERSONS WHO MAY BECOME PARTNERS—TRUSTEES

§ 8A. **Earlier prohibitions on trust investments in partnerships have now largely given way to the prudent man rule and respect for the trust creator's investment authorization and direction. It is therefore possible for a trustee to be a partner in most places, under a proper trust instrument. The liability risks of general partnership make it unlikely that trustees will agree to be anything more than limited partners, unless they are already general partners in their individual capacity.**

There would seem to be no question, from the partnership side, whether a trustee can be a partner.[92] He is a person, and that is enough for U.P.A. § 6(1).[93] However, there are questions from the trust side.[94] While it is clear that a partnership interest is something that can be the res of a trust,[95] there are doubts about its propriety as a trust investment. The doubts do not ordinarily affect the validity of either the trust or the partnership, but they may cause the trustee to be surcharged for improper investment, and thus, at a very practical level, determine whether he is willing to become a partner. Even if he is, the co-partners face a problem in that they may be held liable to the beneficiaries or a successor trustee for knowingly participating in a breach of trust if the trustee's investment in the firm is improper.[96]

Earlier conservatism in trust concepts banned investment in common stocks as unduly risky.[97] Add the element of unlimited liability for partnership debts, imposable either directly or indirectly on the trust corpus, and partnership becomes anathema for the trustee.[98] But the evolution of the prudent man rule of trust investment

92. Something of a trust relation arises when a partner assigns his interest. See Sec. 42(b) below.

93. Cf. Henslee v. Whitson, 200 F.2d 538 (6th Cir. 1952) (trustee can be partner for federal income tax purposes).

94. In general, see Rieman, Trust Participation in a Partnership, 2 Hast. L.J. 24 (Spring 1951); Comment, Trust Participation in Partnership Ventures, 3 Stan.L.Rev. 467 (1951); Duane, Liabilities Arising out of Employment of Trust Funds in Partnerships, 39 Am. L.Reg. (N.S.) 569 (1891).

95. Bogert, Trusts and Trustees § 112 at 573–74 (2d ed. 1960). But cf. Hanson v. Birmingham, 92 F.Supp. 33 (N.D.Iowa 1950), appeal dismissed 190 F.2d 206 (8th Cir. 1951), suggesting that a trust estate, as distinct from a trustee, cannot be a partner. Whatever this formalistic notion means, it must be discounted because of its con-

text; the opinion refused to recognize a family partnership as effective for federal income tax purposes.

96. Penn v. Fogler, 182 Ill. 76, 55 N.E. 192 (1899) (banking partnership); Trull v. Trull, 95 Mass. (13 Allen.) 407 (1866) (executor; manufacturing partnership). The measure of liability is the trustee's investment.

97. See generally Bogert, Trusts and Trustees § 679 (2d ed. 1960).

98. In re Bannin, 142 App.Div. 436, 127 N.Y.S. 92 (1911) (dry goods commission partnership) and cases in n. 96 above. See Kinmonth v. Brigham, 87 Mass. (5 Allen) 270, 279 (1862); dictum: court would not sanction investment as a *special* (limited) partner in trading firm; the only question before the court was allocation of the investment return (which was highly profitable) between principal and income.

brought with it some willingness to let trustees be partners, at least where liability was effectively limited.[99] This has been reinforced by the widely accepted view that the creator of the trust may authorize or direct any kind of investment he wants,[1] a proposition broad enough to cover general partnerships under a suitable trust instrument.[2]

Even where it is clear that a trustee may be a partner and invest in a partnership, the exposure to a partner's liability acts as a deterrent. At least one state has legislated an exemption from such liability.[3] Without exemption, most corporate trustees [3A] (banks and trust companies) will not accept the liability risk, to themselves and perhaps to their other trusts, in becoming general partners. If the trustee is only a limited partner, this concern is assuaged, and ordinary partnerships are sometimes converted to limited partnerships to facilitate a trusteeship. Where conversion is not possible or desirable, the creator may prefer an individual trustee, particularly a co-partner who is already exposed to personal liability.[4]

99. Kimball v. Whitney, 233 Mass. 321, 123 N.E. 665 (1919) (interest in business trust with possible personal liability minimized by business trust acting only as holding unit for corporate stocks); Rhode Island Hospital Trust Co. v. Copeland, 39 R.I. 193, 98 A. 273 (1916) (preferred share interest in business trust, construed not to have partnership liability; see Sec. 33(e) below).

1. Bogert, Trusts and Trustees § 681 (2d ed. 1960); Restatement, Second, Trusts § 227; Uniform Trustees' Powers Act § 3(c) (3), (5).

2. Glaser v. Glaser, 19 App.Div.2d 354, 243 N.Y.S.2d 348 (1963), aff'd 14 N.Y. 2d 895, 252 N.Y.S.2d 93, 200 N.E.2d 776 (1964) (adequate direction to hold interest in family general partnership).

3. S.C.Code § 8–245 (1962) provides that a bank or trust company acting as a trustee of a partnership interest for minors "shall not be liable as a partner except to the extent of the assets in the trust," notwithstanding the U.P.A. The provision impliedly authorizes such trusteeships, within the narrow confines stated for types of trustees and beneficiaries.

Miss.Code § 5554.5 (Supp.1966, enacted 1962) is ambiguous in several ways. Section 2 authorizes any fiduciary to become a limited partner if authorized by the trust or other governing instrument. Section 3, saying nothing about the instrument, says any person acting in a fiduciary capacity may become a limited partner "provided that such person shall not be liable for the debts of the partnership beyond the amount of assets held by such person in his fiduciary capacity pursuant to the provisions of the trust instrument . . . notwithstanding the occurrence of an act or event which otherwise would have the effect to change the partnership into a general one and render the parties consenting thereto liable accordingly." It is not at all clear from the grammar whether the extra liability protection is being enacted by the legislature or is supposed to arise from the trust or partnership agreement and be a condition for the applicability of the statute. Since the trust and partnership agreements would not ordinarily be effective against third persons seeking to impose the liability, the legislature apparently intended to enact the protection itself. To add to the confusion, the reference is to the old limited partnership law, which was repealed two years later on passage of the U.L.P.A.

3A. For corporate trustees, there is the further question whether they have *corporate* power to become partners. See Sec. 9 below.

4. See Bromberg, Selection of a Trustee—Tax and Other Considerations, 19 Sw.L.J. 523, 531–32 (1965). Another alternative is incorporation of the partnership business.

In any event, trustees are rarely tempted to come into partnerships unless they receive partnership interests from the trust creator.[5] But trust transfers of such interests, during life or by will, are common elements in economic and tax planning for partners and their families.[6]

PERSONS WHO MAY BECOME PARTNERS—CORPORATIONS

§ 9. An older view that it was ultra vires for a corporation to be a partner rested on a policy against excessive delegation of corporate management. But decisions often upheld corporate partnerships by use of estoppel, or by calling them joint ventures. Modern corporate statutes largely support corporate partnerships by doing away with the ultra vires doctrine and, in many instances, by expressly or impliedly empowering corporations to be partners. The U.P.A. accepts a corporation as a partner.

We have already noted the clarity with which partnership law accepts a corporation as a partner.[7] This has only occasionally been influential.[8] The matter has usually been viewed as one of corporation law, and the courts have typically said that it is ultra vires for a corporation to be a partner,[9] unless expressly authorized by charter or statute.[10] This is a product of 19th century antipathy to corporate power and diversification, which has survived no longer than most such restrictions. The rationale is primarily that the authority of partners to manage their joint affairs and bind each other is incompatible with the statutory mandate that a corporation be managed by its board of directors. In short, partnership entails excessive delega-

---

5. See generally Annot., Construction and effect of instrument authorizing or directing trustee or executor to retain investments received under such instrument, 47 A.L.R.2d 187, 228–29 (1956).

6. See Sec. 23A(c) below.

7. Sec. 6 n. 59 above.

8. See Memphis Natural Gas Co. v. Pope, 178 Tenn. 580, 586, 161 S.W.2d 211, 213 (1941), aff'd sub. nom. Memphis Natural Gas Co. v. Beeler, 315 U.S. 649, 62 S.Ct. 857, 86 L.Ed. 1090 (1942). Cf. n. 20 below.

9. Brunswick Timber Co. v. Guy, 52 Ga. App. 617, 184 S.E. 426 (1936); Whittenton Mills v. Upton, 76 Mass. (10 Gray) 582, 71 Am.Dec. 681 (Mass.1858); Franz v. William Barr Dry Goods Co., 132 Mo.App. 8, 111 S.W. 636 (1908); Mallory v. Hananer Oil-Works, 86 Tenn. 598, 8 S.W. 396 (1888).

See generally Armstrong, Can Corporations Be Partners?, 20 Bus.Law. 899 (1965); May a Corporation Be a Partner?, 17 Bus.Law. 514 (1962); Note, The Corporate Partner: An Exercise in Semantics, 35 N.Y.U.L.Rev. 548 (1960); Note, Corporation as a Partner, 1955 Wash.U.L.Q. 76; Annot., Corporation's power to enter into partnership or joint venture, 60 A.L.R.2d 917 (1958).

10. Cases finding adequate authorization are collected, Annot., 60 A.L.R. 2d 917, 920 n. 11 (1958). In particular, California presumes authority unless disproved. Coronet Const. Co. v. Palmer, 194 Cal.App.2d 603, 15 Cal. Rptr. 601 (Dist.Ct.App.1961); Universal Pictures Corp. v. Roy Davidge Film Lab, Inc., 7 Cal.App.2d 366, 45 P.2d 1028 (1935).

If corporate partnerships are permitted by statute (see below at nn. 22–23) the courts recognize them. Sterling Builders, Inc. v. Fuhrman, 80 Nev. 543, 396 P.2d 850 (1964).

tion, perhaps even abdication, of corporate management. On the one hand, the rationale overlooks the extent to which corporations are managed and bound by officers and other agents and employees. On the other hand, it ignores the limitations on a partner's authority imposed by the scope of the business and the power to terminate at any time.[11]

But the bark has been worse than the bite. Probably the majority of judicial denunciations have been dicta or alternatives to holdings on a firmer base.[12] The courts have administered liberal doses of estoppel when one partner tried to welsh on a bad deal with the other or to appropriate a good one,[13] and when a third person reasonably relied.[14] And they have not hesitated to uphold arrangements

---

11. Rowley, The Corporate Partner, 14 Minn.L.Rev. 769 (1930). If the co-partner has no management powers, it seems that a corporation can be a de jure partner. Sturm v. Ulrich, 10 F.2d 9 (8th Cir. 1925) (mining partnership —see Sec. 27 below); Bates v. Coronado Beach Co., 109 Cal. 160, 41 P. 855 (1895) (corporation to have all management powers).

12. E. g., J. Robert Neal, Inc. v. McElveen, 320 S.W.2d 36 (Tex.Civ.App. 1959). Cases are collected and analyzed in Armstrong, Can Corporations Be Partners?, 20 Bus.Law. 899 (1965).

13. Boyd v. American Carbon Black Co., 182 Pa. 206, 37 A. 937 (1897) (corporate partner must account to co-partner); J. P. Barnett Co. v. Ludeau, 171 La. 21, 129 So. 655 (1930) (valid against non-corporate partner); Pfeiffer v. Hemisphere International Corp., 153 So.2d 467 (La.App.1963) (accounting between two corporate partners); Snow Hill Banking & Trust Co. v. D. J. Odom Drug Co., 188 N.C. 672, 125 S.E. 394, 37 A.L.R. 1101 (1924) (corporate partner must apply joint property in its hands to payment of joint debts before taking out its share).

14. Traders Loan & Investment Co. v. Butcher, 74 Ind.App. 548, 129 N.E. 257 (1920); Sterling Builders, Inc. v. Fuhrman, 80 Nev. 543, 396 P.2d 850 (1964); Bank of Catskill v. Gray, 14 Barb. 471 (N.Y.1851). But see Mallory v. Hananer Oil-Works, n. 9 above (partially executed agreement).

The corporate partner has been held liable to third persons on partnership obligations. Breinig v. Sparrow, 39 Ind. App. 455, 80 N.E. 37 (1907); Hayes-

Thomas Grain Co. v. A. F. Wilcox Contracting Co., 144 Ark. 621, 223 S.W. 357 (1920); Cleveland Paper Co. v. Courier Co., 67 Mich. 152, 34 N.W. 556 (1887); Hobart-Lee Tie Co. v. Grodsky, 329 Mo. 706, 46 S.W.2d 859 (1931); Stein v. George B. Spearin, Inc., 120 N.J.Eq. 169, 184 A. 436 (1936); Brown v. Leach, 189 App.Div. 158, 178 N.Y.S. 319 (1919); Equitable Trust Co. v. Central Trust Co., 145 Tenn. 148, 239 S.W. 171 (1922); Burton-Lingo Co. v. Federal Glass & Paint Co., 54 S.W.2d 170 (Tex.Civ.App. 1932); Clinchfield Fuel Co. v. Henderson Iron Works Co., 254 F. 411 (5th Cir. 1918). But see Brunswick Timber Co. v. Guy, n. 9 above (denying liability under Workmen's Compensation Law against alleged corporate partner).

An action at law by a corporation against its partner for debts owed it by the partnership was defeated on the ground of inappropriate remedy (see Sec. 69 below) without any question as to the status of a corporate partner. L. H. Heiselt, Inc. v. Brown, 108 Colo. 562, 120 P.2d 644, 168 A.L. R. 1081 (1941).

The debt of a third person to the partnership can be garnished by a creditor of the corporate partner. Ingram v. Clover Leaf Lumber Co., 331 Mo. 739, 55 S.W.2d 295 (1932).

The corporate partner's claim to recover capital contributions and advances is subordinate in bankruptcy to third party creditors. Wallerstein v. Ervin, 112 F. 124 (3d Cir. 1901).

U.P.A. § 16, Sec. 36 below, should be available against a corporation.

by switching the label from partnership to joint venture.[15] The latter, by virtue of its traditionally narrower purpose,[16] has been within a corporation's power. But there is little if any significant difference between the two forms except this result,[17] and careful draftsmen have written their agreements in joint venture language.

The rationale for the old rule fails, and partnerships are valid, if the corporate partner has all the powers of management.[18] A fortiori this is true if the corporation is the sole general partner in a limited partnership.[19] Conversely, if it is a limited partner, its risks are so circumscribed that no significant delegation has occurred, and the partnership is good.[20]

15. "A partnership being the result of intention based upon contract, the fact that the Memphis Cotton Oil Company as a corporation could not legally make a partnership with Patten is a strong circumstance to indicate that they did not intend to enter into such relation." Millers' Indemnity Underwriters v. Patten, 250 S.W. 154 (Tex. Com.App. 1923).

"The defendant as a corporation in the absence of evidence cannot be presumed to have intended to have made an ultra vires contract. If reasonably possible the contract ought to be construed to have established a lawful relation by the defendant." Rosenblum v. Springfield Produce Brokerage Co., 243 Mass. 111, 137 N.E. 357 (1922).

"It is perhaps true that the agreement at bar would have created a partnership if made by individuals, yet it is strange that, so far as I have found, no such contract to which a corporation was a party has been held invalid on the ground that a partnership was intended. The question, certainly as between the parties, being entirely one of intent, the proper rule seems to me to be that parties should not be presumed to intend to create a partnership by a joint venture, when one is a corporation . . . .. Granting that such an intention could be presumed, but for the incapacity of one of the parties, it would be purely gratuitous to impute that purpose, in the face of the incapacity." Luhrig Collieries Co. v. Interstate Coal & Dock Co., 281 F. 265, 274 (S.D.N.Y.1922) (holding the associates liable inter se on executory contract).

Pigg v. Bridges, 352 S.W.2d 28 (Mo.1961) (tort liability to third person); Wilson v. Carter Oil Co., 46 W.Va. 469, 33 S.E.

249 (1899) (liability to third person on executed contract); Salem-Fairfield Tel. Ass'n v. McMahan, 78 Or. 477, 153 P. 788 (1915); Nolan v. J. & M. Doyle Co., 338 Pa. 398, 13 A.2d 59 (1940); McDaniel v. State Fair of Texas, 286 S.W. 513 (Tex.Civ.App.1926); Wyoming-Indiana Oil & Gas Co. v. Weston, 43 Wyo. 526, 7 P.2d 206, 80 A.L.R. 1037 (1932).

See also n. 10 above for the presumption of charter authority used in some states.

16. See Sec. 35 below.

17. Note, The Corporate Partner: An Exercise in Semantics, 35 N.Y.U.L.Rev. 548 (1960).

18. N. 11 above.

19. Note, 35 N.Y.U.L.Rev. 548, 552–53 (1960).

20. Port Arthur Trust Co. v. Muldrow, 155 Tex. 612, 291 S.W.2d 312, 60 A.L.R. 2d 913 (1956), noted 55 Mich.L.Rev. 588 (1957), 35 Texas L.Rev. 265 (1956), involving a corporate trustee with ample trust powers to administer the partnership interests being transferred to it in trust. The court placed some emphasis on the fact that only the trust assets, and not the corporation's own, would be in the partnership and subject to partnership liabilities. It also put some stress on the use of "person" in U.L.P.A. without qualification of the normal meaning of the word which includes corporation. The reasoning is even stronger where U.P.A. is also in force (as it was not then in Texas) since its § 6(2) makes it applicable to limited partnerships and imports the corporation-including meaning of "person" in U.P.A. § 2.

Legislation in the 20th century has largely eliminated ultra vires as a ground for invalidating a corporate act or transfer.[21] A few states expressly grant corporations power to enter partnerships,[22] and many more have presumably accomplished the same thing by the round-about language of the Model Act which empowers corporations "to purchase . . . or otherwise acquire, own, . . . and otherwise use and deal in and with, shares or others interests in . . . associations, partnerships or individuals." [23] In many of the states whose statutes are silent on the subject, the charter may be written to include a partnership power.[24]

While there seems to be no sufficient reason why an ordinary business corporation should not be a partner or joint venturer in an enterprise conforming to its corporate purposes, banks—because of the public interest in protection of depositors—offer a stronger case for strict enforcement of the ultra vires doctrine, particularly if they enter partnerships whose business is not incident to banking.[25]

PERSONS WHO MAY BECOME PARTNERS—INSANE OR INCOMPETENT PERSONS

§ 10. The contract of an insane or incompetent person to be a partner is voidable. Until voided, the partnership continues, and his right to recover his contribution is probably subordinate to claims of partnership creditors.

Direct authority appears to be lacking of the question whether a mentally ill or incompetent person can become a partner. On general principles, if he is adjudicated incompetent by the applicable local

21. Model Business Corp. Act § 6. Statutes are collected, 1 Model Business Corp. Act Ann. 200–01, 208 (1960).

22. N.R.S. (Nev.) 78.070(8) ("to enter into partnerships, general or limited, or joint ventures, in connection with any lawful activities"); McKinney's N.Y. Bus.Corp.Law § 202(a) (15) ("to be a promoter, partner, member, associate or manager of other business enterprises or ventures").

23. Model Business Corp.Act § 4(g). Statutes are collected, 1 Model Business Corp.Act Ann. 84, 92–93 (1960), Armstrong, op. cit. supra n. 9 at 906 n. 58.

24. This appears to be common practice in Delaware charters.

See also n. 10 above.

25. Merchants' Nat. Bank of Cincinnati v. Wehrmann, 202 U.S. 295, 26 S.Ct. 613, 50 L.Ed. 1036 (1906): national bank cannot be held liable to contribute to payment of debts of partnership in which it acquired shares; no liability by estoppel since third persons are presumed to know of bank's incapacity.

Norris v. Oklahoma State Bank, 159 Okl. 51, 14 P.2d 218, 84 A.L.R. 1424 (1932): bank not liable to share losses from taking over frozen assets of another bank under agreement with claimant bank to pool losses equally. See Note, 46 Harv.L.Rev. 519 (1933). Cf. Snow Hill Banking & Trust Co. v. D. J. Odom Drug Co., n. 13 above.

In Marine Bank v. Ogden, 29 Ill. 248 (1862), one banking corporation was found to be the agent of another, not a partner, which would have been ultra vires.

The statutory relaxation of ultra vires rules has generally not extended to banks and other monied corporations.

standard, and his property is put under the control of a guardian or committee, he lacks both the power to enter binding contracts and the power of disposition.   Otherwise, his contracts and other transactions are, by the better view, not void but voidable by him or his guardian under certain conditions.[26]   Whether the transaction is executory or executed, whether the person dealing with him knows of his condition, and whether the transaction is fair are all relevant considerations.

It has been decided that, on a partner's becoming insane, the firm may be dissolved by court decree on petition of any partner,[27] and the U.P.A. codifies.[28]   The wisdom of this as a flat rule is questioned later,[29] and it probably should be applied only when the incapacitated partner cannot bear his proper share of the burdens of management, or his property ought not to be exposed to the hazards of the business. In these circumstances, it seems clear that dissolution is equally appropriate in the case where the partner was incompetent when the firm was formed.

It should follow that an insane person can at least enter into a voidable agreement of partnership, in which he has the status of partner until steps are taken to nullify the agreement.   The incidents of the status, so long as the firm continues, would be somewhat similar to those of a partner who is a minor.[30]   His share in partnership property should be subject to claims of creditors and of co-partners in the absence of fraud or taking conscious advantage of his condition.   His separate property might be held subject to the claims of partnership creditors who give value and deal with the firm in ignorance of his condition, or it might be regarded as immune.

---

26.   See generally Williston, Contracts §§ 249–57 (3d ed. 1959); Weihofen, Mental Incompetency to Contract or Convey, 39 So.Cal.L.Rev. 211 (1966); Comment, Mental Illness and the Law of Contracts, 57 Mich.L.Rev. 1020 (1959); Note, The Mentally Ill and the Law of Contracts, 29 Temple L.Rev. 380 (1956).   Statutes are collected, Lindman & McIntyre, The Mentally Disabled and the Law 275–90 (1961).

27.   Raymond v. Vaughan, 128 Ill. 256, 21 N.E. 566, 4 L.R.A. 440, 15 Am.St.Rep. 112 (1889); Barclay v. Barrie, 209 N.Y.

40, 102 N.E. 602, 47 L.R.A.,N.S., 839, Ann.Cas.1913D, 1143 (1913).   Dissolution is not ipso facto, Raymond v. Vaughan, supra; Pritchett v. Thomas Plater & Co., 144 Tenn. 406, 232 S.W. 961 (1921).   But see McKleroy v. Musgrove, 203 Ala. 603, 84 So. 280 (1919).

28.   U.P.A. § 32(1) (a), Sec. 78(b) below, referring to "lunatic" and "unsound mind".

29.   Sec. 78(b) below.

30.   Sec. 7 above.

PERSONS WHO MAY BECOME PARTNERS— ENEMY ALIENS

§ 11. For reasons of public policy and domestic protection, partnership cannot be created or continued between residents of countries which are at war with each other.

Aliens can be partners with domestics;[31] international partnerships are common. But war changes things. By general principles, contracts with enemy aliens are illegal and unenforceable in most instances.[32] An agreement to be partners would fall under this rule.

An existing partnership is dissolved by war between the nations of its members.[33]

THE BUSINESS ELEMENT

§ 12. "Business" includes every trade, occupation, or profession. U.P.A. § 2.

Joint tenancy, tenancy in common, tenancy by the entireties, joint property, common property, or part ownership does not of itself establish a partnership, whether such co-owners do or do not share any profits made by the use of the property. U.P.A. § 7(2).

Assuming co-owners share profits, the degree of their activity is the logical test to decide whether they are in business.

(a) Scope and Type

A partnership is "to carry on . . . a business."[34] The first part of the phrase, "to carry on," has no arcane significance.[35] Disputes over the existence of a partnership are rarely resolved by finding that there is no "business," for the term is expansively defined to include "every trade, occupation, or profession."[36] Perhaps the only broad class of cooperative profit-seeking[37] activity not embraced is the relatively passive co-ownership or investment considered in (b) below.

---

31. A few states retain prohibitions on ownership of land or certain other kinds of properties by aliens. See generally Sullivan, Alien Land Laws: A Re-Evaluation, 36 Temple L.Rev. 15 (1962). In such states, if a partnership is regarded as an aggregate, and if prohibited property is involved, an alien might not be a valid partner.

32. Corbin, Contracts § 1517 (1962).

33. Sec. 76 below.

34. U.P.A. § 6(1).

35. It is sometimes used to reinforce the continuity aspect of "business," see n. 39 below, or the joint activity or management aspect which we consider as a part of co-ownership and control in Sec. 14(d) below. For an example, see Dills v. Delira Corp., 145 Cal. App.2d 124, 302 P.2d 397, 402 (1956).

36. U.P.A. § 2. For general definitions of business, see 5 Words & Phrases 971–1018 (1940).

37. See Sec. 13 below for the necessity of a profit objective.

A car pool with riders contributing to expenses was not a business. Hence the husband of the driver was not liable as a partner. Rushing v. Polk, 258 N.C. 256, 128 S.E.2d 675 (1962).

"A business is a series of acts directed in a certain manner toward a definite end" said the U.P.A. draftsmen in their commentary.[38] Following this line of thought, at least one court has refused to find partnership for an isolated transaction.[39] Others have discovered business in any profit-oriented undertaking, or chosen to call it a joint venture and apply partnership law with little or no modification.[40] In view of this trend, which seems sensible, it might be well to clarify the Act, perhaps by inserting "or venture" after business in § 6(1), or by including "venture" in § 2's definition of "business."

A partnership may, of course, conduct more than one business.[41] But, at least by an older view, a "business" is lacking if separate businesses merely pool their earnings. In the famous case of Waugh v. Carver,[42] two competing firms of shipping agents agreed to carry on separately their respective trades in different ports, each at its own expense and risk, and to share profits. The court found that, under their agreement, they were not and did not intend to be partners in fact. But by a doctrine, now discarded,[43] that persons sharing the profits of a business should be responsible to third persons for its obligations, one firm was held liable to third persons for debts of the other. Similarly, no partnership exists between several independent carriers, such as stagecoaches [44] or bus lines,[45] who merely agree to pool earnings. But if connecting lines pool earnings and hold themselves out as providing through transportation, there is a unitary business and a partnership may be found to exist.[46] In U.P.A. terms, the missing element in the earlier cases is not "business" so much as co-ownership.[47]

---

38. Commissioners' Note to U.P.A. § 6, 7 Unif.Laws Ann. 12 (1949); Lewis, The Uniform Partnership Act—A Reply to Mr. Crane's Criticism, 29 Harv.L.Rev. 158, 159 (1915).

39. "Carrying on a business is a well-defined term, and means the conduct of a business for a sustained period for the purposes of livelihood or profit, and not merely the carrying on of some single transaction." Walker, Mosby & Calvert, Inc. v. Burgess, 153 Va. 779, 151 S.E. 165 (1930) (construction of buildings on three lots of land). But the results are probably different if the parties are already co-owners; see below at n. 60.

40. Sec. 35 below. Cf. Sec. 9 above for a somewhat comparable use of the joint venture to accommodate corporations in what would otherwise be partnership.

41. See, e. g., Gohen v. Gravelle, 411 Pa. 520, 192 A.2d 414 (1963).

42. 2 H.Bl. 235, 126 Eng.Rep. 525 (1793). Cf. Rosenblum v. Springfield Produce Brokerage Co., 243 Mass. 111, 137 N.E. 357 (1922) (pooling of two businesses did not constitute partnership).

43. See Sec. 14(b) below.

44. Eastman v. Clark, 53 N.H. 276, 16 Am.Rep. 192 (1872).

45. Southern Ohio Public Service Co. v. Public Utilities Com'n, 115 Ohio St. 405, 154 N.E. 365 (1926).

46. Champion v. Bostwick, 18 Wend. 175, 31 Am.Dec. 376 (N.Y.1837). See Hansen v. Adent, 238 Minn. 540, 57 N.W.2d 681 (1953) (owners of trucking equipment pooled operations as well as profits and losses; all held liable for workmen's compensation to driver killed in accident).

47. Borden v. Ellis, 158 Pa.Super. 259, 44 A.2d 530 (1946). Two newspaper proprietors, wanting certain governmental advertising, agreed

On the other hand, it is not essential to the existence of a partnership that business have actually been carried on. An agreement to carry it on creates the partnership, and partnership remedies are available if the business never comes into operation.[48]

(b) Co-ownership

While co-ownership of a *business* is essential to partnership,[49] co-ownership of *property* used in a business is in most places neither a necessary nor a sufficient condition for partnership.

It would be possible to develop or legislate a system making all co-owners partners. But this would radically alter the present law of co-ownership in matters like alienability and lack of fiduciary duty. And it would make little sense if partnership is regarded in its historical setting as a commercial relationship.[50] The present line between co-ownership and business is thus reasonable, and has been

that one should get the contract and divide net profits with the other. The latter, in suing for his share, claimed partnership to avoid the apparent illegality of the arrangement. Held: no partnership since no co-ownership of a business; rather "each party litigant owned its own business, and the appellant invested nothing in the venture, nor did he contribute any services."

48. The draftsmen consciously chose the infinitive in U.P.A. § 6(1) to express this idea. Commissioners' Note to U.P.A. § 6, 7 Unif.Laws Ann. 11–12 (1949). See Thompson v. McCormick, 149 Colo. 465, 370 P.2d 442 (1962) (partnership formed by partnership agreement reciting that one party "is depositing" certain funds, even though he never did; accounting allowed). See also U.P.A. § 21(1), Sec. 68 n. 84 below (partner accountable as fiduciary for transaction connected with formation, conduct or liquidation of firm); R. C. Gluck & Co. v. Tankel, 24 Misc.2d 841, 199 N.Y.S.2d 12 (1960), aff'd 12 App.Div.2d 339, 211 N.Y.S.2d 602 (1961).

If the agreement contains a condition precedent which never occurs, no partnership is formed. Coens v. Marousis, 275 Pa. 478, 119 A. 549 (1923) (agreement with employee that he would be taken into partnership when earnings repaid initial investment); Rowley v. Rowley, 294 Pa. 535, 144 A. 537 (1928); Root v. Tomberlin, 36 S.W.2d 596 (Tex. Civ.App.1931) (agreement between co-

owners of oil lease to be partners if oil produced); Millers' Indemnity Underwriters v. Patten, 250 S.W. 154 (Tex.Com.App.1923) (agreement with employee that he would be given an interest in the enterprise if it proved to be profitable, which was conditional on possibility of paying for interest out of net profits).

Pre-U.P.A. cases often held that partnership came into being only when business was carried on. Sailors v. Nixon-Jones Printing Co., 20 Ill.App. 509 (1886); Meagher v. Reed, 14 Colo. 335, 24 P. 681, 9 L.R.A. 455 (1890) (agreement to acquire mining leases, then engage in partnership operation); Dow v. State Bank, 88 Minn. 355, 93 N.W. 121 (1903) (agreement, accompanied by deposit of capital contributions, to form firm to engage in business at a definite future date). Cf. Kerrick v. Stevens, 55 Mich. 167, 20 N. W. 888 (1884) (contributing of capital and rendering of services in preparation for intended business were given weight in determining the agreement was one of present partnership).

49. U.P.A. § 6(1), Sec. 14 below. "The fundamental requisite of a partnership is co-ownership of a business." Schuster v. Largman, 308 Pa. 520, 529, 162 A. 305 (1932).

50. Contrast the many co-owners by inheritance whose disputes are often in court. They have typically not entered into voluntary collaboration to make money.

affirmed in U.P.A. § 7(2), quoted in the headnote of this Section. But it is a difficult line to draw in many sets of facts.

It is quite clear that co-ownership—in any of its variations, like joint or entirety tenancy—does not by itself create partnership,[51] even if the co-owners share profits from use of their property.[52] However, it is a factor pointing toward partnership, and a partnership is more likely to be found if there is co-ownership than if the property in question is owned by only one of the parties.[53]

An attenuated form of co-ownership of partnership property is a consequence of the existence of partnership,[54] but not helpful in analyzing whether a partnership exists. Indeed, the objective of one who alleges himself a partner is frequently to establish an ownership interest in property. He need not be a co-owner of property at the outset, or even a contributor of property to the firm.[55] Nor is he pre-

51. U. S. v. Farrington, 244 F.2d 111 (7th Cir. 1957) (Ind. law), noted 1957 U.Ill.L.F. 532 (farmer and farm owner each owned half interest in cattle but were not partners; commission broker selling for farmer held liable, in conversion, to farmer's mortgagee); Shelton v. Gaston, 221 Ark. 583, 254 S.W.2d 679 (1953) (one receiving ¼ interest in cattle for raising them was not a partner, had no authority to sell as such; cause of action for conversion stated against third person through whom he sold); Riteway Carriers, Inc. v. Schue, 248 Minn. 299, 79 N.W.2d 505 (1956) (record co-owners of truck not partners in hiring it out).

52. U.P.A. § 7(2).

53. *Compare* Olson v. Olson, 66 Ill.App. 2d 227, 213 N.E.2d 95 (1965) (no partnership in farm on land owned by wife) *with* Raymond S. Roberts, Inc. v. White, 117 Vt. 573, 97 A.2d 245 (1953) (partnership in farm on land owned by wife and husband as entirety tenants).

See also Vlamis v. DeWeese, 216 Md. 384, 140 A.2d 665 (1958); Davis v. Gilmore, 244 S.W.2d 671 (Tex.Civ. App.1951).

54. U.P.A. § 25, Secs. 40–45 below. See also Sec. 37 below, on whether individually owned property becomes partnership property.

55. Stillwell v. Trutanich, 178 Cal.App. 2d 614, 3 Cal.Rptr. 285 (1960) (joint venture between P (seafood company) and owner and captain of boat to sail to Mexico and buy seafood for re-

sale; P entitled to contribution for losses though owned no assets in venture); Brown v. Fairbanks, 121 Cal. App.2d 432, 263 P.2d 355 (1953) (P helped dig a shaft to develop mining claim owned by D but contributed no capital; partnership established); Watson v. Watson, 231 Ind. 385, 108 N.E.2d 893 (1952) (P labored on farms owned by D but contributed no capital; partnership established); Ruta v. Werner, 1 N.J.Super. 455, 63 A.2d 825 (1948) (P levelled and filled land owned by D but contributed no capital; partnership established); Bengston v. Shain, 42 Wash.2d 404, 255 P.2d 892 (1953) (P worked in tavern owned by D, see Sec. 14(g) below; partnership established). See Kaufman-Brown Potato Co. v. Long, 182 F.2d 594 (9th Cir. 1950) (Calif. law). But see Escoe v. Johnson, 110 Ga.App. 252, 138 S.E.2d 330 (1964) (contribution of services insufficient for partnership).

There may be special instances in which it is sensible to regard capital contribution as essential. See Graziani v. Rohan, 10 App.Div.2d 154, 198 N.Y. S.2d 383 (1960), aff'd 8 N.Y.2d 967, 204 N.Y.S.2d 346, 169 N.E.2d 8 (1960). After V was denied a liquor license because he showed a net worth of only $200, he formed a partnership with R (apparently a man of adequate net worth) and applied in the partnership name. The liquor agency denied the application, finding that there was no true partnership; the agreement required R to make no capital contribution and gave him no interest in firm assets (except profits) on dissolution. The courts sustained, ob-

cluded from showing partnership in an undertaking whose purpose is the acquisition of property.[56]

Logically, the criterion for deciding when co-ownership becomes business is the degree of activity carried on or contemplated.[57] Personal occupancy by co-owners is not a business.[58] The purchase of raw land for enhancement by external forces (city growth, highway extension, inflation) is probably the clearest example of a gain-seeking co-ownership that is not a business; it is only an investment.[59] But development by the co-owners (through grading, subdivision, installation of utilities and streets, or construction of buildings) moves into the business category.[60] Similarly, operation of improved property, as a hotel [61] or rooming house,[62] is plainly a business.[63] The trans-

serving that public policy required liquor license holders to have a real stake in the business.

For loss sharing where one partner makes no contribution, see Sec. 65(a) below.

56. Wooten v. Marshall, 279 F.2d 558 (2d Cir. 1960) (N.Y. law).

The issue seems to arise most frequently in Statute of Frauds cases; see Sec. 23 below.

57. Cf. Martin v. Stone, 332 Mass. 540, 126 N.E.2d 196 (1955) holding voting trustees were not partners. Although the court speaks in terms of no control over the affairs of the corporation whose shares were held, the better basis seems to be that neither holding nor voting stock is a business.

A somewhat comparable problem appears in the tax law. An unincorporated organization may elect not to be treated as a partnership if it is used "for investment purposes only and not for the active conduct of a business." Int.Rev.Code of 1954, § 761(a) (1). See also Income Tax Reg. § 1.761–1(a) (2) (1956).

More broadly, the business-investment distinction is a central one in distinguishing ordinary income from capital gain. See Surrey, Definitional Problems in Capital Gains Taxation, 69 Harv.L.Rev. 985, esp. 989–99 (1956).

58. See Austin v. Thomson, 45 N.H. 113 (1863) (two families occupied house, one paying rent and butcher's bill, the second paying other expenses; they were not co-owners).

59. But see Blair v. Scimone, 26 App. Div.2d 751, 272 N.Y.S.2d 75 (1966) holding what appears to be such an investment a joint venture or partnership. No issue was made whether it constituted a "business."

Purchasing corporate stock or other securities for appreciation will normally be investment rather than business, although the number and frequency of transactions may be great enough to make it a business.

60. See Ditis v. Ahlvin Const. Co., 408 Ill. 416, 97 N.E.2d 244 (1951); Harmon v. Martin, 395 Ill. 595, 71 N.E.2d 74 (1947); Wooten v. Marshall, n. 56 above (employed architects, consulted builders, worked on financing; held: joint venture). Cf. Polikoff v. Levy, 55 Ill.App.2d 229, 204 N.E.2d 807 (1965), certiorari denied 382 U.S. 903, 86 S.Ct. 237, 15 L.Ed.2d 156 (1965) (joint venture to buy land, construct and operate a motel).

61. Berg v. King-Cola, Inc., 227 Cal. App.2d 338, 38 Cal.Rptr. 655 (Dist. Ct.App.1964).

62. Boxill v. Boxill, 201 Misc. 386, 111 N.Y.S. 33 (S.Ct.1952).

63. But see M. Lit, Inc. v. Berger, 225 Md. 241, 170 A.2d 303 (1961) where the court fails to distinguish co-ownership of property from operation of a tavern on it. Since the alleged partners were husband and wife, the decision (no partnership) may be explained in terms of its result: protection of the property, which was owned by entireties, from a charging order (see Sec. 43(b) below) by an individual creditor of the husband.

forming activity need not be carried on by all the parties personally. It suffices if one authorizes another to act for him, or they act through a common agent, or if any of these arrangements is planned though not put into effect.[64]

The acquisition of goods in commercial quantity by persons who intend to divide them in specie may be a business transaction, but has been considered only a co-ownership insufficient to constitute partnership.[65] Similarly, the acquisition of property for individual use by the several owners—such as farmers sharing a stallion for stud purposes [66] or a threshing machine [67]—does not alone make a partnership. Nor does the sharing of expenses in such an arrangement.[68] Merely renting the property to someone else would not seem to be a business if it requires little or no activity on the owners' part. But they probably cross the line into business and partnership if they engage in many such transactions, like providing the stallion for a fee, to numerous breeders outside their group. They almost certainly are in business if they put the thresher to joint productive use by handling the crops of others for a charge.[69] Despite a venerable case to the contrary,[70] it can hardly be doubted that purchase of property for resale in the near future is a business sufficient for partnership, or at least for joint venture.[71] This is particularly true if the property is

64. In re Sternberg's Estate, 10 Ill.App. 2d 258, 134 N.E.2d 663 (1956), noted 45 Ky.L.J. 549 (1957), rev'd on other grounds 10 Ill.2d 328, 140 N.E.2d 125 (1957) (power of attorney from co-owners to one of them to run a farm).

65. Hoare v. Dawes, 1 Dougl. 371 (K.B. 1780); Baldwin v. Burrows, 47 N.Y. 199 (1872).

But see R. C. Gluck & Co. v. Tankel, n. 71 below.

66. Croft v. Bain, 49 Mont. 484, 143 P. 960 (1914); Rocky Mountain Stud Farm Co. v. Lunt, 46 Utah 299, 151 P. 521 (1915).

67. Iliff v. Brazill, 27 Iowa 131, 99 Am. Dec. 645 (1869).

68. U. S. v. Farrington, n. 51 above, n. 72 below.

69. For cases on ships, see Croasdale v. Von Boyneburgk, 195 Pa. 377, 46 A. 6 (1900). Cf. Cambra v. Santos, 233 Mass. 131, 123 N.E. 503 (1919) (jury question whether owners of fishing vessel were in partnership); Carver v. Miller & Houghton, Inc., 121 Misc. 707, 201 N.Y.S. 807 (1923) (stating that co-owners are partners as to earnings). But see Thorndike v. De Wolf, 23

Mass. (6 Pick.) 120 (1828); Post v. Kimberly, 9 Johns. 470 (N.Y.1812) (no partnership).

70. Goell v. Morse, 126 Mass. 480 (1879) (co-owners of horse agreed that neither would sell witthout consent of other, and whoever had possession would bear entire expense of maintenance).

71. R. C. Gluck & Co. v. Tankel, 24 Misc. 2d 841, 199 N.Y.S.2d 12 (Sup.Ct.1960), aff'd 12 App.Div.2d 339, 211 N.Y.S.2d 602 (1961) (purchase of stamps in large lots by two wholesale dealers).

But cf. Grober v. Kahn, 47 N.J. 135, 219 A.2d 601, 607–08 (1966). P brought to D's attention the opportunity to buy the assets of a business at a discount. D did so, furnishing substantial funds, and intending to resell. D assigned P a 25% interest in a group of the assets, upon P's payment of a nominal amount; other interests were assigned to D's family. D retained sole power of disposition. They agreed that P's interest was not to be a lien on the assets, and would become void if the agreement were placed of record. The court found it unnecessary to decide whether there was a joint venture, but expressed doubt, describing the ar-

merchandise or if significant personal activity is contemplated in the resale.

Where co-ownership exists but partnership is not desired, one of the best precautions for the co-owners is to have all transactions reflect their separate interests.[72]

Co-ownership and operation of a mineral property present some special problems which are considered in Sec. 27 below.

THE PROFIT ELEMENT

§ 13. **An organization is not a partnership unless its purpose is to make profit, as an organization, for its members. Non-profit civic, religious, and fraternal groups are excluded, as well as labor unions and trade associations.**

A partnership is an association of two or more persons to carry on as co-owners a "business for profit." [73] Section 12 above considered the meaning of "business." Does "profit" add anything? Business seems to connote a profit objective. The U.P.A. draftsmen thought the profit reference gave emphasis and context.[74]

At any rate, the usual non-profit organizations,[75] such as patriotic or civic societies,[76] religious communities,[77] sports clubs,[78] and bene-

---

rangement as common ownership with no business to be conducted. P, who prevailed on his claim for an accounting of the proceeds, was trying on this appeal to obtain counsel fees from a "fund in court" on the theory that a separate entity had been created and its assets were in court; he had sued in behalf of himself and others similarly situated in the alleged joint venture. The court held against him on this shareholder derivative analogy, viewing the controversy as one simply between P and D.

72. Thus, in U. S. v. Farrington, nn. 51, 68 above, it was significant that cattle sales proceeds were remitted separately to each co-owner, and each was billed separately for his part of grain processing.

73. U.P.A. § 6(1).

74. "Lastly, the definition asserts that the business is for profit. Partnership is a branch of our commercial law; it has developed in connection with a particular business association, and it is, therefore, essential that the operation of the act should be confined to associations organized for profit." Commissioners' Notes to U.P.A. § 6, 7 Unif.Laws Ann. 12 (1949).

75. See Sec. 24 at n. 1 below.

76. Ostrom v. Greene, 161 N.Y. 353, 55 N.E. 919 (1900) (patriotic society to erect a soliders' monument; dispute over ouster of officers); McCabe v. Goodfellow, 133 N.Y. 89, 30 N.E. 728, 17 L.R.A. 204 (1892) (citizens' committee to enforce excise laws); Hale v. Hirsch, 205 App.Div. 308, 199 N.Y.S. 514 (1923) (political party); Cousin v. Taylor, 115 Or. 472, 239 P. 96, 41 A.L.R. 750 (1925) (association to secure reduction of telephone rates); Fennell v. Hauser, 141 Or. 71, 14 P. 2d 998 (1932) (political committee).

Non-profit organizations may, to the extent of their business activities, be held to business consequences. See, e. g., Curtis v. Albion-Brown's Post 590 American Legion of Illinois, 74 Ill.App. 2d 144, 219 N.E.2d 386 (1966) (Legion Post sold liquor at retail; no partnership issue).

77. Teed v. Parsons, 202 Ill. 455, 66 N.E. 1044 (1903). But see Thurmond v. Cedar Spring Baptist Church, 110 Ga. 816, 36 S.E. 221 (1900) (church society).

Queen v. Robson, 16 Q.B.D. 137 (1885) (Y.M.C.A. not partnership within stat-

---

78. See note 78 on page 64.

ficial and fraternal orders [79] are not partnerships. Nor are they joint ventures.[80] The joint maintenance of public service for the benefit of associates is not partnership.[81] By a rather fine line, trade and professional associations [82] and unions [83] are generally not partnerships because they do not generate profits in the associations themselves, although they are intended to achieve economic benefits for their organizational and individual members. Similarly, promoters of a proposed corporation are ordinarily not regarded as partners; this is

ute making embezzlement by partner a crime).

78. Florio v. State, 119 So.2d 305, 80 A.L.R.2d 1117 (Fla.App.1960) (not suable as partnership).

79. Security-First Nat. Bank v. Cooper, 62 Cal.App.2d 653, 145 P.2d 722 (1943) (Elks Lodge members liable, but not as partners, on lease signed by officers); Laycock v. State, 136 Ind. 217, 36 N.E. 137 (1894) (not within embezzlement statute directed at partners); Brown v. Stoerkel, 74 Mich. 269, 41 N.W. 921, 3 L.R.A. 430 (1899) (assumpsit maintainable against officer for an accounting); Lafond v. Deems, 81 N.Y. 507 (1880) (partnership dissolution procedures inapplicable); State v. Sunbeam Rebekah Lodge, 169 Or. 253, 127 P.2d 726 (1942) (no implication from U.P.A. that lodge could hold or convey title, hence devise to it failed and escheated); Ash v. Guie, 97 Pa. 493, 39 Am.Rep. 818 (1881) (lodge members not personally liable as partners for debts incurred by officers).

80. Sappenfield v. Mead, 338 Ill.App. 236, 87 N.E.2d 220 (1949). A group of property owners joined in enforcing a zoning law and collected some damages. One member claimed it was a joint venture and demanded equal distribution of the funds collected. Held: not a joint venture; its purpose was not to carry on a business enterprise for profit.

81. Meinhart v. Draper, 133 Mo.App. 50, 112 S.W. 709 (1908) (telephones); Kittrell v. Angelo, 170 Ark. 982, 983, 282 S.W. 363 (1926) (sewers).

82. Burt v. Lathrop, 52 Mich. 106, 17 N.W. 716 (1883) (association of dentists to resist patent infringement claims); State ex rel. Hadley v. Kansas City Live Stock Exchange, 211 Mo. 181, 109 S.W. 675, 124 Am.St.Rep.

776 (1908); Marshalltown Mut. Plate Glass Ins. Ass'n v. Bendlage, 195 Iowa 1200, 191 N.W. 97, 193 N.W. 448 (1922) (merchants sharing losses from breakage of plate glass; not entitled to sue as partnership in firm name; organized to share losses, not profits; also, not carrying on a joint unitary business); Blair v. Southern Clay Mfg. Co., 173 Tenn. 571, 121 S.W.2d 570 (1938) (association of paving brick contractors not a partnership, hence not ultra vires for a corporate member).

A common name statute may be worded broadly enough to include non-profit associations such as stock exchanges and labor unions. Jardine v. Superior Court, in and for Los Angeles Co., 213 Cal. 301, 2 P.2d 756, 79 A.L.R. 291 (1931); F. R. Patch Mfg. Co. v. Capeless, 79 Vt. 1, 63 A. 938 (1906) (union); McKinney's N.Y.Gen. Associations Law, §§ 12, 13. For the reverse proposition of a partnership suable under a statute aimed at unions, see Sec. 5 n. 37 above.

83. Mooney v. Bartenders Union Local No. 284, 302 P.2d 866 (Cal.Dist.Ct. App.1956) (member not entitled to inspection of union books), rev'd on other grounds 48 Cal.2d 841, 313 P.2d 857, 64 A.L.R.2d 1154 (1957); Deeney v. Hotel & Apartment Clerks Union, 57 Cal.App. 2d 1023, 134 P.2d 328 (1943) (union not suable as partnership); Cahill v. Plumbers, etc. Local 93, 238 Ill.App. 123, 135 (1925) (union not suable as an entity); People v. Herbert, 162 Misc. 817, 295 N.Y.S. 251 (1937) (union not partnership for purpose of immunizing officer from embezzlement guilt). Cf. International Brotherhood of Teamsters, etc. v. Santa Fe Packing Co., 300 P.2d 660 (Okl.1956) (union not suable under statute referring to persons who "associate . . . and transact business for gain or speculation").

because they contemplate profit through the corporation rather than through their personal association.[84] The same is true of corporate stockholders.[85]

On the other hand, partnership may exist in a recreational or entertainment activity if the participants expect to earn profits.[86]

It hardly needs saying that the test is profit or expectation of profit. The fact that an organization loses money does not keep it from being a partnership if it was set up for profit,[87] and the other necessary elements are present.

The sharing of profits is discussed in the next Section.

THE CO-OWNERSHIP ELEMENT

§ 14. Business co-ownership (consisting of profit sharing and joint control components) is necessary for partnership.

Sharing of profits is prima facie evidence of partnership except in certain protected relationships described in Secs. 14A–20 below.

Sharing of control is necessary to partnership, unless there is intent or agreement otherwise. But considerable control may be exercised by a creditor without becoming a partner.

Neither loss sharing nor co-ownership of capital or property in the business is necessary for partnership.

(a) Components of Co-ownership

Of all the essential elements of partnership, co-ownership is the most important. It is co-ownership of the business, as distinct from co-ownership of any particular property used in the business.[88] And it goes under diverse names, of which "community of interest" is probably the most widely used.[89]

Certain factors point directly to co-ownership,[90] such as doing business,[91] or holding licenses,[92] or filing assumed name certificates [93]

---

84. Schuster v. Largman, 308 Pa. 520, 162 A. 305 (1932). On promoters' contracts and liabilities generally, see Henn, Corporations 102–14 (1961); Williston, Contracts § 306 (3d ed. 1959).

85. Cf. Sec. 30 below.

86. Bennett v. Lathrop, 71 Conn. 613, 42 A. 634, 71 Am.St.Rep. 222 (1899) (polo team).

87. Persistent losses may be grounds for dissolution. U.P.A. § 32(1)(e), Sec. 78(d) below.

88. Sec. 12(b) above.

89. See below at n. 6.

90. Typically, they point also to the intent necessary for partnership, Sec. 5(a) above.

91. Anderson v. National Producing Co., 253 F.2d 834 (2d Cir.1958), cert. denied 357 U.S. 906 (1959) (N.Y. law); Wurm v. Metz, 162 Cal.App.2d 262, 327 P.2d 969 (1958); Vlamis v. De-Weese, 216 Md. 384, 140 A.2d 665 (1958).

92. Bengston v. Shain, 42 Wash.2d 404, 255 P.2d 892 (1953), discussed Sec. 14(g) below; Wurm v. Metz, n. 91 above; Sterling Builders, Inc. v. Fuhrman, 80 Nev. 543, 396 P.2d 850 (1964). A license in one party's name was evidence against partnership existence in Cullingworth v. Pollard, 201 Va. 498, 111 S.E.2d 810 (1960), discussed Sec. 14(g) below.

93. Brand v. Elledge, 101 Ariz. 352, 419 P.2d 531 (1966); Sterling Builders, Inc. v. Fuhrman, n. 92 above.

in the joint names of the parties, or keeping books which show a capital account for each of them,[94] or filing federal income tax returns as a partnership.[95]

The search for objective evidence of co-ownership logically leads to a break-up of the concept into two components: profit sharing and control, each of which is vital. Both are characteristic of an agreed partnership.[96] Of the two, profit sharing is the more easily identifiable; it is the tip-off to a third party litigant that he has more than one prospective defendant. It is considered further in (b) below and in Secs. 14A–20. Control, as we shall see in (d) below, is more elusive. Other possible elements of co-ownership are considered in the remaining subsections of this Section, and illustrative cases are given at the end.

(b) Profit Sharing

Profit sharing is the primary attribute of partnership.[96A] It is also a necessary condition for the existence of partnership in a disputed case.[97] For most of the 19th century it was a sufficient one,

---

94. Bengston v. Shain, n. 92 above. Absence of a capital account was evidence against partnership existence in Cullingworth v. Pollard, n. 92 above. Semble, Barnes v. Barnes, 355 Mich. 458, 94 N.W.2d 829 (1959).

95. Guthrie v. Foster, 256 Ky. 753, 76 S.W.2d 927 (1934). For many years the U.S. partnership tax return, Form 1065, has required not only the names and profit-loss shares of each partner for the year, but reconciliations of their individual capital accounts in the firm.

Cf. M. Lit, Inc. v. Berger, 225 Md. 241, 170 A.2d 303 (1961) and Cullingworth v. Pollard, n. 92 above (failure to file partnership tax return was evidence against partnership existence); Clauson v. Dept. of Finance, 377 Ill. 399, 36 N.E.2d 714 (1941) (partnership return signed by one partner was evidence against him); Barnes v. Barnes, n. 94 above (recipient's reporting of income from partnership as wages on his personal tax return was evidence against his claim to be a partner).

96. U.P.A. §§ 18(a), 18(e), 9, Secs. 65(a), 65(d), Ch. 6 below.

96A. It is the one singled out for a statutory presumption. See U.P.A. § 7 (4), Sec. 14A below.

97. Instances of not partnership wholly or partly because of no profit sharing

include: Swofford v. Industrial Accident Comm., 121 Cal.App.2d 400, 263 P.2d 129 (1953); Riteway Carriers, Inc. v. Schue, 248 Minn. 299, 79 N.W. 2d 505 (1956); Jones v. Taylor, 401 S.W.2d 183 (Mo.App.1966); Pruitt v. Fetty, 148 W.Va. 275, 134 S.E.2d 713 (1964). See also Haas v. Hodge, 171 Cal.App.2d 748, 340 P.2d 632 (1959) where this was probably a factor though not mentioned as such.

The statement in the text perhaps needs qualification in one respect. It seems possible to have partnership where the profit sharing is contingent or deferred. Thus one person might not share profits until profits pass a certain level, or might be guaranteed a fixed amount regardless of profits. Or profit sharing might begin only after a certain date. Cf. Greenhouse v. Zempsky, 153 Conn. 501, 218 A.2d 533 (1966) where a partnership was found although equitable considerations barred the relief sought. One party received $7,500 a year and 25% of the profits over $27,500. Apparently profits exceeded this level and were being shared. But see Spier v. Lang, 4 Cal.2d 711, 53 P.2d 138 (1935) (agreement to share profits after payback of initial investment; no presumption of partnership since no showing profits were being paid); In re Mission Farms Dairy, 56 F.2d 346 (9th Cir.1932) (Calif. law) (contingent interest in profits after payback of

on the theory that it is fair for persons who take income from a business to bear its obligations. The first expression of the idea in Anglo-American law was probably a dictum in Grace v. Smith: [98] "Every man who has a share of the profits of a trade ought also to bear his share of the loss. And if anyone takes part of the profit, he takes a part of that fund on which the creditor of the trader relies for his payments."

This dictum was used in Waugh v. Carver [99] to impose liability on persons who were admittedly not partners in fact, but who had agreed to pool earnings of their respective shipping agencies. So arose the doctrine of "partners as to third persons"—liability based solely on profit sharing—which had a following in some of the older American states,[1] although it was circumvented in England by holdings that it did not apply unless profits were shared "as such." [2] It was overruled in Victorian England, perhaps because of the importance of capital and financing in that period, by Cox v. Hickman.[3] The resulting rule, as codified in the U.S., makes profit sharing rebuttably presumptive of partnership,[4] and holds associates liable as partners to

original financing did not create partnership).

98. 2 Wm.Bl. 998, 1000, 96 Eng.Rep. 587, 588 (1775) (refusing new trial after jury found that fixed payment to creditor (alleged partner), though higher than allowed by usury law, was not out of profits). Cf. below at n. 9.

99. 2 H.Bl. 235, 126 Eng.Rep. 525 (1793). The agreement was for sharing of gross receipts from certain kinds of transactions but contained an allowance for expenses that probably made it roughly equivalent to a sharing of net profits. In the agreement, each party disclaimed liability for the other's acts and losses.

1. Brandon & Dreyer v. Conner, 117 Ga. 759, 45 S.E. 371, 63 L.R.A. 260 (1903); Leggett v. Hyde, 58 N.Y. 272, 17 Am.Rep. 244 (1874); Wessels v. Weiss, 166 Pa. 490, 31 A. 247 (1895).

One state has made the distinction statutory: "A joint interest in the partnership property, or joint interest in the profits and losses of the business, shall constitute a partnership as to third persons. A common interest in profits alone shall not." Ga.Code, § 75–102 (1964).

See Note, 16 Minn.L.Rev. 115 (1931).

Most U.S. jurisdictions did not accept Waugh v. Carver. Kinney v. Bank of

Plymouth, 213 Iowa 267, 236 N.W. 31 (1931); Beecher v. Bush, 45 Mich. 188, 7 N.W. 785, 40 Am.Rep. 465 (1881), reviewing the decisions.

2. Salary, commission or other payment could thus safely be made "in proportion to a given quantum of profits." See Mollwo v. Court of Wards, L.R. 4 P.C. 419, 17 Eng.Rep. 495, 503 (1872), describing the distinction as "arbitrary."

3. 8 H.L.Cas. 268, 11 Eng.Rep. 431 (1860), discussed more fully Sec. 15 below. The historical development in England is described at length in 1 Rowley, Partnership 105–18 (2d ed. 1960).

4. U.P.A. § 7(4), quoted in the headnote of Sec. 14A below and discussed in that Section.

Nelson v. Seaboard Surety Co., 269 F.2d 882 (8th Cir.1959) (Minn. law) (profit sharing raises inference of partnership, fact question); Greene v. Brooks, 235 Cal.App.2d 161, 45 Cal. Rptr. 99 (Dist.Ct.App.1965); Fyock v. Riales, 251 S.W.2d 102 (Mo.App.1952); Memphis Nat. Gas Co. v. Pope, 178 Tenn. 580, 161 S.W.2d 211 (1942), aff'd 315 U.S. 649, 62 S.Ct. 857, 86 L.Ed. 1090 (1942); Raymond S. Roberts, Inc. v. White, 117 Vt. 573, 97 A.2d 245 (1953).

third persons only if they are partners inter se.[5] On the workings of the presumption, see Sec. 14A below.

Before the U.P.A.'s codified presumptions and non-presumptions, many courts approached the problem by inquiring if the parties had a "community of interest" in profits,[6] or shared them "as such." [7] The semantics were very slippery, and are not greatly improved by the Act.

It has never been necessary that partners share profits equally; they may agree on any proportion or formula. But there may be a question whether an arrangement is profit sharing at all.[8] A loan repayment program with fixed amounts that may yield more than the legal rate of interest can be profit sharing.[9] One court has squarely (if questionably) found profit sharing where real estate agents cooperated with a builder in finding home buyers; of the fixed price received from each buyer, the agents kept a fixed amount and paid certain expenses (including some materials for the construction), and the builder contracted with the buyer for construction, kept the rest of the buyer's payment and paid other expenses.[10] A complex financing arrangement, in which the lender received (in addition to principal and interest) one half the balance in an account debited and credited according to an agreement, was regarded as profit sharing without any effort to analyze the account.[11] In a family setting, the

---

[5] U.P.A. § 7(1). Martin v. Peyton, 246 N.Y. 213, 158 N.E. 77 (1927): "Much ancient learning as to partnership is obsolete. Today only those who are partners between themselves may be charged for partnership debts by others." But see Sec. 4(e) above. A statutory exception is made for cases of holding out as a partner. U.P.A. § 16, Sec. 36 below.

[6] E. g., Florence v. Fox, 193 Iowa 1174, 188 N.W. 966 (1922). See also Malvern Nat. Bank v. Halliday, 195 Iowa 734, 192 N.W. 843 (1923).

[7] See above at n. 2. The habit persists under U.P.A. See First Nat. Bank of Brownwood v. Chambers, 398 S.W.2d 313 (Tex.Civ.App.1965) (profits not shared "as profits").

[8] Cases in the employee-or-partner context are collected, Annot., 137 A.L. R. 6, 28–33 (1942).

[9] Singleton v. Fuller, 118 Cal.App.2d 733, 259 P.2d 687 (1953). Since repayment was to be from proceeds of sale of financed property, it might be viewed as sharing in gross receipts rather than profits, but the usury

argument took precedence.
Concerning the thin line between interest and profits in the usury context, see n. 98 above, n. 40 below, Sec. 5 n. 43 above.

[10] Constans v. Ross, 106 Cal.App.2d 381, 235 P.2d 113 (1951). Since each had separate categories of expenses, this looks more like sharing of gross. See Sec. 14(c) below. A more convincing basis for the result (the agents were held liable to suppliers of material to the builder) was the partnership intent inferred from the language of their agreement.
Cf. Mercer v. Vinson, 85 Ariz. 280, 336 P.2d 854 (1959).

[11] Minute Maid Corp. v. United Foods, Inc., 291 F.2d 577 (5th Cir. 1961), cert. denied 368 U.S. 928 (1961), noted 40 N. C.L.Rev. 355 (1962). The principal debits were interest and warehousing charges on the commodities financed; the main credits were quantity purchase, storage and promotional allowances from the seller of the commodities.
Cf. Air Technology Corp. v. General Electric Co., 347 Mass. 613, 199 N.E.2d

deposit of business receipts in a joint bank account of husband and wife does not necessarily constitute profit sharing.[12]

(c) Gross Sharing

Partners ordinarily share only profits (after expenses), not gross receipts. The sharing of gross raises no presumption of partnership.[13] This is true whether or not the recipients are co-owners of any property involved. Examples include a salesman receiving a percentage commission on his own sales, a sales manager receiving a percentage of all sales, and a landlord receiving a percentage of his tenant's gross receipts.[14] All these would be safe from partnership presumption even if they were getting a share of profits, since wages or rent are involved.[15] Others who might share gross without becoming partners are a franchiser receiving an override (a percentage of the franchisee's sales), co-owners of property dividing rentals,[16] an insurer charging a premium based on gross receipts of the insured,[17] two sales representatives[18] or brokers[19] splitting commissions, and an author receiving royalties.[20]

The distinction between gross returns and net profits is well founded. One who participates in the latter is subjecting himself to the fortunes of the business to a much greater degree.[21]

(d) Control Sharing

Joint control as well as profit sharing is necessary for partnership. Joint control is integral to co-ownership. The only time control need not be proved by one asserting partnership is the rare case in which he

538 (1964). A corporate member of a "team" preparing a proposal for an Air Force prime contract would not have shared profits in the prime contract but would have enjoyed economic benefits as an expected subcontractor. The court held that there was no partnership or joint venture, but recognized a more limited joint undertaking which gave the proposed subcontractor the benefit of fiduciary duties from the prime contractor.

For a comparable problem in determining losses, see Sec. 14(e) at nn. 43–45 below.

12. Anderson v. Evans, 164 Neb. 599, 83 N.W.2d 59 (1954).

13. U.P.A. § 7(3), quoted in the headnote of this Section.

14. Perkins v. Langdon, 231 N.C. 386, 57 S.E.2d 407 (1950) (tobacco warehouse leased for 30% of lessees' commissions on tobacco sales). The de-

cision rests on a special statute described in Sec. 17 below.

Schleicker v. Krier, 218 Wis. 376, 261 N.W. 413 (1935) (apparently dictum since arrangement was farming on shares, which presumably means sharing net rather than gross).

15. U.P.A. § 7(4) (b), Secs. 14A, 16–17 below.

16. Cf. U.P.A. § 7(2), Sec. 12(b) above on sharing of profits by co-owners.

17. Wiersma v. City of Long Beach, 41 Cal.App.2d 8, 106 P.2d 45 (1941).

18. Moore v. DuBard, 318 Mich. 578, 29 N.W.2d 94 (1947) (accounting between them as partners denied).

19. Powell v. Bundy, 38 Tenn.App. 255, 272 S.W.2d 490 (1954).

20. Steinbeck v. Gerosa, 4 N.Y.2d 302, 175 N.Y.S.2d 1, 151 N.E.2d 170 (1958).

21. Cf. Sec. 14(b) at n. 10 above.

shows profit sharing and his opponent offers no credible evidence against the existence of partnership.[22]

The U.P.A. drafters said of their definition (co-ownership of a business): "This distinguishes a partnership from an agency—an association of principal and agent. . . . Ownership involves the power of ultimate control. To state that partners are co-owners of a business is to state that they each have the power of ultimate control." [23] If the magic phrase is the non-statutory "community of interest" or equivalent, control is an equally significant ingredient.[24]

The inquiry, then, is whether each alleged partner had the control of a co-owner or co-principal in the business.[25] This normally entails an equal right to participate in management. Control appears to have no specialized meaning in this area, but to be used in the everyday sense, colored by the business in question.[26] The matter is complicated by recognition that control may be delegated or relinquished in an agreed partnership. How far does this permit finding partnership in a disputed case when actual control by the alleged partner is minimal or absent?

22. See Sec. 14A(a) below.

23. Commissioners' Note to U.P.A. § 6, 7 Unif.Laws Ann. 12 (1949).

24. See Claude v. Claude, 191 Or. 308, 228 P.2d 776, 230 P.2d 211 (1951).

25. Cf. Bullen v. Sharp, L.R. 1 C.P. 86, 111 (1865): "The true question is . . . whether the trade is carried on in behalf of the person sought to be charged as a partner, the participation in profits being a most important element in determining that question, but not being in itself decisive, the test being . . . whether it is such a participation in profits as to constitute the relation of principal and agent between the person taking the profits and those actually carrying on the business." See also Harvey v. Childs & Potter, 28 Ohio St. 319, 22 Am.Rep. 387 (1876).

The U.P.A. and the mercantile view of partnership as an entity required that the partner be thought of as agent for the partnership rather than for his copartners as principals. See Pooley v. Driver, 5 Ch.Div. 458 (1876); Holme v. Hammond, L.R. 41 L.J.Exch. 157, 7 Exch. 218 (1872); Caswell v. Maplewood Garage, 84 N.H. 241, 149 A. 746, 73 A.L.R. 433 (1930).

Analytically, it adds nothing to decide that a person is a partner because he is a principal. The model of a principal only suggests the kind of objective control elements which are relevant.

26. The famous article by Douglas, Vicarious Liability and the Administration of Risk, 38 Yale L.J. 584, 720 (1929) pinpoints the control and provides an economic rationale for its importance. Calling for liability of "enterprisers," he identifies them by four conventional factors: control, ownership, profit participation and loss participation (a majority of the four usually suffice). He refines his analysis and argument by concentrating on two aspects of control—the ability to set prices and to control costs of the enterprise—as justification for imposing liability on those who have them, since these persons can best distribute the risk of loss.

It follows that the necessary control is affirmative—the power to do something—rather than negative—the power to prevent something from being done—so far as this is meaningful. The distinction helps to explain the creditor cases, nn. 31–32 and Secs. 15, 19 below.

As in agency cases, the right to control is equivalent to control for determining the existence of the relationship.[27] However, the available evidence is likely to relate only to actual control unless there is a document setting out rights. So the typical testimony concerns who gave instructions, hired and fired employees, had the say on how money was spent, or made important business decisions. If one participated to a significant degree in these functions, he had sufficient control.[28] If he did not, the normal result is no partnership.[29] But it is still possible to find partnership by emphasizing other elements—especially intent—and taking note the partners may curtail the control of one or more members by agreement or understanding.[30]

To add a final note of confusion, a leading case ignored far-reaching control of a firm by a group which was financing it and sharing its profits; the court concluded from carefully drawn instruments that the control was exercised as creditors rather than as co-owners.[31] Accordingly, the creditors had no liability for debts of the firm. The case suggests the desirability—and the difficulty—of distinguishing kinds of control. An incidental or negative control, typified by veto powers or consultation rights, may be customary and appropriate for a certain relationship, notably debtor-creditor. If so, no partnership results. If it is not customary and appropriate, or if the control is direct or affirmative (including the power to initiate transactions or make internal business decisions), the partnership resemblance grows, and with it the possibility of finding partnership.

27. See Bengston v. Shain, n. 92 above (party had joint right of control although he did not exercise it).

28. Minute Maid Corp. v. United Foods, Inc., n. 11 above: joint control in financing party through (1) power to say what purchases would be acceptable collateral, and (2) right to agree on volume of purchases in anticipation of a price increase. The first is a questionable ground since it is inherent in most credit arrangements. Typical creditor control is usually insufficient to be partnership control; see below at nn. 31–32.

Mere consultation is unlikely to be significant participation. See Anderson v. Evans, 164 Neb. 599, 83 N.W.2d 59 (1954) (farm wife not liable as partner because she talked farm matters over with her husband). A requirement of consultation is a stronger indication of partnership, but far from conclusive.

29. E. g., Swofford v. Industrial Accident Com'n, 121 Cal.App.2d 400, 263 P.2d 129 (1953); Cullingworth v. Pol-

lard, n. 92 above (profit sharing but no partnership); Farbenfabriken Bayer A. G. v. Sterling Drug Co., 307 F.2d 207 (2d Cir. 1962), cert. denied 372 U.S. 929, 83 S.Ct. 872, 9 L.Ed.2d 733 (1963) (profit sharing but no joint venture). See Air Technology Corp. v. General Electric Co., n. 11 above (no joint venture, although a lesser undertaking, with similar duties, recognized).

30. Parks v. Riverside Ins. Co., 308 F. 2d 175 (10th Cir. 1962) (Okl. law); Stillwell v. Trutanich, 178 Cal.App.2d 614, 3 Cal.Rptr. 285 (1960); Greenhouse v. Zempsky, 153 Conn. 501, 218 A.2d 533 (1966); Fenton v. State Industrial Accident Comm., 199 Or. 868, 264 P.2d 1037 (1953); Claude v. Claude, n. 24 above.

Occasional dicta that control must be equal, as in Arthur Venneri Co. v. United States, 169 Ct.Cl. 74, 340 F.2d 337 (1965) must be regarded as overstatements.

31. Martin v. Peyton, discussed Sec. 19 below.

Such distinctions may be useful in giving direction to an inquiry, but they are too elusive to rely on very heavily. The problem is discussed further below.[32]

(e) Loss Sharing

The sharing of losses is a cardinal feature of partnerships unless the partners agree otherwise.[33] And some courts have said it must be present to find partnership in a disputed case.[34] If this means there must be an express agreement to share losses, it is rather naive. Persons casually entering business relations (where most disputed partnership cases arise) are seldom thinking of losses; if they were, they wouldn't be launching the venture. Few jurisdictions insist on an express agreement to share losses.[35] Others will settle for an implied-in-fact agreement,[36] and most require no loss sharing agreement at all. Rather, they soundly regard loss sharing as a consequence of partnership, or as implied by profit sharing, if the partnership relation is otherwise established.[37]

If the parties have contemplated the problem, and explicitly agreed not to share losses, this is entitled to considerable weight as negativing the partnership intent which has been considered above as a separate element.[38] Similarly, if the parties have made a comprehensive agreement which is silent on loss sharing, this has some significance against partnership.[39] Even an express agreement against loss sharing

---

32. Secs. 15 and 19 below. See also n. 26 above.

33. U.P.A. § 18(a), Sec. 65(a) below.

34. Anderson v. Walker, 256 Iowa 1324, 131 N.W.2d 524 (1964) (loss sharing agreement must be clearly shown to establish partnership); Jones v. Taylor, 401 S.W.2d 183 (Mo.App.1966) (sharing of profit and loss necessary, but no profit sharing shown); Hayes v. Killinger, 235 Or. 465, 385 P.2d 747 (1963) (semble; tort case); Steinbeck v. Gerosa, 4 N.Y.2d 302, 175 N.Y.S.2d 1, 151 N.E.2d 170 (1958) (dictum).

35. Iowa is one; see n. 34 above.

36. See First Nat. Bank of Brownwood v. Chambers, 398 S.W.2d 313 (Tex.Civ. App.1965).

37. Parks v. Riverside Ins. Co., 308 F.2d 175 (10th Cir. 1962) (Okl. law); Minute Maid Corp. v. United Foods, Inc., n. 11 above (Tex. law); Anderson v. National Producing Co., 253 F. 2d 834 (2d Cir.1958), cert. denied 357 U.S. 906, 78 S.Ct. 1151, 2 L.Ed.2d 1157

(1958) (N.Y. law); Kaufman-Brown Potato Co. v. Long, 182 F.2d 594 (9th Cir. 1950) (Calif. law); Stillwell v. Trutanich, 178 Cal.App.2d 614, 3 Cal. Rptr. 285 (1960); Rizzo v. Rizzo, 3 Ill. 2d 291, 120 N.E.2d 546 (1954); Arrow Petroleum Co. v. Ames, 128 Ind.App. 10, 142 N.E.2d 479 (1957); Davis v. Gilmore, 244 S.W.2d 671 (Tex.Civ.App. 1951); Bengston v. Shain, n. 92 above; In the Matter of the Estate of Starer, 20 Wis.2d 268, 121 N.W.2d 872 (1963).

See also Brooks v. Warner, 50 Wash.2d 99, 309 P.2d 757 (1957) (loss sharing presumed from profit sharing but rebuttable by substantial evidence).

Opinion is more divided in joint venture cases. See Comment, Joint Adventures —The Sharing of Losses Dilemma, 18 U.Miami L.Rev. 429 (1963).

38. Sec. 5(a) above.

39. Farbenfabriken Bayer A. G. v. Sterling Drug Co., 197 F.Supp. 613, 621 (D.N.J.1961), aff'd 307 F.2d 207 (2d Cir. 1962), cert. denied 372 U.S. 929, 83 S.Ct. 872, 9 L.Ed.2d 733 (1963) (no joint venture).

does not absolutely preclude partnership, especially in a suit among the parties for an accounting.[40]　The significant factor here is an otherwise demonstrable intent to be partners, just as in the situation where they have a written denial of partnership.[41]

An agreement to share losses is obviously strong evidence of co-ownership and of partnership.[42]　The agreement need not be in so many words, but may appear from context, such as an arrangement that an advance be repaid only from the proceeds of sale of property,[43] or an awareness that equipment contributed to a shaky venture (which takes over the instalment debt on it) might be lost through failure to keep up the payments.[44]　Neither of these examples is equivalent to sharing losses of the business in the accounting sense, but only to suffering some economic loss if the business is unsuccessful.[45]　An agreement to share expense, when coupled with one for sharing income, can be equivalent to sharing profits.[46]

(f) Capital or Property Sharing

Another common facet of partnership is co-ownership of property by the partners.[47]　Some statements suggest that co-ownership is a pre-condition to partnership.[48]　But the overwhelming weight of authority is contrary,[49] taking cognizance of the many combina-

---

40.　Gilpin v. Enderbey, 5 Barn. & Ald. 954, 106 Eng.Rep. 1441 (K.B.1822) (not usurious); Robbins v. Laswell, 27 Ill. 365 (1862) (financing partner entitled to accounting against cattle-handling partner; 20% return guaranteed); Clemens v. Crane, 234 Ill. 215, 84 N.E. 884 (1908) (investment in business with guaranteed 15% return was partnership, not loan, hence not usurious; investor allowed to recover); Orvis v. Curtiss, 157 N.Y. 657, 52 N.E. 690, 68 Am.St.Rep. 810 (1899). In these cases the plaintiff investor was guaranteed against loss and, in some instances, guaranteed a minimum rate of profit which was above the legal rate of interest. See also Sec. 5 n. 43 above; Sec. 14(b) at n. 9 above. The resemblance to usury is strong. Cf. Restatement, Contracts, § 527; Williston, Contracts § 1692 (rev. ed. 1938).

41.　See Sec. 5(a) at n. 46 above.

42.　See Penrod v. Smith, 9 Ill.App.2d 257, 132 N.E.2d 675 (1956). There was testimony that a co-trader in a commodity account originally proposed loss sharing and, after losses were incurred, agreed to share them. Although he denied this, he was held liable as a partner to contribute his portion of the losses to the other trader in the account.

43.　Singleton v. Fuller, 118 Cal.App.2d 733, 259 P.2d 687 (1953).

44.　Hansen v. Adent, 238 Minn. 540, 57 N.W.2d 681 (1953).

45.　For a comparable issue in determining profits, see Sec. 14(b) at nn. 8–12 above.

Cases in the employee-or-partner context are collected, Annot., 137 A.L.R. 6, 41–45 (1942).

Cf. In the Matter of the Estate of Starer, 20 Wis.2d 268, 121 N.W.2d 872, 876 (1963) (every lender to a business faces the possibility of loss but does not agree to assume it). See Sec. 15 at nn. 81–83 below.

46.　See Anderson v. Walker, n. 34 above.

47.　U.P.A. §§ 24, 25, Secs. 40–45 below.

48.　E. g., Watson v. Watson, 231 Ind. 385, 108 N.E.2d 893 (1952) (pre-U.P.A.); Anderson v. Walker, n. 34 above.

49.　Sec. 12(b) above.

tions of property or capital of one person with skill and labor of another.

(g) Illustrative Cases

Some concrete examples may help to focus on the problems of disputed partnership among persons who share profits.[50] Here are two cases which fairly typify the problems of informal arrangements [51] and the kinds of evidence adduced. They do not, however, involve every factor which may be of importance in the area.

Cullingworth v. Pollard.[52] H bought cars from P, who sued C for the purchase price. H was in the used car business, and C (formerly a used car dealer) had financed a number of transactions for him over some six months, attending auctions with H, indicating how much he would lend on particular cars, and writing checks directly to the auctioneer. If C didn't agree on a car, H would not buy it since he lacked funds. Car titles were in H's name although C held the title certificates or was shown on them as a lienholder. C received half the profits on resale of cars he financed; H got the other half, and all the 20% dealer reserve from banks who financed buyers from him. After assurance that C would "back" him, H paid all expenses of starting his business. H rented a lot, bought insurance, contracted for utility service, and took out occupational licenses, all in his own name. H paid taxes as a sole proprietor, hired and fired employees, and signed his checks as owner.[53] C wrote some checks, on his own account, to H which "went into the business." There was no testimony on who would bear losses. A capital account was maintained on the books of the business for H, but not for C. C got no profit on cars bought and sold by H but financed by others than C. Some disbursements to C were charged to interest expense. H testified that C stayed on the lot about half the time, answered the telephone, and sold several cars. C and H had no written agreement. There was no representation to third persons that C was a partner. C ended the arrangement after H gave him two bad checks but before H bought the cars being sued on. *Held*: C was not a partner as to H, and not liable for H's debts. There was no co-ownership; C was a creditor. The lower court, which had given judgment for P on a jury verdict, was reversed, and judgment was given for C. The appellate court speaks also, rather generally, in terms of intent, express or implied contract to be partners, community of interest, and joint authority (control) in the business, all of which it finds lacking.

---

50. See also Sec. 19 below.

51. Good examples of more sophisticated arrangements are Martin v. Peyton, Sec. 19 below, and Minute Maid Corp. v. United Foods, Inc., nn. 11, 28 above.

52. 201 Va. 498, 111 S.E.2d 810 (1960).

53. These are to be distinguished from checks C wrote on his own account at auctions to purchase cars for H.

Bengston v. Shain.[54]   B sued S and P to establish his ¼ interest in a tavern partnership.   He had been an employee in S's pawn shop for two years when P proposed to S the purchase of a tavern. B testified that the negotiations included an offer by S for B to work in and become a partner in the tavern.   S testified that he merely asked B if he would work in the tavern with half of S's profits as compensation for his services; P confirmed this version.   B did not participate in any other negotiations and did not know the price paid for the tavern.   S and P furnished the down payment and apparently made a 50–50 partnership agreement.   There was no written agreement with B.   The liquor license was taken in the names of B, S, and P—S explaining that B's inclusion was so he would not have to join the union and would have more respect from customers.   B worked part time in the tavern but drew no money from it, only his regular salary at the pawn shop.   S claimed that B was lending him his (B's) share of the tavern profits to help S build up his equity in the tavern; B had lent him money before.   A third party heard S say (in B's presence but without his objection) that B was not a partner, only working for a share of profits.   Mrs. B testified that S had suggested postponing a car purchase by the Bs until B's share of the tavern was paid off and income available from it.   An accountant, under instructions from P and S prepared an audit report for the tavern at the end of its first calendar year, showing capital accounts (with reconciliations) for B as well as for S and P.   After a few months, S told B to run the pawn shop full time while S worked in the tavern.   Nothing was said about B's interest in the tavern at this time, but a few months later he inquired of S and was told he was out.   *Held*: B was a partner in the tavern, not an employee, and entitled to an accounting.   The necessary intent to form a partnership was present, along with a community of interest or joint ownership of the business.[55]   The oral testimony alone would not have sufficed, but the liquor license in all three names was significant.   The application for it was prepared by P's attorney under a law making licenses issuable only to owners.   The audit report was the other significant piece of evidence.   The court said that B had a joint right of control even though he did not exercise it.[56] The trial court, which had found no partnership, was reversed.

---

54.   42 Wash.2d 404, 255 P.2d 892 (1953).

55.   Washington had recently adopted the U.P.A. but the court used common law language.

56.   It is quite unclear whether the basis for this determination is intent or something else.

PRESUMPTIONS AND NON-PRESUMPTIONS FROM PROFIT SHARING

§ 14A. The receipt by a person of a share of the profits of a business is prima facie evidence that he is a partner in the business, but no such inference shall be drawn if such profits were received in payment:

(a) As a debt by installments or otherwise,

(b) As wages of an employee or rent to a landlord,

(c) As an annuity to a widow or representative of a deceased partner,

(d) As interest on a loan, though the amount of payment vary with the profits of the business,

(e) As the consideration for the sale of a good will of a business or other property by installments or otherwise. U.P.A. § 7(4).

These protected relationships are considered further in Sections 15–20 below.

(a) Presumption; No Protected Relationship

U.P.A. § 7(4) (quoted in the headnote of this Section) creates a presumption of partnership from profit sharing *except* in certain protected relationships: credit, employment, leasing, purchase, etc. Before considering the protected relationships individually in the next six Sections, this Section explores the procedural aspects both of the presumption and of the non-presumption tied to the protected relations.

The draftsmen of the U.P.A. said nothing beyond what appears in the Act, and the courts have said little more. This analysis, then, rests primarily on general principles of procedure and partnership, and on a close reading of the Act.

The statute does not use the word "presumption" in connection with profit sharing, but only the phrase "prima facie evidence." The normal effect of prima facie language is on the burden of producing evidence.[57] If one asserting partnership offers credible evidence of profit sharing,[58] he is entitled to go to the jury (if there is one) on the issue of partnership. Although the U.P.A. does not say it in so many words, he is probably entitled to a directed verdict on the issue if there is no credible opposing evidence and if his evidence is not capable of disbelief. A directed verdict would recognize (as the cases do in other contexts, and as businessmen do) that profit sharing is the central feature of partnership. Since, by the statutory language,

---

57. On presumptions and burdens generally, see James, Civil Procedure, §§ 7.5–7.9 (1965).

58. Reading the Act strictly, it must be evidence of profits already being shared. An agreement to share profits would thus be insufficient, although it is hard to find a good policy reason to sustain this distinction. It would be particularly unfortunate if the distinction applied where the business had operated but failed without earning profit; this is just the time when a potential partner is most needed by creditors and should least be able to escape liability merely because of the lack of profit. Cf. Sec. 14(b) n. 97 above.

the prima facie evidence is that the profit sharer "is a partner in the business," the one asserting partnership seems to be relieved from introducing evidence on other elements of partnership like intent or control.

So far, our analysis is largely theoretical, since it will be an unimaginative party who fails to come up with some evidence against partnership, if only his testimony that "we never intended to be partners" or "it was his business, not mine." Assuming that his evidence is credible and (for the moment) that he does not claim a protected relationship, (1) a directed verdict of partnership is no longer possible, (2) the weighing of the evidence is for the trier of fact, and (3) the burden of persuasion is on the party asserting partnership.[59] If the evidence is evenly balanced in the mind of the trier of fact, the decision is against partnership. The U.P.A. does not say whether the prima facie case is dissipated by the introduction of opposing evidence on intent, control, or other elements of partnership. Traditionally, a presumption is so dissipated, but there are good reasons for a contrary view.[60] However, the complexity of the partnership relation, and the number of elements usually essential to it, probably require that everything be weighed when there is opposing evidence. This means that the one asserting partnership should be prepared to offer evidence on other necessary elements (e. g., intent and control) if he anticipates any credible opposing evidence.[61] The Act, by singling out profit sharing for a presumption, indicates that it is the most important or reliable of the elements.[62]

(b) Non-presumption; Protected Relationship

The U.P.A. language on protected relationships bristles with difficulties.

First, it says that "no such inference" (referring to the one from profit sharing), shall be drawn in the protected relations. The "such" seems almost certainly to refer to the "prima facie evidence" which precedes it; no other inference appears in the paragraph. The effect seemingly is to leave profit sharing as competent evidence, but to make profit sharing alone insufficient to go to the jury. Thus profit sharing must be coupled with other relevant elements of partnership, e. g., control and intent. The burden of persuasion remains on the party asserting partnership.

---

59. See Sec. 4(c) above.

60. See James, Civil Procedure 263–64 (1965).

61. Whether he should offer it in his case in chief or in rebuttal is a tactical question we do not try to answer here.

62. See Wyatt v. Brown, 39 Tenn.App. 28, 281 S.W.2d 64 (1955), stressing that there was no evidence that the profit sharing was rent, interest, debt or wages. Despite some contrary evidence on other elements of partnership, the court found partnership, reversing a contrary determination by the trial court.

Second, what activates the non-presumption (i. e. the statement that "no such inference" shall be drawn from profit sharing in the protected relations)? The key language is: "if the profits were received" in a protected relation. How the profits were received is ordinarily not a matter which can be decided on the pleadings; [63] hence, a pleading that they were received, say, as payment on a loan, does not end the presumption.

A few courts have spoken on the evidence necessary to overcome the presumption from profit sharing, but not too helpfully. One said that it evaporates in the face of "substantial evidence," [64] another that it operates only in the absence of "invalidating" evidence.[65] Obviously, the opponent has the production burden, i. e. to offer credible evidence sufficient (if uncontradicted) to support a finding that the protected relationship exists. This will often be a promissory note, a written lease, a sale contract, or other document, but it may be only testimony of an oral agreement. Logically, it might follow that he also has the burden of persuasion on the issue of the protected relation, but this is less than clear, and is interlocked with the either-or substantive principle discussed below. There is a temptation for the courts, after introduction of evidence on the existence of a protected relation, to conclude that the relation exists and precludes partnership, either as a matter of law, or by examining the incidents of the protected relation found to exist, and holding them inconsistent in fact with partnership. But there is little justification for either course.

Until the opponent satisfies his production burden on the existence of a protected relation, the prima facie evidence stands and permits the party asserting partnership to reach the jury. Once the opponent satisfies his burden, the asserter probably cannot get to the jury on profit sharing alone, but requires evidence of additional elements of partnership.[66] Another unanswered question is whether, if the jury

---

63. No question of fact could be decided on the pleadings. However, the pleadings may be dispositive of the issue if there is a failure to reply (where required by the applicable code) or if there is a demurrer to the defense.

64. Dills v. Delira Corp., 145 Cal.App. ed 124, 130, 302 P.2d 397, 402 (1956) (evidence that transaction was a loan; trial court's finding of no partnership affirmed). The court said that "appellant must show that no substantial evidence supports the finding of non-partnership or that the admitted facts do show a partnership as a matter of law."

Cf. Devereaux v. Cockerline, 179 Or. 229, 170 P.2d 727 (1946), dealing with a pre-

U.P.A. agreement and saying that the presumption from profit sharing is rebutted by a mere showing that the only consideration for the agreement was rendition of services.

65. Blumberg v. Palm, 238 Minn. 249, 56 N.W.2d 412, 415 (1953) (evidence that profit sharing was compensation for services; trial court finding of no partnership affirmed).

66. See Johnson v. Gill, 235 N.C. 40, 68 S.E.2d 788 (1952), where the plaintiff, seeking to show partnership, offered evidence of profit sharing and (through the defendants as adverse witnesses) a protected relation consisting of either lease or sale. A nonsuit at the close of plaintiff's case

rejects the opposing evidence, it can find partnership based on profit sharing alone.

Third, what is the status of one in a protected relation? May he still be a partner? U.P.A. § 7(4) suggests that one is *either* a partner *or* a creditor, lessor, etc. Other parts of the Act point both ways, by recognizing that partners may have dual relations with their firms (e. g., by lending them money), but then by ranking the partner-creditors below outside creditors.[67] The courts have usually assumed the either-or principle without discussion.[68] But U.P.A. § 7(4) does not say that a creditor, etc. cannot be a partner; it merely says profit sharing by him is not prima facie evidence of partnership. At least one court has admitted that a person was a creditor and found also that he was a partner.[69]

Leaving the Act aside, it is analytically correct to determine first whether there is a protected relationship. But doing so in conjunction with the either-or principle leads to some strange results. The most notable is finding that a creditor may have a degree of control (without becoming liable as a partner) which would probably make him a partner if he were not a creditor.[70]

Even without abandoning the either-or principle, it is possible to find that one who is the payee of a note (or one who signed a lease as lessor, or a contract as seller, etc.) is, on consideration of all the evidence, a partner. Otherwise, a partner with full control and partnership intent could escape partnership liability by disguising his relation to fit within the protected group.

It would make sense to examine the evidence initially for profit sharing, control, and some kind of partnership intent, and to decide on this basis whether there is a partnership. This approach has both abstract logic and a kind of realism. To decide first, particularly if from the documents or the designation of themselves by the parties, that there is a protected relation and thus no partnership, may be less logical but is more firmly grounded in the realities of credit and property practice. The latter approach puts a premium on draftsmanship of the legal papers. One entering a profit sharing arrangement which is desired not to be partnership, is well advised to have

---

was affirmed. The decision would not necessarily be controlling if the evidence of protected relation appeared only in defendant's case.

67. U.P.A. § 40(b), Sec. 90 below.

68. Thus, Kaufman-Brown Potato Co. v. Long, 182 F.2d 594 (9th Cir. 1950) (Calif. law) deals with a very ambiguous financing arrangement, seems to accept the either-or idea, and concludes that a partnership existed. See also Sec. 16 n. 99 below, last par.

69. Minute Maid Corp. v. United Foods, Inc., n. 11 above. There was some emphasis that the 100% financing was not a normal credit arrangement.

See also Sterling Builders, Inc. v. Fuhrman, 80 Nev. 543, 396 P.2d 850 (1964) (creditor status doesn't preclude partnership).

70. The classic case is Martin v. Peyton, discussed Sec. 19 below.

the documents deny partnership, assert the relation preferred, and describe the payments as interest, rent or whatever, measured by or equal to a designated portion of the profits, rather than as a share of the profits.[71]

An alternative legal formulation might more rationally reach the results of present case law. It would jettison the either-or principle and regard the establishment of a protected relation as creating a presumption against partnership. (Perhaps this is what the Act intends, although literally it does not go so far.) The presumption would be rebuttable, but only by evidence on elements other than profit sharing, which evidence would have to be stronger than to establish partnership in the absence of a protected relation. In particular, control would have to be more affirmative.

The fundamental problem in this area is how to get from the significant flow of dollars to the proper legal characterization of the relation producing or produced by the dollars. Unfortunately, the Act offers neither a carefully devised theoretical path nor a practical guide to the trial man.

PROFIT SHARING IN PAYMENT OF DEBT

§ 15. **Profit sharing in payment of a debt, by installments or otherwise, does not of itself establish partnership.**

This Section considers profit sharing in payment of the principal of a debt and payment which may cover both interest and principal; Section 19 below considers payment of interest alone. In the cases here, the financing party is accepting risks of the enterprise to a greater degree.

Although profit sharing normally is prima facie evidence that the recipient is a partner,[72] this is not true (i. e. there is no presumption) if the sharing is in payment of a debt by installments or otherwise.[73] The non-presumption in debt cases appears to be a codification of a common law rule developed to protect holders of previously created debt who tried to salvage what they could from a failing debtor by taking some or all of his profits. Ordinarily, of course, a creditor

---

71. A good starting point is the language in the instruments of Martin v. Peyton, n. 70 above, Sec. 19 below, quoted in the intermediate court at 219 App.Div. 297, 302, 220 N.Y.S. 29, 34 (1927): "The parties of the first part [lending securities to a firm] shall not be interested in 'profits' as such. Their interest in profits shall be construed merely as a measure of compensation for loaning . . . securities to [the] firm and granting permission to the firm to hypothecate the same, and for services to be rendered by the trustees [for the lenders]. The parties of the first part shall not be responsible for any losses . . . [nor] in any way be deemed or treated or held as partners . . . nor be under any partnership liability or obligation. It is not the intention of any of the parties of the first part to assume any of the liabilities of the . . firm. . . . ."

72. U.P.A. § 7(4), Sec. 14(b) above.

73. U.P.A. § 7(4) (a), Sec. 14A above.

is entitled to be paid regardless of profits, but enforcement of this right may sink a weakened business and produce a total loss. Creditors are therefore sometimes willing to keep a business afloat, usually under their guidance, in a sort of informal receivership or reorganization. The salvage effort is often unsuccessful, further liabilities accumulate, and the question is whether the creditors are themselves liable as partners to those who extended credit while they were sharing profits.

The leading case is Cox v. Hickman.[74] The owners of an iron works, under financial pressure, transferred the business assets to several of the creditors as trustees for the rest. The trust instrument authorized the trustees to carry on the business and pay the net income to the creditors until their claims were discharged. The trustees were subject to control by vote of the creditors, who (in consideration of the arrangement) agreed not to sue on their claims. The assenting creditors were later sued as partners on a debt contracted by the trustees. They were held not to be partners, and therefore not liable. The exact theory of their exculpation is unclear, since there was no single opinion, but many different ones by the various judges advising the House of Lords. The gist seems to be that the creditors continued to be only creditors, and their rights were derivative.[75] The business was regarded as carried on for the benefit of the debtor (although, in an economic sense, his equity was nil until the creditors were fully paid). The creditors' interest in profits was limited to the amounts of their claims, and they received no compensation for the liability burden plaintiff tried to impose on them (although they received an economic benefit in the form of credit for the business they wanted to keep going). Despite their degree of control over the trustees, and thus over the business, the creditors were held not to be the owners of the business. Several American cases are in accord, as is the U.P.A.[76]

---

74. 8 H.L.Cas. 268, 11 Eng.Rep. 431 (1860). The case is also notable as rejecting the doctrine of partnership as to third persons; see Sec. 14(b) at n. 3 above.

75. For a variant view in terms of agency, and its shortcomings, see Meehan v. Valentine, 145 U.S. 611, 622–623, 12 S.Ct. 972, 974–975, 36 L.Ed. 835 (1892).

76. In re Hoyne, 277 F. 668 (7th Cir. 1922); Wells-Stone Mercantile Co. v. Grover, 7 N.D. 460, 75 N.W. 911, 41 L.R.A. 252 (1898); National Bank of Commerce v. Francis, 296 Mo. 169, 246 S.W. 326 (1922). See Douglas, Vicari-

ous Liability and the Administration of Risk, 38 Yale L.J. 584, 720 (1929).

There are many possible variations in arrangements between creditors and embarrassed debtors. If the debtor transfers his business to the creditors and they hire him as an employee, they may be held liable as partners. Righter v. Farrel, 134 Pa. 482, 19 A. 687 (1890). See also Purvis v. Butler, 87 Mich. 248, 49 N.W. 564 (1891), finding partnership where the creditors controlled the business and made advances necessary for working capital. Sometimes creditors have been held liable as principals without designating them as partners. Furnace Run Saw Mill & Lumber Co. v. Heller Bros.

The non-presumption of partnership is not confined to payments on pre-existing debts or to salvage cases. It is equally applicable to advances initially made to be repaid out of the proceeds or profits of the business.[77] It seems equally applicable to debts created other than by the loan of money, for example as the purchase price of property; arrangements of this sort are more specifically covered by other provisions treated in the following Sections. If repayment of a debt is from the gross proceeds of the business (rather than the net profits), there is even less reason to find partnership.[78]

Despite the non-presumption, it is possible to hold, on other grounds (usually intent and control) that the financing party is a partner,[79] for the economics of a partner's capital contribution and a creditor's loan are quite similar.

It makes a difference whether, by the terms of the financing, the profits or proceeds of the business determine the amount of the repayment or only affect the timing. If there is an absolute obligation to repay, sooner or later, the debt status is firmer.[80] If there is not, it suggests a willingness to risk money on the success of the enterprise, like a partner.[81]

Co., 84 Ohio St. 201, 95 N.E. 771 (1911); Bingaman v. Hickman, 115 Pa. 420, 8 A. 644 (1886).

In Myers v. St. Louis Structural Steel Co., 333 Mo. 464, 65 S.W.2d 931 (1933), D, under contract to erect a bridge, subcontracted part of the work to X. X was unable to finance or furnish a promised surety bond. D waived the bond and agreed to make advances to X and, in return, was given limited powers of supervision over X and a share of his profits. Held: D not a partner liable for X's obligations in the performance of the subcontract. The profit participation and supervision were merely reasonable compensation and protection for D's added risk. Semble, Arthur Venneri Co. v. United States, 169 Ct.Cl. 74, 340 F.2d 337 (1965).

U.P.A. § 7(4) (a), Sec. 14A above.

77. See Spier v. Lang, 4 Cal.2d 711, 53 P.2d 138 (1935) (financing parties repayable from first runs of oil wells, not partners and not liable for debts); Dills v. Delira Corp., 145 Cal.App.2d 124, 302 P.2d 397 (1956) (financing party repayable from first runs of radio shows, not partner and not entitled to any ownership in them); Meisinger v. Johnson, 162 Neb. 360, 76 N.W.2d 267 (1956) (financing party repayable from proceeds of first sales

of lots, not partner and not entitled to accounting); Virginia Hotel Co. v. Dusenberry, 218 S.C. 524, 63 S.E.2d 483 (1951) (financing party repayable from half of profits of operation of hotel lease, not partner and not entitled to permanent interest in profits).

78. Cf. U.P.A. § 7(3), Sec. 14(c) above.

79. E. g., Berg v. King-Cola, Inc., 227 Cal.App.2d 338, 38 Cal.Rptr. 655 (1964) (financing party entitled to accounting as partner); Singleton v. Fuller, 118 Cal.App.2d 733, 259 P.2d 687 (1953) (financing party liable as partner; secret intention to be partners); Black v. Brundige, 125 Cal.App. 641, 13 P.2d 999 (1932) (evidence more substantial for partnership than against it); Davis v. Gilmore, 244 S.W.2d 671 (Tex. Civ.App.1951) (financing party held liable as partner).

80. In the Matter of the Estate of Starer, 20 Wis.2d 268, 121 N.W.2d 872 (1963) (advances to importer for specific merchandise); see n. 83 below.

Sometimes the agreement is ambiguous with respect to the exact relation of profit sharing to total payment; see Virginia Hotel Co. v. Dusenberry, n. 77 above.

81. Davis v. Gilmore, n. 79 above (advances to farmer repayable only out

The usual precautions of a lender—promissory notes, fixed principal and interest, fixed maturity, liens, loan agreements—naturally fortify the financing party against partnership liability. They help to shield him as a creditor from the profit sharing presumption, and they justify a degree of control by him that might otherwise result in partnership.[82] The more he departs from conventional credit terms, the more vulnerable he becomes.[83]

PROFIT SHARING AS WAGES

§ 16. **Profit sharing as compensation for services does not of itself establish partnership.**

One performing services for a share of profits often sues to establish himself as a partner. But, since he is rarely an attractive defendant if the business has gone bad, third persons seldom sue him for the debts of the business, charging that he is a partner. Consequently, the litigation is more homogeneous in this area than in others [84] which turn on profit sharing.[85]

of crop; financing party liable as partner).

See Rubenstein v. Small, 273 App.Div. 102, 75 N.Y.S.2d 483 (1947). P gave D $2,500 to produce vaudeville shows, repayable from profits or unused loans, and not otherwise. The written agreement specified that there was no partnership, joint venture or principal-agent relation. Without classifying the relation beyond saying that it was one of confidence, the court found a cause of action stated for an accounting. Unlike a true loan which is absolutely repayable or adequately secured, this investment was put at hazard of the business and faced all risk of loss.

Cf. Sec. 14(e) at nn. 43–45 above.

82. See Sec. 14(d) at n. 31 above, Sec. 19 below. For example, the holding of automobile titles or liens as security was significant in finding a financing party not liable as a partner. Cullingworth v. Pollard, Sec. 14(g) above. See In re Mission Farms Dairy, 56 F. 2d 346 (9th Cir. 1932) (Calif. law) (note indicated financing was clearly a loan).

However, a fully secured and fully repaid arrangement did not prevent partnership liability for the financing party in Minute Maid Corp. v. United Foods, Inc., n. 11 above, discussed at several points in Sec. 14 above. Nor did notes and mortgages in Davis v. Gilmore, n. 79 above.

83. See Minute Maid Corp. v. United Foods, Inc., n. 82 above, stressing that 100% financing (which was granted) was not a normal financing arrangement. In Kaufman-Brown Potato Co. v. Long, 182 F.2d 594 (9th Cir. 1950) (Calif. law) the party financing a potato crop formally took a 40 or 50% ownership interest in the crop at the time funds were advanced. Although not emphasized by the court, this was probably an element in holding the financier a partner subject to bankruptcy adjudication. Taking title to a fraction of the crop was stated to be a significant factor in holding a landlord liable as a partner, Davis v. Gilmore, n. 79 above.

Cf. In the Matter of the Estate of Starer, n. 80 above. The financier was able to establish his claim as a creditor, but only with some difficulty, when his notes bore no maturity date and, though intended to finance particular merchandise, were not secured by the merchandise or the receivables for them after sale. They were considered demand obligations.

84. Secs. 14–15 above, 17–20 below.

85. In another moderately common context, the person performing services for a share of profits is denying partnership status in order to enjoy benefits which he could not have as a partner, e. g., an action at law for

What difference does it make whether the profits are received as an employee rather than as a partner? Very little as long as they are received.[86] The strife usually starts when the profit sharing stops.[87] The real dispute is likely to be over the assets of the alleged firm. Whether the excluded party has any right to them depends, first, on whether he is a partner, and, second, on whether the assets in question are property of the firm.[88] Merely establishing that he is a 25% partner in a firm does not entitle him to 25% of its assets. Before the division is made, there must be an accounting of all transactions, including outstanding debts,[89] and an allowance to the other parties for any capital contributions they have made.[90] Since the other parties in the typical dispute have usually made substantial capital contributions, the only thing the self-alleging partner is likely to enjoy—besides the nuisance value of the suit—is a share in the appreciation of firm assets, including perhaps some good will or going concern value.[91]

Profit sharing with workers is widely practiced and has a long history.[92] An early example was in whaling and fishing, where it was usual to pay the master and crew, at the end of the voyage, shares of the proceeds or profits of the voyage. This did not make them partners.[93] The same is true for many other profit sharing recipients,

wages (see cases in n. 93 below) or workmen's compensation. Typical of the latter are Herman v. Kandrat Coal Co., 205 Pa.Super. 117, 208 A.2d 51 (1965); Tidwell v. Walden, 205 Tenn. 705, 330 S.W.2d 317 (1959); both involving miners. See also n. 95, last par., below and Sec. 4(c) at n. 59 above.

An unusual case in which one party successfully sought loss contribution from the other (who insisted there was only an employment relation) is Brooks v. Warner, 50 Wash.2d 99, 309 P.2d 757 (1957).

Cases are collected, Annot., Partnership as distinguished from employment (where rights of parties inter se or their privies are concerned), 137 A.L.R. 6–174 (1942).

86. For an attempt to recover an equivalent as compensation when profits were not earned, see Wagner v. Derecktor, 306 N.Y. 386, 118 N.E.2d 570 (1954), holding that existence of a joint venture was a fact question for the jury.

87. See, e. g., Blase v. Pedlow, 183 Cal. App.2d 367, 6 Cal.Rptr. 635 (1960).

If the arrangement is for a fixed term, a compensable breach of contract is equally probable, whether the arrangement is employment or partnership.

88. See Secs. 37, 37A below.

89. See Sec. 72 below.

90. See Sec. 65(a) below.

91. See Sec. 84 below.

92. See, e. g., Metzger, Profit Sharing in Perspective (1964); Council of Profit Sharing Industries, Profit Sharing Manual (1948). In the mass form most common today, profit sharing raises no partnership questions, since it is through trusts with a large number of beneficiaries, under a carefully drawn agreement; no employee receives a direct interest in profits.

93. Mair v. Glennie, 4 M. & S. 240, 105 Eng.Rep. 823 (1815) (captain to share voyage profit as compensation); Wilkinson v. Frasier, 4 Esp. 182 (1803) (whaling crew, to receive share of proceeds of whale oil, not partners; entitled to sue in assumpsit for wages); Brown v. Hicks, 24 F. 811 (D.Mass. 1885) (master contracted for "lay" of 1/15 of net proceeds of whaling voyage, not partner; entitled to sue for wages measured by "lay" of full voyage when

such as agents and brokers [94] and managers and operatives in trade and industry.[95]

voyage cut short by owner); Perrott v. Bryant, 2 Y. & C.Exch. 61, 160 Eng. Rep. 312 (1836) (oyster boat crew compensated by share of catch); Cambra v. Santos, 233 Mass. 131, 123 N.E. 503 (1919) (fishing boat crew received share of gross proceeds after certain expenses, not partners; injured sailor entitled to sue proprietors in tort); Baxter v. Rodman, 20 Mass. (3 Pick.) 435 (1826); Domandich v. Doratich, 165 Wash. 315, 5 P.2d 310 (1931). See Story, Partnership § 42 (3d ed. 1850).

The pattern of compensation continues in the fishing industry, and along with it the question of the legal relation created thereby. The modern question is whether the ship owners are required to pay social security and unemployment taxes on captain and crew as employees. The answer is generally yes. Kirkconnell v. United States, 347 F.2d 260 (Ct.Cl.1965); Cape Shore Fish Co. v. United States, 165 Ct.Cl. 630, 330 F.2d 961 (1964) (discussing the history of compensation in fishing, at 968–69).

94. Heebner v. Senderman, 85 Cal.App. 196, 259 P. 106 (1927); McCarney v. Lightner, 188 Iowa 1271, 175 N.W. 751 (1920) (agent to buy and sell real estate); W. F. Bleck & Co. v. Soeffing, 241 Ill.App. 40 (1926) (agreement of land owner and builder for development and sharing in net proceeds); Las Vegas Machine & Engineering Works v. Roemisch, 67 Nev. 1, 213 P. 2d 319 (1950); Buzard v. First Nat. Bank, 67 Tex. 83, 2 S.W. 54, 60 Am. Rep. 7 (1886) (agent to buy and sell cattle).

95. Kaufmann v. Kaufmann, 222 Pa. 58, 70 A. 956 (1908); Seemann v. Eneix, 272 Mass. 189, 172 N.E. 243 (1930); Klein v. Kirschbaum, 240 Mich. 368, 215 N.W. 289 (1927); F. M. Strickland Printing & Stationery Co. v. Chenot, 45 S.W.2d 937 (Mo.App.1932); Jacobs v. Escoett, 265 App.Div. 111, 37 N.Y.S. 2d 789 (1943); Buchanan & Son v. Ewell, 148 Va. 762, 139 S.E. 483 (1927); Sheldon v. Little, 111 Vt. 301, 15 A.2d 574, 137 A.L.R. 1 (1940).

In Kaufmann v. Kaufmann, supra, four partners originally agreed that, on the death of one, his interest should be bought from his estate; a valuation method was specified. When one partner died, his representative claimed that the original agreement had been superseded by a new one admitting a number of former employees to the firm. The firm had made separate contracts with seven employees, under which each deposited sums with the firm (varying from $35,000 to $120,000), was to perform specified services, and was to receive a percentage of the profits. Held: the original agreement and partnership remained unchanged; the employees did not become partners. Hence the decedent's share was valued in accordance with the original agreement.

See also Frazier v. Mansfield, 305 Pa. 359, 157 A. 798 (1931); Note, 17 St. Louis L.Rev. 339 (1932).

An unusual legislative attempt to encourage profit sharing at a fairly early time was Pa.Act of June 15, 1871, 43 P.S. §§ 321–23 (1964) specifying that employees receiving profit share were not liable as partners, and did not have rights as partners. Because of its title (referring to industrial companies), it was held inapplicable to hotels and liquor selling, Mayer v. Wilson, 242 Pa. 473, 89 A. 685 (1913). Because of its stringent conditions (50% of the profits, after a 10% dividend on common stock, had to be shared with employees) it was little used, and was finally repealed. Pa. Act 1966, Jan. 18 (1965 Reg.Sess.) No. 519, § 50.

A written agreement designating a person as a partner is not conclusive if no partnership element is present beside services compensated by profit sharing. Fenwick v. Unemployment Compensation Comm., 133 N.J.L. 295, 44 A.2d 172 (1945); Peterson v. Eppler, 67 N.Y.S.2d 498 (1946) (junior partner); Scott v. Miller, 260 App.Div. 428, 975, 22 N.Y.S. 981 (1941), aff'd 285 N.Y. 760, 34 N.E.2d 910 (1941). The motive for such arrangements is often to avoid the burden of taxes for unemployment compensation, social security **and other employee welfare benefits.**

In most cases, familiar principles resolve the dispute whether profit sharing for services creates partnership: the intent of the parties, as expressed in their agreement, is clearly one of employment rather than partnership,[96] or there is insufficient control in the asserter to sustain his claim of partnership.[97]

It is possible, however, to find partnership where the person in question has control in only one area[98] or none at all.[99] Partnership intent should be clearly manifested in such instances.[1] While capital

96. Morrow v. McCaa Chevrolet Co., 231 Ark. 497, 330 S.W.2d 722 (1960) (P ran D's used car lot for 50% of profits but admitted he did not consider himself a partner); Frost v. Wells, 388 S.W.2d 235 (Tex.Civ.App.1965) (elaborate contract for ranch manager to receive 50% of profits clearly one of employment); Eder v. Reddick, 46 Wash.2d 41, 278 P.2d 361 (1955) (fact finding affirmed on diverse evidence). On intent generally, see Sec. 5(a) above.

97. Wish v. Small, 1 Camp. 331, 170 Eng.Rep. 975 (1808) (agistor sharing profits of cattle sale not a partner); Dry v. Boswell, 1 Camp. 329, 170 Eng. Rep. 975 (K.B.1808) (lighterman, sharing gross earnings for working lighter not a partner); Mair v. Glennie, n. 93 above; Carpenter v. Lennane, 166 Mich. 610, 132 N.W. 477 (1911) (one performing part of paving contract and receiving percentage of profits not a partner). On control generally, see Sec. 14(d) above.

98. Village of Westby v. Bekkedal, 172 Wis. 114, 178 N.W. 451 (1920); Southern Can Co. v. Sayler, 152 Md. 303, 136 A. 624 (1927).

99. Runo v. Rothschild, 219 Mich. 560, 189 N.W. 183 (1922).

This was a law action, begun by capias, an inappropriate procedure if the parties were partners. P, a physician, had employed D as his assistant in operating his urological laboratory. On P's departure for military service, he agreed with D that D should carry on the business in P's absence, pay expenses from income, and divide the balance equally between them. P claimed D had not complied. Held: the wrong procedure had been used, since P and D were partners. Note that D was in complete control.

See Brown v. Fairbanks, 121 Cal.App.2d 432, 263 P.2d 355 (1953) where P helped D develop a mining claim in D's name by two months work in digging a shaft. There was conflicting testimony over their agreement, but D paid P 50% of the royalties received after D leased the mine. P was found to be a partner, although he apparently had no control even when he was working on the property. D, of course, claimed that the royalty sharing was only compensation for P's labor.

A father-son employer-employee relation can become a partnership without formal agreement and may be shown by admissions of the father and by books crediting the son with half the profits in addition to salary. Matter of Rosenberg, 251 N.Y. 115, 167 N.E. 190 (1929), holding the son entitled to profits as partner. The father's other heirs claimed that the son was only an employee, limited to reasonable compensation for managing the business after the father's death.

See also Dutcher v. Buck, 96 Mich. 160, 55 N.W. 676, 20 L.R.A. 776 (1893) (lumber cutting contract, land-owner sharing in profits); Bengston v. Shain, discussed Sec. 14(g) above; Moseley v. Taylor, 173 N.C. 286, 91 S.E. 1035, L.R.A.1917E, 875 (1917).

By the prevailing view, the relation between parties associated in a business cannot be both partnership and employer-employee. Cook v. Lauten, 335 Ill.App. 92, 80 N.E.2d 280 (1948).

But see Sec. 14A at nn. 68–69 above.

1. For example, in Bengston v. Shain, discussed Sec. 14(g) above, the liquor license was in the name of the alleging partner as well as the others, and an audit report showed a capital account for him.

contribution or co-ownership of property is not essential to partnership,[2] its absence in this context is some evidence against partnership,[3] and its presence is evidence for partnership, the significance varying more or less in proportion to the size of the contribution or co-owner-ship.[4] An agreement to share losses may be explained away on the ground of incentive to an agent or employee,[5] but it is so alien to normal employment relations as to seem a strong indication of partnership.

The U.P.A. has stated the non-presumption of partnership from profit sharing "as wages of an employee." [6] It is probably not limited to employees in the common law sense, but applicable to independent contractors [7] or others who render services for a share of profits.

At common law there is a bootstrap temptation for courts to *assume* that the disputed relation is one of employment, and *conclude*

---

2. Secs. 12(b), 14(f) above.

3. Hunt v. Erikson, 57 Mich. 330, 23 N.W. 832 (1885) (land speculation; one party furnished capital, the other made purchases, taking title in name of the former); Simpson v. Tenney, 41 Kan. 561, 21 P. 634 (1889) (similar).

Where a service contributor shares profit, and it is impossible or very difficult to classify the relation as principal-agent, landlord-tenant, bailor-bailee, or creditor-debtor, the presumption that profit sharing creates partnership may apply. McMurtrie v. Guiler, 183 Mass. 451, 67 N.E. 358 (1903); Runo v. Rothschild, n. 99 above.

McKee v. Capitol Dairies, 164 Or. 1, 99 P.2d 1013 (1940). In a turkey raising project one person was to supply the turkeys and feed, another the range, and a third to do the work; each was to get a third of the profits. Held: joint venture.

Cf. Lomax v. Trull, 232 S.W. 861 (Tex. Civ.App.1921) (writing ambiguous; intent is fact question).

Use of a firm name is evidence of partnership. Phipps v. Little, 213 Mass. 414, 100 N.E. 615 (1913); Laughner v. Wally, 269 Pa. 5, 112 A. 105 (1920) (co-owners of oil lease under common name held not partners). The evidence is much stronger if each party is included in the firm name (see Sec. 14(a) at n. 91 above) or if there is other holding out to third persons as partners.

4. See Zajac v. Harris, 241 Ark. 737, 410 S.W.2d 593 (1967) ($9,000 investment in purchase of inventory, turned over to extent of $73,000; partnership established).

5. Where the agreement is evidently intended to create an agency, the fact that the agent is to share losses (which may be caused by his acts) does not create partnership. Canton Bridge Co. v. City of Eaton Rapids, 107 Mich. 613, 65 N.W. 761 (1895); Hutchinson v. Birdsong, 211 App.Div. 316, 207 N.Y.S. 273 (1925).

6. U.P.A. § 7(4) (b), Sec. 14A above. See also U.P.A. § 7(3), Sec. 14(c) above (no partnership presumption from sharing gross receipts).

7. See Drummy v. Stern, 269 S.W.2d 198 (Ky.1954) (contractor built houses for fixed sum plus 30% of landowner's profit on sale; no reference to U.P.A. which was in force at time of decision but may or may not have been at time of transaction); Foster v. Parker, 282 App.Div. 766, 122 N.Y.S.2d 748 (1953), aff'd 2 N.Y.2d 848, 159 N.Y.S.2d 985, 140 N.E.2d 876 (1957) (patent attorney to receive 50% of profits of an invention); Powell v. Bundy, 38 Tenn.App. 255, 272 S.W.2d 490 (1954) (co-operating real estate brokers splitting commission; U.P.A. in force but not referred to). But cf. Fyock v. Riales, 251 S.W.2d 102 (Mo.App.1952), sustaining a jury finding of partnership between two real estate brokers who agreed to split commissions on properties in one state.

from employee characteristics that no partnership is created or intended. The U.P.A., if anything, strengthens the temptation by its non-presumption of partnership from profit sharing with an employee.[8]

PROFIT SHARING AS RENT

§ 17. **Profit sharing in payment of rent does not of itself establish partnership.**

A business can sometimes be financed as well by furnishing needed land or equipment as by furnishing cash.[9] Profit sharing may be agreed upon in lieu of rent as in lieu of interest. The bargaining motivations are usually the same: the operator of the business wants to avoid or minimize fixed costs; the other party wants a chance at higher returns.[10] The lessor is typically less committed to the business than is the lender, because the leased property is not so subject to dissipation in the business, and can be recovered in kind on default.

Since property owners normally make good defendants, we would expect to find them often alleged as partners when they lease for profit shares to a business which fails to pay its bills. Partnership-existence litigation between the parties to the lease is infrequent. Third party creditors have little success in raising the issue.[11] In deciding whether one is a partner contributing the use of property [12] or a property owner renting it for a share of profit, familiar criteria are employed, mainly intent of the parties [13] and control of the business.[14]

If partnership intent is lacking or denied, a considerable amount of control is permitted a lessor without making him a partner. Thus, he may retain inspection rights and may require daily reporting, banking at a particular place, and cash basis operation.[15] Such inci-

---

8. See Sec. 14A above.

9. See Nelson v. Seaboard Sur. Co., 269 F.2d 882 (8th Cir. 1959) (Minn. law). A firm supplied a contractor with equipment and cash financing; it was held a partner with the contractor. There was substantial evidence to support partnership; much of it is not detailed, but an important element was an express agreement to share losses.

10. There is nothing comparable to the usury-avoiding motive which enters into some cash financing arrangements, since rents can ordinarily be set at any level by agreement of the parties. However, analogous intentions could arise where rents are controlled, as in wartime.

11. Cases are collected, Annot., Lease or tenancy agreement as creating part-

nership relationship between lessor and lessee, 131 A.L.R. 508 (1941). The annotation includes only cases recognizing the agreement as a lease or tenancy and then proceeding to determine the partnership issue; it excludes cases where an ambiguous agreement was held to be a partnership rather than a tenancy, although it cites some of the latter.

12. Secs. 37–38 below.

13. Sec. 5(a) above.

14. Sec. 14(d) above.

15. H. T. Hackney Co. v. Robert E. Lee Hotel, 156 Tenn. 243, 300 S.W. 1 (1927). Other hotel cases held to involve only landlord-tenant relations include Holmes v. Old Colony Railroad Corp., 71 Mass. (5 Gray) 58 (1855); Beecher

dents are viewed as negative checks on the tenant, without giving initiative to the landlord. If his powers are more positive, he may be treated as a co-owner or co-principal in the business, i. e. a partner. This was the result when he nominated a representative to keep books for the business and act as cashier, to receive all money and deposit it in the landlord's name, and to make all payments.[16]

Partnership is more likely to be the result if the landlord retains joint possession with the tenant, since joint activity and control are probable. In Thomas v. Springer,[17] a theatre owner provided his premises complete with services of regular employees (ticket sellers, ushers, orchestra). A producer provided a performance and shared the gross receipts with the owner. The owner was held not liable for the negligence of one of the producer's employees, on the theory the producer was an independent contractor.[18] But, in a rather similar arrangement for auto races at a fair, the producer and the fair owners were held joint venturers, with liability like partners for each other's torts.[19] A concessionaire in a department store, with the store handling collections and providing delivery service and advertising, has been treated as a partner or quasi partner entitled to an accounting against the store.[20] As to third persons unaware of the arrange-

v. Bush, 45 Mich. 188, 7 N.W. 785, 40 Am.Rep. 465 (1881); Austin, Nichols & Co. v. Neil, 62 N.J.L. 462, 41 A. 834 (1898).

Cf. Fuller v. Texas Parking Lot, 133 S. W.2d 605 (Tex.Civ.App.1939). The landowner received 40% of the profits of a filling station and occasionally performed services for it. Held: not a partner. See criticism, Note, 18 Texas L.Rev. 346 (1940).

16. Merrall v. Dobbins, 169 Pa. 480, 32 A. 578 (1895).

Wurm v. Metz, 162 Cal.App.2d 262, 327 P.2d 969 (1958). The landowner of this poultry business had authority to write checks on the business and made some purchases for it. More significantly, the business was carried on in his name along with the tenant's, and they both appeared on occupational licenses as owners. The tenant was his son in law. Held: partnership; landlord liable for debts of business.

See also Wright Co., Inc. v. Green, 196 N.C. 197, 145 S.E. 16 (1928) (hotel); Malvern Nat. Bank v. Halliday, 195 Iowa 734, 192 N.W. 843 (1923) (farming enterprise).

17. 134 App.Div. 640, 119 N.Y.S. 460 (1909).

18. Restatement, Second, Agency § 2(3) defines independent contractor as "a person who contracts with another to do something for him but who is not controlled by the other nor subject to the other's right to control with respect to his physical conduct in the performance of the undertaking." See id. § 220.

19. Ellingson v. World Amusement Service Ass'n, 175 Minn. 563, 222 N.W. 335 (1928).

Cf. Eide v. Skerbeck, 242 Wis. 474, 8 N.W.2d 282, 145 A.L.R. 956 (1943) (carnival operators liable for their negligent placing of tent peg of a concessionaire).

20. Milwaukee Boston Store v. Katz, 153 Wis. 492, 140 N.W. 1038 (1913) (store received 10% of gross).

Cf. Rice v. Smith, 171 Mo. 331, 71 S.W. 123, 124 (1902). One associate worked mine for which other had license. The latter was to hoist ore to surface, prepare for sale and sell; they were to divide proceeds equally. Held: joint enterprise, each liable to third person for tort of other.

ment, the store may be estopped to deny that it is a principal in the business.[21]

A property owner would not normally agree to share losses with the user. If he does, it is significant evidence of partnership.[22] An express agreement not to share losses underscores the usual landlord-tenant relation, and is evidence against partnership.[23]

The property owner sharing gross returns rather than net is less at risk of the business and has a stronger stance against partnership liability.[24] The principle holds in farming cases where the landowner receives a share of the crop.[25] However, if he bears any of the expenses of planting, cultivating and harvesting, he is actually sharing not the gross but something approximating the net profits of the operation. This makes him a bit more susceptible to partnership liability, but he is normally not vulnerable unless he participates in control, say, by designating crops or markets.[26] In the latter situa-

---

21. Hannon v. Siegel-Cooper Co., 167 N.Y. 244, 60 N.E. 597, 52 L.R.A. 429 (1901) (dentist serving patients, apparrently as an employee of store). See Gottlieb Bros., Inc. v. Culbertson's, n. 24 below (store liable for one of concessionaire's purchases but not another).

22. Nelson v. Seaboard Sur. Co., n. 9 above; Giddings v. Harding, 267 S.W. 976 (Tex.1925).

23. Escoe v. Johnson, 110 Ga.App. 252, 138 S.E.2d 330 (1964), in a jurisdiction where loss sharing is apparently essential to partnership.

24. Jarvis v. Wallace, 139 Va. 171, 123 S.E. 374 (1924) (truck owner not partner of trucker who leased for share of gross); Gottlieb Bros., Inc. v. Culbertson's, 152 Wash. 205, 277 P. 447 (1929) (department store not partner or joint venturer of operator of fur concession who paid 15% of his gross).

See also Fredrick v. Cleveland Builders' Supply & Brick Co., 34 Ohio App. 402, 171 N.E. 118 (1929).

25. Smith v. Schultz, 89 Cal. 526, 26 P. 1087 (1891), being a lease for a definite term of years, not terminable at will by the landlord; Florence v. Fox, 193 Iowa 1174, 188 N.W. 966 (1922), landlord not liable to employee of tenant for injury due to unguarded dangerous machinery; Shrum v. Simpson, 155 Ind. 160, 57 N.E. 708, 49 L.R.A. 792 (1900), on death of landlord, his estate may sue for an accounting, tenant not

being a surviving partner; Tomlinson v. Dille, 147 Md. 161, 127 A. 746 (1925), tenant allowed to sue landlord at law for an accounting of proceeds of sales of product; Musser v. Brink, 68 Mo. 242 (1878), landlord could procure an injunction against removal by tenant of part of live stock from premises in violation of agreement; Pestlin v. Haxton Canning Co., 274 App.Div. 144, 80 N.Y.S.2d 869 (1948), injured employee of tenant not entitled to claim workmen's compensation from landlord; Brown v. Jaquette, 94 Pa. 113, 39 Am.Rep. 770 (1880), the tenant's share in the crop could be levied on and sold on execution free of any interest of the landlord; Cedarberg v. Guernsey, 12 S.D. 77, 80 N.W. 159 (1899), landlord not liable for wages of workman hired by tenant; Wagner v. Buttles, 151 Wis. 668, 139 N.W. 425, Ann.Cas.1914B, 144 (1913), same.

Sharing of certain expenses with the tenant was consistent with a landlord relationship where the expenses were separately billed by third parties. United States v. Farrington, 244 F.2d 111 (7th Cir. 1957) (Ind. law), noted 1957 U.Ill.L.F. 532.

26. Anderson v. Walker, 256 Iowa 1324, 131 N.W.2d 524 (1964) (no control or power; no partnership; no liability to contribute to loss); Tomlinson v. Dille, n. 25 above (no participation in management; no partnership); Blue Valley State Bank v. Milburn, 120 Neb. 421, 232 N.W. 777 (1930) (no intent; no partnership; no liability); Davis v.

tion, he may be able to show that the farmer was his employee or servant, thus avoiding partnership but incurring vicarious liability for the farmer's actions in the scope of employment.[27]

The U.P.A. codifies the common law rule by specifying that, while profit sharing is usually prima facie evidence of partnership, "no such inference shall be drawn if such profits were received in payment . . . of . . . rent to a landlord."[28] It should be interpreted broadly enough to include a lessor of equipment or other personal property.[29] At least one state has a separate statute covering lessors generally.[30]

Gilmore, 244 S.W.2d 671 (Tex.Civ.App. 1951) (agreed on crops; partnership; liability to third person). In the Davis case, although it was apparently not significant in the court's decision, the defendant had agreed to pay the kinds of expense represented by plaintiff's claim.

Cases are collected, Annot., 131 A.L.R. 508, 525–28 (1941).

27. Christian v. Crocker, 25 Ark. 327, 99 Am.Dec. 223 (1869).

The "cropper" has been called a "sublimated employee." Union Central Life Ins. Co. v. Audet, 94 Mont. 79, 21 P.2d 53, 92 A.L.R. 571 (1933). See note, 37 Am.Dec. 317.

The crop-sharing agreement has been held to possess delectus personae so that the rights of the occupant are non-assignable. Randall v. Chubb, 46 Mich. 311, 9 N.W. 429, 41 Am.Rep. 165 (1889). See Meyer v. Livesley, 45 Or. 487, 78 P. 670, 106 Am.St. Rep. 667 (1904). Other courts have treated the cropper's rights as assignable without an agreement to the contrary. Dworak v. Graves, 16 Neb. 706, 21 N.W. 440 (1884); Minneapolis Iron Store Co. v. Branum, 36 N.D. 355, 162 N.W. 543, L.R.A.1917E, 298 (1917) (cropper could mortgage his share of crop). See California Packing Corp. v. Lopez, 207 Cal. 600, 279 P. 664, 64 A.L.R. 1412 (1929) (death of cropper did not terminate contract, which could be carried out by his executor or one claiming under him).

Other possible relations have been found in share cropping: Marsh v. Hand, 120 N.Y. 315, 24 N.E. 463 (1890) (independent contractor); Blue v. Leathers, 15 Ill. 31 (1853) (unclassified joint tillage).

28. U.P.A. § 7(4)(b), Sec. 14A above. U.P.A. § 7(3), Sec. 14(c) above, provides similarly for sharing of gross returns.

29. This was the common law rule. Vanderhurst v. DeWitt, 95 Cal. 57, 30 P. 94, 20 L.R.A. 595 (1892). Cases are collected, Annot. 131 A.L.R. 508, 528–31 (1941). It appears to be the rule under U.P.A. See Johnson v. Gill, 235 N.C. 40, 68 S.E.2d 788 (1952) which rests, however, partly on the statute in the next note.

30. "No lessor of property, merely by reason that he is to receive as rent or compensation for its use a share of the proceeds or net profits of the business in which it is employed, or any other uncertain consideration, shall be held a partner of the lessee." G.S. (N.C.) § 42–1 (1966) enacted 1868–69. It was apparently passed to reverse prior cases. For the history, see Keith v. Lee, 246 N.C. 188, 97 S.E.2d 859 (1957). For an application, see Perkins v. Langdon, 231 N.C. 386, 57 S.E. 2d 407 (1950) (tobacco warehouse leased for 30% of tenant's commissions on tobacco sold and tobacco basket rentals received by tenants; no partnership).

PROFIT SHARING AS ANNUITY

§ 18. Profit sharing in payment of an annuity to a deceased partner's widow or representative does not of itself establish partnership.

When a partner dies it is often desirable to preserve going concern values by keeping the business in operation.[31] The widow or estate may prefer to participate in the profits of the business if they are high. The survivors may want to retain in the business the funds which would otherwise have to be paid out in settlement of the decedent's interest. Some such arrangement may be provided by the pre-death agreement among the partners, or by post-death agreement between the surviving partners and the widow or representative. Payments may be gauged in various ways: a fixed percentage of profits, fixed dollar amounts, or some proportion to the capital account of the interest. They may continue for a designated life or lives, or until a certain total is paid, or for a fixed number of years.[32] Such arrangements generally do not constitute partnership with (or for) the recipient of the payments, primarily because he or she has no share in control and is not intended to be a partner, and secondarily because it is usually agreed (explicitly or implicitly) that he or she is not to share losses.[33]

The U.P.A. codification states that no inference of partnership shall be drawn from profit sharing "as an annuity to a widow or representative of a deceased partner."[34] The meaning of annuity in this context has not been determined, but is probably intended to be broad enough to include the variety of payment plans suggested above. The protective provision of the Act appears not to extend to payments made to other dependents, such as children or elderly relatives, although they are probably shielded by their lack of control and the mutual intent that they not be partners. Conceivably, they are embraced by the word "representative." Caution sometimes leads to payments to an executor or trustee for their benefit, in order to take firmer advantage of the insulation of the "representative."

---

31. See Sec. 90A below.

32. See Sec. 86 below, particularly the discussion of liquidating distributions and modified continuation.

33. Holcombe v. Long, 245 Mass. 353, 139 N.E. 633 (1923); Butcher v. Hepworth, 115 N.Y. 328, 22 N.E. 160, 163 (1889); Tisch v. Rockafellow, 209 Pa. 419, 58 A. 805 (1904).

A widow, bequeathed a life interest in a partner's interest in the firm, is not a partner by receipt of a share of profits from the surviving partner. Western shoe Co. v. Neumeister, 258 Mich. 662, 242 N.W. 802 (1922).

The agreement may provide for a fixed annuity to a partner's widow as a minimum, whether earned or not. Kenyon v. Tidey, 314 Mich. 205, 22 N.W.2d 273 (1946).

34. U.P.A. § 7(4) (c), Sec. 14A above. U.P.A. § 42 is in accord by classifying the recipient as an "ordinary creditor" in some circumstances. Id. § 41(10) permits the continued use of the deceased's name without making his "individual property" (presumably his estate) liable.

It may happen that the recipient of payments becomes a member of the firm, usually through participation in management and acceptance by the other partners. If so, he incurs the liabilities and enjoys the rights of a partner.[35]

A retiring partner may also continue to share in profits or receive other payments from the firm by agreement. He enjoys no explicit statutory protection,[36] and runs risks of being held liable for subsequent debts of the firm. (1) He may retain a degree of control and profit sharing which would suffice to make anyone liable. (2) He may fail to give notices which are necessary to cut off his liability.[37] (3) He may continue to hold himself out as a partner, or permit his colleagues to do so.[38]

PROFIT SHARING IN PAYMENT OF INTEREST

§ 19. Profit sharing in payment of interest on a debt does not of itself establish partnership.

We have already considered profit sharing in payment of the principal of a debt, or of mixed principal and interest.[39] The problems and answers are much the same when profit sharing is for interest alone. The justification for separate treatment is that profit sharing for interest alone, which presupposes an absolute promise to repay principal, is (formally at least) a different kind of risk and commitment to the business of the borrower. It is less compatible with partnership intent and more consistent with creditor status. It has a separate historical use as a way around the usury laws.[40] It also happens to be legislated on separately in the U.P.A.[41] In fact, one

---

35. Wild v. Davenport, 48 N.J.L. 129, 7 A. 295, 57 Am.Rep. 552 (1886). Gibboney v. Derreck, 338 Pa. 317, 12 A. 2d 111 (1940) (widow, as sole legatee, became partner hence is not entitled, as executrix, to accounting against co-partners for value at date of death).

On other aspects of a widow's becoming a partner in her husband's firm, see Hamilton v. Johnson, 150 Wash. 312, 272 P. 986 (1928) and Johnson v. Hamilton, 141 Wash. 248, 251 P. 274 (1926).

Cf. Gerding v. Baier, 143 Md. 520, 122 A. 675 (1923).

An estate has been held a partner where the decedent's will provided that a portion of his general estate be held in trust to secure payment of future obligations of the continuing partners. Stearns v. Inhabitants of Brookline, 219 Mass. 238, 107 N.E. 57 (1914).

The partnership agreement may provide that an executor shall become a part-

ner with the surviving partner. If he does so, this may obligate the firm to account to a child born after the dead partner made his will, and so entitled to a fractional share of the estate. Kreinson v. Commercial Nat. Bank, 323 Pa. 332, 185 A. 756 (1936).

36. But see U.P.A. § 7(4) (e), Sec. 20 below.

37. U.P.A. § 35, Sec. 81 below.

38. U.P.A. § 16, Sec. 36 below. See Painter, Partnership by Estoppel, 16 Vand.L.Rev. 327 (1963) and, more broadly on the retiring partner, Comment, Partnerships—Continuing Liability of a Partner Receiving Payments, 20 Sw.L.J. 151 (1966).

39. Sec. 15 above.

40. See Secs. 5 n. 43, 14(b) n. 9, 14(e) n. 40 above.

41. *Compare* U.P.A. § 7(4) (d) *with* § 7 (4) (a).

cannot always tell which situation occurs in the decided cases, since there is often imprecision in the agreement of the parties or in the narration of the courts. Moreover, the difference in economic risk may be slight.

The modern authorities, both at common law and under the U.P.A., hold that the investor for profits in lieu of interest or in addition to interest is not liable as a partner if he does not participate in control or management of the business.[42] His economic position is much the same as a limited partner whose general partners have guaranteed the return of his contribution. His legal position, in light of the authorities just referred to, might seem as strong, but many lawyers would prefer to give him the extra protection from compliance with the limited partnership statutes.[43] There is a disadvantage in that a limited partner is subordinate to outside creditors for the return of his contribution.[44] However, he may make part of his investment as a contribution and part as a loan, and have outside creditor status for the latter.[45] But, whether limited partner or creditor sharing profits for interest, he may become personally liable if he takes part

42. Ex parte Briggs, 3 D. & C. 367 (1833); King & Co. v. Whichelow, 64 L.J.Com.Law, N.S. 801 (1895); Meehan v. Valentine, 145 U.S. 611, 12 S.Ct. 972, 36 L.Ed. 835 (1892) (one year $10,000 loan, renewed several times, for 10% interest plus 10% of profits over $10,-000; insufficent evidence of partnership to go to jury); In re Mission Farms Dairy, 56 F.2d 346 (9th Cir. 1932) (Calif. law) (advance to buy land, cattle and equipment for dairy; principal and 6% interest, evidenced by note, to be paid from 100% of dairy profits; profits to be split with operator after pay back of advance); Arthur Venneri Co. v. U. S., 169 Ct.Cl. 74, 340 F.2d 337 (1965) (contractor's financing of subcontractor); Spier v. Lang, 4 Cal. 2d 711, 53 P.2d 138 (1935) (advances for drilling oil wells); Dills v. Delira Corp., 145 Cal.App.2d 124, 302 P.2d 397 (1956) (advances to produce radio shows); Lintner v. Millikin, 47 Ill. 178 (1863); Smith v. Knight, 71 Ill. 148, 22 Am.Rep. 94 (1873); Thillman v. Benton, 82 Md. 64, 33 A. 485 (1895); Estabrook v. Woods, 192 Mass. 499, 78 N.E. 538 (1906); Myers v. St. Louis Structural Steel Co., 333 Mo. 464, 65 S.W.2d 931 (1933); Curry v. Fowler, 87 N.Y. 33, 41 Am.Rep. 343 (1881); Harvey v. Childs & Potter, 28 Ohio St. 319, 22 Am.Rep. 387 (1876); Waverly Nat. Bank v. Hall, 150 Pa. 466, 24

A. 665, 30 Am.St.Rep. 823 (1892); Boston & C. Smelting Co. v. Smith, 13 R.I. 27, 43 Am.Rep. 3 (1880); Roark v. Hinson, 24 S.W.2d 1109 (Tex.Civ.App. 1930); In the Matter of the Estate of Starer, 20 Wis.2d 268, 121 N.W.2d 872 (1963) (advances to finance specific merchandise importing transactions).

A lender who mistakenly believes he has become a special partner in a limited partnership does not become a partner merely because the limited firm is defectively organized. Giles v. Vette, 263 U.S. 553, 44 S.Ct. 157, 68 L.Ed. 441 (1923), discussed Sec. 32 below. See also Crane, Are Limited Partnerships Necessary, 17 Minn.L. Rev. 351 (1933); Notes, 22 Mich.L.Rev. 588 (1924), 71 U.Pa.L.Rev. 150 (1923).

The lender is not a partner because the agreement describes him as a silent or special partner, if he has no share in control or ownership of property. Petition of Williams, 297 F. 696 (1st Cir. 1924).

43. See generally, Sec. 26 below.

44. U.L.P.A. §§ 16(1), 23(1).

45. U.L.P.A. § 13, which also allows the limited partner to be secured as a creditor if (generally speaking) the firm is solvent when security is given.

in control.[46]   Query whether there is any difference in the amount of control which will trigger liability in the two situations?

Two leading cases under the U.P.A. illustrate the situations which arise in this area, and their legal results.   In Martin v. Peyton,[47] friends of one partner in a stock brokerage and banking firm (which was in financial difficulties) lent the firm $2,500,000 in liquid securities, in return for which the lenders were to receive 40% of the firm's profits, but not less than $100,000 nor more than $500,000.   The creditors had, through trustees and by a series of agreements: (1) the right to be informed of all transactions affecting the loaned securities, (2) the right to be kept advised of the conduct of the business, (3) the right to be consulted on important matters, (4) the right to inspect the firm's books and have any information they thought important, (5) the right to veto any business they thought highly speculative or injurious, (6) security assignments of each member's interest in the firm and of insurance on the life of one, (7) a prohibition on loans and a limitation on distributions to members of the firm, (8) a qualified right to insist that profits be promptly realized (apparently by liquidating securities held by the firm), (9) options to buy up to 50% interest in the firm, and (10) resignations of each member of the firm.

Although the court recognized that the powers had to be viewed cumulatively rather than individually, the lenders were held not to be liable as partners.   This seems formally correct, since their powers were not for affirmative control of the business.   The various clauses were regarded merely as protection for their creditor interests.   The fact that they held unexercised options to become partners added strength (of a sort) to their argument that they had not become partners.

There can be little doubt that, under the circumstances, they could have exercised affirmative control if they chose.   Apparently no issue was made of their actual behavior, and the case was tried on the documents.   Even so, the very extensive veto power, coupled with other rights, might have been considered the substantial equivalent of affirmative control.   The decision demonstrates the considerable power a creditor can have without becoming liable as a partner, if his creditor status is first firmly fixed by the documents.   It is thus a monument to careful draftsmanship.

---

46.   U.L.P.A. § 7, Sec. 26(c) below.

47.   246 N.Y. 213, 158 N.E. 77 (1927), noted 2 St. John's L.Rev. 51 (1927), 2 Ala. L.J. 193 (1927), discussed at various points in Secs. 14, 14A above.

Other cases of limited control for protection of loan not constituting partnership: Mollwo v. Court of Wards, L.R. 4 P.C. 419, 17 Eng.Rep. 495 (1872) (veto power over certain activities); Davis v. Patrick, 122 U.S. 138, 7 S. Ct. 1102, 30 L.Ed. 1090 (1887) (lender appointed manager to exercise control until debt paid); Richardson v. Hughitt, 76 N.Y. 55, 32 Am.Rep. 267 (1879) (lender to receive, in pledge, product of manufacturing enterprise until sold); In re Young, 2 K.B. 484, 65 L.J. Com.Law, N.S. 681 (1896) (lender to take charge of office accounts and finances for limited term, for specified sum payable out of profits).

Although not visibly significant in the court's reasoning, the fact that there was both a maximum and a minimum on the share of profits payable to the lenders added force to the claim that they were creditors rather than partners.

In Southern Can Co. of Baltimore City v. Sayler,[48] the owners of a cannery granted D an exclusive sales agency. In turn, D agreed to provide cans and labels, and to advance funds needed to pay for raw materials and wages. He had the right to determine the scale of wages, and to receive half the net profits. He was held liable as a partner. His control extended to fixing most of the costs as well as the price of the product. He was thus an "enterpriser," in the best possible position to distribute the costs or liabilities imposed on him.[49]

The relevant U.P.A. language is: "The receipt by a person of a share of the profits of a business is prima facie evidence that he is a partner in the business, but no such inference shall be drawn if such profits were received in payment . . . as interest on a loan, though the amount of payment vary with the profits of the business."[50] It appears to cover a fixed rate of interest payable only to

---

48. 152 Md. 303, 136 A. 624 (1927).

See other cases finding partnership between investor and associate over whom investor had a considerable degree of control:

Frowde v. Williams, 56 L.J.Com.Law, N.S. 62 (1886); Pooley v. Driver, 5 Ch.Div. 458 (1876); Buford v. Lewis, 87 Ark. 412, 112 S.W. 963 (1908), the person actively carrying on the business appeared to be the representative of the investor; Kennedy & Shaw Lumber Co. v. Taylor, 3 Cal.Unrep.Cas. 697, 96 Cal. xvii, 31 P. 1122 (1892), assignees of construction contract, who were to finance its completion, keep accounts, and pay bills, collect moneys owing, dividing profits with assignor, who was to supervise and direct completion of work, held to be partners with assignor; San Joaquin Light & Power Corporation v. Costaloupes, 96 Cal.App. 322, 274 P. 84 (1929), facts similar to Southern Can Co. v. Sayler; Nowell v. Oswald, 96 Cal.App. 536, 274 P. 423 (1929), backer of theatrical production, who, through his agent, exercised control, see note 38 Yale L.J. 1152; Fougner v. First Nat. Bank of Chicago, 141 Ill. 124, 30 N.E. 442 (1892) investor to take charge of office, finances, books, accounts, sales, and other matters; Somerby v. Buntin, 118 Mass. 279, 19 Am.Rep. 459 (1875), inventor and person financing application for patent, both to join in promoting its exploitation; Hacket v. Stan-

ley, 115 N.Y. 625, 22 N.E. 745 (1889), investor to assist in promoting business, and further advances were contemplated; Poundstone v. Hamburger, 139 Pa. 319, 20 A. 1054 (1891), investor to purchase entire output of business at prearranged price; Spaulding v. Stubbings, 86 Wis. 255, 56 N.W. 469, 39 Am.St.Rep. 888 (1893), investor, receiving half the net profits in addition to interest, participated in management.

49. See Sec. 14 n. 26 above.

50. U.P.A. § 7(4)(d), Sec. 14A above. For applications, see In re Mission Farms Dairy, 56 F.2d 346 (9th Cir. 1932) (Calif. law); McGurk v. Moore, 234 N.C. 248, 67 S.E.2d 53 (1951); In the Matter of the Estate of Starer, 20 Wis.2d 268, 121 N.W.2d 872 (1963).

It seems obvious that too large a proportion of profits allocated to interest will throw the credit relation in doubt. Both the size of the business and the size of the loan are relevant. But I would be suspicious of any arrangement for the financier to get more than 50% of the profits. On the other hand, the fact that payments of a smaller percentage grow in time to be very large in dollar amount merely reflects the wisdom of the financier's choice and should not push him toward partnership.

The notion of profits as interest carries with it the idea that payments will

the extent earned, as well as a designated share of the profits payable instead of or in addition to a fixed rate of interest.

Many arrangements of the kind described in this Section can be regarded as profit sharing in two directions: (1) by the financier as interest or compensation for the use of money, and (2) by the other party as compensation for services.[51] Examples are the financier who puts up the money to buy a car, while the other man resells it,[52] or the financier who supplies money to buy and develop a property, while the other person does the work and makes the sale.[53]

PROFIT SHARING FOR SALE OF BUSINESS OR GOOD WILL

§ 20. Profit sharing in payment for good will of a business or other property, by installments or otherwise, does not of itself establish partnership.

A business or piece of property is commonly valued in terms of its capacity to produce income. Sometimes the capacity is measured by the past; other times it may be estimated for the future. The uncertainties inherent in valuations, particularly as they pertain to the future, may motivate buyer and seller to agree on a price determined wholly or partly by the future, that is by actual income production in the hands of the buyer. The seller may receive a percentage of gross income, or of net, or there may be a more complicated formula. Typically, the seller makes an absolute transfer, except perhaps for a lien to secure his additional purchase price, and does not expect to share in control of the business or property, or in its losses. By such transactions, no partnership is created.

For example, a perfumer transferred his American business, with a license to use his trademarks, to a buyer who promised a royalty of 25% of the net profits.[54] A holder of options on oil concessions in a foreign country assigned them; part of the consideration was a right to share in gross oil production.[55] A holder of certain rights in a proposed irrigation project transferred them for a share in the profits of the enterprise.[56] In a simpler transaction, one sold a tractor for a share of the buyer's profits from using it.[57]

---

stop when the loan principal is repaid. Whether any proportional reduction is necessary in profits when the principal balance is reduced by installments, is an open question.

51. See Sec. 16 above.

52. See Cullingworth v. Pollard, Sec. 14 (g) above; McGurk v. Moore, n. 50 above. Cf. First Nat. Bank of Brownwood v. Chambers, 398 S.W.2d 313 (Tex.Civ.App.1965).

53. See Black v. Brundige, 125 Cal.App. 641, 13 P.2d 999 (1932).

54. Thomson v. Batcheller, 134 App.Div. 506, 119 N.Y.S. 577 (1909).

55. Hammond Oil Co. v. Standard Oil Co., 259 N.Y. 312, 181 N.E. 583 (1932).

56. Palmer v. Maney, 45 Idaho 731, 266 P. 424 (1928).

57. Johnson v. Gill, 235 N.C. 40, 68 S.E. 2d 788 (1952) (nonsuit in favor of former owner when no evidence of partnership was introduced other than profit sharing; actually, it was not clear from the evidence whether he was receiving a share of the profits or a fixed amount, or whether he had sold or leased).

If X finances the purchase of a property or business for Y, with profits or proceeds to be used first for repaying X and then for sharing between them, the payments to X may be regarded as a loan repayment [58] or as a purchase.[59] Either way, there is no partnership merely because of the use of profits.

Just as in the preceding Sections, there is no clear dividing line between the model under discussion (here a sale) and a partner's contribution for a share of profits. If the transferor of property or business participates in the control necessary to co-ownership,[60] or if appropriate intent is present,[61] there may be a finding of partnership.

The U.P.A. codification is: "The receipt by a person of a share of the profits is prima facie evidence that he is a partner in the business, but no such inference shall be drawn if such profits were received in payment . . . as the consideration for the sale of a good-will or a business or other property by installments or otherwise." [62] The provision appears applicable whether the buyer or seller is an individual, partnership or corporation. Thus it might cover a retiring partner's sale of his interest to a co-partner or stranger, or its liquidation by payments from the firm.[63]

ILLEGALITY

§ 21. If a partnership's purpose or operation is illegal, the partners generally cannot enforce their agreements against one another (by accounting or otherwise) or against third persons, although third persons (if innocent) can enforce against the partners and the firm. A partner may have an accounting if he is not in pari delicto, or if the illegality is incidental or completed. Illegality dissolves the partnership.

Illegality may taint a partnership in various ways. The business itself may violate criminal statutes, like those on dope peddling or usurious loans, or contravene some more general public policy. One or more of the partners may be disqualified from engaging in the business, say, because he lacks a required license as a contractor or liquor dealer.[67] Or the consideration for the partnership agreement may be illicit, like sexual relations. Although the courts regularly say that no partnership comes into existence from such illegal bargains,[68] their view is largely discredited as a matter of contract law,[69] and is incon-

---

58. Sec. 15 above.

59. In re Mission Farms Dairy, 56 F.2d 346 (9th Cir. 1932) (Calif. law).

60. See Sec. 14(d) above.

61. See Sec. 5(a) above.

62. U.P.A. § 7(4) (e), Sec. 14A above. On good will generally, see Sec. 84 below.

63. Cf. Sec. 18 at n. 36 above. [Notes 64–66 omitted.]

67. See Sec. 22A(a) below.

68. On the various kinds of illegal contracts, see Restatement, Contracts §§ 512–609.

69. See Harding, Book Review, 16 Texas L.Rev. 614, 615 (1938); Restatement, Contracts, § 598, Comment.

sistent with the U.P.A.[70] What the courts are doing is denying enforceability to one of the guilty parties. Ironically, it is another guilty party who typically raises illegality to escape his own bargain, from which he has probably benefitted.

In numerous instances, the courts have refused an accounting between partners whose business was illegal.[71] "The Highwaymen's Case" [72] is the earliest we know about; the business was robbery. The parties were hanged and the plaintiff's solicitors were fined. Less colorful examples of accounting denial include: the illegal manufacture or sale of liquor; [73] obtaining public contracts by fictitious bids and suppression of competition [74] or by bids which do not disclose the real parties in interest (one of whom is a public employee, forbidden to make such a contract); [75] illegal restraint of trade; [76] gambling; [77]

---

[70]. See below at n. 6.

[71]. Cases are collected, Annot., Right of partner or joint adventurer to accounting where firm business or transactions are illegal, 32 A.L.R.2d 1345 (1953).

[72]. Everet v. Williams, decided about 1725 and referred to in a note to Ashhurst v. Mason, 20 L.R.Eq. 230 (1875); Lindley, Partnership 135 (12th ed. 1962); Note, 9 L.Q.Rev. 197 (1893); McMullen v. Hoffman, 174 U.S. 639, 654, 19 S.Ct. 839, 845, 43 L.Ed. 1117 (1898).

[73]. Rutkin v. Reinfeld, 229 F.2d 248 (2d Cir.1956) (N.Y. law); Hooper v. Barranti, 81 Cal.App.2d 570, 184 P.2d 688 (1948); Rigo v. De Gutis, 341 Mich. 126, 67 N.W.2d 224 (1954) (P was silent partner, unlicensed); Parise v. Pepe, 270 App.Div. 769, 59 N.Y.S.2d 497 (1946) (partnership liquor store, only one partner licensed); Nahas v. George, 156 Ohio St. 52, 99 N.E.2d 898, 32 A.L.R.2d 1339 (1951) (liquor license required for cafe operation; D had license, P did not); Tucker v. Binenstock, 310 Pa. 254, 165 A. 247 (1933) (large-scale liquor manufacture during Prohibition; "protection" payments to police); Vandegrift v. Vandegrift, 226 Pa. 254, 75 A. 365, 18 Ann.Cas. 404 (1910); Sponholz v. Meyer, 270 Wis. 288, 70 N.W.2d 619 (1955) (P was silent partner, unlicensed).

[74]. McMullen v. Hoffman, n. 72 above; Hunter v. Pfeiffer, 108 Ind. 197, 9 N.E. 124 (1886). See Kennedy v. Lonabaugh, 19 Wyo. 352, 117 P. 1079, Ann. Cas.1913E, 133 (1900) (illegal conspiracy to acquire government coal lands).

Cf. Johnston v. Senecal, 329 Mass. 556, 109 N.E.2d 467 (1952). The illegality was wining and dining municipal officials to induce them to buy parking meters from the partnership. Although this would seem a relatively incidental illegality, the court found it (without stating the basis for the finding) to be a purpose of the partnership, and therefor to bar an accounting suit by one partner against another.

[75]. Woodworth v. Bennett, 43 N.Y. 273, 3 Am.Rep. 706 (1870).

Cf. Miller v. Ousley, 334 Ill. 183, 165 N.E. 629 (1929) (absent a prohibiting statute, a traffic policeman might legally be a partner in a filling station and was entitled to an accounting).

[76]. Farbenfabriken Bayer A. G. v. Sterling Drug Co., 307 F.2d 207 (2d Cir. 1962), cert. denied 372 U.S. 939, 83 S.Ct. 872, 9 L.Ed.2d 733 (1963) (division of markets, suppression of competition); Ful-Vue Sales Co. v. American Optical Co., 118 F.Supp. 517 (S.D. N.Y.1953) (joint venture to acquire stock of a corporation to stifle competition by it); Craft v. McConoughy, 79 Ill. 346, 22 Am.Rep. 171 (1875); Sampson v. Shaw, 101 Mass. 145, 3 Am.Rep. 327 (1869); Morris Run Coal Co. v. Barclay Coal Co., 68 Pa. 173, 8 Am.Rep. 159 (1871).

An arrangement between affiliated corporations for division of markets does not escape the Sherman Anti-Trust Act by labeling it a joint venture. Timken Roller Bearing Co. v. U. S., 341 U.S. 593, 71 S.Ct. 971, 95 L.Ed. 1199 (1951).

[77]. See note 77 on page 100.

leasing of furnished apartments to prostitutes;[78] trading with the enemy;[79] the use by executors of estate funds for their private business;[80] sales above ceiling prices;[81] liquor during Prohibition;[82] practice of law by an attorney and a layman as partners.[83] Generally, the results are the same if the partnership business is a kind requiring licenses, and no one is licensed,[84] or if some partners are licensed but the firm or other partners are not, particularly if plaintiff is unlicensed.[85] By the same token, a court does not impose liability on a party to an illegal partnership contract, for failing to perform.[86] A non-competition covenant in the agreement for an illegal partnership will not be enforced.[87]

77. Central Trust & Safe Deposit Co. v. Respass, 112 Ky. 606, 66 S.W. 421, 56 L.R.A. 479, 99 Am.St.Rep. 317 (1902); McDonald v. Lund, 13 Wash. 412, 43 P. 348 (1896); Shaffner v. Pinchback, 133 Ill. 410, 24 N.E. 867, 23 Am.St.Rep. 624 (1890); Brower v. Johnson, 56 Wash.2d 321, 352 P.2d 814 (1960), citing this text (remanded to determine whether pin ball machines were gambling devices).

Similarly for isolated transactions which are classifiable as joint ventures. Ciampittiello v. Campitello, 134 Conn. 51, 54 A.2d 669 (1949) (forum state's anti-gambling policy barred recovery of joint venture horserace winnings which were legal where made), criticized, Corbin, Contracts § 1530 n. 85 (1962); Bloodworth v. Gay, 213 Ga. 51, 96 S.E.2d 602 (1957) (auto won in lottery).

78. Chateau v. Singla, 114 Cal. 91, 45 P. 1015, 33 L.R.A. 750, 55 Am.St.Rep. 63 (1896).

79. Dunham v. Presby, 120 Mass. 285 (1876). See Snell v. Dwight, 120 Mass. 9 (1876) and Sec. 11 above.

80. Bowen v. Richardson, 133 Mass. 293 (1882), at least where the beneficiaries have not waived their right to demand the profits.

81. Johnson v. Graf, 162 Neb. 396, 75 N.W.2d 916 (1956).

82. Rutkin v. Reinfeld, and Tucker v. Binenstock, both n. 73 above.

83. Waychoff v. Waychoff, 309 Pa. 300, 163 A. 670, 86 A.L.R. 190 (1932); Holland v. Sheehan, 108 Minn. 362, 122 N.W. 1, 23 L.R.A.,N.S., 510, 17

Ann.Cas. 687 (1909) (ambulance chaser P, attorney D).

Cf. Matter of Jackson and Wood, 1 B. & C. 270, 107 Eng.Rep. 101 (1823) (attorney who entered law partnership with clerk was ordered stricken from the rolls. One not admitted to the bar may act as attorney in fact for the collection of claims, and may hire an attorney to render legal services without thereby creating a partnership for the practice of law. Grapel v. Hodges, 112 N.Y. 419, 20 N.E. 542 (1889). See generally on partnerships of lawyers and non-lawyers, A.B.A. Canon of Professional Ethics No. 33; Drinker, Legal Ethics 203–09 (1953).

84. Maslowski v. Bitter, 7 Wis.2d 167, 96 N.W.2d 349 (1959) (real estate brokers).

85. Liquor sales: Hooper v. Barranti; Rigo v. DeGutis; Parise v. Pepe; Nahas v. George; Vandegrift v. Vandegrift; Sponholz v. Meyer; all n. 73 above.

Funeral homes: Thatcher v. Snyder, 308 Ill.App. 325, 31 N.E.2d 333 (1941); Searles v. Haynes, 126 Ind.App. 626, 129 N.E.2d 362 (1955), rehearing denied 130 N.E.2d 482 (1955).

Jitney line: Cerino v. Van Orden, 98 N.J.Eq. 7, 129 A. 704 (1925).

86. Foster v. Driscoll [1929] 1 K.B. 470, 98 L.J.K.B. 282 (contract to export whiskey from England to U. S. during Prohibition).

87. Brower v. Johnson, 56 Wash.2d 321, 352 P.2d 814 (1960) (covenant limited to term of partnership; illegality would end term by dissolution).

The rationales are the ones familiar in general contract cases, especially deterrence of illegal bargains and disinclination to aid wrongdoers who have chosen to operate outside the law.

The hands off doctrine can easily produce inequitable results, and courts have found ways around it, more or less selectively. At least one state allows an accounting on the theory that, even if the partnership agreement is illegal, it is not enforced by accounting.[88] Or the illegality may seem so limited,[89] or so one-sided,[90] that a court will grant relief. The business may be only partially illegal. If it is possible to separate the legal from the illegal phases, an accounting may be had for the proceeds of the legal part, as in a firm to breed race horses and enter them in races (a legal business) although the partners also jointly carry on illegal bookmaking and betting.[91] If the illegality begins or ends during the partnership operations, accounting may be granted for the period of proper operation.[91A] Similarly, if the illegal business has been concluded, and a partner has rendered an accounting for proceeds and holds them under a new agreement as debtor or depositary, he may be compelled to pay over,[92] as may one with whom money has been deposited, but not yet authorized to be

---

88. Peterson v. Tharp, 299 F.2d 434 (5th Cir.1962) (Texas law), cert. denied 371 U.S. 889, 83 S.Ct. 184, 9 L. Ed.2d 122 (1962), and Texas cases there cited.

89. Jones v. Rutherford, 8 Cal.2d 603, 67 P.2d 92 (1937) (joint venturer in dog racing track securing appointment as town solicitor by denying his interest in the venture not barred from an accounting for profits of the venture); Vaszauskas v. Vaszauskas, 115 Conn. 418, 161 A. 856 (1932) (some illegal liquor dealing in an otherwise legal trading business); Kist v. Coughlin, 210 Ind. 622, 1 N.E.2d 602 (1936) (partnership to acquire stock in three newspaper corporations; even if contrary to public policy, a partner could not take advantage of it to withhold property from his co-partners). Cf. n. 6 below.

90. See below at n. 94.

91. Central Trust & Safe Deposit Co. v. Respass, n. 77 above; Sharp v. Taylor, 2 Ph. 801, 41 Eng.Rep. 1153 (1849), disapproved by dictum in Sykes v. Beadon, L.R. 11 Ch.Div. 170, 48 L.J. N.S. 522 (1849).

91A. Searles v. Haynes, n. 85 above (statute changed requirement for licensing); Vaszauskas v. Vaszauskas, n. 89 above.

See Holst v. Butler, 379 Pa. 124, 108 A.2d 740 (1954). Ps were in military service when they became partners in a firm doing business with the government in a way that was illegal because of their conflict of interest. A new agreement was negotiated on their release from service. They sued only under the new agreement (and for the period after release); they prevailed.

92. McDonald v. Lund, n. 77 above (gambling); De Leon v. Manuel Trevino & Bro., 49 Tex. 88, 30 Am.Rep. 101 (1878) (notes given in settlement of accounts arising out of trading with the enemy); Brooks v. Martin, 69 U.S. (2 Wall.) 70, 17 L.Ed. 732 (1864) (preissuance purchase of soldiers' land warrants was illegal, but, before suit, warrants had been issued, and lands mostly located and resold).

But remedy was refused in Mackin v. Shannon, 165 F. 98 (D.Ark.1908) (gambling); Dunham v. Presby, n. 79 above (trading with the enemy, even though there had been a settlement of accounts); McMullen v. Hoffman, n. 74 above (distinguishing Brooks v. Martin, supra this n.).

The degree of illegality of the original transaction may influence the court. See Note, 41 Harv.L.Rev. 650 (1928).

used, for an illegal purpose.[93]   One partner who has been materially guiltier than the other may be called to account; [94] the courts are fond of exercising their Latin and saying that the latter is not *in pari delicto*.[95]   And, of course, a court may be willing to stretch a bit to find that there has been no illegality,[96] or that the illegality was not part of the partnership agreement.[97]

Another device available to ease the harshness of the illegality rule is waiver.   A court occasionally finds the illegality issue waived by failure to raise it in the pleadings or on trial,[98] although most permit it to be raised at any time, or will raise it themselves.[99]

As between the partnership and third persons, the firm is entitled to no remedies to enforce an illegal transaction.   A firm formed for illegal restraint of trade cannot maintain a suit for goods sold.[1]   A partnership not properly licensed to carry on its business cannot (often by specific provision of the licensing statute) enforce contracts which are part of that business.[2]

---

93. Sampson v. Shaw, 101 Mass. 145, 3 Am.Rep. 327 (1869); Keen v. Price, [1914] 2 Ch.Div. 98, 83 L.J.Ch.Div. 865. Cf. Restatement, Contracts § 605; Fryer v. Harker, 142 Iowa 708, 121 N.W. 526, 23 L.R.A.,N.S., 477 (1909).

94. Brand v. Elledge, 89 Ariz. 200, 360 P.2d 213 (1961), subsequent opinion 101 Ariz. 352, 419 P.2d 531 (1966) (older woman (D) induced younger (P) to invest in tavern with liquor license only in D's name; P made full disclosure of recent residence to licensing authority who agreed to reissue in both names after P completed several more months of residence; D lulled P into leaving license in D's name); Morris v. Morris, 117 A. 644 (R.I.1922).

95. See generally, Grodecki, In Pari Delicto Potior Est Conditio Defendentis, 71 L.Q.Rev. 254 (1955).

96. See Thompson v. McCormick, 149 Colo. 465, 370 P.2d 442 (1962) (A.E.C. non-assignability clause in its lease to D was for A.E.C.'s protection and did not bar division of profits of lease with P); Lloyd v. Wiseman, 51 Tenn. App. 401, 368 S.W.2d 303 (1963) (real estate license not necessary since selling own land); Waring v. Lobdell, 69 Wash.2d 972, 416 P.2d 359 (1966), prior opinion 63 Wash.2d 532, 387 P.2d 979 (1964) (pin ball machines held not to be gambling devices; operator allowed to recover from owner (they shared 50-50) half of amount paid U. S. for gaming device license).

97. Fernandez v. Garza, 88 Ariz. 214, 354 P.2d 260 (1960) (agreement to live together not consideration for partnership in rental properties).

98. Penrod v. Smith, 9 Ill.App.2d 257, 132 N.E.2d 675 (1956).

99. Lewis & Queen v. N. M. Ball Sons, 48 Cal.2d 141, 308 P.2d 713 (1957) (may raise on appeal); Greene v. Brooks, 235 Cal.App.2d 161, 45 Cal. Rptr. 99 (1965) (finding, however, no illegality in liquor license only in Ds, construing the agreement as one not to operate illegally, and noting that Ps could have been licensed); Johnson v. Graf, 162 Neb. 396, 75 N.W.2d 916 (1956) (need not be pleaded); Brower v. Johnson, 56 Wash.2d 321, 352 P.2d 814 (1960) (need not be pleaded).

1. Jackson v. Akron Brick Ass'n, 53 Ohio St. 303, 41 N.E. 257, 35 L.R.A. 287, 53 Am.St.Rep. 638 (1895).

Cf. Jeffrey v. Bamford, [1921] 2 K.B. 351, 90 L.J.K.B. (N.S.) 664. Since, in England, gambling is illegal only so far as provided by statute, a bookmaking firm could recover payments made to a customer, pursuant to the Gaming Act.

2. Lewis & Queen v. N. M. Ball Sons, n. 99 above (construction contractor, one partner licensed; statute denied access to courts).

A third person cannot enforce against a partnership formed for an illegal purpose a contract with illegal subject matter.[3] But if the third person makes a contract with a legal subject matter and is without knowledge of the partnership's illegal purpose, he has a remedy at least against the partner who contracts with him, and also against the co-partners if they participate in the making of the contract or authorize it.[4] In favor of the innocent third person the usual incidents of partnership ought to apply, so he should be able to hold the other partners liable on apparent authority, and have a priority in joint assets over separate creditors.[5]

Following the modern view of contract, the U.P.A. does not specify that legality of purpose or object is essential to the existence of a partnership. This was a deliberate choice of the draftsmen,[6] who preferred to make illegality a cause of dissolution. This suggests no adamant hostility toward accounting rights among the partners, although the courts have apparently not used this hint to justify accountings in appropriate cases.[7] A consequence of dissolution by illegality is that a partner's subsequent acts do not bind the firm unless they are for winding up.[8] This may impose an undue hardship on innocent third persons who deal with him.[9]

3. Forsyth v. Woods, 78 U.S. (11 Wall.) 484, 20 L.Ed. 207 (1870) (surety on bond given to effect an illegal partnership cannot recover reimbursement for payments made).

4. Fairlane Estates v. Carrico Const. Co., 228 Cal.App.2d 65, 39 Cal.Rptr. 35 (1964) (owner v. contractors for breach of construction contract; one D licensed, others not; judgment for P affirmed).

5. Patty-Joiner Co. v. City Bank of Sherman, 15 Tex.Civ.App. 475, 41 S.W. 173 (1897), partnership for illegal purpose (cotton buyers, ostensibly competitors); separate creditors deferred to firm creditor in distribution of insolvent estate.

6. "Again, it is not said that the business must be a lawful business. The effect of unlawfulness of the business is dealt with [in U.P.A. § 31(3), Sec. 76 below]. . . . If the business is wholly unlawful, then the partnership is dissolved the moment it is created. The omission of the word 'lawful' in the definition [U.P.A. § 6(1)] does not prevent this result. Very often, however, a business may be in part lawful and in part unlawful. Hotel-keepers may run a 'dive.' Placing the word 'lawful' before the word business in the definition would tend to throw a doubt on the propriety of the orderly winding of such a business as a partnership." Commissioners' Note to U.P.A. § 6, 7 Unif.Laws Ann. 12 (1949).

7. For example, in Brower v. Johnson, n. 99 above, the court refers to dissolution by illegality to hold unenforceable a non-competition covenant written to last for the life of the firm but does not intimate that it may modify in any way the rule on illegality barring an accounting, which was also sought in the action.

8. U.P.A. § 35(3) (a), Sec. 81 below.

9. Crane, The Uniform Partnership Act —A Criticism, 28 Harv.L.Rev. 762, 781 (1915); Note, Partnerships for an Illegal Purpose, 41 Harv.L.Rev. 650 (1928); Lewis, The Uniform Partnership Act—A Reply to Mr. Crane's Criticism, 29 Harv.L.Rev. 291, 302 (1916). See also Recent Case, 37 Harv. L.Rev. 773 (1924).

PARTNERSHIP NAME AND REGISTRATION REQUIREMENTS

§ 22. A partnership name is common but not essential to the existence of a firm. A partnership may do business in the name of one or more of the partners, or in a fictitious name. Statutes require the registration of fictitious names; non-compliance brings diverse sanctions, including fines and inability to sue on partnership contracts and transactions.

The use of a firm name is some evidence of partnership, and the inclusion of an individual's name in the firm name is some evidence that he is a partner.[10] Except for limited partnerships—which must have names [11]—there is no requirement that a partnership have a name.[12] Nor, except for the law of unfair competition and deceptive trade practices, is there any general restriction on the kind of name it can have if it chooses to have one. The name can consist of the names of several or all the partners [13] or of one of them.[14] It can contain last names only, like "Smith and Jones," or add descriptive organizational words, like "Smith, Jones & Co.," "Smith Company," or "Jones and Sons." [15] In most places, a made up or fictitious name, such as "The Corner Grocery," "Swank Shop" or "Investment Opportunities" may

10. See Sec. 14(a) n. 91 above. See also Sec. 36 below.

11. U.L.P.A. § 2(1) (a) (I) clearly implies the need for a name.

12. Partners may carry on business without agreeing on a firm name. Getchell v. Foster, 106 Mass. 42 (1870); Townsend v. L. J. Appel Sons, 164 Md. 255, 164 A. 679 (1933); Meriden Nat. Bank v. Gallaudet, 120 N.Y. 298, 24 N.E. 994 (1890).

A name must be shown on the partnership's income tax return, U. S. Treasury Dept., Internal Revenue Service, Form 1065.

13. Dreyfus v. Union Nat. Bank, 164 Ill. 83, 45 N.E. 408 (1896); Berkshire Woolen Co. v. Juillard, 75 N.Y. 535, 31 Am.Rep. 488 (1879); C. W. West & Co. v. Valley Bank, 6 Ohio St. 168 (1856).

If the entity theory of partnership prevails (see Sec. 3 above), the Statute of Frauds would require that a contract of the partnership be signed in the firm name. Dunbar v. Farnum, 109 Vt. 313, 196 A. 237, 114 A.L.R. 996 (1937), noted 4 U.Pitt.L.Rev. 307.

14. Le Roy, Bayard & Co. v. Johnson, 27 U.S. (2 Pet.) 186, 7 L.Ed. 391 (1829);

Lazarus v. Manufacturers Cas. Ins. Co., 105 U.S.App.D.C. 357, 267 F.2d 634 (1959) (liability policy issued in name of "Rubenstein T/A [trading as] Transport Amoco Service" covered Rubenstein's partner); Daugherty v. Heckard, 189 Ill. 239, 59 N.E. 569 (1901); Bank of Rochester v. Monteath & Keeler, 1 Denio 402, 43 Am. Dec. 681 (N.Y.1845). For the ramifications of the Lazarus case, see Hayden, Does a Garage Liability Policy Survive a "Dead" Partnership?, 1960 Ins.L.J. 495.

15. Application of Seigal, 9 Misc.2d 751, 171 N.Y.S.2d 186 (Sup.Ct.1958) ("Company" all right, but not "Ltd." because of latter's corporate connotation). "Inc." and "Corp." are ruled out on similar grounds. "Ltd." would presumably be acceptable for a limited partnership.

In some states a sole proprietor may not use "Company," e. g., McKinney's N.Y. Penal Law, § 924 (1944). The aim is to avoid the misleading impression that the business has more than one owner. On this ground, a sole owner in N. Y. may not use his name "and Associates." Application of Proctor, 2 Misc.2d 881, 149 N.Y.S. 2d 100 (Sup.Ct.1956).

be used.   Some professions exercise control over use and choice of names.[16]

Doing business in the name of one partner is likely to generate confusion as to when the firm is acting and when he is acting individually.   On the whole, it is a question of fact in any given case, and the burden of proof is one the person asserting a partnership transaction.[17]   But a firm which does business in the name of one partner will have a hard time denying that acts in his name are partnership acts;   the doctrines of estoppel and apparent ownership work against the firm.[18]

A firm name is often an economic advantage and sometimes a practical necessity, particularly when the firm does business with the public.   If nothing else, the opening of a bank account will call for the adoption or designation of some name.   If there is a firm name, transactions are usually made in that name, although this is not compulsory.   The partnership name signed to a contract or promissory note has been said to be the equivalent (for liability purposes) of signatures of all the partners.[19]   However, the statement needs qualification: the results depend on the authority of the person signing the firm name.[20]

Title to personalty may be acquired and disposed of in the firm name.[21]   So may title to realty under the U.P.A.[22] but not under the common law which remains in effect in a few states.   Litigation in

---

16. Broadly speaking, law firms may not have fictitious names, may not include the names of non-lawyers, must drop the name of a member who becomes a judge or leaves the firm to practice elsewhere, but may include (with appropriate indications) the name of a retired or dead member. Many other details are regulated. See A.B.A. Canons of Professional Ethics, No. 33; Drinker, Legal Ethics 206–09 (1953).

17. Yorkshire Banking Co. v. Beason, 4 C.P.D. 204, 48 L.J.Q.B. 422 (1878); Bank of America Nat. Trust & Sav. Ass'n v. Kumle, 70 Cal.App.2d 362, 160 P.2d 875 (1945) (money lent on partner's note is presumably lent to him individually, not to the firm; it is not a loan to the firm merely because the proceeds go to the firm as the partner's capital contribution); Manufacturers' & Mechanics' Bank v. Winship, 22 Mass. (5 Pick.) 11, 16 Am.Dec. 369 (1827); Etheridge v. Binney, 26 Mass. (9 Pick.) 272 (1830); Frederick v. Citizens' Nat. Bank, 231 F. 667 (3d Cir. 1916). See Rumsey v. Briggs, 139 N.Y. 323, 34 N.E. 929 (1893).

If the partner whose name is used has no separate business, this is sometimes prima facie evidence that he is acting for the firm.   Bank of Rochester v. Monteath, n. 14 above; Mifflin v. Smith, 17 Serg. & R. 165 (Pa.1828). But see Burroughs' Appeal, 26 Pa. 264 (1856).

18. Swan v. Steele, 7 East 210, 103 Eng. Rep. 80 (1806); Kallison v. Harris Trust & Sav. Bank, 338 Ill.App. 33, 86 N.E.2d 858 (1949); Kellogg v. Fancher, 23 Wis. 21, 99 Am.Dec. 96 (1868).

See Willey v. Crocker-Woolworth Nat. Bank, 141 Cal. 508, 75 P. 106 (1904) (bank may set off partner's debt against partnership deposit carried in partner's name).

19. Haskins v. D'Este, 133 Mass. 356 (1882).

20. See Secs. 48–53 below.

21. Sec. 38 below.

22. Ibid.

the firm name was not countenanced at common law and is not directly affected by the U.P.A., but is permitted by other laws in many states.[23]

The firm name may acquire considerable value and be the subject of dispute if used by some of the partners after dissolution. This problem can, and usually should, be anticipated by the partnership agreement.[24]

Almost all states have statutes requiring the registration of fictitious or assumed names used in business.[24A] The statutes vary in detail but always call for a filing in the public records (sometimes accompanied by newspaper publication) of the full names and addresses of the individuals doing business in the fictitious name.[24B] The objective, of course, is to make this information available to interested persons for business and credit purposes.[25] The statutes apply to partnerships, along with sole proprietorships and perhaps corporations. By most of the statutes, surnames alone are not fictitious, so that neither "Smith & Jones" nor "Sam S. Smith and John J. Jones" has to be registered if used by Smith and Jones.[26] Under all the statutes, either name is fictitious if the owners of the business are

---

23. Secs. 57, 60 below.

24. See Sec. 84 below.

24A. E. g., West's Ann.Cal.Civ.Code, §§ 2466–2471 (file certificate in county of principal business and publish in newspaper there; may not maintain suit on contract or transaction in fictitious name until certificate filed; must renew every 5 years); Ill.Rev. Stat.1965, c. 96, §§ 4–8a (file certificate in county where business is conducted and publish in newspaper there; $25–$100 fine and 10–30 days jail for each day's violation; non-complying firm may be sued in firm name); M.C.L.A. (Mich.) §§ 445.1–445.5 (file certificate in county where business is conducted; must renew every 5 years; $25–$100 fine and up to 30 days jail for each violation; may not maintain suit on any contract or transaction had in fictitious name until it complies); McKinney's N.Y.Penal Law, §§ 440–440-a (file certificate in county where business is conducted and display at each place of business; failure to file is misdemeanor); see also McKinney's N.Y.Partnership Law, §§ 80–81 on continuation of use of partnership names in certain instances; the N.Y. statutes are the most detailed on firm names; 54 P.S. (Pa.) §§ 28.1–28.13 (file certificate in county where principal business is located and at capitol; notice of intention to file must be published; $25 fine for non-compliance; may not sue on any contract until compliance); Vernon's Ann.Civ.St. (Tex.) arts. 5924–5927, id. P.C. arts. 1067–1070 (file certificate in counties where business is conducted; must renew every 10 years; $25–$100 fine for each day's violation).

24B. They usually require appropriate amendment in case of change of personnel.

25. Accordingly, inclusion of a person who is not a partner does not make him liable to a tort claimant who cannot be said to have detrimentally relied on the registration. Rowland v. Canuso, 329 Pa. 72, 196 A. 823 (1938).

See Lipman v. Thomas, 143 Me. 270, 61 A.2d 130 (1948). An unregistered partnership was allowed to recover for goods sold. "The statute sought to protect the public against fraud and deceit in extending credit. It was not intended to protect those who obtained credit from the partnership."

26. Andrews v. Glick, 205 Cal. 699, 272 P.2d 587 (1928); Cruse v. Wilson, 92 So.2d 270 (Fla.1957); Harris and Lewis v. Ballachino, 106 N.E.2d 174 (Ohio App.1951).

Thomas and King; under most of them, it is fictitious if the owners are Smith, Jones, *and* Thomas and King.[27]

The filing of a fictitious name certificate listing persons as owners of a business is evidence that they are partners,[28] but it is not conclusive.[29]

The statutes are often ignored. Non-compliance invokes varying sanctions, depending on the terms of the statute [30] and the views of the courts.[31] There was a period when a non-complying partnership's contracts were thought illegal and were held unenforceable by the firm.[32] This view has largely disappeared by changing decisions [33] or by statutory amendments.[34] In most states, compliance at any time before bringing suit is sufficient.[35] Elsewhere, non-compliance may

27. As to what are fictitious names, see cases in n. 26 above and Cashin v. Pliter, 168 Mich. 386, 134 N.W. 482, Ann.Cas.1913C, 697 (1912) ("Flint Construction & Realty Company" is fictitious for Cashin and another); Axe v. Tolbert, 179 Mich. 556, 146 N.W. 418 (1914) ("William Axe & Son" not fictitious for William Axe and son); Schwarz & Gottlieb v. Marcuse, 175 Cal. 401, 165 P. 1015 (1917); Befarah v. Spell, 176 N.C. 193, 96 S.E. 949 (1918) ("Aboud Bros." (used by Aboud alone after withdrawal of brother) and "The Raleigh Bargain House, Nassif & Befarah Proprietors" (used by Nassif and Befarah) not fictitious); Walker v. Mason, 272 Pa. 315, 116 A. 305 (1922) ("W. & H. Walker" not fictitious when used by William and Hay Walker, though the firm name was originated by their father and uncle with the same first names).

28. E. g., Leyendecker v. Robertson, 352 S.W.2d 363 (Tex.Civ.App.1961).

29. J. C. Wattenbarger & Sons v. Sanders, 216 Cal.App.2d 495, 30 Cal.Rptr. 910 (Dist.Ct.App.1963).

30. See n. 24A above.

31. Cases are collected, Annot., Construction and effect as to doing business under an assumed or fictitious name or designation not showing the names of the persons interested, 45 A.L.R. 198 (1926), supplemented 42 A.L.R.2d 516 (1955).

32. Hunter v. Big Four Auto Co., 162 Ky. 778, 173 S.W. 120, L.R.A.1915D, 987 (1915); Maurer v. Greening Nursery Co., 199 Mich. 522, 526, 165 N.W. 861, aff'd 168 N.W. 448 (1917); Moyer

v. Kennedy, 76 Pa.Super, 523 (1921); Bristol v. Chas. F. Noble Oil & Gas Co., 273 S.W. 946 (Tex.Civ.App.1925).

33. Piggly-Wiggly Stores, Inc. v. Lowenstein, 197 Ind. 62, 147 N.E. 771 (1925); Hayes v. Providence Citizens' Bank & Trust Co., 218 Ky. 128, 290 S.W. 1028, 59 A.L.R. 450 (1927); Paragon Oil Syndicate v. Rhoades Drilling Co., 115 Tex. 149, 277 S.W. 1036 (1925).

A more recent example of strict application is Sanguin v. Wallace, 205 Okl. 28, 234 P.2d 394, 42 A.L.R.2d 511 (1951). A partnership sued for encroachment on its property by a neighbor's building. It did business in an assumed name and had filed no certificate. Held: suit allowed for damage to land (considered owned by partners as co-tenants) but not for damage to partnership business (despite fact that no contract or transaction in partnership name was involved in the encroachment.)

34. Johnson v. Englebertson, 232 Mich. 518, 205 N.W. 604 (1925); Lamb v. Condon, 276 Pa. 544, 120 A. 546 (1923).

35. Bryant v. Wellbanks, 88 Cal.App. 144, 263 P. 332 (1928); Hill v. Paige Motor Co., 123 Okl. 254, 253 P. 97 (1927); Uhlmann v. Kin Daw, 97 Or. 681, 193 P. 435 (1920); Mellgren Plumbing Shop Inc. v. Lewis & Tinsley, Inc., 77 S.D. 193, 90 N.W.2d 78 (1958).

See Lewis v. Root Paint & Glass Co., 53 Wash.2d 781, 337 P.2d 52 (1959) (may ordinarily comply after filing suit but before trial if no prejudice to other party). Some statutes so specify, e. g., Calif., Mich., and Pa., n. 24A above.

bring a fine but have no effect on the enforceability of contracts.[36] Non-compliance by filing a false certificate usually bars recovery.[37]

LICENSING AND QUALIFICATION REQUIREMENTS

§ 22A.   To engage in certain regulated professions and businesses, either partners or partnerships must be licensed.

Partnerships of one state have not been required to qualify in other states before doing business in the other states.   There is a constitutional question whether they may be required to do so.

(a) Regulated Activities

A partnership which participates in a regulated activity normally becomes subject to licensing and related requirements.   These vary from place to place and from business to business; no detailed coverage is attempted here.   In the legal profession, there is usually no licensing required of the firm if the members are individually licensed.   In the securities business, most jurisdictions require registration or licensing of the firm as an entity.[38]   In other businesses or professions, such as construction contracting, medicine, insurance, engineering, accounting, and liquor, either of these patterns may be followed, or some variant.[39]

(b) Business in Other States

Corporations formed under the laws of one state are required to qualify in other states before doing business there.[40]   Qualification usually consists of filing corporate documents, appointing a local agent for service of process, and paying a fee or tax (which may be annual). Such requirements are statutory and have traditionally not been extended to partnerships.   One probable reason is that partnerships have not represented a big enough section of multi-state business to seem worth regulating.   Another is that partnerships have been thought of as constitutionally protected against such regulation.

---

36. People ex rel. Power v. Rose, 219 Ill. 46, 76 N.E. 42 (1905); Ambro Advertising Agency v. Speed-way Mfg. Co., 211 Iowa 276, 233 N.W. 499 (1930); Bassen v. Monckton, 308 Mo. 641, 274 S.W. 404 (1925); Sinclair Refining Co. v. Smith, 13 F.2d 68 (5th Cir. 1926) (Tex. law).

Cf. Cooper Cotton Co. v. First State Bank, 37 S.W.2d 805 (Tex.Civ.App.1931) where further elements of estoppel were present, Recent Case, 10 Texas L.Rev. 246 (1932).

The registration requirements are typically imposed only on persons doing business in the state. A foreign partnership making a single local transaction through a travelling salesman has been held not to be doing business within the registration requirement. Doll v. Rodgers, 98 Colo. 36, 52 P.2d 1147 (1935).

37. Hixson v. Boren, 144 Cal.App.2d 547, 301 P.2d 615 (1956).

38. E. g., Securities Exchange Act of 1934, §§ 15(a) (1), 3(a) (4), (5), (9), 15 U.S.C.A. §§ 78o(a) (1), 78c(a) (4), (5), (9); Uniform Securities Act §§ 201(a), 401(h). Registration of the firm covers the partners as individuals in most states.

39. See Sec. 21 above. Cf. Sec. 34A below.

40. See Sec. 31 below.

Individuals, who are "citizens" of one state may do business in another state free of such regulation, by force of the "privilege and immunities" clause.[41] By long-standing decision, corporations are not "citizens" for this purpose.[42] If partnerships are regarded as mere aggregates of individuals, they appear to be protected; if they are viewed as separate entities, they appear to be subject to regulation by qualification requirement or otherwise. We have seen that the ordinary partnership partakes of both characteristics [43] and that partnership law gives no clear answer to this taxonomic question. The final test will probably be by more functional criteria.[44]

The issue remained academic until the first requirement for qualification of foreign partnerships was imposed by a 1965 statute,[45] quite similar to that for corporations.[46] The issue may now have to be resolved.[47]

Two other aspects of multi-state partnership operation are discussed elsewhere: personal jurisdiction by service on an agent or under "long arm" statutes,[48] and the doubt whether a limited partner's liability protection is valid without refiling the certificate in each state where the firm does business.[49] It hardly needs saying that if a foreign partnership engages in a regulated activity (of the kind described in (a) above), it must comply with the local requirements for licensing and appointment of an agent for services of process.[50] These usually apply equally to local citizens and thus raise no constitutional issue of privileges and immunities.

41. U.S.C.A.Const. Art. 4, § 2, cl. 1. See Sec. 62 n. 71 below.

42. Paul v. Virginia, 75 U.S. (8 Wall.) 177, 19 L.Ed. 357 (1868).

43. Sec. 3 above.

44. Cf. Hemphill v. Orloff, 277 U.S. 537, 48 S.Ct. 577, 72 L.Ed. 978 (1928) allowing a business trust (an unincorporated organization) to be treated like a corporation for qualification purposes because of its corporate qualities. See generally, Secs. 33(c), 34 below.

45. R.S.A. (N.H.) 305–A:1–305–A:7 (1966).

46. The N.H. provision calls for a registered office and agent in the state, a $50 initial fee and a $25 annual maintenance fee. No filing of the partnership agreement is required, nor even the names of the partners. A non-complying partnership may not sue in the state's courts and may be enjoined from doing business in the state and fined $500. Service of process in any suit may be made on the registered agent or on the secretary of state if the agent is not maintained or cannot be served.

47. See Note, Qualification of Foreign Partnerships, 52 Cornell L.Q. 157 (1966).

48. Sec. 62 below.

49. Sec. 26 at nn. 30–31 below.

50. See Uniform Securities Act § 414 (g), (h); X–L Liquors v. Taylor, 17 N.J. 444, 111 A.2d 753 (1955) (administrative regulation requiring out of state liquor licensee to appoint local agent was valid).

EFFECT OF THE STATUTE OF FRAUDS ON FORMATION AND OPERATION OF PARTNERSHIPS

§ 23. **Some sections of the Statute of Frauds may apply to the formation of partnerships, or their operations. These are the sections on**

(a) **Agreements not performable in a year.**

(b) **Promises to answer for the debt of another.**

(c) **Sale of goods or lands.**

So far as the substantive law of partnership is concerned, no written agreement is necessary to establish or continue the relation. Since most litigation over the existence of a partnership involves arrangements without written agreements, the party denying partnership or trying to avoid an accounting will invoke the Statute of Frauds for whatever it is worth, along with his case on the merits. Several portions of the Statute may be relevant.

(a) Agreements Not Performable in a Year

An agreement to form a partnership for more than one year is within the Statute, and unenforceable between the parties unless in writing.[51] But few unwritten partnership agreements are for any fixed term.[52] As a matter of partnership law, those without fixed terms are for partnerships "at will," subject to dissolution by death or by the will of any partner at any time.[53] Consequently, such agreements are performable within one year and are not within the Statute of Frauds.[54] If partnership business has been undertaken, this may constitute performance sufficient to take the agreement out of the Statute if otherwise within it.[55] Since a partner always has the power

---

51. Morris v. Peckham, 51 Conn. 128 (1883); Wilson v. Ray, 13 Ind. 1 (1859); Wahl v. Barnum, 116 N.Y. 87, 22 N.E. 280, 5 L.R.A. 623 (1889); Pinner v. Leder, 115 Misc. 512, 188 N.Y.S. 818 (Sup.Ct.1921), aff'd 200 App.Div. 894, 192 N.Y.S. 946 (1922).

52. The agreement may be for a partnership to carry out a project too complex to be finished in a year. If the court concentrates on the project rather than on the partnership, the agreement is not performable within one year, is within the Statute and is unenforceable without a writing. See Pemberton v. Ladue Realty & Const. Co., 362 Mo. 768, 244 S.W.2d 62 (1951) (real estate development, 5-year project, within Statute).

53. Sec. 74(b) below.

54. Kist v. Coughlin, 50 N.E.2d 939 (Ind. App.1943), modified on other grounds 222 Ind. 639, 57 N.E.2d 199, 586 (1944);

Stitt v. Rat Portage Lumber Co., 98 Minn. 52, 107 N.W. 824 (1906); Schindler v. Sorbitz, 268 S.W. 432 (Mo.App. 1925); Heathington v. Heathington Lumber Co., 398 S.W.2d 822 (Tex.Civ. App.1966); Howell v. Bowden, 368 S. W.2d 842 (Tex.Civ.App.1963), error ref. n. r. e.; Jordan v. Miller, 75 Va. 442 (1881); Gronvold v. Whaley, 39 Wash. 2d 710, 237 P.2d 1026 (1952) (joint venture); Seeley v. Morris, 137 Wash. 274, 242 P. 359 (1926); Treat v. Hiles, 68 Wis. 344, 32 N.W. 517 (1887).

55. Regan v. Grady, 343 Ill. 423, 175 N.E. 567 (1931); Sanger v. French, 157 N.Y. 213, 51 N.E. 979 (1896). See Hammel v. Feigh, 143 Minn. 115, 173 N.W. 570 (1919).

On the effect of part or full performance on this Statute of Frauds generally, see Corbin, Contracts §§ 457–59 (1950).

(as distinct from the right) to dissolve, it is arguable that even an oral agreement for a several-year partnership is performable within one year. The argument contains an internal inconsistency, since exercise of the dissolution power on these facts would violate the agreement; [56] thus one is really arguing performance by breach.

(b) Promises to Answer for the Debt of Another

One forming a partnership with a sole proprietor or joining an existing partnership as a new member is generally not liable for previous debts of the business unless he assumes them.[57] But assumption may be part of the price he pays to come in. His promise to the former proprietor or partners is a third party beneficiary contract which, by the law of most jurisdictions, is enforceable by the creditor.[58]

It is sometimes objected that such a promise, if not in writing, is unenforceable because of the Statute of Frauds on promises to answer for the debt of another. It does not appear to be within that Statute. The promise is not to the creditor but to the debtor, although a right in favor of the creditor results.[59] Moreover, since the consideration for the promise is the transfer of a property interest to the promisor, his promise is to pay the purchase price, a primary rather than a collateral obligation. If the incoming partner makes a promise directly to the creditor, it may be a novation releasing the prior debtor, or it may be a collateral promise in consideration of an extension of the obligation, which enures to the benefit of the promisor through the partnership's advantage in postponing payment.[60] It appears that such a promise is outside the Statute because it is made to advance an interest of the promisor.[61]

(c) Sale of Goods or Land

An agreement to admit a partner to an existing partnership, or to form a partnership by transferring to him an interest in a going business, would, if performed, result in his acquisition of some rights in partnership property. So far as this is a transfer of ownership of specific partnership property which includes goods, it would seem to be within the portion of the original Statute of Frauds relating to contracts for the sale of goods or within the successor version in the

---

56. See Sec. 74(b) below.

57. Secs. 47(a), 88(b) below.

58. Restatement, Contracts § 136; Corbin, Contracts §§ 787–88 (1951), collecting partnership cases at § 788 n. 75; Williston, Contracts § 381 (3d ed. 1959).

59. To be within the Statute, the promise must be to the creditor. Corbin, Contracts § 357 (1950).

60. A novation is not within the Statute of Frauds. Restatement, Contracts § 183; Corbin, Contracts § 365 (1950); Williston, Contracts § 477 (3d ed. 1960).

61. McCreary v. Van Hook's Ex'rs, 35 Tex. 631 (1872); Restatement, Contracts § 184.

Uniform Sales Act § 4 covering both goods and choses in action. But what the partner acquires is more in the nature of a chose in action: rights against his co-partners to share in profits, to participate in management, to receive the benefit of their services in carrying on the joint undertaking—in short, an interest in a business, not ownership of specific assets in the business.[62] Moreover, unless there is a transfer of an interest in an existing partnership from a partner to the new-comer, the transaction seems more the creation of a chose in action than its transfer. It thus appears that a formation of a partnership should be held outside the sales part of the Statute.[63] If a partner assigns an interest to a third person purchaser, there is an agreement for the sale of a chose in action which would be within the Uniform Sales Act version of the Statute.[64] The latter may be satisfied by part payment, or delivery.[65]

The Statute of Frauds in the sales article of the Uniform Commercial Code has almost entirely superseded both the original and the

62. His rights in specific partnership property are severely limited. See U. P.A. §§ 24–25, Secs. 40–45 below. The agreement may include an understanding that the new partner will receive an undivided interest in each partnership asset proportional to his interest in the partnership, particularly if he is forming a firm with a sole proprietor. Even so, the overriding intent and the net effect is a transfer of business assets to the new partnership rather than to the new partner personally. Cf. Backus Plywood Co. v. Commercial Decal, Inc., 317 F.2d 339 (2d Cir. 1963), cert. denied 375 U.S. 879, 84 S.Ct. 146, 11 L.Ed.2d 110 (1963) (N.Y. law). The court convincingly concluded that the agreement was for transfer of goods from one joint venturer to the other, and found the Statute of Frauds applicable. The assets of one party (a corporation) were to be sold to a subsidiary of the other corporation in the course of a reorganization of the first corporation. Apparently no business was to be carried on jointly.

63. See Corbin, Contracts § 471 (1950): a contract to form a partnership to deal in goods is not within the Statute since it is not for the sale of goods between the partners but binds them to make purchases from and sales to third persons. See also Williston, Contracts § 512 (3d ed. 1960).

It has been held that an oral contract to take stock to be issued by a cor-

poration is not within the Statute. Peninsula Leasing Co. v. Cody, 161 Mich. 604, 126 N.W. 1053 (1910); Farmers' Lumber Co. v. Luikart, 36 Wyo. 413, 256 P. 84 (1927); Ostrander v. Messmer, 315 Mo. 1165, 289 S.W. 609 (1926); Clapp v. Gilt Edge Consol. Mines Co., 33 S.D. 123, 144 N.W. 721 (1913). See Note, 26 Mich.L.Rev. 331 (1928).

A contrary result has been reached in some states. Mayhaw Canning & Preserving Co. v. Cohen, 135 Miss. 378, 99 So. 896 (1924).

Transfers of outstanding corporate stock are within the Statute if it expressly or impliedly includes choses in action. Wheeler v. Barnes, 100 Conn. 57, 122 A. 912 (1923); Illinois-Indiana Fair Ass'n v. Phillips, 328 Ill. 368, 159 N.E. 815, 59 A.L.R. 591 (1927).

64. See Williston, Contracts § 512 (3d ed. 1960).

If the Statute does not include choses in action, a contract for sale of a partner's interest is not within it. Vincent v. Vieths, 60 Mo.App. 9 (1894).

65. Gaisell v. Johnston, 68 Wash. 470, 123 P. 783 (1912) (oral agreement for sale of partner's interest to co-partner, the latter assuming full management and control of the business). See Restatement, Contracts §§ 201–05; Williston, Contracts § 470 (3d ed. 1960).

Uniform Sales Act versions. It does not apply to choses in action,[66] and thus generally does not affect creation or transfers of partnership interests. A residual Statute of Frauds in the U.C.C.[67] requires a writing to enforce an agreement for sales of personal property beyond $5,000 and should govern sales of partnership interests above this relatively large figure, but probably not creations of partnership interests. Since the older sales versions have typically been repealed, the only writing requirement in respect of sales appears to be for transfers of partnership interests involving $5,000 or more.

The effect of the land portion of the Statute of Frauds on creation or transfer of partnership interests is treated in Sec. 39 below.

TAX RECOGNITION OF FAMILY PARTNERSHIPS

§ 23A.   Partnerships among members of a family are appealing devices for the reduction of federal income tax. Their validity for this purpose is a matter of federal law. Past tests of validity focused on the contribution of vital services or original capital by the alleged partner (usually a wife or child) and (later) on bona fide intent.

1951 legislation recognized the tax validity of family partnerships in businesses where capital is a material income producing factor, even though the child's (or other relative's) interest is given to him. The effect of the legislation is to require that (1) the parent receives reasonable compensation for his services, (2) remaining profits are shared in proportion to capital accounts, (3) the child is competent in a practical sense to manage his interest or it is given to a trustee (other than the parent) for his benefit, and (4) the partnership interest (including a share in capital accounts) is completely transferred to the child or trustee free of excessive control by the parent.

(a) Context

Partnerships receive unique treatment in the federal income tax.[68] Although they file annual tax returns showing income and deductions, they pay no tax.[69] Each partner includes his proportional share of partnership income and deductions on his individual income tax return and is taxed on them.[70] The amount of income (if any) actually distributed to him is immaterial. This "conduit" method of taxation— in which the partnership is viewed only as a conduit of income and

---

66. U.C.C. §§ 2–201, 2–105(1). Id. § 8–319 on sale of investment securities seems inapplicable to interests in partnerships owning investment securities for the reasons given in the text.

67. U.C.C. § 1–206: ". . . a contract for the sale of personal property is not enforceable by way of action or defense beyond five thousand dollars in amount or value of remedy unless there is some writing which indicates that a contract for sale has been made between the parties at a defined or stated price, reasonably identifies the subject matter, and is signed by the

party against whom enforcement is sought or by his authorized agent." See generally, Note, The Uniform Commercial Code Section 1–206—A New Departure in the Statute of Frauds?, 70 Yale L.J. 603 (1961).

68. The nearest thing is the Subchapter S corporation, Sec. 34C below. Somewhat similar is the trust; see n. 73 below.

69. Int.Rev.Code of 1954, §§ 701, 6031 (26 U.S.C.A.).

70. Id. §§ 702–04.

deductions to the several partners—escapes the double taxation of corporations,[71] but runs squarely into the individual income tax system, whose rates may be higher or lower. The conduit principle offers an attractive tax reduction device if it channels income away from a person in a high tax bracket (one with a large income) to someone in a low bracket. This is particularly true if it can be done without losing the use of the funds in the business or in the family economic-psychological unit. If a father can divert $10,000 from his top rates, say 50%, to his children who pay 20%, their combined tax is $3,000 less than he would have paid alone, or a saving of 60% of the tax he would otherwise have paid on the $10,000. The technique is equally appealing to a partner in an existing partnership (who subdivides his interest for this purpose) and to a sole proprietor (who forms a partnership with his children for this purpose). The method would work as well if the chosen partner were a stranger, but one is rarely willing to give up a part of his income to anybody but a close relation—hence the family partnership.[72]

The government is understandably unenthusiastic about this method of circumventing the graduated tax rate structure enacted by Congress. A long struggle has been waged, mostly in the courts, over the family partnership as well as over other income-deflecting devices, notably the trust.[73] The family partnership tax cases belong more to the body of anti-tax-avoidance law than to the body of partnership law. But enough of the same elements are employed to repay our survey. Moreover, the family partnership is one of the forms the planning lawyer must have at his command.

The tax law contains its own definition of partnership,[74] suggesting that federal, not state, law determines what is a partnership in the tax context. The case law of taxation has confirmed this, finding that state law validity is neither necessary [75] nor sufficient [76] for tax recog-

---

71. A corporation is taxed on its income, whether or not distributed to shareholders. If it is distributed, shareholders are taxed on dividends received. Id. §§ 11, 61(a) (7), 316.

72. Note, Family Partnerships and the Federal Income Tax, 41 Ind.L.J. 684 (1966) surveys the history and present status of the subject.

The family partnership can also save estate taxes, although we do not consider this aspect further. See Casner, Estate Planning c. XV (3d ed. 1961 & Supp.); Landis, The Utility and Effect of the Partnership in Family Planning, N.Y.U. 24th Inst. on Fed.Tax 339, 354–58 (1966). The creation of a family partnership will usually precipitate a gift tax. Ibid.

73. Generally speaking, a trust's beneficiaries are taxed on income distributed or required to be distributed to them (a conduit approach much like the partnership's) but the trust itself as an entity is taxed at an individual's income tax rates on other income, e. g., that not distributed but retained in the trust (whether by the trustee's discretion or by requirements of the trust instrument). Int.Rev.Code of 1954, §§ 641–63 (26 U.S.C.A.).

74. Id. §§ 761(a), 7701(a) (2), Sec. 4 at n. 35 above.

75. See Felix Zukaitis, 3 T.C. 814 (1944) (husband-wife partnership recognized for tax though not by Mich. law). See also text below at n. 21.

76. See note 76 on page 115.

nition of the partnership, and the Revenue Service has so ruled.[77] Nonetheless, compliance with state law forecloses one line of tax attack on the partnership, and is always advisable.

(b) The Law through Culbertson

The early family partnership cases usually involved partnerships between husband and wife. They were preceded by other income-sharing attempts by spouses, for example, a husband's assignment to his wife of half his interest in an existing partnership. She agreed to share profits and losses with him but had no agreement with the co-partner which would make her a member of the firm. The arrangement failed to pass muster and the income was taxed to the husband rather than the wife,[78] on the then recently confirmed theory that income is taxable to the person earning it, regardless of anticipatory assignment.[79] Subsequent arrangements hoped to remedy the defects of this one by making the wife formally a partner, and transferring to her some "property," [80] i. e. an interest in the partnership or in specific partnership property. But many of them went down to defeat on what appeared to be the rationale of Commissioner v. Tower: [81] "There can be no question that a wife and a husband may, under certain circumstances, become partners for tax, as for other purposes. If she either invests capital originating with her or substantially contributes to the control and management of the business, or otherwise performs vital additional services or does all of these things she may be a partner as contemplated by [the tax law] . . .. A wife may become a general or limited partner with her husband. But when she does not share in the management and control of the business, contributes no vital additional services, and where the husband purports in some way to have given her a partnership interest, the Tax Court may properly take these circumstances into consideration in determining whether the partnership is real within the meaning of the federal revenue laws."

---

76. See Doll v. Commissioner, 149 F.2d 239 (8th Cir. 1945) (state court judgment that partnership existed not bindings for tax). See also Pflugradt v. U. S., 310 F.2d 412, 417 (7th Cir. 1962).

77. Rev.Rul. 58–243, 1958–1 Cum.Bull. 255 (concerning husband-wife firms).

78. Burnet v. Leininger, 285 U.S. 136, 52 S.Ct. 43, 76 L.Ed. 521 (1931); see Sec. 28 at n. 17 below. The cases of this period are discussed by Bruton, Taxation of Family Income, 41 Yale L.J. 1172 (1932); Veron, Taxation of Family Partnerships, 59 Harv.L.Rev. 209 (1945). See also Villere v. Commissioner, 133 F.2d 905 (5th Cir. 1943) (earnings pooling agreement by broth-

ers disregarded as anticipatory assignment).

79. Lucas v. Earl, 281 U.S. 111, 50 S.Ct. 241, 74 L.Ed. 731 (1930).

80. This reflected another basic principle in the case law of taxation: income from property is taxable to the owner of the property. See, e. g., Blair v. Commissioner, 300 U.S. 5, 57 S.Ct. 330, 81 L.Ed. 465 (1937).

81. 327 U.S. 280, 290, 66 S.Ct. 532, 537, 90 L.Ed. 670 (1946). See also the companion case, Lusthaus v. Commissioner, 327 U.S. 293, 66 S.Ct. 539, 90 L.Ed. 679 (1946).

This language received various interpretations. By the Tax Court, and some District Courts, it was taken to establish a formula: if the husband gave the wife her interest and she performs no significant services, no partnership can be recognized. Other federal courts thought it merely pointed to the relevancy of these facts, and afforded support for findings by the trier of fact on the issue of the reality of the intent to form a partnership. There was considerable diversity of result in apparently similar situations.[82]

Some state courts obligingly permitted rescission of family partnerships (and related trusts) which failed to produce the desired tax results.[83]

Meanwhile, pressure built up from another direction. Community property systems in several of the western states with a Spanish legal heritage [84] were interpreted by the Supreme Court [85] as making half their combined income (usually all earned by the husband) taxable to the wife and half to the husband. A number of states began to enact community property laws to take advantage of this benefit, which was proportionately enhanced by the higher and more steeply graduated tax rates enacted during World War II and generally prevalent thereafter.[86] Congress concluded in 1948 to let all spouses split their income, that is to file a joint return and pay the same tax as if each had separately received half the income.[87] This stemmed the spread of community property laws and ended the husband-wife partnership as a tax saving device.[88]

---

82. See jury instruction under which partnership was found to exist among husband, wife, adult sons, and son as trustee for a minor brother. Fretwell v. Bowers, 42 A.F.T.R. 1267, 50–2 U.S. T.C. par. 9396 (E.D.S.C.1950).

Partnerships recognized: Wenig v. Commissioner, 85 U.S.App.D.C. 216, 177 F.2d 62 (1949); Walsh v. Commissioner, 170 F.2d 535 (8th Cir. 1948); Hartz v. Commissioner, 170 F.2d 313 (8th Cir. 1948); Allen v. Knott, 166 F. 2d 798 (5th Cir. 1948); Lawton v. Commissioner, 164 F.2d 380 (6th Cir. 1947); Durwood v. Commissioner, 159 F.2d 400 (8th Cir. 1947).

Partnerships not recognized: Kohl v. Commissioner, 170 F.2d 531 (8th Cir. 1948); Simmons v. Commissioner, 164 F.2d 220 (5th Cir. 1947); Mauldin v. Commissioner, 155 F.2d 666 (4th Cir. 1946).

The Tower case was cited in denying *state* income tax recognition of a partnership between spouses. Thomas v. Wisconsin Dept. of Taxation, 250 Wis. 8, 26 N.W.2d 310 (1947).

83. Miller v. National Bank of Detroit, 325 Mich. 395, 38 N.W.2d 863 (1949); Stone v. Stone, 319 Mich. 194, 29 N.W. 2d 271, 174 A.L.R. 1349 (1947), noted 61 Harv.L.Rev. 553 (1948). See also Farris v. Farris Engineering Corp., discussed Sec. 8 n. 87 above. Cf. Lowry v. Kavanagh, 322 Mich. 532, 34 N. W.2d 60 (1948), refusing rescission where the husband's motive was donative rather than tax saving.

84. See Sec. 45(c) below.

85. Poe v. Seaborn, 282 U.S. 101, 51 S. Ct. 58, 75 L.Ed. 239 (1930).

86. For example, Pennsylvania's Community Property Law of 1947, P.L. 1423, was held unconstitutional in Willcox v. Penn. Mutual Life Ins. Co., 357 Pa. 581, 55 A.2d 521, 174 A.L.R. 220 (1947).

87. Revenue Act of 1948, §§ 103, 301, 62 Stat. 111, 114 (1948). The current provision is Int.Rev.Code of 1954, § 2(a) (26 U.S.C.A.).

88. See Groves, Federal Tax Treatment of the Family 56–69 (1963).

Attention shifted to parent-child partnerships,[89] which were apparently governed by the Tower principles. Such partnerships were granted [90] or denied [91] tax recognition in various states of fact. Parent-child partnerships may have one important factor not present in husband-wife firms: a desire to train children in the business and pave the way for succession by them.[92] These motives are often urged, whether dominant or not. This area of litigation culminated in Commissioner v. Culbertson.[93] Culbertson was in the cattle business with Coon who wanted to retire because of ill health. Most of the assets were liquidated, but they desired to keep the foundation herd intact. Culbertson agreed to buy it but Coon apparently insisted that Culbertson's sons be brought in to provide continuity and aid. Culbertson bought the herd for $100,000 and immediately resold a half interest to his four sons who gave a $50,000 purchase money note. The note was paid partly (about 40%) with gifts from their father and partly from their share of the profits of the firm they formed with him by oral agreement. They shared profits in proportion to their capital accounts. All of the sons (aged 16–24) worked in the business when they could; two were minors still in school; the other two went into

---

Prior to Int.Rev.Code of 1954, § 706(b) (26 U.S.C.A.), a valid husband-wife partnership could have a different fiscal year from the individuals and postpone the time when income was taxable to them. See Beulah H. Nichols, 32 T.C. 1322 (1959), Acq. 1960–2 Cum.Bull. 6.

A partnership between spouses retains some value for self-employment tax and Social Security benefits. See Nickerson v. Ribicoff, 206 F.Supp. 232 (D.C.Mass.1962), decided on ground of intent, and discussed Sec. 8 n. 85, above.

89. "The high water mark in this area is Tinkoff v. Commissioner, 120 F.2d 564 (7th Cir. 1941), involving an accountant who took his son into the accounting firm as a partner on the day the boy was born." Bittker, Federal Income Estate and Gift Taxation 387 (3d ed. 1964).

90. Thomas v. Feldman, 158 F.2d 488 (5th Cir. 1946).

91. Dawson v. Commissioner, 163 F.2d 664 (6th Cir. 1947); Belcher v. Commissioner, 162 F.2d 974 (5th Cir. 1947); Scherf v. Commissioner, 161 F.2d 495 (5th Cir. 1947); Wilson v. Commissioner, 161 F.2d 556 (4th Cir. 1947); Appel v. Smith, 161 F.2d 121 (7th Cir. 1947).

Some of the judicial reactions were sharp. In refusing to recognize a partnership between spouses individually and as trustees for their minor, school-age children who contributed no services, a court said: "The trusts might be said to correspond to a conduit through which money was transferred from a right pocket to a left—here both pockets Zander's and the contents of one as free to his use as the contents of the other. To condone such a procedure, for tax purposes, would hardly be less than establishing a means to tax evasion. . . ." Zander v. Commissioner, 173 F.2d 624, 626–627 (5th Cir. 1949).

92. One court referred approvingly to the "desire of a father . . . with a business that he cherishes and a son that he loves, to have such son with him in his business and to carry it on when he no longer can." Culbertson v. Commissioner, 168 F.2d 979, 984 (5th Cir. 1948), noted 62 Harv.L.Rev. 136 (1948), later reversed; see below at nn. 95–97.

93. 337 U.S. 733, 69 S.Ct. 1210, 93 L. Ed. 1659 (1949). See Bruton, Family Partnerships and the Income Tax— The Culbertson Chapter, 98 U.Pa.L. Rev. 143 (1949).

military service. Their participation was announced by the local newspaper, and all could sign checks on the firm's bank account. The Tax Court, trying to follow Tower, ruled that the sons were not partners for tax purposes, since they contributed neither vital services nor capital originating with them; [94] all the firm's income was taxable to the father. The 5th Circuit reversed,[95] concluding that there was no tax avoidance purpose and that the expectation of future services by the sons was sufficient to validate the partnership for taxation. The Supreme Court rejected the future service argument [96] and remanded to the Tax Court to determine whether there was a bona fide intent that the sons be partners. "If, upon a consideration of all the facts, it is found that the partners joined together in good faith to conduct a business, having agreed that the services or capital to be contributed presently by each is of such value to the partnership that the contributor should participate in the distribution of profits, that is sufficient." [97] The Court made it plain that absence of vital services and original capital would not destroy the tax validity of the firm as a matter of law, though it would put a heavy burden on the taxpayer to establish the essential intent. Finally, the Court denied that capital contributions always must originate with the children, and left open the possibility that they might be gifts from the parent, if the children became the true owners.

The difficulties with the intent test—compared to the relative objectivity of the vital services and original capital tests—were mirrored in the Court's own division in the Culbertson decision. Five justices concurred on diverse grounds set out in four opinions or statements additional to the main opinion. On remand, the Tax Court found that no bona fide partnership was intended.[98] The 5th Circuit again reversed and sustained the partnership.[99]

The Culbertson emphasis on intent has a parallel in substantive partnership law,[1] but the tax law seems to contemplate a more intense variety. While both bodies of law look for some kind of co-ownership, the substantive area concentrates on control, and the tax law on the much milder idea of valuable services or capital contribution.[2] In the substantive law of partnership, either service or capital contribution

---

94. 6 T.C.M. 692 (1947).

95. 168 F.2d 979 (1948), noted 62 Harv. L.Rev. 136 (1948).

The court was convinced that the arrangement was not motivated by tax savings, and this influenced the opinion just cited and the later one, n. 99 below.

96. "The vagaries of human experience preclude reliance upon even good faith intent as to future conduct as a basis for the present taxation of income." 337 U.S. 740, 69 S.Ct. 1213.

97. 337 U.S. 744–45, 69 S.Ct. 1215. See also 337 U.S. at 748, 69 S.Ct. at 1217.

98. 9 T.C.M. 647 (1950).

99. 194 F.2d 581 (5th Cir.1952).

1. Sec. 5(a) above.

2. The tax cases always have the profit sharing component of co-ownership (Sec. 14(a), (b) above)—at least on paper—since this is what the fight is about.

is almost universal, but there is no absolute requirement for them and there is certainly no mandate that the capital originate with the one contributing it.

(c) The 1951 Legislation—In General

While the Culbertson implications were being worked out in the lower courts and the Revenue Service, Congress in 1951 passed a new set of rules.[3] They went into the 1954 Code with no significant change, as follows:

"FAMILY PARTNERSHIPS—

"(1) RECOGNITION OF INTEREST CREATED BY PURCHASE OR GIFT.—A person shall be recognized as a partner for purposes of this subtitle if he owns a capital interest in a partnership in which capital is a material income-producing factor, whether or not such interest was derived by purchase or gift from any other person.

"(2) DISTRIBUTIVE SHARE OF DONEE INCLUDIBLE IN GROSS INCOME.—In the case of any partnership interest created by gift, the distributive share of the donee under the partnership agreement shall be includible in his gross income, except to the extent that such share is determined without allowance of reasonable compensation for services rendered to the partnership by the donor, and except to the extent that the portion of such share attributable to donated capital is proportionately greater than the share of the donor attributable to the donor's capital. The distributive share of a partner in the earnings of the partnership shall not be diminished because of absence due to military service.

"(3) PURCHASE OF INTEREST BY MEMBER OF FAMILY.—For purposes of this section, an interest purchased by one member of a family from another shall be considered to be created by gift from the seller, and the fair market value of the purchased interest shall be considered to be donated capital. The 'family' of any individual shall include only his spouse, ancestors, and lineal descendants, and any trusts for the primary benefit of such persons." [4]

The new rules were intended to reverse a trend that appeared to be evolving to disregard any gratuitous transfer of a partnership interest (or an interest acquired with donated funds) unless the donee was performing significant services.[5] Thus it is no longer necessary for the child to render services to the business or to pretend to do so; an interest can be given to an infant or to a student away at school. A

---

3. For criticism, see Lifton, The Family Partnership: Here We Go Again, 7 Tax L.Rev. 461 (1952); Comment, 61 Yale L.J. 541 (1952).

4. Int.Rev.Code of 1954, § 704(e) (26 U.S.C.A.).

5. S.Rep.No.781, 82d Cong. 1st Sess., 1951-2 Cum.Bull 458, 485-86 (1951).

partnership interest can be given away much like a share of corporate stock, and the income is taxable to the new owner instead of the old.[6] The intent prescribed by Culbertson is immaterial.

The statutory rule operates only if capital is a material income-producing factor in the partnership. Such a partnership is the opposite of one whose income is mainly from personal services—such as entertainers or lawyers. The requirement thus carries forward much of the case law doctrine that income is taxable to one who earns it.[7] There is no doubt of the materiality of capital in firms whose income is mainly from ownership of realty or securities, or if the business requires substantial inventories or substantial investment in fixed assets like plant and machinery.[8] The Revenue Service has taken the litigative position that capital is not a material income-producing factor in businesses with large working capital needs for salaries of employees or for financing of receivables. But the courts have held otherwise.[9]

By the pre-1951 case law, a family partnership was either valid or invalid for tax. Instead of this all-or-nothing position, the statutory rules permit the government to reduce the income taxable to the children and increase the amount taxable to the parent so far as the parent is undercompensated for his services or his capital.[10] What is reasonable compensation for his services is a fact question.[11] What is reasonable compensation for his capital is largely a matter of arithmetic, determined by the ratio of his share of capital to the total capital of the partners.[12] In effect, this makes it requisite that a fair

---

6. S.Rep., n. 5 above.

7. See n. 79 above.

8. Income Tax Reg. (26 C.F.R.) § 1.704–1(e) (1) (iv) (1956, amended 1964), hereafter cited as "Reg."

9. James N. Bennett, 21 T.C.M. 903 (1962) (partnership hired engineers, draftsmen and designers, and furnished them to other employers; up to 300 employees; average payroll $18,000 a week; 6 to 11 weeks between paying employees and collecting from customers); Jeremiah J. O'Donnell, Jr., 23 T.C.M. 210 (1964) (partnership sold woolens on commission and needed to guarantee accounts of some customers; 16 employees); Pearlstone v. Phinney, 5 A.F.T.R.2d 1116, 60–1 U.S. T.C. par. 9360 (W.D.Tex.1960) (auto finance business). Cf. Poggetto v. U. S., 306 F.2d 76 (9th Cir.1962) (capital not material; sale of canned goods on commission; $500 capital sufficed for many years); the opinion gives criteria for deciding whether capital is a material income-producing factor.

10. Int.Rev.Code of 1954, § 704(e) (2) (26 U.S.C.A.), quoted above at n. 4.

11. See Reg. § 1.704–1(e) (3) (i) (c) (consider managerial responsibility, cost of comparable service from non-partner). For examples, in most of which the compensation set seems modest, see Ramos v. U. S., 260 F.Supp. 479 (N.D.Cal.1966); Weller v. Brownell, 240 F.Supp. 201 (M.D.Pa.1965); Ralph C. Gorrill, 22 T.C.M. 804 (1963).

12. If the parent has assets used in the business which are not partnership property (see generally Sec. 37 below), he must be adequately compensated for them too. See Ramos v. U. S., n. 11 above (land, trees and equipment used in partnership almond ranch). Valuation may be more difficult than when capital contributions are credited on the partnership books. Here the court found that 25% of gross income was proper compensation.

salary be provided for the parent (unless all the partners are rendering more or less comparable services) and that profits be shared in proportion to capital accounts.[13]   Therefore, to channel say 30% of the income to the children, they must be given not merely a 30% interest in the profits of the firm, but also a 30% interest in the capital accounts.[14]   No such proportioning of capital to profits is necessary in a non-family partnership.

(d) The 1951 Legislation—Incomplete Transfers

The Committee Reports on the 1951 legislation made clear that Congress left open the possibility of disregarding a family partnership if the purported gift creating it is a sham [15] or is incomplete because of retained control by the donor.[16]   This is the same idea which figures in the Culbertson requirement that the donee be the true owner of the interest given him.   It is also the point which has proved most troublesome, since a degree of control by the donor is inevitable if he remains the moving force in the partnership, as he typically does.   The Revenue Service has published tough Regulations on this point, serving notice that it will look closely at actual operations as well as at legal documents to determine the completeness of a transfer.[17]   Specific factors which, in its eyes, indicate an incomplete transfer include retention by the transferor (usually the parent) of control over distributions from the partnership to the partners or over key assets of the firm; limitations on the transferee's right to liquidate or sell his interest in the firm without financial detriment; and retention by the transferor of unusual management powers in the firm.   As a result, family partnership agreements usually contain clauses requiring distribution of substantially all profits (unless each partner consents to their

---

13. If capital accounts fluctuate disproportionately because of withdrawals, an average balance should probably be used.

14. The necessity that the children have a "capital interest" in the firm is underlined by the statute itself, Int.Rev.Code of 1954, § 704(e) (1) (26 U.S.C.A.), quoted above at n. 4.   The Regs. define a capital interest as "an interest in the assets of the partnership, which is distributable to the owner of the capital interest upon his withdrawal from the partnership or upon liquidation." Reg. § 1.704–1(e) (1) (v).   As a matter of substantive law, a partner has no significant interest in partnership assets (see Secs. 40–45 below).   The language of the Regs. is equated with capital account, since the latter determines the distribution of assets after settlement of liabilities.   U.P.A. § 40(b) (III), Sec. 90 below.

The capital accounts of the children may be established several ways, e. g., by debiting the father's capital account and crediting the children's accounts with the desired amounts, or by contributions from the children to the firm which are credited to their accounts (even though the funds come from the parent).   At the same time, the father, if business circumstances permit, may withdraw funds and correspondingly reduce his capital account and the proportion of income attributable to him on this basis.

15. See Emil Morton, 46 T.C. 723 (1966) (trusts to hold partnership interests found not to exist at time of acquisition of property developed and operated by partnership).

16. S.Rep., n. 5 above.

17. Reg. § 1.704–1(e) (1) (iii), (2).

retention) and permitting relatively free dissolution or sale of interests—both rather inconsistent with the normal concern of the closely held business for continuity and cash conservation.[18]

More positively, the Regulations accept full distribution of income (subject to the sole use of the owner of the partnership interest) and participation in management by the transferee as strong or substantial evidence of the transfer's completeness, and hence of the partnership's validity. Significant supporting evidence arises from treating the transferee as a partner in dealing with the public, creditors, banks and others.[19] The various notions of completed transfer based on control of the interest by the transferee rather than by the transferor presuppose that the transferee has the maturity and understanding to exercise his rights independently. If he is an adult, the partnership will usually withstand attack.[20] He does not have to be of legal age,[21] but must be competent to manage his own affairs. Otherwise (and the burden of proof may be too difficult to risk) the partnership will not be recognized unless the interest is controlled for him by a fiduciary subject to judicial supervision.[22] This usually means a cumbersome and expensive guardianship.[23] On the whole, it is impractical for the partnership interest to belong directly to a minor child unless he is demonstrably capable of dealing with it intelligently, which usually means that he is almost of legal age and is relatively sophisticated.

The solution is often to create for the child a limited partnership interest (which requires less decision making)[24] or put the interest in trust (so the trustee exercises the necessary control)[25] or both. It is difficult for a trustee to have the independence necessary for a completed transfer if he is the parent.[26] The necessary independence of

---

18. Cf. Secs. 41(a), 90A below.

19. Reg. § 1.704–1(e) (2) (iv)–(vi).

20. See Ramos v. U. S., n. 30 below; J. J. O'Donnell, Jr., n. 9 above.

21. Reg. § 1.704–1(e) (2) (viii). In this respect, the tax law may be more liberal than some state law on capacity of minors.

22. Ibid.

23. A guardian does not assure a valid partnership. See Spiesman v. Commissioner, 260 F.2d 940 (9th Cir.1958). Cf. Carl T. Olson, 67–1 U.S.T.C. par. 9239 (C.D.Cal.1966), appeal dismissed, which seems to involve this point although one cannot be sure since only the jury charge and verdict are reported.

24. See Reg. § 1.704–1(e) (2) (ix).

25. See generally Sec. 8A above.

26. See Reg. § 1.704–1(e) (2) (vii), posing the criterion of active representation and protection of the beneficiary's interest.

See Ballou v. U. S., 370 F.2d 659 (6th Cir. 1966) (2–1 decision), cert. denied 388 U.S. 911, 87 S.Ct. 2114, 18 L.Ed.2d 1349 (June 12, 1967), affirming a judgment against the taxpayer on a jury verdict that the partnership interests were not genuinely owned by the trusts for the minor children. The father was the sole trustee, retained the same management of the firm as before, and could not sell the interest in the firm without the consent of the remaining partners (himself and his wife). Neither he (in his trustee capacity) nor the children contributed any services. The court is careful to say that no one factor was conclusive, but that together they afforded a basis for the jury finding. There is a strong dissent.

a trustee other than the parent seems easier to establish.[27] The courts, looking at the partnership agreement, the trust agreement, and the conduct of the parties, have gone both ways, but have upheld the arrangement [28] far more often than they have invalidated it [29] when someone beside the parent is the trustee. This is not the only factor in the decisions, but is one of the more important and one of the easier to plan with.

The 1951 statute did not completely supersede the Culbertson test of intent. The latter remains applicable when the partnership is one in which capital is not a material income-producing factor.[30]

The usefulness of the family partnership has diminished since the advent of the Subchapter S corporation [31] which, despite complications, probably offers an easier way to redistribute taxable income within the family.

CHOICE OF ORGANIZATIONAL FORM

§ 23B. A business may be organized as a corporation, partnership, or proprietorship, as a variant of these basic forms, or in diverse other ways. Many legal, economic and personal factors are relevant to the choice and should be carefully weighed. Each form has traditional characteristics, which may or may not be advantageous in a particular situation. A significant number of the attributes of one form can be given to another by appropriate instrument or agreement. Of the others, the

See also Acuff v. Commissioner, 296 F.2d 725 (6th Cir.1961); Ray R. Offord, Jr., 20 T.C.M. 797 (1961).

However, occasional recognition is given to the partnership interest held by a parent as trustee. See Jack Smith, 32 T.C. 1261 (1959), Acq. 1960–2 Cum. Bull. 7 (same partnership had not been recognized before 1951 legislation).

27. By the Regs., if he is "amenable to the will" of the parent, he must meet the same test as the parent-trustee: active representation and protection of the beneficiary's interest. If he is unrelated and otherwise not subject to the parent's control, he is recognized as the owner of the interest (and the partnership will be recognized as valid), unless the parent retains controls inconsistent with such ownership. Reg. § 1.704–1(e) (2) (vii).

28. E. Ray Jensen, 15 A.F.T.R.2d 234, 65–1 U.S.T.C. par. 9178 (M.D.Ga.1964) (quoting charge to jury and verdict); F. B. Cooper, 60–2 U.S.T.C. par. 9751 (E.D.Wash.1960) (findings and conclusions); Sanford H. Hartman, 43 T.C.

105 (1964), Acq. 1965–2 Cum.Bull. 5 (brother-in-law as trustee sparked the enterprise); James M. Bennett, 21 T.C.M. 903 (1962); Jelindo A. Tiberti, 21 T.C.M. 961 (1962) (quoting trust and partnership agreements in full; trustees were key employee and outside businessman); Pearlstone v. Phinney, n. 9 above (trustee was father's attorney).

29. Henry S. Reddig, 30 T.C. 1382 (1958) (trustee was parent's attorney or latter's partner).

30. See Poggetto v. U. S., 306 F.2d 76 (9th Cir.1962).

The absence of capital as a material income-producing factor (although there was no finding to this effect) may explain why Ramos v. U. S., 260 F.Supp. 479 (N.D.Cal.1966) was decided on the Culbertson rationale without mentioning the 1951 statute. The children-partners were adults and active in the business, the son having been specially trained for it. Thus it was not the typical family case with inactive minors.

31. See Sec. 34C below.

most important will usually be (A) exposure to (or protection from) personal liability, and (B) federal income tax treatment.

(a) Background

The practice of business law consists overwhelmingly of advising on transactions and designing arrangements to carry out clients' objectives. One of the more important problems is choosing the form in which a business is to operate. The question arises not only when a business is started, but periodically thereafter when it may be preferable to shift from one form to another.

Three forms are dominant: the corporation, the partnership, and the sole proprietorship.[32] There are variants on these, e. g., the limited partnership,[33] the joint venture,[34] the Subchapter S corporation,[35] as well as more esoteric and rarely used forms.[36] Moreover, the range of possibilities is broadened by diverse financing, property and employment arrangements which are not usually thought of as creating forms of business organization at all.[37] For example, a manager compensated by a share of the profits may still be an employee of a sole proprietor, but regard the arrangements as an adequate substitute for partnership.[38] An investor who finances a business or project for a promissory note and a share of the profits may prefer this arrangement to partnership.[39] A widow who wants a generous fixed return from a family business may do better to lease assets to it than to be a partner or stockholder in it. A franchise with royalty can be a substitute for traditional forms of organization; so can a lease. Co-owners of an income-producing property may not need anything more elaborate than their fractional undivided interests, perhaps supplemented by a power of attorney to a common agent.

Any intelligent choice among the alternatives depends on an understanding of their characteristics, and of the degree to which they can be modified by agreement. Once this is attained, there is still a problem of evaluating the various factors. This Section offers one approach. Other lawyers and writers use different techniques.[39A]

Aside from a few specific references to the sole proprietorship and other arrangements, we will concentrate our discussion on the corporation and the partnership. At first glance, the corporation seems to have a number of advantages: limited liability, perpetual

---

32. See Sec. 1(c) above. See also the preliminary comparison of the three major forms in Sec. 1(a) above.

33. Secs. 26, 32 below.

34. Sec. 35 below.

35. Sec. 34C below.

36. E. g., business trusts (Sec. 33 below) and joint stock companies (Sec. 34 below).

37. Secs. 15–20 above describe some of these profit sharing arrangements which are close to the boundary of partnership but generally not within it.

38. See generally Sec. 16 above.

39. See generally Secs. 15, 19 above.

39A. See references in n. 87 below.

existence, free transferability of ownership interests, and concentration of management.[40] But these are not the only relevant criteria, nor are they always present or desirable. In the remainder of this Section we examine a number of such factors and their implications.

This Section talks as a business lawyer might. In so doing, it ignores one of the virtues that businessmen sometimes find in partnership or proprietorship: it can be created and operated without seeing a lawyer.[41] Since even the simplest partnership may have serious complexities, lawyers understandably feel that their organizational services should be sought for partnerships as for corporations, and even for proprietorships if the arrangements are complicated.

(b) Number and Kind of Parties

The first question is usually how many people are involved, who are they, and what are they like. If there is only one person, partnership and joint venture are ruled out, since they require two or more participants. If there are two or more, sole proprietorship is eliminated, unless it can be coupled with a financing, property or employment arrangement of the kind suggested in (a) above.

The personalities of the parties, and their economic and bargaining positions, may influence the choice of form, although the correlations are not very direct. If the parties don't really have compatibility and confidence in one another, they probably ought not to be launching a business together. In such situations, it may be desirable to use a form that can be terminated with comparative ease if trouble develops; the partnership is preferable in this respect. An aggressive or domineering person should not be cast as a limited partner since he is unlikely to observe the passivity required for that role.[42]

If one of the parties is a corporation, a joint venture (though virtually indistinguishable from a partnership) has semantic advantages over a partnership; a second, jointly owned corporation may also be used.[43] If one of the parties is a trustee, a limited partnership or corporation is indicated in most cases.[44]

If the parties shun publicity, the limited partnership may be unsuitable;[45] the corporation will provide a higher degree of privacy, and the general partnership usually even more.

---

40. See Sec. 24 below.

41. Some businessmen feel that a lawyer not only charges a fee but introduces unnecessary complication and formality by way of lengthy agreements and elaborate procedures. One of the lawyer's more difficult jobs is to take reasonable precautions but not overburden his clients in this way, particularly if dealing with small business where economy is important and informality is traditional.

42. Sec. 26(c) below.

43. Secs. 9 above, 35 below.

44. Sec. 8A above.

45. Sec. 26(b) below.

(c) Kind and Size of Business

The type of business is highly relevant to the best form of organization, although the connection is usually by way of some other element we are considering separately, such as liability exposure, financing needs, or taxation. It can be very direct in isolated instances, since corporations are often forbidden to practice the learned professions,[46] and limited partnerships to engage in banking and insurance.[47]

If the business is expected to be short-lived, like the performance of a single contract or the development of one piece of property, a non-corporate form may avoid the "collapsible corporation" tax pitfall [48] and the second tax that is usually due on liquidation of a corporation.[49] If the business is primarily passive investment which will yield dividends, interest, royalties and certain other categories of income, the personal holding company tax [50] is a threat which can be averted by not incorporating.

Almost all big businesses are corporations, and this probably is the form best adapted to large scale operation, mainly because of management concentration and protection of owners from liability. But some very sizable firms have operated successfully as partnerships, and others as trusts or joint stock companies, so the size element should not be viewed as conclusive. In any event, the form of organization question typically arises first at the inception of the business, when large size cannot be predicted with confidence.

(d) Needs for and Sources of Financing

Every business needs some kind of financing, although the extent and type vary widely with the nature of the operation. It is often said that the corporate form facilitates financing. By and large, this is true only for one kind of financing: selling stock (or perhaps debt) to the public. It is normally impracticable to market widely a non-corporate ownership interest because of the liability potential it carries.[51]

The availability of other kinds of financing does not depend significantly on the form in which the business is organized. Private and institutional investors tend to be more concerned with the quality of the business and its management. But the attendant liabilities for the business operator-owners may differ radically, depending on the form chosen and the credit practices in use. If the

---

46. Sec. 34A(a) below.

47. Sec. 26(a) below.

48. Int.Rev.Code of 1954, § 341 (26 U.S. C.A.).

49. Sec. 23B(i) n. 78 below.

50. Int.Rev.Code of 1954, §§ 541–47 (26 U.S.C.A.).

51. Other deterrents are the problems— real or imaginary—of transferability and continuity discussed in (g), (h) below.

financing is from banks, the personal credit of the participants will typically have to be committed either as general partners or as endorsers, guarantors or collateral-furnishers of corporate borrowings.   Here the organizational form makes little difference in result.   If financing is via equipment or real estate leases, personal commitment may also be required but is somewhat less common than in bank financing.   If it is not required, the corporate form offers a distinct advantage.   If financing includes a lot of trade credit (which is widely granted without personal commitment), the corporation is even more attractive.

If financing is to be by the participants, other elements come into play.   For example, when the financing is expected to be repaid as soon as the resources of the business permit, there is likely to be a tax advantage in a corporation, which will give promissory notes for a considerable portion of the financing, and stock for the rest. This may permit profit to be applied to repayment of the financing with relatively low tax on the corporation and none on the participant except for the interest factor.   By contrast, partnership profits might be more heavily taxed.[52]   (Similarly, if the profits are expected to be retained in the business for further financing, the corporation may allow this to be accomplished at lower tax cost.)   But calculations in a given situation may show that the non-taxability of distributions from a partnership to partners will bring savings.

If financing is to come from the participants, the effect of the organizational form on losses is also worth considering.   In general partnership, the whole burden of loss falls on the partners; they cannot make any claim as creditors even if they have taken promissory notes for their financing.[53]   But the participants in a more fully recognized entity may attain creditor status for their financing and share with other creditors (or maybe even ahead of them if their claims are secured) in the event of insolvency.   A corporation might accomplish this, or a limited partnership with much of the financing from the limited partners in the form of loans rather than contributions.   However, equitable considerations may be invoked to subordinate the participant-creditors in various situations.

If most of the financing is available on the strength of the assets, as is true in many real estate deals, the choice of form is not very important except for tax purposes.

The corporation is justly admired for the number and variety of financing instruments at its disposal: bonds, notes, subordinated debentures, preferred and common stock (with distinctive voting, dividend and other rights), convertibles, options, warrants, etc.   But partnerships have substantial equivalents, although they are less familiar and appealing to buyers.   On the whole, partnerships are even more flexible because of their complete freedom to contract for

---

52. See Sec. 23B(i) below.   **53.** Sec. 90 and Ch. 9 below.

interests in profits and assets unrelated to fixed shares or class of stock.[54]

(e) Loss and Liability Exposure

The usual motive for starting or continuing business is to make profit. But the possibility of loss has to be faced and may affect the choice of form.

The corporation traditionally gives the protection of limited liability: a shareholder has no personal liability for corporate debts.[55] But he may, as a business necessity, contribute additional money if the business is hard pressed, in hopes of salvaging the investment he has already made. Moreover, as noted in (d) above, he may have to pledge his personal credit to obtain outside financing for the business, on which he becomes liable much as in a partnership or proprietorship.

Tort liabilities are a less predictable cause of loss. Insurance is usually available equally to corporation and partnerships. To the extent tort risks can be (and are) insured against, the corporate advantage is neutralized. But the advantage remains so far as there are uninsured risks. The corporation also shields owners against liability for unauthorized acts of employees or agents, such as misrepresentations by salesmen.[56]

Generally speaking, the riskier the business—in either economic or tort terms—the more advantageous to the owners is the corporate form. It should be understood that a corporation as an entity is liable for contracts, torts, acts of agents and servants, etc. like a partnership or proprietor. The corporate assets are subject to seizure for payment of claims. So long as the business prospers, the corporation will pay valid claims. The diminution of corporate assets will be reflected more or less precisely in the value of the stock. In this sense —loss of their investment—the corporation does not protect stockholders from personal loss. Their shield from personal liability comes significantly into play only when the business cannot pay its debts, i.e. when it has failed.[57]

---

54. For example, the combination of the corporate form and the tax law makes it difficult to provide equitably for a mingling of services and proprietary capital from separate sources. See Herwitz, Allocation of Stock Between Services and Capital in the Organization of a Close Corporation, 75 Harv. L.Rev. 1098 (1962). The flexibility of partnership is useful in such situations.

55. If he has not paid the full purchase price of his shares, he is liable for the unpaid part.

56. Contra in the securities business where statutes make controlling persons (including corporate officials and stockholders) vicariously liable in many instances. Securities Act of 1933, § 15, 15 U.S.C.A. § 77o; Securities Exchange Act of 1934, § 20, 15 U.S.C.A. § 78t; Uniform Securities Act § 410(b).

57. The shield from personal liability can have some importance at an earlier stage. A partnership creditor may (and usually should) sue individual partners as well as the firm. The

Loss and liability exposure is maximum in a general partnership where each partner is potentially liable to pay *all* the debts incurred by the firm.[58] Among the partners, losses or expenditures are usually shared in proportion to their interests in profits.[59] But this does not prevent a creditor from collecting the entire amount from one partner. It merely gives the latter a right of indemnification against his co-partner, which may become worthless just when needed most, i.e. at the failure of the business. The same holds true for what would otherwise be sound adjustments among the partners for differences in ability or willingness to tolerate losses. Thus X may agree to bear all losses above a certain amount. But this is small comfort to his cohorts if X goes broke with the business.

Loss exposure is usually greatest in the early years of a business, for this is when most failures occur.[60] A corporation or limited partnership is correspondingly attractive. If the participants have other income, there is a tax advantage if they can deduct their losses against it. This can be done with a partnership (general or limited) or with a Subchapter S corporation.

The desire to limit liability is naturally greatest among those who have the most to lose. The wealthy backer is likely to insist on a corporation or limited partnership. The latter, or the Subchapter S version of the former, will satisfy his probable tax desire for maximum write-off of losses.

(f) Management and Control Structure

The way the business is to be managed, and how control is to be allocated affect the choice of organizational form.

Typically, in a corporation, the stockholders elect a board of directors who hold the managerial authority, and exercise it largely through officers the board selects. A stockholder as such has no authority to act for the corporation. Thus ownership is separated from control, at least formally. In contrast, partners have equal managerial rights [61] and equal authority to act for the firm.[62] It is impossible to say in the abstract whether the hierarchical pattern of the corporation is better or worse than the direct participation of partnership. For one thing, the differences are not so sharp as this general description indicates. In some states, corporate charters or bylaws may give stockholders managerial rights much like partners, either by

partner may be embarrassed, financially or otherwise, by being named as a party, having his property tied up, or having a judgment entered against him even though the firm assets are sufficient to pay the creditor. All this is generally avoided by corporate shareholders.

58. Secs. 58–60 below.

59. Sec. 65(b) below.

60. See Mayer & Goldstein, Small Business Growth and Survival During the First Two Years, 18 Vand.L.Rev. 1749 (1965).

61. Secs. 48, 65(d) below. See also Sec. 65(f) below.

62. Sec. 49 below.

bypassing the directors and officers or by assuring these positions to the stockholders.[63] In almost all states, the partnership agreement can create management structures very like corporations, e.g., by providing for managing partners (who must act by majority) or a board of directors.[64]

The limited partnership effectively excludes the limited partners from management,[65] and concentrates the latter in the general partners, who share it among themselves as in an ordinary partnership. The limited firm, then, falls between the usual corporate and partnership patterns.

The participants will normally have strong desires about the allocation of control. At the start of a business, they will probably want equal control. But even then, one participant may want to be inactive; more likely, if one provides the bulk of the financing, he will want a veto power or decisive voice. With the passage of time, control desires and needs change, as participants understand their own and each others' capacities better, grow old and less active, bring in new assistants, or die and leave heirs with no competence or interest in the business.

Flexibility is a virtue here, and the partnership usually offers more than the corporation. The partnership is less likely to permit a squeeze-out of one party by the other,[66] and less likely to end in a hopeless deadlock. The reason is the comparative ease of dissolution.

Because of the dominance of the corporation in the American economy, the corporate form has a status value in American society that the partnership lacks. It is a big thing for a man to sign his letter as president, or to be introduced as chairman of the board. Clients are often drawn to the corporate form for this reason, sometimes without admitting it.[67]

(g) Ownership Dispersion or Concentration; Transferability of Interests

There is no theoretical maximum or minimum number for partners or stockholders, except that there must be more than one part-

---

63. See generally, Folk, Corporation Statutes: 1959–1966, 1966 Duke L.J. 875, 896–98, 924–27, 946–57 and references there.

64. Such a partnership agreement is effective within the firm but does not deprive a partner of apparent authority to act for the firm unless the third person with whom he is dealing knows of the agreement. Sec. 53 below. Thus a partner excluded from internal control can still impose liabilities on the firm and its members.

65. Sec. 26(c) below.

66. O'Neal and Derwin, Expulsion or Oppression of Business Associates, esp. c. 6 (1961).

67. If it is really the offices that are coveted, rather than the corporation, they can (by agreement) be created in a partnership. On the other hand, corporate offices are not without their problems. There may not be enough top titles (president, chairman of the board) to go around, and friction may develop in their allocation. One of the nice things about ordinary partnership structure is that everybody is equal.

ner or (perhaps in a few states) stockholder. At the start of the usual business, with only a handful of participants, neither form is preferable in this respect. The situation changes somewhat if many participants—say, more than a dozen or two—are expected. The corporation is well suited to numerous owners. The partnership is less well suited for a variety of reasons: the management authority of each member (leading to too many cooks), the power of each to dissolve the firm, and the dissolution which usually occurs on death or on transfer of interests by gift or sale. But the partnership problems can be solved by appropriate provisions in the partnership agreement. Partnerships with hundreds of members, and trusts and joint stock companies with thousands, do exist. Nonetheless, the corporate form simplifies widespread ownership and is usually dictated when such ownership is foreseen,[68] unless there are compelling reasons (like taxation) for a non-corporate form.

Dispersion can occur gradually and without planning: children acquire interests by gift or inheritance, ex-wives by divorce, key employees by being taken into the firm or allowed to buy stock.

If the participants want (as they often do) to keep ownership concentrated, the conventional partnership is slightly more efficient because of delectus personae—the necessity for consent by existing partners to the admission of a new one.[69] But similar results can be attained by corporate buy-sell agreements and restrictions on transfer of stock.

(h) Continuity and Permanence

The conventional view is that a corporation provides desirable continuity of existence and a partnership does not. But this depends a great deal on the kind of continuity meant, and is more than a little misleading.

It is quite true that the *legal form* of a corporation continues unchanged by events like deaths or transfers of stock. But these events may be just as destructive of the *business* of a corporation as of a partnership. Suppose two men start a business; they guide and dominate it. When one dies and the other is old and ill, the fate of the business is the same regardless of the form, and it is probably just as hard to sell or preserve in one form as in the other.[70] In short, management succession is a separate continuity need of corporate and non-corporate business alike.

68. This is particularly true if interests are to be *sold* to large numbers of people. See (d) above.

69. Sec. 5(c) above.

70. The corporation may be harder to sell. The buyer may fear undisclosed liabilities to which the corporate assets would be subject if he bought stock. If there are assets which have appreciated in value, he would rather buy assets than stock in order to have a higher basis for tax purposes. There are ways (e. g., Int.Rev. of Code of 1954, § 337 (26 U.S.C.A.)) for a corporation to liquidate and sell assets to meet such aspirations, but they only put it about where it would have been if it had been a partnership all along.

On the other hand, the legal form of partnership is traditionally subject to dissolution by death or retirement of a partner, or sale of his interest. But such dissolution can be denied any effect on the business by proper business continuation provisions in the agreement.[71] So in this respect, there is really not much advantage of one form over the other, if adequate care is taken.

Continuity is not necessarily a good thing since it may lock a participant or his heirs into an economically or psychologically destructive relationship. If the parties look far enough ahead to see this possibility and want to plan against it, the partnership without strict continuity provisions is probably indicated. Corporate agreements for easy dissolution are possible in some states but are generally unenforceable or uncertain in outcome.

Transferability of interests, as noted in (g) above, is not always what the participants want. Even if it is, it may be an illusory goal, since the market for interests in a closely held business is virtually non-existent, regardless of the form of organization. The potential buyers are almost inevitably the other participants in the business, to whom it is equally easy to sell partnership interests or corporate stock. The main advantage of transferability in a closely held business is usually to facilitate intra-family gifts for tax and estate planning.[72]

(i) Taxation

Corporate and non-corporate organizations differ more sharply in their federal income tax treatment than in any other respect except perhaps personal liability. For this reason, tax is very often the deciding factor in the choice of form.

Both corporate and partnership tax are complex and this discussion omits many of the refinements.[73] The most prominent feature is that the corporation is taxed as an entity at one set of rates while the partnership is not taxed at all, and each partner is taxed at another set of rates on his pro rata share of partnership income.[74] The corporate rates start higher and end lower than the individual rates. The two sets of rates and their relation to one another have changed from time to time: those which became effective in 1965 were 22 to 48% for corporations and 14 to 70% for individuals; the progression of rates in each category is quite different, as can be seen by examining the rate tables.[75]

---

71. Secs. 83A(c), 90A below.

72. Transferability may also have some tactical value in a struggle within the firm, for example by permitting the threat to bring in an unwanted outsider.

73. For full treatment see Bittker & Eustice, Federal Income Taxation of Corporations and Shareholders (2d ed. 1966); Willis, Handbook of Partnership Taxation (1957), references in Sec. 65(a) n. 18 below.

74. Int.Rev.Code of 1954, § 701 (26 U.S. C.A.)

75. Id. §§ 1, 11.

Partnership profits are taxed to the partners whether or not distributed; there is no additional tax if they are distributed. This is often referred to as conduit treatment.[76] Corporate profits are taxed to the corporation whether or not distributed;[77] if distributed, the dividends are taxable to shareholders at their individual rates.[78] This results in so called double taxation of corporate income.[79] One corollary is that funds and assets can usually be withdrawn from partnerships (but not from corporations) without precipitating a tax; where this kind of mobility of capital is important, the partnership has an advantage.

Another primary feature of partnership taxation is that each partner may deduct his share of partnership losses against any other income he may have.[80] Corporate stockholders are not permitted to do this. However, they do realize losses which are deductible for tax purposes, if they sell their stock for less than it cost them or if it becomes valueless on the collapse of the business. But the loss is typically only a capital loss, of lower tax value than the ordinary loss a partner may deduct as it is incurred by the business.[81] Moreover, the benefit of the deduction is delayed until the stock is sold or becomes worthless, while the partner gets his deduction earlier.

The partnership not only permits "pass-through" of losses but offers greater flexibility in allocating among partners the amounts and kinds of income and loss items,[82] without being tied to stock ownership as in a corporation.

Substantial tax benefits in the form of deferred compensation are available to stockholder-employees of corporations but not to partners.[83] Others, in the form of a deductible buy-out of a dead or

---

76. Conduit treatment also connotes the preservation of the tax character of each item of income and deduction, such as tax-exempt income or capital gain. See id. § 702.

77. If unreasonably accumulated, corporate earnings are subject to a heavy additional tax. Id. §§ 531–37.

78. Id. §§ 61(a) (7), 316.

If the distribution is in dissolution or liquidation, there may also be a tax, but computed differently. The amount received less the shareholder's basis (usually his cost) for his stock is the amount of income. But the applicable tax rates are those for capital gain: half the individual rates, with a maximum of 25%. Id. §§ 331, 1201, 1202.

79. Many techniques are available for reducing double taxation, including the payment of salary, interest or rent to stockholders in their capacities as officers, creditors or landlords. But

all these result in taxation of the income to the stockholder who is no better off as to this income than if he were a partner.

80. Id. §§ 704(d), 705(a), 752(a), (b), 722, 733 provide rather intricate limitations on the deductible loss, which can usually be circumvented (e. g., by borrowing) or made to result only in a delay of the deduction. See Sec. 65(a) n. 18 below.

81. Id. §§ 1211, 1212. If the stock was properly qualified under id. § 1244 before issuance, the loss is ordinary.

82. Id. § 704.

83. Sec. 34A(a) below. Other significant corporate advantages include tax exemption of death benefits (up to $5,000), group life insurance premiums (up to $50,000 in coverage), and medical expenses paid by the employer. Int.Rev.Code of 1954, §§ 101(b), 79, 104–06 (26 U.S.C.A.)

retiring participant's interest by the firm, are available to partnerships but not to corporations.[84]

The sale of a partnership interest or of corporate stock both generally result in capital gain (taxable at a maximum rate of 25%) or capital loss.[85] Exceptions may make part or all of the gain taxable as ordinary income, on quite different terms for corporations and partnerships.[86]

There is no general way to compare taxation of a business in corporate and partnership forms.[87] Which is better will depend on any number of factors; the most important usually are the expected profit or loss of the business, the tax rates of each of the individual participants and the extent to which profits will be distributed or retained. Despite double taxation, the corporation will save taxes in many situations; in many others, the partnership will. One can only predict the specific facts and make calculations.

Certain businesses like oil and gas receive special tax treatment which may influence the choice of form. The special deductions made available in excess of economic loss are more valuable against highly taxed individual income. The general or limited partnership is particularly attractive in these situations.[88]

Since 1958, certain corporations qualifying under Subchapter S of the Internal Revenue Code have been permitted to elect a system of taxation resembling that of partnerships in some but not all important respects.[89] This introduces another complication by increasing the number of alternative forms from which to choose. But it is advantageous in allowing a combination of limited liability (under local law) for all participants, and conduit treatment (under tax law) for ordinary income, losses and capital gains, with concomitant elimination of corporate double taxation.

84. Sec. 86(b) (3) below.

85. Int.Rev.Code of 1954, §§ 1221, 1201, 1202, 741 (26 U.S.C.A.), Sec. 86(b) (1) below.

86. Id. §§ 341, 751 (26 U.S.C.A.). See Sec. 86(b) (1) below on partnerships; Axelrad, Collapsible Corporations and Collapsible Partnerships, 1960 U. of So.Cal.Tax Inst. 269.

87. A brief comparison of corporate and partnership taxation is Bittker & Eustice, op. cit. supra n. 73 at 1–26, esp. 24–26. More comprehensive are Knapp & Semmel, Forms of Business Organization and the Federal Tax Laws (1966); Davies & Lawrence, Choosing the Form of Business Organization (1963); Shockey, Sweeney & Brady, Taxation and Business Planning (1963); Sarner & Shinehouse, Organizational Problems of Small Business (1961); Rohrlich, Organizing Corporate and Other Enterprises (3d ed. 1958); Strecker, When Will the Corporate Form Save Taxes?, 18 Vand. L.Rev. 1695 (1965), 8 Corp.Prac.Comm. 1 (1966); Axelrad, Choice of Form: Partnership, Corporation or In-Between, N.Y.U. 19th Inst. on Fed.Tax 361 (1961).

88. See Sec. 26(d) below.

89. Sec. 34C below. An exhaustive discussion is Dixon et al., Partnerships and Subchapter S: A Comparison of Tax Advantages, N.Y.U. 25th Inst. on Fed.Tax 151 (1967). See also Note, Tax Comparison of the Limited Partnership and the Subchapter S Corporation, 43 Minn.L.Rev. 964 (1959).

A final problem is that the federal tax law has its own definitions of corporation and partnership, and its own criteria for applying them. The results usually, but not always, correspond to the state law classification.[90] Thus, the lawyer forming a business organization must structure it to satisfy the tax requirements as well as those of state law.

Many *states* tax corporations differently from (and typically more heavily than) partnerships and proprietorships. Although the dollar differences are unlikely to be as great as in federal taxation, they too need to be examined and weighed in choosing the form.

(j) Organizational Formality and Cost; Upkeep

Establishment of a corporation entails considerable formality, part of it public (the filing of a charter or articles of incorporation) and part of it private (bylaws, minutes, resolution, etc.). A limited partnership requires the public filing of a detailed certificate rather like a corporate charter.[91] A general partnership calls for no public filing unless under fictitious name statutes;[92] indeed, a written agreement is not legally necessary in most situations, although one is highly advisable. The informality of the partnership, both at the start and through its operative life, has some attraction. But a comprehensive partnership agreement, if one is drawn, can be as formal as corporate documents.[92A]

There is rarely a big difference between corporation and partnership organizational costs if the job is done with equal care. Filing fees are paid by corporations and limited partnerships, but normally not by general partnerships. The amounts vary from place to place, but are usually not very great, e.g., $100 or less for a small business in one state. An attorney's fee is not likely to differ materially for a corporation or a partnership if he considers all the relevant factors, and if he plans and drafts thoughtfully for all the problems which emerge. His fee is usually in the range of several hundred dollars for a small business in most parts of the country. If there is a difference between corporate and partnership legal fees, the former will typically be higher. Businessmen may choose the partnership to bypass the lawyer and avoid his fee, although this may prove more costly in the long run.

A corporation, unlike a partnership, must have (under most state laws) some minimum capital paid in before commencing operation. However, this is usually a modest amount ($1,000 or less) which would be necessary as a practical matter to start business. So it is not a significant factor unless the state law happens to set a very high minimum.

---

90. See Secs. 6(e), 23A above, Secs. 24, 34A below and, more generally, Ch. 3 below.

91. See Sec. 26(b) below.

92. Sec. 22 above.

92A. But see n. 41 above.

Corporations are required to qualify in each state (other than the one where organized) in which they do business; this entails more formality and expense.[93] Partnerships and proprietorships are generally exempt.[94] As a result, corporations face somewhat heavier requirements for annual reports, fees and taxes in states of organization as well as of qualification.

(k) The Final Choice

It should be obvious from a review of this Section that there is no easy criterion for choosing between partnership and corporation. Each has advantages and disadvantages which vary according to the facts known and projected for the particular business being considered. Moreover, it is quite possible that the relative merits will be different for different participants in the same venture. A highly taxed individual may prefer a non-corporate form that will give him usable current deductions, while someone else yearns for the safety of a corporation. One may prefer a corporate control pattern while another thinks partnership is fairer in this respect. Resolving these differences can be as hard as explaining them.

All in all, the partnership is probably the more flexible form, capable of better molding by agreement to the desires of the parties.[95] It is also easier to get out of, under both state and tax law, if personal or business difficulties develop.

Of the many factors considered, two usually turn out to be most important to the participant: limited liability and tax advantages. The former points to limited partnership or corporation (regular or Subchapter S); the latter points to any of these or general partnership, depending on the circumstances. If limited liability is not a major concern, the partnership becomes a much stronger contender.

An either-or choice of form is not always necessary. In some cases two or more may be used, simultaneously or consecutively. A corporation may be formed to hold certain assets and lease them to a partnership which conducts operations, or vice versa. High risk activities may be incorporated and others carried on in partnership. Or a partnership may start a business with the idea of incorporating later when higher profits bring higher taxes on the partners, or when stock is to be sold to the public.[96]

---

93. See Sec. 31 below.

94. See Sec. 22A(b) above.

95. Since the partnership agreement is a private document, it is a little easier to amend than a corporate charter. But partnership amendment requires unanimous agreement unless there is advance provision for change by some lesser proportion. Ordinarily a corporate charter can be amended by a majority (often ⅔) of the shareholders, unless it contains a requirement for a greater proportion. Differences in this respect can thus be made negligible by drafting, but are moderately significant without it. Which pattern is better depends on the situation. Unanimity requirements can lead to deadlock. Low voting proportions can let the majority victimize the minority.

96. See Corneel, Using Partnerships to Solve Close Corporation Problems, N.Y.U. 22d Inst. on Fed.Tax. 629 (1964).

CHAPTER 3

SPECIAL FORMS OF PARTNERSHIP AND RELATED UNINCORPORATED BUSINESS ASSOCIATIONS

Analysis

THE VARIETIES OF BUSINESS ASSOCIATION

§ 24. Besides ordinary partnerships, various types of unincorporated business organizations are known, many from earlier times. Most of them have little contemporary significance, except as given by the federal income tax which tries to treat corporate-like associations as corporations regardless of their formal method of organization. Criteria have evolved to distinguish corporations from other organizations for tax purposes, but they are in dispute. Tax matters aside, unincorporated organizations tend to be treated as partnerships in many respects.

The reader interested solely in conventional partnerships will skip most of this chapter, lingering only over Sections 24A (dealing

137

with terminology), 26 and 32 (limited partnerships) and perhaps 36 (partnership by estoppel). Even he, however, will gain some insight by examining the variety of unincorporated forms considered, for they have developed (to greater or lesser extent) by partnership analogy and they possess partnership features, sometimes in extreme degree.

This book deals only with business associations, i. e. those organized for profit. Except for incidental references, social, fraternal, charitable, religious and other non-profit organizations are excluded by this test, as are labor unions, although the validity and applicability of the test are open to some question.[1]

Many of the forms discussed here have minimal current viability. Some (Secs. 30–32) represent mistakes which can and should be avoided. Those (Secs. 26, 26A, 33) permitting limited liability are less attractive than corporations, which are easily created. Others (Secs. 27, 34, 35) rarely have any advantage over a well-drawn general partnership. In most cases, the explanation (other than sheer history and inertia) for the survival of the older forms and for the origin of the newer ones, is some quirk in the federal income tax which gives special benefit to a particular type of organization.[2] The tax lures are often short-lived, and sometimes illusory, but they require the business lawyer to have at least an elementary knowledge of the diverse forms.

The borderlines among the several sorts of unincorporated associations are indistinct at many points. This is especially true, as we shall see, of joint ventures, mining partnerships, business trusts, joint stock companies and general partnerships. Some of the terminology is loose too. "Syndicate," though widely used, does not refer to any particular legal form.[3] "Firm" usually means partner-

---

1. See Sec. 13 above. Some general references on unincorporated, non-profit associations: Ford, Unincorporated Non-Profit Associations—Their Property and the Liability (1959); Lloyd, Unincorporated Associations (1938) (English law); Oleck, Non-Profit Corporations, Organizations and Associations (2d ed. 1965); Wrighting-ton, Law of Unincorporated Associations and Business Trusts (2d ed 1923); Harth, Legal Nature of Voluntary Associations, 30 Legal Bull. of U. S. Savings & Loan League 71 (Mar. 1964); Crane, Partnership 528–48 (2d ed. 1952).

Some references on particular problems: Note, Exhaustion of Remedies in Private, Voluntary Associations, 65 Yale L.J. 369 (1956); Note, Exclusion from Private Associations, 74 Yale L. J. 1313 (1965); Note, Unincorporated Associations in New England, 37 B.

U.L.Rev. 336 (1957); Note, Diversity Jurisdiction for Unincorporated Associations, 75 Yale L.J. 138 (1965); Comment, Unincorporated Associations: Diversity Jurisdiction and the ALI Proposal, 1965 Duke L.J. 329; Crane, Liability of Unincorporated Association for Tortious Injury to a Member, 16 Vand.L.Rev. 319 (1963); Comment, Liability of Members and Officers of Nonprofit Unincorporated Associations for Contracts and Torts, 42 Calif.L.Rev. 812 (1954); Annot., Sales of memberships in club or similar organization as sale of securities within provisions of securities acts, 87 A.L.R.2d 1140 (1963).

2. See, generally, Bromberg, Tax Influences on the Law of Business Associations, 16 Bayl.L.Rev. 327 (1964).

3. Thus, a syndicate may be a co-ownership, joint venture, partnership,

ship—we normally so use it in this book—but may describe other organizations, corporate or non-corporate.[3A] The dividing line between unincorporated and incorporated associations is not as clear as one might suppose from thinking that a corporation is something organized in accordance with a corporate statute. For one thing, there is the problem—now quite minor—of defective compliance with the statute (see Sec. 30). For another—far more important—there is the long struggle between business and government over substance and form, i. e. whether an organization, though not formally incorporated, is to be taxed or regulated like a corporation (or, conversely, though formally incorporated, to be treated like a partnership).[4] This clash has led to a number of efforts to analyze corporateness, and isolate the essential factors which distinguish it from the opposite. Most of us would agree with this listing of basic corporate characteristics: [5]

(A) Associates

(B) An objective to carry on business for profit

(C) Continuity of organizational life despite changes in personnel

(D) Centralization or delegation of management

(E) Limited liability

(F) Transferability of interests in the organization.

At this point, the agreement abruptly stops. The exact meaning of each element is subject to considerable dispute, as is the completeness of the list, and the proper role of federal and state law (or tax and business associations law) in the decisional process. Some of the characteristics are obviously common to corporate and noncorporate bodies: (A), (B) and (in limited partnerships) (E). Others, by agreement, are often provided in partnerships and eliminated in corporations: (C), (D), (F). In most jurisdictions a corporation can be

---

limited partnership, corporation or something else. See Berger, Real Estate Syndication: Property, Promoters and the Need for Protection, 69 Yale.L.J. 725 (1960).

3A. "Firm" as partnership: Firestone Tire & Rubber Co. v. Webb, 207 Ark. 820, 182 S.W.2d 941 (1944) (one who signed financial statement showing "firm name" was name of other signer, was liable with him as partner by estoppel); Wood v. Universal Creditors Assoc., 112 Ga.App. 203, 144 S.E. 2d 462 (1965) (account receivable validly assigned in firm name); Bufton v. Hoseley, 236 Or. 12, 386 P.2d 471 (1963) (pleading that Ds operated under a certain "firm name" allowed proof of partnership).

But see U. S. v. Cook, 384 U.S. 257, 261, 86 S.Ct. 1412, 16 L.Ed.2d 516 (1966)

(18 U.S.C.A. § 660, prohibiting embezzlement from "any [common carrier] firm, association or corporation" applies to a sole proprietorship).

4. Int.Rev.Code of 1954, § 7701(a) (3) (26 U.S.C.A.) defines "corporation" to include "associations" and joint stock companies; partnerships are separately defined, id. §§ 761(a), 7701(a) (2). Since these provisions determine whether an organization is subject to the corporate or non-corporate tax systems, most of the battles have been fought over these sections and their predecessors.

5. Income Tax Reg. § 301.7701-2 (1960, amended 1965). See also Morrissey v. Commissioner, 296 U.S. 344, 56 S.Ct. 289, 80 L.Ed. 263 (1935).

one-man in the sense that an individual owns all the stock (or all but qualifying shares); in a few he can be the whole board of directors; [6] this further undermines (D). Suffice it to say that there is no consensus, and no intellectually respectable set of guides, on which of the listed attributes are essential and which are merely customary, nor on the proper application to a given organization when some factors point one way and some the other. Such questions must be resolved in a larger context, and are treated somewhat further in particular Sections of this chapter.[7]

Clarity on the corporate-noncorporate characterization has not been promoted by the curious but economically understandable role reversal which has occurred. In the 1920–30s the tax authorities were seeking corporate treatment of many unincorporated organizations which resisted it. In the 1950–60s the tax authorities were resisting corporate treatment of many unincorporated organizations which sought it. In each period, of course, it was a matter of which form produced higher taxes for the organizations involved.

Congress has made some well-intentioned efforts to relieve the tax problems and organizational disparities by permitting some unincorporated associations to be taxed as if they were incorporated, and conversely.[8] Naturally, each eligible unit chooses the method generating the lesser tax, and no fundamental solution evolved. Nor will one as long as corporate and non-corporate businesses are subject to entirely different rates and methods of taxation.[9]

While the income tax continues to treat corporate and other businesses very differently (however much trouble it may have distinguishing them), other areas of law take a more unitary approach. In securities regulation and blue sky law, it typically makes no difference whether the issuer is incorporated or not.[10] So also with most regula-

---

6. E. g., 8 Del.C.Ann. § 141(b). Statutes are collected, Folk, Corporation Statutes: 1959–66, 1966 Duke L.J. 875, 896–98; 1 Model Business Corp. Act Ann. 587 (1960 and Supp.).

7. See, e. g., Secs. 33–34C below.

8. Secs. 34A, 34B below.

We do not consider here the election granted certain partnerships to be taxed as co-ownerships. Those eligible include some mineral operations and investment firms not actively conducting a business. Int.Rev.Code of 1954, § 761(a) (26 U.S.C.A.) and Reg. thereunder. See Taubman, Oil and Gas Partnerships and Section 761(a), 12 Tax L.Rev. 49 (1956).

9. See Bromberg, op. cit. supra n. 2. Scallen, Federal Income Taxation of Professional Associations and Corporations, 49 Minn.L.Rev. 603, 609–25 (1965) traces the legislative development of tax distinctions between corporations and partnerships. Strecker, When Will the Corporate Form Save Taxes?, 18 Vand.L.Rev. 1695 (1965) explores the problems indicated by its title. See also Secs. 23A, 23B above.

10. Securities Act of 1933, § 2(1), (2), (4), 15 U.S.C.A. § 77(b) (1), (2), (4); Pawgan v. Silverstein, 265 F.Supp. 898 (S.D. N.Y.1967) (general partnership interests held securities).

Uniform Securities Act § 401(g), (i) (l); McKinney's N.Y.Gen.Business Law, § 352–e (real estate syndications); Annot., Blue Sky Law, 87 A.L.R. 42, 65–71 (1933). See Note, Sale of Limited Partnership Interests, 14 Hast.L.J. 176 (1962).

tion of business activities.[11] The Uniform Commercial Code generally treats all forms of business organization alike. For example, it defines person—on which many of its operative provisions depend—to include an individual or an organization, and the latter to include "corporation, . . . business trust, . . . partnership or association, two or more persons having a joint or common interest, or any other legal or commercial entity." [12]

SOME PARTICULAR KINDS OF PARTNERS

§ 24A. **Partners are sometimes referred to with qualifying terms.** We describe here for future use the more important ones:

(a) **General and limited partners**

(b) **Ostensible partners or partners by estoppel**

(c) **Dormant or secret partners**

(d) **Incoming partners**

(e) **Retiring or outgoing partners**

(f) **Continuing or ongoing partners**

(g) **Surviving partners**

(h) **Liquidating or winding-up partners**

(i) **Managing partners**

(j) **Senior and junior partners**

(k) **Co-partners.**

Limited partners (special partners in older terminology) are members of statutory limited partnerships, typically sharing profits, immune from personal liability for firm debts, and not participating in management.[13] General partners, in either limited or general partnerships, also share profits but have full management powers and full personal liability.[14] "Partner" normally means general partner unless otherwise indicated.

Partners by estoppel (or ostensible partners) are not actually partners but represent themselves to be partners, or consent to their being so represented by others. The result is that third persons who are led to act upon the representations may hold them liable as though they were partners.[15]

A dormant partner (or secret partner) is one whose name is not used and who is so inactive that his association with the firm is generally unknown. He is nonetheless a partner, liable for firm obliga-

---

11. See, e. g., U. S. v. A & P Trucking Co., 358 U.S. 121, 79 S.Ct. 203, 3 L.Ed. 2d 165 (1958) (regulation of motor carriers); U. S. v. The Brookman Co., 229 F.Supp. 862 (N.D.Calif.1964) (Sherman Anti-Trust Act).

12. U.C.C. § 1—201(28), (30).

13. Sec. 26 below.

14. U.P.A. §§ 18(e), 15; Secs. 65(d), 58, 64 below.

15. Sec. 36 below.

tions like other partners.[16]   However, on his retirement from the firm, he may not need to give the notice required of other partners to avoid liability for obligations incurred by the firm thereafter.[17]

Incoming partners are ones who enter a going firm as new partners. They are not personally liable on old obligations, unless they assume them, but their shares in partnership property are liable.[18]

Retiring or outgoing partners are those who cease to be partners in the business, which is carried on by others. They remain liable for obligations incurred by the firm while they were partners. But they are not liable for new obligations, unless they fail to give appropriate notice and so are held as partners on estoppel principles.[19]

Continuing or ongoing partners are those who continue a partnership business after one or more partners die or retire.

Surviving partners are continuing partners after a death. They succeed to the ownership of certain rights in partnership property, and have a duty to liquidate unless there is an agreement for continuation of the business.

Liquidating or winding-up partners settle the firm's affairs after dissolution unless there is a continuation agreement.[20]

Managing partners have special responsibilities and control delegated to them by the other partners.[21]

Senior and junior partners are often so designated, formally or informally, in law and other professional firms. The phrases have no fixed legal content but depend on the allocation of powers, duties and profit shares by the particular partnership agreement.[21A]

"Co-partnership" is a pompous legalism meaning nothing more than "partnership." The same is true of "co-partners" when referring to all the partners. However, "co-partners" is a convenient shorthand for distinguishing fellow partners, i. e. "A partner sued his co-partner(s)."

16.   Schwaegler Co. Inc. v. Marchesottl, 88 Cal.App.2d 738, 199 P.2d 331 (1948); Warner v. Modano, 340 Mass. 439, 164 N.E.2d 904 (1960); Dygert v. Hansen, 31 Wash.2d 858, 199 P.2d 596 (1948).

17.   Sec. 81(c) below.

18.   Sec. 88 below.

19.   Sec. 81 below, Sec. 18 at nn. 36–38 above.

20.   Secs. 83, 86 below.

21.   White v. Houston, 103 S.W.2d 1073 (Tex.Civ.App.1936). McEvoy v. Grant, 302 Pa. 539, 153 A. 763 (1931) (managing partner analogized to executive committee of corporate board of directors). See also Sec. 65(d) at nn. 56–57 below.

21A.   See Provident Trust Co. of Philadelphia v. Rankin, 333 Pa. 412, 5 A.2d 214 (1939) (junior partner in architectural firm expressly liable for firm debts). Cf. City of Wheeling v. Chester, 134 F.2d 759 (3d Cir. 1943) ("junior member" in engineering firm, which was a sole proprietorship, was an employee and not liable to proprietor for share of losses). See also Sec. 65 at n. 3 below.

SOME UNUSUAL TYPES OF PARTNERSHIP

§ 25. The term "partnership" has been applied to some forms of organization which do not have the same incidents as normal partnerships. These include:

(a) Limited partnerships—Sec. 26

(b) Limited partnership associations—Sec. 26A

(c) Mining partnerships—Sec. 27

(d) Sub-partnerships—Sec. 28.

LIMITED PARTNERSHIPS

§ 26. A limited partnership is formed by compliance with statutory requirements. It consists of (a) general partners, who manage the business and have the same liability as in an ordinary partnership, and (b) limited partners, who take no part in management, share profits, and do not share losses beyond their capital contributions to the firm. A limited partner may forfeit his limited liability by taking part in control of the business. In most other respects, limited partnerships are like general partnerships.

Since limited liability is more easily and surely attained by incorporation, the limited partnership finds its main use where the conduit or aggregate treatment of partnerships by the tax law is preferred to the entity treatment of corporations.

(a) Background

Since business employs both capital and services, with relative importance varying according to the kind of business, a need exists for a form of association permitting capital investment without responsibility for management and without liability for losses beyond the amount invested. A creditor has such a position, but may feel that a fixed return (particularly if restricted by the usury laws) is incommensurate with the risk. The need encompasses, then, a right to share profits with limited liability for losses.

During the middle ages, the need was met by the *commenda*.[22] This was an arrangement under which the *commendator* supplied money to the *commendatarius* (or *tractator*) to be employed in trade. The *commendator* received the major portion of the profits, but had no

---

22. 8 Holdsworth, History of English Law 195; Mitchell, Early Forms of Partnership, 3 Select Essays, Anglo-American Legal History 183 (1909). On limited partnerships in the U. S., see Ames v. Downing, 1 Bradf. 321 (N.Y.1850); Troubat, Commandatary and Limited Partnership in the United States (1853); Comment, The Limited Partnership, 45 Yale L.J. 895 (1936).

The first acts were adopted in N.Y. (1822), Conn. (1822) and Pa. (1836). This was said to be the first instance of an American state deriving its statutory law from a country other than England. 3 Kent, Commentaries *36.

On the early history of the commenda, see Lobingier, The Natural History of the Private Artificial Person, 13 Tul.L.Rev. 41, 56 (1938). See also Sec. 2 above. For a modern version, see Comment, Partnership in Commendam—Louisiana's Limited Partnership, 35 Tul.L.Rev. 815 (1961).

liability for losses.   He had no claim against the *commendatarius* for loss of the capital investment not caused by the latter's fault.   The institution was sanctioned by the French Commercial Code of 1807, Sections 23–28.   It suggested the basic characteristics of the U.S. limited partnership, which was first provided for by legislation over a century ago.[23]   The impetus for adoption here was the desire to avoid the doctrine of partnership liability to third persons, based on profit-sharing, which followed in the wake of Waugh v. Carver.[24]   Corporate charters, which equally satisfy the need, were not easily obtained; limited partnership acts preceded by several decades the general corporation acts.

Limited partnership statutes have been enacted in all states. Earlier versions suffered from strict wording and from common law hostility to limited liability;   courts imposed full liability for rather trivial failures in compliance.[25]   The predominant statute now is the

---

23.   See n. 22 above.

24.   H.Bl. 235 (1793).   See Sec. 14(b) above, and Douglas, Vicarious Liability and the Administration of Risk, 38 Yale L.J. 720 (1929).

25.   The older acts were strictly construed on immunity from liability. The common view was that a special or limited partner was essentially a general partner with immunity only on condition of full and exact compliance with the statutory details. Andrews v. Schott, 10 Pa. 47 (1848); Rathke v. Griffith, 36 Wash.2d 394, 218 P.2d 757, 18 A.L.R.2d 1349 (1950), noted 26 Wash.L.Rev. 222 (1951), citing this text; In re Merrill, 17 Fed.Cas. 82, 83 (No. 9,467) (N.D.N.Y.1874).   But see criticism of this view in President, etc. of Manhattan Co. v. Laimbeer, 108 N.Y. 578, 581, 15 N.E. 712, 713 (1888).   See also Crane, Are Limited Partnerships Necessary?, 17 Minn.L. Rev. 351–355 (1933); Comment, 45 Yale L.J. 895 (1936); Note, 36 Harv. L.Rev. 1016 (1923), Comment, 48 Mich. L.Rev. 347 (1950).

Gradually the courts took a less rigid attitude, and shifted to the view that special partners were to be liable only to the extent and under the circumstances expressly required by the statutes. White v. Eiseman, 134 N.Y. 101, 103, 31 N.E. 276, 277 (1892); Chick v. Robinson, 95 F. 619, 52 L.R.A. 833 (6th Cir. 1899).   The statutes imposed liability, in case of false statements in the certificate, upon persons interested in the partnership, Richardson v.

Hogg, 39 Pa. 153 (1861);   Crehan v. Megargel, 234 N.Y. 67, 136 N.E. 296 (1922), discussed in Warren, Corporate Advantages without Incorporation 311 et seq. (1929).   Liability was imposed for failure to file the certificate, Henkel v. Heyman, 91 Ill. 96 (1878);   or for failure to file in the right offices, O'Connor v. Graff, 186 App.Div. 116, 173 N.Y.S. 730 (1919).

Relaxation of the older view was apparent in decisions holding the special partner not liable to creditors who dealt with the firm as a limited partnership, Allegheny Nat. Bank v. Bailey, 147 Pa. 111, 23 A. 439 (1892);   not liable for torts, McKnight v. Ratcliff, 44 Pa. 156 (1863);   not liable as a partner by estoppel after withdrawal from the firm without notice, Tilge v. Brooks, 124 Pa. 178, 16 A. 746, 2 L.R.A. 796 (1889).

See also Sec. 32 below and cases collected, Comment, 65 Colum.L.Rev. 1463, 1464 (1965);   Lewis, The Uniform Limited Partnership Act, 65 U.Pa.L.Rev. 715, 720–22 (1917).

For a recent comparison of U.L.P.A. and an earlier statute still in force, see Basye, A Survey of the Limited-Partnership Form of Business Organization, 42 Ore.L.Rev. 35 (1962).   See also Hurd and Mayer, Ohio Limited Partnerships—Business Use and Effect, 27 Ohio St.L.J. 373 (1966) (surveying U.L.P.A.);   Comments, The Limited Partnership, 2 U.C.L.A. L.Rev. 105 (1954), Partnership in Commendam— Louisiana's Limited Partnership, 35 Tul.L.Rev. 815 (1961).

Uniform Limited Partnership Act (U.L.P.A.),[26] which expressly provides protection against technical defects if there is good faith attempt at compliance.[27] England's limited partnership legislation dates from 1907.[28]

Under the U.L.P.A., a limited partnership can carry on any business which can be carried on by a general partnership, unless specific exception is stated in the statute. About half the states except banking and insurance.[28A]

(b) Formation

The creation of a limited partnership is not a mere private, informal, voluntary agreement such as may suffice for a general partnership, but is a public and formal proceeding which must follow the statutory requirements. The associates must sign a certificate setting forth the firm name, character, duration,[28B] and location of business, the identity of the general and limited partners, the amount and character of the limited partners' contributions and their shares in profits, and the methods (if any) for change of personnel and subsequent continuance of the business.[29] A simple limited partnership certificate appears in Appendix VII. In content and method of filing it somewhat resembles a corporate charter. There is usually a separate, private limited partnership agreement covering matters (like profit shares of general partners) not required to be stated in the certificate.

Curiously, there is no requirement that a limited firm so identify itself in its name or dealings, although this would be the most effective way of communicating its status to third persons trading with it. Many firms do, in fact, display their limited character on their stationery or in their formal contracts with outsiders.

The certificate must be filed with a designated official,[29A] where it is typically open to public inspection. Many states designate an official in the county where the principal business of the firm is to be carried on. Controversies naturally arise if the firm does substantial business in several counties. Cautious firms record in each county

---

26. See Table in Sec. 2 above.

27. U.L.P.A. § 11, Sec. 32 below. See also U.L.P.A. § 6, Sec. 32 below, which limits liability for false statements in the certificate so that it runs only in favor of persons relying on them and only against signers knowing of the falsity. U.L.P.A. § 2(2) provides that a limited partnership is formed if there has been substantial compliance in good faith with the requirements for signing and filing the certificate.

28. Limited Partnerships Act, 7 Edw. VII., ch. 24 (1907).

28A. U.L.P.A. § 3. State variations are listed, 8 Unif.Laws Ann. 14 (1922 & Supp.).

28B. There is no limit to the duration in most states, although at least one requires annual renewal. F.S.A. (Fla.) § 620.31 (1956), largely gutted by Vulcan Furniture Mfg. Corp. v. Vaughan, discussed Sec. 32 n. 47 below.

29. U.L.P.A. § 2(1) (a).

29A. U.L.P.A. § 2(1) (b). State variations on the place of filing are collected in 8 Unif.Laws Ann. 6–8 (1922 & Supp.).

where they operate, to avoid claims of non-compliance which might forfeit limited liability. Some states require multiple filings. Others eliminate the problem by requiring filing only at a single, central point (normally the capitol). The U.L.P.A. does not expressly recognize the existence of a firm whose certificate has been filed in another state, although the courts may do so through their choice of law rules.[30] Since constructive notice is almost nil for something filed in another state, a court could easily rule that failure to file locally makes the firm a general one. For this reason, certificates are often refiled in each state where the partnership does business.[31]

A few states require newspaper publication of the certificate (or a summary), as well as filing.[32]

The certificate contents and filing present some negative features. Disclosure of limited partners' contributions and profit shares is resented by some businessmen; comparable information is not generally required of corporations. Capitalization is relatively rigid, since limited partners' contributions must be itemized in the certificate. However, no minimum capitalization is required, nor must the contributions be paid at any particular time. Moreover, the contribution may be changed by amendment. So may, or must, a number of other things in the certificate,[33] calling for a sequence of amendments which may be a nuisance.

Although the limited partnership was conceived to accommodate only a few limited partners, there is no statutory limit, and some very large groups have been assembled.[33A]

(c) Liability and Role of Limited Partner

General partners conduct the business as in a general partnership, and are personally liable to creditors. The necessity for at least one general partner [34] reflects a policy that someone have personal liability.

---

30. See Cheyenne Oil Corp. v. Oil & Gas Ventures, Inc., —— Del. ——, 204 A.2d 743 (Del.1964) (certificate filed in N.J.; failure to file in Ark., Tex., no bar to suit by firm on transactions in those states; loss of limited liability is only U.L.P.A. sanction for failure to file certificate); Gilman Paint and Varnish Co. v. Legum, 197 Md. 665, 80 A.2d 906, 29 A.L.R.2d 286 (1951) (certificate filed in Md., where all members lived; Md. law controlled liability of limited partner for goods delivered in Tenn. for use in Ga.). Older cases are collected, Annot., 29 A. L.R.2d 295, 306–08 (1953).

F.S.A. (Fla.) § 620.41 (1959) has a procedure for domestication and recognition of foreign limited partnerships.

31. This is cumbersome because of the frequent need for amendment, U.L.P.A. § 24.

If the firm carefully identifies itself, in dealing with others, as a limited partnership under the laws of State X, it gets a good deal of protection since third persons in State Y doing business with it on this basis are probably estopped to assert general partnership liability because of non-filing in State Y. However, multiple filing is likely to be safer.

32. McKinney's N.Y. Partnership Law § 91.

33. U.L.P.A. § 24.

33A. See, e. g., n. 52 below.

34. U.L.P.A. § 1

However, it is easily circumvented in states where a corporation (with limited liability by virtue of corporate laws) can be the general partner.

Limited partners are exempt from personal liability on condition that they do not participate in management.[35] There is no express bar to their participation, but the threat of personal liability is a strong deterrent. Neither the Act nor the decisions [36] under it are very helpful on the critical question of how much review, advisory, management selection, or veto power a limited partner may have without being regarded as taking part in control.[37] The resulting uncertainty is probably the greatest drawback of the limited partnership form.

35. U.L.P.A. § 7: "A limited partner shall not become liable as a general partner unless, in addition to his rights and powers as a limited partner he takes part in the control of the business." Holzman v. De Escamilla, 86 Cal.App.2d 858, 195 P.2d 833 (1948), n. 36 below. See also Russell v. Warner, 96 Cal.App.2d 986, 217 P.2d 43 (1950), and Sec. 65(d) n. 59 below.

36. Holzman v. De Escamilla, n. 35 above. Limited partners who determined what crops should be planted in the farming venture, and who signed checks on firm bank accounts were sufficiently participating in business to be held liable as general partners.

Grainger v. Antoyan, 48 Cal.2d 805, 313 P.2d 848 (1957), noted 56 Mich.L.Rev. 285 (1957). A limited partner was sales manager of the firm's new car department. He signed checks occasionally but had no authority to hire or fire, to buy new cars, or to set sale prices or trade-in values. He was not liable as a general partner.

Silvola v. Rowlett, 129 Colo. 522, 272 P. 2d 287 (1954), noted 27 Rocky Mt.L. Rev. 98. A limited partner was repair shop foreman and sometimes discussed major problems with the general partner. But exclusive control was in the latter, and the former was not liable as a general partner.

Plasteel Products Corp. v. Helman, 271 F.2d 354 (1st Cir. 1959) (Mass. law). Trustee limited partners did not take part in control by designating general sales manager of firm and providing for his joint financial control with the general partner; latter could have discharged general sales manager at any time.

Rathke v. Griffith, 36 Wash.2d 394, 218 P.2d 757, 18 A.L.R.2d 1349 (1950),

noted 26 Wash.L.Rev. 222 (1951). A limited partner did not take part in control by being named to the board of directors of the firm where he never functioned as such. (The board of directors is a rare device in limited firms; a limited partner's participation on one would be highly dangerous to his immunity from liability).

Cf. De Long v. Marston, 308 Mich. 63, 13 N.W.2d 209 (1944). The limited partner was in fact a straw man in whose name investment was made by one who actively participated in management of the business by agreement between the general and the ostensible limited partner. On the latter's exclusion from management, a suit was filed in the name of the limited partner. The court refused to dismiss and suggested that the real party in interest be substituted as plaintiff. This, of course, involves no issue of liability to creditors.

Cf. Garter v. Metzdorf Associates, 217 Cal.App.2d 812, 32 Cal.Rptr. 113 (1963). The facts raise issues whether the limited partners took part in control, but the issues were left undecided.

37. California, by 1963 amendments (which were said to be clarifications rather than changes of existing law) recognizes that limited partners may have and exercise powers to vote on certain matters without being deemed to partake in control. The matters are: election or removal of general partners, termination of the firm, amendment of the agreement, and sale of all or substantially all the firm's assets. The voting powers must be in the certificate. The list is not exclusive of other powers which a limited partner might enjoy without losing his protection against liability. West's Ann.Cal.Corp.Code, § 15507. If these

Even without taking part in control, a limited partner may lose his immunity if his name appears in the firm name,[38] if he knows of falsity in the certificate,[39] or if he holds himself out as a general partner.[40] And, generally, he is liable to creditors to the extent of any contribution he has promised the firm but not made, and to the extent of any part of his contribution he has withdrawn from the firm.[41] Finally, he may be liable if the firm is defectively organized and he fails to make the appropriate renunciation on discovery of the situation.[42]

Apart from his contribution to the firm (on which there is no minimum) and his share in its profits (on which there is no maximum), the limited partner plays a negligible role in the partnership. He may not take part in control;[43] his contributions may not be services;[44] his name may not appear in the firm name.[45] He ordinarily has no auhority to bind the firm.[46] Indeed, although he is a "member" of the firm, it is very doubtful whether he is a "partner" in the U.L.P.A. sense.[47] But he is entitled to inspect the books and have an accounting,[48] and to have creditor status for loans to the firm apart from his contribution.[49] He is entitled to the return of his contribu-

---

powers include the right to initiate the matters, and to decide them entirely within the group of limited partners, they give very substantial control to the limited partners. To the extent they are confined to approval of actions of the general partners, they are no greater than shareholders usually have, and are not very substantial.

38. U.L.P.A. § 5(2).

39. U.L.P.A. § 6, n. 27 above, Sec. 32 below.

40. U.P.A. § 16, Sec. 36 below, Cf. J. C. Wattenbarger & Sons v. Sanders, 191 Cal.App.2d 857, 13 Cal.Rptr. 92 (1961), noted 14 Hast.L.J. 62 (1962), subsequent opinion 216 Cal.App.2d 495, 30 Cal.Rptr. 910 (1963).

41. U.L.P.A. § 17. A creditor of the firm can proceed against a limited partner (to the extent of his liability) before pursuing general partners or the firm. Kittredge v. Langley, 252 N.Y. 405, 169 N.E. 626 (1930). See Annot., Liability of special partner who has withdrawn his capital, to creditors of the firm, 67 A.L.R. 1096 (1930).

42. U.L.P.A. § 11, Sec. 32 below.

43. Above at nn. 35–37.

44. U.L.P.A. § 4. He is not barred from performing services for some compensation other than a share of profits. Silvola v. Rowlett, n. 36 above. But doing so raises the question whether he is taking part in control.

45. Above at n. 38.

46. Berman v. Herrick, 231 F.Supp. 918 (E.D.Pa.1964) (Pa. law); Skolny v. Richter, 139 App.Div. 534, 124 N.Y.S. 152 (1910) (under statute prior to U.L.P.A.). *Compare* U.L.P.A. § 9 giving general partners broad rights and powers (including representative capacity) *with* § 10 giving limited partners narrow rights (not including representative capacity).

47. See Bromberg, Partnership Dissolution—Causes, Consequences and Cures, 43 Texas L.Rev. 631, 640 (1965); Lewis, The Uniform Limited Partnership Act, 65 U.Pa.L.Rev. 715, 724–25 (1917).

A limited partner does not breach any fiduciary duty by becoming a limited partner in another firm engaged in the same business in the same community. Skolny v. Richter, n. 46 above. See also n. 51 below.

48. U.L.P.A. § 10(1).

49. U.L.P.A. § 13.

tion in accordance with the certificate or on dissolution, but only if the firm is solvent.[50] His interest is assignable to a degree controlled partly by the certificate.[51]

The extensive use of limited partnerships in investment syndications of real estate in the 1950s and 1960s has raised serious questions of a limited partner's right to sue, either individually or in behalf of the firm, for economic injury to the firm by the general partners or by outsiders. His right to do so seems fully recognized in the jurisdictions which have considered the matter; [52] the analogy to shareholder derivative suits is persuasive and gives more leverage than a traditional accounting action for breach of fiduciary duty,[53] which would normally not be maintainable against anyone but a partner. Related questions concern the applicability of investor protection legislation like the securities laws.[53A]

---

50. U.L.P.A. § 16.

51. U.L.P.A. § 19, Sec. 42(b) below.

It may be questioned whether a limited partner is a co-owner of specific partnership property to even the slight extent that general partners are. Lacking power to participate in management, it seems that he has no right to dispose of or possess firm property, even for firm purposes, as against the general partners. Despite his inspection right, it has been stated that he is not co-owner of the books or of any other specific partnership asset. Sanderson v. Cooke, 256 N.Y. 73, 175 N.E. 518 (1931).

The nature of a limited partner's interest was an issue in Alley v. Clark, 71 F. Supp. 521 (E.D.N.Y.1947). The general partner was an enemy alien and the firm property was seized by the Alien Property Custodian. The limited partner tried by bill in equity to assert an interest in the property. Held: he could proceed (under the Trading with the Enemy Act, 50 U.S. C.A. §§ 9(a), 33–35) only by administrative action as for the collection of a debt owed by the alien.

52. Klebanow v. New York Produce Exchange, 344 F.2d 294 (2d Cir.1965) (N.Y. brokerage firm; alleged injury to firm from third parties' violations of federal antitrust and securities laws); Riviera Congress Associates v. Yassky, 18 N.Y.2d 540, 277 N.Y.S. 2d 386, 223 N.E.2d 876 (1966) (350-member real estate syndicate; alleged injury to firm by general partners). See also Lichtgyer v. Fran-

chard Corp., 18 N.Y.2d 528, 277 N.Y. S.2d 377, 223 N.E.2d 869 (1966) (class action permitted by limited partners of real estate syndicate with several hundred members; alleged injury to firm by general partners and outsiders). But cf. Sloan v. Clark, 18 N. Y.2d 570, 277 N.Y.S.2d 411, 223 N.E.2d 893 (1966) (limited partners may not sue on partnership cause of action being litigated by firm's bankruptcy trustee). See Comment, Standing of Limited Partners to Sue Derivatively, 65 Colum.L.Rev. 1463 (1965).

U.L.P.A. § 26, speaking in terms of a contributor, seems to say that a limited partner is not a proper party to a suit by or against the firm. However, a variety of reasons have been given why it does not bar a derivative suit by limited partners. Klebanow v. New York Product Exchange, supra; Riviera Congress Associates v. Yassky, supra; Comment, 65 Colum. L.Rev. 1463, 1474–76 (1965). Cf. Sec. 57 n. 7 below.

53. See n. 53B below.

53A. See Berger, Real Estate Syndication: Property, Promotion and the Need for Protection, 69 Yale L.J. 725 (1960); Note, 14 Hast.L.J. 176 (1962). Cf. West's Ann.Cal.Corp. Code, § 25100(m) exempting from the blue sky law partnership interests (both general and special) "except...when offered to the public;" McKinney's General Business Law (N.Y.), § 352–e (real estate syndications treated alike regardless of corporate, partnership, trust or other form of organization).

In other respects, the limited partnership is much the same as a general partnership in the rights of creditors and the relations of the associates inter se; [53B] the U.P.A. is applicable to matters not covered by the U.L.P.A.[54] Special problems arising in dissolution [55] and bankruptcy [56] are separately treated below.[57]

(d) Use of the Limited Partnership

The limited partnership form of association is a less effective liability shield [58] than the corporation, which is created with equal facility (and perhaps greater privacy), is better understood, may offer more flexibility of structure, and does not require such frequent amendment.[59] And a creditor arrangement, with a share in profits is (under later decisions [60] and the U.P.A.[61]) relatively free from the threat of partnership liability. Thus, one might conclude that the limited partnership now has little utility, except perhaps for the formation of firms which, for some special reason, cannot incorporate (like brokerage houses when corporations could not be members of the major stock exchanges).

Although no statistics are available, it seems probable that limited partnerships were sparingly used until World War II. A considerable increase then came about largely because of high federal income tax rates. The limited partnership is unique in combining (A) direct deduction of expenses or losses by members against their other income,[62] and (B) protection from personal liability. Thus, it has become popular with high-income individuals investing in high-risk enterprises (e. g., Broadway plays). The popularity is even greater if there are special tax benefits like deduction of drilling costs and percentage depletion in oil and gas ventures [63] or accelerated deprecia-

---

53B. Fiduciary duties of general partners (treated in Sec. 68 below) are equally applicable in limited firms. See Homestake Mining Co. v. Mid-Continent Exploration Co., 282 F.2d 787 (10th Cir.1960). But limited partners apparently have fewer or lighter duties; see n. 47 above.
General partners may agree to indemnify special partner against loss of their capital investment. Lanier v. Bowdoin, 282 N.Y. 32, 24 N.E.2d 732 (1939); Herrick v. Guild, 257 App. Div. 341, 13 N.Y.S.2d 115 (1939).

54. U.P.A. § 6(2); Horn v. Builders Supply Co., 401 S.W.2d 143 (Tex.Civ. App.1966).

55. Sec. 90B below.

56. Sec. 96A below.

57. See also Secs. 37(h) 91(f) below.

58. Sec. 26(c) above.

59. Sec. 26(b) above.

60. E.g., Cox v. Hickman, 8 H.L.Cas. 268, 11 Eng.Rep. 431 (1860), discussed Sec. 15 above; Giles v. Vette, 263 U.S. 553, 44 S.Ct. 157, 68 L.Ed. 441 (1923), discussed Sec. 32 below.

61. U.P.A. § 7(4) (a), (d), Secs. 15, 19 above.

62. This is the conduit principle of partnership taxation. Int.Rev.Code of 1954, §§ 701–02 (26 U.S.C.A.). See Sec. 23B(i) above.

63. Id. §§ 263(c), 613. The limited partnership is also used in hard mineral ventures, where percentage depletion is available. For a complex example, see Homestake Mining Co. v. Mid-Continent Exploration Co., 282 F.2d 787 (10th Cir.1960).

tion in construction or leasing activities.[64]

Limited partnerships are often employed when a partnership interest is to be held in trust (for family tax planning or testamentary disposition) since trustees, especially corporate fiduciaries, are unwilling to risk the liabilities they might have as general partners.

LIMITED PARTNERSHIP ASSOCIATIONS

§ 26A.   A limited partnership association is a statutory form of organization in which no associate has personal liability.   Permitted in only a few states, these organizations resemble corporations more than partnerships.

In a few states limited partnership associations (sometimes called partnership associations) were authorized by statute at a time when incorporation was difficult or impossible.[65] Pennsylvania originated the form in 1874, making the subscribed capital alone responsible for debts of the association, except in certain circumstances.[66] The Pennsylvania Act was repealed in 1966 except as to professions not permitted to incorporate.[67] Similar laws exist in three other states,[68]

---

64. Int.Rev.Code of 1954, § 167(b) (26 U.S.C.A.). In general, see Taubman, Limited Partners, 3 Corp.Prac.Comm. 15 (Feb. 1962). Taubman usefully considers whether a limited partnership will be treated as a corporation for tax purposes, thus forfeiting the direct deductions by investors. Tracing the vagaries of this area, he concludes that there is no present danger. See also Driscoll, The Limited Partnership and the Association Question, U. of So. Cal. 12th Inst. on Tax 539 (1960); Income Tax Reg. § 301.7701–3(b) (1960); Glensder Textile Co., 46 B.T.A. 176 (1942), acq. 1942–1 Cum.Bull. 8.

65. Schwartz, The Limited Partnership Association—An Alternative to the Corporation for the Small Business with "Control" Problems, 20 Rutgers L.Rev. 29 (1965) is a comprehensive discussion.

66. 1874 Pa.Laws 271, now 59 P.S. §§ 341–461 (1964). Hill v. Stetler, 127 Pa. 145, 13 A. 306, 17 A. 887 (1889) said the act was passed "to relieve against the risk and inconvenience attending general partnerships, by providing a mode by which individuals might invest a fixed sum in a business enterprise, without liability to loss beyond the sum so invested. The method provided is the creation

of a new artificial person to be called a joint stock association [sic], having some of the characteristics of a partnership and some of a corporation."

One state imposes on members a liability for labor claims (as do a few corporate statutes). M.C.L.A. (Mich.) § 449.302.

Following the early line of limited partnership cases (Sec. 26 n. 25 above), immunity in Pa. was conditional on close compliance with organizational requirements of the statutes. Eliot v. Himrod, 108 Pa. 569 (1885); Lee & Bacchus v. Burnley, 195 Pa. 58, 45 A. 668 (1900).

Elsewhere, the de facto corporation analogy and estoppel have given shelter where there was a good faith attempt to comply with the statute, and creditors have dealt with the association as such. Staver & Abbott Mfg. Co. v. Blake, 111 Mich. 282, 69 N.W. 508, 38 L.R.A. 798 (1896); Deckert v. Chesapeake Western Co., 101 Va. 804, 45 S.E. 799 (1903).

67. Pa.Act 1966, Jan. 18 (1965 Reg. Sess.) No. 519, § 50(g). The preservation for professionals is related to the problem discussed in Sec. 34A below.

68. M.C.L.A. (Mich.) §§ 449.301–449.316, 449.351; N.J.S.A. §§ 42:3–1–42:3–29;

but little use appears to have been made of them save in Pennsylvania and Michigan.

The capital of the association is fixed by its organizational document (which is publicly filed) and may be changed by amendment. There is no minimum or maximum amount. Each member subscribes for a designated part of the capital, is usually required to pay some of it within a short time, and is liable for any unpaid portion.

The duration of the association is restricted, typically to 20 years. Ordinarily there must be at least three members, and one state has a maximum of 25.[69] "Limited" must be the last word in the association name, and (on pain of general partnership liability) must be conspicuously used in advertisements, stationery and signs. Dissolution occurs by expiration of the prescribed term or by majority action of the members.[70]

While partnership associations possess the corporate attributes of concentration of management,[71] some transferability of shares, right to sue and be sued [72] (and to own property) in the association name, and limited liability, they are not corporations. They retain to a degree the delectus personae feature of partnership,[73] and, at least in the past, have not been regarded as entities for purpose of diversity jurisdiction in the federal courts.[74] But they closely resemble cor-

---

R.C. (Ohio) §§ 1783.01–1783.12 (1964). Virginia had one from 1874 to 1918; see Schwartz, op. cit. supra n. 65 at 29 n. 3.

69. R.C. (Ohio) § 1783.01.

70. The action may be informal, Stevens v. Delaware, L. & E. R. Co., 278 Pa. 284, 122 A. 504 (1923). Continuation of business after dissolution by expiration converts the firm into a general partnership. Leventhal v. Atlantic Rainbow Painting Co., Ltd., 68 N.J.Super. 406, 172 A.2d 710 (1961).

71. The usual provision is for members to elect designated managers. One state specifies cumulative voting. M.C.L.A. (Mich.) § 449.351.

72. The privilege of suing and being sued in the common name has been held local, and not extended into another state than that where the association is organized. Edwards v. Warren Linoline & Gasoline Works, 168 Mass. 564, 47 N.E. 502, 38 L.R.A. 791 (1897).

73. The association is not dissolved by the death or assignment of a member. But delectus personae is provided by the statute (effective unless modified by the agreement of association): no assignee of shares becomes a member except by consent of the majority. If consent is refused, he is entitled to payment of the value of his shares. M.C.L.A. (Mich.) § 449.304; N.J.S.A. § 42:3–11; R.C. (Ohio) § 1783.05 (1964); 59 P.S. (Pa.) § 383 (1964). Goodspeed v. Wayne, 199 Mich. 273, 165 N.W. 943, 166 N.W. 899 (1917).

74. Great Southern Fireproof Hotel Co. v. Jones, 177 U.S. 449 (1900). The court permitted amendment of the association's complaint to show that it was brought by the members as partners; jurisdiction was found to exist upon a showing of the requisite complete diversity between the members and the defendants. Great Southern Fireproof Hotel Co. v. Jones, 193 U.S. 532, 20 S.Ct. 690, 44 L.Ed. 842 (1904). Query whether this non-entity view would prevail today. See Sec. 34 at n. 30 below.

porations and they may be taxed [75] and regulated [76] as such. It is doubtful whether they should be regarded as partnerships.[77]

MINING PARTNERSHIPS

§ 27. In some states, development of mineral property by co-owners does not alter their co-ownership status. In other states it is regarded as creating a mining partnership, a distinct form of association. This differs from ordinary partnership in that delectus personae is generally lacking and power of representation is much less extensive.

In some jurisdictions, the development of mining property by co-owners, sharing expenses and proceeds of operation, does not create a partnership, since there is no manifested intent to become partners.[78] With suitable intent, it is, of course, possible for mine co-owners to form an ordinary partnership,[79] a limited partnership,[80] a joint stock company,[81] or a business trust.[82]

In many jurisdictions intent is ignored or inferred, and a distinct status—the mining partnership—results from the joint operation by co-owners of a mining property,[83] including an oil and gas lease.[84] The

75. Whitney Realty Co., Ltd. v. DeLand, 228 Mich. 96, 199 N.W. 669 (1924); Tide-Water Pipe-Line Co. v. Berry, 52 N.J.Law 308, 19 A. 665 (1890); Tide Water Pipe Co. v. State Board of Assessors, 57 N.J.Law 516, 31 A. 220, 27 L.R.A. 684 (1895).

For treatment as a corporation under federal income tax, see Giant Auto Parts, Ltd., 13 T.C. 307 (1949), 14 T.C. 579 (1950). The result is probably the same under Income Tax Reg. §§ 301.7701–2 (1960, 1965) and 301.7701–3(c) (1960).

76. Registration or qualification may be required for doing business in another state. Hemphill v. Orloff, 277 U.S. 537, 48 S.Ct. 577, 72 L.Ed. 978 (1928) (business trust; statute referred to "all associations, partnership associations and joint stock companies having any of the powers and privileges of corporations"). In re Hercules Atkin Co., 133 F. 813 (E.D.Pa.1904) (bankruptcy adjudication as a corporation).

77. U.P.A. § 6(2) suggests that the Act is inapplicable to partnership associations.

78. See Sec. 12 above, discussing co-ownership v. partnership.

79. Decker v. Howell, 42 Cal. 636 (1872); Thompson v. Crystal Springs Bank, 21 F.2d 602 (8th Cir. 1927).

80. Stowe v. Merrilees, 6 Cal.App.2d 217, 44 P.2d 368 (1935).

81. Fairman Bros. v. Ogden Gas Co., 106 Pa.Super. 130, 161 A. 634 (1932).

82. Haskell v. Patterson, 165 Ark. 65, 262 S.W. 1002 (1924); McCamey v. Hollister Oil Co., 241 S.W. 689 (Tex. Civ.App.1922).

83. Kahn v. Central Smelting Co., 102 U.S. 641, 26 L.Ed. 266 (1881); Skillman v. Lachman, 23 Cal. 198, 83 Am. Dec. 96 (1863), citing many cases; Wagner Supply Co. v. Bateman, 118 Tex. 498, 18 S.W.2d 1052 (1929), discussed in Jones, Mining Partnerships in Texas, 12 Texas L.Rev. 410 (1934).

For a mining partnership to exist, co-owners must join in operation. One co-owner developing the property by himself does not establish a mining partnership. Peterson v. Beggs, 26 Cal.App. 760, 148 P. 541 (1915); McAnally v. Cochran, 170 Okl. 368, 46 P.2d 955 (1935). The requisite participation by co-owners can, of course, be through agents; the owners needn't appear with picks and drills.

A mining partnership does not arise from profit sharing or production sharing to compensate a lender of money or equipment, Seifert v. Brown, 53

84. See note 84 on page 154.

mining partnership is a product of the common law but has been partially codified in some statutes.[85] No particular agreement or formality is necessary to create a mining partnership.

The mining partnership differs from the ordinary partnership in that membership is freely transferable by assignment (i.e. of the co-owner's interest in the property). Transfer does not effect a dissolution,[86] nor does the bankruptcy[87] or death[88] of a partner. Because of the absence of delectus personae,[89] and because of the limited scope of the enterprise, a partner's power of representation is limited.[90] He has implied power to charge co-partners with expenses incurred in the necessary operation or development of the enterprise, such as buying equipment and supplies.[91] Within this area, a partner

S.W.2d 117 (Tex.Civ.App.1932); Gardner v. Wesner, 55 S.W.2d 1104 (Tex.Civ.App.1933); or an employee or person rendering services, Dunigan Tool & Supply Co. v. Carroll, 60 S.W.2d 296 (Tex.Civ.App.1933).

There must be co-ownership of property, not merely contribution of funds by investors. Kuser v. Cooke, 112 N.J.Eq. 553, 165 A. 292 (1933), dealing with a Missouri operation and citing Freeman v. Hemenway, 75 Mo.App. 611 (1898).

The issuance by a partnership owning and operating mineral properties of shares of beneficial interest to investors (described as "well beneficiaries") who had no participation in management, no ownership of properties, and no liability (according to their agreement) for losses, did not constitute them partners. Stewart v. Angle, 315 Pa. 135, 172 A. 898 (1934).

The leading oil and gas state stresses in its version of U.P.A. § 7 that operation of a mineral property under a joint operating agreement does not of itself establish an ordinary partnership. Vernon's Ann.Civ.St. (Tex.) art. 6132b, § 7(5). This does not preclude a finding of mining partnership.

84. Much recent litigation and most current writing on mining partnerships concerns oil and gas. See Mud Control Laboratories v. Covey, 2 Utah 2d 85, 269 P.2d 854 (1954); McKay, Joint Ventures and Mining Partnerships, 7 Kan.L.Rev. 22 (1958); Comment, Mining Partnerships, 12 Bayl.L.Rev. 103 1960). It is no accident that the most comprehensive treatment is

Summers, Law of Oil and Gas §§ 721–724 (1962). Also extensive is 2 Rowley, Partnership §§ 56.1–56.16 (2d ed. 1960).

85. Ala.Code 1940, Tit. 43, §§ 36–47 (1960); West's Ann. Cal. Public Resources Code, §§ 2351–2361 (inapplicable to oil and gas); I.C. (Idaho) §§ 53–401 – 53–412 (1957); R.C.M.1947 (Mont.) §§ 63–1001 – 63–1010 (1962); N.R.S. (Nev.) 520.160 – 520.260 (1956). These require express authority from a member to bind him by written contract, but say nothing of oral contracts.

86. Childers v. Neely, 47 W.Va. 70, 34 S.E. 828, 49 L.R.A. 468, 81 Am.St.Rep. 777 (1899). Cf. Kell v. Commissioner, 88 F.2d 453 (5th Cir.1937) (intra-family assignment of interest in mining partnership effective to divert income for tax purposes).

87. Sturm v. Ulrich, 10 F.2d 9 (8th Cir.1925).

88. Park v. Adams, 114 W.Va. 730, 173 S.E. 785 (1934), discussed 41 W.Va. L.Q. 144.

89. Sec. 5 above.

90. See Annot., Powers, duties and accounting responsibilities of managing partner of mining partnership, 24 A.L. R.2d 1359 (1952).

91. Manville v. Parks, 7 Colo. 128. 2 P. 212 (1883); Manufacturers Light & Heat Co. v. Tenant, 104 W.Va. 221 139 S.E. 706 (1927), noted 34 W.Va. L.Q. 199.

has full personal liability, just as in a general partnership.[92] A partner paying necessary expenses has a lien on the shares of co-partners for contribution, which is effective against purchasers [93] or mortgagees [94] of their shares. But a partner cannot bind his co-partners to negotiable instruments or otherwise borrow money on partnership credit without express authority.[95]

A fiduciary duty exists between the partners, so one is accountable to the others for secret profits.[96] Dissolution is not as easy as in an ordinary firm,[97] but after it occurs, an accounting may be had in equity.[98] As in regular partnerships, one partner cannot sue another for services rendered or any component of the partnership accounts.[99]

The mining partnership concept has little to distinguish it from joint venture or other narrow purpose partnership.[1] The restricted representative capacity is a function of the narrow purpose. The other prominent features of a mining partnership—transferability of interests and continuity despite death—can as easily be accommodated within the ordinary partnership via agreement or custom, as by devising a separate type of organization.[2] Although joint ownership and operation of ordinary real estate does not establish a partnership, even with the sharing of profits [3] or gross return,[4] the extrac-

---

92. Arrow Petroleum Corp. v. Ames, 128 Ind.App. 10, 142 N.E.2d 479 (1957) (Ill. law); Mikel Drilling Co. v. Dunkin, 318 P.2d 435 (Okl.1957).

93. Duryea v. Burt, 28 Cal. 569 (1865); Kinne v. Duncan, 383 Ill. 110, 48 N.E.2d 375 (1943); Kennedy v. Beets Oil Co., 105 Okl. 1, 231 P. 508 (1924).

94. Sturm v. Ulrich, 10 F.2d 9 (8th Cir. 1925), collecting cases on mining partnerships. The lien may be enforced without dissolution. Gilbert v. Fontaine, 22 F.2d 657 (8th Cir.1927).

95. Skillman v. Lachman, 23 Cal. 198, 83 Am.Dec. 96 (1863); Decker v. Howell, 42 Cal. 636 (1872); Boonville Nat. Bank v. Thompson, 339 Mo. 1049, 99 S.W.2d 93 (1936); Wilkinson v. Bell, 118 Mont. 403, 168 P.2d 601 (1946).

96. Johnson v. Ironside, 249 Mich. 35, 227 N.W. 732 (1929). Zogg v. Hedges, 126 W.Va. 523, 29 S.E.2d 871, 152 A.L.R. 991 (1944) (secret profits in acquisition of firm's property). But see Neill v. Shamburg, 158 Pa. 263, 27 A. 992 (1893) (no disclosure duty among co-tenants developing mining property; not partners). Cases involving

constructive trust remedies are collected, Annot., 44 A.L.R.2d 519, 526–29 (1955).

97. Blackmarr v. Williamson, 57 W.Va. 249, 50 S.E. 254, 4 Ann.Cas. 265 (1905) (buyer of share in mining partnership, not shown to be a losing venture, not entitled to dissolution and sale of entire property because of disharmony over development methods).

98. Childers v. Neely, n. 86 above. See Gray, Mining Partnerships, 3 Wis.L. Rev. 13 (1924).

99. Elder v. Tucker, 116 W.Va. 94, 178 S.E. 629 (1934).

1. See Yeager v. Graham, 150 Kan. 411, 94 P.2d 317 (1939) (immaterial whether arrangement regarded as mining partnership or joint venture).

2. West's Ann.Cal.Corp.Code, § 15006 includes mining partnerships (like limited partnerships) under U.P.A. except so far as governed by other and inconsistent statutes.

3. U.P.A. § 7(2).

4. U.P.A. § 7(3).

tion and sale of minerals is much more a business and can be regarded as presumptively creating a regular partnership for this purpose.[5]

SUB-PARTNERSHIPS

§ 28.   "Sub-partnership" is the relation between a partner and a non-partner who agree on the sharing of profits and losses of the partner from his partnership.   Sub-partnership is not properly a partnership relation.

The term "sub-partnership" is applied to the relation resulting from a contract by a partner in a firm (called the common partner) with a third person (called the sub-partner) to share profits and losses from the common partner's membership in the firm.   The sub-partner does not become a partner with the non-common partners in the firm because there is no agreement with them.[6]   The sub-partner is, therefore, not directly liable to firm creditors.[7]   Consequently, the sub-partnership has been said to be a possible method of risk evasion by investors.[8]   In a jurisdiction which allows creditor beneficiaries to recover from promisors,[9] if the sub-partner has promised the common partner to pay part of the latter's share of losses to the firm or its creditors, the promise should be enforceable in behalf of creditors.   If the sub-partner has promised the common partner to pay to the latter a part of any losses he may sustain (or which may be chargeable to him, as in the leading case of Burnett v. Snyder[10]), it is a contract of indemnity, enforceable only by the promisee.

Since the sub-partner is not a partner with the non-common partners, his primary remedies (by way of accounting or otherwise) are against the common partner.[11]   However, he has been allowed remedies against the non-common partners when necessary to protect his

---

5.   U.P.A. § 7(4).

6.   Mathewson v. Clarke, 47 U.S. (6 How.) 122, 12 L.Ed. 370, 371 (1848); Burnet v. Leininger, 285 U.S. 136, 52 S.Ct. 345, 76 L.Ed. 665 (1931); O'Connor v. Sherley, 107 Ky. 70, 52 S.W. 1056 (1899); Lovejoy v. Bailey, 214 Mass. 134, 101 N.E. 63 (1913); Burnett v. Snyder, 76 N.Y. 344 (1879); Haines & Co.'s Assigned Estate, 176 Pa. 354, 35 A. 237 (1896); Riedeburg v. Schmitt, 71 Wis. 644, 38 N.W. 336 (1888).

7.   Bybee v. Hawkett, 12 F. 649 (D.Or. 1882); Burnett v. Snyder n. 6 above; Quadrangle Petroleum Co. v. Kendrick & Eason Lumber Co., 120 Okl. 246, 249 P. 910 (1926); Keystone Nat. Bank v. Randle, 1 Pa.Co.Ct.R. 354 (1885); Setzer v. Beale, 19 W.Va. 274, 287 (1882).

Nor can the non-common partner enforce contribution from the sub-partner.

Murray v. Bogert & Kneeland, 14 Johns. 318, 7 Am.Dec. 466 (N.Y.1817). The sub-partner has been held liable on the now discarded theory that one who shares profits should be responsible for losses. See Fitch v. Harrington, 79 Mass. (13 Gray) 468, 74 Am. Dec. 641 (Mass.1859).

8.   Rowley, Risk Evasion through Sub-Partnership, 30 Colum.L.Rev. 674 (1930).

9.   Restatement, Contracts § 136.

10.   N. 6 above.

11.   Henry v. Evans, 95 Iowa 244, 63 N.W. 687 (1895); Lovejoy v. Bailey, 214 Mass. 134, 101 N.E. 63 (1913); Nirdlinger v. Bernheimer, 133 N.Y. 45, 53, 30 N.E. 561, 562 (1892); Replogle v. Neff, 176 Okl. 333, 55 P.2d 436 (1936); Mathewson v. Clarke, n. 6 above.

interests.[12] This is particularly appropriate where the non-common partners know of and recognize the sub-partnership.[13]

The sub-partner has been described as a partner with the common partner with respect to the latter's interest in the firm.[14] This seems erroneous since they are not carrying on a business together as co-owners.[15] They cannot be co-owners of any specific partnership property, since this would require consent of the non-common partners. They may be co-owners of an interest in the firm, by virtue of a partial assignment.[16] But sharing the income from the interest is not carrying on a business. The relation usually calls for no acts on the part of the sub-partner, nor has he authority to act in the firm's affairs. On the other hand, he may advance funds or give advice. There is good reason to impose on the sub-partnership such partnership features as fiduciary duties (especially on the part of the common partner who typically has an opportunity to divert profits from his sub-partner) and dissolution procedures.

The sub-partnership is rarely found because it accomplishes little. As a protection against liability it is inferior to the limited partnership and the corporation. If the sub-partner gives value for his interest, he would normally prefer to negotiate his way into the firm, with consequent protection of his position. The sub-partnership, then, is useful mainly when the sub-partner doesn't want the non-common partners to know of his participation, or the common partner doesn't want to upset them, or the arrangement is gratuitous.

So far as is known, the only extensive use made of the sub-partnership in modern times was for attempted federal income tax savings. A partner entered a sub-partnership with close relatives, hoping to divert income from his higher tax brackets into their lower ones. These efforts were largely unsuccessful, with the courts taxing the common partner as the earner of the income.[17] They have become

---

12. Replogle v. Neff, n. 11 above.

As an assignee of a partnership interest, the sub-partner has accounting rights at dissolution, U.P.A. § 27(2), Sec. 42 (b) below. See cases in n. 11 above.

13. See Silberfeld v. Swiss Bank Corp., 266 App.Div. 756, 41 N.Y.S.2d 470 (1943). This complex litigation is recapitulated in id., 99 N.Y.S.2d 888 (S. Ct.1950), aff'd 278 App.Div. 676, 103 N.Y.S.2d 130 (1951), app. dism. 302 N.Y. 878, 100 N.E.2d 54 (1951).

14. Henry v. Evans, n. 11 above (plaintiff supplied part of capital invested by A and B, as partners, with C, D, and E who did not know of plaintiff's interest; while plaintiff was held not to be a member of the larger firm, he was a member with A and B, entitled

to an accounting against them); Nirdlinger v. Bernheimer, n. 11 above. See also Frost v. Moulton, 21 Beav. 596, 52 Eng.Rep. 990 (1856); Ex parte Barrow, 2 Rose 255 (1815).

15. Cohan v. Commissioner, 39 F.2d 540 (2d Cir. 1930). See also Burnet v. Leininger, n. 6 above.

16. See Sec. 42 below.

17. E. g., Burnet v. Leininger, n. 6 above, subsequent opinion 86 F.2d 791 (6th Cir. 1936); Cohan v. Commissioner, n. 15 above. But see Forman v. Commissioner, 199 F.2d 881 (9th Cir. 1952) (sub-partner made substantial investment). The early cases are discussed by Bruton, Taxation of Family Income, 41 Yale L.J. 1172, 1188–91 (1932).

unnecessary because of tax legislation recognizing family partnerships and permitting spouses to split incomes.[18]

A situation somewhat similar to the sub-partnership may result from a partner being an agent for an undisclosed principal who has furnished the capital contribution and expects to receive all the profits of the nominal partner's interest. A partnership relation does not exist between the principal and the other partners who are ignorant of the circumstances, because of the absence of agreement among them. If the facts are known, he should be treated as a partner; [19] under the agency doctrine of undisclosed principal he should be held liable to partnership creditors on partnership obligations.[20]

SOME APPLICATIONS OF PARTNERSHIP LAW TO OTHER TYPES OF ASSOCIATIONS

§ 29. **In many instances, persons associate to carry on a business or to share its profits, intending to form an organization other than partnership. The courts sometimes apply partnership law to the relations of the associates among themselves, and to their liabilities to third persons, as though the associates were partners.**

It has been the tendency of the common law to classify all business associations as corporations or partnerships, with the latter the residual class. An association is likely to be called a partnership by the courts for purpose of imposing a liability to creditors upon the associates for whose benefit the business is carried on, regardless of their intent not to be partners and not to bear such liabilities. Personal liability has been the traditional price for profit-sharing.

Examples of this rather mechanical judicial process have been cases of defective incorporation, failure to qualify foreign corporations to do business in a state, defectively formed limited partnerships, and business trusts. Joint stock companies and some forms of business trusts are regarded as partnerships with the corporate features of concentration of management and transferability of shares by

---

18. Sec. 23A above.

19. Morrison v. Dickey, 122 Ga. 353, 50 S.E. 175, 69 L.R.A. 87 (1905). The real party at interest (the principal of the nominal partner) was at first unknown to the other partner. After disclosure, she was treated as a partner, as between her and the other partner.

However, the fact that a partner is a straw man, contributing capital supplied by a principal who conceals his interest to defraud creditors, does not justify the other partner in refusing to account to the nominal partner. The firm is legal and there is no fraud on the partners. Stein v. Bieber, 342 Ill.App. 583, 98 N.E.2d 156 (1951). In an accounting suit, the alleged principal disclaimed any interest.

20. Webb v. Johnson, 95 Mich. 325, 54 N.W. 947 (1893). A partner was an agent for a third person who provided the capital and intended to exercise control through him; the other partner knew and agreed. The third person was liable as a partner.

Cf. Bullen v. Sharp, 1 C.P. 86 (1865), where the backer of a partner was to receive from him an annuity and a contingent interest in profits, but was held not liable as a partner.

agreement of the associates. Joint ventures are essentially partner-ships for less extensive purposes than ordinary partnerships. Professional associations and corporations, formed under a rash of tax-motivated statutes in the 1960s, have a confused mixture of corporate and partnership characteristics. Partnership by estoppel is not really a form of association, but it appears so to third persons, who may enforce personal liability as though a partnership existed.

These several situations are considered separately in the remaining sections of this chapter.

DEFECTIVELY ORGANIZED OR TAX-DELINQUENT CORPORATIONS

§ 30. **Under older statutes, associates who try to incorporate but fail to satisfy fully the formal requirements, do not have a de jure corporation. If they have in good faith attempted to comply with the requirements of a law under which they might have incorporated, and have dealt with third persons as a corporation, they are generally treated by the courts as a de facto corporation. This gives them immunity from personal liability for the obligations incurred in the course of the business. They are not partners because they do not intend to form an association which the law classifies as a partnership. They are not liable as partners to third persons who deal with them as a corporation.**

Modern statutes largely eliminate the problem by providing for the conclusiveness of the certificate of incorporation issued by a state official.

Officers and directors of corporations delinquent in their taxes may have partnership liability imposed on them by statute.

A business corporation is, like a partnership, an association to carry on a business for profit for the benefit of the associates and subject to their ultimate control. It differs from a partnership in that it cannot be created by mere exercise of the will of the associates but must be authorized by an appropriate statute and organized in compliance therewith. When created, a corporation usually has attributes not possessed by partnerships, including concentration of management in directors and officers, assignability of ownership interests, continuity despite assignments or deaths, and immunity of associates from personal liability for corporate obligations.[21]

In family corporations and others with few members, some of these features (particularly concentration of management) may be unattractive. Stockholder agreements to modify them, and to carry

---

21. See Sec. 24 above.

Statutes have added to shareholder liability in some corporations, especially banks because of the importance of protecting depositors against insolvency. The technique was largely abandoned after the experience of the 1920s and 1930s when it proved futile in some cases and oppressive in others. Some states once imposed personal lia-bility on shareholders in all corporations. Today the only significant exception to stockholder immunity is the rare one in favor of employees' wages and salaries, e. g. McKinney's N. Y. Business Corp. Law, § 630. See Henn, Corporations 79 (1961); Vincens, On The Demise of Double Liability of Bank Shareholders, 12 Bus.Law 275 (1957).

on business more like partners, have been grudgingly accepted by the courts if no third party interests were affected.[22] To a degree, such agreements have been authorized by legislation.[23] On the other hand, limited liability is highly cherished and never waived by stockholders except under economic pressure. To what extent may it be lost by failure to comply with the statutory requirements for incorporation? The procedure is fairly technical, especially in older statutes. It often happened (and sometimes still does) that a detail is neglected so that the organization fails to become a *de jure* corporation, i. e. one properly incorporated in all respects. A common defect is failure to record the charter or certificate (issued by a state official) in a designated office of the county or city where the principal place of business is to be.[24] Modern corporation statutes are eliminating this problem by providing that the corporate existence conclusively begins with the issuance of the certificate.[25] But they often impose joint and several liability on officers and directors who commence corporate business before the required minimum capital has been paid in to the company.[26]

Consequences of defective compliance with the older statutes turned on the courts' view of incorporation. Some regarded immunity from personal liability for group action as a statutory privilege obtainable only by exact conformity to the statute, and thus available only to *de jure* corporations.[27] Other groups would be liable as partnerships. This approach makes effective the supposed legislative intent to restrict corporate privileges to those who comply exactly.[28] Such a solution ignores the intent of the organizers and share purchasers not to be partners and not to authorize their officers and other rep-

---

22. *Compare* Clark v. Dodge, 269 N.Y. 410, 199 N.E. 641 (1936) *with* McQuade v. Stoneham, 263 N.Y. 323, 189 N.E. 234 (1934). See also references in n. 23 below.

23. See Folk, Corporation Statutes 1959–66, 1966 Duke L.J. 875, 946–57; Bradley, Toward a More Perfect Close Corporation—The Need for More and Improved Legislation, 54 Geo.L.J. 1145 (1966); O'Neal, Developments in the Regulation of the Close Corporation, 50 Cornell L.Q. 641 (1965); Henn, Corporations 400–47 (1961).

24. See Burks v. Cook, 225 Ark. 756, 284 S.W.2d 855 (1955), noted 10 Ark. L.Rev. 217 (1956).

25. Model Business Corp.Act § 50. Statutes are collected, 2 Model Business Corp.Act Ann. 174, 181–82 (1960).

Quite apart from the helpful statutes, defective incorporation has diminished

as a result of better communications and greater familiarity with corporate law.

26. Model Business Corp.Act § 43. Statutes are collected, 2 Model Business Corp.Act Ann. 15–17, 31–33 (1960).

27. Arkansas has been the most vigorous proponent in recent years. Burks v. Cook, n. 24 above; Whitaker v. Mitchell Mfg. Co., 219 Ark. 779, 244 S.W.2d 965 (1952).

A similar attitude toward limited partnerships is outlined in Sec. 26 n. 25 above and Sec. 32 below.

28. Bigelow v. Gregory, 73 Ill. 197 (1874); Kaiser v. Lawrence Savings Bank, 56 Iowa 104, 8 N.W. 772, 41 Am.Rep. 85 (1881); Bergeron v. Hobbs, 96 Wis. 641, 71 N.W. 1056, 65 Am.St. Rep. 85 (1897).

resentatives to bind them personally (i. e. beyond the joint assets they have contributed or promised).

Other courts, less strictly inclined, came to recognize the *de facto* corporation. It results from a real and bona fide attempt to organize under an existing statute (which would have permitted the desired incorporation), followed by user (i. e. carrying on business and conducting internal affairs in a corporate-like manner).[29] In such situations, third persons were generally denied the right to challenge the corporate existence and hold the associates liable as partners.[30] Some jurisdictions relaxed the *de facto* doctrine even further [31] but most have enforced it in substantially the form stated.[32] By another line of reasoning which winds up at the same place, third persons who deal with the organization as a corporation may be estopped to treat it as a partnership; [33] they have no reasonable expectation of securing the benefits of personal liability.

Third persons who deal with an organization which is defectively incorporated, but who are not aware of any attempt to incorporate

29. Henn, Corporations 196–200 (1961); Warren, Corporate Advantages without Incorporation 683–839 (1929). *De facto* corporations appear to be peculiarly American and not judicially recognized in other common law jurisdictions. Lloyd, Law of Unincorporated Associations 9 (1938).

30. Di Francesco v. Kennedy, 114 Conn. 681, 160 A. 72 (1932); Inter-Ocean Newspaper Co. v. Robertson, 296 Ill. 92, 129 N.E. 523 (1920); Tisch Auto Supply Co. v. Nelson, 222 Mich. 196, 192 N.W. 600 (1923); Interstate Airlines, Inc. v. Arnold, 127 Neb. 665, 256 N.W. 513 (1934).

In the Tisch case, articles were not filed with the secretary of state or with the county clerk. The court nevertheless held, in a creditor's suit against members as partners, that organization was *de facto* and subject to attack only by the state.

See also Aetna Life Ins. Co. of Hartford, Conn. v. Weatherhogg, 103 Ind. App. 506, 4 N.E.2d 679 (1936) (*de facto* corporation though it used name slightly different from that in its charter, which it failed to record locally); Staver & Abbott Mfg. Co. v. Blake, 111 Mich. 282, 69 N.W. 508, 38 L.R.A. 798 (1896) (*de facto* doctrine applied to limited partnership association).

31. Baker v. Bates-Street Shirt Co., 6 F.2d 854 (1st Cir. 1925) (no colorable compliance with statute because of failure to file in certain offices); Fay v. Noble, 61 Mass. (7 Cush.) 188 (1851) (defects not apparent).

32. Davis v. Stevens, 104 F. 235 (D.S.D. 1900) (no law under which such a corporation could be formed); Eaton v. Walker, 76 Mich. 579, 43 N.W. 638, 6 L.R.A. 102 (1899) (law unconstitutional); Beck v. Stimmel, 39 Ohio App. 510, 177 N.E. 920 (1931) (charter issued but no organizational steps amounting to user; also, since tort case, no estoppel element); Provident Bank & Trust Co. v. Saxon, 116 La. 408, 40 So. 778 (1906) (no good faith). Cf. Kinney v. Bank of Plymouth, 213 Iowa 267, 236 N.W. 31 (1931), noted 16 Minn.L.Rev. 115 (innocent subscriber to stock in bank whose incorporation was not even attempted, not liable to creditors).

33. Cranson v. International Business Mach. Corp., 234 Md. 477, 200 A.2d 33 (1964). The articles of incorporation were signed but, through an attorney's oversight, were not filed until six months later. It would be difficult (though perhaps not impossible) to find a *de facto* corporation in this instance, but estoppel achieved the same result. The estoppel approach presupposes a good faith attempt to incorporate; without it, there is no protection from partnership liability even though third parties treated the group as a corporation. See Thompson v. Robinson Tube Fabricating Co., 238 Ark. 996, 386 S.W.2d 926 (1965).

and who reasonably suppose that they are dealing with a partnership, may impose personal liability on the associates.[34] If a partnership incorporates under the same name, third persons not knowing of the change may use estoppel principles to hold the partners as such on post-incorporation contracts.[35]

Some state statutes impose personal liability on the officers or directors of a defectively incorporated company.[36]

Partnership-type liability may also be decreed by statute for officers and directors (and occasionally for shareholders) of corporations which have dissolved (e. g., by expiration of the term set in the charter) or become delinquent in paying taxes.[37] Similarly, courts may "pierce the corporate veil" and hold officers, directors or shareholders liable when they have misused the corporation; this falls outside our scope.[38]

34. Guckert v. Hacke, 159 Pa. 303, 28 A. 249 (1893); Slocum v. Head, 105 Wis. 431, 81 N.W. 673, 50 L.R.A. 324 (1900).

Cf. Guilford Builders Supply Co. v. Reynolds, 249 N.C. 612, 107 S.E.2d 80 (1959) (third person who refused to extend credit to corporation but insisted on dealing individually with a shareholder, could not hold other shareholders liable on discovery that corporate status had lapsed for failure to file reports and pay franchise taxes).

35. Ogden Packing & Provision Co. v. Wyatt, 59 Utah 481, 204 P. 978, 22 A. L.R. 359 (1922); Mulkey v. Anglin, 166 Okl. 8, 25 P.2d 778, 89 A.L.R. 980 (1933), noted 33 Mich.L.Rev. 132 (1934).

Cf. Overlock v. Hazzard, 12 Ariz. 142, 145, 100 P. 447, 448 (1909): "ordinarily, a change from a partnership to a corporation is attended with such change of name and frequently with such other changes as not to require personal notice of such change."

Some states require publication of a notice of incorporation without change of name, on penalty of continued personal liability for later transactions, e. g., Vernon's Ann.Civ.St. (Tex.) art. 1302–2.02 (1962); Hobbs v. Triangle Supply Co., 378 S.W.2d 726 (Tex.Civ. App.1964).

36. O. S. Richardson Fueling Co. v. Seymour, 235 Ill. 319, 85 N.E. 496 (1908); the state has since adopted the conclusive certificate approach, Ill.Rev. Stat.1965, c. 32, § 157.49. Hessig-Ellis Drug Co. v. Wilkerson, 115 Miss. 668, 76 So. 570 (1917) (statute imposing personal liability on those who do business without full compliance applied to shareholders as well as officers and directors).

General references on shareholder liability in defective corporations: Burdick, Are Defectively Incorporated Associations Partnerships?, 6 Colum.L. Rev. 1 (1906); Baldwin, Partnership Liability of Stockholders in De Facto Corporations, 8 Ill.L.Rev. 246 (1913); Dodd, Partnership Liability of Stockholders in Defective Corporations, 40 Harv.L.Rev. 521 (1927); Magruder, A Note on Partnership Liability of Stockholders in Defective Corporations, 40 Harv.L.Rev. 733 (1927); Carpenter, Are the Members of a Defectively Organized Corporation Liable as Partners?, 8 Minn.L.Rev. 409 (1924).

37. Matter of Hare, 205 F.Supp. 881 (D. Md. 1962); V.A.T.S. Tax.–Gen.(Tex.) art. 12.14 (1960) ("liable . . . as if such directors and officers . . . were partners") applied in Sheffield v. Nobles, 378 S.W.2d 391 (Tex.Civ.App. 1964) (joint and several liability). Cf. Guilford Building Supply Co. v. Reynolds, n. 34 above.

38. See Henn, Corporations 203–17 (1961) and references there; Stevens, Corporations 95–99 (2d Ed. 1949); Ballantine, Corporations 287–332 (rev. ed. 1946).

UNQUALIFIED FOREIGN CORPORATIONS

§ 31. Statutes require qualification of foreign corporations (those organized under the laws of other states or countries) before doing business in a state. Violation may cause the offending corporation to be regarded as a partnership with resultant personal liability for its officers, directors or stockholders. The weight of authority is against such liability if it is not expressly imposed by legislation.

A corporation organized under the laws of one state or country generally cannot do business (other than purely interstate or foreign business) in another without qualifying under the laws of the latter. This typically entails filing its organizational documents with an official, appointing an agent for service of process, submitting financial information, and paying taxes or fees in the latter jurisdiction. Doing business in a state without such qualification is widely prohibited by statute, and fines or other penalties are usually provided against the offending corporation and those who act for it in the state.

What happens to the limited liability of shareholders in corporations which do business in a state without qualifying? The courts may reason that the manifested legislative policy against unauthorized corporate activity compels disregard of the corporate existence as a shield to liability. Officers and agents may suffer personal liability based on breach of warranty of existence or capacity of their principal (the corporation).[39] Alternatively, disregard of the corporation makes the shareholders principals or partners and liable as such; this result has been reached in a few states.[40] However, in most jurisdictions, the existence of the foreign corporation and the validity of its contracts are recognized, without personal liability of shareholders or any penalty other than those expressly imposed by the statutes.[41]

39. Joseph T. Ryerson & Son v. Shaw, 277 Ill. 524, 115 N.E. 650 (1917); Peacock Coal Co. v. Gaines Coal Co., 206 Iowa 1228, 219 N.W. 24 (1928); Lasher v. Stimson, 145 Pa. 30, 23 A. 552 (1892). Cf., under later statute, Bala Corp. v. McGlinn, 295 Pa. 74, 144 A. 823 (1929).

See Restatement, Second, Agency §§ 326, 332.

40. Taylor v. Branham, 35 Fla. 297, 17 So. 552, 39 L.R.A. 362, 48 Am.St.Rep. 249 (1895); Cunnyngham v. Shelby, 136 Tenn. 176, 188 S.W. 1147, L.R.A.1917B, 572 (1916). See Booth v. Scott, 276 Mo. 1, 205 S.W. 633 (1918). Cf. Herbert H. Pape, Inc. v. Finch, 102 Fla. 425, 136 So. 496 (1931) (where foreign corporation had power to buy land, it alone was liable on mortgage notes); Towle v. Beistle, 97 Ind.App. 241, 186 N.E. 344 (1933) (no liability of non-participating stockholders of In-diana corporation which had no charter authorization to do business in Tennessee but did act and incur liabilities there).

41. Beal v. Childress, 92 Kan. 109, 139 P. 1198 (1914); Shawmut Commercial Paper Co. v. Auerbach, 214 Mass. 363, 101 N.E. 1000 (1913); Martin Bros. v. Nettleton, 138 Wash. 102, 244 P. 386 (1926).

The statutory sanctions commonly include denial of access to the state's courts, either as plaintiff or as defendant. Model Business Corp.Act, § 117. Statutes are collected, 2 Model Business Corp.Act Ann. 666–71, 674–75 (1960). See generally, Note, Sanctions for Failure to Comply with Corporate Qualification Statutes: An Evaluation, 63 Colum.L.Rev. 117 (1963); Note, The Legal Consequences of Failure to Comply with Domestication Statutes, 110 U.Pa.L.Rev. 241 (1961).

Some statutes expressly impose personal liability on officers and directors for corporate obligations incurred while doing business in violation of the qualification requirements.[42]

There appears to be less reason for imposing liability upon associates (shareholders) not participating in management than in the case of defectively organized corporations. In the latter case, defects may be considered due to the neglect of incorporators or their agents who are subject to their control and for whom they should be responsible. But after a *de jure* corporation has been created, the responsibility for complying with the requirements for doing business belongs to the directors and officers, not the shareholders, whose control is much more remote than that of promoters and incorporators.

DEFECTIVE LIMITED PARTNERSHIPS

§ 32. Under earlier limited partnership statutes, failure to comply with the organizational requirements made the special (limited) partners liable as general partners. Today, under the U.L.P.A., it is recognized that the limited partner is not essentially a general partner, regardless whether he complies with the statutory technicalities, and is not liable unless he conducts himself as a general partner. Nor is his relationship to the general partners such as to make him a partner under the U.P.A. if organization as a limited firm is defective in some respect.

By express provisions of some of the earlier limited partnership acts, full liability was imposed on would-be limited partners in cases of defects in organization, such as false statements in the certificate filed, failure to file the certificate, or failure to file again where a branch was established.[43] Aside from express statutory provision, the view was taken that a limited partner was essentially a general partner, with immunity from personal liability conditional on compliance with the statutory formalities of organization. Non-compliance left him a general partner.[44] In time, the New York courts (whose decisions were especially important because many statutes were patterned after that state's) shifted to imposing liability only if the statute expressly required it;[45] the unique status of the limited partner was recognized as a corollary.[46]

---

42. E. g., I.C. (Idaho) § 30–508 (1948); M.G.L.A. (Mass.) c. 181, § 5; Va.Code § 13.1–119 (1964) (joint and several liability for contracts and torts). See Bachman v. Doerrie, 70 N.M. 277, 372 P.2d 951 (1962). Until its 1961 repeal, W.S.1957 (Wyo.) § 17–34 imposed liability on shareholders as well.

43. Sec. 26 n. 25 above.

44. "The question therefore is, have the members of the firm complied with the terms prescribed by the statute? For, unless the conditions of the act are substantially observed, all the defendants are general partners." Andrews v. Schott, 10 Pa. 47 (1848). Madison County Bank v. Gould, 5 Hill. 309 (N.Y.1843); Richardson v. Hogg, 38 Pa. 153 (1861). See also Sec. 26 n. 25 above.

45. Buck v. Alley, 145 N.Y. 488, 40 N.E. 236 (1895). See also Sec. 26 n. 25 above.

46. Tilge v. Brooks, 124 Pa. 178, 16 A. 746, 2 L.R.A. 796 (1889) discusses the status of a limited partner at some length.

One of the major purposes of the U.L.P.A. was to ease the earlier strictures on limited liability.[47] It emphasizes broadly that a limited partner is not liable as a general partner unless he takes part in control of the business.[48] Liability for false statements in a certificate runs only in favor of persons relying on them and only against members who signed the certificate and knew of the falsity.[49] A limited partnership is formed by substantial, good faith—though perhaps incomplete or defective—compliance with the requirements for signing and filing the certificate.[50] And there is explicit shelter for one who erroneously believes himself a limited partner, provided he renounces his interest in profits on discovery of his error.[51] U.P.A. is complementary in stating that persons who are not partners as to each other are not partners as to third persons.[52]

---

47. Commissioners' Note to U.L.P.A. § 1, 8 Unif.Laws Ann. 2–5 (1922); Lewis, The Uniform Limited Partnership Act, 65 U.Pa.L.Rev. 715 (1917); In re Marcuse, 281 F. 928, 934–35 (7th Cir. 1922), discussed below at nn. 53–56; Comment, 48 Mich.L.Rev. 347 (1950).

See also Vulcan Furniture Mfg. Corp. v. Vaughn, 168 So.2d 760 (Fla.App. 1964) dubiously finding a *de facto* limited partnership sufficient to shield a limited partner from liability for firm debts contracted more than 3 years after failure to obtain required annual renewal of the firm's status. The decision makes a mockery of the expressed legislative "policy . . . that the rights, privileges and benefits granted to limited partners . . are on an annual basis and are granted only after [the] limited partnership has met the requirements . . . regarding securing certificate of authority or renewal thereof." F.S.A. § 620.31.

48. U.L.P.A. § 7, Sec. 26 above; see also U.L.P.A. § 1 (limited partners, as such, not bound by obligations of the firm).

49. U.L.P.A. § 6. See Walraven v. Ramsay, 335 Mich. 331, 55 N.W.2d 853, 34 A.L.R.2d 1449 (1953). Cases are collected, Annot., 34 A.L.R.2d 1454 (1954).

50. U.L.P.A. § 2(2). This is a statutory *de facto* doctrine resembling the judicial one for corporations, Sec. 30 above.

51. U.L.P.A. § 11. U. S. v. Coson, 286 F.2d 453 (9th Cir. 1961) (Nev. law).

Cases are collected, Annot., 18 A.L.R. 2d 1360 (1951).

Its context suggests strongly that a limited partner seeking relief under § 11 must have been acting in good faith. This is recognized in J. C. Wattenbarger & Sons v. Sanders, 191 Cal. App.2d 857, 13 Cal.Rptr. 92 (1961), noted 14 Hast.L.J. 62 (1962) (summary judgment for limited partner reversed, remanded for trial of good faith and erroneous belief issues); subsequent opinion 216 Cal.App.2d 495, 30 Cal. Rptr. 910 (1963) (judgment on merits for limited partner affirmed). The alleged lack of good faith resulted from the filing and publication of a fictitious name certificate showing the limited partner as a member of the firm without indication of his limited status. However, the court found that this did not preclude good faith. It laid some emphasis on the fact that the name certificate did not come to plaintiff's attention until after the transactions sued on; this is relevant to estoppel under U.P.A. § 16, Sec. 36 below, but not to good faith.

Reading U.L.P.A. §§ 2(2) and 11 together indicates that the latter is intended to operate mainly when no certificate has been filed, or only a grossly defective one. It also seems applicable when a moderately defective certificate was filed and his associates (but not he) acted in such bad faith that § 2(2) is inoperative. If § 2(2) is applicable, renunciation under § 11 seems unnecessary.

52. U.P.A. § 7(1).

Two of the lines of escape afforded a limited partner by these Acts are illustrated in Giles v. Vette.[53] Marcuse and Morris proposed to form a limited partnership to succeed a stock brokerage partnership in which Marcuse had been a partner. They intended to have several limited partners, but discovered that the rules of the N.Y. Stock Exchange then forbade affiliated firms having more than two. They decided to organize with Hecht and Finn as limited partners, holding their interests partially in trust for others who contributed.[54] An agreement was executed and filed in supposed compliance with the Illinois Act. The Act had been repealed and superseded by the U.L.P.A. two days earlier. The new Act (of which the parties had no knowledge and with which they had no intent to comply) excluded stock brokerage firms. When the business became insolvent, bankruptcy petitions were filed against the general and limited partners and their trust beneficiaries, as all constituting a partnership. The limited partners, with an eye to U.L.P.A. § 11, paid into court the profits they had received. Reversing the District Court, the Circuit held that the general partners were the only ones who could be adjudicated bankrupt;[55] the Supreme Court affirmed.[56] The limited partners were entitled to the benefits of § 11 although they did not intend to organize under the U.L.P.A. and could not have done so by reason of the nature of their business. It was also held that the limited partners and their beneficiaries, not being co-owners of the business, under U.P.A. definitions and rules, were not general partners or liable as such under that Act.

53. 263 U.S. 553, 44 S.Ct. 157, 68 L.Ed. 441 (1923), affirming In re Marcuse & Co., 281 F. 928 (7th Cir. 1922).

54. See also, on combination of limited partnership and trust, Crehan v. Megargel, 234 N.Y. 67, 136 N.E. 296 (1922).

Cf. Cohen v. Hughes, 38 N.Y.S.2d 874 (Sup.Ct.1942). A's funds were invested by B in the limited partnership of which she was a member. The court concluded there was no partnership between A and B. Although B had a duty to account to A, the action was barred by limitations. On the latter ground, the decision was affirmed 266 App.Div. 658, 41 N.Y.S.2d 210 (1943), 291 N.Y. 698, 52 N.E.2d 591 (1943). This is a form of subpartnership, discussed generally in Sec. 28 above.

55. In re Marcuse & Co., 281 F. 928 (7th Cir. 1922), discussing, among other things, U.P.A. §§ 6 and 7 and the detachment of an investing limited partner from the firm.

56. Giles v. Vette, 263 U.S. 553, at 561–63, 44 S.Ct. 157, 160, 68 L.Ed. 441 (1923): "Hecht and Finn did not intend or agree to become general partners. The things intended and done do not constitute a partnership. They did nothing to estop them from denying liability as such. The case is not doubtful. But if it were their intent should be followed. . . . Moreover, we think that . . . [U.L. P.A. § 11] was applicable, and was properly invoked. . . . Section 11 is broad and highly remedial. The existence of a partnership—limited or general—is not essential in order that it shall apply. The language is comprehensive, and covers all cases where one has contributed to the capital of a business conducted by a partnership or person erroneously believing that he is a limited partner."

Both appellate courts construed U.L. P.A. as applicable to an association ignorant of it and not intending to organize under it. This is proper for § 11 which is not by its terms limited to arrangements intending to comply with the Act.

The decision establishes two rules. (1) Under the U.P.A., one who participates in the business only as a limited partner is not a general partner.   (2) Under the U.L.P.A., if the firm can be held subject to it, the limited partner can avoid personal liability by renouncing his interest in profits or other compensation promptly on ascertaining the mistake in believing himself a *de jure* limited partner. Whether he must return profits previously received was not decided in Giles v. Vette. A later case held that return was not required. One could not renounce an interest in profits already received but only in a right to receive profits.[57]

It does not follow that a person can escape liability merely by claiming to be a limited partner. He must show compliance with U.L.P.A.[57A] or establish one of the exceptions just described.[58]

Since filing of the certificate is primarily for the protection of third persons, it is not essential to the validity or enforceability of the agreement among the members of the firm.[59]

BUSINESS OR MASSACHUSETTS TRUSTS

§ 33. Businesses may be organized as trusts, with trustees as managers, and beneficiaries as investors and holders of transferable shares. The trust instrument is usually comprehensive, and fixes internal and some external relationships. The business trust has many corporate features and once enjoyed them without corporate taxation and regulation. Currently it is taxed and regulated like corporations, and consequently little used except where special tax privileges happen to be available. Beneficiaries are generally not liable for trust debts unless they have control over the trustees, in which case partnership or principalagent analogies apply. The requisite degree of control, and the elements comprising it, are not very clear. Trustees are personally liable, but may and do relieve themselves by appropriately contracting with third persons.

(a) Character and Use

The business trust is an adaptation of the traditional common law (or equitable) trust to the purpose of carrying on a business. Non-statutory in origin, it is usually formed by a trust instrument which prescribes the pattern of operation. Typically, title to the property used in the business is held by managers (trustees) who

---

57. Gilman Paint & Varnish Co. v. Legum, 197 Md. 665, 80 A.2d 906, 29 A.L. R.2d 286 (1951), at least as to profits paid out before any defect existed and before complainant became a creditor. The case is noted, 31 B.U.L.Rev. 561, 26 N.Y.U.L.Rev. 717 (1951).

57A. Refinite Sales Co. v. Fred R. Bright Co., 119 Cal.App.2d 56, 258 P. 2d 1116 (1953) (reversing non-suit in favor of one who testified she was a limited partner but offered no other proof of her status).

58. See Arrow Petroleum Corp. v. Ames, 128 Ind.App. 10, 142 N.E.2d 479 (1957) (certificate not filed; no renunciation).

59. Hoefer v. Hall, 75 N.M., 751, 411 P. 2d 230 (1966).

See Sponholz v. Meyer, 270 Wis. 288, 70 N.W.2d 619 (1955) (parties admitted that failure to file certificate did not affect rights inter se).

conduct the business and divide the profits among the beneficiaries. The latter are usually contributors of capital and hold transferable shares evidencing their interest.

"These organizations, commonly denominated 'Massachusetts trusts,' originated because of the hostility of some states towards corporations, and due to the desire [for] . . . advantages that would be secured by incorporating, without incurring the burdens and restrictions resulting therefrom. Due to statutory provisions in Massachusetts, prohibiting corporations from dealing in real property, this type of organization reached its fullest development and most extensive use in that state, but . . . has been adopted for use in many other states. The chief advantages of such organizations . . . are that until recently, they were, in most states, free from regulation, enjoyed freedom from corporation taxation, and [the] members enjoyed the freedom from personal liability that is imposed upon partners." [60]

The business trust started in England but gained its greatest vitality in Massachusetts in the later 19th century.[61] It retained considerable vogue until the 1920s, after which it declined in popularity.[62] There were several reasons, discussed in (c) and (e) below: (1) decisions in a number of states imposing personal liability on beneficiaries, (2) decisions exposing the trusts to federal income taxation as corporations, and (3) gradual enactment of legislation subjecting trusts to many of the other burdens of corporations.

Except in Massachusetts, business trusts were rarely formed after the 1920s, and most of those in existence faded away through dissolution or incorporation.[63] To a modest degree, investment companies (mutual funds) survived or were born as trusts, and some of

---

60. Goldwater v. Oltman, 210 Cal. 408, 292 P. 624, 71 A.L.R. 871 (1930).

On the Massachusetts origin, see also Bogert, Trusts and Trustees § 292 (2d ed. 1964); Comment, 37 Yale L.J. 1103, 1106 (1928).

61. For a discussion of the origin of the business trust and a historical comparison with the corporate form, see Wilgus, Corporations and Express Trusts as Business Organizations, 13 Mich.L. Rev. 71, 205 (1914). At the turn of the century, the business trust had become so well established that there was speculation it would replace the corporation as the most popular type of business organization, Powell, Passing of the Corporation in Business, 2 Minn.L.Rev. 401 (1918).

62. Bogert, Trusts and Trustees § 292 (2d ed. 1964).

Comprehensive legal studies of the business trust include Bogert, op. cit. §§ 291–310; Warren, Corporate Advantages without Incorporation (1929); Hildebrand's series of articles, The Massachusetts Trust, 1 Texas L.Rev. 127 (1923), Liabilities of the Trustees, Property and Shareholders of a Massachusetts Trust, 2 Texas L.Rev. 139 (1924), and Massachusetts Trust—A Sequel, 4 Texas L.Rev. 57 (1925); Annot., 156 A.L.R. 22–231 (1945). See also references in n. 92 below.

Brief recent surveys are Comment, 31 Tenn.L.Rev. 471 (1964); Henn, Corporations §§ 58–67 (1961).

63. No statistics have been found, but these are my observations from work as a business lawyer and from review of the reported cases, which diminished almost to nothing.

the largest members of the industry are trusts.[64] Federal tax laws go far to explain this, since the favorable conduit treatment (taxation of income to the shareholders but not to the company) is available to investment companies equally in the corporate and trust forms.[65] The business trust experienced an unexpected revival from a tax law enacted in 1960 to give real estate investment trust conduit treatment.[66] Many states responded with authorizing legislation.[67] A number of realty trusts were formed, and their shares sold to the public.[68]

64. Massachusetts Investors Trust is the second largest, with more than $2 billion of assets and 200,000 shareholders. Insurance Securities Trust Fund is fifth, with $1.3 billion and 190,000. Moody, Bank and Finance Manual 1272–73, 1251, a50 (1966). See, generally, Bogert, Trusts and Trustees §§ 249, 270.30 (2d ed. 1964).

Mesabi Trust is listed on the N. Y. Stock Exchange and has over 7,000 holders; it owns hard mineral royalties and was formed for tax reasons. See Moody, Industrial Manual 925 (1966). A venerable, widely-held, land-owning trust is Texas Pacific Land Trust, id. at 440; see n. 71 below.

65. Int.Rev.Code of 1954, §§ 851–55 (26 U.S.C.A.). Income Tax Reg. § 301.-7701–4(c) (1960).

The conduit treatment of regulated investment companies distinguishes only capital gain and ordinary income, and does not preserve for shareholders the special character of other items. e. g. tax-exempt income from municipal bonds (Int.Rev.Code of 1954, § 103 (26 U.S.C.A.)). Investment companies holding municipal securities have therefore organized as fixed investment trusts (without power to change the portfolio securities) so they will qualify as ordinary trusts (with more thorough-going conduit treatment) rather than business trusts treated as corporations. Income Tax Reg. § 301.-7701–4(c) (1960); Commissioner v. North American Bond Trust, 122 F.2d 545 (2d Cir. 1941), cert. denied 314 U.S. 701, 62 S.Ct. 479, 86 L.Ed. 560 (1942). In effect, they avoid corporate status by eliminating centralized management through having virtually nothing to manage. Recent examples are the Nuveen Tax-Exempt Bond Funds; see Moody, Bank and Finance Manual 462–68 (1967).

66. Int.Rev.Code of 1954, §§ 856–858 (26 U.S.C.A.). Among the requirements are transferable shares held (with some degree of dispersion) by 100 or more persons, income derived at least 90% from rent, interest, dividends, etc. and distributed at least 90% to beneficiaries. See, generally, Dawson, The Real Estate Investment Trust, 40 Texas L.Rev. 886 (1962); Grant, Developments in Real Estate Investment Trust Field, U. of So. Cal. 14th Tax Inst. 805 (1962) (with emphasis on trust instrument); Lynn, Real Estate Investment Trusts: Problems and Prospects, 31 Fordham L.Rev. 73 (1962); Note, The Real Estate Investment Trust—Past, Present, and Future, 23 U.Pitt.L.Rev. 779 (1962).

Although ostensibly modelled on the regulated investment company provisions, n. 65 above, the REIT sections are limited to trusts. The reason was no better than that those pushing the legislation represented, or were interested in, organizations which happened to be trusts. Congress has been urged to extend the applicability to real estate corporations as well as trusts, which would be reasonable.

67. Vernon's Ann.Civ.St. (Tex.) art. 6138A. See also n. 82 below. Texas had been one of the strictest states in imposing liability on trust beneficiaries (below at n. 91), thereby virtually killing the form of organization. But it was quick to revive the form, and give it limited liability by statute, when tax savings became possible.

68. "REITs"—$1 Billion Operation, 123 Financial World 11 (Apr. 7, 1965) refers to 65 trusts with assets valued at more than $1 billion. The number of investors is not given, nor any indication of the completeness of the data. The formation of an REIT is described in Real Estate Trusts—A Different Breed, 122 id. 5–7 (May 29, 1963).

Business trusts, particularly in earlier periods, were created by property owners who became the beneficiaries and perhaps also the trustees. The trusts served primarily management or (hopefully) liability-limiting functions. Although numerous owners or investors might assemble in a single trust, the entrustment often represented only the holdings or operations of an individual or family enterprise with the individual or family members filling the trusteeship(s).[69] Frequently, and more so in later years, trusts are formed by promoters for the purpose of selling beneficial interests to others. In either case, the settlor may be technically a beneficiary, although in the latter version it is not for long. Both differ from the usual common law trust which entails a gratuitous transfer by one person to a trustee for the benefit of another, and which is more concerned with investment than with business operation.

(b) Creation

A business trust is created by agreement between the settlor(s) and the trustee(s). Normally there is a formal trust instrument covering all phases of the enterprise: a description of the trust property and the business to be conducted, designation of the trustees, provision for their succession,[70] specification of their powers,[71] authorization of the shares of beneficial interest to be issued, provision for their transferability, rights of holders, rights of creditors dealing with the trustees and whether their remedies are restricted to trust assets.[72] The instrument spells out the control (if any) of the trustees by the beneficiaries—a matter which is influential in deciding whether beneficiaries are liable to trust creditors. There is usually a procedure

69. A recent example: Hayes' Case, 348 Mass. 447, 204 N.E.2d 277 (1965).

The reluctance of courts to accept limited liability of beneficiaries (Sec. 33 (e) below) is best understood against this pattern in which there has been no change of economic position or power but only legal legerdemain shifting outright ownership to trusteeship and beneficial interest in essentially the same group.

A father's conveyance of a business to his sons as trustees for themselves and their heirs was regarded as a private trust rather than a business one, despite a provision for transferable shares. Berry v. McCourt, 1 Ohio App. 2d 172, 204 N.E.2d 235 (1965). At issue was the trustees' compensation; there was no question of liability to third parties dealing with the trust.

70. 860 Lake Shore Drive Trust v. Gerber, 19 Ill.App.2d 1, 153 N.E.2d 253 (1958) illustrates a succession provi-sion and suggests the complexities which may arise if it is not followed. See also Plymouth Securities Co. v. Johnson, 335 S.W.2d 142, 144, 149–50 (Mo.1960).

71. For example, the instrument of Texas Pacific Land Trust calls for meetings of shareholders when the trustees "deem it necessary." The rules of the N. Y. Stock Exchange (on which the Trust's shares are listed) were held not to require annual meetings of shareholders. Kroese v. New York Stock Exchange, 227 F.Supp. 519 (S. D.N.Y.1964). The trustees' power in this respect was complete, as stated in the instrument.

72. Annot., 156 A.L.R. 65 (1945) has a specimen trust instrument and discussion of the various clauses which may be used. A trust is quoted at length in Rhode Island Hospital Trust Co. v. Copeland, 39 R.I. 193, 98 A. 273 (1916).

for amending the instrument, and perhaps for dissolving the trust, by prescribed vote of the beneficiaries. In many states the instrument must be recorded, which may put the world on notice of its contents.[73]

The factors which distinguish a business trust from other unincorporated associations are largely formal and found in the trust instrument. Foremost is the use of trust language,[74] which will ordinarily not appear in any of the other organizational types. Express provision for free transferability of interests [75] and for delegated, centralized management and title holding differentiate from partnership but are similar to joint stock companies. If the trustees fill their own vacancies, management is (at least on paper) more self-perpetuating than in a joint stock company where the shareholders typically elect management periodically. An election arrangement may be included in a business trust. Trusts commonly (and other organizations rarely) include statements that the beneficiaries or members are not personally liable; however, their effectiveness depends on elements considered later in this section.

A trust is customarily drawn to endure for a limited number of years, although in most states this is unnecessary to avoid the rules against perpetuities or restraints on alienation.[76] The trustees have power to transfer corpus and the legal interest is fully vested in them, the equitable interest in the beneficiaries.[77]

(c) Corporate Features and Consequences

The attributes already mentioned (e. g., transferable interests and centralized management)—plus the continuity of life which makes the trust's existence independent of change in, or occurrences to, beneficiaries—give the business trust a close resemblance to the corporation. The trust at one time seemed to offer most or all the corporate advantages without corporate drawbacks such as taxation, financial control and other regulation.[78]

The reaction was predictably negative, though slow. A few courts held the business trust subject to dissolution by the state in quo

---

73. E. g., RCWA (Wash.) 23.90.040(1) (1961). See below at n. 99.

74. But see Darling v. Buddy, n. 92 below.

75. See discussion in State Street Trust Co. v. Hall, 311 Mass. 299, 41 N.E.2d 30, 156 A.L.R. 13 (1942).

76. Hart v. Seymour, 147 Ill. 598, 35 N.E. 246 (1893); Baker v. Stern, 216 N.W. 147, 194 Wis. 233, 58 A.L.R. 462 (1927). Contra, Johnson v. Fitzmaurice, 127 N.W.2d 497 (N.D.1964); Carl-son v. Tioga Holding Co., 72 N.W.2d 236 (N.D.1955).

77. Hart v. Seymour, n. 76 above; Howe v. Morse, 174 Mass. 491, 55 N.E. 213 (1899); Liberty Nat. Bank & Trust Co. v. New England Investors Shares, 25 F.2d 493 (D.Mass.1928); Bogert, Trusts and Trustees § 304 (2d ed. 1964); Whiteside, Restrictions on the Duration of Business Trusts, 9 Cornell L.Q. 422 (1924).

78. See above at n. 60. Tax cases are collected, Annots., 108 A.L.R. 340 (1937), 144 A.L.R. 1050 (1943).

warranto proceedings for usurpation of the corporate form.[79] Others interpreted their tax and regulatory statutes to apply to business trusts as well as corporations,[80] notably the federal corporate income tax.[81] Elsewhere, legislatures amended their laws to bring business trusts under the same rules as corporations.[82] But the business trust, as a voluntary association, is not subject to all the statutory requirements for corporations. For example, two trusts may informally merge if their trust instruments give the necessary power.[83] Internally, the trust is governed by its instrument, supplemented (when needed) by general principles of trust law. Its external relations are considered in (e) and (f) below.

79. State ex rel. Range v. Hinkle, 126 Wash. 581, 219 P. 41 (1923); State ex rel. Colvin v. Paine, 137 Wash. 266, 243 P. 2, 46 A.L.R. 165 (1926). See Warren, Corporate Advantages without Incorporation 526–41 (1929). Washington later reversed its position by statute, n. 82 below.

80. Taxed as corporations: Nedeau v. United Petroleum, 251 Mich. 673, 232 N.W. 202 (1930); City Bank Farmers Trust Co. v. Graves, 272 N.Y. 1, 3 N.E.2d 612, 108 A.L.R. 333 (1936). Contra, In re Opinion of the Justices, 266 Mass. 590, 165 N.E. 904, 63 A.L.R. 952 (1929) (no special privilege or franchise as corporations). See references in n. 78 above.

Regulated as corporations: Hemphill v. Orloff, 277 U.S. 537, 48 S.Ct. 577, 72 L.Ed. 978 (1928) (qualification as a foreign corporation before doing business); Nedeau v. United Petroleum, above, this n. (annual reports); Forgan v. Mackie, 232 Mich. 476, 205 N.W. 600 (1925) (may sue only in common name); Home Lumber Co. v. Hopkins, 107 Kan. 153, 190 P. 601, 10 A.L.R. 879 (1920) and State v. Cosgrove, 36 Idaho 278, 210 P. 393 (1922) (subject to blue sky law provisions for corporations); Coleman v. McKee, 162 Ark. 90, 257 S.W. 733 (1924) and Barrett v. Gore, 88 Cal.App. 372, 263 P. 564 (1928) (subject to blue sky law provisions for associations). But cf. Bouchard v. First People's Trust, 253 Mass. 351, 148 N.E. 895 (1925) (not subject to suit in common name under statute referring to associations).

81. Burk-Waggoner Oil Ass'n v. Hopkins, 269 U.S. 110, 46 S.Ct. 48, 70 L.Ed. 183 (1925) and Helvering v. Combs,

296 U.S. 365, 56 S.Ct. 287, 80 L.Ed. 275 (1935) (oil production); Swanson v. Commissioner, 296 U.S. 362, 56 S.Ct. 283, 80 L.Ed. 273 (1935), Helvering v. Coleman-Gilbert Associates, 296 U.S. 369, 56 S.Ct. 285, 80 L.Ed. 278 (1935) and Mann-Hammond Land Trust v. Commissioner, 200 F.2d 308 (6th Cir. 1952) (apartment house ownership and operation); Morrissey v. Commissioner, 296 U.S. 344, 56 S.Ct. 289, 80 L.Ed. 263 (1935) (suburban development and operation of golf course and clubhouse). See Sec. 24 above.

82. Ga.Code § 108–608; Ind.Stat.Ann. § 25–4809; M.S.A. (Minn.) § 318.03–318.04 (securities and insurance regulation); T.C.A. (Tenn.) § 48–1804(3) (1964); RCWA (Wash.) 23.90.040(3)–(4) (1961); Pacific American Realty Trust v. Lonctot, 62 Wash.2d 91, 381 P.2d 123 (1963) (foreign trust entitled to sell securities in Wash. on compliance with statute just cited and with the state's securities laws). The Wash. statute is discussed 34 Wash.L. Rev. 305 (1959).

Statutes are collected, Bogert, Trusts and Trustees § 293 n. 34 (2d ed. 1964). Many of the statutes affirmatively authorize business trusts, resolving doubts that may have existed about their validity. Some, directly or indirectly, prescribe non-liability of shareholders, e. g., M.S.A. (Minn.) § 318.02 Subd. 4; T.C.A. (Tenn.) § 48–1802 (1964); RCWA (Wash.) § 23.90.-020 (1961). Most of the statutes were enacted after the trust form was given new blood by the tax law discussed above at nn. 66–68.

83. Page v. Arkansas Natural Gas Corp., 53 F.2d 27 (8th Cir. 1931).

(d) Powers and Duties of Trustees

The trust instrument commonly states the kind of business to be conducted. Like the purpose clauses in a corporate charter, it may be liberally construed with respect to implied powers of management, here the trustees.[84] The instrument often says that the trustees must act as a group (or by majority) or that more than one trustee must join in making a contract. A trustee who violates such a clause may be subject to removal or loss of compensation, or may forfeit his right of reimbursement from the trust corpus for liabilities incurred by him.[85]

Without enabling provisions in the instrument, trustees have no power to create a partnership between the trust and another business organization.[86] Trustees are, of course, fiduciaries and must not divert trust property to their personal use,[87] or otherwise profit at the expense of the trust. A trustee's separate creditor who knowingly receives trust property in payment of a trustee's personal obligation can be held accountable for it to the trust.[88] A trustee proposing an amendment of the instrument substantially affecting the rights of beneficiaries has a duty to disclose fully all material facts.[89]

(e) Liability of Beneficiaries

The business trust has had varying degrees of effectiveness in giving shareholders (beneficiaries) immunity from personal liability for obligations of the business.[90] Some courts hold them liable as partners, regardless whether they retain any control over the trustees, because they have established the business and authorized the trustees to conduct it for their benefit. The statutes provide ways for such persons to enjoy immunity from liability, viz. by incorporating or forming a limited partnership. If they do not avail themselves of the statutory methods, they must be deemed to have formed the only other sort of voluntary business association known to the law: general partnership. The trust device is not to be expanded to include a business enterprise established by the beneficiaries. Such, in substance, is

---

84. Bomeisler v. M. Jacobson & Sons Trust, 118 F.2d 261 (1st Cir. 1941).

85. It follows that a creditor is deprived of any remedy by subrogation to the trustee's reimbursement right. The Downey Co. v. The 282 Beacon Street Trust, 292 Mass. 175, 197 N.E. 643 (1935).

86. Phoenix Oil Co. v. McLarren, 244 S.W. 830 (Tex.Civ.App.1922).

87. See Flynn v. LaSalle Nat. Bank, 9 Ill.2d 129, 137 N.E.2d 71 (1956) (fiduciary duty of trustee, managing agents

and majority owners of beneficial interests, in selling trust property to themselves).

88. Wichita Royalty Co. v. City Nat. Bank, 127 Tex. 158, 89 S.W.2d 394, 93 S.W.2d 143 (1935).

89. Shapiro v. Chicago Title & Trust Co., 328 Ill.App. 650, 66 N.E.2d 731 (1946).

90. A recent review which is nationwide, despite its title, is Jones, Business Trusts in Florida—Liability of Shareholders, 14 U.Fla.L.Rev. 1 (1961).

the basis on which many states have rejected limited liability in all business trusts.[91]

In other states investor immunity from personal liability has not seemed so contrary to public policy. It has not been objectionable that beneficiaries created trusts to carry on a business. The distinction between the trust (in which there is no personal liability) and the partnership (in which there is) has been held to depend on whether the beneficiaries have power of control of management by the trustees.[92] The concern is whether management is vested in the trustees

---

91. Willey v. W. J. Hoggson Corp., 90 Fla. 343, 106 So. 408 (1925); McClaren v. Dawes Electric Sign & Mfg. Co., 86 Ind.App. 196, 156 N.E. 584 (1927); Weber Engine Co. v. Alter, 120 Kan. 557, 245 P. 143, 46 A.L.R. 158 (1926); Ing v. Liberty Nat. Bank, 216 Ky. 467, 287 S.W. 960 (1926); Thompson v. Schmitt, 115 Tex. 53, 274 S.W. 554 (1925).

The Texas decision was of great significance because hundreds of trusts had been formed there, especially for oil and gas development. After the decision, the device was practically abandoned in the state. Hildebrand, Massachusetts Trust—A Sequel, 4 Texas L.Rev. 57 (1925); Comment, 37 Yale L.J. 1103, 1107 n. 19 (1928). Because the beneficiaries' expectation of limited liability was frustrated by the decision, they were permitted in other cases to dissolve trusts before the date specified in the instrument. O'Dell v. Grubstake Inv. Ass'n, 38 S.W.2d 151 (Tex.Civ.App.1931).

Texas law was applied to a trust organized in Oklahoma and doing business in Texas, Means v. Limpia Royalties, 88 S.W.2d 1080 (Tex.Civ.App.1936) but not to a trust organized in Texas and doing business in Iowa, Farmers' & Merchants Nat. Bank v. Anderson, 216 Iowa 988, 250 N.W. 214 (1933), noted 32 Mich.L.Rev. 559. See Restatement, Conflict of Laws, §§ 343, 345.

"Freedom from personal responsibility for breach of their business contracts is not a matter which a group of men can confer upon themselves by the creation of a trust, without the sanction of a statute to that effect, or without the intelligent contractual consent of the parties with whom they deal." Linn v. Houston, 123 Kan. 409, 412, 255 P. 1105, 1107 (1927).

92. Betts v. Hackathorn, 159 Ark. 621, 252 S.W. 602, 31 A.L.R. 847 (1923); Schumann-Heink v. Folsom, 328 Ill. 321, 159 N.E. 250, 58 A.L.R. 485 (1927); Goldwater v. Oltman, 210 Cal. 408, 292 P. 624, 71 A.L.R. 871 (1930), noted 19 Calif.L.Rev. 42; Krey Packing Co. v. Hitchings, 18 S.W.2d 123 (Mo.App. 1929), commented on, 28 Mich.L.Rev. 931.

"The true test of such a trust seems to be to determine whether the relation between the parties is that of principal and agent or trustee and beneficiary; whether the subscribers are separated from direct interest, ownership and control of the property and affairs of the trust. A trustee is a principal, not an agent in the management of the trust property. . . . The trustees should therefore be a self-perpetuating body, owning the property of the syndicate, with all powers of control over it. The shareholders should have no rights except to receive dividends and to share in the final distribution when the business is wound up. . . . The agreement is one of joint adventure when the subscribers retain some degree of ownership and control over the property which they put into the pool . . . whether the syndicate is the one or the other depends upon the way in which the trustees are to conduct the affairs committed to their charge. If they act as principals, owners of the sums subscribed free from the control of the subscribers, a trust is created; but if the trustees are subject to the control of the subscribers as co-owners of a business for profit, . . . a partnership or joint undertaking exists as to third persons, although otherwise as to the subscribers among themselves. . . . A partnership is a joint undertaking wherein the partners agree to share in profits and losses. A business trust,

as principals or as agents of the beneficiaries. Liability naturally follows if the beneficiaries are regarded as the principals.[93] What degree of control renders the beneficiaries principals is not altogether certain. Important factors are powers to instruct the trustees,[94] to remove them,[95] to alter, amend or terminate the trust,[96] to elect trustees periodically or fill vacancies.[97] (Ironically, some of these are enjoyed by corporate shareholders without sacrificing their limited

---

like a corporation, has its own profits and losses. The subscribers as such, like stockholders have none. Yet here the subscribers agreed to share personally in the profits and losses of the syndicate. The managers act as agents of the subscribers subject to an accounting to them." Pound, C. J., in Brown v. Bedell, 263 N.Y. 177, 188 N.E. 641 (1934).

Note that the court has in mind the non-partnership type of trust.

Trust and beneficiary language is not essential to immunity from liability. If the agreement is in substance one of trust, other verbiage may be used, e. g., "syndicate managers" and "syndicate subscribers." Darling v. Buddy, 318 Mo. 784, 1 S.W.2d 163, 58 A.L.R. 493 (1927).

Cox v. Hickman, 8 H.L.Cas. 268, 11 Eng. Rep. 431 (1860), summarized in Sec. 15 above, is an early example of trustees doing business. The trust was in effect a mortgage. The beneficiaries included the debtor as well as the creditors, who were beneficiaries only to the extent of their claims. Trust deed provisions for creditors' meetings and power to make rules for carrying on the business (or to order its discontinuance) did not amount to sufficient participation in management to make the creditors principals and partners. The arrangement differed from the usual business trust in the limited monetary interest of the alleged partners (who were only trying to salvage bad debts) and the limited time therefor contemplated for the trust operation.

Much has been written on the liability of beneficiaries. Among the leading works are: Judah, Possible Partnership Liability under the Business Trust, 17 Ill.L.Rev. 77 (1922); Aaron, Massachusetts Trust as Distinguished from Partnership, 12 Ill.L.Rev. 482 (1918); Magruder, The Position of Shareholders in Business Trusts, 23 Colum.L.Rev. 423 (1923); Rowley, The

Influence of Control in the Determination of Partnership Liability, 26 Mich. L.Rev. 290 (1928); Stevens, Limited Liability in Business Trusts, 7 Cornell L.Q. 116 (1922); Comment, 37 Yale L.J. 1103 (1928); Dunn, Trusts for Business Purposes (1922); Sears, Decline of Trust as Effective Substitute for Incorporation (1911); Wrighting-ton, The Law of Unincorporated Associations and Business Trusts (2d ed. 1923); and references in n. 62 above.

93. Restatement, Second, Agency, § 14B.

94. Williams v. Inhabitants of Milton, 215 Mass. 1, 102 N.E. 355 (1913). See Krey Packing Co. v. Hitchings, 18 S. W.2d 123 (Mo.App.1929) (no control in beneficiaries by virtue of required consultation of trustees with "advisory committee" of beneficiaries whose advice needn't be followed).

95. Horgan v. Morgan, 233 Mass. 381, 124 N.E. 32 (1919).

96. Simson v. Klipstein, 262 F. 823 (D. N.J.1920).

97. Rand v. Morse, 289 F. 339 (8th Cir. 1923).

But see the more persuasive view in Levy v. Nellis, 284 Ill.App. 228, 1 N. E.2d 251 (1936): "We do not believe it can be logically argued, where the trustees have exclusive and full control of every detail of a business, that merely the power under certain circumstances to fill vacancies among the trustees or to elect trustees at stated intervals, or even to alter or amend the trust agreement, turns the trust into a partnership contrary to the intent of the parties."

See also Goldwater v. Oltman, and Krey Packing Co. v. Hitchings, n. 92 above; Rhode Island Hospital Trust Co. v. Copeland, 39 R.I. 193, 98 A. 273 (1916); Bank of America v. Scully, 18 F.Supp. 182 (D.Colo.1937).

liability.) Under this more liberal view, the terms of the trust instrument are important, although actual operation (as distinct from formal power) will be scrutinized in the search for control.

The trust instrument usually states that beneficiaries are not liable for trust debts, or that trustees have no power to bind the beneficiaries but only to create obligations enforceable against the trust corpus. Such provisions are effective as to third persons with knowledge or notice of them, even in states which otherwise hold the beneficiaries liable with or without control.[98] Courts often find the third party knowledge or notice necessary to make these liability-limiting clauses work;[99] compulsory recording statutes may assist in the process.[1] There is, of course, no problem if the liability limitation is written into the contract under which the third party's claim arises; he has waived.[1A]

(f) Liability of Trustees

By the usual trust rule, trustees (if they are not considered agents of the beneficiaries) are the principals in trust transactions and are personally liable for their contracts and torts as well as those of trust employees and agents within the scope of the trust's business.[2] They are entitled to reimbursement from trust assets unless they have been guilty of certain kinds of misconduct. The trust instrument commonly negatives personal liability of trustees as well as of beneficiaries. Such a provision is ineffective against third persons who do not know

---

98. Farmers' State Bank & Trust Co. v. Gorman Home Refinery, 3 S.W.2d 65 (Tex.Com.App.1928).

99. Commercial Cas. Ins. Co. v. North, 320 Ill.App. 221, 50 N.E.2d 434 (1943); Roberts v. Aberdeen-Southern Pines Syndicate, 198 N.C. 381, 151 S.E. 865, 71 A.L.R. 885 (1930); McCarthy v. Parker, 243 Mass. 465, 138 N.E. 8 (1923); Brown v. Bedell, 263 N.Y. 177, 188 N.E. 641 (1934).

Contra, Victor Refining Co. v. City Nat. Bank of Commerce, 115 Tex. 71, 274 S.W. 561 (1925); Sessums v. Citizens' Nat. Bank, 72 S.W.2d 403 (Tex.Civ. App.1934).

Downey Co. v. Whistler, 284 Mass. 461, 188 N.E. 243 (1933) third person dealing with trust is chargeable with notice of limitations in instrument recorded pursuant to statutory requirement. If recording is not required, it gives no constructive notice, McClaren v. Dawes Electric Sign & Mfg. Co., 86 Ind.App. 196, 156 N.E. 584 (1927); Hayes Motor Truck Wheel Co. v. Wolff, 175 Wis. 501, 185 N.W. 512 (1921).

A liability limitation in the instrument is ineffective where it is unknown to a third person. Case v. McConnell & Forrester, 37 P.2d 190 (Cal.App.1934). A contrary dictum appears in In re Conover's Estate, 295 Ill.App. 443, 14 N.E.2d 980 (1938), criticized 27 Geo. L.Rev. 103.

A provision limiting liability to the trust assets does not create a lien on the assets in favor of a creditor prior to some legal action by him. Ballentine v. Eaton, 297 Mass. 389, 8 N.E.2d 808 (1937).

1. Above at nn. 73, 99.

1A. The agreed limitation need not be in the instrument creating the obligation. Shelton v. Montoya Oil & Gas Co., 292 S.W. 165 (Tex.Com.App.1927).

2. Bogert, Trusts and Trustees § 300 (2d ed. 1964); Scott, Liabilities Incurred in the Administration of Trusts, 28 Harv.L.Rev. 725 (1915); Taylor v. Davis' Adm'x, 110 U.S. 330, 4 S.Ct. 147, 28 L.Ed. 163 (1883).

of and assent to it.[3] The trustee may avoid personal liability by contracting against it in dealing with third persons.[4]

The trustee is not liable on a negotiable instrument which shows on its face that it is executed as an obligation of the trust, and not of the trustee save in a representative capacity.[5] It has been questioned whether an instrument collectible only out of trust assets (on which neither trustees nor beneficiaries are personally liable) is enough of an unconditional promise to pay money that it will qualify as a negotiable instrument.[6] However, corporate notes are similar and regularly regarded as negotiable. Those of a joint stock company have been held negotiable [7] and only some reticence about the trust as an entity presents any obstacle. Some courts still refuse to see the business trust as an entity, despite its functional similarity to the corporation.[8] The Uniform Commercial Code [9] confirms the negotiability of a trust's instrument limited to payment out of trust assets.

If a trust is treated as a partnership (because of agency attributes) trustees who are also beneficiaries are liable as partners unless protected by contract with the third party claimant. If not beneficiaries, they appear free from liability under the usual rules of agency, unless they are considered as acting for partially disclosed principals (whose existence is disclosed but whose identity is not),[10] or unless they are

---

3. Betts v. Hackathorn, and Goldwater v. Oltman, n. 92 above; Hildebrand, Liability of Trustees, Property and Shareholders of a Massachusetts Trust, 2 Texas L.Rev. 139, 145 (1924); Williston, Contracts § 313A (3d ed. 1959).

4. Shoe & Leather Nat. Bank v. Dix, 123 Mass. 148, 25 Am.Rep. 49 (1877) ("We as trustees but not individually promise to pay."). The mere addition of "trustee" after signature may not be sufficient to prevent liability. Philip Carey Co. v. Pingree, 223 Mass. 352, 111 N.E. 857 (1916). But see Pennsylvania Co., etc. v. Wallace, 346 Pa. 532, 31 A.2d 71, 156 A.L.R. 1 (1943) (trustees' mortgage bond sufficiently indicated they were signing only in trust capacity; promisee-lender knew it was dealing with Mass. trust without liability of beneficiaries or trustee).

5. Uniform Commercial Code § 3—403. based on Negotiable Instruments Law § 20. The N.I.L. was applied to relieve trustees in Charles Nelson Co. v. Morton, 106 Cal.App. 144, 288 P. 845 (1930); Hamilton v. Young, 116 Kan. 128, 225 P. 1045, 35 A.L.R. 496 (1924); Adams v. Swig, 234 Mass. 584, 125 N.E. 857 (1920). The same result was reached without the N.I.L. in Brown v. Smith, 73 F.2d 524 (2d Cir. 1934), noted 34 Mich.L.Rev. 121. See also Pennsylvania Co., etc. v. Wallace, n. 4 above; Note, The Liability of an Authorized Trustee under Section 20 of the Negotiable Instruments Laws, 7 U.Cin.L.Rev. 288 (1933)

6. Bonds of the International Hydro-Electric System of Mass. were held non-negotiable on this ground, Lorimer v. McGreevy, 229 Mo.App. 970, 84 S.W. 2d 667 (1935), criticized 49 Harv.L.Rev. 478 (1936), 45 Yale L.J. 176 (1935).

7. Hibbs v. Brown, 190 N.Y. 167, 82 N. E. 1108 (1907). See also Page v. Arkansas Natural Gas Corp., 53 F.2d 27 (8th Cir. 1931).

8. E. g., Hayes' Case, 348 Mass. 447, 204 N.E.2d 277 (1965) (trustee not covered by workmen's compensation; trust not his employer).

9. § 3—105(1) (h).

10. Restatement, Second, Agency § 321. Disclosure of the trust by name should be sufficient without disclosure of the beneficiaries. See Notes, 27 Harv.L. Rev. 83 (1913); 33 id. 591 (1920); 42 id. 123 (1927).

understood by the third person to be parties to the contract in question.[11] Trustees in all cases are liable for their own torts.

JOINT STOCK COMPANIES

§ 34. A joint stock company is created by agreement providing for centralized management and transferable shares. It does not give limited liability (except by agreement with creditors) and has therefore fallen into disuse. Although it is often spoken of as a partnership, it more closely resembles a corporation (except for liability), and is usually so taxed and regulated.

The joint stock company (JSC) or joint stock association is another non-statutory business organization.[12] It is created by agreement among participants which has as its most conspicuous feature a provision for transferable shares of ownership or membership.[13] Membership is usually large: dozens, hundreds or even thousands. The JSC originated in a period when corporate charters were hard to get, and was primarily a capital-pooling (or capital-raising) and management-centralizing device.[14] The principal users in 19th century America were the express companies [15] but they, like nearly everyone else, have by now abandoned the form for the greater safety of incorporation.[16]

The JSC agreement (sometimes called the constitution or articles of association) typically provides for concentration of management in designated officers or directors elected by the shareholders. The agreement also covers name, duration, capitalization (on which there

---

11. Restatement, Second, Agency § 320.

12. Henn, Corporations, §§ 50–57 (1961) and Note, The Joint Stock Company and the Problems of the Close Corporation, 50 Iowa L.Rev. 118 (1964) are recent surveys of JSCs. Older and more comprehensive are Cook, Corporations §§ 504–10 (8th ed. 1923); Wrightington, The Law of Unincorporated Associations and Business Trusts (2d ed. 1923).

13. Gleason v. McKay, 134 Mass. 419 (1883); Townsend v. Goewey, 19 Wend. 424, 32 Am.Dec. 514 (N.Y.1838). See Warren, Corporate Advantages without Incorporation 333 (1929).

14. See Ballantine, Corporations § 5 (rev. ed. 1946). Early history, in England and on the Continent, is traced in Schmitthoff, The Origins of the Joint Stock Company, 3 U.Toronto L.J. 74 (1939); Warren, Safeguarding the Creditors of Corporations, 36 Harv.L.Rev. 509 (1923).

15. Note their dominance of the litigation discussed in Warren, Corporate Advantages without Incorporation 458–507 (1929).

16. American Express Co., with 27,000 shareholders, was probably the largest and most widely held of the JSCs. After operating as a JSC under N.Y. since 1858, it finally incorporated in 1965 when massive liability of a corporate subsidiary raised the spectre of suits against members on their personal liability. See Bromberg, Partnership Dissolution—Causes, Consequences and Cures, 43 Texas L.Rev. 631, 668 n. 184 (1965). However, most of its express business, along with that of Adams, Wells Fargo and other major express companies, had been consolidated in 1918 into American Railway Express Co. (after 1929, Railway Express Agency, Inc.). Moody, Bank and Finance Manual 883 (1966). Adams Express Co. became an investment company but remains a JSC with 19,000 shareholders. Id. 504; Jones v. Healy, n. 25 below.

is no externally imposed maximum or minimum), and internal organizational matters in much the same way as a business trust instrument or corporate charter and bylaws. The agreement is private in the sense that it need not be publicized or filed with a government office in most places.[17] However, the fictitious or assumed name statutes may require identification of the members.

A JSC has the corporate characteristics which can be created by agreement, particularly centralization of management, continuity of life,[18] and transferability of interests. But, without trust precedents to employ, it cannot achieve limited liability for the members. The partnership model of joint (or joint and several) liability is imposed on the theory that the members, by virtue of their control over the managers, are co-owners of the business.[19] They or their management may, of course, expressly contract with third persons that only the joint or company property shall be responsible.[20] The partnership model is not wholly applicable since delectus personae has been relin-

17. McKinney's N.Y. General Associations Law, § 4 requires annual filing.

18. Id. § 5: "A joint-stock association shall not be dissolved except in pursuance of its articles of association, or by consent of all its stockholders, or by judgment of a court for fraud in its management, or for good cause shown."

19. Ashley v. Dowling, 203 Mass. 311, 89 N.E. 434, 133 Am.St.Rep. 296 (1909); Brown v. Bedell, 263 N.Y. 177, 188 N. E. 641 (1934); Carter v. McClure, 98 Tenn. 109, 38 S.W. 585, 36 L.R.A. 282, 60 Am.St.Rep. 842 (1897); C. D. Hartnett Co. v. Shirah, 116 Tex. 154, 287 S.W. 902 (1926).

The JSC differs from the business trust in that the managers are chosen by and responsible to the members who have power of control. Brown v. Bedell, above; Goubeaux v. Krickenberger, 126 Ohio St. 302, 185 N.E. 201 (1933); Earlsboro Gas Co. v. Vern H. Brown Drilling Co., 175 Okl. 320, 52 P.2d 730 (1935).

On retirement from a JSC, a well-known member should give notice in order to avoid liability for subsequent transactions, as in partnership. Dinsmore v. J. H. Calvin Co., 214 Ala. 666, 108 So. 583 (1926); Tyrrell v. Washburn, 88 Mass. (6 Allen) 466 (1863).

If coverture bars liability as a partner, it also bars liability as a JSC member. Flint v. Culbertson, 159 Tex. 243, 319 S.W.2d 690 (1958).

Limited liability might have been secured by compliance with the limited partnership association statutes (Sec. 26A above); failing that, the members are liable as partners. The treasurer, however, has no power to bind them by a judgment note. Fairman Bros. v. Ogden Gas Co., 106 Pa. Super. 130, 161 A. 634 (1932).

Absent a statute for suits in the common name, suit must be brought against all the members, as in ordinary partnership, if the liability is regarded as joint. Pettis v. Atkins, 60 Ill. 454 (1871); Van Aernam v. Blustein, 102 N.Y. 355, 7 N.E. 537 (1886).

In some states there is no remedy against members until remedies against the JSC and its assets are exhausted. Reinig v. Nelson, 199 Wis. 482, 227 N.W. 14 (1929).

In N. Y. a creditor can sue the members in the first instance, but if he elects to sue the association he must exhaust this remedy before pursuing the members. Hibbs v. Brown, 190 N.Y. 167, 82 N.E. 1108 (1907); N.Y. Gen. Assoc. Law §§ 16–17.

Similarly in Texas, members may be sued along with the JSC, and judgment taken against them, but execution will not issue against individual property until the joint property has been exhausted. Vernon's Ann.Civ. St. (Tex.) art. 6137.

20. Hibbs v. Brown, 190 N.Y. 167, 82 N.E. 1108 (1907); Note, 8 Colum.L.Rev. 215 (1908).

quished by the choice of transferable shares.[21] This indicates that the members have agreed to be represented not by anyone who happens to be a member, but only by the designated officers or directors.[22] The courts have so recognized, and persons dealing with a JSC with knowledge of its character acquire rights against it only through the acts of its officials.[23]

A member's personal liability for obligations properly incurred during his membership does not terminate when he dies or transfers his shares.[24] But he is not liable for obligations incurred later.

The preponderance of corporate characteristics has led to taxation and regulation of JSCs as corporations in most respects.[25]

21. If restrictions are placed on share transfers, the organization is classified as an ordinary partnership, dissolved by a member's death. Hammond v. Otwell, 170 Ga. 832, 154 S.E. 357 (1930); Haiku Sugar Co. v. Johnstone, 249 F. 103 (9th Cir. 1918). See also Reinig v. Nelson, 199 Wis. 482, 227 N.W. 14 (1929).

22. Oliver's Estate, 136 Pa. 43, 20 A. 527, 9 L.R.A. 421, 20 Am.St.Rep. 894 (1890); Oil Lease & Royalty Syndicate v. Beeler, 217 S.W. 1054 (Tex.Civ.App. 1920).

For limits on an officer's authority, see Amerada Petroleum Corp. v. Mexia Big Pool Royalty Co., 220 S.W.2d 497 (Tex.Civ.App.1949). Cf. Campsey v. Jack County Oil & Gas Association, 328 S.W.2d 912 (Tex.Civ.App.1959) (title cleared for JSC; one purporting to convey for it was not officer or agent). See also n. 23, below.

23. Limitations on officers' authority are effective like those on other agents. Spotswood v. Morris, 12 Idaho 360, 85 P. 1094, 6 L.R.A.,N.S., 665 (1906). See also n. 22 above.

Without express authorization, JSC officers have no power to make it a partner with another firm. Phoenix Oil Co. v. McLarren, 244 S.W. 830 (Tex.Civ.App.1922).

24. Lindley v. Seward, 103 Ind.App. 600, 5 N.E.2d 998 (1937); Tyrrell v. Washburn, 88 Mass. (6 Allen 466) (1863). The estate of a deceased member may be liable for post-death obligations, as where his personal representative succeeds to this membership in the JSC. Phillips v. Blatchford, 137 Mass. 510 (1884). The JSC agreement may provide that, among the members, a trans-

fer of shares discharges the transferor from existing obligations and charges the transferee. Smith v. Virgin, 33 Me. 148 (1851). Creditors would not be bound by such a provision unless they knew and consented.

25. Taxation: Roberts v. Anderson, 226 F. 7 (2d Cir. 1915). Int.Rev.Code of 1954, § 7701(a) (3) (26 U.S.C.A.) defines corporation to include JSC. But see Gleason v. McKay, 134 Mass. 419 (1883) (excise tax on JSC unconstitutional since JSC had no statutory powers or privileges, only those created by agreement); People ex rel. Winchester v. Coleman, 133 N.Y. 279, 31 N.E. 96, 16 L.R.A. 183 (1892) (JSC not taxable under law applicable only to corporations)

Regulation: Brown v. Farmer & Ochs Co., 209 F.2d 703 (6th Cir. 1954) (JSC subject to Mich. statute barring use of courts by unqualified foreign corporation); In re Tidewater Coal Exchange, 280 F. 638 (2d Cir. 1922) and In re Poland Union, 77 F.2d 855 (2d Cir. 1935) (bankruptcy procedures); Securities Act of 1933, § 2(1), (2), 15 U.S.C.A. § 77b(1), (2); Uniform Securities Act § 401(i), (l) (securities regulation). See also last par. of n. 27 below.

See also the realistic opinion in Jones v. Healy, 184 Misc. 923, 55 N.Y.S.2d 349 (Sup.Ct.1945), aff'd 270 App.Div. 895, 62 N.Y.S.2d 605 (1946). A JSC's articles gave shareholders dissenting from an amendment to the articles the right to receive the "true cash value" of their shares. Noting that the company (Adams Express Co.) had long since converted from an operating express company to a closed end investment company (with 12,000 sharehold-

Some states have statutes reversing the common law by permitting JSCs to hold land,[26] or to sue and be sued,[27] either in the company name or that of an officer. New York has legislated more comprehensively.[28]

An earlier view that no JSC is an entity for diversity jurisdiction in the federal courts [29] is now being superseded by a careful scrutiny for corporate attributes which, if found, will support entity treatment.[30]

PROFESSIONAL ASSOCIATIONS AND CORPORATIONS

§ 34A. **For federal tax reasons, most states have enacted professional corporation or professional association statutes for learned profes-**

ers), the court opted for a corporate measure of appraisal as a going concern rather than a partnership measure in terms of liquidation value; the latter would have been higher.

26. McKinney's N.Y.Gen.Associations Law, § 6. Land holding in the firm name would be permitted under U.P.A. § 8(3), Sec. 38 below.

For the confusing history, in one jurisdiction, see Morita v. Public Utilities Commission, 40 Haw. 579 (1954).

27. McKinney's N.Y.Gen.Associations Law §§ 12–13; Pa.R.Civ.P. 2176, 2177, applied in Van Sant v. American Express Co., 169 F.2d 355, 371–72 (3d Cir. 1948); Tex.Rev.Civ.Stat.Ann. art. 6133 (1962). Id. arts. 6134, 6137 provide for service on an officer and any member against whom individual liability is sought. See Port Terminal R. R. Authority v. Leonhardt, 289 S.W.2d 649 (1956).

Under such statutes, a member can prosecute a claim against the JSC by suit against an officer. Westcott v. Fargo, 61 N.Y. 542, 19 Am.Rep. 300 (1875). Such statutes are not extraterritorial in operation. Taft v. Ward, 106 Mass. 518 (1871). But see Adams Express Co. v. State, 55 Ohio St. 69, 44 N.E. 506 (1896).

JSCs have been held suable under partnership common name statutes. Goubeaux v. Krickenberger, 126 Ohio St. 302, 185 N.E. 201 (1933). But the statute has been construed to require service on one or more members, and was **not** complied with by service on the **principal** agent in the state. Bloom v. American Express Co., 222 Minn. 249, 23 N.W.2d 570 (1946).

A JSC is indictable in the company name for violation of the Interstate Commerce Act (49 U.S.C.A. § 1 et seq.) U. S. v. Adams Express Co., 229 U.S. 381, 33 S.Ct. 878, 57 L.Ed. 1237 (1913).

28. E. g., McKinney's N.Y.Gen. Associations Law §§ 7 (amending articles), 7–a (incorporation), 9 (receivership), 18 (designation of secretary of state as agent for service of process). Other provisions are in nn. 17–19, 26–27 above.

29. Chapman v. Barney, 129 U.S. 677, 9 S.Ct. 426, 32 L.Ed. 800 (1899); Brocki v. American Express Co., 279 F.2d 785 (6th Cir. 1960), cert. denied 364 U.S. 871, 81 S.Ct. 113, 5 L.Ed.2d 92 (1960).

30. Mason v. American Express Co., 334 F.2d 392 (2d Cir. 1964), noted 65 Colum. L.Rev. 162, 53 Geo.L.J. 513, 78 Harv. L.Rev. 1661 (1965). The opinion reviews developments undermining the earlier view. The defendant, a JSC under N.Y.Gen.Assoc.Law, had ample corporateness for diversity jurisdiction. But see United Steelworkers of America v. Bouligny, Inc., 382 U.S. 145, 86 S.Ct. 272, 15 L.Ed.2d 217 (1965) declining to extend this approach to labor unions. More generally, see Note, Diversity Jurisdiction for Unincorporated Associations, 75 Yale L.J. 138 (1965); Comment, Unincorporated Associations: Diversity Jurisdiction and the ALI Proposal, 1965 Duke L.J. 329.

The older view meant that widely held JSCs might not be suable anywhere in federal diversity cases, since a member could always be found with the same citizenship as the plaintiff, thus destroying the necessary complete diversity. The express companies enjoyed this benefit for some time.

sions unable to incorporate. The statutes gives a number of corporate characteristics but qualify them with traditional professional patterns of licensing and of relationships with clients or patients. The tax authorities have resisted corporate status for professionals, and the tax efficacy of the association and corporation laws is still in doubt.

(a) Tax Context

In the early 1960's, some thirty states passed laws authorizing professional associations or professional corporations.[31] This extraordinary development—probably the greatest burst of legislative activity in the history of business associations—was part of a long struggle by professional men (principally doctors) for tax benefits available to employees.[32] The desired benefits were primarily [33] deferred compensation via qualified pension and profit sharing plans, which permit funds to be set aside without tax to the employee (but with a deduction for the employer), to be invested without tax before distribution on the income or appreciation, and, under appropriate circumstances, to be distributed to the employee at lower capital gain tax rates.[34] Shareholder-officer-directors of corporations are eligible for such benefits, subject to general bars on discrimination in their favor and against lower employees.

But such benefits were unavailable to most professionals: [35] doctors, lawyers, accountants, etc. As sole proprietors or practitioners, they were clearly nobody's employees. As partners, in the long-standing opinion of the Internal Revenue Service, they were not employees either.[36] These were basically the only organizational forms in which they could practice, since incorporation was forbidden by licensing laws or professional tradition.

31. Statutes are collected currently in the CCH annotation to Int.Rev.Code of 1954, § 7701 (26 U.S.C.A.); the latest at this writing is 6 CCH Stand. Fed.Tax.Rep. par. 5943.0973 (1967). Law review coverage has been too extensive to cite in full; perhaps the best are Scallen, Federal Income Taxation of Professional Associations and Corporations, 49 Minn.L.Rev. 603 (1965) (listing references at 605 n. 6); Bittker, Professional Associations and Federal Income Taxation: Some Questions and Comments, 17 Tax L.Rev. 1 (1961); Grayck, Professional Associations and the Kintner Regulations: Some Answers, More Questions, and Further Comments, 17 Tax.L.Rev. 469 (1962); Comment, 16 Sw.L.J. 462 (1962) (tabulating statutory provisions on continuity, centralization, transferability and liability); Note, 75 Harv. L.Rev. 776 (1962).

32. Historically, the professional has been an independent contractor, and has fought to remain such.

33. For others, see Int.Rev.Code of 1954, §§ 79, 101(b), 104–06, 119 (26 U.S.C.A.), Sec. 23B(i) n. 83 above.

34. Id. §§ 401–04. Estate tax exemption is also available, id. § 2039(c).

35. Whether they are really worth the price of corporate taxation, with its many bothersome features, is a serious question which was rarely asked or answered. See Note, Professional Corporations and Associations, 75 Harv. L.Rev. 776, 790–92, 794 (1962). More generally, see Strecker, When Will the Corporate Form Save Taxes?, 18 Vand. L.Rev. 1695 (1965).

36. Rev.Rul. 65–178, Part 2(j) (1), 1965–2 Cum.Bull. 94, 102; I.T. 3350, 1940–1 Cum.Bull. 64.

Taking advantage of the Internal Revenue Code's broad definition of corporation [37] which includes association, some enterprising doctors formed (and agreed to be employees of) associations which, by contract, had most of the characteristics identified by the courts as corporate in earlier litigation subjecting unwilling associations to corporate tax.[38] The doctors were successful, at least in the short run, in turning the tables on the government.[39] The government countered with Regulations which relied heavily on local law characteristics and stated that most unincorporated associations (particularly those under U.P.A. and U.L.P.A.) lacked sufficient corporate features to qualify as corporations under the tax laws.[39A] Those conspicuously missing, in its eyes, were continuity of organizational life, centralized management, limited liability, and free transferability of interests—at least three of which would have to be present.

The response was a well organized campaign for state legislation permitting professional organizations with several or all of the necessary attributes. As noted above, many states complied. The laws differ considerably in detail, but are fairly clearly divided into corporation and association patterns. Representatives of each class are discussed in (b) and (c) below.

The statutes had at least a fighting chance of satisfying the then Regulations and achieving corporate tax status. However, they provoked a new set of Regulations [40] which, largely ignoring local law, redefined corporate characteristics so that they were out of reach not only of professional associations but of professional organizations fully incorporated under general laws.[41] There the matter rests at this writing. Much litigation over the validity of the Regulations is probably in the offing. The courts will be called on to choose between the specific but strained Regulations and the rather general case law. One of the issues at stake is the extent to which local law classification and characteristics will determine federal tax results. Another is the essence of corporateness in the tax context.

The events to date have been one of the most convincing examples of how tax law influences business associations law.[42]

---

37. Int.Rev.Code of 1954, § 7701(a) (3) (26 U.S.C.A.).

38. Sec. 24 above.

39. U. S. v. Kintner, 216 F.2d 418 (9th Cir. 1954); Foreman v. U. S., 232 F. Supp. 134 (D.Fla.1964); Galt v. U. S., 175 F.Supp. 360 (N.D.Tex.1959), noted 14 Okla.L.Rev. 99 (1961). The government conceded victory for 1961–64 to those who filed tax returns as corporations. Rev.Proc. 65–27, 1965–2 Cum. Bull. 1017.

39A. Income Tax Reg. § 301.7701–2 (1960).

40. Income Tax Reg. §§ 301.7701–1(c), 301.7701–2(h) (2) (1965).

41. The 1965 revisions (and the whole history of the controversy) are exhaustively discussed in Scallen, Federal Income Taxation of Professional Associations and Corporations, 45 Minn. L.Rev. 603, esp. 694–708 (1965).

42. Bittker, op. cit. supra n. 31, notes the parallel to the adoption of community property statutes by states before income splitting was permitted by the tax Code in 1948. See Sec. 23A(b) above. The professional association

(b) Professional Corporations

About two thirds of the 1960s legislation [43] authorizes the formation of professional corporations, usually subject to the general business corporation statutes to the degree not covered by the professional corporation statutes themselves.[44] However, officers, directors, stockholders and professional employees must be duly licensed to practice.[45] Special provision is made for supervision by the professional regulatory body,[46] which may disqualify the corporation if any of such persons loses his license or engages in unethical professional conduct and is not promptly removed or discharged.[47] The corporate statutes (in contrast to the association variety) usually permit one-man organizations.[48]

Although purporting to create corporations, the statutes shy away from letting an organization call itself a corporation, typically authorizing the name to include such words as "chartered" or "limited;" [49] some flatly prohibit "corporation." [50] Formally, at least, organizations of this type provide centralized management and continuity of life (via the general corporate statutes), modified transferability of interests and partial limited liability.[51] The real extent of management centralization will depend on the rules and traditions of the particular profession [51A] and on the actual operation of the particular organization. Since most professions pride themselves on (and need) the independence of their members in carrying out their activities, they are not too likely to subject themselves to thorough-going control of

and corporation statutes may end similarly in repeal if their objectives are attained in other ways, e. g., by liberalization of deferred compensation benefits for proprietors and partners. A meagre beginning in the Self-Employed Individuals Retirement Act, 76 Stat. 809 (1962) was enhanced by P.L. 89–809, § 204 (1966), both amending parts of Int.Rev.Code of 1954, §§ 401, 404 (26 U.S.C.A.).

43. Scallen, op. cit. supra n. 41, at 607–08 lists 10 states with association statutes and 24 with corporate.

44. E. g., Ill.Rev.Stat.1965 (hereafter "Ill.") c. 32, § 632 (limited to medical; for other professions, associations are authorized, see c. 106½, §§ 101–110); M.C.L.A. (Mich.) § 450.233.

45. Ibid.

46. M.G.L.A. c. 156A (Mass.) §§ 2, 7, 15, 17. For implementation in the case of lawyers, see Re Florida Bar, 133 So. 2d 554, 4 A.L.R.2d 375 (Fla.1965) and authorities collected in Annot., 4 A.L. R.3d 383 (1965).

47. Ill.Rev.Stat.1965, c. 32, § 640. There is also a catch-all provision for disqualification for non-compliance with the Act. F.S.A. § 621.11 makes explicit a matter implicit in some statutes: stock can be transferred only to a licensed professional.

48. C. 32, (Ill.) § 632; M.C.L.A. (Mich.) § 450.224.

49. C. 32, (Ill.) § 634, which also permits "service corporation" or its abbreviation. F.S.A. (Fla.) § 621.12 and M.C. L.A. (Mich.) § 450.231 require "professional corporation" or "professional association" but lets the organization drop the phrase in doing business.

50. F.S.A. (Fla.) § 621.11.

51. F.S.A. (Fla.) § 621.07, similar to association provisions discussed at n. 67 below.

51A. Cf. A.B.A.Comm. on Professional Ethics, Opinion No. 303, 48 A.B.A.J. 159 (1962) cautiously approving law practice in organizations with corporate attributes.

anyone, even a group of their colleagues.[52]   Both continuity of life and transferability of interests are attenuated by provisions designed to prevent fee-splitting.   Thus, a member's interest cannot be transferred to anyone but a licensed professional,[53] and must be relinquished by his estate within a reasonable time after his death.[54]

(c) Professional Associations

The remaining Acts authorize some sort of professional association.   In areas not covered by these Acts, the associations may be subject to the general corporate law [55] or to unspecified general law. In the latter instance, confusion is compounded by occasional statements that the Acts create associations which are distinct from corporations and from partnerships,[56] thus intimating that neither body of general law is applicable.   Except perhaps in such cases, the courts may be expected to use partnership principles to fill the gaps,[57] presuming that corporate laws would have been referenced by the legislatures if intended to operate.   The association statutes resemble the professional corporation statutes in many respects: restriction of participation to licensed professionals,[58] supervision by the professional regulatory body (with related powers of disqualification) [59] continuity of life despite changes in membership,[60] and transferability of interests

---

52. See Note, 75 Harv.L.Rev. 776, 782 (1962).

53. C. 32 (Ill.) § 643. Additional restrictions may be imposed by the organization. F.S.A. (Fla.) § 621.11 requires, in addition, majority stockholder approval of any transfer. M.C. L.A. (Mich.) §§ 450.228, 450.230.

54. C. 32 (Ill.) § 646. N.J.S.A. § 14:19–13 expressly imposes the same requirement on an associate who loses his professional qualifications.

55. Ga.Code (hereafter "Ga.") § 84–4318 (Supp.1966). T.C.A. (Tenn.) § 61–105(3) (Supp.1966) does not affirmatively authorize the creation of professional associations but recognizes them and provides that corporate law is applicable and U.P.A. is inapplicable if they have certain designated corporate characteristics.

56. C. 106½ (Ill.) § 101. Vernon's Ann. Civ.St. (Tex.) art. 6132b, § 6(3) states that professional associations which take certain steps are not subject to U.P.A. Presumably they remain subject to the common law of partnership.

Bromberg, Source and Comments, 17 Tex.Rev.Civ.Stat.Ann. 240–41 (1962).

57. See Sec. 29 above.

58. Ga. §§ 84–4303, 84–4314; c. 106½ (Ill.) § 101.

59. This usually is accomplished by continuing supervision over individuals through the licensing laws, and a requirement that each professional in an association remain licensed. C. 106½ (Ill.) § 105; Ga. § 84–4311.

Inherent judicial jurisdiction over the practice of law is superimposed here as with professional corporations. State ex rel. Green v. Brown, 173 Ohio St. 114, 180 N.E.2d 157 (1962). Some statutes expressly recognize it, c. 106½ (Ill.) § 110.

60. Ga. § 84–4309; c. 106½ (Ill.) § 107. These typically specify that the association shall continue until the expiration of its term, unless dissolved sooner by a designated majority of its members, notwithstanding a member's death, insanity, withdrawal, transfer of interest, etc. Individual members are denied power to dissolve; cf. Sec. 75(a) below.

within the profession (subject to any restrictions imposed by the oganization.)[61]

Usually two or more persons are necessary to create an association. An association can hold title, contract, sue and be sued in its own name as an entity.[62] The name must ordinarily include "association" or some similar word or phrase.[63] There is provision for a centralized management through a board of directors or other governing body,[64] often buttressed by a denial of a mere member's representative capacity to bind the association.[65] Liability sometimes goes unmentioned; [66] more often it is covered by a general statement that no change is intended in the relation between the professional and the client or patient, including liability,[67] and at least one state substantially preserves partnership liability [68] while others deny liability of an associate or members for the acts or obligations of the association or the other associates.[69]

Neither the association nor the corporation statutes have been used or interpreted enough to pass seasoned judgment on them. But it is obvious that they are preoccupied with tax objectives and reflect little thought on the other problems of converting a traditionally non-corporate professional practice into a corporate one.[70]

---

61. Ga. §§ 84–4314, 84–4310; the latter permits either stock or non-stock structures. C. 106½ (Ill.) § 107.

62. Ga. § 84–4316.

63. Ga. § 84–4304; c. 106½ (Ill.) § 103. Cf. 14 P.S. (Pa.) § 197–15 (any name not contrary to law or professional ethics). Pa. professionals may also use the limited partnership association, which was preserved for them when repealed for everyone else; see Sec. 26A above at n. 67.

64. C. 106½ (Ill.) § 108 ("so that centralization of management will be assured"); Va.Code (hereafter "Va.") § 54–882 (1967), which was tightened by a 1966 amendment.

65. Ga. § 84–4308; c. 106½ (Ill.) § 108.

66. C. 106½ (Ill.) §§ 101–110.

67. Ga. § 84–4307; Va. § 54–886. The import of this language is obscure. It may preserve partnership liability; see Bittker, op. cit. supra n. 31 at 8–13; but see Note, 75 Harv.L.Rev. 776, 781 (1962).

68. 14 P.S. (Pa.) § 197–17.

69. Va. § 54–892, imposing liability on the associate for his own acts and those of persons under his direct supervision and control, and liability on the association for acts of associates and employees to the same extent as a corporation. Query whether centralized management requires that all the associates be under the direct supervision and control of the board of directors (or equivalent group), who therefore become personally liable like partners?

70. Cf. Bromberg, Tax Influences on the Law of Business Associations, 16 Bayl. L.Rev. 327, 335–36 (1964).

SUBCHAPTER R (TAX OPTION) PARTNERSHIPS

§ 34B. For a time, certain partnerships were allowed by legislation to elect corporate tax status. In all other respects they remained partnerships.

In deference to the tax aspirations of some businesses (or at least one [70A]) which wanted to be taxed as corporations but were prevented by local law or custom from incorporating, Congress in 1954 gave certain entities an election to be taxed as corporations.[71] However, it withheld the most desired corporate tax attribute: employee status of officer-director-shareholders for deferred compensation purposes.[72] Perhaps for this reason, the provision was little used, and was repealed in 1966, effective partly that year and partly in 1969.[73]

These Subchapter R organizations were, for all local law purposes, genuine partnerships.[74]

SUBCHAPTER S (TAX OPTION) CORPORATIONS

§ 34C. Since 1958 certain corporations have had a statutory election to be taxed like partnerships to the extent that capital gain, ordinary income and losses are passed through to the shareholders pro rata, on a conduit basis, and the firm is not taxed. Corporate double taxation is avoided. In other tax respects, and in all substantive law matters, they are corporations.

The corporate pattern of taxation has its negative side, and is not universally desired by those who incorporate for liability protection or other non-tax reasons. Concern for this group and, more generally, concern over the arbitrary differences between corporate and non-corporate taxation, led Congress in 1958 to permit certain corporations to elect taxation on a system modelled after that of partnerships.[75] However, the resemblance is quite incomplete.[76] The

---

[70A]. See Surrey, The Congress and the Tax Lobbyist—How Special Provisions Get Enacted, 70 Harv.L.Rev. 1145, 1149 n. 4(i) (1957); Cary, Pressure Groups and the Revenue Code: A Requiem in Honor of the Departing Uniformity of the Tax Laws, 68 Harv. L.Rev. 745, 750–51 (1955).

[71]. Int.Rev.Code of 1954, Subch. R, § 1361 (26 U.S.C.A.). Membership was limited to 50; capital had to be a material income producing factor, or 50% of gross income derived from trading in realty, securities or commodities for others. See Bittker & Eustice, Federal Income Taxation of Corporations and Shareholders 45–47 (2d ed. 1966) and references there.

[72]. Int.Rev.Code of 1954, § 1361(d) (26 U.S.C.A.). Professionals were thus not

given what they wanted. see Sec. 34A above, even if they were eligible.

[73]. P.L. 89–389, § 4(a) (1966).

[74]. They might, in theory, also have been sole proprietorships.

[75]. Int.Rev.Code of 1954, Subch. S, §§ 1371–78 (26 U.S.C.A.). See, in general, Bittker & Eustice, Federal Income Taxation of Corporations and Shareholders 709–39 (2d ed. 1966). Other concerns which may enjoy different versions of conduit treatment are regulated investment companies and real estate investment trusts, discussed Sec. 33, at nn. 64–68 above.

[76]. The differences are detailed in Caplin, Subchapter S v. Partnership: A Proposed Legislative Program, 46 Va.L.

conduit principle (on which the entity is not taxed and the partners individually report and pay tax on their shares of each item of partnership income and deduction) is followed (with some modification) for three major classes of items: (A) capital gains, (B) operating losses, and (C) all other income. In addition, as with partnerships, since income is taxed whether or not distributed, there is no tax on distributions from the firm to the shareholders. Hence, double taxation is avoided. In other features, these Subchapter S corporations are taxed as regular corporations.[77]

To be eligible to elect, a corporation can have only one class of stock and no more than 10 stockholders. It must satisfy a number of other requirements, but there are no limits on the size of its income or assets, and, broadly speaking, no limitation on the kind of business it can conduct, except that (after the first two years), a maximum of 20% of its income can be passive (i.e. from investments, as through dividends, interest, royalties and rents).

The rules of Subchapter S are far more technical and full of pitfalls than this short summary can indicate.[78] Nonetheless, it has been quite popular, and some 10% of all corporations are using it.[79]

Most entities electing Subchapter S are formally organized as corporations under state law.[80] Presumably nothing in the election alters that status for local purposes, and they continue to enjoy limited liability and other corporate features.[81]

Rev. 61 (1960). See Dixon et al., Partnerships and Subchapter S: A Comparison of Tax Advantages, N.Y.U. 25th Inst. on Fed.Tax 151–227 (1967).

77. As a corollary, employee benefits (including deferred compensation, see Sec. 34A(a) above) are available to officer-director-shareholders, although their relative value may be offset by having to pay individual tax on all the corporate income. Subchaper S is not the solution for the professionals since it presupposes corporate tax status before the election.

78. See Bittker & Eustice, op. cit. supra, n. 75; Hewitt, Some Intriguing Recent Developments in Subchapter S, 44 Taxes 848 (1966); Hoffman, Let's Go Slow with Tax Option Corporations, 37 Taxes 21 (1959).

79. U. S. Treasury Dept., Internal Revenue Service, Statistics of Income 1962 —Corporation Income Tax Returns 4, Table A (1966).

80. However, any organization taxable as a corporation can elect if it otherwise meets the requirements (which include the one that it be domestic, i. e. U.S.). So it is possible that some unincorporated association (perhaps a business trust or joint stock company, see Secs. 33–34 above) would employ the Subchapter.

81. It is conceivable that a plaintiff seeking to "pierce the corporate veil" (see, generally, Henn, Corporations 203–17 (1961)) may have an easier time if, in addition to other suitable facts, he can argue that the company behaved non-corporately by making the Subchapter S election. The argument might be in terms of diverting a corporate benefit to the shareholders, or in terms of destroying what has probably come to be the most important economic feature of the corporation, its taxation as a separate entity. In the only remotely relevant case so far, corporate creditors in bankruptcy sought to claim for the corporation the value of a tax loss (as a carryback justifying a refund). But the court sustained the sole shareholder as entitled to the loss (and its value) through a proper Subchapter S election. Hauptman v. Director of In-

JOINT VENTURES

§ **35. A joint venture is an association created by co-owners of a business undertaking, differing from partnership (if at all) in having a more limited scope. In all important respects, the joint venture is treated as a partnership.**

A joint venture (JV) or joint adventure is a business association distinguishable from partnership (if at all) only by narrowness of purpose and scope.[82] A partnership may be formed for a single undertaking,[83] but is usually intended to encompass an indefinite number of transactions within a relatively broad line of business for an indefinite duration. Typically, some or all of the partners devote their entire time to the business. A JV is commonly a single undertaking or series of related undertakings, not requiring the entire attention of the participants, and having a fairly short duration. A wide variety of formal and informal financial and business arrangements may be JVs,[84] whether or not the phrase is used by the parties. JVs are com-

---

ternal Revenue, 309 F.2d 62 (2d Cir. 1962), cert. denied 372 U.S. 909, 83 S. Ct. 723, 9 L.Ed.2d 718 (1963). The separate corporate entity was not considered eroded in any way by the election

82. In general, see Comment, Joint Adventures—The Sharing of Losses Dilemma, 18 U.Miami L.Rev. 429 (1963); Jaeger, Partnership of Joint Venture? 37 Notre Dame Law. 138 (1961); Jaeger, Joint Ventures: Organization, Nature and Development, 9 Am.U.L.Rev. 1 (1960); Jaeger, Joint Ventures: Membership, Types and Termination, 9 Am.U.L.Rev. 111 (1960); Taubman, What Constitutes a Joint Venture, 41 Cornell L.Q. 640 (1956); Nichols, Joint Ventures, 36 Va.L.Rev. 425 (1950); Comment, The Joint Venture: Problem Child of Partnership, 38 Calif.L.Rev. 860 (1950); Comment, Joint Venture or Partnership, 18 Fordham L.Rev. 114 (1949); Mechem, The Law of Joint Adventures, 15 Minn.L.Rev. 644 (1931).

Jaeger and, to a lesser degree, Taubman argue that the JV should not be treated as a species of partnership. Taubman at 649–55 lists practical characteristics which tend to distinguish it, e. g., mobility of association and diversity of factual patterns.

83. Cornelius v. Holland, 102 Cal.App. 136, 282 P.2d 539 (1929); Tiedeck v. Pedrick, 122 N.J.Eq. 20, 191 A. 751 (1937).

84. JV examples include:

Real estate speculation, Adams v. Bruce, 265 Mich. 137, 251 N.W. 328 (1934); Saunders v. McDonough, 191 Ala. 119, 67 So. 591 (1914); Fitzhugh v. Thode, 221 Iowa 533, 265 N.W. 893 (1936); Cecil v. Montgomery, 95 Okl. 184, 218 P. 311 (1923).

Subdivision and sale of real estate, Fishback v. U. S., 215 F.Supp. 621 (D.C. S.D.1963). By agreement with landowner, real estate agent advanced funds for improvement and subdivision, and sold lots. Proceeds were allocated to pay landowner $400 per lot, to reimburse him for certain earlier improvements, and to reimburse the agent for funds advanced; any surplus was to be divided equally between them. Held: landowner not entitled to capital gain on $400 per lot; land passed to joint venture created by them, and was held primarily for sale to customers.

Production of a play, Selwyn & Co. v. Waller, 212 N.Y. 507, 106 N.E. 321, L.R.A.1915B, 160 (1914).

Co-authorship of a play, Losch v. Marcin, 251 N.Y. 402, 167 N.E. 514 (1929).

Building construction, Zech v. Bell, 94 Wash. 344, 162 P. 363 (1917).

Purchase, holding and sale of bank stock, Chisholm v. Gilmer, 81 F.2d 120 (4th Cir. 1936), aff'd 299 U.S. 99, 57 S.Ct. 65, 81 L.Ed. 63 (1936).

monly used to carry out a single transaction (such as constructing a single building) or to develop and lease or sell a particular property. The participants may number in the dozens or hundreds when they are mainly suppliers of capital, or there may be only two. There is no easy dividing line between JV and partnership, whether the question is to classify the operation or to find the consequences of its classification one way or the other.[84A] If anything, a court is more likely to find a JV than a partnership when a plaintiff tries to enforce vicarious liability on a member of a loose group with which he dealt.

As in partnership, there is confusion about the essential elements, similarly attributable to the effort to do equity in a variety of situations. Sometimes an outsider is urging the existence of the relation in order to find a solvent defendant he can hold liable. Other times the dispute is among the alleged venturers themselves, one claiming

Acquiring, financing and operating utility projects by banking firms, Smith, Landeryou & Co. v. Hollingsworth, 218 Iowa 920, 251 N.W. 749 (1934).

Association of fighter and manager, Safro v. Lakofsky, 191 Minn. 532, 255 N.W. 94 (1934).

Cotton hauling, Garner v. Maxwell, 50 Tenn.App. 157, 360 S.W.2d 64 (1962). Truck-tractor owner, trailer owner, driver and person named on bill of lading for cotton all shared profits and were held liable for compensatory and punitive damages to driver injured by running into truck which was left parked on highway at night without lights or warning devices required by statute. The terms of the relationship are not discussed in the opinion beyond the statement of profit-sharing. In tort cases, especially those involving vehicles, JV edges over into joint enterprise which includes some non-business activities as well. See Prosser, Torts § 71 (3d ed. 1964), Restatement, Second, Torts § 491.

Construction and operation of a uranium mill, Homestake Mining Co. v. Mid-Continent Exploration Co., 282 F.2d 787 (10th Cir. 1960).

Jaeger, Joint Ventures: Membership, Types and Termination, 9 Am.U.L.Rev. 111, 117–27 (1960) exhaustively lists the kinds of enterprises which have appeared in JV litigation.

See also Butler v. Attwood, 369 F.2d 811 (6th Cir. 1966) (Mich. law) recognizing the enforceability of an agreement for 50–50 acquisition by two persons of all stock in a closely held corporation which might become available. The court does not describe it as a JV, although it might be so regarded.

84A. "It is sometimes a difficult question whether a transaction constitutes a partnership or just a joint adventure. One of the principal distinctions between a partnership and a joint adventure lies in the fact that a partnership, ordinarily, is formed for the transaction of a general business of a particular kind, while a joint adventure relates to a single transaction of a particular kind, though it may continue for years. There are other more important distinctions, viz., a partner acts as a principal for himself and as agent for his copartners in the transaction of the partnership business, whereas, in a joint adventure, no one of the parties thereto can bind the joint adventure. On the other hand, the resemblance between a partnership and a joint adventure is so close that the rights, as between the adventurers, are practically governed by the same rules that govern partnerships. Accordingly, a joint adventurer has a right to, and may sue for an accounting of profits, in accordance with the agreement therefor, and the obligations growing out of the agreement between the parties are governed by the same rules of law applicable to partnerships." Tufts v. Mann, 116 Cal.App. 170, 2 P.2d 500 (1931) (JV for sale of real estate). The statement about a venturer's inability to bind seems wrong; see below at n. 97.

a right to profits or property in the hands of another, or to contribution for losses incurred by him. Speaking generally, a JV, like a partnership, requires a business purpose as distinct from a social one,[85] or from an incidental economic benefit. For example, an effort to enforce a zoning law, joined in by several property owners, resulting in a settlement and payment of damages, is not a JV for the purpose of requiring an equal division of the funds received.[86] There must be co-ownership of the enterprise, as distinguished from a principal and agent relation,[87] and probably a degree of common control (although this may be unimportant where one person is conducting the entire activity with others as investors). There must be an intention to submit the capital investment (if any) of each associate to the risks of the enterprise, as distinguished from a loan to be returned absolutely.[88] The sharing of profits is presumptive of joint venture, but not conclusive, as for partnership.[89] No express agreement to share losses

85. Krause v. Hall, 195 Wis. 565, 217 N.W. 290 (1928). On the broader view taken in automobile cases, see comment following Garner v. Maxwell, n. 84 above.

86. Sappenfield v. Mead, 338 Ill.App. 236, 87 N.E.2d 220 (1949).

87. Ross v. Burrage, 233 Mass. 439, 124 N.E. 267 (1919) (employer had no fiduciary duty to disclose as he would in a JV).

Foster v. Parker, 282 App.Div. 766, 122 N.Y.S.2d 748 (1953), aff'd 2 N.Y.2d 848, 159 N.Y.S.2d 985, 140 N.E.2d 876 (1957). An inventor agreed to pay a patent attorney 50% of the profits from an invention realized through arrangements negotiated by the attorney. This transferred no proprietary interest in the invention and created no JV or partnership. Accordingly, the inventor had no duty, in terminating the agreement, to disclose that he had obtained $20,000 by his own efforts from a prospect with whom the attorney was authorized to negotiate.

Custis v. Serrill, 321 Pa. 154, 183 A. 774 (1936).

Chapman v. Dwyer, 40 F.2d 468 (2d Cir. 1930). Arrangement between attorneys for mutual assistance in certain cases held not to show intent to enter a JV so that accounting in equity (as distinct from law action for compensation) would be maintainable.

The essentials of a JV have been said to be at least (a) community of interest in the object of the undertaking, (b) equal right to direct and govern the conduct of each other therein, (c) share in loss, (d) close and even fiduciary relation. Beck v. Cagle, 46 Cal.App.2d 152, 115 P.2d 613 (1941). Some of these elements are consequences rather than prerequisites. Another judicial formulation and extended discussion is Ford v. McCue, 163 Ohio St. 498, 127 N.E.2d 209 (1955) (owner of truck and bakery route not in JV with one who took them over for several weeks during his vacation; no sharing of receipts or expenses, no control). Cf. Zorich v. Petroff, 152 Cal.App.2d 806, 313 P.2d 118 (1957) (no JV for production of film; plaintiff, by agreement, was to be associate producer and share profits but did not assume financial risks or have right of control, hence he had no property interest in the film).

88. Treat v. Murdock, 55 P.2d 547 (Cal. App.1936); Waldman v. Shoemaker, 367 Pa. 587, 80 A.2d 776 (1951) (P lent $18,000 to operator of turkey raising project and was to receive share of profits; held: P entitled to repayment of loan though project was unsuccessful; Ds retained sole title to turkeys, eggs and proceeds of sale; Ps had no voice in control; no express or implied agreement to share losses).

89. See Garner v. Maxwell, n. 84 above and, generally, U.P.A. § 7, Secs. 14–20 above. Mere royalty payments or commissions are not enough, Nizuk v. Gorges, 180 Cal.App.2d 699, 4 Cal.Rptr. 565 (1960) (furniture store with franchised thrift plan paid franchiser fix-

seems necessary, since this will be a consequence if the JV exists.[90] And no express agreement to form a JV is requisite; the relation may be inferred from conduct.[91] A JV may exist by estoppel, when one holds himself out as a joint venturer or consents to another's doing so.[92]

Whether a JV is considered a partnership or merely analogized to one, the venturers are governed by the rules applicable to partners.[93] The U.P.A. applies, e. g., to the results of wrongful dissolution.[94] There are the usual fiduciary duties to account for profits and joint property,[95] although the more limited purpose and part-time

ed fee per member and fixed percentage of gross sales to members); Bates v. Simpson, 121 Utah 165, 239 P.2d 749 (1952) (used car dealers operating on same lot and sharing expenses; each received $25 for selling a car belonging to the other, and a commission for arranging any financing).

90. The conflict and confusion on this point are traced in Comment, Joint Adventures—The Sharing of Losses Dilemma, 18 U.Miami L.Rev. 429 (1963).

Of course, within the firm, an agreement (express or implied) for one member to bear all the losses is binding. Allison v. Dilsaver, 387 S.W.2d 206 (Mo. App.1965).

91. Ditscher v. Booth, 13 N.J.Super. 568, 80 A.2d 648 (1951); Stein v. George B. Spearin, Inc., 120 N.J.Eq. 169, 184 A. 436, 437 (1936); Ditis v. Ahlvin Const. Co., 408 Ill. 416, 97 N.E.2d 244 (1951).

A husband-wife relationship in operating a household is said to be not the result of contract but of status under which he must provide her with a home. Accordingly, it is not a JV, and he is not responsible for her negligent performance of household chores injuring a third person. State ex rel. McCrory v. Bland, 355 Mo. 706, 197 S.W.2d 669, 168 A.L.R. 929 (1946). Cf. Lemon v. Lonker, 97 Pa.Super. 240 (1929).

92. John's, Inc. v. Long Island Garden Center of Nassau, Inc., 49 Misc.2d 1086, 269 N.Y.S.2d 231 (Dist.Ct.1966). See Garrison v. Place, 92 Ohio App. 239, 109 N.E.2d 569 (1952). See generally Sec. 36 below.

93. Few v. Few, 239 S.C. 321, 122 S.E. 2d 829 (1962). See Homestake Mining Co. v. Mid-Continent Exploration Co.,

282 F.2d 787 (10th Cir.1960) (N.M. law) (this limited partnership could be more accurately described as several JVs among subgroups of its members, but same fiduciary duties apply either way).

The assignment of an interest in a JV is similar to that in partnership. Meinhard v. Salmon, n. 95 below.

Comment, 18 Fordham L.Rev. 114 (1949) suggests that tenancy in partnership (U.P.A. § 25, Secs. 40–45 below) should not be applied to JVs. But see Comment, 38 Calif.L.Rev. 860 (1950).

94. Zeibak v. Nasser, 12 Cal.2d 1, 82 P. 2d 375 (1938). Although a JV's purpose has not been accomplished, a member has power to dissolve, exposing himself to liability for breach of contract. See Comment, 38 Calif. L.Rev. 860, 868 (1950).

A JV without a fixed term can be ended without liability by any party at any time. Harrington v. Sorelle, 313 F.2d 10 (10th Cir.1963) (N.M. law).

See also Annot., Rights in profits earned by partnership or joint adventure after death or dissolution, 55 A.L.R.2d 1391 (1957).

95. Homestake Mining Co. v. Mid-Continent Exploration Co., n. 93 above; Allen v. Steinberg, 244 Md. 119, 223 A.2d 240 (1966).

Smith, Landeryou & Co. v. Hollingsworth, 218 Iowa 920, 251 N.W. 749 (1934); Mendelsohn v. Leather Mfg. Corp., 326 Mass. 226, 93 N.E.2d 537 (1950) (one venturer buying out interest of the other); Johnson v. Ironside, 249 Mich. 35, 227 N.W. 732 (1929) (dealings in property within scope of JV); Selwyn & Co. v. Waller, 212 N.Y. 507, 106 N.E. 321, L.R.A.1915B, 160 (1914) (joint venturer in play produc-

participation may shrink the area in which non-competition aspects of fiduciary duty are operative.[95A] Quite generally, the agreement among joint venturers has the same central role as in partnership.[96] It fully binds the members, though not ignorant outsiders.

JV members are personally liable for debts, like partners. Each venturer has authority to act and bind within the scope of the business.[97] Such authority is limited to the actual or apparent scope of

tion must disclose that he has share of author's royalties); Losch v. Marcin, 251 N.Y. 402, 167 N.E. 514 (1929); Meinhard v. Salmon, 249 N.Y. 458, 164 N.E. 545, 62 A.L.R. 1 (1928) (JV member accountable for obtaining renewal of leasehold on JV's hotel property; this is perhaps the leading case on fiduciary duties and widely followed in partnership; the opinion is quoted in part, Sec. 68 n. 55 below); R. C. Gluck & Co. v. Tankel, 12 A.D.2d 339, 211 N.Y.S.2d 602 (1961); McIver v. Norman, 187 Or. 516, 213 P.2d 144, 13 A.L.R.2d 749 (1949); Horne v. Holley, 167 Va. 234, 188 S.E. 169 (1936); William Goldstein Co. v. Greenberg, Inc., 352 Pa. 259, 42 A.2d 551 (1945).

See also Air Technology Corp. v. General Electric Co., 347 Mass. 613, 199 N.E.2d 538 (1964), involving a "team" proposal to the Air Force for a prime contract for complex scientific equipment. No JV resulted, for reasons including: P was to be only a subcontractor if D got the prime contract, P was not to share in profits of the prime contract, and P would have no control over performance of the prime contract. Nonetheless, the court viewed the arrangement as "a more limited joint undertaking" with duties which D breached by not pressing for inclusion of P as a subcontractor and by competing with P in the area for which it was to be subcontractor.

As in ordinary partnership, illegality of the undertaking may preclude judicial relief. Ciampittiello v. Campitello, 134 Conn. 51, 54 A.2d 669 (1949) (forum state's anti-gambling policy barred recovery of JV horserace winnings which were legal where made), criticized 6A Corbin, Contracts § 1530 n. 85 (1962). See Sec. 21 above and cases collected, Annot., Right of partner or joint adventurer when firm business or transactions are illegal, 32 A.L.R.2d 1345 (1953).

95A. See Homestake Mining Co. v. Mid-Continent Exploration Co., n. 93 above, finding no usurpation of "partnership opportunity" in one partner's building a uranium mill similar to the firm's. In a general partnership the result might well have been different. Members entering a JV of narrow scope may impliedly waive some of the non-competitive phases of fiduciary duty, although the court in Homestake did not employ this theory.

96. If the existence of a JV depends entirely on the effect of a written agreement, it must be sufficiently definite and complete in its terms to be a valid contract in general. Mason v. Rose, 176 F.2d 486 (2d Cir. 1949), noted 18 Geo.Wash.L.Rev. 559, 48 Mich.L.Rev. 701 (1950), 1950 U.Ill. L.F. 136 (actor-movie producer contract incomplete). A very sketchy agreement that "any future purchase of stock shall be made on a 50-50 basis" was recognized as valid and enforceable, without calling it a JV, in Butler v. Attwood, 369 F.2d 811 (6th Cir. 1966) (Mich. law).

97. Bushman Const. Co. v. Air Force Academy Housing, Inc., 327 F.2d 481 (10th Cir. 1964) Colo. law) (payment and lien waiver certificates in construction subcontracting JV); Foote v. Posey, 164 Cal.App.2d 210, 330 P.2d 651 (1958) (note and mortgage in real estate JV); Deicher v. Corkery, 205 Cal.App.2d 654, 23 Cal.Rptr. 270 (1962) (agreement with selling agent to reimburse him for crediting part of his commission against sale price in order to avoid revision of escrow documents when acreage discrepancy discovered; real estate JV); Bond v. O'Donnell, 205 Iowa 902, 218 N.W. 898, 63 A.L.R. 901 (1928); Daily v. Scott, 74 S.W.2d 881 (Mo.App.1934) (collection of JV debt); Keiswetter v. Rubenstein, 235 Mich. 36, 209 N.W. 154, 48 A.L.R. 1049 (1926) (tort within

the venture. The usual narrow purpose puts constraints on actual authority and, to a lesser extent, on apparent authority. Agreements to limit authority further are affective only among members and against third parties with notice.[97A] It is a great mistake to think (as some businessmen do) that a joint venture offers significant protection from liability).

A joint venturer may have an accounting in equity.[98] This remedy is not always exclusive, and he may be allowed a suit at law for delivery of joint property or contribution to expenses incurred.[99] But, as in partnership, if there are many transactions and the financial relations are complicated, component claims will not be passed on piecemeal by the courts, and an accounting is necessary.[1]

If not considered technically a partnership, a group of joint venturers could not be adjudicated bankrupt as a single entity. Rules of creditor priority in joint and separate property[2] would not apply. But, in the many states where JVs are deemed partnerships, there is no reason why they should not be so treated in bankruptcy.[3]

Where JVs are distinguished from partnerships, they are likely to be accorded less entity status. Even so, there is recognition of an equivalent of the partners' equities doctrine at common law.[4]

While the death of a joint venturer will normally bring about a technical dissolution, the typical limited objective of the firm makes it easier to find an implied agreement that the objective be carried out,

scope of JV); State ex rel. Crane Co. v. Stokke, 65 S.D. 207, 272 N.W. 811, 110 A.L.R. 761 (1937); Burton-Lingo Co. v. Federal Glass & Paint Co., 54 S.W.2d 170 (Tex.Civ.App.1932); Manatee Loan & Mortgage Co. v. Manley's Estate, 106 Vt. 356, 175 A. 14 (1934) (members liable on purchase money note for JV land, but not on clause in note for attorney's fee in event of default).

N.Y. courts tend to confine a member's authority closely to what is necessary to carry on the particular venture. Jones v. Gould, 209 N.Y. 419, 103 N.E. 720 (1913).

See Note, 33 Harv.L.Rev. 852, 854 (1920) distinguishing JV from partnership on the ground that in partnership there is an entity of which partners are the agents, but in JV there is no entity, and mutual agency must be proved.

97A. Taylor v. Brindley, 164 F.2d 235 (10th Cir. 1947) (Okl. law; constructive knowledge of limitation from instrument recorded in chain of title).

98. Saunders v. McDonough, 191 Ala. 119, 67 So. 591 (1914); Butler v. Union Trust Co., 178 Cal. 195, 172 P. 601 (1918); Waldo Lumber Co. v. Metcalf, 132 Me. 374, 171 A. 395 (1934); Adams v. Bruce, 265 Mich. 137, 251 N.W. 328 (1934). See generally Sec. 72 below.

99. Clark v. Sidway, 142 U.S. 682, 12 S.Ct. 327, 35 L.Ed. 1157 (1892); Brudvik v. Frosaker Blaisdell Co., 56 N.D. 215, 216 N.W. 891 (1927); Cecil v. Montgomery, 95 Okl. 184, 218 P. 311 (1923); Kingsley Clothing Mfg. Co. v. Jacobs, 344 Pa. 551, 26 A.2d 315 (1942).

1. See Sec. 69 below.

2. See Sec. 93–94 below.

3. Despite federal pre-emption of bankruptcy, local law determines what is a partnership for bankruptcy purposes. Sec. 91B(a) below.

4. Twyford v. Sonken-Galamba Corp., 177 Okl. 486, 60 P.2d 1050 (1936) (venturer's mortgage of his interest held subject to co-venturer's equities). On partners' equities, see Sec. 43(a) below.

and the firm continued by the survivors. Such a conclusion is strengthened if the survivor was given powers of representation by the original agreement,[5] or if there are a number of venturers and they have agreed that the majority can make decisions [6] and take action. If the firm is to be wound up, the job should, as in partnership,[7] devolve on the survivors.[7A]

A JV is a partnership for income tax purposes.[8] In particular, profits are taxable to the members as earned, whether or not distributed.[9]

Where corporations are not permitted to be partners, the JV takes on added significance since corporations may nonetheless enter JVs.[10] The distinction is made that a JV involves less delegation of managerial authority of the board of directors.[11] Corporate joint ventures are now often themselves incorporated, so that the vehicle is technically a commonly-owned subsidiary rather than a JV.[12]

While JV interests are sometimes said not to be securities subject to the blue sky laws,[13] this view depends on some practical equality among participants,[14] and the supposed protection afforded by fiduciary duties. Since these tend to disappear with increasing size of the membership, there is good reason to regard publicly offered JV interests as securities and to compel compliance with the laws applicable to corporate and other interests.[15]

---

5. Pownall v. Cearfoss, 129 W.Va. 487, 40 S.E.2d 886 (1946). If the decedent was to participate personally in the venture, his death should dissolve. Roberts v. Weiner, 137 Conn. 668, 81 A.2d 115 (1951).

6. Harmon v. Martin, 395 Ill. 595, 71 N. E.2d 74 (1947).

7. Sec. 83 below.

7A. Roberts v. Weiner, n. 5 above. But see Pfingstl v. Solomon, 240 Ala. 58, 197 So. 12 (1940).

8. Int.Rev.Code of 1954, § 761(a) (26 U.S.C.A.).

9. First Mechanics Bank v. Commissioner, 91 F.2d 275 (3d Cir. 1937).

10. For the resulting tax problems, see Winger, Joint Ventures with Corporate Participants, N.Y.U. 22d Inst. on Fed. Tax 611 (1964).

11. See Sec. 9 above.

12. See Note, Joint Venture Corporations: Drafting the Corporate Papers, 78 Harv.L.Rev. 393 (1964); Adkins et al., Corporate Joint Ventures in Action, 41 Bus.Law. 285 (1959); Berle,

Developments in the Pattern of Corporate Joint Enterprises, 14 Bus.Law. 309 (1959).

13. Brown v. Cole, 155 Tex. 624, 291 S. W.2d 704, 59 A.L.R.2d 1011 (1956).

14. Hill, Pitfalls in the Texas Securities Act, 10 Sw.L.J. 265 (1956); Polikoff v. Levy, 55 Ill.App.2d 229, 204 N.E.2d 807 (1965), cert. denied 382 U.S. 903, 86 S.Ct. 237, 15 L.Ed.2d 156 (1965).

15. West's Ann.Cal.Corp.Code, § 25100 (m) so mandates by exempting JV interests (like general and limited partnership interests, id. (*l*)) only if not sold to the public. See Jahn, When Is a Security a Security?, 40 L.A. B.Bull. 75 (1964). Mich.Comp.L.1948 § 451.105(j) was similar but set a maximum of 25 associates. It was repealed in 1964 in favor of a small offering exemption covering all types of issuers (see M.C.L.A. § 451.802(b) (9)). The Calif. and Mich. statutes reflect earlier decisions that JV interests are not securities. See Loss & Cowett, Blue Sky Law 371 (1958).

There is no federal securities exemption for JVs, and they must be registered if sold to the public.

PARTNER BY ESTOPPEL

§ 36.   (1) When a person, by words spoken or written or by conduct, represents himself, or consents to another representing him to any one, as a partner in an existing partnership or with one or more persons not actual partners, he is liable to any such person to whom such representation has been made, who has, on the faith of such representation, given credit to the actual or apparent partnership, and if he has made such representation or consented to its being made in a public manner he is liable to such person, whether the representation has or has not been made or communicated to such person so giving credit by or with the knowledge of the apparent partner making the representation or consenting to its being made.

> (a) When a partnership liability results, he is liable as though he were an actual member of the partnership.

> (b) When no partnership liability results, he is liable jointly with the other persons, if any, so consenting to the contract or representation so as to incur liability, otherwise separately.

(2) When a person has been thus represented to be a partner in an existing partnership, or with one or more persons not actual partners, he is an agent of the persons consenting to such representation to bind them to the same extent and in the same manner, as though he were a partner in fact, with respect to persons who rely upon the representation. Where all the members of the existing partnership consent to the representation, a partnership act or obligation results; but in all other cases it is the joint act or obligation of the person acting and the persons consenting to the representation.   U.P.A. § 16.

Partnership by estoppel is not a form of business association. Rather, it is a technique for fixing liability on one who has let it appear that he is in a business association.   It is not a voluntary arrangement, except in the sense that the alleged partner acted voluntarily when he did whatever it was that precipitates the liability.

There are many ways in which a non-partner may be held out as a partner in a proprietorship or partnership,[16] for example, by his name forming part of the firm name (or appearing on signs, letterheads, advertisements or other lists of partners) or simply by being referred to, by himself or by persons in the business, as a partner.[17]

---

16. Cf. U.P.A. § 16(1) and pars. (a), (b) thereof.

17. The representation may be of the forthright, "I am a partner" type, in which case there is little to argue about.   For examples, see Branscome v. Schoneweis, 361 F.2d 717 (7th Cir. 1966) (Ill. law); Lazarus v. Goodman, 412 Pa. 442, 195 A.2d 90 (1963); Buehner Block Co. v. Glezos, 6 Utah 2d 226, 310 P.2d 517 (1957).

Or the representation may be ambiguous, as in Hunter v. Croysdill, 169 Cal.App.2d 307, 337 P.2d 174 (1959).

Here D (the alleged partner) wrote the plaintiff manufacturer describing the advantages that "the association" of himself and C would provide as a distributorship, and emphasized that "business and financial guidance" would be in D's hands, while C would handle promotion and sales.   The letter avoided describing the form of association, except to say that it would have a separate identity.   D also visited the manufacturer's home office for several days and stated he would be the financial backer of the distributorship.   The business was

Principles of estoppel and apparent authority [18] naturally come into play if the alleged partner has participated in or consented to the representation.[19] The result is personal liability for the ostensible partner.[20] If the representation is privately made, it may be taken advantage of only by persons to whom it was made; [21] if it was publicly made, anyone (roughly speaking) can make use of it.[22] However, in

formally set up as C's sole proprietorship, but D was held liable, under U.P.A. § 16(1), for goods sold by the manufacturer. The trial court's finding that D had represented himself as a partner was affirmed. C's statement that D would be his partner was not binding, but was admissible as corroboration.

See also Clay v. Sandal, 369 P.2d 890 (Alaska 1962) (defendant left ex-husband in charge for 6 months; liquor license was in both their names).

But the filing of an assumed name certificate showing D as one of the persons conducting and composing a business, without identifying him as a limited partner, was not a representation that he was a general partner. J. C. Wattenbarger & Sons v. Sanders, 216 Cal.App.2d 495, 30 Cal. Rptr. 910 (1963). The proposition is questionable. Elsewhere, the filing of an assumed name or similar certificate constitutes not only a representation of partnership but one made in a public manner (see below at n. 22). West Side Trust Co. v. Gascoigne, 39 N.J.Super. 467, 121 A.2d 441 (1956).

Representation may occur by signing checks or notes for the alleged firm. Branscome v. Schoneweis, 361 F.2d 717 (7th Cir. 1966) (Ill. law); Gustafson v. Taber, 125 Mont. 225, 234 P.2d 471 (1951).

Representation need not name the ostensible partner if he is adequately identifiable. Thus the owner of "The Jacqueline Shop," who dealt personally only in dresses, was liable for shoes sold to Jones who sold shoes on the same premises without any distinction of name. Shoes were advertised in the Shop's ads and were invoiced and shipped to the Shop without protest from the owner who must have known of the practice because of access to the mail. Boone v. General Shoe Corp., 219 Ark. 340, 242 S.W.2d 138 (1951), noted 6 Ark. L.Rev. 63 (1951–52).

18. Boone v. General Shoe Corp., n. 17 above, found liability as partner or principal, without need to decide which relation was created.

19. X's representation that Y is his partner does not bind Y if he is unaware of it and does not consent. Bates v. Simpson, 121 Utah 165, 239 P.2d 749 (1952). See U. S. v. Coson, 286 F.2d 453 (10th Cir. 1961) (Nev. law) (no estoppel by listing one as a partner on a tax return without his knowledge or consent).

U.P.A. § 4(2) broadly preserves in partnership the law of estoppel.

A comprehensive analysis is Painter, Partnership by Estoppel, 16 Vand.L. Rev. 327 (1963). He particularly notes the problems of the retiring partner who is potentially subject to liability under U.P.A. § 35, Sec. 81 below, as well as under § 16, discussed here. See also Comment, Partnerships—Continuing Liability of a Partner Receiving Payments, 20 Sw.L.J. 151 (1966), and Secs. 18, 20 above.

For a general treatment in a non-U.P.A. state, see Note, Partnership by Estoppel, 13 Drake L.Rev. 87 (1963).

20. U.P.A. § 16(1).

Triangle Machine Co. v. Dutton & Adams, 13 La.App. 14, 127 So. 54 (1930); Speer v. Bishop, 24 Ohio St. 598 (1874); Fletcher American Nat. Bank v. Wells, 282 Pa. 164, 127 A. 468 (1925); International Harvester Co. v. Graber, 59 S.D. 601, 241 N.W. 726 (1932); Hobbs v. Virginia Nat. Bank, 147 Va. 802, 128 S.E. 46, 133 S.E. 595 (1926).

21. U.P.A. § 16(1). See Warner v. Modano, 340 Mass. 439, 164 N.E.2d 904 (1960) (no liability to persons unaware of representations; trial court found publicly made but appellate court disagreed).

22. U.P.A. § 16(1). The line between public and private representations is inevitably blurred. Appellate courts

either case, it appears that the person seeking to enforce liability must show that he relied on the representation.[23] This means it must have come to his attention in some way;[24] the particular way need not have been with the ostensible partner's consent so long as he made or consented to some sort of public representation.[25]

It is a disputed question whether consent is inferrible from knowledge and failure to contradict a representation made by someone

have tended to require more dissemination than trial courts. See Warner v. Modano, n. 21 above; Gilbert v. Howard, n. 25 below. A representation in a publicly filed document, like an assumed name certificate, is likely to be considered publicly made; see n. 17, 4th par., above. So is an application for a license and display of the latter on the premises. Brown & Bigelow v. Roy, 132 N.E.2d 755 (Ohio App.1955), noted 45 Ky.L.J. 553 (1957).

In Brown & Bigelow, the court, by a dubious reading of U.P.A. § 16(1), excused the third party from any need to know or rely on the representation. The Act seems to make it immaterial whether the ostensible partner knows of the transmission of the representation, once it is publicly made. But the phrase "such person" as a back reference in § 16(1), suggests strongly that the third person must have acted on the faith of the representation in giving credit. See Painter, op. cit. supra n. 19 at 338–39.

23. U.P.A. § 16(1): "on the faith of such representation [gave] credit to the actual or apparent partnership." See the last par. of the preceding note.

Presumably the reliance must be reasonable. The character, scope and proof of the reliance are all troublesome. See Painter, op. cit. supra n. 19 at 332–35; Morgan v. Farrel, 58 Conn. 413, 20 A. 614, 18 Am.St.Rep. 282 (1890) (third person must act in reliance on representation, in good faith with due diligence). See Swantner v. Meek, 77 F.2d 822 (5th Cir. 1935) (bank not allowed to recover against clerk it knew to be only an ostensible partner). Cf. Merchants' Nat. Bank v. Wehrmann, 69 Ohio St. 160, 68 N.E. 1004 (1903) (third persons, charged with knowledge that national bank cannot be a partner, could not legally rely on its holding out as such).

The third person need rely only on the existence of the partnership, not on

the financial condition of the apparent partner. Hunter v. Croysdill, n. 17 above (only casual credit inquiries made).

Some courts stress the detrimental element in the reliance. Active Co. v. Slate, 10 Wis.2d 340, 103 N.W.2d 46 (1960); Wisconsin Telephone Co. v. Lehmann, 274 Wis. 331, 80 N.W.2d 267 (1957), noted 56 Mich.L.Rev. 139 (1957). In both cases there were prior dealings which would apparently have continued on the same basis without the advent of the ostensible partner.

Sometime the reliance requirement is imposed without using the word "reliance." West Side Trust Co. v. Gascoigne, n. 17 above (no liability where third person is aware of facts [here an incomplete financial statement, not signed by the alleged partner] which call for inquiry into the verity of the representation, and fails to make a reasonable investigation).

24. Orofino Rochdale Co. v. Fred A. Shore Lumber Co., 43 Idaho 425, 252 P. 487 (1927); Eastern Electric Supply Co. v. Ekdahl Bros., 84 N.H. 339, 150 A. 549, 550 (1930); Denithorne v. Hook, 112 Pa. 240, 3 A. 777 (1886).

See Gilbert v. Howard, n. 25 below (no liability for representation *after* credit granted). Semble, J. C. Wattenbarger & Sons v. Sanders, n. 17 above.

25. U.P.A. § 16(1).

Some older cases presume reliance from a public holding out. Thompson v. First Nat. Bank, 111 U.S. 529, 4 S.Ct. 689, 28 L.Ed. 507 (1884); Webster v. Clark, 34 Fla. 637, 16 So. 601, 27 L.R.A. 126, 43 Am.St.Rep. 217 (1894); Poillon v. Secor, 61 N.Y. 456 (1875). U.P.A. does not say anything explicit on this point, but does not forbid the presumption, though Gilbert v. Howard, 64 N. M. 200, 326 P.2d 1085, 1087 (1958) seems to find in it a waiver of reliance. In any event, reliance almost always is a question of fact.

else. It has been said: "if [one] is held out as a partner and he knows it, he is chargeable as one, unless he does all that a reasonable and honest man should do under similar circumstances, to assert and manifest his refusal, and thereby prevent innocent persons from being misled."[26] A duty to disclaim has been imposed in some cases,[27] particularly if the representation is made in the ostensible partner's presence.[28] Other cases have held that there is no duty to deny false representations, to the making of which one was not a party.[29] U.P.A. is designed to impose liability only if there is consent in fact.[30] In one case, a person represented to be a member of a banking partnership without his consent, did enough to avoid liability when he directed those who published the representation to stop doing so.[30A]

The elements of a partnership by estoppel (such as representation, consent, reliance and reasonableness) are fact questions for the jury if there is one.[31]

In tort cases, liability is imposed only if there is dealing by the third person with the supposed partnership in reliance upon its apparent membership, whereby he exposes himself or his property to the risk of injury.[32] If there is no such reliance before the tort, the

---

26. Parsons, Partnership *134 (3d ed. 1878).

27. Tanner & DeLaney Engine Co. v. Hall, 86 Ala. 305, 5 So. 584 (1889); E. L. Martin & Co. v. A. B. Maggard & Son, 206 Ky. 558, 267 S.W. 1102 (1925); Fletcher v. Pullen, 70 Md. 205, 16 A. 887, 14 Am.St.Rep. 355 (1889); Bivins v. Oldham, 224 S.W. 240 (Tex.Civ.App. 1920).

28. Wirta v. Vergona, 195 Cal.App.2d 365, 15 Cal.Rptr. 804 (1961); Singh v. Kashian, 124 Cal.App.2d Supp. 879, 268 P.2d 768 (1954); Clarke v. Woodward, 76 Ga.App. 181, 45 S.E.2d 473 (1947).

29. Bishop v. Georgeson, 60 Ill. 484 (1871); Standard Oil Co. of New York v. Henderson, 265 Mass. 322, 163 N.E. 743 (1928); Munton v. Rutherford, 121 Mich. 418, 80 N.W. 112 (1899); Hartford Acc. & Indem. Co. v. Oles, 152 Misc. 876, 274 N.Y.S. 349 (1934). See also Wilkerson v. Wood, 81 Ind.App. 248, 143 N.E. 166 (1924).

30. Commissioners' Note to U.P.A. § 16, 7 Unif.Laws Ann. 94–95 (1949); Lewis, The Uniform Partnership Act, 24 Yale L.J. 617, 625 (1915).

Brocato v. Serio, 173 Md. 374, 196 A. 125 (1937), decided after the state's adoption of U.P.A., seems to find

knowledge of holding out sufficient without consent. See Comment, 3 Md. L.Rev. 189 (1939). It was followed by McBriety v. Phillips, 180 Md. 569, 26 A.2d 400 (1942): one knowing he is being held out is liable "unless he does all that a reasonable and honest man would do under similar circumstances to assert his denial." Note, 6 Md.L. Rev. 337 (1942) suggests that the court means failure to contradict under certain circumstances may be evidence of consent to holding out. See Painter, op. cit. supra n. 19 at 330–31.

30A. Anfenson v. Banks, 180 Iowa 1066, 163 N.W. 608, L.R.A.1918D, 482, 505 (1918).

31. Lazarus v. Goodman, 412 Pa. 442, 195 A.2d 90 (1963).

32. Sherrod v. Langdon, 21 Iowa 518 (1866) (deceit in sale of goods); Maxwell v. Gibbs, 32 Iowa 32 (1871) (injury to horse rented to supposed partnership); Cook v. Coleman, 90 W.Va. 748, 111 S.E. 750 (1922) (injury to patient in hospital in which D was apparently a partner). For tort liability of retired partners, see Sec. 81 at n. 93 below.

See Kell v. Nainby, 10 B. & C. 20, 19 Eng.Rep. 474 (1829) stating that ostensible partner in law firm would be liable for negligence; Rhone v. Try

ostensible partner is not liable; there is no basis for estoppel.[33]

Just as the represented partner may be bound, so may he bind, e. g., by acts to which the third person is a party in reliance on the supposed partnership.[34] The apparent authority is mutual, like actual authority in a regular partnership.

Among the apparent partners, there is no basis for estoppel, and their relations should be governed by the terms of their actual contract[35] (if any). However, X's holding out of Y as a partner is evidence of partnership between them when Y seeks an accounting.[36]

Where there is no partnership in fact, rules of joint creditor priority in joint property, and separate creditor priority in separate property,[37] are not applicable because there is no joint property.[38]

The real owner(s) of a business can maintain an action against third persons for the enforcement of contract or other rights without joining the ostensible partner as co-plaintiff.[39]

Like a partnership, a joint venture may exist by estoppel.[40]

Me Cab Co., 62 D.C.App. 201, 65 F.2d 834 (1934), imposing liability for a taxi accident on a non-profit corporation holding itself out as providing cab service on call.

Frye v. Anderson, 248 Minn. 478, 493, 80 N.W.2d 593, 603 (1957), criticized 55 Mich.L.Rev. 1190 (1957) by dictum indicates liability for negligence in partnership by estoppel. Cases are collected in Painter, op. cit. supra n. 19 at 336–37; Recent Decision, 55 Mich. L.Rev. 1190 (1957). Painter correctly observes the improbability that plaintiff has "given credit" in the language of U.P.A. § 16. However, that section does not deal with most torts, which may therefore come under general law of estoppel via § 4(2)

33. Shapard v. Hynes, 104 F. 449, 52 L. R.A. 675 (8th Cir. 1900) (wrongful levy); Rowland v. Canuso, 329 Pa. 72, 79, 196 A. 823, 826 (1938) (fictitious name registration does not bar denial of partnership in traffic accident case; the purpose of registration is to acquaint persons with the identity of those with whom they do business); Pruitt v. Fetty, 148 W.Va. 275, 134 S.E.2d 713 (1964); Meehan v. Hesselgrave, 121 Wash. 568, 210 P. 2 (1922) (traffic accident).

See also Restatement, Second, Agency § 265(2).

34. U.P.A. § 16(2).

Dettloff v. Langkau, 214 Wis. 367, 253 N.W. 170 (1934) (payment to ostensible partner).

35. Lord v. Plumer, 237 Mass. 176, 129 N.E. 387 (1921) (one who lets his name be used as nominal partner, after retirement, cannot object to admission of new partners). But see Paul v. Paul, 266 Pa. 241, 109 A. 674 (1920); limited partner named in certificate entitled to accounting which the sole proprietor had filed to preserve his property from creditors; the transaction was regarded as an executed fraudulent conveyance. See also Stein v. Bieber, 342 Ill.App. 583, 98 N.E. 2d 156 (1951) (ostensible partner, alleged to be straw man for a principal trying to defraud his creditors, entitled to accounting).

36. Demmert v. Demmert, 14 Alaska 425, 115 F.Supp. 430 (D.Alaska 1953) (holding out for 23 years; Y successful). See also n. 35 above.

37. Secs. 91, 91A, 94, 94 below.

38. Commissioners' Note to U.P.A. § 16, 7 Unif.Laws Ann. 95 (1949). *Compare* U.P.A. § 16(1) (b) *with* id. § 16(1) (a).

39. Kell v. Nainby, n. 32 above.

40. Sec. 35 at n. 92 above.

CHAPTER 4

PARTNERSHIP PROPERTY AND INTERESTS IN PARTNERSHIP

Analysis

DISTINGUISHING PARTNERSHIP PROPERTY FROM SEPARATE PROPERTY

§ 37.   Whether property belongs to the partnership or to one or more of the partners has a significant bearing on the rights of partners, creditors, heirs and others.   The partners' agreement is usually determinative, if there is one; if not, their intention, as inferred from their conduct, is controlling.   Certain presumptions operate with varying force. The most important is codified in U.P.A. § 8(2): "Unless the contrary intention appears, property acquired with partnership funds is partnership property."

(a) Background

There are no limitations on the kinds of property a partnership may own.   But the subject of partnership property is beset with two generic problems.   One is conceptual: distinguishing partnership property from the related property called a partner's interest in the partnership.   The difference is as fundamental as that between a telephone and a share of AT&T stock.   It is a matter of two sorts of property and is treated in Sections 40–45 below.

The other problem is more factual: distinguishing partnership property from property of individual partners.   It is a question of who owns a particular property—the firm or one or more partners—rather than of the nature of the property, and is largely a matter of intent.   It is important in many contexts, e. g., (1) is gain or loss on disposition of the property, or income from it, to be shared by the partners?   (2) who gets it on dissolution of the firm or divorce of a partner?   (3) who may convey or devise it?   (4) are partnership or individual creditors entitled to priority against it in satisfying their claims? (5) can homestead or other exemption claims be made upon it?   Since questions like this usually entail strong economic or psychological clashes, it is no surprise that issues of partnership v. individual ownership arise often and are fought fiercely.   The methods of distinguishing firm property are covered in this Section and (for special types of intangibles) the next one.   The rest of the Chapter deals with other attributes of partnership property.

A firm usually begins business with property derived from the partners.[1]   It may be real estate, tangible personalty, money or other intangible.   It may be contributed to the firm (becoming firm prop-

---

1.   See cases collected in Annot., When real estate owned by a partner before formation of partnership will be deemed to have become asset of firm, 45 A.L.R.2d 1009 (1956); Note, Farm Partnership: Ownership and Use of Real Property, 47 Iowa L.Rev. 689 (1962).

erty), or lent (remaining individual property), or made available in a more ambiguous way.[2] Property of a partner may similarly enter the firm at a later stage.

The partners can decide what shall and shall not be partnership property. Their decision binds creditors and third persons unless overridden by rules of estoppel or apparent ownership.[3] Speaking more broadly, the partners' intent controls the question of ownership.[4] Often there will be a specific written agreement that expresses their intent beyond any reasonable doubt. Such an agreement will customarily control as a matter of law,[5] and one finds understandably few of them in the reported cases.[6] This is the sensible way for foresighted partners to deal with the matter.[6A]

All too frequently, however, there is no such agreement, a dispute arises, and the problem must be settled by inferring their intent from their behavior. This typically involves a question of fact,[7] within the province of the jury if there is one. The rest of this Section and the next one survey the more common situations and the inferences which have been raised from them with varying degrees of force. Some of them have less cogency than they would in non-partnership cases. Thus, possession or use is not very significant because of the tendency to mix personal and partnership affairs, especially in family firms. And "title" is inconclusive because of reluctance to place it in the

---

2. Fazio v. Tracy, 39 Misc.2d 172, 240 N.Y.S.2d 412 (1963) was a dispute whether a partner's $5,000 payment on the formation of a firm was a contribution to the firm or a payment to his co-partner for an interest in the business. Although the check and note were payable to the co-partner personally, and deposited and used by him individually, the written agreement was construed in favor of contribution. After specifying that the co-partner was to "contribute" certain paid memberships in the business (a health club), it provided that the partner would "contribute" the $5,000. Although the agreement didn't say to whom the contributions were being made, the court read in the partnership, taking "contribution" to mean "to give in common with others; give to a common stock or for a common purpose." This correctly reflects the etymology of the word; the prefix means "with." As a result, the co-partner was required to account for the $5,000 as partnership property on dissolution of the firm.

See also Homestake Mining Co. v. Mid-Continent Exploration Co., 282 F.2d 787, 794–97 (10th Cir. 1960) (N.M. law),

concluding that uranium ore which a limited partner held under lease was not a capital contribution to the firm, although it was "dedicated" or committed to the mill built by the firm to the extent of the mill's capacity as allocated by contract. Restrictions in the lease prevented the ore from being contributed, and the limited partnership agreement was construed against the capital contribution.

3. Cf. Note, Notice: Occupancy by a Partnership as Notice of Its Claim to Land, 11 Okla.L.Rev. 462 (1958).

4. Pendleton v. Strange, 381 S.W.2d 617 (Ky.1964) citing this text; Price v. McFee, 196 Md. 443, 77 A.2d 11 (1950); McCormick v. McCormick, 342 Mich. 525, 70 N.W.2d 706 (1955); Littleton v. Littleton, n. 13 below.

5. There may be statute of frauds questions; see Sec. 39 below, Sec. 23 above.

6. Curtis v. Campbell, 336 S.W.2d 355 (Ky.1960) is an example.

6A. See Appendix V, pars. 4.1, 4.2 below.

7. Pluth v. Smith, 205 Cal.App.2d 818, 23 Cal.Rptr. 550 (1962).

firm as a result of concern (largely unjustified under U.P.A.) over ability to convey good title later.

U.P.A. § 8(1), quoted in the margin,[8] is only a feeble guide to ownership, since it depends critically on two rather vague terms. The partnership "stock" probably has the older meaning of all assets used in the business,[9] but this is far from clear. In present parlance, "stock" usually refers to inventory, a much narrower term. In addition, the property must be brought into the firm "on account of" the partnership. This might refer to ownership, in which case it is redundant. Or it may refer to purpose, in which case it leaves open all the same questions of intent that would exist without it. Another possible meaning refers to the books of account, and whether the property is listed there. This would do little for those firms with adequate accounting systems, which create logical presumptions without benefit of the statute,[10] and would have no applicability to those without.

The Act's draftsmen can, of course, be forgiven for failing to pin down something so elusive. The cases demonstrate that there is no universal formula. Nor would we expect one, so great is the diversity of circumstances in property handling by partners and partnerships. All we can hope to do is illustrate some of the elements which have been weighed. We can also realize—as few courts admit [11] but most are aware—that the relationship of the litigants is a major element. On the same facts, a dispute among partners might reach a quite different result from one involving heirs or creditors. The equities, as seen by the trier of fact, are of major importance.

(b) Use, Occupancy or Possession

Real estate owned by a partner, or by the partners as co-tenants, before formation of the firm may be occupied and used by the firm without any agreement that it shall become partnership property. It remains separate property, hence subject to the prior rights of separate creditors of the owning partner in the event of distribution of insolvent estates.[12] Thus, mere use or occupancy by the partnership does little

---

8. "All property originally brought into the partnership stock or subsequently acquired by purchase or otherwise, on account of the partnership, is partnership property." U.P.A. § 8(1).

9. See Vlamis v. DeWeese, 216 Md. 384, 140 A.2d 665 (1958) (land, garage, salesroom and equipment for car agency, as well as cars, are part of "stock").

10. See Sec. 37(e) below at n. 61.

11. A rare example is Kook v. American Sur. Co., 88 N.J.Super. 43, 210

A.2d 633 (1965) discussed in n. 42 below.

12. Robinson Bank v. Miller, 153 Ill. 244, 38 N.E. 1078, 27 L.R.A. 449, 46 Am.St.Rep. 883 (1894); Jones v. Dugan, 124 Md. 346, 92 A. 775 (1914); Taber-Prang Art Co. v. Durant, 189 Mass. 173, 75 N.E. 221 (1905); Goepper v. Kinsinger, 39 Ohio St. 429 (1883); Picetti v. Orcio, 58 P.2d 1046 (Nev. 1936).

A leasehold owned by a partner does not become partnership property by reason of occupation by the partnership.

or nothing to show that land or other fixed assets have become partnership property,[13] whether at the start of the firm or later on.

A typical situation of this sort is Taber-Prang.[14] Land and buildings were owned as tenants in common by Charles L. and Henry E. Jones. They conducted a manufacturing business on the premises as partners under a firm name. On the death of Charles, he devised his half share of the land, buildings and fixtures to Frank H. Jones. Thereafter Henry and Frank carried on the business on the premises under the same name as before. There was no conveyance to themselves as a firm (nor to the firm in its name), nor was there evidence of any agreement that the land should be regarded as firm property. It was held that the land and original buildings remained separate property; on insolvent dissolution, the proceeds were to be distributed among the separate creditors of the partners according to the dual priorities rule.[15] Buildings, fixtures and other improvements added to the land with partnership funds and used for partnership purposes were held to be partnership property, and distributable to partnership creditors.

In re Welch, 77 Misc. 427, 137 N.Y.S. 941 (1912); Quinn v. Reed, 85 Misc. 510, 148 N.Y.S. 801 (1914).

Where a lease of premises occupied by the partnership is negotiated for by the partnership, the rent paid by the use of partnership funds, and the profit arising from its assignment to a third person treated as a partnership profit, the lease is to be regarded as partnership property, although it is executed by the partners in their individual names, and not in the firm name, Bratton v. Morris, 54 Idaho 743, 37 P.2d 1097 (1934). See also In re Allen Street in City of New York, 148 Misc. 488, 266 N.Y.S. 277 (1933).

"Whether real estate upon which a partnership transacts its business is firm property or the property of individual members of the firm is oftentimes a difficult question to determine, and one upon which the authorities are not altogether uniform. The mere fact of use of land by a firm does not make it partnership property. . . . Nor is real estate necessarily the individual property of the members of a firm because the title is held by one member, or by the several members in individual interests. 1 Bates, Partn. § 280. Whether real estate is partnership or individual property depends largely upon the intention of the partners. That intention may be expressed in the deed conveying the land, or in the articles of partnership; but when it is not so expressed the circumstances usually relied upon to determine the question are the ownership of the funds paid for the land, the uses to which it is put, and the manner in which it is entered in the accounts upon the books of the firm." Magruder, J., in Robinson Bank v. Miller, supra.

13. Ellis v. Mihelis, 60 Cal.2d 206, 218–19, 32 Cal.Rptr. 415, 384 P.2d 71 (1963) noting that it is not unusual for a partnership to have use of property (here a ranch) without ownership.

See Littleton v. Littleton, 341 S.W.2d 484 (Tex.Civ.App.1960) error ref. n. r. e. L. T., to buy his divorcing wife's community property interest in land, borrowed from his brother, O.L., deeded the land to O.L. (by what the court found to be an equitable mortgage, apparently payable from the proceeds of a dairy operated on the land) and commenced partnership with O.L. in the dairy. Held: the land belongs to L.T., subject to the equitable mortgage, not to O.L. or the partnership; intent controls.

14. N. 12 above.

15. Sec. 91 below.

Where two persons enter partnership and at the same time one conveys to the other a half interest in land to be used as the firm's place of business, it may be shown that their intention is to remain owners of the premises as tenants in common. As a result, after solvent dissolution, there may be a partition proceeding between them,[16] rather than a liquidation of the property as partnership property. The more logical result is contrary, especially if the conveyance covers equipment and inventory as well as land and buildings, i. e. an interest in a whole business.[17]

Tangible personalty owned by a partner may be used in the partnership business without becoming firm property. A member of a law firm may retain ownership of his law books. A partner in a commercial firm may retain ownership of a truck loaned for firm deliveries.[18] A partner in a construction firm may retain ownership of his tools.[19] Often, however, the express agreement, or the conduct of the parties, indicates an intention that tangible personalty shall pass to the firm.[20] A strong presumption to this effect should arise when the property is of a kind sold in the ordinary course of business (inventory) or consumed in its operation (supplies).[21]

Intangible property of a partner may be contributed to the firm, or it may be merely lent. It seems that money used as working capital of the firm would have to be considered partnership property. However, some courts have unconvincingly regarded the partner as contributing only the use of money.[22] Intangibles which are not consumed but remain in specie may or may not become partnership property, according to the intent of the parties.[23]

16. Blakeslee v. Blakeslee, 265 Ill. 48, 106 N.E. 470 (1914); Zucaro v. Pepe, 299 Pa. 354, 149 A. 650 (1930).

17. Vlamis v. DeWeese, 216 Md. 384, 140 A.2d 665 (1958). As a result, the heirs of the first partner to die took no interest in the land.

18. Hartigan v. Casualty Co., 227 N.Y. 175, 124 N.E. 789 (1919).

19. Summa v. Masterson, 215 App.Div. 159, 213 N.Y.S. 177 (1926).

20. Rankin v. Trickett, 75 Kan. 306, 89 P. 698 (1907) (abstract outfit); Hillman v. King, 258 Mich. 400, 242 N.W. 767 (1932) (tools and machinery used in operating gravel pit).

21. See Sher & Bromberg, Texas Partnership Law in the 20th Century— Why Texas Should Adopt the Uniform Partnership Act, 12 Sw.L.J. 263, 289 (1958).

22. Id. at 291–92. Meadows v. Mocquot, 110 Ky. 220, 61 S.W. 28 (1901).

23. In general, see Sec. 37A below.

A buyer of an automobile business took a covenant not to compete from his seller and later formed a partnership. Held: the benefit of the covenant passed to the partnership by implied assignment and it could sue to enjoin a breach. Wright v. Scotton, 13 Del. Ch. 402, 121 A. 69, 31 A.L.R. 1162 (1923).

In re Kennedy's Estate, 321 Pa. 225, 183 A. 798 (1936) (agreement provided that title to business and good will would remain in senior partner while others would merely share profits during the life of the firm).

(c) Purchase with Partnership Funds or Credit

As indicated by the Taber-Prang case,[24] there is a presumption that property purchased with partnership funds is partnership property. This is both logical and statutory.[25] It closely resembles the purchase money resulting trust.[26] The presumption is a powerful one,[27] especially when coupled with partnership use of the property [28] or collection of rentals from it.[29]

There is little need for the presumption if title has been taken in the firm name.[30] It operates on title in the name of one partner,[31] or several or all the partners,[32] or a third person.[33] The presumption will cover partnership-paid improvements on land owned by a partner.[34] Partnership use of the property is not indispensable to the

---

24. At n. 14 above.

25. U.P.A. § 8(2) quoted in the headnote of this Section. See also Bratton v. Morris, n. 12 above.

There is something of a contrary presumption when individual funds are used. Cf. below at nn. 43–44, and cases collected in Annot., Constructive trust in favor of partnership when one partner purchases real estate with his own funds, 44 A.L.R.2d 519 (1955).

26. Restatement, Second, Trusts §§ 440 et seq. Cf. Kurtz v. Kurtz, 10 Ill.App. 2d 310, 134 N.E.2d 609 (1956) effectively equating the partnership presumption and the trust doctrine.

27. Occasionally a court gets carried away with the presumption. In one instance a co-partner (father of the partner) was allowed a lien on property set aside to the partner's wife on divorce. The dubious rationale was that it had been bought with funds overdrawn from the firm by the partner. Conyers v. Conyers, 386 P.2d 633 (Okl.1963). Since the co-partner's consent was inferable, the funds should have been treated as a loan to the partner, hence his property, not the firm's. See below at nn. 43–44.

28. In re Gerlach's Estate, 364 Pa. 207, 72 A.2d 271, 16 A.L.R.2d 1397 (1950).

29. Foster v. Sargent, 72 N.H. 170, 55 A. 423 (1903). Cf. below at n. 35.

30. See Sec. 37(d) below.

31. Proctor v. Hearne, 100 Fla. 1180, 131 So. 173 (1931); McDonald v. Dabney, 161 Ga. 711, 132 S.E. 547 (1926); People v. Sholem, 244 Ill. 502, 91 N.E.

704 (1910) (compare Nehrkorn v. Tissier, 352 Ill. 181, 185 N.E. 227 (1933)); Todd v. Todd, 250 Iowa 1084, 96 N.W. 2d 436 (1959) (non-U.P.A.); Cyrus v. Cyrus, 242 Minn. 180, 64 N.W.2d 538, 45 A.L.R.2d 1002 (1954); Berliner v. Roberts, 226 Or. 350, 360 P.2d 533 (1961) (personalty); Smith v. Brown, 294 Pa. 203, 143 A. 913 (1928); In re Gerlach's Estate, n. 28 above; Savings & Loan Corp. v. Bear, 155 Va. 312, 154 S.E. 587, 75 A.L.R. 980 (1930). See also Sec. 37(d) below.

The presumption was extended, with somewhat less force, to cover property purchased partially with funds contributed by the partners individually, on the theory that the firm was the sole source of their income. Rizzo v. Rizzo, 3 Ill.2d 291, 120 N.E.2d 546 (1954). There is a danger here of proving too much. See n. 27 above and text at nn. 43–44 below.

32. Lewis v. Buford, 93 Ark. 57, 124 S. W. 244 (1910); Foster v. Sargent, n. 29 above; Magen v. Neiman, 301 Pa. 164, 151 A. 796 (1930); J. E. Ervine & Co. v. U. S., 3 F.Supp. 334 (Ct.Cl.1933). See also Sec. 37(d) below.

33. Korziuk v. Korziuk, 13 Ill.2d 238, 148 N.E.2d 727 (1958) (trustee); Bacon v. Bacon, 7 N.J.Super. 182, 72 A.2d 879 (1950), aff'd 6 N.J. 117, 77 A.2d 802 (1951) (partner's wife).

34. Marston v. Marston, 277 Mass. 129, 177 N.E. 862 (1931); Clark's Appeal, 72 Pa. 142 (1872). See also above at n. 14 and Sneed v. Kanelos, 150 Cal.App. 2d 684, 310 P.2d 706 (1957). But see Taber-Prang Art Co. v. Durant, nn. 12, 14 above where some improvements remained individual on the theory that

presumption; the property may be regarded as an investment of surplus.[35]

The usual form of the presumption relates to purchases with partnership funds.[36] But the presumption is just as cogent if the property is acquired for or derived from some other partnership asset.[37] The same result should follow from a purchase on partnership credit. Even though the partners have individual liability, the partnership obligation—which represents a commitment of future partnership funds —deserves primacy.[38] If, as often happens, only the partners sign, and do not formally obligate the firm, there is less reason to presume partnership property, but still a substantial basis if they have signed jointly and severally.[39] The latter is more consistent with partnership than with mere co-ownership.

The presumption from source of funds is the strongest of the lot, but is not absolute. The Act qualifies it by "unless the contrary intention appears," [40] and the courts have been willing to find contrary intention in appropriate cases,[41] particularly when the rights of non-partners are at stake.[42] Moreover, not every partnership check

the partnership was reimbursed for its expenses out of rentals.

35. Sargent v. Blake, 160 F. 57, 64, 17 L.R.A., N.S., 1040, 15 Ann.Cas. 58 (8th Cir. 1908); Buzianis v. Buzianis, 81 Utah 1, 16 P.2d 413 (1932). See also above at n. 29.

36. The purchase sometimes takes the form of transfer of funds to a corporation in exchange for its shares, or an advance to a corporation already owned. The presumption is equally applicable. See Farris v. Farris Engineering Corp., 8 N.J.Super. 475, 73 A.2d 617 (1950), modified on other grounds 7 N.J. 487, 81 A.2d 731 (1951) and Fortugno v. Hudson Manure Co., 51 N.J.Super. 482, 144 A.2d 207 (1958).

37. See Attaway v. Stanolind Oil & Gas Co., 232 F.2d 790 (10th Cir. 1956) (property received in partial satisfaction of debt owing to partnership; N.M. law); Pearson v. Norton, 230 Cal. App.2d 1, 40 Cal.Rptr. 634, 644 (1964) (realty transferred to partners in exchange for partnership realty); Meinhard v. Salmon, 249 N.Y. 458, 164 N.E. 545, 62 A.L.R. 1 (1928) (renewal of partnership lease); Fortugno v. Hudson Manure Co., n. 36 above (corporations whose assets were received from partnership or bought with partnership funds). See also Sec. 68 below concerning "partnership opportunities"

and other matters of fiduciary breach connected with partnership property.

38. This contingency is not covered by U.P.A., which refers only to partnership funds, § 8(2).

39. Emerson v. Campbell, 32 Del.Ch. 178, 84 A.2d 148 (1951) (partners gave joint notes and mortgage, took title as tenants in common; property, notes and mortgage carried on partnership books; held: partnership property).

40. U.P.A. § 8(2). This shifts at least the burden of going forward with the evidence. Oswald v. Dawn, 143 Colo. 487, 354 P.2d 505 (1960), subsequent opinion (aff'g holding that property was not partnership's), 154 Colo. 572, 391 P.2d 878 (1964).

41. Block v. Schmidt, 296 Mich. 610, 296 N.W. 698 (1941) (realty and personalty in joint tenancy with right of survivorship). See also Sec. 37A at n. 89 below. Now and then a court wholly ignores the presumption, e. g., Gertz v. Fontecchio, 331 Mich. 165, 49 N.W.2d 121 (1951) (leasehold for which partnership paid rent).

42. Kook v. American Sur. Co., 88 N.J. Super. 43, 210 A.2d 633 (1965) faces the issue forthrightly and says the presumption must be applied with considerable caution to outsiders. The

represents partnership funds. It may represent a distribution to partners who are then using individual funds; proper books will indicate this by debiting as asset account (for partnership property) or capital or drawing accounts (for withdrawals or distributions).[43] Conversely, a partner's check in payment for property may represent partnership funds when his capital account (or a payable to him) is credited and a property account debited.[44]

(d) Record Title

If the property is a kind which has a record title (such as real estate, motor vehicles or stock certificates) or is carried in a given name (like a checking or savings account), there is a presumption of some vigor that the named owner is the beneficial owner.[44A] However, the presumption is not symmetrical. Record title in the firm is much more indicative of firm ownership [45] than is individual title of individual ownership.[46] The explanation for the lopsided presumption is

question was whether liability insurance covered a multiple-family dwelling. The dwelling was allegedly acquired with partnership funds but title was taken in the names of the partners. The policy was issued to the partnership, not the partners. The firm was in the plumbing business, not real estate ownership or management. A judgment for the insurer on other grounds was reversed and remanded for further proof on the ownership issue. The court noted that there had been no evidence from the partnership books, documents or tax returns, and suggested that the partnership funds used for purchase might have been charged to individual partners' accounts and thus become individual funds.

43. See the preceding note and Sec. 37 (f) below.

44. In re Gerlach's Estate, n. 28 above.

44A. Pendleton v. Strange, 381 S.W.2d 617 (Ky.1964) (record title in individual partner creates presumption of individual ownership which can be rebutted only by a clear manifestation of partnership intent).

45. See Brown v. Brown, 45 Tenn.App. 78, 320 S.W.2d 721 (1958) (dispute among heirs and kin).

46. Ownership by the firm has often been found despite record title in one

or more partners. See, in addition to the cases in nn. 31–32 above:

Smith v. Dixon, 238 Ark. 1018, 386 S.W. 2d 244 (1965) (record title in numerous relatives who had formed partnership to farm and lease it);

Vineland Homes v. Barish, 138 Cal.App. 2d 747, 292 P.2d 941 (1956) (title in four partners "each as to an undivided one-fourth of interest as his separate property");

Rizzo v. Rizzo, 3 Ill.2d 291, 120 N.E.2d 546 (1954) (premises of family business, in which all sons worked and shared profits, deeded by father to oldest son without consideration; influencing factors were understanding of partners (and presumably of father) and fiduciary obligation of eldest son (who was general manager) which would bar him from taking individually);

McCormick v. McCormick, 342 Mich. 525, 70 N.W.2d 706 (1955) (title successively in 2 partners, 3 partners, 1 partner and another); Ewing v. Caldwell, 243 N.C. 18, 89 S.E.2d 774 (1955); Stark v. Reingold, 18 N.J. 251, 113 A.2d 679, 687 (1955) (title in one partner and wife); Wiseman v. Martorano, 405 Pa. 369, 175 A.2d 873 (1962). Most of these involved disputes among the partners.

Cf. Belton v. Buesing, 240 Or. 399, 402 P.2d 98 (1965). Three partners held title to tracts in their individual names as joint tenants or as partners. One, in anticipation of marriage, conveyed

easy. Title would rarely be placed in the partnership unless the ownership were intended to be there too. But title is often taken in individual names when ownership by the firm is intended, in anticipation of real or imagined difficulties in later transferring good title to a buyer.[47]

Individual ownership is often upheld against a claim that ownership is in the firm, e.g., if there is no partnership financing or use of the property,[48] or if there is a clear expression of intent for individual ownership.[49]

A lease between partners and partnership strengthens the inference that the record owner (lessor) retains beneficial ownership.[50]

Where property belongs to the firm but record title is in one or more of the partners, the firm has only equitable title. Creditors of the record title holders may have superior rights in the property (compared to creditors of the firm) by operation of the recording acts and the doctrine of apparent ownership.[51] So may purchasers.

his interest to another. When some of the tracts were later sold, the proceeds were deposited in the firm's bank account. Held: on the death of the conveying partner, his estate was subject to inheritance tax on the value of the interest he conveyed as though he had not. The court speaks of express trust and resulting trust, not clearly choosing one over the other. Nor is it clear whether the trust is regarded as for the conveying partner or for the firm. Nonetheless, the result is quite correct; the property continued to be used by the firm and to be treated as its property.

47. See Sec. 38 below. Title may be in a partner merely for convenience, McCormick v. McCormick, n. 46 above.

48. Nehrkorn v. Tissier, 352 Ill. 181, 185 N.E. 227 (1933). "The title to this property was in the name of Charles A. Tissier, and there is no showing that in the deed by which he obtained title there was any declaration that he was to hold the lot as the property of the partnership. The presumption therefore is that the lot was his individual property. . . . There is absolutely no showing that the lot was purchased with partnership money or for partnership purposes or that it was entered and carried on the books of the partnership as the property of the partnership, or that there was any contract or understanding between the partners that the lot was the property of the partnership. In the absence of evidence of one or more of these con-

trolling factors to show that the lot was partnership property, a finding that it was partnership property cannot be sustained."

49. Block v. Schmidt, 296 Mich. 610, 296 N.W. 698 (1941) (record title of joint tenancy with right of survivorship was conclusive on partners and heirs). See Pendleton v. Strange, 381 S.W.2d 617 (Ky.1964) (taking of title to several tracts in joint names of partners implies that tract taken in name of one partner alone was his individual property).

Picetti v. Orcio, 57 Nev. 52, 58 P.2d 1046 (1936); Wheatley's Heirs v. Calhoun, 12 Leigh (39 Va.) 264, 273, 37 Am.Dec. 654 (1841).

See Gertz v. Fontecchio, 331 Mich. 165, 49 N.W.2d 121 (1951) (leasehold in name of one partner who assigned half interest to other dubiously held cotenancy, not partnership property, though used for partnership business with rents paid by partnership).

Cf. Littleton v. Littleton, n. 13 above.

50. People ex rel. Dept. of Public Works v. Dickinson, 230 Cal.App.2d 932, 41 Cal.Rptr. 427 (1964) (separate parcels, with record title in separate partners, all leased to firm, were not partnership property, hence not entitled to severance damages on condemnation of one and part of another); Sneed v. Kanelos, n. 34 above.

51. Roy E. Hays & Co. v. Pierson, 32 Wyo. 416, 234 P. 494 (1925). See also Sec. 38 below, at nn. 23, 24.

(e) Other Indicia

Numerous other factors may be clues to the intent of the parties. All of the following point to partnership ownership: [52] partnership payment of taxes,[53] repairs,[54] or insurance,[55] and deduction of the same on the partnership income tax return; improvements at partnership expense; [56] partnership payment of mortgage; [57] mortgage by partnership of crops and rentals; [58] listing on partnership financial statements submitted for credit purposes, or other admissions by partners that the property belongs to the firm; [59] disproportionality between funds in dispute and agreed value of partnership interest.[60] Such factors tend to be cumulative of other evidence, not conclusive alone. They are of unequal weight. Thus, tenants frequently have express obligations to insure, repair and pay property taxes. Accordingly these are weaker indicia of ownership than mortgaging the property, making payments on a mortgage, or deducting depreciation of the property on an income tax return.[61]

Any well-kept set of books for a partnership will identify the firm's assets. Property included on the books should be strongly presumed to belong to the firm [61A] unless there is reason to think they were improperly kept. If the books seem otherwise complete, there

---

52. Similar factors and reasoning, mutatis mutandi, indicate that ownership is in a partner. Sneed v. Kanelos, 150 Cal.App.2d 684, 310 P.2d 706 (1957) is a good example. The property was acquired by a partner before formation of the firm; it did not appear on the firm's books; the partner individually mortgaged it and collected rents from tenants (including the partnership). These outweighed promises to convey half to his co-partner, and the expenditure of partnership funds for improvements (the latter were treated as partnership property).

53. Smith v. Dixon, n. 46 above; Swarthout v. Gentry, 62 Cal.App.2d 68, 144 P.2d 38 (1944); Cyrus v. Cyrus, n. 31 above.

54. Smith v. Dixon, n. 46 above; Emerson v. Campbell, 32 Del.Ch. 178, 84 A. 2d 148 (1951); Stark v. Reingold, n. 46 above.

55. Smith v. Dixon, n. 46 above; Klingstein v. Rockingham Nat. Bank, 165 Va. 275, 182 S.E. 115 (1935).

56. Cyrus v. Cyrus, n. 31 above. But see Sneed v. Kanelos, n. 52 above; Taber-Prang Art Co. v. Durant discussed at n. 14 above.

57. Smith v. Dixon, n. 46 above.

58. Ibid.

59. McKinnon v. McKinnon, 56 F. 409 (8th Cir. 1893); Cyrus v. Cyrus, n. 31 above. Cf. Vlamis v. DeWeese, 216 Md. 384, 140 A.2d 665 (1958), noted 19 Md.L.Rev. 141 (1959) (treatment by deceased partner's attorney, executrices and bank as partnership property).

60. Kelso v. Kelso, 40 Tenn.App. 681, 292 S.W.2d 483 (1955).

61. Depreciation properly goes with ownership. Ellis v. Mihelis, n. 13 above, at 60 Cal.2d 219 mentions depreciation on tax returns but does not pass on the question since the returns were not introduced in evidence. Nor does it clarify whether the depreciation was on all improvements on the property, or only those made by the firm.

61A. Emerson v. Campbell, n. 54 above; Einsweiler v. Einsweiler, 390 Ill. 286, 61 N.E.2d 377 (1945); In re Gerlach's Estate, n. 28 above. See quotation from Robinson Bank v. Miller, n. 12 above.

should be a corresponding (but perhaps weaker) presumption that property not shown there is not property of the firm.[62]

(f) Change from Partnership to Individual Property

Just as individual property may become the firm's, the process may be reversed. Firm property may be distributed in kind on dissolution,[63] passing to the members separately. Without dissolution there may be a distribution in kind rather than in money as a share of profits or return of capital, as where partnership property is sold and purchase money notes are distributed to the partners,[64] or shares of stock are purchased with partnership funds but registered in the names of individual partners.[65] Where partnership funds are used to purchase a dwelling and, with the consent of all partners, title is taken in the name of one partner who uses it as a family residence, it is regarded as his separate property.[66] A partner may waive his right to share in a particular asset on dissolution,[67] thus effectively permitting the asset to shift from partnership status to ownership by the other partners.

(g) Liabilities

Distinguishing between firm and individual liabilities involves some of the same questions of intent and conduct as distinguishing between firm and individual property. The liability problems are discussed elsewhere.[68] The emphasis on external and objective factors is greater, because of the important participation of the creditor who is an outsider in most cases.

(h) Limited Partnerships

The capacity of limited partnerships to hold property, and the possible confusion between property of the firm and that of the general partners is the same as in general partnerships. However, there is less likely to be confusion with regard to property of limited part-

62. Sneed v. Kanelos, n. 52 above.

63. Shafer's Appeal, 106 Pa. 49 (1884). Cf. U.P.A. § 38(1) requiring liquidation of the firm on dissolution "unless otherwise agreed;" see Secs. 83A, 90A below. Cf. Phillips v. Krensky, 98 So. 2d 788 (Fla.1957) discussed Sec. 68 n. 84 below.

64. Green v. Whaley, 271 Mo. 636, 197 S.W. 355 (1917); Diversified Fruit Farms v. Johnson, 58 S.W.2d 73 (Tex. Com.App.1933).

65. Azevedo v. Sequeira, 132 Cal.App. 439, 22 P.2d 745 (1933).

66. State Bank of Wheatland v. Bagley Bros., 44 Wyo. 244, 11 P.2d 572 (1932).

67. Berliner v. Roberts, 226 Or. 350, 360 P.2d 533 (1961) (claim against third party, with whom two partners agreed not to sue). See Stroh v. Dumas, 117 Vt. 13, 84 A.2d 408 (1951) (under survivorship agreement for firm's bank account (and controlling bank statutes), surviving partner took bank account individually and free from claims of deceased's estate).

68. Sec. 91A(b) at n. 39 below. Cf. Buckner v. Prairie County Bank, 235 Ark. 307, 359 S.W.2d 443 (1962) (partner's bank borrowing to make capital contribution to firm was individual liability, not firm's).

ners. Their contribution to the firm must be described in the certificate [69] which is commonly a public record. Other property of a limited partner which comes into the hands of the firm is presumptively a loan, with ownership retained by him.[70] The presumption would logically not apply to money, consumables or inventory, but would to fixed assets.

DISTINGUISHING PARTNERSHIP PROPERTY FROM SEPARATE PROPERTY—SPECIAL KINDS OF PARTNERSHIP PROPERTY

§ 37A. The basic criteria for determining partnership ownership are somewhat modified for types of intangible property like stock exchange seats (which are not freely transferable and may be held only subject to certain restrictions), insurance policies (in which numerous parties may have different contractual or other interests), and inventions and good will (which are created within the firm).

(a) Stock Exchange Seats

While there is some conflict of authority as to the nature of a membership ("seat") in a stock exchange, the federal courts hold it to be property available to creditors in bankruptcy proceedings against the owner.[71] Rules of the exchanges commonly restrict membership to individuals.[72] A seat is typically not transferable without the approval of the exchange. Nonetheless, a seat in the name of a partner as legal owner may be equitably the property of the firm, so that proceeds of its sale are partnership property.[73] If the partnership agreement provides that a partner's seat is firm property, such evidence of intention is controlling, particularly where the seat has been purchased with partnership funds,[74] or where there was agreement on formation of the firm that the seat would be the capital contribution of the partner in whose name it stood.[75] The same result is reached

---

69. U.L.P.A. § 2(a) (VI), Sec. 26(b) above. See Appendix VII, par. 6.

70. Cf. id. § 13.

71. Page v. Edmunds, 187 U.S. 596, 23 S.Ct. 200, 47 L.Ed. 318 (1902); In re Stringer, 253 F. 352 (2d Cir. 1918).

72. Partnerships can, with Exchange approval, be member firms. Corporations have had a similar right since the 1950s. Leffler & Farwell, The Stock Market 115–20 (3d ed. 1963) describes New York Stock Exchange membership rules and common methods of financing the purchase of seats. See also N.Y.S.E. Rules 301–02 and annotations thereto in C.C.H. N.Y.S.E. Guide, pars. 2301–02.

73. Rubin v. Whitney, 162 Misc. 821, 295 N.Y.S. 255 (1937). The text of the agreement does not appear in the opinion, which merely states that the seat-holder's "share" was to be his seat on the N. Y. Stock Exchange. However, the agreement was explicit that he would use the seat to further the interests of the firm, and that the proceeds of the seat, when sold, would be applied to the firm debts and repayment of the limited partner's contribution with interest.

74. In re Hearns, 214 N.Y. 426, 108 N. E. 816 (1915), affirming 163 App.Div. 897, 147 N.Y.S. 447 (1914).

75. In re Swift, 118 F. 348 (D.Mass.1902) (agreement silent but bookkeeping entries indicated that seat was regarded as partnership asset); In re Hurlbutt, Hatch & Co., 135 F. 504 (2d Cir. 1905) (express provision for contribution of seat as capital investment); In re Stringer, 253 F. 352 (2d Cir. 1918).

when there is express agreement for use of the seat in the firm business and treatment of the proceeds of its sale as firm property, even though the agreement nowhere specifies in haec verba that the seat will be partnership property.[76]

However, as with other items of property, it may be the intention of the parties, as shown by their partnership agreement and conduct, that the seat shall remain the separate property of a partner, with merely the use thereof vested in the firm.[77]

(b) Property Insurance

A partner as co-owner has an insurable interest in partnership property which he may insure with loss (if any) payable to him as his separate property.[78] But if the policy is issued in the firm name and the premiums paid with firm funds, the proceeds are partnership property even though by terms of the policy payable to a partner.[79] It is sometimes a question of construction as to what interest is insured by a policy on firm property. A partner who takes out a policy in his own name may find his recoverable loss limited to his proportional interest in the firm property,[80] however that is calculated. If by mistake the policy names one partner as the insured, but the actual intent of the parties is to cover the entire interest of the partners,

76. In re Snow, 252 App.Div. 369, 299 N.Y.S. 287 (1937), aff'd 277 N.Y. 660, 14 N.E.2d 208 (1938); Rubin v. Whitney, n. 73 above. But cf. Hyney v. Nielsen, n. 77 below.

77. Burleigh v. Foreman, 130 F. 13 (1st Cir. 1904); In re Atwater, 266 F. 278 (2d Cir. 1920); In re Amy, 21 F.2d 301 (2d Cir. 1927); In re Strassburger, 12 F.Supp. 420 (S.D.N.Y.1935). In the last case, the seat owner expressly agreed that it should be available for the payment of the firm's debts. Since it was held out to a limited partner as a firm asset, the limited partner was entitled to share in the proceeds of the seat sale for repayment of his contribution, in priority to the separate creditors of the seat owner.

The seat was found to be individual property in Hyney v. Nielsen, 140 N.Y. S.2d 111 (S.Ct.1955) rev'd on other grounds, 286 App.Div. 891, 142 N.Y.S. 2d 446 (1955), aff'd 1 N.Y.2d 823, 153 N.Y.S.2d 77, 135 N.E.2d 606, 153 N.Y.S. 2d 77 (1956). In addition to firm use, the agreement stated that proceeds of the seat would be partnership property so far as "necessary for the protection of the creditors of the firm." This is less than a general appropriation to the firm. Another indicator of

individual ownership is that the partners apparently made equal capital contributions apart from the seat.

But where it was expressly agreed that the partner's seat should be his property, subject to the payment of claims of firm creditors, it was not subject to the repayment of a limited partner's capital contribution. Chalmers v. Weed, 175 Misc. 740, 25 N.Y.S.2d 195 (1940).

78. Cassidy & Hogard v. Jenkins & Cassidy, 226 Ky. 828, 11 S.W.2d 946, 61 A.L.R. 1198 (1928), treated as insuring the partner's separate interest, and payable to the assignee of his interest, although by mistake the policy named the partnership as the insured. Compare dictum in Manhattan Insurance Co. v. Webster, 59 Pa. 227, 98 Am.Dec. 332 (1868), "It is plain, then, each partner has an insurable interest in the entire stock, and on receipt of a loss on insurance must account therefor to the partnership."

79. Tebbetts v. Dearborn, 74 Me. 392 (1883).

80. Graves & Barnewall v. Boston Marine Ins. Co., 6 U.S. 419, 2 L.Ed. 324 (1804).

the policy may be equitably reformed to fulfill the intention, and the proceeds treated as partnership property.[81]

(c) Life Insurance

Life insurance is more complex than most property because of the number of different interests and persons possibly involved: the applicant for the policy, the person whose life is insured, the payer of premiums, the beneficiary, the assignee and the person authorized to exercise inter vivos rights like changing the beneficiary or borrowing against the policy. Moreover the policy may build up substantial values before the insured event occurs. Since life insurance is often employed by partners in conjunction with buy-sell or similar agreements,[81A] questions of ownership occur frequently in partnership cases.[82] Some of the basic principles established in the previous Section are applicable, but the numerous elements of a life policy may necessitate certain changes.

A partnership has an insurable interest in the life of each of its members, as does each partner in the life of his co-partners.[83] Dissolution of the firm or withdrawal of the insured partner does not, in most jurisdictions, terminate the interest as to a policy already taken out.[84]

If the ownership dispute materializes before the death of the insured, only the cash surrender value (if any) is at issue. The presumption from source of payment [85] of premiums is likely to be deci-

---

81. Manhattan Ins. Co. v. Webster, 59 Pa. 227, 98 Am.Dec. 332 (1868), by mistake of the insurance agent, to whom a partner applied for insurance on the partnership goods in behalf of the partnership paying a premium on the entire value, a policy was issued in the name of one partner. He was allowed to recover the entire loss for the benefit of the partnership in an action in his own name.

See also Snell v. Atlantic F. & M. Ins. Co., 98 U.S. 85, 25 L.Ed. 52 (1878), where reformation of a policy issued in the name of a partner, but intended to cover the firm was decreed by a court of equity, despite the fact that the mistake was regarded as one of law as to the proper form for an insurance policy on partnership property.

81A. Cf. Sec. 90A below.

82. See, in general, Appleman, Insurance Law and Practice § 871.

83. Rush v. Howkins, 135 Ga. 128 68 S.E. 1035 (1909). Vance, Insurance 198 (3d ed. 1951). Cases are collected in Annot., Insurable interest of partner or partnership in life of partner, 70 A.L.R.2d 577 (1960). Query whether a firm (or a general partner) has an insurable interest in the life of a limited partner who has made his agreed contribution and thus is only a quasi-creditor. Perhaps there is an insurable interest if the contribution is repayable at the limited partner's death.

84. Gerstel v. Arens, 143 Fla. 20, 196 So. 616 (1940). Cf. Ryan v. Andrewski, 206 Okl. 199, 242 P.2d 448 (1952). But cf. Ruth v. Flynn, 26 Colo.App. 171, 142 P. 194 (1914).

Nor does dissolution necessarily shift the proceeds to the contingent beneficiary when the primary beneficiary is the firm and the policy provides that the contingent beneficiary shall take if the primary dies before the policy matures. Brammer v. Wilder, 122 Tex. 247, 57 S.W.2d 571 (1933). Semble, Gersten v. Arens, n. 84 above.

85. Sec. 37(c) above.

sive. Thus a partner who contracted to sell all his interest in assets of the firm was liable for failing to transfer a policy on his life which had been paid for with firm funds.[86] Where each partner took out two policies on his life, one payable to his wife and one to his co-partner, and all the premiums were paid by the firm, all the policies were partnership assets to be accounted for on dissolution.[87]

More will be at stake if the dispute arises at the death of the insured, for the face amount of the policy will then be payable.[88] In such cases, the beneficiary designated in the policy commonly prevails,[89]

86. Wise v. Nu-Tone Products Co., 148 Colo. 574, 367 P.2d 346 (1962). The primary beneficiary was a co-partner who had already died, the contingent beneficiary was the firm as constituted at the insured's death. The insured retained the right to change beneficiaries. The measure of liability was the cash surrender value.

87. Miller v. Hall, 65 Cal.App.2d 200, 150 P.2d 287 (1944). A specific provision for a different disposition on death was inapplicable since the partners were still alive. The court awarded each insured the policy on his life, valued as the cash surrender value, adjusted for differences in premiums paid. The court noted that this would give each partner full control over his own insurance, independent of any action or inaction of the other. The younger partner was contending for equal interests in each policy to each partner. This would very probably have been to his advantage since the other partner was considerably older and had suffered a paralytic stroke which left him permanently incapacitated.

88. Cases are collected, Annot., Relative rights of surviving partner and the estate of the deceased partner in proceeds of life insurance acquired pursuant to partnership agreement, 83 A.L.R.2d 1347 (1962).

89. Sneed v. Kanelos, 150 Cal.App.2d 684, 310 P.2d 706 (1957) (each partner planned to take out insurance payable to his wife; only one did, since the other was uninsurable); Price v. McFee, 196 Md. 443, 77 A.2d 11 (1950).

Continental American Life Ins. Co. v. Malkin, 237 N.Y.S.2d 520 (Sup.Ct.1963), aff'd 20 A.D.2d 627, 245 N.Y.S.2d 957 (1963), appeal denied 14 N.Y.2d 482, 198 N.E.2d 371, 249 N.Y.S.2d 1025 (1964). Each partner took out insurance on the other, payable to the latter's wife. The court found that the purpose was to free the survivor from claims of the widow. The widow-beneficiary won despite the fact that her husband had secretly cashed in the policy he held on the surviving co-partner, thus depriving the latter's wife of her expected reciprocal benefit at his death. The decision left open the possibility of a claim by the surviving partner against the estate of the deceased.

Fidelity Trust Co. v. Travelers' Ins. Co., 320 Pa. 161, 181 A. 594 (1935). Each partner took out insurance on himself, payable to his wife. The purpose was to avoid the difficulty of valuing good will in the firm. One partner, without knowledge of the other, changed the beneficiary in the policy on his life from his wife to a trustee for his girl friend. The latter prevailed; nothing in the partnership arrangement (there was nothing formally agreed in this respect) gave the wife vested status as a beneficiary.

But see Quinn v. Leidinger, 107 N.J.Eq. 188, 152 A. 249 (1930), aff'd 110 N.J.Eq. 663, 160 A. 537 (1932). Partners had wanted firm as beneficiary so survivor would have money to wind up or carry on. But insurance agent erroneously told them it was impossible to name firm as beneficiary, whereupon they designated their respective estates. Proceeds payable to the insured's estate were treated as partnership property by the decision. This is as much a case of mistake as of overriding intent.

See also Harrel's Admr. v. Harrel, 232 Ky. 469, 23 S.W.2d 922 (1930) (intent established in favor of co-partner, who was uncle and creditor, against partner's estate, which was named beneficiary).

because of the contractual feature of the policy and because the designation is a clear expression of intent, at least of the person who named the beneficiary. These factors usually outweigh premium payment by the firm.[90] If the firm is the beneficiary, the proceeds are partnership property, subject to accounting to the estate of the insured partner [91] unless the partners have agreed otherwise.[92] If a copartner is the beneficiary, he takes individually without any duty to account.[93] even though he is described in the policy as partner of the insured,[94] unless, of course, an express or implied agreement to the contrary can be shown. Since the loser in these cases is typically the insured partner's widow or estate, they suggest that the consequences of the insurance arrangements were not fully understood or were not made clear to all concerned.

Insurance is often tied into an agreement for continuation of the business by the survivors. This subject is discussed generally in Sec. 90A below. In larger firms, the insurance is usually owned by and payable to the firm or a trustee under clear instructions as to disposition. Arrangements in smaller firms tend to be more casual, often initiated by insurance salesmen whose concern is more to make a sale than to adjust post-death interests in the firm. In 2-man firms, the parties seldom think of the partnership as surviving the death of either, so insurance is normally made payable to individual beneficiaries. Two patterns are common. In one, the proceeds are payable to the surviving partner for the purpose of buying out the interest of the deceased. In the other, the proceeds are payable to the estate

90. But cf. Holmes v. Gilman, 138 N.Y. 369, 34 N.E. 205, 20 L.R.A. 566, 34 Am. St.Rep. 463 (1893) (constructive trust of proceeds because of wrongful conversion of partnership fund to pay premiums). But the beneficiary prevails when partnership funds are used with consent, e. g., Sneed v. Kanelos, n. 89 above.

91. Rubel v. Rubel, 221 Miss. 848, 75 So.2d 59, 47 A.L.R.2d 1410 (1954) (proceeds includible as partnership assets in determining book value for survivor purchase option); Block v. Mylish, 351 Pa. 611, 41 A.2d 731 (1945).

92. See Filcher v. Cox, n. 3 below. Often such an agreement is made partly to avoid increasing the dead partner's federal estate tax valuation. The desirability of lower tax must be weighed against greater benefits for the dead partner's estate or heirs in planning such disposition.

93. Esswein v. Rogers, 216 Cal.App.2d 91, 30 Cal.Rptr. 738 (1963) (firm owned policies, paid premiums); Silva v. Cohn, 200 Cal.App.2d 651, 19 Cal.Rptr. 469 (1962) (cross-ownership of policies, partners paid premiums individually through partnership disbursements charged to their separate accounts); Rush v. Howkins, n. 83 above; Hutchinson v. Goceliak, 73 N.J.Super. 550, 180 A.2d 359 (1962) (apparently each partner owned the policy on his life, and premiums on both policies were paid individually by the surviving partner). See also Oglesby-Barnitz Bank, v. Clark, n. 96 below. The cases are normally supported by evidence of intent to benefit the survivor. Sometimes, as in Silva v. Cohn, this is by reference to a desire to provide for firm creditors, which could equally be done by making the firm the beneficiary.

94. All cases in the preceding note, except Silva v. Cohn (where the point was not involved), so hold. The additional language serves merely to show insurable interest on the face of the policy, and does not make the beneficiary a trustee for the firm.

or widow of the deceased *as* purchase price (whole or part) of the interest, so that the interest passes at death to the survivor.[95] A classically inept version of the first pattern appears in the Oglesby-Barnitz case.[96] An otherwise apparently comprehensive 2-man partnership agreement provided that "the life" of each partner should be insured for $10,000 with premiums paid by the firm and the other partner designated as beneficiary, and "the surviving party shall use the proceeds of said insurance to purchase the deceased party's interest in the firm." Insurance paid at death was actually $40,000 due to a later doubling of the life policy by the partners (without alteration of the agreement), and addition of $20,000 accident insurance. The courts concluded that the agreement pegged the price of the dead partner's interest at $10,000 and the remaining $30,000 belonged to the surviving partner individually.[97] The estate of the dead partner claimed unsuccessfully that the price under the agreement was whatever insurance was in force, i.e. $40,000. The survivor claimed unsuccessfully that he was free to keep all the insurance proceeds except an amount equal to the $2,846 "interest" of the deceased in the firm (apparently book value). In the court's view, "life" insurance did not include accident insurance, and the doubling of the life insurance without amendment of the agreement did not appropriate the additional life insurance to the purchase of the interest. But the initially specified $10,000 was so appropriated, regardless of any other measure of value of the interest. A few thoughtful sentences in the agreement could easily have anticipated these problems of setting the price and disposing of the insurance proceeds.

As a matter of insurance law, the assignee of a policy typically has superior rights to a beneficiary.[98] Partnership instances include assignment of a partnership policy to a purchaser of the firm [99] and of a partner's policy to his co-partner.[1] An assignment as security to a creditor of the firm will similarly override, to the extent of the debt. A buy-sell agreement may be treated as an assignment of the related policies when necessary to carry out its purpose.[2] Once an assignment

95. Coe v. Winchester, 43 Ariz. 500, 33 P.2d 286 (1934); First Nat. Bank of Rome v. Howell, 195 Ga. 72, 23 S.E.2d 415 (1942); More v. Carnes, 309 Ky. 41, 214 S.W.2d 984 (1948). For a vain attempt to prove such an agreement, see Winfrey v. State Life Ins. Co., 227 Ind. 449, 85 N.E.2d 821 (1949).

96. Oglesby-Barnitz Bank v. Clark, 112 Ohio App. 31, 15 Ohio Op.2d 415, 175 N.E.2d 98, 83 A.L.R.2d 1337 (1959).

97. Accord, Kavanaugh v. Johnson, 290 Mass. 587, 195 N.E. 797 (1935).

98. Vance, Insurance 681–82 (3d ed. 1951).

99. Brand v. Erisman, 84 U.S.App.D.C. 194, 172 F.2d 28 (1948).

1. Smith v. Hessey, 63 Tex.Civ.App. 478, 134 S.W. 256 (1911). Here the co-partner's right to the proceeds was held limited to the debt owed him by the insured partner.

A partner's policy does not become firm property by virtue of its assignment to secure a firm creditor. Hiscock v. Varick Bank, 206 U.S. 28, 27 S.Ct. 681, 51 L.Ed. 945. (1907).

2. In re Ferrero's Estate, 142 Cal.App. 2d 473, 298 P.2d 604 (1956) (assignee co-partner prevails over named beneficiaries).

is released, the status quo ante (including the right of the designated beneficiary) is restored.[3]

(d) Patents, Inventions and Ideas

A patent obtained by a partner on his invention is his separate property in the absence of express or implied agreement to the contrary. If the business of the partnership does not include making inventions, no agreement to assign the application or the patent to the partnership is implied, even though the inventing partner uses partnership premises and equipment and time which should be devoted normally to partnership duties while making his invention.[4] If the business of the partnership does include the making of inventions, patents obtained as a result of the inventive activities of one or all of the partners in the course of the business would presumably be partnership property like any other product of the partnership business.[5] However, the circumstances of the invention (even though it is the first) may put the partnership in the invention business.[6] There is no

---

3. Esswein v. Rogers, 216 Cal.App.2d 91, 30 Cal.Rptr. 738 (1963) (co-partner, named as beneficiary, prevailed over insured's estate which claimed that assignment of partnership-owned policy to bank to secure debt (since released) extinguished the right of the named beneficiary). Semble, Filcher v. Cox, 4 Cal.App.2d 486, 40 P.2d 864 (1935) (individually owned policy, assigned to firm and made payable to it when insurance protection needed for the business, reverted to individual property when no longer needed by the firm and partners agreed that each was free to change beneficiary; immaterial that insured died before making the change).

Cf. Ryan v. Andrewski, 206 Okl. 199, 242 P.2d 448 (1952) (assignment of insured's interest in firm to co-partners on his withdrawal did not affect designation of firm as beneficiary in policy on his life; firm was named beneficiary and policy owner).

4. Belcher v. Whittemore, 134 Mass. 330 (1883). Compare Restatement, Agency, Second § 397. As to rights of employers in inventions of employees, see United States v. Dubilier Condenser Corporation, 289 U.S. 178, 53 S.Ct. 554, 77 L.Ed. 1114, 85 A.L.R. 1488 (1933); E. F. Drew & Co. v. Reinhard, 170 F.2d 679 (2d Cir. 1948).

5. Blood v. Ludlow Carbon Black Co., 150 Pa. 1, 24 A. 348 (1892): "The minds are individual, but the results are joint, and the results of joint action by the members are the results of action by the firm, and if in the course of the partnership business, the result becomes partnership property." But it has been held that issuance of a patent to partners jointly, even though the expenses of application are paid out of partnership funds, vests the legal title in them as cotenants, and the partnership has no equitable interest in the patent in the absence of express agreement. Levy v. Dattlebaum, 63 F. 992 (C.C.N.Y.1894); Drake v. Hall, 220 F. 905 (7th Cir. 1914). The fact of co-ownership of a patent does not of itself establish partnership. Williams v. Knibbs, 213 Mass. 534, 100 N.E. 666 (1913); Drake v. Hall, supra; Pitts v. Hall, 19 Fed.Cas. p. 758, No. 11,193 (C.C.N.Y.1854).

6. Gohen v. Gravelle, 411 Pa. 520, 192 A.2d 414 (1963). The invention was a device for filling-station nozzles. The factors were (1) financial co-mingling of the affairs of the nozzle development operation with the others conducted by the partners (filling-stations and auto parts shop), (2) use of partnership assets (employees and premises) in the nozzle operation, (3) inventing partner spent almost all his time on the nozzle while co-partner handled other matters, (4) admissions by the inventing partner that nozzle business was included in the partnership, and (5) reporting of nozzle receipts on partnership income tax return.

doubt that a partnership, like a corporation or any other business association, may be the legal or equitable owner of a patent.[7] As in the situation of employer and employee, the respective rights and obligations of partnership and partner with respect to the inventions of a partner depend on the express and implied terms of the contract of partnership. If a partner is made such by reason of his inventive ability, and if the business of the partnership includes the making of inventions, it would seem evident that the intention of the parties is that the benefit of the inventions should belong to the partnership, and that any patents issued thereon should belong to the partnership.[8]

If it cannot be found to be the intention of the partners that an invention made by a partner belongs to the partnership in its entirety, it may be more readily inferred that the partnership, as in the case of an employer [9] is vested with an implied non-exclusive license to utilize the invention, though it be patented by the partner, for partnership purposes during the duration of the partnership.[10] On dissolution of the partnership and withdrawal of the patentee partner, the license continues in those who take over partnership property as to existing machinery and appliances.[11]

7. Freeman v. Freeman, 136 Mass. 260 (1884); Id., 142 Mass. 98, 7 N.E. 710 (1886). A partner assigned to the partnership the invention he had made while a partner and patent was issued to the partnership. It was held that on dissolution by death the patent was partnership property, not joint property, so that the surviving partner was accountable for profits derived from its use.

See also Hill v. Miller, 78 Cal. 149, 20 P. 304 (1889), a partnership is the equitable owner of a patent issued to a partner on an invention he had contributed to the firm on its formation; Freeman v. Lowell Specialty Co., 174 Mich. 59, 140 N.W. 572 (1913); Spears v. Willis, 151 N.Y. 443, 45 N.E. 849 (1897); Whitcomb v. Whitcomb, 85 Vt. 76, 81 A. 97, Ann.Cas.1913E, 1015 (1911); Bussey v. Porter, 182 Ga. 727, 186 S.E. 826 (1936).

By express agreement the partnership may be entitled to a share in inventions made by a partner in collaboration with a third person. Burr v. De La Vergne, 102 N.Y. 415, 7 N.E. 366 (1886).

8. During the life of a partnership a partner invented and patented machines used by the partnership and manufactured and sold by it. Expenses of developing the inventions and securing the patents were paid out of partnership funds. It was held on dissolution that the patents were partnership property. Zanetti v. Zanetti, 77 Cal.App.2d 553, 175 P.2d 603 (1947).

See also Adams v. Silfen, 337 Ill.App. 654, 86 N.E.2d 288 (1949).

9. United States v. Dubilier Condenser Corporation, 289 U.S. 178, 53 S.Ct. 554, 77 L.Ed. 1114, 85 A.L.R. 1488 (1933), dealing with the employer's implied license, known as "shop-rights."

10. Mulhens & Kropff v. Fred Muelhens, Inc., 38 F.2d 287 (S.D.N.Y., 1929), a case presenting the analogous situation of a registered trademark for a product made by a partner by a secret process.

11. Such license or "shop-right" terminates on dissolution. Haffcke v. Clark, 50 F. 531 (4th Cir. 1892); Elgin Wind Power & Pump Co. v. Nichols, 65 F. 215 (7th Cir. 1895); Carroll v. Goldschmidt, 80 F. 520 (C.C. N.Y., 1897). It continues as to existing machinery and appliances taken over by continuing partners. Keller v. Stolzenbach, 20 F. 47 (C.C.Pa., 1884); Id., 28 F. 81 (C.C.Pa., 1886); Mueller v. Mueller, 95 F. 155 (3d Cir. 1899). See also Slemmer's Appeal, 58 Pa. 155, 98 Am.Dec. 248 (1868).

An idea for a radio program, carried into execution by a partnership may become the property of the firm. contributed thereto by the partner who conceived it.[12]

(e) Good Will

Goodwill is a kind of property a partnership may own. Sometimes it is purchased in connection with a business or tangible assets; if so, the usual presumptions arise as to whether it belongs to the firm or the members. There is a further complication in the more common case where good will is not purchased but is generated in the operation of the business. Particularly if it is a service business, one or more partners may claim that it was created by, and belongs to, them as individuals. The problem usually comes up at dissolution, and is discussed in detail there.[13]

LEGAL TITLE TO PARTNERSHIP PROPERTY

§ 38. Any estate in real property may be acquired in the partnership name. Title so acquired can be conveyed only in the partnership name.

A conveyance to a partnership in the partnership name, though without words of inheritance, passes the entire estate of the grantor unless a contrary intention appears. U.P.A. § 8(3, 4).

The common law rule was otherwise, with partners holding legal title to real estate in individual names, subject to a sort of trust for the firm. But legal title to personalty could be held in the firm name.

The U.P.A. authorization to take legal title in the firm name eliminates many complexities of the split between legal and equitable ownership. But there has been some tendency to cling to past practice in conveyancing.

Personal property and choses in action have long been capable of holding by a partnership in the firm name.[14] But, at common law, the title to real estate had to be held by recognized legal persons. Reluctance of the courts to accept the partnership as a legal person[15] resulted in holding that a partnership could not take title to realty in the firm name.[16] A conveyance designating a grantee firm by its artificial name, such as "American Stove & Lumber Co." did not pass legal

---

12. Lyon v. MacQuarrie, 46 Cal.App.2d 119, 115 P.2d 594 (1941).

13. Sec. 84(a) below; see also sec. 52(b).

14. Hendren v. Wing, 60 Ark. 561, 31 S.W. 149, 46 Am.St.Rep. 218 (1895); Kellogg v. Olson, 34 Minn. 103, 24 N.W. 364 (1885); Harris, Woodson, Barbie Co. v. Gwathmey, 130 Va. 277, 107 S.E. 658 (1921).

15. See Sec. 3 above.

16. "A partnership can really own no property. The property of the firm is owned by the members thereof." Adams v. Blumenshine, 27 N.M. 643, 204 P. 66, 20 A.L.R. 369 (1922); Woodward v. McAdam, 101 Cal. 438, 35 P. 1016 (1894); Bankers Trust Co. v. Knee, 263 N.W. 549 (Iowa 1935). Earlier cases are cited in Crane, The Uniform Partnership Act—A Criticism, 28 Harv.L.Rev. 762, 770 n. 65 (1915).

title.[17] A mortgage to a partnership in its artificial name has been held effective as constituting a lien but not a conveyance of title.[18] Other methods were devised to give the firm some protection against loss of its interest. A conveyance to a partnership whose name included the surname of a partner vested legal title in that partner in trust for the firm.[19] A few courts held that membership of the firm could be shown by parol evidence, and that the grant vested title in them as tenants in common.[20]

Additional common law complications arose from the prima facie presumption that the record title indicates the real or beneficial ownership.[21] Among partners it is possible to overcome the presumption by showing intent for ownership by the firm.[22] But third parties are generally not bound by such intent if they are ignorant of it. The partnership may lose its equitable interest to third persons dealing with the partner who has record title, as in other cases of a trustee's sale of trust assets to a bona fide purchaser for value.[23] Similarly a

---

17. Africa v. Trexler, 232 Pa. 493, 81 A. 707 (1911). Accord, Spaulding Mfg. Co. v. Godbold, 92 Ark. 63, 121 S.W. 1063, 29 L.R.A.,N.S., 282, 135 Am.St. Rep. 168, 19 Ann.Cas. 947 (1909) (though equity will reform deed on grounds of mistake); Curtis v. Reilly, 188 Iowa 1217, 177 N.W. 535 (1920) (semble); Holmes v. Jarrett, Moon & Co., 54 Tenn. (7 Heisk.) 506 (1872); Silverman v. Kristufek, 162 Ill. 222, 44 N.E. 430 (1896) (deed did not give firm legal title but amounted to contract to convey, and vested equitable title in the firm).

For an exhaustive collection of authorities on how legal title is affected by various forms of grants to partners and partnerships, see Sackman, Law of Titles § 2.25 (1959). See also Powell, Land Capacity of Natural Persons as Unincorporated Groups, 49 Colum.L.Rev. 297, 314–15 (1949).

18. Barber v. Crowell, 55 Neb. 571, 75 N.W. 1109 (1898).

19. Holmes v. Jarrett, Moon & Co., n. 17 above; Gille v. Hunt, 35 Minn. 357, 29 N.W. 2 (1886); Schlake v. Healey, 108 Neb. 35, 187 N.W. 427 (1922); Berg v. Johnson, 139 Ark. 243, 213 S.W. 393, 8 A.L.R. 489 (1919); Riddle v. Whitehill, 135 U.S. 621. 10 S.Ct. 924, 34 L.Ed. 232 (1890).

See Attaway v. Stanolind Oil & Gas Co., 232 F.2d 790 (10th Cir. 1956) reaching the same result under N. M. law without emphasizing the existence of a partner's name in the firm name.

For other partnership-protecting devices in case of failure of legal title, see n. 17 above.

20. Kentucky Block Cannel Coal Co. v. Sewell, 249 F. 840, 1 A.L.R. 556 (6th Cir. 1918), noted 17 Mich.L.Rev. 190 (1918); Walker v. Miller, 139 N.C. 448, 52 S.E. 125, 1 L.R.A.,N.S., 157, 111 Am.St.Rep. 805, 4 Ann.Cas. 601 (1905); Wray v. Wray, 2 Ch. 349, 74 L.J.Ch. 687 (1905); Kelley v. Bourne, 15 Or. 476, 16 P. 40 (1887); Hoffman v. Porter, Fed.Cas.No.6,577, 2 Brock. 156 (1824).

21. Sec. 37(d) above. Failure to designate whether the title is taken as joint tenants or as tenants in common results in a holding of the latter, by the majority American view. Williams v. Dovell, 202 Md. 351, 96 A.2d 484 (1953). See Sec. 40 below at n. 48. Cases are collected in 2 Am.L. of Prop. 36 (1952).

22. Sec. 37 above.

23. McNeil v. First Congregational Soc., 66 Cal. 105, 4 P. 1096 (1884); Seeley v. Mitchell's Assignee, 85 Ky. 508, 4 S.W. 190 (1887); Hammond v. Paxton, 58 Mich. 393, 25 N.W. 321 (1885); Gwinner v. Union Trust Co., 226 Pa. 614, 75 A. 856 (1910) (semble). See also Sec. 37(d) above at n. 51. A fuller discussion is Sher & Bromberg, Texas Partnership Law in the 20th Century—Why Texas Should Adopt the Uniform Partnership Act, 12 Sw. L.J. 263, 285–87 (1958). Cf. U.P.A. § 10(3), Sec. 50A below.

creditor of the record holder may be able to establish priority over a partnership creditor against the property, reversing the usual order of priorities.[24]

The obvious solution to the common law non-entity view was to authorize partnerships to take legal title (or any other estate) in the firm name, and this is what the U.P.A. has done.[25] There can be little doubt that the Act means what it says,[26] or that this is one of the more profound theoretical changes it has made.

The practicalities are another matter. For one thing, tradition dies hard, especially in the property field. An eminent Texas land lawyer, officer of a leading title company, wrote in the 1960s after examining the U.P.A. which had just been adopted in that state (although in force many other places for half a century): "A partnership cannot acquire the *legal* title to real estate under the partnership name. Fundamentally a partnership is not a legal entity, and no act of the Legislature can make it so." [27] One early commentator [28] ventured that partners might be reluctant to take title in the name of the firm because of the comparative ease with which any partner could then convey good title to a third person. There is, of course, some risk although perhaps no greater than in having one partner sign checks on the firm's bank account.

Still another concern is whether good title can be conveyed later when the partners want to sell or mortgage. There is apprehension that title companies or examiners may require elaborate curative work

But if the buyer has notice of the partnership's interest, he takes subject to it. Hartnett v. Stillwell, 121 Ga. 386, 49 S.E. 276, 104 Am.St.Rep. 151 (1904); Martin v. Carlisle, 46 Okl. 268, 148 P. 833, 6 A.L.R. 154 (1915); Magen v. Neiman, 301 Pa. 164, 151 A. 796 (1930). Partnership possession of the land has dubiously been held not to constitute notice. Hammond v. Paxton, above. See Note, Notice: Occupancy by a Partnership as Notice of Its Claim to Land, 11 Okl.L.Rev. 462 (1958).

24. See Sec. 91 below, Sec. 37(d) above at n. 51.

25. U.P.A. § 8(3); see also id. § 8(4). One state reduces confusion as to the nature of the grantee by specifying "A conveyance to a partnership in the firm name shall recite that the grantee is a partnership." R.C. (Ohio) § 1775.-07 (1964), which is otherwise U.P.A. § 8. No identification of partners is required.

Words of inheritance, though commonly used, are largely superfluous. U.P.A. § 8(4). The justification for their continued use is as an antidote to any intention which might otherwise appear to contradict the general rule of the cited Section that a conveyance passes the grantor's entire interest.

26. Among the cases recognizing its validity are Palkovitz v. Second Fed. Sav. & Loan Assoc., 412 Pa. 547, 195 A.2d 347 (1963); Brown v. Brown, 45 Tenn.App. 78, 320 S.W.2d 721 (1950).

One state has provided a statutory form of acknowledgment for conveyances of title held in the firm name. Calif. Civil Code § 1190a.

27. Letter, Aug. 17, 1961 to Alan R. Bromberg. It seems kinder not to disclose the writer's name.

28. Lewis, The Uniform Partnership Act, 24 Yale L.J. 617, 624 (1915), referring to U.P.A. § 10(1), Sec. 50A below.

on all changes in membership of the firm between the grants to and from it.[29]

For these reasons, or others which may have more substance, there has been some reluctance to take advantage of the U.P.A. provision for conveyances to the firm. Many conveyances are still made to some or all the partners as individuals, with or without mention of the partnership.[30] They thus needlessly preserve all the confusions and complications of the common law.

If property belongs beneficially to the firm, partners' rights in it [31] are the same whether legal title is in the firm or someone else, except insofar as all their rights may be cut off by an unauthorized conveyance or other third party rights.

If a partnership has taken title to land in its name, the U.P.A. provides that title can be conveyed only in that name.[32] However, a conveyance by one or more of the partners, if a firm act,[33] would convey at least an equitable title of the partnership. Such title would probably be bad against a later B.F.P. taking a conveyance in the firm name, unless the local recording acts caused the prior deed to be indexed in the firm name. It would similarly be bad against an execution creditor if, by the recording acts, he is in the position of a B.F.P. as regards unrecorded equitable interests.

EFFECT OF STATUTE OF FRAUDS ON REAL ESTATE BECOMING PARTNERSHIP PROPERTY

§ 39. The land portion of the Statute of Frauds may nullify an oral agreement to create a partnership interest in real estate. But it is usually inapplicable to a partnership agreement which requires no specific conveyance. The Statute is also mitigated by the doctrines of resulting and constructive trust. The Statute does not bar an accounting for the proceeds of an executed partnership in real estate.

The fourth section of the historic Statute of Frauds,[34] some form of which is ubiquitous in the U.S., generally requires a written memorandum for the enforceability of a contract for the transfer of an interest in land. It gives rise to several problems in agreements for

---

29. This is, from the partnership viewpoint, an unnecessary precaution, unless perhaps there has been a change in firm name. A conveyance in the firm name, executed by one partner recited to be such, is ordinarily enough. U.P.A. § 10(1), Sec. 50A below. Simes, Model Title Standards 66–67 (1960).

In any event, comparable difficulties are present when several partners are grantees, or the firm is mentioned in the conveyance to them.

30. The most common form of reference to the firm is probably "To X and Y

doing business as the XY Co." Query: is legal title in X and Y or in the firm?

31. U.P.A. § 25, Secs. 40–45 below.

32. See Karesh, Partnership Law and Uniform Partnership Act in South Carolina, 3 S.C.L.Rev. 366, 395 (1951).

33. U.P.A. § 10(2).

34. 29 Chas. II (1677). Other portions of the Statute are discussed in Sec. 23 above.

the formation of partnerships and joint ventures, and in real estate acquired pursuant to such agreements.

An oral agreement to create a partnership is valid; if acted on by conducting a business, a partnership legally exists even though it is intended that the partnership own or deal in real estate.[35] No transfer of an interest in land between the parties is required by such an agreement; they are only making a partnership (or joint venture) contract.[36] If real property is acquired with partnership funds for partnership purposes, it is partnership property.[37] Though title is taken in the name of one or more of the partners, the Statute of Frauds does not prevent partnership ownership.[38] The situation is in effect

35. "An agreement to become partners in dealing in real estate is neither a contract to buy nor a contract to sell real estate as between the parties to it. So far as the formation of the co-partnership is concerned, title to real estate is in no wise affected by the making of the agreement. The terms of the agreement, the mutual undertakings of the partners as between themselves as to what each will contribute, and the interests of each in the profits of their undertaking, are matters not necessarily affected by the statute." Garth v. Davis & Johnson, 120 Ky. 106, 85 S.W. 692, 27 Ky.Law Rep. 505, 117 Am.St.Rep. 571 (1905). "But suppose two persons, by parol agreement, enter into a partnership to speculate in lands, how do they come in conflict with the statute of frauds? No estate or interest in land has been granted, assigned or declared. When the agreement is made no lands are owned by the firm, and neither party attempts to convey or assign any to the other. The contract is a valid one, and in pursuance of this agreement they go on and buy, improve and sell lands. While they are doing this, do they not act as partners and bear a partnership relation to each other? Within the meaning of the statute in such case, neither conveys or assigns any land to the other, and hence there is no conflict with the statute." Chester v. Dickerson, 54 N.Y. 1, 8, 9, 13 Am. Rep. 550, 553, 554 (1873).

36. N. 35 above. Workman v. Harrison, 282 F.2d 693 (10th Cir. 1960) (N.M. law) (joint venture for development of a shopping center); Hunt v. Hammonds, 257 Ala. 586, 60 So.2d 355 (1952) (P agreed to furnish land, D to erect drive-in theatre and cafe for P to

manage and share profits); Potucek v. Blair, 176 Kan. 263, 270 P.2d 240 (1954) (joint ownership and operation of oil and gas leases); Appleby v. Buck, 351 S.W.2d 494 (Ky.1961) (semble; constructive trust applied). Cases are collected in Corbin, Contracts § 411 (1950).

Cf. Summers v. Hoffman, 341 Mich. 686, 69 N.W.2d 198, 48 A.L.R.2d 1033 (1955). A joint venture for acquiring, title-clearing, developing and selling land, with equal sharing of profits, was not within Statute of Frauds provision requiring written agreement "to pay any commission . . . upon the sale of any interest in real estate." Specific performance was granted.

The limited rights of a partner in partnership property (U.P.A. § 25, Secs. 40–45 below) and the personal property character of his interest in the partnership (U.P.A. § 26, Ch. 4A below) reinforce the conclusion that no transfer of an interest in land is inherent in a partnership agreement for using or dealing in land or making it partnership property.

37. Sec. 37 above.

38. Bates v. Babcock, 95 Cal. 479, 30 P. 605, 16 L.R.A. 745, 29 Am.St.Rep. 133 (1893); Van Housen v. Copeland, 180 Ill. 74, 54 N.E. 169 (1899); Fitch v. King, 279 Ill. 62, 116 N.E. 624 (1917); Ottaviano v. Lorenzo, 169 Md. 51, 179 A. 530 (1935); Richards v. Grinnell, 63 Iowa 44, 18 N.W. 668, 50 Am.Rep. 727 (1884); Greenwood v. Marvin, 111 N.Y. 423, 19 N.E. 228 (1888); Ihmsen v. Huston, 247 Pa. 402, 93 A. 601 (1915); Bruce v. Hastings, 41 Vt. 380, 98 Am.Dec. 592 (1868); McElroy v. Swope, 47 F. 380 (C.C.Mo., 1891).

a resulting trust, which is outside the Statute.[39] If a partner in a going firm, in the course of carrying on the business, has a duty to acquire land for the firm but acquires it in his own name (even though he uses his own funds), the partnership may enforce an equitable claim to the property by way of a constructive trust,[40] which is also outside the Statute.[41] The courts are fairly well agreed on these propositions.

The situations which produce greater difficulties and conflicts of authority are those of oral agreements to join in a future partnership or joint venture to buy and sell land. Typically, then, one partner makes the deal in his own name with his own money or credit, and the other claims his share. In most states an oral agreement to give another an interest in land owned or to be acquired by the promisor does not give the promisee an enforceable legal or equitable interest in the land.[42] That the disappointed promisee has rendered services in connection with the transaction is often insufficient part performance to take the agreement out of the Statute and permit its specific enforcement. However, if the promisee brings an action for an accounting of

---

39. Restatement, Second, Trusts, § 406.

40. Dikis v. Likis, 187 Ala. 218, 65 So. 398 (1914); Regan v. Grady, 343 Ill. 423, 175 N.E. 567 (1931); Garth v. Davis & Johnson, 120 Ky. 106, 85 S.W. 692, 27 Ky.Law Rep. 505, 117 Am.St. Rep. 571 (1905); Lurie v. Pinanski, 215 Mass. 229, 102 N.E. 629 (1913); Mattikow v. Sudarsky, 248 N.Y. 404, 162 N.E. 296 (1928), noted in 6 N.Y.U.L. Rev. 208; 77 U.Pa.L.Rev. 293; Smith v. Brown, 294 Pa. 203, 143 A. 913 (1928).

41. Restatement, Second, Trusts, § 40, comment *d*.

A constructive trust may be imposed on property taken in the names of a partner and wife as joint tenants. Miller v. Ousley, 334 Ill. 183, 165 N.E. 629 (1929).

Cf. Nester v. Sullivan, 147 Mich. 493, 111 N.W. 85, 9 L.R.A.,N.S., 1106 (1907); Mullholland v. Patch, 205 Mich. 490, 171 N.W. 422, 18 A.L.R. 468 (1919) allowing an accounting for profits from dealing in options on farm lands.

42. Morton v. Nelson, 145 Ill. 586, 32 N.E. 916 (1893); Rieike v. Kowalsky, 207 Misc. 254, 138 N.Y.S.2d 711 (Sup. Ct.1954), aff'd 285 App.Div. 1009, 139 N.Y.S.2d 299 (1955); Edgcomb v. Clough, 275 Pa. 90, 118 A. 610 (1922), noted 23 Colum.L.Rev. 378 (1923), 32 Yale L.J. 504 (1923); Burgwyn v.

Jones, 113 Va. 511, 75 S.E. 188, 41 L.R.A.,N.S., 120, Ann.Cas.1913E, 564 (1912); Seymour v. Cushway, 100 Wis. 580, 76 N.W. 769, 69 Am.St.Rep. 957 (1898); White v. McNeil, 294 S.W. 928 (Tex.Civ.App.1927).

Contra, Perelli-Minetti v. Lawson, 205 Cal. 642, 272 P. 573 (1928); Bastjan v. Bastjan, 215 Cal. 662, 12 P.2d 627 (1932); Sadugor v. Holstein, 199 Cal. App.2d 477, 18 Cal.Rptr. 859 (1962) (trust imposed on land acquired by one proposed joint venturer (D) who excluded other (P) from the purchase after agreeing orally to make it jointly; P was willing and able to put up his share of the purchase price, but D appropriated the deal when P refused to sign a note and mortgage on the property to finance D's half; the latter was not part of the agreement); Eubank v. Richardson, 353 S.W.2d 367 (Ky.1962).

It has been held that an oral agreement for a real estate joint venture is so invalid under the Statute that one participant is not liable for the acts of the other as his representative. Goodsitt v. Richter, 216 Wis. 351, 257 N.W. 23, 95 A.L.R. 1238 (1934). See Morrison v. Meister, 212 Mich. 516, 180 N.W. 395 (1920). Contra, Chester v. Dickerson, 54 N.Y. 1, 13 Am.Rep. 550 (1873) (misrepresentation in course of the business).

profits derived from the venture, or a breach of contract action at law, it seems he is entitled to a remedy. He is not seeking to establish an interest in land or to enforce a promise to transfer to him such an interest, but is claiming a share of money due him by agreement. The weight of authority gives him relief.[43]

The Statute may operate more vigorously to prevent property previously owned by a partner from becoming partnership property without a conveyance or other writing.[44] This looks more like an agreed transfer of an interest in land. However, intent is usually found to control, with trust theories available to circumvent the Statute if necessary.[45]

43. Wooten v. Marshall, 279 F.2d 558 (2d Cir. 1960) (N.Y. law, noting the distinction between an agreement for a commercial venture, here a real estate development, which is outside the Statute, and one for mere co-ownership, which is within; the evolution of N.Y. law is traced). Eads v. Murphy, 27 Ariz. 267, 232 P. 877 (1925); Bates v. Babcock, 95 Cal. 479, 30 P. 605, 16 L.R.A. 745, 29 Am.St.Rep. 133 (1892); Von Trotha v. Bamberger, 15 Colo. 1, 24 P. 883 (1890); Lane v. Lodge, 139 Ga. 93, 76 S.E. 874 (1912), action for damages for breach of contract to enter into a partnership which was to acquire a business part of the assets of which were real estate; Blythe, Markley, Rule & Smith v. Cummings, 190 Iowa 1239, 176 N.W. 688 (1920); Fencer v. Wills, 259 Mass. 546, 156 N.E. 841 (1927); Snyder v. Wolford, 33 Minn. 175, 22 N.W. 254, 53 Am.Rep. 22 (1885); Newell v. Cochran, 41 Minn. 374, 43 N.W. 84 (1889), the associate who in breach of his fiduciary duty has received secret profits is accountable for them; Scott v. Kempland, 264 S.W.2d 349 (Mo.1954); Ruta v. Werner, 1 N.J.Super. 455, 63 A.2d 825 (1948); Huson v. Portland & S. E. Ry. Co., 107 Or. 187, 211 P. 897, 213 P. 408 (1923); Howell v. Kelly, 149 Pa. 473, 24 A. 224 (1884); Huntington v. Burdeau, 149 Wis. 263, 135 N.W. 845 (1912), transaction being fully executed, save for accounting for profits; Hoge v. George, 27 Wyo. 423, 200 P. 96, 18 A.L.R. 484 (1921); Dale v. Hamilton, 5 Hare 369 (1846).

But see cases reaching a contrary result in a minority of jurisdictions: Schultz v. Waldons, 60 N.J.Eq. 71, 47 A. 187 (1900); Silberman v. Angert, 101 N.J. Eq. 477, 138 A. 529 (1927); Raub v. Smith, 61 Mich. 543, 28 N.W. 676, 1 Am.St.Rep. 619 (1886); Davis v. Hillman, 288 Pa. 16, 135 A. 254 (1927).

See also Redditt v. Horn, 361 Pa. 533, 64 A.2d 809 (1949). An architect by oral agreement undertook to plan and supervise a building construction project and was to receive a share of the net profits. He was denied an accounting in equity as this would by specific enforcement recognize an interest in land. It was, however, indicated that he could recover in an action at law restitution for the value of his services.

Assignment to a co-partner of a partner's interest, where the firm assets include real estate has generally been held to fall within the Statute of Frauds as to dealings in real estate, King v. Northern Pac. R. R. Co., 27 Wash.2d 250, 177 P.2d 714, 171 A.L.R. 190 (1947).

One claiming a share of profits of a real estate development as compensation for services, has been allowed an accounting (without alleging partnership) outside the Statute of Frauds. Berne v. Keith, 361 S.W.2d 592 (Tex. Civ.App.1962) error ref., n. r. e.

44. Pappas v. Gounaris, 168 Tex. 355, 311 S.W.2d 644 (1958). Cases are collected, Annot., 45 A.L.R.2d 1009, 1015–17 (1956). Substantial injustice can result in widely varying situations, e. g., Weatherford v. Lee, 364 S.W.2d 730 (Tex.Civ.App.1963), error ref. n. r. e. (campsite for longtime neighbors); Ideal Structures Corp. v. Levine, Huntsville Development Corp., 251 F. Supp. 3, 10 (N.D.Ala.1966) (multimillion dollar shopping center financing and development; Ala. law).

45. Sec. 37 above; Annot., 45 A.L.R.2d 1009 (1956).

DISTINGUISHING PARTNERSHIP PROPERTY FROM INTEREST IN PARTNERSHIP

§ 40. At common law, partners were regarded as tenants in common with some features of joint tenants. The share of each partner was subject to his co-partners' enforceable right to have the common property held for partnership purposes and for the payment of partnership debts. This hybrid arrangement was often called "partners' equities."

The property rights of a partner are (1) his rights in specific partnership property, (2) his interest in the partnership, and (3) his right to participate in the management. U.P.A. § 24.

A partner is co-owner with his partners of specific partnership property holding as a tenant in partnership. U.P.A. § 25(1). The incidents of this tenancy are so negligible that ownership of the property is, for all practical purposes, in the partnership, not in the partners.

A partner's interest in the partnership is his share of the profits and surplus, and the same is personal property. U.P.A. § 26.

(a) Common Law

Since the common law did not recognize the capacity of a partnership to hold title to land,[45a] title was usually taken in the name of the partners. The form of co-ownership which evolved to meet the special needs of partners was a modification, by the courts of equity and the law merchant, of the simpler forms of joint tenancy and tenancy in common,[46] both of which were non-commercial in origin and operation. One of the earliest cases held that a normal incident of joint tenancy—the right of survivorship in the beneficial as well as the legal title—did not apply to partnerships.[47] Valuable economic rights which the deceased presumably expected to preserve for his heirs, rather than give to his partners, were thereby protected. Similarly, tenancy in common (which is often described as the way partners hold realty[48]) was modified by the pivotal doctrine of "partners'

Other references on partnership application of Statute of Frauds: Lilienthal, Oral Agreements for Real Estate Co-partnerships, 13 Harv.L.Rev. 455 (1900); Brightman, Oral Partnership Agreements Concerning an Interest in Land, 9 Cornell L.Q. 97 (1924); Notes 42 Harv.L.Rev. (1929), 77 U.Pa.L.Rev. 293 (1928), Notes cited in n. 42 above, and Corbin, Contracts § 411 (1950).

45a. Sec. 38 above.

46. "The legal characteristics of partnership property, and the interests, powers and rights of the partners relative to the same, are peculiar, and cannot well be assimilated to any other class of property. . . . While it has many characteristics of estates in common and joint tenancies, yet the interest of partners in the firm prop-

erty is neither that of joint tenants nor that of tenants in common, but is sui generis." Morrison v. Austin State Bank, 213 Ill. 472, 480, 72 N.E. 1109, 1111, 104 Am.St.Rep. 225 (1905). Semble, Lueth v. Goodknecht, 345 Ill. 197, 177 N.E. 690, 79 A.L.R. 780 (1931).

47. Martin v. Crump, 2 Salkeld 444, 91 Eng.Rep. 385 (1698): "Two joint merchants make B their factor; one dies, leaving an executor; this executor and the survivor cannot join, for the remedy survives but not the duty; and therefore on recovery he must be accountable to the executor for that." This is the complete reported opinion.

48. Woodward v. McAdam, 101 Cal. 438, 35 P. 1016 (1894); Curtis v. Reilly, 188 Iowa 1217, 177 N.W. 535 (1920); Whit-

equities." The latter stands for the right of each partner to have all partnership property, both real and personal, applied for partnership purposes including the payment of partnership debts. This recognizes (1) the business primacy of the relationship, which would be disrupted if a partner were free to transfer his property interest out of the firm, and (2) the personal liability of each partner for the firm debts, which might be magnified for any one partner if he could not insist that the joint property be used to pay joint debts. Another feature is that the successor to a partner's share as co-owner, whether by assignment, execution sale, or inheritance, does not become a partner, owing to *delectus personae*.[49] Whatever title he takes is subject to the right of the other partners, as was the title of the partner through whom he claims, to use and apply the entire property for partnership purposes.[50]

The common law, then, was twisted up with the difficulty of trying to reconcile two essentially different kinds of ownership—organizational (or collective) and individual—in a single concept.

A few common law jurisdictions cut the Gordian knot by declaring the partnership a legal entity or person capable of holding property.[51] But it was still necessary to fashion some device for implementing the individual partner's derivative or secondary rights relative to the firm's property. This usually took the form of recognizing that he had some "equity" in the property, encompassing at least a residual right to share it (or its proceeds) on dissolution and after payment of debts.[52]

man v. Boston & Maine R. R., 3 Allen 133 (Mass.1861); Buchan v. Sumner, 2 Barb.Ch. 165, 47 Am.Dec. 305 (N.Y. 1847); Kentucky Block Cannel Coal Co. v. Sewell, 249 F. 840, 1 A.L.R. 556 (6th Cir. 1918).

Personal property has been said to be held by partners as joint tenants: Nixon & Chatfield v. Nash & Atkinson, 12 Ohio St. 647, 80 Am.Dec. 390 (1861); Deal v. Bogue, 20 Pa. 228, 57 Am.Dec. 702 (1853); Anderson v. Tompkins, Fed.Cas.No.365 (D.Va.1820).

See also Sec. 38 n. 21 above.

49. Sec. 5 above.

50. Western Shoe Co. v. Neumeister, 258 Mich. 662, 242 N.W. 802 (1932); Hammond Oil Co. v. Standard Oil Co. of New Jersey, 259 N.Y. 312, 181 N.E. 583 (1932); Horton's Appeal, 13 Pa. 67 (1850).

51. Parker v. Rolfe, 167 Ark. 245, 267 S.W. 775 (1925), noted 39 Harv.L.Rev. 247 (1925); Johnson v. Shirley, 152 Ind. 453, 53 N.E. 459 (1899); Jensen v. Wiersma, 185 Iowa 551, 170 N.W. 780, 4 A.L.R. 298 (1919); Pratt v. McGuinness, 173 Mass. 170, 53 N.E. 380 (1899); Menagh v. Whitwell, 52 N.Y. 146, 11 Am.Rep. 683 (1873); Richard v. Allen, 117 Pa. 199, 11 A. 552, 2 Am.St.Rep. 652 (1887).

See also Sec. 43 n. 15 below.

In Helvering v. Walbridge, 70 F.2d 683 (2d Cir. 1934), the entity approach was applied to determine gain on sale of partnership property transferred to the firm as part of a partner's capital contribution. Gain was computed on the basis of the value when acquired by the firm. In response, the law was amended to make the tax basis to the partnership the same as in the partner's hands. Revenue Act of 1934, § 113(a) (13). See Rabkin & Johnson, The Partnership under the Federal Tax Laws, 55 Harv.L.Rev. 908, 915–20 (1942). The basis carryover provision is now Int.Rev.Code of 1954, § 723 (26 U.S.C.A.)

52. See Sec. 43(a) below.

(b) U.P.A.

The distinction between the firm's ownership of its property and the partner's ownership of an interest in the firm is taken over by the U.P.A. and refined into a sharp division.[53]

The U.P.A. draftsmen first embraced, then shrank from a complete entity treatment of the firm.[54] They reached workable results consistent with the entity theory, but not identical,[55] by creating a newly labelled "tenancy in partnership" in which the partners are said to own the partnership property. In this tenancy, the co-ownership rules developed at common law are codified and stiffened in their entity features. The net effect is self-contradictory. Although stating that each partner is a co-owner of partnership property,[56] the Act systematically destroys the usual attributes of ownership.[57] The process is described in the next five Sections and, incidentally, makes no distinction between real and personal property of the firm.[58] Functionally, despite the literal language, the partnership owns its property [58A] and the partners do not.[59] The Act would be better if it conceded this rather than accomplishing it by indirection.

Since a limited partner is probably not a partner in the statutory sense,[60] he apparently lacks even the attenuated rights in specific partnership property that a general partner has.

The Act is more coherent in its structuring of a partner's interest in the firm. This is a property right of the particular partner,[61] is necessarily intangible, and is personalty.[62] It is defined as his share of the firm's profits and surplus,[63] and is primarily an economic right. It has most of the qualities of ownership that are expressly denied to

---

53. See Bynum v. Sands, Inc., n. 65 below; Ellis v. Ellis, 415 Pa. 412, 203 A.2d 547 (1964).

54. Sec. 3(e) above.

55. "While objection has been made in some of the cases to holding that a partnership is a separate entity, like a corporation, no appropriate word has been suggested which will express the true idea accurately.

"As to such property the co-partners are neither joint tenants nor tenants in common, but possessors of their respective interests as partners as defined by law, based upon and limited by the contract, but subject first of all to the co-partnership debts." Harris, Woodson, Barbie Co., v. Gwathmey, 130 Va. 277, 107 S.E. 658 (1921).

56. U.P.A. § 25(1). Cf. id. § 24(1).

57. U.P.A. § 25(2). The byproducts include inability of a partner to sue in-

dividually on a partnership cause of action. See Fuqua v. Watson, 107 U.S.P.Q. 251 (N.Y.S.Ct. Dec. 10, 1955) (partner cannot sue for unlawful use of firm name). This appears to be the same case affirmed without opinion 7 A.D.2d 900, 182 N.Y.S.2d 336 (1959). For contract cases, see Sec. 57 below at n. 7.

58. Cf. Casner v. Oldham, 279 S.W.2d 252 (Ky.1955) (pre-U.P.A.)

58A. U.P.A. § 8, Secs. 37, 38 above, adds support to the argument by recognizing partnership ownership.

59. See Bynum v. Sands, Inc. and Ellis v. Ellis, n. 53 above.

60. Sec. 90B(a) below.

61. U.P.A. § 24(2).

62. Id. § 26; U.L.P.A. § 18.

63. U.P.A. § 26.

a partner in specific partnership property, and is a suitable surrogate for them. We examine these aspects too in the next five Sections, each of which successively treats partnership property and the interest in the firm.

—— *Relation Between Partnership Property and Interest in Firm*

A partner's interest in the firm bears roughly the same relation to the firm's property as a share of General Motors stock does to a Chevrolet on the assembly line. One is an ownership interest in the whole business organization; the other is a particular item owned by the organization.

Another way to visualize the difference is by reference to a partnership balance sheet:

ASSETS		LIABILITIES & CAPITAL	
Cash in banks	$ 10	Notes and accounts payable	$ 50
Accounts receivable	20	Capital accounts:	
Inventory	30	Partner X	30
Land, building, equipment	40	Partner Y	20
	$100		$100

The assets are partnership property, the things with which it does business. The capital (or equity) accounts are not exactly the interests of the partners in the firm, but represent the value the interests would bring on immediate liquidation of the firm.[64] In accounting terms, the capital accounts equal the excess of assets over liabilities, divided according to the partners' respective shares. This is why businessmen and accountants would be likely to say X had a $30 interest in the firm.[65]

Another connection between partnership property and the interest in the firm is via transfers. When a partner puts money or property into the firm, it normally becomes firm property.[66] His capital account is credited with the value of the property and his interest in the firm increases in value accordingly; the value of the property appears

---

64. This assumes that the assets could be sold for the values shown for them, which will rarely be true.

65. Another common way of describing a partner's interest, say a 50% interest, usually refers to his share of the profits, and may not (owing to differences in contributions and withdrawals) be in the same proportion as his capital account. It is not the same as his "interest in the partnership" as defined in the U.P.A. because of these differences. See Bynum v. Sands, Inc., 70 Nev. 191, 264 P.2d 846 (1953) (assignee of 20% of profits af-

ter repayment of assignors' advances had no interest in partnership leasehold).

In the example given, X may have a 50% interest in profits, but have contributed $10 more (or withdrawn $10 less) than Y. Or he may have a 60% interest in profits with no disparity in contributions and withdrawals. Various other combinations could produce the proportions shown in the capital accounts.

66. It may be that only the use of the property is transferred; see Sec. 37 (a) above.

on the other side of the balance sheet as an asset. The reverse processes occur when a partner withdraws money or property as a distribution of earnings or return of capital contribution.

Rights in partnership property, tenancy in partnership, and a partner's interest in the partnership are best understood by their specific attributes, which are examined in the following Sections 41–45.

(c) Income Tax

For many years, one of the more tormented questions in federal income tax law was the nature of ownership in a partnership. The problem commonly arose when a partner sold what he asserted was an interest in the firm—a single, intangible asset—and claimed favorable capital gains treatment for the profit. The tax authorities countered that he sold his share of each property owned by the firm, including ordinary income items like inventory or uncollected fees for services. The taxpayers consistently won in the courts which, often relying on U.P.A., found that an interest in the firm was sold, not shares in underlying assets of the firm.[67] However, the Treasury won in Congress which, since 1954, has provided tax law's own hybrid concept of the interest in a partnership. It is treated as a single (capital) asset in the main, but with ordinary income attributes when the underlying assets of the firm are, to a significant degree, appreciated inventory or unrealized receivables.[68]

POSSESSION

§ 41. A partner, subject to the provisions of this act and to any agreement between the partners, has an equal right with his partners to possess specific partnership property for partnership purposes; but he has no right to possess such property for any other purpose without the consent of his partners. U.P.A. § 25(2)(a). The common law was in accord.

(a) Partnership Property

Ordinarily, each partner has the right to possess partnership property for partnership purposes. The right may be surrendered by agreement. In some firms, such as joint stock companies with large membership, management and possession are concentrated in designated managers.[69] During a firm's existence, actions between part-

---

67. E. g., Hatch's Estate v. C. I. R., 198 F.2d 26 (9th Cir. 1952); Swiren v. C. I. R., 183 F.2d 656 (7th Cir. 1950), cert. denied 340 U.S. 912, 71 S.Ct. 293, 95 L.Ed. 659 (1951) (law partner; 70% of value represented unbilled fees). Cases are collected, Annot. 44 A.L.R. 354 (1943).

68. Int.Rev.Code of 1954 §§ 745, 751(a) (26 U.S.C.A.). See further discussion Sec. 86(b) (1) below; Jackson et al.,

The Internal Revenue Code of 1954: Partnerships, 54 Colum.L.Rev. 1183, 1215–18 (1954); Bromberg, Taxable Income Without Gain on the Sale of a Deceased Partner's Interest: Code, Common Law and Community Property, 13 Sw.L.J. 343 esp. 347–48 (1959).

69. Oliver's Estate, 136 Pa. 43, 20 A. 527, 9 L.R.A. 421, 20 Am.St.Rep. 894 (1890).

ners cannot usually be maintained on claims arising out of partnership affairs.[70] Thus, though it may be a wrong to deprive a partner of possession of firm property, he cannot maintain a possessory action, such as replevin, against a co-partner.[71] A partner must answer for his wrongful possession in an accounting action, typically on dissolution; in particular, he must account for any profits from the use of the property.[72]

A partner has sufficient possessory and other rights in a partnership bank account to justify a federal tax lien on it for taxes owed by him individually.[73] His right to claim unreasonable search and seizure [74] or privilege against self-incrimination [75] with respect to partnership books or records is more confused. He has generally been permitted to do so in small or family firms where his personal interest looms large,[76] but not in bigger, impersonal firms.[77]

---

70. Secs. 70, 72 below.

71. Buckley v. Carlisle, 2 Cal. 420 (1852); Amusement Syndicate Co. v. Martling, 108 Kan. 798, 196 P. 1058 (1921); Few v. Few, 239 S.C. 321, 122 S.E.2d 829, 837 (1961). Cases are collected, Annots. 21 A.L.R. 21, 124–25 (1922), 168 id. 1088, 1117 (1947).

A partner is not justified in forcibly resisting an attempt of his co-partner to take possession. State v. Roby, 43 Idaho 724, 254 P. 210 (1927).

A partner cannot properly register a partnership automobile in his own name. Kilduff v. Boston Elevated Ry. Co., 247 Mass. 453, 142 N.E. 98 (1924).

72. Ligare v. Peacock, 109 Ill. 94 (1884); Adams v. Kable, 45 Ky. (6 B.Mon.) 384, 44 Am.Dec. 772 (1846); Kraus v. Kraus, 250 N.Y. 63, 164 N.E. 743 (1928). See Sec. 72 below.

Under the U.P.A., a partner's interest is too slight to entitle him to tie up firm realty by a lis pendens when he sues for dissolution and accounting. Rosen v. Rosen, 126 Misc. 37, 212 N.Y.S. 405 (1925), noted 26 Colum.L.Rev. 488 (1926).

73. U. S. v. Balanovski, 131 F.Supp. 898, 907–08 (S.D.N.Y.1955) aff'd on this point, rev'd in part on other grounds, 236 F.2d 298 (2d Cir. 1956), cert. denied 352 U.S. 968, 77 S.Ct. 357, 1 L.Ed.2d 322 (1957). The partners and the partnership were Argentine, but they stipulated that Argentine law governing interests in partnership property was the same as New York's. The income in question was earned through the partnership. The lien statute, creating quasi in rem jurisdiction, referred to "all property and rights to property . . . belonging to" the taxpayer. Int.Rev.Code of 1939, § 3670, now Int.Rev.Code of 1954 § 6321 (26 U.S.C.A.). The court distinguished seemingly contra opinions on the ground they involved rights of partnership creditors with superior claims (over a partner or his creditors) to partnership assets, not questions of jurisdiction. Because of the peculiar nature of the case (particularly the pressure to collect tax on U.S. earnings from non-resident aliens with no other U.S. assets), it should not be regarded as precedent for liens against partnership assets in favor of partners' individual creditors. See Sec. 43 below.

74. U.S.Const. amend. IV.

75. U.S.Const. amend. V.

76. In re Subpoena Duces Tecum, 81 F. Supp. 418 (N.D.Calif.1948) (partner not compelled to produce partnership papers which might be used against him; 6-member family firm). See U. S. v. Lawn, 115 F.Supp. 674 (S.D.N.Y. 1953) (indictments dismissed; partnership records had been procured without warning partners of self-incrimination privilege); U. S. v. Linen Service Council, 141 F.Supp. 511 (D.N.J. 1956) (granting immunity to partners under 15 U.S.C.A. § 32 if partnership documents produced; information on character of firm not given).

77. U. S. v. Onassis, 133 F.Supp. 327 (S.D.N.Y.1955) (partner compelled to

Just as a partner has a right to possess property of the firm for firm purposes, he has no right to possess it for personal purposes unless, of course, his co-partners consent.[78] This serves to keep the property in the firm when needed, but can lead to a clash over distributions. If they are viewed as a partner's right to his share of profits, he apparently has an absolute right to them as against his co-partners.[79] But if they are viewed as a disposition of firm property (cash in the bank), no partner has an individual right to them except by agreement with his associates. The latter view should probably prevail because of its specificity, compared to the rather loose statutory language supporting the other position.[80] This makes it particularly important for the members of the firm to agree in advance when and how profits will be distributed.[80A]

Courts have repeatedly held that a partner cannot be guilty of larceny, embezzlement or similar crimes against partnership property. Various reasons are given, typically that he has sufficient ownership rights so it is not property "of another," or so there is no "taking", or that his initial possession is rightful.[81] Decisions of this kind rest on

produce documents which might incriminate co-partner; 8 general and 2 limited partners in firm with several offices and international ship-brokering activities; partner's right to possess books for partnership purposes was sufficient to support subpoena against him since proceedings related to partnership business; co-partner's right was insufficient to claim books were his private property); U. S. v. Silverstein, 314 F.2d 789 (2d Cir. 1963), cert. denied 374 U.S. 807, 83 S.Ct. 1696, 10 L.Ed.2d 1031 (1963) (partner compelled to produce partnership document which might incriminate him; 3 general partners in 5 firms, each with 25 to 147 limited partners and total capitalization over $5 million); U. S. v. Silverstein, 237 F.Supp. 446 (S.D. N.Y.1965), aff'd, 344 F.2d 1016 (2d Cir. 1965), cert. denied 382 U.S. 823, 86 S.Ct. 65, 15 L.Ed.2d 73 (1965) (semble; 3 managing general partners and 17 nonmanaging general partners). The first Silverstein case is noted 63 Colum.L.Rev. 1319 (1963); 62 Mich.L. Rev. 526 (1964); 7 So.Tex.L.J. 155 (1964); 15 Syr.L.Rev. 92 (1963).

78. U.P.A. § 25(2) (a).

79. U.P.A. § 18(a); id. § 26, U.L.P.A. §§ 10(2), 15, Sec. 40(b) above.

80. N. 79 above. The problem is discussed Sec. 65 below at n. 10.

80A. See Appendix V, par. 2.7 below.

81. State v. Quinn, 245 Iowa 846, 64 N.W.2d 323, 43 A.L.R.2d 1240 (1954) (false pretenses; not property of another); Stark v. Commonwealth, 295 S.W.2d 337 (Ky.1956) (larceny; possession rightful); State v. Peterson, 232 La. 931, 95 So.2d 608 (1957), noted 18 La.L.Rev. 182 (1957), 3 Vill.L.Rev. 215 (1958) (theft; not property of another); People v. Dudley, 97 N.Y.S.2d 358 (County Ct.1950) (dictum). State v. Elsbury, 63 Nev. 463, 175 P.2d 430, 169 A.L.R. 364 (1946) (larceny) is a loose opinion which somehow seems to reach opposite conclusions: (1) no taking of property of another (in the definition of the offense) and (2) no taking of property partly of another and partly of the accused (in the prohibition of a defense of joint ownership).

See Adams v. State, 189 So.2d 354 (Ala. App.1966) (conviction for embezzlement; no partnership existed). Cases are collected, Annots., 17 A.L.R. 982 (1922) (embezzlement), 169 id. 372 (1947) (larceny), 43 A.L.R.2d 1253 (1955) (false pretenses and allied crimes). See also Sec. 69 at n. 25 below.

There is, of course, nothing in this reasoning to keep a third party from being convicted of larceny of partnership funds. See State v. Snow, 98 N.H. 1, 93 A.2d 831 (1953).

technicalities of ownership which may be proper for the criminal law when a person's liberty is at stake, but are hardly consistent with the pro-entity pattern of the U.P.A.[82] A better justification for them is probably the inappropriateness of criminal charges between partners in settling their characteristically complicated accounts, for which adequate civil means are available.[83]

Except perhaps for the criminal aspect just mentioned, a partner's right to possession of partnership property is substantially the same under U.P.A. as it was at common law.

(b) Interest in Firm

Since the interest in the partnership is an intangible owned by the partner, no significant possession questions appear.

ASSIGNABILITY

§ 42. At common law, a partner's share in partnership property was assignable, but the assignee took subject to equitable rights of co-partners to have the property applied for partnership purposes (including debts of the firm). Assignment produced dissolution of the firm.

A partner's right in specific partnership property is not assignable except in connection with the assignment of rights of all the partners in the same property. U.P.A. § 25(2)(b).

(1) A conveyance by a partner of his interest in the partnership does not of itself dissolve the partnership, nor, as against the other partners in the absence of agreement, entitle the assignee, during the continuance of the partnership, to interfere in the management or administration of the partnership business or affairs, or to require any information or account of partnership transactions, or to inspect the partnership books; but it merely entitles the assignee to receive in accordance with his contract the profits to which the assigning partner would otherwise be entitled. (2) In case of a dissolution of the partnership, the assignee is entitled to receive his assignor's interest and may require an account from the date only of the last account agreed to by all the partners. U.P.A. § 27.

(a) Partnership Property

Attempted assignments relating to partnerships take various guises. One may be a partner's conveyance of the firm's entire interest in an asset. The problems here are those of his authority to act for the firm, and are treated in another chapter.[84] A second may be a partner's transfer of his entire interest in the partnership. The re-

---

82. The only case which seems to have taken a hard look at the U.P.A. in this context sustained an indictment for embezzlement. State v. Sasso, 20 N.J. Super. 158, 89 A.2d 489 (1952).

Cf. Larceny Act, 1916, 6 & 7 Geo. 5, c. 50, § 40(4): "If any person who is a member of a co-partnership . . . steals or embezzles any such property of or belonging to such co-partnership . . . he shall be liable to be dealt with, tried and punished as if he had not been or was not a member of such co-partnership. . . ."

83. State v. Peterson, n. 81 above, so suggests.

84. Secs. 49, 50A below.

lated questions center on the nature of the interest and the rights of the assignee, and are considered in the second half of this Section. Another may be a partner's assignment of *his* interest in a particular asset of the firm. This is the subject of the present sub-Section.

These types of transactions are easily illustrated. Suppose X is a 50% partner (in all respects) with Y in the XY firm which owns two 100-share certificates of corporate stock. The three kinds of assignment by X would then be: (1) of 200 shares, normally represented as firm property, (2) of his interest in the XY firm, mentioning the shares (if at all) only by inclusion in the firm assets, and (3) of 100 shares, normally represented as his individual property. It will not always be simple to distinguish the three types of assignments. If the firm has only one asset, the second and third tend to blur (especially if there are no debts).[84A] And the representation by X, express or implied, and the related question of whether he purports to act for the firm or for himself, can make the first and third shade into each other. Similar possibilities exist for land, cash, tangible personalty and other sorts of property, although matters of record title may vary the results somewhat. Most of the problems are caused by imprecision.

X (particularly in a firm with informal operations or few members) has an understandable tendency to think he owns a fraction of any particular firm asset, say 50% of the 200 shares in our example, and can sell his 100-share portion when he wants or mortgage it when he is pressed. Two questions arise in dealing with an attempt by him to do so: (a) Has he the power to make any disposition of his share in specific property? (b) If so, what are the relative rights of the assignee and of the firm? The U.P.A. says no on the first question.[85]

84A. Cf. n. 85 below, last par.

85. U.P.A. § 25(2) (b). Windom Nat. Bank v. Klein, 191 Minn. 447, 254 N.W. 602 (1934), noted 19 Minn.L.Rev. 252 (1935); Smithfield Oil Co. v. Furlonge, 257 N.C. 388, 126 S.E.2d 167 (1962) (alternative holding or dictum). Cases are collected, Annot., 39 A.L.R.2d 1365 (1955).

To put it differently, the Act has destroyed the quality of assignability except for partnership purposes. Commissioners' Note to U.P.A. § 25, 7 Unif. Laws Ann. 148 (1949); Lewis, The Uniform Partnership Act, 24 Yale L.J. 617, 634 (1915).

See Salomon Bros. & Hutzler v. Pedrick, 105 F.Supp. 210 (S.D.N.Y.1952) (death, withdrawal and admission of partners produced no transfer or ownership of securities held by the firm, hence no liability for stamp taxes on transfers; referring to U.P.A. § 25, the court concludes that a partner's rights in partnership assets fall short of individual ownership of undivided interest; consequently, he has no right in specific partnership property which he alone can transfer). From 1947 to 1958 the tax in such a case was limited in proportion to the capital interest in the firm transferred on the change in membership. P.L. 387, 61 Stat. 921, 922 (1947) amending Int. Rev.Code of 1939, § 1802(b), later Int. Rev.Code of 1954, § 4352, repealed in 1958, P.L. 85–859, 72 Stat. 1299 (1958). Since then, Int.Rev.Code of 1954, § 4383 (26 U.S.C.A.) has provided that no stamp tax is due on partnership-owned securities because of changes in membership of the firm unless there is a transfer of a 50% or greater interest in the firm in a period of 12 months (the same test used in id. § 708 for income-tax continuity of the firm).

There were a number of reasons for so doing. One already familiar is the preservation of the property for the business, both in the operational and in the financial sense. Another important one is the difficulty of evaluating a partner's interest in a particular piece of property which may be equitably encumbered for the payment of firm debts.[86] Thus a 50% partner cannot realistically be said to have a 50% interest in Blackacre or a stock certificate if another partner has a right to force its sale or mortgage to discharge obligations of the firm.

The common law generally said yes on the first question.[86A] Facing the second, equity undertook to preserve the rights of other partners (and of the firm) by asserting continuance of partners' equities in the entire property of the firm, and their right to have it applied in payment of debts and adjustment of accounts.[87] The net result was very similar to an assignment of an interest in the firm. However, at common law, dissolution usually resulted.[88]

Where all partners have simultaneously or successively assigned their respective shares in partnership property, the persons who com-

---

A purported transfer of rights in specific partnership property may be treated as an assignment of a partner's interest in the firm, in order to give a transferee an interest in the firm's surplus. An example is Johnston v. Ellis, 49 Idaho 1, 285 P. 1015 (1930).

86. Commissioners' Note to U.P.A. § 25, 7 Unif.Laws Ann. 145–50 (1949); Lewis, The Uniform Partnership Act, 24 Yale L.J. 617, 630–34 (1915).

86A. Keith v. Ham, 89 Ala. 590, 7 So. 234 (1890); Stokes v. Stevens, 40 Cal. 391 (1870).

In many cases, a contrary doctrine has been asserted. It is not clear whether the courts are interpreting the assignment and determining the intent of the parties, or setting forth the final result of the transaction in equity, or denying a legal power of disposition. Parker v. Rolfe, 167 Ark. 245, 267 S.W. 775 (1925).

But see Tuller v. Leaverton, 143 Iowa 162, 121 N.W. 515, 136 Am.St.Rep. 756 (1909); Deeter v. Sellers, 102 Ind. 458, 1 N.E. 854 (1885); Pratt v. McGuinness, 173 Mass. 170, 53 N.E. 380 (1899); National Citizens' Bank of Mankato v. McKinley, 129 Minn. 481, 152 N.W. 879 (1915).

In re Cutler & Horgan, 204 Iowa 739, 212 N.W. 573, 54 A.L.R. 527 (1927),

held that a chattel mortgage of his interest by a partner in a newly formed firm, with the consent of his co-partner, was a lien superior to that of subsequent firm creditors, the mortgage being duly recorded.

87. Fyffe v. Skaggs, 246 Ky. 5, 54 S.W. 2d 369 (1932). See Note, 39 Harv.L. Rev. 247 (1924). Cf. In re Cutler & Horgan, 204 Iowa 739, 212 N.W. 573, 217 N.W. 448, 54 A.L.R. 527 (1927) (co-partner consented). Valaske v. Wirtz, 106 F.2d 450, 124 A.L.R. 889 (6th Cir. 1939) held that a partner's assignment, by mortgage of all his two thirds interest in the property of the firm, whether consented to or ratified by his co-partner, not purporting to be a partnership act, created no lien on firm property.

If the partnership agreement requires that firm realty be held not only to pay debts but to settle respective rights of partners inter se (a common provision), the assignee of a partner obtains no better rights than the assignor. He does not become a co-tenant of specific realty but has merely an interest in personalty. He cannot obtain partition. Altman v. Altman, 271 App.Div. 884, 67 N.Y.S.2d 119 (1946), aff'd 297 N.Y. 973, 80 N.E. 2d 359 (1948).

88. N. 6 below.

plain are unpaid partnership creditors. The creditors, as such, have no lien on partnership property. They are entitled to obtain judgment against the partners jointly, and to levy execution on joint property, in priority to separate creditors. If the partnership property has become the property of third persons without any fraudulent conveyance, the right of partnership creditors to have it applied in payment of their claims is gone.[89] According to some decisions, which fail to recognize the existence of the partnership as a person, and consider the rights of partnership creditors in partnership property as merely derivative, the rights of creditors are gone if no partner is in a position to demand the application of partnership property to partnership debts. If each partner has assigned, then all have extinguished their equities, and there is no partnership property right to be reached by partnership creditors.[90] But if the partnership, as a group entity or person, is considered to be the owner of partnership property, and the partner has the power to assign only his interest in surplus after payment of debts, the assignments of all do not affect the partnership ownership in the property and its availability for partnership creditors.[91] The Uniform Partnership Act appears to have adopted this latter view.

The U.P.A. ban on a partner's transfer of rights in specific partnership property has been relaxed by interpretation in one instance: when the transfer is to a co-partner. Although this disregards the literal statutory language, it has been justified by strong inference from other parts of the Act,[92] and by demonstration that the protection of the firm and its creditors sought by the ban is not impaired by a transfer between partners.[93] The result is consistent with the common law. It could have been reached with less violence to the Act by

89. Creditors' rights would attach to the proceeds (if any) from the sale of the partnership property. But if, as usually happens in such a case, the proceeds are distributed to the partners because the firm has broken up, the partnership creditors would not only lose the priority they have in partnership assets but perhaps become inferior claimants against the assets of the individual partners.

90. Case v. Beauregard, 99 U.S. 119, 25 L.Ed. 370 (1878); First Nat. Bank of Indianola v. Brubaker, 128 Iowa 587, 105 N.W. 116, 2 L.R.A.,N.S., 256, 111 Am.St.Rep. 209 (1905); Stahl v. Osmers, 31 Or. 199, 49 P. 958 (1897).

91. Johnson v. Shirley, 152 Ind. 453, 53 N.E. 459 (1899); Menagh v. Whitwell, 52 N.Y. 146, 11 Am.Rep. 683 (1873).

92. U.P.A. § 41(1), (2), both referring to a retiring partner's assignment to oth-

er partners of his rights in the partnership property. Stilgenbaur v. U. S., 115 F.2d 283 (9th Cir. 1940) (Calif. law; withdrawing partner's transfer of rights in specific partnership property to ongoing partners was sale for capital loss tax purposes); Goldberg v. Goldberg, n. 93 below.

A transfer to a co-partner inter vivos by agreement is consonant with the transfer to co-partners at death by operation of U.P.A. § 25(2) (d), Sec. 45 below. Transfers by agreement, at death, are recognized too. Sec. 90A (b) below.

93. Goldberg v. Goldberg, 375 Pa. 78, 99 A.2d 474, 39 A.L.R.2d 1359 (1953) containing a thoughtful evaluation of the problem. Becker v. Hercules Foundries, Inc., 263 App.Div. 991, 33 N.Y.S. 2d 367 (1942), appeal denied 264 App. Div. 721, 34 N.Y.S.2d 524 (1942).

regarding the partner's transfer as one of his interest in the firm, which carries with it (to another partner) rights in specific partnership property.[94] The Act probably should be amended to codify the exception for transfers to co-partners.

(b) Interest in Firm

A partner's interest in the firm is assignable [95] like any chose in action.[96] The assignee does not become a partner without consent of the other partners.[97] But he does succeed to the assignor's right to profits [98] and—on dissolution, which the assignee may cause in certain instances [99]—to the assignor's right to surplus.[1] In addition to receiving profits and liquidating distributions, an assignee may realize on the value of his interest by selling or mortgaging it, although there may not be any takers.

Some damper on assignments is provided by the U.P.A. which denies inspection and accounting rights to the assignee.[2] Without them, he is very much at the mercy of the other partners. Assignees of limited partners are given more protection if they become substitute limited partners.[3] At least one state has extended similar inspection

94. This will not be feasible if a partner has purportedly assigned his interest in only an isolated asset, which may have been the case in Becker v. Hercules Foundries, Inc., n. 93 above. But it will be appropriate if he has assigned his interest in all firm assets as in Stilgenbaur v. U. S. and Goldberg v. Goldberg, nn. 92–93 above.

Cf. above, n. 85, last par.

95. U.P.A. § 27, U.L.P.A. § 19(1). A part of a partner's interest may be assigned; the last clause of U.P.A. § 27(1) ("in accordance with his contract") so contemplates. For an example of a partial assignment in profits (and none in capital), see Bynum v. Sands, Inc., Sec. 40 n. 65 above.

96. An unrecorded assignment may fall before a lien creditor or bankruptcy trustee. Kerry v. Schneider, 239 F.2d 896 (9th Cir. 1956) (Wash. law).

97. U.P.A. § 18(g), Sec. 5(c) above. A limited partner's assignee becomes a substituted limited partner with such consent, or if the certificate so authorizes. U.L.P.A. § 19(4). In either case, the certificate must be amended, id. §§ 19(5), 24(2)(b). A limited partner may assign fully, without consent, a debt owing from the firm, as distinguished from his interest in the firm. See Myerson v. Lampl, 19 Misc.2d 206,

191 N.Y.S.2d 599 (S.Ct.1959). Cf. U.L. P.A. § 13(1).

98. U.P.A. § 27(1), U.L.P.A. §§ 19(3), 19(6), 10(2), 15.

99. U.P.A. § 32(2), Sec. 78(e) below. An assignee has no right to dissolve as such, but only as a purchaser, i. e. for value.

The assignee-purchaser's right to dissolve presupposes the validity of the assignment. If the partnership agreement prohibits assignment of an interest without co-partners' consent, a purported assignment is invalid. Pokrzywnicki v. Kozak, 354 Pa. 346, 47 A.2d 144 (1946).

A substituted limited partner has the same rights as his assignor to dissolve, U.L.P.A. § 19(6), but these are slight, Sec. 90B(b) below.

1. U.P.A. § 27(2) ("interest" here must mean the same as "surplus" in id. §§ 26, 38); U.L.P.A. §§ 19(3), 19(6), 10(2). On an assignee's right to maintain an accounting action, see Chatten v. Martell, 166 Cal.App.2d 545, 333 P.2d 364 (1958).

2. U.P.A. § 27(1). A limited right is granted at dissolution, covering only the period since the last accounting agreed on by the partners. Id. § 27(2).

3. See n. 97 above. Compare U.L.P.A. §§ 19(6), 10(1)(a) with id. § 19(3).

right to the assignee of a general partner.[4] Another possible deterrent to assignment is the right of the other partners to dissolve the firm [5] which they may well do if they resent the assignee having an interest. The greatest practical restraint on assignments is the difficulty of finding a buyer who will pay well to put himself in such an insecure position. This has no bearing on gratuitous assignments. Despite these limitations, partnership interests have a fairly high degree of assignability.

The assignment of a partner's interest does not of itself cause a dissolution of the firm.[6]

It hardly needs to be said that an assignee has no right to interfere in the management of the business.[7]

CREDITORS' RIGHTS

§ 43. At common law, a creditor of a partner could subject his share in partnership property to attachment or execution. Rights of co-partners to have the property applied for partnership purposes and derivative rights of partnership creditors were given varying degrees of protection by courts of equity and by legislation.

A partner's right in specific partnership property is not subject to attachment or execution, except upon a claim against the partnership. U.P.A. § 25 (2) (c).

On due application to a competent court by any judgment creditor of a partner, the court which entered the judgment, order, or decree, or

---

4. Vernon's Ann.Civ.St.(Tex.) art. 6132b, § 27(1), allowing the assignee "for any proper purpose, to require reasonable information or account of partnership transactions and to make reasonable inspection of the partnership books." Among the reasons given for the Texas modification are: the frequency of assignments (e. g., for tax and family financial planning purposes, or as security for loans), the fact that the assignee is generally a partner for U. S. income tax purposes and needs information in this respect, and the inspection rights given corporate shareholders whose status is somewhat similar. Bromberg, Source and Comments, 17 Vernon's Annotated Texas Statutes 259 (1962).

5. U.P.A. § 31(1) (c), Sec. 74(c) below.

6. U.P.A. § 27(1).

It has been held in some jurisdictions prior to the U.P.A. that an unqualified assignment of his interest by a partner causes a dissolution, whether it be to a third person: Haworth v. Jackson, 80 Or. 132, 156 P. 590 (1916); Horton's Appeal, 13 Pa. 67 (1850); Fourth Nat.

Bank v. New Orleans & Carrollton Railroad Co., 11 Wall. 624, 20 L.Ed. 82 (1870); or to a co-partner: Durham v. Edwards, 50 Fla. 495, 38 So. 926 (1905); Sherk v. First Nat. Bank, 152 S.W. 832 (Tex.Civ.App.1913); Sandberg v. Scougale, 75 Wash. 313, 134 P. 1051 (1913); In re Suprenant, 217 F. 470 (N.D.N.Y.1914).

See also authorities in Sec. 78(e), n. 78 below.

But an assignment to a third person by way of collateral security, without interruption of the assigning partner's activities in partnership affairs, does not of itself operate as a dissolution. Power Grocery Co. v. Hinton, 187 Ky. 171, 218 S.W. 1013 (1920); Dupont v. McLaran, 61 Mo. 502 (1876); Brown v. Beecher, 120 Pa. 590, 15 A. 608 (1888). Nor does an assignment to a partner for security. Monroe v. Hamilton, 60 Ala. 226 (1877).

7. U.P.A. § 27(1). See Beckley v. Speaks, discussed Sec. 43 n. 45 below; Hazen v. Warwick, 256 Mass. 302, 152 N.E. 342 (1926); Valley Springs Holding Corp. v. Carlson, 56 S.D. 163, 227 N.W. 841 (1929).

any other court, may charge the interest of the debtor partner with payment of the unsatisfied amount of such judgment debt with interest thereon; and may then or later appoint a receiver of his share of the profits, and of any other money due or to fall due to him in respect of the partnership, and make all other orders, directions, accounts and inquiries which the debtor partner might have made, or which the circumstances of the case may require. U.P.A. § 28(1).

(a) Partnership Property

—— Common Law

No partnership property question has been more confused by the decisions than the right of a partner's separate creditor to attach or levy execution on his share or interest in the firm's property.

The English courts at first treated the partners in the aggregate as co-owners of partnership property with the usual incidents, including the right of a separate creditor to reach his debtor's share. Heydon v. Heydon,[8] describing the proper course for a sheriff holding an execution against the partner, said "the sheriff must seize all, because the moieties are undivided; for if he seize but a moiety and sell that, the other [partner] will have a right to a moiety of that moiety; but he must seize the whole, and sell a moiety thereof undivided, and the vendee will be tenant in common with the other partner." Since execution at common law reached only tangible things, and choses in action could not be subjected to *fieri facias*,[9] the only method of reaching a partner's interest was by physically seizing specific partnership property. The partnership thus lost possession and use value.[10] The chancery courts later recognized and enforced, against separate creditors and execution purchasers, the co-partners' right to apply firm property to firm purposes (including discharge of firm obligations). In Fox v. Hanbury,[11] Lord Mansfield quoted from his note of a judgment of Lord Hardwicke in Skipp v. Harwood: [12] "If a creditor of one partner takes out execution against the partnership effects he can only have the undivided share of his debtor; and must take it in the same manner the debtor himself had it, and subject to the rights of the other partner." Soon the law courts as well began to distinguish the ownership of the partnership in specific partnership property from the interest of the partner, the distinction so clearly made in the

---

8. 1 Salkeld 392, 91 Eng.Rep. 340 (1693). See also Nixon & Chatfield v. Nash, 12 Ohio St. 647, 80 Am.Dec. 390 (1867): "Each partner has a legal interest and right of possession as to all the joint assets, and it would be strange indeed and contrary to public policy if such an interest could not be seized and subjected to any judgment against him." See Note, 27 Colum.L.Rev. 436 (1927).

9. 7 Holdsworth, History of English Law 541 (1925); Glenn, Fraudulent Conveyances and Preferences § 24 et seq. (rev. ed. 1940).

10. See quotation from Brown Jansen & Co. v. Hutchinson & Co., n. 40 below.

11. 2 Cowp. 445, 98 Eng.Rep. 1179 (1776).

12. 2 Swanst. 586, 36 Eng.Rep. 739 (1747).

Uniform Partnership Act, §§ 24–28. In Pierce v. Jackson [13] Parsons, C. J., said: "At common law, a partnership stock belongs to the partnership, and one partner has no interest in it, but his share of what is remaining after all the partnership debts are paid, he also accounting for what he may owe to the firm. Consequently, all the debts due from the joint fund must first be discharged, before any partner can appropriate any part of it to his own use, or pay any of his private debts; and a creditor to one of the partners cannot claim any interest but what belongs to his debtor, whether his claim be founded on any contract made with his debtor, or on a seizing of the goods on execution." While the earlier cases protecting the partnership from the separate creditor were based on the non-debtor partners' equities in partnership property,[14] many later decisions have expressed the theory that the ownership of specific partnership property is in the partnership as a distinct legal person.[15]

As in Heydon v. Heydon, the weight of authority has been that the officer proceeding under a separate creditor's execution should seize the whole of the leviable partnership property [16] and actually take possession.[17] What he sells to the purchaser on execution sale, is

13. 6 Mass. 242 (1810).

14. Taylor v. Fields, 4 Ves.Jun. 396, 31 Eng.Rep. 201 (1799); Warren, Corporate Advantages without Incorporation 52–55 (1929).

15. Sec. 40 n. 51 above. Richard v. Allen, 117 Pa. 199, 11 A. 552, 2 Am.St. Rep. 652 (1887): "A partnership is a distinct entity, and the joint effects belong to it, and not to the several partners."

Johnson v. Wingfield, 42 S.W. 203 (Tenn. Ch.App.1897). "The earlier cases were determined when partnerships were regarded as mere co-tenancies. Hence, those cases, and such modern cases as have been controlled by them, place sales under execution for the separate debts of a co-partner very much on the same ground as a sale for a separate debt of a co-tenant.

Therefore according to this view, an officer can, under such an execution, levy upon a part as well as upon the whole of the chattels of the firm; and it can, by his sale, transfer a moiety of the legal title, together with the right to take and hold possession against the other partners, leaving them without any other means of enforcing the rights of the partnership than by proceedings in chancery. But the courts have gradually progressed toward a realization of the true nature of part-nerships and have therefore come to understand that they are materially different from co-tenancies. A co-partner has no right to any specific chattel belonging to the firm, nor has he any right as against the firm to take and hold exclusive possession of any such chattel. The real ownership of all the chattels is vested in the firm. The real interest of each partner is merely a right to share in the proceeds of these chattels after all the partnership obligations have been satisfied."

See also the comprehensive discussion in R. A. Myles & Co. v. A. D. Davis Packing Co., 17 Ala.App. 85, 81 So. 863 (1919) (sheriff guilty of conversion if he levies on partnership property for individual debt).

16. Daniel v. Owens, 70 Ala. 297 (1881); Weber v. Hertz, 188 Ill. 68, 58 N.E. 676 (1900); Ernest v. Woodworth, 124 Mich. 1, 82 N.W. 661 (1900); Whigham's Appeal, 63 Pa. 194 (1869).

In some states it has been permissible to seize part of the partnership property, Wiles v. Maddox, 26 Mo. 77 (1857); Hershfield v. Claflin, 25 Kan. 166, 37 Am.Rep. 237 (1881) semble; Fogg v. Lawry, 68 Me. 78, 28 Am.Rep. 19 (1878).

17. Andrews v. Keith, 34 Ala. 722 (1859) (although the purchaser at execution is

not a title to an undivided share of the property, or the entire title to any part of the property, but only the debtor partner's interest in the partnership property.[18] To have that interest determined and realized in cash, the purchaser must proceed in equity to have a partnership accounting.[19] In the meantime, the partners retain the power of disposition of the partnership property,[20] and an execution by a partnership creditor is effective and entitled to priority as to the specific property.[21]

Following the "partners' equities" analysis to a conclusion, dictum in a leading case, Doner v. Stauffer,[22] states that executions against each of the partners, and sales pursuant thereto, destroy the rights of the partners to apply firm property to the payment of firm debts; consequently, the firm creditors can neither share in the sale proceeds nor pursue the property into the hands of the buyers. This is similar

not entitled to exclusive possession); Clark v. Cushing, 52 Cal. 617 (1878); White v. Jones, 38 Ill. 159 (1865); Wickham v. Davis, 24 Minn. 167 (1877); Smith v. Orser, 42 N.Y. 132 (1870) (purchaser entitled to possession); Atkins v. Saxton, 77 N.Y. 195, 197 (1879).

Cf. Rogers v. Landers, 128 Misc. 208, 218 N.Y.S. 98 (1926), noted 27 Colum. L.Rev. 426 (1927).

18. Deal v. Bogue, 20 Pa. 228, 57 Am. Dec. 702 (1853); Rainey v. Nance, 54 Ill. 29 (1870).

19. Story on Partnership, § 263 (3d ed. 1850); Johnson v. Wingfield, n. 15 above; Eighth Nat. Bank v. Fitch, 49 N.Y. 539 (1872).

20. The remaining partner can have it applied to payment of firm debts. Harney v. First Nat. Bank, 52 N.J. Eq. 697, 29 A. 221 (1894).

21. Peck v. Fisher, 7 Cush. 386 (Mass. 1851); Swan v. Gilbert, 175 Ill. 204, 51 N.E. 604, 67 Am.St.Rep. 208 (1898); Darnell v. State Nat. Bank of Oklahoma City, 59 Okl. 204, 158 P. 921, L.R.A.1916F, 1279, (1916); Richard v. Allen, 117 Pa. 199, 11 A. 552, 2 Am.St. Rep. 652 (1887).

Remaining partners can enjoin sale by sheriff on execution against one partner of entire property in the firm property. Williams v. Lewis, 115 Ind. 45, 17 N.E. 262, 7 Am.St.Rep. 403 (1888); Romey v. Shearer, 139 Wash. 621, 247 P. 949 (1926).

A partner could not proceed alone against a partnership debtor. (See Sec. 57 below.) Therefore a separate creditor of a partner cannot garnish a partnership debtor, Springfield Fire & Marine Ins. Co. v. Huntington Nat. Bank, 229 Ky. 674, 17 S.W.2d 726, 71 A.L.R. 70 (1929); Rader v. Goldoff, 223 App.Div. 455, 228 N.Y.S. 453 (1928) (referring to charging order under U. P.A. § 28); F. B. Scott Co. v. Scheidt, 35 N.D. 433, 160 N.W. 502 (1916); Sartain v. Cowherd, 103 Okl. 72, 229 P. 408 (1924), 34 Yale L.J. 559; Myers v. Smith, 29 Ohio St. 120 (1876); First Nat. Bank v. Davidson, 67 S.W.2d 456 (Tex.Civ.App.1934).

In Midland Nat. Bank of Minneapolis v. Douglas, 199 Iowa 1190, 203 N.W. 44 (1925), the partners had directed the garnishee (prior to garnishment by a separate creditor) to divide the funds in his hands to remit to each partner his share. Since the division had not occurred, the fund was partnership property at the time of garnishment, so could not be reached by the creditor.

22. 1 Pen. & W. 198, 21 Am.Dec. 370 (Pa.1829). Contra, Menagh v. Whitwell, 52 N.Y. 146, 11 Am.Rep. 683 (1873).

In Stahl v. Osmers, 31 Or. 199, 49 P. 958 (1897), the share of one partner was sold under a separate creditor's execution and the other partner assigned his share. Firm creditors were held unable thereafter to reach the specific partnership property or its proceeds.

to the result reached in Case v. Beauregard,[23] where there were successive assignments by each of the partners. The Doner case was approved but distinguished in Richard v. Allen,[24] where the firm creditors levied execution on partnership property after separate executions against all the partners, but before any sale; the firm creditors were accorded priority.

Pre-U.P.A. legislation in many states arranged for separate creditors to reach a partner's interest with the least possible disturbance of the rights of the partners in carrying on their business.[25]

——U.P.A.

The need for a solution which would properly protect partners and separate creditors was the principal reason why the Commissioners of Uniform State Laws directed Dean Ames (the original U.P.A. draftsman) to proceed on the entity theory.[26] While this direction was later changed,[27] the Act as finally adopted produces the same result as the entity theory.[28] It does so by prohibiting any attachment or execution of specific partnership property by a creditor of an in-

23. 99 U.S. 119, 25 L.Ed. 370 (1878). See also Fitzpatrick v. Flannagan, 106 U.S. 648, 654, 1 S.Ct. 369, 373, 374, 27 L.Ed. 211 (1882).

24. 117 Pa. 199, 11 A. 552, 2 Am.St.Rep. 652 (1887).

In Rogers v. Landers, n. 17 above, a separate creditor got judgment and execution against each partner and bought in the firm property. The U. P.A., then in effect, was ignored. Later a receiver for the firm was held entitled to recover the firm property remaining in the buyer's possession, but not allowed to recover (in conversion) the proceeds of the buyer's resale of part of the property.

See Drexel Furniture Co. v. Bank of Dearing, 178 Ga. 33, 172 S.E. 30 (1933). A creditor who recovered judgment against each of two partners (one as maker, the other as endorser of a note) was deferred to general creditors of the firm in enforcement of a judgment lien against firm property.

25. In Georgia, it is reached by garnishment. Blakeney v. Franklin, 26 Ga. App. 305, 105 S.E. 872 (1921); Citizens' Bank & Trust Co. v. Pendergrass Banking Co., 164 Ga. 302, 138 S.E. 223 (1927); Ga.Code (1914), § 3190.

In Massachusetts, it was reached by bill in equity to reach a debtor's property which cannot be attached or seized on execution in an action at law. Gordon v. Borans, 222 Mass. 166, 109 N.E. 950 (1915).

In Texas, a constructive seizure was made by serving notice on a member of the partnership. J. M. Radford Grocery Co. v. Owens, 161 S.W. 911 (Tex.Civ.App.1913).

In Pennsylvania, a statute provided for a levy upon the interest of a partner in the partnership, which did not materially change the procedure which had developed under the equitable limitations put upon the process of execution under the general statutes. Dengler's Appeal, 125 Pa. 12, 17 A. 184 (1889).

Garnishment was held to be unavailable because the partner's interest is unliquidated. Horne v. Petty, 192 Pa. 32, 43 A. 404 (1899).

26. Lewis, The Uniform Partnership Act—A Reply to Mr. Crane's Criticism, 29 Harv.L.Rev. 158, 162 (1915). See Sec. 3(e) above.

27. Id. at 173.

28. U.P.A. § 25. Crane, The Uniform Partnership Act—A Criticism, 28 Harv.L.Rev. 762, 772 (1915).

dividual partner.[29] This follows from a partner's inability to assign his rights in specific partnership property;[30] a creditor should not be allowed an involuntary assignment.[31] Although the statute mentions only two forms of compulsory seizure, it has been broadly construed to include other varieties.[32] The firm's property remains subject to seizure by creditors of the firm.[33]

The creditor of an individual partner is given a more circuitous remedy in the form of a charging order.[34] If it fails, for example, because the debtor partner cannot be reached for local jurisdiction to impose a charging order, some states permit a sort of foreign attachment, a proceeding like garnishment in which there is no seizure of partnership property and no interference with the partnership business.[35] Although predicating quasi in rem jurisdiction on the local presence of partnership assets, it is more like a proceeding against the partner's interest in the firm.

Some pre-U.P.A. decisions allowed partnership property to be seized and sold free of equities on execution after judgment against *all* the partners on a non-partnership debt. New York courts suggest that the same can be done under the Act.[36] It seems, however, that

---

29. U.P.A. § 25(2) (c). An extreme example is Wiseman v. Martorano, 405 Pa. 369, 175 A.2d 873 (1962); the individual creditor was the co-partner, and the claim was for purchase price of partnership property advanced by the co-partner for the account of the debtor-partner.

It follows that quasi in rem jurisdiction based on attachment of a debtor's property in the jurisdiction cannot be maintained with an attachment of partnership property. Dalinda v. Abegg, 175 Misc. 945, 25 N.Y.S.2d 612 (S.Ct.1941). But see below at n. 35 and Sec. 41 above at n. 73.

Richardson, Creditors' Rights and the Partnership, 40 Ky.L.J. 243 (1951) argues that an individual creditor may levy on *all* partnership assets as distinct from specific partnership assets. This reader was not convinced.

30. U.P.A. § 25(2)(b), Sec. 42(a) above.

31. Commissioners' Note to U.P.A. § 25, 7 Unif.Laws Ann. 150 (1949).

32. Fish v. Wood, 203 Ark. 539, 158 S. W.2d 267 (1942) (garnishment) (pre-U.P.A.); Hilke v. Bank of Wash., 251 S.W.2d 963 (Mo.App.1953) (garnishment); Rader v. Goldoff, n. 21 above (injunction against bank transfer of partnership funds, equivalent to a levy); Northeastern Real Estate Securities Corp. v. Goldstein, 267 App. Div. 832, 45 N.Y.S.2d 848 (1944), appeal dism'd 292 N.Y. 720, 56 N.E.2d 125 (1944) (restraining provision in 3d party subpoena for examination of partnership in supplementary proceeding); Northampton Brewery Corp. v. Lande, 133 Pa.Super. 181, 2 A.2d 553 (1938) (garnishment).

M.S.A. (Minn.) § 323.24(3) adds "garnishment" to U.P.A. § 25.

33. Cf. L. C. Jones Truck Co. v. Superior Oil Co., 68 Wyo. 384, 234 P.2d 802, 814 (1951) (judgment against one partner on partnership note).

34. Sec. 43(b) below.

35. Rankin v. Culver, 303 Pa. 401, 154 A. 701 (1931); Luick v. Luick, 164 Pa. Super. 378, 64 A.2d 860 (1949) (deserted wife by bill in equity can reach her absconding husband's interest in partnership, for her separate maintenance; analogy to foreign attachment). See Townsend v. L. J. Appel Sons, 164 Md. 255, 164 A. 679 (1933), denying an attachment procedure in which specific partnership property would be seized.

36. Geitner v. United States Fidelity & Guaranty Co., 251 N.Y. 205, 167 N.E. 222 (1929), stating that U.P.A. § 25(2)

if a partner's share in specific partnership property cannot be attached or executed for a non-partnership liability (which the New York Court of Appeals clearly distinguishes from a liability of all the partners), the same inhibition should apply to the shares of several or all of the partners. This is certainly true if there are partnership creditors, since their priority in partnership assets—part of the dual priorities rule [37]—is an important concomitant of the partners' equities doctrine and of the U.P.A. scheme.

(b) Interest in Firm (Charging Order)

Since partnership property is shielded from the attack of a partner's individual creditor, his natural target is the interest in the firm. This is assignable,[38] and extralegal pressures may induce the partner to assign to the creditor, either absolutely or as security. Or, once he has reduced his claim to judgment, the creditor may employ the charging order,[39] a device derived from the English Partnership Act,[40] and very sketchily presented there and in the American ver-

(c) "provides merely that a partner's interest (not the interest of all the partners) in specific partnership property is not subject to attachment or execution, except on a claim against the partnership." But see opinion in Appellate Division, 225 App.Div. 451, 233 N.Y.S. 378 (1929). It was held that an automobile liability insurance policy issued to the firm did not cover a nonpartnership joint and several liability of the partners.

Rhoades v. Robles, 1 Misc.2d 43, 145 N. Y.S.2d 286 (S.Ct.1955), aff'd 285 App. Div. 1139, 142 N.Y.S.2d 360 (1955), permitting levy against partnership bank account on judgment against partners individually. The court stated that the funds in the account appeared on the facts presented to belong to the individual partners. If so, they were not partnership property, and § 25(2) (c) was inapplicable. The facts suggest that the judgment was at least partially on a claim against the partnership, in which case a levy on firm property would be easy to justify. Cf. n. 33 above.

Attachment of firm property for a debt of all the partners individually, may garner some slight support from the assignability among partners of rights in specific partnership property, which some jurisdictions have accepted. Sec. 42 above at nn. 92–93.

37. Secs. 91, 91A, 93 below.

38. Sec. 42(b) above.

39. U.P.A. § 28. Sherwood v. Jackson, 121 Cal.App. 354, 8 P.2d 943 (1932) (tort claimant).

Semble U.L.P.A. § 22(1) with some unexplained differences. It applies only to a limited partner's interest. A general partner in a limited firm would be subject to U.P.A. § 28 by virtue of id. § 6(2) and perhaps U.L.P.A. § 9.

The right to an effective charging order cannot be defeated by a fraudulent dissolution of the firm. Spitzer v. Buten, 306 Pa. 556, 160 A. 444 (1932) (debtor partner was ostensibly eliminated from the firm but continued to receive a salary and installment payments, as a creditor, for the value of his interest).

40. 53–54 Victoria, ch. 29, § 23.

"(1) After the commencement of this Act a writ of execution shall not issue against any partnership property, except on a judgment against the firm.

"(2) The High Court, or a judge thereof, or the Chancery Court of the county palatine of Lancaster, or a county court, may, on the application by summons of any judgment creditor of a partner, make an order charging that partner's interest in the partnership property and profits with payment of the amount of the judgment debt and interest thereon, and may by the same or a subsequent order appoint a receiver of that partner's share of profits (whether already declared or accruing), and of any other money which

sion.[41] It is a judicial proceeding leading to a sort of lien on the interest in the firm.[42] By logical consequence, payments (particularly distributions of earnings or withdrawals of capital) which would otherwise go to the debtor partner should be made to the creditor. However, the Act is not quite so explicit. Undoubtedly the court has power to issue such a payment order.[43] A creditor would be wise to ask for it (and a corresponding order against payments to the debtor partner), as well as for notice to the debtor, his co-partners, and the firm, and opportunity for hearing.

may be coming to him in respect of the partnership, and direct all accounts and inquiries, and give all other orders and directions which might have been directed or given if the charge had been made in favor of the judgment creditor by the partner, or which the circumstances of the case may require."

The act has been applied in several cases.

Brown Jansen & Co. v. Hutchinson & Co., [1895] 1 Q.B. 737, approves issuance of charging order and appointment of receiver. Discussing situation under old law, "the first thing was to issue a fi. fa. and the sheriff went down to the partnership place of business, seized everything, stopped the business, and drove the solvent partners wild, and caused the execution creditor to bring an action in Chancery in order to get an injunction to take an account and pay over that which was due by the execution creditor. A more clumsy method of proceeding could hardly have grown up."

Later, an order was granted to the execution creditors directing the defendant partners to render an account of the share of profits accruing to the debtor partner, and to pay over to receiver. An appeal was allowed, [1895] 2 Q.B. 126, on the ground that the act did not give to the creditor any rights in excess of those of the debtor partner, who was not entitled to an account during the continuance of the partnership. Peake v. Carter, [1915] 1 K.B. 652, 85 L.J.K.B. 761, interpleader will lie by other partners to prevent seizure by sheriff of partnership property on execution against one partner.

Further on the English charging order, see Lindley, Partnership 387–92 (12th ed. 1962).

41. Gose, The Charging Order under the Uniform Partnership Act, 28 Wash.L. Rev. 1 (1953) explores the gaps. See also Note, 9 Wyo.L.J. 112 (1955).

42. U.P.A. § 28(1). Kerry v. Schneider, 239 F.2d 896 (9th Cir. 1956) (Wash. law) treats a charging order as a lien for purposes of giving a bankruptcy trustee the status of a charging creditor under Bankruptcy Act § 70c, 11 U.S.C.A. § 110(c), which grants the trustee the rights of a lien creditor under state law.

Taylor v. S & M Lamp Co., 190 Cal.App. 2d 700, 12 Cal.Rptr. 323 (1961) treats a charging order as a lien for purposes of imposing tort liability on one who acquires assets of a firm without payment of fair consideration, knowing of the charge and that the transfer would diminish the value of the lien. This is not conversion, since the charging creditor has no right to possession of partnership property, but the result is strikingly similar. Cf. Central Petroleum Corp. v. Korman, Sec. 46 n. 28 below.

U.P.A. § 28(1), U.L.P.A. § 22(1) also authorize the appointment of a receiver for the charged interest, and give the court broad power to make appropriate orders and inquiries. The sections give no authority for appointment of a receiver for the partnership or its property.

One state extends the charging order procedure to any owner of a partnership interest, e. g., an assignee. Vernon's Ann.Civ.St. (Tex.) art. 6132b, § 28(1).

43. Last clause of U.P.A. § 28(1) and U.L.P.A. § 22(1).

While the charge is in effect, the partner presumably continues to be a partner in all respects except distributions and withdrawals from the firm. And the charging creditor is not the owner of the interest.[44] He may become so by foreclosing.[45] The Act is vague about this too, not explicitly authorizing foreclosure sale, much less setting standards for it, but only recognizing it obliquely.[46] But there can be no doubt that the Act gives the court enough general power to cover foreclosure.[47] However, consistency with the Act's general concern for the partnership as a going business and as a group of associates suggests that foreclosure should be decreed only if the charged interest is not likely to pay off the debt within a reasonable time.[48] The advantage to a charging creditor in foreclosing and buying is that he becomes the owner of the interest, gaining psychological leverage as well as the improved position of an owner over a lienor.[49] Moreover, he then acquires the right to dissolve the firm if it is one at will.[50] If he presses this far, he will be able to get his hands on partnership assets: whatever share would have come to his debtor after payment of all partnership creditors and claims of co-partners. It is a roundabout route to partnership assets, and one which may yield little or nothing.[51]

44. Taylor v. S & M Lamp Co., n. 42 above.

45. The interest may be sold at foreclosure to a third party. One purchased in Beckley v. Speaks, 39 Misc. 2d 241, 240 N.Y.S.2d 553 (S.Ct.1963), aff'd 21 A.D.2d 759, 251 N.Y.S.2d 1015 (1964), app. dismissed 15 N.Y.2d 546, 254 N.Y.S.2d 362, 202 N.E.2d 906 (1964), but got very little, in particular no right to apply for renewal of the liquor license which was the firm's only valuable asset. This was partnership property, subject to management by the partners (and by the surviving partners after one died); the buyer of an interest had no ownership in the property or right to interfere in the management. Under such circumstances, the creditor is likely to be the only buyer.

46. See U.P.A. § 28(2).

47. Last clause of U.P.A. § 28(1), U.L. P.A. § 22(1). See Taylor v. S & M Lamp Co., n. 42 above, considering but not deciding whether a sheriff can hold an execution sale without a foreclosure order (i. e. based only on the charging order and the debt judgment).

48. See City of New York v. Bencivenga, 8 Misc.2d 29, 169 N.Y.S.2d 515 (Sup.Ct.1955), granting charging order and appointing receiver, but denying authority to sell charged interest, without prejudice to a later application "upon a showing of the necessity for such foreclosure."

49. He may cause to be set aside a partner's attempted assignment of a share in specific partnership property. Windom Nat. Bank v. Klein, 191 Minn. 447, 254 N.W. 602 (1934).

50. U.P.A. § 32(2). His right is more restricted if his debtor is only a limited partner; see Sec. 90B below.

51. A charging order has no priority in partnership property over a later levy by a partnership creditor, but, rather, is subject to it. Shirk v. Caterbone, 201 Pa.Super. 544, 193 A.2d 664 (1963). The unofficial report confusingly says "The court below properly held that the changing [sic] order has priority." 193 A.2d at 665. The official version corrects and reverses the sense by including "no such" before "priority," 201 Pa.Super. at 546.

The case suggests that partnership debts incurred after the charging order have priority too. This seems correct since the value of the interest could not very well be frozen without impeding the partnership business in a way the U.P.A. seeks to avoid.

The other partners may not like a partner's individual creditor breathing down their necks, and are authorized to dissolve the firm,[52] or to redeem the charged interest (before foreclosure).[53] If they dissolve, they must account to the charging creditor for the debtor partner's interest.[54] If they want to redeem, there is no express statutory procedure for determining the price at which they can do so. Perhaps the price is the amount of the creditor's claim. This would make redemption uneconomic if the claim were greater than the value of the partner's interest. The court probably has general authority in such a case to value the interest and permit redemption at the value.[55]

Although the U.P.A. nowhere says that a charging order is the exclusive process for a partner's individual creditor, the courts have generally so interpreted it.[56] This seems consistent with the Act, but (since the charge is wholly post-judgment) may not harmonize with the policy of allowing pre-judgment attachment in many states. Against a limited partner's interest, the charging order is cumulative of other remedies which may exist apart from the partnership Acts.[57]

A charging order has also been granted claimants who are not strictly judgment creditors, such as spouses seeking alimony or child support.[58]

EXEMPTIONS AND HOMESTEAD RIGHTS

§ 44. **The common law usually rejected exemption claims in partnership property.**

When partnership property is attached for a partnership debt, the partners, or any of them, or the representatives of a deceased partner, can-

---

52. U.P.A. § 31(1) (c), Sec. 78(e) below.

53. U.P.A. § 28(2). U.L.P.A. § 22(2) is similar but does not allow redemption with partnership property. Gose, op. cit. supra n. 41 at 17–18 argues forcefully that the redeemed interest should be held in trust for the debtor partner because of the fiduciary relation among the partners.

54. Cf. Spitzer v. Buten, n. 39 above, where an attempted dissolution did not defeat the charging order. Cf. U.P.A. § 27(2).

55. The last clause U.P.A. § 28(1), U.L. P.A. § 22(1) affords a statutory basis for such authority.

56. Baum v. Baum, 51 Cal.2d 610, 335 P.2d 481 (1959); Sherwood v. Jackson, 121 Cal.App. 354, 8 P.2d 943 (1932); Metropolitan Cas. Ins. Co. v. Cimino, 108 N.J.L. 243, 157 A. 152 (1931); Rader v. Goldoff, n. 21 above; Weisinger v. Rae, 19 Misc.2d 341, 188 N.Y.S.2d 10 (1959); Northampton Brewery Corp. v. Lande, 133 Pa.Super. 181, 2 A.2d 553 (1938), noted 38 Mich. L.Rev. 421 (1940), 23 Minn.L.Rev. 538 (1939).

57. U.L.P.A. § 22(3). There is reason for treating a limited partner's interest differently. His position carries neither personal liability nor right of management, and is primarily that of an investor, somewhere between a creditor and a preferred equity holder. However, there is nothing in his status, or in the U.L.P.A., which suggests that his creditor may proceed directly against partnership property contrary to U.P.A. § 25(2) (c). The upshot probably is that the creditor may use attachment or execution to reach and sell the interest, without employing the charging order.

58. Baum v. Baum, n. 56 above.

not claim any rights under the homestead or exemption laws. U.P.A. § 25(2)(c).

Nothing in this act shall be held to deprive a partner of his right, if any, under the exemption laws, as regards his interest in the partnership. U.P.A. § 28(3).

(a) Partnership Property

Exemption and homestead laws permit a debtor to retain certain property free from attachment, execution or bankruptcy proceedings by his creditors.[59] Exemption statutes usually apply to individuals only, and hence not to partnerships.[60]

Can a partner personally claim exemption in specific partnership property? The pre-U.P.A. authorities were in conflict. In the majority of jurisdictions, no exemption was allowed. In some cases it was denied because the ownership of partnership property was considered to be in the firm as an entity, not in the partners.[61] Other cases held that a partner's interest was confined to the surplus after payment of partnership debts and adjustment of partners' accounts. Consequently, he could claim exemption only in his share of that

---

[59]   Exemptions are created almost entirely by state law. But they are accepted in federal bankruptcy. See Sec. 95A below.

[60]   Thurlow v. Warren, 82 Me. 164, 19 A. 158, 17 Am.St.Rep. 472 (1889); Pond v. Kimball, 101 Mass. 105 (1869) (statute exempted tools and equipment, material and stock of debtor "necessary for carrying on his trade and business"); Rogers v. Raynor, 102 Mich. 473, 60 N.W. 980 (1894); Lynch v. Englehardt-Winning-Davison Mercantile Co., 1 Neb. (Unof.) 528, 532, 96 N.W. 524 (1901) ("a partnership is a legal, not a social entity"); Bonsall v. Comly, 44 Pa. 442 (1863) (statute referring to "defendant and his family"); In re Lentz, 97 F. 486 (D.S.D., 1899).

In re Deadwiler & Fortson, 293 F. 762 (N.D.Ga.1923), under a Georgia statute granting homestead to "head of family"; the court held a partner entitled to homestead to be taken equally out of two funds, the firm and separate estate.

See Sec. 95A below.

A statute (no longer in force) explicitly covering partnerships was applied in Noyes v. Belding, 5 S.D. 603, 59 N.W. 1069 (1894).

[61]   Porch v. Arkansas Milling Co., 65 Ark. 40, 45 S.W. 51, 67 Am.St.Rep.

895 (1898) ("the title and ownership of partnership property are in the partnership, and neither partner has any exclusive right to any part of it"); Commercial Bank of Thomasville v. Watt, 178 Ga. 615, 173 S.E. 394 (1934); Jensen v. Wiersma, 185 Iowa 551, 170 N.W. 780, 4 A.L.R. 298, with extensive annotations on partner's right to exemption (1919) ("the property does not belong separately to the individual partners, but to the distinct entity").

Green v. Taylor, 98 Ky. 330, 32 S.W. 945, 56 Am.St.Rep. 375 (1895), "in case of a partnership neither member has title to firm property, but the title is in the firm." It was held that a sole proprietor of a business, ostensibly carried on as a partnership, was estopped to deny partnership for the purpose of claiming exemption.

Clegg v. Houston, 1 Phila. 352 (Pa.1852), "no one of the members of a copartnership has a separate property in the partnership effects".

Brindle v. Hiatt, 42 F.2d 212 (8th Cir. 1930), "There can be no question that in partnership property there is no individual ownership until at least, the partnership has ceased activity and all of the debts have been paid so that there remains nothing but a division of the property."

surplus (usually regarded as a composite intangible), not in any specific partnership property before payment of firm creditors.[62] This reflects the overriding commitment of the firm's property to the fortunes of the business. Another reason is the partner's disability to possess firm property for personal purposes.[63]

Some exemption statutes were construed to let partners claim exemption against partnership creditors, with emphasis on the view that the firm property is owned by the partners as co-tenants.[64] Elsewhere it was held that partners could sever their joint ownership in firm property, convert it into separate ownership, and claim exemption therein.[65] The same result has been reached where, after bankruptcy, partners agree to set apart to themselves part of the firm property for purpose of exemption.[66] But the more usual result is a nullification of the conversion as a fraudulent conveyance.[67]

Under the U.P.A. there is no right in partners to exemption or homestead in specific partnership property, and the adoption of the Act changed the law in a number of states.[68] Although the Act, literally read, bars exemption only when partnership property is "attached" for a partnership debt, it should have the same effect irrespective of the process used by the creditor.[69] The U.P.A. does not interfere with an exemption claim in non-partnership property, and tends to intensify disputes over whether property belongs to the firm or to some or all of the partners.[70]

62. Giovanni v. First Nat. Bank, 55 Ala. 305, 28 Am.Rep. 723 (1876); State ex rel. Peck v. Bowden, 18 Fla. 17 (1881); State ex rel. Billingsley v. Spencer, 64 Mo. 355, 27 Am.Rep. 244 (1877); Gaylord v. Imhoff, 26 Ohio St. 317, 20 Am.Rep. 762 (1875).

63. Sec. 41 above. Since personal possession is permitted by consent of all the partners, a claim of exemption may be supportable with unanimous consent. See below at nn. 65–66.

64. Stewart v. Brown, 37 N.Y. 350, 93 Am.Dec. 578 (1867); Pennell v. Robinson, 80 S.E. 417, Ann.Cas.1915D 77 (1913) (other partners agreed); In re Solomon & Johnson, 254 F. 503 (E.D. Mich.1918) (Mich. statutes).

65. Lee v. Bradley Fertilizer Co., 44 Fla. 787, 33 So. 456 (1903). But see In re David, 54 F.2d 140 (S.D.Fla. 1931) (exemption denied in property divided on dissolution with assumption of firm debts; under Florida law, a debtor cannot claim exemption out of the consideration for his promise to pay the purchase price for property).

Mortley v. Flanagan, 38 Ohio St. 401 (1882). But cf. Casci v. Evans, 21 Ohio App. 288, 152 N.E. 764 (1921) where bad faith was found to exist.

Davis v. Smith, 113 N.C. 94, 18 S.E. 53 (1893) (general assignment with reservation of exemptions); Crawford v. Sternberg, 220 F. 73 (8th Cir. 1915).

66. O'Gorman v. Fink, 57 Wis. 649, 15 N.W. 771, 46 Am.Rep. 58 (1883); In re Aurora Hardware Co., 287 F. 164 (E.D. N.C.1923). Cf. Phillips v. C. Palomo & Sons, 270 F.2d 791 (5th Cir. 1959), discussed Sec. 95A n. 70 below.

67. Casci v. Evans, n. 65 above. Secs. 46, 91B(f), 95A below.

68. U.P.A. § 25(2) (c). In re Safady Bros., 228 F. 538 (W.D.Wis.1915); Schefman v. De Groot, 35 F.2d 950 (6th Cir. 1929); In re Clark, 11 F.2d 540 (E.D.Mich.1926); State v. Elsbury, 63 Nev. 463, 175 P.2d 430, 169 A.L.R. 364 (1946).

69. Cf. Sec. 43 n. 32 above.

70. Cf. Sec. 37 above.

(b) Interest in Firm

The partners are entitled to claim any applicable exemption out of their respective interests in the firm after firm debts have been paid.[71] Such an exemption is rarely provided. It is good, of course, only against individual creditors since, by hypothesis, the interest is defined only by the net remaining after satisfaction of partnership creditors.

INHERITABILITY; MARITAL RIGHTS; DEATH TAXES

§ 45. At common law, the legal title to a partner's share in partnership real estate passed to his heirs or devisees and was subject to dower interests. But in equity the rights of the surviving partners to apply the property for partnership purposes were protected.

On the death of a partner, his right in specific partnership property vests in the surviving partner or partners, except where the deceased was the last surviving partner, when his right in such property vests in his legal representative. Such surviving partner or partners, or the legal representative of the last surviving partner, has no right to possess the partnership property for any but a partnership purpose. U.P.A. § 25(2)(d).

A partner's right in specific partnership property is not subject to dower, curtesy, or allowances to widows, heirs or next of kin. U.P.A. § 25(2)(e).

A partner's interest in the partnership passes as he provides, or by intestacy, and may be subject to marital rights.

Interests in partnership property may be community property, but partnership property cannot.

A partner's interest in the firm is subject to inheritance taxation as intangible personalty.

(a) Partnership Property

—— *Common Law*

At common law, the title to specific partnership personalty held by the firm, both tangible and intangible, passed on death of a partner to the surviving partners for the purpose of winding up.[72] Complications arose with respect to realty, as might be expected from the historical importance of land, and the special family provisions made in land which may conflict with business use.

---

71. U.P.A. § 28(3). Semble, U.L.P.A. § 22(4).

72. "As surviving partner he administers, or rather manages and controls, his own property. He owns in his own right a partner's share in the partnership assets, and he has legal title to the whole as trustee for the purpose of winding up the partnership business." Groves v. Aegerter, 226 Mo. App. 128, 42 S.W.2d 974 (1931).

See also Knox v. Gye, L.R. 5 H.L. 656, 42 L.J.Ch. 234 (1872); Casey v. Hurley, 115 Conn. 341, 161 A. 518 (1932); Hewitt v. Hayes, 204 Mass. 586, 90 N. E. 985, 27 L.R.A.,N.S., 154 (1910); Poy v. Allan, 247 Mich. 385, 225 N.W. 532 (1929); Nehrboss v. Bliss, 88 N.Y. 600 (1882); In re Dunn, 53 F.2d 516 (E.D. N.Y.1931).

Assuming the title to be in the partners, the legal title of a dead partner's share as co-tenant descended to his heirs, subject to dower rights of his widow. But the surviving partners retained their equities in the property for partnership purposes. By the so-called "equitable conversion" doctrine, a court of equity treated the realty as if it were personalty to enable the surviving partners to use it or its proceeds in winding up the firm. Surviving partners had the power to sell realty, and the chancery court would compel the heirs of the deceased partner to join in any conveyance necessary for the passing of legal title.[73]

After winding up and ascertainment of the dead partner's share, part of it might consist of realty or its proceeds. Whether such part went to the personal representative (as personalty) or descended to the heirs subject to dower (as realty), depended on whether the equitable conversion was considered complete ("out and out") or *pro tanto* (operative only so far as necessary in the interest of firm creditors and co-partners). The English cases and the English Partnership Act favored out and out conversion,[74] as did some of the American deci-

---

73. Walling v. Burgess, 122 Ind. 299, 22 N.E. 419, 23 N.E. 1076, 7 L.R.A. 481 (1889); Merritt v. Dickey, 38 Mich. 41 (1878); Barton v. Lovejoy, 56 Minn. 380, 57 N.W. 935, 45 Am.St.Rep. 482 (1894) (proceeding to determine adverse claims to real estate conveyed by surviving partner); Easton v. Courtwright, 84 Mo. 27, 39 (1884); Delmonico v. Guillaume, 2 Sandf.Ch. 366 (N.Y. 1845); Tillinghast v. Champlin, 4 R.I. 173, 210, 67 Am.Dec. 510 (1856), semble; Weld v. Johnson Mfg. Co., 86 Wis. 552, 57 N.W. 374 (1893); Shanks v. Klein, 104 U.S. 18, 26 L.Ed. 635 (1881).

Some pre-U.P.A. statutes provided for the surviving partner's succession to the title to all partnership property, both real and personal. See Gardner Hotel Co. v. Hagaman, 47 N.D. 434, 182 N.W. 685 (1921); McPherson v. Swift, 22 S.D. 165, 116 N.W. 76, 133 Am.St. Rep. 907 (1908).

74. "Where land or any heritable interest therein has become partnership property, it shall, unless the contrary intention appears, be treated as between the partners (including the representatives of a deceased partner), and also as between the heirs of a deceased partner and his executors or administrators, as personal or moveable and not real or heritable estate." English Partnership Act, 1890, 53–54 Victoria, ch. 39, § 22.

Darby v. Darby, 3 Drewry 495, 61 Eng. Rep. 992 (Ch.1856); Ex parte Corbett, L.R. 14 Ch.Div. 122 (1880); Wray v. Wray, L.R. [1905] 2 Ch. 349, 79 L.J.Ch. 687.

Burdick, Partnership Realty, 9 Colum.L. Rev. 197 (1909).

The prevailing common law view of the effect of a partner's death on firm realty is set forth in Perin v. Megibben, 53 F. 86, 92 (6th Cir. 1892):

"First. The legal title to partnership real estate held in the names of the partners descends to the widow and heirs of each exactly as it would were the partners tenants in common.

"Second. Where real estate is purchased with partnership funds for partnership purposes, it is partnership property, to which the surviving partner has an equitable title, and which he may sell to pay partnership debts or settle partnership equities, compelling, by aid of a court of equity, the heirs of the deceased partner to perfect the sale by deeding such title.

"Third. In the absence of any agreement between the partners, express or implied to the contrary, both the legal title and the beneficial interest in the surplus of such partnership real estate, after the debts and the equities of the partnership are satisfied, decend to the heir at law.

sions.[75] But the weight of U. S. common law was for *pro tanto* conversion.[76] The results affected not only the wife's dower, but also intestate takers, who might be different for realty and personalty.[77] The chief difficulty with *pro tanto* conversion is that it may leave rights in suspense (while the firm is wound up) and somewhat at the mercy of the surviving partners (who may decide which of the firm's assets to sell).[78]

     The wife of a partner retains her dower interest in property owned by him in severalty during marriage, though later transferred by him to his firm.[79] Whatever right of dower is incident to property acquired by the partnership from other sources is subject to the rights of partners and firm creditors.[80] Consequently, the wife need not join in a partnership conveyance (for firm purposes) either before or

---

"Fourth. When, however, there is an express agreement between the partners, or one which can be clearly implied from the circumstances, to consider and treat such real estate as part of the personal property stock of the partnership, then, though the legal title to the deceased partner's interest descends to the heir under the statutes of descent, the equitable title, and the full beneficial interest after the payment of the partnership debts and adjustment of the equities between the partners, vest in the personal representatives of the deceased partner for distribution as personal property, and to this end a court of equity may force a conveyance of the legal title from the heirs to the vendee of the personal representatives."

75. Miller v. Ferguson, 107 Va. 249, 57 S.E. 649, 122 Am.St.Rep. 840, 13 Ann. Cas. 138 (1907), citing earlier Va. cases; McAlister v. Montgomery, 4 Tenn. (3 Hayw.) 94 (1816); Hoxie v. Carr, Fed.Cas.No.6,802 (D.R.I.1832), opinion by Judge Story reviewing earlier English and American cases. Story, Partnership § 93 (3d ed. 1850).

76. Lenow v. Fones, n. 82 below. See also, in favor of reconversion, Shearer v. Shearer, 98 Mass. 107 (1867); Foster's Appeal, 74 Pa. 391, 15 Am.Rep. 553 (1873); Account of C. H. Welles, 191 Pa. 239, 43 A. 207 (1889).

Cases are collected, Comment, Characterization of Partnership Property Upon Death of One of the Partners, 16 U.Miami L.Rev. 92, 94 (1961). Williams v. Dovell, 202 Md. 351, 96 A.2d 484 (1953) discusses the reasons for the two conflicting views.

77. Cases are collected, Annot., Partnership land as real or personal property for purposes of descent and distribution. 25 A.L.R. 389 (1923).

78. Lewis, The Uniform Partnership Act, 24 Yale L.J. 617, 637 (1916).

79. Chase v. Angell, 148 Mich. 1, 108 N. W. 1105, 118 Am.St.Rep. 568 (1906); Shupe v. Rainey, 255 Pa. 432, 100 A. 138 (1917); Grissom v. Moore, 106 Ind. 296, 6 N.E. 629, 55 Am.Rep. 742 (1886).

80. Hauptmann v. Hauptmann, 91 App. Div. 197, 86 N.Y.S. 427 (1904); Sleeth v. Taylor, 82 W.Va. 139, 95 S.E. 597 (1918); Duhring v. Duhring, 20 Mo. 174 (1854) (insolvent firm conveyed the real estate to a creditor, widow need not release dower).

A widow of a deceased partner is not entitled to a statutory widow's allowance out of specific partnership property, the firm creditors being unpaid, McLerkin v. Schilling, 192 Ark. 1083, 96 S.W.2d 445 (1936), on the ground that the allowance is to be taken only from the assets of the deceased person, and partnership assets do not belong to the partner until creditors are paid; Wood v. Brown, 121 Ga. 471, 49 S.E. 295 (1904); Julian v. Wrightsman, 73 Mo. 569 (1881); Burroughs v. Knutton, 13 A. 108 (R.I.1888); In re F. Dobert & Son, 165 F. 749 (N.D.Tex.1908).

It has been held that on the death of a surviving partner liquidating firm property, a widow's allowance may be made, though it reduce the property of the insolvent firm. Hewitt v. Hayes, 204 Mass. 586, 90 N.E. 985, 27 L.R.A.,N.S. 154 (1910).

after dissolution.[81] But after partnership purposes are satisfied, the widow takes by right of dower as realty (*pro tanto* conversion) rather than as personalty, according to the prevailing common law rule.[82] The rule can be modified by the partners' agreement; if they provide that the survivors shall buy out the deceased's interest, a complete conversion is effected, and the widow takes her distributive share as personalty.[83]

---

81. Welch v. McKenzie, 66 Ark. 251, 50 S.W. 505 (1899); Barton v. Wamsley, 194 Iowa 591, 190 N.W. 18 (1922); Woodward-Holmes Co. v. Nudd, 58 Minn. 236, 59 N.W. 1010, 27 L.R.A. 340, 49 Am.St.Rep. 503 (1894). See Parrish v. Parrish, 88 Va. 529, 14 S.E. 325 (1892).

In Woodward-Holmes, above, denying dower in partnership realty sold after dissolution, the court said: "the land in the hands of the purchaser is not subject to any inchoate interest of the wives of the partners. The error which lies at the foundation of the whole argument of defendant's counsel is in the assumption that, at the time of the purchase of this property, it became the individual real estate of the husband, and that the inchoate right of the wife under the statute immediately attached, subject only to a lien for the payment of partnership debts. This is not correct, and none of the authorities that we have found so hold. The fact is that only so much of it becomes the individual real estate of the partner as remains in specie, unconverted, after all the purposes of the partnership have been entirely fulfilled, and it is only to such of it that any inchoate interest of the wife ever attaches. If counsel's contention is correct the partners could never, even during the active life of the co-partnership, convey perfect title to partnership land without their wives joining, except to the extent actually necessary to pay existing debts of the firm. This would practically involve, in every case where one of the wives refused to join in a conveyance, the necessity of a suit to which she is made a party, in order to determine whether the sale was necessary to pay debts. Any such rule would hamper the business of the firm to an extent that might practically defeat the purposes of the partnership."

82. Lenow v. Fones, 48 Ark. 557, 4 S.W. 56 (1887) (widow takes life estate, as dower, instead of absolute distributive share, as if personalty). But see French v. Vanatta, 83 Ark. 306, 104 S.W. 141 (1907).

Cf. Faust v. Heckler, 359 Pa. 19, 58 A.2d 147 (1948). Partnership land, after payment of firm creditors and settlement of accounts between partners, reverted to tenancy in common. Hence one could not by purchase at tax sale destroy the interest of the other. No reference was made to the U.P.A. The result, it seems, would have been the same if the land were regarded as unliquidated partnership property.

Cultra v. Cultra, 188 Tenn. 506, 221 S.W.2d 533 (1949), noted 21 Tenn.L. Rev. 202 (1950), 298 U.Pa.L.Rev. 269 (1949), held that firm realty under the U.P.A., though not needed to pay debts, was to be treated as personalty for competing claims of partner's widow and after-born child. Semble, Brown v. Brown, 45 Tenn.App. 78, 320 S.W.2d 721 (1959).

83. In re Hall's Estate, 266 Pa. 312, 109 A. 697 (1920), based on the partnership agreement rather than the U.P.A. See note to decision below, 28 Pa.Dist. R. 312, in 19 Colum.L.Rev. 404 (1919).

A similar result obtained for a firm whose business was trading in lots of land. The real estate was treated as stock in trade and distributed as personalty, as between widow and heirs. Patrick v. Patrick, 71 N.J.Eq. 347, 63 A. 848 (1906).

Cases on dower in partnership property are collected 25 A.L.R. 389, 411–14 (1923). See also Note, 47 Iowa L.Rev. 689, 709–10 (1962) citing this text.

————U.P.A.

The U.P.A. follows a modern trend of eliminating significant distinctions between real and personal property. It also dispenses with any need for the confusing discussion of whether realty is really personalty. These advances are achieved by the careful separation of the partnership property from the partner's interest in the firm.[84] The former belongs to the partnership, not to the partner. Any ownership rights he has in it are molded to partnership purposes and pass to the other partners on his death.[85] These rights, and the underlying property itself, are exempt from dower and related marital claims.[86] The logic for this is as compelling as for saying a wife has no dower in property owned by a corporation in which her husband holds stock.

The surviving partners may dispose of the partnership property (including realty) without joinder by heirs, devisees or widow of the dead partner. The surviving partners need no aid from the court in liquidating realty of the firm.[87]

(b) Interest in Firm

What remains to the dead partner's estate is what he owned during life: his interest in the partnership.[88] The transfer of his rights in specific partnership property to the surviving co-partners by operation of the Act is entirely consistent, since the survivors take for partnership purposes [89] and subject to the same duty of accounting they had before the partner's death. The economic value of the partner's interest in the firm can be realized in various ways, primarily by sale or by an accounting action [90] which will usually involve liquidation of the firm and distribution of the proceeds unless the agreement provides otherwise. The interest itself is personalty.[91] So will be any

---

84. Sec. 40 above.

85. U.P.A. § 25(2) (d). Beckley v. Speaks, discussed Sec. 43 n. 45 above; Ellis v. Ellis, 415 Pa. 412, 203 A.2d 547 (1964).

86. U.P.A. § 25(2) (e). In re Ostler's Estate, 4 Utah 2d 47, 286 P.2d 796 (1955), remanding for determination whether the property belonged to the partnership or the partner.

87. Wharf v. Wharf, 306 Ill. 79, 137 N. E. 446 (1922). A probate court cannot authorize the personal representative to participate in winding up the firm, In re Sage's Estate, 31 Misc.2d 715, 221 N.Y.S.2d 414 (Sur.Ct.1961) (signing partnership checks and conveyances); Ellis v. Ellis, n. 85 above (sale of partnership property).

88. Ellis v. Ellis, n. 85, above. Cf. U.P.A. § 42, Sec. 86(c) below. U.L.P.A. § 21 does not provide precisely for passage of a limited partner's interest at death, but seems operationally equivalent in giving the personal representative all the rights of the limited partner.

89. U.P.A. § 25(2) (d), second sentence.

90. Sec. 72 below.

91. U.P.A. § 26, U.L.P.A. § 18. Sec. 40 above. One state stresses out and out conversion by adding to § 26: "for all purposes." Vernon's Ann.Tex.Civ.St. (Tex.) art. 6132b, § 26. The personal character of a limited partner's interest is reinforced in that he has a right to the return of his contribution only in cash, regardless of the form in which it was made, unless the certificate provides otherwise or all the members consent. U.L.P.A. § 16(3).

sale proceeds or liquidating distribution in satisfaction of it—even though in the form of realty—since the character of the interest at death is determinative, not the method used to pay it out.

Who eventually enjoys the interest in the firm, or its value, depends on other factors. It may pass by the partnership agreement to one or more surviving partners, often upon payment to a designated person such as the widow or personal representative. Such an agreement is valid, even if there is no additional consideration at death, unless the agreement is shown unfair at the time it was made.[92] Without provision in the agreement, the interest passes according to the decedent's will, if any, or by intestacy laws.

There is nothing in the U.P.A. to prevent dower in the interest, if applicable law grants it in intangible personalty.[93]

Since the interest in the firm is personalty, it will in most states come initially into the hands of the executor, administrator or other personal representative (unless its transfer is specified by the partnership agreement). As long as the estate is subject to administration, the personal representative alone (rather than the heirs or legatees) can deal with the interest, whether by sale or by accounting action.[94]

The Act was intended to reverse the dominant American pattern of *pro tanto* conversion and reach the result of the out and out conversion theory.[95] With minor exception, the courts have so construed it,[96] although some of them persist in using the self-contradictory conversion language which the Act makes unnecessary.

92. Sec. 90A(b) below. Such an agreement is not precluded by the U.P.A. specification that a survivor takes rights in partnership property solely for partnership purposes (n. 89 above). Jones v. Schellenberger, 225 F.2d 784, 792–94 (7th Cir. 1955), cert. denied 350 U.S. 989, 76 S.Ct. 476, 100 L.Ed. 855 (1956) (Ill. law); In re Ilg's Estate (Lynch v. Ilg), 348 Ill.App. 545, 109 N.E.2d 362 (1952), appeal denied 413 Ill. 633 (1953), both noted 34 Chi-Kent L.Rev. 239 (1956). This is a reasonable conclusion, entirely harmonious with the separate transferability of a partner's interest in the firm.

93. This was the result in Re Estate of Abraham Binkow, n. 96 below.

94. Taylor v. Lint, 338 Mich. 673, 62 N. W.2d 453 (1954); LaRusso v. Paladino, 109 N.Y.S.2d 627 (1951), aff'd 280 App. Div. 988, 116 N.Y.S.2d 617 (1952); Ewing v. Caldwell, 243 N.C. 18, 89 S.E. 2d 774 (1955).

95. Lewis, The Uniform Partnership Act, 24 Yale L.J. 617, 637 (1915).

96. Wharf v. Wharf, n. 87 above; Vlamis v. DeWeese, 216 Md. 384, 140 A.2d 665 (1958), noted 19 Md.L.Rev. 141 (1959); Ewing v. Caldwell, n. 94 above; Cultra v. Cultra, n. 82 above. Cases are collected, Comment, 16 U. Miami L.Rev. 92, 96 (1961); Note, 45 Ky.L.J. 650 (1957); Annot., 80 A.L.R. 2d 1107 (1961).

Contra, Hannold v. Hannold, 4 N.J. Super. 381, 67 A.L.R.2d 352 (1949), giving only scant attention to the U. P.A. Cf. Faust v. Heckler, n. 82 above.

Re Estate of Abraham Binkow, 120 So. 2d 15, 80 A.L.R.2d 1100 (Fla.App.1960) reached a perverse result. It first concluded that a Florida decedent's interest in Michigan and Maryland partnerships were personalty under the laws of those states (where U.P.A. was in force). It then applied Florida law to give the widow dower (applicable in that state equally to personalty and realty) in the proceeds of the partnership interests, one of which had been liquidated and the other bought by the surviving partner pursuant to the agreement.

(c) Community Property

In the eight states [97] which have community property, each spouse typically has an undivided half interest in the community but the husband has full control while both live and stay married. Each half is separately subject to testamentary disposition by its owner or passes by intestacy at his or her death.[98] On divorce, the community can be partitioned. In general community concepts apply equally to real and personal property and, unlike dower, are operative throughout the marriage rather than just at death or divorce.

Where the common law aggregate theory of partnership prevails, whatever direct ownership rights an individual partner has in specific partnership property can be regarded as belonging to his marital community.[99] Regardless of the theory of partnership, there is no obstacle to finding that property belongs to the marital communities of the partners if it is not property of the partnership.[1] The presence of community property, with its strong presumption that property acquired during marriage is community, is more likely to lead to holdings that property does not belong to the partnership, and hence is community.[2]

---

97. Ariz., Calif., Ida., La., N.M., Nev., Tex., Wash., all with a Spanish or French civil law heritage.

98. Norris v. Vaughan, n. 99 below, pitted the wife's heirs against the husband.

99. See Coe v. Winchester, 43 Ariz. 500, 33 P.2d 286 (1934) suggesting that partnership property may be community property. Another case talks of partnership property being community property: Norris v. Vaughan, 152 Tex. 491, 260 S.W.2d 676 (1953). Oil and gas wells drilled on leases acquired after partner's marriage, using "community effort, skill and labor" (i. e. of the husband-partner) were community property. The wife's half descended to her heir. On the other hand, partnership interests owned and wells drilled on partnership leases before marriage remained separate property. The decision draws no distinction between partnership property and the husband's property, or between either and the interest in the firm. Both cited cases preceded the adoption of U.P.A. in the jurisdictions.

Difficult allocation problems arise when a partnership interest is owned before marriage and is thus separate property, but increases in value through appreciation of partnership properties, accumulation of partnership income, or application of community funds or effort, and thus may become partially community. See Comment, 36 Texas L.Rev. 187 (1957). From the partnership viewpoint, at least where U.P.A. is in effect, there is no justification for treating any of the partnership property as community. The proper analysis is that the interest in the firm becomes partially community, or that the community is entitled to reimbursement (from the separate estate of the partner) for its contributions to the enhancement of the interest held by the separate estate.

1. Adams v. Blumenshine, 27 N.M. 643, 204 P. 66, 20 A.L.R. 369 (1922) (pre-U.P.A.). A controlling factor here seems to have been that families of both partners lived wholly on the property as well as using it for business of the firm. Record title was in the partners individually, acquired after marriage and formation of the firm.

2. See Porter v. Porter, 101 Ariz. 131, 416 P.2d 564, 571–72 (1966). The property was initially acquired in the name of husband and wife rather than of the firm to which the husband belonged. This gave the court good reason to apply first the community presumption.

Under the U.P.A., partnership property belongs to the firm, not to husband, wife or their community.[3] Other marital rights, like dower, are inapplicable to partnership property, and it is logical to treat community property the same way. Several states have done so in versions of the Act which announce that rights in specific partnership property are not community.[4]

What may be community under the Act is the interest in the partnership.[5] It can be reached by a charging order to enforce alimony or support payments [5A] or divided between the spouses on divorce.[6] (The non-partner spouse can receive distributions from it, or realize upon it by sale or accounting action.) However, courts are naturally reluctant to split an interest in the firm—which would inevitably intrude the ex-spouse into firm affairs to some degree—and have devised ways to avoid this, commonly by awarding other property of equal value to the non-partner in exchange for a release of claims against the partnership interest.[7]

Similarly, on death of the non-partner spouse, her (or his) community share of the interest in the firm may pass separately by will or intestacy.[8] This, too, may bring strangers into the partnership affairs, and is almost always worth avoiding by appropriate provision in the partnership agreement for purchase or retirement of the non-partner spouse's interest at death. Unless the non-partner spouse joins in the agreement for this purpose, its enforceability is questionable.

(d) Inheritance Taxation

State inheritance taxes normally apply to realty in the state (wherever the owner lives) and to intangible personalty of a domi-

3. Hill v. Hill, 82 Cal.App.2d 682, 187 P.2d 28, 38 (1947) (partnership property not subject to division between spouses on partner's divorce); In re Dumarest's Estate, 146 Misc. 442, 262 N.Y.S. 450 (Sur.1933) (Ecuadorian community property applied to a partnership law presumed to be the same as New York's).

4. West's Ann.Cal.Corp.Code § 15025(2) (e); N.M.1953 Comp. § 66–1–25(2) (e) (1960); Vernon's Ann.Civ.St. (Tex.) art. 6132b, § 28–A(1). Id. § 28–A(3) adds what is probably true anyway as a matter of interpretation: a partner's right to participate in management (U.P.A. § 18(e), Sec. 65(d) below) of the firm is not community. It is inherently incapable of transfer to a non-partner.

5. Id. § 28–A(2) so specifies. See Lovetro v. Steers, 234 Cal.App.2d 461, 44 Cal.Rptr. 604, 610 (1965), concerning a note received on sale of a partnership interest found to be community.

5A. Baum v. Baum, 51 Cal.2d 610, 335 P.2d 481 (1959); Porter v. Porter, n. 2 above (dissenting opinion).

6. Vernon's Ann.Civ.St. (Tex.) art. 6132b, § 28–B(1) (A), giving the non-partner the status of a purchaser and assignee of the fractional interest. See Bromberg, Source & Comments, 17 Vernon's Annotated Texas Statutes 262–63 (1963).

7. Spector v. Spector, 94 Ariz. 175, 382 P.2d 659 (1963); Rosenthal v. Rosenthal, 240 Cal.App.2d 927, 50 Cal.Rptr. 385 (1966); Carmichael v. Carmichael, 216 Cal.App.2d 674, 31 Cal.Rptr. 514 (1963); Polanski v. Polanski, 193 Or. 429, 238 P.2d 739 (1951) (here it appears that the spouses were the only partners).

8. Vernon's Ann.Civ.St. (Tex.) art. 6132b, § 28–B, giving the takers the same status described in n. 6 above; see the reference there.

ciliary of the state (wherever the underlying property is). The nature of partnership realty affects the applicability of both. Suppose a partner dies a domiciliary of State X, and the firm owns realty in State Y; which state can levy an inheritance tax? If X regards the interest in the firm as personalty, it taxes the entire value of that interest including the portion attributable to the foreign realty. If X regards the partner as owning a direct interest in the realty, and applies no common law conversion doctrine, it will typically exempt the interest in foreign realty as beyond its jurisdiction to tax. A comparable analysis is necessary in Y. If that state treats the partnership interest as personalty, no tax is due since the owner is a non-resident. If the state looks on a partner as owning an interest in the realty, it will tax the value of the interest in the realty (usually without any offset for partnership debts except for mortgage on the particular property) as property within its borders.

The applicable view of partnership, then, is controlling. If the relevant law is the U.P.A., the domiciliary state (X) taxes the entire value of the decedent's interest in the firm, no matter what its properties are or where they are located.[9] The same result should follow if the governing law is not U.P.A. but accepts out and out conversion.[10] But the reverse will probably be true if there is only *pro tanto* conversion.[10A]

At the other end, the state where the property is (Y) will tax the value of the local property if it follows *pro tanto* conversion [11] but not if it accepts out and out conversion or has the U.P.A.[12] The two states may have different but equally revenue-enhancing views, so that each levies a tax; this is constitutional [13] and happens with some frequency

---

9. Blodgett v. Silberman, 277 U.S. 1, 48 S.Ct. 410, 72 L.Ed. 749 (1928); Lynch v. Kentucky Tax Commission, 333 S. W.2d 257 (Ky.1960); In the Matter of the Estate of Horace Havemeyer, Dec'd., 17 N.Y.2d 216, 270 N.Y.S.2d 197, 217 N.E.2d 26 (1966). The result is the same under U.L.P.A.; cf. n. 91 above.

10. Cf. Sugar v. State, 243 La. 217, 142 So.2d 401 (1962) (Louisiana partner's share of Texas partnership's sale of physical assets in Texas *held* subject to Louisiana income tax, not within exclusion for sales of capital assets outside Louisiana; both states regard a partner as owning merely an intangible right in surplus). The flaw in the reasoning is equating the firm's sale of some of its assets (not all) with a partner's sale of an interest.

10A. Consistency suggests that the domiciliary state should tax only that part

of the land needed to pay debts at death since, by theory, no more than this portion is converted into personalty. By the same reasoning, only the balance would represent realty and would be the maximum taxable by the location state. The effect would be complementary fractions, each taxable in a single state. Any allocation would necessarily be somewhat arbitrary. No state seems to be using such a refined approach, perhaps because conversion is thought to take place totally, with reconversion at a later date, after settlement of the firm.

11. In re Perry's Estate, 121 Mont. 280, 192 P.2d 532 (1948) (pre-U.P.A.). See also n. 10A above.

12. In re Arbuckle's Estate, 252 Pa. 161, 97 A. 186 (1918).

13. Blodgett v. Silberman, n. 9 above.

when the domiciliary state has the U.P.A. and the location state does not.[14]

The applicable law, depending on the conflicts rule used by the forum, can be that of the state where the partnership agreement was made,[15] the state having the most significant contacts with the partnership,[16] or the state where the property lies.[17] By analogy to decisions on corporations, still another state—where the firm has a business situs—may tax.[18] The possibilities for multiple taxation are quite real but may be eased by reciprocal statutes.

Shares in a business trust, if regarded as personalty, would doubtless be subject to inheritance taxation by the state of domicile of a deceased holder. They are so regarded, though the trust operates and owns realty in another state, if the realty is equitably converted by the terms of the trust instrument or by inclusion in the trust corpus of a large amount of personalty.[18A] If the trust property is all realty and not regarded as equitably converted, the shares are treated as foreign realty and not taxed at the holder's domicile.[19] The state where the property is located may tax the shares of a non-resident if it regards his interest as realty[20] but not if it treats them as equitably converted.[21]

14. In the Matter of the Estate of Horace Havemeyer, Dec'd., n. 9 above. It occurred in Lynch v. Kentucky Tax Commission, n. 9 above, where both states had the Act, although the reported litigation was only in the domiciliary state; there may have been no contest in the location state.

15. Blodgett v. Silberman, n. 9 above (without discussion of the choice of law; the firm also operated partly or wholly in the state where the agreement was made); In the Matter of the Estate of Horace Havemeyer, Dec'd., n. 9 above.

16. Ibid.

17. Wooten v. Oklahoma Tax Commission, 185 Okl. 259, 91 P.2d 73 (1939); Op.Att'y Gen. (Tex.) WW–911 (1960) (Texas inheritance tax applies to interest of Texas resident in partnership owning foreign realty if partnership interest is intangible under the foreign law).

18. Curry v. McCanless, 307 U.S. 357, 59 S.Ct. 900, 83 L.Ed. 1339, 123 A.L.R. 162 (1939); State Tax Commission of Utah v. Aldrich, 316 U.S. 174, 62 S.Ct. 1008, 86 L.Ed. 1358, 139 A.L.R. 1436 (1942), overruling prior decisions which had invalidated taxation of non-resident decedents by the state of incorporation. See Note, Effect of the Uniform Partnership Act on Death Taxation of a Non-Resident Partner's Interest, 45 Ky.L.J. 190 (1956). Cases are collected, Annot., 144 A.L.R. 1134, 1137–38 (1943).

18A. Dana v. Treasurer & Receiver General, 227 Mass. 562, 116 N.E. 941 (1917).

19. Bates v. Decree of Judge of Probate, 131 Me. 176, 160 A. 22 (1932).

20. Priestley v. Treasurer & Receiver General, 230 Mass. 452, 120 N.E. 100 (1918); Baker v. Commissioner of Corporations & Taxation, 253 Mass. 130, 136, 148 N.E. 593, 596 (1925).

21. Priestley v. Treasurer & Receiver General, n. 20 above.

FRAUDULENT CONVEYANCES BY PARTNERSHIPS

§ 46. **Every conveyance of partnership property and every partnership obligation incurred when the partnership is or will be thereby rendered insolvent, is fraudulent as to partnership creditors, if the conveyance is made or obligation incurred,**

(a) **To a partner, whether with or without a promise by him to pay partnership debts, or**

(b) **To a person not a partner without fair consideration to the partnership as distinguished from consideration to the individual partners. U.F.C.A. § 8.**

In determining whether a partnership is insolvent there shall be added to the partnership property the present fair salable value of the separate assets of each general partner in excess of the amount probably sufficient to meet the claims of his separate creditors, and also the amount of any unpaid subscription to the partnership of each limited partner, provided the present fair salable value of the assets of such limited partner is probably sufficient to pay his debts, including such unpaid subscription. U.F.C.A. § 2(2).

Partnerships, like other persons, are generally free to dispose of their property in any way desired.[22] But, like others, they may run afoul of the fraudulent conveyance laws. These are designed to protect creditors against concealment or dissipation of assets by debtors leaving insufficient property to satisfy the creditors' claims. The subject is governed by the rather widely adopted Uniform Fraudulent Conveyance Act[23] (U.F.C.A.), by other state statutes and common law, and by the National Bankruptcy Act.[24] The U.P.A. leaves fraud-

---

[22] A leading case is Ex parte Ruffin, 6 Ves.Jr. 119, 31 Eng.Rep. 970 (Ch. 1801), quoted in part n. 36 below. While the partnership was solvent, one of two partners transferred his interest to the other, who assumed the firm's debts. The continuing partner became bankrupt. The unpaid firm creditors were held entitled to no priority in the distribution of the proceeds of the former partnership property held by the continuing partner at the time of his bankruptcy.

Accord, Warner v. Grafton Woodworking Co., 210 F. 12 (4th Cir. 1913); Rapple v. Dutton, 226 F. 430 (9th Cir. 1915), holding that the retired partner has no right, on the later bankruptcy of the continuing partner, to require the application of the former partnership assets to the payment of partnership debts in the absence of agreement segregating property for the purpose. The case is noted 16 Colum.L.Rev. 355 (1916). See Wade v. National Bank of Commerce, 221 S.W. 364 (Mo.1920).

See also, on the power of partners to turn firm property into separate prop-

erty, Edwards v. Commercial Union Assur. Co., 218 S.W. 87 (Tex.Civ.App. 1920); Green v. Whaley, 271 Mo. 636, 197 S.W. 355 (1917); Titus v. Maxwell, 281 F. 433 (6th Cir. 1922).

Quite apart from creditors, the firm may recover transfers for inadequate or no consideration made by a partner without authority. See U.P.A. § 10(1), Sec. 50A below; Strickler v. Goldman, 155 N.Y.S.2d 132 (S.Ct.1956) (gratuitous transfer to partner's wife). Insolvency is irrelevant.

[23] 9B Unif.Laws Ann. 73 (1966). The chief draftsman for the Act, which was promulgated in 1918, was the same as for the U.P.A., Prof. William Draper Lewis. By 1966, 24 states had adopted the U.F.C.A., including major commercial states like Calif., Mich., N. Y., Ohio and Pa. Adopting states and citations are given id. at 70 and kept current by pocket parts.

[24] Bankruptcy aspects, though similar, are separately treated in Sec. 91B(f) below.

ulent conveyances largely to these other laws; [25] the U.L.P.A. has some provisions of its own. [26]

The usual ingredients of a fraudulent conveyance are (1) the debtor is insolvent or will become so as a result of the transfer, and (2) the transfer is made without fair consideration [27] or with intent to delay or defraud creditors. [28] Its usual consequences are rights in the creditor to have the conveyance rescinded or to pursue the property into the hands of the transferee and attach or execute it there. [29]

Partnership problems center on determination of insolvency, and transfers from firm to partners.

25. U.P.A. § 41(9). § 41 provides generally that creditors of a firm continue as such despite changes in membership of the firm or transfers of the firm's property to individual or corporate successors in the business. These resemble fraudulent conveyance laws in leaving the transferred assets subject to creditors' claims, but are independent of insolvency and (in some cases) of intent. See Sec. 47 below.

26. U.L.P.A. § 13(2) (payment or security to a limited partner *as creditor* is fraudulent if received when firm has insufficient assets to pay third party creditors). For transactions with limited partners which withstood attack under § 13(2), e. g., because the firm was solvent when they were made, see **Hughes v. Dash,** 309 F.2d 1 (5th Cir. 1962) (Fla. law); **Grainger v. Antoyan,** 48 Cal.2d 805, 313 P.2d 848 (1957).

Wrongful repayment of a limited partner's *capital contribution* (in essence when the firm is insolvent, U.L.P.A. § 16) results both in personal liability and in a constructive trust resembling the sort imposed on fraudulent transfers, id. § 17(2), (4). The latter subsection makes the limited partner liable even though the firm was solvent at the time his contribution was withdrawn, for claims then existing. This will become critical if the other partners dissipate the assets instead of using them to pay firm debts. For a painful example, under earlier law, of which § 17(4) is said to be declaratory, see Kittredge v. Langley, 252 N.Y. 405, 169 N.E. 626, 67 A.L.R. 1087 (1930). Cases are collected, Annot., id. at 1096.

Wrongful payment of *profits* to a limited partner has no specific consequence in U.L.P.A. and is presumably left to general law.

27. U.F.C.A. § 4.

28. Id. § 7. Other common situations are transfers in contemplation of incurring debts beyond the debtor's ability to pay, id. § 6, and transfers by a businessman leaving his remaining property unreasonably small for the business being conducted, id. § 5.

The facts in Taylor v. S & M Lamp Co., 190 Cal.App.2d 700, 12 Cal.Rptr. 323 (Dist.Ct.App.1961) are illustrative. The partnership property was assigned to a customer of the firm in consideration of $500 (which was not paid) and a promise of employment of one of the partners (which was not carried out). If the firm had been insolvent, the transaction would have fallen squarely within U.F.C.A. §§ 8(b) and 4, and probably § 7. However, these questions were not reached since the plaintiff was a charging creditor of two of the partners, rather than a creditor of the firm. This aspect is discussed Sec. 43 above, n. 42.

Semble, Central Petroleum Corp. v. Korman, 15 Misc.2d 245, 177 N.Y.S.2d 761 (S.Ct.1958), appeal dism'd 8 A.D.2d 782, 190 N.Y.S.2d 314 (1959). Creditors of general partners attacked a transfer of all the limited partnership's property to a corporation in exchange for its stock. The court viewed the incorporation as delaying and defrauding the creditors in their statutory right to obtain a charging order against the partners' interests in the firm. Accordingly, the court denied the partners' motion for summary judgment dismissing the complaint.

29. U.F.C.A. § 9 for creditors with matured claims. Those whose claims are unmatured are given somewhat less direct rights to injunction, receivership and rescission, id. § 10.

In measuring partnership insolvency, account is taken of the partners' joint or joint and several liability for the firm's debts.[30]   Since the partners are obligated to pay the bills, the solvency of the firm alone, as an entity, is not very important if they are solvent individually.   The U.P.A. points this way by treating as partnership assets the partners' obligations to contribute to the firm for payment of its liabilities.[31]   The U.F.C.A. deals more precisely with the issue by incorporating the dual priorities rule, which gives partnership creditors priority in partnership assets and individual creditors in individual assets.[32]   The logical result is that only the individual partners' assets in excess of their respective individual debts are available to partnership creditors.   It is only this excess which is added to assets held by the firm in calculating the firm's insolvency for fraudulent conveyance purposes.[33]

Assuming the firm is insolvent, can its creditors effectively object to use of its property to pay separate debts of the partners, or the transfer of its property to the partners?   Are these fraudulent conveyances, i. e. infringements of the creditor's right to realize upon the available assets of the debtor? [34]

The answer depends in part on how partners' rights in partnership property are regarded.   According to some courts, the creditors' rights are only derivative from the partners' equities,[35] subject to destruction by the partners.   "The right of the creditors of the partnership to payment out of the partnership property in preference to the individual creditors is a mere right by subrogation or derivation to enforce this right of one of the partners after the partnership property has been placed in the custody of the law.   Until it has been so placed each partner has plenary power at any time to release or waive this right, and if each partner has done so and at the time the property comes within the jurisdiction of the court no partner has this right, then no creditor of the partnership has it, for a stream cannot rise higher than its source." [36]

---

30.   Sec. 58 below.

31.   U.P.A. § 40(a)(II), Sec. 90 below, dealing with priorities on distribution but not insolvency for fraudulent conveyance purposes.   U.P.A. § 40(d), (h), (i) treats various aspects of insolvency and dual priorities.

32.   Sec. 91 below.

33.   U.F.C.A. § 2(2).   The Bankruptcy Act has a similar provision; see Sec. 91B(c) below.

34.   See Glenn, Fraudulent Conveyances and Preferences 374–82 (rev. ed. 1940) discussing partnership problems.

35.   Sec. 40(a) above.

36.   Sargent v. Blake, 160 F. 57, 17 L.R.A.,N.S., 1040, 15 Ann.Cas. 58 (8th Cir. 1908).   See also Titus v. Maxwell, 281 F. 433, 437 (6th Cir. 1922); Case v. Beauregard, 99 U.S. 119, 124, 25 L.Ed. 370 (1878).   The cases derive their doctrine from the language of Ex parte Ruffin, n. 22 above: "In all these ways the equity is not that of the joint creditors, but that of the partners with regard to each other that operates to the payment of the partnership debts.   The joint creditors must of necessity be paid, in order to the administration of justice to the partners themselves."

Warren, Corporate Advantages without Incorporation, 65 et seq. (1929): "At any time before firm creditors acquire

Other cases have held that the firm creditor has an expectation of applying partnership property to his claim which cannot be defeated by act of the partners when insolvent. Some decisions regard the partners' equities as indestructible, where the rights of firm creditors would be injuriously affected.[37] Others proceed on the ground that the firm is a legal person owing debts and owning property, and that it is a fraudulent conveyance for it to apply its property, when insolvent, to any purpose other than the payment of its debts.[38] This view is most consistent with the U.P.A., which treats

a lien upon partnership assets, the partners acting in good faith may sever this joint ownership of the property by dividing it among themselves in severalty so that it becomes individual property." In re David, 54 F.2d 140 (S.D.Fla.1931); Hays v. Harris, 78 F.2d 66 (8th Cir. 1935); Lanier v. Wallace, 116 Ind. 317, 17 N.E. 923, 1 L.R.A. 179 (1888).

37. Arnold v. Hagerman, 45 N.J.Eq. 186, 17 A. 93, 14 Am.St.Rep. 712 (1889):

"Growing out of the right of partners, has arisen a corresponding equity in partnership creditors to have their debts first satisfied out of the firm property, which is now deemed a substantial element of their demands. Generally it may be said that this equity of creditors continues only so long as the right of the partners against each other subsists, and perishes when that terminates; but this is not universally true, for this equity may survive the right to which it is ordinarily attached. In this respect it resembles the claim which the general creditors of an individual have upon his property. It is neither an estate nor a lien. It is ordinarily but a right, by lawful procedure, to acquire a lien during the ownership of the debtor. Yet under certain circumstances that lien may be acquired after the debtor's ownership has ended. This results from the provisions of the ancient statute for the prevention of frauds and perjuries by force of which, when a person has aliened his property, with intent to hinder, delay or defraud his creditors, the rights of those creditors remain as if no alienation had taken place, except against the claims of bona fide purchasers, for good consideration, without notice."

Ex parte Mayou, 4 De Gex J. & S. 664 (1865).

Wilson v. Robertson, 21 N.Y. 587 (1860), "an appropriation of the firm property to pay the individual debt of one of the partners, is in effect, a gift from the firm to the partner—a reservation for the benefit of such a partner, or his creditors, to the direct injury of the firm creditors".

Jackson Bank v. Durfey, 72 Miss. 971, 18 So. 456, 31 L.R.A. 470, 48 Am.St. Rep. 596 (1895).

Wilson v. Robertson, supra, was distinguished in Citizens' Bank of Perry v. Williams, 128 N.Y. 77, 28 N.E. 33, 26 Am.St.Rep. 454 (1891), sustaining an assignment for the benefit of creditors, in which the partnership preferred a creditor of all of the partners, who was not a partnership creditor.

In Darby v. Gilligan, 33 W.Va. 246, 10 S.E. 400, 6 L.R.A. 740 (1889), it was said that, "according to the better reason and the weight of authority, if the firm is insolvent, or on the eve of insolvency, and both of the partners are insolvent, a purchase by one partner of the interest of the other, in consideration of the former's assumption of all the debts of the firm, will be regarded as a purchase upon a consideration which is of no value whatever; and, no equivalent having been given, the transfer is in effect voluntary, and its only effect, if sustained, would be to hinder partnership creditors, and hence is deemed ineffectual to convert the joint property into separate property, as against the firm creditors."

Cases are collected, Crane, The Uniform Partnership Act—A Criticism, 28 Harv.L.Rev. 762, 774 (1915).

38. Roop v. Herron, 15 Neb. 73, 78, 17 N.W. 353 (1883), "a partnership is a distinct entity, having its own property, debts and credits, there is an

the firm functionally as an entity for property purposes [39] and evinces a particular concern for partnership creditors.[40]

The U.F.C.A. accepts the entity view by making fraudulent a transfer by the partnership to a separate creditor or to a partner while the firm is insolvent, or which renders it such.[41] Note, however, that a solvent firm cannot become insolvent merely by a transfer of property to a solvent partner, since the property continues to be counted in measuring the firm's solvency.[42] If the recipient partner is insolvent, and the property is allowed to become his, his separate creditors will obtain priority in it, so that some or all is lost to partnership creditors, and to the calculation of firm solvency. The U.F.C.A. makes actual intent to defraud firm creditors immaterial. The transfer is treated as fraudulent unless there is fair consideration moving to the partnership, as distinguished from consideration moving to the partners. The former is not fully defined by the statute. It seems clear that the following would not come within this description: (A)

implied agreement that all its assets shall, if necessary, be applied to the payment of the firm debts, and any diversion of such assets of an insolvent firm is a fraud upon its creditors".

Bulger v. Rosa, 119 N.Y. 459, 24 N.E. 853 (1890), "the partnership as such has its own property and its own creditors, as distinct from the individual property of its members and their individual creditors".

Note, 39 Harv.L.Rev. 247 (1925). Cowles, The Firm as a Legal Person, 57 Cent. L.J. 343 (1903).

39. Sec. 40(b) above.

40. U.P.A. § 25(2)(c), Secs. 43(a), 44(a) above.

41. U.F.C.A. § 8.

"The act seems to us to be an adoption of the entity theory for the purpose of determining whether a conveyance is fraudulent under the act, except as it defers the claim of the partnership against the partners to claims by their other creditors." Warren, Corporate Advantages without Incorporation 79 (1929).

An insolvent partnership's transfer to a corporation formed by the partners, and the corporation's subsequent mortgage (without consideration) of the transferred property, are frauds on partnership creditors. The mortgage cannot be enforced by an assignee for value who is aware of the facts.

Liebowitz v. Arrow Roofing Co., 259 N.Y. 391, 182 N.E. 58 (1932).

Young v. Mayfield, 316 P.2d 162 (Okl. 1957) (transfer to trustee for some partners void under pre-U.F.C.A. statute referring to delaying and defrauding creditors).

Hartnett v. Doyle, 16 Tenn.App. 302, 64 S.W.2d 227 (1933) (diversion of partnership property to partners' wives fraudulent as to firm creditors).

In re Jacobs, 21 F.2d 1006 (W.D.Mich. 1927), noted 41 Harv.L.Rev. 664 (1928) (insolvent partners cannot dissolve firm on eve of bankruptcy, divide the property and secure exemptions therein). Accord, In re Turnock & Sons, 230 F. 985 (7th Cir. 1916). Contra, Crawford v. Sternberg, 220 F. 73 (8th Cir. 1915); Lee v. Bradley Fertilizer Co., 44 Fla. 787, 33 So. 456 (1903).

It has been held that a transfer by insolvent partners of separate property to the firm in payment or security for overdrafts is not necessarily a fraudulent conveyance voidable by the separate creditors. Lanier v. Wallace, n. 36 above. With the firm insolvent, the effect was paying partnership debts with separate property, which does not appear fraudulent, although it defeats the expectation of separate creditors.

On comparable Bankruptcy Act provisions derived from U.F.C.A. § 8, see Sec. 91B(f) below.

42. Above at n. 33.

assumption of partnership debts by continuing or incoming partner or partners on retirement of a partner,[43] (B) payment of or security for a partner's separate obligation.[44] Payment of or security for a partnership obligation by the transferee, though the partners or some of them may be separately bound therefor, would seem to be fair consideration moving to the partnership, though it might constitute a preference under other laws.[45] The question should be whether the result of the transaction is to disturb the balance between partnership liabilities and partnership property to which partnership creditors have a primary right to resort for payment.

BULK SALES AND TRANSFERS

§ 47. **Statutes make ineffective against creditors the bulk sale or transfer of inventory, not in the ordinary course of business, unless certain notices are given. The conversion from a proprietorship to a partnership, changes in membership of a partnership, and conversion from partnership to proprietorship or corporation all may involve bulk transfers subject to the statutes. The statutes add nothing of significance if the successor voluntarily assumes the debts or if (as is true in many cases) there is an assumption by operation of partnership law.**

Many states formerly had "Bulk Sales Acts" for the purpose of making voidable, in favor of unpaid creditors, the transfer by a merchant of a stock of goods outside the usual course of business. Without such statutes, creditors might be frustrated by debtors disappearing with, or quickly using up, the liquid proceeds of the transfer, while the merchandise itself passes out of the creditors' reach.

The Uniform Commercial Code [46] (U.C.C.), Article 6, has now almost completely superseded the Bulk Sales Acts, but is similar in many respects. The thrust of both is to give creditors recourse against the transferred assets (even though the transferee does not assume the debts) unless creditors are notified in advance of the transfer. To the extent there is insolvency, intent to delay or defraud creditors, or lack of fair consideration, the transfer may also fall under the fraudulent conveyance laws.[47]

Several partnership situations typically arise.

(a) Change from Proprietorship to Partnership

A merchant takes in a partner and the newly formed firm continues his business with the same stock in trade. Unless the firm assumes the prior debts, the old creditors have no remedy against the partnership at common law. They are restricted to the separate assets of the former proprietor, including his interest in the new firm after paying partnership creditors. The assets, now in the hands of the

---

43. Cf. U.F.C.A. § 8(a).

44. Cf. id. § 8(b).

45. See Sec. 91B(e) below.

46. By 1966 the Code was adopted in 47 states. Unif.Laws Ann., U.C.C. 9 (Supp.1966).

47. Sec. 46 above.

partnership, are exposed to the hazards of the business; in event of insolvency, partnership creditors will have priority over claimants against the individual partners (including those of the former proprietor).

In some cases this sort of transaction has been held in violation of the Bulk Sales Acts unless the Act's formalities have been complied with.[47A] In other cases, taking on a partner has been regarded as outside the scope of the Bulk Sales Acts.[48] The normal thing is for the partnership to assume the trade debts of the former proprietor. Failure to do so is within the evil intended to be remedied by the statutes,[49] particularly if the former proprietor receives a cash consideration.[50] The conclusion is reinforced by the U.P.A. which requires that the firm be recognized as distinct from the sole proprietorship and from the partners. Although there is a possibility that the property in question will remain that of the former proprietor, merely being used in the new firm, the presumption is strong that the inventory or merchandise, at least, becomes firm property.[51]

The U.C.C. excludes certain transactions from its bulk transfer provisions,[52] particularly "A transfer to a new business enterprise

---

47A. Daly v. Sumpter Drug Co., 127 Tenn. 412, 155 S.W. 167, Ann.Cas. 1914B, 1101 (1913); Brownson v. Lewis, 233 Or. 152, 377 P.2d 327 (1962) (emphasizing that the newcomer paid the sole proprietor for an interest rather than contributing to the capital of the new firm; creditor, however, held to have waived his rights under the Act); Spokane Merchants' Assoc. v. Koska, 118 Wash. 445, 203 P. 969 (1922); Marlow v. Ringer, 79 W.Va. 568, 91 S.E. 386, L.R.A.1917D, 619 (1917).

See also Watkins v. Angus, 241 Mich. 690, 217 N.W. 894 (1928), voiding transfer by merchant of half interest in business, followed a year later by transfer to the partner of the other half. Virginia-Carolina Chemical Co. v. Bouchelle, 12 Ga.App. 661, 78 S.E. 51 (1913) has similar facts with 3-month interval between transfers.

In C. M. Miller Co., Inc. v. Lunceford, 54 Ga.App. 21, 186 S.E. 766 (1936), the taking in of a partner was held not to be within the Act. But the Act applied where this was followed by sale of the original proprietor's interest to his co-partner two months later.

Cases are collected, Annot., 96 A.L.R. 1213 (1935).

48. In addition to dicta in cases in n. 47A above, see Weiner v. Everglades, 33 Del.Co. 280 (Pa.1945). Authorities are reviewed in Note, The Application of Bulk Sales Acts to Partnership, 22 Va.L.Rev. 689 (1936). Cf. Sec. 23(b), (c) above.

49. The contrary view is based on the outmoded practice of strictly interpreting legislation changing the common law.

50. See Brownson v. Lewis, n. 47A above.

51. Sec. 37(b) above at n. 21.

52. The U.C.C. defines a bulk transfer as "any transfer in bulk and not in the ordinary course of the transferor's business of a major part of the materials, supplies, merchandise or other inventory * * * of an enterprise subject to this Article." § 6–102(1). The enterprises "are all those whose principal business is the sale of merchandise from stock, including those who manufacture what they sell." § 6–102(3). A transfer of equipment is a bulk transfer if accompanied by a bulk transfer of inventory. § 6–102(2). There is no specific applicability to partnerships or any other types of business arrangement or association. But the

organized to take over and continue the business, if public notice of the transaction is given and the new enterprise assumes the debts of the transferor and he receives nothing from the transaction except an interest in the new enterprise junior to the claims of creditors." [53] While potentially applicable to a conversion from a proprietorship to a partnership, it will in fact often be inapplicable, either because there is no express assumption of debts or because there is no public notice.[54] The transfer to the new firm will then be ineffective against prior creditors,[55] unless they have been individually notified 10 days in advance of the transfer [56] and certain other steps are taken.[57] Many transfers will forego compliance with the U.C.C., as they did with prior acts, because there is express assumption of debts, because the transferee prefers the risk of some claims to the expense and delay of notification, or because the transferee trusts the transferor to satisfy creditors.

(b) Change in Membership of Partnership

The admission or retirement of a partner may have created a new firm at common law, thereby involving a transfer of assets from one to the other, and a resulting bulk sale problem. By the better modern view, there is continuity of the firm.[58] Continuity of liability and creditor status follows, and the U.P.A. so provides.[59] It makes resort

whole pattern of the Code is to avoid organizational distinctions of this sort. Thus a "person" includes an individual or an organization, § 1–201(30), and the latter term includes "a corporation, government or governmental subdivision or agency, business trust, estate, trust, partnership or association, two or more persons having a joint or common interest, or any other legal or commercial entity," § 1–201(28). In this vein, the bulk transfer provisions are written in terms of "transfer" or "transferor." There can be no doubt that they apply generally to partnerships.

53. U.C.C. § 6–103(7).

54. Neither the content of the notice nor the method of giving it is spelled out in the U.C.C.

55. U.C.C. §§ 6–104(1), 6–109. The result is to let creditors reach the transferred assets by execution levy, receivership or other remedy available by local law. Comment, par. 2, to U.C.C. § 6–104, Unif.Laws Ann. (U. C.C.) 149 (1962). Except as provided in the optional § 6–106, n. 57 below, the transferee has no personal liability, as he did under some of the older statutes. A later transferee for value without knowledge that the first transfer failed to comply, is protected. § 6–110.

Non-compliance with Article 6 does not affect the validity of the agreement between transferor and transferee, unless the agreement calls for compliance. Macy v. Oswald, 198 Pa.Super. 435, 182 A.2d 94 (1962) (transfer from partnership to third party).

56. U.C.C. §§ 6–105, 6–107 (10 days before possession or payment, whichever is earlier).

57. U.C.C. § 6–104 (schedule of creditors and transferred property). An optional § 6–106, omitted by most of the adopting states, imposes on the transferee the duty to see that the consideration paid the transferor is applied to discharge the scheduled debts.

58. Sec. 78A below and references there.

59. U.P.A. § 41(1), (3), (5), (6), Sec. 88 below. An incoming partner's liability for prior debts is limited to partnership property, id. §§ 41(7), 17, Sec. 88 below.

to the Bulk Sales Acts or U.C.C. unnecessary.[60]

(c) Change from Partnership to Proprietorship or Corporation

Either of these metamorphoses will entail asset transfers falling within the old Bulk Sales Acts [61] or Article 6 of the U.C.C. if inventory is present. The U.C.C. exclusion provision [62] may be claimed for an incorporation if the partners take only stock or subordinated debt, the new entity assumes the debts, and proper public notice is given. It is doubtful whether a transfer to a stranger or a partner as sole proprietor merits the exclusion, since neither fits very well the statutory description of "a new business enterprise organized to take over and continue the business."

In most of these cases, the U.P.A. decrees that old creditors become creditors of the ongoing owners or entity,[63] so that neither the Bulk Sales Acts nor the U.C.C. add anything significant. The latter will have their major role in an area not occupied by the U.P.A.: incorporation without assumption of debts.

Only creditors of the seller or transferor are entitled to complain of a bulk sale or transfer. The separate creditors of a partner are not creditors of the firm, and are not entitled to direct remedies against partnership property.[64] It follows that they are not within the protection of the Bulk Sales Acts as to sales by the partnership [65] nor as to transfers of a partner's interest to a co-partner.[66] On the other

60. By giving proper public notice, the firm may take advantage of the U.C.C. exclusion, above at n. 53. But little will have been accomplished since the new or continuing firm is liable, by force of U.P.A., on the old debts.

61. Cases are collected, Annot., 96 A.L.R. 1213 (1935).

62. Above at n. 53.

63. U.P.A. § 41(2) (one partner continues, alone or with new partners), § 41(4) (third party, including corporation formed by partners, continues but only if there is an express assumption), discussed Sec. 89 below.

64. U.P.A. § 25(2)(c), Sec. 43 above.

65. Ellis Jones Drug Co. v. Coker, 151 Miss. 102, 117 So. 545, 59 A.L.R. 285 (1928); Schoeppel v. Pfannensteil, 122 Kan. 630, 253 P. 567, 51 A.L.R. 398 (1927), noted 75 U.Pa.L.Rev. 787 (1927), 11 Minn.L.Rev. 668 (1927); Garner v.

Thompson, 161 Wash. 317, 296 P. 1043 (1931); First Nat. Bank v. Davis, 147 So. 93 (La.App.1933); M. System Stores v. Johnston, 124 Tex. 238, 76 S.W.2d 503 (1934); Peterson Co. v. Freeburn, 204 Iowa 644, 215 N.W. 746 (1927).

But see Gilbert v. Ashby, 133 Tenn. 370, 181 S.W. 321 (1915), where the court apparently considered that separate creditors should have been given notice of a transfer of partnership property to a partner. However, the transaction was not voidable where firm creditors exhausted the entire purchase price. See Note, 64 U.Pa.L.Rev. 639 (1916).

Cases are collected, Annots., 84 A.L.R. 1406, 1416–17 (1933), 102 id. 565, 568–69 (1936), 85 A.L.R.2d 1211, 1242–43 (1962).

66. Citizens' Trust Co. of Birmingham v. Merselis, 148 Misc. 676, 266 N.Y.S. 353 (1933), aff'd 244 App.Div. 845, 279 N.Y.S. 324 (1935), aff'd 271 N.Y. 539, 2 N.E.2d 684 (1936).

hand, partnership creditors are creditors of a partner, and are entitled to the benefits of the Acts on a bulk sale by a partner of his separate property.[67]   These results should be the same under U.C.C. Article 6.

67.   Mahoney-Jones Co. v. Sams Bros.,
128 Tenn. 207, 159 S.W. 1094 (1913).

CHAPTER 5

POWERS OF PARTNERS TO ACT FOR THE PARTNERSHIP

Analysis

MANAGEMENT OF THE BUSINESS BY THE PARTNERS

§ 48. **The business of the partnership is managed by the partners, who are empowered to act for and bind the partnership within the scope of the business. Although it is sometimes said that a partner is a principal for himself and an agent for the other partners, the better view is that he is an agent for the partnership.**

Partnerships are formed so that partners may carry on a business. This requires various acts: the transfer of property, the creation of obligations, and, as an inevitable incident to a going business, the commission of torts. All partners may be actors, since, in the absence of agreement to the contrary, "All partners have equal rights in the management and conduct of the partnership business."[1] Since partners are jointly or jointly and severally liable on firm contracts,[2] and jointly and severally liable for firm torts,[3] it has been said that when a partner performs an act within the scope of his real or apparent authority he is both principal, as to himself, and agent, as to his copartners. "Each constituted the other his agent for the purpose of entering into all contracts for him, and for the partnership, within the scope of the partnership business. The law of agency, mainly, although not exclusively, governs the relation of the partners as to each other and to the persons who deal with the partnership. Each partner acts as to himself, as a principal, having a joint interest in the partnership property, and as to each other partner, as a general agent."[4] Such an analysis is in accordance with the aggregate view of the partnership relation.

The statement that a partner when acting is both principal and agent of his co-partners is misleading. In the making of a contractual obligation within the scope of his authority he creates, in the third person, a right for the vindication of which the third person has the power to obtain a judgment collectible out of the firm property and out of the separate property of all of the partners.[5] The power of the active partner to create such a right is not impaired by the dissent of a minority of the partners, who, so long as the partnership relation continues, cannot prevent their shares in partnership property and their own separate property being chargeable by an act within the scope of the business.[6] An ordinary principal can revoke his agent's authority at any time[7] but a partner cannot by revocation terminate the power of a co-partner to bind him unless he dissolves the partnership.

---

1. U.P.A. § 18(e), Sec. 65(d) below. In joint-stock companies and business trusts, there is by agreement concentration of management in a managerial group, designated as directors, trustees, managers, or officers, as in the case of a corporate form of organization. Such an arrangement is a natural incident in a form of association in which delectus personae as to membership is lacking.

2. U.P.A. § 15(b), Sec. 58 below. Limited partners have no right to participate in management. This is not explicitly stated in U.L.P.A. but is strongly implied by the whole concept of the Act, especially §§ 4, 7, 9, and 10. See Sec. 26(c) above.

3. U.P.A. §§ 13, 14.

4. First Nat. Bank of Ann Arbor, Mich., v. Farson, 226 N.Y. 218, 123 N.E. 490 (1919); Caswell v. Maplewood Garage, 84 N.H. 241, 149 A. 746, 73 A.L.R. 433 (1930).

See also Schumann-Heink v. Folsom, 328 Ill. 321, 159 N.E. 250, 58 A.L.R. 485 (1927); Burgan v. Lyell, 2 Mich. 102, 55 Am.Dec. 53 (1851); Bonneau v. Strauss Brothers, 72 Okl. 110, 179 P. 10, 4 A.L.R. 255 (1919); Vrabel v. Acri, 156 Ohio St. 467, 103 N.E.2d 564, 30 A.L.R.2d 853 (1952); Egner v. States Realty Co., 223 Minn. 305, 26 N. W.2d 464, 170 A.L.R. 500 (1947).

5. Sec. 59 below.

6. Sec. 53 below.

7. Restatement, Second, Agency § 118.

The entity view leads to the better result of describing the partner as the agent of the partnership.[8] This is the thrust of the Uniform Partnership Act in stating the representative power of a partner: "Every partner is an agent of the *partnership* for the purpose of its business . . .." [9] A partner binds his co-partners through their joint or joint and several liability for partnership debts.[10]

If a partner does an act not within the scope of the business, and not expressly authorized by the others, such as the making of an admission pertaining to partnership matters when not at the time engaged in partnership affairs,[11] his act is not binding on his co-partners individually; and it is not binding on partnership property, i.e., it may not be used to enable the third person to charge partnership property, or even the acting partner's share therein,[12] but it is binding on the acting partner individually with respect to his separate property.[13] Any normal person is responsible for his own acts. The prob-

---

8. See Pooley v. Driver, 5 Ch.Div. 458, 476 (1876). Jessel, M. R., said, in part: "You cannot grasp the notion of agency properly speaking, unless you grasp the notion of the existence of the firm as a separate entity from the existence of the partners; a notion which was well grasped by the old Roman lawyers, and which was partly understood in the Courts of Equity before it was part of the whole law of the land as it is now. But when you get that idea clearly you will see at once what sort of agency it is. It is one person acting on behalf of the firm. He does not act as agent, in the ordinary sense of the word, for the others so as to bind the others; he acts on behalf of the firm of which they are members; and as he binds the firm and acts on the part of the firm, he is properly treated as the agent of the firm. If you cannot grasp the notion of a separate entity for the firm, then you are reduced to this, that inasmuch as he acts partly for himself and partly for the others, to the extent that he acts for the others he must be an agent, and in that way you get him to be an agent for the other partners, but only in that way, because you insist upon ignoring the existence of the firm as a separate entity."

9. U.P.A. § 9(1), emphasis added. See also §§ 11–14; in each case it is "the partnership" which is bound or affected.

State v. Sasso, 20 N.J.Super. 158, 89 A.2d 489 (1952) sustaining indictment, (under criminal statute dealing with agent and principal) of partner for embezzlement from partnership.

10. U.P.A. § 15, Sec. 58 below.

The Restaters have made a curious, partial and unexplained shift on this point. Initially they said: "The partnership relation differs from that of the principal-agent relation since a partner, although he has power to bind his co-partner, is not subject to the other's control. A partner is, however, an agent of the partnership considered as a group, and is normally subject to the control of the majority of the group." Restatement, Agency, § 14, comment, quoted in Crane, Partnership 238 (2d ed. 1952). However Restatement, Second, Agency § 14A, comment, describes a partner as "a general agent for the other members of the group" and, in the same breath, "a servant of the partnership."

11. U.P.A. § 11.

12. Caswell v. Maplewood Garage, 84 N.H. 241, 149 A. 746, 73 A.L.R. 433 (1930), opinion discussing desirability of adopting entity view of partnership in dealing with representative powers of partner. Compare Treon v. Shipman & Son, 275 Pa. 246, 249, 119 A. 74 (1922).

13. In the making of a contract, the partner purports to bind and does bind himself, even though he does not bind any one else so as to permit a remedy against property other than his own. Taft v. Church, 162 Mass. 527, 39 N.E.

lem of partnership law is the extent to which a partner can charge the partnership property and his co-partners individually.

POWER OF A PARTNER TO ACT AS AGENT

§ 49. Every partner is an agent of the partnership for the purpose of its business, and the act of every partner, including the execution in the partnership name of any instrument, for apparently carrying on in the usual way the business of the partnership of which he is a member binds the partnership, unless the partner so acting has in fact no authority to act for the partnership in the particular matter, and the person with whom he is dealing has knowledge of the fact that he has no such authority. U. P.A. § 9(1).

"A power is an ability on the part of a person to produce a change in a given legal relation by doing or not doing an act." [14] Power exists by virtue of actual or apparent authority.[15] "As to third persons the authority of a partner must be found in the actual agreement of the partners, or through implication in the nature of the business according to the usual and ordinary course in which it is carried on by those engaged in it in the locality which is its seat, or as reasonably necessary or fit for its successful prosecution. If it cannot be found in these, it still may be inferred from the actual, though exceptional course, and conduct of the particular partnership itself, as personally carried on, with the knowledge, actual or presumed of the partner sought to be charged. The power or authority of a partner in a commercial partnership is to be tested and measured, when the actual agreements between the partners are unknown, by the ordinary usages and methods customarily used in partnerships conducting a business like unto, or by the usages and methods of his own partnership." [16] It thus ap-

---

283 (1895); Gimbel Bros., New York, v. Martinson, 157 N.Y.S. 458 (Sup. 1916); York Bank's Appeal, 36 Pa. 458 (1860).

At one time in Pennsylvania, it was held that a partner executing a power of attorney to confess judgment on a partnership obligation created a power to enter a judgment collectible out of his own property and also out of partnership property, but not out of the separate property of co-partners. Funk v. Young, 254 Pa. 548, 99 A. 76 (1916).

This power does not exist under the U.P.A. § 9(3). Fairman Bros. to Use of First Nat. Bank of Clarion v. Ogden Gas Co., 106 Pa.Super. 130, 161 A. 634 (1932).

As to an agent's liability for his own torts, see Restatement, Second, Agency § 343.

14. Restatement, Second, Agency § 6.

15. "Authority is the power of the agent to affect the legal relations of the principal by acts done in accordance with the principal's manifestations of consent to him." Restatement, Second, Agency § 7.

"Apparent authority is the power to affect the legal relations of another person by transactions with third persons, professedly as agent for the other, arising from and in accordance with the other's manifestations to such third persons." Restatement, Second, Agency § 8.

16. First Nat. Bank of Ann Arbor, Mich., v. Farson, 226 N.Y. 218, 123 N.E. 490 (1919).

See also Irwin v. Williar, 110 U.S. 499, 505, 4 S.Ct. 160, 28 L.Ed. 225 (1883); Iroquois Rubber Co. v. Griffin, 226 N.Y. 297, 123 N.E. 369 (1919); Swanson v. Webb Tractor & Equipment Co., 24 Wash.2d 631, 167 P.2d 146 (1946).

pears that there are three kinds of evidence of authority: (1) the agreement of the partners inter se, (2) the course of business of the particular partnership, and (3) the course of business of similar partnerships in the locality.

The partnership agreement typically recites the business of the partnership.[17] Since it is an objective manifestation of the partners' intent, it forms the natural starting point for determining the scope within which a partner's acts are binding. The business stated in the agreement may be more or less specific and subject to interpretation. Unlike a corporation, whose purpose clause can be changed by a prescribed majority of shareholders despite minority opposition,[18] a partnership's purpose or business (like any other provision of the partnership agreement) can be altered only by unanimous approval.[19] Subject to this requirement, however, the partnership business may be changed formally (by written instrument) or informally (by oral or behavioral consent). In particular, enlargement of the scope of the business confers new powers of representation upon the partners.[20]

The business of similar partnerships is emphasized by the English Partnership Act, stating that authorized acts include "any act for carrying on in the usual way business of the kind carried on by the firm of which he is a member."[21] Many American cases approve the inclusion of this class of evidence.[22] The U.P.A. in using the phrase

---

17. See Appendix V, par. 1.4 below.

18. 2 Model Bus.Corp.Act Ann. 227–28 (1960).

19. It is, of course, possible to provide in the agreement that it may be amended by a specified non-unanimous vote or by a certain class of partners. In becoming parties to such an agreement, the partners give their unanimous consent to the method of modification.

20. Boardman v. Adams, 5 Iowa 224 (1857), partners in a printing and publishing business took on the agency for the sale of pianos. The court said: "Where a partnership firm, embarked in a particular business to which their engagements are confined, and to which alone their partnership contracts extend, by mutual agreement, enlarge the sphere of their operations, and include another branch of business, the power of each partner to bind the firm by his contracts is coextensive with the whole business of the partnership; and the acts of each member are as binding on the firm in the new branch of business in which they are engaged as they are

in the former regular and ordinary business."

21. 53–54 Vict. ch. 39, § 5.

22. Irwin v. Williar, n. 16 above, dealing in futures not, as a matter of law, incident to business of grain dealing; Woodruff v. Scaife, 83 Ala. 152, 154, 3 So. 311 (1887), member of farming partnership not, as matter of law, apparently authorized to contract for medical services for laborer; Alley v. Bowen-Merrill Co., 76 Ark. 4, 88 S.W. 838, 113 Am.St.Rep. 73, 6 Ann.Cas. 127 (1905), buying of law books incident to business of law partnership; Smith v. Collins, 115 Mass. 388 (1874); Wexford Tp. v. Seeley, 196 Mich. 634, 163 N.W. 16 (1917), banking partnership a public depository, partner signing firm name as surety on treasurer's bond; Commercial Hotel Co. v. Weeks, 254 S.W. 521 (Tex.Civ.App. 1923), purchase, by partner in firm carrying on a hotel, of lease of dining room and kitchen, firm not theretofore having operated eating facilities; Hoskinson v. Eliot, 62 Pa. 393 (1869), note in payment of debt given by partner in manufacturing firm; Reid v. Linder, 77 Mont. 406, 251 P. 157 (1926),

"for apparently carrying on in the usual way the business of the partnership of which he is a member," is ambiguous. "Usual way" may be interpreted as meaning usual for the particular partnership, or usual for similar partnerships. The draftsman of the Act, Dean Lewis, has correctly maintained that the former should be included.[23] The latter may also be included under the usual rule of construction in accordance with the common law.[24]

If the partner has the requisite authority, he binds the partnership whether he acts in its name or his own.[25]

giving note for money borrowed by member of farming and stock raising partnership, considered a trading partnership; Miller Pub. Co. v. Orth, 133 Minn. 139, 157 N.W. 1083 (1916), contract for advertising within scope of milling business; Sweet v. Wood, 18 R.I. 386, 28 A. 335 (1893), hiring of horse by partner in general store.

Some decisions emphasize the negative application of this test, i. e., that the act was not within the course of the business as carried on by the particular partnership, but without any suggestion that other similar partnerships engaged in such acts. J. F. Beasley Lumber Co. v. Sparks, 169 Ark. 640, 276 S.W. 582 (1925), building contract by lumber partnership; Delta Asbestos Co., Inc. v. Sanders, 259 Mich. 317, 243 N.W. 16 (1932), purchase of roofing material by "Security Storage and Transfer Co.," Uniform Partnership Act cited; Shambleau v. Hoyt, 265 Mich. 560, 251 N.W. 778 (1933), evidence showing that a brokerage firm undertook to hold its customers harmless in case of loss on purchases of a certain stock the firm was distributing; Barry v. Mattocks, 156 Miss. 424, 125 So. 554 (1930), subscription to corporate stock by mercantile partnership; First Nat. Bank of Ann Arbor, Mich., v. Farson, 226 N.Y. 218, 123 N.E. 490 (1919): "The implied powers of a partner rest in the usages and business methods of those conducting commerce and trade, and grew out of the necessities of commercial business. They do not extend broadly to partners in non-trading partnerships. As to third persons, the authority of a partner must be found in the actual agreement of the partners, or through implication, in the nature of the business according to the usual and ordinary course in which it is carried on by those engaged in it in the locality which is its seat, or as rea-

sonably necessary or fit for its successful prosecution. If it cannot be found in these, it may still be inferred from the actual, though exceptional, course and conduct of the business of the particular partnership itself, as personally carried on with the knowledge, actual or presumed, of the partner sought to be charged." The court found no evidence of a power to guarantee securities sold by a partner in a firm of investment dealers.

23. Lewis, The Uniform Partnership Act—A Reply to Mr. Crane's Criticism, 29 Harv.L.Rev. 291, 299 (1915). See Jacobson v. Lamb, 91 Cal.App. 405, 267 P. 114 (1928); Bailey v. Triplett Bros., 286 S.W. 914 (Tex.Civ.App.1926).

24. The broader construction seems to be followed in U.P.A. cases. Boise Payette Lumber Co. v. Sarret, 38 Idaho 278, 221 P. 130 (1923) (not citing Act); Lawer v. Kline, 39 Wyo. 285, 270 P. 1077 (1928) (taking lease of premises for firm business; construing U.P.A. § 9 as being in accord with common law rule to effect that the power of a partner includes acts "within the scope of the firm business as that is ordinarily conducted").

It has been said that the U.P.A. is "an attempt to codify the existing common law on the subject, rather than to change that system; but where the rules are conflicting it chooses the one supposed to be the better." In re Safady Bros., 228 F. 538 (D.Wis.1915).

See also U.P.A. § 4(3) ("The law of agency shall apply under his Act") and Restatement, Second, Agency § 36 (". . . an agent is authorized to comply with relevant usages of business. . . .").

25. Lemon v. Montgomery, 288 P.2d 407 (Okl.1955); Warner v. Modano, 340 Mass. 439, 164 N.E.2d 904 (1960),

CERTAIN USUAL POWERS

§ 50. Whether such common acts as borrowing money, executing negotiable or sealed instruments, purchasing property and hiring employees are partnership acts when done by a partner, depends upon the nature of the business.

A partner may have express authority for a particular act by the terms of the partnership agreement, by consent of his co-partners or otherwise. If he does, his act binds the partnership. If he does not, he may still have apparent authority sufficient to bind it. The following discussion focusses on the latter point and assumes that express authority is lacking. Even without apparent authority, his acts will be binding if they are later ratified.[26]

(a) Borrowing Money and Issuing Negotiable Instruments

The Partnership Act makes no distinction between a partner's authority to borrow and his authority to do other acts.[27] Abstractly, there may be no reason to make such a distinction. Nonetheless, courts have tended to do so, perhaps because borrowing can impose such staggering liability on co-partners and (since it usually produces cash) is capable of much abuse.

For determining whether there is implied or apparent power to borrow money or execute negotiable instruments by reason of the nature of the business, some courts have distinguished trading and non-trading partnerships. In trading partnerships, such powers are held to exist,[28] but not in non-trading partnerships.[29] "A trading partnership or association is, generally speaking, one doing business commercially (a business of buying or selling for profit) while those in which the business done is something other than buying and selling for profit constitute the non-trading class."[30] Non-trading partner-

---

citing this text; Edwards Feed Mills, Inc. v. Johnson, 158 Tex. 313, 311 S.W. 2d 232 (1958); Raymond S. Roberts, Inc. v. White, 117 Vt. 573, 97 A.2d 245 (1953).

Cf. McHaney v. Hackleman, 347 S.W.2d 822 (Tex.Civ.App.1961) permitting specific performance against C of a contract made by H although the other party to the contract was unaware of the partnership between C and H when the contract was made.

26. Restatement, Second, Agency § 82.

27. Indeed, in describing his acts which bind the partnership, the statute expressly includes "the execution in the partnership name of any instrument." U.P.A. § 9(1). This covers a promissory instrument used in borrowing.

28. United Drug Co. v. Gramling-Belcher Drug Co., 216 Ala. 79, 112 So. 357 (1927); Smith v. Collins, 115 Mass. 388 (1874); First Nat. Bank of St. Paul v. Webster, 130 Minn. 277, 153 N.W. 736 (1915); First Nat. Bank of Ann Arbor, Mich., v. Farson, 226 N.Y. 218, 123 N.E. 490 (1919); Maasdam v. Van Blokland, 123 Or. 128, 261 P. 66 (1927); Hobbs v. Virginia Nat. Bank of Petersburg, 147 Va. 802, 128 S.E. 46, 133 S.E. 595 (1926); Winship v. Bank of United States, 30 U.S. (5 Pet.) 529, 8 L.Ed. 216 (1831).

29. See nn. 31–36 below.

30. Schumacher v. Sumner Telephone Co., 161 Iowa 326, 142 N.W. 1034, 1036, Ann.Cas.1916A, 201 (1913). See Dowling v. National Exch. Bank of

ships (in which a power to borrow and execute negotiable instruments presumably does not exist) include professional partnerships (such as lawyers,[31] physicians [32]), partnerships to operate theatres [33] and farms,[34] and partnerships to pave, grade and curb city streets,[35] and to carry on a real estate, insurance, and loan business.[36] The test applied in these cases is generally: Does the business include buying and selling? With the increasing number of businesses other than those which are strictly merchandising, in which working capital is necessary, the category of trading partnerships has been expanded to include tailors,[37] plumbing contractors,[38] manufacturers,[39] con-

Boston, 145 U.S. 512, 12 S.Ct. 928, 36 L.Ed. 795 (1892).

Compare the division under the civil law between associations subject to the civil code or the commercial code. Gibbons, Inc. v. S. & B. Stable, 144 So. 641 (La.App.1932).

31. Worster v. Forbush, 171 Mass. 423, 50 N.E. 936 (1898); Roe v. Cooke, 350 Ill.App. 183, 112 N.E.2d 511 (1953) involving authority to endorse a check.

32. Crosthwait v. Ross, 20 Tenn. (1 Humph.) 23, 34 Am.Dec. 613 (1839).

33. Pease v. Cole, 53 Conn. 53, 22 A. 681, 55 Am.Rep. 53 (1885).

In Higgins v. Beauchamp, [1914] 3 K.B. 1192, Lush, J., said in part: "There was no actual authority to Milles to borrow money, it being a term of the partnership deed that he should not do so without the express consent of the other partners. Therefore the plaintiff must prove that he was justified under the circumstances in assuming that Milles had authority. He might show that in either of two ways: first, by shewing that the defendant had so conducted himself as to lead him to believe that Milles had authority, and there was no suggestion of any such case here; or secondly, by shewing that an authority was to be implied from the nature of the business carried on. It was this that the plaintiff endeavored to prove. The judge below did not go upon the ground that this was a trading business. He has not so found, and in my opinion there was no evidence on which he could find it." Compare Hale v. Giesea, 84 Cal.App. 430, 258 P. 407 (1927).

34. Gordon v. Marburger, 109 Wash. 496, 187 P. 354, 9 A.L.R. 369 (1920).

Compare Reid v. Linder, 77 Mont. 406, 251 P. 157 (1926).

35. Harris v. City of Baltimore, 73 Md. 22, 17 A. 1046, 20 A. 111, 985, 8 L.R.A. 677, 25 Am.St.Rep. 565 (1890).

36. Lee v. First Nat. Bank of Ft. Scott, 45 Kan. 8, 25 P. 196, 11 L.R.A. 238 (1890).

37. Ah Lep v. Gong Choy & Gong Wing, 13 Or. 205, 9 P. 483 (1886).

38. Marsh, Merwin & Lemon v. Wheeler, 77 Conn. 449, 59 A. 410, 107 Am. St.Rep. 40 (1904): "If we turn now to the case of Wheeler & Co., we find a partnership whose business was the taking and execution of plumbing contracts. It conducted no store, over whose counter articles it had bought were sold. Whatever buying and selling it did was that incident to the execution of plumbing contracts, as a stated business. It is common knowledge, however, that the execution of plumbing contracts in these modern days involves extensive purchases in the market of fixtures and fittings, of large cost. These are not bought for use by the buyer, but to be disposed of for money. The value of that which is bought enters as a large factor into the receipts of the contractor. The value of labor necessary to the adaptation of the purchased articles to their intended uses will also become a factor. But that makes no difference. The sale is not required to be of the articles in the same form as when purchased. It thus appears that the firm carried on a business which contemplated frequent and extensive purchases, not as incidental to an occupation or for use, but for the distinct purpose of sell-

39. See note 39 on page 280.

struction contractors,[40] and dairy farming.[41]   Though a business may be classed as non-trading, it may appear, as a matter of fact, that borrowing money and issuing negotiable instruments is within the usual course of business of the particular partnership, and therefore power to engage in such transactions exists in fact.[42]

In recent years the dichotomy between trading and non-trading partnerships has appeared less frequently.   It is doubtful whether the distinction, as originally drawn, is now useful in view of the growing diversity of business and the increasing variety of financing methods. It takes no account of the needs or customs of the particular partnership and thus may conflict with agency law's more analytical approach to apparent authority.[43]   Often the logical and commercial connection between buying-selling and borrowing is obscure.

The terms "trading" and "non-trading" are not employed in the Uniform Partnership Act.   However, they are sufficiently established in the case law that they may persist under the Act, though with changing content.[44]   If the partnership appears to the court to be a commercial or trading partnership, it will rule as a matter of law that certain powers exist in the partners.   If not, then it is a question for the jury as to what are the powers of the partners, in the light of the nature of the business of the particular partnership and the manner and usages in accordance with which it is in fact carried on, the burden being on the person claiming the power to exist to establish its existence.[45]

ing again in an adapted or applied, if not the original, shape, and that its business, therefore, carried it frequently into the market, and brought it into contact with the commercial world in transactions naturally involving the use of credit and the usual instrumentalities of trade. Its business being of such a character, it was a commercial or trading partnership, within the meaning of that term as used in this connection."

39.   Phipps v. Little, 213 Mass. 414, 100 N.E. 615 (1913). Contra: Bole v. Lyle, 39 Tenn.App. 679, 287 S.W.2d 931 (1955) involving selling rather than borrowing.

40.   Alabama Cabinet Works v. Benson Hardware Co., 220 Ala. 336, 125 So. 214 (1929).

41.   Vancouver Nat. Bank v. Katz, 142 Wash. 306, 252 P. 934 (1927).

See also Edwards v. Dunlap, 97 S.W.2d 978 (Tex.Civ.App.1936), holding that a partner in a partnership to operate a general farming and stock raising business had power to execute a note

for the purchase of farm implements; White v. Houston, 103 S.W.2d 1073 (Tex.Civ.App.1936), cattle raising; Wurm v. Metz, 162 Cal.App.2d 262, 327 P.2d 969 (1958), poultry raising.

42.   Hoskinson v. Eliot, 62 Pa. 393 (1869), manufacturing; Pooley Barnum & Co. v. Whitmore, 57 Tenn. (10 Heisk.) 629, 633, 27 Am.Rep. 733 (1873), newspaper publishers; Vetsch v. Neiss, 66 Minn. 459, 69 N.W. 315 (1896).

43.   Sec. 49 above. For an approach via U.P.A., see Holloway v. Smith, 197 Va. 334, 88 S.E.2d 909 (1955); Thompson v. Williams, 190 Cal.App.2d 56, 12 Cal.Rptr. 9 (1961).

44.   Jacobson v. Lamb, 91 Cal.App. 405, 267 P. 114 (1928); Rue v. Merrill, 42 Wyo. 497, 297 P. 375 (1931).

45.   Alsop v. Central Trust Co., 100 Ky. 375, 380, 38 S.W. 510, 511 (1897); Dowling v. National Exch. Bank of Boston, 145 U.S. 512, 12 S.Ct. 928, 36 L.Ed. 795 (1892); Vetsch v. Neiss, 66 Minn. 459, 69 N.W. 315 (1896).

Normally a partner will borrow in the partnership name.[46] If he does so, partnership and co-partner liability follows from any kind of authority.[47] Even if authority is totally lacking—but the money is used for the benefit of the partnership—it seems that the lender should have a remedy in quasi-contract for benefits conferred (in misreliance on the express contract) or on the common counts.[48] If the partner borrows in his own name, the partnership and co-partners ordinarily will not be liable.[49] However, they may be if it is shown that the firm is doing business in the name of the borrowing partner [50] or if the partner appears to be acting in behalf of the firm.[51] But no liability is created by the mere fact that the funds are used for partnership purposes.[52]

If a partner has authority to borrow, he has incidental authority to give promissory notes.[53]

46. His authority to issue negotiable paper, as to execute other written contracts, is presumably an authority to do so in the partnership name. U.P.A. § 9(1).

47. Sec. 49 above. See Zander v. Larson, n. 53 below; Brewer v. Big Lake State Bank, 378 S.W.2d 948 (Tex.Civ. App.1964).

48. First Nat. Bank of Browerville v. Stadden, 103 Minn. 403, 115 N.W. 198 (1908), semble.

Compare First Nat. Bank of Las Vegas v. Oberne, 121 Ill. 25, 7 N.E. 85 (1886), where a partnership repudiated a negotiable instrument issued by an agent in excess of his authority, but was held liable to the extent that the proceeds were applied for the benefit of the partnership.

See Woodward, Quasi Contracts, § 75; Restatement, Second, Agency § 141; Restatement, Restitution § 15.

Quasi-contractual relief may be denied because it is not properly pleaded. Cf. Plains State Bank v. Ellis, 174 Kan. 653, 258 P.2d 313 (1953), suit brought solely on note signed by one partner individually.

An accommodation party to a note made by a partner in the name of the partnership without authority is liable to the payee who has acted in good faith. Stewart v. Behm, 2 Watts 356 (Pa.1834). He is, of course, liable to a transferee for value before maturity without notice. Dalrymple v. Hillenbrand, 62 N.Y. 5, 20 Am.Rep. 438 (1875). But in Russell v. Annable, 109 Mass. 72, 12 Am.Rep. 665 (1871), it was held that a bond to obtain dissolution of an attachment on partnership property executed by one partner without authority was invalid as to the surety, whose undertaking was construed as one to perform the obligation of the firm, which obligation was non-existent.

49. See N.I.L. § 18: "No person is liable on the instrument whose signature does not appear thereon . . . ." U.C.C. § 3–401(1) has the same language.

50. Rumsey v. Briggs, 139 N.Y. 323, 34 N.E. 929 (1893). See N.I.L. § 18: "But one who signs in a trade or assumed name will be liable to the same extent as if he had signed his own name." The effect of U.C.C. § 3–401(2) is similar.

51. Mills v. Riggle, 83 Kan. 703, 112 P. 617, Ann.Cas.1912A 616 (1911), allowing the lender to treat the note as collateral security and hold the partnership for the money lent. Cf. Hoeflinger v. Wells, 47 Wis. 628, 3 N.W. 589 (1879), credit given to the firm.

52. First State Bank of Riesel v. Dyer, 151 Tex. 650, 254 S.W.2d 92 (1953); Gay's Jewelry, Inc. v. Goldberg, 129 Ind.App. 356, 156 N.E.2d 637 (1959); Ravold v. Fred Beers, Inc., 151 Misc. 628, 270 N.Y.S. 894 (1933).

53. Zander v. Larson, 41 Wash.2d 503, 250 P.2d 531 (1952). In such a case it is immaterial that the partnership did not receive the borrowed funds.

(b) Sealed Instruments

Under the common law, authority of an agent to execute a sealed instrument otherwise than in the presence of the principal must be conferred by an instrument of equal formality.[54] This rule has occasionally been applied to partnerships.[55] But by the weight of authority, a partner may be authorized by parol to execute sealed instruments,[56] and his act in so doing may be similarly ratified.[57]

Lacking express authority or ratification, it has been held that the power to execute sealed instruments is not within the implied or apparent authority of a partner. "The law of partnership is part of the law merchant, which has respect exclusively to the business of commerce; and as sealed instruments do not ordinarily enter into it, the authority of a partner, being restricted to the scope of the trade, is held to be incompetent to the execution of them." [58]

Under the U.P.A., including within the implied power of a partner "the execution in the partnership name of any instrument," [59] it ap-

54. Restatement, Second, Agency § 28.

55. Trimble v. Coons, 9 Ky. (2 A. K. Marsh) 375, 12 Am.Dec. 441 (1820); Gordon v. Funkhouser, 100 Va. 675, 42 S.E. 677 (1812).

56. Mackay v. Bloodgood, 9 Johns. 285 (N.Y.1902); Edwards v. Dillon, 147 Ill. 14, 35 N.E. 135, 37 Am.St.Rep. 199 (1893).

Restatement, Second, Agency § 28(2) (b) recognizes that the common law agency rule is not well adapted to partnerships: "Sealed authority is not necessary to execute an instrument under seal where . . . the instrument is authorized by a . . . partnership in accordance with the rules relating to the authorization of such instruments by such associations . . . ."

57. Tischler v. Kurtz, 35 Fla. 323, 17 So. 661 (1895); Swan v. Stedman, 45 Mass. (4 Metc.) 548 (1842); National Citizens' Bank v. McKinley, 129 Minn. 481, 152 N.W. 879 (1915); Miller v. Royal Flint Glass Works, 172 Pa. 70, 33 A. 350 (1895); McDonald v. Eggleston, 26 Vt. 154, 60 Am.Dec. 303 (1853).

58. Hart v. Withers, 1 Pen. & W. 285, 21 Am.Dec. 382 (Pa.1830). See Mautner v. Eitingon, 197 App.Div. 756, 189 N. Y.S. 567 (1921); Larkin Co. v. Faggen, 71 Pa.Super. 430, 432 (1919).

In Harrison v. Jackson, 17 T.R. 207, 101 Eng.Rep. 935 (1797), another effective

objection was expressed, that the obligees of a covenant would have a preference. This objection does not exist in the U. S. McDonald v. Eggleston, 26 Vt. 154, 60 Am.Dec. 303 (1853).

59. U.P.A. § 9. This section was applied to sustain a lease to a partnership in Lawer v. Kline, 39 Wyo. 285, 270 P. 1077 (1928).

Referring to U.P.A. § 9, the court said: "The provision does not, so far as the point here involved is concerned, seem to have received any judicial construction heretofore. Those who drafted it doubtless had in mind the conflicting authorities on that point, and seem to have definitely settled the dispute in favor of what we have stated to be the prevailing view. The controlling point in this case, accordingly, seems to be as to whether or not the lease in question is within the limitations expressed in the section; namely, that it was executed to carry on the business of the partnership in the usual way. We think it is. The partnership needed some lease to carry on its business. We do not think that leases lasting for five years are at all out of the ordinary, as is indicated in the case above cited. Past transactions may be taken into consideration in determining this point. . . . And, as we have seen, the partnership had a lease lasting for five years previous to the time that the lease in question was taken. In fact leases

pears that the only question in the case of the sealed instrument is whether its execution is within the apparent scope of the business.

lasting only a short time could, in the nature of things, not be satisfactory unless perchance in those cases in which a partnership is formed for only a short and definite period of time. We conclude that David Kline had implied authority to execute the lease in question, which was binding upon the partnership in the absence of knowledge by plaintiff of his actually limited power. . . ." As to the power to execute a written contract within the Statute of Frauds, the court again referred to section 9 of the U.P.A., "which authorizes a partner to sign any instrument, if executed in connection with the usual course of business of the partnership. The framers of that provision knew, of course, the existence of the statute of frauds in every state in the Union, and they knew, further, that innumerable leases are constantly made for terms lasting longer than one year, and it would be strange indeed, that, while making such sweeping provision as above mentioned, they should not have intended to include leases of the character in question here. . . . "

Sealed notes, executed by a partner, have been held to be binding on the partnership under a statute declaring that there is authority for the execution of "any writing or bond in the course of business." Maynard v. Rawlins, 45 Ga.App. 91, 163 S.E. 269 (1932).

It should be noted that U.P.A. § 9 is specifically concerned with the execution of written instruments only when executed in the partnership name. The act of a partner, done in his own name, may be binding on the partnership, because his name is the firm name, generally or for the particular transaction, Rumsey v. Briggs, 139 N.Y. 323, 34 N.E. 929 (1893); or, in case of a concealed partnership, or concealment of the partnership character of the transaction, by application of the agency doctrine of liability of the undisclosed principal, Reynolds v. Cleveland, 4 Cow. 282, 15 Am.Dec. 369 (N.Y.1825). This rule applies to informal contracts, and not to sealed instruments and negotiable instruments, where only the persons who are parties thereto can be bound. Williams v. Gillies, 75 N.Y. 197 (1878); Pope v. Jennings, 34 Ga.App. 496, 130 S.E. 348 (1925); North Pennsylvania Coal Co's Appeal, 45 Pa. 181, 84 Am. Dec. 487 (1863), sealed instruments; and Holmes v. Burton, 9 Vt. 252, 31 Am.Dec. 621 (1837), negotiable instrument.

If the transaction is one in which the firm is regarded as the person to whom credit is given as the principal debtor, the partner's note may be regarded as collateral security. Hoeflinger v. Wells, 47 Wis. 628, 3 N.W. 589 (1879), was an action to recover from a partnership on account of money loaned for which the note of a partner was given. The court said: "If upon the trial the plaintiff can show that the money was borrowed for the firm, that he was at the time advised that it was for the firm, and that he loaned it to the firm and upon its credit, then the mere taking of the individual note of the one partner for the money so loaned will not defeat the action. The taking of such note may be evidence tending to show that the money was not loaned to the firm, and that the sole credit was given to Stafford; but it is not conclusive of that fact; and if the jury or the court should find as a fact that the money was borrowed by and loaned to the firm and upon its credit, then the taking of the individual note of one member of the firm could not be a payment of such firm debt, unless it was affirmatively shown that such note was taken in payment of the same."

See Mills v. Riggle, 83 Kan. 703, 112 P. 617, Ann.Cas.1912A, 616 (1911). Compare Meyer v. Hegler, 121 Cal. 682, 54 P. 271 (1898).

If an instrument is signed in the names of all the partners, it may be shown by extrinsic evidence to be intended as a partnership instrument. Frederick v. Citizens' Nat. Bank, 231 F. 667 (3d Cir. 1916); Davis v. Turner, 120 F. 605 (4th Cir. 1903).

For a fuller treatment of the subject of seals (which are declining in importance), the reader is referred to the predecessor of this work.[60]

(c) Hiring and Firing Employees

A partner has implied power to hire employees whose services are necessary for the carrying on of the business of the partnership.[61] He may make reasonable agreements for compensation.[62] He may discharge an employee.[63]

(d) Purchase of Property

A partner can bind the partnership for the purchase of property reasonably incident to the business.[64] This is clearly true of a com-

---

60. Crane, Partnership 248–52 (2d ed. 1952).

61. Rice v. Jackson, 171 Pa. 89, 32 A. 1036 (1895). There is no implied authority to employ for purposes outside the ordinary course of business, as to draw plans for a hotel to be erected on land held by a partnership for the purpose of sale, Palliser v. Erhardt, 63 App.Div. 617, 71 N.Y.S. 563 (1901); or hiring of a physician to treat employees of a farming partnership, Woodruff v. Scaife, 83 Ala. 152, 3 So. 311 (1887). Felice v. Felice, 34 N.J. Super. 388, 112 A.2d 581 (1955); Dygert v. Hansen, 31 Wash.2d 858, 199 P. 2d 596 (1948).

62. Miller v. Miller, 118 Pa.Super.Ct. 38, 179 A. 248 (1935).

An agreement to pay to four employees half of the net profits is so far unreasonable as to be void. Warren v. Mosher, 31 Ariz. 33, 250 P. 354, 49 A.L.R. 1311 (1926).

But profit-sharing compensation per se is not void and a partner can engage an employee on this basis. Lieberman v. Dubin, 62 N.Y.S.2d 880 (City Ct. 1946).

63. First Nat. Bank of Ann Arbor, Mich. v. Farson, 226 N.Y. 218, 123 N.E. 490 (1919).

64. Iroquois Rubber Co. v. Griffin, 226 N.Y. 297, 123 N.E. 369 (1919).

This was an action to recover the price of a lot of automobile supplies purchased by a member of a partnership which was engaged in the business of operating an automobile sales agency.

"The judge . . . directed a verdict for the amount of the May purchase, because it was ordered on the letterhead of the defendants, and this representation of the business authorized Griffin's act. . . . Considering the nature of the agency, the letterheads, the business as previously conducted and explained by this defendant, was the partnership merely to sell automobiles, or did it include their fixing and repair, thus requiring accessories? This was for the jury. . . . A man who enters a partnership for only one purpose is not liable for the purchases of the other partner unless used in that business or the articles are of the kind usually and customarily bought for such an undertaking existing or represented to exist."

Boise Payette Lumber Co. v. Sarret, 38 Idaho 278, 221 P. 130 (1923) held that the question whether it was within the scope of a partnership formed for sheep raising and selling to purchase lumber, fence posts, wire, nails, etc., was properly submitted to the determination of the jury, and that evidence of what was usual in such purchases by such partnerships in the community was properly admitted.

If the purchase is within the scope of the business, the fact that the purchasing partner converts the property to his own use does not prevent the partnership from remaining liable to the bona fide seller. Bond v. Gibson, 1 Camp. 185 (1808), P. Hoffmaster Sons Co., Ltd. v. Hodges, 154 Mich. 641, 118 N.W. 484 (1908); Phillips v. Stanzell, 28 S.W. 900 (Tex.Civ.App. 1895).

mercial partnership, and it is also true of other partnerships as to property necessary for the business, as in the case of law books for a law firm.[65]

A partner who has the authority to acquire property for the firm also has the authority to enter into a binding agreement to acquire it and satisfy the Statute of Frauds by executing a memorandum in the firm name.[66]

(e) Waiver of Statute of Limitations

It was held at one time in England that a joint debtor had the power to bind his co-obligors by a part payment or by an express or implied new promise so as to bar the defense of Statute of Limitations. This was changed by statute,[67] and in this country many states have statutory provisions to the effect that payment or acknowledgment by one joint contractor shall not toll the running of the statute as to other joint contractors who do not join therein. In other states, this result has been reached by judicial decision.[68] But if the part payment [69] or new promise expressed or implied from acknowledgment [70]

A partner, in a partnership engaged in sales of real estate, has authority from the nature of the business to purchase an automobile to aid him in making sales. Allison v. Campbell, 35 S.W.2d 776 (Tex.Civ.App.1931).

A partner does not have apparent authority to purchase goods not reasonably appropriate for the carrying on of the business such as a purchase by a partner in a general merchandising firm whose place of business is in dry territory, where it cannot legally sell liquor, of a lot of liquor from a seller in another state. Cummings v. S. Funkenstein Co., 17 Ala.App. 7, 81 So. 343 (1919).

An employee, placed in charge of a general store by a partnership with authority to buy merchandise, on credit, but ordered not to buy more than $50 at one time, can bind the firm to a purchase of costume jewelry in amount of $284, to a seller unaware of the limitation on his authority and of the fact that the store had not theretofore handled costume jewelry, Mason v. Rice, 47 Ga.App. 502, 170 S.E. 829 (1933).

65. Alley v. Bowen-Merrill Co., 76 Ark. 4, 88 S.W. 838, 113 Am.St.Rep. 73, 6 Ann.Cas. 127 (1905).

66. Lawer v. Kline, 39 Wyo. 285, 270 P. 1077 (1928), supra, note 59.

67. Lord Tenterden's Act, 9 Geo. IV c. 14 (1828).

68. Williston, Contracts, § 191. (3d ed. 1957).

69. Harding v. Butler, 156 Mass. 34, 30 N.E. 168 (1892); Tappan v. Kimball, 30 N.H. 136 (1855), after dissolution of which creditor was uninformed; Carlton v. Coffin, 28 Vt. 504 (1856).

An incoming partner, not being liable as such for the debts of the former partnership, is not affected by a part payment by a continuing partner. If he has assumed liability, it would seem that the obligation is to be regarded as that of the new partnership, and he should be bound by a part payment, as regards the tolling of the statute of limitations. It has, however, been held that the payment by the co-partner in such a case is presumably for his own account, not as a firm act, and that it does not affect the incoming partner who has not assumed the debts. Stephens v. Neely, 161 Ark. 114, 255 S.W. 562, 45 A.L.R. 1236 (1923). If the partnership is subject to the U.P.A. § 41, under which creditors retain their status as partnership creditors after a change in personnel, though without recourse to the separate property of the incoming partner who does not

70. See note 70 on page 286.

is made by a partner in the course of carrying on the business, it is a partnership act, and effectively tolls the statute as to all of the partners. The same rule applies to joint venturers.[71]

(f) Payment, Delivery, and Enforcement of Claims

A partner presumably has the power to receive performance of obligations due to the partnership. Delivery or payment to a partner is delivery or payment to the partnership, unless the third person is aware of restrictions on his authority.[72] A partner has the implied power to institute actions for the collection of claims due to the partnership.[73]

assume liability, it would seem that the incoming partner would be bound by acts of his co-partners which toll the statute, so far as partnership property is concerned.

70. Furlow Pressed Brick Co. v. Balboa Land & Water Co., 186 Cal. 754, 200 P. 625 (1921); Abrahams v. Myers, 40 Md. 499 (1874).

The acknowledgment is effective to renew the indebtedness though the statute has run. Sears v. Starbird, 78 Cal. 225, 20 P. 547 (1889); Walsh v. Mayer, 111 U.S. 31, 4 S.Ct. 260, 28 L. Ed. 338 (1884).

The statutes making part payments and acknowledgments of joint debtors ineffective as to co-debtors do not apply to partnerships. Vermont-People's Nat. Bank v. Parker, 269 Mass. 387, 169 N.E. 154 (1929); Carlton v. Coffin, 28 Vt. 504 (1856). But see Blethen v. Murch, 80 Me. 313, 14 A. 208 (1888), where the statute was held applicable to a payment made by a continuing partner after dissolution, out of his own funds to a creditor uninformed of the dissolution. The court said: "A payment made before dissolution, from partnership funds, might, perhaps, be regarded as payment by all the partners, and thus affect them all."

After the partnership has been discharged in bankruptcy, a promise by a partner to pay a discharged obligation is binding on him. Vachon v. Ditz, 114 Wash. 11, 194 P. 545 (1921). But it should not be held binding on the co-partners, the powers of representation having been extinguished by the dissolution and complete winding up in bankruptcy.

71. Reinig v. Nelson, 199 Wis. 482, 227 N.W. 14 (1929). In this case the part

payment of the joint obligation by the managing associate, by the use of funds borrowed on his own credit, was held to be binding on the co-adventurers.

72. Effective delivery may be made to a partner who is presumably entitled to possess partnership property. Crosswell v. Lehman, Durr & Co., 54 Ala. 363, 25 Am.Rep. 684 (1875); Bunnell v. Ward, 241 Mich. 404, 217 N.W. 68 (1928), after dissolution; Kenney v. Altvater, 77 Pa. 34 (1874).

A payment, to a partner, of a debt due the firm is payment to the firm. Major v. Hawkes, 12 Ill. 298 (1850); Huffman Farm Co. v. Rush, 173 Pa. 264, 33 A. 1013 (1896); Van Billiard v. Croft & Allen Co., 302 Pa. 349, 153 A. 555 (1931); Mosby v. United States, 194 F. 346 (6th Cir. 1912). See also Sec. 52 n. 53 below.

The partners may agree among themselves that payments shall be received by one partner exclusively, and this would be binding on a debtor with notice. Clark v. Lauman, 63 Ill.App. 132 (1895).

As to whether one of two partners may, by notice to a debtor forbidding payment to the other partner, cut off his power to receive payment, see Noyes v. New Haven, N. L. & S. Railroad Co., 30 Conn. 1 (1861); Steele v. First Nat. Bank of Joliet, 60 Ill. 23 (1871).

In Markee v. Philadelphia, 270 Pa. 337, 113 A. 359 (1921), each of two partners gave such a notice. It was held that interest did not run against the debtor, pending settlement of their disagreement.

73. Kuhn v. Weil, 73 Mo. 213 (1880), holding the partnership liable **for a**

(g) Other Incidents of the Business

A partner has apparent authority to indorse checks and notes.[74]

It is reasonably incident to the business of selling that representations should be made to customers,[75] and that advertising should be contracted for by a partner.[76]

It is not incident to the business of selling lumber to enter into a contract to construct a building, and a partnership engaged in the lumber business is not bound by such a contract made by a partner without express authority.[77]

It has been suggested that a partnership may "deputize" a partner to represent it on a corporate directorate so as to make the partnership a "director" for purposes of the federal statute [78] imposing liability for certain short-term security transactions by directors and others. However, no such authority was found from the mere fact

wrongful attachment; Clarke v. Slate Val. R. Co., 136 Pa. 408, 20 A. 562, 10 L.R.A. 238 (1890), suit instituted by authority of majority of partners; Henson v. First Security & Loan Co., 164 Wash. 198, 2 P.2d 85 (1931).

A partner has no power to dismiss an action brought with the authority of the majority, Lunt Farm Co. v. Hamilton, 217 Iowa 22, 250 N.W. 698 (1933). See also Sec. 52(d) below.

A partner has the power to defend actions brought against the partnership, McCord Co. v. Callaway, 109 Ga. 796, 35 S.E. 171 (1900); but may not by his appearance for the partnership subject partners not served with process to the jurisdiction of the court as individuals, Beaver Board Cos. v. Imbrie, 47 F.2d 271 (D.C.N.Y.1922). Maglo v. Weaver, 11 N.J.Super. 32, 77 A.2d 499 (1950).

Haslet v. Street, 2 McCord's Law (S.C.) 310, 13 Am.Dec. 724 (1823), acceptance of service and appearance bound only the partners so acting. In South Carolina service on a partner gives the court no jurisdiction over the partnership or nonresident partner, Duncan v. Pearson, 35 F.Supp. 631 (D.S.C. 1940). In such a situation there may be a judgment against the partner served and the partnership property. See Karesh, Partnership Law and the Uniform Partnership Act in South Carolina, 3 S.C.L.Rev. 414 (1951).

74. Stauffer v. Ti Hang Lung & Co., 29 Cal.App.2d 121, 84 P.2d 209 (1938).

Roe v. Cooke, 350 Ill.App. 183, 112 N.E. 2d 511 (1953); Kallison v. Harris Trust & Sav. Bank, 338 Ill.App. 33, 86 N.E.2d 858 (1949); Link v. First Nat. Bank, 312 Ill.App. 502, 38 N.E. 2d 815 (1941).

Lycoming Trust Co. v. Allen, 102 Pa. Super. 184, 156 A. 707 (1931).

There is some older authority denying such authority in a non-commercial firm, e. g., a farming partnership, Ulery v. Gingrich, 57 Ill. 531 (1871).

See also U.C.C. § 3–508(5): notice (of dishonor of a negotiable instrument) to one partner is notice to each although the firm is dissolved.

75. Griffin v. Bergeda, 152 Tenn. 512, 279 S.W. 385 (1926).

Wyatt v. Brown, 39 Tenn.App. 28, 281 S.W.2d 64 (1955), guarantee that water would be fit for human consumption was incident to digging of well.

76. Miller Pub. Co. v. Orth, 133 Minn. 139, 157 N.W. 1083 (1916). Compare G. H. Haulenbeck Advertising Agency v. November, 27 Misc. 836, 60 N.Y.S. 573 (1899), where an advertising contract was held to be invalid as against one of two partners who had notified that agency that he revoked the authority of his co-partner to enter into such a contract.

77. J. F. Beasley Lumber Co. v. Sparks, 169 Ark. 640, 276 S.W. 582 (1925).

78. Securities Exchange Act of 1934, § 16(b), 15 U.S.C.A. § 78(p)(b).

that the partnership was in the investment banking business and its partners sat on the boards of many corporations.[79]

TRANSFERS OF PARTNERSHIP PROPERTY

§ 50A. **Whether a partner's transfer of partnership property is a partnership act depends not only upon the nature of the business and of the transfer but also (in the case of land) upon the manner in which record title to the property is held.**

The transfer of personal property is governed largely by the rules already discussed.[80] Thus, in a commercial partnership (whose business consists of buying and selling) a partner has authority to sell goods in the ordinary course of business.[81] But it is not within his power to sell property other than that held for purpose of sale.[82] Nor can he sell the entire property of the partnership,[83] since this would break up the partnership business.[84]

79. Blau v. Lehman, 368 U.S. 403, 82 S.Ct. 451, 7 L.Ed.2d 403 (1962). Cf. Higgins v. Shenango Pottery Co., discussed Sec. 54(b) n. 5 below.

80. Secs. 49–50 above.

81. Crites v. Muller, 65 Cal. 559, 4 P. 567 (1884), sale, by a member of a cattle dealing partnership, of forty-six head from the herd of sixty-five; Blaugrund v. Mogel, 53 S.W.2d 315 (Tex.Civ.App.1932); Little v. Britton, 189 Ala. 10, 66 So. 694 (1914), sale of mechanics' lien by member of a building partnership;

After dissolution, the power to make contracts of sale is limited to goods on hand. Bass Dry Goods Co. v. Granite City Mfg. Co., 116 Ga. 176, 42 S.E. 415 (1902).

82. In re Messenger, 32 F.Supp. 490 (E.D.Pa.1940) (Pa. law); Ellis v. Mihelis, 60 Cal.2d 206, 384 P.2d 7, 32 Cal.Rptr. 415 (1963) citing this text; Lowman v. Sheets, 124 Ind. 416, 24 N.E. 351, 7 L.R.A. 784 (1890); Steele v. Estabrook, 232 Mass. 432, 122 N.E. 562 (1919); Cayton v. Hardy, 27 Mo. 536 (1858); Kotsakis v. Williamson, 72 Mont. 158, 231 P. 1104 (1924); Sloan v. Moore, 37 Pa. 217 (1860); McGrath v. Cowen, 57 Ohio St. 385, 49 N.E. 338 (1898).

83. Hunter v. Waynick, 67 Iowa 555, 25 N.W. 776 (1885), retail grocery; Bender v. Hemstreet, 12 Misc. 620, 34 N.Y.S. 423 (1895); Ditzel v. Kent, 131 Mont. 129, 308 P.2d 628 (1957), ranch;

Freeman v. Abramson, 30 Misc. 101, 61 N.Y.S. 839 (S.Ct.1899), cigar dealers.

Contra: Arnold v. Brown, 41 Mass. (24 Pick.) 89, 35 Am.Dec. 296 (Mass.1831), partner in retail firm could sell entire stock of goods in one transaction.

Incorporating partnership property is a transfer beyond the authority of a single partner (or any number less than all). Fortugno v. Hudson Manure Co., 51 N.J.Super. 482, 144 A.2d 207 (1958); MacDonald v. Trojan Button-Fastener Co., 9 N.Y.S. 383 (S.Ct. 1890) aff'd. 56 Hun 648, 10 N.Y.S. 91 (1890).

Corporate law offers an analogy: except in the regular course of business, a sale of substantially all the assets requires stockholder approval, 2 Model Bus. Corp. Act 374–75 (1960). Occasional statutes deal specifically with this aspect of partnerships; for an example, see Kotsakis v. Williamson, 72 Mont. 158, 231 P. 1104 (1924).

84. Petrikis v. Hanges, 111 Cal.App.2d 734, 245 P.2d 39 (1952), cocktail lounge. U.P.A. § 9(3) (c), Sec. 52 below.

Cf. Watson v. Oregon Moline Plow Co., 112 Or. 414, 227 P. 278 (1924), Sec. 52 n. 39 below, partner could not rescind dealership contract which was basis of entire partnership business.

Herr v. Brakefield, 50 Wash.2d 593, 314 P.2d 397 (1957), citing this text, is a well-reasoned holding that a partner in a beef cattle and farming firm had authority to sell the entire herd of 53

In apparent contradiction to the foregoing principles, there are many holdings that a partner does have authority to mortgage property not held for purpose of sale,[85] or even the entire property of the firm.[86] However, the inconsistency dissolves upon realization that these are almost invariably mortgages to secure antecedent debts. The partner's authority derives from his general authority to pay firm debts.[87] It does not encompass mortgages to secure a partner's individual debts.[88]

Just as with personal property, a partner can transfer real estate in the ordinary course of the partnership business.[89] The U.P.A., which enables a partnership to own legal title to realty,[90] also expands the rights of partners to deal with it.[91] In so doing it favors grantees who rely on the record title over the co-partners of a partner who exceeds his actual authority. Results vary considerably, depending on who is the record owner.

If record title is in the partnership and a partner conveys in the partnership name, legal title passes. But the partnership may recover the property (except from a bona fide purchaser from the grantee) if it can show (A) that the conveying partner was not apparently carry-

cattle. Its conclusion is that such sales "were not unusual and were appropriate and not ordinarily detrimental to enterprises of this kind."

85. McCarthy v. Seisler, 130 Ind. 63, 29 N.E. 407 (1891); Rock v. Collins, 99 Wis. 630, 75 N.W. 426, 67 Am.St.Rep. 885 (1898).

86. Nelson v. Wheelock, 46 Ill. 25 (1867); Tapley v. Butterfield, 1 Metc. 515, 35 Am.Dec. 374 (Mass.1840); Beckman v. Noble, 115 Mich. 523, 73 N.W. 803 (1898); Settle v. Hargadine-McKittrick Dry-Goods Co., 66 F. 850 (5th Cir. 1894).

87. There are surprisingly few cases on mortgages not involving prior debts. Jones v. Davis, 25 A. 370, (N.J.Ch. 1892) holds that a partner has no authority to mortgage.
Cf. Bender v. Hemstreet, 12 Misc. 620, 34 N.Y.S. 423 (Sup.Ct.1895), partner has authority to transfer partnership assets to creditor in satisfaction of existing debt although he could not sell them to a stranger. See Schneider v. Schmidt, 82 N.J.Eq. 81, 88 A. 179 (1913), partnership property, though not held for sale, may be transferred to creditor in payment of debt.
A partner's mortgage which produced funds used in the firm business was held valid in Salinas v. Bennett, 33

S.C. 285, 11 S.E. 968 (1890); however, there was acquiescence by the co-partner.
A partner's mortgage to secure unmatured debts whose owners have not requested security is outside the ordinary course of business and invalid. McGrath v. Cowen, 57 Ohio St. 385, 49 N.E. 338 (1898).

88. Pride v. Brandon, 227 S.W.2d 385 (Tex.Civ.App.1950). See also Sec. 51 (b) n. 5 infra. A partner may mortgage his interest in the partnership to secure his personal debt. Sec. 51(b) below discusses the use of partnership property to pay an individual debt.

89. Harmon v. Martin, 395 Ill. 595, 71 N.E.2d 74 (1947); Chester v. Dickerson, 54 N.Y. 1, 13 Am.Rep. 550 (1873); partnerships in real estate business. Authority to make contracts and conveyances is incidental to the authority to sell or transfer.
Cf. Robinson v. Daughtry, 171 N.C. 200, 88 S.E. 252 (1916), partner has authority to sell real estate taken in course of trade.

90. U.P.A. § 8(3), Sec. 38 above.

91. In re George & John Hurt, 129 F. Supp. 94 (S.D.Calif.1955), California law. This opinion discusses the meaning and purposes of all of U.P.A. § 10.

ing on business in the usual way or (B) that he had in fact no authority and the grantee had knowledge of that fact.[92] The burden of proof with respect to authority is thus on the partnership.

If record title is in the partnership and a partner conveys in his own name, only equitable title passes and then only if the partner had actual or apparent authority.[93] Here the burden is on the grantee, for his grantor is not the record owner.

If record title is in some of the partners individually and they convey in their own names, legal title passes to a holder for value without knowledge.[94] Since the grantee has a conveyance from all persons shown by the records to have an interest, he is accorded a high degree of protection. The use of nominees is facilitated by such a rule.

A prospective grantee is well advised to require a conveyance in the name or names shown by the title records and, where feasible, to obtain consents or authorizations from all the partners.

Leases and mortgages are subject to the same rules as other conveyances of land.[95]

The transfer of stock certificates is regulated by special statutes which protect the transferee and have the effect of expanding a partner's authority.[96]

92. U.P.A. § 10(1). See U.P.A. § 3 for the relevant definition of knowledge.

93. U.P.A. § 10(2). There is no conflict with U.P.A. § 8(3) which states that title acquired in the partnership name "can be conveyed only in the partnership name"; it refers only to legal title.

94. Dodson v. Webb, 74 S.D. 166, 50 N.W.2d 92 (1951).

U.P.A. § 10(3). From any other grantee the partnership may recover if the conveyance was without actual or apparent authority. Ibid.

If record title is in all the partners and they all convey, all their rights pass. U.P.A. § 10(5). Other situations are covered by U.P.A. § 10(4). Although record title was in all the partners, a contract of sale in the firm name (signed by one partner) was enforced. Smith v. Dixon, 238 Ark. 1018, 386 S.W.2d 244 (1965). The signing partner had at least apparent authority.

95. U.P.A. §§ 2 (5th sentence) and 10.

96. Uniform Stock Transfer Act § 1, making an indorsement sufficient if "by the person appearing by the certificate to be the owner of the shares." "Person" includes "partnership", id. § 22. Rescission is permitted only in very limited instances, id. § 7. It is the custom in the securities business to accept indorsements in the firm name without indication of the partner or agent who signs. N. Y. Stock Transfer Assoc. Rules 150, 201. For other provisions concerning partnership, see id. Rules 32, 64, 72, 129. The Uniform Stock Transfer Act provisions cited are rapidly being superseded by Uniform Commercial Code §§ 8–308(1) and (3) (a), 1–201(30) and (28), and 8–315 which produce essentially the same result.

ACTS NOT WITHIN APPARENT AUTHORITY

§ 51.   An act of a partner, which is not apparently for the carrying on of the business of the partnership in the usual way, does not bind the partnership unless authorized by the other partners.   U.P.A. § 9(2).

Examples of acts not within the apparent authority of a partner, as partnerships are usually conducted, include contracts of suretyship and guaranty, payment of separate debts with partnership property, making of stock subscriptions, and gratuitous undertakings.

(a) Suretyship and Guaranty

It is generally outside the scope of business for a partner to assume, in the name of the partnership, liability for the debt of another.[97]   But the nature of the business may be such that such acts are within its scope.[98]   There may be actual authority as indicated by past

97. Duncan v. Lowndes, 3 Camp. 478 (1813); Bank of Fort Madison v. Alden, 129 U.S. 372, 9 S.Ct. 332, 32 L.Ed. 725 (1889); Mayberry, Pollard & Co. v. Bainton & Bancroft, 2 Har. 24 (Del.1835); Megunticook Nat. Bank v. Knowlton Bros., 125 Me. 480, 135 A. 95 (1926); Nat. Security Bank v. McDonald, 127 Mass. 82 (1879); Heffron v. Hanaford, 40 Mich. 305 (1879); Foot v. Sabin, 19 Johns. 154, 10 Am.Dec. 208 (N.Y.1821); Jones & Brindisi, Inc. v. Breslaw, 250 N.Y. 147, 164 N.E. 887 (1928); Jamestown Banking Co. v. Conneaut Lake Dock & Dredge Co., 339 **Pa. 26, 14 A.2d 325 (1940).**

The same rule applies to executing firm paper to be discounted and proceeds made available for use of a third person. Back Bay Nat. Bank v. Brickley, 254 Mass. 261, 150 N.E. 11 (1926).

"It is not usual for persons in business to make themselves answerable for the conduct of other people; and it is settled law that the party who takes a promissory note bearing the indorsement of a firm, whether as guarantors or as sureties, takes it burdened with the presumption that the firm name was not signed in the usual course of partnership business, and no recovery can be had by simply showing the instrument." Clarke v. Wallace, 1 N.D. 404, 48 N.W. 339, 26 Am.St.Rep. 636 (1891).

See Note, 20 Mich.Law Rev. 678 (1922).

While a guaranty executed by a partner in the partnership name may not be a partnership act, because of lack of authority, the partner signing the guaranty is personally liable. Jones

& Brindisi, Inc. v. Breslaw, supra; Bonneau v. Strauss Bros., 72 Okl. 110, 179 P. 10, 4 A.L.R. 255 (1919); Dillingham v. Cantrell, 54 Ga.App. 622, 188 S.E. 605 (1936).

Compare the limitations on a corporation's power to guarantee or become surety; Ballantine, Corporations 231–34 (rev. ed. 1946); Baker & Cary, Cases and Materials on Corporations 367–68 (3rd ed. unabr. 1959).

98. It may be the ordinary course of business for a securities selling partnership to guarantee securities sold by it. First Nat. Bank of Ann Arbor, Mich., v. Farson, 226 N.Y. 218, 123 N.E. 490 (1919).

Compare Shambleau v. Hoyt, 265 Mich. 560, 569, 251 N.W. 778 (1933), broker's guarantee that customer would not lose on purchase of a stock; authority was express as well as implied by the nature of the business.

See Note, 20 Mich.Law Rev. 678 (1922).

It has been held that a partner has implied authority to guarantee the obligation of a corporation in which the partnership is interested. Rodabaugh v. Kauffman, 53 Cal.App. 676, 200 P. 747 (1921).

See also Stauffer v. Ti Hang Lung & Co., 29 Cal.App.2d 121, 84 P.2d 209 (1938), endorsement of note of corporation owned in part by firm and whose business was distribution of goods imported by firm.

Where a banking partnership is a depositary, it has been held to be within the scope of business to guarantee the town treasurer's bond. Wexford

dealings of the partnership,[99] or there may be ratification.[1]

Under the law of Negotiable Instruments, a holder in due course may enforce an instrument against a partnership whose name was signed on it by a partner having general authority to execute negotiable instruments for firm purposes, though in the particular instance he signed the firm name as an accommodation party without authority.[2]

Township v. Seeley, 196 Mich. 634, 163 N.W. 16 (1917).

Where a partnership has undertaken the purchase of property, and a portion of the price is due, it is within the course of business for the majority of the partners to execute a guarantee of the loan of the vendor from a bank, thus securing from him an extension of the maturity of the partnership debt to him. Wolff v. First Nat. Bank of Winslow, 47 Ariz. 97, 53 P.2d 1077 (1936).

Rediscounting of commercial paper with unrestricted endorsement may be within the scope of business of a banking partnership. McNeal v. Gossard, 6 Okl. 363, 50 P. 159 (1897).

Arrangement for an attachment bond for a non-resident client may be within the scope of business of a law partnership, so as to render it liable for money received by a partner for the purpose of procuring a surety. Fornes v. Wright, 91 Iowa 392, 59 N.W. 51 (1894).

99. Steuben County Bank v. Alburger, 101 N.Y. 202, 4 N.E. 341 (1886).

The partners may authorize by express assent in advance. Seeberger v. Wyman, 108 Iowa 527, 79 N.W. 290 (1899).

1. Sweetser v. French, 56 Mass. (2 Cush.) 309, 48 Am.Dec. 666 (1848); Kneisley Lumber Co. v. Edward B. Stoddard Co., 131 Mo.App. 15, 109 S.W. 840 (1908); McNeal v. Gossard, 6 Okl. 363, 50 P. 159 (1897); Nicolai-Neppach Co. v. Abrams, 116 Or. 424, 240 P. 870 (1925).

In Marsh v. Gold, 19 Mass. (2 Pick.) 285 (1824), a member of a partnership of attorneys undertook to indemnify an officer serving a writ of execution. It was held that while such a contract was presumably unauthorized as a partnership act, there was sufficient evidence of ratification by the co-partner.

2. "As a general principle, partners are agents for each other, and each is bound by the act of the other, when the act is within the scope of the partnership purposes and business, but the execution of notes for the accommodation of another, or the acceptance and indorsement of the accommodation paper of another, is not within the implied powers of a partner, and a partner is not authorized, in the absence of a contract, or of special authority, to execute such paper for the partnership. . . . However, if the partnership is one engaged in trade, and the paper, executed for accommodation, is negotiable and executed by the managing member, and the accommodation character of the signature does not appear upon the face of the paper, the partnership will be bound upon it when it is negotiated and in the hands of a bona fide holder without notice of its infirmity by reason of its unauthorized execution." Power Grocery Co. v. Hinton, 187 Ky. 171, 218 S.W. 1013 (1920).

Accord, Wait v. Thayer, 118 Mass. 473 (1875); Catskill Bank v. Stall, 15 Wend. 364 (N.Y.1836).

The fact that several signatures, including that of the firm, appear as co-makers, is not notice that it is accommodation paper. Union Nat. Bank of Kansas City, Mo. v. Neill, 149 F. 711, 10 L.R.A.,N.S., 426 (5th Cir. 1906).

The fact that a note made by a partner for the accommodation of himself and another is by him endorsed in the firm name, is not notice, of itself. Feigenspan v. McDonnell, 201 Mass. 341, 87 N.E. 624 (1909).

The firm is not bound on an unauthorized instrument, unless the making of such instruments is apparently within the course of business. Dowling v. National Exchange Bank of Boston, 145 U.S. 512, 12 S.Ct. 928, 36 L. Ed. 795 (1892); Pooley, Barnum &

The form of the instrument and the surrounding circumstances may be such as to prevent the taker from becoming a holder in due course.[3]

(b) Paying or Assuming Separate Debt of a Partner

Partnership property is by agreement of the partners devoted to partnership purposes. Its use for the payment of a separate debt is only indirectly of benefit to the partnership, in that it may serve to maintain partnership credit.[4] Whatever the nature of the business, it is presumably unauthorized for a partner to apply partnership property to the payment of his own debt or for any other purely personal advantage.[5] The giving of a partnership obligation to a separate creditor is likewise not within the apparent authority.[6] Co-partners may be estopped to deny the validity of a transfer by a partner for his separate purposes if they have allowed the business to be carried on in his name,[7] or if they allow him to hold the title to partnership

Co. v. Whitmore, 57 Tenn. (10 Heisk.) 629, 633, 27 Am.Re. 733 (1873).

If the purchaser of the paper is aware of its accommodation character, he is not a bona fide purchaser, and cannot hold the partnership unless it was authorized. Megunticook Nat. Bank v. Knowlton Bros., 125 Me. 480, 135 A. 95 (1926).

3. Back Bay Nat. Bank v. Brickley, 254 Mass. 261, 150 N.E. 11 (1926), form of transaction such that bank taking note given for accommodation of a third party might have been put on inquiry, question of fact for jury; Smith v. Weston, 159 N.Y. 194, 54 N.E. 38 (1899), second endorsement in name of firm held to put holder taking from payee and first endorser on notice; Winona Nat. Bank v. Brackens Creek Coal Land Co., 109 W.Va. 362, 154 S.E. 872 (1930).

4. Ex parte Bonbomus, 8 Ves.Jr. 541, 32 Eng.Rep. 465 (1803).

5. Miller v. Yates, 171 Ark. 958, 287 S.W. 179 (1926); Morrison v. Austin State Bank, 213 Ill. 472, 72 N.E. 1109, 104 Am.St.Rep. 225 (1904); Janney v. Springer, 78 Iowa 617, 43 N.W. 461, 16 Am.St.Rep. 460 (1889); Brickett v. Downs, 163 Mass. 70, 39 N.E. 776 (1895); McIntosh v. Detroit Sav. Bank, 247 Mich. 10, 225 N.W. 628 (1929); Jones v. Turner, 249 Mich. 403, 228 N.W. 796 (1930); Mastley v. Moe, 193 Minn. 411, 258 N.W. 591 (1935); Great Southwest Life Ins. Co. v. Pruitt & Harp, 177 Okl. 544, 61 P.2d 683 (1936); Morgenthaler v. Cohen, 103

Ohio St. 328, 132 N.E. 730 (1921); Todd v. Lorah, 75 Pa. 155 (1874); Crilly v. Fitzsimmons, 73 S.Dak. 646, 48 N.W.2d 62 (1951).

A partner cannot pledge or mortgage firm property to secure a separate debt. Gold Fork Lumber Co. v. Sweany & Smith Co., 35 Idaho 226, 205 P. 544 (1922); Post v. Kimberley, 9 Johns. 470 (N.Y.1812). See also Sec. 50A n. 88 above.

See also Uniform Fiduciaries Act, § 4, cited in Norristown-Penn Trust Co. v. Middleton, 300 Pa. 522, 150 A. 885 (1930).

A creditor of the partnership and of a partner, receiving partnership funds with knowledge, must apply it to the partnership debt. Mastley v. Moe, supra.

See, on application of payments, Restatement, Contracts § 388.

Because of the legal power which a partner has in the disposition of partnership property, including choses in action, the remedy of a co-partner, where partnership assets have been diverted to a partner's use, may be limited to a suit in equity to rescind the transaction, rather than a suit at law which assumes that no transaction had taken place. See Horner v. Bennett, 241 Ill.App. 134 (1926).

6. Lutz v. Miller, 102 W.Va. 23, 135 S.E. 168, 50 A.L.R. 426 (1926); Maxfield v. J. L. Heishman & Sons, 209 Iowa 1061, 229 N.W. 681 (1930).

7. Locke v. Lewis, 124 Mass. 1, 26 Am. Rep. 631 (1878); Morgenthaler v. Co-

property [8] and the transferee is ignorant that he is taking partnership property.

The partnership may authorize the payment of a separate debt with partnership property,[9] or ratify such a transaction.[10] Partnership creditors may void such a transfer or assumption of obligation if it is a fraud on creditors.[11]

(c) Stock Subscriptions

Partnership capital is presumably to be employed by the partnership directly in carrying on business. Therefore subscribing for stock in a corporation has been held outside the scope of the business,[12] even though its activities would be of incidental benefit to the partnership. One may question the wisdom of such a rule today when multiple entities and diversified operations are common and often have tax and other advantages.[13]

A stock subscription or purchase may be within the course of business, as where the partnership is engaged in the sale of stocks,[14] or where the firm is used for investing. It may be expressly authorized or ratified.[15] A partner may be found to have apparent authority to enter into a joint adventure with a third person in behalf of the partnership.[16]

hen, 103 Ohio St. 328, 132 N.E. 730 (1921).

Compare F. E. Nellis & Co. v. Green & Stallworth, 36 Ga.App. 684, 137 S.E. 843 (1927).

8. Robinson Bank v. Miller, 153 Ill. 244, 38 N.E. 1078, 27 L.R.A. 449, 46 Am. St.Rep. 883 (1894).

9. Larzelere & Son v. Tiel & Tooley, 3 Pa.Super. 109 (1896); Gansevoort v. Williams & Johnson, 14 Wend. 133 (N. Y.1835).

10. Miller v. Yates, 171 Ark. 958, 287 S.W. 179 (1926); Marine Co. of Chicago v. Carver, 42 Ill. 66 (1866); Feigenspan v. McDonnell, 201 Mass. 341, 87 N.E. 624 (1909), semble.

11. Hartley v. White, 94 Pa. 31 (1880); Uniform Fraudulent Conveyance Act, § 8; Bankruptcy Act, § 67d(4), 11 U. S.C.A. § 107d(4). See Sec. 46 above on fraudulent conveyances.

12. Barnard v. Lapeer & Port Huron Plank Road Co., 6 Mich. 274 (1859); Barry v. Mattocks, 156 Miss. 424, 125 So. 554 (1930); Patty v. Hillsboro Roller Mill Co., 4 Tex.Civ.App. 224, 23 S.W. 336 (1893).

It is likewise outside of the actual and apparent authority of a partner in a partnership not engaged in dealing in securities, such as a lumber company, to purchase shares of stock and give a note secured by the shares as collateral in payment therefor. A verdict for the non-participating partner, who has not authorized or ratified the transaction, may be directed by the court. Bank of Commerce v. Phillips, 24 Ga.App. 9, 100 S.E. 22 (1919).

13. The converse policy, restricting the right of corporations to enter partnerships (discussed Sec. 9 above), is gradually eroding under the same economic pressures. See Baker & Cary, Cases and Materials on Corporations 368–69 (3rd ed. unabr. 1959); 2 Model Bus. Corp.Act Ann. 83–93 (1960).

14. Maltby v. Northwestern Virginia R. Co., 16 Md. 422 (1860).

15. Livingston v. Pittsburgh & Stubenville R. Co., 2 Grant Cas. 219 (Pa. 1858).

16. McEvoy v. Grant, 302 Pa. 539, 153 A. 763 (1931), arrangement being made by managing partner.

It is not within the power of trustees of a business trust to enter into a partnership with other trusts, as they would thereby divest themselves of the personal duty to manage and control the trust estate committed to their care.[17]

(d) Gratuitous Undertakings

As partnerships are formed for the purpose of carrying on business for profit, a partner is presumably without authority to engage the partnership in a charitable undertaking, or to give away partnership property.[18] If a member of a partnership of druggists dispenses a free prescription, the partnership is not liable for his negligence in compounding it.[19] If a member of a partnership of attorneys transfers a chose in action of which he personally is the owner, and promises his assignee that the firm will furnish legal services for its collection free of charge, it is not a partnership transaction, and no liability is imposed upon the co-partner.[20] But if a partner for personal reasons undertakes to render professional services free of charge, no fee can be collected by the partnership, since no contract for the payment of compensation was created.[21] It would seem that some gratuitous services might come within the scope of the business, as a matter of business usage, as where a member of a brokerage firm furnishes market information to a customer or prospective customer, or where a member of a partnership operating a filling station inflates tires, or inspects oil in crank case or water in batteries. Such acts though not immediately charged for, may be within the scope of authorized methods of building up good will and seeking business, customary for like firms in the community.

---

17. Phoenix Oil Co. v. McLarren, 244 S.W. 830 (Tex.Civ.App.1922).

The powers of the trustees of a business trust are to be tested by the provisions of the articles of association, as in the case of a corporation. West Side Oil Co. v. McDorman, 244 S.W. 167 (Tex. Civ.App.1922); Martin v. Security Nat. Bank, 257 S.W. 645 (Tex.Civ.App.1924).

18. A similar restriction on corporate powers has now largely given way. See Henn, Corporations 281–82 (1961); Baker & Cary, Cases and Materials on Corporations 366–67 (3rd ed. unabr. 1959).

19. Gwynn v. Duffield, 66 Iowa 708, 24 N.W. 523, 55 Am.Rep. 286 (1885). It would seem that custom of the business might afford a basis for finding that the dispensing of free samples, as a part of an advertising campaign, might be within the scope of a retail business such as a drug store or grocery. Compare Aetna Life Ins. Co. v. Matthews, 47 S.W.2d 667 (Tex.Civ. App.1932), holding that the new accounts executive of a national bank was not acting in the course of business so as to be within the protection of a Workmen's Compensation Act, while dealing with cashier's checks deposited with him as stakeholder for the purposes of an election bet.

20. Davis v. Dodson & Moon, 95 Ga. 718, 22 S.E. 645, 29 L.R.A. 496, 51 Am. St.Rep. 108 (1895)

21. Stone v. Hart, 66 S.W. 191, 23 Ky. Law Rep. 1777 (1902). It was held, however, that the client having assented to an assignment by the attorney of his fee to the latter's creditor, the assignee could claim a fee on principles of estoppel.

(e) Miscellaneous

It is a transaction outside of the ordinary course of business to sell property which is a part of the capital assets and not held for purposes of sale,[22] or which is entirely outside the partnership business.[23]

In a close case on the facts, a lawyer's misappropriation of funds of a third party was held outside the course of business of the law firm to which he belonged.[23A]

ACTS WHICH ARE UNAUTHORIZED UNDER THE UNIFORM PARTNERSHIP ACT

§ 52. Unless authorized by the other partners or unless they have abandoned the business, one or more but less than all the partners have no authority to:

(a) Assign the partnership property in trust for creditors or on the assignee's promise to pay the debts of the partnership,

(b) Dispose of the good will of the business,

(c) Do any other act which would make it impossible to carry on the ordinary business of the partnership,

(d) Confess a judgment,

(e) Submit a partnership claim or liability to arbitration or reference. U.P.A. § 9(3).

The Uniform Partnership Act has departed from general statement of principle and gone into detail in enumerating certain acts which are generally held to be outside the implied power of a partner. It might better be subject to variation according to local usage or changing methods of doing business. What is within the ordinary course of business may vary with the time and place; the attempt to crystallize it is one of the defects of codification. The corresponding advantage is the constructive notice to the business community that certain extraordinary acts require unanimous authorization. A particular firm hindered by these rules can avoid them by express agreement, in the articles of partnership or elsewhere.

(a) Assignment for Creditors

"While the contract of partnership constitutes each of its members an agent for the others, it is only for the purpose of carrying on

---

22. In re Messenger, 32 F.Supp. 490 (E.D.Pa.1940), a sale of a truck owned by a plumbing partnership. It was also held that the transaction was a fraudulent conveyance, as the firm was insolvent and the payment by the buyer enured for the most part to the benefit of the selling partner. The sale was voided by the trustee in bankruptcy of the firm.

Rutherford v. McDonnell, 66 Ark. 448, 51 S.W. 1060 (1899), sale by a partner in a farming partnership of live stock and farm equipment. See also Sec. 50A above.

23. Bole v. Lyle, 39 Tenn.App. 679, 287 S.W.2d 931 (1955), timber sold by member of partnership manufacturing wood products.

23A. Douglas Reservoir Water Users Ass'n v. Maurer & Garst, 398 P.2d 74 (Wyo.1965).

the partnership, not for destroying it. Denuding the firm of all its property is a thing not contemplated, and consequently no agency for such a purpose was intended to be created. When therefore, one partner is at hand and might assent, but does not, it is quite unreasonable to presume that he has empowered his partner to do an act destructive of the purposes for which the firm was established." [24] In general, an assignment by a partner of all the partnership property for the benefit of creditors is invalid, and may be voided by creditors or by the other partners.[25] If the other partners have absconded,[26] or are absent and inaccessible,[27] the power exists. The act may be authorized by parol,[28] or it may be ratified.[29] Assignments for benefit of creditors are comparatively rare. The modern procedure is bankruptcy. The power of a partner to take his firm into bankruptcy is discussed later.[30] It may well be questioned whether it is not in accord with public policy (and with the interests of creditors and all of the partners) that a partner in an insolvent partnership should have the power to submit its affairs to an orderly liquidation through the appropriate channels.

(b) Disposition of the Good Will of the Business

It is often said that a partner, acting alone, cannot dispose of the good will of the firm.[31] Such a statement becomes meaningful only through a careful analysis of what good will is and how it may be disposed of.

Good will often means a "well founded expectation of continued public patronage." [32] It is not a separate and distinct item of property but is generally attached to such items as place of business, name or

24. Sloan v. Moore, 37 Pa. 217 (1860).

Similar reasoning appears in cases dealing with sale or mortgage of all the assets. Sec. 50A n. 84 above.

25. U.P.A. § 9(3) (a). Parker v. Brown, 85 F. 595 (8th Cir. 1898); Richlin v. Union Bank & Trust Co., 197 Cal. 296, 240 P. 782 (1925); Mills v. Miller, 109 Iowa 688, 81 N.W. 169 (1889); Shattuck v. Chandler, 40 Kan. 516, 20 P. 225, 10 Am.St.Rep. 227 (1889); Welles v. March, 30 N.Y. 344 (1864); Fox v. Curtis, 176 Pa. 52, 34 A. 952 (1896); Hill v. Postley, 90 Va. 200, 17 S.E. 946 (1893).

26. Sullivan v. Smith, 15 Neb. 476, 19 N.W. 620, 48 Am.Rep. 354 (1884); Deckard v. Case, 5 Watts 22, 30 Am. Dec. 287 (Pa.1836); Voshmik v. Hartmann, 91 Wis. 513, 65 N.W. 60 (1895).

27. Harrison v. Sterry, 5 Cranch 289, 3 L.Ed. 104 (1809); H. B. Clafflin Co. v. Evans, 55 Ohio St. 183, 45 N.E. 3,

60 Am.St.Rep. 686 (1896); Hennessy v. Western Bank, 6 Watts & S. 300, 40 Am.Dec. 560 (Pa.1843).

28. Bumb v. Bennett, 51 Cal.2d 294, 333 P.2d 23 (1958) citing this text; In re Grant, 106 F. 496 (S.D.N.Y.1901).

29. Hodenpuhl v. Hines, 160 Pa. 466, 28 A. 825 (1894).

30. Sec. 91B(b) below.

31. U.P.A. § 9(3)(b); Commissioner v. Whitney, 169 F.2d 562 (2d Cir. 1948), cert. denied 335 U.S. 892, 69 S.Ct. 247, 93 L.Ed. 429 (1948); Young v. Cooper, 30 Tenn.App. 55, 203 S.W.2d 376 (1947).

32. Dodge Stationery Co. v. Dodge, 145 Cal. 380, 78 P. 879 (1904). For other definitions, see Foreman, Conflicting Theories of Goodwill, 22 Colum.L.Rev. 638 (1922).

Good will is further discussed Sec. 84 below.

records. When an asset to which good will is an incident is transferred, the vendor often undertakes that the vendee shall be protected in the enjoyment of the good will by freedom from competition on the part of the vendor. This may be by express agreement, or it may be implied as a matter of interpretation from an assignment of good will in connection with the transfer of business assets.[33] If a partner has the authority to transfer any item of partnership property in which good will is inherent, such as a place of business, there is no reason why the purchaser should not enjoy its use to the fullest extent. Whether its enjoyment may be enhanced by an undertaking, express or implied, that the purchaser shall be free from competition by the partnership is another question. For a partner to restrict the right of the partnership to continue to carry on business, even partially, would appear to be in excess of his implied authority. The statement that he cannot dispose of the good will of the business must be taken to mean that he cannot bind the partnership by an undertaking not to compete.[34] A fortiori, he cannot bind his co-partners not to compete individually. "Assent of all partners would be necessary to an agreement which would forfeit each individual partner's right to engage in a particular line of business." [35]

Even before the U.P.A., statutes in several states provided that a partner has no implied power to dispose of the good will of the business; such statutes have been applied to invalidate express agreements not to compete with the purchaser of assets.[36] It is probable that the

33. Williston, Contracts, § 1640 (rev. ed. 1937); Crane, Partnership Goodwill, 18 Va.Law Rev. 651, 656 (1932); Note, 11 Va.Law Rev. 392, (1925).

34. Petrikis v. Hanges, 111 Cal.App.2d 734, 245 P.2d 39 (1952) illustrates a contract for the sale of a business and an express covenant not to compete, signed by less than all the partners and therefore ineffectual.

But see Moreau v. Edwards, 2 Tenn.Ch. 347 (1875), partner can sell good will but can't bind co-partner not to compete. The former is probably no longer good law.

35. Laskey Bros. of W. Va., Inc. v. Warner Bros. Pictures, Inc., 130 F. Supp. 514, 521 (S.D.N.Y.1955), aff'd 224 F.2d 824 (2d Cir. 1955), cert. denied 350 U.S. 932, 76 S.Ct. 300, 100 L.Ed. 814 (1956). A stipulation of disqualification of attorneys (arising out of conflict of interest from former employment of the partner who signed in the firm name) was not binding on his co-partner after dissolution of the firm.

Cf. Hanson v. Wirtz, 52 N.Dak. 604, 204 N.W. 672 (1925), express covenant made in partnership name by one partner is enforceable against that partner individually; voidness could be claimed only by co-partners.

36. Cowan v. Tremble, 111 Cal.App. 458, 296 P. 91 (1931); Kelly v. Pierce, 16 N.D. 234, 112 N.W. 995, 12 L.R.A.,N.S., 180 (1907) (holding invalid an agreement by a partner selling trade assets that the partnership would discontinue its entire business); Griffing v. Dunn, 23 S.D. 141, 120 N.W. 890, 20 Ann.Cas. 579 (1909) (holding invalid a partner's agreement not to compete, in connection with sale of harness stock by a hardware partnership).

In Kidder Equity Exchange v. Norman, 42 S.D. 229, 173 N.W. 728, 5 A.L.R. 1180 (1919), a partner in a grain-dealing partnership sold an elevator, his own property, in which the partnership had carried on business as one of its four branches. The sales agreement provided for the inclusion in the transaction of the "good will of the business, as well as the described prop-

section of the U.P.A. quoted in the heading of this section pertaining to good will, was copied from such statutes.

(c) Any Other Act Which Would Make it Impossible to Carry on the Ordinary Business of the Partnership

It is beyond the implied power of a partner to do any act which would make it impossible to carry on the ordinary business of the firm.[37] The power to sell or mortgage the entire mass of partnership property has already been discussed.[38] Where the entire business of the partnership consists in the performance of a contract, the act of less than all of the partners in cancelling the contract is unauthorized.[39] An agreement by a partner that the partnership will withdraw from competition would seem to be subject to the ban of this theory, as well as of the preceding one relating to good will. A question of interpretation of the clause "ordinary business of the partnership" would arise if a partner were to dispose of business premises constituting a branch of the business, or a stock of goods constituting a department.[40] Suppose a partner in a firm having an automobile sales agency covering a considerable territory were to close out a branch, or suppose he were to discontinue the sale of some accessory, such as tires or radios. Such acts would not make it impossible to resume the discontinued activity. But if the selling partner were to agree with the vendee not to compete, the stipulation would fall under the ban against disposing of good will.

(d) Confession of Judgment

The conduct of litigation for or against a partnership is a transaction within the scope of the business. A partner may initiate proceedings for the collection of an obligation owing to the partnership.[41]

---

erty." Held: the vendee could not enjoin the firm from engaging in competing business in the locality, since the partner had no authority to dispose of partnership goodwill.

In Gewirtz v. Abraham & Vinik, 171 Ill.App. 433 (1912), there being no statute applicable, it was held that a partner could bind the partnership to a contract for the sale of a part of a bakery route, with a contract not to compete, so that liquidated damages (equal to the purchase price) could be recovered after competition took place.

37. U.P.A. § 9(3) (c); U.L.P.A. § 9(1) (b).

38. Sec. 50A above.

39. W. D. Reeves Lumber Co. v. Davis, 124 Ark. 143, 187 S.W. 171 (1916); Watson v. Oregon Moline Plow Co., 112 Or. 414, 227 P. 278 (1924).

Compare Harper v. McKinnis, Davis & Co., 53 Ohio St. 434, 42 N.E. 251 (1895), as to power of a partner who negotiated a firm contract of agency to cancel it while executor.

As to power to dismiss a suit brought by firm, see Lunt Farm Co. v. Hamilton, 217 Iowa 22, 250 N.W. 698 (1933).

40. Cf. Herr v. Brakefield, 50 Wash.2d 593, 314 P.2d 397 (1957), discussed Sec. 50A, n. 84 above.

41. Jones v. Hurst, 67 Mo. 568 (1878); McCluny & Co. v. Jackson, 47 Va. (6 Grat.) 96 (1849); Henson v. First Security & Loan Co., 164 Wash. 198, 2 P.2d 85 (1931).

As to power of majority to sue, see Clarke v. Slate Valley R. Co., 136 Pa. 408, 20 A. 562, 10 L.R.A. 238 (1890).

It is so far the duty of a partner to utilize legal process to enforce a part-

A partner may defend actions brought against the partnership.[42] But he has no power to submit a co-partner personally to the jurisdiction of a court, as by appearing for a partner who has not been served.[43]

A partner, in defending actions brought against the partnership, should act with good faith and diligence in the interests of the firm. He should not abandon defenses. An offer of judgment by a partner is unauthorized, and does not bar the creditor from the right to costs, on recovering a judgment in a lesser sum than that offered.[44] The partner has no power to confess a judgment binding on a co-partner,[45] the partnership,[46] or the partnership property.[47] In Pennsylvania, prior to the U.P.A., it was possible for a partner, when entering into

nership demand that his failure, when sued on a partnership obligation, to plead the demand as a counterclaim extinguishes it. It cannot later be maintained in an action by a co-partner not served in the former action, and so not a party thereto. Bowdish & Degarmo Bros. v. Groscup, 70 W.Va. 758, 74 S.E. 950 (1912). See also Sec. 50 n. 73 above.

42. Wheatley v. Tutt, 4 Kan. 240 (1867); McCord Co. v. Callaway, 109 Ga. 796, 35 S.E. 171 (1900); Bowdish & Degarmo Bros. v. Groscup, n. 41 above.

43. Hall v. Lanning, 91 U.S. 160, 23 L. Ed. 271 (1875); Hills v. Ross, 3 U.S. (3 Dall.) 331, 1 L.Ed. 623 (1796); Beaver Board Cos. v. Imbrie, 47 F.2d 271 (S.D.N.Y.1922); Phelps v. Brewer, 63 Mass. (9 Cush.) 390, 57 Am.Dec. 56 (1852).

44. In Friedman v. Blauner, 227 N.Y. 327, 125 N.E. 443 (1919), a partner, after the partnership was sued on a contract claim, made an offer of judgment in behalf of the partners. This was rejected and the case proceeded to trial, the plaintiff recovering less than the amount offered. It was held that the plaintiff was entitled to costs, since the offer of judgment was not to be presumed to be authorized by the firm.

45. Scanlon v. Kuehn, 225 App.Div. 256, 232 N.Y.S. 592 (1929), under U.P.A. The non-assenting partner can have the judgment opened. Hier v. Kaufman, 134 Ill. 215, 25 N.E. 517 (1890); Remington & Parry v. Cummings & Goodrich, 5 Wis. 138 (1856). He may cause execution against his separate property to be set aside.

Morgan v. Richardson, 16 Mo. 409, 57 Am.Dec. 235 (1852); Ellis v. Ellis, 47 N.J.Law 69 (1885); Feighan v. Sobers, 239 Pa. 284, 86 A. 857 (1913); or may have enforcement enjoined, Davenport Mills Co. v. Chambers, 146 Ind. 156, 44 N.E. 1109 (1896).

It has been held that a partner has no authority to insert into a contract a stipulation for liquidated damages. Waldron v. Hughes, 44 W.Va. 126, 129, 29 S.E. 505, 506 (1897). But see Gewirtz v. Abraham & Vinik, 171 Ill.App. 433 (1912).

46. U.P.A. 9(3)(d); U.L.P.A. 9(1)(c).

47. Soper v. Fry, 37 Mich. 236 (1877); Ellis v. Ellis, 47 N.J.Law 69 (1885); Hoffman v. Spokane Jobbers' Ass'n, 54 Wash. 179, 102 P. 1045 (1909).

The courts have held, prior to the U.P.A., that the power to object to a judgment by confession of one partner is vested in the co-partners, and that if they do not object other firm creditors are without power to do so. Farwell v. Huston, 151 Ill. 239, 37 N.E. 864, 42 Am.St.Rep. 237 (1894); Rosenberg v. Boehm, 25 N.Y.S. 936 (Sup.1893); George W. McAlpin Co. v. Finsterwald, 57 Ohio St. 524, 49 N.E. 784 (1898); Grier v. Hood, 25 Pa. 430 (1855).

Since adoption of the U.P.A., a similar decision has been made in Dixonville Deposit Bank v. Marshall Federal Bakery, 102 Pa.Super. 308, 156 A. 629 (1931), the Act not being referred to in the opinion. It would seem that the common law rule as to who may object to the judgment should be considered to remain operative; nothing is expressly provided to the contrary in the U.P.A.

a partnership obligation, to include a power of attorney permitting the creditor, on default, to confess judgment against the partnership. Such a judgment was binding on the partner who executed the instrument and on the partnership property, but not on the co-partners separately, if they had not authorized it.[48] Such a transaction as a method of providing a creditor with security on partnership property seems no more objectionable than that of giving a mortgage on partnership property, for which transaction the judgment note in some jurisdictions is an alternative method of giving security, particularly where a creditor cannot begin an ordinary contract action by attachment. It has been recognized in Pennsylvania that the giving of a judgment note by a partner is no longer impliedly authorized,[49] nor is a power to confess judgment for rent of chattels [50] or realty [51] leased to the partnership.

(e) Submission of Partnership Claim or Liability to Arbitration or Reference

A partner has the power to receive payment of partnership demands and to release debtors to the partnership.[52] A partner, acting in good faith, may compromise with third persons demands of or against the partnership.[53] This power cannot be delegated to a third person.[54] In a few states, absent U.P.A., it has been held that a partner has the implied power to submit a controversy to arbitration, by a parol agreement, and that an award made in such a proceeding is binding.[55] But by the weight of authority, such power is lacking.[56] Arbitration

---

48. Boyd v. Thompson, 153 Pa. 78, 25 A. 769, 34 Am.St.Rep. 685 (1893); Funk v. Young, 241 Pa. 72, 88 A. 291 (1913); Hurshman, The Power of a Partner to Confess Judgment in Pennsylvania, 62 U.Pa.L.Rev. 621 (1914).

49. Fairman Bros. to Use of First Nat. Bank of Clarion v. Ogden Gas Co., 106 Pa.Super. 130, 161 A. 634 (1932), permitting judgment to be opened for the purpose of making defense by the partnership; Jamestown Banking Co. v. Conneaut Lake Dock & Dredge Co., 339 Pa. 26, 14 A.2d 325 (1940), stating that the act of confessing judgment is voidable by the other partners. In Sterle v. Galiardi Coal & Coke Co., 168 Pa.Super. 254, 77 A.2d 669 (1951), the act is held to be voidable, but capable of ratification, as by affirming a lease containing a power to confess judgment in ejectment at termination.

50. Mullen v. Slupe, 360 Pa. 485, 62 A. 2d 14 (1948).

51. Garcia v. Burke Display Institute, 52 Lack.Jur. 129 (Pa.Com.Pl.1950).

52. Lodewick v. Cutting, 121 Misc. 348, 201 N.Y.S. 276 (1923); Bachman v. H. R. Ennis Real Estate & Inv. Co., 199 Mo.App. 674, 204 S.W. 1115 (1918); Van Billiard v. Croft & Allen Co., 302 Pa. 349, 153 A. 555 (1931); Mosby v. United States, 194 F. 346 (6th Cir. 1912).

53. Mortimore v. Atkins, 98 Ark. 183, 135 S.W. 865 (1911); Webber v. Webber, 146 Mich. 31, 109 N.W. 50 (1906); L. O. & H. L. Street v. Arnold, 170 Okl. 389, 40 P.2d 1050 (1935). See also Sec. 50 n. 72 above.

If the partner colludes with the third person to make a fraudulent settlement, the injured partner is not bound by it. Sweet v. Morrison, 103 N.Y. 235, 8 N.E. 396 (1886).

54. Sweet v. Morrison, n. 53 above.

55. Hallack v. March, 25 Ill. 48 (1860); Taylor v. Coryell, 12 Serg. & R. 243 (Pa.1824); Gay v. Waltman, 89 Pa. 453 (1879).

56. U.P.A. § 9(3) (e).

has been jealously regarded by many courts, since it is a procedure which tends to oust the courts of jurisdiction.[57] It has been said that agreements to arbitrate are unusual, outside the ordinary course of business, and unnecessary as a method of procuring the settlement of controversies. The partnership is not bound to perform an award unless all partners agreed to the submission,[58] nor can it enforce an award against the third person.[59] The agreement to arbitrate and an award made pursuant thereto are binding on the partner who agreed to it.[60] If an award is made against the third person and he performs it, payment being received by a partner, there is a discharge of the obligation by accord and satisfaction, since a partner has the authority to compromise a partnership demand.[61]

By assenting to a particular contract, the partnership may be bound by an arbitration provision contained therein.[62] Authority to enter into a general arbitration agreement may be inferred from knowledge and acquiescence.[63] Since arbitration is now looked upon with greater favor and is being used more frequently as a substitute for litigation, it seems unfortunate that the old rule was crystallized by adoption in the U.P.A. Many partnerships effectually avoid the rule by including in their partnership agreements provisions for arbitration of disputes among themselves [64] or between the partnership and

---

57. Williston, Contracts, § 1919 (rev. ed. 1938); Restatement, Contracts § 550.

58. Horton v. Wilde, 74 Mass. (8 Gray) 425 (1857); Walker v. Bean, 34 Minn. 427, 26 N.W. 232 (1886); Hoffman v. Westlecraft, 85 N.J.L. 484, 89 A. 1006 (1914); Fancher v. Bibb Furnace Co., 80 Ala. 481, 2 So. 268 (1886).

59. Buchoz v. Grandjean, 1 Mich. 367 (1850); Tillinghast v. Gilmore, 17 R.I. 413, 22 A. 942 (1891).

60. Karthaus v. Ferrer, 26 U.S. (1 Pet.) 222, 7 L.Ed. 121 (1828).

61. Buchanan v. Curry, 19 Johns. 137, 10 Am.Dec. 200 (N.Y.1821).

62. Stein-Tex, Inc. v. Scappatillio, 193 Misc. 402, 87 N.Y.S.2d 317 (S.Ct.1948), modified on other grounds 275 App. Div. 749, 88 N.Y.S.2d 270 (1949), assent found in acceptance of and payment for part of goods covered by contract, and in failure to urge lack of authority in the arbitration proceeding sought by the other party to the contract.

63. Chickasha Cotton Oil Co. v. Chapman, 4 F.2d 319 (5th Cir.1925), cert.

den. 268 U.S. 700, 45 S.Ct. 636, 69 L.Ed. 1164 (1925), arbitration required by rules of trade association to which partnership belonged by acts of managing partner.

It cannot be doubted that a partner would have the power to insure partnership property under a standard form of fire insurance policy containing an appraisal clause. See Brink v. New Amsterdam Fire Ins. Co., 28 N.Y.Super.Ct. (5 Rob.) 104 (1867). If a partnership business is such that contracts are frequently entered into by partners which include arbitration clauses, such as construction contracts, authority may be inferred from the course of business.

Compare as to ratification, Sterle v. Galiardi Coal & Coke Co., n. 49 above, holding that a partnership affirming a lease affirms the power to confess judgment included therein.

64. Silberfeld v. Swiss Bank Corp., 99 N.Y.S.2d 888 (Sup.Ct.1950), aff'd without opinion 278 App.Div. 676, 103 N.Y. S.2d 130 (1951), app.dism. 302 N.Y. 878, 100 N.E.2d 54 (1951); Lipschutz v. Gutwirth, 278 App.Div. 132, 103 N.Y. S.2d 732 (1951), app.dism. 303 N.Y. 670, 102 N.E.2d 830 (1951); Gutwirth

third persons.[65]

The Uniform Limited Partnership Act contains limitations upon the powers of a general partner or all of the general partners to do certain acts in violation of the certificate of association or outside of the usual course of business without the consent of the limited partners. Acts so prohibited include confession of judgment, admitting additional general or special partners, continuing the business after a general partner has ceased to be such.[66]

KNOWN EXCESS OF AUTHORITY

§ 53. **No act of a partner in contravention of a restriction on authority shall bind the partnership to persons having knowledge of the restriction. U.P.A. § 9(4).**

A provision of U.P.A. already discussed [67] recognizes that apparent authority does not bind the partnership if actual authority is lacking and the third person concerned knows it. The rule has its obvious root in the fact that the third person is not misled and cannot reasonably rely on the appearance of authority. The provision quoted in the headnote of this section affirms the rule when the partner's lack of authority results from an express restriction. Restrictions of this sort are usually found in the partnership agreement and are of the form that certain acts shall not be done at all, or shall not be done without unanimous consent (or, perhaps, a specified vote). Such limitations are ineffective against third persons dealing with a partner in ignorance of their existence.[68] They are, however, effective as between the partners [69] and as to third persons who have knowledge of them.[70]

v. Carewell Trading Corp., 20 Misc.2d 64, 187 N.Y.S.2d 949 (1959), aff'd 12 App.Div.2d 920, 211 N.Y.S.2d 732 (1961). Lowengrub v. Meislin, 376 Pa. 463, 103 A.2d 405 (1954).

65. Baker v. Board of Education, 309 N.Y. 551, 132 N.E.2d 837 (1956); Application of Damsker, 283 App.Div. 719, 127 N.Y.S.2d 355 (1954).

66. U.L.P.A. § 9.

67. U.P.A. § 9(1), Sec. 49 above.

68. Shackelford v. Williams, 182 Ala. 87, 62 So. 54 (1913); Crane Co. v. Tierney, 175 Ill. 79, 51 N.E. 715 (1898); Burgan v. Lyell, 2 Mich. 102, 55 Am. Dec. 53 (1851); Picone v. Commercial Paste Co., 215 Miss. 114, 60 So.2d 590 (1952); McGovern v. Mattison, 116 N.Y. 61, 22 N.E. 398, 5 L.R.A. 589 (1889); Rice v. Jackson, 171 Pa. 89, 32 A. 1036 (1895); Dobie v. Southern Trading Co. of Texas, 193 S.W. 195 (Tex. Civ.App.1917).

69. People v. Esrig, 240 App.Div. 300, 270 N.Y.S. 372 (1934), was a prosecution for forgery against a partner. The articles provided that funds should be deposited in a checking account, checks to be signed by both partners. After a check was so signed, one partner fraudulently altered it by raising the amount. It was held that she was guilty of forgery. See also State v. Sotak, 100 W.Va. 652, 131 S.E. 706, 46 A.L.R. 1523 (1926); People v. Van Skander, 20 Cal.App.2d 248, 66 P.2d 1228 (1937).

A member of a joint-stock company contracting with it, is subject to a provision in the articles of association to the effect that no member shall be personally liable for the obligations of the company. Dunning v. Gibbs, 213 Ky. 81, 280 S.W. 483 (1926).

The managers of a joint-stock company or business trust who execute a note without including therein a stipulation

70. See note 70 on page 304.

In this context, a person has "knowledge" of a fact not only when he has actual knowledge of it but also when he has knowledge of such other facts as in the circumstances shows bad faith.[71]

A partnership, having a checking account, informs the bank of a rule requiring signatures of all the partners. The bank, cashing a check signed by one partner, cannot charge it against the account.[72] But if the money so drawn is applied to a legitimate partnership purpose, such as the payment of firm obligations, the bank can defend on that ground.[73] If the third person is notified of a limitation, on a partner's power, to purchase only for cash, he cannot recover for goods sold on credit, in the absence of ratification with knowledge by the other partner.[74]

Normally, the majority of the members of a partnership have the power to decide matters within the scope of the business, but they do not have the power to override the minority in the doing of an act which is outside the scope of the business they have agreed to carry on or which is in violation of a provision of the articles.[75] The minority

---

limiting liability to the joint funds, as they are required to do by the articles of association, when sued on the note are not permitted to bring in the members of the association as parties primarily liable. Barnett v. Cisco Banking Co., 253 S.W. 339 (Tex.Civ. App.1923).

70. U.P.A. § 9(4). Wilson v. Bramblett, 151 Cal.App.2d 369, 311 P.2d 22 (1957); Ditzel v. Kent, 131 Mont. 129, 308 P. 2d 628 (1957). For the corresponding agency law, see Restatement, Second, Agency §§ 160–62.

71. U.P.A. § 3(1). Cf. Picone v. Commercial Paste Co., n. 68 above, which raises but does not decide whether public filing of the partnership agreement would constitute sufficient constructive notice of restrictions contained in it. Cf. Restatement, Second, Agency § 167 and the different definition of "notice" in id. § 9.

72. Granby Mining & Smelting Co. v. Laverty, 159 Pa. 287, 28 A. 207 (1893).

73. Granby Mining & Smelting Co. v. Laverty, n. 72 above. It is questionable whether the third person should on equitable grounds recover for an enrichment conferred upon another against his manifested will. In Dawson, Blakemore & Co. v. Elrod, 105 Ky. 624, 49 S.W. 465, 88 Am.St.Rep. 320 (1899), goods were sold and delivered to a partnership, which made use of

them, though the seller was notified by one of the two partners not to make the sale. It was held that the dissenting partner was not liable.

74. Sladen, Fakes & Co. v. Lance, 151 N.C. 492, 66 S.E. 449 (1909). See also Baxter v. Rollins & Co., 90 Iowa 217, 57 N.W. 838, 48 Am.St.Rep. 432 (1894). See, on ratification, Cowan v. Tremble, 111 Cal.App. 458, 296 P. 91 (1931); Samstag & Hilder Bros. v. Ottenheimer & Weil, 90 Conn. 475, 97 A. 865 (1916); Porter v. Curry, 50 Ill. 319, 99 Am.Dec. 520 (1869).

75. "Any difference arising as to ordinary matters connected with the partnership business may be decided by a majority of the partners; but no act in contravention of any agreement between the partners may be done rightfully without the consent of all the partners." U.P.A. § 18(h); Nick v. Craig, 301 Pa. 50, 151 A. 573 (1930). The majority may retract by notice to third persons, a power which could otherwise be exercised by a partner, Carr v. Hertz, 54 N.J.Eq. 127, 33 A. 194 (1895) (implied power to mortgage); Steele v. First Nat. Bank of Joliet, 60 Ill. 23 (1871) (power to receive payment of debt to firm).

The majority can act or authorize action only in the usual course of business. A sale of the entire assets of the partnership to the majority to the exclusion of the dissenting minority is

may not hamper the majority in carrying on the business in accordance with the articles or other partnership agreement.[76]

In cases of an even division of the partners as to whether or not an act within the scope of the business should be done, of which disagreement a third person has knowledge, it seems that logically no restriction can be placed upon the power to act. The partnership being a going concern, activities within the scope of the business should not be limited, save by the expressed will of the majority deciding a disputed question; half of the members are not a majority.[77] In practical operation application of such a solution to projected transactions might be inconvenient and costly. If each of two partners wishes to buy goods, or hire employees, to an extent needed for the transaction of business, and if on disagreement known to third persons, each is to be considered as capable of acting so as to bind the other, the firm might become disastrously overstocked with goods, services, or other things. In its practical workings the better rule appears to be that in case of even disagreement, known to third persons, no action new or positive can be taken until the partners themselves reach a solution.[78]

outside the course of business and unauthorized. Flint v. Codman, 247 Mass. 463, 142 N.E. 256 (1924).

If by articles of association powers of management are vested in certain members of the association, to the exclusion of others, the majority of the members cannot in violation of the articles authorize the hiring of an employee at a stipulated salary, Kentucky Distilleries & Warehouse Co. v. Louisville Public Warehouse Co., 19 F.2d 866 (6th Cir. 1927).

In Cotton Plant Oil Mill Co. v. Buckeye Cotton Oil Co., 92 Ark. 271, 122 S.W. 658 (1909), a partnership agreement delegated the entire management to one of the partners. The others having become dissatisfied, it was held that they could revoke his exclusive powers and act in opposition to him in the sale of partnership property. This decision seems to give insufficient effect to the terms of the original agreement of association.

As to the relation between corporate directors and shareholders, see Stevens, Corporations, § 143 (2d ed. 1949).

76. Johnston & Co. v. Dutton's Adm'r, 27 Ala. 245 (1855); Wilkins & Rollins v. Pearce, 5 Denio 541 (N.Y.1848); Reiser v. Johnston, 65 Okl. 307, 166 P. 723, L.R.A.1918A, 924 (1917); Clarke v. Slate Valley R. Co., 136 Pa. 408, 20 A. 562, 10 L.R.A. 238 (1890). There is

some scattered authority to the contrary, which appears to be due to an ignoring by the courts of the distinction between a dissenting minority and an equally divided group of associates. Bradley Fertilizer Co. v. Pollock & Co., 104 Ala. 402, 16 So. 138 (1893), semble; O. L. Standard Dry Goods Co. v. Hale & Pressley, 148 Va. 640, 139 S.E. 300 (1927), a decision which makes no reference to U.P.A. § 18(h), quoted above.

77. Coggeshall v. McKenney, 114 S.C. 1, 103 S.E. 30 (1920); Wipperman v. Stacy, 80 Wis. 345, 50 N.W. 336 (1891); Canadian Bank of Commerce v. Patricia Syndicate, 20 Ont.Weekly Notes 529 (1922).

National Biscuit Co., Inc. v. Stroud, 249 N.C. 467, 106 S.E.2d 692 (1959), quoting this text.

See Notes, 12 Colum.Law Rev. 85 (1912); 29 Colum.Law Rev. 66 (1929); 35 Harv.Law Rev. 770 (1922).

78. Leavitt v. Peck, 3 Conn. 124, 125, 8 Am.Dec. 157 (1819); Knox v. Buffington, 50 Iowa 320 (1879); Dawson, Blakemore & Co. v. Elrod, 105 Ky. 624, 49 S.W. 465, 88 Am.St.Rep. 320 (1899); Monroe v. Conner, 15 Me. 178, 32 Am. Dec. 148 (1838); St. Louis Brewing Ass'n v. Elmer, 189 Mo.App. 197, 175 S.W. 102 (1915); Haulenbeck Advertising Agency v. November, 27 Misc. 836, 60 N.Y.S. 573 (1899); Yeager v.

An act may be evidently outside the scope of the business. such as the purchase by a mercantile partnership of goods which have no relation to the business.[79] The transaction may be of a kind similar to those apparently authorized within the scope of the business, but of such a degree as to be evidently unauthorized; as where a partner in a drug business, authorized to purchase coal for consumption purposes in carrying on the business, buys an excessive quantity;[80] or a partner authorized to borrow money, borrows an amount out of all proportion to the needs of the business;[81] or a partner, authorized to fix the compensation of employees, fixes them at an unreasonable amount, undertaking to divide with four of them half the profits as a bonus.[82]

Wallace, 57 Pa. 365 (1868); Bank of Bellbuckle v. Mason, 139 Tenn. 659, 202 S.W. 931 (1918), holding that receipt of goods purchased by a partner without authority is not ratification.

If the dissent is uncommunicated it is ineffective as to the third person. Phipps v. Little, 213 Mass. 414, 100 N.E. 615 (1913).

De Santis v. Miller Petroleum Co., 29 Cal.App.2d 679, 85 P.2d 489 (1939); O. L. Standard Dry Goods Co. v. Hale & Pressley, 148 Va. 640, 139 S.E. 300 (1927).

If the question arises not with respect to new business, but the performance of an existing contract, the interest of a third person in prompt and orderly completion of a transaction to which the partnership is committed as a party should disable a dissenting partner from effective interference. In Coggeshall v. McKenney, 114 S.C. 1, 103 S.E. 30 (1920), a partnership having purchased lumber, one of the two partners gave the seller shipping directions. Held: the other partner could not effectively revoke the directions. In Lodewick v. Cutting, 121 Misc. 348, 201 N.Y.S. 276 (1923), it was held that one partner could receive payment of a partnership claim and give the debtor a valid release, though notified by the other partner not to make payment to the one to whom payment was made. See, to same effect, Burns v. Treadway & Webb, 174 Ky. 123, 191 S.W. 868 (1917). In Markee v. City of Philadelphia, 270 Pa. 337, 113 A. 359 (1921), each partner having notified the debtor not to pay the other, the debtor withheld payment. Held: this was not a default, so that interest would run, though the debtor might have been justified in paying either. In Donaldson v. Williams, 1 C. & M. 345, 149 Eng.Rep. 432 (1833), one of two partners discharged a servant, while the other told him to remain. Held: the partner who discharged him was not privileged to forcibly eject him from the premises.

In Dinkelspeel v. Lewis, 50 Wyo. 380, 65 P.2d 246 (1937), where the evidence was that a partner asked that a purchase made by his copartner be not charged to the former, it was interpreted as not a disclaimer of liability but as an effort to keep his connection with the business undisclosed to the public.

79. Sargent v. Henderson, 79 Ga. 268, 5 S.E. 122 (1888).

80. Reed Coal Co. v. Fain, 171 N.C. 646, 89 S.E. 29 (1916).

81. Hobbs v. Virginia Nat. Bank of Petersburg, 147 Va. 802, 133 S.E. 595 (1926).

82. Warren v. Mosher, 31 Ariz. 33, 250 P. 354, 49 A.L.R. 1311 (1926).

POWER TO SUBJECT THE PARTNERSHIP
TO TORT LIABILITY

§ 54. Partnership Bound by Partner's Wrongful Act. Where, by any wrongful act or omission of any partner acting in the ordinary course of the business of the partnership or with the authority of his co-partners, loss or injury is caused to any person, not being a partner in the partnership, or any penalty is incurred, the partnership is liable therefor to the same extent as the partner so acting or omitting to act. U.P.A. § 13.

Partnership Bound by Partner's Breach of Trust. The partnership is bound to make good the loss:

(a) Where one partner, acting within the scope of his apparent authority, receives money or property of a third person and misapplies it; and

(b) Where the partnership in the course of its business receives money or property of a third person, and the money or property so received is misapplied by any partner while it is in the custody of the partnership. U.P.A. § 14.

(a) Negligence

The most frequent examples of tort liability are cases of negligent conduct. The partners are liable for the negligent operation of a vehicle by a partner, acting in the course of the business, which results in a traffic accident.[83] It is often a disputed question as to whether the partner is acting in the course of business. If he is driving a partnership-owned vehicle for purposes of his own, though with the consent of his partners, the acting partner alone is liable; it is not a partnership tort.[84] If he is driving his own vehicle for partnership purposes, the

---

83. Eule v. Eule Motor Sales, 34 N.J. 537, 170 A.2d 241 (1961); Treon v. Shipman & Son, 275 Pa. 246, 119 A. 74 (1922); Dixon v. Haynes, 146 Wash. 163, 262 P. 119, 55 A.L.R. 1218 (1927) (intoxicated partner driving load of coal to residence of partners for their use).

84. For the corresponding rule in agency, see Restatement, Second, Agency §§ 219, 243.

See Wallan v. Rankin, 173 F.2d 488 (9th Cir. 1949) (cause of action stated against partnership and surviving partner for co-partner's negligent airplane crash).

See Buckley v. Chadwick, 45 Cal.2d 183, 288 P.2d 12 (1955), jury was correctly instructed that any negligence of partner operating crane would be imputed to co-partner who was killed by the crane, and would constitute contributory negligence by the deceased partner preventing recovery for his death under the wrongful death statute.

Teague v. Martin, 228 Mass. 458, 117 N.E. 844 (1917); Bunnell v. Vrooman, 250 Mass. 103, 145 N.E. 58 (1924); Morris v. Raymond, 101 Wash. 34, 171 P. 1006 (1918).

But slight evidence may show the transaction to be in the course of business, as in Treon v. W. A. Shipman & Son, supra, note 83.

Compare Tarlecka v. Morgan, 125 Ohio St. 319, 181 N.E. 450 (1932): the "jury might have inferred that use of (a taxi cab) for transportation of members of their (the partners') families was privilege common to both," and a directed verdict for defendant was refused.

In Zutter v. O'Connell, 200 Wis. 598, 229 N.W. 73 (1930), the surviving partner of a partnership which owned a truck, instructed an employee to use the truck on a non-business errand, in the course of which a traffic collision occurred caused by the concurring negligence of both drivers. It was held that damages to the truck could be recovered

partnership is liable.[85]   In some states there are statutes providing that a person other than the owner operating a motor vehicle with consent of the owner is deemed to be the latter's agent for purposes of liability.   It has been held, under such a statute, that partnership liability results from operation for nonpartnership purposes by a partner with consent of his co-partner.[86]   A furnishing of medicine by a partner in a firm of druggists as a gratuity is outside the scope of a business carried on for profit, and the non-participating co-partners are not liable for the acting partner's negligence in compounding the medicine.[87]

Liability for negligent acts applies to professional partnerships.   A law partnership is subject to liability for improper advice culpably furnished a client by one of their number,[88] or for furnishing a defective abstract of title.[89]   A partnership of physicians is liable for a partner's negligent treatment of a patient.[90]   It is sometimes a question whether the act of the partner is in the course of the business.   It has been held to be a partnership act to allow a patient, being moved after an opera-

in behalf of the partnership, the negligence of the truck driver not being imputed.

85. Melosevich v. Cichy, 30 Wash.2d 702, 193 P.2d 342 (1948).   Even if partner was going home, he was on call to service partnership pinball machines during the evening.   It was immaterial whether the partnership paid his car expenses.

86. Kangas v. Winquist, 207 Minn. 315, 291 N.W. 292 (1940).

A similar result was reached in Bachand v. Vidal, 328 Mass. 97, 101 N.E.2d 884 (1951) under a statute providing that evidence of car registration in the name of a person is prima facie evidence that the car is under control of one for whose conduct the registered owner is legally responsible.   The car was found to be "registered" in the partnership name because license plates of the partnership (which dealt in used cars) were placed on the vehicle when it was bought a few hours before the accident.   The jury could have found that the partner was testing the car when he drove it home and parked it in the position from which the collision occurred.

A contrary result was reached in Wadsworth v. Webster, 237 App.Div. 319, 261 N.Y.S. 670 (1932), on the ground that the partner acting was a co-owner, and the statute creating a new liability must be strictly construed.

87. Gwynn v. Duffield, 66 Iowa 708, 24 N.W. 523, 55 Am.Rep. 286 (1885).

88. Blyth v. Fladgate, 1 Ch. 337 (1891).

89. Priddy v. Mackenzie, 205 Mo. 181, 103 S.W. 968 (1907).

90. Hess v. Lowery, 122 Ind. 225, 23 N.E. 156, 7 L.R.A. 90, 17 Am.St.Rep. 355 (1890); Hyrne v. Erwin, 23 S.C. 226, 55 Am.Rep. 15 (1885).   In Whittaker v. Collins, 34 Minn. 299, 25 N.W. 632, 57 Am.Rep. 55 (1885), it was held that the gravamen of the action was contract, and therefore both partners must be joined as defendants.

See Wolfsmith v. Marsh, 51 Cal.2d 832, 337 P.2d 70, 82 A.L.R.2d 1257 (1959), malpractice cause of action stated against medical partners.

Where the only negligence alleged was the treatment by physician-partners (which would, if proved, have been malpractice and barred by a 2-year statute of limitations), no cause of action could be maintained against the partnership for negligently permitting the patient to be treated by incompetent agents (which would have been permitted under a 3-year statute of limitation for negligence).   Golia v. Health Insurance Plan, 6 App.Div.2d 884, 177 N.Y.S.2d 550 (1958), reversing on this point 7 Misc. 919, 166 N.Y.S.2d 889 (S.Ct.1957).

tion with the assistance of a physician partner, to fall down an open elevator shaft.[91] Such conduct may be held not to be too far removed from the scope of the partnership act of performing an operation. With the increasing use by members of professional partnerships, such as attorneys and physicians, of their individually owned and maintained automobiles in traveling on firm business from office to hospitals, patients' homes, courthouses, clients' places of business, and the like, there arises the question of whether the operation of the automobile is a partnership act so as to create partnership liability for negligent injury to person or property of a stranger on the highway. It does not seem that a partner while engaged in travel from one arena of operations to another by means of an instrumentality which is subject to his exclusive control and ownership, and which is chosen by him for his own convenience or comfort out of many available modes of conveyance should be considered to be acting in the course of business.[92]

---

91. Haase v. Morton & Morton, 138 Iowa 205, 115 N.W. 921, 16 Ann.Cas. 350 (1908).

92. Iron v. Sauve, 27 Wash.2d 562, 179 P.2d 327 (1947), citing this text. A partner, or joint adventurer in turkey raising had a traffic accident while driving from the turkey ranch to the co-partner's ranch to see about mixing some feed. It was his own car and he paid for the repairs. It was not shown that his co-partner knew in advance of the trip or would have approved of it. The co-partner was not liable.

An insurance solicitor, and collector of premiums, drove his own automobile at his own expense while making calls within his territory. It was held that his employer was not liable for a traffic accident resulting from his negligent driving, since the instrumentality was not furnished by the employer and not subject to its control. Wesolowski v. John Hancock Mut. Life Ins. Co., 308 Pa. 117, 162 A. 166, 87 A.L.R. 783 (1932). As to the employer's liability for the negligence of messenger boys running along the streets, see Note, 45 Harv. Law Rev. 376 (1931).

Even if an employer were to be held responsible for the errors in locomotion of a servant, the situation in a professional partnership is generally different. How a partner gets about is normally regarded as his own affair, and no concern of his partners, provided he travels with a reasonable degree of speed and safety.

In particular, they have no control over the physical details of his movement. This is the distinction used in holding that a principal is not liable for the negligence of an agent who is not also a servant. Restatement, Second, Agency § 250 and Comment thereto. However, there are situations in which a professional firm might well be liable for a partner's negligence while using his own car to go to and from patients, clients, etc., e. g. (1) if the firm pays the expenses or makes an allowance for the operation of the car; (2) if the partner's transportation time enters into the calculation of fees charged by the firm, or (3) if this is the only means of transportation which will reasonably permit the partnership work to be accomplished. Compare Melosevich v. Cichy, n. 85 above. Many businesses maintain liability insurance on "non-owned" automobiles to protect against this sort of risk. Might such insurance estop the firm to deny liability? Cf. Bachand v. Vidal, n. 86 above.

Cf. Rigutto v. Italian Terrazzo Mosaic Co., 93 F.Supp. 124 (W.D.Pa.1950). The allegation was that a partner in a Florida firm, while driving his car in Pennsylvania on partnership business, negligently caused a death. Jurisdiction over the partnership by service on a Pennsylvania state official under the Nonresident Motorist Act, was sustained. The decision is merely on the point of jurisdiction and the substantive law question of partnership liability is not discussed.

A partnership may be liable for a partner's negligent maintenance of property.[93]

An association of pilots which maintains weather forecasting services for the members, regulates the order in which they secure employment, distributes their pooled earnings among the members, may be a partnership, but the negligent act of a member pilot in causing the vessel piloted to go to sea in an unseaworthy condition, and subsequent negligent navigation may not be a partnership act, within the scope of the partnership business, so as to make the association liable to a seaman injured by the negligence.[94]

(b) Fraud and Breach of Fiduciary Duty

The partnership is liable for misrepresentation by a partner in the course of selling goods [95] or real estate [96] which it is within the scope of his authority to sell.[97] The partnership is liable for the loss

---

93. Peterson v. Brune Realty Co., 273 S.W.2d 278 (Mo.1954). Here, however, it was found that the partner was acting in his individual capacity as landlord and not for partnership as property manager.

94. McGrath v. Nolan, 83 F.2d 746 (9th Cir. 1936).

95. Morehouse v. Northrop, 33 Conn. 380, 89 Am.Dec. 211 (1866); Wolf v. Mills, 56 Ill. 360 (1870) (substitution of inferior goods by partner for those by partnership); White v. Sawyer, 82 Mass. (16 Gray) 586 (1860); Locke v. Stearns, 42 Mass. (1 Metc.) 560, 35 Am.Dec. 382 (1840); Brundage v. Mellon, 5 N.D. 72, 63 N.W. 209 (1895).

In Re A. F. Hardie & Co., 143 F. 607 (D. C.Tex.1906), a materially false statement made in purchase of goods was imputed to the firm, so as to bar partners not participating in the misrepresentation from discharge in bankruptcy.

For the corresponding agency rules, see Restatement, Second, Agency, e. g. §§ 249, 257, 261–63.

A similar result was reached in Griffin v. Bergeda, 152 Tenn. 512, 279 S.W. 385 (1926), where a discharge in bankruptcy was pleaded as a defense to an action by the defrauded buyer seeking a rescission, and return of the price paid.

96. Monmouth College v. Dockery, 241 Mo. 522, 145 S.W. 785 (1912), obtaining mortgage money from investor; Gannon, Goulding & Thies v. Hausa-

man, 42 Okl. 41, 140 P. 407, 52 L.R.A., N.S. 519 (1914); Chester v. Dickerson, 54 N.Y. 1, 13 Am.Rep. 550 (1873).

97. For an interesting example of the scope problem see Mading v. McPhaden, 50 Wash.2d 48, 308 P.2d 963 (1957). A lending firm was liable for the premium paid it for a loan in a transaction arranged by a partner, but not for the secret profit obtained by the partner acting as agent for the purchase of the building on which the loan was made. The loan was within the scope but the purchase was not. See also n. 87 above.

Compare Blackburn v. Witter, 201 Cal. App.2d 518, 19 Cal.Rptr. 842 (1962) (securities broker-dealer was bound by agent's selling regular customer securities in a non-existent corporation) with Rouse v. Pollard, 130 N.J.Eq. 204, 21 A.2d 801, 136 A.L.R. 1105 (1941) (law firm was not bound by partner's taking client's money for investment).

See Coffin v. Fidelity-Philadelphia Trust Co., 374 Pa. 378, 97 A.2d 857, 39 A.L. R.2d 625 (1953). A partner had partnership checks drawn to the order of customers of the firm for securities sold. He then forged endorsement of the payees' signatures and cashed the checks. His action was not chargeable to the firm so as to prevent recovery by the firm from the drawee bank. The opinion is preoccupied with the bank-depositor relationship and gives scant attention to the partnership question. On the latter point the court merely cites U.P.A. § 12 which states

to a third party caused by a partner procuring property for the partnership by means of misrepresentations,[98] by obtaining a loan through misrepresentations,[99] or by writing checks without sufficient funds on deposit.[1] The partnership is also liable if a partner with authority receives money for the firm but misappropriates it.[2] But the non-participating partner is not subject to the extraordinary remedy of arrest and imprisonment, such remedy being given only for actual fraud of a defendant.[3]

The partnership is liable when a partner is involved in a breach of fiduciary duty, for example: (1) where the partnership is an agent and a partner colludes with third persons to secure a secret profit at the expense of the principal;[4] (2) where a partner is a fiduciary and breaches his trust to the benefit of the partnership, e. g., diverting to the partnership the business of a corporation which he serves as officer and director;[5] (3) where a partner participates in a third person's breach of trust, e. g., by bribing him to disclose his employer's trade secrets,[6] or by paying him "kickbacks" on contracts between his employer and the partnership.[7]

(c) Willful Trespasses to Personal or Property Interests

The fact that a tort is willful does not necessarily take it out of the course of the business,[8] but it is a factor to be considered.[9] It has

that notice to a partner is not notice to the firm in the case of fraud; it has nothing to do with authority of a partner to act for the firm.

98. Banner v. Schlessinger, 109 Mich. 262, 67 N.W. 116 (1896).

99. Strang v. Bradner, 114 U.S. 555, 5 S.Ct. 1038, 29 L.Ed. 248 (1885), liability surviving bankruptcy.

1. Sam & Sons Produce Co. v. Campese, 14 A.D.2d 487, 217 N.Y.S.2d 275 (1961). Apparently the funds obtained with the checks were used in the partnership business. The court also holds that this liability based on fraud is not discharged by bankruptcy. See also n. 95 above.

2. Zander v. Larsen, 41 Wash.2d 503, 250 P.2d 531 (1953).

3. Stewart v. Levy, 36 Cal. 159 (1868).

4. Philips v. U. S., 61 App.D.C. 206, 59 F.2d 881 (1932), partner falsified prices at which sales for the principal were made. See Mading v. McPhaden, supra n. 97.

5. Higgins v. Shenango Pottery Co., 256 F.2d 504 (3rd Cir. 1958) and 279 F.2d

46 (3d Cir. 1960), cert. denied 364 U.S. 899, 81 S.Ct. 232, 5 L.Ed.2d 193 (1960) (Pennsylvania law). (The court observes that similar liability flows from constructive trust theory.) Compare Blau v. Lehman, 368 U.S. 403, 82 S.Ct. 451, 7 L.Ed.2d 403 (1962) discussed Sec. 50(g) at n. 79 above. Compare Cady, Roberts & Co., SEC Sec. Exch. Act Rel. 6668 (Nov. 8, 1961), noted 75 Harv. L.Rev. 1449 (1962) employee (knowing of dividend reduction by corporation of which he was director) informed employer who sold shares of the corporation; employer suspended from Stock Exchange for violation of SEC fraud rules.

6. Hamlyn v. Houston, (1903) 1 K.B. 81.

7. B. F. Goodrich Co. v. Naples, 121 F. Supp. 345 (S.D.Cal.1954) (California law).

8. For the corresponding rule in agency, see Restatement, Second, Agency § 244 (trespass and conversion), § 245 (intended tortious harm).

9. See K & G Oil Tool & Service Co. v. G & G Fishing Tool Service, 158 Tex. 594, 314 S.W.2d 782 (1958), cert. denied 358 U.S. 898, 79 S.Ct. 223, 3 L.Ed.

been held that the commission of assault and battery by a partner, in the course of an altercation with a landlord over the removal of alleged partnership property, is not within the scope of the business.[10] Where a partner takes upon himself the task of watching the premises at night on the lookout for burglars and shoots a person whom he discovers trying the door, the act has been held to be outside of the scope of the business.[11] The partnership has been held not liable for false

2d 149 (1958): "A non-participating partner is ordinarily not personally liable for the wrongful, tortious or criminal acts of the acting partner unless such acts are within the scope of the partnership's business, or were consented to, authorized, ratified or adopted by the non-participating partner." Non-participating partner was not liable for co-partners' violation of trade secret and copying of a magnetic tool.

For the rule in agency concerning interference with business relations, see Restatement, Second, Agency, § 248.

[10] Polis v. Heizmann, 276 Pa. 315, 120 A. 269, 27 A.L.R. 948 (1923). See 72 U.Pa.L.Rev. 197 (1924). Sustaining a compulsory non-suit, the court said: "The injury here is charged and shown to have been maliciously and wantonly inflicted by wilful and intentional violence, and extent and character such as would constitute the crime of aggravated assault and battery. A partnership relation in a lawful enterprise will not render one partner liable for the intentional criminal act of another. . . . Knocking a man down, as in this case, with the fist, and then again with an automobile, both done wilfully, cannot be said to come within the scope of the business of raising pigs."

Schloss v. Silverman, 172 Md. 632, 192 A. 343 (1937), was another case of non-liability of the absent, non-assenting partner for assault and battery.

[11] Idom v. Weeks & Russell, 135 Miss. 65, 99 So. 761, 40 A.L.R. 668 (1924), sustaining a peremptory instruction in favor of the partner of the one who committed the act, the court said: "It was not within the scope of the partnership business, and the ordinary partnership agreement does not contemplate, that one partner, when the place of business is closed for the night, shall go to the store and there

conceal himself and try and capture burglars." A dissent said that: "If therefore one partner is the agent of the other partner for the purposes of the partnership, then Russell had the right to protect the assets of the partnership from being burglarized, and if, in attempting to do this he negligently and unnecessarily killed the plaintiff's intestate, then both members of the partnership are clearly liable for such wrongful killing. It seems to me that it could not be contended that Russell did not have the authority to employ a person to go in the store and guard it, and, if he had done so, and such person so employed to guard the property had negligently killed the parties who were killed in this case, both partners would have been liable; Russell having full authority to make any contract for such purpose. It seems to me it could not be disputed that a partner is under duty to preserve and take care of partnership property, and if he had knowledge of the burglary or theft which would lead him reasonably to believe that such would be committed, and failed to take some action to prevent the burglary or theft, that he would be liable to his partner for the damages or theft, unless he gave due notice to the other partner so that he would take proper steps to protect his own interests."

Where a partner in course of argument with a person with whom the firm has dealings kills him and is indicted for murder, payment of expenses for his defense by the firm is not deductible as an ordinary and necessary business expense. Sturtivant, 15 Tax Court 880 (1950).

The partnership has been held liable for the acts of a partner in employing unlawful force in evicting a former tenant from partnership premises, it being within the scope of the acting partner's duties to regain possession. Ray v. Dyer, 20 S.W.2d 328 (Tex.Civ.App. 1929).

imprisonment of a customer suspected of shoplifting.[12] Such decisions are somewhat questionable. It would appear to be clearly within the scope of business for a partner to use reasonable efforts for the protection of partnership property. If his over-zealousness or bad judgment leads him to use excessive force or to apply force to the wrong person, such mistakes are part of the risks of the business which should be assumed by the partnership to the extent of providing the injured third person with compensation. If the co-partner is present, and does not manifest objection or attempt to interfere with acts of violence committed for the supposed benefit of the partnership, he is considered to authorize the acts.[13]

The partnership is not liable for the act of a partner in knowingly purchasing stolen goods.[14] But the partnership is liable for the act of a partner in making the partnership a party to a conspiracy in restraint of trade to the injury of a third person.[15]

The partnership is liable for defamation [16] committed in the course of business, such as slander of title,[17] libel by letter [18] or by newspaper publication,[19] slander by accusing an employee of theft,[20] libel by asserting in an advertisement that a judgment, pursuant to which execution sale of firm property is about to be held, was obtained by fraud and perjury.[21] If the act was not in the course of business, as where a partner in a hotel partnership slanders or libels a former guest, not in furtherance of the business, the partnership is not liable.[22]

Where all partners join in an action which constitutes a malicious prosecution, it is a partnership act and damages are collectible out of

A co-partner is not liable when a partner makes an unprovoked assault "to vent his own spleen or malevolence." Vrabel v. Acri, 156 Ohio St. 467, 103 N.E.2d 564, 30 A.L.R.2d 853 (1952). See Annot., Liability for assault by partner or joint adventurer, 30 A.L.R. 2d 859 (1953).

12. Bernheimer Bros. v. Becker, 102 Md. 250, 62 A. 526, 3 L.R.A.,N.S., 221, 111 Am.St.Rep. 356 (1905).

13. Mehlstaub v. Michael, 221 Mo.App. 807, 287 S.W. 1079 (1926), assault on salesman in the course of ejecting him from store; Dulchevsky v. Soloman, 136 Wash. 645, 241 P. 19 (1925), assault on customer.

14. Prairie Oil & Gas Co. v. Shanblum, 294 F. 894 (5th Cir. 1923).

15. Dietrich v. Cape Brewery & Ice Co., 315 Mo. 507, 286 S.W. 38 (1926).

16. For the corresponding rule in Agency, see Restatement, Second, Agency §§ 247, 254.

17. Haney Mfg. Co. v. Perkins, 78 Mich. 1, 43 N.W. 1073 (1889), attack on patent rights of a competitor.

18. Henry Myers & Co. v. Lewis, 121 Va. 50, 92 S.E. 988 (1917), a case of ratification, even if the libel was originally unauthorized.

19. Lothrop v. Adams, 133 Mass. 471, 43 Am.Rep. 528 (1882).

20. Gordon v. Hyman, 129 Misc. 351, 221 N.Y.S. 429 (1927).

21. Barnett v. McClain, 153 Ark. 325, 240 S.W. 415 (1922).

22. Wheless v. W. L. Davis & Son, 122 S.W. 929 (Tex.Civ.App.1909).

Under a statute providing that, "Partners are not responsible for torts committed by a co-partner," a partnership was held not liable for slander. Ozborn v. Woolworth, 106 Ga. 459, 32 S.E. 581 (1899).

See also Duquesne Distributing Co. v. Greenbaum, 135 Ky. 182, 121 S.W.

partnership property.[23] But it appears that the institution of criminal proceedings has been generally regarded as outside the scope of business, and hence only the active partners are liable in their individual capacity.[24]

The partnership is liable for the conversion of property entrusted to the partnership by a third person, which is converted by the act of a partner.[25] This liability of the innocent partner is not barred by his discharge in bankruptcy.[26]

Under general principles of the law of agency, the partnership is liable for the tort of an employee within the scope of his employment.[27] No provision for such liability is made in the U.P.A. other than the general statement that "the law of agency shall apply under this Act," [28] but a joint and several liability is imposed, as in the case of torts by partners.[29]

(d) Injury to Any Person Not Being a Partner

The liability extends to injuries to employees by partners; the fellow servant rule has no application.[30] The partnership is not liable

---

1026, 24 L.R.A.,N.S., 955, 21 Ann.Cas. 481 (1909). See Note, 19 Yale L.J. 293 (1910).

23. Page v. Citizens' Banking Co., 111 Ga. 73, 36 S.E. 418, 51 L.R.A. 463, 78 Am.St.Rep. 144 (1900).

Compare Martin v. Simkins & Co., 116 Ga. 254, 42 S.E. 483 (1902), holding that the partnership was not liable for the act of a partner, citing the statute referred to in preceding note.

For the rule in agency, see Restatement, Second, Agency §§ 246, 263.

24. Marks v. Hastings, 101 Ala. 165, 13 So. 297 (1893); Rosenkrans v. Barker, 115 Ill. 331, 3 N.E. 93, 56 Am.Rep. 169 (1885); Noblett v. Bartsch, 31 Wash. 24, 71 P. 551, 96 Am.St.Rep. 886 (1903), "prosecution of larceny is not within the scope of the business of a mercantile partnership."

25. Clark v. Ball, 34 Colo. 223, 82 P. 529, 2 L.R.A.,N.S., 100, 114 Am.St.Rep. 154 (1905); In re Peck, 206 N.Y. 55, 99 N.E. 258, 41 L.R.A.,N.S., 1223, Ann. Cas.1914A, 798 (1912); Brokaw v. Lage, 203 App.Div. 155, 196 N.Y.S. 531 (1922); Guillou v. Peterson, 89 Pa. 163 (1879); Blaustein v. Shapiro, 73 Pa. Super. 235, 236 (1919); Model Building & Loan Ass'n of Mott Haven v. Reeves, 201 App.Div. 329, 194 N.Y.S. 383 (1922), embezzlement by partner in law firm of client's funds.

26. McIntyre v. Kavanaugh, 242 U.S. 138, 37 S.Ct. 38, 61 L.Ed. 205 (1916). See also Griffin v. Bergeda, 152 Tenn. 512, 279 S.W. 385 (1925).

27. Linton v. Hurley, 80 Mass. (14 Gray) 191 (1859); Champion v. Bostwick, 18 Wend. 175, 31 Am.Dec. 376 (N.Y. 1837); Zondler v. Foster Mfg. & Supply Co., 277 Pa. 98, 120 A. 705 (1923).

The partnership is not liable for acts of an employee outside the scope of his employment, such as misrepresentations. Orvis v. George, 47 F.2d 1045 (5th Cir. 1931).

28. U.P.A. § 4(3).

29. Longmotti v. Rhodes, 215 Ark. 380, 220 S.W.2d 812 (1949), assault; Miller v. Long, 126 Ind.App. 482, 131 N.E.2d 348, 132 N.E.2d 272 (1956), conversion; Soberg v. Sanders, 243 Mich. 429, 220 N.W. 781 (1928), negligence.

30. Ashworth v. Stanwix, 3 El. & El. 701 (1860).

The partnership may be subject to liability to the employee exclusively under the provisions of a Workmen's Compensation Act. In that case there is no personal liability of the partner, owner of defective premises causing the employee's injury, Williams v. Hartshorn, 296 N.Y. 49, 69 N.E.2d 557 (1946); or of the partner whose negligent operation of an automobile caused

for an injury to a partner.[31] He is not within the workmen's compensation acts, as generally interpreted.[32] By express provision, partners receiving wages may be included within the benefits of some such acts.[33]

The section of the U.P.A. quoted at the beginning of this section, states that the partnership is liable for a tort committed by a part-

the injury, Klein v. Pepe, 99 N.Y.S.2d 794 (Sup.1950). See Sec. 3(c) n. 64 above.

31. This immunity from liability of the group is on the theory that a partner is a co-principal, and the negligence or other wrongful act of a partner or employee is imputed to all. See De Villars v. Hessler, 363 Pa. 498, 70 A.2d 333, 14 A.L.R.2d 470 (1950), a case of joint enterprise. Cases are collected, Annot., 98 A.L.R.2d 345 (1964). The wrongful actor himself is of course liable.

See also Hromek v. Gemeinde, 238 Wis. 204, 298 N.W. 587 (1941), member of a labor organization injured by defective condition of meeting premises. Liability was not imposed on members not at fault, as wrongdoing agents were agents of plaintiff, as well as of other members.

It has been held that a partner may recover for the death of a spouse employed by the partnership. Keegan v. Keegan, 194 Minn. 261, 260 N.W. 318 (1935), noted 49 Harv.L.Rev. 155 (1935). See further discussion of this case at Sec. 70 below.

This denial of protection to a partner represents a dubious policy and should be reversed by deleting "not being a partner in the partnership" from U.P.A. § 14; Crane, Liability of Unincorporated Association for Tortious Injury to a Member, 16 Vand.L.Rev. 319 (1963).

32. Ellis v. Jos. Ellis & Co., [1905] 1 K. B. 324; Cooper v. Industrial Accident Commission, 177 Cal. 685, 171 P. 684 (1918); In re W. A. Montgomery & Son, 91 Ind.App. 21, 169 N.E. 879 (1930); Wallins Creek Lumber Co. v. Blanton, 228 Ky. 649, 15 S.W.2d 465 (1929); James W. Ryder's Case, 341 Mass. 661, 171 N.E.2d 475 (1961); Lyle v. H. R. Lyle Cider & Vinegar Co., 243 N.Y. 257, 153 N.E. 67, 47 A. L.R. 840 (1926); McMillen v. Industrial Commission of Ohio, 13 Ohio App.

310; Id., 32 O.C.A. 285 (1920); Gerbers v. Murfreesboro Laundry Co., 159 Tenn. 51, 15 S.W.2d 737 (1929); Superior Ins. Co. v. Kling, 160 Tex. 155, 327 S.W.2d 422 (1959) (holding, however, for partner because he was expressly included in policy); Rockefeller v. Industrial Com. of Utah, 58 Utah 124, 197 P. 1038 (1921).

See contra, De Martini v. Industrial Accident Comm., 90 Cal.App.2d 139, 202 P.2d 828 (1949); Kramer v. Charlevoix Beach Hotel, 342 Mich. 715, 71 N.W.2d 226 (1955); Ohio Drilling Co. v. State Industrial Commission, 86 Okl. 139, 207 P. 314, 25 A.L.R. 367 (1922); Rodgers v. Blair, 201 Okl. 249, 204 P. 2d 867 (1949).

See Pederson v. Pederson, 229 Minn. 460, 39 N.W.2d 893 (1949), for a full discussion of the authorities. It is stated that under the U.P.A., whatever may be the case as to third persons, as between themselves the partners are not to be regarded as an entity. See also Sec. 3(c) above.

Compare International Brotherhood etc. v. Hanke, 339 U.S. 470, 70 S.Ct. 773, 94 L.Ed. 995, 13 A.L.R.2d 631 (1950), upholding an injunction against picketing a business carried on by a partnership without employees, to induce joining a union, as a picketing of "self employed". The decision of the Supreme Court of Washington, 207 P. 2d 206, applying a statute forbidding picketing of "self employed" to a business carried on by a partnership was affirmed.

33. Johnson v. Industrial Accident Commission, 198 Cal. 234, 244 P. 321 (1926); Wilcox v. Wilcox Bros., 332 Mich. 140, 205 N.W. 90 (1925); Swalley v. Department of Labor and Industries, 154 Wash. 432, 282 P. 905 (1929).

See also N.R.S. (Nev.) 616.055, "employee" includes working partner receiving wages; 85 Okl.Stat.Ann. § 3(4) (as amended 1959), firm may elect to include partner by policy indorsement.

ner, "to the same extent as the partner so acting or omitting to act." As an affirmative statement of liability to make compensation, this is in accordance with the common law. It has on occasion been given a restrictive application in situations where the acting partner has a personal immunity from liability by reason of a family relation to the injured person. In Caplan v. Caplan,[34] the wife of a partner, injured by the latter's negligent operation of an automobile in the course of the partnership business, was held to have no right of action against the partnership or any of the partners. The court rejected the entity theory of partnership as applied to tort liabilities, and held that liability, when imposed, was joint and several.[35] Joint liability could not be imposed, as the husband was immune, and as no joint liability existed, separate liability could not be imposed upon the other partners. The same court had previously held that immunity of an agent for a tort, by reason of family relation to the injured person, did not relieve his corporate principal, the rule of respondeat superior imposing liability for a wrongful act in the course of the employment.[36] This case was distinguished on the ground that in partnership transactions a partner is both agent and co-principal. In further discussion, the predecessor of this work [37] stated:

> "It is possible that a different result would be reached by a court which gave more attention to the provision in the

34. 268 N.Y. 445, 198 N.E. 23, 101 A. L.R. 1223 (1935). In accord with this decision are Wadsworth v. Webster, 237 App.Div. 319, 261 N.Y.S. 670 (1932); Belleson v. Skilbeck, 185 Minn. 537, 242 N.W. 1 (1932), noted in 16 Minn.Law Rev. 872; Mahaffey v. Mahaffey, 15 Tenn.App. 570 (1933), noted in 19 Va.Law Rev. 730; David v. David, 161 Md. 532, 157 A. 755, 81 A.L.R. 1000 (1932), noted in 8 Wis. Law Rev. 82. A contrary result was reached in Wait v. Pierce, 191 Wis. 202, 209 N.W. 475, 210 N.W. 822, 48 A.L.R. 276 (1926), under a statute permitting married women to sue as though sole.

See comments on Caplan v. Caplan in 21 Cornell L.Q. 157; 45 Yale L.J. 528; 22 Va.L.Rev. 473.

Interspousal immunity was eliminated in New York by the 1937 amendment to N. Y. Domestic Relations Law § 57 (See McKinney's General Obligations Law, § 3–313). Accordingly, a wife can maintain an action against her husband's partnership for his negligence. Jacobs v. U. S. Fidelity & Guaranty Co., 2 Misc.2d 428, 152 N.Y.

S.2d 128 (S.Ct.1956), partner's wife (with unsatisfied judgment against co-partner for injuries caused by partner-husband) entitled to summary judgment against partnership's liability insurer. The opinion, like Eule v. Eule Motor Sales, infra n. 40, traces the history of New York cases and statutes in this area. See also Travelers Indem. Co. v. Unger, 4 Misc.2d 955, 158 N.Y.S.2d 892 (S.Ct. 1956), partner's wife can sue partnership alone.

35. Compare Sumner v. Brown, 312 Pa. 124, 167 A. 315 (1933), holding that tort liability being that of partners, rather than of the partnership as an entity, is at common law discharged by the death of all of the partners.

36. Schubert v. August Schubert Wagon Co., 249 N.Y. 253, 164 N.E. 42, 64 A.L. R. 293 (1928). See, in accord, Miller v. J. A. Tyrholm & Co., Inc., 196 Minn. 438, 265 N.W. 324 (1936), explaining Belleson v. Skilbeck, as based on the terms of the U.P.A.

37. Crane, Partnership 290 (2d ed. 1952).

Uniform Partnership Act that 'the law of agency shall apply under this Act' [38] and as regards traffic accidents, at least to the factor generally present in cases of business enterprises of coverage by liability insurance." [39]

The prophecy is being fulfilled. New Jersey, carefully construing the Act and realistically considering how businessmen anticipate tort risks and provide for them, has permitted a wife to maintain an action against her husband's partnership for an injury negligently caused by him.[40] Iowa, which does not have the Act, has reached a similar result.[41]

(e) Punitive Damages

If the partnership is liable to the same extent as the guilty partner,[42] and punitive damages are recoverable against him, it would seem to follow that punitive damages would be recoverable against the partnership, regardless of the innocence of other partners. A contrary result has been reached in a jurisdiction which had adopted the Uniform Act.[43] In the absence of statute, there is a diversity of authority

38. U.P.A. § 4(3). Restatement, Second, Agency § 217(b), has adopted the view that a principal is not entitled to the benefit of his agent's personal immunity from suit.

39. The existence of liability insurance has been held to be a factor which eliminates the principal reason for the immunity arising out of the domestic relation, Lusk v. Lusk, 113 W.Va. 17, 166 S.E. 538 (1932), child injured by father's negligent operation of school bus; Dunlap v. Dunlap, 84 N.H. 352, 150 A. 905, 71 A.L.R. 1055 (1930), employer parent who carried liability insurance subject to liability to employee son. Though the ultimate bearing of the burden of liability by an insurance company would dispose of the "domestic tranquility" argument as a basis for immunity from liability for torts between persons in domestic relations to one another, to recognize an exception in such cases might create a danger of "domestic fraud and collusion." See McCurdy, Torts between Persons in Domestic Relations, 43 Harv.Law Rev. 1030, 1076 (1930).

40. Eule v. Eule Motor Sales, 34 N.J. 537, 170 A.2d 241 (1961), citing this text. A summary judgment for the partnership was reversed. "Although a number of rationales of *respondeat superior* have been suggested, the final basis is a public policy that one who expands his operation by the employment of others should bear the incidental losses. The employer is better able than the employee to bear the burden, and he can pass it along as a cost of his product or service." The court accepted the precedent of Felice v. Felice, 34 N.J.Super. 388, 112 A.2d 581 (1955), employee-wife entitled to workmen's compensation from partnership of which her husband was a partner. Eule is noted 10 Kan.L.Rev. 478 (1962), 14 Stan.L.Rev. 150 (1961), 47 Va.L.Rev. 1450 (1961).

41. Cody v. J. A. Dodds & Sons, 252 Iowa 1394, 110 N.W.2d 255 (1961), noted 47 Iowa L.Rev. 1159 (1962). The court relies on Iowa precedents to the effect that a partnership is a separate entity, and on Iowa rules permitting suit in the firm name without joinder of individual partners. Here and in Eule v. Eule Motor Sales, n. 40 above, the suit was solely against the firm; no partner was named or served as a party.

See other cases in Sec. 3(c) nn. 63, 67 above.

42. U.P.A. § 13, quoted at beginning of section.

43. Broudy-Kantor Co. v. Levin, 135 Va. 283, 116 S.E. 677, 32 A.L.R. 249 (1923). The opinion makes no reference to the

as to whether punitive damages are recoverable from a partnership or from the innocent partner.[44] If the partners ratify the act with knowledge, as by retention of benefits, the same measure of damages is recoverable as against the guilty partner.[45]

(f) Penalties

At common law, acts so contrary to public policy as to be subject to statutory penalties are generally considered outside the scope of business, so that a non-participating partner is not liable. The innocent partner has been held not liable to an action of trover for the security furnished on a usurious loan.[46] The non-participating partners are not liable for the statutory penalty recoverable for unlicensed use of a copyrighted picture.[47] The penal liability imposed by statute for wilfully cutting timber on another's land cannot be recovered from an innocent partner.[48] But where a partnership neglects to enter satisfaction for a mortgage which has been paid, the statutory penalty can be imposed on all the partners,[49] as this is a non-feasance which is more nearly in the course of business than is a malfeasance.

A more modern view scrutinizes carefully the character of the partnership business. If the improper transaction is clearly enough related to the business, there is good reason to impose liability on the firm and its members, e. g. a usury penalty against a partnership engaged in the loan business.[50] This is the approach of the U.P.A. which makes the partnership liable equally for "loss or injury" and

U.P.A. As punitive damages are somewhat of an anomaly in civil cases, not universally allowed, it may be possible to construe the U.P.A. provision as applicable only to liability for compensatory damages. Or a court might apply its general rules of agency law, as in the case of personal defence of the acting partner by reason of family relationship.

44. Punitive damages have been allowed in Heirn v. McCaughan, 32 Miss. 17, 66 Am.Dec. 588 (1856); Robinson v. Goings, 63 Miss. 500 (1886). They have been denied as against the innocent partner in Grund v. Van Vleck, 69 Ill. 478 (1873); Henry Myers & Co. v. Lewis, 121 Va. 50, 92 S.E. 988 (1917), semble. See also Gill v. Selling, 125 Or. 587, 267 P. 812, 58 A.L.R. 1556 (1928), associated physician.

45. United States v. Baxter, 46 F. 350 (D.Wash.1891), action for cutting timber, applying against the partnership the value of the timber after preparation for shipment, rather than value

in place, partner cutting having guilty knowledge; Henry Myers & Co. v. Lewis, n. 44 above. If all partners are equally culpable, punitive damages may be recovered from all. Cosgriff Bros. v. Miller, 10 Wyo. 190, 68 P. 206, 98 Am.St.Rep. 977 (1902).

46. Graham v. Meyer, Fed.Cas.No.5,673, 4 Blatchf. 129 (S.D.N.Y.1858).

47. Schreiber v. Sharpless, 6 F. 175 (E. D.Pa.1881).

48. Williams v. Hendricks, 115 Ala. 277, 22 So. 439 (1897), annotated in 41 L.R. A. 650, 67 Am.St.Rep. 32; Watson v. Hinchman, 42 Mich. 27, 3 N.W. 236 (1879).

49. Renfro v. Adams, 62 Ala. 302 (1878).

50. See Wright v. E–Z Finance Co., 267 S.W.2d 602 (Tex.Civ.App.1954) holding, however, that a partner's death dissolved the firm and terminated the liability for the penalty. See the next note.

for "any penalty . . . incurred" by a partner acting in the ordinary course of business or with the authority of his co-partners.[51]

(g) Criminal Liability

Criminal liability is generally personal and co-partners who do not participate are not liable for crimes of which guilty intent is an element.[52] "While partners may act for one another in civil matters this is not true so far as criminal liability is concerned, which is personal. In criminal cases a partner is not chargeable with acts of his co-partners unless he has knowledge."[53] If all partners participate in a criminal act, all are guilty.[54] If the act is in the course of a criminal business in which they are engaged, they have actually authorized acts incident to the business and are guilty.[55] A statute may create a crime in the nature of *malum prohibitum* in which guilty intent is not a necessary element, and if the crime is committed by a partner in the course of the business, all may be found guilty.[56]

The Supreme Court has somewhat broadened the criminal liability of partnerships. It recognizes that the legislature can make a

---

51. U.P.A. § 13, quoted at the beginning of this section. The provision was applied in Calimpco, Inc. v. Warden, 100 Cal.App.2d 429, 224 P.2d 421 (1950) to hold a partnership and individual partners liable for the statutory usury penalty. The partnership was one of several creditors who furnished building supplies and materials to the developers of a housing project. By voluntary arrangement, the creditors through trustees took over the development and received for themselves certain lots whose value (plus agreed interest at 4%) was found to exceed the 10% statutory limit. For the corresponding rules in agency, see Restatement, Second, Agency § 217D (penalties), 217C (punitive damages).

52. State v. Maurisky, 102 Conn. 634, 129 A. 714 (1925); Munoz v. State, 87 Fla. 220, 99 So. 555 (1924); Acree & Kinman v. Com., 76 Ky. (13 Bush.) 353 (1877); Sleight v. United States, 65 App.D.C. 203, 82 F.2d 459 (1936). U. S. v. Ward, 168 F.2d 226 (3d Cir. 1948), defrauding U. S. by padded payrolls on government contracts.

The expense paid by a partnership in defending a partner indicted for murder in situation where no liability attached to the partnership is not a deductible business expense. B. W. Sturtivant v. Commissioner, 15 Tax Court 880 (1950).

53. U. S. v. Quinn, 141 F.Supp. 622 (S.D.N.Y.1956). A federal statute made it unlawful for a Member of Congress to receive, directly or indirectly, any compensation for services by him or another in any proceeding to which the U. S. is a party. Congressman Quinn's law partners handled tax matters before the Bureau of Internal Revenue. The court held that there was no evidence upon which a jury could find actual knowledge by Quinn; accordingly, his motion for acquittal was granted.

54. Levin v. United States, 5 F.2d 598 (9th Cir. 1925), false income tax return.

55. State v. O'Kelley, 258 Mo. 345, 167 S.W. 980, 52 L.R.A.,N.S., 1063 (1914), business of partnership included illegal sales of liquor.

56. People v. Berridge, 212 Mich. 576, 180 N.W. 381 (1920) (illegal possession of liquor); Spokane v. Patterson, 46 Wash. 93, 89 P. 402, 8 L.R.A.,N.S., 1104, 123 Am.St.Rep. 921, 13 Ann.Cas. 706 (1907) (blasting in violation of city ordinance); Robinson v. State, 38 Ark. 641 (1882) (sale of liquor to a minor); Ex parte Casperson, 69 Cal.App.2d 441, 159 P.2d 88 (1945).

penal law applicable to partnerships, regardless of their entity or aggregate character for other purposes. This can be accomplished expressly through the definition of such operative words as "whoever" or "any person" used in describing the offense. Even if this is not done, a court will be reluctant to conclude that the legislature intended to exclude partnerships from an otherwise comprehensive regulatory scheme (in this case safety measures for motor carriers). Nor is there any insuperable obstacle to finding that a partnership acted "knowingly" or "wilfully". Like a corporation, it can do so vicariously through its representatives. However, ". . . the conviction of a partnership cannot be used to punish the individual partners, who might be completely free of personal guilt. As in the case of corporations, the conviction of the entity can lead only to a fine levied on the firm's assets." [57]

Torts by a partner against his co-partner or the partnership are discussed later.[58]

ADMISSIONS

§ 55.　An admission or representation made by any partner concerning partnership affairs within the scope of his authority as conferred by this act is evidence against the partnership. U.P.A. § 11.

Admissions by a party, as testified to by third persons, are admissible in evidence against him in litigation.[59] Admissions by another are admissible against a party to litigation, if, in making such statement the person speaking is acting in the capacity of agent of the party against whom the admission is offered in evidence.[60] Statements made by a partner with reference to partnership affairs are admissible against the partnership, if the partner speaking is acting within the scope of his authority as partner, speaking for the partnership while engaged in carrying on the business of the partnership.[61] Where a partner is speaking for himself, and not purporting to act for the partnership, his admission binds himself alone. Though a partner purports to speak for the partnership, his statements are not admissions of the partnership unless he is acting for the partnership in speaking. This problem of admissions frequently arises after a tort, such

57.　U. S. v. A & P Trucking Co., 358 U. S. 121, 79 S.Ct. 203, 3 L.Ed.2d 165 (1958), noted 1 Bos.Coll.Ind. & Comm. L.Rev. 109 (1959), 47 Geo.L.J. 807 (1959), 8 Kan.L.Rev. 486 (1960), 33 St. John's L.Rev. 404 (1959).

58.　Sec. 69 below.

59.　Morgan, Admissions as an Exception to the Hearsay Rule, 30 Yale L. J. 355 (1921); 2 Wigmore, Evidence, § 1048, et seq. (3rd ed. 1940). That one is a partner may be proved by his own admissions. Benoliel v. Homac, 87 N. J.Law, 375, 94 A. 605 (1915).

60.　Morgan, Rationale of Vicarious Admissions, 42 Harv.Law Rev. 461 (1929). 2 Wigmore § 1077 et seq. Restatement, Second, Agency §§ 284–91.

61.　Bank of Italy Nat. Trust & Sav. Ass'n v. Johnson, 7 Cal.App.2d 463, 46 P.2d 244 (1935); Bisel v. Hobbs, 6 Blackf. 479 (Ind. 1843); Bell v. Porter, 261 Mich. 97, 246 N.W. 93 (1932).

as a traffic accident, has been committed by a partner, or alleged servant of the partnership, and a partner subsequently admits that the wrongful act was committed in the course of business. A well considered opinion was rendered in Caswell v. Maplewood Garage.[62] A son of a partner had a traffic accident while driving a motor vehicle owned by the partnership. Evidence was admitted of statements made by each of the partners, from which it might be inferred that the driver was about partnership business at the time of the accident. It was held that such statements were inadmissible, lacking evidence that the occasions on which they were made were partnership transactions. The court adopted the entity view of partnership and held that the agency of a partner for the firm existed only when he was acting in the carrying on of partnership business. Further, the court held, under the aggregate view of partnership, treating each partner as a co-principal, there was no joint act of the partners as co-principals, unless they acted jointly or jointly authorized one of their number to act for them.

The existence of the partnership relation, as distinguished from some fact relating to partnership business, can be proved by the separate admissions of each and all of the partners.[63] A person's admission that another is his partner can be used against himself [64] but not against the other person.[65] But if existence of the partnership is proven by prima facie evidence, admissions of alleged partners are admissible against all in corroborative proof.[66] A partner can *testify* that transactions were partnership transactions [67] but his prior admissions to that effect cannot be received against the partnership as the sole

62. 84 N.H. 241, 149 A. 746, 73 A.L.R. 433 (1930), noted 17 Va.Law Rev. 295 (1931).

Accord, Samstag & Hilder Bros. v. Ottenheimer & Weil, 90 Conn. 475, 97 A. 865 (1916); Boor v. Lowery, 103 Ind. 468, 3 N.E. 151, 53 Am.Rep. 519 (1885); Heffron v. Hanaford, 40 Mich. 305 (1879); Mansfield v. Howell, 218 Mo. App. 557, 279 S.W. 1058 (1926); Union Nat. Bank of Rahway, N. J. v. Underhill, 102 N.Y. 336, 7 N.E. 293 (1886); Folk v. Schaeffer, 180 Pa. 613, 37 A. 104 (1897); Princess Ring Co. v. Read, 58 R.I. 178, 192 A. 173 (1937); Looney v. Bingham Dairy, 75 Utah 53, 282 P. 1030, 73 A.L.R. 427 (1929).

But see King v. Rieth, 341 Mo. 467, 108 S.W.2d 1 (1937); Osbun v. De Young, 99 N.J.Law, 204, 122 A. 809 (1923); Treon v. Shipman & Son, 275 Pa. 246, 119 A. 74 (1922); Muench v. Heinemann, 119 Wis. 441, 96 N.W. 800 (1903).

63. Huron v. Schomaker, 123 Pa.Super. 82, 185 A. 859 (1936). See the closely related problem of partnership by estoppel, Sec. 36 above, esp. n. 17.

64. Hutchison v. Brown, 277 App.Div. 130, 97 N.Y.S.2d 757 (1950).

65. Boise Payette Lumber Co. v. Sarret, 38 Idaho, 278, 221 P. 130 (1923) semble; Daugherty v. Heckard, 189 Ill. 239, 59 N.E. 569 (1901); Robertson v. Cambon, 176 La. 753, 146 So. 738 (1933).

A partner may testify to the existence of the partnership, and may testify to admissions of his co-partner, a co-defendant in the action, Huron v. Schomaker, 123 Pa.Super. 82, 185 A. 859 (1936).

66. Dimon v. Romeo, 99 Conn. 197, 121 A. 352 (1923); Daugherty v. Heckard, n. 65 above; Henderson v. Trammell Oil Co., 159 Okl. 250, 15 P.2d 44 (1932).

67. Slattery v. Labbitt, 120 Mont. 183, 181 P.2d 601 (1947).

evidence on that point.[68] But where an act is apparently within the scope of the business, admissions by the partner while acting in the transaction that it is for partnership purposes are admissible against the partnership.[69]

When a partner is engaged in a partnership transaction his incidental admissions are admissible against the partnership. This rule applies to receipts given for goods delivered to the partnership,[70] or to an account stated, rendered by a partner to a creditor.[71]

The provision of the Act quoted at the beginning of this section is capable of two different constructions. If the phrase "within the scope of his authority" modifies "made", the partner must be acting within his authority in making the admission. If the phrase modifies "affairs", the admission must relate to matters over which the partner has authority. The grammar suggests that the latter (and somewhat broader) meaning is intended. The draftsmen have hinted in both directions.[72]

NOTICE TO PARTNER AS NOTICE TO PARTNERSHIP

§ 56. Notice to any partner of any matter relating to partnership affairs, and the knowledge of the partner acting in the particular matter, acquired while a partner, or then present to his mind, and the knowledge of any other partner who reasonably could and should have communicated it to the acting partner, operate as notice to or knowledge of the partnership, except in the case of a fraud on the partnership committed by or with the consent of that partner. U.P.A. § 12.

Clearly a third person desiring to give notice to a partnership of some matter pertaining to the partnership business need not communicate with all of the partners. If notice is delivered to a partner, that is an effective communication to the partnership.[73] There is more dif-

68. Tuttle v. Cooper, 22 Mass. (5 Pick. 414) (1827); Taft v. Church, 162 Mass. 527, 39 N.E. 283 (1895); Slipp v. Hartley, 50 Minn. 118, 52 N.W. 386, 36 Am. St.Rep. 629 (1892); Mansfield v. Howell, 218 Mo.App. 557, 279 S.W. 1058 (1926), 21 Ill.Law Rev. 181; Thorn v. Smith & Wright, 21 Wend. 365 (N.Y. 1839); Princess Ring Co. v. Read, 58 R.I. 178, 192 A. 173 (1937); Kaiser v. Fendrick, 98 Pa. 528 (1881); Boise Payette Lumber Co. v. Sarret, 38 Idaho 278, 221 P. 130 (1923).

69. Treon v. Shipman & Son, 275 Pa. 246, 119 A. 74 (1922). Compare Deater v. Penn Machine Co., 311 Pa. 291, 166 A. 846 (1933); Sweet v. Wood, 18 R.I. 386, 28 A. 335 (1893).

70. Bisel v. Hobbs, 6 Blackf. 479 (Ind. 1843).

71. Milwaukee Harvester Co. v. Finnegan, 43 Minn. 183, 45 N.W. 9 (1890).

So as to other admissions of amount of debt due to creditors. Burgan v. Lyell, 2 Mich. 102, 55 Am.Dec. 53 (1851); Nichols v. Lane, 192 N.Y.S. 362 (Sup.Ct. 1922).

72. Commissioners' Note, 7 Unif.Laws Ann. 76 (1949).

73. Stork Restaurant v. Sahati, 166 F. 2d 348 (9th Cir. 1948), notice to discontinue use of trade name; Bulldog Concrete Forms Sales Corp. v. Taylor, 195 F.2d 417, 49 A.L.R.2d 1 (7th Cir. 1952) (Indiana law), notice of sale of goods repossessed under conditional sales contract.

Observe the distinction between notice (express statement affirmatively

ficulty in determining whether to impute to the partnership knowledge acquired by a partner otherwise than by communication made to him for the purpose of informing the partnership. If a partner acting in a particular matter has acquired pertinent knowledge while a partner, it is imputed to the partnership.[74] Knowledge actually present in

given) and knowledge (which may be either actual or constructive, i. e. from knowledge of such other facts as in the circumstances shows bad faith). U.P.A. § 3.

A demand, the making of which is necessary to create a duty immediately to do an act, is effectively made of the partnership when made to a partner. Johnson v. Frix, 177 Ala. 251, 58 So. 427 (1912), demand that partnership as mortgagee satisfy of record a mortgage that has been paid; Carstensen v. Gottesburen, 215 Cal. 258, 9 P.2d 831 (1932), demand by lessor for possession of real estate occupied by partnership is effectively made on partner; Spencer v. Collins, 156 Cal. 298, 104 P. 320, 20 Ann.Cas. 49 (1909), notice of termination by client of retention of partnership as attorneys.

Claflin v. Wolff, 88 N.J.Law, 308, 96 A. 73 (1915), notice of bankruptcy proceedings against a firm debtor to one partner is notice to the partnership; Gates v. Beecher, 60 N.Y. 518, 19 Am. Rep. 207 (1875), demand of payment of a partnership note is sufficient if made to one partner, the situation being distinguishable from mere joint makers on the ground that "partners are but one person, in legal contemplation."

A notice to partners, as owners of real estate, to make an improvement pursuant to municipal ordinance, is effective when delivered to one of the partners. City of Philadelphia, to Use of Lupowitz v. Black, 120 Pa. Super. 550, 182 A. 752 (1936).

Cf. Restatement, Second, Agency §§ 272, 275.

74. Southern Chemical Co. v. Bass, 175 N.C. 426, 95 S.E. 766 (1918); Patterson v. Seaton, 70 Iowa 689, 28 N.W. 598 (1886); Brooks v. Davis, 294 Mass. 236, 1 N.E.2d 17 (1936); McClurkan v. Byers, 74 Pa. 405 (1873); Anthony v. Jeffress, 172 N.C. 378, 90 S.E. 414 (1916) semble.

Lee v. Durango Music Co., 144 Colo. 270, 355 P.2d 1083 (1960), expiration date of partnership lease.

Bauman v. Citizens Trust Co., 248 App. Div. 9, 289 N.Y.S. 606 (1936), modified on other grounds on reargument 249 App.Div. 369, 293 N.Y.S. 45 (1937), aff'd 276 N.Y. 623, 12 N.E.2d 608 (1938), premature delivery of funds from stockholders to aid bank's capital impairment.

Higgins v. Shenango Pottery Co., 256 F.2d 504 (3d Cir. 1958) and 279 F.2d 46 (3d Cir. 1960), cert. denied 364 U. S. 899, 81 S.Ct. 232, 5 L.Ed.2d 193 (1960) (Pennsylvania law), knowledge of three partners (that, by diverting business from corporation to partnership, they were breaching fiduciary duty as directors and officers of the corporation) was knowledge of the partnership and sufficient to hold the partnership and all the co-partners, including limited partners, liable for the profits realized by the breach.

Though the partner acting in the transaction is ignorant of a pertinent fact, the knowledge of his co-partners, who know the fact is of interest to the partnership, is imputed to the firm. Darrow v. Blake, 58 Iowa 750, 13 N. W. 50 (1882), purchase by a partner, who was innocent, of a note known by the other partners to have been procured by fraud.

In Fererira v. Silvey, 38 Cal.App. 346, 176 P. 371 (1918), knowledge of a partner of the vicious character and habits of a mule owned by the partnership and used in its business was imputed to the partnership for the purpose of establishing a duty to inform an employee of the peril.

In Moskowitz v. A. B. Kirschbaum Co., 89 Pa.Super. 274 (1926), a written contract of employment was executed by one member of a partnership of four, one other partner having knowledge of it. The partnership was later incorporated, and the four partners became the executive officers of the corporation, which continued the busi-

his mind when acting, however acquired, is also imputed.[75]

Whether knowledge of a partner acquired by him in a non-partnership transaction is to be imputed to the partnership is a more difficult question. If a partner in one banking partnership, against which a check has been drawn and payment thereof ordered stopped by the drawer, fails to communicate the fact of stoppage of payment to another partnership of which he is a member, which acquires the check in due course without his knowledge of or participation in the transaction, his knowledge is not imputed to the transferee partnership so as to prevent its being a holder in due course.[76]   It is not to be expected,

ness, the employee continuing to work for the corporation. It was held that the four partners having "legal knowledge" of the contract, they were also charged with knowledge of it in their capacity of officers of the corporation, and that the corporation was bound by the terms of the contract. Perhaps the fact that the corporation may be regarded as the "alter ego" of the partnership justifies the apparently double application of the technique of constructive notice.

As to constructive notice to corporations, see Stevens, Corporations, § 166 (2d ed. 1949).

In a proceeding to forfeit an automobile used in illegal transportation of intoxicating liquors, under the federal revenue laws, to sustain the claim of a partnership as conditional vendor of the vehicle, it must be shown that no one of the partners knew of the buyer's reputation as a bootlegger. United States v. Cook & Border Motor Co., 89 F.2d 648 (8th Cir. 1937).

75. Higgins v. Shenango Pottery Co., n. 74 above.

This is an application of the agency rule prevailing in the majority of jurisdictions. 2 Mechem, Agency, §§ 1808–13 (2d ed. 1914); Restatement, Second, Agency §§ 274–76, 278. It was deliberately chosen by the draftsmen of the U.P.A., see Commissioners' Note, 7 Unif.Laws Ann. 77–78 (1949).

See, in general, Seavey, Notice Through an Agent, 65 U.Pa.L.Rev. 1 (1916), reprinted Seavey, Studies in Agency 29 (1949).

76. Flynn v. Bank of Mineral Wells, 53 Tex.Civ.App. 481, 118 S.W. 848 (1909).

But where a partnership is the drawer of a bill of exchange which is dis-

counted and held until maturity and dishonor by a bank in which a partner of the drawer firm is cashier, his knowledge of dishonor is imputed to the partnership. Hays v. Citizens' Savings Bank, 101 Ky. 201, 40 S.W. 573 (1897). The interest of the partnership in the matter is obvious to the cashier, and it is to be expected that he would advise his co-partner and see that proper action was taken.

Cf. Hale v. Depaoli, 33 Cal.2d 228, 201 P.2d 1, 13 A.L.R.2d 183 (1948), injured tenant could not charge landlord with knowledge of latent defect in building merely because, some years earlier, landlord's then partner had superintended construction of the building and should have had knowledge.

Smith v. Norman Motors Co., 84 Ga.App. 186, 65 S.E.2d 699 (1951), knowledge of partner's private transaction not imputed to co-partner relative to his private transaction.

In Baldwin v. Leonard, 39 Vt. 260, 94 Am.Dec. 324 (1867), a person acting as agent for another approached a partner in a hay-raising partnership with a view to buying hay for his principal. No contract was made. Later the agent bought the hay from another partner without disclosing his agency. It was held that he was in the position of agent for an undisclosed principal, and that the first partner's knowledge of agency was not imputed, since no transactions resulted from their conversations, and they were not of such a character that it should be presumed that he would communicate them to his co-partners.

In states which have not adopted the Act, there is some authority for the rule that knowledge of a partner

under the circumstances, that he will communicate such knowledge to his co-partners. If an owner of land has created an easement and subsequently the land becomes the property of a partnership of which he is a member, the knowledge of the easement is imputed to the partnership, this being a fact which he would naturally communicate.[77] It is not to be expected that a partner will communicate to his co-partners the fact that he is committing a fraud against the partnership. If a partner deposits checks which belong to the partnership to his separate account, the partnership is not chargeable with knowledge of the transaction.[78] It is not to be expected that a partner will communicate to the partnership the fact that he is committing a fraud upon a third person in a non-partnership transaction, as where a partner acquires funds by forgery of a check, and uses a part thereof to make a capital contribution to the partnership.[79] Where a partner deals with the partnership as a stranger, having an obvious adverse interest, as where he sells to the partnership a negotiable instrument unenforceable by him because of some defect such as fraud or lack of consideration, the partnership should be regarded as a holder in due course without notice.[80]

gained in non-partnership transactions is not to be imputed to the partnership, despite the fact that the circumstances are such that it would be natural for him to communicate it. In Anthony v. Jeffress, 172 N.C. 378, 90 S.E. 414 (1916), the court refused to impute to a partnership continuously dealing with a corporation, as customer in the purchase of goods, knowledge of the affairs of the corporation possessed by a partner who was a corporate director and officer.

77. Buckles Irvine Coal Co. v. Kennedy Coal Corporation, 134 Va. 1, 114 S.E. 233 (1922). See Tucker v. Cole, 54 Wis. 539, 11 N.W. 703 (1882), imputing to partnership engaged in buying timber fact of notice to one of them that certain timber which had been cut and was subsequently purchased by the firm was his property.

78. McIntosh v. Detroit Sav. Bank, 247 Mich. 10, 225 N.W. 628 (1929), citing U.P.A. § 12.

Cf. Adams v. Harrison, 34 Cal.App.2d 288, 93 P.2d 237 (1939), partner's knowledge not chargeable to co-partner he is defrauding.

Cf. Restatement, Second, Agency § 282, principal not affected by knowledge of agent secretly acting adversely, except in specified situations.

79. Gilruth v. Decell, 72 Miss. 232, 16 So. 250 (1894).

In a criminal prosecution for defrauding the United States actual knowledge of a partner must be proven to make him liable for the fraudulent conduct of a co-partner. United States v. Ward, 168 F.2d 226 (3d Cir. 1948). Accord U. S. v. Quinn, 141 F.Supp. 622 (S.D.N.Y.1956) discussed Sec. 54(g) n. 53 above.

See also Bienenstok v. Ammidown, 155 N.Y. 47, 49 N.E. 321 (1898); Liddell, Johnson & Garmany v. Crain, 53 Tex. 549 (1880); Englar v. Offutt, 70 Md. 78, 16 A. 497, 14 Am.St.Rep. 332 (1889).

If a partner has actual knowledge that his co-partner is employing trust funds in the partnership business, he is accountable to the extent of the enrichment so received as a constructive trustee. Penn v. Fogler, 182 Ill. 76, 55 N.E. 192 (1899).

80. This is the agency rule, as stated in Restatement, Second, Agency § 279; 2 Mechem, Agency, § 1815 (2d ed. 1914). Adams v. Ashman, 203 Pa. 536, 53 A. 375 (1902), appears to be contrary to this proposed solution. Doty, a member of a banking partnership, held a note unenforceable because of misrepresentations and lack of consideration. It was discounted by the banking partnership. It was held

Still another difficulty is posed by the knowledge of a partner who is not acting for the firm in the matter to which the knowledge relates. His knowledge is imputed if he reasonably could and should have communicated it, i. e. if he had reason to believe it related to partnership affairs and was so situated that he was able to communicate it to the partner acting in the matter.[81]

that the latter could not enforce it, but was affected by Doty's knowledge. In Boston Box Co. v. Shapiro, 249 Mass. 373, 144 N.E. 233 (1924), a partnership was not allowed to enforce an accommodation note given ultra vires by a corporation to a partner and by him transferred to the partnership without consideration. In this case the partnership was, of course, not a purchaser for value.

81. U.P.A. § 12, quoted at the beginning of this Section; Commissioners' Note, 7 Unif.Laws Ann. 78 (1949).

Cf. Restatement, Second, Agency §§ 275, 278.

CHAPTER 6

ENFORCEMENT OF PARTNERSHIP RIGHTS AND LIABILITIES

Analysis

ENFORCEMENT OF PARTNERSHIP RIGHTS

§ 57. An obligation running to the partnership is regarded at common law as the joint right of the partners, and an action to enforce it must be brought in the names of all of the partners. Suit cannot be brought in the partnership name, unless such procedure is permitted by statute. Many states have such statutes.

(a) Joinder of Partners

In accordance with the mercantile conception of the partnership as a unit, partnership dealings are usually carried on in the partnership name. The common law conception of partnership as an aggregate persists in the matter of procedure. Only legal persons may be named as the parties to litigation. In the absence of statutory changes, the choses in action of a partnership are regarded as substantive rights of the partners,[1] and litigation for their enforcement must be carried on in the names of the partners as joint owners.[2] A dormant partner

---

1. Restatement, Contracts § 128 and Comment *a* thereto.

2. "An action to enforce a joint right under a contract must be brought by

327

occupies a position of undisclosed principal, and need not be joined as co-plaintiff,[3] though he may be joined.[4] A nominal or ostensible partner need not be joined in an action on an informal contract,[5] but if his name appears as party to a formal contract, such as a negotiable instrument,[6] his name must appear as co-plaintiff in an action on the instrument.

A partner cannot sue alone on a contractual right of the partnership without joining, as co-plaintiffs, the active known partners,[7] ex-

or in the name of all surviving obligees." Restatement, Contracts § 129.

See Clark, Code Pleading 348–72 (2nd ed. 1947) for a discussion of joinder of plaintiffs at common law, in equity, and under modern codes.

See Wilson v. Wallace, 8 Serg. & R. 53 (Pa.1822).

See Grant County Deposit Bank v. McCampbell, 194 F.2d 469 (6th Cir. 1952) (each partner is indispensable party plaintiff).

Under Pa.R.Civ.P. 2127(a) (1958) actions by a partnership should be brought in the following manner, "A, B and C, trading as X & Co." In many jurisdictions the form is "A, B, and C dba [doing business as] X & Co."

3. Shoaff v. Gage, 168 F.Supp. 161 (D. C.Neb.1958); Desha v. Holland, 12 Ala. 513, 46 Am.Dec. 261 (1847); Goble v. Gale, 7 Blackf. 218, 41 Am.Dec. 219 (Ind.1844); Wood v. O'Kelley, 8 Cush. 406 (Mass.1851); Sharp v. Simons, 49 Barb. 407 (N.Y.1867); Brown v. Globe Laboratories, Inc., 165 Neb. 138, 84 N.W.2d 151 (1957); Wilkes v. Clark, 12 N.C. 178 (1827); Dwyer v. Wiley Hotel Co., 91 Ohio App. 525, 108 N.E. 2d 859 (1952); Nashville, C. & St. L. Ry. v. Davis, 21 Tenn.App. 663, 114 S.W.2d 830 (1938); American Nat. Bank v. Haggerton, 250 S.W. 279 (Tex. Civ.App.1923); Waite v. Dodge, 34 Vt. 181, 182 (1861).

4. Rogers v. Kichline's Adm'rs, 36 Pa. 293 (1860), semble; Cothay v. Fonnell, 10 B. & C. 671 (1830).

5. Lasher v. Colton, 225 Ill. 234, 80 N. E. 122, 8 Ann.Cas. 367 (1906); Wheelock v. Zevitas, 229 Mass. 167, 118 N.E. 279 (1918). It has been said that the nominal partner cannot be joined, Furstman v. Frank, 206 Mich. 619, 173 N.W. 342 (1919).

6. Guidon v. Robson, 2 Camp. 302, 170 Rep. 1163 (1809). That a non-partner may be joined, see Waite v. Dodge, n. 3 above.

7. Fred Gray Cotton & Gin Co. v. Smith, 214 Ala. 606, 108 So. 532 (1926); Illinois Oil Co. v. Block, 129 Okl. 122, 263 P. 650 (1928); Hood v. Warren, 205 Ala. 332, 87 So. 524 (1921), partner cannot sue alone for breach of warranty of hogs bought by partnership, though he has purchased copartner's share in the hogs; Frumes v. Glaser, 127 N.Y.S. 321 (Sup.1911); Godwin v. Vinson, 251 N.C. 326, 111 S.E.2d 180 (1959), non-suit proper; Thomas v. Benson, 264 Mass. 555, 163 N.E. 181 (1928), the defect being one of substance, can be raised under an answer of general denial.

The assignee of a partner cannot sue on a contract right of the partnership. Shapira v. Budish, 275 Mass. 120, 175 N.E. 159 (1931).

Where, as in Vermont, a partnership is regarded as a legal entity, the addition of a co-partner to an action brought by a partner on a partnership-owned cause of action cannot be allowed. It would be substituting a different party plaintiff. Brooks v. Ulanet, 116 Vt. 49, 68 A.2d 701 (1949).

As to the running of the statute of limitations prior to joinder of the co-partner, see Morris v. Gwaltney, 215 S.W. 473 (Tex.Civ.App.1919); Midland Oil Co. v. Moore, 2 F.2d 34 (8th Cir. 1924).

A special partner in a limited partnership is not a necessary party plaintiff or defendant. U.L.P.A. § 26; Spalding v. Black, 22 Kan. 55 (1879); In re Dunn & Bro., 115 La. 1084, 40 So. 466 (1906); Wetherill v. McCloskey, 28 W.Va. 195 (1886). See Sec. 26(c) n. 52 above.

cept in actions on contracts made with the partner in his own name.[8] The partner fares no better if he sues only for his proportional share rather than for the entire claim of the firm.[9] However, some procedural codes permit a partner to litigate a partnership claim in full by joining a reluctant co-partner as a defendant.[10]

Strict application of joinder rules can produce hardship; recognizing this, courts permit some relaxation. Thus, a suing partner can make his fellow partners co-plaintiffs if they will not voluntarily join or if their whereabouts are unknown.[11] And defendant's failure to make timely objection will operate as a waiver.[12] But further liberalization is desirable and is justified by each partner's important representative capacity. "The partnership will be bound by the act of the single partner in bringing suit and any recovery will discharge the partnership's claim against the defendants. On the other hand, if defendants prevail with a judgment for costs, that judgment will bind the partnership assets and at the very least the assets of the individual partner who has caused the action to be brought."[13] It would be strange if a partner could not litigate a partnership claim in which he

As to extraterritorial effect of the disabilities of the special partner, see Lawrence v. Batcheller, 131 Mass. 504 (1881).

8. Rock Creek Oil Corp. v. Wolfe, 35 S. W.2d 1072 (Tex.Civ.App.1930); Meyers v. Zahn, 136 Kan. 49, 12 P.2d 727 (1932); Brown v. Globe Laboratories, Inc., n. 3 above; Bryant v. Phillips, 189 Mo.App. 278, 176 S.W. 294 (1915).

9. Vinal v. West Virginia Oil & Oil Land Co., 110 U.S. 215, 4 S.Ct. 4, 28 L.Ed. 124 (1884); Anable v. McDonald Land & Mining Co., 144 Mo.App. 303, 128 S.W. 386 (1910); Coast v. Hunt Oil Co., 195 F.2d 870 (5th Cir. 1952) cert. denied 344 U.S. 836, 73 S.Ct. 46, 97 L.Ed. 651 (1952) (Applying Louisiana law which strongly recognizes the partnership as an entity). These holdings reflect the very limited individual rights of a partner in specific partnership property, here a cause of action. See Secs. 40–45 above.

10. E. g., Fed.Rules Civ.Proc., rule 19 (a), 28 U.S.C.A.; C.G.S.A. (Conn.) § 52–101.

11. Rose v. Beckham, 264 Ala. 209, 86 So.2d 275 (1956), setting out the pleading used for this purpose. F.R.Civ. P. 19(a) (involuntary plaintiff).

If originally defective, the pleadings can usually be amended to add the co-partners as plaintiffs; see Shoaff v. Gage, 168 F.Supp. 161 (D.Neb.1958). See also Sheffield v. Alexander, 194 N.C. 744, 140 S.E. 726 (1927).

12. Hutchinson v. Dubois, below, n. 23. See Ginsberg Tile Co. v. Faraone, 99 Cal.App. 381, 278 P. 866 (1929); Vogel v. Bushnell, 203 Mo.App. 623, 221 S. W. 819 (1920).

13. Leh v. General Petroleum Corp., 165 F.Supp. 933, 937 (S.D.Calif.1958), noted 73 Harv.L.Rev. 411 (1959). See also U.P.A. § 9(1), above secs. 49–50. The partner will hold in trust for the firm any recovery, U.P.A. § 21(1), below Sec. 68.

If the plaintiff partner loses on the merits, his co-partners should be barred from suing again, in order to protect the defendant from multiple actions on the same claim. A partner's representative capacity should be sufficient to assure this, but courts have sometimes failed to recognize this, occasionally permitting second suits. See Annot., Judgment for or against a partner as res judicata in favor of or against co-partner, 11 A.L.R.2d 847, 863–65 (1950).

has a very immediate interest, while a shareholder could litigate a corporate claim in which he has a very remote interest.[14]

Actions for damages for torts injuring partnership property or business should be brought by the partners jointly, and actions for torts injuring a partner with respect to his personal interests should be brought by him separately. Actions for trespass to partnership property, as by wrongful attachment,[15] are properly brought by the partners jointly, and not by a partner.[16] An action for deceit, causing a loss of partnership assets, is properly brought by the partners.[17] The partners may maintain an action for assault on the partners on the business premises, causing a public brawl, disabling the partners from carrying on business, and thereafter deterring customers from coming to the premises.[18] The partners jointly may sue for libel or slander of the partnership causing damage to the business.[19] For injuries to the partner personally, as by slander or libel,[20] or in-

14. For general discussion of shareholder derivative suits, see Henn, Corporations 559–612 (1961); Ballantine, Corporations 333–74 (rev. ed. 1946).

For derivative suits by limited partners, see Sec. 26(c) at n. 52 above.

15. Robinson v. Mansfield, 30 Mass. (13 Pick.) 139 (1832); Russell v. Cole, 167 Mass. 6, 44 N.E. 1057, 57 Am.St.Rep. 432 (1896).

16. Midland Oil Co. v. Moore, 2 F.2d 34 (8th Cir. 1924); Posey v. Kirk, 112 Kan. 682, 212 P. 667 (1923); Bigelow v. Reynolds, 68 Mich. 344, 36 N.W. 95 (1888); Buch v. Newsome, 129 N.J.L. 585, 30 A.2d 579 (1943).

It has been held that where a partner makes an unauthorized sale of partnership property, the co-partner may maintain an action of trover to recover the value of his share as co-owner. Phillips v. Thorp, 12 Okl. 617, 73 P. 268 (1903); McNair v. Wilcox, 121 Pa. 437, 15 A. 575, 6 Am.St.Rep. 799 (1888). But see Reed v. Gould, 105 Mich. 368, 63 N.W. 415, 55 Am.St.Rep. 453 (1895), holding that a partner could not maintain an action at law, because of the difficulty of establishing the value of his interest, and stating further that he could not join as co-plaintiff the partner who was guilty of the unauthorized act.

In the case of a business trust, the trustees, in whom is vested the legal title to the property of the association, can maintain an action to enjoin a tort threatening injury to the property.

Wesson v. Galef, 286 F. 621 (S.D.N.Y. 1922). A suit to quiet title to land belonging to the trust has been allowed to be maintained by the trustees in whom the legal title is vested. Denny v. Cascade Platinum Co., 133 Wash. 436, 232 P. 409 (1925). The fact that business trusts were then regarded as illegal in Washington did not deprive the plaintiffs of a remedy. See Sec. 33 nn. 79, 82 above.

17. Medbury v. Watson, 47 Mass. (6 Metc.) 246, 39 Am.Dec. 726 (1843).

18. Seidell v. Taylor, 86 Wash. 645, 151 P. 41 (1915).

19. Weitershausen v. Croatian Printing & Pub. Co., 151 F. 947 (C.C.N.Y.1907); Melcher v. Beeler, 48 Colo. 233, 110 P. 181, 139 Am.St.Rep. 273 (1910); Wright v. Afro-American Co., 152 Md. 587, 137 A. 273, 52 A.L.R. 908 (1927) semble; Vogel v. Bushnell, 203 Mo. App. 623, 221 S.W. 819 (1920); Wilson v. Sun Pub. Co., 85 Wash. 503, 148 P. 774, Ann.Cas.1917B, 442 (1915); Forster v. Lawson, 3 Bing. 452, 12 Eng. Rep. 209 (1826).

The special damage due to loss of business can only be recovered in an action by the partners jointly. Lewis v. Hayes, 177 Cal. 587, 171 P. 293 (1918); Kornblum v. Commercial Advertiser Ass'n, 183 App.Div. 615, 170 N.Y.S. 249 (1918). Contra, Wills v. Jones, 13 App. D.C. 482 (1898).

20. Constitution Pub. Co. v. Way, 94 Ga. 120, 21 S.E. 139 (1894); Collier v.

In federal court, a partnership may always sue in its common name on a substantive right arising under the U.S. Constitution or laws,[32] for example, patent [33] or anti-trust [34] matters.   And in an action based on diversity of citizenship, the partnership may sue in its firm name if it could do so in a state court where the federal court is held.[35]   However, diversity is determined by reference to the citizenship of each partner; thus, no partner may reside in the same state as any defendant.[36]   This denies many partnerships access to federal court; a better rule would treat a partnership as a citizen of the place where its principal business is located.[37]

The trustees of a business trust, even though it may be classified as a partnership for the purposes of personal liability of its members, may maintain an action in their own names for breach of contract or injury to the trust property; if they are of diverse citizenship from that of the defendant, they are entitled to sue in the federal courts, regardless of the citizenship of the beneficiaries.[38]   In some states, by statute, suits may be instituted by business trusts in the common name.[39]

32.   Fed.Rules Civ.Proc. rule 17(b), 28 U.S.C.A.

33.   Gregory v. Royal Typewriter Co., 27 F.Supp. 160 (S.D.N.Y.1939).

34.   Leh v. General Petroleum Corp., 165 F.Supp. 933 (S.D.Calif.1958).

35.   Fed.Rules Civ.Proc. rule 17(b), 28 U.S.C.A.

36.   Great Southern Fireproof Hotel Co. v. Jones, 177 U.S. 449, 20 S.Ct. 690, 44 L.Ed. 842 (1900) (Pennsylvania limited partnership association); Rosendale v. Phillips, 87 F.2d 454 (2d Cir. 1937) (unincorporated membership association).

A partner cannot create the desired diversity by suing individually, omitting his co-partner (with the same residence as one of the defendants) for the co-partner is an indispensable party. Charne v. Essex Chair Co., 92 F.Supp. 164 (D.N.J.1950), citing this text. However, the opposite result has been reached where the omitted partner disclaimed his interest in the action, Grant County Deposit Bank v. McCampbell, 194 F.2d 469, 31 A.L.R.2d 909 (6th Cir. 1952).

37.   3 Moore, Federal Practice par. 17.25 (2d ed).

38.   Simson v. Klipstein, 262 F. 823 (D. N.J.1920); Wesson v. Galef, 286 F. 621 (S.D.N.Y.1922).   See, also, Simson v. Klipstein, 88 N.J.Eq. 229, 102 A. 242 (1917).

As to suits by trustees as parties to contracts of leasing, see Hull v. Newhall, 244 Mass. 207, 138 N.E. 249 (1923); as to suits to quiet title, see Denny v. Cascade Platinum Co., 133 Wash. 436, 232 P. 409 (1925). In Willey v. W. J. Hoggson Corp., 90 Fla. 343, 106 So. 408 (1925), it was held that beneficiaries, being partners, should join in an action to procure a transfer of corporate stock, part of the property of the association.

In the absence of statutory recognition of the trust as an entity, entitled to sue in the common name, it seems that action could be brought only by the trustees in their own names, and not in the name of the trust. Denny v. Cascade Platinum Co., supra. If a lease is executed in the names of the trustees, it seems that no action on it can be maintained in the name of the trust. Hull v. Newhall, supra. Action on a note in the name of "H. Kempner" as payee, the name in which a trust carries on its business, should be maintained in the names of the trustees, and not in the name of "H. Kempner, a trust company." H. Kempner v. Welker, 36 Ariz. 128, 283 P. 284 (1929).

39.   General American Oil Co. v. Wagoner Oil & Gas Co., 118 Okl. 183, 247 P.

In some states statutes permit actions to be maintained by joint stock companies in the common name.[40] In some states they may be maintained in the name of the president or treasurer.[41]

ENFORCEMENT OF PARTNERSHIP OBLIGATIONS—PROCEDURAL CHARACTERISTICS OF A PARTNERSHIP CONTRACT AT COMMON LAW

§ 58. A joint obligation of the partners normally results from a contract made by the partnership. Save as affected by statutory changes, or by equitable doctrines, the characteristics of a partnership contractual obligation in accordance with the common law of joint obligations are:

(a) In an action to enforce such an obligation all the partners should be named as defendants;

(b) A release of one partner releases all;

(c) A judgment upon a partnership contract in favor of the obligee operates as a merger, discharging all partners from the obligation, including those not subject to the jurisdiction of the court;

(d) In case of death of a partner the liability rests upon the surviving partners, and, upon the death of all, upon the representative of the one last dying;

(e) A judgment creditor of the partnership can levy execution on either joint or separate property, but in some states execution against separate property is conditional on the joint property being insufficient.

Most states have made some statutory modification, particularly of (a).

A partnership entity can have a liability even where it cannot be sued as such. Thus, the U.P.A., in force in practically all states, makes the partnership initially responsible for acts of the partners as agents,[42] as well as for their admissions,[43] knowledge or notice,[44] wrongful acts,[45] and breaches of trust.[46] The liability of the partners is for the debts and obligations *of the partnership.*[47]

The threshold inquiry, then, is the nature of the partner's liability for a partnership obligation: joint, several, or joint and several. The main procedural differences among the alternative types of liability

99 (1925); Graham v. Omar Gasoline Co., 255 S.W. 896 (Tex.Civ.App.1923).

An action having been brought in the common name of the trust, on its withdrawal from the action, it cannot be continued by the trustees in their names. Forgan v. Mackie, 232 Mich. 476, 205 N.W. 600 (1925).

40. Wichita County Lumber Co. v. Maer, 235 S.W. 990 (Tex.Civ.App.1921).

Such a statute also includes a business trust. Graham v. Omar Gasoline Co., 255 S.W. 896 (Tex.Civ.App.1923).

41. McKinney's N. Y. General Associations Law, § 12.

42. U.P.A. § 9.

43. U.P.A. § 11.

44. U.P.A. § 12.

45. U.P.A. § 13.

46. U.P.A. § 14.

47. U.P.A. § 15. On the unique situation in Louisiana, see Sec. 3(f) n. 7A above.

have been summarized this way: "At common law joint obligors must be sued jointly, subject to a few exceptions where jurisdiction over all could not be obtained. Several obligors must be severally sued, while as to joint and several obligors, the plaintiff might choose how he would sue." [48]

U.P.A., in its original form and as enacted in most states, codifies the common law view that the partners' liabilities are joint in contract,[49] but concedes that a partner may enter into a separate obligation to perform a partnership contract.[50] The latter, if it occurs, has the effect of making the obligation several as to him. A several obligation is sometimes expressly created by careful draftsmen who desire maximum flexibility in enforcement against the partners.[51] Or it may arise by implication, e. g., where a partner individually signs a partnership note.[52]

Beyond this, some states have made all partnership liability joint and several, either by decision [53] or by statute.[54]

Unless otherwise indicated, the following discussion relates to the common law view of partnership contractual obligations, i. e. joint liability.

(a) Joinder of All Partners as Defendants

"A partnership at common law is not a legal entity, but only a contractual status. Suits affecting partnership matters must be brought by or against the members of the firm." [55]   Each person

---

48. Clark, Code Pleading 373 (2d ed. 1947).

49. U.P.A. § 15(b); Commissioners' Note to U.P.A. § 15, 7 Unif.Laws Ann. 86–87 (1949). The language has been altered to specify joint and several liability in some states; see n. 54 below. The draftsmen of the Act anticipated this development, although it is not certain that they were correct in their view that it lacked substantive significance; Commissioners' Note to U.P.A. § 15, 7 Unif.Laws Ann. 86–87 (1949).

50. U.P.A. § 15(b).

51. The agreement need merely recite that it is made by the partners jointly and severally, and be signed by each. Or, one or more partners may be asked to guarantee performance of the partnership; this produces a similar result.

52. International Trust Co. v. Myers, 252 Mass. 94, 147 N.E. 591 (1925).

53. Coates v. Milner, 134 Ark. 311, 203 S.W. 701 (1918); Brown v. Belches, 1

Va. (1 Wash.) 9 (1791); Roberts v. Toney, 100 W.Va. 688, 131 S.E. 552 1926).

Many of the statutes cited in the next note codify prior decisional law.

54. Ala.Code 1940, Tit. 43, § 7 (by implication); A.R.S. (Ariz.) § 29–215; V.A.M.S. (Mo.) § 358.150; G.S. (N.C.) § 59–45; T.C.A. (Tenn.) § 61–114; Vernon's Ann.Civ.St. (Tex.) art. 6132b, § 15. Statutes of this kind are urged by Campbell, Partnership Obligations and their Enforcement, 32 Chi-Kent L.Rev. 127 (1954).

The number of states with such statutes seems to have diminished since promulgation of the U.P.A. Its draftsmen in 1914 cited 12 jurisdictions, Commissioners' Note, 7 Unif.Laws Ann. 86 (1949). Many states reach a substantial equivalent of joint and several liability by their common name statutes, Sec. 60 below. See also below at nn. 63–64.

55. Kent v. National Supply Co. of Texas, 36 S.W.2d 811 (Tex.Civ.App.1931),

bound by a joint obligation is bound for the whole obligation, but by making appropriate objection can prevent recovery of judgment against him unless the other joint promisors are joined with him, save those who are deceased, or beyond the jurisdiction.[56] As to those beyond the jurisdiction, the old English practice was to join all joint debtors and proceed to outlawry against those who were absent, and then obtain judgment in due course against those subject to the jurisdiction.[57] Outlawry is unknown in this country, but the same result (i. e., permitting the action to proceed against the partners served), has followed a return of "non est inventus" as to those without the jurisdiction.[58]

Non-joinder of a non-dormant partner, in an action on the partners' joint liability, can be taken advantage of by plea in abatement,[59]

prior to adoption of U.P.A.; Lewis v. West Side Trust & Savings Bank, 377 Ill. 384, 36 N.E.2d 573 (1941); Thompson v. Corn, 102 Ind.App. 6, 200 N.E. 737 (1936); Haney v. Thomson, 339 Mo. 505, 98 S.W.2d 639 (1936); Brown & Bigelow v. Roy, 71 O.L.A. 438, 132 N.E.2d 755 (Ohio App.1955); Wheatley v. Carl M. Halvorson, Inc., 213 Or. 228, 323 P.2d 49 (1958).

Dismissal of partners originally joined prevents judgment against the rest. Balley v. Davis, 75 Idaho 73, 267 P.2d 631, 44 A.L.R.2d 575 (1954).

A consequence of the view quoted in the text is that, on recovery of judgment against the partners, execution may be levied on the separate property of a partner personally bound by the judgment, regardless of the amount of joint property available. Dean v. Phillips, 17 Ind. 406 (1861); Randolph v. Daly, 16 N.J.Eq. 313 (1863).

A lien against the separate property resulting from a judgment against the partners is superior to a subsequently obtained lien resulting from proceedings by a separate creditor. Meech v. Allen, 17 N.Y. 300, 72 Am.Dec. 465 (1858).

An attachment of separate property by a partnership creditor is superior to a subsequent attachment by a separate creditor. Allen v. Wells, 39 Mass. (22 Pick.) 450, 33 Am.Dec. 757 (1839).

A lien on separate property resulting from a judgment in behalf of a partnership creditor is not avoided by bankruptcy within four months of the partnership, but not of the partners.

Liberty Nat. Bank of Roanoke, Va., v. Bear, 276 U.S. 215, 48 S.Ct. 252, 72 L.Ed. 536 (1928); Savings & Loan Corporation v. Bear, 155 Va. 312, 154 S.E. 587 (1930), annotated as to relative rank of judgment, attachment and execution liens on the partnership and individual property, in 75 A.L.R. 980, 997.

The lien resulting from a judgment applies only to the property of those who are personally parties to the judgment. If the action be regarded as against the partnership as a distinct legal entity, the judgment resulting does not constitute a lien on the property of a partner. Bankers Trust Co. v. Knee, 222 Iowa 988, 270 N.W. 438 (1936).

56. Seligman v. Friedlander, 199 N.Y. 373, 92 N.E. 1047 (1910), 11 Colum.L. Rev. 101, 114 (1911). The case is a fine example of the resistance of common law to statutory change.

New York's vacillation between joint and joint-and-several liability for partners is described in Friedman v. Gettner, 6 A.D.2d 647, 180 N.Y.S.2d 446 (1958) aff'd 7 N.Y.2d 764, 194 N.Y.S.2d 35, 163 N.E.2d 141 (1959).

57. Hall v. Lanning, 91 U.S. 160, 23 L. Ed. 271 (1875); Blessing v. McLinden, 81 N.J.Law, 379, 79 A. 347, 35 L.R.A., N.S., 312 (1911).

58. Tappan v. Bruen, 5 Mass. 193 (1809); Dillman v. Schultz, 5 Serg. & R. 35 (Pa.1818).

59. Page v. Brant, 18 Ill. 37 (1856); Alexander v. McGinn, 3 Watts 220 (Pa.

or, if it appears on the plaintiff's declaration, by demurrer.[60] Failure to make timely objection operates as a waiver and permits a judgment against fewer than all the partners.[61]

In some states, the requirement of joinder has been changed by statutes making partnership obligations joint and several,[62] or specifically providing that a partner may be sued on a partnership obligation.[63] The effect of general joint debtor statutes on partnerships is discussed below.[64]

In a federal court action, based on diversity of citizenship, to enforce a partnership obligation, all the defendant partners must have citizenship different from the plaintiffs.[65] Apparently, a plaintiff cannot avoid this barrier by suing only the partner with diverse citizenship.[66] These results need reconsideration in two respects, both based on the premise that capacity to sue or be sued is determined by state law.[67] Where the partnership can be sued as an entity, it would be better to accord it citizenship distinct from its members.[68] And where a partner, as a matter of substantive law, can be sued severally on a

1834); Barry v. Foyles, 26 U.S. (1 Pet.) 311, 7 L.Ed. 157 (1822).

"The general rule is, that the plaintiff must join as parties defendant all who are jointly liable upon the contract sued on, and if he does not, the nonjoinder being pleaded in abatement, he cannot recover against any. And in actions in form ex contractu against partners, although the plaintiff need not join dormant or secret partners not known to him at the time of the contract, he must sue all who are ostensible and public members of the firm at the time of making the contract sued on." Page v. Brant, supra.

60. Sandusky v. Sidwell, 173 Ill. 493, 50 N.E. 1003 (1898); Bowen v. Crow, 16 Neb. 556, 20 N.W. 850 (1884); Cox v. Gille Hardware & Iron Co., 8 Okl. 483, 58 P. 645 (1899).

61. Brown & Bigelow v. Roy, 132 N.E.2d 755 (Ohio App.1955).

62. See n. 54 above.

But in order to be able to levy execution on partnership property it is necessary that the judgment be obtained in an action against the partnership or against all of the partners. Lewis v. Tyler Hotel Co., 257 S.W. 704 (Tex. Civ.App.1924).

63. Iowa R.Civ.P. 4 (1958); 1953 Comp. (N.Mex.) § 21–6–5 (1954); Pa.R.Civ.P.

2128(a) (1951); Vernon's Ann.Civ.St. (Tex.) arts. 2033, 2223.

64. Sec. 59, below.

Statutes making joint obligations joint and several in some states have not been construed as applying to partnership obligations for the purpose of permitting suit against a partner. First Nat. Bank of Abbeville v. Capps, 208 Ala. 207, 94 So. 109 (1922); Erskine v. Russell, 43 Colo. 449, 96 P. 249 (1908); Fleming v. Ross, 225 Ill. 149, 80 N.E. 92, 8 Ann.Cas. 314 (1907); Seligman v. Friedlander, 138 App.Div. 784, 123 N.Y.S. 583 (1910). See note 81 below.

65. Brocki v. American Express Co., 279 F.2d 785 (6th Cir. 1960) (joint stock company). Similarly, complete diversity of partners is required where the suit is to enforce a partnership right; see discussion at n. 36 above.

66. Eastern Metals Corp. v. Martin, 191 F.Supp. 245 (S.D.N.Y.1960). But see Cooper v. North Jersey Trust Co., 250 F.Supp. 237 (S.D.N.Y.1965).

67. Fed.Rules Civ.Proc. rule 17(b), 28 U.S.C.A.

68. See the similar argument at n. 37 above, concerning the partnership as plaintiff.

partnership obligation, the other partners should not be regarded as indispensable parties, and their citizenship should be ignored.

(b) Effect of Release of One Partner

In accordance with the law of joint obligations,[69] release by a partnership creditor of a partner discharges the joint liability of the others,[70] including dormant partners.[71] As in the case of other joint obligations, there may be a covenant not to sue, or a release so qualified as to save rights against the other partners.[72] Such a transaction is sometimes provided for by statute.[73]

The release of one jointly and severally liable released the co-obligors from all their liabilities at common law.[74] The Contracts Restatement has adopted the view that such a release discharges only the joint liability.[75] Under this view release of a partner, where the obligation is expressly, or by operation of law, joint and several, would not discharge the several liability of other partners.[76]

(c) Effect of Judgment Against a Partner

"A judgment rendered by a court of competent jurisdiction within the United States against one or more joint promisors, or against one

69. Williston, Contracts, § 333 (3rd ed. 1959). Restatement, Contracts §§ 121–124.

70. Gray's Ex'rs v. Brown, 22 Ala. 262 (1853); Clark v. Mallory, 185 Ill. 227, 56 N.E. 1099 (1900); Williamson v. McGinnis, 50 Ky. (11 B.Mon.) 74, 52 Am.Dec. 561 (1850); Hale v. Spaulding, 145 Mass. 482, 14 N.E. 534, 1 Am. St.Rep. 475 (1888); Rocky Mountain Stud Farm Co. v. Lunt, 46 Utah 299, 151 P. 521 (1915); Blodgett v. Inglis, 63 Wash. 513, 115 P. 1043 (1911).

See Annot., Release of one of several joint or joint and several contract obligors as affecting liability of other obligors, 53 A.L.R. 1420 (1928).

Many questions concerning the validity of a release are treated in Freedman v. Montague Associates, 18 Misc.2d 1, 187 N.Y.S.2d 636 (Sup.Ct.1959), reversed 9 A.D.2d 936, 195 N.Y.S.2d 392 (1959), motion for leave to appeal denied, 10 A.D.2d 637, 197 N.Y.S.2d 441 (1960). The lower court opinion cites and discusses some two dozen cases.

71. Harbeck v. Pupin, 145 N.Y. 70, 39 N.E. 722 (1895); Willings v. Consequa, Fed.Cas.No.17,767 (D.Pa.1816).

72. Haney & Campbell Mfg. Co. v. Adaza Coop. Creamery Co., 108 Iowa 313, 79 N.W. 79 (1899); Goodnow v. Smith, 35 Mass. (18 Pick.) 414, 29 Am.Dec.

600 (1836); Greenwald v. Kaster, 86 Pa. 45 (1878); Restatement, Contracts §§ 121(2), 122.

73. Orr v. Read Phosphate Co., 215 Ala. 562, 112 So. 145 (1927); Harbeck v. Pupin, 123 N.Y. 115, 25 N.E. 311 (1890); Sprague v. Childs, 16 Ohio St. 107 (1865).

Model [formerly Uniform] Joint Obligations Act, §§ 4–5, in force in Hawaii, Maine, Nevada, N. Y., Utah, Wisconsin.

Miss.Code 1942, § 334. McKinney's N.Y. Debtor and Creditor Law, § 237, provides: "A release of a partner from a partnership liability shall release his co-partners from the same liability to the creditor giving the release, but after a partnership has been dissolved, by consent or otherwise, any partner may make a separate composition or compromise shall discharge from such liability the partner making it, and him only."

74. Williston, Contracts, § 334 (3rd ed. 1959). Corbin, Contracts, § 931 (1951).

75. Restatement, Contracts § 123.

76. Singer v. Ritter, 167 Pa.Super. 154, 74 A.2d 520 (1950), citing this text. Reclamation Co. v. Western Brokerage & Supply Co., 57 S.W.2d 274 (Tex.Civ. App.1933).

or more joint and several promisors, upon a joint promise, discharges the joint duty of the other joint promisors." [77] This rule of merger and res adjudicata applies to joint partnership obligations.[78]

But some courts have held that the rule does not apply to partners outside the jurisdiction,[79] following the rule of many courts as to joint obligations in general.[80] Such a result, non-merger, follows from joint debtor statutes applicable to partnerships.[81]

If the obligation is joint and several, a judgment against one partner on his several liability does not bar the enforcement of the several liability of the other partners.[82] This appears to be the common law rule and it has been incorporated into several statutes.[83] The judgment against one partner does not personally bind co-partners not party to the suit.[84] Therefore, a new action must be brought against them, but the prior judgment may be determinative of partnership liability.[85]

77. Restatement, Contracts § 119(1).

78. Blythe v. Cordingly, 20 Colo.App. 508, 80 P. 495 (1905); Fleming v. Ross, 225 Ill. 149, 80 N.E. 92, 8 Ann.Cas. 314 (1903); Ward v. Johnson, 13 Mass. 148 (1816); Candee & Scribner v. Clark & Brown, 2 Mich. 255, 256 (1851); Davison v. Harmon, 65 Minn. 402, 67 N.W. 1015 (1896); Ryckman v. Manerud, 68 Or. 350, 136 P. 826, Ann.Cas. 1915C, 522 (1913); McFarlane v. Kipp, 206 Pa. 317, 55 A. 986 (1903); Warren v. Rickles, 129 Wash. 443, 225 P. 422 (1924).

See Annot., Judgment for or against partner as res judicata in favor of or against copartner not a party to the judgment, 11 A.L.R.2d 847, 850 (1950).

But see McLelland v. Ridgeway, 12 Ala. 482 (1847).

79. Crehan v. Megargel, 234 N.Y. 67, 136 N.E. 296 (1922).

Draisner v. Liss Realty Co., 97 U.S.App. D.C. 77, 228 F.2d 48 (1955) (suggesting that the same rule would apply if the partner were within the jurisdiction but not a party to the suit).

Contra: Fleming v. Ross, 225 Ill. 149, 80 N.E. 92, 8 Ann.Cas. 314 (1903).

80. Field v. Layton & Layton, 16 Del. Ch. 135, 141 A. 818 (1928); Merriman v. Barker, 121 Ind. 74, 22 N.E. 992 (1889); Dennett v. Chick, 2 Greenl. 191, 11 Am.Dec. 59 (Me.1823); Olcott v. Little, 9 N.H. 259, 32 Am.Dec. 357 (1838).

81. Uniform Joint Obligations Act, § 2, see n. 64 above. See 13 Cornell L.Q.

640, as to effect of this statute on New York law. See Corbin, Contracts, § 929 (1951). Ill.Rev.Stat.1965, c. 110, § 27; M.G.L.A. (Mass.) c. 227 § 15 (1955). As to the Michigan statute, see Mason v. Eldred, 73 U.S. (6 Wall.) 231, 18 L. Ed. 783 (1867). McKinney's CPLR (N.Y.) § 1502. Other statutes are collected in note, 1 A.L.R. 1601, 1608 (1919).

See Williston, Contracts, § 336; Burdick, Joint and Several Liability of Partners, 11 Colum.L.Rev. 101 (1911).

82. Restatement, Contracts § 119(3). Ablon v. King, 279 S.W. 563 (Tex.Civ. App.1926).

See Annot., Judgment for or against partner as res judicata in favor of or against copartner not a party to the judgment, 11 A.L.R.2d 847, 856 (1950).

83. Model [formerly Uniform] Joint Obligations Act, § 2, see n. 73 above; 12 P.S. (Pa.) § 806 (1953).

84. Kittredge v. Langley, 252 N.Y. 405, 169 N.E. 626, 67 A.L.R. 1087 (1930), reargument denied 253 N.Y. 555, 171 N.E. 780 (1930). See Draisner v. Liss Realty Co., 97 U.S.App.D.C. 77, 228 F.2d 48 (1955).

85. Lamar-Rankin Drug Co. v. Copeland, 7 Ga.App. 567, 67 S.E. 703 (1910); International Shoe Co. v. Hawkinson, 73 N.D. 677, 18 N.W.2d 761 (1945).

The copartners may still show affirmative defenses (e. g. payment, accord and satisfaction) or that they were not members of the partnership.

If a claimant sues one partner and loses on the merits, it appears that he can later maintain an action against the other partners.[86]

(d) Survivorship

Unless the contract is of such a personal nature that the death of one partner renders it impossible of substantial performance,[87] the liability on a contract after death of a partner rests upon the survivors, and not upon the estate of the deceased partner, according to the common law.[88] Equity at an early time relieved against this rule, where the deceased obligor had shared in the benefit of the consideration for the obligation (as would be the case with partners) and the surviving co-obligors were insolvent.[89] Many states have by statute provided for a remedy against the estate of a deceased joint obligor.[90]

---

86. McLelland v. Ridgeway, 12 Ala. 482 (1847); Lindsay v. Gager, 11 App.Div. 93, 42 N.Y.S. 851 (1896). Contra: Taylor v. Sartorious, 130 Mo.App. 23, 108 S.W. 1089 (1908).

87. It has been held that a contract whereby a partnership employs an agent is terminated by death of a partner. Tasker v. Shepherd, 6 H. & N. 575, 158 Eng.Rep. 237 (1861); Griggs v. Swift, 82 Ga. 392, 9 S.E. 1062, 5 L. R.A. 405, 14 Am.St.Rep. 176 (1889); Shumate v. Sohon, 56 U.S.App.D.C. 290, 12 F.2d 825, 59 A.L.R. 291 (1926). Compare Phillips v. Hull Alhambra Palace Co., 1901, 1 Q.B. 59, 70 L.J. Q.B. 26 (contract by firm of theatre producers with group of performers); Hughes v. Gross, 166 Mass. 61, 43 N.E. 1031, 32 L.R.A. 620, 55 Am.St.Rep. 375 (1896) (business carried on by surviving partners); Fereira v. Sayres, 5 Watts & S. 210, 40 Am.Dec. 496 (Pa. 1843).

88. Grant v. Shurter, 1 Wend. 148 (N.Y. 1828); 2 Williston, Contracts, § 344 (3rd ed. 1959).

89. Doggett v. Dill, 108 Ill. 560, 48 Am. Rep. 565 (1884): "Doggett, in his lifetime, was individually liable for this debt, and if he had been sued, and a judgment obtained against him, any of his individual property would have been liable to be taken and sold in satisfaction of the debt. It is true, if he had been sued at law in his lifetime, it would have been necessary to join his partners as defendants in the action; but after judgment it was not necessary to exhaust the partnership assets before individual property could

be taken, but the creditor could resort to such property in the first instance, if he saw proper. Did the death of Doggett in any manner change the liability which existed on this contract before his death? We think not. The liability continued as before, but the remedy to enforce that liability was changed from a court of law to a court exercising equitable powers. Before his death the liability could only be enforced by a joint action against Doggett and his partners. After his death the liability continued, but could only be enforced in the probate court, which in the allowance of claims exercises equitable powers. The death of a debtor may extinguish a legal remedy on a joint contract; but we are not aware that it has ever been held that the death of a debtor could extinguish the debt or discharge the estate of the deceased."

90. Hawkes v. First Nat. Bank, 264 Mass. 545, 163 N.E. 249, 61 A.L.R. 1408 (1928): "The question whether a creditor must exhaust his remedies against the surviving partner before proceeding against the estate of a deceased partner, has never been discussed in our decisions. The rule in England seems to be settled that creditors of the firm may first sue the estate of the deceased partner, regardless of the question whether the surviving partner is solvent or bankrupt. . . . This appears to be the view of the Supreme Court of the United States. . . . There are other authorities to the same effect. . . . There are authorities to the contrary and there is some conflict among the decisions. . . . Since there is no

This remedy is generally available against a partner's estate without the necessity of seeking recovery from the surviving partners, or showing the futility of such procedure.[91] In New York, the deceased partner's estate cannot be held liable unless the survivors are insolvent.[92] The rule is followed in a few other states.[93]

limitation in G.L. c. 197, § 8, and since that section has been held applicable to partnerships, it must follow that in this commonwealth the firm creditor is not required first to sue the surviving partner, but may at his election sue first the estate of the deceased partner. . . . "

"On the death of a joint obligor in contract, his executor or administrator shall be bound as such jointly with the surviving obligor or obligors." Model [formerly Uniform] Joint Obligations Act, § 6, see n. 73 above.

2 Williston, Contracts § 344A (3rd ed. 1959) cites statutes in 30 jurisdictions providing some sort of survival of joint obligations in general.

91. Nelson v. Hill, 46 U.S. (5 How.) 127, 133, 12 L.Ed. 81, 84 (1847); Camp v. Grant, 21 Conn. 41, 54 Am.Dec. 321 (1851); Union Trust Co. v. Shoemaker, 258 Ill. 564, 101 N.E. 1050 (1913); Hawkes v. First Nat. Bank, n. 90 above; Blair v. Wood, 108 Pa. 278 (1885) (see 59 P.S. (Pa.) § 151 (1930)); In re Bloomer's Estate, 2 Wis.2d 623, 87 N.W.2d 531 (1958); Devaynes v. Noble, 1 Merriv. 529, 566–70, 35 Eng. Rep. 767, 779, 780 (Ch. 1816). Cases are collected, Annot., 61 A.L.R. 1410 (1929).

See 20 P.S. (Pa.) § 320.603 providing that representatives may be sued either alone or jointly with surviving joint obligors for decedent's obligations. It is not mandatory that the representative of a deceased partner be joined. The creditor may still proceed against the surviving partner alone, Lipschutz v. Lipschutz, 124 Pa.Super. 380, 188 A. 556 (1936).

92. Seligman v. Friedlander, 199 N.Y. 373, 92 N.E. 1047 (1910): "At common law the liability of copartners was joint, although it was several in equity. The fundamental principle upon which the partnership relation is founded is that of a joint adventure, with joint ownership of assets and only joint liability for debts, unless

the property held jointly is insufficient to pay the firm debts, or it appears that there can be no effective remedy without resort to individual property. [Citations omitted]. Hence for time out of mind the representatives of a deceased partner could not be sued at law unless the surviving partners were insolvent, or some other special reason of an equitable nature existed. The theory of the law was that the joint liabilities should be paid from the joint property if possible, and not until that remedy was exhausted, or resort thereto shown to be useless could payment from the individual property be exacted. . . . No reason is apparent for leaving all the assets in the possession of the survivors upon the death of one of the partners and yet making the representatives of the latter liable in the first instance without touching the partnership assets."

This result is not altered by the Uniform Joint Obligations Act as passed in New York, for it adds that "nothing in this article shall be construed as repealing any of the provisions . . . of the partnership law." McKinney's N.Y. Debtor and Creditor Law, § 240. Friedman v. Gettner, 6 A.D.2d 647, 180 N.Y.S.2d 446 (1958), aff'd. 7 N.Y.2d 764, 194 N.Y.S.2d 35, 163 N.E.2d 141 (1959).

See Burdick, Joint and Several Liability of Partners, 11 Colum.L.Rev. 101 (1911).

93. Sale v. Dishman's Ex'rs, 30 Va. (3 Leigh) 548 (Va.1832); Marr's Ex'x v. Southwick, 2 Port. 351 (Ala.1835); De Monco v. Means, 47 Colo. 457, 107 P. 1107 (1910); Robert Morton Organ Co. v. Armour, 173 Wash. 462, 23 P.2d 887, 27 P.2d 1119 (1933). See Horsey v. Heath, 5 Ohio 353 (1832).

See Restatement, Contracts § 125: "Survivorship of Joint Duties. On the death of a joint promisor in a contract when one or more of the joint promisors are still surviving, the estate of the deceased promisor is not bound by the joint promise unless all of the

By statute in almost all states, the individual property of a deceased partner is liable for partnership obligations incurred while he was a partner.[94]

(e) Execution on Judgment Against Partners

The generally prevailing common law rule is that the partnership creditor having obtained a judgment may at his option proceed against joint or separate property or both simultaneously in his efforts to collect by means of execution.[94A] In some states the judgment creditor is not permitted to proceed against separate property until he has exhausted his remedies against partnership property, or shown that such remedies are non-existent.[95]

ENFORCEMENT OF PARTNERSHIP OBLIGATIONS—SUITS AGAINST PARTNERS WITH SERVICE ON LESS THAN ALL, AT COMMON LAW AND UNDER JOINT DEBTOR ACTS

§ 59. In some states at common law, in others under joint debtor acts, the partnership creditor can bring suit against the partners with service on less than all and obtain a judgment collectible out of partnership property and the property of the partners subject to the personal jurisdiction of the court by service or appearance.

Normally, the proper parties defendant in an action on a partnership contract are all the partners.[96] This follows from the view that it is a joint obligation,[97] unless expressly entered into as a joint and several obligation, or made joint and several by statute. The judgment obtained by the plaintiff in an action on a joint obligation is ordinarily against the parties originally jointly bound. But if the court has no jurisdiction over one of the defendants, judgment cannot be given against him, but can be given against the others.[98]

surviving joint promisors are insolvent; nor in that event if the deceased promisor was a surety."

94. U.P.A. § 36(4), discussed below, Sec. 79(d). See Note, Partnerships, Claims of Creditor on Death of Partner, 11 Okla.L.Rev. 229 (1958). However, separate creditors have priority by § 36(4) over partnership creditors in the deceased's separate assets.

94A. See Richardson, Creditors' Rights and the Partnership, 40 Ky.L.J. 243, 254–60 (1951) and references there.

95. Seligman v. Friedlander, 199 N.Y. 373, 92 N.E. 1047 (1910). May v. McGowan, 194 F.2d 396 (2d Cir. 1952) (N. Y. law). See Sec. 60 below on suits under Common Name Statutes.

The separate property of a partner can be attached in an action to collect a claim against a non-resident partnership. Gomez v. Vazquez, 177 Misc. 874, 32 N.Y.S.2d 34 (1941).

In some states, a creditor with a judgment against the partners (but not against the firm) can levy execution against partnership property, at least if the judgment grows out of a partnership debt. Palkovitz v. Second Federal Sav. and Loan Ass'n, 412 Pa. 547, 195 A.2d 347 (1963).

96. See Sec. 58(a) above.

97. See Sec. 58 above.

98. "In an action on a joint promise the judgment must be for or against all the defendants who were originally bound unless judgment against one or more of the defendants is precluded by

"(a) Death

"(b) Lack of jurisdiction

In some jurisdictions, the plaintiff who has been able to serve less than all of the partner-defendants can obtain judgment against all of them, including those not subject to the jurisdiction of the court, the judgment being enforceable against the joint property and that of the partners served.[99]

The courts have apparently reached this result on the ground that the partners are vested with a power to apply firm property to payment of partnership debts, that each partner is under a duty to creditors so to deal with the property, and a court having jurisdiction of one partner can, through him, reach and apply the partnership property to the purpose to which the partners have devoted it by agreement, a sort of specific performance of the partnership contract. "For the separate debt of a partner, I admit, only his separate estate can be sold. . . . But for a partnership debt, the entire property in the specific thing must be sold, even on a judgment against one of the partners; because through the medium of the execution, the law compels him to make the same application of the joint funds to the joint debts, that it was undoubtedly competent for him to make voluntarily."[1] It has, moreover, prior to the U.P.A. been held in Pennsylvania that a partner can confess a judgment good against firm property, but not against the property of the other partners who have not given him authority.[2] "If a partner can bind the partnership by confessing a judgment against the firm why may not the firm be equally bound if the judgment is obtained by adverse process and not by confession? . . . We think it is clear on both reason and authority that service upon one or more members of a partnership in a suit instituted against the firm is a good service for the purpose of affecting the partnership with notice and in the event of recovery of binding the partnership property."[3]

"(c) Contractual incapacity

"(d) A discharge in bankruptcy

"(e) A discharge or barring of the claim by the Statute of Limitations.

"In any of these cases judgment may be given for or against the others." Restatement, Contracts § 118.

See Sec. 58(c) above concerning res judicata, merger, and collateral estoppel as to partners not served.

99. Johnston v. Mathews, 32 Md. 363 (1870), semble; Powers v. Braley, 41 Mo.App. 556 (1890); Winters v. Means, 25 Neb. 241, 41 N.W. 157, 13 Am.St. Rep. 489 (1888); Dwiggins v. Parkway Bus Co., Inc., 230 N.C. 234, 52 S.E.2d 892 (1949) (tort); Walsh v. Kirby, 228 Pa. 194, 77 A. 452, 20 Ann.Cas. 1237 (1910).

1. Taylor & Fitzsimmons v. Henderson, 17 Serg. & R. 453 (Pa.1828).

2. Harper v. Fox, 7 Watts & S. 142 (Pa. 1844): "A judgment may be recovered against a less number than all the members, if there be not a plea in abatement; and the effects of the partnership may consequently be seized in execution of it. What matters it, then, whether the judgment has been obtained adversely or by confession if it be against the firm."

But see U.P.A. § 9(3), followed in Fairman Bros. to Use of First Nat. Bank v. Ogden Gas Co., 106 Pa.Super. 130, 161 A. 634 (1932).

3. Walsh v. Kirby, 228 Pa. 194, 77 A. 452, 20 Ann.Cas. 1237 (1910), an action of trespass.

Statutes have been enacted in several states known as joint debtor acts. The first was in New York in 1788,[4] and, as subsequently amended, has served as a model in other states. The form in which it has been most widely imitated[5] is as follows: "Where the action is against two or more defendants and the summons is served on one or more of them but not on all of them, the plaintiff may proceed as follows: 1. If the action be against the defendants jointly indebted upon contract, he may proceed against the defendant served, unless the court otherwise direct; and if he recover judgment it may be entered against all the defendants thus jointly indebted, so far only as that it may be enforced against the joint property of all and the separate property of the defendants served. . . ."[6] Such a statute applies only to contract claims, and not to tort liabilities.[7] In some other states, similar statutes apply to all partnership obligations.[8]

Pennsylvania R.Civ.P. 2131(a), Pa.Stat. Ann. tit. 12 Appx., carries this practice somewhat further by providing as follows, "Service of process upon a partner or a registered agent of a partnership, or upon the manager, clerk or other person for the time being in charge of any regular place of business of a partnership shall be deemed service upon the partnership and upon each partner individually named in the action, provided the person served is not a plaintiff in the action." See Darby v. Philadelphia Transp. Co., 73 F.Supp. 522 (E.D.Pa.1947). It is further provided in Rule 2132(c), "No judgment shall be entered against a partner individually named in the action, who has not been personally served or who has not appeared as a party or as a witness in the action until the plaintiff has given such partner such notice of the pendency of the action as the court by general rule or special order shall direct." The judgment entered in an action against a partnership sued in the names of the partners supports execution against partnership property and property of a partner named as defendant if jurisdiction has been obtained as above provided. Rule 2132(b).

4. N.Y.Laws 1788, chapter 46, § 23.

5. See, e. g. West's Ann.Calif. Code Civ. Proc. § 414; G.S. (N.C.) § 1–113 (1953); R.C. Ohio § 2703.25 (1954). The Ohio provision has been applied to partners, James Talcott, Inc. v. Burke, 145 F. Supp. 389 (N.D. Ohio 1956).

6. N.Y.Laws 1866, chapter 824, § 5. See McKinney's (N.Y.) CPLR §§ 1501–1502.

Under such a statute it is improper to enter judgment against less than all the partners joined as co-defendants. Heaton v. Schaeffer, 34 Okl. 631, 126 P. 797, 43 L.R.A.,N.S., 540 (1912): "The common law doctrine as to joint obligations survives in this state, except so far as it has been modified by § 5619, Comp.Laws 1909, [12 Okl.St. Ann. § 178] quoted above. That section enables a creditor to obtain judgment against joint obligors by service against only one, so far as the judgment affects joint property, thus changing the rule at common law that all the joint obligors must be summoned (4 Minor's Inst. 650; 1 Tidd Pr. 420), but prevents judgment from being enforced against the individual property of the obligors not served. The statute does not permit an individual judgment to be rendered in a suit against the partnership. The theory is that, the debt being a joint one, the judgment must be joint."

7. Kittredge v. Grannis, 244 N.Y. 182, 155 N.E. 93 (1926); Kittredge v. Langley, 252 N.Y. 405, 169 N.E. 626, 67 A. L.R. 1087 (1930).

As to waiver of tort and claim in quasi contract, see Notes 36 Yale L.J. 1179 (1927), 26 Colum.L.Rev. 771 (1926).

In its present form the New York statute is applicable to tort as well as contract claims. Comment, Service of Summons on Co-partnership, 15 St. John's Law Rev. 131 (1940).

8. Uniform Joint Oblig. Act § 1 defines obligation to include tort liability for purposes of the Act.

The property of the partner not served cannot be reached by execution on the judgment, as the judgment is not against him personally,[9] but the property of the partner served can be reached.[10] To obtain a judgment collectible from the partnership property, it is necessary to name all the partners as defendants; [11] and in some states, it must appear from process and pleading that they are sued as partners.[12]

Such procedure might raise constitutional questions if it purported to permit a personal judgment against a non-resident defendant, not personally served or appearing in the proceeding.[13] It could probably be justified on the ground that the partner served is the agent of the absent partner for carrying on a business within the jurisdiction, and has been thereby authorized to receive service.[14] An action based on service on the resident agent of a non-resident partnership has been sustained.[15] The proceeding is clearly one in personam, rather than in

9. Griffin v. Langley, 40 S.W.2d 1100 (Tex.Civ.App.1931); Hirsch v. Samulan, 93 Pa.Super. 49 (1927).

10. Heaton v. Schaeffer, 34 Okl. 631, 126 P. 797, 43 L.R.A.,N.S., 540 (1912); Walsh v. Kirby, 228 Pa. 194, 77 A. 452, 20 Ann.Cas. 1237 (1910); Amarillo-Panhandle Development Corp. v. Ellis, 10 S.W.2d 733 (Tex.Civ.App.1928) (no judgment can be rendered against partnership as a whole, without judgment against the partner served); Yakima Sash & Box Co. v. Kopp, 140 Wash. 420, 249 P. 786 (1926).

11. Fenner, Beane & Ungerleider v. Donosky, 62 S.W.2d 269 (Tex.Civ.App. 1933).

12. To obtain a judgment good against partnership property, the partners must be sued as co-partners. Speight v. Horne, 101 Fla. 101, 133 So. 574 (1931).

13. See the fuller discussion of constitutional and jurisdictional issues in Sec. 62 below.

In Neustadter v. United Exposition Service Co., 14 N.J.Super. 484, 82 A.2d 476 (1951), a partner excluded from the partnership by reason of nonpayment of an assessment, of which he had insufficient notice, sought an injunction in an action in which, under Rule 3:4–4, service was made on less than all of the partners. Held: the relief sought was against the partners jointly, and not against a partnership entity, and the partners not served were not subject to the decree granted.

14. Davidson v. Henry L. Doherty & Co., 214 Iowa 739, 241 N.W. 700, 91 A. L.R. 1308 (1932); Goodman v. Henry L. Doherty & Co., 218 Iowa 529, 255 N.W. 667 (1934), aff'd 294 U.S. 623, 55 S.Ct. 553, 79 L.Ed. 1097 (1935), under a statute providing for jurisdiction by service on an agent of a non-resident defendant, who was carrying on business in the state.

See Prashker, Service of Summons on Non-Resident Natural Persons Doing Business in New York, 15 St. John's L. Rev. 1 (1940); Notes, 46 Harv.L.Rev. 153 (1932); 48 Harv.L.Rev. 1433 (1935); 33 Mich.L.Rev. 963 (1935); 83 U.Pa.L.Rev. 921 (1935); 13 Miss.L.J. 559 (1941), commenting on Miss.Laws of 1940, ch. 246, constituting the doing of business by a non-resident person or partnership in the state an appointment of the secretary of state as agent on whom process may be served.

Compare Flexner v. Farson, 248 U.S. 289, 39 S.Ct. 97, 63 L.Ed. 250 (1919).

15. Stoner v. Higginson, 316 Pa. 481, 175 A. 527 (1934), noted 83 U.Pa.L.Rev. 683, 2 U.Pitt.L.Rev. 115. The action was against the partners rather than against the firm as an entity. Service was under a statute authorizing it upon the clerk or agent of non-residents engaged in business in the state, now 12 P.S. (Pa.) §§ 296, 297.

In New York service on the resident agent of a partnership formed in another state, all of whose members are non-residents of New York, has been held to give personal jurisdiction of

rem, lacking any attachment of property at the outset.[16]

It has been suggested that the joint debtor statute involves a recognition of the partnership as a legal entity.[17] The decisions do not support such a view, except possibly in Oklahoma.[18] In other states, the courts applying the Joint Debtor Acts have said that the partnership is not an entity,[19] although the opinions often distinguish between suits and judgment against the partnership and against the partners.[20]

The most acceptable explanation of the statutory procedure appears to be that jurisdiction over a partner gives the court the power to compel him to apply partnership property to the partnership purpose of paying debts,[21] and that the other partners are joined as parties to the suit and to the judgment merely to satisfy the common law rule as to suits on joint obligations and the rule that the execution should follow the judgment. The constitutionality of such a procedure might well be objected to in cases of joint debtors not partners, and no case is found in which it has been so employed.[22]

Apart from the joint debtor acts, some states have changed the common law rules by statutes declaring that joint obligations shall be joint and several[23] or making joint obligors suable separately.[24]

the partners under Civil Practice Act, § 229–b. (See McKinney's CPLR §§ 301, 302(1)). Melvin Pine & Co. v. McConnell, 298 N.Y. 27, 80 N.E.2d 137 (1948), affirming 64 N.Y.S.2d 814, and 273 App.Div. 218, 76 N.Y.S.2d 279, 10 A.L.R.2d 194.

See Sec. 62 below for jurisdiction over a partnership by service on an agent.

16. Warren, Corporate Advantages without Incorporation 240 (1929); Magruder & Foster, Jurisdiction over Partnerships, 37 Harv.Law Rev. 793, 807 (1924).

But see Hoffman v. Wight, 1 App.Div. 514, 37 N.Y.S. 262 (1896).

17. Magruder & Foster, op. cit. 804. Compare Warren, op. cit. 240.

18. Heaton v. Schaeffer, 34 Okl. 631, 126 P. 797, 43 L.R.A.,N.S., 540 (1912); W. B. Johnston Grain Co. v. Self, 344 P.2d 653 (Okl.1959).

A somewhat similar statute, expressly authorizing judgment against the partnership and the partners served (now Vernon's Ann.Civ.Stat. (Tex.) art. 2223), recognizes the partnership as an entity. Sugg v. Thornton, 132 U.S. 524, 10 S.Ct. 163, 33 L.Ed. 447 (1889).

19. State ex rel. Palmer v. Gray, 92 Fla. 1123, 111 So. 242 (1927); Feldman v. Seay, 291 S.W. 350 (Tex.Civ.App.

1927); Parker Motor Co. v. Hamilton, 9 S.W.2d 426 (Tex.Civ.App.1928); Beaver Board Cos. v. Imbrie, 47 F.2d 271 (S.D.N.Y.1922).

20. See Oklahoma cases cited in n. 18; Amarillo-Panhandle Development Corporation v. Ellis, 10 S.W.2d 733 (Tex. Civ.App.1928); State ex rel. Palmer v. Gray, 92 Fla. 1123, 111 So. 242 (1927), distinguishing between suing "A and B partners" and "A and B as partners."

21. Brooks & Ellis v. McIntyre, 4 Mich. 316 (1856), discussing the English process of outlawry, for which the act is a substitute; Oakley v. Aspinwall, 4 N.Y. 513 (1851). As to outlawry, see 9 Holdsworth, History of English Law, 254.

Constitutionality of the statute was approved in Sugg v. Thornton, 132 U.S. 524, 10 S.Ct. 163, 33 L.Ed. 447 (1889), in which the court characterized the judgment as one "treating the partnership as a distinct legal entity." See also Thomas v. Nathan, 65 Fla. 386, 62 So. 206 (1913).

22. A California decision holding the process unconstitutional stands alone. Tay, Brooks & Backus v. Hawley, 39 Calif. 93 (1870).

23. E. g., Ill.Rev.Stat.1967, c. 76, § 3; M.S.A. (Minn.) § 548.20 (1947); V.A.M.

24. See note 24 on page 347.

ENFORCEMENT OF PARTNERSHIP OBLIGATIONS— COMMON NAME STATUTES

§ 60. **In the absence of an enabling statute, it is improper to sue partners in the partnership name. Many states have statutes permitting suit on a partnership obligation against the partnership in the partnership name, resulting in a judgment collectible out of partnership property, and out of the separate property of the partners served or personally appearing in the action.**

A partnership is not enough of a legal person at common law as to be a party to court proceedings.[25] If it is sued in the partnership name, the error in procedure can be objected to, and if seasonable objection is made, the action can be dismissed.[26] In many cases, the defect has been treated as merely formal, and if objection is not made at the outset of the proceeding, it is considered as waived, and a judgment collectible out of partnership property may result.[27]

In many states, statutes have been enacted permitting suit against the partnership in the partnership name. A typical statute is that of California. "When two or more persons, associated in any business, transact such business under a common name, whether it comprise the names of such persons or not, the associates may be sued by such common name, the summons in such cases being served on one or more of the associates; and the judgment in the action shall bind the joint property of all the associates and the individual property of the party or parties served with process in the same manner as if all had been named defendants, and had been sued upon their joint li-

S. (Mo.) § 431.110. The Missouri provision appears inapplicable to partnership because of the subsequent enactment of U.P.A. § 15 specifying joint liability for partnership contracts; see Comment, 15 Mo.L.Rev. 176 (1950).

24. E. g., I.C.A. (Iowa) § 613.1; G.S. 1949 (Kan.) 16–104; N.J.S.A. 2A:55–1; Vernon's Ann.Civ.St. (Tex.) art. 1986. A tabulation of statutory changes in joint obligations for each state appears in 2 Williston, Contracts § 336A (3rd ed. 1959).

25. X–L Liquors, Inc. v. Taylor, 17 N.J. 444, 111 A.2d 753 (1955). See Sec. 3 above.

26. I. Epstein & Bro. v. First Nat. Bank, 92 Fla. 796, 110 So. 354 (1926); Werner v. W. H. Shons Co., 341 Ill. 478, 173 N.E. 486 (1930) (referring to a statute, later omitted, permitting jurisdiction over nonresident partnership by action

in the firm name; see Comment, Service on Partnerships in Illinois, 42 Ill. Law Rev. 72 (1947)); Thompson v. Corn, 102 Ind.App. 6, 200 N.E. 737 (1936); Calumet & Hecla Mining Co. v. Equitable Trust Co., 186 App.Div. 328, 174 N.Y.S. 317 (1919); Dunham v. Shindler, 17 Or. 256, 20 P. 326 (1889); Sturges, Unincorporated Associations as Parties to Actions, 33 Yale L.J. 383 (1924); Dodd, Dogma and Practice in the Law of Associations, 42 Harv.Law Rev. 977 (1929).

27. Seitz v. Buffum & Co., 14 Pa. 69 (1850); Tonge v. Item Publishing Co., 244 Pa. 417, 91 A. 229 (1914); Shelansky v. A. Weinfeld & Son, 82 Pa.Super. 180 (1923); Meyer v. Wilson, 166 Ind. 651, 76 N.E. 748 (1906). See Ord v. Neiswanger, 81 Kan. 63, 105 P. 17, 29 L.R.A.,N.S., 287 (1909). But see Lewis v. West Side Trust & Sav. Bank, 377 Ill. 384, 36 N.E.2d 573 (1941), noted 42 Ill.Law Rev. 72, 73 (1947).

ability." [28]   Other states have statutes varying in some details.[29] It is generally agreed that under these statutes, the right to sue the partnership in the firm name is permissive, not mandatory.[30]   The statutes do not constitute the partnership a legal person, but permit it to be treated as such for this procedural purpose.[31]   The object of their

28.   West's Ann.Cal.Code Civ.Proc. § 388. See collection of statutes and decisions in Warren, Corporate Advantages without Incorporation 152–233 (1929).

New York by adopting § 222a of the Civil Practice Act, N.Y.Laws 1945, c. 842 (now McKinney's CPLR § 1025 (1963)), provided that partners might sue or be sued in the partnership name.   This statute is noted in 20 St. John's Law Rev. 109 (1946).

29.   Colo., Conn., Ga., Iowa, Mich., Neb., N.M., N.Y., Ohio, Tex., Wyo., Vt. provisions cited in Sec. 57 above, n. 28.

Ala.Code 1940, Tit. 7, § 141; R.L.H.1955 (Haw.) § 230–10; I.C. (Idaho) § 5–323 (1948); Ill.Rev.St.1967, c. 110, § 27.1 (1); LSA–C.C.P. (La.) art. 737; M.S.A. (Minn.) § 540.15; R.C.M.1947 (Mont.) § 93–2827; N.R.S. (Nev.) 12.110; Pa. R.Civ.P. 2128(a) (1951); Utah R.Civ.P. 17(d) (1953); W.S.A. (Wis.) 301.07 (only when members are unknown). In addition, some fictitious name statutes (see Sec. 22 above) make noncomplying partnerships suable in the firm name.

Cf. F.S.A. (Fla.) § 47.15 (1943): "When . . . process is sued out against several persons composing a mercantile or other firm, the service . . . on any one member . . . shall be valid as if served upon each . . .; and the plaintiff may, after service upon any one member . . . proceed to judgment and execution against them all." Although not purporting to permit suits in the firm name, this does allow judgment binding on partnership property, Florida Brewing Co. v. Sendoya, 73 Fla. 660, 74 So. 799 (1917). Although purporting to permit judgment and execution against partners not served, it does not do so. Ibid., First Nat. Bank v. Greig, 43 Fla. 412, 31 So. 239 (1901). There is a similar provision for limited partnerships. F.S.A. (Fla.) § 620.30.

"Long arm" statutes authorizing service of process on a state official against an out of state individual or business

may be written to permit suits against partnerships in the firm name.   See generally Sec. 62 below.

In England, suits by and against firms in the firm name are permitted by court order. Lindley, Partnership 301–03, 879–81 (12th ed. 1962).

30.   Peabody v. Oleson, 15 Colo.App. 346, 62 P. 234 (1900); Hotchkiss v. Di Vita, 103 Conn. 436, 130 A. 668 (1925); Gardiner v. Eclipse Grocery Co., 72 Mont. 540, 234 P. 490 (1925); Hamner v. B. K. Bloch & Co., 16 Utah 436, 52 P. 770, 67 Am.St.Rep. 643 (1898).

But in Louisiana a commercial partnership is an entity which must be sued or sue in the firm name, though the partners can be joined as co-defendants in a proceeding against the firm. Empire Rice Mill Co., Ltd. v. K. & E. Neumond, 199 F. 800 (D.La.1912).

In Hamsmith v. Espy, 13 Iowa 439 (1862), an action was brought against "Thomas S. Espy, Charles Baker and John Robinson, doing business as partners, in the name and style of Espy, Barker & Robinson." On judgment for the plaintiff he was allowed to levy execution on the individual property of Espy. The court said: "Our Code changes the common law, in providing that a partnership may be sued in its firm name. If thus sued, a scire facias is necessary in order to reach individual property. If, however, a plaintiff follows, as he may, the common law requirement, of giving the individual names, and thus serving and suing all, he may take the property of either partner in satisfaction of his writ." But see Bankers Trust Co. v. Knee, 263 N.W. 549 (Iowa 1935).

31.   Artana v. San Jose Scavenger Co., 181 Cal. 627, 185 P. 850 (1919); Rudnick v. Delfino, 140 Cal.App.2d 260, 294 P.2d 983 (1956); Ungerleider v. Ewers, 20 Ohio App. 79, 153 N.E. 191 (1925). But see Gale v. Townsend, 45 Minn. 357, 47 N.W. 1064 (1891), under a statute permitting "associates" to be sued by common name.

enactment is to serve the convenience of persons having claims against associations who might find it difficult or impossible to ascertain the names of all of the associates. In their operation, however, such statutes have a tendency to cause the courts to consider partnerships and other associations within their scope as entities.[32]

Several of the statutes or rules specify [33] or imply [34] that the partnership may be sued with or without the partners as parties. Many of them provide that service may be made on one or more partners [35] and that the judgment binds partnership property [36] as

Proceeding against the partnership in the partnership name does not prevent the running of the statute of limitations in favor of a partner. John Bollman Co. v. S. Bachman & Co., 16 Cal.App. 589, 117 P. 690, 122 P. 835 (1911). Porter v. Hardin, 164 F.2d 401 (5th Cir. 1947).

For the complications in a non-U.P.A. state with a common name statute but so little entity theory that an individual partner's creditor may levy on partnership property, see Hutchison, Enforceability of Iowa Creditors' Judgments Against Partnership and Partners' Assets, 44 Iowa L.Rev. 643 (1959).

The death of a partner pending the proceeding against the partnership does not make a revivor necessary. Comer & Trapp v. Reid, 93 Ala. 391, 9 So. 620 (1891).

The Pennsylvania Rule of Civil Procedure 2128(c), dealing with actions against the liquidator of a dissolved partnership, has been construed like the rules for actions in the firm name, as permitting judgment enforcible only against firm property. Billow v. Billow, 360 Pa. 343, 347, 61 A.2d 817, 819 (1948).

Judgment cannot be entered against the partnership when the partners are the defendants sued, Ferry v. North Pacific Stages, 112 Cal.App. 348, 296 P. 679 (1931); Good v. Red River Valley Co., 12 N.M. 245, 78 P. 46 (1904).

32. An action was brought against a defendant described as a corporation. After the statute of limitations had run, an amendment was allowed, describing defendant as a partnership, sued in the common name. This was not a change of parties, as "the defendant newly named **under the** amendment was merely the partnership *entity*." As with a corporation,

judgment could be enforced only against the property of the entity sued. Gozdonovic v. Pleasant Hills Realty Co., 357 Pa. 23, 53 A.2d 73 (1947).

The opinion in Darby v. Philadelphia Transp. Co., 73 F.Supp. 522 (E.D.Pa. 1947), states that the jural entity of the partnership is recognized in the Pennsylvania Rules of Civil Procedure, which permit action against the partnership in the firm name. It was held that there was proper venue in the district where the firm had its principal place of business.

33. Iowa, Neb., Ohio, above n. 29.

34. Ill., Mich., N.M., Pa., above n. 29.

35. Ala., Calif., Fla., Ga. (if returned non est inventus as to other partners), Haw., Idaho, Minn., Mont., Nev., N.M., Vt., above n. 29.

Iowa R.Civ.P. 56(f) (Supp.1966); Minn. R.Civ.P. in D.Ct., 4.03(b) (1958); McKinney's CPLR (N.Y.) § 310 (1963); R.C. (Ohio) § 2703.08 (1954); Pa.R.Civ. P. 2131 (1951); Vernon's Ann.Civ. Stat. (Tex.) art. 2033.

Where suit can be brought in federal court against a partnership in the firm name, service can be made on any managing or general agent, Fed. Rules Civ.Proc. rule 4(d) (3), 28 U.S. C.A.; this term includes a partner, Porter v. Hardin, 164 F.2d 401 (5th Cir. 1947).

Appearance by a partner is equivalent to service upon him, Hardy & Newsome, Inc. v. Whedbee, 244 N.C. 682, 94 S.E.2d 837 (1956). This, of course, is true of defendants generally, e. g., McKinney's CPLR (N.Y.) § 320(b) (1963).

36. Ala., Colo., Fla., Ga., Haw., Ida., Iowa, Minn., Mont., Neb., Nev., N.M., Utah, Vt., above n. 29; Calif., above n. 28. Pa.R.Civ.P. 2132(a).

well as the individual property of partners served.[37]

Common name statutes allowing service on less than all partners and individual judgment against those served,[38] effectively produce joint and several liability. Accordingly, they should permit subsequent actions against partners not parties to the initial suit.[39] Some statutes so specify[40] and a few go to the point of making the second action essentially a suit on the first judgment.[41] Indeed, it is arguable that this last result should follow from U.P.A. § 15 which makes partners liable for partnership debts.[42] The reason is that partnership liability was determined in the first suit; the partner participating in it had adequate representative capacity for the partnership to be bound. If so, all that is left for the second suit are such questions

---

37. Fla., Ga., Haw., Iowa, N.M., above n. 29; Calif., above n. 28. Pa.R.Civ. P. 2132(b), (c) (provided partner has been named as a defendant); Vernon's Ann.Civ.St. (Tex.) art. 2223.

In some instances, it is erroneous to give judgment against a non-served partner. Hamner v. B. K. Bloch & Co., 16 Utah 436, 52 P. 770, 67 Am. St.Rep. 643 (1898); Baldridge v. Eason, 99 Ala. 516, 13 So. 74 (1893); Lansing v. Bever Land Co., 158 Iowa 693, 138 N.W. 833 (1912); Ford Motor Co. v. Sylte, 188 Minn. 578, 248 N.W. 55 (1933).

In others, it is necessary to give judgment against all partners, but it is ineffective as to the individual property of non-served partners, Spencer Kellogg & Sons, Inc. v. Bush, 31 Misc. 2d 70, 219 N.Y.S.2d 453 (Sup.Ct.1961). To this extent, a court may acquire jurisdiction even though one of the partners is a nonresident and not served, Eastex Poultry v. Benefield, 268 S.W.2d 270 (Tex.Civ.App.1954); see Sec. 59 above at n. 22.

On the constitutional question of jurisdiction over unserved partners, see Sec. 62 below.

The individual liability of a partner can be determined in the state of his residence, even though no other partner resides there and no partnership business was done there, Fidelity and Cas. Co. of New York v. Homan, 116 So. 2d 444 (Fla.App.1959). See, concerning many of the matters discussed in this Section, Annot., Right to judgment, levy or lien against individual in action under statute permitting persons associated in a business under a common name to be sued in that name, 100 A.L.R. 997 (1936).

38. Nn. 28, 29 above.

39. Sec. 58 nn. 82–83 above; Annot., Judgment for or against partner as res judicata in favor of or against copartner not a party to the judgment, 11 A.L.R.2d 847, 857–59 (1950).

40. Ill.Rev.Stat.1967, c. 110, § 27.1(2); Iowa R.Civ.P. 4 (1951); R.R.S.1943 (Neb.), § 25–316; N.M.1953 Comp. § 21–6–5; NDCC (N.D.) 32–30–01 (1960); Ohio R.C. § 2325.21 (1954); Pa.R.Civ. P. 2134 (1951).

41. Neb. (if partnership property insufficient), N.D., Ohio, n. 40 above; Leach v. Milburn Wagon Co., 14 Neb. 106, 15 N.W. 232 (1883); International Shoe Co. v. Hawkinson, 73 N.D. 677, 18 N.W.2d 761 (1945); Hall v. Oldfield Tire & Rubber Co., 117 Ohio St. 247, 158 N.E. 191 (1927).

The same result can be reached under statutes, applicable to joint debtors generally, which permit a party to be brought in after judgment, Waterman v. Lipman, 67 Cal. 26, 6 P. 875 (1885); Sherburne v. Hyde, 185 Ill. 580, 57 N.E. 776 (1900); Magrini v. Jackson, 17 Ill.App.2d 346, 150 N.E.2d 387 (1958); Daniel v. Bethell, 167 N.C. 218, 83 S.E. 307 (1914).

However, some of the partnership statutes explicitly contemplate that the whole issue be relitigated, Iowa ("A new action . . . on the original cause of action"), Pa. ("subsequent action on same cause of action"), n. 40 above, and others have been interpreted this way, Lewinson v. First Nat. Bank, 11 N.M. 510, 70 P. 567 (1902).

42. Sec. 58 n. 47 above.

as whether the later defendant was a partner or has personal defenses.[43]

Common name statutes do not operate, like incorporation, to make the partnership a citizen of the state where organized regardless of the citizenship of the partners, for the purpose of diversity jurisdiction of federal courts.[44]

ENFORCEMENT OF PARTNERSHIP OBLIGATIONS—EXTRATERRITORIAL EFFECT OF JUDGMENTS OBTAINED UNDER COMMON NAME STATUTES

§ 61. A judgment obtained against the partnership sued under a common name can be given extraterritorial effect by suit thereon in another state, but no greater effect than in the state where rendered.

One who has obtained a judgment is entitled to have that judgment given full faith and credit in another state, under the Federal Constitution.[45] To be entitled to such effect in personam, it must be a judgment based on personal jurisdiction. A court does not obtain jurisdiction over a partnership, so as to render a judgment against it in the partnership name entitled to extraterritorial enforcement, merely by reason of service on a partner temporarily in the state wherein the partnership does not carry on business.[46] If the partnership is carrying on business in the state, a judgment against it can be obtained,[47] jurisdiction being based on personal service of a partner. This judgment is entitled to some extraterritorial recognition.[48] In the case of East Denver Municipal Irrigation District v. Doherty,[49] actions

---

43. Contra, Detrio v. U. S., 264 F.2d 658 (5th Cir. 1959) (N.Y. and Fla. law, with overtones of due process: for personal liability a partner "must have an opportunity to contest the claim on its merits"); Ratchford v. Covington County Stock Co., 172 Ala. 461, 55 So. 806 (1911) (must be sued on original obligation). Compare Sec. 59 above at nn. 13–14.

44. Empire Rice Mill Co. v. K. & E. Neumond, 199 F. 800 (D.C.La.1912).

See Sec. 57 above at nn. 32–37.

Compare Puerto Rico v. Russell & Co., 288 U.S. 476, 53 S.Ct. 447, 77 L.Ed. 903 (1933), holding that a sociedad en comandita organized under the Code of Puerto Rico possesses jurisdictional citizenship as a legal person.

45. U.S.C.A.Const., Art. 4, § 1.

See Kincade v. Jeffery-DeWitt Insulator Corp., 242 F.2d 328 (5th Cir. 1957) (Tenn. judgment enforceable against partner in federal court in Miss.;

partner was not named in Tenn. complaint or judgment, nor was he served, but he did appear and defend).

46. Snyder v. Davison, 15 La.App. 695, 129 So. 185, 131 So. 64 (1930); Snyder v. Davison, 172 La. 274, 134 So. 89 (1931). However, jurisdiction can be obtained over the partner individually, Fidelity and Cas. Co. of New York v. Homan, 116 So.2d 444 (Fla.App.1959).

47. Restatement, Conflict of Laws, § 86 (1) (jurisdiction over causes of action arising out of business in that state).

48. Id. § 86(2) (binding adjudication with respect to partnership assets in any other state).

49. 293 F. 804 (S.D.N.Y.1923). See discussion in Magruder & Foster, Jurisdiction over Partnerships, 37 Harv. Law Rev. 793 (1924); Warren, Corporate Advantages without Incorporation, 251–262 (1929); Beale, Conflict of Laws, § 86–1; Note, 24 Colum.L. Rev. 540 (1924).

were brought against a foreign partnership in the common name, service was made upon a partner, appearance was made in the partnership name and the actions were contested. Judgments were rendered against the partnership, which under the statutes of Colorado, where the proceedings were brought, were enforceable against partnership property, and that of the partners served. Judgment being unsatisfied, suit was brought in the Federal District Court in New York, in which state there was no common name statutes, against the partners for the purpose of enforcement out of the partnership property. A judgment was rendered, to be collected only out of firm assets. The court appeared to consider the Colorado judgment as imposing an obligation upon the partners limited in effect to the firm property, a personal obligation, enforceable extraterritorially as any other personal judgment, subject to the same limitation. The difficulty is that the obligation is imposed upon the partnership as a legal person distinct from the partners, and not upon the partners not served and not personally appearing. In some other states, such a judgment imposes no personal obligation upon the partners.[50] The result of the case is just, since the partnership did appear in Colorado and defend, and had a "day in court" with respect to the partnership's duty to answer to the original obligation out of partnership property. Differing views as to the nature of the partnership, and procedural diversities, were not allowed to stand in the way of interstate collection of claims adequately defended and adjudicated.[51]

---

50. Ratchford v. Covington County Stock Co., 172 Ala. 461, 55 So. 806 (1911).

51. Restatement, Conflict of Laws § 86, comment *b*.

Under a joint debtor statute, a judgment obtained against the partners after service on one, collectible out of partnership property, has been held not to be entitled to extraterritorial effect, even as to partnership property, where service in the latter action on the judgment was only on a partner not a party to the former proceeding. Hoffman v. Wight, 1 App.Div. 514, 37 N.Y.S. 262 (1896). See criticism, Magruder & Foster, op. cit. n. 49 supra, at 806.

Such a judgment has been held to have no personal effect upon the partner not a party thereto, and he cannot be sued on it in another state. D'Arcy v. Ketchum, 52 U.S. (11 How.) 165, 13 L.Ed. 648 (1850).

A statute could probably permit a court to make absent partners individually parties to actions brought in states where the partnership is doing business, personal jurisdiction being obtained by service on a partner, or other agent of the partnership. If it is due process of law to render a judgment against a non-resident trader after service on his resident agent, as in Goodman v. Henry L. Doherty & Co., 218 Iowa 529, 255 N.W. 667 (1934), aff'd 294 U.S. 623, 55 S.Ct. 553, 79 L.Ed. 1097 (1935), or on a non-resident partnership after service on a local agent, Stoner v. Higginson, 316 Pa. 481, 175 A. 527 (1934), it would seem to be due process of law to assume jurisdiction over an absent partner, the court having jurisdiction of a co-partner and of the partnership. If it is due process to render a personal judgment, it should be given extraterritorial recognition, at least to the extent that it could be enforced in the jurisdiction in which it was rendered.

Jurisdiction over a partnership is further discussed in Sec. 62 below.

ENFORCEMENT OF PARTNERSHIP OBLIGATIONS—JURISDICTION OVER A PARTNERSHIP BY SERVICE ON AN AGENT

§ 62.   If a non-resident partnership does business in a state whose statutes provide for service on a resident agent, jurisdiction can be obtained by such means, at least as to causes of action arising out of business done in the state.

At common law, all partners were necessary parties to a suit on a partnership obligation; [52] for personal jurisdiction, each had to be personally served.   We have seen that many statutes which permit partnerships to be sued in the common name also allow process to be served on any partner.[53]   Some go farther and permit service on an agent of the partnership.[54]   In general, jurisdiction can be obtained by service on an agent,[55] but questions arise in the case of non-resident partners or partnerships and transitory causes of action arising outside the forum.   The answers depend on the exact language of the statute, on the constitutional issue of due process, and on whether partnerships are treated as entities or aggregates.

Some statutes operate only if the defendant is "doing business" in the state;   this phrase naturally requires interpretation [56] and the results have been diverse.[57]   Other terms of the statutes tend to be strictly construed.[58]

---

52.   Sec. 58(a) above.

53.   Sec. 60 n. 35 above.

54.   E. g., Ariz.R.Civ.P. 4(d) (6) (1956); Iowa R.Civ.P. 56(f), (g) (Supp.1966); Minn.R.Civ.P. in Dist.Ct. 4.03(b) (1958) (managing agent); R.R.S.1943 (Neb.) § 25–314 (1956) (clerk, general agent); Pa.R.Civ.P. 2131 (1951) (registered agent;   manager, clerk or other person in charge); Vernon's Ann.Civ.St. (Tex.) art. 2033(b) (1964) (any agent or clerk); 12 V.S.A. (Vt.) § 814.   The Ariz., Iowa and Vt. provisions are modeled on Fed.Rules Civ.Proc. rule 4(d) (3), 28 U.S.C.A. (managing or general agent, or any other agent authorized by appointment or by law to receive service of process).   Among the agents held to have the necessary authority are truck dispatchers, Gerut v. Poe, 11 F.R.D. 281 (N.D.Ill.1951) and football coaches, American Football League v. National Football League, 27 F.R.D. 264 (D.Md.1961).

By U.P.A. § 9, a partner is an agent of the firm.   Service on him would therefore be good under these provisions as well as under those relating specifically to him.   See also U.P.A. § 12

(partnership charged with notice to partner), discussed Sec. 56 above.

55.   A statute is necessary to confer jurisdiction over a partnership by service on an agent;   none exists at common law.   Matson v. Mackubin, 61 U.S.App.D.C. 102, 57 F.2d 941 (1932).

See generally, Campbell, Partnership Obligations and Their Enforcement, 32 Chi-Kent L.Rev. 127, 131–40 (1954), reviewing venue, service and jurisdiction.

56.   Compare Lewis Manufacturing Co. v. Superior Court, 140 Cal.App.2d 245, 295 P.2d 145 (1956) (doing business), noted 45 Calif.L.Rev. 93 (1957), *with* Modern Contract Furnishings, Inc. v. Bishop International Engineering Co., 165 N.E.2d 703 (Ohio C.P.1960) (not doing business).

57.   Annot., What amounts to doing business in a state, 10 A.L.R.2d 200 (1950); see also Annot., 42 A.L.R.2d 516, at 556 (1955).   Decisions involving corporations are collected in Corporation Trust Co., What Constitutes Doing Business (1963).

58.   Thornburg v. James E. Bennett & Co., 206 Iowa 1187, 221 N.W. 840

There is ordinarily no jurisdiction over a non-resident in the absence of a statute.[59] The constitutionality of such statutes has been the subject of numerous decisions, recognizing gradually expanding bases for jurisdiction: "domicile", "presence", "consent", and "minimum contacts".[60] The subject is too complex for full treatment here,[61] and we attempt only to sketch the jurisdiction arising out of partnership contacts in the state. Recent cases have mainly involved corporations, but should provide precedents for partnerships so far as they are considered entities (i. e. for judgments binding on the partnership and on the partners to the extent of their interests in partnership property).[62] The regular activity and presence of a local agent, and service on him, will suffice for jurisdiction over a partnership on a cause of action arising within the forum.[63] In some in-

(1928); Rorick v. Stilwell, 101 Fla. 4, 133 So. 609 (1931).

59. Rosenblum v. Judson Engineering Corp., 99 N.H. 267, 109 A.2d 558 (1954). By express contract, a party may consent to jurisdiction. Emerson Radio & Phonograph Corp. v. Eskind, 32 Misc.2d 1038, 228 N.Y.S.2d 841 (S.Ct. 1957); Green Mountain Jr. College v. Levine, 120 Vt. 332, 139 A.2d 822 (1958).

60. See, e. g. Pennoyer v. Neff, 95 U.S. 714, 24 L.Ed. 565 (1877); International Shoe Co. v. Washington, 326 U.S. 310 (1945); Travelers Health Ass'n v. Virginia, 339 U.S. 643, 70 S.Ct. 927, 94 L.Ed. 1154 (1950); McGee v. International Life Ins. Co., 355 U.S. 220, 78 S.Ct. 199, 2 L.Ed.2d 223 (1957).

61. See, e. g., Developments in the Law —State-Court Jurisdiction, 73 Harv.L. Rev. 909 (1960); Transient Jurisdiction—Remnant of Pennoyer v. Neff— A Round Table, 9 J.Pub.L. 281 (1960).

62. Under the entity theory, it is questionable whether a partner has the necessary jurisdictional connection with a particular state merely because the partnership does. Under the aggregate theory, it seems clear that he does. Under either theory, if the partner has the necessary connection, the partnership does because of his agency for the firm, U.P.A. § 9(1).

63. One fairly early case points the other way, Flexner v. Farson, 248 U.S. 289, 39 S.Ct. 97, 63 L.Ed. 250 (1919).

This case has been followed in Andrews Bros. v. McClanahan, 220 Ky. 504, 295

S.W. 457 (1927); Knox Bros. v. E. W. Wagner & Co., 141 Tenn. 348, 209 S.W. 638 (1919); Matson v. Mackubin, U.S., 61 App.D.C. 102, 57 F.2d 941 (1932). It has been criticized in Scott, Jurisdiction over Non-Residents Doing Business within a State, 32 Harv.L.Rev. 871 (1917). See also Burdick, Service as a Requirement of Due Process of Actions in Personam, 20 Mich.L.Rev. 422 (1922); Notes, 3 Minn.L.Rev. 277 (1918); 28 Yale L.J. 512 (1919).

Flexner v. Farson is easily distinguishable on the ground that the local agent had ceased to be an agent before he was served. Moreover, it utilizes a more restrictive concept of jurisdiction ("consent") than now prevails.

See Stoner v. Higginson, 316 Pa. 481, 175 A. 527 (1934). Service, in an action based on a Pennsylvania transaction, was made upon one who had been designated by the non-resident partnership doing business in Pennsylvania as its agent when it complied with the Fictitious Names Act (54 P.S. § 21) by registration. It was found by the court that at the time of service the partnership was still doing business in the State through this agent. Flexner v. Farson was not followed on the grounds that (1) in that case the person served was not at the time an agent; (2) the case appeared to have been overruled by the decisions such as Hess v. Pawloski, 274 U.S. 352, 47 S.Ct. 632, 71 L.Ed. 1091 (1926), sustaining substituted service on non-resident motorists; and (3) being a rule of procedure, not of property, it ought to be overruled in the light of changing views of public policy. See notes 83 U. of Pa.Law

stances a single, isolated act may suffice.[64]

Where the partnership is treated as an aggregate, there is also precedent for jurisdiction by service on an agent.[65] The chief case concerned an individual principal with local office and agent, but the result is easily extended to partners regarded as co-principals.

Rev. 683; 2 U. of Pittsburgh Law Rev. 115.

See Eastex Poultry Co. v. Benefield, 268 S.W.2d 270 (Tex.Civ.App.1954) (jurisdiction over partnership by service on resident partner despite non-residence of co-partner).

Melvin Pine & Co., Inc. v. McConnell, 298 N.Y. 27, 80 N.E.2d 137 (1948), affirming 273 App.Div. 218, 76 N.Y.S.2d 279 (1948) (valid service on non-resident partners through resident corporate manufacturer's agent).

64. A few statutes so specify, e. g. Ill. Rev.Stat. 1967, c. 110, § 17(1); 1953 Comp. (N.M.) § 21–3–16 (Supp.1961); (N.Y.) McKinney's CPLR § 302; Vernon's Ann.Civ.St. (Tex.) art. 2031b, § 4; RCWA (Wash.) 4.28.185; Unif. Securities Act § 414(h). See also W.S.A. (Wis.) 262.05. Their validity has not been fully determined, but there should not be much question in view of McGee v. International Life Ins. Co., 355 U.S. 220, 78 S.Ct. 199, 2 L. Ed.2d 223 (1957).

65. Goodman v. Henry L. Doherty & Co., 218 Iowa 529, 255 N.W. 667 (1934), affirmed 294 U.S. 623, 55 S.Ct. 553, 79 L.Ed. 1097 (1935), an action against a non-resident principal, jurisdiction being based on service on this resident agent. See also Davidson v. Henry L. Doherty & Co., 214 Iowa 739, 241 N. W. 700, 91 A.L.R. 1308 (1932); Culp, Process in Actions against Non-Residents, 32 Mich.Law Rev. 909; notes, 46 Harv.Law Rev. 153; 20 Iowa Law Rev. 53.

The United States Supreme Court's opinion distinguished Flexner v. Farson on the ground that the person there served was not then an agent of the non-resident partnership. The opinion appears to be based, in part, upon the fact that the business of the defendant was dealing in securities, an activity, like that of operating motor vehicles on the highway, which is properly subject to special regulation. The statute of Iowa, under which the service was made, was not confined to persons engaged in any particular line of business. It read: "When a corporation, company or individual has for the transaction of any business an office or agency in any county other than that in which the principal resides, service may be made on any agent or clerk employed in such office or agency, in all actions growing out of or connected with the business of that office or agency." Iowa Code 1927, § 11079.

Note that the Iowa and Pennsylvania statutes, and the Kentucky statute involved in Flexner v. Farson, were by their terms applicable to actions both against partnerships and individuals. It might be questioned whether a statute applicable only to suits against partnerships, or a Rule such as Pa.R. Civ.P. 2131 (jurisdiction based on service upon an agent not a partner), would be constitutional. The ordinary partnership exists as a matter of common right of the partners, who as citizens may do business in several states. Unless treated as a legal person, could partners be subjected to jurisdiction by means other than those necessary for other joint debtors or single individuals? It has been held that an excise tax, based on the privilege of doing business, applicable to corporations, business trusts, and partnerships, but not to individuals, is unconstitutional as to partnerships. Corn v. Fort, 170 Tenn. 377, 95 S.W.2d 620, 106 A.L.R. 647 (1936). To subject foreign partnerships, engaged in extensive interstate operations, to substituted service, or service on actual agents, in the interest of local creditors, is probably no more excessive burden on their migratory rights than in the case of a foreign corporation engaged in interstate commerce. Compare International Harvester Co. v. Commonwealth of Kentucky, 234 U.S. 579, 34 S.Ct. 944, 58 L.Ed. 1479 (1914).

Where the cause of action arises entirely outside the state, doubt has been expressed over local jurisdiction.[66] Most statutes expressly provide that service on a local agent is valid for local causes of action,[67] thereby excluding foreign causes of action by negative implication. One may question whether this limitation is constitutionally necessary,[68] if there is contact between the defendant and the state.[69]

The foregoing discussion relates to agents employed in the ordinary course of business. The situation appears to be no different if the agent is appointed pursuant to a statutory requirement. Although it is common for legislation to require designation of resident agents by foreign corporations doing local business [70] it is rare for partnerships.[71] However, it does occur in regulated businesses like securities,[72] liquor,[73] and motor carriers [74] and in some fictitious name statutes.[75]

What if the required agent has not been appointed or cannot be found? To deal with these situations, and those where the requirement is inapplicable, some states specify that doing business in the

---

66. Interchemical Corp. v. Mirabelli, 269 App.Div. 224, 54 N.Y.S.2d 522 (1945).

67. E. g., Ill.Rev.Stat.1967, c. 110, § 17 (3). Semble, Restatement, Conflicts § 86(1) (jurisdiction over causes of action arising out of business in that state).

68. See Developments in the Law— State-Court Jurisdiction, 73 Harv.L. Rev. 909, 945–47, 930–32 (1960). At least one state has attempted to extend jurisdiction beyond purely local causes of action; see W.S.A. (Wis.) 262.05(1). Although personal service outside the state is authorized in general, it is not authorized against partners when jurisdiction is based on the cited provision, id. 262.06(6).

69. Cf. Hanson v. Denckla, 357 U.S. 235, 78 S.Ct. 1228, 2 L.Ed.2d 1283 (1958) (no jurisdiction since minimum contacts lacking).

70. See Sec. 31 above and 1 Model Business Corp.Act Ann. 229–36 (1960).

71. West's Ann.Cal.Corp.Code, § 15700, M.G.L.A. (Mass.) c. 227 § 5 are among the rare requirements for appointment of agents by partnerships. RSA (N. H.) 305–A:1—305–A:7 (Supp.1966) is an even rarer example of a full qualification requirement for a foreign partnership; it is discussed Sec. 22A nn. 45–46 above.

One reason for the disparate treatment of partnerships and corporations is that the latter are not citizens within the meaning of the privileges and immunities clause, U.S.C.A.Const. Art. 4, § 2, Paul v. Virginia, 75 U.S. (8 Wall.) 168, 19 L.Ed. 357 (1869). Therefore, their entry into a state may be denied (subject to the commerce clause) or qualified by such requirements as the payment of taxes or the appointment of an agent for process. As individuals, partners are citizens and entitled to the privileges and immunities, although this does not necessarily free them from such requirements if imposed nondiscriminatorily. Query, whether a partnership regarded as an entity is a citizen and has privileges and immunities? The implication in the cases is yes, The Bank of Augusta v. Earle, 13 U.S. (13 Pet.) 517 (1839); Flexner v. Farson, 248 U.S. 289, 293, 39 S.Ct. 97, 98, 63 L.Ed. 250 (1919). But neither reveals a clear consideration of partnership as entity. See also Sec. 22A(b) above.

72. See Unif.Securities Act §§ 202(a), 414(g).

73. See X–L Liquors, Inc. v. Taylor, 17 N.J. 444, 111 A.2d 753 (1955).

74. 49 U.S.C.A. § 321(c).

75. See Stoner v. Higginson, n. 63 above; Brown v. Ingraham, 11 F.R.D. 522 (W.D.Pa.1951).

state will constitute a designated governmental official as agent for service for process.[76] The validity of these substitute service procedures depends on the considerations already discussed.[77] In addition, they must give the defendants notice reasonably calculated to apprise them of the pendency of the action and afford them an opportunity to appear.[78] This is usually done by serving extra copies of the complaint on the official and requiring him to mail them to the defendants.[79]

Judgments based on valid jurisdiction are entitled to full faith and credit (i. e. by extraterritorial enforcement).[80]

We have suggested that personal jurisdiction over partners can be obtained by service on a partnership agent.[81] We have also noted that under common name statutes, designed to facilitate actions against partners, service on a partner normally gives jurisdiction only over the partnership and the partner served.[82] The two views collide in the paradox of giving more jurisdiction in the case of an agent although a partner has greater representative capacity. The anomaly occurs because the common name statutes expressly or impliedly exclude jurisdiction over the unserved partners.[83] It is thus a matter of statutory language rather than constitutional necessity. There appears to be no reason why statutes could not provide for personal jurisdiction over all partners by service on one partner as fully as by service on an agent.[84]

76. See, e. g., Vernon's Ann.Civ.St. (Tex.) art. 2031b, §§ 1, 3; Unif. Securities Act § 414(h). Such statutes are modeled on the non-resident motorist statute held constitutional in Hess v. Pawlowski, 274 U.S. 352, 47 S.Ct. 632, 71 L.Ed. 1091 (1927); for the background of the Texas provision, see Wilson, In Personam Jurisdiction Over Non-Residents: An Invitation and a Proposal, 9 Baylor L.Rev. 363 (1957).

Another solution to the no-local-agent problem is personal service outside the state. This is authorized by such legislation as Ill.Rev.Stat.1967, c. 110, § 17(1); 1953 Comp. (N.M.) § 21–3–16; RCWA (Wash.) 4.28.185 (1962). Further treatment of this point is beyond our scope.

77. Lewis Mfg. Co. v. Superior Court, 140 Cal.App.2d 245, 295 P.2d 145 (1956); noted 45 Calif.L.Rev. 93 (1957); State v. Ritholtz, 257 Minn. 201, 100 N.W.2d 722 (1960) (service on Secretary of State valid against non-resident partnership).

78. Mullane v. Central Hanover Bank & Trust Co., 339 U.S. 306, 70 S.Ct. 652, 94 L.Ed. 865 (1950).

79. Vernon's Ann.Civ.St. (Tex.) art. 2031b, § 5; Unif. Securities Act § 414(h). Service by mail has been upheld where other jurisdictional requirements are met. International Shoe Co. v. Washington; Travelers Health Ass'n v. Virginia; McGee v. International Life Ins. Co., all n. 60 above.

80. See Sec. 61 above.

81. At nn. 54–55 above.

82. Sec. 60 above, nn. 36–37.

83. Also, common name statutes have entity features, Sec. 60 at n. 31 above. Personal jurisdiction over partners by service on a partnership agent is much less clear under the entity theory than under the aggregate; see n. 62 above.

84. See Sec. 61 n. 51 above. Pennsylvania has done so, Pa.R.Civ.P. 2131 (service on partner or agent), 2132 (execution against partner named and

Jurisdiction in rem or quasi in rem raises no problems peculiar to partnerships. Even though the property involved belongs to the partnership, the partners have sufficient rights in it [85] to be bound by the judgment.

SET-OFF AND COUNTERCLAIM

§ 63. Set-off requires mutuality of parties. In four common situations, set-off or counterclaim is not allowed, in the absence of special circumstances, because of lack of mutuality:

(a) When a partnership sues a third person on a partnership demand, the third person cannot set off the debt of a partner;

(b) When a partner sues a third person on a separate demand, the latter cannot set off a debt of the partnership;

(c) When a third person sues a partnership, the defendants cannot set off a demand of a partner; and

(d) When a third person sues a partner, the latter cannot set off a demand of the partnership.

(a) Suit by Partnership Against Third Person

When a partnership sues a third person on a partnership demand, the defendant cannot set off a debt due from a partner, for there is not only want of mutuality usually necessary for set-off, but it would be inequitable to compel the partnership to pay the debt of a partner.[86] This disability exists, though the third person, when contracting, did not know that his creditor was a partnership; [87] but if it is a secret partnership, dormant partners allowing one to carry on as ostensible sole trader, set-off is allowed, in accordance with the agency rules as to actions by agents of undisclosed principals.[88]

Set-off is allowed against a partner suing as assignee of a partnership demand,[89] or against a surviving partner.[90] Set-off is allowed

served under 2131, if given notice of the action).

85. U.P.A. § 25.

86. Yankelewitch v. Beach, 115 Cal.App. 629, 2 P.2d 498 (1931); Lovelace v. Reliable Garage, 33 Ga.App. 289, 125 S.E. 877 (1924); Williams v. Brimhall, 79 Mass. (13 Gray) 462 (1859); Holton v. American Pastry Products Corp., 274 Mass. 268, 174 N.E. 663 (1931); Kentling & Kentling v. Magers, 256 S.W. 528 (Mo.App.1923); Ladue v. Hart, 4 Wend. 583 (N.Y.1830); Ravold v. Fred Beers, Inc., 151 Misc. 628, 270 N.Y.S. 894 (1933); Prescott v. Buckwalter & Boyer, 1 Wkly.Notes Cas. 58 (Pa. 1874); Zucht v. Jorrie, 294 S.W. 687 (Tex.Civ.App.1927).

Counterclaims of causes of action against each member of the plaintiff partnership have been allowed under Federal Rule 13 in Abraham v. Selig, 29 F.Supp. 52 (S.D.N.Y.1939), noted 7 U.Chi.L.Rev. 394 (1940).

87. Kleinschmidt v. White, 159 Okl. 234, 15 P.2d 127 (1932).

88. Dixon Livery Co. v. Bond, 117 Va. 656, 86 S.E. 106, L.R.A.1916A, 1211 (1915); Restatement, Second, Agency, §§ 306, 307.

89. Carter v. Mizell, 214 Ala. 182, 106 So. 846 (1926).

90. Holbrook v. Lackey, 54 Mass. (13 Metc.) 132, 46 Am.Dec. 726 (1847).

against a partnership which has assumed liability for the debt of a partner.[91]

(b) Suit by Partner Against Third Person

When a partner sues a third person on a separate demand, the **de-fendant cannot set off** a claim against the partnership, for that would be compelling a partner to pay an obligation for which he is only liable jointly.[92] Set-off may be maintained if agreed to in advance by all parties,[93] or if the partnership obligation is joint and several,[94] or if statutes expressly permit.[95] It has been allowed in cases of insolvency of the partnership.[96] Where a partnership is indebted to a bank on a joint note or other joint obligation, the bank is generally not allowed to set it off against the deposit account of a partner.[97] Collateral pledged by a partner to secure his personal loan is applicable to partnership indebtedness [98] or not,[99] according to the interpretation of the agreement under which it is pledged.

(c) Suit by Third Person Against Partnership

When a third person sues the partnership on a partnership obligation, one partner cannot plead a separate demand as a defense.[1] But

91. Dishon v. Schorr, 19 Ill. 59 (1857).

92. Metcalf v. People's Grocery Co., 24 Ga.App. 663, 101 S.E. 768 (1920); Raymond v. Palmer, 41 La.Ann. 425, 6 So. 692, 17 Am.St.Rep. 398 (1889); Rath v. Kelly, 246 Mich. 25, 224 N.W. 377 (1929); Spofford v. Rowan, 124 N.Y. 108, 26 N.E. 350 (1891); Simon v. Rudner, 43 Ohio App. 38, 182 N.E. 650 (1932); Mintz v. Tri-County Nat. Gas Co., 259 Pa. 477, 103 A. 285 (1918); Elliott v. Bell, 37 W.Va. 834, 17 S.E. 399 (1893).

93. Stinson v. Lanier, 223 Ala. 62, 134 So. 793 (1931).

94. Davis v. Bessemer City Cotton Mills, 178 F. 784 (4th Cir. 1910). But see First Nat. Bank of Abbeville v. Capps, 208 Ala. 207, 94 So. 109 (1922); contra, Bradley Fertilizer Co. v. Cooke, 104 Ala. 402, 16 So. 138 (1894).

95. M. M. Bryant & Bro. v. Reamer, 211 Ky. 503, 277 S.W. 826 (1925).

96. Hoover's Ex'rs v. Bowers, Hoover, & Co., 146 Va. 84, 135 S.E. 698 (1926), criticized in 27 Colum.L.Rev. 746 (1927).

97. First Nat. Bank v. Capps, n. 94 above; Raymond v. Palmer, n. 92 above; Adams v. First Nat. Bank, 113

N.C. 332, 18 S.E. 513, 23 L.R.A. 111 (1893). Contra, Boeger & Buchanan v. Hagen, 204 Iowa 435, 215 N.W. 597, 55 A.L.R. 562 (1927) (partners jointly and severally liable by statute).

98. Hallowell v. Blackstone Nat. Bank, 154 Mass. 359, 28 N.E. 281, 13 L.R.A. 315 (1891); Bennett v. North Philadelphia Trust Co., 66 Pa.Super. 261 (1917); In re William Hill & Sons, 186 F. 569 (E.D.Pa.1911).

99. Bank of Buffalo v. Thompson, 121 N.Y. 280, 24 N.E. 473 (1890); New Bethlehem Trust Co. v. Spindler, 315 Pa. 250, 172 A. 309 (1934); Wolstenholm v. Banking Co., 54 L.T.,N.S., 746 (1886).

1. Omaha Crockery Co. v. Cleaver, 104 Kan. 642, 180 P. 273, 5 A.L.R. 1537 (1919); McGuinness v. Kyle, 208 Mass. 443, 94 N.E. 700 (1911) semble; Pophan v. Rubin, 134 N.Y.S. 1065 (Sup.1912); Sanford v. Pike, 87 Or. 614, 170 P. 729, 171 P. 394 (1918).

See also Jordison v. Jordison Bros., 215 Iowa 938, 247 N.W. 491 (1933), where wife of a partner, suing partners as well as partnership for money loaned, could not be met by set-off for necessities furnished her family by partnership, not being a right of all of the partners.

in many jurisdictions, set-off is allowed by reason of equitable considerations, such as insolvency of the plaintiff.[2] If the partnership obligation is joint and several, the partner can plead his set-off;[3] or if, in a suit against the partnership, only one partner is served, he may set off his separate demand;[4] and so may a surviving partner.[5]

(d) Suit by Third Person Against Partner

When a third person sues a partner on a separate debt, the partner cannot set off a partnership claim against the third person.[6] Aside from the technical objection of lack of mutuality, to allow a partner indebted to a third person to set off a partnership demand would allow him to divert partnership property to the payment of a separate debt. Such procedure is presumably unauthorized, and in the absence of evidence of assignment to him of the partnership demand, or of consent by his co-partner, set-off is not permitted.[7] If the other partners assign their claim to the debtor partner, or (without the formality of assignment) consent to his using it as a defense, and if the third person, creditor of the partner, is solvent, the courts generally allow equitable set-off.[8] If the third person is insolvent, especially if it is a bank, equities of other creditors are to be considered. It is no longer merely a matter of avoiding circuity of action and relaxation of technical requirements of mutuality, but involves the

---

2. Youmans v. Moore, 11 Ga.App. 66, 74 S.E. 710 (1912); Jack v. Klepser, 196 Pa. 187, 46 A. 479, 79 Am.St.Rep. 699 (1900); Willing v. Binenstock, 88 F.2d 474 (3rd Cir. 1937). See notes, 5 A.L.R. 1541; 10 A.L.R. 1252; 81 A.L.R. 781.

3. Merchants' Nat. Bank of Los Angeles v. Clark-Parker Co., 215 Cal. 296, 9 P.2d 826, 81 A.L.R. 778 (1932); McKinnon v. Palen, 62 Minn. 188, 64 N.W. 387 (1895); Seaman v. Slater, 49 F. 37 (S.D.N.Y.1892).

See also Fox Chase Knitting Mills, Inc. v. Handal, 232 App.Div. 498, 250 N.Y.S. 416 (1931).

4. Alpaugh v. Battles, 235 App.Div. 321, 257 N.Y.S. 126 (1932), noted 18 Corn. L.Q. 110; Mott v. Mott, 5 Vt. 111 (1833). See Morey v. State ex rel. Mothersead, 129 Okl. 136, 263 P. 1098 (1928).

5. Lewis v. Culbertson, 11 Serg. & R. 48, 14 Am.Dec. 607 (Pa.1824).

A surviving partner sued for an accounting by the administrator of a deceased partner can set off a debt owed him by the decedent. Overbeck v. Overbeck, 354 Pa. 142, 47 A.2d 264 (1946).

A partner sued after dissolution for a personal debt can set off the amount due him from plaintiff, liquidating the affairs of the partnership, Sooy v. Cerf, 220 Cal. 611, 32 P.2d 365, 93 A.L.R. 287 (1934).

6. Kennedy v. Schultz, 105 Ga.App. 522, 125 S.E.2d 87 (1962); Powell v. Dowrning, 225 S.W.2d 952 (Mo.App. 1950); Rose v. Motes, 220 S.W.2d 734 (Tex.Civ.App.1949).

See Pruett v. Ralston Purina Co., 273 Ala. 594, 143 So.2d 309 (1962) (co-partners lacked sufficient interest to intervene in action against partner on separate obligation).

7. Jones v. Blair, 57 Ala. 457 (1876); Dehon v. Stetson, 50 Mass. (9 Metc.) 341 (1845); Wrenshall v. Cook, 7 Watts 464 (Pa.1838), semble.

8. Montz v. Morris, 89 Pa. 392 (1879); Edelman v. Scholl, 65 Pa.Super. 357 (1916).

question of preferences. The more equitable view would seem to be that set-off is to be refused in such circumstances.[9]

In special circumstances set-off may be properly allowed, as where the debtor partner is a surviving partner,[10] or where his interest in the partnership is substantially complete ownership.[11]

TORT AND CRIMINAL LIABILITY

§ 64. Tort liability of partners is joint and several, whether for torts committed by a partner, or by a servant or agent of the partnership.

Partners are jointly and severally liable for torts committed by a partner within the scope of the business.[12] They may be sued joint-

---

[9] Fralick v. Coeur d'Alene Bank & Trust Co., 35 Idaho 749, 208 P. 835, 27 A.L.R. 110 (1922); Wolcott v. Pierre, 100 Ind.App. 16, 188 N.E. 596 (1934); In re Bank of Sampson, 205 N.C. 333, 171 S.E. 436 (1933), noted 47 Harv.L. Rev. 1069.

In Wolcott v. Pierre, supra, the court said: "If the joint deposit in this case should be set off against the individual debt, it would have to be upon the theory of an assignment of the deposit to appellee. In other words, the consent of the appellee's partner to the use of their joint deposit as a set-off, in effect, amounts to an assignment of his interest in such deposit to appellee. If this were permitted, then one who is indebted to an insolvent bank and does not have a deposit in the bank at that time could, after receivership, obtain an assignment of a deposit from some other depositor, and set this off against his own indebtedness. This principle, if adopted in this state, would work an injustice upon the other depositors who were unable to obtain assignments of deposits to set off against their debts."

Contrary results have been reached in some states. Jack v. Klepser, 196 Pa. 187, 46 A. 479, 79 Am.St.Rep. 699 (1900), a bank case, opinion citing a line of Pennsylvania cases in accord; Burns v. Lopez, 256 N.Y. 123, 175 N.E. 537 (1931), debtor partner's interest in partnership claim exceeding his indebtedness to plaintiff, an individual. Where there is fraud on plaintiff's part set-off has been allowed, as where a banker induces the partnership to continue its deposit, representing that he still holds notes of a partner, which he has in fact assigned to another, and agrees that they may be paid through the deposit. Second Nat. Bank of Cincinnati v. Hemingray, 34 Ohio St. 381 (1878).

Immediately before the closing of an insolvent bank, the senior partner in a law firm assigned to a copartner indebted to the bank on a note a claim of the partnership against the bank for legal services. It was held that the assignee partner could set off the assigned claim for services against the note. People ex rel. Nelson v. Roseland Sav. Bank, 282 Ill.App. 289 (1935).

Where a bank refused to make further loans to a firm which had a deposit account, but did lend to a partner on his note, the proceeds being credited to the firm, on the bank's insolvency, set-off of the firm's deposit balance was allowed in favor of the partner, the maker of the note. Marcum v. Wilhoit, 290 Ky. 532, 162 S.W.2d 10 (1942), noted in 31 Ky.L.J. 201.

[10] Hughes v. Trahern, 64 Ill. 48 (1872); Heiden v. Beuttler, 11 F.Supp. 290 (D. Iowa 1935).

[11] Morey v. State ex rel. Mothersead, 129 Okl. 136, 263 P. 1098 (1928).

Two partners jointly liable on a non-partnership obligation have been allowed to set off a partnership demand. Oliver v. Godley, 38 Ga.App. 66, 142 S.E. 566 (1928).

[12] The partnership is liable on the theory of respondeat superior, codified in U.P.A. § 13, analyzed above in Sec. 54. By U.P.A. § 15(a), all partners are liable jointly and severally for liabilities under § 13.

ly,[13] or severally.[14] They are severally, as well as jointly, liable for the tort of a servant or agent of the partnership within the course of the employment.[15] If the cause of action is in substance contractual, the liability is joint only,[16] if that is the prevailing view of partners' contract liability in the jurisdiction.

A distinction exists between tort and contract liability with respect to discharge. Liability for a willful tort may not be discharged in bankruptcy, even as against a morally innocent partner.[17] Since liability for a personal injury at common law ceases with the death of tort-feasors, on death of all of the partners one who has suffered a personal injury is without remedy.[18]

The abatement of the action as against the deceased partner does not affect the remedy for a negligent tort against the surviving partner.[19]

In a jurisdiction where tort liabilities survive against the deceased tort-feasor, liability may be imposed on the partnership, the surviving partner and the representative of the negligent deceased partner.[20]

13. Phillips v. Lyon, 109 Cal.App. 264, 292 P. 711 (1930).

14. Mode v. Penland, 93 N.C. 292 (1885): "Although the partners are all liable in such cases and may be sued, it does not follow that all of them must be sued. The law treats all torts as several, as well as joint, and the party injured may, at his election, sue all the partners, or any one or more of them, for the injury done him. This rule of law is not peculiar to partnership—it extends to all cases of joint torts and trespasses at the common law, whether positive or constructive."

Roux v. Lawand, 131 Me. 215, 160 A. 756 (1932); Dancy v. Missouri-Kansas-Texas R. R. Co. of Texas, 49 S.W.2d 910 (Tex.Civ.App.1932).

Weaver v. Marcus, 165 F.2d 862, 175 A.L.R. 1305 (4th Cir. 1948), diversity of citizenship for purpose of Federal jurisdiction exists when suit is against nonresident partners for a traffic accident, although one partner, not sued, is a resident. This case is annotated at 175 A.L.R. 1310 (1948) on Tort Liability of Partners.

15. Soberg v. Sanders, 243 Mich. 429, 220 N.W. 781 (1928), calling attention to the gap in the U.P.A. on this point; see Note, 4 Va.Law Rev. 315 (1917); Right Way Laundry v. Davis, 98 Okl. 264, 225 P. 345 (1924); Weaver v. Marcus, n. 14 above, citing this text.

See Note 34 Va.Law Rev. 614–616 (1948).

After a joint judgment for the tort of a servant, a partner is subject to capias ad satisfaciendum. Baxter v. Wunder, 89 Pa.Super. 585 (1926).

16. Whittaker v. Collins, 34 Minn. 299, 25 N.W. 632, 57 Am.Rep. 55 (1895).

Partnership liability under a Workmen's Compensation Act has been held not to be joint and several under §§ 13 and 14 of the U.P.A., dealing with wrongful acts, and necessarily joint under § 15(b). Palle v. Industrial Commission of Utah, 79 Utah 47, 7 P.2d 284, 81 A.L.R. 1222 (1932).

17. McIntyre v. Kavanaugh, 242 U.S. 138, 37 S.Ct. 38, 61 L.Ed. 205 (1916).

18. Sumner v. Brown, 312 Pa. 124, 167 A. 315 (1933); 82 U. of Pa.L.R. 166.

Liability for a conversion of property is joint and several, and a joint action in the form of money had and received may be maintained against the surviving partners jointly with the representative of the deceased partner. State Bank of Binghamton v. Bache, 156 Misc. 503, 282 N.Y.S. 187 (1935).

19. Kangas v. Winquist, 207 Minn. 315, 291 N.W. 292 (1940).

20. Wallan v. Rankin, 173 F.2d 488 (9th Cir. 1949).

A judgment against a partner in a tort action is not generally res judicata in a later action against his copartners. Copartners might be collaterally estopped if it were shown that they had actually participated in the defense of the first action.[21]

Criminal responsibility is, of course, essentially individual. However, in certain instances, a partnership can be guilty of a crime.[22] The resulting monetary obligation (i. e. fine or penalty) would appear to be a joint and several liability of the partners.[23]

---

21. Dillard v. McKnight, 34 Cal.2d 209, 209 P.2d 387, 11 A.L.R.2d 835 (1949). Griffin v. McBrayer, 252 N.C. 54, 112 S.E.2d 748 (1960).

See Annot., Judgment for or against partner as res judicata in favor of or against copartner not a party to the judgment, 11 A.L.R.2d 847 (1950).

22. Sec. 54(g) above.

23. U.P.A. §§ 13, 15(a).

CHAPTER 7

RIGHTS AND DUTIES OF PARTNERS INTER SE AND ACTIONS FOR BREACH OF DUTIES

Analysis

RIGHTS AND DUTIES OF PARTNERS INTER SE

§ 65. **The rights and duties of the partners in relation to the partnership shall be determined, subject to any agreement between them, by the following rules:**

    (a) **Each partner shall be repaid his contributions, whether by way of capital or advances to the partnership property, and share equally in the profits and surplus remaining after all liabilities, including those to partners, are satisfied; and must contribute towards the losses, whether of capital or otherwise, sustained by the partnership, according to his share in the profits.**

    (b) **The partnership must indemnify every partner in respect of payments made and personal liabilities reasonably incurred by him in the ordinary and proper conduct of its business, or for the preservation of its business, or property.**

    (c) **A partner who, in aid of the partnership, makes any payment or advance beyond the amount of capital which he agreed to contribute, shall be paid interest from the date of the payment or advance.**

    (d) **A partner shall receive interest on the capital contributed by him only from the date when repayment should be made.**

    (e) **All partners have equal rights in the management and conduct of the partnership business.**

364

(f) No partner is entitled to remuneration for acting in the partnership business, except that a surviving partner is entitled to reasonable compensation for his services in winding up the partnership affairs.

(g) No person can become a member of a partnership without the consent of all the partners.

(h) Any difference arising as to ordinary matters connected with the partnership business, may be decided by a majority of the partners; but no act in contravention of any agreement between the partners may be done rightfully without the consent of all the partners. U.P.A. § 18.

Partnership typically results from contract between the partners.[1] The incidents of the relation as between the partners are subject to such agreements as they may make.[1A] They may include in their partnership articles or other form of agreement provisions for sharing of profits and losses, rights and responsibilities as to participation in management, and compensation other than profit sharing for contributions of capital and services. Provisions are often made for unequal or variable sharing of profits, for unequal voting power (sometimes proportioned to shares in profits), and for salaries or guaranteed minimum income to some of the partners.[2] Different classes of members (such as junior and senior partners) may be created with different rights and duties.[3] If the partners make no specific agreement with regard to certain details, the law applies rules which are in accordance with mercantile usage, and which may be presumed to be in accordance with the intention of associates who have neglected to manifest any agreement concerning the matters. The following discussion assumes that the partners have made no agreement on the point in question.

Since the order of this treatise is roughly chronological, we consider here the rights and duties of partners during the life of the firm, even though they are rarely litigated until dissolution.

---

1. See Sec. 5(b) above.

1A. Meyer v. Sharp, 341 Ill.App. 431, 94 N.E.2d 510 (1950).

U.P.A. § 18, 1st sentence.

2. The partnership agreement in Appendix V should be read with this chapter. A well-drafted agreement avoids many of the problems treated here, and U.P.A. § 18 is a useful checklist for preparing such an agreement. See Moulin v. Der Zakarian, 191 Cal. App.2d 184, 12 Cal.Rptr. 572 (1961) for an agreement with many variations from the norm.

In general, there is no requirement that a partnership agreement be in writing, but there are obvious difficulties in establishing its terms if it is not. Moreover, the statute of frauds may require a writing; see Secs. 23, 39 above.

3. This is common practice, particularly in law and accounting firms. See, e. g., Carrington & Sutherland, Articles of Partnership for Law Firms 49–50 (1961). It is specifically authorized in at least one statute, Vernon's Ann. Civ.St. (Tex.) art. 6132b, § 18(2) (1962). See also Sec. 24A above.

(a) Repayment of Contributions; Sharing in Profits and Losses
_____ *Profits and Losses*

Profit sharing is the essence of partnership. In general, the partners share equally [4] even though they may have contributed unequally to capital or services.[5] The obligation to share losses is a corollary to the right to share profits, and is in the same proportions,[6] even though the partners may have contributed capital or services in different proportions.[7] Thus, if there is no agreement on the point, the partners share profits and losses equally. If there is an agreement to share profits 2 to 1 and nothing is said about losses, they are also shared 2 to 1.

Implicit in sharing is the question of what is to be shared. There is little doubt that profits (i. e. net profits) of ordinary business operations are to be shared. Non-recurring gains, e. g. on the sale of fixed assets, would normally be shared too.[8] Profits earned between dissolution and termination are generally to be shared.[9]

Also implicit in sharing is the question when profits are to be shared. Distribution or retention in the business is normally a matter to be determined by the partners under the partnership agreement or by majority decision.[10] In dissolution, profits rank low in priority

4. U.P.A. § 18(a). Carlson v. Phillips, 326 Ill.App. 594, 63 N.E.2d 193 (1945), joint preparation of radio script.

5. Greenberg v. Rose, 173 Cal.App.2d 532, 342 P.2d 522 (1959). If one of the partners abandons the business, he may forfeit some or all of his share of profits. Davis v. Spengler, 93 So.2d 348 (Fla.1957). This edges over into the question whether the remaining partners are entitled to additional compensation; see Sec. 65(e) below.

6. U.P.A. § 18(a).
A limited partner shares losses only to the extent of his contribution, U.L.P.A. §§ 17, 7.

7. Below at n. 15. It is not uncommon to find provisions for sharing profits in different ratios from losses, e. g., where the economic positions of the parties are such that one needs to protect another against risks beyond a certain point. They may agree that one partner shall bear a smaller percentage of losses, or his regular percentage up to some specified dollar amount.

8. Contra where the gain is realized in winding up and the partners had agreed to distribute assets in propor-

tion to capital account, Vollet v. Pechenik, 380 Pa. 342, 110 A.2d 221 (1955).

Contra also where the gain is from the sale of an asset which belongs, not to the partnership, but to a partner who has given only the "use" of it to the firm. See Annot., When real estate owned by partner before formation of partnership will be deemed to have become asset of firm, 45 A.L.R.2d 1009 (1956).

9. U.P.A. § 21. The reasons customarily given are that the partnership continues until termination, U.P.A. § 30, and that the profits are generated by partnership assets in which each partner continues to have an interest. This area has been the subject of extensive litigation. See, e. g. Vangel v. Vangel, 116 Cal.App.2d 615, 254 P.2d 919 (1953); Annot., Accountability of partner or joint adventurer for profits earned subsequently to death or dissolution, 80 A.L.R. 12 (1932), supplemented 55 A.L.R.2d 1391 (1957). See also Vollet v. Pechenik, n. 8 above.

10. The time of distribution may be left to the decision of a managing partner, by the terms of the articles. Commissioner v. Olds, 60 F.2d 252 (6th Cir. 1932). In the absence of agreement as to when profits shall be distributed,

and can be distributed only after payment of debts, partners' advances, and partners' capital.[11]

The sharing of losses may require a partner to contribute additional funds.[12]

For example, suppose A, B, and C have contributed respectively $10,000, $5,000 and $2,000 to the firm's capital of $17,000, and share profits equally. On dissolution, after paying debts there remains $5,000, reflecting a loss of $12,000.[13] Sharing this loss equally means a debit to each of $4,000. A would receive $6,000, B would receive $1,000, and C would pay in $2,000 to meet the deficiency.[14] This rule has been applied where one or more partners have contributed no capital, but only their services.[15] Prior to the U.P.A. there was con-

or who shall decide the question, it would probably be "ordinary matter connected with the partnership business", the decision of which is within the powers of the majority. U.P.A. § 18(h). Of course an attempt in bad faith to unreasonably exclude a partner from his right to participate in profits in a cause for dissolution and accounting by decree of court. U.P.A. § 32(d), (f); Herman v. Pepper, 311 Pa. 104, 166 A. 587 (1933).

A limited partner cannot effectively insist on a distribution of earnings where the general partners find it necessary to retain them for working capital. Wolcheck v. Wecher, 66 N.Y.S.2d 384 (Sup.Ct.1946), aff'd without opin. 272 App.Div. 912, 72 N.Y.S.2d 273 (1947).

Distributions to a limited partner may not be made unless partnership assets exceed liabilities to third persons, U.L.P.A. § 15.

Lissman v. McDonald, 119 Cal.App.2d 228, 258 P.2d 1057 (1953) (agreement required distribution).

At this point the semantics shift, and we are really concerned about assets (money). Since the money belongs to the partnership, no partner can take it without consent of the others, U.P. A. § 25(2) (a), Sec. 41(a) above. But see Sonksen v. Primm, 71 Nev. 120, 281 P.2d 987 (1955) (assignee of 1% of profits "distributable" to a partner held entitled to accounting for profits capable of distribution, not merely those which were distributed by agreement of the partners).

11. U.P.A. § 40(b).

12. This will usually be true when his share of losses exceeds his capital account.

13. Such a loss is "capital" in the sense that the original capital has been consumed by it. In modern tax-influenced parlance, "capital loss" is the kind incurred by the sale, below cost, of a "capital asset", typically a fixed asset as distinguished from inventory. Int. Rev.Code of 1954 §§ 1221, 1222 (26 U.S.C.A.). The former meaning refers to effect, the latter to cause; both are subject to sharing by the partners.

14. Whitcomb v. Converse, 119 Mass. 38, 20 Am.Rep. 311 (1875); Shirley v. Straub, 50 N.D. 872, 198 N.W. 675 (1924); Raymond v. Putnam, 44 N.H. 160 (1862); Wischmeyer v. Siebeneck, 46 Ohio App. 486, 189 N.E. 509 (1933) (several liability of each solvent partner); Rosenberger v. Kuesel, 292 Pa. 184, 140 A. 860 (1928).

But see Glenn v. Weill, 319 Pa. 380, 179 A. 563 (1935), applying for some reason not clear a rule that capital losses should be shared proportionately to capital contribution.

In Greiss v. Platzer, 131 N.J.Eq. 160, 24 A.2d 408 (1942), the firm never commenced business. Proceeds of liquidation of property contributed as capital, less than stated value, were distributed in proportions in which originally owned by partners. The property was the assets of a corporation of which the partners were stockholders.

15. Whitcomb v. Converse, n. 14 above; Moseley v. Taylor, 173 N.C. 286, 91 S.E. 1035, L.R.A.1917E, 875 (1917), semble; Bivins v. Proctor, 125 Tex. 137, 80 S.

siderable authority to the contrary, based on the ground that the contributor of capital contributes its use merely, and it should not be presumed that the other partners intended not only to risk receiving nothing as compensation for services, but also to assume a duty of indemnifying another against capital losses.[16] It may be answered that such a partnership, in which some partners contribute nothing to capital, is an unusual situation in a partnership where a substantial amount of capital is employed. In entering an association with unusual features, the associates should foresee that application of the usual rules may bring about unusual results, and take advantage of their power to vary by agreement the rules which in the absence of agreement are implied. It doubtless appears to be a hardship that the contributor of services and a relatively small amount of capital, or none at all, should be obligated to contribute toward the loss of the large contributor, who according to the agreement of association contributed no services. As a practical matter the obligation to contribute anything beyond the working partner's original investment, if any, is probably in most cases a nominal one. The partner who contributes little or no capital is generally without resources wherewith to share losses. He may be execution proof.

The proportional sharing of losses is purely an internal matter and does not prevent a partnership creditor from recovering his entire claim against one partner through his joint or joint and several liability. The partner's way of prorating his loss is by indemnification from his co-partners.[17] For federal income tax purposes, a partner is taxable on his share of income and may deduct his share of loss regardless whether it is distributed to him, and may deduct his share of loss regardless whether he has contributed toward it.[18]

W.2d 307 (1935) (distinguishing capital invested in permanent things, such as real estate and equipment, from capital invested in consumable or disposable property, such as cattle); Richert v. Handly, 53 Wash.2d 121, 330 P.2d 1079 (1958). See Note, 24 Colum.L. Rev. 508 (1924).

16. Meadows v. Mocquot, 110 Ky. 220, 61 S.W. 28 (1901); In re Liquidation of Mitchell-Borne Constr. Co., note 26 below; Baker v. Safe Deposit & Trust Co., 90 Md. 744, 45 A. 1028, 78 Am. St.Rep. 463 (1900); Hasbrouck v. Childs, 16 N.Y.Super. 105 (1858).

Other rationales have been offered, e. g., that the loss of one's services balances the other's capital, and that the partners have agreed upon the equal value of their services and capital, and thus the loss has been shared according to their expectations. Kovacik v. Reed, 49 Cal.2d 166, 315 P.2d 314 (1957).

Such a decision conflicts with U.P.A. § 18(a) unless based on factual finding of the partners' intent; see Sher and Bromberg, Texas Partnership Law in the 20th Century, 12 Sw.L.J. 263, 288–94 (1958). This article analyzes and sharply criticizes the "use" and "labor" exceptions to the sharing of "capital" losses.

It may be agreed that respective rights in capital shall be different from the respective contributions thereto. Lavoine v. Casey, 251 Mass. 124, 146 N.E. 241 (1925). See 8 Wis.L.Rev. 84.

17. See Sec. 65(b) below.

18. Int.Rev.Code of 1954, §§ 702(a), 704 (26 U.S.C.A.). Note, however, that a partner's loss deduction may not exceed his basis in the partnership, id. § 704(d). This has the effect of denying him a deduction for a loss which has not been economically absorbed

The tax law treats the partnership as an entity in requiring it to file a return,[19] and as an aggregate in taxing the income to the partners rather than the partnership.[20]

_____ *Capital Contributions and Advances*

Before profits are shared on dissolution, payments must be made to creditors, and partners must be repaid their advances and their capital contributions.[21] Presumably the partner making advances is entitled to interest thereon until paid.[22] If the partnership property is

by his share of income, capital contribution or borrowings. However, he may take the loss later when he does absorb it in any of these ways. Since undistributed profits are taxed, it is only fair that distributions not be taxed; this is generally the case, id. § 731. On partnership taxation in general see Aronsohn, Partnerships and Income Taxes (1966); McDonald, Dohan & Phillips, Federal Income Taxation of Partners and Partnerships (1957); Willis, Handbook of Partnership Taxation (1957); Jackson et al., The Internal Revenue Code of 1954: Partnerships, 54 Colum.L.Rev. 1183 (1954).

19. Int.Rev.Code of 1954 § 6031 (26 U.S. C.A.).

Other entity features include computation of tax by the partnership like an individual (including the making of elections on the partnership return), id. § 703. Partnership property is not subject to distraint for taxes of a partner, I.T. 3356, 1940–1 Cum.Bull. 72. But see U. S. v. Balanovski, 236 F.2d 298 (2d Cir. 1956), cert. denied 352 U.S. 968, 77 S.Ct. 357, 1 L.Ed.2d 322 (1957) (quasi in rem jurisdiction over partnership bank account to enforce taxes against non-resident partners). The case is discussed Sec. 41, n. 73 above.

20. Int.Rev.Code of 1954 § 701 (26 U.S. C.A.). For further analysis of entity and aggregate concepts in taxation, see Sec. 3(d) at nn. 74–75 above; Bromberg, Taxable Income Without Gain on the Sale of a Deceased Partner's Interest: Code, Common Law, and Community Property, 13 Sw.L.J. 343, 362 (1959); Bromberg, Error Seen in Taxing Partner on Firm's Installment Notes at Gift of His Interest, 14 J.Tax. 36 (1961); Surrey and Warren, Federal Income Taxation—Cases

and Materials 1124–26 (1960). For a general comparison of partnership under local and tax law, see Sullivan, Conflicts Between State Partnership Laws and the Internal Revenue Code, 15 Tax L.Rev. 105 (1959) and 229 (1960).

21. U.P.A. § 40(b) sets the priorities of distribution in this order. Section 18 (a) reinforces the rights to receive them. The terminology of the two sections is not identical but presumably the significance is the same. Thus, "advances" in § 18(a) are equivalent to "those owing to partners other than for capital and profits" in § 40(b) (II).

A contribution of property is credited at its market value when contributed, Bass v. Daetwyler, 305 S.W.2d 339 (Mo.App.1957).

22. Kraus v. Kraus, 250 N.Y. 63, 164 N.E. 743 (1928); Levy v. Leavitt, 257 N.Y. 461, 178 N.E. 758 (1931).

Annot., Right of Partners Inter Se in Respect of Interest, 66 A.L.R. 3, 17–22 (1930).

The interest continues until dissolution, Vaughan v. Caldwell, 200 Cal. 572, 253 P. 929 (1927).

Prior to the U.P.A., the presumption was against interest in some states. Ice v. Kilworth, 84 Kan. 458, 114 P. 857, 35 L.R.A.,N.S., 220 (1911); Miller v. Lord, 28 Mass. (11 Pick.) 11 (1831); Godfrey v. White, 43 Mich. 171, 5 N.W. 243 (1880).

Compare Drudge v. Citizens' Bank, 209 Ind. 638, 196 N.E. 111 (1935); Munroe, Boyce & Co. v. Ward, 207 Mich. 369, 174 N.W. 285 (1919).

The distinction between a capital contribution and an advancement or loan to the partnership by a partner was made in Nye v. United States, 84 F.2d 457 (1st Cir. 1936). A federal revenue

insufficient to repay advances, the deficiency, like any other loss, is charged against all the partners in the proportion in which they share profits.[23]

After repayment of advances, the partners are to be repaid their capital contributions. As a general proposition, no interest is payable on capital [24] except from the time when repayment should have been made; [25] but this rule may be modified by agreement of the partners, and a partner may be entitled to interest on capital at some specified rate. Where the capital contributions are unequal, an agreement that partners shall be "equal partners," presumably relates to profits only, and not to capital.[26]

The bookkeeping and accounting methods used by the partnership are vitally important to the matters treated in this section. Although they may not have the force of law, they will be evidence of intent (particularly if accepted by all the partners) and influential in computing profits and losses, in distinguishing capital from advances, and in many other respects. Simple accounting normally closes each partner's profit and loss account to his capital account at the end of the year, thus telescoping the two concepts.[27] To keep the two accounts

---

act provided for a tax on profits allowing a credit of certain percentages on "invested capital," which was defined as not including "money or other property borrowed" (40 Stat. 306, § 207). It was held that on reorganization of a partnership with a fixed capital of $100,000, contributions of additional amounts, derived from undistributed profits of a former partnership, on which interest was to be paid to the contributing partners, and which were to be repaid before distribution of capital and profits, were "borrowed money." The relation of creditor and debtor between partner and partnership was recognized for this purpose.

Funds are advances (not capital) if the partners do not contemplate that they are irrevocably risked in the business. M. & C. Creditors Corp. v. Pratt, 172 Misc. 695, 17 N.Y.S.2d 240 (1938), aff'd 255 App.Div. 838, 7 N.Y.S.2d 662 (1938), aff'd 281 N.Y. 804, 24 N.E.2d 482 (1939).

Whether an advance by the partner to the firm is a loan or an added contribution to capital is a question of fact. Rodgers v. Clement, 162 N.Y. 422, 56 N.E. 901, 76 Am.St.Rep. 342 (1900).

As to charging a partner with interest on his withdrawals, see Underdown v. Underdown, 279 Pa. 482, 124 A. 159

(1924); Kaufman v. Catzen, 108 W.Va. 1, 150 S.E. 371 (1929), co-adventurer.

23. U.P.A. §§ 40(c), 18(a).

24. Luchs v. Ormsby, 171 Cal.App.2d 377, 340 P.2d 702 (1959).

25. Taft v. Schwamb, 80 Ill. 289 (1875); Keiley v. Turner, 81 Md. 269, 31 A. 700 (1895); Jackson v. Johnson, 11 Hun 509 (N.Y.1878).

Annot., Right of Partners Inter Se in Respect of Interest, 66 A.L.R. 3 (1930).

26. Gillespie v. Gillespie, 124 Misc. 881, 210 N.Y.S. 303 (1924); Glenn v. Weill, 319 Pa. 380, 179 A. 563 (1935).

See Hillock v. Grape, 111 App.Div. 720, 97 N.Y.S. 823 (1906); Johnson v. Jackson, 130 Ky. 751, 114 S.W. 260, 17 Ann.Cas. 699 (1908); In re Liquidation of Mitchell-Borne Constr. Co., 145 La. 379, 82 So. 377 (1919); In re Adams & Lester's Estate, 215 Mo.App. 606, 257 S.W. 142 (1923); Buie v. Kennedy, 164 N.C. 290, 80 S.E. 445 (1913); Farris v. Farris Engineering Corp., 7 N.J. 487, 81 A.2d 731 (1951). But see Taft v. Schwamb, 80 Ill. 289 (1875); Thrall v. Trout, 107 Kan. 509, 192 P. 750 (1920).

27. On partnership accounting see: Finney & Miller, Principles of Accounting—Introductory 106-13, 226-41 (4th

separate, it may be advisable so to specify in the partnership agreement;[27A] however, if the books have been well kept, it will usually be possible to reconstruct the capital accounts as distinct from the profit and loss accounts.

(b) Indemnification

A partner's joint or joint and several liability may force him to pay an entire partnership debt.[28] But losses are shared by all partners equally or in agreed proportions.[29] Any apparent conflict between these two principles is resolved by noting that the liability is external (to third persons) and the sharing is internal (among partners). The equilibrating mechanism, by which one partner recovers from the partnership or his co-partners any amounts he has paid in excess of his share, is variously called indemnification, contribution [30] and reimbursement. If a partner fails to obtain indemnification (e. g. if his co-partners are absent or insolvent), the entire economic burden falls on him; this is one of the risks of the partnership form.

The right to indemnification exists not only when a partner is compelled to pay more than his share of a partnership debt, but also when he does so voluntarily.[31] To protect a partner from having to expend his own money first and then seek indemnity, the right extends not only to payments made but to liabilities incurred by him.[32]

ed. 1953),—Advanced 1–87 (4th ed. 1952). Graham & Katz, Accounting in Law Practice 101–29 (2d ed. 1938); Wixon, Accountants' Handbook, 24.1–24.24 (4th ed. 1961).

27A. See Appendix V, pars. 2.3–2.6 below.

28. Sec. 58 above.

29. Sec. 65(a) above.

30. This is to be distinguished from contribution to losses, UPA § 18(a), Sec. 65(a) above. The three terms are closely related, and may arise from the same economic circumstances, as where one partner incurs the expenditure which constitutes the loss. Indemnification may arise apart from losses, e. g., in one partner's paying for a valuable asset. On the other hand, a partner must contribute to losses incurred entirely with partnership funds and therefore creating no indemnification right. To avoid confusion, it is preferable to follow the statute and use "contribution" in connection with UPA § 18(a) and "indemnification" in connection with UPA § 18(b). Note that the former is an income concept and the latter an asset-liability concept. The possible overlap should not make a partner liable twice for the same economic sum.

31. UPA § 18(b) makes no distinction between voluntary and compulsory payments.

32. UPA § 18(b). Bass v. Daetwyler, 305 S.W.2d 339 (Mo.App.1957). But see Burstein v. Zelman, 182 Cal.App. 2d 1, 5 Cal.Rptr. 829 (1960) (partner not entitled to indemnity for losses without proof that he paid them); Barron v. Koenig, 80 Idaho 28, 324 P.2d 388 (1958) (contribution only for partner who has paid obligation or otherwise relieved firm from it).

For an example of the rudimentary application of indemnification, see Smith v. Shetter, 38 Tenn.App. 642, 277 S.W. 2d 464 (1955). On dissolution, the total contributions of each of the two partners were totalled. The one who contributed more was entitled to recover, from the other, half the excess. The situation is typical of small partnerships in several respects: (1) some contributions were made in kind, (2) their value was not agreed upon at the time and was disputed later, (3) ap-

A partner is entitled to indemnification first from the partnership.[33] If the partnership fails to pay, the obligation falls on his co-partners,[34] since he becomes a creditor of the partnership to the extent of his claim.[35]

If the partners share losses in the same ratios as profits, these ratios will govern their contributions toward indemnification. If the loss ratios differ from the profit ratios, it is not clear which will govern. (1) If the payment being indemnified is considered in isolation from other partnership transactions, and can be traced to a loss or expense item, the loss ratios perhaps should control.[36] (2) If the payment is considered in isolation and can be traced to a capital outlay, probably the profit ratios should control. (3) If the payment is not considered in isolation, or if it cannot be traced to any particular expenditure, it appears that the results for the entire accounting period should be determinative: if there is an overall loss, the loss ratios should apply and if there is a gain, the gain ratios should.[37]

The indemnification right has been explained as an implied contract arising out of the agreement to share profits and losses in designated proportions.[38] It can also be justified by viewing the paying partner as subrogated to the rights of the creditors (whom he has paid) against the partnership and the partners.[39] Or it can be regarded as an incident of the partners' representative and fiduciary relation to one another.[40]

Indemnification is available only for expenses reasonably incurred in the ordinary and proper conduct of the partnership business or for the preservation of its business or property.[41] Examples of indemnifiable expenses include: costs of litigation to recover partnership property,[42] damages to a partner's truck used in the partnership busi-

parently there was no written partnership agreement, (4) adequate books were not kept. Bass v. Daetwyler, supra, involves a similar reconstruction from inadequate records at the end of the partnership.

33. UPA § 18(b).

34. UPA § 40(d).

35. UPA § 40(b) (II).

36. See Barron v. Koenig, 80 Idaho 28, 324 P.2d 388 (1958), tracing borrowed funds into operating expenses.

37. There is virtually no authority directly in point. UPA § 18(b) and § 40 (d) call for sharing per profit ratios, but these are subject to any agreement among the partners. A different set of loss ratios probably would be a controlling agreement where a loss in fact occurs.

38. Vaughan v. Caldwell, 200 Cal. 572, 253 P. 929 (1927).

39. See Paggi v. Quinn, 179 S.W.2d 789 (Tex.Civ.App.1944).

40. See Restatement, Second, Agency §§ 438–39 (agent's indemnity from principal); Restatement, Second, Trusts §§ 244–47 (trustee's indemnity from trust estate).

41. UPA § 18(b). The idea is similar to that of UPA § 9(1) designating the circumstances in which a partner binds the partnership to third persons; see Secs. 49–50 above. However, UPA § 18(b) contains far more restrictions since there are no third persons to be protected.

42. Evan v. Boggs, 35 Tenn.App. 354, 245 S.W.2d 641 (1951).

ness,[43] and even living expenses if closely enough related to the partnership business.[44]   Indemnification has been allowed for expenses incurred prior to formation of the partnership.[45]

At common law, the traditional way of enforcing indemnification was in an accounting at dissolution.   The partner need not wait this long if the claim is isolated [46] or if all other partnership affairs have been accounted for.[47]   Moreover, he may now have an accounting without dissolution whenever circumstances render it just and reasonable.[48] This will often be the case when he has paid or incurred a substantial partnership liability without prospect of prompt indemnification except through an accounting.

(c) Interest on Capital and Advances

Subject always to specific agreement, a partner is entitled to interest on payments to or for the partnership in excess of his agreed capital contribution.[49]   But he is not entitled to interest on his capital contribution itself except from the date when it should be repaid to him.[50]

---

43. Smith v. Hensley, 354 S.W.2d 744, 98 A.L.R.2d 340 (Ky.1962).

44. See Hurst v. Hurst, 86 Ariz. 242, 344 P.2d 1001 (1959).   But see Bass v. Daetwyler, 305 S.W.2d 399 (Mo.App. 1957), dubiously holding that a partner who agreed to furnish his land to the partnership rent-free was not entitled to reimbursement for taxes and road repairs on the land.   A more logical approach would have been to inquire whether the payments benefited the land in the capacity in which the partnership used it.

45. Hargett v. Miller, 235 Ark. 523, 361 S.W.2d 83 (1962); the court reasoned that the partnership would have had to incur the expense (laying the foundation for a building completed after formation of the firm) itself. The case questionably denies reimbursement for expenses and depreciation of a partner's truck used in partnership business, confusing reimbursement with "remuneration" which UPA § 18(f) denies in the absence of specific agreement.   The distinction is recognized in Hurst v. Hurst, n. 44 above.

46. Smith v. Hensley, 354 S.W.2d 744, 98 A.L.R.2d 340 (Ky.1962) (tort claim).

47. Taylor v. Richman, 395 Pa. 162, 149 A.2d 69 (1959).

48. UPA § 22(d), discussed Sec. 72 below.

49. UPA § 18(c).

50. UPA § 18(d); Luchs v. Ormsby, 171 Cal.App.2d 377, 340 P.2d 702 (1959).

The time when repayment should be made will usually be when winding up would have been completed in the normal course of events.   Thus, interest has been allowed from the date when partnership assets were sold, Thompson v. Beth, 14 Wis.2d 271, 111 N.W. 2d 171 (1961), and from six months after the date of dissolution, Evans v. Gunnip, 36 Del.Ch. 589, 135 A.2d 128 (1957).   But see Berliner v. Greenberg, 37 Wash.2d 308, 223 P.2d 598, 65 A.L.R.2d 513 (1950) (interest from date of dissolution decreed by court).

Interest has been allowed a partner on profits, where distributions to him were delayed by his co-partner's excessive withdrawals, Morris v. Redak, 124 Colo. 27, 234 P.2d 908 (1951).   See also Hargas v. Tipsword, 335 S.W.2d 137 (Mo.1960) (partner entitled to interest where co-partner failed to make required capital contribution).   The allowance of interest is influenced by a jurisdiction's general statutory and case law on interest; often these give substantial discretion to the trial court.   See Greenan v. Ernst, 408 Pa. 495, 184 A.2d 570 (1962).

The rationale is that capital contributions are an agreed aspect of the partnership business, and that one kind of compensation (interest) will not be inferred where another (profit-sharing) is express or necessarily and primarily implied.[51] However, interest on capital overdue for repayment is not for its expected use in the business but for delay in discharge of a matured obligation. Similarly, interest on advances recognizes their unexpected or exceptional character.

(d) Participation in Management

All partners have the right to participate in management, and no partner may be excluded from participation.[52] The management right is described as a property right,[53] although the significance of this classification is obscure. Each partner's management rights are equal,[54] subject to majority rule in ordinary matters.[55]

By agreement, these arrangements may be varied, and management concentrated in one or more partners.[56] This is a common feature of large professional partnerships [57] and of joint stock companies.

In a limited partnership, management is in the general partners as though there were no others.[58] Limited partners are not expressly

51. This theory is further discussed in connection with compensation to partners, Sec. 65(e) below.

52. Strickland Printing & Stationery Co. v. Chenot, 45 S.W.2d 937 (Mo.App. 1932); Harris v. Harris, 132 Ala. 208, 31 So. 355 (1902); Batson v. Drummond, 158 Ark. 29, 249 S.W. 547 (1923); Katz v. Brewington, 71 Md. 79, 20 A. 139 (1889); Wilcox v. Pratt, 125 N.Y. 688, 25 N.E. 1091 (1890). In the above cases it was held that exclusion was a cause for dissolution.

National Biscuit Co. v. Stroud, 249 N.C. 467, 106 S.E.2d 692 (1959), noted 1960 Duke L.J. 150; Parks v. Riverside Ins. Co. of America, 308 F.2d 175 (10th Cir. 1962) (Okla. law).

It follows that a court will not enjoin the exercise of a partner's management rights, Hauke v. Frey, 167 Neb. 398, 93 N.W.2d 183 (1958).

53. U.P.A. § 24(3).

54. U.P.A. § 18(e).

55. U.P.A. § 18(h); Sec. 65(h) below.

56. McAlpine v. Millen, 104 Minn. 289, 116 N.W. 583 (1908); Trigg v. Shelton, 249 S.W. 209 (Tex.Com.App.1923).

Agreement to commit control to one partner may be inferred from a long continued assumption of such control acquiesced in by the others. Miller v. Ashley & Rumelin, 127 Or. 215, 271 P. 596 (1928).

Reservation of control in one partner is not binding on third persons dealing with other partners without notice. Wilke v. Simon, 46 S.D. 422, 193 N.W. 666 (1923).

Though one partner has a "controlling" power of management by agreement, he cannot exclude the others from all participation, or from possession of partnership property or right to accounting. Groth v. Payment, 79 Mich. 290, 44 N.W. 611 (1890).

If one partner to whom management of a transaction is intrusted abandons it, the others may assume control and conclude the business. Sweet v. Morrison, 103 N.Y. 235, 8 N.E. 396 (1886).

57. See n. 3 above.

58. U.L.P.A. § 9; Sec. 26 above.

barred from management, but they lose their limited liability if they take part in the control of the business.[59]

(e) Right to Compensation for Services and Use of Property

Without an agreement, a partner's services in carrying on the firm's business entitle him to no compensation other than his share of the profits.[60] "The reason is that the partner is but attending to his own affairs." [61] A more cogent rationale is that one kind of compensation will not be inferred where another (profit-sharing) has been expressed.[62] A fuller explanation follows:

"In the business of a partnership the services of a partner are rendered for the common benefit in the performance of an obligation

---

59. U.L.P.A. § 7. A limited partner's contribution may not be services, U.L.P.A. § 4. This does not prevent him from performing services otherwise than as his contribution, but any services run the risk of being treated as participation in control, thus forfeiting limited liability. See Secs. 26(c), above, 90B below.

But see Executive Hotel Associates v. Elm Hotel Corp., 41 Misc.2d 354, 245 N.Y.S.2d 929 (Civ.Ct.1964), aff'd per curiam 43 Misc.2d 153, 250 N.Y.S.2d 351 (Sup.Ct.App.T.1964). The opinion asserts, on pre-U.L.P.A. authority, that a limited partner is as much a partner as a general partner, and can take an active part if he chooses to face the consequence of personal liability. It is very doubtful that this is a correct interpretation under U.L.P.A. One of the Act's purposes was to dispose of the notion that a limited partner was basically just another partner. Indeed, he is probably not a "partner" at all, only a "member." See Secs. 26(a), 26(c), 32 above.

The result of the cited case is proper: allowing a limited partner to bring a suit in behalf of the firm against a corporation indebted to it and controlled by general partners who had breached their fiduciary duty. The same result has been reached by higher authority applying fiduciary principles without discussing the limited partner's management capacity. Riviera Congress Associates v. Yassky, 18 N.Y.2d 540, 277 N.Y.S.2d 386, 223 N.E.2d 876 (1966).

60. U.P.A. § 18(f).

Hurst v. Hurst, 86 Ariz. 242, 344 P.2d 1001 (1960) ; Wind v. Herbert, 186

Cal.App.2d 276, 8 Cal.Rptr. 817 (1960) ; Engelstein v. Mackie, 35 Ill.App.2d 276, 182 N.E.2d 351, 361 (1962) ; A. Willmann & Associates v. Penseiro, 159 Me. 319, 192 A.2d 469 (1963) ; Mousseau v. Walker, 356 Mich. 373, 97 N.W.2d 110 (1959) ; Cohen v. Erdle, 282 App.Div. 569, 126 N.Y.S.2d 32 (1954) ; Rosenfeld v. Rosenfeld, 390 Pa. 39, 133 A.2d 829, 66 A.L.R.2d 1013 (1957) ; Waagen v. Gerde, 36 Wash.2d 563, 219 P.2d 595 (1950) noted 49 Mich. L.Rev. 905 (1951).

An apparently contrary rule applies in income taxation of the family partnership. Reasonable compensation for services *must*, in effect, be paid. Int.Rev.Code of 1954, § 704(e) (2) (26 U.S.C.A.) The purpose, of course, is to prevent deflection of income from the one whose efforts are instrumental in generating the income (usually the father, in high tax brackets) to other members of the family (usually children in low income brackets). See Sec. 23A above.

61. Lindsey v. Stranahan, 129 Pa. 635, 18 A. 524 (1889). A similar explanation is that the partner is a principal, not an employee, Heilbron v. Stubblefield, 203 S.W.2d 986, 989 (Tex.Civ. App.1947) error ref. n. r. e.

62. The implication is even stronger in the case of a limited partner, whose compensation is restrictively set forth in U.L.P.A. § 15. The same negative implication supports the disallowance of interest to a partner on his capital contribution, U.P.A. § 18(d), Sec. 65(c) above.

created by the partnership agreement, and the resultant benefit is divided pro rata as provided in the partnership contract. These profits constitute, in the absence of other agreement, the stipulated reward for services to be rendered, and there is no right to other compensation based on the reasonable value of the services actually rendered.[62A] Inequality of the value of services rendered, even the fact that the services were extraordinary and that, at the time the contract was made, the parties did not contemplate that such services would be required in the course of the partnership business, would not alone justify the award of compensation outside the share of profits accruing to the partner rendering the services. True, such circumstances, though insufficient alone to give rise to an implied promise to pay for the services rendered, may give significance and color to other evidence, tending to establish that the parties intended that special payment should be made for special services and expressed that intention— though perhaps somewhat equivocally, either in words or deeds." [63]

The agreement which varies the basic rule may be either express [64] or implied.[65] The existence of an implied agreement, and its terms, are questions of fact. An agreement to pay wages for services would be natural where some partners devote their entire time to the business, while others are inactive,[66] though such a situation could also be cared

---

62A. It has been so held even where the other partner prevented the realization of expected profits by terminating the arrangement between them. White v. Lemley, 328 S.W.2d 694 (Mo. 1958), noted 26 Mo.L.Rev. 84 (1961).

63. Levy v. Leavitt, 257 N.Y. 461, 178 N.E. 758 (1931). Even if unusual services of a professional nature are rendered, as where a member of a commercial partnership who is an attorney collects claims owing the firm, he is not entitled to compensation except by special agreement. Vanduzer v. McMillan, 37 Ga. 299 (1867).

See also: Cole v. Cole, 119 Ark. 48, 177 S.W. 915 (1915), noted 64 U.Pa.L.Rev. 326 (1916) (applying the rule to a case of illness of a partner requiring additional services by a copartner); In re McConnell's Estate, 6 Cal.2d 493, 58 P.2d 639 (1930); Street v. Thompson, 229 Ill. 613, 82 N.E. 367 (1907) (joint venture); Condon v. Moran, 11 N.J. Super. 221, 78 A.2d 295 (1951) (refusing compensation other than profits to partner who furnished major part of services, but allowing copartner compensation for use of premises where business was carried on and for board and room furnished active partner);

Baker v. McGrane, 198 Wis. 512, 224 N.W. 737 (1929).

Where partners have agreed to go "50–50" with a provision that one partner, who contributes services, not capital, shall have a drawing account of $60 per week, it is not salary but an advance on profits. Boyer v. Bowles, 310 Mass. 134, 37 N.E.2d 489 (1941).

64. Chambers v. Sims, 13 Utah 2d 371, 374 P.2d 841 (1962) (written agreement specified "reasonable" compensation; amount was set by court after testimony on value). See Rosenfeld v. Rosenfeld, 390 Pa. 39, 133 A.2d 829, 66 A.L.R.2d 1013 (1957) (agreement setting salary but not specifying duration was, like partnership, terminable at will). See Annot., Construction and effect of agreement relating to salary of partners, 66 A.L.R.2d 1023 (1959).

65. McBride v. Fitzpatrick, 224 Or. 457, 356 P.2d 947 (1960).

Salary or interest paid to a partner is treated for income tax purposes as though he were a stranger. Int.Rev. Code of 1954, § 707 (26 U.S.C.A.).

66. This will usually be true in a joint stock company in which there is a concentration of management.

for by agreement as to respective shares of profits. Where shares of profits are proportioned to shares of capital, and some partners serve while others are inactive, as in a mining partnership, agreement to pay wages or salaries may be implied, in view of custom as well as of circumstances.[67] The same inference has been drawn in the case of a manufacturing partnership, where profits were shared equally, but one partner was inactive.[68] That wages have been paid over a considerable

See also Greenan v. Ernst, 408 Pa. 495, 184 A.2d 570 (1962). Here the services were "beyond normal partnership functions", continued for several decades, and produced millions in profits. In addition, there was agreement for *some* compensation, in the form of a contract for salary for the first six months, to be readjusted thereafter.

67. Rains v. Weiler, 101 Kan. 294, 166 P. 235, L.R.A.1917F, 571 (1917): "So here the plaintiff was an active partner who organized the business and advanced money to start it. He was made general manager and gave his entire time to the management of the business. During the continuance of the business the plaintiff performed this unusual service, while the defendant was engaged in another line of business and gave no time to the partnership business. There was testimony of statements by defendant that he left the management of the business to the plaintiff and that whatever plaintiff did was satisfactory to him. A case where an active and managing partner devotes his whole time and attention to a partnership business at the instance of other partners who are attending to their individual business and giving no time or attention to the business of the firm presents unusual conditions which take the case out of the general rule as to compensation and warrants the implication of an agreement to pay compensation. . . . Complaint is made of the introduction of evidence that a custom or usage existed in the mining district to the effect that partners who devote their time to managing a mine where other partners do not give the business any time or attention are given compensation for their services. . . . The custom being general and well settled the defendant is presumed to have known of it and to have contracted with reference to it. It is not opposed to law, and cannot be said to be unreasonable. It appears to ac-

cord with the other testimony in the case; that is, the facts and circumstances were such as to show a mutual intention to pay for the exceptional services of the plaintiff. . . ."

Duthweiler v. Hanson, 54 Idaho 46, 28 P.2d 210 (1933), oral agreement showed two of three partners to labor in mine at going wages, the third, who contributed larger share of capital, to receive salary for supervision, agreement to share profits equally, which was held to mean profits after paying agreed compensation to partners.

68. Emerson v. Durand, 64 Wis. 111, 24 N.W. 129, 54 Am.Rep. 593 (1885); In re Levy's Estate, 125 Wash. 240, 215 P. 811 (1923), mercantile partnership of two members, one of whom was absent for a long period leaving management to the others.

Davis v. Spengler, 93 So.2d 348 (Fla.1957) (partner entitled to compensation for services when co-partner abandoned business).

But in Leslie v. Oakley, 108 W.Va. 64, 150 S.E. 226 (1929), a partner in a jewelry business, who attended to its affairs while his co-partner sold automobiles, (but who was apparently not overworked) was held not to be entitled to compensation for his services; there was no agreement to that effect.

See Thompson v. Beth, 14 Wis.2d 271, 111 N.W.2d 171 (1961). This decision seems to allow a partner compensation on the absurd theory that his services were his contribution to partnership capital. The result, which took the form of letting him share in the proceeds of the sale of the partnership assets, appears equitable. It could apparently have been reached, without the absurdity, by allowing the partner to share in the profits on the sale or even by finding an implied agreement for compensation.

A related problem, the sharing of losses by a partner who contributes only

period of time, and duly entered in the books, is evidence of assent by the partners, who are presumably familiar with partnership books.[69]

If a partner's services are the kind which would not normally be performed by a partner, it is reasonable to allow compensation on a quantum meruit theory.[70]

With monotonous regularity, partners in disputed dissolutions pad their demands with claims for compensation. While it is important that equity be done, the courts should insist on convincing evidence to overcome the non-compensation rule. Otherwise a basic principle is violated when a partner, by a dubious salary claim, is permitted double compensation (once in profits and once in salary) or insulation from loss (by offset of the salary claim). The frequency of this kind of litigation emphasizes the importance of explicit, written agreement on compensation.[71]

The presumption against additional compensation should normally prevent a partner from collecting rent for property which he permits the partnership to use,[72] unless there is an agreement [73] or the use was not contemplated when the partnership was formed.

---

services is discussed Sec. 65(a) above at n. 15.

In a business trust the trustees, who are expected to perform services in carrying on the enterprise, although they may also be beneficiaries, are entitled to compensation, even in the absence of express contract, so that their compensation is a proper expense in determining the net income of the trust for the purpose of taxation. Trust No. 5522 and Trust No. 5644, Bellehurst Syndicate v. Commissioner, 83 F.2d 801 (9th Cir. 1936).

69. Dugan v. Forster, 104 Cal.App. 117, 285 P. 384 (1930); Mondamin Bank v. Burke, 165 Iowa 711, 147 N.W. 148 (1914), tacit understanding between partners found to exist; Hoag v. Alderman, 184 Mass. 217, 68 N.E. 199 (1903); Fortugno v. Hudson Manure Co., 51 N.J.Super. 482, 144 A.2d 207 (1958); Ashe v. Webb, 142 Tenn. 436, 217 S.W. 654 (1919).

See, as to express agreements, Jones v. Jones, 254 Ky. 475, 71 S.W.2d 999 (1934); Arthur v. McCallum, 195 Mich. 618, 162 N.W. 118 (1917); Will v. Domer, 134 Wash. 576, 236 P. 104 (1925); Notes, 24 Colum.L.Rev. 508 (1924); 17 L.R.A.,N.S., 385 (1909); L. R.A.1917F, 575.

See also Cole v. Cole, 119 Ark. 48, 177 S.W. 915 (1915), noted 64 U.Pa.L.Rev. 326 (1916).

Where it is uncertain whether amounts withdrawn by a partner are wages or advance on account of profits, the fact that no social security, federal old age benefits or other compulsory deductions were made is indicative of their treatment as advances. Midler v. Heinowitz, 6 N.J.Super. 359, 71 A.2d 540 (1950), aff'd 10 N.J. 123, 89 A.2d 458 (1952).

70. Waldor v. Bruey, 24 N.J.Misc. 354, 49 A.2d 151 (1946), aff'd 139 N.J.Eq. 238, 50 A.2d 646 (1949) (partner, in his separate establishment, performed secondary work (which the firm was unable or unwilling to do) on jobs undertaken by the firm). Montgomery v. Burch, 11 S.W.2d 545 (Tex.Civ.App. 1928) error dismissed (partner did work which was expected to be done by hired help). See also Madigan v. McCann, 346 Mass. 62, 190 N.E.2d 215 (1963) (purchase of partnership interest rescinded for fraud; purchaser entitled to compensation for services to the partnership while he was a partner).

71. For example, see Appendix V, par. 3.4.

72. Barron v. Koenig, 80 Idaho 28, 324 P.2d 388, 397 (1958); Waagen v. Gerde, 36 Wash.2d 563, 219 P.2d 595 (1950),

---

73. See note 73 on page 379.

At common law, a partner engaged in liquidation of partnership affairs after dissolution was entitled to no additional compensation, in the absence of special circumstances.[74] It is a risk he assumes in entering the partnership.[75] But if the surviving partner, in order to conserve partnership property and fulfill obligations to third persons, carries on the business for a time, and so does more than merely liquidate and distribute, he may be entitled to additional compensation.[76] Extraordinary services may be compensated at their fair value.[77] A receiver may hire a partner to assist him in continuing the business.[78] The U.P.A., in creating a presumption that a surviving partner is entitled to compensation for winding up partnership affairs,[79] goes somewhat beyond the common law rule.[80]

noted 49 Mich.L.Rev. 905 (1951). This point is not covered by U.P.A.

A related problem involves depreciation (a non-cash expense) on a partner's property used by the partnership. Without an agreement, a partner may not charge such depreciation to the firm, Sundstrom v. Sundstrom, 75 S.D. 555, 70 N.W.2d 65 (1955). A different result might be reached if this were regarded as an expenditure for the partnership, entitling the partner to indemnification; see U.P.A. § 18(b) and Sec. 65(b) above. The court considered, and rejected, depreciation as analogous to interest on capital. But see Hargett v. Miller, 235 Ark. 523, 361 S.W.2d 83 (1962) (U.P.A. § 18(f) precludes reimbursement for cash operating expenses and depreciation of partner's truck used in partnership business).

73. Meier v. Murphy, 207 S.W.2d 947 (Tex.Civ.App.1948), error ref. n. r. e.

74. Magullion v. Magee, 241 Mass. 360, 135 N.E. 560 (1922); Lacey v. Rutter, 366 Pa. 17, 76 A.2d 389 (1950). This is especially true where the partner does no more than he would have done under the original partnership contract. Consaul v. Cummings, 222 U.S. 262, 32 S.Ct. 83, 56 L.Ed. 192 (1911).

75. Justice v. Lairy, 19 Ind.App. 272, 49 N.E. 459, 65 Am.St.Rep. 405 (1898); Smith v. Knight, 88 Iowa 257, 55 N.W. 189 (1893).

76. Clifton v. Clark, 83 Miss. 446, 36 So. 251, 66 L.R.A. 821, 102 Am.St.Rep. 458, 1 Ann.Cas. 396 (1904); Babbitt v. Riddell's Ex'rs, 1 Grant Cas. 161 (Pa.

1854); Puffer v. Merton, 168 Wis. 366, 170 N.W. 368, 5 A.L.R. 1288 (1919).

But see Leary v. Kelly, 277 Pa. 217, 120 A. 817 (1923), overlooking provision of U.P.A. § 18f; noted, 33 Yale L.J. 216 (1923).

77. Maynard v. Richards, 166 Ill. 466, 46 N.E. 1138, 57 Am.St.Rep. 145 (1897); Zell's Appeal, 126 Pa. 329, 17 A. 647 (1889); Bracht v. Connell, 313 Pa. 397, 170 A. 297 (1933).

78. Efner v. Reynolds, 109 Neb. 275, 190 N.W. 864 (1922); Herman v. Pepper, 317 Pa. 349, 176 A. 201 (1935).

79. U.P.A. § 18(f); Murdock v. Murdock, 300 Pa. 280, 150 A. 599 (1930). Jacobson v. Wikholm, 29 Cal.2d 24, 172 P.2d 878 (1946), discussing the factual problem of determining what is reasonable compensation and holding that the estate of the deceased partner is not to be limited to interest on capital employed or profits attributable only to its use, under U.P.A. § 42, which is held to apply to continuance of the business without liquidation.

Compare Johnson v. Munsell, 170 Neb. 749, 104 N.W.2d 314 (1960) (surviving partner entitled to compensation out of deceased partner's share of profits). This is a dubious result under U.P.A. § 18(f) which is not conditional on profits.

A surviving partner may forfeit his right to compensation by breach of his fiduciary duties in winding up. Lee v. Dahlin, 399 Pa. 50, 159 A.2d 679, 81 A.L.R.2d 442 (1960).

In general, see Annot. Construction and application of § 18(f) of Uniform Part-

80. See note 80 on page 380.

(f) Duty to Render Services

The question of duty to serve often arises with the question of right to compensation: a partner claims compensation for his services on the ground that his co-partner breached a duty to serve. He is more likely to succeed in establishing the co-partner's duty than his own right to remuneration.[81] A partner is normally obliged to render services to the firm in carrying on its business.[82] There is no statutory basis for this view, and its rationale in the cases is not very clear.[83] It is probably rooted in the expectation of the parties, and arose when active participation by all partners was more customary than it is now. Even today, with numerous firms in which partners invest funds but perform no services, it is likely that the great majority of partners do give active service. Thus, the rule has a real (if declining) basis in terms of expectation. But it should be applied less rigidly against a financing partner, or one in whose inactivity the other partners have acquiesced.

An express agreement requiring or exempting services will, of course, prevail.[84] An implied agreement can be found on appropriate facts, like the acquiescence mentioned in the previous paragraph, or in the joint stock company where there is a customary concentration of management.

A partner who breaches a duty to serve may suffer various consequences. He may be charged with the cost of hiring an employee to take his place,[85] or with the value of the services he failed to perform.[86]

nership Act as to surviving partner's right to compensation for services in winding up partnership, 81 A.L.R.2d 445 (1962).

"Surviving partner" in U.P.A. § 18(f) means one surviving after death, not after other forms of dissolution (here dissolution at will). Chazan v. Most, 209 Cal.App.2d 519, 25 Cal.Rptr. 864 (1962).

80. Note, 24 Colum.L.Rev. 508 (1924). In re Higgins' Estate, 69 Pa.D. & C. 489 (Pa.Com.Pl.1949).

81. Sec. 65(e) above.

82. Condon v. Moran, 11 N.J.Super. 221, 78 A.2d 295 (1951). Contra for a limited partner; he is under pressure not to render services. Services may not be his contribution, U.L.P.A. § 4. If performed, they may be deemed taking part in control, thus sacrificing his limited liability, U.L.P.A. § 7.

83. It does not arise out of fiduciary duties, which prohibit competition but do not affirmatively require support; see Sec. 68 below.

84. See, e. g. Hall v. Hall, 288 S.W.2d 51 (Ky.1956) (express agreement to devote full time); Balian v. Rainey, 115 Cal.App.2d 10, 251 P.2d 731 (1953) (express agreement to serve, specifying rate of charges against partners who failed to serve).

It is wise for the partners to reach a clear understanding on their service obligation and embody it in their agreement. See Appendix V, par. 5.3 below.

85. Hart v. Myers, 59 Hun 420, 13 N.Y. S. 388 (Sup.Ct.1891), aff'd 128 N.Y. 578, 28 N.E. 250 (1891). In general, see Annot., Liability of partner for failure to perform personal services, 165 A.L.R. 981 (1946).

86. Olivier v. Uleberg, 74 N.D. 453, 23 N. W.2d 39, 165 A.L.R. 974 (1946); Appeal of Marsh, 69 Pa. 30, 8 Am.Rep. 206 (1871).

Alternatively, his co-partners may be allowed compensation for their services.[87] His inaction may be ground for dissolution of the partnership.[88]

If a partner is permanently disabled and unable to render services as contemplated when the partnership was formed, there may be a right to dissolution by decree of court.[89] If the disability is temporary and not due to the partner's fault, it would seem that he is not chargeable for his failure to serve, since absence of a partner from time to time due to illness or other disability is a foreseeable risk. His right to profits should be unimpaired. If he is receiving a salary it should continue, in the absence of agreement to the contrary.[90]

(g) Consent of Partners Necessary for Admission to Partnership

This rule has been discussed previously in dealing with formation of partnerships.[91]

(h) Majority Rule

As discussed in dealing with the powers of partners,[92] the democratic principle of majority rule prevails.[93] However, it extends only to ordinary matters connected with the partnership business,[94] and not to matters which are extraordinary,[95] enumerated by statute,[96] or in

---

87. Davis v. Spengler, 93 So.2d 348 (Fla.1957); Valentin v. Sarrett, 25 Idaho 517, 138 P. 834 (1914).

88. U.P.A. § 32(1) (b), (d), Sec. 78 below.

89. See U.P.A. § 32(1) (b); Sec. 78, below.

90. Quillen v. Titus, 172 Va. 523, 2 S.E. 2d 284 (1939). Where the partner's temporary disability, during which his salary continues to be paid, is due to the tort of a third person, loss of earnings during disability is not a recoverable item of damage. Pensak v. Peerless Oil Co., 311 Pa. 207, 166 A. 792 (1933).

Even if the disability is long continued, if the disabled partner continually seeks a dissolution, which is contested by the other partner, the latter is not entitled to additional compensation for services in carrying on the business. Lacey v. Rutter, 366 Pa. 17, 76 A.2d 389 (1950).

Even if during a long period of disability a partner might be charged with the cost of providing a substitute, if the other partners continue to pay him his share of profits and receive and approve annual statements showing the fact that and that no charge has been made against him for the cost of substitutes,

any right to charge him is waived. Blut v. Katz, 14 N.J.Super. 121, 81 A. 2d 406 (1951), on other grounds, rev'd and remanded, 24 N.J.Super. 165, 93 A.2d 775 (1952), aff'd 13 N.J. 374, 99 A.2d 785 (1953).

91. See Sec. 5(c) above.

92. Sec. 53 above.

93. U.P.A. § 18(h). This is a characteristic of corporate directors and shareholders.

Latta v. Kilbourne, 150 U.S. 524, 545, 14 S.Ct. 201, 209, 37 L.Ed. 1169 (1893).

Church v. Collier, 71 Ariz. 353, 227 P.2d 385 (1951) (two partnerships with common majority members were controlled by the same interests so as to be a single "employing unit" under the local unemployment compensation statute).

94. U.P.A. § 18(h).

95. Fortugno v. Hudson Manure Co., 51 N.J.Super. 482, 144 A.2d 207 (1958), noted 4 Vill.L.Rev. 457 (1959) (incorporation of part of the partnership business).

96. U.P.A. § 9(3), Sec. 52 above (e. g., assignment for the benefit of creditors,

violation of the partnership agreement;[97] for these, unanimity is required. These results may be varied by agreement in numerous ways. Less than a majority may be authorized to act[98] or a greater proportion may be required.[99] Votes need not be one per partner; they may be based on capital accounts, income shares, seniority or other factors.[1]

Members of a joint-stock company commonly have voting rights similar to shareholders in a corporation, primarily for the election of directors or managers. What rights they have is a matter of agreement, and is expressed in the articles of association.[2] The voting rights of the beneficiaries in a business trust are set forth in the declaration of trust or articles of association. There is an unlimited variety as to such rights, from the extreme of no voting rights whatever,[3] to voting rights so extensive as to give them complete control over the personnel of the board of trustees and their conduct of the business.[4] Even where the beneficiaries have complete control over the conduct of the business, and can authorize sale of the property or termination of the business, the majority cannot authorize a sale to themselves of the entire property.[5] In this respect the association is treated as a partnership, rather than a corporation. In the absence of fraud or imposition upon minority shareholders, the majority shareholders in a corporation, under the corporation laws of most of the states, can bring about a dissolution and liquidation, and themselves purchase the corporate property.[6]

A limited partner in a limited partnership probably has no right to participate in management. If he does so, he subjects himself to liability as a general partner.[7] Provisions in articles of association

---

disposition of firm's good will, confession of judgment).

97. U.P.A. § 18(h).

98. Sec. 65(d) above.

99. This is true of corporate voting requirements (both directors and shareholders) in a growing number of jurisdictions. Henn, Corporations 415–17 (1961); 1 Model Bus.Corp.Act Ann. 626–27 (1960), 2 id. 759–69.

1. For examples, see Lowengrub v. Meislin, 376 Pa. 463, 103 A.2d 405 (1954) (requirement for approval of majority of each of two units of partners gave veto power to partner with 1/30th of investment); Carrington & Sutherland, Articles of Partnership for Law Firms 46–49 (1961) (vote according to participating units in profits).

2. See articles quoted in Tyrrell v. Washburn, 88 Mass. (6 Allen) 466

(1863); Hibbs v. Brown, 112 App.Div. 214, 98 N.Y.S. 353 (1906).

As to methods of electing directors of a joint-stock company, see Spraker v. Platt, 158 App.Div. 377, 143 N.Y.S. 440 (1913).

3. Betts v. Hackathorn, 159 Ark. 621, 252 S.W. 602, 31 A.L.R. 847 (1923); Thompson v. Schmitt, 115 Tex. 53, 274 S.W. 554 (1925).

4. Dana v. Treasurer & Receiver General, 227 Mass. 562, 116 N.E. 941 (1917); Morehead v. Greenville Exch. Nat. Bank, 243 S.W. 546 (Tex.Civ. App.1922).

5. Flint v. Codman, 247 Mass. 463, 142 N.E. 256 (1924).

6. See O'Neal, Expulsion or Oppression of Business Associates esp. 78–81 (1961).

7. U.L.P.A. § 7.

which give to limited partners the right to elect directors are dangerous to the formation of a statutory limited partnership.[8] Certain acts of the general partners, outside of the ordinary scope of the business, require for their validity the assent of all of the limited partners.[9]

PARTNERSHIP BOOKS

§ 66. The partnership books shall be kept, subject to any agreement between the partners, at the principal place of business of the partnership, and every partner shall at all times have access to and may inspect and copy any of them. U.P.A. § 19.

It is obvious that any business needs adequate financial records for determining the results of its past operations and planning its future ones.[10] Because the interests of several owners are involved, proper books are more vital for a partnership than for a sole proprietorship;[11] because the interests are more intimate and direct, the partnership's need may be even greater than the corporation's. Like corporation law,[12] a partnership law requires that books be kept.[13] Also like corporation law (but unlike commercial codes in many civil law countries), the requirement is not at all specific about the type of records and books.[14] However, considerable specificity is provided by the income tax law. Each taxpayer is required to maintain "such accounting records as will enable him to file a correct return,[15] and "such permanent books of account or record, including inventories, as are sufficient to establish the amount of gross income, deductions, credits or other matters required to be shown" in the return.[16] For a partnership, the return is Form 1065[17] which requires a statement of income and deductions (each classified into about a dozen categories, some with supplementary schedules) as well as each partner's share of these items, a rather detailed balance sheet, and a reconciliation of partners' capital accounts.[18]

---

8. See Strang v. Thomas, 114 Wis. 599, 91 N.W. 237 (1902).

9. U.L.P.A. § 9, similar to U.P.A. § 9(3) discussed n. 96 above.

10. Thus, in partnership, adequate books are essential to each partner's right to participate in management, U.P.A. § 18(e), Sec. 65(d) above.

11. Each partner has a right to an account, U.P.A. § 22, Sec. 72 below.

12. A common requirement is that every corporation maintain "complete and correct books and records of account", Model Bus.Corp.Act. § 46. For other provisions, see 2 Model Bus.Corp.Act Ann. 112–134 (1960).

13. U.P.A. § 19. Even this is rather oblique, since the statement is primarily *where* they shall be kept, and only secondarily *that* they shall be kept.

14. On partnership accounting in general, see references in Sec. 65(a) n. 27 above.

15. Income Tax Regs. § 1.446–1(a) (4) (1957, amended 1961).

16. Id. § 1.6001–1 (1959).

17. Id. § 1.6031–1(a) (1959).

18. See also Int.Rev.Code of 1954, § 446 (a) (26 U.S.C.A.) (taxable income computed under the method of accounting

With this background, we might expect to find that partnerships keep adequate books. No doubt many of them do, but it is shockingly common to find inadequate records or none at all.[19] To a degree, this can and should be corrected by provisions in the partnership agreement.[20]

A partner need not be an expert bookkeeper, or qualified to cause books to be kept in accordance with standard accounting practice.[21] But books should be kept in a manner adequate to the needs of the business, and if a partner charged with the duty is incompetent, he should hire a competent employee.[22] It may appear that all partners have acquiesced in failure to keep proper records and so are barred from demanding an accounting after original vouchers are lost.[23]

If a partner undertakes to keep books, it is his duty to do so accurately and adequately, according to his ability.[24] If he fails to do so, he may have breached his fiduciary duty,[25] and the presumptions are against him on an accounting.[26] If all partners permit neglect in

on the basis of which the taxpayer regularly computes income in keeping his books), id. § 446(c) (if no method of accounting regularly used, or if method used does not clearly reflect income, Commissioner shall specify method which does clearly reflect income). An element of relaxation is Income Tax Regs. § 1.446–1(a) (2) (1957): "Each taxpayer shall adopt such forms and systems as are, in his judgment, best suited to his needs."

19. See, e. g., Hurst v. Hurst, 86 Ariz. 242, 344 P.2d 1001 (1959) ("a model of disarray"); Luchs v. Ormsby, 171 Cal. App.2d 377, 340 P.2d 702, 705 (1959) (slipshod, many transactions not accounted for, some entries contrary to fact); Hansen v. Hansen, 130 Mont. 175, 297 P.2d 879, 881 (1956) ("utterly unreliable"); Wikstrom v. Davis, 211 Or. 254, 315 P.2d 597, 601 (1957) ("amazingly inadequate financial record"); Hairston v. Richie, 338 S.W.2d 263, 265 (Tex.Civ.App.1960) ("poorly conceived, poorly kept, wholly inadequate . . . devoid of the hallmarks of reliability . . . To attempt to determine the profit . . . for any single year or from any particular project would be an impractical and futile undertaking").

It is no accident that inadequate books turn up so frequently in litigated cases; they are bound to create doubts and suspicions, and contribute to disputes. And it is probably no accident that so many of the cases involve farming and ranching partnerships.

20. For example, see Appendix V, pars. 2.3–2.6, 2.8, 3.1, 5.4 below.

21. Bracht v. Connell, 313 Pa. 397, 170 A. 297 (1933).

22. Charles v. Charles, 199 Ky. 208, 250 S.W. 855 (1923).

It is a proper item of expense to hire an expert accountant to examine and audit books and prepare balances. Godfrey v. White, 43 Mich. 171, 5 N.W. 243 (1880).

23. Wooley v. Mattingly, 204 Ky. 699, 265 S.W. 302 (1924).

See, on acquiescence in inefficient bookkeeping, Morris v. Griffin, 83 Iowa 327, 49 N.W. 846 (1891); Shoemaker v. Shoemaker, 92 S.W. 546, 29 Ky. Law Rep. 134 (1906); Poulette v. Chainay, 236 Mass. 602, 129 N.E. 290 (1921); Knapp v. Edwards, 57 Wis. 191, 15 N.W. 140 (1883). See also Corr v. Hoffman, 256 N.Y. 254, 176 N.E. 383 (1931).

24. Bracht v. Connell, note 21, above; Dale v. Dale, 57 N.M. 593, 261 P.2d 438 (1953); Duncan v. Bartle, 188 Or. 451, 216 P.2d 1005 (1950).

25. Adams v. Mason, 358 S.W.2d 7 (Mo. 1962).

26. Katz v. Brewington, 71 Md. 79, 20 A. 139 (1889); Wilson v. Moline, 229 Minn. 164, 38 N.W.2d 201 (1949), subsequent appeal 234 Minn. 174, 47 N.W. 2d 865 (1951); Hansen v. Hansen, 130

the keeping of books, a court may refuse to decree any relief in a bill for accounting.[27] But, on the whole, courts go to great pains to correct or reconstruct records in order that an accounting may be had.[28]

If there is a managing partner, the duty to keep books falls on him.[29]

Books should be kept at the place of business [30] and all partners are entitled to access to them.[31] It is presumed, though subject to

Mont. 175, 297 P.2d 879 (1956); Glazer v. Kurman, 384 Pa. 283, 120 A.2d 892 (1956); Dial v. Martin, 37 S.W.2d 166 (Tex.Civ.App.1931); Sweatt v. Johnson, 97 Vt. 177, 122 A. 501 (1923); Benedetto v. Di Bacco, 83 W.Va. 620, 99 S.E. 170 (1919); Simich v. Culjak, 27 Wash.2d 403, 178 P.2d 336 (1947).

27. Donaldson v. Donaldson, 237 Ill. 318, 86 N.E. 604 (1908); Clarke's Adm'r v. Clarke, 125 Va. 68, 99 S.E. 664 (1919). See Bass v. Daetwyler, 305 S.W.2d 339 (Mo.App.1957) (court costs assessed against partner who undertook to keep accurate records but failed to do so).

28. See, e. g., cases cited n. 19 above and Adams v. Mason, 358 S.W.2d 7 (Mo. 1962); Dale v. Dale, 57 N.M. 593, 261 P.2d 438 (1953); Berliner v. Roberts, 226 Or. 350, 360 P.2d 533 (1961).

29. Rogers v. Stacy, 63 N.M. 317, 318 P.2d 1116 (1957).

30. Greatrex v. Greatrex, 1 Deg. & Sm. 692, 63 Eng.Rep. 1254 (1847). U.P.A. § 19. This may be varied by agreement.

31. In Sanderson v. Cooke, 256 N.Y. 73, 175 N.E. 518 (1931), the court said: "The general rule regarding business partnerships is that books should be kept, open to the inspection of any partner at all reasonable times, even after dissolution, subject, however, to special agreement. . . . Even under these broad statements of the law, a partner's rights are not absolute. He may be restrained from using the information gathered from inspection for other than partnership purposes. . . . The employment of an agent to make the inspection does not authorize the selection of anybody he may choose for the purpose. The agent employed must be a person to whom no reasonable objection can be taken, and the purpose for which he seeks to use the right of inspection must be one

consistent with the main purposes and the well being of the whole partnership. . . . The right of inspection by an agent is not so absolute as the right to a personal inspection, and may be refused if the court is satisfied that the assistance of an agent is not reasonably required, or that the inspection is wanted for an improper purpose. . . ." The right of a partner to inspect the books is an absolute right, by reason of his joint ownership. Stebbins v. Harmon, 17 Hun 445 (N.Y.1879).

Price v. Briggs, 160 Cal.App.2d 524, 325 P.2d 573 (1958) (former partner).

A partner is entitled to physical possession of the books, People v. Phillips, 207 Misc. 205, 137 N.Y.S.2d 697 (County Ct.1955). This accords with the general rule that a partner is entitled to possess partnership property for partnership purposes, U.P.A. § 25(2) (a), Sec. 41(a) above.

The right of a shareholder in a joint-stock company to inspect the company's books has been dealt with in a manner similar to such a demand by a corporate shareholder. He is entitled to a writ of mandamus only for an inspection for a purpose shown to be proper, and only after demand on the officers refused after a reasonable time. Matter of Hatt, 57 Misc. 320, 108 N.Y.S. 468 (1908).

On inspection rights of corporate directors and shareholders (which are quite similar to partners') see Henn, Corporations, 325–30, 346–47 (1961), 2 Model Bus.Corp.Act Ann. 112–34 (1960).

Inspection rights are denied the assignee of a partner's interest, see U.P.A. § 27(1); but see the more liberal treatment in Vernon's Ann.Civ.St. (Tex.) art. 6132b, § 27(1) (reasonable inspection).

A limited partner has the same rights as a general partner in respect to keeping

rebuttal, that partners have knowledge of the contents of the partnership books.[32] The books are presumed to state accurately the state of accounts,[33] but errors can be corrected.[34]

DUTY OF PARTNERS TO RENDER INFORMATION

§ 67. Partners shall render on demand true and full information of all things affecting the partnership to any partner or to the legal representative of any deceased partner or partner under a legal disability. U.P.A. § 20.

A partner's duty to render information is closely related to his duty to account,[35] and may be enforced in an accounting action.[36] The duty is owed by all partners,[37] but is especially heavy for managing

and inspecting the books. U.L.P.A. § 10(1) (a).

The right of a partner to make use of information contained in the partnership books is confined to partnership purposes and protection of his rights as partner. If, by reason of the terms of a dissolution agreement, goodwill and the exclusive right to solicit former customers passes to one partner, a co-partner is not entitled to copy the books for the purpose of using customer lists in violation of the agreement. Trego v. Hunt, [1896] A.C. 7; Chamberlain v. Hemingway, 97 Conn. 156, 115 A. 632 (1921).

A court of equity may decree a discovery in aid of a partner wishing to inspect. Seeley v. Dunlop, 157 Md. 378, 146 A. 271 (1929).

32. Geddes' Appeal, 80 Pa. 442 (1876) (a partner, selling his interest in the partnership to a co-partner, cannot claim concealment of facts open to him from an inspection of the books); United States Bank v. Binney, Fed.Cas.No. 16,791, 5 Mason 176, (D.Mass.1828).

But where a partner is under a known physical disability and the copartner undertakes to provide information as to the state of partnership affairs as a basis for a dissolution and settlement, the incapacitated partner, though represented by counsel, is entitled to trust his co-partner to make a full disclosure and is not charged with a knowledge of the contents of the books. Smith v. Rosson, 233 Ala. 219, 171 So. 375 (1936).

33. McKleroy v. Musgrove, 203 Ala. 603, 84 So. 280 (1920); Darlington v. Per-

ry, 354 Ill. 22, 187 N.E. 796 (1933); Topliff v. Jackson, 78 Mass. (12 Gray) 565 (1859); Cronk v. Crandall, 137 App.Div. 440, 121 N.Y.S. 805 (1910).

34. Hurter v. Larrabee, 224 Mass. 218, 112 N.E. 613 (1916); Donovan v. Clark, 138 N.Y. 631, 33 N.E. 1066 (1893).

The books are not even admissible in evidence against a partner who has been excluded from access to them, Adams v. Funk, 53 Ill. 219 (1870); Saunders v. Duval's Adm'r, 19 Tex. 467 (1857).

It can be shown that the books were not kept in the manner provided for by the partnership agreement. Lewis v. Loper, 54 F. 237 (6 Cir. 1893).

If the books have been made the basis of an account stated, equity will not interfere to correct error, it has been held, in the absence of fraud. Belt v. Mehen, 2 Cal. 159, 56 Am.Dec. 329 (1852); Corr v. Hoffman, 256 N.Y. 254, 176 N.E. 383 (1931). Compare Restatement, Contracts § 422.

Books are admissible as evidence of the terms of the partnership contract. Darlington v. Perry, 354 Ill. 22, 187 N.E. 796 (1933).

On self-incrimination and related Constitutional privileges of a partner in partnership books, see Sec. 41 at nn. 74–77 above.

35. U.P.A. § 21, Sec. 68 below.

36. Fernandez v. Garza, 88 Ariz. 214, 354 P.2d 260 (1960).

37. U.P.A. § 20. A similar duty is owed by agents and trustees, Restatement, Agency, Second § 381; Restatement, Second, Trusts § 173.

partners.[38] Like the duty to account, it applies not only to the partnership's operations,[39] but to transactions connected with its formation (such as the cost of property to a partner [40] or his interest in it) [41] and liquidation.[42] It is owed equally to general and to limited partners.[43]

The duty also exists in the purchase [44] or sale [45] of an interest between partners. There is no duty of disclosure of facts of which all partners have an equal opportunity to be informed, such as facts appearing on the books.[46] But a partner who refuses access to the

38. Dale v. Dale, 57 N.M. 593, 261 P.2d 438 (1953).

39. Dale v. Dale, n. 38 above.

40. Fuller v. Pierce, 92 Fla. 129, 109 So. 238 (1926); Axton v. Kentucky Bottlers' Supply Co., 159 Ky. 51, 166 S.W. 776, Ann.Cas.1915D, 74 (1914), semble; Bloom v. Lofgren, 64 Minn. 1, 65 N.W. 960 (1896) semble, disapproved in Walker v. Patterson, 166 Minn. 215, 208 N.W. 3, 7 (1926); R. C. Gluck & Co. v. Tankel, 12 A.D.2d 339, 211 N.Y.S. 2d 602 (1961). Contra, Densmore Oil Co. v. Densmore, 64 Pa. 43 (1870); Uhler v. Semple, 20 N.J.Eq. 288 (1869).

The same rule is applicable to a joint adventure. Moe v. Lowry, 69 Colo. 371, 194 P. 363 (1920), noted 21 Colum. L.Rev. 387 (1921).

If one is induced by fraudulent misrepresentations of value of property contributed by his copartner to enter the partnership, he is entitled to rescission without proof of pecuniary damage. Harlow v. La Brum, 151 N.Y. 278, 45 N.E. 859 (1897). See also U.P.A. § 39, Sec. 85 below.

41. Selwyn & Co. v. Waller, 212 N.Y. 507, 106 N.E. 321, L.R.A.1915B, 160 (1914), two theatrical producers agreed as joint adventures to produce a play, on a profit-sharing basis, paying the author certain royalties; one concealed from the other an agreement with the author whereby he was the assignee of a share of the royalties, and was held accountable to his fellow adventurer for a pro rata share thereof.

42. Vogel v. Brewer, 176 F.Supp. 892 (E.D.Ark.1959); Alexander v. Sims, 220 Ark. 643, 249 S.W.2d 832 (1952) (partner, failing to disclose knowledge of co-partner's malignant cancer, in-

duced co-partner to agree that survivor would be sole owner of partnership property; agreement unenforceable); Vai v. Bank of America, 56 Cal.2d 329, 15 Cal.Rptr. 71, 364 P.2d 247 (1961) (community property settlement; partnership analogy); Weidlich v. Weidlich, 147 Conn. 160, 157 A.2d 910 (1960).

U.P.A. § 20 specifies that the duty is owed also to the representative of a deceased or disabled partner; this contemplates liquidation situations.

43. U.L.P.A. § 10(1) (b).

44. DeLorma Brooks v. Martin, 69 U.S. (2 Wall.) 70, 17 L.Ed. 732 (1864); Caldwell v. Davis, 10 Colo. 481, 15 P. 696, 3 Am.St.Rep. 599 (1887); Gilbert & O'Callighan v. Anderson, 73 N.J.Eq. 243, 66 A. 926 (1907), semble; Wright v. Duke, 91 Hun 409, 36 N.Y.S. 853 (1895); Kelly v. Delaney, 136 App. Div. 604, 121 N.Y.S. 241 (1910); Guggenheim v. Guggenheim, 95 Misc. 332, 159 N.Y.S. 333 (1916); Poss v. Gottlieb, 118 Misc. 318, 193 N.Y.S. 418 (1922). See Hagan v. Dundore, 187 Md. 430, 50 A.2d 570 (1947).

Of course actual fraud is a cause for setting aside a purchase of a partner's interest, Sachs v. Karos, 310 Mich. 577, 17 N.W.2d 759 (1945), presenting numerous breaches by a partner of his fiduciary duties.

45. Sexton v. Sexton, 9 Grat. 204 (Va. 1852).

As to duty of disclosure as between partners preparing to dissolve, see Shelley v. Smith, 271 Mass. 106, 170 N.E. 826 (1930).

46. Aronhime v. Levinson, 119 Va. 394, 89 S.E. 893 (1916), noted 16 Colum.L. Rev. 693 (1916); Dorsett v. Ormiston, 25 Misc. 570, 55 N.Y.S. 1037 (1898). See

books to other partners cannot take advantage of their ignorance of facts contained therein.[47] After a contract for the sale of a partner's interest has been entered into, there is no duty of disclosure of facts thereafter learned by the purchasing partner.[48] When a partner is selling his interest in the partnership to a third person, while not under a fiduciary duty of disclosure, he is under a duty to refrain from false representations as to the collectibility of accounts receivable, and if the purchaser relies on such representations the sale is voidable.[49]

At common law, a partner is not only bound to give information on demand but, in certain circumstances, he is under a duty of voluntary disclosure.[50] UPA § 20 expresses the duty to render information "on demand." Strict statutory construction would find a negative implication where no demand is made. But this should be outweighed by the high fiduciary duties of partners.[51] In consequence, voluntary disclosure shoud be considered as necessary under the Act as at common law.[51A]

also Notes, 33 Harv.Law Rev. 852 (1920); 6 Minn.Law Rev. 397 (1922); 58 U. of Pa.Law Rev. 309 (1910).

47. Joseph v. Mangos, 192 Iowa 729, 185 N.W. 464 (1921).

48. Patrick v. Bowman, Use of Slattery, 149 U.S. 411, 13 S.Ct. 811, 866, 37 L.Ed. 790 (1893), discovery of ore deposit on mining property after agreement had been entered into for the purchase by one partner of co-partner's interest.

Compare Power v. Wood, 200 Iowa 979, 205 N.W. 784, 41 A.L.R. 1452 (1925), where, after dissolution, it was discovered that an employee had embezzled funds of the partnership, which he was compelled to repay to the continuing partner. On the ground of mutual mistake, a reformation of the dissolution agreement was decreed. "Where there are outstanding assets of a firm unknown to either partner at the time of the dissolution of the firm, one partner may recover his proportionate share of said assets from the other partner who has received and collected the same after the dissolution."

As to the duty of full disclosure in settlement of accounts in a joint venture see Goldstein Co. v. Joseph J. & Reynold H. Greenberg, Inc., 352 Pa. 259, 42 A.2d 551 (1945).

49. Bailey v. Smith, 57 App.D.C. 369, 23 F.2d 977 (1928).

50. Johnson v. Peckham, 132 Tex. 148, 120 S.W.2d 786, 120 A.L.R. 720 (1938).

51. Sec. 68 below.

51A. See Berg v. King-Cola, Inc., 227 Cal.App.2d 338, 38 Cal.Rptr. 655 (1964) holding, without discussion of the point, that there was fiduciary breach by non-disclosure even though no express demand was made. However, an implied demand might be found from the facts.

PARTNER ACCOUNTABLE AS A FIDUCIARY

§ 68. (1) **Every partner must account to the partnership for any benefit, and hold as trustee for it any profits, derived by him without the consent of the other partners from any transaction connected with the formation, conduct, or liquidation of the partnership or from any use by him of its property.**

(2) **This section applies also to the representatives of a deceased partner engaged in the liquidation of the affairs of the partnership as the personal representatives of the last surviving partner. U.P.A. § 21.**

Fiduciary duties are among the most important aspects of partnership. Such duties arise in many situations where one person has another's property, authority or confidence. They are recognized in relationships like principal and agent, trustee and beneficiary, director and corporation. The unique feature they have in partnership is their symmetry; each partner is, roughly speaking, both a principal and an agent, both a trustee and a beneficiary, for he has the property, authority and confidence of his co-partners, as they do of him. He shares their profits and losses, and is bound by their actions. Without the protection of fiduciary duties, each is at the others' mercy.

Fiduciary duties are essentially the same in general partnerships,[51B] limited partnerships,[52] and joint ventures.[53]

We often say that a partner is accountable (or has a duty to account) as a fiduciary. This means a number of different things:

(1) He must keep accounts or books, discussed in Sec. 66 above.

(2) He must render information, discussed in Sec. 67 above.

(3) He must submit to financial review, discussed in Sec. 72 below.

(4) He must answer for any breach of fiduciary duty, discussed in this Section.

There is no easy formulation of fiduciary duties; the most comprehensive [54] and the most eloquent [55] are quoted in the margin. The main

---

51B. See generally, Note, Fiduciary Duties of Partners, 48 Iowa L.Rev. 902 (1963).

52. Allen v. Steinberg, 244 Md. 119, 223 A.2d 240 (1966); Soffer v. Glickman, 27 Misc.2d 721, 209 N.Y.S.2d 743 (1960); Homestake Mining Co. v. Mid-Continent Exploration Co., 282 F.2d 787 (10th Cir. 1960).

53. Van Stee v. Ransford, 346 Mich. 116, 77 N.W.2d 346 (1956); Lipinski v. Lipinski, 227 Minn. 511, 35 N.W.2d 708 (1949). Joint ventures have somewhat narrower scopes within which fiduciary duties operate.

54. It is "well settled that one partner cannot, directly or indirectly, use partnership assets for his own benefit; that he cannot in conducting the business of a partnership, take any profit clandestinely for himself; that he cannot carry on the business of the partnership for his private advantage; that he cannot carry on another business in competition or rivalry with that of the firm, thereby depriving it of the benefit of his time, skill, and fidelity, without being accountable to his copartners for any profit that may accrue to him therefrom; that he can-

55. See note 55 on page 390.

elements are well recognized: utmost good faith, fairness, loyalty. But the specific applications must be gleaned from a vast number of cases like those discussed below. The cases also demonstrate how frequently and how far human behavior deviates from the legal norm.

A partner must account for any profit acquired in a manner injurious to the interests of the partnership,[56] such as commissions on the purchase [57] or sale [58] of partnership property. Such profits are almost always secret so far as the co-partners are concerned, and this is part of their vice. Not only may secrecy cloak the partner's guilty intent; it deprives the co-partners of a contemporaneous chance to assert their interests.

A partner cannot, without consent of his partners, acquire for himself a partnership asset, e. g., by substituting a contract with himself for one with the partnership,[59] personally taking a renewal of a

---

not be permitted to secure for himself that which it is his duty to obtain, if at all, for the firm of which he is a member; nor can he avail himself of knowledge or information which may be properly regarded as the property of the partnership, in the sense that it is available or useful to the firm for any purpose within the scope of the partnership business." Latta v. Kilbourn, 150 U.S. 524, 541, 14 S.Ct. 201, 207, 37 L.Ed. 1169 (1893).

55. "Joint adventurers, like copartners, owe to one another . . . the duty of finest loyalty. Many forms of conduct permissible in a workaday world for those acting at arm's length, are forbidden to those bound by fiduciary ties. A trustee is held to something stricter than the morals of the market place. Not honesty alone, but the punctilio of an honor the most sensitive is then the standard of behavior. As to this there has developed a tradition that is unbending and inveterate. Uncompromising rigidity has been the attitude of courts of equity when petitioned to undermine the rule of undivided loyalty by the 'disintegrating erosion' of particular exceptions . . . Only thus has the level of conduct for fiduciaries been kept at a level higher than that trodden by the crowd. It will not consciously be lowered by any judgment of this court." Cardozo, C. J. in Meinhard v. Salmon, 249 N.Y. 458, 164 N.E. 545, 546, 62 A.L.R. 1 (1928).

See also Bakalis v. Bressler, 1 Ill.2d 72, 115 N.E.2d 323, 327 (1953): "The fiduciary relation prohibits all forms of

trickery, secret dealings and preference of self in matters relating to and connected with a partnership and joint venture."

56. Waring v. Cram, 1 Pars.Eq.Cas. 516 (Pa.1850).

57. Prince v. Harting, 177 Cal.App.2d 720, 2 Cal.Rptr. 545 (1960) (partner secretly owned partnership's source of supply); Stenian v. Tashjian, 178 Cal. 623, 174 P. 883 (1918); Esmond v. Seeley, 28 App.Div. 292, 51 N.Y.S. 36 (1898); Liggett v. Lester, 237 Or. 52, 390 P.2d 351 (1964) (partner liable for gross amount of secret commissions or discounts on sales to partnership, even though secret operation as a whole resulted in a loss to him).

See as to joint venture, Fitch v. Ingalls, 271 Mass. 121, 170 N.E. 833 (1930); Hodge v. Twitchell, 33 Minn. 389, 23 N.W. 547 (1885).

58. Poss v. Gottlieb, 118 Misc. 318, 193 N.Y.S. 418 (1922). See Van Hooser v. Keenon, 271 S.W.2d 270 (Ky.1954) (consideration for secret option to buy shares of corporation into which partnership was to be converted).

59. Holmes v. Darling, 213 Mass. 303, 100 N.E. 611 (1913); Shelley v. Smith, 271 Mass. 106, 170 N.E. 826 (1930).

See Sorenson v. Nielsen, 240 N.Y.S. 250 (Sup.1930), noted 30 Colum.L.Rev. 896 (1930).

Bracht v. Connell, 313 Pa. 397, 170 A. 297 (1933) (new contract to be performed after dissolution of firm).

partnership lease,[60] mortgaging partnership property and lending the proceeds to his entity,[60A] or causing the partnership to default on a mortgage and then acquiring the property on foreclosure.[61] Nor may he divert to his own use or profit a "partnership opportunity." [62] This includes an activity necessary [63] or clearly related [64] to the partnership's operations, one offered to [65] or learned about through[66] the partnership, and one developed with partnership funds and facilities.[67]

A partner is under a duty not to compete with the partnership within the scope of its business.[68] He is accountable for profit from trading in property in which the partnership also trades,[69] and for acquiring the reversion of premises leased to the partnership,[70] since this

---

60. Ferry v. McNeil, 214 Cal.App.2d 411, 29 Cal.Rptr. 577 (1963); Lurie v. Pinanski, 215 Mass. 229, 102 N.E. 629 (1913) (plaintiff partner was not barred of a remedy in accounting because of the fact that he had himself previously sought to renew the lease in his own right); Ladas v. Psiharis, 241 Mich. 101, 216 N.W. 458 (1927); Mitchell v. Reed, 61 N.Y. 123, 19 Am.Rep. 252 (1874); Johnson's Appeal, 115 Pa. 129, 8 A. 36, 2 Am.St.Rep. 539 (1886) (lease expired after dissolution); Smith v. Bolin, 153 Tex. 486, 271 S.W. 2d 93 (1954), subsequent appeal 294 S.W.2d 280 (Tex.Civ.App.1956) error ref. n. r. e. Meinhard v. Salmon, n. 55 above (joint venture), noted 29 Colum.L.Rev. 367 (1929), 42 Harv.L. Rev. 953 (1929), 38 Yale L.J. 782 (1929).

60A. Allen v. Steinberg, 244 Md. 119, 223 A.2d 240 (1960).

61. Seligson v. Weiss, 222 App.Div. 634, 227 N.Y.S. 338 (1928).

62. On the parallel corporate opportunity concept, see Henn, Corporations 371–74 (1961); Comment, The Corporate Opportunity Doctrine, 18 Sw.L.J. 96 (1964)

63. Bakalis v. Bressler, 1 Ill.2d 72, 115 N.E.2d 323 (1953) (acquisition of realty leased to the partnership). See also n. 70 below).

64. Fortugno v. Hudson Manure Co., 51 N.J.Super. 482, 144 A.2d 207, 216 (1958), noted 4 Vill.L.Rev. 457 (1959).

65. Fouchek v. Janicek, 190 Or. 251, 225 P.2d 783 (1950), noted 23 Rocky Mt.L. Rev. 479 (1951) (war surplus firm; op-

portunity for additional financing of same kind of business). This opinion contains a good discussion of the whole area.

66. Stark v. Reingold, 18 N.J. 251, 113 A.2d 679 (1955) (rental car firm; similar franchises in neighboring counties).

67. Homestake Mining Co. v. Mid-Continent Exploration Co., 282 F.2d 787 (10th Cir. 1960), discussed n. 78 below; In re Wilson's Estate, 50 Wash. 2d 840, 315 P.2d 287 (1957), subsequent appeal 53 Wash.2d 762, 337 P.2d 56 (1959) (tractor purchased with partnership credit).

68. Jones v. Jones, 254 Ky. 475, 71 S.W.2d 999 (1934); Shulkin v. Shulkin, 301 Mass. 184, 16 N.E.2d 644, 118 A.L.R. 629 (1938) (approving the principle but declining to apply it because of insufficient evidence of profits derived within the scope of the firm's business). See also cases on substitution for contracts of the firm, n. 59 above.

69. Watson v. Kellogg, 129 Cal.App. 592, 19 P.2d 253 (1933). See Abramson v. Davis, 100 N.J.Eq. 563, 135 A. 774 (1927).

70. Maas v. Goldman, 122 Misc. 221, 203 N.Y.S. 524 (1924); Id., 210 App.Div. 845, 206 N.Y.S. 930 (1924). But compare Thanos v. Thanos, 313 Ill. 499, 145 N.E. 250 (1924), holding that a partner could hold for himself a reversion of premises occupied by the firm, purchased with his own funds. This case was distinguished and greatly weakened by Bakalis v. Bressler, 1 Ill.2d 72, 115 N.E.2d 323 (1953). As a

creates a conflict of interest. He may be enjoined from opening a competing store in the same neighborhood.[71]

The partnership relation does not extend to all affairs and transactions between partners.[72] While a partner ordinarily owes to the partnership the benefit of his business activities,[73] he is not considered to have violated his obligation, or to be competing with the partnership, if he accepts employment of a nature different from the partnership business, not requiring a great deal of his time, and hence he is not accountable for the earnings. A partner in a law firm need not account for fees received as executor or administrator.[74] A partner need

result, Illinois now follows the rule stated in the text.

In Stewart v. Ulrich, 117 Wash. 109, 201 P. 16 (1921), a partner in a firm which operated a billiard room on leased premises arranged with the landlord to decline to renew the lease on its expiration, but to take over the business and run it in association with him. It was held that there was no liability, in the absence of any fraudulent or wrongful acts in preventing the renewal of the lease. See criticism in Note, 35 Harv.L.Rev. 622 (1922).

Where the partnership fails to carry out an agreement to purchase premises of which it is lessee a partner may purchase subject to the lease and without fraud upon his co-partners. Sonek v. Hill Building & Loan Ass'n, 138 N.J. Eq. 534, 49 A.2d 303 (1946). Cf. Gertz v. Fontecchio, 331 Mich. 165, 49 N.W. 2d 121 (1951) (semble; lease belonged to partners, not to firm).

See also cases on individual renewal of partnership lease, n. 60 above, and cases collected in Annot., Constructive trust in favor of partnership where one partner purchases real estate with his own funds, 44 A.L.R.2d 519 (1955).

71. Crownfield v. Phillips, 125 Md. 1, 92 A. 1033, Ann.Cas.1916E, 991 (1915).

72. McDonald v. McDonald, 408 Ill. 388, 97 N.E.2d 336 (1951) (partition of land by five co-owners was distinct from farming on it by two of them in partnership).

Phillips v. Krensky, 98 So.2d 788 (Fla. 1957) (questionable holding that partners dealt separately in disposing of partnership land to third persons, and that one need not disclose to the

other that he was receiving different amount and payment terms for his share).

73. An undertaking by a partner in a law firm to render services of a legal nature to a client, in a matter in which the attorney has a personal interest, is effective in so far that it bars the partnership from claiming a fee for the services, though it is a wrong as between the partners. Stone v. Hart, 66 S.W. 191, 23 Ky.Law Rep. 1777 (1902).

Where the partnership agreement calls for devotion of entire time to business, a partner may be compelled to discontinue engaging in another business. Murrell v. Murrell, 33 La.Ann. 1233 (1881).

Permission may be given to engage in other business. Dennis v. Gordon, 163 Cal. 427, 125 P. 1063 (1912); Winchester v. Glazier, 152 Mass. 316, 25 N.E. 728, 9 L.R.A. 424 (1890).

74. Metcalfe v. Bradshaw, 145 Ill. 124, 33 N.E. 1116, 36 Am.St.Rep. 478 (1893).

But see Starr v. Case, 59 Iowa 491, 13 N.W. 645 (1882) (agreement of law partners expressly permitted holding of other offices or agencies); Deeds v. Gilmer, 162 Va. 157, 174 S.E. 37, 75 (1934) (agreement permitted partner to engage in a semi-competitive business, on sharing the commissions earned thereby).

It does not afford a basis for a claim of the partnership to share in the profits of non-competitive activities outside the scope of the partnership business to show that the partner was given the opportunity to engage therein because of his reputation, experience, and knowledge acquired as a partner.

not refrain from employing his financial resources in the purchase of property which he is under no duty to purchase from the partnership. If a partnership is engaged in buying and selling real estate for others on commission as brokers, a partner may purchase real estate with his own funds.[75] A partner in the business of operating an oil and gas lease may procure another lease for his own account.[76] A partner in a fishing venture may acquire land along the shore useful for fishing purposes, in which partnership has no interest, and has made no effort to acquire any.[77]

Consent to competition may be inferred from actions of the partners [78] or from facts known when the partnership is formed. A partner in a firm organized to operate a hotel, who owns another hotel on adjacent land, is not guilty of breach of his fiduciary duties as partner in improving and enlarging the hotel he owns.[79]

In determining the scope of the partnership business (within which competition is not permitted), courts apply the same factors as in fixing the scope within which a partner has authority to bind the partnership.[80] However, there is a tendency to find a somewhat broader scope in the first context than in the second. The scope depends on the

Very likely a lawyer is appointed executor of a will or to some other office by reason of his standing as an attorney. In Aas v. Benham, [1891] 2 Ch. 244, a partner in a firm of ship brokers assisted in the formation of a joint-stock company for the non-competitive business of shipbuilding, and in so doing made use of information acquired as a ship broker. It was held that he was under no duty to account for the profits and salaries received from the company.

See also Evans v. Gunnip, 36 Del.Ch. 76, 125 A.2d 378 (1956), modified on other grounds 36 Del.Ch. 589, 135 A.2d 128, 65 A.L.R.2d 513 (1957). Partner in accounting firm did not breach fiduciary duty by buying stock in a corporate client; even though he used partnership funds, they were ultimately debited to him, and he did not conceal the transaction.

75. Shrader v. Downing, 79 Wash. 476, 140 P. 558, 52 L.R.A.,N.S., 389 (1914);

Latta v. Kilbourn, 150 U.S. 524, 14 S.Ct. 201, 37 L.Ed. 1169 (1893), not accountable for profits though defendant violated agreement to advise of investment opportunities.

See Annot., Constructive trust in favor of partnership where one partner purchases real estate with his own funds, 44 A.L.R.2d 519 (1955).

76. More v. Burroughs, 111 Kan. 28, 205 P. 1029 (1922); Dennis v. Gordon, 163 Cal. 427, 125 P. 1063 (1912); Jennings v. Rickard, 10 Colo. 395, 401, 15 P. 677 (1887).

Similarly for a mining and milling firm, Homestake Mining Co. v. Mid-Continent Exploration Co., 282 F.2d 787 (10th Cir. 1960) (N.M. law).

77. Lipinski v. Lipinski, 227 Minn. 511, 35 N.W.2d 708 (1949).

78. Levine v. Personnel Institute, Inc., 138 N.Y.S.2d 243 (Sup.Ct.1954), aff'd without opin. 2 A.D.2d 964, 158 N.Y. S.2d 740 (1956).

Cf. Homestake Mining Co. v. Mid-Continent Exploration Co., n. 76 above. Copartners were not entitled to a constructive trust on a partner's high-cost, high-risk competing venture when they made no claim on it until it was successful, although they had known generally of its development. For the limited relief granted, e. g., reimbursement of diverted funds, see 282 F.2d at 798 n. 21.

79. Holmes v. Keets, 80 App.D.C. 327, 153 F.2d 132 (1946).

80. Secs. 49–51 above.

agreement of association, as interpreted by the conduct of the parties in its performance. It may be shown that the parties "agreed to limit their joint undertakings to those mutually approved, leaving each free to undertake other privately.[81]

At common law, there was some question when fiduciary duties begin and end. Earlier cases held that, in the formation of a partnership, the parties deal at arm's length, and there is no fiduciary duty of disclosure.[82] The problem often arises where a partner already has an interest (such as an option) in property to be acquired by the firm in such manner as to yield him a concealed profit. If there is positive misrepresentation, such as a statement that the property is being acquired at the lowest possible price, he is accountable.[83] If there is no misrepresentation, apparently there is no liability. This rule has been reversed by the U.P.A. which covers any transaction connected with the formation, conduct or liquidation of the partnership.[84]

Partners are not relieved of fiduciary duties by strained relations between them.[85] If this were true, "a designing fiduciary could easily bring about such relations to set the stage for a sharp bargain." [86]

It is ordinarily not necessary to distinguish a partner's fiduciary duties to the partnership from those to his co-partners. However, the latter have a separate existence, particularly when he is buying a co-

81. Meyer v. Sharp, 341 Ill.App. 431, 94 N.E.2d 510 (1950).

82. Densmore Oil Co. v. Densmore, 64 Pa. 43 (27 L.I. 20, 1870); Walker v. Patterson, 166 Minn. 215, 208 N.W. 3 (1926); Uhler v. Semple, 20 N.J.Eq. 288 (1869)

83. Seehorn v. Hall, 130 Mo. 357, 32 S.W. 643 (1895); Kroll v. Coach, 45 Or. 459, 78 P. 397 (1904).

84. U.P.A. § 21(1). Allen v. Steinberg, 244 Md. 119, 223 A.2d 240 (1966). R. C. Gluck & Co. v. Tankel, 12 A.D.2d 339, 211 N.Y.S.2d 602 (1961); Fouchek v. Janicek, 190 Or. 251, 225 P.2d 783 (1950) (formation); Claude v. Claude, 191 Or. 308, 228 P.2d 776 (1951) (termination).

But see Phillips v. Krensky, 98 So.2d 788 (Fla.1957). Partners sold their equal interests in the principal partnership asset to the same buyer, one for cash, the other for deferred payments at a higher price, and immediately terminated the firm. Held: no fiduciary breach; each partner dealt with his interest separately and not as partnership property. U.P.A. not in force.

On the fiduciary duties of a surviving partner, see Sec. 86 below. The same duties extend to the representative of the last surviving partner if he winds up the firm, U.P.A. § 21(2).

The N.Y. courts are fond of saying that a partnership or joint venture cannot be carried on through a corporation. After incorporation, the parties have only the rights and duties of stockholders. Weisman v. Awnair Corp., 3 N.Y.2d 444, 165 N.Y.S.2d 745, 144 N.E.2d 415 (1957) (accounting denied); Bing v. Morgan Guaranty Trust Co., 17 A.D.2d 132, 232 N.Y.S.2d 832 (1962). The N.J. courts have a more fluid view; see n. 91 below. So does Calif., Berg v. King-Cola, Inc., 227 Cal.App.2d 338, 38 Cal.Rptr. 655 (1964) (partnership fiduciary duties with respect to incorporated venture).

85. Karle v. Seder, 35 Wash.2d 542, 214 P.2d 684 (1950).

86. Johnson v. Peckham, 132 Tex. 148, 120 S.W.2d 786, 788, 120 A.L.R. 720 (1938).

partner's interest. He is then obliged to make full disclosure and pay a fair price.[87]

Once a fiduciary breach is established, numerous remedies are available to fit the equities of the case. Money recovery is allowed for actual losses,[88] for profits earned as a result of the breach,[89] and perhaps even for exemplary damages.[90] Property involved in the breach may be traced[91] and subjected to constructive trust.[92] In addition, breaches may be enjoined.[93]

Although a partner owes a duty of faithful services to the best of his ability, he is not held to possess the degree of knowledge and skill of a paid agent.[94] In the absence of special agreement, no partner guarantees his own capacity.[95] He is not liable to his partnership for the whole burden of losses caused by errors of judgment and failure to use ordinary skill and care in the supervision and transaction of business.[96] He may be held liable for loss caused by hasty action which

87. Alexander v. Sims, 220 Ark. 643, 249 S.W.2d 832 (1952); Vai v. Bank of America, 56 Cal.2d 329, 15 Cal.Rptr. 71, 364 P.2d 247 (1961) (community property settlement; partnership analogy); Inman v. Parr, 311 S.W.2d 658 (Tex.Civ.App.1958) error ref. n. r. e.

Cases cited Sec. 67, nn. 45–46 above.

88. Prince v. Harting, 177 Cal.App.2d 720, 2 Cal.Rptr. 545 (1960).

89. In re Kohn's Estate, 26 Misc.2d 659, 116 N.Y.S.2d 167 (Surr.1952), aff'd without opin. 282 App.Div. 1045, 126 N.Y.S.2d 897 (1953); In re Wilson's Estate, 50 Wash.2d 840, 315 P.2d 287 (1957).

90. See International Bankers Life Ins. Co. v. Holloway, 368 S.W.2d 567 (Tex. 1963) (exemplary damages for breach of fiduciary duty by corporate directors and officers).

91. Fortugno v. Hudson Manure Co., 51 N.J.Super. 482, 144 A.2d 207 (1958), noted 4 Vill.L.Rev. 457 (1959) (partnership property traced into corporations, which would be liquidated if necessary). But cf. n. 84, last par., above.

92. Bufalini v. DeMichelis, 136 Cal.App. 2d 452 and 458, 288 P.2d 934 and 937 (1955); Annot., Constructive trust in favor of partnership where one partner purchases real estate with his own funds, 44 A.L.R.2d 519 (1955). See also U.P.A. § 21(1) which specifies that a partner holds as trustee any

profits derived by him, without consent, from partnership transactions or property.

93. Crownfield v. Phillips, 125 Md. 1, 92 A. 1033, Ann.Cas.1916E 991 (1915).

94. A paid agent is under a duty to his principal to act with standard care and with the skill standard in the locality for the kind of work which he is employed to perform, and in addition to exercise any special skill which he has. He is liable for losses caused by failure to conform to this duty. Restatement, Second, Agency §§ 379, 400–402.

95. Hurter v. Larrabee, 224 Mass. 218, 112 N.E. 613 (1916), not liable for loss caused by faulty bookkeeping.

96. Northen v Tatum, 164 Ala. 368, 51 So. 17 (1909) (managing partner liable only for losses caused by fraud, bad faith, or culpable negligence); Snell v. De Land, 136 Ill. 533, 27 N.E. 183 (1891) (partner not an insurer, and liable only for loss resulting from wilful disregard of duty); Thomas v. Milfelt, 222 S.W.2d 359 (Mo.App.1949) (partner only liable for losses caused by fraud, culpable negligence or bad faith).

Knipe v. Livingston, 209 Pa. 49, 57 A. 1130 (1904) (not liable for laxity in collections). "We see no fair reason to criticize his business management. He can only be held liable for the loss, if any, upon proof that he has been culpably negligent. Even if a loss sustained by a firm is imputed

would have been avoided by consultation with his partners,[97] for extraordinary capital expenditures incurred over the objection of his partners,[98] or for loans made to a corporation in obvious financial difficulties, in which he is interested.[99] If he undertakes to act in a way exposing the firm to liabilities to the public, as by operating a motor vehicle, he may (as between the partners) be held liable for the whole loss caused by injury to a third person in a traffic accident.[1] For a loss due to joint negligence, contribution may be had as between the partners.[2]

to the conduct of one partner more than to that of another, still, if the former acted bona fide, with a view to the benefit of the firm, and without culpable negligence, the loss must be equally born by all. Lindley on Partnership, § 386." See also Lyons v. Lyons, 207 Pa. 7, 56 A. 54, 99 Am.St. Rep. 779 (1903).

Compare the rule as to responsibility of corporate directors. The Uniform Corporations Act (now withdrawn) § 33, imposed, in accordance with the weight of authority, an obligation on officers and directors to "discharge the duties of their respective positions in good faith and with that diligence, care and skill which ordinary prudent men would exercise under similar circumstances in their personal affairs." Such a provision exists in many corporate laws. It would appear that the same standard should be applied to the officers of joint stock companies and business trusts, in the absence of some provisions to the contrary in the articles of association. See Exchange Bank of Leon v. Gardner, 104 Iowa 176, 73 N.W. 591 (1897).

The articles of business trusts often contain provisions limiting the liability of trustees to "the result of his own gross negligence or bad faith." See a case construing this provision, Digney v. Blanchard, 226 Mass. 335, 115 N.E. 424 (1917). Since such persons are commonly compensated for their services [Trust No. 5522 and Trust No. 5644, Bellehurst Syndicate, v. Commissioner of Internal Revenue, 83 F.2d 801 (9th Cir. 1936)], in the absence of agreement to the contrary they should be subject to the standards of responsibility of paid agents. See Restatement, Second, Agency §§ 379, 400–402.

97. Yorks v. Tozer, 59 Minn. 78, 60 N.W. 846, 28 L.R.A. 86, 50 Am.St.Rep. 395

(1894). Cf. Looney v. Gillenwaters, 1 Tenn. 384, 11 Heisk. 133 (1872) (partner accountable for price paid for goods in excess of that which partners had fixed by agreement between themselves as a maximum).

A partner should consult with his co-partner, and secure his permission, before engaging professional assistance out of the usual course of business. Townsend v. Meyers, 142 App. Div. 851, 127 N.Y.S. 451 (1911) held that a member of a law partnership who engaged associate counsel for the conduct of litigation, without consultation, could not charge the co-partner with his share in the expense so incurred.

Before mortgaging the entire partnership stock to creditors whose claims are not matured and who are not pressing for security, a partner should consult with his co-partner who is available. McGrath v. Cowen, 57 Ohio St. 385, 49 N.E. 338 (1898).

98. Gordon v. Moore, 134 Pa. 486, 19 A. 753 (1890).

99. Watt v. German Sav. Bank, 183 Iowa 346, 165 N.W. 897 (1917).

A partner has been held liable for sales on credit, contrary to partnership agreement, to impecunious relatives. McCoy v. Crosfield, 54 Or. 591, 104 P. 423 (1909).

1. Kiffer v. Bienstock, 128 Misc. 451, 218 N.Y.S. 526 (1926); United Brokers' Co. v. Dose, 143 Or. 283, 22 P.2d 204 (1933); Note, The Permissible Conduct of a Partner in Carrying on of Firm Business, 29 Colum.L.Rev. 66, 74 (1929).

2. In re Ryan's Estate, 157 Wis. 576, 147 N.W. 993, L.R.A.1917A, 443, Ann. Cas.1916D, 840 (1914); 1 Iowa Law Bul. 45.

The trustee of a business trust, though the declaration of trust states that he shall be liable only "for the result of his own gross negligence or bad faith," is under a duty to reimburse the trust for diversion of funds into ultra vires enterprises.[3] The trustees and majority shareholders may be enjoined, on complaint of the minority, from a sale of the trust property to a corporation created by the majority.[4]

A sale by trustees of a business trust to a corporation, in exchange for stock, may be set aside at the complaint of minority shareholders, and, following the analogy of shareholders' bills in corporations, it is not a condition precedent that the plaintiffs first go through the obviously futile formality of applying to the trustees for relief.[5]

Where the articles of agreement in a business trust require the trustees to include in every contract with third persons a stipulation restricting liability to the joint funds, and the trustees neglect to do so, they cannot, when sued by third persons, cause the beneficiaries to be made parties defendant, as being primarily liable.[6]

OBLIGATIONS BETWEEN PARTNERS AND REMEDIES FOR THEIR NON-PERFORMANCE

§ 69. Partners, and persons intending to become partners, enter into contractual and other obligations with each other. For the nonperformance of such obligations, the usual common law remedies are available. For the breach of obligations between a partner and the partnership, the appropriate remedy is an accounting.

If persons agree to become partners, and one of them commits an inexcusable breach, he is subject to liability. Remedies for breach of contract in general include damages, restitution, and specific per-

---

Where a partner has dealt with the firm as a customer and been subjected to a property loss through the tort of an employee for which the partners are jointly liable, he must bear his share of the loss as partner in collecting his claim as customer. Farney v. Hauser, 109 Kan. 75, 198 P. 178 (1921).

3. Digney v. Blanchard, 226 Mass. 335, 115 N.E. 424 (1917). The trust was organized for the purpose of investing in real estate and mortgages, with power to erect buildings and otherwise improve land belonging to the trust. The trustee was held personally liable for losses caused by entering into a building-contracting business, erecting and repairing buildings on land of others.

4. Flint v. Codman, 247 Mass. 463, 142 N.E. 256 (1924). The trust was organized to acquire land and wharf property and improve it. Three corporate tenants of the property acquired the majority of the stock and agreed with the trustees to purchase all of the property with a view to winding up the trust. It was held, in accordance with the rule applicable to ordinary partnerships, that the majority of the associates could not authorize a sale to themselves of the entire property, though at a fair price. The situation was distinguished from that of a corporation on the theory (now very doubtful) that shareholders owe no such fiduciary duty to themselves or to the corporation as are owed by partners to the partnership and to each other.

5. Greer Inv. Co. v. Booth, 62 F.2d 321 (10th Cir. 1932).

6. Barnett v. Cisco Banking Co., 253 S. W. 339 (Tex.Civ.App.1923).

formance.[7] Specific performance of a contract to become partners is not allowed as a remedy because of the personal element of the contract, and because it would be futile, since any partner can dissolve the partnership at any time.[8] The injured party is entitled to restitution of what he has paid, by way of part performance of his agreement, to the contract breaker, in the form of property, money, or services.[9] He is entitled to damages as compensation for the gains prevented,[10] but the recovery of such damages is dependent on the possibility of proving their amount with the necessary degree of certainty.[11] If the injured party was, by the contract, to be admitted to a going business, past experience may furnish adequate evidence of the value of an interest in it.[12] If the contract breaker carries on the enterprise contemplated with profitable results, this is evidence of the loss caused to the excluded party.[13] But if the agrement called for the undertaking of a new venture which was abandoned, lack of certainty that the outcome would have been profitable precludes the recovery of substantial damages as compensation for gains prevented.[14] For fraud in the formation of the partnership, as by misrepresenting the past experience

---

7. Restatement, Contracts, § 326.

8. Clark v. Truitt, 183 Ill. 239, 55 N.E. 683 (1899); Maxa v. Jones, 148 Md. 459, 129 A. 652 (1925); Pater v. Schumaker, 21 Ohio App. 528, 153 N.E. 230 (1926); Hyer v. Richmond Traction Co., 168 U.S. 471, 18 S.Ct. 114, 42 L.Ed. 547 (1897). See Saunders v. McDonough, 191 Ala. 119, 67 So. 591 (1914) (joint venture).

In some cases, where the agreement to form a partnership and to transfer a share in certain property has been considered divisible, courts have decreed specific performance of the agreement to transfer property: Elliott v. Jones, 11 Del.Ch. 343, 101 A. 874 (1917) (race horse); Somerby v. Buntin, 118 Mass. 279, 19 Am.Rep. 459 (1875) (patent).

9. Coens v. Marousis, 275 Pa. 478, 119 A. 549 (1923), the owner of a shoe shine parlor installed plaintiff as manager, under an agreement to take him into partnership when the earnings had paid for the initial outlay. On breach of the agreement by the owner, plaintiff was entitled to recover the value of his services.

Cook v. Canny, 96 Mich. 398, 55 N.W. 987 (1893); Eastman v. Dunn, 34 R.I. 416, 83 A. 1057 (1912).

10. No partnership being formed, the injured partner is not entitled to an accounting of profits of the venture

carried on by the contract-breaker defendant: Powell v. Maguire, 43 Cal. 11 (1872); Haskins v. Burr, 106 Mass. 48 (1870); Armstrong v. Rickard, 199 App.Div. 880, 192 N.Y.S. 502 (1932).

11. Restatement, Contracts § 331; McCormick, Damages §§ 25–32 (1935).

12. Where defendant, who wrongfully refused to admit plaintiff as partner in his business, later sold it to another, the price obtained is evidence of the value of an interest in the business. Maxwell v. Persons, 150 Ga. 339, 103 S.E. 816 (1920).

13. Ramsay v. Meade, 37 Colo. 465, 86 P. 1018 (1906).

14. Eastman v. Dunn, 34 R.I. 416, 83 A. 1057 (1912); Webster v. Beau, 77 Wash. 444, 137 P. 1013, 51 L.R.A., N.S., 81 (1914).

But see the more liberal view of Perry v. Lambourne, 177 Cal.App.2d 662, 2 Cal.Rptr. 441 (1960): anticipated profits need not be established with complete certainty. Also, the value of services was taken into account. Semble, Gross v. Raeburn, 219 Cal.App.2d 792, 33 Cal.Rptr. 432 (1963).

Overstreet v. Merritt, 186 Cal. 494, 200 P. 11 (1921) (plaintiff could recover for his loss in giving up his existing business for the purpose of entering the partnership).

of a business or the cost or character of property to be employed therein, an action for deceit can be brought,[15] or the injured party may procure a dissolution and restitution.[16]

Rights of action between partners in a going partnership depend upon whether the breach of contract or other wrong is an injury to the complaining partner in his individual interest, or an injury to the partnership. For reasons of convenience and economy of litigation, and in accordance with the presumed intentions of partners, rights and duties which are a part of a partner's relations to the partnership as a partner are not litigated until a complete accounting takes place. At common law, this was necessarily at dissolution. Under U. P. A. it is normally at dissolution, but may be whenever circumstances make it just and reasonable.[17] If a partner lends his co-partner money to enable him to pay in his agreed capital contribution, or for any other purpose, though relating to the partnership affairs, that is a transaction between partner and partner, (not part of the partnership affairs) and an action may be brought to enforce payment.[18] But for the breach of the undertaking of a partner to pay in to the partnership his agreed capital contribution, or to perform any other duty to the partnership, there is no remedy in the other partner, except in the course of partnership accounting.[19] A partner may bring an action to recover for a debt

---

15. Bowman v. Sedgwick, 82 N.W. 491 (Iowa 1900); Oswalt v. Cronk, 195 Iowa 230, 190 N.W. 162, 191 N.W. 978 (1923).

16. U.P.A. § 39, Sec. 85 below. Long v. Newlin, 144 Cal.App.2d 509, 301 P.2d 271 (1956) (rescission; money had and received).

17. U.P.A. § 22, Secs. 70, 72 below.

18. Bull v. Coe, 77 Cal. 54, 18 P. 808, 11 Am.St.Rep. 235 (1888); Haskins v. Curran, 4 Idaho 573, 43 P. 559 (1895); Hartzell v. Murray, 224 Ill. 377, 79 N.E. 674 (1906); Wetherbee v. Potter, 99 Mass. 354 (1868); Seanor v. Fitt, 263 Pa. 389, 106 A. 792 (1919), defendant agreed to pay plaintiff his share of the value of a stock of goods supplied to partnership.

A partner who loans money to another to pay a partnership debt, taking his note for repayment, may enforce the note. Chamberlain v. Walker, 92 Mass. (10 Allen) 429 (1865); Crater v. Bininger, 45 N.Y. 545 (1871); Hopkins v. Adey, 92 Md. 1, 48 A. 41, 50 L.R.A. 498 (1900).

A partner who pays a firm debt with his own funds, upon the express promise of his co-partner to contribute, may recover on that promise. Cilley v. Van Patten, 58 Mich. 404, 25 N.W. 326 (1885).

If a partner is obliged to pay an obligation wrongfully given by his co-partner for a private purpose, he may recover the amount paid in an action at law against the wrongdoing partner. Cross v. Cheshire, 7 Exch. 43 (1851).

A partner is liable to a co-partner for breach of contract to pay and hold him harmless as to certain partnership debts. Simpson v. Ritchie, 110 Me. 299, 86 A. 124 (1913).

19. "The general, if not universal, rule is that, in the absence of an express agreement, an action in assumpsit, as distinguished from a suit in equity, cannot be maintained in respect to partnership transactions, unless there has been an accounting or settlement of the partnership affairs. . . . It is just as well settled that an action at law may be maintained by a party to an executory agreement to form a partnership to recover damages for the breach by other parties to the agreement. . . . Here the partnership was formed, it commenced business, and for aught appearing in the pleadings or evidence it is still

incurred quite outside of the partnership business.[20]

A partner is subject to liability to his co-partner for the tortious injury by him of the latter's property which has been loaned to the partnership for use in its business.[21] For an injury to or conversion of partnership property by a partner, ordinarily no action (short of accounting) can be maintained by the co-partner.[22] In some cases, where

in business. The purpose of the action is to recover for the cost of stock and equipment which, under the partnership articles, were sold by plaintiffs to the partnership consisting of plaintiffs and defendant, or to put it differently, to recover for a contribution which defendant agreed to make to the partnership. However stated the action will not lie at law." Stephens v. Lehnert, 310 Pa. 412, 165 A. 651 (1933).

Accord, Jones v. Cade, 19 Ala.App. 27, 94 So. 255 (1922); Green v. Mulkey, 142 Ark. 124, 218 S.W. 201 (1920); Ivy v. Walker, 58 Miss. 253 (1880); Miller v. Kemper, 107 Wash. 274, 181 P. 859 (1919); Sadler v. Nixon, 5 Barn. & Ald. 936 (1834); L. H. Heiselt, Inc. v. Brown, 108 Colo. 562, 120 P.2d 644, 160 A.L.R. 1081 (1941), annotated, and showing the cases in which actions lie as between partners.

The same rule has been applied to members of a business trust. One who sold goods to the trust could not recover from a fellow member prior to dissolution and accounting. He might even then be barred by the terms of association, which provided that no member shall be subject to any personal liabilities, a stipulation which is effective inter se, regardless of its validity as to third persons. Hardee v. Adams Oil Ass'n, 254 S.W. 602 (Tex. Civ.App.1923). So in the case of a joint-stock company, it has been held that there is no remedy available to a member against a fellow member prior to dissolution. Bullard v. Kinney, 10 Cal. 60 (1858). There is no reason, it seems, to bar a beneficiary in a business trust from suing the trustees, or the trust itself, if it can be sued in the common name, or to bar the member of a joint stock company from suing it in its common name or its officers in a representative suit, on an obligation which is in default prior to dissolution.

20. A partner may recover for money loaned to his co-partner, Collins v.

Meis, 139 Cal.App. 233, 33 P.2d 472 (1934); Chung Gee v. Quan Wing, 103 Cal.App.2d 19, 229 P.2d 50 (1951); Hartzell v. Murray, 224 Ill. 377, 79 N.E. 674 (1906); McIntosh v. McIntosh, 79 Mich. 198, 44 N.W. 592 (1890); Houghton v. Grimes, 100 Vt. 99, 135 A. 15 (1926), a joint-stock company relation; Elder v. Hood, 38 Ill. 533 (1865).

A partner can recover for goods sold to his co-partner. Martin v. McBryde, 182 N.C. 175, 108 S.E. 739, annotated, as to actions at law by partner against partner, in 21 A.L.R. 12 (1921); Zimmerman v. Lehr, 46 N.D. 297, 176 N.W. 837, 21 A.L.R. 8 (1920).

He may recover for services performed, Parker v. Day, 155 N.Y. 383, 49 N.E. 1046 (1898), executor of an estate engaged his partner as counsel. He may maintain an action on an agreement with his partner for the joint purchase, as individuals, of property. Rosenblum v. Arbitman, 81 N.Y.S.2d 478 (Sup.Ct.1948).

21. Haller v. Williamowicz, 23 Ark. 566 (1861); Smith v. Hensley, 353 S.W.2d 744, 98 A.L.R.2d 340 (Ky.1962); Newby v. Harrell, 99 N.C. 149, 5 S.E. 284, 6 Am.St.Rep. 503 (1888). Cases are collected, Annot., 98 A.L.R.2d 345 (1964).

A partner may recover for an injury to his person and effects by wrongfully evicting him from premises occupied by the partnership, Grabowski v. Benzsa, 80 Ind.App. 214, 140 N.E. 76 (1923). Cases are collected, Annot., 98 A.L.R.2d 345 (1964).

22. Bertozzi v. Collaso, 21 Ariz. 388, 188 P. 873, 21 A.L.R. 5 (1920); Bohmfalk v. Vaughn, 89 Ariz. 33, 357 P.2d 617 (1960); Grace v. Johnson, 209 Ky. 170, 272 S.W. 392 (1925); Ruschoff v. Wachsmuth, 185 Minn. 579, 242 N.W. 296 (1932), noted 17 Minn.L.Rev. 225 (1933); Duncan v. Bruce, 179 Misc. 992, 43 N.Y.S.2d 447 (1943); Masterson v. Allen, 69 S.W.2d 539 (Tex.Civ. App.1934), semble, allowing action against liquidating partner.

an action has been allowed, the conduct of the defendant was such as to bring about a wrongful dissolution or ouster of the complaining partner, by diverting the entire partnership stock from partnership purposes.[23] And equity, as distinct from law, may entertain a suit between partners that does not involve an accounting.[24]

Whether a partner appropriating partnership property is guilty of larceny depends on the interpretation of applicable statutes. It has been held that he is not taking property "partly the property of another and partly the property of the accused", in a jurisdiction where property rights are governed by the Uniform Act.[25]

The right to have the business of the partnership continued and to participate therein results from the agreement of partnership. The acts of a partner in wrongfully forcing a premature dissolution or in ousting a partner from the partnership business are breaches of the contract between the partners for which actions at law for damages are appropriate remedies.[26] If the wrongful act of a partner does not

---

23. Newsom v. Pitman, 98 Ala. 526, 12 So. 412 (1893); Oswalt v. Cronk, 195 Iowa 230, 190 N.W. 162, 191 N.W. 978 (1923); Enloe v. Ragle, 195 N.C. 38, 141 S.E. 477 (1928); Mills v. Williams, 113 Or. 528, 233 P. 542 (1925).

The managing partner of an oil producing partnership produced and sold oil in excess of amounts permitted by a state probation act. He was held accountable for the proceeds. Turnbow v. Lamb, 95 F.2d 29 (5th Cir. 1938). While he sold at less than the market prices for legitimately produced oil, it may be questioned whether he should not have been liable for more than what he actually received. See Note 4 U.Pitt.L.Rev. 304 (1938).

24. Kelly v. Tracy, 209 Or. 153, 305 P.2d 411 (1956) (constructive trust on shares of corporation (to which partnership assets were transferred) wrongfully taken by partner in her own name).

25. State v. Elsbury, 63 Nev. 463, 175 P.2d 430, 169 A.L.R. 364 (1946). A partner's rights in partnership property are set out in U.P.A. § 25; see Secs. 40–45, esp. Sec. 41(a) on criminal offenses.

A partner who signs his co-partner's name to a check on the firm account, without authority, the terms of deposit requiring two signatures, may be convicted of forgery. People v. Van Skander, 20 Cal.App.2d 248, 66 P.2d 1228 (1937).

People v. Esrig, 240 App.Div. 300, 270 N.Y.S. 372 (1934), citing other cases

dealing with embezzlement and larceny.

26. Karrick v. Hannaman, 168 U.S. 328, 18 S.Ct. 135, 42 L.Ed. 484 (1897); Williams v. Hildebrand, 220 Ark. 202, 247 S.W.2d 356 (1952). Barlow v. Collins, 166 Cal.App.2d 274, 333 P.2d 64 (1958) (not only breach of contract but tortious destruction of the partnership, by appropriation of all the partnership assets); Lupton v. Horn, 193 Ind. 499, 139 N.E. 177, 141 N.E. 49 (1923); Berkule v. Feldman, 39 Misc.2d 250, 240 N.Y.S.2d 462 (1963), aff'd 20 A.D.2d 761, 247 N.Y.S.2d 550 (1964); Enloe v. Ragle, 195 N.C. 38, 141 S.E. 477 (1928); McCollum v. Carlucci, 206 Pa. 312, 55 A. 979, 98 Am. St.Rep. 780 (1903).

As to damages, there is the problem of certainty similar to that raised in actions for breach of contract to engage in partnership. The question in this situation, too, is what is the value of the contract. Experience of the business before and after the breach may furnish evidence of value of an interest of a partner therein. Bagley v. Smith, 10 N.Y. 489, 61 Am.Dec. 756 (1853).

There is no right to specific performance of the partnership contract. McCollum v. McCollum, 67 S.W.2d 1055 (Tex.Civ.App.1934).

Injured partners may continue the business under certain circumstances without winding up, see Sec. 75 below.

amount to a dissolution of the partnership, but merely prevents a co-partner's enjoyment of his rights to participate in profits and management, the matter is considered as an item in partnership affairs, for which no remedy is available other than accounting in the course of dissolution.[27]

This is also true in case of a joint adventure, in which the rights and remedies between the adventurers are similar to those between partners.[28]

After dissolution, or conclusion of business, a partner may maintain an action at law for assets which were concealed, overlooked or misappropriated,[29] or for isolated claims outstanding.[30]

TRANSACTIONS BETWEEN PARTNERSHIP AND PARTNER, AND REMEDIES OTHER THAN DISSOLUTION AND ACCOUNTING FOR ENFORCEMENT OF OBLIGATIONS

§ 70. Transactions between partner and partnership may create obligations. The remedy for the non-performance of such obligations is usually deferred until accounting in the course of dissolution. If it is apparent that an obligation between partner and partnership is intended to be segregated from partnership accounts and to be immediately performed, there is no reason why it should not be enforced by action at law, other than the procedural difficulty of common party plaintiff and defendant in a legal action. The procedural difficulty is removed by transfer to one who may sue in his own right, as a holder of a negotiable instrument.

The conduct of partnership business gives rise to rights of the partner against the partnership and duties of the partner to the partnership. Ordinarily the adjustment of such matters is made in the course of accounting of partnership affairs and no judicial remedies can be obtained other than the formal accounting which is normally at dissolution, but may be granted whenever just and reasonable.[31] Without an accounting, a partner may not enforce his right to contribution or indemnification,[32] even though he has made advancements

---

27. Wills v. Andrews, 73 Fla. 384, 75 So. 618 (1917); Milligan v. Mackinlay, 209 Ill. 358, 70 N.E. 685 (1904); Ryder v. Wilcox, 103 Mass. 24 (1869); Swartz v. Biben, 87 Pa.Super. 270 (1926).

See Mitchell v. Tonkin, 109 App.Div. 165, 95 N.Y.S. 669 (1905).

28. Cunningham v. De Mordaigle, 82 Cal.App.2d 620, 186 P.2d 423 (1947).

29. Mumm v. Adam, 134 Colo. 493, 307 P.2d 797 (1957).

30. Taylor v. Richman, 395 Pa. 162, 149 A.2d 69 (1959) (indemnification from co-partner for partnership note paid by partner); Pilch v. Milikin, 200 Cal.App.2d 212, 19 Cal.Rptr. 334 (1962).

31. U.P.A. § 22; see Secs. 69 above and 72 below. U.P.A. § 22 gives accounting rights to the partners but not to partnership. The action can always be brought in the name of a partner, even though it is primarily for the benefit of the firm against a particular partner.

32. Sadler v. Nixon, 5 Barn. & Ald. 936 (1834); Miller v. Kemper, 107 Wash. 274, 181 P. 859 (1919).

for partnership purposes.[33] Similarly, damages from a partner's failure to render required services to the partnership are recoverable in an accounting,[34] but not in a separate action.[35] In general, then, so far as law is distinguished from equity (where accounting traditionally lies), an action at law is not maintainable between partner and partnership.[36]

Frequently, however, a transaction occurs between partner and partnership which is intended not to be merely an item in partnership accounts, but to create an obligation similar to that which would result from dealings between the partnership and a third person. If a partner deposits grain in an elevator operated by the partnership, he is entitled to compensation for its conversion by an employee, and to share in the benefits of a blanket policy of insurance in the event of its loss by fire.[37] If a partner makes a deposit in a partnership bank, he is entitled to the rights of an ordinary depositor.[38] A partner has been permitted to recover from her partnership (and its insurance carrier) under a Workmen's Compensation Act, for the death of her husband who was an employee of the partnership.[39] The fact that the loss rested ultimately on the insurer may have helped.[40] Under a few Workmen's Compensation statutes, a partner may sue the partnership for his own injuries.[41] Another forthright decision, brushing away "legalistic con-

---

33. U.P.A. § 18(a)–(b), Sec. 65(b) above.

34. Sec. 65(f) above.

35. Miller v. Freeman, 111 Ga. 654, 36 S.E. 961, 51 L.R.A. 504 (1900); Capen v. Barrows, 67 Mass. (1 Gray) 376 (1854).

36. Cases are collected in Annots., Actions at law between partners and partnerships, 21 A.L.R. 21 (1922), 58 A.L.R. 621 (1929), 168 A.L.R. 1088 (1947).
But see Pa.R.Civ.P. 2129 authorizing actions at law by partnership against partners and vice versa.

37. Farney v. Hauser, 109 Kan. 75, 198 P. 178 (1921), the claims were adjusted in the courts of dissolution and final accounting. As to the transaction, the court said: "There is nothing illegal, or at variance with the theory of a partnership, for plaintiff to deal with it as an ordinary customer. It would be absurd to hold that in this commercial age, when partnerships are so common, that a man could not buy from, sell to, trade with, or patronize a business partnership as any other person might do, and with the same rights and liabilities, merely because he had a partner's interest

in the firm business. If the partnership gets into financial difficulties with third parties, a partner who is a creditor of the firm may have his claim postponed until third parties are satisfied. But for all practical purposes a partnership may be considered as a business entity."

38. Lingner v. Gaines, 244 S.W. 205 (Tex.Civ.App.1922), an action at law was allowed against the co-partners, a procedure which may be explained by the fact that, in Texas, partnership obligations are joint and several.

39. Keegan v. Keegan, 194 Minn. 261, 260 N.W. 318 (1935), noted 49 Harv.L. Rev. 155 (1935). See also Sec. 3(c) above.

40. The presence of liability insurance protection has been held to remove the objections to imposing liability for torts between members of a family. Dunlap v. Dunlap, 84 N.H. 352, 150 A. 905, 71 A.L.R. 1055 (1930); Lusk v. Lusk, 113 W.Va. 17, 166 S.E. 538 (1932).

41. See the "contra" cases, Sec. 54(d) n. 32 above, the statutes in Sec. 54(d) n. 33 above, and Sec. 3(c) at nn. 60–62 above.

cepts", has permitted a partner to recover from the partnership for damage to his truck which was used in the partnership business.[42] These are all sensible applications of the entity concept of partnership.[43]

Considerable conflict exists as to the effect of an express contract between partner and partnership, such as a promise to pay money in the form of a negotiable instrument. Questions arise as to whether there is any legal contract (because of common parties obligor and obligee), whether such a contract is legally enforceable between the parties (in view of the procedural difficulty of a party suing himself), and whether the procedural difficulties are removed by transfer to a third person.

It has been said that a man cannot make a contract with himself, and therefore cannot make a contract with himself and another as joint obligors or obligees.[44] If the partnership may be personified as a group entity, there is no difficulty on this score. "A partnership, or joint stock company, is just as distinct and palpable an entity in the idea of the law, as distinguished from the individuals composing it as is a corporation; and can contract as an individualized and unified party, with an individual person who is a member thereof, as effectually as a corporation can contract with one of its stockholders. The obligation and the liability inter partes are the same in the one case as the other. The only practical difference is a technical one having reference to the forum and form of remedy." [45] Even if the partnership is not treated as an entity, there is a growing tendency to regard such contracts as having legal validity. "A contract may be formed between two or more persons acting as a unit and one or more but fewer than all of these persons, acting either singly or with other persons." [46]

The procedural difficulty of a person suing himself is not dealt with by the Model [formerly Uniform] Interparty Agreement Act nor by the Contracts Restatement. The enactment of legislation validating such contracts implies that a remedy for their enforcement shall

---

42. Smith v. Hensley, 354 S.W.2d 744, 98 A.L.R.2d 340 (Ky.1962). See also cases in Sec. 69, n. 21.

Compare the growing willingness to permit suits against the partnership by a partner's spouse who has been negligently injured, Sec. 54(d) above at nn. 34–41. And see Shea v. Yanof, 288 S.W.2d 575 (Tex.Civ.App.1956) error dism. (partner's wife, who made loan to partnership, can recover from copartner on his joint and several liability).

43. See Sec. 3 above.

44. Warren, Corporate Advantages Without Incorporation 88 (1929).

45. Walker v. Wait, 50 Vt. 668 (1878).

46. Restatement, Contracts § 17. See also Explanatory Notes by Samuel Williston, published by the A.L.I. with Contracts O.D. 1, Sept. 15, 1928.

The Model [formerly Uniform] Interparty Agreement Act, adopted in Maryland, Nevada, Pennsylvania, and Utah, provides, in section 1: "A conveyance, release or sale may be made to or by two or more persons acting jointly and one or more, but less than all, of these persons acting either by himself or themselves or with other persons; and a contract may be made between such parties."

be available. The courts may minimize the procedural technicality. In Laughner v. Wally,[47] co-tenants, held not to be partners, sold oil-drilling equipment to one of their number and sued for the price as A, B and C versus C. On appeal from a judgment for the plaintiffs, the court said: "We express no opinion on the right of such an association to bring suit against one of its members, as the question is not raised. The right of one co-tenant to bring suit against another is undoubted, and even if the insertion of Wally's name as a plaintiff was a misjoinder it was waived by going to trial upon the merits." In the cases in which the objection has been made, it has been held that a partner cannot sue a partnership,[48] nor a partnership a partner[49] at law on a joint right or obligation. If the partnership obligation is joint and several, the partner can maintain an action against his co-partners on an obligation such as a promissory note, intended to be isolated from the partnership accounts.[50] Careful reading reveals that many of the cases cited for the broad proposition that no suit can be maintained between partners and partnership, actually say only that the suit cannot be maintained without an accounting.[51] This is a much narrower and sounder approach, but has occasionally been carried to ridiculous extremes.[52] Other decisions perpetuate the ancient conceptualism of impossible duality.[53] In most instances,

---

47. 269 Pa. 5, 112 A. 105 (1920).

The procedural difficulty in actions between partnership and partner in Pennsylvania is removed by Pa.R.Civ. P. 2129, but the substantive objection to litigating isolated transactions between partner and going partnership is still effective.

48. Moore v. Denslow, 14 Conn. 235 (1841). See Hanley v. Elm Grove Mut. Tel. Co., 150 Iowa 198, 129 N.W. 807 (1911); Newsom v. Pitman, 98 Ala. 526, 12 So. 412 (1893); Warren, Corporate Advantages Without Incorporation 85 (1929).

49. Kalamazoo Trust Co. v. Merrill, 159 Mich. 649, 124 N.W. 597 (1910); Burley v. Harris, 8 N.H. 233, 29 Am.Dec. 650 (1836).

50. Mayer v. Lane, 33 N.M. 24, 262 P. 180 (1927); Willis v. Barron, 143 Mo. 450, 45 S.W. 289, 65 Am.St.Rep. 673 (1898). The action in this case was on a promissory note, and plaintiff partner sued for and recovered judgment for only one-half of its face value.

Compare other Missouri cases, all involving negotiable instruments: Boyce v. Howell, 210 S.W. 89 (Mo.App.1919); Powell Hardware Co. v. Mayer, 110 Mo.App. 14, 83 S.W. 1008 (1904);

Hindman v. Secoy, 218 S.W. 416 (Mo. App.1920).

51. Malott v. Seymour, 101 Cal.App.2d 245, 225 P.2d 310 (1950); Cohen v. Erdle, 282 App.Div. 569, 126 N.Y.S.2d 32 (1953); Nixon v. Morse, 194 N.C. 225, 139 S.E. 170 (1927).

52. The most absurd is Cohen v. Ziskind, 290 Mass. 282, 195 N.E. 346 (1935). D borrowed from and gave a note to a cooperative society (similar to a savings and loan association) of which he was a member along with 200 others. Held: the assignee of the note could not sue on it, since the society was a partnership and could not have sued without an accounting.

See also State v. Quinn, 245 Iowa 846, 64 N.W.2d 323, 43 A.L.R.2d 1240 (1954) (partner can't be guilty of obtaining money by false pretenses; the implication is that an accounting is necessary to determine whether the taking is wrongful).

53. Duplis v. Rutland Aerie, etc., 118 Vt. 438, 111 A.2d 727 (1955) (member suing fraternal association for negligent injury would be on both sides of the case; this is not allowed).

Generally joint enterprisers are treated as co-principals and one cannot hold

convenience and justice will be served by permitting actions between partners and partnerships (with accounting when appropriate); this is particularly true if there is insurance, if the partnership can be sued in its common name, or if the partner's interest in the partnership is small relative to the claim in question.[54]

The procedural difficulty can be removed by the transfer of a negotiable instrument to the holder who may sue in his own name.[55] Where the endorsee is a holder in due course, he is allowed to enforce the instrument.[56] Some decisions appear to indicate that the instrument is incomplete until endorsed,[57] but this view could not be taken in a jurisdiction which recognized the capacity of a partner to enter into a contract with the partnership. If the endorsement is after maturity, there is a conflict as to the rights of the endorsee. The preferable view is that it is to be enforced, subject only to equities existing against the paper at the time of endorsement, and that the general right to accounting between partners is not such an equity where the partnership is still a going concern.[58] Decisions to the

the group liable for a personal injury received in the course of the enterprise, since negligence is imputed equally to all, including the plaintiff. However, any individual actor is liable for his wrongful conduct. De Villars v. Hessler, 363 Pa. 498, 70 A.2d 333, 14 A.L.R.2d 470 (1950). In this case a member of a grange was participating in operating a concession for preparing and selling food granted the grange at a county fair. While she was preparing and serving food, she was injured by reason of a defective steam table. The grange was a nonprofit unincorporated association.

Compare McClean v. University Club, 327 Mass. 68, 97 N.E.2d 174 (1951), holding that a member of a club (apparently incorporated) could recover from the club for damages suffered through the negligence of the manager in forcing him to vacate a bedroom and leave the club in a helpless condition. The action was in contract. A member of a club, whether incorporated or not, which has officers directing its employees, cannot fairly be considered a co-principal when patronizing the club.

See Crane, Liability of Unincorporated Association for Tortious Injury to a Member, 16 Vand.L.Rev. 319 (1963) tracing and criticizing the application of the co-principal doctrine to labor unions, and discussing one of the pivotal cases permitting a union member to sue the union, Marshall v. International Longshoremen's & Warehousemen's Union, 57 Cal.2d 781, 22 Cal. Rptr. 211, 371 P.2d 987 (1962). See Annot., Recovery by member from unincorporated association for injuries inflicted by tort of fellow member 14 A.L.R.2d 473 (1950).

54. Arguing for the entity theory in this connection is Crane, Liability of Unincorporated Association for Tortious Injury to a Member, 16 Vand.L.Rev. 319 (1963).

55. Moore v. Denslow, n. 48 above. Contra: Cohen v. Ziskind, n. 52 above, where the indorsee had notice and gave no value.

56. Thayer v. Buffum, 52 Mass. (11 Metc.) 398 (1846); Kipp v. McChesney, 66 Ill. 460 (1872); Smith v. Lusher, 5 Cow. 688 (N.Y.1825). See Woodman v. Boothby, 66 Me. 389 (1876): "It is obvious that an action could not be maintained upon this note by the payees (note given by partner to partnership) for the promisors could not sue one of their number as a maker. But this affects the remedy, not the right and when the note is duly endorsed to a third person, he acquires a legal title, and may sue upon it in his own name. . . . A firm is to be regarded as a distinct personality."

57. Thayer v. Buffum, n. 56 above.

58. "While there is a difficulty in a suit at law in the name of a party against

contrary unduly ignore the intention of the partners to take this transaction out of the course of partnership accounts.[59]

TRANSACTIONS BETWEEN PARTNERSHIPS HAVING COMMON MEMBERS

§ 71. **Unless aided by statute, a partnership cannot enforce, by action at law, obligations incurred by another partnership having a common member. Endorsees and assignees may enforce such obligations. A remedy is afforded in equity, between the two partnerships, without the necessity of accounting among the members.**

himself, yet if this is the only difficulty, it goes only to the form of the remedy, and not to its existence. There never was any legal or equitable reason why a partner should not have specific dealings with his firm as well as any other person; and unless those dealings from their nature, are intended to go into the general accounting, and wait for their adjustment till dissolution, they give a right to have a remedy according to their exigency, and can be dealt with like any other claims. The only reason why they must, under the old practice, be prosecuted in equity instead of at law, rose from the necessity at law of having plaintiffs capable of suing the defendants. In such a case the failure of a remedy at law justified a resort to equity. But equity could grant relief in such cases, and under our present rules there can be no difficulty at law. Where parties have seen fit to deal with each other without reference to the final accounting the transaction is not subject to the necessity or delay of such an accounting. The note was by its terms negotiable. It is elementary doctrine that negotiability does not cease when paper matures. It is only subject to such equities as exist against the paper at the date when it is negotiated. And the equities which affect the indorsee are only such as attach directly to the note itself, and do not include collateral matters. . . . When this note was indorsed there could be no accounting, because the firm continued its ordinary business. The debt was for a loan, and not for investments in the capital. It was distinct from the mutual relations among the partners, and stood as a separate contract." Carpenter v. Greenop, 74 Mich. 664, 42 N.W. 276, 4 L.R.A. 241, 16 Am.St. Rep. 662 (1889).

Accord, Nevins v. Townsend, 6 Conn. 5 (1825); Roberts v. Ripley, 14 Conn. 543 (1842), transfer after dissolution for purpose of collection; Knaus v. Dudgeon, 110 Mo. 58, 19 S.W. 535 (1892); Caldwell v. Dismukes, 111 Mo. App. 570, 86 S.W. 270 (1905).

59. Nixon v. Morse, 194 N.C. 225, 139 S.E. 170 (1927) (denying remedy by partner as endorsee of note given partnership by co-partner); Summerson v. Donovan, 110 Va. 657, 66 S.E. 822, 19 Ann.Cas. 253 (1910) (partner's note not enforceable by trustee in liquidation of partnership); Tipton v. Nance, 4 Ala. 194 (1842) (partner, as endorsee from partnership, not allowed to sue co-partner as indorser of instrument purchased by partnership); Thompson v. Lowe, 111 Ind. 272, 12 N.E. 476 (1887) (continuing partner, sued on obligation given in purchase of retired partner's interest, cannot set-off a note given by latter to partnership).

In Cutting v. Daigneau, 151 Mass. 297, 23 N.E. 839 (1890), a note was given by a partnership to a partner. Two years later, after the partnership became insolvent and was dissolved, the payee partner endorsed the note to a third person, under an agreement that he should seek to recover on it and divide the net proceeds with the payee. It was held that the endorsee was not entitled to recover, since he stood in no better position than the payee, it not being a bona fide transfer, and the payee was entitled to nothing, firm creditors not being paid.

See also Hill v. McPherson, 15 Mo. 204, 55 Am.Dec. 142 (1851), under a statute permitting defenses against transferees which could be made against transferors.

A contract between partnerships with common members is subject to the same considerations concerning its substantive validity as a contract between a partner and his partnership.[60] An early English case, Bosanquet v. Wray,[61] said that no contract could legally exist in such a situation, and held that the removal of the procedural difficulty by the death of the common partner did not enable the survivors to maintain an action at law. Other cases agree that there is no common law remedy because of the common party plaintiff and defendant.[62] Legislation sometimes affords relief.[63] Third parties, as endorsees of negotiable instruments,[64] and even as assignees of non-negotiable choses in action where they are allowed to sue in their own names,[65] have been permitted to recover. Equity provides a remedy between the two partnerships,[66] and a remedy is readily obtainable in code jurisdictions where legal and equitable remedies are merged.[67] Where the obligation of a partnership is joint and several, non-common partners can be sued at law.[68]

60. Sec. 70 above.

61. 6 Taunt. 597 (1815).
Lacy v. Le Bruce and Prince, 6 Ala. 904 (1844), allowed a remedy at law after the death of the common partner.

62. Thompson v. Young, 90 Md. 72, 44 A. 1037 (1899); Green v. Chapman, 27 Vt. 236 (1855); Taylor v. Thompson, 176 N.Y. 168, 68 N.E. 240 (1903) (semble, action for deceit); Newport Constr. Co. v. Porter, 118 Or. 127, 246 P. 211 (1926). See Annots., Actions at law between partners and partnerships, 21 A.L.R. 21, 130–33 (1922), 58 A.L.R. 621, 634 (1929).

63. Pa. Act of April 14, 1838, P.L. 457, 12 Pa.Stat.Ann. § 150. Grubb v. Cottrell, 62 Pa. 23 (1869) said that the Act removed all legal procedural difficulties and the case between two partnerships was to be considered "as though the parties plaintiffs and defendants were separate and distinct persons." See also Pa.R.Civ.P. 2129 (partnership may sue partners, together with others, at law).

64. Murdock v. Caruthers, 21 Ala. 785 (1852).

65. Beacannon v. Liebe, 11 Or. 443, 5 P. 273 (1884); Manatee Loan & Mortgage Co. v. Manley's Estate, 106 Vt. 356, 175 A. 14 (1934) (joint venture). But see Aylett v. Walker, 92 Va. 540, 24 S.E. 226 (1896), under a statute permitting assignees to maintain only such actions as the original obligee might have brought.

66. Rose v. Beckham, 264 Ala. 209, 86 So.2d 275 (1956); Burrows v. Leech, 116 Mich. 32, 74 N.W. 296 (1898); Crosby v. Timolat, 50 Minn. 171, 52 N.W. 526 (1892). As to proof in bankruptcy, see Sec. 93(f) below.

67. Cole v. Reynolds, 18 N.Y. 74 (1858); Mangels v. Shaen, 21 App.Div. 507, 48 N.Y.S. 526 (1897); Townsend v. Whitacre, 190 App.Div. 716, 180 N.Y.S. 368 (1920).

68. Alexander Bros. v. Jones, 90 Ala. 474, 7 So. 903 (1890). After discussing the procedural and substantive objections to causes of action between firms having common partners, the court said: "Whether the rule is referable to one or the other, or both of these reasons, it is a pure technicality, as is demonstrated by the fact that such contracts have always been upheld and enforced in equity. Its existence, even in those cases where the reasons stated apply, has been deplored by eminent jurists who approve as a better doctrine of abstract law, that which obtains in every system of jurisprudence except that of common-law countries, and which accords to partnerships something of an entity, like that of corporations, separate and apart from the individuals who compose them, in such sort that contracts and actions between them are in nowise affected by the fact of a common membership."

Here, as in actions between partners and partnerships,[69] utilization of the entity theory will permit prompter disposition of issues on their merits.

A transaction between two corporations with a common director is often treated as voidable, particularly if its fairness is not shown.[70] The result is based on fiduciary duties similar to those of partners.[71] It could equally well be applied to transactions between partnerships having a common member, or between a partnership and a corporation having a common member-director. No cases have been found directly doing so.[72]

RIGHT TO AN ACCOUNT; ACTION FOR ACCOUNTING

§ 72. Any partner shall have the right to a formal account as to partnership affairs:

(a) If he is wrongfully excluded from the partnership business or possession of its property by his co-partners.

(b) If the right exists under the terms of any agreement.

(c) As provided by section 21.

(d) Whenever other circumstances render it just and reasonable. U.P.A. § 22.

He may enforce his right by an action for an accounting, an equitable proceeding for comprehensive investigation of transactions and adjudication of rights of the partners.

We have already considered the partner's right to inspect the books,[73] be informed about partnership affairs,[74] and have his partners account for breaches of trust.[75] These relate mainly to specific transactions and do not necessarily provide systematic financial review.[76]

---

69. Sec. 70 above.

70. Ballantine, Corporations 179–84 (rev. ed. 1946); Henn, Corporations 374–77 (1961) and references there cited.

71. Sec. 68 above.

72. Compare Jungk v. Reed, 9 Utah 49, 33 P. 236 (1893), subsequent appeals 12 Utah 196, 42 P. 292 (1895), 15 Utah 198, 49 P. 305 (1897) implying that conflict of interest might invalidate the transactions between two partnerships with a common member, if co-partners had not acquiesced, and holding that it did invalidate guarantees by non-partners of the partnership obligations. The court carefully considers that the best possible deal may not have been made because of the conflict of interest.

Morris v. Owen, 143 S.W. 227 (Tex.Civ. App.1912) (surviving partner, in course of winding up, may sell partnership assets to another partnership of which he is a member, if he acts in good faith; price appears to have been fair).

The more conventional sort of case is one in which a dual partner is held liable to his co-partners in one firm for profits derived in the second firm from transactions between the two, Van Deusen v. Crispell, 114 App.Div. 361, 99 N.Y.S. 874 (1906). This is merely an extension of his fiduciary duty not to compete, see Sec. 68 above, and does not affect the validity of the inter-firm transactions.

73. Sec. 66 above.

74. Sec. 67 above.

75. Sec. 68 above.

76. Partnership income tax returns, discussed in Sec. 66 above, should be fair-

To assure full review, each partner is entitled to a formal account in certain circumstances, e. g., when provided by agreement,[77] when there is a breach of fiduciary duty,[78] when a partner is wrongfully excluded from partnership business or property,[79] and (quite broadly) when other circumstances render it just and reasonable.[80]

A formal account or (as it is sometimes called) an accounting is more than a presentation of financial statements. It encompasses a review of all transactions, including alleged improprieties, which should be reflected in the financial statements. It resembles a trustee's accounting.

If a partner asks his co-partners for an account and does not get it, or is not satisfied with it, he may bring an action for an accounting. This is a comprehensive investigation of transactions of the partnership and the partners, and an adjudication of their relative rights. It is conducted by the court or, more commonly, by an auditor, referee or master,[81] subject to the court's review. Equitable throughout most of its long history, this action is well adapted to the complexity of partners' relations.[82] But its origins lie in the mutual fiduciary obligations of the partners.[83]

An accounting action is designed to produce and evaluate all testimony relevant to the various claims of the partners.[84] It results in a money judgment for or against each partner according to the balance struck. Ancillary relief, like injunction,[85] receivership,[86] and partition[87] may be granted in appropriate cases. Since all activities

---

ly comprehensive, but they are not prepared primarily to show the relative rights of the partners. All too often, they are not accurately prepared; see, e. g., Mumm v. Adam, 134 Colo. 493, 307 P.2d 797 (1957).

77. U.P.A. § 22(b). Carefully prepared partnership agreements usually provide for annual or more frequent accounting; see Appendix V, pars. 2.8, 3.2.

78. U.P.A. § 22(c) referring to U.P.A. § 21, Sec. 68 above.

79. U.P.A. § 22(a).

80. U.P.A. § 22(d). Accord U.L.P.A. § 10(1)(b).

Agents and trustees have a duty to keep and render accounts, Restatement, Second, Agency § 382; Restatement, Second, Trusts § 172.

81. Brandenburg v. Brandenburg, 234 Ark. 1117, 356 S.W.2d 625 (1963) (error not to refer to master if transactions are complicated).

82. See Donatelli v. Carino, 384 Pa. 582, 122 A.2d 36 (1956). See also Couder v. Gomez, 378 S.W.2d 14 (Tex.1964) (suit to recover business assets held to state cause of action for accounting though evidence was insufficient to show conversion).

Equitable defenses are available, e. g., laches, Silver v. Korr, 392 Pa. 26, 139 A.2d 552 (1958).

83. See McClintock, Equity 537–39 (2d ed. 1948).

84. Weidlich v. Weidlich, 147 Conn. 160, 157 A.2d 910 (1960) ("the one great occasion for a comprehensive and effective settlement of all partnership affairs").

85. Johann v. Johann, 232 Ind. 40, 111 N.E.2d 473 (1953).

86. Jones v. Schellenberger, 201 F.2d 29 (7th Cir. 1953) (Ill. law).

87. Willman & Assoc. v. Penseiro, 159 Me. 319, 192 A.2d 469 (1963); Chase v. Angell, 148 Mich. 1, 108 N.W. 1105, 118

related to the partnership are subject to scrutiny, a wide variety of matters may be determined,[88] for example:

(1) Questions of conventional accounting, such as cash or accrual method of reporting, application of payments, valuation of inventories, type of depreciation, expenses v. capital expenditures, and other factors in computing profit and loss as well as assets and liabilities.

(2) Questions of reconstruction of inadequate records.[89]

(3) Questions of agreement, such as whether a partner was to have a salary, or was to treat an advance to the partnership as a loan (rather than a contribution).

(4) Questions of fiduciary duty, such as whether a partner must account for profits from an outside transaction or holds property in trust for the partnership.[90]

(5) Questions of scope of the partnership business, such as whether a particular expenditure was proper, or whether certain profits belong to the partnership or to another business.[91]

(6) Questions of ownership of property, e. g. whether individual or partnership.[91A]

(7) Questions of valuation of assets, such as good will.[91B]

The character of an accounting is concisely conveyed by the court's compilation in a relatively simple case involving the construction and sale of a motel by partners Hargett and Miller.[92] It is easy to visualize the dispute generated by almost every item.

Am.St.Rep. 568 (1906). But see U.P.A. § 38(1) giving each partner, on dissolution, the right to have the surplus distributed in *cash;* this obviously precludes partition unless all partners agree.

88. Perhaps the largest and most complex accounting in the reports is Greenan v. Ernst, 408 Pa. 495, 184 A.2d 570 (1962) concerning numerous transactions in oil properties over several decades and involving millions of dollars.

89. Adams v. Mason, 358 S.W.2d 7 (Mo. 1962) (reconstruction of income by reference to comparable or expected yield for type of property involved); Hairston v. Richie, 338 S.W.2d 263 (Tex.Civ.App.1960) (net worth method). See also cases cited Sec. 66 nn. 19 and 28 above.

90. Sec. 67 above.

91. Gohen v. Gravelle, 411 Pa. 520, 192 A.2d 414 (1963).

91A. Few v. Few, 239 S.C. 321, 122 S.E. 2d 829, 836 (1961).

91B. Sec. 84 below (good will). See Smith v. Smith, 149 Cal.App.2d 29, 307 P.2d 644 (1957) (inventory); McBride v. Fitzpatrick, 224 Or. 457, 356 P.2d 947 (1960) (dealer's reserves against automobile installment paper; building).

92. Hargett v. Miller, 235 Ark. 523, 361 S.W.2d 83, 85 (1962).

Another example of calculations is Yeomans v. Lysfjord, 162 Cal.App.2d 357, 327 P.2d 957 (1958).

Sale price of Motel	$120,000.00	
Cash in cash drawer (admitted by Hargett)	300.00	
Cash in cash drawer (additional amount found by chancellor from testimony)	2,035.39	

A—TOTAL ASSETS OF PARTNERSHIP ------------------ $122,335.39

Payments from Assets:

(1) To Lovett in discharge of loan	53,417.75	
(2) To Bank in discharge of loan	11,920.80	
(3) To Hargett in additional salary	2,219.91	
(4) To Miller, reimbursement for loan payments & other advances	20,875.00	
(5) To Miller, interest on advances beyond capital	92.23	
(6) Cash paid for property improvement by Hargett (capital contribution)	2,398.96	

B—TOTAL OBLIGATIONS --------------------------------- 90,924.65

C—BALANCE TO DIVIDE --------------------------------- 31,410.74

D—AMOUNT DUE EACH PARTNER FROM BALANCE -- $ 15,705.37

Amount due Miller from above calculation:

(4) Reimbursement for loan payments & other advances	$ 20,875.00	
(5) Interest on advances beyond capital	92.23	
(D) Amount due Miller from balance	15,705.37	

E—TOTAL DUE MILLER -------------------------------- $ 36,672.60

Amount in Miller's possession ----- 36,912.25

F—OVERPAYMENT TO MILLER ---------------------- $ 239.65

Amount due Hargett from above calculation:

(3) Additional salary	$ 2,219.91	
(6) Cash paid (capital contribution)	2,398.96	
(D) Amount due Hargett from balance	15,705.37	

G—TOTAL DUE HARGETT --------------------------- $ 20,324.24

Amount in Hargett's possession ----- 20,084.59

H—BALANCE DUE HARGETT -------------------------- $ 239.65

At common law an action for an accounting was generally denied except incident to dissolution.[93] The feeling was that partners should not seek to have the courts operate their affairs; if they cannot get along together amicably, they should dissolve and wind up. Moreover, no finality could be reached while business activities and financial re-

---

[93.] An accounting for an isolated transaction will generally be denied, Lord v. Hull, 178 N.Y. 9, 70 N.E. 69, 102 Am.St.Rep. 484 (1904), and so will an accounting for a limited period, leaving the partnership relation intact, Young v. McKenney, 197 Ky. 768, 247 S.W. 964 (1923); Childers v. Neely, 47 W.Va. 70, 34 S.E. 828, 49 L.R.A. 468, 81 Am.St.Rep. 777 (1901).

Failure to demand an accounting for a long period of time, the existence of the partnership not being denied, is not laches such as to bar the right to an accounting, and settlement of partnership affairs after death of the partner in whose name real estate was purchased with partnership funds. Einsweiler v. Einsweiler, 390 Ill. 286, 61 N.E.2d 377 (1945). See n. 95 below. See also Secs. 69–70 above.

lations continued. A partner could have his accounting if he dissolved, which he might do as of right if it were a partnership at will, or on subjecting himself to damages for wrongful dissolution if it were not.[94] In either case, he paid the price of destroying the going business. To relieve this dilemma, the framers of U.P.A. deliberately broadened the grounds for accounting, so that they are no longer contingent on dissolution.[95] The feasibility of periodic accounting has long been demonstrated in trust and related proceedings; where necessary, it can be applied to partnerships.

Even without U.P.A., non-dissolution accounting has been decreed when the partnership agreement calls for annual accounts [96] or when a partner has been excluded from participation and profit sharing.[97] Accounting has been granted where the existence of the partnership was denied.[98]

If an account is agreed to by the partners as a final settlement of partnership affairs, showing what is owing by one partner to another, an action can be maintained at law by one partner against another to enforce payment.[99] Though there is no express promise to pay, one

94. See Secs. 74–75 below. A partner's breach of agreement or duty does not forfeit his right to an accounting, Thompson v. McCormick, 149 Colo. 465, 370 P.2d 442 (1962); Bowen v. Velliquette, 153 Cal.App.2d 847, 315 P.2d 95 (1957).

Various kinds of illegality may preclude an accounting. See Annot., 32 A.L.R. 2d 1345 (1953).

The refusal of a partner to render an accounting when due is a sufficiently serious breach to warrant dissolution by court decree.

Under U.P.A. § 32(1) (d), a court may decree a dissolution where a partner willfully or persistently commits a breach of the partnership agreement. Refusal to render annual account, as expressly provided for in the agreement of partnership, is such a breach, and the court may decree dissolution and accounting on petition of the aggrieved partner. Lavoine v. Casey, 251 Mass. 124, 146 N.E. 241 (1925).

95. Commissioners' Note to U.P.A. § 22, 7 Unif.Laws Ann. 125 (1949).

The right to an account accrues at dissolution, in the absence of contrary agreement, U.P.A. § 43, Sec. 87 below. This appears to conflict with U.P.A. § 22 which specifies the right exists on the specified occasions. The conflict disappears if we accept that the limit-

ed purpose of § 43 is to bar a defense of laches or limitations, so long as the partnership has not dissolved. If so, it does not affect the assertion of a right to an accounting before dissolution. Amendment to this effect is desirable.

96. Miller v. Freeman, 111 Ga. 654, 36 S.E. 961, 51 L.R.A. 504 (1900). See McLauthlin v. Smith, 166 Mass. 131, 44 N.E. 125 (1896) (action between co-owners of ship for balances due may be maintained after each voyage, which may be treated as a separate venture).

97. Tarabino v. Nicoli, 5 Colo.App. 545, 39 P. 362 (1895); Maloney v. Crow, 11 Colo.App. 518, 53 P. 828 (1898); Hogan v. Walsh, 122 Ga. 283, 50 S.E. 84 (1905); Pirtle v. Penn, 33 Ky. (3 Dana) 247, 28 Am.Dec. 70 (1835); Hirshfield v. Robins, 99 Pa.Super. 217 (1930) semble.

98. Bailly v. Betti, 241 N.Y. 22, 27, 148 N.E. 776 (1925). Of course, if the court finds that no partnership exists, there is no basis for an accounting, Shaffer v. Ross, 143 So.2d 568 (Fla. App.1962).

99. Davenport v. Witt, 212 Ala. 114, 101 So. 887 (1924); Burns v. Nottingham, 60 Ill. 531 (1871), semble.

is implied, as in an account stated.[1] A partial settlement will not afford a basis for an implied promise,[2] but if an express promise is made by one partner to another to pay over what is found to be due on a partial accounting, such a promise may be enforced by an action at law.[3]

1. Knerr v. Hoffman, 65 Pa. 126 (1870). (But see Lawrence v. Mangold, 1 Walk. 202 [Pa.1880]); Purvines v. Champion, 67 Ill. 459 (1873); Fanning v. Chadwick, 3 Pick. 420, 15 Am.Dec. 233 (Mass.1826).

2. Davenport v. Gear, 3 Ill. (2 Scam.) 495 (1840).

3. A note given by a partner to his co-partner, in performance of a duty to contribute, to reimburse him for a particular item of expense, may be enforced by an action at law. Clamp v. Nolan, 300 S.W. 105 (Tex.Civ.App. 1927); Collamer v. Foster, 26 Vt. 754 (1854).

CHAPTER 8

DISSOLUTION AND WINDING UP OF SOLVENT PARTNERSHIPS

Analysis

"DISSOLUTION" v. "TERMINATION."

§ 73.   The "dissolution" of a partnership is the change in the relation of the partners caused by any partner ceasing to be associated in the carrying on, as distinguished from the winding up, of the business.   U.P. A. § 29.

On dissolution the partnership is not terminated, but continues until the winding up of partnership affairs is completed.   U.P.A. § 30.

The terms "dissolution," "winding up," and "termination" are often confused.   As the terms are used in the U.P.A., dissolution "designates the point in time when the partners cease to carry on the business together; termination is the point in time when all partnership affairs are wound up; winding up, the process of settling partnership affairs after dissolution." [1]   Winding up is often called liquidation, in business as well as legal parlance.   Despite the relative precision of the statutory language, the terms continue to be used indiscriminately by many courts and lawyers.

The statute is imprecise, not in the relative meaning of the three phrases, but in the incomplete coordination between the general definition of dissolution (in terms of a partner ceasing to be associated) and the specific causes of dissolution.[2]   Thus there are dissolu-

---

[1] Commissioners' Notes to U.P.A. § 29,   [2] U.P.A. §§ 31–32, Secs. 74–78 below.
      7 Uniform Laws Ann. 165–66 (1949).

tions not covered by specific causes [3] and disassociations of partners which are not dissolutions.[4] Moreover, the defintion confuses cause and effect.[5] There is room for improvement of the U.P.A. in this respect.[6]

After brief discussion in this Section, the causes of dissolution are considered in greater detail in Sections 74–78 below, and the consequences, both inside and outside the partnership, in the remainder of the chapter. Limited partnerships are treated separately in section 90B.

In the ordinary partnership, the ceasing of any partner to be associated in the carrying on of the business is a significant event, having the consequence, usually, of winding up or the formation of a new partnership to carry on the business. This is not true of all partnerships. In the joint-stock company with transferable shares, perpetual succession or continuity of existence is preserved, as in the case of a corporation. This is likewise true of the business trust with transferable shares. In a limited partnership the retirement, death or insanity of a general partner may dissolve the partnership as in the case of a partner in an ordinary partnership, but does not do so if the business is continued by one or more general partners pursuant to the

---

3. See Shearer v. Davis, 67 Cal.App.2d 878, 155 P.2d 708 (1945) (failure to furnish additional funds).

Retirement is an obvious cause of dissolution not specified, although it may fall within one of the specific causes. Admission of a new partner is not specified as a cause although it is often said to be. The better view is that it is not. Bromberg, op. cit. infra n. 4 at 636–37.

See also O'Donnell v. McLoughlin, 386 Pa. 187, 125 A.2d 370 (1956).

4. E. g., on death of a partner, when the agreement specifies no dissolution. This result has been reached by decision, Zeibak v. Nasser, 12 Cal.2d 1, 82 P.2d 375 (1938); Beller v. Murphy, 139 Mo.App. 663, 123 S.W. 1029 (1909) (pre-U.P.A.); Storer v. Ripley, 12 Misc.2d 662, 178 N.Y.S.2d 7 (1958) (dictum); Schenk v. Lewis, 125 S.C. 228, 118 S.E. 631 (1923) (dictum) (pre-U.P.A.). It is also statutory in some places, West's Ann.Cal.Corp.Code § 15031(4); G.S. (N.C.) § 59–61(4); 54 Okl.Stat.Ann. § 231(4); Vernon's Ann.Civ.St. (Tex.) art. 6132b § 31(4). Apparently this result is reached in cases of death and all other disassociations by Ark.Stats. § 65–129 which appends to U.P.A. § 29 "provided that

this change in the relation of the partners shall not effect a dissolution of the partnership in contravention or violation of the agreement between the partners." The statute is noted 15 Ark.L.Rev. 440 (1961) as a codification of common law.

Cf. Ga.Code § 75–110 (1964): "If the [partnership] contract specifies the term for which the partnership is formed, it shall continue for that time, or until the death of a partner. If it is desired to continue notwithstanding the death of a partner, it shall be so specified."

For a fuller discussion, see Bromberg, Partnership Dissolution—Causes, Consequences, and Cures, 43 Texas L.Rev. 631 (1965).

5. For example, a partner expressing his will to dissolve per U.P.A. §§ 31 (1) (b) or 31(2) is disassociating himself and causing a dissolution. But the disassociation results from the dissolution when it is caused, e. g., by judicial decree under U.P.A. § 32(1) (c)–(f) and 32(2), Sec. 78 below, and perhaps by illegality or bankruptcy under U.P.A. §§ 31(3), 31(5), Secs. 76, 77 below.

6. See Sec. 77 below, and Bromberg, op. cit. supra n. 4 at 646.

certificate or with the consent of all members.[7] Nor does dissolution result from the death or assignment of interest of a limited partner.[8] In all these cases, the death, incapacity or assignment of a member does not result in winding up or in any material change in the affairs of the firm, other than perhaps the substitution of a successor to the rights and duties of the former members.[9]

In fact, it is equally true that no dissolution occurs in a large partnership whose articles specify that there is no dissolution on death, retirement, incapacity, etc. Examples include accounting, law, and investment firms with dozens or hundreds of partners, and frequent changes in membership. There is no reason why legal theory should not accept this practical result, and it has done so.[10] And there is no reason to limit it to larger firms.[11]

The older view of inevitable dissolution depended on delectus personae [12] and the non-transferability of interests in partnership.[13] But both these roots are matters of partnership agreement and can be varied by agreement. Moreover, it is now common to provide that a deceased or withdrawing partner's interest is not transferred to

---

7. U.L.P.A. §§ 20, 2(1) (a) (XIII), Sec. 90B below.

8. U.L.P.A. § 19 so implies.

9. "In a joint-stock company the members have no right to decide what new members shall be admitted to the firm; on the other hand the right of delectus personarum is an inherent quality of the ordinary partnership. . . . A joint-stock company often consists of a large number of persons, between whom there is no special relationship of confidence; the retirement or death of a member works no dissolution." Haiku Sugar Co. v. Johnstone, 249 F. 103, 108 (9th Cir. 1918).

"An unincorporated company, fundamentally a large partnership, may be said to be an association, and with certain provisions may be said to be a joint-stock company, and it will differ mainly from a partnership in that it is not bound by the acts of the individual partners but only by those of its managers; that its shares are transferable; and that it is not dissolved by the retirement, death, bankruptcy, etc. of its individual members." Burk-Waggoner Oil Ass'n v. Hopkins, 296 F. 492, 497 (N.D.Tex.1924), aff'd 269 U.S. 110, 46 S.Ct. 48, 70 L.Ed. 183 (1925).

By U.L.P.A. § 19, the assignee of a limited partner receives his rights to profits and capital, but does not become a full-fledged limited partner without a formal substitution pursuant to the certificate or by agreement of all the members. Id. § 21 makes the executor or administrator of a limited partner, in effect, an assignee of his interest.

10. N. 4 above; West's Ann.Cal.Corp. Code § 15031(7) (admission or retirement).

11. A fuller discussion is in Bromberg, op. cit. supra n. 4 at 637–38.

12. Secs. 5 above and 77 below.

13. Even so, the courts gave recognition to the practical result of non-dissolution pursuant to agreement by saying that dissolution could be postponed. "The articles of partnership contained an express provision that the firm should not be dissolved by the death, withdrawal, failure or pleasure of any of its members, nor in any way but by the consent of all the members thereof. A method of continuing the business after the death of a member is also provided. That such stipulations are perfectly valid and binding cannot be doubted." Leaf's Appeal, 105 Pa. 505, 513 (1884).

See also Rand v. Wright, 141 Ind. 226, 39 N.E. 447 (1895); Williams v. Schee, 214 Iowa 1181, 243 N.W. 529 (1932).

someone else, but surrendered to the firm in exchange for certain payments.[14] When this occurs, neither delectus nor transferability is involved.

The older view regarded continuation provisions in this way: "Where there are provisions in the articles or will for the continuance of the business after the death of one of the partners, it is sometimes inaccurately said that the death of a partner does not dissolve the partnership. If the business is carried on after the death of the partner, under such an arrangement or by the agreement of the heirs or personal representatives of the deceased, there is in effect and in law a new partnership, of which the survivors and the executors or the heirs are the members becoming liable as the old to the creditors of the firm".[15]

The debate whether dissolution occurs on certain events is somewhat artificial. The operative significance of dissolution is that it may require the business to be wound up and liquidated, and each partner to be paid off in cash.[16] Going concern values are typically destroyed in the process. Consequently, in most cases where the problem is foreseen, the partners take advantage of one of the exceptions to the rule of forced liquidation on dissolution.[17] This is customarily by way of a continuation agreement, permitting some or all of the remaining partners to keep the partnership property and carry forward its business, making some kind of settlement with the outgoing partner.[18] In such instances, where the principal consequence of dissolution is properly avoided, it makes little sense to say there is a dissolution, especially where the agreement says there is not. On the other hand, little harm results other than the waste of a concept.[19]

If the partnership business is not continued, but is liquidated, the firm's legal existence nevertheless continues during the period of winding up.[20] The partnership property is still held by the partners

---

14. Income tax provisions have encouraged this development. See Secs. 86 (a) (3), 86(b) below. One of the essential features of the partnership (as opposed to the corporation) is that it has no fixed capital structure; profit and capital interests can be continually rearranged by agreement.

15. Andrews v. Stinson, 254 Ill. 111, 124, 98 N.E. 222, 225, Ann.Cas.1913B, 927 (1912).

Neither the partnership agreement nor the will of a deceased partner so operate as to make the representative a partner automatically. There must be some act of assent on the part of both the representative and the surviving partners. Western Shoe Co. v. Neumeister, 258 Mich. 662, 242 N.W.

802 (1932); Exchange Bank v. Tracy, 77 Mo. 594 (1833).

16. U.P.A. § 38(1); Secs. 83A, 86 below.

17. Sec. 83A below.

18. See 86, 90A below.

19. Creditors are adequately protected, U.P.A. § 41, Secs. 88–89 below.

20. U.P.A. § 30. An option to buy out a co-partner's interest at its book value "at any time during the life of this partnership agreement" can be exercised within a reasonable time after dissolution of a partnership at will. Hagan v. Dundore, 185 Md. 86, 43 A.2d 181, 160 A.L.R. 517 (1945), annotated 160 A.L.R. 523 as to provi-

as tenants in partnership. The partnership and partners can sue and be sued for the enforcement of partnership rights and obligations.[21] The partners retain their power of representation for the purpose of transactions incident to the process of winding up the business.[22] If dissolution really occurs, no new partnership business should be undertaken thereafter, but affairs should be liquidated and distribution made to the proper parties. New business may be undertaken by a partner for his own account[23] where it does not involve the unauthorized use of partnership property (including good will) or other breach of a partner's fiduciary duties, which continue through this period.[24]

DISSOLUTION WITHOUT VIOLATION OF THE PARTNERSHIP AGREEMENT

§ 74. **Dissolution is caused without violation of the agreement between the partners—**

(a) **By the termination of the particular term or particular undertaking specified in the agreement;**

(b) **By the express will of any partner when no definite term or particular undertaking is specified;**

(c) **By the express will of all the partners who have not assigned their interests or suffered them to be charged for their separate debts, either before or after the termination of any specified term or particular undertaking;**

(d) **By the expulsion of any partner from the business bona fide in accordance with such a power conferred by the agreement between the partners. U.P.A. § 31(1).**

Partnerships can be dissolved by a variety of different causes. Some are in contravention of the partnership agreement,[25] some are not,[26] and some are not clearly classified with reference to this criterion.[27] The distinction is important because of the statutory right of

sions in articles giving one partner the option to buy out the co-partner.

21. Process can be served after dissolution on a managing agent of the partnership who was authorized to receive it before dissolution. Scaglione v. St. Paul-Mercury Indemnity Co., 28 N.J. 88, 145 A.2d 297 (1958). A fortiori, it can be served on a partner. Cotten v. Perishable Air Conditioners, 18 Cal.2d 575, 116 P.2d 603 (1941), annotated on this point, 136 A.L.R. 1068 at 1071 (1942).

22. Sork v. C. Trevor Dunham, Inc., 107 Pa.Super. 77, 163 A. 315 (1932).

U.P.A. §§ 33, 35, Secs. 80–81 below.

23. Meyer v. Sharp, 341 Ill.App. 431, 94 N.E.2d 510 (1950).

24. U.P.A. § 21(1), Sec. 68 above.

25. U.P.A. § 31(2), Sec. 75 below.

26. U.P.A. § 31(1), this Sec.

27. U.P.A. §§ 31(3)–(5), 32, Secs. 76–78 below. Most of these, by inspection, are not in contravention. For a detailed classification of dissolution causes for general and limited partnerships, see Bromberg, Partnership Dissolution—Causes, Consequences, and Cures, 43 Texas L.Rev. 631 (1965). For the pre-U.P.A. situation, see Annot. What is Sufficient Cause for the Dissolution of a Partnership, 69 Am. St.Rep. 410 (1899).

the other partners to continue the business after a dissolution in contravention.[28] In addition, the general definition of dissolution is self-executing and recognizes dissolution by causes not specified.[29]

(a) Termination of Term or Undertaking

Partnership, being a consensual relation, can be ended by the will of the parties thereto. Since it is an informal relation, no judicial procedures are necessary as may be in the dissolution of a corporation, or the divorce of a married couple.[30] Consent to dissolve the relation may be manifested in advance by the terms of the agreement which creates the relation. A provision in the agreement that the relation shall end on a future date is operative when that date arrives.[31] An agreement that the relation shall continue unless or until some condition occurs is operative upon the happening of the condition.[32] An agreement to carry on a farming business in partnership on a particular farm expires when the farm is taken away from the partners by foreclosure proceedings.[33] A partnership to carry on a bank is ended when the bank is closed.[34] So with other partnerships for purposes which are accomplished, or can no longer be pursued.[35] Continuance of the business after the expiration of the agreed term operates as an implied in fact agreement for a partnership at will under the original terms, so far as applicable.[36]

---

28. U.P.A. § 38(2), Sec. 83A below.

29. U.P.A. § 29, Sec. 73 above at n. 3.

30. A limited partnership's certificate, filed in the public records, is to be cancelled by a subsequent filing at dissolution. U.L.P.A. § 24(1). It is doubtful that a failure to do so would affect rights among the members.

31. U.P.A. § 31(1) (a). Morrill v. Weeks, 70 N.H. 178, 46 A. 32 (1900).

32. Cominos v. Kalkanes, 37 Wash.2d 843, 226 P.2d 863 (1951) (managing partner authorized to sell out if profits averaged less than $400 a month for five successive months).

33. Fuller v. Laws, 219 Mo.App. 342, 271 S.W. 836 (1925).

34. Potter v. Tolbert, 113 Mich. 486, 71 N.W. 849 (1897).

35. Kennedy v. Porter, 109 N.Y. 526, 17 N.E. 426 (1888) (partnership to deal with stock of a certain railroad for the purpose of getting control); Seufert v. Gille, 230 Mo. 453, 131 S.W. 102, 31 L.R.A.,N.S., 471 (1910) (mercantile partnership transferred all its prop-

erty to a corporation and ceased to engage in trade).

For the reverse proposition, see text at nn. 44–45 below, discussing when a partnership is for a fixed term or particular undertaking not yet completed.

36. Houseman v. Waterhouse, 191 App. Div. 850, 182 N.Y.S. 249 (1920); Corr v. Hoffman, 219 App.Div. 278, 219 N.Y.S. 656 (1927); Id., 256 N.Y. 254, 176 N.E. 383 (1931); Mifflin v. Smith, 17 Serg. & R. 165 (Pa.1827); Robbins v. Laswell, 27 Ill. 365 (1862); Steele v. Estabrook, 232 Mass. 432, 122 N.E. 562 (1919).

"Continuance of partnership beyond a fixed term. (1) When a partnership for fixed term or particular undertaking is continued after the termination of such term or particular undertaking without any express agreement, the rights and duties of the partners remain the same as they were at such termination, so far as is consistent with a partnership at will. (2) A continuance of the business by the partners or such of them as habitually acted therein during the term, without settlement or liquidation of the part-

(b) Dissolution by Will of Any Partner of Partnership at Will

As will be seen later, the weight of authority and the Uniform Partnership Act are to the effect that any partnership can be dissolved by a partner who so elects and manifests his election, though the term for which it was formed has not expired or the particular purpose been accomplished. The significance of the partnership being one at will, i. e. without any definite term or undertaking to be accomplished, is that the termination by the election of a partner is not a breach of contract.[37] If the partnership is one at will (i. e. without any definite term or undertaking), any partner may freely dissolve[38] without breach of contract.[39] This is sometimes expressed as the right to dissolve as distinct from the power.[40] When the right exists, it would seem that there is no liability for its exercise, whatever the motive and whatever the injurious consequences to co-partners who have neglected to protect themselves by an agreement to continue for a definite term.[41] Some authorities, however, have held that there is liability for acting with "unfair design or for selfish purposes,"[42] or stated that the power to dissolve, like any other held by a fiduciary, must be exercised in good faith.[43]

nership affairs, is prima facie evidence of a continuation of the partnership." U.P.A. § 23. This section is applied in Corr v. Hoffman, supra, holding that a preemptive right of a partner to purchase the co-partner's interest on dissolution is not inconsistent with the relation of partnership at will.

37. Watson v. Kellogg, 129 Cal.App. 592, 19 P.2d 253 (1933), referring to U. P.A. § 31(1); Thanos v. Thanos, 313 Ill. 499, 145 N.E. 250 (1924); Steele v. Estabrook, 232 Mass. 432, 122 N.E. 562 (1919); Bayer v. Bayer, 215 App. Div. 454, 214 N.Y.S. 322 (1926); Dolenga v. Lipka, 224 Mich. 276, 195 N.W. 90 (1923).

38. Harrington v. Sorelle, 313 F.2d 10 (10th Cir. 1963); Posner v. Miller, 356 Mich. 6, 96 N.W.2d 110 (1959) (joint venture); Bevins v. Harris, 380 S.W. 2d 345 (Mo.1964).

39. See n. 37 supra.

40. Straus v. Straus, 254 Minn. 234, 94 N.W.2d 679, 686 (1959); Collins v. Lewis, 283 S.W.2d 258 (Tex.Civ.App. 1955) (pre-U.P.A).

41. There is no legal wrong in a third person inducing a partner to terminate a partnership at will and enter into another association with the third

person. Harris v. Hirschfeld, 13 Cal. App.2d 204, 56 P.2d 1252 (1936).

See, as to non-liability of partner withdrawing from a partnership at will: Salter v. Condon, 236 Ill.App. 17 (1925); Johnson v. Jackson, 130 Ky. 751, 114 S.W. 260, 17 Ann.Cas. 699 (1908); Freund v. Murray, 39 Mont. 539, 104 P. 683, 25 L.R.A.,N.S., 959 (1909); Walker v. Whipple, 58 Mich. 476, 25 N.W. 472 (1885); Blomquist v. Roth, 173 Wash. 79, 21 P.2d 279 (1933).

42. Howell v. Harvey, 5 Ark. 270, 39 Am.Dec. 376 (1843); Beller v. Murphy, 139 Mo.App. 663. 123 S.W. 1029 (1910); McMahon v. McClernan, 10 W.Va. 419 (1877).

See also Trigg v. Shelton, 249 S.W. 209 (Tex.Com.App.1923), stating that an express power of one partner to dissolve at any time would have to be exercised in good faith.

43. Page v. Page, 55 Cal.2d 192, 10 Cal. Rptr. 643, 359 P.2d 41 (1961) (dictum: dissolution is wrongful if partner attempts to appropriate business without adequate compensation to co-partner; this is violation of implied agreement not to exclude co-partner wrongfully from partnership business opportunity). Trigg v. Shelton, 249 S.W. 209 (Tex.Com.App.1923). To the same effect as Page v. Page, see How-

Running through much of this area is the difficult question—usually one of fact—whether the partnership is at will or for a particular term or undertaking, when neither has been expressed. A term or undertaking may be inferred from various circumstances, such as an agreement to repay certain debts from partnership profits,[44] or the terms of leases under which the partnership is lessee.[45]

(c) Dissolution by Agreement of All of the Partners

Like other bilateral executory contracts,[46] a contract of partnership may be ended by mutual agreement of the parties.[47] The agreement must be unanimous. The majority alone cannot dissolve the partnership unless a partnership at will, without breach of contract,[48] unless, of course, the agreement expressly permits dissolution by less than all.[49] This is a form of unanimous agreement, only it is given in advance rather than at the moment of dissolution. A partnership can be dissolved without breach of the partnership agreement by less than all the partners where the other partners have assigned their interests, or they have been subjected to a charging order.[50] The

ell v. Bowden, 368 S.W.2d 842 (Tex. Civ.App.1963) (damages for wrongful appropriation of partnership business by one partner though partnership was at will; pre-U.P.A.).

44. Owen v. Cohen, 19 Cal.2d 147, 119 P.2d 713 (1941); Zimmerman v. Harding, 227 U.S. 489, 33 S.Ct. 387, 57 L. Ed. 608 (1913); Drashner v. Sorenson, 75 S.D. 247, 63 N.W.2d 255 (1954).

But see Page v. Page, n. 43 above, finding that there was "no more than a common hope that the partnership earnings would pay for all the necessary expenses," insufficient to imply a definite term or undertaking. The opinion distinguishes Owen v. Cohen and other cases. Semble, Frey v. Hauke, 171 Neb. 852, 108 N.W.2d 228 (1961).

45. Zeibak v. Nasser, 12 Cal.2d 1, 82 P.2d 375 (1938). See also Bates v. McTammany, 10 Cal.2d 697, 76 P.2d 513 (1938) (partnership to operate radio station as long as government would license it).

46. Restatement, Contracts § 406.

47. French v. Mulholland, 218 Mich. 248, 187 N.W. 254, 21 A.L.R. 1 (1922) (dissolution effected by sale of interest from one partner to the other); Simpson v. Shadwell, 264 Ill.App. 480 (1932); First Nat. Bank v. White, 268 Ill.App. 414 (1932) (consent of partner

whose interest has been subjected to execution unnecessary).

48. Fitts v. Mission Health & Beauty Shop, 58 Cal.App. 362, 208 P. 691 (1922); Patterson v. Bonner, 73 Okl. 224, 175 P. 826 (1918).

In the articles of business trusts it is often provided that there may be a termination and winding up of the business before the expiration of the agreed term, upon vote of the majority or some other greater proportion of the shares of beneficial interest.

49. It is fairly common for agreements to provide that a majority or some other designated proportion may dissolve. See Appendix VI, par. 6.1. An example of a dissolution right given to one partner is Trigg v. Shelton, n. 42 above.

50. U.P.A. § 31(1) (c). This is designed to let the remaining partners dissolve the firm after a stranger has acquired an interest by assignment per U.P.A. § 27, Sec. 42(b) above, or charging order per U.P.A. § 28, Sec. 43(b) above. The stranger does not become a partner without unanimous consent of the remaining partners, U.P.A. § 18(g). His rights as a non-partner are quite limited by U.P.A. §§ 27–28, Sec. 42(b) above, but the remaining partners may find intrusive the ones he does have. If they do dissolve, they must settle with him as with the partner from

same would apply to joint ventures, since the relations between the venturers are determined in accordance with the law of partnership. Dissolution is optional with the partners or joint venturers who retain their interests and does not follow ipso facto from assignment or charging order.[51] In a 2-man partnership, dissolution occurs when one partner sells his interest to the other.[52] This may be regarded either as a unanimous agreement to dissolve, or as a termination of the particular joint undertaking.[53]

Dissolution agreements are commonly in writing, setting the time when they shall become effective, and providing the method to be followed in winding up and how property shall be disposed of. The agreement may be informal, however, in separate writings,[54] or oral,[55] or merely evidenced by conduct.[56]

The original partnership agreement may permit withdrawal or retirement of a partner on notice after a stated interval. In such case no reason for withdrawal need be stated.[57] This is another form of

---

whom he derived his interest. They have the alternative, if he holds a charging order, of redeeming the interest with their own or firm property. U.P.A. § 28(2).

51. See Meinhard v. Salmon, 249 N.Y. 458, 164 N.E. 545, 62 A.L.R. 1 (1928), where a joint venture was held not dissolved by assignment of a member to his wife, the other party recognizing the assignment and proceeding as manager with the conduct of the enterprise.

52. Dillingham v. Schipp, 154 Cal.App. 2d 553, 316 P.2d 1014 (1957) (subject to approval of third party). See Brownback v. Nelson, 122 Mont. 525, 206 P.2d 1017 (1949). However, at least for federal income tax purposes, the partnership continues until all payments due the outgoing partner from the partnership are completed. Income Tax Reg. §§ 1.708–1(b) (1) (a), 1.736–1 (a) (6) (1956).

53. U.P.A. § 31(1) (a), Sec. 74(a) above.

54. Frear v. Lewis, 166 App.Div. 210, 151 N.Y.S. 486 (1915). If the entire dissolution agreement is in writing, it is the measure of the partner's rights and liabilities, e. g., as to good will, Hilton v. Hilton, 89 N.J.Eq. 182, 104 A. 375, L.R.A.1918F, 1174 (1918); or as to the scope of the property or business included in its operation, Trexler v. Reynolds, 232 Pa. 173, 81 A. 194 (1911).

If the agreement of dissolution appears to be comprehensive in its scope, the parol evidence rule precludes showing additional oral undertakings not covered in the written agreement, e. g., an agreement by a retiring partner not to compete for a term. O'Brien v. O'Brien, 362 Pa. 66, 66 A.2d 309, 10 A.L.R.2d 714 (1949).

55. Pilch v. Milikin, 200 C.A.2d 212, 19 Cal.Rptr. 334 (1962) (oral agreement and unsigned written agreement; part performance); Ferguson v. Baker, 116 N.Y. 257, 22 N.E. 400 (1889) (oral part of dissolution agreement not merged in writing which was not inconsistent); In re Kahane, 6 Misc.2d 575, 160 N.Y.S.2d 252 (1957).

56. Beck v. Cagle, 46 Cal.App.2d 152, 115 P.2d 613 (1941); Kennedy v. Porter, 109 N.Y. 526, 17 N.E. 426 (1888); Bayer v. Bayer, 215 App.Div. 454, 214 N.Y.S. 322 (1926); Brand v. Erisman, 84 U.S.App.D.C. 194, 172 F.2d 28 (1948) (sale of all the property of the partnership).

"The abandonment or dissolution of a partnership or joint adventure may take place by conduct inconsistent with its continuance." Beck v. Cagle, 46 Cal.App.2d 152, 115 P.2d 613, 619 (1941). See also Pilch v. Milkin, n. 55 above.

57. Young v. Cooper, 30 Tenn.App. 55, 203 S.W.2d 376 (1947).

unanimous agreement in advance.[58] The agreement may provide for settlement with the withdrawing partner, for example, by the partners or the partnership paying him the amount of his original capital contribution plus his share of accumulated profits. This makes liquidation unnecessary.[59]

The parties may agree upon terms of dissolution differing from those originally provided in partnership articles.[60] But once a dissolution agreement has been reached, all partners are bound, and one cannot change his mind and back out.[61]

The fiduciary duty of disclosure of material facts is applicable, and a dissolution agreement may be avoided for non-disclosure [62] or misrepresentation.[63]

The fact that a dissolution agreement is in part illegal, as where it contemplates continuance by a partner of a trucking business under a license issued to the partnership, does not nullify the dissolution, since a party cannot secure judicial aid when, to establish his case, he must show his own wrong.[64]

Where a dissolution agreement provides for payment to a retiring partner of his interest according to the state of accounts on the firm books, a payment of an erroneous amount by reason of mistake as to the true state of books can be corrected.[65]

(d) Expulsion in Accordance with Power Conferred by Agreement

The partnership agreement may provide for expulsion of a partner, either automatically or by vote of a designated portion of the re-

58. See Appendix V, par. 6.2; Appendix VI, par. 7.3 below.

59. Turken v. Olshanski, 237 Mich. 623, 212 N.W. 961 (1927); Wathen v. Brown, 200 Pa.Super. 620, 189 A.2d 900 (1963), citing this text.

Whether this constitutes a dissolution is open to argument. See sec. 73 above at nn. 4, 10–11.

60. Guenther v. Kutz, 270 Pa. 144, 112 A. 919 (1921); LeMaine v. Seals, 47 Wash.2d 259, 287 P.2d 305, 313 (1955) quoting this text.

61. Pritzker v. Stern, 187 Md. 499, 51 A.2d 69 (1947).

62. Shelley v. Smith, 271 Mass. 106, 170 N.E. 826 (1930), partner in a firm of accountants withheld information as to his prospects of retainers for which he was negotiating.

A partner defrauded by the settlement may recover at law for deceit, if he elects to let the transaction stand. Curry v. Windsor, 22 Ariz. 108, 194

P. 958 (1921); French v. Mulholland, n. 47 above.

This is a fortiori true when a partner induces a dissolution agreement by fraudulently causing a notice from a creditor threatening garnishment to be served, and so exerts unjustified pressure. Reed v. Wood, 190 Okl. 169, 123 P.2d 275 (1942).

Spencer v. Wilsey, 330 Ill.App. 439, 71 N.E.2d 804 (1947) (joint venture); Johnson v. Peckham, 132 Tex. 148, 120 S.W.2d 786, 120 A.L.R. 720 (1938), annotated on disclosure in purchase of partner's interest.

63. McBride v. Fitzpatrick, 224 Or. 457, 356 P.2d 947 (1960).

64. Slater v. Slater, 365 Pa. 321, 74 A.2d 179 (1950).

65. Cobb v. Cole, 44 Minn. 278, 46 N.W. 364 (1890). In absence of fraud or excusable mistake of fact a dissolution agreement cannot be upset. Close v. Derbyshire, 169 Pa.Super. 344, 82 A.2d 301 (1951).

maining partners.[66] The expulsion may be conditioned on specific causes,[67] which must be shown to exist in fact to justify the exercise of the power. Or it may be authorized when the other partners deem it desirable in the interests of the partnership,[68] or entirely without cause.

Expulsion provisions are rare because of each partner's fear that the others may gang up on him. However, if properly limited, they are useful, especially for professional firms which might be disqualified by the actions of a member. Whatever their merit, expulsion provisions carry the significant consequence that the expelled partner is entitled only to a cash settlement, without liquidation of the business.[69]

Expulsion of a partner not pursuant to the agreement is a wrongful dissolution; see Sec. 75 below.

DISSOLUTION IN CONTRAVENTION OF THE AGREEMENT, AND ITS CONSEQUENCES

§ 75. Dissolution is caused in contravention of the agreement between the partners, where the circumstances do not permit a dissolution under any other provisions of the section, by the express will of any partner at any time. U.P.A. § 31(2).

When dissolution is caused in contravention of the partnership agreement, each partner who has not caused the dissolution wrongfully shall have the right as against each partner who has caused the dissolution wrongfully to damages for breach of the agreement.

When dissolution is caused in contravention of the partnership agreement, the partners who have not caused the dissolution wrongfully if they all desire to continue the business in the same name, either by themselves or jointly with others, may do so, during the agreed term for the partnership and for that purpose may possess the partnership property, provided they secure the payment by bond approved by the court, or

---

66. See Appendix VI, par. 7.4, below.

67. Ross v. Cornell, 97 Ga. 340, 22 S.E. 394 (1895), privilege of dissolving on business becoming unprofitable; to justify exercise of power, the condition named would have to exist.

It is sometimes provided that a partner may be excluded by his co-partners for certain specified acts of misconduct. Krigbaum v. Vindquest, 10 Neb. 435, 6 N.W. 631 (1880) (becoming dissipated and neglecting business, both of which facts would have to be shown); Neustadter v. United Exposition Service Co., 14 N.J.Super. 484, 82 A.2d 476 (1951) (expulsion for nonpayment of an assessment, under articles, could be enjoined where it did not appear that the delinquent partner had due notice of the assessment);

Barnes v. Youngs, [1898] 1 Ch. 414, 67 L.J.Eq. 263 (immorality, partners could not act summarily without opportunity to explain); Carmichael v. Evans, [1904], 1 Ch. 486, 73 L.J.Eq. 329 (addicted to conduct detrimental to business); Clifford v. Timms, [1908] A.C. 12, 77 L.J.Eq. 91 (professional misconduct by member of firm of dentists, improper advertising); Green v. Howell, [1910] 1 Ch. 495, 79 L.J.Eq. 549 (flagrant breach of duties of partner, stated that unfair advantage should not be taken by a partner exercising such a power).

68. Smart v. Hernandez, 95 N.H. 492, 66 A.2d 643 (1949).

69. U.P.A. 38(1), 2d sentence, Sec. 83A (b) below.

pay to any partner who has caused the dissolution wrongfully, the value of his interest in the partnership at the dissolution, less any damages recoverable under clause (2 a II) of this section, and in like manner indemnify him against all present or future partnership liabilities. U.P.A. § 38(2) (a II), (b).

Any dissolution which is wrongful in a general sense may be deemed in contravention of the agreement for the purpose of applying the damages and business continuation provisions.

(a) Power to Dissolve

Where a partnership has been formed to continue for a definite term, or to accomplish a certain undertaking, it has been held that no partner has the right to dissolve the partnership until the term has ended or the undertaking been accomplished.[70] This has been the English view at common law, and it has not been changed by the English Partnership Act.[71] There has been some support for this view in the American cases.[72] It is of course a hardship on partners who have invested their capital and services in a venture to have it brought to a premature close. As to the partnership property it might be considered that there is a power coupled with an interest, given to secure the performance of the contract.[73] As to the power to continue to create personal obligations of the withdrawing partner, there seems to be no reason, under agency principles, why it should not be capable of revocation, though in breach of contract.[74] "Each partner is the general agent of the firm, and the firm is the agent of each partner, with power to bind him to a personal liability in favor of partnership creditors. Whoever acts as another's agent must base his authority on the other's consent. Such assent, if given, may be retracted at any time as regards future transactions. This doctrine in the law of agency rests on reasons which apply fully to the partnership relation."[75] This view is followed in the majority of American courts

70. The difficult question of an implied term or undertaking is considered in Sec. 74 at nn. 44–45 above.

71. Moss v. Elphick, [1910] 1 K.B. 846, 79 L.J.K.B. 631.

72. Howell v. Harvey, 5 Ark. 270, 39 Am.Dec. 376 (1843); Williamson v. Wilson, 1 Bland, 418, 424 (Md.1826); Dobbins v. Tatem, 25 A. 544 (N.J.Ch. 1892); Cole v. Moxley, 12 W.Va. 730 (1878).

73. Restatement, Second, Agency §§ 138, 139.

74. Restatement, Second, Agency § 118.

75. Lapenta v. Lettieri, 72 Conn. 377, 44 A. 730, 77 Am.St.Rep. 315 (1890).

In Karrick v. Hannaman, 168 U.S. 328, 18 S.Ct. 135, 42 L.Ed. 484 (1897), the court stated the reasons for the view favoring the power of dissolution as follows: "A contract of partnership is one by which two or more persons agree to carry on a business for their common benefit, each contributing property or services, and having a community of interest in the profits. It is in effect a contract of mutual agency, each partner acting as a principal in his own behalf and as agent for his copartner. Meehan v. Valentine, 145 U.S. 611, 12 S.Ct. 972 [36 L.Ed. 835]. Every partnership creates a personal relation between the partners, rests upon their mutual consent, and exists between them only . . . .. No partnership can efficiently or beneficially carry on its business without the mutual confidence and cooperation of all the partners. Even when, by the partnership

and has been incorporated in the U.P.A.[76]   It recognizes a power to dissolve where a right to dissolve does not exist.[77]

(b) Damages

The partner who has wrongfully caused a dissolution is subject to liability for damages, which may be charged against him on accounting or recovered by an action at law.[78]

articles, they have covenanted with each other that the partnership shall continue for a certain period, the partnership may be dissolved at any time, at the will of any partner, so far as to put an end to the partnership relation and to the authority of each partner to act for all; but rendering the partner who breaks his covenant liable to an action at law for damages, as in other cases of breaches of contract. [numerous citations omitted] According to the authorities just cited, the only difference, so far as concerns the right of dissolution by one partner, between a partnership for an indefinite period and one for a specified term, is this: In the former case, the dissolution is no breach of the partnership agreement, and affords the other partner no ground for complaint. In the latter case, such a dissolution before the expiration of the time stipulated is a breach of the agreement, and as such to be compensated in damages. But in either case the action by one partner does actually dissolve the partnership."

Accord, Solomon v. Kirkwood, 55 Mich. 256, 21 N.W. 336 (1884); Cahill v. Haff, 248 N.Y. 377, 162 N.E. 288 (1928); McCollum v. McCollum, 67 S.W.2d 1055 (Tex.Civ.App.1934) (injunctive relief against dissolution refused); Crossman v. Gibney, 164 Wis. 395, 160 N.W. 172 (1916), under U.P.A. § 31(a)

76.   U.P.A. § 31(2), 38(2) quoted at the head of this section.

Notice to dissolve must be unequivocal. Where a partnership was to continue until terminated by 30 days notice and an appraisal, the giving of such notice did not forthwith dissolve, being accompanied by an offer to sell. Johnson v. Moreau, 323 Mass. 481, 82 N.E. 2d 802 (1948).

77.   Sec. 74 at n. 40 above.   For a fuller treatment, see Sher & Bromberg, Texas Partnership Law in the 20th Century, 12 Sw.L.J. 263, 304–07 (1958).

78.   U.P.A. § 38(2) (a II).   See Sec. 69 above.   Burnstine v. Geist, 257 App. Div. 792, 15 N.Y.S.2d 48 (1939) (law action).

Although a partner has the power to cause a dissolution before the end of the term if his so doing is wrongful, a receiver may be appointed on petition of the other partners, the business ordered liquidated and damages caused by the seceding partner assessed against him.   Kurtzon v. Kurtzon, 339 Ill.App. 431, 90 N.E.2d 245 (1950).

If the partner bringing about a dissolution would have been able to secure a dissolution by decree of court, because of the other partner's breach of his agreement, the latter is not entitled to damages, Schnitzer v. Josephthal, 122 Misc. 15, 202 N.Y.S. 77 (1923), affirmed 208 App.Div. 769, 202 N.Y.S. 952 (1924); Reiter v. Morton, 96 Pa. 229, 240 (1880).   See also Lavoine v. Casey, 251 Mass. 124, 146 N.W. 241 (1925).

As to accountability for profits after dissolution, Annot., 80 A.L.R. 12, 41, and Sec. 86(c) below.

The measure of damages is complicated, as with any business interest.   If the other partners exercise their right to continue the business, they apparently give up any claim for destruction of the business, although they may still recover for injury to it (or to their interests in it).   If they exercise their further right to keep all the partnership property, by securing to the dissolving partner the amount due him, they can hardly claim injury resulting from withdrawal of partnership assets or funds, and thus they further reduce the damages they may recover.

(c) Continuation Right

To protect the innocent partners from the hardship which would be caused by a summary winding up of the business with a sacrifice of good will and property values, they are permitted by the U.P.A. to continue the business by themselves or with new partners. They are then entitled to possess the firm property and use the firm name. To do this, they must (1) pay or secure to the dissolving partner the value of his interest [79] less any damages from his breach, and less any value attributable to good will,[80] and (2) indemnify him against all partnership liabilities.[81] While this provision is comforting to innocent partners, it has too many uncertainties to rely on for planning purposes. There will almost inevitably be litigation over the value of the interest, the extent of the good will and the amount of damages for breach. Lesser issues, such as the proper method of indemnification, are likely to be troublesome too.[82] If literally read, the Act might permit the innocent partners to continue the business only for the "agreed term" of the partnership,[83] which might be quite short. The more reasonable interpretation, giving effect to all parts of the statute, is that the innocent partners may continue the business

---

79. U.P.A. § 38(2) (b) suggests that the other partners may possess the property and continue the business merely by securing to the dissolver the value of his interest by a court-approved bond. This can only be a temporary measure, i. e. pending final accounting and valuation or, possibly, completion of the "agreed term" of the partnership. The dissolver is entitled to be paid cash sooner or later. Dow v. Beals, 149 Misc. 631, 268 N.Y.S. 425 (1933) (if partner seeking to purchase under U.P.A. § 38(2) (b) cannot pay cash, liquidation will be ordered).

On payment for his interest, see Secs. 83A(a), 86(c) below.

80. See Sec. 84 below.

81. U.P.A. § 38(2) (b), (c). Vangel v. Vangel, 116 Cal.App.2d 615, 254 P.2d 919 (1953), aff'd in part, rev'd in part, and remanded 45 Cal.2d 804, 291 P.2d 25, 55 A.L.R.2d 1385 (1955). Valuation is as of the date of dissolution. The wrongfully dissolving partner continues to share in profits from then until he is paid off; his proportion is determined by the value of his interest at dissolution relative to the other partners' interests. Ibid.

An early decision, Crossman v. Gibney, 164 Wis. 395, 160 N.W. 172 (1916) has not been followed in its unjustifiably strict interpretation of U.P.A. § 38(2) (b). It states that the business would have to be continued in the same name for the section to apply, and that the partnership property must be used to pay the dissolver (though the statute says nothing at all about what property is used for payment). These statements are unnecessary to the disposition of the case, which permits the dissolver to eject his copartner from the partnership farm, primarily on the ground that the farm was not partnership property.

82. See Vangel v. Vangel, n. 81 above (leading case illustrating a host of problems under U.P.A. § 38(2) (b)); Drashner v. Sorenson, 75 S.D. 247, 63 N.W.2d 255 (1954) (valuation and good will questions).

83. "A trial on the merits will determine whether plaintiff [dissolving partner] is in a position to question the length of time the remaining partners may continue in the partnership business and whether the applicable statute limits the continuation of the partnership business by the remaining partners to the agreed term." Straus v. Straus, 254 Minn. 234, 246, 94 N.W. 2d 679, 687 (1959). The court goes on to cite authors to the effect that the dissolver may be completely bought out.

either indefinitely (by paying the dissolver for his interest) or, at their option, for the agreed term (by properly securing him).[84]

(d) When Is Dissolution in Contravention?

The U.P.A. grants damages for wrongful dissolution and the right to continue the business only when the dissolution is "in contravention" of the partnership agreement. The sole cause of dissolution explicitly so characterized is "by the will of any partner" where "the circumstances do not permit a dissolution under any other provision of this section."[85] Literally, this appears to relate only to dissolutions at will when the partnership is for a fixed term or undertaking,[86] since other contingencies seem to be covered by other parts of the section. However, the courts have wisely tended to treat any dissolution that is "wrongful" in a general sense as the equivalent of one "in contravention," and thus permitted continuation or damages.[87] The rationale may be that the quoted phrases are used interchangeably in the Act[88] or that the particular causes involve violations of the partnership agreement in the contract sense regardless of the Act.[89] A litigant seeking damages or continuation rights would do well to try for a trial court finding that the dissolution was both "wrongful" and "in contravention."

---

84. See n. 79 above. Under the second alternative, liquidation would have to be accomplished at the end of the agreed term, when the dissolver would receive the value of his interest as of the date of his dissolution. During the interim, he would have the option to receive interest on this value or the profits attributable to its use by the firm, U.P.A. § 42, Sec. 86 below.

85. U.P.A. § 31(2).

86. On this point, see Sec. 74 at nn. 44–45 above.

87. Zeibak v. Nasser, 12 Cal.2d 1, 82 P.2d 375 (1938) (obstruction of agreed incorporation, refusal to pay share of deficit, refusal to cooperate in other ways; trial court characterized partner's conduct as prejudicially affecting the carrying on of the business and making it impracticable to carry on the partnership with him); Vangel v. Vangel, n. 81 above (exclusion of co-partners from management); Drash-

ner v. Sorenson, n. 82 above (neglect of business, frequenting bars during business hours).

This may extend to partnerships at will, at least for purpose of damages; see Page v. Page and Howell v. Bowden, Sec. 74, n. 43 above.

In most of these cases, the technical dissolution was by judicial decree under U.P.A. § 32(1), but the courts have looked through to the underlying cause (i. e. the partner's behavior) to determine whether it was wrongful or in contravention.

88. "In contravention" appears in U.P.A. §§ 31(2), 38(1) and 38(2); "wrongfully" in §§ 37 and 38(2) (a), (b) and (c). The functional equivalence is particularly close in § 38(2).

89. See cases in n. 87 above. The Act appears to use "violation" and "contravention" equivalently; compare U.P.A. § 31(1) with 31(2).

DISSOLUTION BY SUPERVENING ILLEGALITY

§ 76. Dissolution is caused by any event which makes it unlawful for the business of the partnership to be carried on or for the members to carry it on in partnership. U.P.A. § 31(3).

A partnership agreement, like other contracts,[90] is subject to discharge, as regards future performance, by supervening illegality. It may be that the business itself has become illegal,[91] or that it has become illegal for the partners to carry it on together. A state of war between the countries of which the partners are respectively residents makes it illegal for them to continue to maintain commercial relationships with each other, and their partnership is immediately dissolved.[92] This result follows for the domestic partner, even though the law of the country in which the partnership was organized permits its continuance.[93] The election of a lawyer to the position of judge, thereby incapacitating him from the practice of law, dissolves a partnership of attorneys of which he is a member.[94] Where wives can-

---

90. Restatement, Contracts § 608. Compare Restatement, Second, Agency §§ 115, 116.

For the effect of illegality on a partner's right to an accounting, see Annot., 32 A.L.R.2d 1345 (1953); Sec. 21 above.

91. This occurred on a broad scale when Prohibition went into effect. On criminal acts of partners generally, see Sec. 64(g) above.

92. Sutherland v. Mayer, 271 U.S. 272, 46 S.Ct. 538, 70 L.Ed. 943 (1925), noted 40 Harv.L.Rev. 138 (1926); Griswold v. Waddington, 16 Johns. 438 (N.Y. 1819); Comment, Effect of War on Business Associations, 28 Yale L.J. 680 (1919).

Though a dissolution is effected, the domestic members of the partnership may use the name of the alien enemy partner as co-plaintiff in an action for the purpose of getting in the assets in the course of liquidation. Rodriguez v. Speyer Brothers, [1919] A.C. 59. Compare Continental Tyre Co. v. Daimler Co., [1916] 2 A.C. 307.

If the business is continued by the domestic partner, the alien enemy partner will be entitled, at the end of the war, to receive not only the value of his interest at the time of dissolution, but a share in the profits earned thereafter attributable to the use of his property. Stevenson v. Aktiengesellshaft fur Cartonnagen-Industrie, [1918] A.C. 239. Compare U.P.A. § 42, Sec. 86 below.

Under the U. S. Trading with the Enemy Act, 50 U.S.C.A.App. §§ 1, 6, the interest of the enemy alien partner would be subject to vesting by the Alien Property Custodian.

See Joring v. Harriss, 292 F. 974 (2d Cir. 1923), noted 37 Harv.L.Rev. 773 (1924). A joint adventure between American and Austrian associates for the importation of American cotton into Austria was interrupted by the war. The Americans sold the cotton. The Austrians were not entitled to share in the profit derived from the sale, because the ownership of the cotton, at the time of the dissolution of the adventure, was still in the American associates.

93. Rossie v. Garvan, 274 F. 447 (D. Conn.1921), noted 35 Harv.L.Rev. 337 (1922).

94. Justice v. Lairy, 19 Ind.App. 272, 49 N.E. 459, 65 Am.St.Rep. 405 (1898). See Restatement, Second, Agency § 111.

Compare Attorney General v. Tufts, 239 Mass. 458, 131 N.E. 573, 17 A.L.R. 274, 132 N.E. 322, 17 A.L.R. 274 (1921), commenting on impropriety of a district attorney remaining a member of a law partnership which engaged in criminal court practice in another county.

On the effects of illegality in general, see Note, Partnerships for an Illegal Purpose, 41 Harv.L.Rev. 650 (1928).

not be partners,[95] marriage of a female partner works a dissolution.[96] These results may be explained either on the theory of illegality or on the ground of the partner's incapacity to perform.[97]

A firm of brokers some of whose members are members of a stock exchange may by operation of rules of the exchange be subject to dissolution as a result of findings of violations of the rules of the exchange.[98]

It has been held that induction into military service of a partner who is drafted terminates the partnership,[99] unless the agreement provides otherwise.[1] No illegality is involved in such a situation.

DISSOLUTION BY DEATH OR BANKRUPTCY

§ 77. Dissolution is caused by the death of a partner, and by the bankruptcy of any partner or the partnership. U.P.A. § 31(4) (5).

(a) Death

There can be no doubt that "dissolution" in the general sense in which the term is used in the U.P.A.—a ceasing of a partner to be associated in carrying on the business—results from his death.[2] By the older view,[3] "The delectus personarum lies at the foundation of the agreement of the parties, and is one of the main considerations on which it rests. The personal qualities of each member of a firm enter largely into the inducements which lead parties to form a co-partnership; and if the abilities and skill, or the character and credit of any one are withdrawn, the contract between them is terminated and

---

95. They can under most modern legislation; see Sec. 8 above.

96. Bassett v. Shepardson, 52 Mich. 3, 17 N.W. 217 (1883) (marriage of partners to each other); Little v. Hazlett, 197 Pa. 591, 47 A. 855 (1901); R. A. Brown & Co. v. Chancellor, 61 Tex. 437 (1884); King v. Matney, 259 S.W. 2d 606 (Tex.Civ.App.1953). For the tax consequence of the last case (nondeductibility of her share of the partnership loss), see Harry F. Shannon v. Commissioner of Internal Revenue, 29 T.C. 702 (1958).

97. This is a separate ground for judicial dissolution, U.P.A. § 32(1) (b), Sec. 78 below.

98. Avery v. Moffatt, 187 Misc. 576, 55 N.Y.S.2d 215 (1945). Compare Restatement, Contracts § 576, declaring illegal a contract the performance of which involves breach of a contract with a third person.

99. J. C. H. Service Stations, Inc. v. Patrikes, 180 Misc. 401, 46 N.Y.S.2d 228 (1944). Under the Selective Service Act the drafted partner could avoid further liability as to himself and his interest in the partnership on a lease.

Compare the dissenting opinion in Ginsberg v. Arnold, 176 F.2d 879 (5th Cir. 1949) alluding to the job retention policy of the Selective Service Act.

1. See Linden v. Hoshal, 307 Mich. 568, 12 N.W.2d 385 (1943), where two physicians who practised in partnership agreed that upon one of them going into military service he should receive 25% of the net income derived by the remaining partner who remained and carried on. An accounting was ordered. The partners apparently treated the partnership as continuing.

In Lacey v. Rutter, 358 Pa. 502, 57 A.2d 679 (1948), a dissolution of a partnership at will was ordered on petition of a partner. Both partners had been in military service, and in their absence their business, that of a restaurant and bar, was voluntarily operated by friends. There is no suggestion in the opinion that the partners' being in the army effected a dissolution ipso facto.

2. U.P.A. § 29, Sec. 73 above.

3. See also Sec. 73 at nn. 12–13.

the co-partnership is dissolved."[4]   This is an application of the rule of contracts as to the effect of impossibility due to death of a person whose performance is necessary.[5]   The rule was followed by a long current of decision.[6]   Where courts said that the rule may be varied by agreement, the result was sometimes interpreted to mean merely that dissolution was not followed immediately by the usual consequence, i. e. winding up of the business.[7]

The more modern view sees that there is no impossibility of performance when the agreement specifies an alternative performance or ceases to require performance.   It abandons the notion of a mystical union of partners, destroyed by any change in the group.   The idea is reminiscent of the extreme aggregate view of partnership (not merely a collection of individuals, but a unique collection) and of the strict joint liability of partners at early common law.   Neither of these prevail today,[8] and there is is little justification for the union concept when the emphasis is on the business operation and when the partners expressly agree to the changes and deny the dissolution. This view has been adopted for general partnerships by some decisions [9] and, in several states, by statute.[10]   It is the law almost everywhere for limited partnerships.[11]   Where it is decisional, there is an inconsistency with the general definition of dissolution.[12]   This can be reasonably reconciled by regarding the general definition, like so many other relations among the partners,[13] as subject to modification by their agreement.   The logic of this development suggests the desirability of modifying U.P.A. § 29.[14]

The older view rested also on the non-transferability of partnership interests.   This made it possible to accept non-dissolution on the death of a member of a joint stock company or business trust with transferable shares.[15]   But transferability by agreement of the part-

---

4. Marlett v. Jackman, 85 Mass. (3 Allen) 287, 290 (1861).

5. Restatement, Contracts § 459.

6. Hammond v. Otwell, 170 Ga. 832, 154 S.E. 357 (1930), 29 Mich.L.Rev. 259; Parish v. Bainum, 306 Ill. 618, 138 N.E. 147 (1923); Williams v. Schee, 214 Iowa 1181, 243 N.W. 529 (1932); Spalding v. Spalding's Adm'r, 248 Ky. 259, 58 S.W.2d 356 (1933); Casey v. Hurley, 112 Conn. 536, 152 A. 892 (1931); Winget v. Grand Trunk Western Ry. Co., 210 Mich. 100, 177 N.W. 273 (1920); Stem v. Warren, 227 N.Y. 538, 125 N.E. 811 (1920); McGrath v. Cowen, 57 Ohio St. 385, 49 N.E. 338 (1898); Froess v. Froess, 284 Pa. 369, 131 A. 276 (1925); Martin v. Dial, 57 S.W.2d 75, 89 A.L.R. 571 (Tex.Com.App.1933) (pre-U.P.A.); Ben-

edict v. Price, 38 F.2d 309 (E.D.N.Y. 1929).

7. See Sec. 73 above.

8. See Secs. 58–60 above.

9. Sec. 73, n. 4 above.

10. Ibid.

11. Sec. 73, nn. 7–8 above, Sec. 90B(b), below.

12. U.P.A. § 29, Sec. 73 above.

13. E. g., U.P.A. §§ 18, 19, 22(b), 25(2) (a), 37, 38(1) and 42.

14. See Sec. 73 above and Bromberg, Partnership Dissolution—Causes, Consequences, and Cures, 43 Texas L.Rev. 631, 645–46 (1965).

15. Sec. 73 above.

ners has always been recognized. Moreover, modern practice is frequently for the surrender or liquidation of a deceased partner's interest, rather than for its transfer.[16] Today, the older view has little support in theory or in practice.

The difference between the two views may become critical where the partners have manifested a desire for continuity, but have not expressly authorized the continuation of the business in all possible contingencies.[17] Under the older view, any partner would have the right to force liquidation of the firm after a technical dissolution, perhaps destroying values in the process. The non-dissolution agreement might be interpreted to permit continuation of the business by the survivors, but this called for some stretching of the older view. It is a natural consequence of the modern one.[18] It may be that the answer lies in more foresight and better partnership agreements, rather than a shift of legal rules.

A few cases have held that the adjudicated insanity of a partner dissolves the partnership.[19] The prevailing view is that insanity is not a self-operating cause of dissolution, but a reason for applying to the court for a dissolution by decree.[20]

(b) Bankruptcy

The bankruptcy of a partnership results in its property being taken out of the hands of the partners and in their inability to continue the business, which necessarily amount to a dissolution.[21] The bankruptcy of one partner disables him from the further enjoyment of his interest in the partnership, which passes to his trustee for the bene-

---

16. See Secs. 73 above, 86(a)(3) below.

17. See, e. g., Young v. Cooper, discussed Sec. 90A(e) below.

18. The difference between the two views may turn out to be important in determining whether a partnership has the characteristics which cause it to be treated as a corporation for federal income tax. In an effort to prevent certain partnerships from voluntarily obtaining corporate tax status, the Treasury has adopted the older view. Income Tax Reg. § 301.7701–2 (b), (e) (1960 amended 1965). Its validity remains to be tested. See Secs. 24, 34A above.

The difference may also be significant on the admission or retirement of a partner. If dissolution results, some other partner may be able to force a liquidation of the firm.

19. McKleroy v. Musgrove, 203 Ala. 603, 84 So. 280 (1919); Isler v. Baker,

Johnson & Co., 25 Tenn. (6 Humph.) 85 (1845), criticized in Pritchett v. Thomas Plater & Co., 144 Tenn. 406, 232 S.W. 961 (1921).

20. U.P.A. § 32(1) (a), (b), Sec. 78(b) below. Raymond v. Vaughn, 128 Ill. 256, 21 N.E. 566, 4 L.R.A. 440, 15 Am. St.Rep. 112 (1889); Pritchett v. Thomas Plater & Co., note 19 above.

21. U.P.A. § 31(5).

In re Malschick, 217 F. 492 (E.D.Pa. 1914), holding that the admissions of a partner during examination in the course of bankruptcy are not binding on co-partners, since not made in the course of business, the partnership being dissolved; Lesser v. Gray, 8 Ga. App. 605, 70 S.E. 104 (1911).

Compare U.P.A. § 32(1) (e), Sec. 78(d) below: a partnership may be judicially dissolved when its business can only be carried on at a loss.

fit of his creditors. Dissolution results.[22] The authority of the bankrupt partner to act for the partnership and the authority of the other partners so to act as to bind him are terminated.[23]

The special problems of bankrupt partners and partnerships are discussed in Chapter 9 below.

Dissolution occurs not only when a partner or partnership is bankrupt under the federal Bankruptcy Act but also when he or it is insolvent under any state insolvency statute.[24]

DISSOLUTION BY DECREE OF COURT

§ 78.   (1) **On application by or for a partner the court shall decree a dissolution whenever:**

    (a) **A partner has been declared a lunatic in any judicial proceeding or is shown to be of unsound mind,**

    (b) **A partner becomes in any other way incapable of performing his part of the partnership contract,**

    (c) **A partner has been guilty of such conduct as tends to affect prejudicially the carrying on of the business,**

    (d) **A partner willfully or persistently commits a breach of the partnership agreement, or otherwise so conducts himself in matters relating to the partnership business that it is not reasonably practicable to carry on the business in partnership with him,**

    (e) **The business of the partnership can only be carried on at a loss,**

    (f) **Other circumstances render a dissolution equitable.**

  (2) **On the application of the purchaser of a partner's interest under sections 27 or 28:**

    (a) **After the termination of the specified term or particular undertaking,**

    (b) **At any time if the partnership was a partnership at will when the interest was assigned or when the charging order was issued.** **U.P.A. § 32.**

---

22. U.P.A. § 31(5). Brandt & Brandt Printers, Inc. v. Klein, 220 F.2d 935 (2d Cir. 1955); King v. Leighton, 100 N.Y. 386, 3 N.E. 594 (1885); Stickney v. Kerry, 55 Wash.2d 535, 348 P.2d 655 (1960).

Closely related is one of the grounds for judicial dissolution: a partner becoming incapable of performing his part of the partnership contract, U. P.A. § 32(1) (b), Sec. 78 below.

23. Compare Restatement, Second, Agency §§ 113, 114 (bankruptcy of agent or principal).

For the somewhat peculiar rules on a partner's authority after dissolution by bankruptcy, see Secs. 80–82 below.

24. U.P.A. § 2, 4th par. In view of the federal dominance of the bankruptcy field, it is not clear what state insolvency statutes are operative for this purpose. To the extent there are any, they may present different patterns of procedure and tests of insolvency, complicating the determination whether and when the partnership is dissolved. Under federal law, it is probably the adjudication of bankruptcy which is the decisive event in an involuntary proceeding, although the filing of a petition may be in a voluntary one. Stickney v. Kerry, n. 22 above.

(a) In General

This section analyzes the judicial causes of dissolution, i. e. those requiring a court decree. Judicial action is appropriate because they involve the determination of difficult matters (such as lunacy, persistent breach, or, in the last analysis, impossibility of performance) or because the would-be-dissolver is not a partner. However, the distinction is not clear-cut, and lawsuits easily materialize over such supposedly non-judicial causes of dissolution as whether a business has become unlawful, whether an expulsion is bona fide, or whether the partnership is one at will or for a particular term or undertaking.[25] Indeed, as we have seen,[26] that most objective of events—death—does not inevitably cause dissolution, and litigation may arise concerning the agreement which prevents it. And any dissolution may become judicial to the extent that a partner seeks a court-supervised accounting,[27] winding up,[28] or receivership.[29]

Nothing appears more rightful than a court order. But we have seen that a judicial dissolution may be considered "in contravention" of the partnership agreement in order to allow damages and continuation of the business.[30]

The non-judicial causes appear to operate ipso facto, and dissolution dates from the occurrence of the event. But a judicial dissolution dates from the court decree,[31] unless there is equitable reason for the court to set an earlier date.[32] These rules fix the time when partners' rights and powers are modified,[33] and when their rights to an accounting accrue.[34]

The U.P.A. language is mandatory: "a court shall decree dissolution" whenever any of the judicial causes occur. However, a court desiring to avoid dissolution has considerable leeway to hold that some of the more generally stated causes have not, in fact or in law, occurred. In addition, it may find equitable grounds for refusing dissolution.[35]

---

25. Sec. 74, nn. 44–45 above.

26. Secs. 73, 77(a) above.

27. U.P.A. § 22, Sec. 72 above.

28. U.P.A. § 37, Sec. 83 below.

29. Annot., Appointment of receiver in proceedings arising out of dissolution of partnership or joint adventure, otherwise than by death of partner or at instance of creditor, 23 A.L.R.2d 583 (1952).

30. Sec. 75 above.

31. Zeibak v. Nasser, 12 Cal.2d 1, 82 P.2d 375 (1938); Scheckter v. Rubin, 349 Pa. 102, 36 A.2d 315 (1944); Kirby v. Kalbacher, 373 Pa. 103, 95 A.2d

535 (1953) (decree nisi). Compare James v. Fabrikant, 3 A.D.2d 895, 162 N.Y.S.2d 215 (1957) appeal denied 3 A.D.2d 1004, 165 N.Y.S.2d 434 (1957) (partnership at will; dissolution no later than filing of accounting action).

32. Roberts v. Mariner, 195 Or. 311, 245 P.2d 927 (1952) (effective on cancellation of real estate license which was essential to operation of the firm).

33. U.P.A. §§ 33–35, Secs. 80–82 above describe how they are modified.

34. U.P.A. § 43, Sec. 87 below.

35. Bates v. McTammany, 10 Cal.2d 697, 76 P.2d 513 (1938) ("clean hands"). See also n. 50 below and Collins v.

Judicial dissolution is particularly suited to facts which may amount to impossibility of performance or total breach of the partnership agreement, but which are so disputed or equivocal that automatic dissolution by operation of law, or self-help by partners would be reckless.

(b) Lunacy and Other Incapacity

Such an equivocal fact is incapacity of a partner due to insanity or other form of illness or physical disability. It is a principle of the law of contracts that a "duty that requires for its performance action that can be rendered only by the promisor or some other particular person is discharged by his death or by such illness as makes the necessary action by him impossible or seriously injurious to his health, unless the contract indicates a contrary intention or there is contributing fault on the part of the person subject to the duty." [36] The contract of partnership normally contemplates participation in management by each of the partners, both for the purpose of rendering services necessary for the accomplishment of the enterprise and for the purpose of safeguarding his investment and the personal liabilities which may result from business transactions.

If the physical or mental incapacity of a partner substantially prevents his rendering any significant services expected from him, fairness to the other partners requires that they should be permitted to have the partnership dissolved. Fairness to the disabled partner who is no longer able to take care of his own interests may require that his property, both that invested in the business and his separate property, should no longer be subject to the hazards of the enterprise. On the other hand, it may be unfair to an incapacitated partner, and a windfall to his co-partners, if he can be forced out of a profitable enterprise to which he has already contributed agreed capital and for which he has no significant obligation to render services. Thus the disability of a limited partner is not a cause of dissolution.[37] The same result would be equitable for an inactive, capital-contributing partner in an ordinary firm, although it might be hard to reach in the face of the apparent statutory mandate.[38]

Partnership for a definite term or purpose is not a single transaction; it involves a business, a series of acts extending over a period of time. Partial or temporary incapacity, not such as to materially frus-

---

Lewis, 283 S.W.2d 258 (Tex.Civ.App. 1955). Compare U.P.A. § 32(1) (f).

36. Restatement, Contracts § 459. See also § 10 above.

37. U.L.P.A. § 20 provides that the retirement, death or insanity of a general partner does not dissolve if the business is continued pursuant to the certificate or by unanimous consent. A fortiori, the acts of a limited partner ought not to bring about dissolution unless the agreement specifies that they will. There is a more fundamental reason, too; see Sec. 90B below.

38. But see above at n. 35, below at n. 42.

trate the purposes of the association, should not warrant the drastic remedy of dissolution.

Permanent insanity will warrant dissolution by decree of court on petition by either the incapacitated partner,[39] or by his co-partners.[40] It must be shown to be permanent, which means not incurable, but apparently for the duration of the partnership agreement.[41] Adjudication of lunacy is proof of incapacity as of the time of adjudication, but not necessarily proof that it exists at time of hearing of a bill for dissolution, or that it is permanent. Commitment for mental illness may or may not establish legal incapacity, depending on the local law.[42]

Incapacity due to other causes than insanity will warrant a decree if it is "lasting rather than merely temporary, and the prospect of recovery . . . is remote, continued or reasonably certain to continue during so substantial a portion of the partnership period as to defeat or materially affect and obstruct the purpose of the partnership."[43] Accounting on dissolution for this cause has been granted as of a date prior to the decree, so that the partner who has carried on the business might have the benefits of his sole efforts,[44] although the incapacitated partner in the meantime was subject to the risks of the business.[45] But, under U.P.A., the dissolution would date from the

---

39. Jones v. Lloyd, 18 Eq. 273, 43 L.J. Eq. 826 (1874).

40. Raymond v. Vaughan, 128 Ill. 256, 21 N.E. 566, 4 L.R.A. 440, 15 Am.St. Rep. 112 (1889); Pritchett v. Thomas Plater & Co., 144 Tenn. 406, 232 S.W. 961 (1921), semble.

41. If the partner has recovered at the time of the hearing, no dissolution will be decreed, Sayer v. Bennet, 1 Cox 107, 29 Eng.Rep. 1084 (1784); Anonymous, 2 K. & J. 441, 69 Eng.Rep. 855 (1856).

42. See, e. g., Vernon's Ann.Civ.St. (Tex.) art. 5547–83(b) (judicial determination of mental illness or commitment to mental hospital is not a determination of mental incompetence unless a finding is made to that effect). Statutes are collected, Lindman & McIntyre, The Mentally Disabled and the Law 230–51 (1961). See Sec. 77 at n. 19 above.

43. Barclay v. Barrie, 209 N.Y. 40, 102 N.E. 602, 47 L.R.A.,N.S., 839, Ann.Cas. 1913D, 1143 (1913). "As has already been stated, independent of express provision a partner impliedly undertakes to advance the success of the copartnership by devoting to it, within

reasonable limits, his time, efforts, and ability. His co-partners are entitled to this contribution, and if for any reason he fails to fulfill his duties, they are thereby deprived, in greater or less degree, according to the extent of his failure, of the benefits of the contract which they have made, and of the fruits thereof to which they are legitimately entitled. With entire justice, therefore, the principle has been well established that courts of equity have power to decree dissolution of a co-partnership because of permanent incapacity of a partner which materially affects his ability to discharge the duties imposed by his partnership relation and contract." Noted 62 U.Pa. L.Rev. 46 (1913).

44. Barclay v. Barrie, n. 43 above, accounting as of date of filing petition.

45. On this ground, accounting was not made retroactive in Besch v. Frolich, 1 Ph. 172, 41 Eng.Rep. 597 (1842).

The incapacity of a partner does not affect the power of copartners to engage in partnership transactions binding on him and his share in partnership property. Jurgens v. Ittmann, 47 La.Ann. 367, 16 So. 952 (1895).

court decree [46] and the incapacitated partner would probably share profits until his interest is paid off.[47]

Partnership agreements often anticipate these problems by providing that incapacity shall not dissolve, and that the incapacitated partner shall receive a settlement of his interest or perhaps a reduced share of profits.[48]

(c) Misconduct or Breach

Misconduct of a partner which will materially interfere with the conduct of the business is a cause for dissolution by decree on petition of the injured,[49] but not of the guilty partner.[50]

Among the acts which warrant a decree are exclusion of one partner from participation in management,[51] substantial overdraft of his

---

[46]. N. 31 above.

[47]. See U.P.A. § 42, Sec. 86 below, granting an option for profits or interest on the value of the partnership interest, when any partner "retires or dies." Incapacity might be considered a retirement.

[48]. See Appendix VI, pars. 7.9, 7.10.

[49]. U.P.A. § 32(1) (c), (d), (f). Wallace v. Sinclair, 114 Cal.App.2d 220, 250 P. 2d 154 (1953) illustrates numerous forms of misconduct. Cases (many pre-U.P.A.) are collected in Annot., Misconduct of or dissensions among partners or joint adventurers as ground for dissolution by court, 118 A.L.R. 1421 (1939).

[50]. "A party who is the author of the ill-feeling between himself and his partners ought not to be permitted to make the relation he has induced the ground of a dissolution of the partnership. His conduct may have been taken with a view to that very result, and it would be inequitable to allow him advantage from his own wrongful acts. It would allow one partner, at his election, to put an end to his own deliberate contract, while the other has been guilty of no wrongful act or omission of duty." Gerard v. Gateau, 84 Ill. 121, 25 Am.Rep. 438 (1876). A partner may, however, in breach of his contract, dissolve the partnership at any time. U.P.A. § 31(2), Sec. 75 above.

"The jurisdiction of a court of equity in cases of co-partnership flowing from the peculiar trusts and duties growing out of that connection, is of the most extensive and beneficial character. It often declares partnerships utterly void, in cases of fraud, imposition, and oppression in the original agreement; or decrees a dissolution of a partnership which was unobjectionable in its origin, but which subsequent causes have rendered onerous or oppressive; gross misconduct, want of good faith, or criminal want of diligence, or such cause as is productive of serious and permanent injury in the partnership concerns, or renders it impracticable to carry on the business, is good ground for a dissolution at the suit of the injured partner. Habitual drunkenness, great extravagance or unwarrantable negligence in conducting the business of the partnership, justifies a dissolution; but then it must be a strong and clear case of positive or meditated abuse to authorize such a decree. For minor misconduct and grievances, if they require redress the court will interfere by way of injunction to prevent the mischief." Howell v. Harvey, 5 Ark. 270, 39 Am.Dec. 376 (1843).

However, dissolution may be ordered where "the relations have become so strained and the mutual confidence so impaired, through the contributing fault of *both partners*, that it is no longer just or equitable that the partnership be continued." Stark v. Reingold, 18 N.J. 251, 113 A.2d 679, 685 (1955) (emphasis added).

[51]. Herman v. Pepper, 311 Pa. 104, 166 A. 587 (1933); Dow v. Beals, 149 Misc. 631, 268 N.Y.S. 425 (1933); Heyman v. Heyman, 210 Ill. 524, 71 N.E. 591

account by a partner,[52] fraudulent conduct in dealings with a corporation in which the partner is interested,[53] fraudulent retention or disposition of funds collected for the partnership property,[54] neglect of business causing injury to partnership assets,[55] irreconcilable dissensions and disagreements between the partners, endangering the partnership goodwill and property,[56] conveyance of his separate property and notice to mercantile agencies with effect of impairing firm's credit,[57] and refusal of an accounting at times when it should be had according to the provisions of the partnership articles.[58]

The court will not decree a dissolution for a breach of the agreement it considers immaterial, such as a want of courtesy to firm customers; [59] or withholding of funds due to bona fide differences of opinion; [60] or causing slight losses due to errors of judgment; [61] friction between senior partner in whom wide powers of management are vested and junior partners, not affecting success of business [62] or using partnership property to pay separate debts openly without impairment of his share of capital contribution,[63] or, in general, minor or

(1904); Groth v. Payment, 79 Mich. 290, 44 N.W. 611 (1890); Howell v. Harvey, 5 Ark. 270, 39 Am.Dec. 376 (1843).

52. Darlington v. Perry, 354 Ill. 22, 187 N.E. 796 (1933).

53. Gianuso v. Weis, 195 N.Y.S. 279 (Sup.1922); Hanna v. McLaughlin, 158 Ind. 292, 63 N.E. 475 (1902); Frankfort Const. Co. v. Meneely, 62 Ind.App. 514, 112 N.E. 244 (1916).

54. Brooke v. Tucker, 149 Ala. 96, 43 So. 141 (1907); Clay v. Palmer, 104 Neb. 476, 177 N.W. 840 (1920); Smith v. Jeyes, 4 Beav. 503, 49 Eng.Rep. 433 (1841); Cheesman v. Price, 35 Beav. 142, 55 Eng.Rep. 849 (1865).

55. Lisco v. Husmann, 98 Neb. 276, 152 N.W. 383 (1915).

56. Creel v. Creel, 63 App.D.C. 384, 73 F.2d 107 (1934); Crim v. Crim, 194 Iowa 1137, 191 N.W. 157 (1922); Jones v. Jones, 229 Ky. 71, 16 S.W.2d 503 (1929) Ferrick v. Barry, 320 Mass. 217, 68 N.E.2d 690 (1946). See Harrison v. Tennant, 21 Beav. 482, 52 Eng. Rep. 945 (1856). In such situations the courts frequently appoint a receiver to take over the partnership property and operate the business, as a preliminary measure of relief, pending the decision of the question of whether a dissolution shall be ordered. The appointment of a receiver rests in the sound discretion of the

court. Moffett v. Peirce, 344 Pa. 16, 24 A.2d 448 (1942); Dolenga v. Lipka, 224 Mich. 276, 195 N.W. 90 (1923). See also n. 29 above.

57. Sutro v. Wagner, 23 N.J.Eq. 388 (1873).

58. Lavoine v. Casey, 251 Mass. 124, 146 N.E. 241 (1925).

59. Gerard v. Gateau, 84 Ill. 121, 25 Am.Rep. 438 (1876).

60. Young v. McKenney, 197 Ky. 768, 247 S.W. 964 (1923).

61. Cash v. Earnshaw, 66 Ill. 402 (1872).

62. Potter v. Brown, 328 Pa. 554, 195 A. 901, 118 A.L.R. 1415 (1938). "Differences and discord should be settled by the partners themselves by the application of mutual forbearance rather than by bills in equity for dissolution. Equity is not a referee of partnership quarrels. A going and prosperous business will not be dissolved merely because of friction among the partners; it will not interfere to determine which contending faction is more at fault." Id., 195 A. at 904. Accord: Lunn v. Kaiser, 76 S.D. 52, 72 N.W.2d 312 (1955) (short time left for partnership to run).

63. Page v. Vankirk & Marshall, 1 Brewst. 282 (Pa.1866).

trifling matters.[64]   If the firm is financially successful, dissolution is less likely to be ordered for misconduct or dissension.[65]

It is safer for a partner having a cause for dissolution, by reason of the co-partner's misconduct or breach of the agreement, to petition a court for a decree of dissolution and accounting.   But if he proceeds to exercise self-help in such a situation, and excludes the erring partner or dissolves by notice, he is not liable for damages for his justifiable termination of the partnership agreement.[66]

If the misconduct amounts to fraud and occurs in the formation of a partnership, the innocent partner has the alternate remedy of rescission, which may be more powerful than dissolution.[67]

In a business trust, fraudulent or other seriously improper conduct on the part of trustees may be a sufficient reason for their removal by a court of equity, but it is not necessary that the trust be wound up.   Other trustees can be appointed for the purpose of carrying out the enterprise according to the terms of the articles of organization.[68]   It may be provided in the trust articles that the beneficiaries by majority vote may remove trustees and fill the vacancies so created.[69]

(d) Losses

Since the purpose of a partnership is to make profit, it may be dissolved by decree of court when it becomes apparent that it is unprofitable, with no reasonable prospects of success.[70]

Troublesome definitional problems may arise in considering whether partnerships should be dissolved because of losses.   Some ventures are planned to operate at a loss in the tax and accounting sense, but to provide a cash "throw-off" as a result of depreciation or other non-cash deductions.   In such a case, loss should be interpreted in cash terms according to the partners' frame of reference, and dissolution denied on this ground if their expectations are being reasonably fulfilled.   At the other extreme, a business with heavy

---

64. N. 62 above.   Roberts v. Mariner, 195 Or. 311, 245 P.2d 927 (1952).

65. See, e. g., cases in n. 62 above.

66. Schnitzer v. Josephthal, 122 Misc. 15, 202 N.Y.S. 77 (1923), affirmed 208 App.Div. 769, 202 N.Y.S. 952 (1924); Reiter v. Morton, 96 Pa. 229, 240 (1880).   See Lavoine v. Casey, 251 Mass. 124, 146 N.E. 241 (1925).

67. U.P.A. § 39, Sec. 85 below.

68. Burnett v. Smith, 240 S.W. 1007 (Tex.Civ.App.1922).   See also Phoenix Oil Co. v. McLarren, 244 S.W. 830 (Tex.Civ.App.1922).

69. Douglass v. Safe Deposit & Trust Co., 159 Md. 81, 150 A. 37 (1930). Such a provision may be construed as vesting in the beneficiaries a measure of control sufficient to constitute them partners.

70. Rosenstein v. Burns, 41 F. 841, (D. Mass.1892) aff'd on other grounds, 135 U.S. 449, 10 S.Ct. 817, 34 L.Ed. 193 (1890); Wallace v. Sinclair, 114 Cal. App.2d 220, 250 P.2d 154 (1953); Thomson v. Langton, 51 Cal.App. 142, 196 P. 103 (1921); Sieghortner v. Weissenborn, 20 N.J.Eq. 172 (1869); Willis v. Chapman, 68 Vt. 459, 35 A. 459 (1896).

See n. 71 below.

debt may have profits in the tax or accounting sense but be unable to generate enough cash to meet its obligations. This might well be considered a loss situation, though dissolution is not likely to help much. If this method of financing was reasonably in contemplation of the parties, they presumably were thinking of income in the accounting sense, and dissolution on the ground of losses should normally be denied.[71]

Dissolution for losses is closely related to dissolution for bankruptcy.[72]

(e) Assignments and Their Consequences

There is a conflict of authority as to the effect of an assignment by a partner of his interest in the partnership. Under the U.P.A., he is incapable of assigning a share in the title to specific partnership property,[73] and can only assign his interest, i.e. his share of profits and surplus.[73A] The assignment of his interest does not necessarily operate as a dissolution,[74] although it may if it comes within either the

---

71. Collins v. Lewis, 283 S.W.2d 258 (Tex.Civ.App.1955) illustrates a heavily financed venture, all of whose revenues would be consumed by debt retirement for many years. The effect of the long-term debt on profits never became an issue; the jury found that profits were possible but for the interference of the partner who was seeking dissolution.

72. U.P.A. § 31(5), Sec. 77(b) above.

73. U.P.A. § 25(2) (b), Sec. 42(a) above.

73A. Sec. 42(b) above.

74. U.P.A. § 27, Sec. 42(b) above. Annot., Sale or transfer of interest by partner as dissolving partnership, 75 A.L.R.2d 1036 (1961).

In tax law, where termination, not dissolution, is significant, a partnership terminates only if no part of its business is carried on by any of the partners in partnership, or 50% or more of the interest in capital and profits is sold within a 12-month period. Int. Rev.Code of 1954, § 708(b) (1) (26 U. S.C.A.). Semble, on the 50%, Investment Advisers Act of 1940, § 202(a) (1), 15 U.S.C.A. § 80b–2(a) (1); Investment Company Act of 1940, § 2 (a) (4), 15 U.S.C.A. § 80a–2(a) (4).

A mortgage or pledge of a partner's interest to a third person to secure a debt does not necessarily operate

as a dissolution, and does not impair the assigning partner's right to participate in management, and exercise the rights of a partner as to calling for a dissolution and accounting if the occasion arises. Kist v. Coughlin, 210 Ind. 622, 1 N.E.2d 602 (1936); Power Grocery Co. v. Hinton, 187 Ky. 171, 218 S.W. 1013 (1920); Dupont v. McLaran, 61 Mo. 502 (1876); Brown v. Beecher, 120 Pa. 590, 15 A. 608 (1888); Herman v. Pepper, 311 Pa. 104, 166 A. 587 (1933). On the assignee's rights, see Sec. 42(b) above.

A partner may assign to his co-partner his interest by way of mortgage without a dissolution. Monroe v. Hamilton, 60 Ala. 226 (1877); Donnelly v. McArdle, 120 App.Div. 871, 105 N. Y.S. 331 (1907).

Whether transactions between partners in dealing with a partner's interest result in severance of his relation as partner is a matter of intent, Stockhausen v. Johnson, 173 Iowa 413, 155 N.W. 823 (1916); Taft v. Buffum, 31 Mass. (14 Pick.) 322 (1833).

Even though a partner may retire on disposing of his interest to his co-partners, the terms of the dissolution may be such that he is not entitled to a winding up, and the others may continue the business. Lobdell v. Baldwin, 93 Mich. 569, 53 N.W. 730 (1892).

general definition [75] or the specific causes.[76]   However, the non-assigning partners are entitled to dissolve by agreement without breach of contract.[77]   Prior to the U.P.A., many courts held that the assignment by a partner of his share in partnership property amounted to a dissolution *ipso facto*.[78]

If the partnership is one at will, either by original agreement or by expiration of the stated term for its duration, the assignee of a partner's interest is entitled to a dissolution by decree of court.[79] A similar right is vested in the purchaser of a partner's interest as a result of a charging order.[80]

EVENTS WHICH DO NOT CAUSE DISSOLUTION

§ 78A. By the better view, changes in membership pursuant to agreement do not necessarily cause dissolution.

---

75. E. g., if the partner ceases to be associated with the firm after the assignment, U.P.A. § 29, Sec. 73 above.

76. E. g., willful breach of the agreement, U.P.A. § 32(1) (d), Sec. 78(c) above.

77. U.P.A. § 31(1) (c), Sec. 74(c) above.

78. Fourth Nat. Bank v. New Orleans & Carrollton R. Co., 78 U.S. (11 Wall.) 624, 20 L.Ed. 82 (1870); Karrick v. Hannaman, 168 U.S. 328, 18 S.Ct. 135, 42 L.Ed. 484 (1897), semble; Morss v. Gleason, 64 N.Y. 204 (1876); Flett v. Willeford, 114 Or. 80, 234 P. 802 (1925); Horton's Appeal, 13 Pa. 67 (1850).

The entire transaction may be such as to indicate that the intent of the parties is to substitute the assignee for the assignor as a member of the partnership, in which case there is, perhaps, a technical dissolution though without winding up. McCall v. Moss, 112 Ill. 493 (1885); Morss v. Gleason, supra. See also authorities in Sec. 42(b) above.

U.P.A. § 27(1) has changed the law of many states as to the effect of assignment as working a dissolution per se, Meinhard v. Salmon, 249 N.Y. 458, 164 N.E. 545, 62 A.L.R. 1 (1928), joint venture; White v. Long, 289 Pa. 525, 137 A. 673 (1927); Rossmoore v. Anderson, 1 F.Supp. 35 (S.D.N.Y.1932).

However, it has been ignored occasionally in judicial opinions, First Nat. Trust & Sav. Bank of San Diego v. Industrial Accident Commission, 213 Cal. 322, 2 P.2d 347, 78 A.L.R. 1324 (1931).

79. U.P.A. § 32(2), if he is a "purchaser." Murdoch v. Murdoch, 279 Pa. 97, 123 A. 683 (1924).

A partnership formed to operate a radio station so long as a license could be obtained from the Federal Government was not treated as a partnership at will which could be dissolved by decree of court on prayer of a partner. Bates v. McTammany, 10 Cal.2d 697, 76 P. 2d 513 (1938).

If the partnership agreement provides that one partner cannot assign his interest without the consent of his co-partner, an attempted assignment does not entitle the assignee to secure a dissolution, Pokrzywnicki v. Kozak, 354 Pa. 346, 47 A.2d 144 (1946).

80. U.P.A. § 31(4). Beckley v. Speaks, 39 Misc.2d 241, 240 N.Y.S.2d 553 (1963), aff'd 21 A.D.2d 759, 251 N.Y.S.2d 1015 (1964), appeal dismissed 15 N.Y.2d 546, 202 N.E.2d 906, 254 N.Y.S.2d 362 (1964) (dictum). See Sherwood v. Jackson, 121 Cal.App. 354, 8 P.2d 943 (1932), dictum permitting a charging order in favor of a co-partner's tort claimant, during the course of dissolution.

As to the rights of a separate creditor to obtain a charging order despite a sham dissolution, see Spitzer v. Buten, 306 Pa. 556, 160 A. 444 (1932).

Dissolution is not necessarily caused by some things which would have caused dissolution at common law, e.g. an accounting,[81] or the assignment of a partner's interest.[82]   It is not caused by a creditor's charging order on a partner's interest in the firm, or a foreclosure thereof.[83]   Nor is it caused by minor frictions among partners.[84]   Admission of a new partner, since it requires unanimous consent of the other partners,[85] and does not involve any partner ceasing to be associated, should not be regarded as dissolving the firm.[86]   By the better view, a partnership is not necessarily dissolved by the withdrawal or death of a partner, if the agreement so provides.[87]

Partnerships have evolved with the economy.   Concepts which were appropriate in a simpler day for 2- or 3-man firms without written agreements need modification today for larger firms with elaborate structures and continuity agreements.   In the latter cases, dissolution is an empty and useless notion.   It is time we recognize in this respect, as we do in so many others, that the partnership is what the partners make it.[88]

Limited partnerships are subject to dissolution in far fewer instances than general partnerships.[89]

EFFECT OF DISSOLUTION ON EXISTING LIABILITIES OF THE PARTNERSHIP

§ 79.   **(1) The dissolution of the partnership does not of itself discharge the existing liability of any partner.**

(2) A partner is discharged from any existing liability upon dissolution of the partnership by an agreement to that effect between himself, the partnership creditor and the person or partnership continuing the business; and such agreement may be inferred from the course of dealing between the creditor having knowledge of the dissolution and the person or partnership continuing the business.

(3) Where a person agrees to assume the existing obligations of a dissolved partnership, the partners whose obligations have been as-

---

81.   U.P.A. §§ 21–22 (by implication). See the tortured last sentence in Commissioners' Note to U.P.A. § 22, 7 Uniform Laws Ann. 126 (1949).

82.   See Sec. 78(e) above.

83.   U.P.A. § 28 (by implication), Sec. 43 above.

84.   See Sec. 78(c) at nn. 62, 64 above.

85.   U.P.A. § 18(g), Sec. 5(c) above.

86.   Dubious authority to the contrary is analyzed in Bromberg, Partnership Dissolution — Causes, Consequences, and Cures, 43 Texas L.Rev. 631, 636–37 (1965).

87.   Sec. 73 at nn. 4, 10–11 and Sec. 77(a) above.

88.   See Sec. 73 at nn. 12–14 above, noting that the older view rests on delectus personae and non-tranferability of partnership interests, both of which are modifiable by agreement, and that outgoing partners' interests are often surrendered rather than transferred. See also Sec. 77(a) above, attacking the ideas of mystical union and of impossibility of performance.

A middle ground is the idea of "partial dissolution", Adams v. Jarvis, 23 Wis. 2d 453, 127 N.W.2d 400 (1964), noted 48 Marq.L.Rev. 253 (1964).

89.   Secs. 90B below, 73 above.

sumed shall be discharged from any liability to any creditor of the partnership who, knowing of the agreement, consents to a material alteration in the nature or time of payment of such obligations.

(4) The individual property of a deceased partner shall be liable for all obligations of the partnership incurred while he was a partner but subject to the prior payment of his separate debts. U.P.A. § 36.

Contracts of insurance and of suretyship to which partnerships are parties, if construed strictly, will cease to be operative after change in membership of the partnership involved. The modern trend in cases of corporate commercial sureties and insurers is to regard as immaterial a change which does not substantially alter the risk, as where the business of the partnership is continued by some of the former partners.

(a) In General

Dissolution of itself has no effect on existing liabilities of the partnership.[90] If it did, partners could escape their obligations by dissolving. But the cause of dissolution, e.g., impossibility, may discharge executory contracts. "A duty which requires for its performance action that can be rendered only by the promisor is discharged by his death or by such illness as makes the necessary action by him impossible or seriously injurious to his health, unless the contract indicates a contrary intention or there is contributing fault on the part of the persons subject to the duty."[91] A contract whereby a 2-man partnership employs a general manager is discharged by the death of a partner;[92] and so it has been held with other employment

90. U.P.A. § 36(1). Western Spring Service Co. v. Andrew, 229 F.2d 413 (10th Cir. 1956) (tort liability for post-dissolution injury resulting from negligent pre-dissolution welding); Credit Bureaus of Merced County, Inc. v. Shipman & Davis Lumber Co., 167 Cal. App.2d 673, 334 P.2d 1036 (1959) (demurrage on containers not returned at dissolution persisted and continued to accrue).

Dissolution does not of itself discharge any existing liability of the *partnership*, for the partnership continues through the period of winding up. U.P.A. § 30, Sec. 73 above. Emerson Radio & Phonograph Corp. v. Eskind, 32 Misc.2d 1038, 228 N.Y.S.2d 841 (1957) (service valid against dissolved partnership); Carter v. Love, 394 P. 2d 472 (Okl.1964) (partnership may, but need not be, a party). However, at the end of that period, when the partnership is terminated, it may be that partnership liability ceases, or no judgment can be recovered against it. See Moore v. Diehm, 200 Okl. 664, 199 P.2d 218 (1948). The liability of the individual partners continues. Ibid.; Yellow Cab Co. v. Allen, 377 P.2d 220 (Okl.1962).

Within the partnership, a dissolution *agreement* may terminate obligations, e. g., to make further capital contributions. Wathen v. Brown, 200 Pa.Super. 620, 189 A.2d 900 (1963) (implied rescission or settlement of contribution obligation). Absent such an agreement, dissolution does not affect partners' existing obligations to the partnership, since it is a continuing organization until wound up. In particular, dissolution *per se* does not alter a partner's obligation to share losses, indemnify his co-partners, or account as a fiduciary with respect to past transactions. U.P.A. §§ 18(a)–(c), 40(d), (g), 21(1).

91. Restatement, Contracts § 459.

92. Shumate v. Sohon, 56 App.D.C. 290, 12 F.2d 825, 59 A.L.R. 291 (1926). The unjustifiable aspect of this decision is that it ignores the partnership agreement for continuation of the business and of the manager's employment by the surviving partner.

contracts.[93]

But where the contract lacks a sufficient personal element on the partnership side, the result is otherwise. A contract for the performance of a vaudeville act for a partnership which operated a theatre is not discharged by the death of a partner.[94] Where a trading partnership of several members engaged an agent to represent it in a foreign port, and after the death of a partner, the business was continued by the survivors, the employment contract was not discharged.[95] As a rule, the greater the continuity of the partnership in fact or by internal agreement, the greater is the continuity of its obligations.

The results are similar when the partnership is being employed or engaged, rather than employing or engaging. If personal services are not central to the arrangement, it is not discharged by the death of a partner.[96] The contrary is true if the contract requires the special skill of one partner.[97] The relation between a client and a law partnership may contemplate the services of a particular partner, so that his death will terminate the relation not only with him, but with the survivors,[98] or it may contemplate the services of the partnership, or any of the partners, or power to delegate. It seems to be generally held that retainers of lawyers,[99] or other professional part-

93. Griggs v. Swift, 82 Ga. 392, 9 S.E. 1062, 5 L.R.A. 405, 14 Am.St.Rep. 176 (1889); Greenburg v. Early, 4 Misc. 99, 23 N.Y.S. 1009 (1893); Tasker v. Shephard, 6 H. & N. 575, 158 Eng. Rep. 237 (1861).

Rights of the partnership may be made contingent on the existence of the firm, and thus be extinguished by its dissolution or termination. See Frederick C. Smith Clinic v. Lastrapes, 111 Ohio App. 42, 170 N.E.2d 497 (1959) (non-competition covenant of employee unenforceable after change in firm membership; contract provided for automatic termination on dissolution of firm).

94. Phillips v. Alhambra Palace Co., [1901] 1 K.B. 59. It might well have been discharged by the death or incapacity of a member of the vaudeville team, depending on his importance to the show, and the intent of the parties. See nn. 97–98 below.

A contract of a California merchandising firm with a New York agent for services in connection with New York buying of merchandise, for a definite term, was not a contract for personal services and was not terminated by death of a partner. Yahr-Donen Corp.

v. Crocker, 80 Cal.App.2d 675, 182 P.2d 209 (1947).

95. Fereira v. Sayres, 5 Watts & S. 210, 40 Am.Dec. 496 (Pa.1843). See Hughes v. Gross, 166 Mass. 61, 43 N.E. 1031, 32 L.R.A. 620, 55 Am.St.Rep. 375 (1896), where the business was continued by survivors and services thereafter accepted.

96. Burkle v. Superflow Mfg. Co., 137 Conn. 488, 78 A.2d 698 (1951). The partnership solicited orders for plumbing supply manufacturers. The court states that the contract would not be discharged, and holds that it is consequently within the statute of frauds. Hentges v. Wolff, 240 Minn. 517, 61 N.W.2d 748 (1953) (listing with real estate broker firm).

97. George v. Richards, 361 Pa. 278, 64 A.2d 811 (1949) (tunnel construction).

98. Clifton v. Clark, Hood & Co., 83 Miss. 446, 36 So. 251, 66 L.R.A. 821, 102 Am.St.Rep. 458, 1 Ann.Cas. 396 (1904), semble; Wright v. McCampbell, 75 Tex. 644, 13 S.W. 293 (1890), semble. Compare In re Lichtblau's Estate, 146 Misc. 278, 261 N.Y.S. 863 (1933).

99. Little v. Caldwell, 101 Cal. 553, 36 P. 107, 40 Am.St.Rep. 89 (1894); Felt

nerships,[1] are binding upon the surviving member of the partnership after the death of a partner, but it is optional with the client whether or not to continue the relation.[2]

When a partnership is voluntarily dissolved and the business is continued by some of the partners, obligations incurred before dissolution are binding on both the continuing and the retiring partners.[3] A retired partner in a law partnership is liable to a client for collections made under a retainer before dissolution.[4] A retired partner in a commercial partnership is liable to the vendor of goods contracted for before the dissolution and delivered to the continuing partners after the dissolution.[5] Where partners incorporate and turn over their business to the corporation, a person from whom goods were ordered by the partnership before incorporation, who delivers after incorporation without knowledge thereof, is entitled to collect the price from the partners.[6]

v. Mitchell, 44 Ind.App. 96, 88 N.E. 723 (1909); Clifton v. Clark, n. 98 above; Puffer v. Merton, 168 Wis. 366, 170 N.W. 368, 5 A.L.R. 1288 (1919).

1. Stem v. Warren, 227 N.Y. 538, 125 N.E. 811 (1920), obligation of survivors to complete architectural work being provided for in contract of employment.

Voluntary dissolution of a firm of real estate brokers was held to terminate their power to sell land of a client. Schlau v. Enzenbacher, 265 Ill. 626, 107 N.E. 107, L.R.A.1915C, 576 (1914); Egner v. States Realty Co., 223 Minn. 305, 26 N.W.2d 464, 170 A.L.R. 500 (1947).

The dissolution of a partnership of automobile sales agents justifies the manufacturer in terminating the agency. Wheaton v. Cadillac Automobile Co., 143 Mich. 21, 106 N.W. 399 (1906).

2. Cf. Platt v. Henderson, 227 Or. 212, 361 P.2d 73 (1961), Sec. 83 n. 39 below, where the younger partner walked out on the older one, took the clients' files with him, and continued to serve and bill them without objection from the clients. On the related problem of sharing in fees earned partly or wholly after dissolution, see Annot., 78 A.L.R.2d 280 (1961).

3. See n. 90 above. Contra: Menenberg v. Carl R. Sams Realty Co., 337 Mich. 143, 59 N.W.2d 125 (1953). A 3-man partnership was agent for a builder, and agreed to pay a lawyer-

accountant $40 for each sale made by the partnership as agent. The partnership was dissolved and wound up. Two of the partners formed a new firm which continued to act as agent for the builder. *Held*: the new partnership is not liable to lawyer-accountant; his agreement terminated (impliedly without liability) on the dissolution of the old partnership, and was not assumed by the new partnership. The decision has conflict-of-interest overtones since the lawyer-accountant worked for the builder. Compare Shunk v. Shunk Mfg. Co., n. 8 below, where the contract was for a fixed term.

4. McCoon v. Galbraith, 29 Pa. 293 (1857).

5. Henry v. Seiberling Rubber Co., 265 Ky. 241, 96 S.W.2d 590 (1936); Clinchfield Fuel Co. v. W. M. Lundy & Son, 130 Tenn. 135, 169 S.W. 563, L. R.A.1915B, 418 (1914).

Goldman v. General Supply Co., 6 So.2d 778 (La.App.1942). An additional basis of the liability was that no notice of dissolution was given.

But notice does not relieve the outgoing partner unless the seller agrees to hold responsible only the continuing partner. Martinez v. McGregor-Doniger, Inc., 173 A.2d 221 (D.C.Mun.App.1961).

6. Herring v. Mishawaka Rubber & Woolen Mfg. Co., 192 Ark. 1055, 95 S.W.2d 1141 (1936). As to liability of the corporation, see Sec. 89 below.

If partners have engaged an employee to act as controller, "for and during the balance of the term of the partnership" which by its articles has a stated number of years to run, the employee's contract does not terminate on incorporation of the partners to carry on their business and he is entitled to damages for wrongful discharge.[7]   Where partners engaged an employee for a term of years, the subsequent dissolution of the partnership (by changes in membership) without notice to him has been treated as a termination of his contract without fault on his part.[8]

A contract of continuing guaranty, such as a fidelity bond or a guaranty of payment of goods sold in the future, being subject to construction *strictissimi juris,* at least in cases of accommodating parties other than paid sureties, is usually discharged as to future transactions by a change in the membership of a partnership which is the creditor[9] or the debtor.[10]   Such changes are likely to alter the risk

---

7.   Helmick v. Rankin, 166 Pa.Super. 189, 70 A.2d 362 (1950).

8.   Shunk v. Shunk Mfg. Co., 86 Ohio App. 467, 93 N.E.2d 321 (1949). The precedent value of the case is limited because of the peculiar situation. Although the successor partnership continued to pay the employee for a time, it finally discharged him for failure to perform duties. In order to recover, he had to establish that there were no duties for him to perform, i. e. that the contract had already terminated. Since the contract was regarded as partial consideration for his sale of the business to the predecessor partnership, the court "reached" for a holding in his favor. If he had been an ordinary employee, the result probably would have been that his contract was taken over by the successor partnership, and he would have been properly discharged for failure to perform duties to it. Compare Menenberg v. Carl R. Sams Realty Co., n. 3 above, where the contract was not for a fixed term.

9.   Black v. Albery, 89 Ohio St. 240, 106 N.E. 38 (1914), surety for purchaser of entire output of creamery operated by 3-man partnership from which one partner retired, was held to be not liable for the deliveries subsequently made.

John H. Lyon & Co. v. Plum, 75 N.J. L. 883, 69 A. 209, 14 L.R.A.,N.S., 1231, 127 Am.St.Rep. 858, 15 Ann.Cas. 1019 (1908), creditor partnership took in an additional member and later incorporated;   Schoonover v. Osborne,

108 Iowa 453, 79 N.W. 263 (1899), partner retired;   Bennett v. Draper, 139 N.Y. 266, 34 N.E. 791 (1893), partner died and another was substituted; Jordan Marsh Co. v. Beals, 201 Mass. 163, 87 N.E. 471 (1909), partnership was incorporated.   In these cases an unduly arbitrary effect is given to a single fact.   The question should have been whether the risk to the surety is so substantially changed that it is inequitable or in violation of the original contractual intention to hold him bound to further transactions.

Annot., Who may enforce guaranty, 41 A.L.R.2d 1213, 1230–33 (1955).

A fire insurance policy issued to a partnership on partnership property is not avoided by retirement of a partner, Powers v. Guardian Fire & Life Ins. Co., 136 Mass. 108, 49 Am.Rep. 20 (1883); First Nat. Trust & Sav. Bank of San Diego v. Industrial Accident Commission, 213 Cal. 322, 2 P.2d 347, 78 A.L.R. 1324 (1931), workmen's compensation insurance policy.   Contra, Buckley v. Garrett, 47 Pa. 204 (1864). An assignment of a partner's interest to a stranger does not avoid a fire policy, Wood v. American Fire Ins. Co., 149 N.Y. 382, 44 N.E. 80, 52 Am.St. Rep. 733 (1896).   See Vance Insurance 835–36 (3d ed. 1951).

Workmen's compensation insurance issued to a single insured does not lapse on his taking in a partner, but it does not cover the liability of the partner, Zimmerman v. Industrial Accident Commission, 119 Cal.App. 253,

---

10.   Footnote 10 on page 449.

assumed by the surety. He is not to be held for a risk differing from that which he intended to assume when entering into the accommodation contract. It may appear, however, to be the intention of the parties that changes in personnel (the group and the business risks remaining substantially unchanged) shall not affect the guarantor's continuing obligations. If so, the court interpreting the contract may hold it still operative.[11]

(b) Novation

It is possible for a retiring partner to be discharged from his existing liabilities by reason of a novation, effected on or after dis-

---

6 P.2d 291 (1931). Insurance of a firm does not lapse with the retirement of a partner, or substitution of a new partner, Ardolino v. Ierna, 225 App. Div. 439, 233 N.Y.S. 477 (1929); United States Fidelity & Guaranty Co. v. Booth, 164 Tenn. 41, 45 S.W.2d 1075 (1932). In the latter case the insurance was held to cover an accident to the retired partner who became an employee.

10. Dupee v. Blake, 148 Ill. 453, 35 N.E. 867 (1893); Byers v. Hickman Grain Co., 112 Iowa 451, 454, 84 N.W. 500, 501 (1900); Hunt Oil Co. v. Killion, 299 S.W.2d 316 (Tex.Civ.App.1957); Lumberman's Bank & Trust Co. v. Sevier, 149 Wash. 118, 270 P. 291 (1928).

A change in membership of the obligor partnership does not affect the obligation of a surety contract entered into before dissolution, Gargan v. School Dist. No. 15, 4 Colo. 53 (1877). See note, 29 Colum.L.Rev. 97 (1929); Williston, Contracts, § 1240 (rev. ed. 1936).

Similarly, the guarantor of the bank debt of three partners remained liable despite renewal by two of them after bankruptcy of the third. National Bank of La Crosse v. Funk, 216 Wis. 412, 256 N.W. 786 (1934).

11. In Richardson v. County of Steuben, 226 N.Y. 13, 122 N.E. 449 (1919), reversing 174 App.Div. 491, 160 N.Y.S. 445 (1916) which affirmed Richards [sic] v. Steuben County, 155 N.Y.S. 571 (Sup.Ct.1915), noted 29 Harv.L.Rev. 460, plaintiff became surety for a county deposit in the "Hallock Bank." This was a partnership, the membership was changed from time to time during the period for which the undertaking was given. It was held that

this did not impair the effect of the guaranty. The court said that the rule of strict construction of suretyship contracts "does not mean that in interpreting the undertaking of a surety we are to be governed by different fundamental rules than those which are applicable to the construction of another contract. . . . There seems to stand out with perfect clearness from the terms of the instrument the thought and guaranty that here was an institution engaged in receiving deposits and that it—the bank, the institution—would continue to repay for the few years of a county treasurer's term the deposits which were thus received. If as we think this was the intent of the sureties, and this is the fair interpretation of their engagement, then their liability was continuing and is not to be measured or limited by the rules which control an ordinary guaranty of a copartnership." Accord, Elliott-Lewis Electric Co., Inc. v. Hausman, 104 Pa.Super. 322, 158 A. 626 (1931).

As to changes in the membership of the creditor partnership, see Metcalf v. Bruin, 12 East 400, 104 Eng.Rep. 156 (1810), holding that the guaranty of the fidelity of a clerk employed by the Globe Insurance Company was not affected by changes in the membership of the group who did business under that name.

Semble Kitt v. Home Indemnity, 153 Ohio St. 505, 92 N.E.2d 685 (1950) (indemnity policy against dishonesty of partnership employees was enforceable by partnership despite change in members; policy was issued in firm's assumed name, manifesting intent to cover the unincorporated body, however constituted).

solution, with the continuing partners and the creditor. The mere fact of agreement between the retiring partner and the continuing partner, whereby the latter assumes the duty of performance of existing obligations and notice of such agreement to the creditor, does not effect a novation.[12] There must be an agreement by the creditor for sufficient consideration to release the retiring partner.[13] The consideration may be found in the incurring by the continuing partner or partners of an obligation differing from that to which they were previously subject. Changing a joint obligation as partners into a separate obligation, thereby giving the creditor a parity with other creditors of the separate estate, will operate as consideration.[14] If, as under the U.P.A., the creditor by operation of law becomes the creditor of the partnership or persons continuing the business,[15] it may be questioned whether an express promise to him is effective consideration, but it appears that it is under section 36(2) quoted above.[16]

The consent of the creditor to a novation is sometimes express, but more often implied by his conduct. Whether his dealings with the continuing partners after dissolution amount to a novation is a fact question of intent. The receipt from the continuing partner of partial payments,[17] delayed payments,[18] interest,[19] or negotiable instruments [20] is insufficient. But it has been held that there is assent to a novation in taking a negotiable instrument in full settlement of the

12. Credit Bureaus of Merced County, Inc. v. Shipman, n. 90 above; Phillips v. Schlang, 139 App.Div. 930, 124 N.Y.S. 40 (1910). See Comment 10 Colum.L.Rev. 550 (1910).

Notice to, or knowledge by, the creditor does not by itself relieve the outgoing partner, even from future liability under existing contracts. See Martinez v. McGregor-Doniger, Inc., n. 5 above.

13. A promise by the creditor to the retiring partner to release him from his obligation without any consideration is ineffective as *nudum pactum*. Walstrom v. Hopkins, 103 Pa. 118 (1883). See State ex rel. J. B. Speed & Co. v. Traylor, 98 Ind.App. 290, 173 N.E. 461 (1930); Motley v. Wickoff, 113 Mich. 231, 71 N.W. 520 (1897).

14. Ludington v. Bell, 77 N.Y. 138, 33 Am.Rep. 601 (1879); Hayward v. Burke, 151 Ill. 121, 37 N.E. 846 (1894), semble; Henry v. Seiberling Rubber Co., 265 Ky. 241, 96 S.W.2d 590 (1936), semble; Collyer & Co. v. Moulton, 9 R.I. 90, 98 Am.Dec. 370 (1868); Lyth

v. Ault, 7 Exch. 669 (1852); Restatement, Contracts §§ 427, 428.

15. U.P.A. § 41(1), Sec. 89 below. In re Hess, 1 F.2d 342 (E.D.Pa.1923).

16. Drake v. Hodgson, 118 Misc. 503, 194 N.Y.S. 874 (1922).

17. Chapin v. Brown, 4 Cal.Unrep.Cas. 300, 34 P. 525 (1893); Walker v. Wood, 170 Ill. 463, 48 N.E. 919 (1897).

18. Credit Bureaus of Merced County, Inc. v. Shipman, n. 90 above.

19. Hayward v. Burke, n. 14 above; Campbell v. Floyd, 153 Pa. 84, 25 A. 1033 (1893).

20. State ex rel. J. B. Speed & Co. v. Traylor, n. 13 above; Marshall Field & Co. v. Fishkin, 180 Wis. 149, 192 N. W. 463 (1923), not referring to U.P.A. § 36(3); Michelin Tire Co. v. Akers, 32 N.M. 234, 255 P. 388, 52 A.L.R. 494 (1927). In such cases there might have been a discharge by reason of altering the maturity of the obligation.

claim.[21] The creditor's knowledge of the changes is essential in holding him to an implied novation.[22]

(c) Assumption and Alteration

On retirement of a partner and sale of his interest in the partnership to his co-partners who continue the business, it is possible for the parties to agree who among them shall pay the creditors. It is natural that the continuing partner or partners, who take over the partnership property, should assume the burden, and that this should be taken into consideration in fixing the price paid to the retiring partner for his interest. If the agreement of dissolution is silent on the matter, it is presumed that the continuing partners assume the debts.[23] Thereafter, *inter se,* the assuming partners are principal debtors and the outgoing partner is surety.[24] Whether the creditor

---

21. Venable v. Stevens, 94 Ga. 281, 21 S.E. 516 (1894), retiring partner insisting that goods ordered before dissolution should not be received from carrier, until seller assented to take acceptance of new partnership on drafts drawn for the price; Hauge v. Bye, 51 N.D. 848, 201 N.W. 159, 36 A.L.R. 613 (1924); Saint Louis Perfection Tire Co. v. McKinney, 212 Mo. App. 355, 245 S.W. 1100 (1922).

22. U.P.A. § 36(2). See n. 28 below.

23. "The interest of a partner in the assets of a firm of which he is a member consists of his portion of the residue left after payment of the liabilities of the firm and the adjustment of their partnership claims against each other. . . . In determining the value of Benedict's interest, all the parties must have adopted this rule of law in determining that value. The sale operated as a dissolution of the partnership. The interest of Benedict in the assets was transferred to Cobb and Wilson. If nothing whatever was said on the subject of the discharge of the then existing liabilities of the firm, all must have contemplated, according to the statement of Cobb and Wilson, that they were to discharge such liabilities. They received the assets. From that source they were to discharge the liabilities. It was Benedict's interest in these assets after the debts were paid, which they purchased. Having assumed the entire control of the property of the firm, and agreed to pay Benedict a sum certain for what, in their judgment, his net interest was worth, it was, in

effect, an accounting between the members of the firm of partnership matters, from which it would naturally be inferred that the purchasing partners assumed the firm debts." Cobb v. Benedict, 27 Colo. 342, 62 P. 222 (1900). Accord: Pendleton v. Foley, 21 Ohio App. 118, 152 N.E. 778 (1925); State ex rel. J. B. Speed & Co. v. Traylor, 98 Ind.App. 290, 173 N.E. 461 (1930). See Kavanaugh v. Johnson, 290 Mass. 587, 195 N.E. 797 (1935) (where a partner takes over the assets and continues the business, proof of assumption of debts requires only slight evidence).

The creditor, as a third party beneficiary, can enforce the assumption contract. Byvesky v. Agins, 100 N.J.L. 75, 125 A. 574 (1924); Bellas v. Fagely, 19 Pa. 273 (1852).

Without assumption, an incoming partner is not personally liable. U.P.A. § 17, Sec. 88 below.

24. If the retired partner is compelled to pay, he is entitled to reimbursement, Robinson v. Roos, 138 Ill. 550, 28 N.E. 821 (1891); Price v. Parker, 197 Mass. 1, 83 N.E. 323, 125 Ann.St.Rep. 326 (1907); Nelson v. Century Indemnity Co., 65 F.2d 765 (9th Cir. 1933), subrogation to creditor's security.

The retired partner has a right of action for breach of the continuing partner's contract of assumption. Gillen v. Peters, 39 Kan. 489, 18 P. 613 (1888). Pursuant to his right of exoneration, the retired partner may compel the assuming incoming partner to pay by making him a party to a suit

who is notified of the arrangement becomes subject to the law of suretyship in his dealings with the principal debtor, the authorities are in conflict. It has been maintained that the creditors' rights are fixed by the original contract, and that they should not thereafter be altered without his consent. But the burden on the creditor is relatively slight, no more serious than to compel an obligor to recognize the effect of an assignment by his obligee.[25] U.P.A., § 36(3) has adopted the view supported by the majority of the decisions that the creditor with notice must be held to the same limitations as if the situation had existed from the outset. He is subject to the suretyship relation, so that alteration of the nature and time of payment, as between the creditor and the continuing partner, discharges the retired partner.[26] However, there is no relief if the continuing partners

brought against him by the creditor, under some procedural statutes. Carpenter v. Park, 19 Cal.App.2d 567, 66 P.2d 224 (1937).

25. Williston, Contracts, § 1258.

26. Lenger v. Hulst, 259 Mich. 640, 244 N.W. 187 (1932) (creditor taking renewal notes from continuing partners). Semble Heller v. Mattar, 135 F.Supp. 767 (W.D.Ark.1956).

McClatchy Newspapers v. Robertson, 68 Cal.App.2d 138, 155 P.2d 882 (1945); Associates Discount Corp. v. Greisinger, 103 F.Supp. 705 (W.D.Pa.1952) (refinancing agreement for bailment leases).

Cases giving the retired partner the benefit of a surety's position as against the creditor with notice who deals with the continuing partner— Faricy v. J. S. Brown Mercantile Co., 87 Colo. 427, 288 P. 639 (1930) (citing U.P.A. § 36(3), as persuasive evidence of the better rule, though the statute had not yet been adopted in Colorado); Hall v. Johnston, 6 Tex.Civ.App. 110, 24 S.W. 861 (1894), criticized in 8 Harv.L.Rev. 56; Preston v. Garrard, 120 Ga. 689, 48 S.E. 118, 102 Am.St. Rep. 124, 1 Ann.Cas. 724 (1904); Smith v. Shelden, 35 Mich. 42, 24 Am. Rep. 529 (1876); Millerd v. Thorn, 56 N.Y. 402 (1874); Johnson v. Jones, 39 Okl. 323, 135 P. 12, 48 L.R.A.,N.S., 547 (1913); Goldfarb v. Bartlett, [1920] 1 K.B. 629.

A creditor with knowledge of the dissolution and assumption of debts by continuing partners can only hold the retired partner to a secondary liability after exhausting his remedies against

the continuing partners. Stikeman v. Whitman, Requardt & Smith, 272 App. Div. 627, 75 N.Y.S.2d 73 (1947).

See notes, 9 L.R.A.,N.S., 49; 48 L.R.A., N.S., 547; 10 Colum.L.Rev. 550 (1910).

Cases holding that the creditor need not recognize a suretyship relation—National Cash Register Co. v. Brown, 19 Mont. 200, 47 P. 995, 37 L.R.A. 515, 61 Am.St.Rep. 498 (1897), release of attachment of property of insolvent continuing partner; Marshall Field & Co. v. Fishkin, 180 Wis. 149, 192 N.W. 463 (1923), taking of postdated checks from continuing partner, the court not noting the application to the situation of the Act.

A middle ground was adopted by White v. Brown, 110 U.S.App.D.C. 232, 292 F.2d 725 (1961) (pre-U.P.A.). The court accepted the retiring partner as a surety, but held him to the obligation of a commercial (rather than a gratuitous) one. The test, then, is whether he was harmed by the alteration of the obligation (here the acceptance of a series of notes for an open-account indebtedness for services). The case is noted 3 Bos.Coll.Comm. & Ind.L.Rev. 306 (1962) which sharply criticizes the U.P.A. rule.

In Clinchfield Fuel Co. v. W. M. Lundy & Son, 130 Tenn. 135, 169 S.W. 563, L.R.A.1915B, 418 (1914), a partnership had prior to dissolution contracted to purchase a quantity of coal. The retiring partner was held liable for the purchase price of coal delivered after notice to the seller of the dissolution and the assumption of firm liabilities by the continuing partner.

Though the estate of a deceased partner, who has guaranteed a partnership ob-

do not assume the obligations,[27] if the creditor is unaware of the change,[28] or if there is no material alteration.[29] The retired partner may also be entitled to other defenses incident to the law of suretyship, as against a creditor who is advised of the changed situation.[30]

ligation, is entitled to the status of a surety, an extension with reservation of rights against the surety does not operate as a discharge. See Negotiable Instruments Law, § 120; Uniform Commercial Code § 3–606. The withholding of a partnership note guaranteed by a partner, now deceased, as collateral for a new note given by the surviving partners who continue the business, operates as a reserving of rights against the deceased partner's estate. In re DeRoy's Estate, 305 Pa. 541, 157 A. 800 (1931).

See also First Nat. Bank of Anniston v. Cheney, 114 Ala. 536, 21 So. 1002 (1897); Stump v. Wilson, 100 W.Va. 227, 130 S.E. 463 (1925); In re Heller's Estate, 319 Pa. 135, 178 A. 681 (1935).

27. Kaydee Sales Corp. v. Feldman, 14 Misc.2d 793, 183 N.Y.S.2d 151 (Sup. Ct.1958).

28. Sorenson v. U. S., 226 F.2d 460 (9th Cir. 1955) (Calif. law); Marsh Wall Products, Inc. v. Henry Marcus Bldg. Specialties, 16 Cal.App.2d 371, 328 P.2d 259 (1958). The burden of proof is on the retiring partner. Cameron & Hawn v. La Porte, 216 App. Div. 579, 215 N.Y.S. 543 (1926).

Although U.P.A. § 36(3) speaks of "knowing" while § 36(2) refers to "knowledge", the terms are presumably equivalent and governed by § 3 which includes not only actual knowledge of the fact in question, but also knowledge of such other facts as in the circumstances shows bad faith. Notice, e. g., pursuant to § 35, does not ipso facto establish knowledge of the recipient although it goes a long way. The retiring partner who wants to play it safe will get some sort of acknowledgement of the notice, or talk directly to the creditor.

29. Kaydee Sales Corp. v. Feldman, n. 27 above (assignment of collateral to secure existing debt was not material alteration).

30. The mere forbearance to sue the continuing partner by the creditor does not discharge the retired partner.

Hall & Long v. Jones, 56 Ala. 493 (1876); McAreavy v. Magirl, 123 Iowa 605, 99 N.W. 193 (1904); Michelin Tire Co. v. Akers, 32 N.M. 234, 255 P. 388, 52 A.L.R. 494 (1927); Advance Rubber Co. v. Bershad, 125 Misc. 826, 211 N.Y. S. 574 (1925).

The creditor is not bound to exhaust his remedies against the continuing partner before bringing a joint action against the continuing and retired partners. Phillips v. Schlang, 139 App.Div. 930, 124 N.Y.S. 40 (1910), reversing Phillips v. Mendelsohn, 67 Misc. 142, 121 N.Y.S. 913 (1910), noted 10 Colum.L.Rev. 550 (1910).

In jurisdictions which adhere to the rule that a surety is released if on demand the creditor refuses to sue the principal, and the surety is damaged thereby (Arant, Suretyship, 315; Williston, Contracts, § 1236), a failure of the creditor to sue the continuing partner on demand of the retired partner may result in the latter's release, Colgrove v. Tallman, 67 N.Y. 95, 23 Am.Rep. 90 (1876); Advance Rubber Co. v. Bershad, supra, semble. But see Faricy v. J. S. Brown Mercantile Co., 87 Colo. 427, 288 P. 639 (1930), denying any effect to the surety partner's demand. The court said: "He had the legal right without the company's consent, to pay the debt and thereupon sue Davis. Or, without paying the debt and without the company's consent, Faricy had the right to bring suit to compel Davis to satisfy the debt due the company."

The retired partner in the position of surety should be entitled to a defense on the ground that the creditor has surrendered securities to the continuing partner. It is clear that the retired partner is entitled to the benefit of such security. Nelson v. Century Indemnity Co., 65 F.2d 765 (9th Cir. 1933).

Where the continuing partner incurs additional indebtedness to a firm creditor who is notified of the dissolution it may be the duty of the creditor to apply any payments made after the dissolution to the prior indebtedness

(d) Death

Death of a partner, who was a joint obligor, left the obligation a burden of the survivors only, at common law, and the decedent's estate was not liable.[31] Courts of equity provided a remedy against the decedent's estate in such situations as partnerships where the estate had been enriched by the consideration for the obligation, and owed a duty of contribution to the survivors.[32] By statute in most states, there is a remedy against the deceased partner's estate,[33] though in some states, this remedy is not available unless remedies against the survivors have been exhausted or are of no value.[34]

When partnership creditors proceed against the estate of the deceased partner, the "dual priorities" rule subordinates them to the claims of the individual creditors.[35]

EFFECT OF DISSOLUTION ON POWERS OF PARTNERS

§ 80. **Except so far as may be necessary to wind up partnership affairs or to complete transactions begun but not then finished, dissolution terminates all authority of any partner to act for the partnership,**

> (1) **With respect to the partners:**
>
>> (a) **When the dissolution is not by the act, bankruptcy or death of a partner; or**
>>
>> (b) **When the dissolution is by such act, bankruptcy or death of a partner, in cases where section 34 so requires.**
>
> (2) **With respect to persons not partners, as declared in section 35.**

U.P.A. § 33.

(a) In General

On the dissolution of a partnership, several needs arise: (1) the need to wind up the business and distribute its assets, unless it is to be continued by agreement, (2) the need to protect third persons who have done business with the partnership, e.g., in future transactions which appear to be part of a continuous course of dealing, and (3) the need to protect outgoing partners from new liabilities. There is some

---

which the continuing partner is under a duty to the retired partner to discharge. Texas Co. v. Genetski, 291 Mich 569, 289 N.W. 257 (1939). See also Restatement, Contracts, § 394, illus. 2.

31. "On the death of a joint promisor in a contract when one or more of the joint promisors are still surviving, the estate of the deceased promisor is not bound by the joint promise unless all of the surviving joint promisors are insolvent, nor in that event if the deceased promisor was a surety." Restatement, Contracts § 125; see Williston, Contracts, § 344 (3d ed. 1959);

Sec. 58(d) above; Note, Partnerships: Claim of Creditor at Death of Partner, 11 Okla.L.Rev. 229 (1958).

32. Williston, op. cit. § 344; 4 Corbin, Contracts, § 930 (1951).

33. U.P.A. § 36(4). Semble U.P.A. § 40 (g). See summary of statutes in Williston, op. cit. § 344A; Note, 11 Okla. L.Rev. 229 (1958).

34. See Sec. 58(d) above.

35. U.P.A. § 36(4). Semble § 40(h), (i), Sec. 90 below. See also Secs. 91, 91A below on dual priorities.

conflict among these needs, and their resolution necessarily requires compromises, depending sometimes on the specific cause of the dissolution. The results are quite intricate, perhaps unnecessarily so. The first need generates actual authority, discussed in this section. The second need generates apparent authority, discussed in the next section. The last need generates limitations on both kinds of authority, as well as rights to indemnification, discussed in the section after next.

If there is no authorization (by agreement or statute [36]) for continuation of the business, a partnership ceases to be a going concern on dissolution, and no new business should be undertaken. Unless expressly enlarged,[37] actual authority to charge the firm property and create personal liabilities of co-partners is confined to acts appropriate for winding up,[38] and does not extend to new business.[39]

(b) Executory Contracts

Since existing contracts are usually unaffected by dissolution,[40] there is authority to complete their performance in a usual way. A partnership contract to cut and haul timber is not of a personal nature, and may be completed by a partner after dissolution.[41] So may construction contracts.[42] A contract to buy securities may be completed by the usual method of pledging to one who lends the money necessary to pay the purchase price.[43] Performance of a

---

36. See Sec. 83A below.

37. Merchants' Bank v. Holland, 4 Hun. 420 (N.Y.Sup.Ct.1875) aff'd 66 N.Y. 648 (1876) (renewal of commercial paper); Annot., 60 A.L.R.2d 826, 832 (1958).

38. U.P.A. §§ 33, 35(1) (a), 35(3). Compare § 9. In general, see Annot., Powers of liquidating partner with respect to incurring of obligations, 60 A.L.R.2d 826 (1958).

39. Froess v. Froess, 284 Pa. 369, 131 A. 276 (1925); Id., 289 Pa. 69, 137 A. 124 (1927).

Day v. Wilson, n. 42 below (surviving partner who used partnership equipment to perform non-partnership contracts was surchargeable (by decedent's estate) for the fair rental value of the equipment); Credit Bureau v. Beach, 144 Cal.App.2d 439, 301 P.2d 87 (Dist.Ct.App.1956).

If the surviving partner in a professional partnership carries on business, taking new retainers which were only in prospect of the time of dissolution, the proceeds are his, and the estate of the deceased partner has no share in

them. Groves v. Aegerter, 226 Mo.App. 128, 42 S.W.2d 974 (1931).

See also George v. Richards, 361 Pa. 278, 64 A.2d 811 (1949), firm of construction engineers on whose services a coal company had an option. As the work required a high degree of skill, the contract was ended by death of a partner, and further work orders were solely for account of surviving partner.

40. U.P.A. § 36, Sec. 79 above.

41. W. D. Reeves Lumber Co. v. Davis, 124 Ark. 143, 187 S.W. 171 (1916).

42. Day v. Wilson, 286 F.2d 274 (10th Cir. 1961); Glassell v. Prentiss, 175 Cal.App.2d 599, 346 P.2d 895 (Dist.Ct. App.1959).

43. Butchart v. Dresser, 4 De G. M. & G. 542 (1853). See on completing contract of purchase, Asbestos Mfg. & Supply Co. v. Lennig-Rapple Engineering Co., 26 Cal.App. 177, 146 P. 188 (1914). Demand of payment of a partnership note is effectively made on one partner after dissolution. Gates v. Beecher, 60 N.Y. 518, 19 Am.Rep. 207 (1875).

contract to buy goods may be completed, although the agreement is oral and the defense of the statute of frauds might have been made.[44]

(c) Sales

Winding up involves reducing assets to cash to pay creditors and distribute to partners the value of their respective interests. A partner may sell partnership property, such as a judgment.[45] His authority is limited to the amount of the partnership stock, and a contract to sell more than the partnership has is not binding.[46] A partner may transfer property to a creditor by way of mortgage.[47]

While ordinarily sales are made for cash a partner liquidating firm assets which include mineral rights can dispose of them by executing a lease, that being a usual way of realization on such assets.[48]

(d) Debts

A partner may receive payment of obligations due to the partnership,[49] may compromise with firm debtors,[50] and release them.[51] If necessary for collection, a partner may cause suit to be brought in the names of the partners against a debtor.[52]

44. Lorborbaum v. Leviy, 228 Ill.App. 338 (1923).

45. Robbins v. Fuller, 24 N.Y. 570 (1862).

46. Bass Dry Goods Co. v. Granite City Mfg. Co., 116 Ga. 176, 42 S.E. 415 (1902). But see n. 56 below.

47. Amunategui v. Spokane Cattle Loan Co., 36 Idaho 688, 214 P. 211 (1923); Smith v. Dennison, 101 Ill. 531 (1882), liquidating partner; First Nat. Bank v. Parsons, 128 Ind. 147, 27 N.E. 486 (1891), surviving partner; Engelhard v. Schroeder, 92 N.J.Eq. 663, 116 A. 717, 21 A.L.R. 957 (1921); State Bank v. Bagley Bros., 44 Wyo. 303, 11 P.2d 590 (1932); In re Bourne [1906] 2 Ch. 427, surviving partner; 60 A.L.R.2d at 844.

48. Martin v. Dial, 57 S.W.2d 75, 89 A.L.R. 571 (Tex.Com.App.1933).

49. Heartt v. Walsh, 75 Ill. 200 (1874), misapplication by collecting partner does not affect the discharge given by him.

50. Hawn v. Seventy-Six Land & Water Co., 74 Cal. 418, 16 P. 196 (1887); De Mott v. Kendrick, 65 Hun. 623, 20 N.Y. S. 195 (1892).

51. Gordon v. Albert, 168 Mass. 150, 46 N.E. 423 (1897), partner, as joint obligee, may release his own interest, and in absence of fraud, that is effective as to the entire interests of the obligees. See Restatement, Contracts §§ 130, 131.

But see Atlas Assur. Co. Ltd. v. Cotter, 226 Ky. 554, 11 S.W.2d 427 (1928), holding that after dissolution a partner had no power to cancel an insurance policy on partnership property issued before dissolution. The partner who arranged the cancellation with the agent of the insurer did not have the policy, and as the agent knew he had sold out his interest to the continuing partner, this may be considered a fraudulent act.

52. Voss v. Arthurs, 129 Ark. 143, 195 S.W. 680 (1917); Sork v. C. Trevor Dunham, Inc., 107 Pa.Super. 77, 163 A. 315 (1932).

The right to sue for the enforcement of a partnership claim after dissolution is vested in the partnership, and not in a single partner or his assignee. Shapira v. Budish, 275 Mass. 120, 175 N.E. 159 (1931).

See also Peck v. Better Business Standards Ass'n, Inc., n. 72 below.

After dissolution the power of a partner to borrow money and obligate the partners to repay is normally not necessary and appropriate for winding up. But where as a result of the transaction, the partners are benefitted, (e.g. the money borrowed is applied in the reduction of firm indebtedness), the lender should be entitled to a remedy. It has been held that the lender to a surviving partner, who subsequently assigns the partnership property for the benefit of creditors, including the loan as a debt to be paid, is entitled to share in the distribution of the assigned estate, and the inclusion of his claim in the schedule of debts to be paid was not a fraud on the partnership creditors.[53] Where a liquidating partner borrows money, which he uses to pay firm debts, and gives the lender a note for the money, if the partners are not liable on the note, they are liable under the common count for money loaned.[54] In general, strictures on the partner's post-dissolution authority yield to the necessity for winding up. Thus, a partner may borrow to finance the completion of pending business or the performance of existing contracts,[55] and to augment inventory [56] or process raw material [57] to make it more saleable.

After dissolution, a partner has no power to appear for a copartner in an action brought against the partnership. Hall v. Lanning, 91 U.S. 160, 23 L.Ed. 271 (1875); Bowler v. Huston, 71 Va. (30 Grat.) 266, 32 Am.Rep. 673 (1878).

53. Durant v. Pierson, 124 N.Y. 444, 26 N.E. 1095, 12 L.R.A. 146, 21 Am.St.Rep. 686 (1891): "It appears to us that the conclusion is warranted from the authorities referred to that where a person in good faith loans money to a surviving partner, and where the money is faithfully applied by such partner in satisfaction of the liabilities of the firm, the claim becomes one which in equity should be paid out of the assets of the firm; and in an accounting between the survivor with the personal representatives of the deceased partner equity will recognize the right of the surviving partner to have the money so borrowed and applied by him repaid out of the assets of the firm, and an assignment so directing is not fraudulent."

A liquidating partner can pledge firm property to secure a loan made to him, the proceeds of which are applied to pay firm debts. Smith v. Dennison, 101 Ill. 531 (1882). See also n. 47 above.

A liquidating partner would ordinarily be entitled to contribution for advances made by him for the payment of partnership liabilities. But where the liability is not personal but merely a charge on partnership property, as where an assessment is levied on bank stock owned by the partnership, the right of a liquidating partner to pay the assessment and charge a share of it to his co-partner depends upon whether he acted reasonably in paying it rather than abandoning the bank stock. Jones v. Mitchell, 47 S.W.2d 371 (Tex.Civ.App.1932).

54. Steinbach v. Smith, 34 Cal.App. 223, 167 P. 189 (1917). But see Kilgour v. Finlyson, 1 H.Bl. 155, 126 Eng.Rep. 92 (1789), criticized in Keener, Quasi-Contracts, 116.

55. Whitesell v. Pioneer Const. Co., 2 S.W.2d 147 (Mo.App.1928); Feucht v. Corbett, 214 Ind. 103, 12 N.E.2d 957 (1938) criticized 13 Ind.L.J. 574 (1938).

56. Gardner v. Thrall, 107 Kan. 509, 192 P. 750 (1920); Big Four Implement Co. v. Keyser, 99 Kan. 8, 161 P. 592, L.R.A.1917C, 166 (1916); Watumull v. Ettinger, 39 Haw. 185 (1952).

57. Calvert v. Miller, 94 N.C. 600 (1886).

A partner is held, by the weight of authority, to have no authority after dissolution to make, renew, or endorse negotiable instruments.[58] He can transfer a negotiable instrument by endorsement without recourse.[59] Demand for payment of a partnership instrument, as well as notice of dishonor of an instrument to which the partnership is a party, is effective when made to a partner.[60]

A partner has the power to pay partnership creditors.[61] The usual effect of a partial payment by a debtor to a creditor is to toll the statute of limitations, i.e., the period of the statute begins anew as of the date of the payment. This is because a promise to pay the balance is implied from a part payment, and on that promise an action may be brought within the statutory period.[62] Whether such payment by a partner after dissolution tolls the statute as to any one but himself depends on whether it is considered that the making of a promise after dissolution to perform a partnership obligation is an appropriate incident in the process of winding up the affairs of the partnership. The prevailing view is that it is not, and the part payment affects the running of the statute only as regards the partner making the payment.[63] In a few states it is held that a payment by a

---

58. Hignite v. Nantz, 254 Ky. 214, 71 S.W.2d 442 (1934); Bank of Monroe v. E. C. Drew Inv. Co., 126 La. 1028, 53 So. 129, annotated in 32 L.R.A.,N.S., 255 (1910); Aetna Casualty & Surety Co. v. Wofford, 296 P.2d 967 (Okl. 1956). Marlett v. Jackman, 85 Mass. (3 Allen) 287 (1861); Potter v. Tolbert, 113 Mich. 486, 71 N.W. 849 (1897); First Nat. Bank of Antigo v. Larsen, 146 Wis. 653, 132 N.W. 610 (1911).

It has been held that authority to execute a renewal note is vested in a liquidating partner. Meyran v. Abel, 189 Pa. 215, 42 A. 122, 69 Am.St.Rep. 806 (1899). But see Palmer v. Dodge, 4 Ohio St. 21, 62 Am.Dec. 271 (1854).

See Note, 60 U.Pa.L.Rev. 338 (1912); Annot., 60 A.L.R.2d 826, 833–41 (1958).

As to a surviving partner, see In re Heller's Estate, 319 Pa. 135, 178 A. 681 (1935).

59. Yale v. Eames, 42 Mass. (1 Metc.) 486 (1840).

60. N.I.L. §§ 77, 99; Uniform Commercial Code §§ 3—504(3), 3—508(5); Kensington Nat. Bank v. Ware, 32 Pa. Super. 247 (1906).

61. Barnes v. Northern Trust Co., 169 Ill. 112, 48 N.E. 31 (1897). It is doubtful whether the partner has the power to compromise with creditors after dissolution. It has been held that an

agreement of a partner to indemnify a landlord against loss due to reentry and releasing of premises leased to the partnership is not binding on his co-partner. Locke v. Fahey, 288 Mass. 341, 193 N.E. 26 (1934). The court regarded the undertaking of the partner as new business, not appropriate for winding up.

62. As to the effect of part payments by a partner before dissolution, see Sec. 53 above.

63. Bell v. Morrison, 26 U.S. (1 Pet.) 351, 7 L.Ed. 174 (1828); Gates v. Fisk, 45 Mich. 522, 8 N.W. 558 (1881); Davis v. Poland, 92 Va. 225, 23 S.E. 292 (1895). This is especially so after the statute has run. See Mayberry v. Willoughby, 5 Neb. 368, 25 Am.Rep. 491 (1877).

The law of the forum was applied, notwithstanding a different rule as to the authority of the liquidating partner at the place where he made the new promise, in Kerper v. Wood, 48 Ohio St. 613, 29 N.E. 501, 15 L.R.A. 656 (1891). See Crane, Conflict of Laws under the Uniform Partnership Act and the Uniform Limited Partnership Act, 66 U.Pa.L.Rev. 310, 317 (1918).

A contrary result has been reached in many states, some holding that an acknowledgment or new promise be-

liquidating partner may operate as a new promise binding on the other partners.[64] It would be beneficial to the partnership to induce a creditor to forbear to take legal action, and that would be the expected result of a part payment; such forbearance would be conducive to an orderly and economical liquidation.

(e) Other Matters

Admissions of a partner, made to a partnership creditor in the course of discussing his claim, appear to be incident to winding up, assuming that there was a claim and that the partner was authorized to deal with the creditor in the matter. Many courts have held such admissions to be admissible in evidence as against co-partners, though not conclusively binding.[65] Other courts have held that admissions of one partner after dissolution, not actually authorized by co-partners, are not admissible against them.[66]

A partner has authority to engage an accountant to take inventory and audit partnership books.[67] He may take out fire insurance on

fore the statute has run is effective, Burr v. Williams, 20 Ark. 171 (1859); Parker v. Butterworth, 46 N.J.Law 244, 50 Am.Rep. 407 (1884); Clement v. Clement, 69 Wis. 599, 35 N.W. 17, 2 Am.St.Rep. 760 (1887); some that the new promise is effective as a partnership act even after the statute has run, Wheelock v. Doolittle, 18 Vt. 440, 46 Am.Dec. 163 (1846).

If the creditor does not know of the dissolution, the partner's acknowledgment and implied promise is binding on the partnership, Craig Bros. v. Ellsaesser & Henry, 113 Kan. 416, 215 P. 454 (1923); Vermont-People's Nat. Bank v. Parker, 269 Mass. 387, 169 N.E. 154 (1929); Pottash Bros. v. Burnet, 60 App.D.C. 167, 50 F.2d 317 (1931) (waiver of limitation on income tax assessment).

64. Jack v. McLanahan, 191 Pa. 631, 43 A. 356 (1899). The Pennsylvania rule is followed in First State Bank of Max v. Steinhaus, 61 N.D. 336, 237 N.W. 852 (1931). See Note, 31 Colum.L. Rev. 1370 (1931); 1 Williston, Contracts § 192 (3d ed. 1957).

65. Maxwell v. Massachusetts Title Ins. Co., 206 Mass. 197, 92 N.E. 42 (1910); Bell v. Porter, 261 Mich. 97, 246 N.W. 93 (1932).

Feigley v. Whitaker, 22 Ohio St. 606, 10 Am.Rep. 778 (1872):

"It cannot be disputed that the implied authority of a general partner to bind

his copartners to any new engagement, contract, or promise, although within the scope of the partnership business is absolutely revoked by the dissolution of the partnership. But it is nevertheless true, when not otherwise agreed upon, that an implied authority continues in each partner after the dissolution to act for himself and his copartners in the matter of winding up and adjusting the business of the firm; and while acting within the scope of such limited authority, we can see no reason why the several members of the firm should not be bound by the acts and admissions of each other, as in other cases of agency." Wilson & Griffith v. McCormick, 86 Va. 995, 11 S.E. 976 (1890); Wood v. Braddick, 1 Taunt. 104, 127 Eng.Rep. 771 (1818); Annot., 73 A.L.R. 447, 465–72 (1931).

66. Miller v. Neimerick, 19 Ill. 172 (1857); Mackintosh v. Kimball, 101 App.Div. 494, 92 N.Y.S. 132 (1905); Lieberman v. Dubin, 62 N.Y.S.2d 880 (Sup.Ct.1946); Hogg v. Orgill, 34 Pa. 344 (1859); Burdett v. Greer, 63 W. Va. 515, 60 S.E. 497, 15 L.R.A.,N.S., 1019, 129 Am.St.Rep. 1014, 15 Ann. Cas. 935 (1908), criticized in Note, 8 Colum.L.Rev. 481 (1908). See Annot. 73 A.L.R. 447, 459–65 (1931).

67. Lichenstein v. Murphree, 9 Ala.App. 108, 62 So. 444 (1913). There is no power to execute a guaranty of the correctness of partnership bills receivable on firm books, in the course of

partnership property,[68] and collect proceeds of life insurance payable to the partnership.[69] If he commits a tort in the course of winding up, it is a liability of the partnership.[70] Differences between the partners as to alternative courses of conduct in the course of winding up may be settled by the decision of the majority.[71]

Litigation of claims by and against the partnership is a part of winding up. A partner has the same authority over litigation after dissolution as before,[72] and can incur necessary legal expenses.[73]

The partners may appoint one or more of their number as liquidating or winding up partner or partners. If they publish the appointment, as in a notice of dissolution, third persons must deal only with the liquidating partner in matters having to do with winding up, and the authority of other partners is non-existent as to persons chargeable with knowledge of the appointment.[74]

assigning them to a purchaser, Wise v. Cobb, 135 Miss. 673, 100 So. 189 (1924).

68. Conrad v. Buck, 21 W.Va. 396 (1883).

69. Hutchinson v. Goceliak, 73 N.J.Super. 550, 180 A.2d 359 (1962).

70. Voss v. Arthurs, 129 Ark. 143, 195 S.W. 680 (1917), damages assessed against partners as plaintiffs in unsuccessful foreclosure suit instituted by partner; Powell v. Roberts, 116 Mo. App. 629, 92 S.W. 752 (1906), wrongful retention by law partner of funds collected under a retainer of partnership before dissolution, collection being after dissolution.

Compare Blanchard v. Farmers' State Bank, 158 Ga. 780, 124 S.E. 695 (1924), indicating that partnership property was not subject to liability for a tort committed after dissolution by surviving partner in dealing with property entrusted to the partnership.

71. Western Stage Co. v. Walker, 2 Iowa 504, 65 Am.Dec. 789 (1856).

72. See Sec. 57 above.

Leh v. General Petroleum Corp., 165 F. Supp. 933 (S.D.Cal.1959). Cheyenne

Oil Corp. v. Oil & Gas Ventures, Inc., 204 A.2d 743 (Del.1964) (general partner of limited partnership has authority to sue for pre-dissolution injury to partnership). But see Peck v. Better Business Standards Ass'n, Inc., 44 Wash.2d 804, 271 P.2d 697 (1954) holding that an ex-partner alone cannot bring suit on a partnership cause of action without showing an assignment of it from the partnership. Apparently the partnership had terminated as well as dissolved. See also n. 72 above. See Sec. 73, n. 21 above concerning service of process on a partnership after dissolution.

73. Magullion v. Magee, 241 Mass. 360, 135 N.E. 560 (1922) (to conserve property). Cahill v. Haff, 248 N.Y. 377, 162 N.E. 288 (1928). Murdock v. Murdock, 300 Pa. 280, 150 A. 599 (1930).

74. U.P.A. § 35(3) (c), quoted at beginning of Sec. 83 above; Hilton v. Vanderbilt, 82 N.Y. 591 (1880).

See also Singleton v. Moore, 262 F. 357 (2d Cir. 1919); Bank of Montreal v. Page, 98 Ill. 109 (1881).

ESTOPPEL TO DENY POWERS OF PARTNERS AFTER DISSOLUTION (APPARENT AUTHORITY)

§ 81.   (1) After dissolution a partner can bind the partnership except as provided in paragraph (3),

(a) By any act appropriate for winding up partnership affairs or completing transactions unfinished at dissolution;

(b) By any transaction which would bind the partnership if dissolution had not taken place, provided the other party to the transaction

(I) Had extended credit to the partnership prior to dissolution and had no knowledge or notice of the dissolution; or

(II) Though he had not so extended credit, had nevertheless known of the partnership prior to dissolution, and, having no knowledge or notice of dissolution, the fact of dissolution had not been advertised in a newspaper of general circulation in the place (or in each place if more than one) at which the partnership business was regularly carried on.

(2) The liability of a partner under paragraph (1b) shall be satisfied out of partnership assets alone when such partner had been prior to dissolution

(a) Unknown as a partner to the person with whom the contract is made; and

(b) So far unknown and inactive in partnership affairs that the business reputation of the partnership could not be said to have been in any degree due to his connection with it.

(3) The partnership is in no case bound by any act of a partner after dissolution,

(a) Where the partnership is dissolved because it is unlawful to carry on the business, unless the act is appropriate for winding up partnership affairs; or

(b) Where the partner has become bankrupt; or

(c) Where the partner has no authority to wind up partnership affairs; except by a transaction with one who

(I) Had extended credit to the partnership prior to dissolution and had no knowledge or notice of his want of authority; or

(II) Had not extended credit to the partnership prior to dissolution, and, having no knowledge or notice of his want of authority, the fact of his want of authority has not been advertised in the manner provided for advertising the fact of dissolution in paragraph (1bII).

(4) Nothing in this section shall affect the liability under section 16 of any person who after dissolution represents himself or consents to another representing him as a partner in a partnership engaged in carrying on business.   U.P.A. § 35.

The event of dissolution terminates the actual authority of a partner to act for the partnership (except for purposes of winding up [75]). But apparent authority or power to bind, within the scope of the partnership business, may continue as to persons subsequently dealing with him who previously knew of the partnership but do not know of its dissolution.[76] Although notice to such persons is not affirmatively required,[77] it is encouraged. Ostensibly, this is to protect the third persons, although they are already protected by the apparent authority. The main function of the notice is to protect the outgoing partner against new liabilities.[78]

(a) Type of Dissolution

Notice of dissolution is unnecessary where the third person knows of it or is legally presumed to know it. The U.P.A. does not require notice where the partnership is dissolved because it is unlawful to carry on the business.[79] It may be questioned whether this rule is a fair one, if the facts making the business illegal are not such that the third person should know them.[80] The only cases on the point so far decided are cases of dissolution caused by war, a fact of which every one engaged in business doubtless has knowledge, though it may be doubted whether an outsider should be charged with knowledge of the nationality of all the members of a partnership with which he is dealing.

It was formerly held that dissolution by reason of death of a partner was effective as to third persons regardless of lack of knowledge or notice; [81] but this is not so under the Act.[82] It was also unnecessary to give notice of dissolution by reason of the bankruptcy of a partner.[83] But notice in such cases is apparently necessary un-

---

75. U.P.A. §§ 35(1) (a), 33, Sec. 80 above.

76. U.P.A. §§ 35(1) (b), 9. § 35 and its relationship to § 16 are discussed critically in Painter, Partnership by Estoppel, 16 Vand.L.Rev. 327 (1963). Marsh Wall Products, Inc. v. Henry Marcus Building Specialties, 162 Cal. App.2d 371, 328 P.2d 259 (1958).

Accord: Restatement, Second, Agency §§ 124A–136.

77. At least one state has an express requirement of publication of dissolution. West's Ann.Cal.Corp.Code, § 15035.5.

78. Notice can also help relieve an outgoing partner of liability on an existing obligation. This occurs if it is assumed by a continuing partner, and the creditor knows and consents to a material alteration. U.P.A. § 36(3), Sec. 79(c) above.

79. U.P.A. § 35(3) (a). Even here, actual authority for winding up continues.

80. See the end of Sec. 21 above.

81. "As the fact of death was not in its nature private or confined within the knowledge of the members of the firm, the presumption is that third persons also had notice of it. They ought not to be held liable for omitting to give notice of that which others are supposed to know." Marlett v. Jackman, 85 Mass. (3 Allen) 287 (1861); Bass Dry Goods Co. v. Granite City Mfg. Co., 116 Ga. 176, 42 S.E. 415 (1902); National Union Bank of Maryland v. Hollingsworth, 135 N.C. 556, 47 S.E. 618 (1904).

82. U.P.A. § 35; Crane, The Uniform Partnership Act—A Criticism, 28 Harv. L.Rev. 762, 782 (1915); Note, 41 Harv. L.Rev. 650 (1928).

83. Eustis v. Bolles, 146 Mass. 413, 16 N.E. 286, 4 Am.St.Rep. 327 (1888).

der the U.P.A. However, where the third person after dissolution by bankruptcy deals with the bankrupt partner himself, he acquires no right against the other partners, since he is bound to know the status of the person with whom he is actually dealing.[84] No third person can be misled by the failure to give notice of dissolution, unless he was informed of the existence of the partnership prior to dissolution.[85]

(b) Prior Creditors

Persons who had extended credit to the partnership prior to dissolution are entitled to notice of the dissolution;[86] and if they have no notice or knowledge, are entitled to hold a retired partner for obligations incurred by continuing partners after the dissolution.[87] "Notice," as defined in the U.P.A.,[88] requires either a verbal statement to the party notified,[89] or actual delivery of the statement, and not

---

84. U.P.A. § 35(3) (b).

85. Simmel v. Wilson, 121 S.C. 358, 113 S.E. 487 (1922); Puritan Trust Co. v. Coffey, 180 Mass. 510, 62 N.E. 970 (1902); First International Bank of Portal, N. D. v. Brown, 130 Minn. 210, 153 N.W. 522 (1915); Thompson v. Harmon, 207 S.W. 909 (Tex.Com.App. 1919); Morris v. Brown, 115 Conn. 389, 162 A. 1 (1932).

86. The U.P.A. does not specify how recently the person must have extended credit in order to need notice. Obviously, a reasonable time is contemplated. One state has specified two years. Vernon's Ann.Civ.St. (Tex.) art. 6132(b), § 35(1) (b) and (3) (c) (1963).

87. U.P.A. § 35(1) (b) (I); see also § 35 (3) (c) (I).

Security State Bank of Benson v. Nelson, 171 Minn. 332, 214 N.W. 51 (1927); Epley v. Hiller, n. 89 below; Torvend v. Patterson, 136 Cal.App. 120, 28 P.2d 413 (1933); Schwartz Bros. & Co. v. Beacham, 157 Miss. 93, 127 So. 689 (1930).

Formal written notice is unnecessary where the former dealer through his agent has information orally communicated by a former partner. Miller v. Pfeiffer, 168 Ind. 219, 80 N.E. 409 (1907). In this case it was doubtful whether the person sued had ever been a partner, as distinguished from a partner by estoppel. Notice is as necessary to terminate the effect of the estoppel as where a real partnership existed.

Newspaper publication, not read by the former dealer, is insufficient, Lyon v. Johnson, 28 Conn. 1 (1859); Crowley Trust & Savings Bank v. Hollier, 161 La. 1079, 109 So. 907 (1926).

Recording of a conveyance by retiring partner of an interest to continuing partner is not notice. American Wholesale Corp. v. Cooper, 194 N.C. 557, 140 S.E. 210 (1927); Bluff City Lumber Co. v. Bank of Clarksville, 95 Ark. 1, 128 S.W. 58 (1910).

Registration of a taxicab in his own name by a retired partner who continued the business in the old firm name and bought tires from a dealer who attached them to the cabs, is not notice of dissolution. Johnson Tire Co. v. Maddux, 188 Tenn. 626, 221 S. W.2d 948 (1940).

For corporations, requirements of notice of dissolution vary widely. See, e. g., Model Business Corp. Act § 80(a) (actual notice to each creditor); 8 Del.Code § 275(a), (b) (newspaper notices).

88. U.P.A. § 3.

89. U.P.A. § 3(2) (a). There are obvious difficulties in relying on verbal notice, and the partner denying liability may not be able to meet his burden of proof that notice was given, Epley v. Hiller, 128 Cal.App.2d 100, 274 P.2d 696 (1954), or when it was given, Kaydee Sales Corp. v. Feldman, 14 Misc.2d 793, 183 N.Y.S.2d 151 (Sup.Ct.1959).

merely a reasonable effort to make delivery.[90]   The notice is effective if given to an agent of the creditor whose duty it is to deliver it.[91] The U.P.A. requires actual notice only to persons who have extended credit in previous dealings with the partnership.   Only such persons are likely to have their names and addresses recorded on the partnership books.[92]   The liability extends to torts committed by the continuing partners or their employees, if the plaintiff can be found to have been exposed to the risk of injury in reliance upon the retired partner.[93]

Where the members of a partnership form a corporation, knowledge by former dealers with the partners of the incorporation is not necessarily knowledge of dissolution of the partnership.[94]

90.   The burden of proving that notice has been given is not satisfied by evidence that a postal card containing the information was prepared for mailing.   Reading Braid Co. v. Stewart, 19 Misc. 431, 43 N.Y.S. 1129 (1897).

Evidence that notice was mailed is not conclusive when its receipt is denied, Poage Milling Co. v. Joseph Howard & Co., 227 Ky. 353, 13 S.W.2d 266 (1929); Austin v. Holland, 69 N.Y. 571, 25 Am. Rep. 246 (1877); Meyer v. Krohn, 114 Ill. 574, 2 N.E. 495 (1885); Reid-Murdock & Co. v. Model Meat & Grocery Co., 204 Ky. 795, 265 S.W. 322 (1924).

91.   Haines v. Starkey, 82 Minn. 230, 84 N.W. 910 (1901), semble; Hurst Boillin Co. v. Jones, 152 Tenn. 535, 279 S.W. 392, 43 A.L.R. 742 (1926); Williams v. Penick-Hughes Co., 36 S.W.2d 1060 (Tex.Civ.App.1931); Jenkins Bros. Shoe Co. v. G. V. Renfrow & Co., 151 N.C. 323, 66 S.E. 212, 25 L.R.A.,N.S. 231 (1909).

In Haines v. Starkey, supra, plaintiffs made a sale after dissolution as undisclosed principals through an agent who had previously dealt with defendants in behalf of other principals, and who had no notice of the dissolution. Held: plaintiffs were entitled to notice; having none, they could recover.

92.   Austin v. Holland, 69 N.Y. 571, 25 Am.Rep. 246 (1877), employee of partnership; Lyon v. Johnson, 28 Conn. 1 (1859), single sale of goods; Rose v. Coffield, 53 Md. 18, 36 Am.Rep. 389 (1879), holder of note given before dissolution took a check after dissolution; Thayer v. Goss, 91 Wis. 90, 64 N.W. 312 (1895), single loan of money.

One who deals with the partnership for the first time after dissolution, with-

out notice, is included with prior dealers, as to future dealings. Amidown v. Osgood, 24 Vt. 278, 58 Am. Dec. 171 (1852).

Persons who have merely purchased goods from the partnership before dissolution are not included.   Askew v. Silman, 95 Ga. 678, 22 S.E. 573 (1895).

The fact that a bank has discounted notes of a partnership for the payee does not constitute it a prior dealer so as to be entitled to actual notice, but it is entitled to enforce notes made after dissolution if no publication thereof was made.   Vernon v. Manhattan Co., 22 Wend. 183, 195 (1839); City Bank of Brooklyn v. McChesney, 20 N.Y. 240 (1859); Hutchins v. Bank of State, 27 Tenn. (8 Humph.) 418 (1847); Rocky Mountain Nat. Bank v. McCaskill, 16 Colo. 408, 26 P. 821 (1891).

93.   Jewison v. Dieudonne, 127 Minn. 163, 149 N.W. 20 (1914), plaintiff, a former customer, came upon premises on business and was injured by negligent act of employee; Middleton v. Frances, 257 Ky. 42, 77 S.W.2d 425 (1934), patron of taxi company.

94.   Letellier-Phillips Paper Co. v. Fiedler, 32 Tenn.App. 137, 222 S.W.2d 42 (1949), approves a charge to the jury, in part as follows: "The Chancellor then charged fully and correctly that the important thing was whether the complainant had notice or knowledge of the dissolution of the partnership. That mere notice or knowledge of the formation of the corporation standing alone is immaterial because there is no inconsistency in the continued existence of the partnership alongside the newly created corporation.   That

(c) Others With Knowledge

As to persons who have not had dealings with the partnership prior to dissolution, but who have known of its existence and do not know of its dissolution, liability is imposed upon the partners for contracts thereafter made unless notice of dissolution is published in newspapers.[95] A person claiming on the basis of lack of publication must show that he knew of the partnership prior to dissolution.[96] If the third person has knowledge of the dissolution, though no publication

the creation and existence of the corporation were important and material only when it should further appear that it had become known to complainant that such corporation had taken over the business formerly operated by the partnership and had supplanted the latter."

As to incorporation of partnership, see Mulkey v. Anglin, 166 Okl. 8, 25 P.2d 778, 89 A.L.R. 980 (1933), noted 8 Temple L.Q. 551.

95. U.P.A. § 35(1) (b) (II); see also § 35(3) (c) (II).

Citizens' Nat. Bank of Corry v. Weston, 162 N.Y. 113, 56 N.E. 494 (1900), "The great weight of authority in this state is to the effect that the only safe rule, in order to make the general notice of dissolution legally effective, is to seasonably publish it in one or more of the newspapers in the immediate vicinity." It was also held that notice to commercial agencies was insufficient. See, also, as to notice to agencies, Bank of Monongahela Valley v. Weston, 159 N.Y. 201, 54 N.E. 40, 45 L.R.A. 547 (1899).

The paper must be one of general circulation, and the notice must be published more than once. Ellison v. Sexton, 105 N.C. 356, 11 S.E. 180, 18 Am.St.Rep. 907 (1890).

The U.P.A. requires newspaper publication, as to those who have no actual knowledge. Prior to the Act many decisions were rendered in which other methods of giving the fact notoriety, though not coming to the knowledge of the third person, were held to be sufficient: Lovejoy v. Spafford, 93 U.S. 430, 440, 442, 23 L.Ed. 851 (1876); Askew v. Silman, 95 Ga. 678, 22 S.E. 573 (1895).

Recording of a bill of sale, whereby one partner sells out his interest to the other partner, is not sufficient as public notice. Braun v. Bellini, 203 N.Y.S. 109 (Sup.1924).

"Ordinarily a change from a partnership to a corporation is attended with such change of name and frequently with such other changes as not to require personal notice of such change. Where, as in the present case, there is no change of name or place of business or other change which might reasonably be presumed to impart notice, some kind of notice reasonably adapted for that purpose ought to be given. The question whether personal notice is reasonably required must be determined from the circumstances of each case." Overlock v. Hazzard, 12 Ariz. 142, 100 P. 447 (1909). See Mulkey v. Anglin, 166 Okl. 8, 25 P.2d 778, 89 A.L.R. 980 (1933), noted 8 Temple L.Q. 551; Adkins v. Hash, 190 Va. 86, 56 S.E.2d 60 (1949).

Notice to an agent of the third person, whose duty it is to convey it to the principal, is sufficient: Hendley & Co. v. Bittinger, 249 Pa. 193, 94 A. 831, L.R.A.1915F, 711 (1915), semble; Westinghouse Electric & Mfg. Co. v. Hubert, 175 Mich. 568, 141 N.W. 600, Ann.Cas.1915A, 1099 (1913); Union Nat. Bank v. Dean, 154 App.Div. 869, 139 N.Y.S. 835 (1913).

In Pennsylvania advertisement must also be published in the legal periodical designated by rule of court in the place or places of business of the partnership. 59 P.S. (Pa.) § 97(1) (b) (II) (1964).

In general there is no express requirement of publication, only a potential liability for later debts. But see n. 77 above.

96. U.P.A. § 35(1) (b) (II); see also § 35(3) (c) (II), Vogler v. Ingrao, 123 Cal.App.2d 341, 266 P.2d 826 (1954).

was made, he cannot hold retired partners. Evidence of knowledge may be found in general notoriety in the community.[97]

On retirement of a dormant partner, i.e. secret and inactive, no notice is necessary to terminate the power of continuing partners to bind him personally, for there is no basis for estoppel.[98] But if a third person knew of his membership in the partnership, though his connection is generally unknown, notice must be given to that person.[99]

After dissolution, as before, one can make himself liable for the acts of another by representing that the other person is his partner, or by allowing someone else to do so.[1]

RIGHT TO CONTRIBUTION FOR LIABILITIES INCURRED AFTER DISSOLUTION

§ 82. Where the dissolution is caused by the act, death, or bankruptcy of a partner, each partner is liable to his co-partners for his

---

97. Bush & Hattaway v. W. A. McCarty Co., 127 Ga. 308, 56 S.E. 430, 9 Ann. Cas. 240 (1907).

98. U.P.A. § 35(2). However, he is bound to the extent of his interest in partnership assets. Ibid. See Van Andel v. Smith, 248 F.2d 915 (10th Cir. 1957).

Grosvenor v. Lloyd, 42 Mass. (1 Metc.) 19 (1840); Nussbaumer v. Becker, 87 Ill. 281, 29 Am.Rep. 53 (1877); Hornaday v. Cowgill, 54 Ind.App. 631, 101 N.E. 1030 (1913); Warner v. Modano, 340 Mass. 439, 164 N.E.2d 904 (1960) citing this text; Kelley v. Hurlburt, (5 Cow.) 534 (1826); Baptist Book Concern v. Carswell, 46 S.W. 858 (Tex. Civ.App.1898); In re Stoddard Bros. Lumber Co., 169 F. 190 (D. Idaho 1909); Crane, The Uniform Partnership Act—A Criticism, 28 Harv.L.Rev. 762, 783 (1915); Lewis, The Uniform Partnership Act—A Reply to Mr. Crane's Criticism, 29 Harv.L.Rev. 158, 291, 311 (1916).

It has been held that persons doing business under an artificial name are not dormant partners, Clark v. Fletcher, 96 Pa. 416 (1880); Rowland v. Estes, 190 Pa. 111, 42 A. 528 (1893), "T. W. Estes & Company"; Elmira Iron & Steel Rolling-Mill Co. v. Harris, 124 N.Y. 280, 26 N.E. 541 (1891), "Blood & Co.," but here defendant was not entirely inactive, and his membership was known to some persons. But compare Hornaday v. Cowgill; Gros-

venor v. Lloyd, supra; Warren v. Ball, 37 Ill. 76 (1865).

If active, though unknown to the third persons, the retiring partner must give notice. Elkinton v. Booth, 143 Mass. 479, 10 N.E. 460 (1887).

99. Milmo Nat. Bank v. Bergstrom, 1 Tex.Civ.App. 151, 20 S.W. 836 (1892); Benjamin v. Covert, 47 Wis. 375, 2 N.W. 625 (1879). It may be questioned whether there can be a dormant partner in a partnership which has registered the names of all its members under a Fictitious Names Act. See Fisher v. Colorado Central Power Co., 94 Colo. 218, 29 P.2d 641 (1934).

On the subject of notice of dissolution in general, see Notes, 13 Colum.L.Rev. 423 (1913); 60 U.Pa.L.Rev. 338 (1912); 8 Temple L.Q. 551 (1934).

1. U.P.A. §§ 35(4), 16, sec. 36 above.

See also U.P.A. § 41(10): "The use by the person or partnership continuing the business of the partnership name, or the name of a deceased partner as part thereof, shall not of itself make the individual property of the deceased partner liable for any debts contracted by such person or partnership." The implication is that a retiring partner is liable if his name continues to be used. See U.P.A. § 16 above. Compare U.L.P.A. § 5 permitting a general partner's name to remain in the firm name, without liability, if he becomes a limited partner.

share of any liability created by any partner acting for the partnership as if the partnership had not been dissolved unless

> (a) The dissolution being by act of any partner, the partner acting for the partnership had knowledge of the dissolution; or

> (b) The dissolution being by the death or bankruptcy of a partner, the partner acting for the partnership, had knowledge or notice of the death or bankruptcy. U.P.A. § 34.

An agent or partner is entitled to contribution or indemnification for expenses incurred in the normal course of the business.[2] After dissolution, this right continues for prior transactions but is modified for later ones. In essence, a partner retains contribution rights for later transactions within his actual authority, i.e. those for winding up.[3] But for later transactions outside his actual authority, though within his apparent authority or power to bind the firm, his contribution right depends on additional factors discussed below.

Under the older agency rule, an agent who acts after termination of his authority, though without knowledge or notice thereof, is not entitled to indemnity, in the absence of agreement to that effect.[4] The Commissioners on Uniform State Laws felt that the rule for partners should be otherwise, and have so provided in the section above quoted.[5]

Several situations may arise. The third person dealing with a partner after dissolution may or may not have knowledge or notice thereof. If not, he has an obligation of the partnership under Section 35 of the U.P.A.[6] if he was a prior creditor.[7] The duty of contribution to meet the obligation so created should normally rest on each of the partners, as in the case of any other firm obligation. However, if the acting partner has knowledge or notice of the dissolution, the ultimate burden of an obligation which he has a power, but not a privilege, to create, should rest on him. Section 34 in effect states that a partner has a privilege to act (and therefore a right to contribution) when he is ignorant of a dissolution caused by act of a partner, death, or bankruptcy of a partner. But the acting partner has no privilege to act if he is possessed of knowledge of dissolution by the act of a partner, or notice or knowledge of dissolution by death or bankruptcy. In these cases, although he still has power to bind the partnership, the responsibility should ultimately be his. Accordingly, the right of

---

2. U.P.A. § 18(b), Sec. 65(b) above. Restatement, Second, Agency §§ 438–39.

3. This is the significance of the language "as if the partnership had not been dissolved" in U.P.A. § 34; see also §§ 9(1), 33, 35(1) (a) describing actual authority.

4. Restatement, Second, Agency § 451, comment c.

5. Commissioners' Notes to U.P.A. § 34, 7 Unif. Laws Ann. 190–92 (1949).

6. See Sec. 81(b) above.

7. An obligation may also arise to other third persons if notice is not published. See Sec. 81(c) above.

contribution exists against him and in favor of the innocent partners.

If the third person dealing with a partner after dissolution has the knowledge or notice of the dissolution, but the acting partner does not, and the transaction is not within the scope of the winding up of the partnership, it seems that, in the absence of fraud by the third person, the transaction would create an obligation on the part of the acting partner. In such a case it should follow, under section 34, that the innocent acting partner may call upon his co-partners for contribution.

In the third party has not previously heard of the partnership, he is not entitled to notice; and if he is now, after dissolution, dealing with a partner for the first time, he does not obtain a partnership obligation but at least he obtains the obligation of the acting partner. If the latter was acting innocently, under this section he would be entitled to contribution.

It should be noted that a distinction between dissolution by act of a partner, and dissolution by death or bankruptcy, is made as to the existence of a privilege of a partner to act for the firm and the accompanying right to indemnity. In the former case, the privilege exists when the acting partner has no knowledge of the fact; in the latter, when he has neither knowledge nor notice. Knowledge and notice are defined in the preliminary sections of the Uniform Act,[8] and the terms as used in section 34 should be so understood.

The post-dissolution contribution provision of U.P.A. does not take into account all forms of dissolution. Ignored are dissolution by termination of the term or undertaking, illegality of the business, all of the judicial causes, and perhaps some others. It is doubtful that the draftsmen intended to deny contribution rights in all these instances. Rights should be recognized by analogy to the cases which are covered. In any event, it seems clear that contribution rights exist, regardless of the cause of dissolution, for transactions properly incident to winding up.[9]

RIGHT TO WIND UP

§ 83. Unless otherwise agreed, the partners who have not wrongfully dissolved the partnership, or the legal representative of the last surviving partner, not bankrupt, has the right to wind up the partnership affairs; provided, however, that any partner, his legal representative, or his assignee, upon cause shown, may obtain winding up by the court. U.P.A. § 37.

Compensation to a partner for winding up is allowed only by agreement or where he is the survivor after death.

---

8. See U.P.A. § 3.

9. One exception may be a wrongfully dissolving partner who is specifically

denied authority to wind up. U.P.A. § 37, Sec. 83 below.

(a) After Death

At common law the surviving partner succeeds to the title to partnership property and has the right and duty to wind up the partnership affairs.[10] In some states a desire to provide full protection to the interests of those entitled to share in the estate of the deceased partner has led to statutory provisions for winding up by the representative of the deceased partner; but whether by him or by the surviving partner, the process may be under the control of a probate court, or the estate of the deceased partner protected by a bond with satisfactory security or surety.[11]

The surviving partner, at common law, has the right to continue to administer the partnership affairs so long as he acts honestly and with due diligence.[12] On the death of the last surviving partner, the

---

10. In re McCormick's Estate, 286 Ill. App. 90, 2 N.E.2d 967 (1936); Tennant v. Dunlop, 97 Va. 234, 33 S.E. 620 (1899). A similar result is produced by U.P.A. § 25(2) (d), Sec. 45 above. However, it is phrased in terms of the deceased partner's rights in partnership property (rather than his title to or interest in it) vesting in the survivor.

11. The statutory provisions and their effect are discussed in Ickes v. Gazzam, 65 App.D.C. 346, 83 F.2d 603 (1936), holding that the surviving partner of a partnership of the state of Washington could not continue an action instituted by the partnership before the death of his co-partner without being appointed administrator of the partnership by the proper probate court.

Tannenbaum v. Rosenbaum, 141 N.Y.S. 2d 708 (Sup.Ct.1955) (under N.Y.Partnership Law § 75). See Dow v. Simpson, 17 N.M. 357, 132 P. 568 (1912); Simon v. Levy, 114 Wash. 556, 195 P. 1025 (1921).

Compare McCaughan v. Brown, 76 Miss. 496, 25 So. 155 (1898); Goodson v. Goodson, 140 Mo. 206, 41 S.W. 737 (1897); Gardner Hotel Co. v. Hagaman, 47 N.D. 434, 182 N.W. 685 (1921); Thomas v. Mann, 22 Wyo. 99, 135 P. 1088 (1913); Davis v. Hutchinson, 36 F.2d 309 (9th Cir.1929).

In Ohio complete jurisdiction over the winding up of a partnership dissolved by death is in the probate court in which the estate of the deceased partner is administered. Nahas v. George, 85 Ohio App. 328, 88 N.E.2d 429 (1949). In North Carolina the surviving part-

ner is required to post a bond for the protection of the estate of the deceased partner, and file an inventory of partnership assets. In re Johnson's Estate, 232 N.C. 59, 59 S.E.2d 223 (1950).

In re Kohn's Estate, 26 Misc.2d 659, 116 N.Y.S.2d 167 (1952) aff'd 282 App.Div. 1045, 126 N.Y.S.2d 897 (1953) illustrates the conflict between a surviving joint venturer and the personal representative of the co-venturer. The survivor prevails with respect to further winding up, but the personal representative is free from liability for actions taken with the property prior to the determination that it belonged to the venture. See also Ellis v. Ellis, 415 Pa. 412, 203 A.2d 547 (1964), recognizing the jurisdiction of the general court (Common Pleas) over the winding up of the partnership; when this is completed, and the accounting and payment are made to the estate, the estate then acquires an asset within the jurisdiction of the probate (Orphans') court.

One state has resolved its conflicting statutes by an amendment specifying that the probate provisions (for control by the executor or administrator) shall apply, notwithstanding conflict with the U.P.A. A.C.L.A.Supp. (Alaska) § 13.20.325.

12. Hewitt v. Hayes, 204 Mass. 586, 90 N.E. 985, 27 L.R.A.,N.S. 154 (1910); Comstock v. McDonald, 113 Mich. 626, 71 N.W. 1087 (1897); Thompson v. Flynn, 102 Mont. 446, 58 P.2d 769 (1936).

Absent contrary statutes, an action by the representative of a deceased partner for an accounting by the surviving

right to take over partnership property and to finish winding up passes to his representative.[13] If the surviving partner is not acting diligently and in good faith, the court may, on petition of the representative of the deceased partner's estate, appoint a receiver.[14] The U.P.A. substantially codifies all the rules stated in this paragraph, as well as the duty of a surviving partner to wind up and account for the interest of the decedent.[15]

Under the U.P.A., title to partnership real estate remains in the partnership. The decedent's limited rights in it pass to the surviving partner,[16] so that he can convey in the course of liquidation, without joinder of the decedent's heirs or representatives.[17] Under the common law prior to the Uniform Act, the share in the legal title held by a partner would descend to his heirs, and it would be necessary for them to convey (which a court of equity would compel them to do) if necessary to make payments to creditors.[18]

The power of the surviving partner to convey a good record legal title would exist as to real estate which stood in the firm name, or in the names of all the partners. As to real estate in the name of the deceased partner alone, or in a third person in trust for the firm, the surviving partner could convey the equitable title, but would probably need to have the record owner (or his heirs, if he were the deceased) execute a deed if demanded by a purchaser. A purchase would be well-advised so to demand.

partner should be brought in a court of general equity jurisdiction and not in a probate court. See In re Kalik's Estate, 178 Misc. 607, 35 N.Y.S.2d 16 (1942), noted 28 Cornell L.Q. 223 (1943).

13. Churchill v. Buck, 102 F. 38 (8th Cir. 1900). If there are conflicting interests between the representatives of the deceased partners, a court may appoint a receiver. Blumer Brewing Corp. v. Mayer, 223 Wis. 540, 269 N. W. 693, 111 A.L.R. 1087 (1936).

14. Ekberg v. Lancaster, 105 Neb. 510, 181 N.W. 160 (1920); Mosher v. Lount, 29 Ariz. 267, 240 P. 1027 (1925); Jay v. Clark, 85 Cal.App.2d 88, 192 P.2d 462 (1948).

Such judicial action, whether common law or statutory, is discretionary and will be taken only when some purpose will be served thereby. Yanakeff v. George, 207 Ind. 703, 194 N.E. 329 (1935).

Judicial winding up of corporations is similarly available. See Model Business Corp. Act § 80(c).

15. U.P.A. § 37. Englestein v. Mackie, 35 Ill.App.2d 276, 182 N.E.2d 351

(1962); Hutchinson v. Goceliak, 73 N. J.Super. 550, 180 A.2d 359 (1962); Ewing v. Caldwell, 243 N.C. 18, 89 S.E. 2d 774 (1955); Spivak v. Bronstein, 367 Pa. 70, 79 A.2d 205 (1951); Hume v. Ricketts, 69 Wyo. 222, 240 P.2d 881 (1952).

The right to wind up is in the surviving partners even though their interests have been sold under foreclosure of charging orders. Beckley v. Speaks, 39 Misc.2d 241, 240 N.Y.S.2d 553 (1963) aff'd 21 App.Div.2d 759, 251 N.Y.S.2d 1015 (1964), app. dism. 15 N.Y.2d 546, 202 N.E.2d 906, 251 N.Y.S.2d 1029, 254 N.Y.S.2d 362 (1964).

16. U.P.A. § 25(2) (d). Ellis v. Ellis, 415 Pa. 412, 203 A.2d 547 (1964).

17. Wharf v. Wharf, 306 Ill. 79, 137 N. E. 446 (1922); Davis v. Hutchinson, 36 F.2d 309 (9th Cir.1929).

18. Shanks v. Klein, 104 U.S. 18, 26 L. Ed. 635 (1881); Bonner v. Coburn, 163 Ark. 274, 260 S.W. 28 (1924); Dyer v. Clark, 46 Mass. (5 Metc.) 562, 39 Am. Dec. 697 (1843); Delmonico v. Guillaume, 2 Sandf.Ch. 366 (N.Y.1845).

Title to personalty of the firm stays in the firm, and is subject to control by the surviving partner.[19] He is the proper party plaintiff to sue for the enforcement of partnership claims.[20]

By agreement, the partners may designate someone else to wind up.[21] And in any situation, for good cause, judicially-supervised winding up may be had.[22]

(b) After Other Dissolution

Where a partnership is ended by agreement, or by expiration of its agreed term, the right to wind up is vested in all the partners.[23] They may agree that one or more of their number shall act as liquidating partner thereby vesting in him exclusively their powers, save as to transactions with third persons without notice.[24] His status has been compared to that of a surviving partner.[25]

If the partners cannot agree as to who shall wind up, and the articles make no provision for such a situation, the court may appoint a receiver.[26]

19. Barry v. Briggs, 22 Mich. 201 (1871); Gratwick v. Smith, 202 App.Div. 600, 195 N.Y.S. 568 (1922).

20. Goode v. Weaver, 214 Ala. 333, 107 So. 861 (1926), account by agent; Rosenberg v. J. C. Penney Co., 30 Cal.App. 2d 609, 86 P.2d 696 (1939), action for libel committed before dissolution by death of a partner; Friesen v. Hiatt, 129 Kan. 470, 283 P. 644 (1930); Poy v. Allan, 247 Mich. 385, 225 N.W. 532 (1929).

An administratrix of a deceased partner has no right to sue for an accounting from a corporation with which the firm had entered into a joint venture. The right vests solely in the surviving partner. Silberfeld v. Swiss Bank Corp., 273 App.Div. 686, 79 N.Y.S.2d 380 (1948), aff'd 298 N.Y. 776, 83 N.E. 2d 468 (1948).

Hayden v. Hayden, 354 Pa. 11, 46 A.2d 502 (1946); Hawkins v. Capron, 17 R. I. 679, 24 A. 466 (1892); Thomas v. Mann, 22 Wyo. 99, 135 P. 1088 (1913).

21. U.P.A. § 37. Smith v. Wayman, 148 Tex. 318, 224 S.W.2d 211 (1949) (trustees) (pre-U.P.A.).

22. U.P.A. § 37. This usually means a receivership.

A request for a disinterested person is not sufficient ground for appointment of a receiver. Orem v. Moore, 224 Ark. 146, 272 S.W.2d 60 (1954).

See also Straus v. Straus, 254 Minn. 234, 94 N.W.2d 679 (1959) (denying receivership and permitting continuation of the business by the partners other than the one who caused the dissolution; the court notes the expense and damage to a business caused by receivership).

23. Smith v. Hovland, 11 F.2d 9 (9th Cir.1926); Bennett v. Buchan, 61 N.Y. 222 (1874).

24. Singleton v. Moore, 262 F. 357 (2d Cir.1919); Hilton v. Vanderbilt, 82 N. Y. 591 (1880).

If the designated liquidator dies, the authority to wind up reverts to the surviving partners. No one of them loses his authority by transferring his interest in the firm to someone else, nor does the latter acquire the authority by the transfer. Weidlich v. Weidlich, 151 Conn. 471, 199 A.2d 336 (1964).

25. Adams v. Carmony, 44 Ind.App. 291, 87 N.E. 708, 89 N.E. 327 (1909).

26. McKinley v. Long, 227 Ind. 639, 88 N.E.2d 382 (1940) (pre-U.P.A.).

U.P.A. § 37. See n. 22 above and Annot., 23 A.L.R.2d 583 (1952). See also Note, Receivers—Appointment on Dissolution of Partnership Other Than by Death, 8 S.C.L.Q. 473 (1956).

If dissolution is by bankruptcy of a partner,[27] the power to wind up is vested in the non-bankrupt partner,[28] though he may consent to liquidation by the other partner's trustee in bankruptcy. If dissolution results from bankruptcy of the partnership, winding up is by its trustee in bankruptcy.[29]

For obvious reasons, a wrongfully dissolving partner is expressly denied authority to wind up.[30]

(c) Compensation for Winding Up

In the absence of statute, it has generally been held that the surviving partner is not entitled to compensation for his services in winding up.[31] But in exceptional cases, compensation has been allowed.[32] In professional partnerships, special circumstances may exist. Since the client has the power to terminate a retainer calling for personal services, some courts have held that the survivor need not account for earnings under a re-employment.[33] But if the contract is for

---

27. U.P.A. § 31(5), Sec. 77(b) above. See Annot., 81 A.L.R.2d 445 (1962).

28. Bankruptcy Act § 5i, 11 U.S.C.A. § 23(i); Marnet Oil & Gas Co. v. Staley, 218 F. 45 (5th Cir. 1914); Hart v. Ronan, 58 N.D. 516, 226 N.W. 620 (1929); American Steel & Wire Co. v. Coover, 27 Okl. 131, 111 P. 217, 30 L.R.A.,N.S. 787 (1910); Stickney v. Kerry, 55 Wash.2d 535, 348 P.2d 655 (1960) (non-bankrupt partner may wind up partnership, must account to bankrupt estate for partner's interest, and cannot use funds to pay himself a non-partnership debt owing by the bankrupt partner).

Though all the members of a partnership are adjudicated bankrupt, but there is no adjudication of the partnership, the trustee for the partners has no right to administer the partnership affairs. In re Mercur, 122 F. 384 (3d Cir.1903).

If the dormant partner of an ostensible sole trader makes no objection to the latter's trustee in bankruptcy taking over the partnership property, he is held to have consented. In re Harris, 108 F. 517 (N.D.Ohio 1899).

"Where all the general partners are adjudged bankrupts, the partnership shall also be adjudged a bankrupt." Bankruptcy Act, § 5i; 11 U.S.C.A. § 23(i).

29. Bankruptcy Act § 5c, 11 U.S.C.A. § 23(c).

30. See Sec. 75 at n. 87 above, concerning the meaning of "wrongful" in connection with dissolution.

31. Caughy v. Hearn, 158 Md. 597, 149 A. 295 (1930); Magullion v. Magee, 241 Mass. 360, 369, 135 N.E. 560 (1922); Leary v. Kelly, 277 Pa. 217, 120 A. 817 (1923); Johnson v. Hamilton, 141 Wash. 248, 251 P. 274 (1926); Ruggles v. Buckley, 175 F. 57, 27 L.R.A.,N.S. 541, 20 Ann.Cas. 1057 (6th Cir. 1910).

Compare Jewell v. Harper, 205 Or. 1, 285 P.2d 133 (1955), noted 34 Chi-Kent L. Rev. 169 (1956). Both partners died simultaneously. The widow of one wound up the firm and was allowed compensation for her services.

32. Where the business is continued with authority, Schenkl v. Dana, 118 Mass. 236 (1875); Condon v. Callahan, 115 Tenn. 285, 89 S.W. 400 (1905), annotated in 1 L.R.A.,N.S. 643, 112 Am. St.Rep. 833, 5 Ann.Cas. 659; or where extraordinary services are rendered, as in prosecuting litigation to realize on a partnership asset, Maynard v. Richards, 166 Ill. 466, 46 N.E. 1138, 57 Am.St.Rep. 145 (1897); Zell's Appeal, 126 Pa. 329, 17 A. 647 (1889).

33. Puffer v. Merton, 168 Wis. 366, 170 N.W. 368 (1919), annotated in 5 A.L.R. 1288; see also 80 A.L.R. 87; Stearns v. Blevins, 262 Mass. 577, 160 N.E. 417 (1928).

George v. Richards, 361 Pa. 278, 64 A.2d 811 (1949), open contract with engineering firm to dig tunnels when

a specific service, and the survivor does no more in completing the transaction that he would have been under a duty to do had there been no dissolution, he must share the fee received with the decedent's estate.[34]   Where he is compelled to do more than was intended, he has been held entitled to extra compensation for his services.[35]

Under the U.P.A., the surviving partner after death is entitled to reasonable compensation for his services in winding-up.[36]   The principle has been applied in a case of a joint venture.   Two authors agreed to collaborate in writing a play.   The one who had conceived the plot and the idea died when the play was partly finished.   It was completed and delivered to the producer by the survivor.   The estate of the deceased author was held entitled to share the royalties with the survivor, making an allowance for the extra work done by the latter.[37]

ordered.   This was regarded as matter requiring special skill of a personal nature and survivor could make new contract without accountability to decedent's estate.

But it has been held that the earnings from the continued service, though under a new contract, must be divided as though there had been no dissolution.   Stem v. Warren, 227 N.Y. 538, 125 N.E. 811 (1920), noted 33 Harv. L.Rev. 1070 (1920).

See also Little v. Caldwell, 101 Cal. 553, 36 P. 107, 40 Am.St.Rep. 89 (1894).

34.   Consaul v. Cummings, 222 U.S. 262, 32 S.Ct. 83, 56 L.Ed. 192 (1911).

35.   Roth v. Boies, 139 Iowa 253, 115 N.W. 930 (1908); Clifton v. Clark, 83 Miss. 446, 36 So. 251, 66 L.R.A. 821, 102 Am.St.Rep. 458, 1 Ann.Cas. 396 (1904).

36.   U.P.A. § 18(f), Sec. 65(e) above; Annot., 81 A.L.R.2d 445 (1962).   Section 18(f) authorizes compensation for "a surviving partner" winding up, suggesting that two or more surviving partners may not be eligible.   Cf. § 37 which permits "the partners" to wind up.   Multiple surviving partners were allowed compensation in Johnson v. Munsell, 170 Neb. 749, 104 N.W.2d 314, 327 (1960) (apparently pre-U.P.A.) although the survivors were really continuing rather than winding up.

Cahill v. Haff, 248 N.Y. 377, 162 N.E. 288 (1928); Jacobson v. Wikholm, 29 Cal.2d 24, 172 P.2d 878 (1946); Murdock v. Murdock, 300 Pa. 280, 150 A. 599 (1930).

A partnership of lawyers was dissolved by death of a partner.   The survivor completed litigation in which the firm was engaged prior to the dissolution.   Applying U.P.A. § 18(f), the survivor was entitled to reasonable compensation for his post-dissolution services in the pending cases.   As to new matters brought in by former clients, compensation earned by the surviving partner was entirely outside of partnership accounts, and the deceased partner's estate had no share in it.   Faries v. McDowell, Cal.Super.Ct. 1950, 18 U.S.Law Week 2489.   See Annot., 78 A.L.R.2d 280 (1961) for decisions (mostly pre-U.P.A.) involving law firms.

In Jacobson v. Wikholm, supra, in applying the statute, the court distinguished liquidation from completion of a pending construction contract, and allowed no more than the surviving partner's half share in profits for his services in carrying on the contract.   The winding up of law partnerships by completion of pending cases was distinguished.

37.   Losch v. Marcin, 251 N.Y. 402, 167 N.E. 514 (1929).

The analogy of surviving partners has been applied to the case of a partner who, after dissolution inter vivos, carried through to completion a contract secured by the partnership before dissolution.   The non-participating partner was entitled to share in the profits, but with an allowance for the services of the partner who conducted the transaction (road building).   Bracht v. Connell, 313 Pa. 397, 170 A. 297 (1933).

No compensation is allowed if the surviving partners improperly continue the business instead of winding it up.[38]

If dissolution is not by death, a winding-up partner is not entitled to compensation for his services unless otherwise agreed.[39]

RIGHT TO CONTINUE

§ 83A. **The remaining partners have the right to continue the partnership business (a) after dissolution in contravention of the agreement, (b) after expulsion of a partner, and (c) by agreement.**

The legal existence of a partnership continues after dissolution.[40] But the operation of the business normally continues only to the extent necessary for winding up.[41] The reason is that dissolution gives each partner the right (subject to limited exceptions) to have the business liquidated, and his share of the surplus paid in cash.[42] Since this often results in the sacrifice of going concern values,[43] it is important to understand when and how liquidation can properly be avoided and the business continued indefinitely. The following possibilities are recognized by statute.[44]

---

38. Hurst v. Hurst, 1 Ariz.App. 227, 401 P.2d 232 (1965), modified on other grounds, 1 Ariz.App. 603, 405 P.2d 913 (1965); Wikstrom v. Davis, 211 Or. 254, 315 P.2d 597 (1957). These were not dissolutions by death.

39. The authorization for compensation in U.P.A. § 18(f) applies only in case of death. Chazan v. Most, 209 Cal. App.2d 519, 25 Cal.Rptr. 864 (1962); Frates v. Nichols, 167 So.2d 77 (Fla. App.1964); Geist v. Burnstine, 19 N.Y. S.2d 76 (Sup.Ct.1940); Platt v. Henderson, 227 Or. 212, 361 P.2d 73 (1961). In the latter case, a younger law partner withdrew, took most of clients' files, and completed the work on them. This interfered with the older partner's equal right to participate in liquidation, which he was willing and able to do. The court divided the fees for the work according to the partners' previous ratios, without compensation to the younger partner who did substantially all the work.

40. U.P.A. § 29, Sec. 73 above.

41. Sec. 80 above.

42. U.P.A. § 38(1). Young v. Cooper, 30 Tenn.App. 55, 203 S.W.2d 376 (1947).

Fortugno v. Hudson Manure Co., 51 N.J.Super. 482, 144 A.2d 207 (1958), noted 4 Vill.L.Rev. 457 (1959). The court held that the liquidation right extended to the assets of corporations whose shares were owned by the partnership and whose operations were an integral part of it. However, recognizing the destruction of values that might result, the court authorized a decree (if agreed to by all the partners) for appraisal of the enterprise and payment by the other partners for the complaining partner's interest in that valuation. 144 A.2d at 218–19 cites cases authorizing distribution of assets in kind where equitable.

See also Rinke v. Rinke, 330 Mich. 615, 48 N.W.2d 201 (1951) (court could distribute assets in kind (not pro rata) where there were no creditors and ex-partners went into separate businesses).

43. Fortugno v. Hudson Manure Co., n. 42 above.

44. A similar result may occur when some of the partners acquire the partnership assets at liquidation and continue the business, or when they continue in the same line of business claiming some continuity with the partnership by name or otherwise. These problems are explored in Secs. 86 and 84 below.

Sec. 84 also discusses the statutory right of surviving partners to continue in a few states.

(a) Dissolution in Contravention of the Agreement

Dissolution at the will of a partner is in contravention of the agreement if the latter is for a fixed term or particular undertaking.[45] So, probably, is judicial dissolution for a partner's breach or misconduct.[46] When dissolution is in contravention, the dissolving partner cannot force the liquidation of the firm. His co-partners can liquidate if they choose, and collect damages for his breach.[47] Alternatively, they may possess the firm property and continue the business by themselves or with new partners. To do so, they must pay off the dissolving partner (offsetting their damages), or secure a future payment to him.[48] These rights are less attractive to the remaining partners than they first appear. There are numerous complications and doubts concerning the amount and method of payment, and some question about how long the partnership can be continued.[49] For these reasons, this continuation right is something to use when nothing else is possible, but it is a very incomplete form of relief. Moreover, it is inapplicable to dissolution by death, disability and other non-wrongful causes, and generally inapplicable to partnerships at will.[50]

(b) Expulsion

A partner expelled pursuant to an express provision of the partnership agreement [51] cannot force the liquidation of the firm. He is entitled only to be paid in cash the net amount due him from the firm [52] and to be protected from firm liabilities.[53] The remaining partners have the clearly implied right to continue the business as long as they like.

This right of continuation is even more limited than the one discussed in the previous subsection, particularly since expulsion

---

45. The term or undertaking may be express or implied; see Sec. 74 at nn. 44–45 above.

46. Sec. 75(d) above.

47. Sec. 75(b) above.

48. Secs. 75(c) above, 86(c) below.

49. Ibid.

50. Damages may be allowed for certain types of dissolutions of partnerships at will; see Sec. 74 at n. 43 above. But it is questionable whether a continuation right would be recognized in the absence of agreement.

51. See Sec. 74(d) above for the different types of expulsion provisions.

52. U.P.A. § 38(1), second sentence. See also Sec. 86(c) below. The expulsion must be bona fide, whatever that means in such a case.

53. U.P.A. § 38(1). This must be by payment of the liabilities (which is rarely practicable in a short time) or by release or novation from creditors under U.P.A. § 36(2), discussed Sec. 79(b) above (which is rarely practicable if the creditors are numerous). If neither of these methods is practicable, a court might permit expulsion (or the partner might be persuaded to accept it) with suitable indemnification (including surety) rather than release or novation. This is done under U.P.A. § 38(2) (discussed Sec. 75(c) above) which, however, specifically authorizes it. See Vangel v. Vangel, 116 Cal.App.2d 615, 254 P.2d 919 (1953), aff'd in part, rev'd in part, and remanded 45 Cal.2d 804, 291 P.2d 25, 55 A.L.R.2d 1385 (1955) (indemnification against liabilities under long term loan and marketing agreement).

clauses are so seldom used in partnership agreements. In addition, the statute does not state how the amount due him is to be computed.[54] The valuation provisions for use in wrongful dissolution, by negative implication, suggest that good-will (or appreciation in assets over book value) should be included for an expelled partner. If the agreement specifies a method of valuation (which it should because of the statutory omission), it ought to be conclusive.

(c) Agreement

A partner may compel liquidation after dissolution "unless otherwise agreed."[55] The agreement may be made at the time of dissolution, although this presents practical obstacles.[56] Or it may be embodied in the partnership agreement, where dissolution can usually be considered long in advance and therefore treated with more detachment.

Continuation agreements are most commonly drawn for dissolution by death, and these are considered further in Section 90A below. But they can be made equally applicable to any kind of dissolution, and even to a partnership at will.[57] The main elements in such an agreement are the events on which it comes into effect, the method of disposition of the outgoing partner's interest,[58] and the compensation to him.[59]

An agreement of this sort is the only reliable way of assuring the preservation of a partnership business. It is likely to offer the best

54. For no apparent reason, U.P.A. § 38(1) refers to "the net amount due him" while § 42, discussed Sec. 86(c) below, speaks of "the value of his interest at dissolution" (plus profits or interest on that amount). It is doubtful that a different measure is intended, particularly since § 42 is applicable to an expulsion through its cross-reference to § 41(6). The proper interpretation of "the net amount due him" appears to be (1) the value of his interest at dissolution (i. e. expulsion, U.P.A. § 31(1)(d), Sec. 74(d) above), plus (2) any profits or interest to which he is entitled, plus or minus (3) any other amounts owing by the partnership to him or vice versa. Section 42 precedents should be valid in calculating the first and second items.

55. U.P.A. § 38(1).

56. See Sec. 90A(a) below. Probabilities are high that the partners and other interested parties will see things differently in most dissolutions. If there has been a death, the estate or widow may have objectives that differ sharply from the surviving partners'. The same may be true when one partner retires at an advanced age. If dissolution results from dissension or misconduct, the partners are almost bound to be in conflict.

57. Napoli v. Domnitch, 14 N.Y.2d 508, 248 N.Y.S.2d 228, 197 N.E.2d 623 (1964) affirming 18 App.Div.2d 707, 236 N.Y.S.2d 549 (1962) (partner had right to dissolve, subject to co-partners' right to buy his interest per agreement).

58. See Secs. 86(a), 90A below.

59. See Appendix V, pars. 6.1, 6.7, 6.8; Appendix VI, pars. 6.1, 7.3–7.10 below. Continuation agreements are discussed more fully in Bromberg, Partnership Dissolution—Causes, Consequences, and Cures, 43 Texas L.Rev. 631 (1965); Bromberg, Partnership Dissolution—Causes, Consequences and Cures, Including Special Problems of Law Firms, 7 Law Office Economics & Management 27 and 158 (1966).

price to the outgoing interest. In addition, it can have important income tax effects,[60] and can (contrary to general impression) provide almost any desired degree of continuity for the partnership entity.

GOOD WILL IN DISSOLUTION AND WINDING UP

§ 84. **Good will is an attribute which adds value to partnership property, and therefore is to be considered in determining what is payable to a retiring partner, or to the estate of a deceased partner, by a partner who takes over the property and continues the business. The good will may be enhanced in value by a retiring partner undertaking to refrain from competition. Many aspects of good will are importantly affected by the partnership agreement.**

(a) Nature and Source of Good Will; Duty to Account for It

Good will is a slippery intangible. It is so elusive that a cynic may wonder whether it serves any purpose beyond the padding of one partner's claim against another when there is a disputed dissolution and no arms length valuation of the business.

Conventionally, good will has been defined as a "well founded expectation of continued public patronage." [61] In part, at least, it represents the going concern value of a business in contrast to its break-up value.[62] It is occasionally described in terms of above-average success of the business, and is almost always related in some

---

60. Sec. 86(b) below.

61. Dodge Stationery Co. v. Dodge, 145 Cal. 380, 78 P. 879 (1904).

Lord Eldon, in Cruttwell v. Lye, 17 Ves. 335, 346, 34 Eng.Rep. 129, 134 (1810), defined "good will" rather narrowly as "nothing more than the probability that the old customers will resort to the old place."

Justice Story, in his treatise on Partnership, § 99 (3d ed. 1850), describes it as a benefit or advantage "which is acquired by an establishment beyond the mere value of the capital, stock, funds or property employed therein, in consequence of the general public patronage and encouragement, which it receives from constant or habitual customers on account of its local position, or common celebrity, or reputation for skill or affluence, or punctuality, or from other accidental circumstances or necessities, or even from ancient partialities or prejudices."

See also Foreman, Conflicting Theories of Good-Will, 22 Colum.L.Rev. 638 (1922); Wright, Nature and Basis of Legal Good-Will, 24 Ill.Law Rev. 20 (1929); Note, 33 Colum.L.Rev. 900 (1933).

In Stanton v. Commissioner, 189 F.2d 297 (7th Cir. 1951), the court referred to definitions of good will quoted in 2 Paul, Federal Estate and Gift Taxation, sec. 18.16, and noted that "the various definitions quoted all appear to relate to some advantage in the competition for *customers*, not for commodities to sell to those customers." This seems a rather narrow view. A business organization by reason of its credit rating, volume and stability of demand may have a competitive advantage in purchasing, which may make its business or an interest therein more valuable to a transferee, even though, as in the Stanton case, firm commitments of particular suppliers are lacking. Such an expectation in the case of a partnership may be (as was found in the Stanton case) personal to the partners, and not transferable.

62. But see Marso v. Graif, 226 Minn. 540, 33 N.W.2d 717 (1948) distinguishing good will from going concern value.

way to profitability.[63] Its more objective components include name, location, customer records [64] and contacts, and employment relationships.[65]

A going partnership, as much as any other business, generally has good will. If it does, no partner can dispose of it during the life of the business without unanimous consent.[66] The apparent purpose of the rule (to preserve the value of the business) disappears in a dissolution followed by liquidation. In fact, the purpose of liquidation is more likely to be achieved by selling the good will with the physical assets. Probably for these reasons, it is commonly said that good will is to be converted into cash on dissolution. In any event, it must be accounted for like any other element of value.[67]

It often happens, after dissolution, that one or more of the partners (or persons succeeding to their rights in the business) continue in the same line of business and try to use the good will of the partnership. This benefit they seek to secure by creating an appearance of continuity of the business and, in some cases, by preventing or limiting competition by retired partners. Questions arise as to the extent to which continuing partners may create the appearance of continuity of the business, as to their accountability to retired partners or to a deceased partner's representatives for such a benefit, and as to the existence and scope of obligations of retired partners not to compete.

The partnership considered as a group entity may have good will, or the good will may be solely that of the partners individually. This appears to be largely a question of fact, although it is not always so regarded. In a professional or personal service partnership, good will is likely to be personal to the several partners and incapable of transfer.[68] Good will is generally not a group asset of and there is no duty

63. See n. 99 below. Kennedy v. Yost, 32 Del.Ch. 386, 88 A.2d 297 (1952) (no good will for restaurant which failed to make a profit); Farwell v. Huling, 132 Ill. 112, 23 N.E. 438 (1890) (no good will for firm which had been in business less than a year and lost heavily). See also Johnson v. Munsell, 170 Neb. 749, 104 N.W.2d 314 (1960) (no good will for speculative and unstable mineral products business). But see Engstrom v. Larson, 77 N.D. 541, 44 N.W.2d 97 (1950) (failure of cafe profit, explainable by other factors, doesn't preclude good will when profit was previously earned).

64. See In re Arnay's Estate, 18 Misc.2d 266, 187 N.Y.S.2d 782 (Surr.1959).

65. See Smith v. Bull, nn. 79, 91 below.

66. U.P.A. § 9(3) (b).

67. See, in general, Annot., Accountability for good will on dissolution of partnership, 65 A.L.R.2d 521 (1959).

68. "Ability, skill, experience, acquaintanceship, personal clientele, and other personal characteristics and qualification do not constitute goodwill." Stanton v. Commissioner, n. 61 above. See also Vanderplow v. Fredricks, 321 Mich. 483, 32 N.W.2d 718 (1948) (good will personal to sole general partner of beer distributor).

For many years, the position of the Internal Revenue Service was that good will of a professional was so personal that it could not be transferred at all. See Hock, Personal Good Will, 37 Taxes 825 (1959). This view ignored the fact that it was bought

to account for it on dissolution of partnerships of lawyers,[69] physicians and dentists,[70] architects,[71] accountants,[72] and weighers and gaugers.[73] "Ordinarily good will is partnership property, but whether or not partnership good will exists in any particular case depends upon the particular facts and circumstances involved, and one test of determining its existence is whether a reasonable person would pay anything for it." [74] Good will has been recognized as an asset of partnerships conducting such business as a sanitarium,[75] a stockholder's office,[76] an architect's office,[77] a stockbroker's office,[78] an advertising agency,[79] a dancehall,[80] a scrap metal business,[81] and a canning business.[82] Some of these firms are as much professional or personal service as they are mercantile. As a result, it becomes more difficult to make the traditional distinction and say that only the latter can have partnership

and sold daily by doctors, accountants and other professionals. Finally, the I.R.S. relented, and recognized the transferability of good will. Rev.Rul. 64–235, 1964–2 Cum.Bull. 18. However, it continued to assert that there is no transfer of good will when a professional admits a partner, since the good will of the former continues to be available to him through the firm.

Good will is important for tax purposes in that payments for good will are capital gain to the recipient and non-deductible by the payor, Karan v. Commissioner, 319 F.2d 303 (7th Cir. 1963) (CPAs), noted 19 J.Tax. 198 (1963), Aaron Michaels, 12 T.C. 17 (1949) (laundry), while payments for non-competition agreements (which may be functionally indistinguishable) are ordinary income and deductible, respectively. See n. 18B below.

69. Siddall v. Keating, 8 A.D.2d 44, 185 N.Y.S.2d 630 (1959) aff'd 7 N.Y.2d 846, 196 N.Y.S.2d 986, 164 N.E.2d 860 (1959) and cases there cited. Compare Burchell v. Wilde, [1900] 1 Ch. 551, 69 L.J.Ch. 314.

70. Foss v. Roby, 195 Mass. 292, 81 N.E. 199, 10 L.R.A.,N.S., 1200, 11 Ann. Cas. 571 (1907); Freund v. Murray, 39 Mont. 539, 104 P. 683, 25 L.R.A., N.S., 959 (1909); Slack v. Suddoth, 102 Tenn. 375, 52 S.W. 180, 45 L.R.A. 589, 73 Am.St.Rep. 881 (1899).

71. Rutan v. Coolidge, 241 Mass. 584, 136 N.E. 257 (1922); Hunt v. Street, 182 Tenn. 167, 184 S.W.2d 553 (1945).
72. Cook v. Lauten, 1 Ill.App.2d 255,

117 N.E.2d 414 (1954). But see Evans v. Gunnip, n. 83 below.

73. Lloyd v. Rahe, 234 App.Div. 626, 252 N.Y.S. 135 (1931). See Laube, Good Will in Professional Partnerships, 12 Cornell L.Q. 303 (1927); Crane, Partnership Goodwill, 18 Va. L.Rev. 651 (1932).

74. Spalding v. Spalding's Adm'r., 248 Ky. 259, 58 S.W.2d 356 (1933).

75. Williams v. Wilson, 4 Sandf.Ch. 379 (N.Y.1846).

76. In re Brown's Will, 242 N.Y. 1, 150 N.E. 581, 44 A.L.R. 510 (1926), noted 41 Harv.L.Rev. 803.

77. Rutan v. Coolidge, n. 71 above. But in Hunt v. Street, 182 Tenn. 167, 184 S.W.2d 553 (1945), it was declared that there was no good will in a partnership formed to practice architecture which survived voluntary dissolution; the court refused to enjoin use by one partner of the firm name or to order it to be sold.

78. Re Estate of Spingarn, 5 Misc.2d 36, 159 N.Y.S.2d 532 (1956); Miller v. Hall, 65 C.A.2d 200, 150 P.2d 287 (1944).

79. Smith v. Bull, 50 Cal.2d 294, 325 P.2d 463 (1958).

80. Driskill v. Thompson, 141 Cal.App. 2d 479, 296 P.2d 834 (1956).

81. In re Glant's Estate, 57 Wash.2d 309, 356 P.2d 707 (1960).

82. Taormina v. Culicchia, 355 S.W.2d 569 (Tex.Civ.App.1962)

good will. Indeed, one recent case has recognized good will in a firm of certified public accountants.[83]

In some cases, it would be a fraud on the public to attempt to conserve the good will of a former partner which is personal to him by attempting to create an appearance of continuity. A quartet of musicians performed publicly and sought engagements under the name of "Flonzaley Quartet." On dissolution three of the quartet attempted to continue under the same name, but the name was held not transferable, and its use was enjoined at the suit of the retired member.[84] In the case of lawyers, if the practice is continued, using a firm name which includes that of a retired or deceased partner, care should be taken "that no imposition or deception is practiced by this use." [85]

In virtually all cases finding that no good will existed, the court mentions that none appeared on the firm's books. This is largely irrelevant and perhaps misleading. Tax and financial accounting theories—which determine the content of most books—permit the inclusion of good will in a balance sheet only if it is purchased, and usually require its amortization then.[86] Self-generated good will would never appear on a "proper" set of books, yet this is the kind of good will regularly alleged by a retiring partner or decedent's representatives. Courts must look beyond the books to do justice in this respect.

(b) Appropriation and Valuation

Once it has been determined that good will existed, and that it belonged to the partnership rather than the partners, the next question is whether it has been used by a partner in such a way that he must account for it. If it has been sold to a stranger, the proceeds must be shared.[87] And if it has been appropriated by one partner, he must pay his co-partner the latter's share of its value. Such appropriation may take various forms, such as continuing at the same location with the same name,[88] advertising as the successor of the firm,[89] describing the firm as moved to a new location where the

83. Evans v. Gunnip, 36 Del.Ch. 589, 135 A.2d 128, 65 A.L.R.2d 513 (1957), noted 35 U.Det.L.J. 388 (1958).

84. Bailly v. Betti, 241 N.Y. 22, 148 N.E. 776 (1925); Bailey v. Betti, 126 Misc. 45, 212 N.Y.S. 455 (1925), noted 11 Cornell L.Q. 256 (1926); 24 Mich. L.Rev. 515 (1926); Comment 35 Yale L.J. 496 (1926).

See also, as to musical associations, The Fadettes, 168 Mass. 140, 46 N.E. 407 (1897); Blakely v. Sousa, 197 Pa. 305, 47 A. 286, 80 Am.St.Rep. 821 (1900).

85. Canons of Professional Ethics No. 33, 53 Am.Bar Assn.Rep. 495. The

ethical problem is considered in Siddall v. Keating, n. 69 above.

Compare Burchell v. Wilde, [1900], 1 Ch. 551, 69 L.J.Ch. 314.

86. See Wixon, Accountants' Handbook 19.14–19.19 (4th ed. 1962).

87. Engstrom v. Larson, n. 63 above.

88. Re Estate of Spingarn, n. 78 above. See also Richter v. Richter, 202 Ga. 554, 43 S.E.2d 635, 173 A.L.R. 436 (1947) (incorporating under a similar name).

89. Evans v. Gunnip, n. 83 above.

ex-partner operates alone,[90] representing that the business is being continued with only a change of name,[90A] taking files, employees and the business of the main client,[91] or generally continuing the same business operation.[92] Conversely, no accounting is required if the good will is not appropriated.[93] If the appropriation is alleged to result from competition, no accounting is required if competition is permitted by the terms of the agreement.[94] A partner is sometimes permitted to continue in business under the partnership name without accounting, usually where the other partner is not planning to compete.[95] Nor is accounting for good will required when innocent partners continue the business after a dissolution in contravention of the agreement.[96]

Valuation of good will is a complex matter of fact. It may be based on sales of comparable businesses, offers for or by the business in question,[97] or expert testimony.[98] The latter, in turn, is usually grounded on various approximation formulas applied to earnings.[99]

90. Pilch v. Millikin, n. 15 above (no liability because of agreement).

90A. Miller v. Hall, 65 Cal.App.2d 200, 150 P.2d 287 (1944).

91. Smith v. Bull, n. 79 above.

92. Taormina v. Culicchia, n. 82 above. Cf. Annot., Rights as to business unfinished or fees uncollected upon withdrawal or death of partner in law firm, 78 A.L.R.2d 280 (1961).

93. See Barron v. Koenig, 80 Idaho 28, 324 P.2d 388 (1958).

94. Stranges v. Fliehman, 88 Ohio L. Abstr. 150, 182 N.E.2d 19 (1961). See also Behn v. Shapiro, 8 Ill.App.2d 25, 130 N.E.2d 295 (1955) (denying injunction against solicitation of former customers).

95. Speka v. Speka, 124 Cal.App.2d 181, 268 P.2d 129 (1954), suggesting that each partner has some right to use the firm name, and distinguishing firm name from good will. McKinney's N.Y. Partnership Law, § 80 broadly permits use of the firm name by any partners continuing the business. See also Annot., Right to use firm name on dissolution of partnership, 173 A.L.R. 444 (1948).

96. U.P.A. § 38(1), Secs. 75(c), 83A above. Zeibak v. Nasser, 12 Cal.2d 1, 82 P.2d 375 (1938); Vangel v. Vangel, 45 Cal.2d 804, 291 P.2d 25, 55 A.L.R.2d 1385 (1955); Drashner v. Sorenson, 75 S.D. 247, 63 N.W.2d 255 (1954).

If the dissolution is in contravention, the innocent partners are authorized to continue the partnership name as well as its business. U.P.A. § 38(2) (b).

97. Evans v. Gunnip, n. 83 above.

98. Smith v. Bull, n. 79 above; In re Glant's Estate, n. 81 above; Taormina v. Culicchia, n. 82 above.

99. Driskill v. Thompson, n. 80 above (two times excess earnings); Blut v. Katz, 36 N.J.Super. 185, 115 A.2d 119 (1955) (three times earnings averaged over 4 years); In re Welch, 77 Misc. 427, 137 N.Y.S. 941 (1912); Re Estate of Spingarn, n. 78 above (three times excess earnings determined by deducting from total earnings a specified rate of return on capital investment); In re Glant's Estate, n. 81 above (formula not described); Taormina v. Culicchia, n. 82 above (capitalization of excess earnings according to a tax rule, A.R.M. 34, 2 Cum. Bull. 31 (1920)). See Comment, Partnerships—Valuation of Assets on Death of a Partner, 53 Mich.L.Rev. 972, 974–77 (1955).

(c) Non-competition Agreements

A method of enhancing the good will of continuing partners in professional, as well as commercial, partnerships is to secure forbearance from competition by a retired partner. He may agree not to compete, within reasonable limits of time and space, and such an undertaking may be enforced by injunction.[1] Without an express promise not to compete, such an obligation may be implied from the purported transfer of the good will of a professional partnership, as by no other means can it be preserved for the benefit of the continuing partner.[2] In Massachusetts, a promise not to compete is implied in any

---

1. Proctor v. Hansel, 205 Iowa 542, 218 N.W. 255, 58 A.L.R. 153 (1928); Glover v. Shirley, 169 Mo.App. 637, 155 S.W. 878 (1913); Marvel v. Jonah, 83 N.J.Eq. 295, 90 A. 1004, L.R.A. 1915B, 206, Ann.Cas.1916C, 185 (1914); McClurg's Appeal, 58 Pa. 51 (1868).

A contract by a retiring partner not to compete with the continuing partner is not waived or discharged by a subsequent formation of a new partnership between the parties. After dissolution of the second partnership, the restrictive agreement in the former dissolution is still in effect and its violation may be enjoined. Faust v. Rohr, 166 N.C. 187, 81 S.E. 1096 (1914). See also Scudder v. Kilfoil, 57 N.J.Eq. 171, 40 A. 602 (1898).

A contrary result was reached in McLeod v. Schluter, 221 S.W. 961 (Tex. Com.App.1920), noted 30 Yale L.J. 305.

On consolidation of three large accounting firms, with offices in ten cities, it was agreed that a partner voluntarily withdrawing should not within four years compete within one hundred miles of any of the firm's offices. This agreement was held invalid, being unreasonably broad. It was described as a Draconian forfeiture which savored of servitude. Lynch v. Bailey, 275 App.Div. 527, 90 N.Y.S.2d 359 (1949), reversing 194 Misc. 280, 86 N.Y.S.2d 783, affirmed per curiam 300 N.Y. 615, 90 N.E.2d 484 (1949). The decision of the Supreme Court is noted in 62 Harv.L. Rev. 1409 (1949), 14 Albany L.Rev. 62 (1950). The opinion in the Appellate Division refers to statutes making such agreements illegal restraints of trade; Comp.Laws Michigan, 1929 §§ 16661, 16667, 16672, now M.C.L.A. §§ 445.731, 445.761, 445.766; West's Ann.Cal.Bus. & Prof.Code, §§ 16600–16602. In a sub-

sequent proceeding it was held that the bona fide assertion by the partners of the validity of the restrictive covenants, held to be unreasonable, was not an act so wrongful as to constitute a cause of action. Lynch v. Bailey, 99 N.Y.S.2d 585 (1950).

An offer executed in the firm name to sell the business, and containing an undertaking that "we the undersigned, will not directly or indirectly" engage in a competitive business, later renewed over the signatures of all the partners, and accepted by the offeree, results in an obligation which is breached by the competitive activities of a partner. Trenton Potteries Co. v. Oliphant, 58 N.J.Eq. 507, 43 A. 723, 46 L.R.A. 255, 78 Am.St.Rep. 612 (1899). But see Streichen v. Fehleisen, 112 Iowa 612, 84 N.W. 715, 51 L.R.A. 412 (1900), holding that an undertaking by the partnership was broken only by partnership action. It is a question of interpretation of the contract made by the parties in each case. It would seem the more reasonable interpretation in cases of small businesses, where the good will is personal to the individuals carrying on the enterprise, that the vendee intends to secure protection not only against a recreation of the dissolved partnership, but protection against what would be almost equally injurious, a resumption of business by any of the partners.

See 4 Corbin, Contracts, § 926.

See, on the general question of validity of promises not to compete, Carpenter, Validity of Contracts not to Compete, 76 U.Pa.L.Rev. 244 (1928).

2. Brown v. Benzinger, 118 Md. 29, 84 A. 79, Ann.Cas.1914B, 582 (1912); Yeakley v. Gaston, 50 Tex.Civ.App. 405, 111 S.W. 768 (1908).

case of voluntary transfer of good will, in the absence of a stipulation to the contrary, as otherwise the vendor of the good will would be derogating from his grant.[3] The majority of courts have permitted a partner, who has on dissolution agreed to a transfer of good will to continuing partners, to compete but not to solicit directly the continued patronage of former customers.[4]

Though entitled to compete after relinquishing good will on dissolution the retiring partner commits a tort against the continuing partner's property rights if he holds himself out as still carrying on the business of the former firm.[5]

In a manufacturing or trading partnership, good will may also pass to one who acquires the property and right to continue the business.[6] It is an attribute which adds value to the partnership property and must be considered in determining the amount for which the continuing partner must account to the retired partner or deceased partner's estate.[7] The transferee of good will is entitled to use

3. Foss v. Roby, 195 Mass. 292, 81 N.E. 199, 10 L.R.A.,N.S., 1200, 11 Ann.Cas. 571 (1907). It has even been implied where good will was not mentioned. Tobin v. Cody, 343 Mass. 716, 180 N.E. 2d 652 (1962) (sale of half interest in scrap metal corporation to owners of other half interest).

See Notes, 40 Harv.L.Rev. 319 (1926); 34 Yale L.J. 557 (1925); annotations, 11 Ann.Cas. 573; 19 L.R.A.,N.S., 762; 82 A.L.R. 1030, which collect fully the cases on implied agreements not to compete.

A general release given by the buyer to the seller of good will may relieve the seller from the obligation not to compete. Pitman v. J. C. Pitman & Sons, Inc., 324 Mass. 371, 86 N.E.2d 649 (1949).

4. Gibbons v. Hansch, 185 Minn. 290, 240 N.W. 901, 82 A.L.R. 1027 (1932); Burnham v. Burnham, 153 Md. 147, 137 A. 860 (1927); Hilton v. Hilton, 89 N.J.Eq. 182, 104 A. 375, L.R.A. 1918F, 1174 (1918); Von Bremen v. MacMonnies, 200 N.Y. 41, 93 N.E. 186, 32 L.R.A.,N.S., 293, 21 Ann.Cas. 423 (1910); White v. Trowbridge, 216 Pa. 11, 64 A. 862 (1906); Notes, 10 Colum. L.Rev. 649 (1910); 16 Minn.L.Rev. 106, 712 (1931–32).

But see Warp v. Warp, 307 Ill.App. 205, 30 N.E.2d 146 (1940), holding that a retiring partner in a manufacturing partnership who sold out his interest,

including good will, was entitled to compete and solicit customers in the absence of any prohibiting agreement. Semble, Behn v. Shapiro, n. 94 above.

See also Stranges v. Fliehman, n. 94 above (right to compete unless agreement contra; may solicit customers so long as doesn't represent himself as firm's successor).

5. O'Brien v. O'Brien, 362 Pa. 66, 66 A. 2d 309, 10 A.L.R.2d 714 (1949), holding that the claim for damages for the unfair competition was a tort claim which could not be set off against the retired partner's action in assumpsit for profits due him under the dissolution agreement.

See also Stranges v. Fliehman, n. 94 above.

6. See Annot., Sale of business or of real estate upon which business is conducted as transferring good will by implication, in absence of covenant not to compete, 65 A.L.R.2d 502, 508–13 (1959).

7. Moore v. Rawson, 185 Mass. 264, 70 N.E. 64 (1904); Whitman v. Jones, 322 Mass. 340, 77 N.E.2d 315 (1948); Slater v. Slater, 175 N.Y. 143, 67 N.E. 224, 61 L.R.A. 796, 96 Am.St.Rep. 605 (1903); Macfadden v. Jenkins, 40 N.D. 422, 169 N.W. 151 (1918).

There can be no charge for good will as against partners continuing the business after dissolution in the absence of evidence as to its value. Moffett v. Peirce, 344 Pa. 16, 24 A.2d 448 (1942).

the firm name,[8] and trademarks and trade names.[9] Good will may, however, be attached to a specific asset which by agreement is to revert to a partner who contributed merely the use of it for partnership purposes, and so good will value is not an item in accounts. This may occur in the case of real estate,[10] or patent rights.[11]

Relying on a policy favoring free enterprise, the courts have been rather reluctant to enforce express non-competition agreements. It is strange that they have found and enforced implied agreements as frequently as they have. A strong factual basis should be required for such implications. Often the parties are better left to their remedies, if any, under the law of unfair competition.[12]

Where a partnership dissolution is not the result of the voluntary agreement of the partners, the limitations on the right to compete are different from those imposed in cases of a dissolution accompanied by a voluntary transfer of good will. On sale of the partnership property and good will by a receiver or trustee in bankruptcy, or by a surviving partner, there is no limitation imposed upon the carrying on of business and solicitation of former customers by the former partners, other than the duty incident to the law of fair competition in general, that one may not falsely represent his business to be a continuation of the business of another person or group of persons.[13]

8. Twin City Brief Printing Co. v. Review Pub. Co., 139 Minn. 358, 166 N.W. 413, L.R.A.1918D, 154 (1918); Snyder Mfg. Co. v. Snyder, 54 Ohio St. 86, 43 N.E. 325, 31 L.R.A. 657 (1896); Notes 33 Colum.L.Rev. 900 (1933), 13 Minn.L. Rev. 733 (1929).

Unless he expressly agrees otherwise, a person may use his own personal name, even though it is similar to the partnership name. See Annots., 44 A.L.R. 2d 1156 (1955), 173 A.L.R. 444, 457–61 (1948), 47 A.L.R. 1189 (1927).

9. Menendez v. Holt, 128 U.S. 514, 9 S. Ct. 143, 32 L.Ed. 526 (1888).

10. Salter v. Condon, 236 Ill.App. 17 (1925), partner ousted from partnership engaged in conducting a public golf course on land owned by wrongdoing co-partner not entitled to any allowance for good will, which was an attribute of the land in which the partnership as such had no ownership.

11. In re Ulrici's Estate, 111 Misc. 55, 182 N.Y.S. 516 (1920).

A partnership agreement provided that one of the partners might at any time take over the business, paying to the others the value of the property, excluding good will. He later transferred to them his interest at a valuation which took no account of good will. It was held to be a taxable gift of the value of the good will made in contemplation of death. See In re Deutz's Estate, 105 N.J.Eq. 671, 149 A. 257 (1930).

12. See Potter v. Colvin, 302 S.W.2d 105, 65 A.L.R.2d 496 (Ky.1957) (not a partnership case, but a sale of a motel to strangers).

13. Smith v. Everett, 27 Beav. 444, 54 Eng.Rep. 175 (1859); Hutchinson v. Nay, 187 Mass. 262, 72 N.E. 974, 68 L.R.A. 186, 105 Am.St.Rep. 390 (1905); Marmaduke v. Brown, 254 Pa. 18, 98 A. 769 (1916); Underdown v. Underdown, 279 Pa. 482, 124 A. 159 (1924).

The above were cases of dissolution by death. The same right of continuing in business with unrestrained competition exists in other cases of involuntary dissolution. "The good will which the owner thereof parts with in invitum, as in bankruptcy proceedings or by operation of law, as in the liquidation of a partnership by lapse of time or its termination pursuant to the articles of partnership, is a lesser property than the good will which is the subject of a voluntary sale and trans-

(d) Effect of Partnership Agreement

Partnership articles or dissolution agreements may control the disposition of good will on dissolution and winding up. They may provide that good will shall be completely ignored in determining the value of a deceased [14] or outgoing [15] partner's interest, or that it shall be arbitrarily appraised at a fixed sum [16] or at a certain percentage of inventoried value of tangible property and bills receivable.[17]　Non-

fer by the owner for valuable consideration. In the first case the former owner remains under no legal obligation restricting competition on his part in the slightest degree . . . The necessity for the distinction which the law thus makes may be readily illustrated. If the sale of the good will upon the ordinary dissolution and liquidation of a partnership imported the same obligation as that which arises upon a voluntary sale, not to solicit trade from customers of the old firm, merchants who had been in trade as partners of undesirable associates would constantly find themselves, by the mere fact of the dissolution of the firm they desired to leave, disqualified from seeking business from those who might be their most desirable customers." Von Bremen v. MacMonnies, n. 4 above.

It may be doubted whether there is any good will of insurance agents where they have no firm name, and where after dissolution each has the right to continue business for himself. Rice v. Angell, 73 Tex. 350, 11 S.W. 338, 3 L. R.A. 769 (1889).

But where they agree that one partner shall purchase the policy records, with expiration dates, the other has no right to derogate from the value of his grant by attempting to make copies of the records for the purpose of using them in soliciting former customers. Chamberlain v. Hemingway, 97 Conn. 156, 115 A. 632 (1921) noted 31 Yale L.J. 666 (1932).

As to the duty not to hold oneself out as continuing the business of another, see White v. Trowbridge, 216 Pa. 11, 64 A. 862 (1906).

14. Douthart v. Logan, 190 Ill. 243, 60 N.E. 507 (1901); Minoff v. Margetts, 14 N.J.Super. 30, 81 A.2d 369 (1951); In re Moore's Estate, 228 Pa. 523, 77 A. 902 (1910); Lanshe v. Lanshe, 95 Pa.Super. 390 (1928); Hirschberg v. Bacher, 159 Wis. 207, 149 N.W. 383

(1914). See Withers v. Mills, 168 App. Div. 209, 153 N.Y.S. 1016 (1915) (partner not entitled to accounting for good will where agreement provided that he would have no interest in it).

Succession of Jurisich, 224 La. 325, 69 So.2d 361 (1953) (right to purchase decedent's interest at book value relieved survivor from accounting for good will; no good will was carried on the books).

If, pursuant to the partnership articles, the surviving partners acquire the deceased partner's interest in good will without paying for it, there is a transfer taking effect in possession and enjoyment at death and it is subject to inheritance tax. Minoff v. Margetts, 14 N.J.Super. 30, 81 A.2d 369 (1951).

Arbitrary valuations of good will passing from the estate of deceased partners, while effective for purposes of partnership accounting are not necessarily binding on the tax collector.

15. Pilch v. Milikin, 200 Cal.App.2d 212, 19 Cal.Rptr. 334 (1962) (meat packing); O'Donnell v. McLoughlin, 386 Pa. 187, 125 A.2d 370 (1956).

Cf. Haas v. Hodge, 171 Cal.App.2d 478, 340 P.2d 632 (1959). An agreement between two doctors contained a clause by which one of them disclaimed any right to their professional practice and "to the good will thereof." The disclaiming doctor thus had no interest in good will, and a restrictive covenant in the agreement was not enforceable against him since, under Calif. law, such covenants are valid only in connection with the sale of good will. The court did not decide whether the agreement was one of partnership or employment; the agreement denied that it was either.

16. Murphy v. Murphy, 217 Mass. 233, 104 N.E. 466 (1914).

17. Kaufmann v. Kaufmann, 222 Pa. 58, 70 A. 956 (1908); Id., 239 Pa. 42, 86 A. 634 (1913).

payment for good will in a series of prior admissions and dissolutions negates any implied agreement to pay for good will.[18]

In light of the uncertainties and complications in this area, it is most important that specific agreement be reached on disposition and valuation of good will, and on specific incidents such as use of firm name, disposition of files and customer information, and right to compete. [18A]

The agreement can have important income tax consequences too. In particular, it may determine whether the outgoing or his copartners bear the tax on the portion of payments classed by them as good will.[18B]

DISSOLUTION FOR FRAUD IN FORMATION OF PARTNERSHIP

**§ 85.	Where a partnership contract is rescinded on the ground of the fraud or misrepresentation of one of the parties thereto, the party entitled to rescind is, without prejudice to any other right, entitled,**

> **(a)	To a lien on, or right of retention of, the surplus of the partnership property after satisfying the partnership liabilities to third persons for any sum of money paid by him for the purchase of an interest in the partnership and for any capital or advances contributed by him; and**
>
> **(b)	To stand, after all liabilities to third persons have been satisfied, in the place of the creditors of the partnership for any payments made by him in respect to the partnership liabilities; and**
>
> **(c)	To be indemnified by the person guilty of the fraud or making the representation against all debts and liabilities of the partnership. U.P.A. § 39.**

If one is induced by fraud to become a partner, the transaction, like other acts induced by fraud, is voidable and the victim is entitled to rescission and restitution.[19]

In re Randall's Estate, 29 Wash.2d 447, 188 P.2d 71 (1947). The articles gave the survivors on death an option to purchase the decedent's interest in the business, assets and good will by paying the value thereof as determined by the last annual inventory. Although the most valuable assets of the business (good will and a liquor license) had never been valued and placed on the books, the deceased partner's estate was held entitled only to payment in accordance with what appeared in the inventory. "Partners have the right, in the absence of fraud or overreaching, to make a valid and binding contract among themselves for the purchase . . . of the interest of a deceased or withdrawing partner. In the absence of fraud, the fact that they may have agreed that such

an interest may be purchased for a sum less (or more) than the actual value of the interest at some subsequent date, does not render the partnership contract subject to attack . . ."

18.	Siddall v. Keating, n. 69 above.

18A.	See Appendix VI, pars. 7.7, 7.12.

18B.	Sec. 85(b) below. Note, Tax Aspects of Good Will and Covenants not to Compete in the Transfer of Partnership Interests, 16 U.Fla.L.Rev. 440 (1963).

19.	Restatement, Contracts § 476.

U.P.A. § 39 deals with the consequences of rescission but does not expressly authorize it; contract law therefore controls. Damages may be available as an alternative to rescission. Long

Dissolution necessarily results.[20] The relation and status of partnership has been created, however, and until it is dissolved, the defrauded partner is subject to the creation of liabilities to third persons; but in a decree of dissolution he is entitled to indemnity against such liability.[21] He is entitled to restoration of whatever he has paid in or advanced for partnership purposes, less allowance for what he has received.[22]

v. Newlin, 144 Cal.App.2d 509, 301 P.2d 271 (1956). See also n. 29 below. But this will be true only in the relatively rare case where no accounting is necessary to take care of other claims of partners and third parties. If accounting is sought, the innocent partner is likely to be in a stronger position, by virtue of U.P.A. § 39, if he elects rescission rather than damages.

The partner guilty of fraud is a trustee ex maleficio pending a bill to rescind the partnership agreement. Levin v. Hurwitz, 148 Md. 249, 129 A. 218 (1925).

If the misrepresentation consists merely in overestimates of the value of things of indeterminate worth, such as machinery, it is not regarded as so material as to warrant rescission. Gerard v. Gateau, 84 Ill. 121, 25 Am. 438 (1876).

Misrepresentations as to the specific fact of costs of property, although the share purchased is worth as much as is paid for it, are sufficient basis for rescission since partnership is a fiduciary relation. Harlow v. La Brum, 151 N.Y. 278, 45 N.E. 859 (1897); Jones v. Weir, 217 Pa. 321, 66 A. 550, 10 Ann.Cas. 692 (1907).

"The question of whether a money damage has been sustained by the party, who has been induced to enter into a partnership relation through fraudulent representations, has nothing to do with the decision of the case presented for the avoidance of the partnership agreement. The true principle by which the court is to be guided in such a case is, that the party deceived has a right to have the agreement set aside; if it has been obtained by fraud he is entitled to say that the misrepresentations vitiate the contract . . . . The relation of partners is one implying the highest degree of mutual confidence, as it was well observed in the opinion below, and if the contract of partnership was initi-

ated by fraud, it is thereby avoided and annulled. The person fraudulently induced to enter into the partnership is entitled to a degree canceling the partnership agreement ab initio, and he can, also, have an action for the deceit." Harlow v. La Brum, above.

See also, Notes 18 Mich.L.Rev. 62 (1919); 4 Minn.L.Rev. 299 (1920).

Representation (by promoters of a Texas business trust) that beneficiaries are not personally liable, shown by subsequent judicial decisions to have been erroneous, has been regarded as a ground for dissolution on petition of the beneficiaries. O'Dell v. Grubstake Inv. Ass'n, 38 S.W.2d 151 (Tex.Civ. App.1931).

A dissolution agreement procured by fraud may be rescinded. Shelley v. Smith, 271 Mass. 106, 170 N.E. 826 (1930).

20. It may fall under the general definition, U.P.A. § 29, Sec. 73 above, or under such specific causes as U.P.A. §§ 32(1) (c), 32(1) (f), Sec. 78(c) above.

21. U.P.A. § 39(c). Van Andel v. Smith, 248 F.2d 915 (10th Cir. 1957), noted 11 Vand.L.Rev. 942 (1958); Hynes v. Stewart & Owens, 49 Ky. (10 B.Mon.) 429 (1850); Grossman v. Lewis, 226 Mass. 163, 115 N.E. 236 (1917); Richards v. Todd, 127 Mass. 167 (1879).

Courts sometimes say that rescission of a partnership contract renders it void ab initio, but they hasten to add that liabilities to third persons may accrue in the interval. See Weltman v. Kaye, 167 Cal.App.2d 607, 334 P.2d 917 (1959); Long v. Newlin, 144 Cal.App. 2d 509, 301 P.2d 271 (1957). What they really mean is that the contract is void ab initio as to the defrauder, but not as to innocent third parties.

22. Smith v. Everett, 126 Mass. 304 (1879); Madigan v. McCann, n. 27 below.

He is subrogated to the rights of creditors he may have paid, but may not enforce the rights until all creditors have been satisfied.[23] Since he has been defrauded in a fiduciary relation [24] rather than an ordinary commercial one, he is given some extra protection.[25] For his payments to creditors, as well as for his capital contributions and advances, he has a lien on the partnership property remaining after payment of creditors.[26] He is also entitled to compensation for services rendered by him in carrying on the business.[27] To be entitled to the remedy of rescission and restitution, the defrauded partner must act promptly on discovery of the fraud.[28] The same remedy is available to persons who have participated in a joint adventure.[29]

One who by false pretenses induces another to invest as a member of a partnership may be convicted of theft by false pretenses. The fact that the defrauded person acquires a partner's interest in the capital contributed does not bar liability of the defrauder.[30]

---

23. U.P.A. § 39(b).

24. U.P.A. § 21, Sec. 68 above, extends fiduciary obligations to any transaction connected with the formation, conduct or liquidation of the firm.

25. Actually, it may be no more than he would have under the rules of constructive trusts.

26. U.P.A. § 39(a). Apparently the lien extends also to payments made to another partner (rather than to the partnership) for the acquisition of an interest. This, and other aspects of the section, suggest that it was drawn with 2-man partnerships in mind, and may not work well when there are more, some of whom are involved in the fraud and others not.

The defrauded partner's subordination to third party creditors may mean nothing is left for him. See S. E. C. v. DuPont, Homsey & Co., 204 F.Supp. 944 (1962), appeal dism'd sub nom. Legate v. Maloney, 308 F.2d 228 (1st Cir. 1962), cert. denied 372 U.S. 912, 83 S.Ct. 726, 9 L.Ed.2d 720 (1963). The lower court held that the innocent limited partner was subordinated according to the statute. A subsequent appeal, Legate v. Maloney, 334 F.2d 704 (1st Cir. 1964), cert. denied 379 U.S. 973, 85 S.Ct. 662, 13 L.Ed.2d 564 (1965) indicates that the claims of creditors (customers of the firm, which was a stock broker) exceeded the assets and could not be satisfied. The

last opinion also affirmed a master's finding that the innocent partner showed only "puffing" and "prophecy" which were an insufficient basis for rescission.

27. Richards v. Todd, n. 21 above; Weltman v. Kay, n. 21 above; Madigan v. McCann, 346 Mass. 62, 190 N.E. 2d 215 (1963).

28. Levin v. Hurwitz, 148 Md. 249, 129 A. 218 (1925), allowing a bill for a dissolution; Andriessen's Appeal, 123 Pa. 303, 16 A. 840 (1888). A partner does not lose his right to rescind merely because he is in breach of the agreement. Alcorn v. Kohler, 203 Or. 19, 277 P.2d 1009 (1954) (nature of breach unspecified).

29. Menefee v. Oxnam, 42 Cal.App. 81, 183 P. 379 (1919), noted 18 Mich.L.Rev. 62; 4 Minn.L.Rev. 299. Damages may be recovered from the fraudulent party. Fitch v. Ingalls, 271 Mass. 121, 170 N.E. 833 (1930); Hey v. Duncan, 13 F.2d 794 (7th Cir. 1926).

The fraudulent adventurer who has concealed a secret interest in the subject matter of the adventure may be compelled to account for it. Selwyn & Co. v. Waller, 212 N.Y. 507, 106 N.E. 321, L.R.A.1915B, 160 (1914).

See U.P.A. § 21, Sec. 68 above.

30. People v. Jones, 36 Cal.2d 373, 224 P.2d 353 (1950).

PROFIT SHARING AND DISPOSITION OF INTERESTS AFTER DISSOLUTION

§ 86. By agreement, an outgoing partner's interest may be purchased by the remaining partners, liquidated by distributions from the firm, or continued in modified or temporary form. Or, the firm may be wound up and the proceeds distributed. The income tax results of the various methods are different, and will normally determine which is the best to use. In any case, fiduciary duties continue after dissolution.

If the partnership is wound up, an outgoing partner shares in profits and losses until termination.

When any partner dies or retires, and the business is continued under any of the conditions set forth in section 41(1, 2, 3, 5, 6) or section 38(2b) without any settlement of accounts as between him or his estate and the person or partnership continuing the business, unless otherwise agreed, he or his legal representative as against such persons or partnership may have the value of his interest at the date of dissolution ascertained, and he shall receive as an ordinary creditor an amount equal to the value of his interest in the dissolved partnership with interest, or, at his option or at the option of his legal representative, in lieu of interest, the profits attributable to the use of his right in the property of the dissolved partnership; provided that the creditors of the dissolved partnership as against separate creditors or the representative of the retired or deceased partner, shall have priority on any claim arising under this section, as provided by section 41(8) of this act. U.P.A. § 42.

After dissolution, a partnership continues until liquidated.[31] Unless there is a right to continue the business, the remaining partners have the right and duty to wind up and liquidate the firm.[32] Fiduciary duties persist during this period.[33]

In combination, these principles raise questions concerning the partners' roles in liquidation or continuation, the different ways of handling an outgoing interest (and their tax consequences), and the sharing of post-dissolution profits and losses.

(a) Patterns of Disposition of Outgoing Interests

Theoretically, liquidation calls for a sale of partnership property to strangers, payment of debts, and division of proceeds among the partners. Factually, the most logical buyers are often the remaining partners. They have knowledge of the business, experience in its

31. U.P.A. §§ 29–30, Sec. 73 above.

32. Secs. 83, 83A above; U.P.A. § 38(1).

"Unless the articles of partnership provide otherwise, the surviving partner must proceed at once to wind up the partnership affairs, because there can be only a limited continuance of the business and that for the sole purpose of winding it up. He must wind it up within a reasonable time and account to the heirs for any surplus remaining in his hands after payment of the partnership debts, . . . The surviving partner is, by construction of law, a trustee holding the assets of the firm in trust for the purpose of paying firm debts and settling and winding up the partnership affairs." Dial v. Martin, 37 S.W.2d 166, 177 (Tex.Civ.App.1931) (pre-U.P.A.).

33. U.P.A. § 21, Sec. 68 above.

operations, and (perhaps) confidence in its future. They have an existing financial and psychological stake in it, and the corollary opportunity to acquire the entire business by purchasing the outgoing partner's fractional interest. The substantial problems of selling a business to a stranger for a good price [34] may be avoided by sale to remaining partners. On the other hand, the remaining partners may be in a position to take advantage of the outgoing interest, particularly at death. Fiduciary obligations therefore come into play.[35] If the remaining partners desire to continue operations without liquidation of the business (as distinct from liquidation of the firm as a legal entity), they must settle with the outgoing interest and acquire its rights. Assuming proper agreement, this can be done in various ways. The following, which are analyzed further in the next subsection, and in sec. 90A, are the major alternatives.

(1) *Sale of Interest.* Purchase by other partners of the outgoing interest in the partnership.[36]

(2) *Sale of Assets.* Purchase by other partners of the partnership property, as in a liquidating sale, with distribution of the proceeds to themselves as well as the outgoing interest.[37] They would naturally offset the distributions due them against the purchase price, paying only the net amount due the outgoing interest.

(3) *Liquidating Distributions.* Liquidation or discharge of the outgoing interest by payments from the continuing partnership.[38]

(4) *Modified Continuation.* Continuation of the outgoing interest on a modified or temporary basis in the hands of the original partner or his designated successor. Thus, the share of profits may be reduced, or the interest continued only for a limited period.

Although the methods are structurally and formally different, and have different tax consequences, they present basically the same fiduciary problems. A surviving partner, in particular, has a duty to disclose all facts having a bearing on value. If he conceals such facts, the sale may be voided.[39] If the surviving partner attempts to take over the business by selling the partnership property to himself or to

---

34. See Bunn & Terflinger, Buying and Selling a Small Business (Small Business Management Research Reports 1963).

35. Legal theories are often slight protection against actual abuse. An interesting study of this problem is O'Neal and Derwin, Expulsion or Oppression of Business Associates (1961), esp. ch. VI on partnerships.

36. This is his share of profits and surplus, distinguished from his rights in specific partnership property. U.P.A. 24–26, Secs. 40–45 above.

37. A variant is to distribute the assets from the firm to the partners, and let the partners sell them.

38. This method is tax-motivated; see below at Sec. 86(b) (3) and nn. 64–66. It is not specifically authorized by U.P.A., although § 38(1), last sentence, seems to contemplate it in the case of expulsion.

39. Malden Trust Co. v. Brooks, 276 Mass. 464, 177 N.E. 629, 80 A.L.R. 1028 (1931); Cotton v. Stevens, 79 N.H. 224, 107 A. 602 (1919). See also Tennant v. Dunlop, 97 Va. 234, 33 S.E. 620 (1889), where the court refused to rescind the

someone acting for him, the transaction may be voidable by the representative.[40] A few states, recognizing that the survivor is the natural purchaser, have not only authorized him to buy but given him a preferential and enforceable right to do so. In return, they have imposed safeguards such as judicial determination of price and terms.[41] Good arguments can be made for allowing surviving partners to purchase in any court-supervised winding up under U.P.A.[42] But they are not entirely convincing and should hardly be relied on if the matter is still at a stage where specific agreement can be reached.

Advance agreements for continuation after dissolution are fully authorized.[43] They may use any of the forms described above for handling the outgoing interest; they may be either options or binding obligations. They are generally valid and enforceable.[44] For the special problems of agreements operative on dissolution by death, see sec. 90A below.

sale, but required payment of the fair value of the interest.

40. Didlake v. Roden Grocery Co., 160 Ala. 484, 49 So. 384, 22 L.R.A.,N.S., 907, 18 Ann.Cas. 430 (1909); Valentine v. Wysor, 123 Ind. 47, 23 N.E. 1076, 7 L.R.A. 788 (1890); Dewey v. Chapin, 156 Mass. 35, 30 N.E. 223 (1892); Rowell v. Rowell, 122 Wis. 1, 99 N.W. 473 (1904).

Alternatively, of course, an accounting may be had. See, e. g., Grigg v. Hanna, 283 Mich. 443, 278 N.W. 125 (1938). On a partner's accountability for appropriating the intangible partnership property known as good will, see Secs. 84(a), (b) above.

The surviving partner cannot use partnership property to pay his separate debts. Hill v. Draper, 54 Ark. 395, 15 S.W. 1025 (1891). The property cannot be reached by execution on behalf of a separate creditor, Farley v. Moog, 79 Ala. 148, 58 Am.Rep. 585 (1885); Maddock's Adm'x v. Skinker, 93 Va. 479, 25 S.E. 535 (1896). Cf. U.P.A. § 25(2) (c).

If the surviving partner goes bankrupt, the partnership property must be kept separate for partnership purposes, Hewitt v. Hayes, 204 Mass. 586, 90 N.E. 985, 27 L.R.A.,N.S., 154 (1910); and he cannot claim a personal exemption out of partnership property. In re Mosier,

112 F. 138 (D.Vt.1901). Cf. U.P.A. § 25(2) (c), Sec. 44 above.

41. R.C. (Ohio) § 1779.04 (1964) (maximum time for payment 9 months); R.C.W. (Wash.) 11.64.030 (1967), applied In re Wilson's Estate, 50 Wash. 2d 840, 315 P.2d 287 (1957). Such provisions do not operate where the agreement calls for a different method, such as purchase at book value. In re Squeri's Estate, 37 Ohio Op. 316, 80 N.E.2d 733 (Ohio Prob.1948). Both statutes are discussed Comment, 62 Mich.L.Rev. 106, 119–21 (1963).

See also McKinney's N.Y.Partnership Law, § 75, providing broadly for continuation and settlement among partners under court supervision.

42. Comment, Right of a Surviving Partner to Purchase a Deceased Partner's Interest under the Uniform Partnership Act, 62 Mich.L.Rev. 106 (1963). Part of the argument is that U.P.A. § 38(1), on dissolution, gives to "each partner" the right to force liquidation, but says nothing about "legal representatives" of a deceased partner.

43. U.P.A. § 38(1), Sec. 83A(c) above.

44. See, e. g., Crofton v. Bargreen, 53 Wash.2d 243, 332 P.2d 1081 (1958); Sec. 90A below; Annot., Provision of partnership agreement giving one partner option to buy out other partner, 160 A.L.R. 523 (1946).

(b) Tax Differences in Patterns of Disposition

Partnership dissolution of itself has no tax consequences. But the subsequent events have very different tax effects, depending on the pattern used to handle the outgoing interest. Putting it more realistically, the choice of the pattern will usually depend on the tax results.

(1) *Sale of Interest.* An interest in a partnership is, by and large, a capital asset. Upon its sale to another partner or to a stranger, capital gain or loss is recognized by the seller.[45] The capital character extends to values represented by good will. An important exception occurs if the partnership has inventories which are substantially appreciated (20% or more over cost) or receivables which are unrealized. In these cases, the part of the price attributable to the inventory appreciation and the unrealized receivables is ordinary income.[46] If a partner has died, the fair market value of his interest is subject to estate tax, and the value becomes its cost for tax purposes.[47] The usual result, if it is sold for that value, is no gain and no tax.[48]

The purchaser's outlay is a non-deductible capital expenditure. However, he offsets future ordinary income insofar as he may get an increased basis in the partnership's receivables and inventory through an appropriate inside basis adjustment.[49]

Income from the interest until the date of sale is taxable to the seller, after that to the buyer.

(2) *Sale of Assets.* If the whole partnership property (rather than one partner's interest in the partnership) is sold, gain or loss is computed on each class of assets separately,[50] and taxed to each partner pro rata.[51] Thus any gain attributable to inventory (even though appreciated less than 20%), receivables or other ordinary-income assets is ordinary income. In this respect, sale of assets is less advantageous than sale of an interest. But the reverse is true if there is loss rather than gain on such assets, for sale of an interest generates capital loss while sale of assets may generate ordinary losses which are fully deductible.[52]

---

45. Int.Rev.Code of 1954, § 741 (26 U.S. C.A.).

46. Id. § 751(a).

47. Id. § 1014(a).

48. On the special problems here, see Bromberg, Taxable Income Without Gain on the Sale of a Deceased Partner's Interest: Code, Common Law and Community Property, 13 Sw.L.J. 343 (1959).

49. Int.Rev.Code of 1954, §§ 743, 754 (26 U.S.C.A.). He also offsets ordinary income to the extent that the adjustment increases his basis in depreciable partnership property, thereby generating extra future deductions for him.

50. Williams v. McGowan, 152 F.2d 570, 162 A.L.R. 1036 (2d Cir. 1945).

51. Int.Rev.Code of 1954, § 702 (26 U.S. C.A.).

52. See Jones v. Phinney, 1 A.F.T.R.2d 1555, 58–1, U.S.T.C. par. 9484 (W.D. Tex.1958).

The results of sale of assets will be similar whether the buyers are strangers or partners. However, in the latter case, certain losses may be disallowed, and certain gains (which would otherwise be capital) may be treated as ordinary.[53] For this reason, it may be better to have the outgoing partner sell his interest in the partnership to the remaining partners rather than have the firm sell property to them.[54]

Distribution of sale proceeds will ordinarily involve no additional tax.[55]

The purchasers' outlay is a non-deductible capital expenditure. However, they offset ordinary income insofar as they get an increased basis in receivables, inventory or other ordinary income items.

(3) *Liquating Distributions.* Instead of selling his interest, the outgoing partner may relinquish or surrender it in return for payment from the partnership (as distinct from the individual partners). This is somewhat like selling the interest to the partnership as an entity.[56] But the tax results are different from selling to anyone else. First, payment for the partner's interest in partnership property (other than unrealized receivables and substantially appreciated inventory) [57] is tax-free return of capital to the extent of the basis for his interest in the firm, and capital gain in excess of that.[58] Good will is consider-

---

53. Int.Rev.Code of 1954, § 707(a), (b) (26 U.S.C.A.).

54. The situation is essentially the same if the partnership sells its assets, or distributes them pro rata in kind to the partners who sell them. Id. § 735. If only one of the distributees sells his interest to the others, who then form a new firm, there has been no sale by the ongoing partners, and they are not faced with the problems described at n. 53 above. However, the outgoing partner may not be as well off as if he had sold his interest in the firm without going through the distribution rigamarole.

55. In the rare case where the proceeds exceed a partner's basis for his interest in the partnership, he will be taxable. Id. § 731(a) (1).

56. The analogy to a corporation's purchase of its own shares is somewhat misleading. It conflicts with the flexible capitalization of a partnership, which is not divided into fixed shares like a corporation, but can be continuously rearranged (by agreement)

as to profits, or surplus (capital), or both.

The proper view of a relinquishment or surrender, as a matter of partnership law, seems to be that all the partner's property rights (e. g. U.P.A. §§ 24–26, 18(e)) are given up. The rights of the remaining partners are correspondingly enlarged, but not by direct transfer from him to them. See n. 38 above.

For some of the accounting methods used to record this type of transaction, see Finney & Miller, Principles of Accounting—Advanced 31–38 (4th ed. 1952); Wixon, Accountant's Handbook 24.14–24.16 (4th ed. 1960). These authors do not consider payments contingent on future developments. The latter may be handled in similar ways or as a continuing share of profits.

57. Payments for these assets result in ordinary income. Int.Rev.Code of 1954 §§ 736(b) (2) (A), 751 (26 U.S.C.A.).

58. Id. § 736(b) (1). On death, basis typically rises enough, per id. § 1014 (a), to cancel any capital gain. See sec. 90A at n. 72 below concerning estate tax.

ed property for this purpose if the partnership agreement so provides.[59] This payment is not deductible by the partnership or the other partners. Second, any other payment is ordinary income to the recipient and deductible (or excludable, which comes to the same thing) by the other partners.[60] Thus, payments based on a partner's capital account or attributable to book value or appraised value of the underlying firm assets (other than unrealized receivables and substantially appreciated inventory) will be either tax-free or capital gain but non-deductible. The same is true of payment for good will (whether a fixed sum, capitalized earnings or otherwise) if the agreement classifies it as property. While this is attractive for the outgoing interest, it usually is not for those who continue. It is to their advantage that the payments to the outgoing interest be classed as ordinary income, for their ordinary income is reduced correspondingly. They intensify this advantage by placing a low valuation on the assets and not treating good will as property for this purpose. The outgoing interest may be agreeable to such an arrangement since it (e.g. a widow or retired partner) is typically in a lower tax bracket.[61]

All this amounts to a rare opportunity for the remaining partners to acquire a business interest partly or largely with funds generated by the business and not taxed to them or to the business. This opportunity is usually too good to refuse, and argues strongly for this method (including not classifying good will as property) in preference to other methods.

(4) *Modified Continuation.* If the outgoing partner or his estate retains a partnership interest, there are normally no tax consequences even though the form of the interest is modified. He or his estate continues to be taxed on his distributive share of income.

Any of these methods (except perhaps the third) can be combined with (a) payment for good will, which may be capital gain to the recipient and non-deductible by the payor, and (b) payment for an agreement not to compete, which is ordinary income to the recipient and deductible by the payor over the life of the agreement.[62]

Each of these methods may involve questions of allocating the payments between two (or more) categories, such as good will, other property, and agreements not to compete. Any allocation agreed upon by the parties is likely to be accepted.[63] This is largely because they have conflicting tax interests, and are assumed to bargain knowledge-

59. Id. § 736(b) (2) (B).

60. Id. § 736(a).

61. For a judicial explanation of the tax ramifications of a sale or liquidation of a partnership interest, and the freedom the parties have to choose whichever they agree upon, see David A. Foxman, 41 T.C. 535 (1964), affirmed 352 F.2d 466 (3d Cir. 1965).

A comprehensive discussion is Swihart, Tax Problems Raised by Liquidations of Partnership Interests, 44 Texas L. Rev. 1209 (1966).

62. Sec. 84 at n. 18B above.

63. E. g., Income Tax Reg. § 1.736–1(b) (1) (1956).

ably for the final result. Fiduciary responsibilities have an important role to play in seeing that one side does not take advantage of the other by proposing a pattern without disclosing its tax consequences.

No one of the methods is inevitably superior. The third has the greatest internal flexibility, and is probably best in the greatest number of instances. But there is no substitute, in a given situation, for a complete analysis of all alternatives before the choice is made.

The third method may appear novel to the lawyer who is not a tax specialist, and would probably not occur to him, especially for a two-man partnership where one partner dies or withdraws. Even in this situation, the third method can be used. Until payment to the outgoing interest is completed, the partnership continues to exist both in tax law,[64] and under U.P.A.[65] Persons claiming the advantages of the third method are frequently defeated by inadequate draftsmanship which creates an agreement among partners rather than one between a partner and a partnership.[66]

(c) Profits and Losses; Payment for Partner's Interest

If a partnership is seasonably wound up after dissolution, profits and losses during the liquidation are shared by the partners in proportion to their pre-dissolution ratios,[67] unless they have agreed otherwise. This is a corollary of the continued existence of the firm during the period,[68] and of the partners' representative authority in winding up.[69]

The situation changes if the business is not wound up, but continued, whether with or without agreement. In either case, the non-continuing partner (or his representative) has a *first election* between two basic alternatives, either of which can be enforced in an action for an accounting.[70] He can force a liquidation, taking his part of the proceeds and thus sharing in profits and losses after dissolution.[71]

---

64. Income Tax Reg. § 1.708–1(b) (i) (1956).

65. The payout of the retiring interest is part of the winding up. The partnership therefore continues until its completion, U.P.A. 30, Sec. 73 above.

66. Karan v. Commissioner, 319 F.2d 303 (7th Cir. 1963); David A. Foxman, 41 T.C. 535 (1964) aff'd 352 F.2d 466 (3d Cir. 1965); Charles F. Phillips, 40 T.C. 157 (1963).

67. Day v. Wilson, 286 F.2d 274 (10th Cir. 1961); Harstad v. Metcalf, 56 Wash.2d 239, 351 P.2d 1037 (1960) (including profits on post-dissolution contracts resulting from pre-dissolution preliminary studies). But see Couder v. Gomez, 378 S.W.2d 14 (Tex. 1964) (losses are shared in proportion to relative value of interests at dissolution) (pre-U.P.A.).

68. U.P.A. § 30, Sec. 73 above.

69. U.P.A. §§ 33, 35, Secs. 80–81 above.

70. U.P.A. § 22, Sec. 72 above.

See, in general, Annots., 55 A.L.R.2d 1391 (1957), 80 A.L.R. 12 (1932). See also, as to law firms, Annot., 78 A.L.R. 2d 280 (1961).

71. Essay v. Essay, 175 Neb. 689, 123 N.W.2d 20 (1963) modified to require consideration of managing partner's right to extra profits because of his special skills and services, 175 Neb. 730, 123 N.W.2d 648 (1963); Young v. Cooper, 30 Tenn.App. 55, 203 S.W.2d 376 (1947).

Alternatively, he can permit the business to continue (or accept the fact that it has continued [72]) and claim as a creditor (though subordinate to outside creditors) the value of his interest at dissolution.[73] This gives him a participation in all values at dissolution,[74] including asset appreciation and good will,[75] and means he is unaffected by later changes in those values.[76] If he takes the latter route, he has a *second election* to receive in addition either interest (presumably at the local legal rate) or profits from date of dissolution.[77] This second election

A partner expelled pursuant to the agreement, or one who has dissolved in contravention of it, cannot force liquidation. U.P.A. § 38, Secs. 75, 83A above. He is entitled to the value of his interest (with appropriate offset for damages in wrongful dissolution), and an election between profits and interest on that value to date of payment, under the second election described in the text.

72. But see Blut v. Katz, 13 N.J. 374, 99 A.2d 785 (1953) strictly and dubiously construing the statute to require consent of the outgoing interest to the continuation of the business. The decision was widely noted and roundly criticized, e. g., 23 Fordham L.Rev. 211 (1954), 67 Harv.L.Rev. 1271 (1954), 38 Minn.L.Rev. 553 (1954), 29 N.Y.U. L.Rev. 1151 (1954), 63 Yale L.J. 709 (1954).

73. U.P.A. § 42. Hurst v. Hurst, 1 Ariz. App. 227, 401 P.2d 232 (1965), revised 1 Ariz.App. 603, 405 P.2d 913 (1965); Wanderski v. Nowakowski, 331 Mich. 202, 49 N.W.2d 139 (1951); Sarner v. Sarner, 62 N.J.Super. 41, 162 A.2d 117 (1960) (judgment for profits alone reversed and remanded for valuation of interest).

Wikstrom v. Davis, 211 Or. 254, 315 P. 2d 597 (1957). The outgoing partner is regarded as a creditor as of the date of dissolution, not as of the later receiver's sale of the partnership property.

Although subordinate to third party creditors of the firm, he is still a creditor of the firm and therefore prior (as to firm assets) to individual creditors of the continuing partners. U.P.A. § 40(h), Sec. 90 below; Wanderski v. Nowakowski, above.

Cases under U.P.A. § 42 are collected in Annot., 2 A.L.R.2d 1084 (1948).

74. Hurst v. Hurst, n. 73 above.

75. Young v. Cooper, n. 71 above. These values are apparently shared according to pre-dissolution profit percentages. See Hurst v. Hurst, n. 73 above.

76. Casida v. Roberts, 51 Cal.2d 583, 337 P.2d 829 (1959). This was a 2-man partnership which operated for only five days, after which one partner continued for two months. The other was entitled to use U.P.A. § 42.

M. & C. Creditors Corp. v. Pratt, 172 Misc. 695, 17 N.Y.S.2d 240 (1938), aff'd 255 App.Div. 838, 7 N.Y.S.2d 662 (1938), aff'd on other grounds, 281 N.Y. 804, 24 N.E.2d 482 (1939).

The protection against subsequent declines in value of partnership assets is only against the other partners, not the creditors. The outgoing partner continues liable for pre-dissolution debts, U.P.A. § 36, Sec. 79 above, and may be called on to pay them if the firm fails. Cf. Kittredge v. Langley, 252 N.Y. 405, 169 N.E. 626, 67 A.L.R. 1087 (1930) (pre-U.L.P.A. limited partner withdrew his contribution when firm was apparently solvent; he was liable to creditor existing at dissolution when later decline in value of assets made the firm insolvent).

77. U.P.A. § 42; Casida v. Roberts, n. 76 above; Froess v. Froess, 284 Pa. 369, 131 A. 276 (1925), id. 289 Pa. 69, 137 A. 124 (1927).

The right to interest is cognate with U.P.A. § 18(d), Sec. 65(c) above.

See Taormina v. Culicchia, 335 S.W.2d 569 (Tex.Civ.App.1962) (outgoing partner must prove what the profits are before he can share in them) (pre-U.P.A.).

The profits shared include those from unauthorized use of partnership property. Bracht v. Connell, 313 Pa. 397, 170 A. 297 (1933).

shields him from losses, at least vis-à-vis the continuing partners. He need not make the second election until an accounting has disclosed the comparative figures and he sees which is more favorable to him.[78] However, he may elect earlier, either deliberately or by inept pleading or handling of his case.[79] He may not have interest for part of the time and profits for the rest, but must take one or the other consistently.[80]

The second election may seem one-sided. It serves as "a species of compulsion . . . to those continuing the business . . . to hasten its orderly winding up."[81] In part it is compensation to the outgoing partner for his liability on partnership obligations existing at dissolution; this liability continues until satisfaction,[82] which would normally occur in the process of winding up. The election is also compensation to the outgoing partner for his exposure to additional liability through the continuing partners' apparent authority.[83] Where the continuation of the business is without the consent of the outgoing partner, his option parallels a beneficiary's right to share in the profits of a fiduciary's unauthorized transactions.[84]

The second election rests partly on the use of the outgoing partner's assets in the conduct of the business. For this reason, the share of profits he may elect to take is based not on his pre-dissolution profit percentage but on the proportion of his value to the total value at date of dissolution.[85] In consequence, his right to profits ends when the value of his interest is properly paid to him.[86] This theory has oc-

78. Moseley v. Moseley, 196 F.2d 663 (9th Cir. 1952); Casida v. Roberts, n. 76 above; Wikstrom v. Davis, n. 73 above; Kreinson v. Commercial Nat. Bank, 323 Pa. 332, 185 A. 756 (1936).

79. See Vangel v. Vangel, 116 Cal.App. 2d 615, 254 P.2d 919 (Dist.Ct.App. 1953) aff'd in this respect, rev'd in other respects, and remanded, 45 Cal. 2d 804, 291 P.2d 25, 55 A.L.R.2d 1385 (1955), subsequent appeal n. 86 below.

80. Hurst v. Hurst, 86 Ariz. 242, 344 P.2d 1001 (1959).

81. Wikstrom v. Davis, 211 Or. 254, 315 P.2d 597, 608 (1957). Accord, Casida v. Roberts, n. 76 above.

82. U.P.A. § 36, Sec. 79 above.

83. U.P.A. § 35, Sec. 81 above.

84. Cf. U.P.A. § 21, Sec. 68 above; Hamilton Co. v. Hamilton Tile Corp., 23 Misc.2d 589, 197 N.Y.S.2d 384 (1960).

85. Moseley v. Moseley, n. 78 above; Vangel v. Vangel, n. 79 above; Yeomans v. Lysfjord, 162 Cal.App.2d 357, 327 P.2d 957 (1958); Wood v. Wood, 312 Pa. 374, 167 A. 600 (1933) (emphasizing investment rather than operational character of the profits); Douthart v. Logan, 190 Ill. 243, 60 N.E. 507 (1901); Robinson v. Simmons, 146 Mass. 167, 15 N.E. 558, 4 Am.St. Rep. 299 (1888) (both pre-U.P.A.).

Interest, if elected, is based on the same value at dissolution. In either case, the election is relatively little help to a partner whose capital interest is small relative to his share of profits, e. g., because he contributed services while others contributed capital, or because his profits went to pay for his interest in the firm.

86. Vangel v. Vangel, 51 Cal.2d 510, 334 P.2d 863 (1959) (deposit in escrow sufficed for payment in this case); Johnson v. Munsell, 170 Neb. 749, 104 N.W.2d 314, 326 (1960) (pre-U.P.A.).

casionally been extended to deny him profits when his interest at dissolution has little or no value.[87]

Both the first and the second elections are subject to any agreement the partners may have made.[88] Not every agreement automatically eliminates the second option. If the agreement merely sets the price, the outgoing partner may claim profits to the date of payment.[89]

While the conceptual distinction between liquidation (which does not allow the first election) and continuation (which allows the first and the second) is clear, it may be hard to tell in some cases which has in fact occurred, i. e. whether there has been a continuation or only a slow winding up.[90] Where each of the partners continues some phase of the business, neither the purposes nor the mechanics of the elections are very applicable. The best solution in such a case is usually to treat the partnership as terminated, with an appropriate accounting based on assets taken, liabilities paid or assumed, and profits and losses from pre-dissolution business.[91]

---

87. Hall v. Watson, 73 Cal.App.2d 735, 167 P.2d 210 (1946); Frey v. Hauke, 171 Neb. 852, 108 N.W.2d 228 (1961). Normally, a partner who abandons the firm forfeits his rights to share in subsequent profits. Herren v. Harris, Cortner & Co., 201 Ala. 577, 78 So. 921 (1918) (dictum). Forbes v. Becker, 150 Okl. 281, 1 P.2d 721, 80 A.L.R. 1 (1931) (pre-U.P.A.). Contra, Pownall v. Cearfoss, 129 W.Va. 487, 40 S.E.2d 886 (1946).

88. U.P.A. § 42 (election "unless otherwise agreed"). McClennen v. Commissioner, 131 F.2d 165, 144 A.L.R. 1127 (1st Cir. 1942); Harris v. Klure, 205 Cal.App.2d 574, 23 Cal.Rptr. 313 (1962) (agreement for 5% interest from death; profits not allowed); Smith v. Smith, 149 Cal.App.2d 29, 307 P.2d 644 (1957) (agreement for net book value without interest); Lyon v. Sanger, 107 N.Y.S.2d 300 (Sup.Ct. 1951) (agreement for actual investment plus profit share for current six months); Young v. Young, 233 N.C. 247, 63 S.E.2d 535 (1951) (post-dissolution agreement for each partner to take separate group of properties); Clark v. Allen, 215 Or. 403, 333 P.2d 1100 (1958); Tucker v. Tucker, 370 Pa. 8, 87 A.2d 650 (1952); In re Prins' Estate, 33 Wash.2d 831, 207 P. 2d 909 (1949).

The agreement may take any of the forms discussed in Sec. 86(a), (b) above. But see Young v. Cooper, n. 71 above (agreement for right of first refusal on sale of partner's interest didn't preclude his right to dissolve and terminate).

89. In re Streck's Estate, 35 Ill.App.2d 473, 183 N.E.2d 26 (1962); In re Prins' Estate, n. 88 above.

90. See Hurley v. Hurley, 33 Del.Ch. 231, 91 A.2d 674 (1952) (business operated for over 2 years after dissolution, but only for purpose of liquidating at better price; outgoing interest entitled only to share of liquidation proceeds, not to value at dissolution or interest thereon).

See also Eardley v. Sammons, 8 Utah 2d 159, 330 P.2d 122 (1958) (financing partner who took charge of cafe when operating partner was drunk and neglecting it, did not elect to take it over permanently so as to give operating partner election under U.P.A. § 42; financing partner immediately filed suit for accounting and, apparently, dissolution).

91. See Harstad v. Metcalf, n. 67 above; Rinke v. Rinke, 330 Mich. 615, 48 N.W. 2d 201 (1951) (hardware business and two automobile dealerships split among three partners).

ACCRUAL OF ACTIONS

§ 87. **The right to an account of his interest shall accrue to any partner or his legal representative, as against the winding-up partners or the surviving partners or the person or partnership continuing the business, at the date of dissolution, in the absence of any agreement to the contrary. U.P.A. § 43.**

After dissolution a partner, or one who represents him as owner of his interest, is entitled to an account, i. e. to a statement of the partnership affairs,[92] and, in the due course, to a payment of the amount of his interest.[93] As to when the statute of limitations begins to run, there is some diversity of authority. It would seem that so long as there is no apparent neglect, or wrongful withholding of information or of property, there is no occasion for resorting to legal remedies, and no reason for commencing the running of the statutory period. This has been held to be the law as to dissolution inter vivos, where no partner is appointed a liquidating partner.[94] Other courts have held that the statute does not being to run so long as there are unsettled debts due to or by the partnership.[95] Other courts have held that it runs from the date of dissolution.[96] An accounting begun within the limitations period after dissolution can extend back over the entire span of partnership operations.[97]

For an action against a surviving partner or liquidating partner,[98]

92. U.P.A. § 43. Long v. Mertz, 21 N. J.Super. 401, 91 A.2d 341 (1952). The section does not preclude an earlier accounting when appropriate. U.P.A. § 22, Sec. 72 above esp. at n. 95.

93. Hayden v. Hayden, 354 Pa. 11, 46 A.2d 502 (1946).

The right to an accounting may be non-existent by reason of terms in the partnership agreement. In Hermes v. Compton, 260 App.Div. 507, 23 N.Y. S.2d 126 (1940), the articles provided that survivors should continue the business, that the deceased partner's estate should have no interest in assets but merely a right to receive for five years certain percentage of profits. It was held that there was no right to an accounting under this section of the U.P.A., and that the remedy at law was adequate.

94. Riddle v. Whitehill, 135 U.S. 621, 10 S.Ct. 924, 34 L.Ed. 282, 283 (1890); Gray v. Green, 142 N.Y. 316, 37 N.E. 124, 40 Am.St.Rep. 596 (1894).

95. Prentice v. Elliott, 72 Ga. 154 (1883); Easley v. Clay, 16 S.W.2d 888 (Tex.Civ.App.1929); Jordan v. Miller, 75 Va. 442 (1881); or until the amount due from partner to partner is ascertained, Clark v. Moffett, 136 Kan. 711, 714, 18 P.2d 555, 556 (1933).

96. Eddy v. Fogg, 192 Mass. 543, 78 N. E. 549 (1906). See note, Ann.Cas. 1918D, 1107.

97. See Sec. 72 above; Greenan v. Ernst, 408 Pa. 495, 184 A.2d 570 (1962) (38 years).

98. Gopala Chetty v. Vijayaraghava-chariar, [1922] 1 A.C. 488. In absence of agreement to the contrary the right to an accounting accrues as against liquidating partner at date of dissolution, Trecker v. Trecker, 334 Ill.App. 263, 78 N.E.2d 843 (1948). Guldin v. Lorah, 141 Pa. 109, 21 A. 504 (1891). But see McPherson v. Swift, 22 S.D. 165, 116 N.W. 76, 133 Am.St.Rep. 907 (1908), holding that the statute does not begin to run in favor of the surviving partner in the absence of some breach of duty by him. In Zell's Appeal, 126 Pa. 329, 17 A. 647 (1889), the statute was held not to run in favor of the surviving partner as to an asset acquired thirteen years after dissolution. See also

as stated in the Uniform Act,[99] the statute begins to run on the date of dissolution.[1]

The U.P.A. section quoted at the beginning of this paragraph serves also to identify the persons entitled to an accounting at dissolution. These include partners and their legal representatives, but not their heirs.[2] Assignees of partners' interests are given limited rights to accounting.[3]

LIABILITY OF ONGOING AND INCOMING PARTNERS

§ 88. When any new partner is admitted into an existing partnership, or when any partner retires and assigns (or the representative of the deceased partner assigns) his rights in partnership property to two or more of the partners, or to one or more of the partners and one or more third persons, if the business is continued without liquidation of the partnership affairs, creditors of the first or dissolved partnership are also creditors of the partnership so continuing the business. U.P.A. § 41(1).

A person admitted as a partner into an existing partnership is liable for all the obligations of the partnership arising before his admission as though he had been a partner when such obligations were incurred, except that this liability shall be satisfied only out of partnership property. U.P.A. § 17.

Duncan v. Westerlund, 110 S.C. 94, 96 S.E. 531 (1918). See 28 Harv.L.Rev. 787; 29 Harv.L.Rev. 309.

An action for accounting by the surviving partner against the estate of the deceased partner is not barred by the lapse of the statutory period since dissolution, but the period runs from the time when liquidation should have been finished. Burris v. Burris, 140 Kan. 208, 34 P.2d 127, 96 A.L.R. 432 (1934).

99. U.P.A. § 43, applied as a binding statutory rule in Manley v. Belew, 190 Tenn. 698, 231 S.W.2d 353 (1950). La Russo v. Paladino, 109 N.Y.S.2d 627 (Sup.Ct.1952), aff'd 280 App.Div. 988, 116 N.Y.S.2d 617 (1952), appeal denied 281 App.Div. 753, 118 N.Y.S.2d 557 (1953).

In England, rights of third party creditor beneficiaries not being recognized, a novation is necessary to bind the incoming partner to former creditors. See Turner, Pollock on Partnership, 56, 57 (1944).

1. A decision which might have applied U.P.A. § 43 to reach an opposite result,

fails even to mention it. A firm ceased operations in 1929; one partner took over its land and had occasional timber cuttings through the years and gave an option on some of the land in 1952. Although another of the partners had died in 1932, an accounting action was permitted in 1953 under a statute of limitations permitting actions for settlement of partnerships until five years after "cessation of dealings in which they are interested together." Hodge v. Kennedy, 198 Va. 416, 94 S.E.2d 274 (1956). Semble, Brand v. Elledge, 101 Ariz. 352, 419 P.2d 531 (1966).

2. La Russo v. Paladino, n. 99 above. See Peller v. Katz, 15 Misc.2d 1093, 181 N.Y.S.2d 519 (1959), recognizing some exceptions. Ewing v. Caldwell, 243 N.C. 18, 89 S.E.2d 774 (1955).

3. U.P.A. § 27(2), Sec. 42 above (only since the last account agreed to by all the partners). One state has broadened this to the right "to require reasonable information or account." Vernon's Ann.Civ.St. (Tex.) art. 6132b, § 27(2) (1962).

An incoming partner may become personally liable by assumption or novation.

(a) Ongoing Partners

It is often said that any change in the members of a partnership involves a technical dissolution, although the business is continued without apparent change.[4] By the better view, this is not necessarily so.[5] If dissolution does occur, and the old firm's property is transferred to a new firm, to a single continuing partner or to a stranger, there is no property left to the old firm. Unless this is a fraudulent conveyance (because of the old firm's insolvency) or in violation of bulk sale or transfer acts, the power of old firm creditors to reach directly the former firm property by attachment or execution is gone.[6] With it goes their priority over individual creditors. Without novation or assumption they are, at common law, not creditors of the new firm; they are only individual creditors of the former partners, subordinate to the rights of creditors of the new firm in the new firm's property (including that transferred from the old firm).[7] They encounter procedural difficulties in trying to collect; in event of insolvency, they have little chance of getting anything. That this result seems seldom to have occurred is probably due to the fact that the firm or person continuing the business usually assumes the old debts, or there is a novation.

The U.P.A. has effected a significant change by providing that, when a business of a dissolved partnership is continued by a former

---

4. Shunk v. Shunk Mfg. Co., 86 Ohio App. 467, 93 N.E.2d 321 (1949).

5. Secs. 78A, 73, 77(a) above.

6. Ex Parte Ruffin, 6 Ves.Jr. 119, 30 Eng.Rep. 988 (1801), holding that former partnership creditors had no priority in the partnership assets in the hands of an insolvent continuing partner; Freeman v. Huttig Sash & Door Co., 105 Tex. 560, 153 S.W. 122, Ann. Cas.1916E, 446 (1913), the old firm creditor could not attach the property in the hands of the new firm composed of continuing and incoming partners.

Compare Reddington v. Franey, 124 Wis. 590, 102 N.W. 1065 (1905), where a retiring partner assumed the payment of the old firm debts and promised to hold the incoming partner harmless. The latter paid the old creditors. It was held that he could not recover reimbursement from the retired partner, since he was under no necessity of payment of the debts to protect the property in the hands of the new firm.

In Locke v. Hall, 9 Greenl. 133 (Me. 1832), a creditor, in ignorance of assumption by new firm, sued the old firm. It was held that he could not, after judgment, levy execution on property attached in the possession of the new firm.

See Secs. 46 and 47, above, on fraudulent conveyances and bulk transfers, Sec. 91B(d)–(f) below on transfers voidable in bankruptcy. See Remedies of Partnership Creditors on Transfer of Firm Assets to One Partner, 49 Yale L.J. 686 (1940).

7. The former partners continue liable on obligations existing at dissolution. Sec. 79 above. But this may be of little help to the partnership creditor, who faces the dual obstacles of joint liability (where it prevails, Secs. 58–60 above) and possible priority of each partner's individual creditors in his individual assets (Sec. 90 below). See Sher & Bromberg, Texas Partnership Law in the 20th Century—Why Texas Should Adopt the Uniform Partnership Act, 12 Sw.L.J. 263, 280–83 (1958).

partner or partners, with or without new partners, the old creditors are creditors of the person or partnership continuing the business.[8] Under such a statute the old creditors are on a parity with the new in that they can bring suit against the new firm, levy execution on its property, and share in its distribution in the event of insolvency. The results are substantially the same despite variations in the pattern of membership changes.[9] No agreement of assumption is necessary; it is supplied by the statute.

The liability of the outgoing partner is considered elsewhere.[10]

(b) Incoming Partners

The incoming partner is not, at common law, liable on old debts.[11] The Act does not impose any such liability on him beyond his share in partnership property.[12] The incoming partner may, in consideration of his acquiring an interest in the new partnership, promise to his co-partners or to a retiring partner that old creditors will be paid. As third party beneficiaries, the old creditors are entitled to enforce such a promise in the majority of jurisdictions.[13] The U.P.A. does not deal

---

8. See extended Commissioners' Notes to U.P.A. §§ 17 and 41, 7 Uniform Laws Ann. 100 and 229 (1944).

9. U.P.A. § 41(1) (admission of new partner; retirement of partner and transfer two or more partners; retirement of partners and transfer to one or more partners and one or more strangers); 41(2) (retirement of all but one, who continues alone or with strangers); 41(3) (retirement or death without assignment); 41(5) (continuation after wrongful dissolution; Sec. 83(a) above); 41(6) (continuation after expulsion; Sec. 83A(b) above).

The firm creditors have priority over a retiring or deceased partner who has become a creditor for the value of his interest by U.P.A. § 42, Sec. 86 above, or otherwise. U.P.A. § 41(8). And their rights under the law of fraudulent conveyances are preserved. U.P. A. § 41(9).

For continuation entirely by strangers, see U.P.A. § 41(4), Sec. 89 below.

10. Secs. 79–81 above.

11. Tuller v. Leaverton, 143 Iowa 162, 121 N.W. 515, 136 Am.St.Rep. 756 (1909); Freeman v. Huttig Sash & Door Co., n. 6 above, holding, however, that the incoming partner was liable for goods ordered before his admission and delivered after his admission,

while he was a partner; Wolff v. Madden, 6 Wash. 514, 33 P. 975 (1893).

An incoming partner is held liable for rent accruing after his admission under a lease for a term of years entered into prior to his admission. He is in effect a co-tenant. Ellingson v. Walsh, O'Connor & Barneson, 15 Cal. 2d 673, 104 P.2d 507 (1940), noted 29 Calif.L.Rev. 252 (1941).

12. U.P.A. §§ 17, 41(7).

13. Wood v. Macafee, 172 N.Y.S. 703 (Sup.1918); Townsend v. Long, 77 Pa. 143, 18 Am.Rep. 438 (1874); Pierce Butler Radiator Corp. v. Luongo, 87 F.Supp. 56 (E.D.Pa.1949), citing U.P.A. § 17. See Note, 19 Colum.L.Rev. 66–68 (1919).

If the incoming partner agrees to assume certain specified obligations, he cannot be held liable for others. McGilvery v. McGilvery & Seeley, 23 Idaho 116, 128 P. 978 (1912).

As to proof in bankruptcy against a continuing firm which has assumed old firm debts, see In re Stringer, 234 F. 454 (S.D.N.Y.1916).

As to third party creditor beneficiaries in general, see Restatement, Contracts, § 136.

As to the enforcement of the partnership promise of assumption of the trade debts of a member whose business is

with this situation, and it may be assumed that old creditors, as third party beneficiaries, are entitled to the same remedies as before the adoption of the Act.[14] The incoming partner may become personally liable as a result of novation between the old creditor and the new firm.[15]

Similarly, an incoming partner is not personally bound by non-monetary partnership contracts unless there is assumption or novation.[16]

The U.P.A. provisions, by their terms, do not apply when a sole proprietor and a stranger become partners to operate the business formerly conducted by the proprietor. In such a case, neither the firm [17] nor the new participant [18] is liable. Naturally, either may become so by novation or assumption of prior obligations of the business.[19]

LIABILITY OF PURCHASERS AND CORPORATE SUCCESSORS OF BUSINESS

§ 89. When all the partners or their representatives assign their rights in partnership property to one or more third persons who promise to pay the debts and who continue the business of the dissolved partnership, creditors of the dissolved partnership are also creditors of the person or partnership continuing the business. U.P.A. § 41(4).

Where, for valuable consideration (such as the transfer of the property and business of a partnership) a third person expressly assumes the payment of a part or all of the partnership obligations, it is a creditor beneficiary contract which is generally held to be enforcible by the creditor.[20] The result is the same whether the purchaser is an

taken over by the partnership, see Arnold v. Nicols, 64 N.Y. 117 (1876).

14. Cf. Magrini v. Jackson, n. 18 below.

15. First Nat. Bank of Winfield v. Perfected Curing & Storage Co., 280 S.W. 737 (Tex.Com.App.1926).

16. Fields v. City of Oakland, 137 Cal. App.2d 602, 291 P.2d 145 (1956) (exculpatory provisions of lease).

17. Arnold Barber & Beauty Supply Co. v. Provance, 221 Ark. 385, 253 S.W.2d 367 (1953). However, their may be liability under "bulk sales" statutes; see Sec. 47 above.

18. Hargis v. Hargis, 221 Ark. 654, 255 S.W.2d 663 (1953). This was a federal income tax liability which was probably personal then and clearly is now. See Int.Rev.Code of 1954 § 701 (26 U.S. C.A.) (partners, not partnerships, subject to tax). Griffin v. Williamson, 137 Cal.App.2d 308, 290 P.2d 361 (1956). Magrini v. Jackson, 17 Ill. App.2d 346, 150 N.E.2d 387 (1958), noted 1958 U.Ill.L.F. 661.

19. Pecarovich v. Becker, 113 Cal.App. 2d 309, 248 P.2d 123 (1952) (newcomer's agreement with sole owner for acquisition of half interest in "contracts" and other specified items was an assumption of liabilities under the contracts; creditor as third party beneficiary could enforce).

Magrini v. Jackson, n. 18 above (agreement among partners to make mortgage payments from partnership funds, use of mortgaged property in partnership business, and some actual payments on mortgage from partnership funds amounted to an assumption).

20. Restatement, Contracts § 136; Williston, Contracts, § 381 (3d ed. 1959).

individual, a corporation, or another partnership.[21] The problem frequently arises where a business has been carried on by a partnership and the partners, desiring the advantages of the corporate form, create a corporation,[22] transfer to it the partnership property, and become shareholders, directors and officers rather than partners. For the protection of the partners it is common to include in the transaction an express assumption of the partnership obligations, as a part of the price paid for the property. In such case the corporation is subject to recovery by the partnership creditors whose claims are assumed, under the U.P.A. provision quoted above, and at common law in jurisdictions recognizing the rights of third party creditor beneficiaries.[23]

In the absence of express assumption, in some jurisdictions no assumption is implied, and the corporation, regarded as a distinct entity, is under no liability.[24] The situation is different from a transfer by one corporation to another with identical membership, where the original debtor is stripped of its assets, and the creditors left without remedy except as they may pursue the assets under the law of fraudulent conveyances.[25] The remedy against the partners personally remains, and if they are solvent, is adequate. If they are insolvent, the transaction may be attacked as a fraudulent conveyance.[26] In the majority

---

21. U.P.A. §§ 41(4), 2 (definition of persons). If the purchaser is a partnership including one or more of the former partners, see Sec. 88 above.

22. The shift is often made for tax reasons. For the special problems involved, see Paul & Kalish, Transition from a Partnership to a Corporation, N.Y.U. 18th Inst. on Fed.Tax. 639 (1960); Gifford, Changing a Partnership into a Corporation, 16 Vand.L. Rev. 351 (1963).

23. In re Stone-Moore-West Co., 292 F. 1004 (M.D.Ga.1923); Modern Dairy & Creamery Co. v. Blanke & Hauk Supply Co., 116 S.W. 153 (Tex.Civ.App. 1909), semble; Schufeldt v. Smith, 139 Mo. 367, 40 S.W. 887 (1847).

There may in the case of executory bilateral contracts, such as employment contracts, be a novation manifested by the corporation accepting services from employees of the former partnership, so that the corporation becomes the employer in substitution for the partnership. Stowell v. Garden City News Corp., 143 Kan. 840, 57 P.2d 12 (1936); Moskowitz v. A. B. Kirschbaum Co., 89 Pa.Super. 274 (1926).

24. Rodgers v. Lincoln Hospital, 239 Mich. 329, 214 N.W. 88 (1927), noted

26 Mich.L.Rev. 449; Schufeldt v. Smith, 139 Mo. 367, 40 S.W. 887 (1897), semble; Taylor Lumber Co. v. Clark Lumber Co., 33 Ga.App. 815, 127 S.E. 905 (1925); Martin v. Culpeper Supply Co., 88 W.Va. 471, 107 S.E. 183 (1921). See also Commissioners' Note to U.P.A. § 41(4), 7 Unif.Laws Ann. 231 (1949).

25. See Stevens, Corporations, § 193 (2d ed. 1949); Note, 3 U.Pitt.L.Rev. 62 (1936). Compare Aetna Ins. Co. v. Bank of Wilcox, 48 Neb. 544, 67 N.W. 449 (1896); Hibernia Ins. Co. v. St. Louis & N. O. Transp. Co., 13 F. 516, 518 (E.D.Mo.1882).

26. Mulford v. Doremus, 60 N.J.Eq. 80, 45 A. 688 (1900). See also Secs. 43, 44 above.

As to whether transfer of partnership property to a corporation in exchange for stock issued to the partners, who are otherwise without substantial resources, is a fraudulent conveyance, note the provisions of the Uniform Fraudulent Conveyance Act, § 8, making a conveyance by a partnership, thereby rendered insolvent, for a consideration moving to the individual partners, a fraudulent conveyance.

See also Bankruptcy Act, § 67d(4), Sec. 91B(f) below.

of jurisdictions liability is imposed on the grounds of assumption implied in fact from the circumstances in accordance with the presumed intention of the partners,[27] or a liability is imposed on the corporation as the *alter ego* of the partners who have formed it; the legal entity of the corporation as a distinct person is disregarded in the interests of justice to the creditors who might otherwise be hindered.[28] When liability is imposed on this ground, it is doubtful whether it should extend beyond the property received from the partners.[29]

U.P.A. § 41(8) provides that partnership creditors have a priority over separate creditors of the retired partner in the consideration received. Accordingly, when a partnership transfers its property to a corporation which assumes the liabilities, partnership creditors can reach the corporate shares received by a partner for his interest even if he was not a partner when the obligation was incurred to the credi-

U.P.A. § 41(9) provides that nothing in the section shall be held to modify any right of creditors to set aside any assignment on the ground of fraud. Bulk sale or transfer acts may be applicable to the process of incorporating partnerships. Partners cannot be allowed to circumvent their creditors by the use of the corporate device. The court in bankruptcy may disregard the corporate entity to administer as partnership property the assets of a corporation created by the bankrupt partnership as a means of defrauding creditors. In re Rieger, Kapner & Altmark, 157 F. 609 (S.D. Ohio 1907). See comment by Wormser, The Disregard of the Corporate Fiction and Allied Corporate Problems, pp. 49, 50. See also O'Neal v. Jones, 34 S.W.2d 689 (Tex.Civ.App. 1931).

27. Du Vivier & Co. v. Gallice, 149 F. 118 (2d Cir. 1906); Hall v. Herter Bros., 90 Hun 280, 35 N.Y.S. 769 (1895), aff'd 157 N.Y. 694, 51 N.E. 1091 (1898); Andres v. Morgan, 62 Ohio St. 236, 56 N.E. 875, 78 Am.St.Rep. 712 (1900); Modern Dairy & Creamery Co. v. Blanke & Hauk Supply Co., 116 S.W. 153 (Tex.Civ.App.1909); Ziemer v. C. G. Bretting Mfg. Co., 147 Wis. 252, 133 N.W. 139, Ann.Cas.1912D, 1275 (1911). See 8 Fletcher, Corporations, § 4014, note 3 U.Pitt.L.Rev. 62 (1936).

In some jurisdictions it has been held that there is a rebuttable presumption of assumption. Curtis, Jones & Co. v. Smelter Nat. Bank, 43 Colo. 391, 96 P. 172 (1908); Reed Bros. Co. v. First

Nat. Bank, 46 Neb. 168, 64 N.W. 701 (1895).

No assumption is to be implied either as a matter of fact or of law if membership in the corporation is not identical with membership in the partnership. Cooper Bros. Co. v. Putnam, 122 Me. 495, 120 A. 624 (1923); Adams v. Empire Laundry Mach. Co., 52 Hun 610, 4 N.Y.S. 738 (1889).

28. Kulka v. Nemirovsky, 321 Pa. 234, 182 A. 692 (1936); In re W. J. Marshall Co., 3 F.2d 192 (S.D.Ga.1924); In re Johnson-Hart Co., 34 F.2d 183 (D.C.Minn.1929).

Compare Coaldale Coal Co. v. State Bank, 142 Pa. 288, 21 A. 811 (1891), where the partners retained assets apparently sufficient to meet the claims of unsecured creditors, which assets subsequently became valueless, and also pledged the corporate stock to other creditors, who would have been defeated had the claim of the unsecured partnership creditors against the corporation been sustained.

In some cases, partners remain liable for debts incurred after incorporation, unless some kind of notice is given. See Vernon's Ann.Civ.St. (Tex.) art. 1302–2.02 (1962) (newspaper notice required if no change of name). For pre-incorporation notice requirements in general, see 2 Model Bus.Corp.Act Ann. 169–70 (1960).

29. Compare Allen v. North Des Moines M. E. Church, 127 Iowa 96, 101, 102 N.W. 808, 810, 69 L.R.A. 255, 109 Am. St.Rep. 366, 4 Ann.Cas. 257 (1905), a

tor seeking to enforce a judgment, as an incoming partner he is liable to the extent of partnership property, and the shares received by the partner in exchange for the partnership property are treated as partnership property.[30]

RULES FOR DISTRIBUTION

§ 90. In settling accounts between the partners after dissolution, the following rules shall be observed, subject to any agreement to the contrary:

(a) The assets of the partnership are;

    (I) The partnership property.

    (II) The contributions of the partners necessary for the payment of all the liabilities specified in clause (b) of this paragraph.

(b) The liabilities of the partnership shall rank in order of payment as follows:

    (I) Those owing to creditors other than partners,

    (II) Those owing to partners other than for capital and profits,

    (III) Those owing to partners in respect of capital,

    (IV) Those owing to partners in respect of profits.

(c) The assets shall be applied in the order of their declaration in clause (a) of this paragraph to the satisfaction of the liabilities. U.P.A. § 40(a), (b), (c).

The process of winding up, where the business is not continued,[31] consists in reducing the property to cash and distributing the proceeds. The property of the partnership must be liquidated and distributed. Partners severally have the authority to sell partnership property and to collect obligations due to the partnership.[32] Property available for distribution includes, in addition to the partnership property, contributions which may be collected from the partners for the payment of partnership obligations to creditors and to partners. The U.P.A., as quoted above, defines partnership assets to include these contributions, which is quite consistent with the entity theory of partnership.[33] The

case of one corporation succeeding to the assets and business of another.

30. Stein v. Andron, 55 Cal.App.2d 510, 131 P.2d 39 (1943).

31. If the business is continued, the rules for settlement are described in Sec. 86(c) above.

32. Secs. 80, 83A above; U.P.A. § 38(1).

33. "This language in section 40 recalls the thought advanced by Cory, an advocate of the entity theory (pp. 36–38, referring to Cory on Accounts, 2d Ed.

pp. 124 et seq.), and with which we have now become familiar, that the partnership will have as one of its assets a claim against the partner to supply to it the funds necessary to pay its obligations." Warren, Corporate Advantages without Incorporation 297 (1929).

In 29 Harv.L.Rev. 165, 166 (1916) Dr. Lewis, the draftsman of the Uniform Act, referring to the method of imposing liability on partners for firm obligations, under the entity theory, said: "The only practical solution under the legal person theory was the one to

effect is to make the assets equal the liabilities, except where all the partners are insolvent, or will become so through their contribution.[34] This duty of contribution [35] to effect a proper sharing of losses and expenditures has already been discussed.[36] The duty may be enforced by any of the partners or their legal representatives,[37] or by appropriate representatives of creditors.[38]

The order of distribution of assets is carefully specified by statute.[39] First payment must go to creditors other than partners. Then come the claims of partners other than for capital contributions or profits, such as claims for advancements or loans. The presumption is that interest is payable on such advancements.[40] After this, partners are entitled to return to their respective capital contributions.[41] If the partnership property is insufficient to repay capital contributions, the loss is to be shared by the solvent partners, like other losses, in the proportions in which they would share profits.[42] Finally, any remaining balance of partnership property is distributable as profits.

Statutory rules of dissolution and liquidation may be varied by agreement of the partners, either in original articles or in a dissolution agreement.[43] It may be agreed that one partner can on notice

which all of the advocates of that theory to whom he had talked adhered, namely, that the partner should be regarded as a contributor to the partnership and as having an obligation to the partnership to furnish it with the necessary funds to meet its obligations to third persons, but that those having claims against the partnership have, as such claimants, no claims against the partners."

34. See Comment, 23 Rocky Mt.L.Rev. 331 (1951).

35. U.P.A. § 40(d); Caldwell v. Herrick, 328 Pa. 128, 114 A.2d 130 (1955). The obligation extends to the individual property of a deceased partner. U.P. A. § 40(g). U.P.A. § 36(4), Sec. 79(d), above, preserves the priority of individual creditors in the individual property. Semble U.P.A. § 40(i).

36. Sec. 65(a), (b) above.

37. U.P.A. § 40(f).

38. U.P.A. § 40(e).

39. U.P.A. § 40(b).

40. U.P.A. § 18(c), Sec. 65(c) above.

41. Sinman v. Mezoff, 327 Mass. 285, 98 N.E.2d 263 (1951); Bass v. Daetwyler,

305 S.W.2d 339 (Mo.App.1957); Eardley v. Sammons, 8 Utah 2d 159, 330 P. 2d 122 (1958).

42. U.P.A. §§ 40(d), 18(a), Sec. 65(a) above. Where the fund remaining after payment of debts is less than one partner's capital contribution (and the co-partner made no capital contribution), it all goes to the partner. Lyman v. Wood, 169 Pa.Super. 512, 83 A.2d 420 (1951). The partner did not seek contribution from the co-partner toward the deficiency.

43. U.P.A. § 40, 1st clause. Wallner v. Schmitz, 239 Minn. 93, 57 N.W.2d 821 (1953) (release). Wathen v. Brown, 200 Pa.Super. 620, 189 A.2d 900 (1963) (dissolution agreement presumed to settle all claims between partners). Of course, no agreement among partners can change the rights of third persons without their consent.

Other examples of agreements are given in Secs. 86(a) above and 90A below and Bromberg, Partnership Dissolution—Causes, Consequences, and Cures, 43 Texas L.Rev. 631, 653–69 (1965).

Disagreement on the method of distribution is arbitrable. Vogel v. Simon, 26 Misc.2d 436, 201 N.Y.S.2d 877 (1960).

buy out all or a part of the interest of another partner for a sum not exceeding its book value.[44]

It may be agreed that any partner may dissolve the partnership on notice, whereupon the other partners may buy out the interest of the retiring partner at a price based on market value of properties, excluding goodwill.[45]

It may be agreed that on dissolution by death the survivor will take all the partnership property, without any duty to share with the representatives of deceased partners.[46] On formation of a partnership, conventional valuations may be put upon capital contributions in the form of property for the purpose of fixing the relative capital rights of partners, so that on dissolution return of capital may be on a different basis in fact than were contributions.[47] Partners may agree that they are owners of capital in proportions different from their contributions.[48]

A dissolution agreement may work a reconversion of partnership real estate so that partners thereafter hold as tenants in common with a right to partition.[49]

44. Hagan v. Dundore, 185 Md. 86, 43 A.2d 181, 160 A.L.R. 517 (1945).

45. Wood v. Gunther, 89 Cal.App.2d 718, 201 P.2d 874 (1949).

46. Ottaviano v. Lorenzo, 169 Md. 51, 179 A. 530 (1935); In re Karlinski's Estate, 38 N.Y.S.2d 297 (Sur.1942) (subject to statutory rights of a spouse in decedent's estate). Partners may invest their profits in a manner clearly indicating joint tenancy with right of survivorship, Block v. Schmidt, 296 Mich. 610, 296 N.W. 698 (1941). Partners may carry their cash in a joint bank account, survivor to take all, Collier v. Benjes, 195 Md. 168, 73 A.2d 21 (1950), subject however to its application to reimburse deceased partner's estate for payment made to a firm creditor.

Where the partnership carried life insurance on the life of each partner they may by dissolution agreement provide that each partner shall take by assignment the policy on his own life. Elliott v. Metropolitan Life Ins. Co., 116 Ind.App. 404, 64 N.E.2d 911 (1946). See Sec. 37A(c) above.

Partners may each insure, naming co-partners as beneficiaries, with agreement that proceeds shall be used to buy out a deceased partner's interest, and that survivor shall become successor beneficiary of policy on his life. In such a situation each partner is the ultimate beneficiary and cannot deduct the premiums paid by him as business expense for income tax purposes. Ernest J. Keefe v. Commissioner, 15 T.C. 947 (1950). See Int.Rev. Code of 1954, § 264 (26 U.S.C.A.).

47. Kennedy v. Hill, 89 S.C. 462, 71 S.E. 974 (1911).

48. Groth v. Kersting, 23 Colo. 213, 47 P. 393 (1896); Smiley v. Smiley's Adm'x, 112 Va. 490, 71 S.E. 532, Ann. Cas.1913B, 1159 (1911). See also Burnett v. Hopwood, 187 Minn. 7, 244 N.W. 254 (1932).

49. Webber v. Rosenberg, 318 Mass. 768, 64 N.E.2d 98 (1945).

ANTICIPATING DEATH AND OTHER CHANGES
IN MEMBERSHIP

§ 90A. Without an advance agreement, partnership dissolution typically brings unnecessary economic loss to one or both sides. Agreements may be validly made for continuation of the business with a wide variety of dispositions or retentions of partnership interests, or substitutions of partners. They may be made effective at death, withdrawal or other events which normally produce dissolution.

(a) Background

We have previously considered (A) the ease of dissolution of partnerships,[50] (B) the basic right of any partner to force liquidation after dissolution,[51] (C) the continuation agreement as the only reliable exception to the liquidation right,[52] (D) the different patterns for handling an outgoing partner's interest,[53] and (E) their tax consequences.[54]

Without an agreement, the alternatives at dissolution may be bleak.[55] If the business is liquidated, there is typically a sacrifice of economic values in a going concern, not to mention the livelihood of the other partners. Recognizing this, an outgoing partner may demand an exorbitant price to forego his liquidation right. If the business is continued too long after dissolution pending negotiations for an agreement, the continuing partners are at the mercy of the outgoing interest's election to be paid its full value at dissolution, plus either profits or interest on that amount until final settlement.[56] On the other hand, if the outgoing partner is ill or dead, it is in practice all too easy for the other partners to take advantage of the situation.

For these reasons, most partnerships which anticipate the problem at all wish to provide some sort of continuation agreement. The usual variety deals only with dissolution by death, but provision can and often should be made for withdrawal, disability, dissension and other types of dissolution. The financial obligation to settle with the outgoing interest must be provided for, either by insurance or reserves, or by a payment schedule that can be met from partnership credit or profits. Attention must be given to the diverse tax problems.[57]

---

50. Secs. 74–78 above.

51. Secs. 83A, 86 above.

52. Sec. 83A(c) above.

53. Secs. 86(a), (b).

54. Sec. 86(b) above.

55. See Sec. 83A(c) above. The problems of law partnerships are particularly difficult because of ethical limitations on sale of a practice or split-

ting of fees (e. g., with widows, heirs, or even retired lawyers). Proper continuation agreements may solve all these problems. See Bromberg, Partnership Dissolution—Causes, Consequences and Cures, Including Special Problems of Law Firms, 7 Law Office Economics & Management 27, esp. 162 n. 100a, 163–65, 185 n. 182a, 187–89 (1966).

56. Sec. 86(c) above, esp. at n. 90.

57. See Sec. 86(b) above.

Of the many aspects of continuation agreements,[58] the most critical is valuation, but this is more a business matter than a legal one.[59] We consider here the diverse forms such agreements can take, and the particular problems of those intended to take effect after death.

(b) Disposition of Interest at Death

Articles may provide that on death of a partner survivors shall purchase his interest for an amount determined in accordance with a prescribed method, e. g., by placing an arbitrary value on good will equal to a percentage of the net assets.[60] Or survivors may have an

---

58. See Fuller, Partnership Agreements for Continuation of an Enterprise after the Death of a Partner, 50 Yale L.J. 202 (1940); Rohrlich, Organizing Corporate and Other Business Enterprises, § 13.03 (3d ed. 1958); Note, Partnership Continuation Agreements, 72 Harv.L.Rev. 1302 (1959) (emphasizing property and trust aspects); Bromberg, Partnership Dissolution—Causes, Consequences and Cures, 43 Texas L. Rev. 631, 653–68 (1965) (listing a dozen variables in such agreements); the very comprehensive Polasky, Planning for the Disposition of a Substantial Interest in a Closely Held Business, Part II—Planned Disposition of a Partnership Interest, 45 Iowa L.Rev. 46 (1959). See also Mulder & Volz, The Drafting of Partnership Agreements 18–24, 35–37, 50–51, 81–116, 129–31 (1955). On professional firms see Carrington & Sutherland, Articles of Partnership for Law Firms 49–82 (A. B.A. Economics of Law Practice Series No. 6, 1961), and n. 55 above; Hirsh, The Medical Partnership, 13 DePaul L.Rev. 28 (1963); Favaloro, Retirement of Partners, 103 J.Accountancy 66 (1957) (accountants).

59. See Bromberg, op. cit. supra n. 58 at 656–59. Litigation over value is reviewed in Comment, Partnerships— Valuation of Assets on Death of a Partner, 53 Mich.L.Rev. 972 (1955).

60. Kaufmann v. Kaufmann, 222 Pa. 58, 70 A. 956 (1908). Purchase is the method described in Sec. 86(a) (1) above.

It may be agreed that the surviving partner shall determine what shall be due to the decedent's estate, which will preclude a right to an account, in the absence of bad faith or fraud on the part of the surviving partner. Casey v. Hurley, 112 Conn. 536, 152 A. 892 (1931).

Partnership articles may provide for arbitration of the value of deceased partner's interest and an option in survivor to purchase at the price so determined, McDevitt v. McDevitt, 365 Pa. 18, 73 A.2d 394 (1950). See also Johnson v. Munsell, 170 Neb. 749, 104 N.W.2d 314 (1960) (alternative methods of appraisal).

It may be agreed that on dissolution by death the entire partnership property shall become legally and equitably that of the survivors without any liability to the decedent's estate. Hale v. Wilmarth, 274 Mass. 186, 174 N.E. 232, 73 A.L.R. 980 (1931); In re Mildrum's Estate, 108 Misc. 114, 177 N. Y.S. 563 (1919).

But such an agreement was held to be testamentary hence ineffective against the claim of the widow for her statutory rights in the deceased partner's estate in Fleming v. Fleming, 194 Iowa 71, 174 N.W. 946, 180 N.W. 206, 184 N.W. 296 (1919).

An agreement whereby the surviving partner becomes entitled to all the partnership property, although oral, is effective as to real estate as well as personal property, despite the Statute of Frauds. Ottaviano v. Lorenzo, 169 Md. 51, 179 A. 530 (1935).

It may be agreed that the survivor shall take over the good will, patents, and firm name without payment, and shall purchase the other assets at a valuation as shown by an audit. Pailthorpe v. Tallman, 87 N.Y.S.2d 822 (1949), aff'd 276 App.Div. 823, 93 N.Y. S.2d 712 (1949).

If the agreement merely sets the price, the retiring partner or legal representative may claim profits to the date of payment. In re Streck's Estate, 35 Ill.App.2d 473, 183 N.E.2d 26 (1962). This right can be denied or limited by agreement.

option to purchase the decedent's interest for a stated sum, regardless of the then condition of the partnership accounts.[61] The agreement may also specify the method of payment.[62] Life insurance may be used to finance the transaction.[63]

It may be agreed that on death of a partner the surviving partner shall become sole owner of the partnership property without payment.[64] Such agreement is not invalid and may be specifically enforced if it does not involve an attempt to defeat the statutory rights of the deceased partner's widow.[65] Presumably it would not stand up if his estate were insolvent and it was made to defraud creditors.

Such agreements are not testamentary in character. Although they are performed after the death of a party thereto the agreements are dispositive for consideration of present property rights.[66] A wide variety of options and obligations, reciprocal or non-reciprocal, with or without consideration at death, have been upheld.[67] It hardly

61. Daub's Estate, 313 Pa. 35, 169 A. 379 (1933). Provision may be made that the surviving partner shall purchase the decedent's interest at a fixed price, Murphy v. Murphy, 217 Mass. 233, 104 N.E. 466 (1914); Gerding v. Baier, 143 Md. 520, 122 A. 675 (1923); or that the value of the interest shall consist in a right to a certain share of the profits for a limited period. Benedict v. Price, 38 F.2d 309 (E.D. N.Y.1929).

62. In re Eisenlohr's Estate, 258 Pa. 431, 102 A. 115 (1917); Holcombe v. Long, 245 Mass. 353, 139 N.E. 633 (1923); In re Prins' Estate, 33 Wash.2d 831, 207 P.2d 909 (1949) (90-day, 5% note and mortgage).

As to the nature of the right of the deceased partner's representatives where (in accordance with the articles) the decedent's interest is to be retained by continuing partners as a "deposit," to be paid for over a term of years, and as to the status of the claim as regards personal property taxation, see In re Arbuckle's Estate, 324 Pa. 501, 188 A. 758 (1937). The case was unusual, in that the two surviving partners were also the executrices and legatees under the deceased partner's will. They determined to do away with the accruing of interest on the "deposit," with the result that it was held not to be within the personal property tax law as either "an account bearing interest" or as "moneys loaned or invested in other states."

A contract among three partners that on the death of one, his widow shall receive from the survivors the sum of $500 per month so long as they and she live is enforceable by her, after her husband's death, as a third party beneficiary. Garratt v. Baker, 5 Cal. 2d 745, 56 P.2d 225 (1936).

63. See Sec. 37A(c) above. See also Hutchinson v. Goceliak, 73 N.J.Super. 550, 180 A.2d 359 (1962) (policy payable to partner not partnership property); Annot., 83 A.L.R.2d 1347 (1962).

64. Note 60 above

65. In re Karlinski's Estate, 38 N.Y.S.2d 297 (Sur.1942). See also Fleming v. Fleming, n. 60 above

66. Michaels v. Donato, 4 N.J.Super. 570, 67 A.2d 911 (1949), citing numerous cases from other jurisdictions. A decision to the contrary, Ferrara v. Russo, 40 R.I. 533, 102 A. 86 (1917), was followed by a statute providing that no partnership agreement in writing shall be deemed testamentary because it contains a provision regulating, in event of death of a partner, (1) disposition of assets of the partnership to surviving partners or estates of deceased partners, (2) use of firm name or (3) disposition of life insurance proceeds. R.I.Gen.Laws 1956, § 7–12–1.

67. E. g., McKinnon v. McKinnon, 56 F. 409 (8th Cir. 1893) (non-reciprocal, no contemporaneous consideration); Bear v. Bear, 151 Colo. 188, 377 P.2d

needs to be added that the agreements must have been fair when made.[68]   There is some danger of unenforceability if they have become grossly unfair with the passage of time or the change of circumstances.[69]

The agreement may specify that on death of a partner the business shall be taken over by trustees for the purpose of orderly liquidation within a term of years.[70]

(c) Retention of Interest at Death

In a professional or personal service partnership employing little capital, the deceased partner's interest beyond his share in fixed assets and cash in hand may be difficult to evaluate.   A law partnership may have pending litigation or other retainers which produce income after the partner's death and in which his estate should share, by reason of his ability as a business getter and the good will retained by the continuing survivors.   Such payments are often thought of as mutual insurance among the partners.   It is not unusual in such cases to provide in the articles that an annuity shall be paid to the widow of the deceased partner in the amount of a share in profits.[71]   Often it is agreed that a share in profits shall be paid the deceased partner's estate for a specified period.[72]

538 (1962) (reciprocal, no contemporaneous consideration); Murphy v. Murphy, 217 Mass. 233, 104 N.E. 466 (1914) (non-reciprocal obligation); Silverthorne v. Mayo, 238 N.C. 274, 77 S.E.2d 678 (1953) (reciprocal obligations); Rohrbacher's Estate, 168 Pa. 158, 32 A. 30 (1895) (reciprocal options to buy). An unwritten agreement has been upheld where proved as an implied-in-fact contract. Balafas v. Balafas, 263 Minn. 267, 117 N.W.2d 20 (1962) (reciprocal, no contemporanous consideration). The opinion reviews the relevant UPA provisions and finds them all subject to the partners' agreement. Authorities are collected in Annot., 1 A.L.R.2d 1178, 1265–69 (1948); Annot., 160 A.L.R. 523 (1946); Annot., 73 A.L.R. 983 (1931). See also Smith v. Wayman, n. 70 below.

68. This is a function of the partners' fiduciary duties. See Alexander v. Sims, 220 Ark. 643, 249 S.W.2d 832 (1952) (reciprocal agreement for continuation without payment invalid because one partner had, and failed to disclose, knowledge of the other's illness when the agreement was signed).

69. See Helms v. Duckworth, 101 U.S. App.D.C. 390, 249 F.2d 482 (1957), 72

Harv.L.Rev. 555 (1959). A corporation's only two shareholders agreed that, on the death of the older one, the younger could buy his shares at $10 each, their value at the time of the agreement. Eight years later, when the older man died, the shares were worth approximately $80 each. The administratrix sought to cancel the agreement. Summary judgment for the younger man was reversed. He had, on the partnership analogy, a fiduciary duty to bargain in good faith periodically to renegotiate the price.

70. Smith v. Wayman, 148 Tex. 318, 224 S.W.2d 211 (1949). The possible difficulties of administration by trustees is discussed in Note, 63 Harv. L.Rev. 1074 (1950).

71. This does not make the widow a partner. U.P.A. § 7(4) (c), Sec. 18 above.

72. This is one form of the method described in Sec. 86(a) (3) above.

For a time, there was doubt whether the value of such payments was subject to federal estate tax. See Bull v. U. S., 295 U.S. 247, 55 S.Ct. 695. 79 L.Ed. 1421 (1935). The doubts have

Specific enforcement of continuation agreements is generally available against the outgoing interest.[73]

(d) Substitution of Executor or Nominee

The partners in any type of firm may desire that after the death of one or more, the business should be continued with the use of all of the partnership property, the interest of the deceased being left in the business and a share in profits paid to the beneficiary of the deceased. This is a valid contract between the partners,[74] though its specific performance might not be compelled against the survivors if personal services by them are involved.[75] They would, of course, be liable for damages. It would be binding against the decedent's estate.[76] The nature of his interest is what the partnership agreement has made it.[77] The decedent's representative or beneficiary does not become a partner, nor is any of his estate subject to risk of losses beyond the interest in the partnership.[78]

A variation of the method is for the articles to prescribe that a deceased partner be succeeded by his executor or some other person nominated by him (either by the articles or by his will) as a substituted partner.[79] Such an agreement may be contractually valid and binding on the survivors and the estate of the deceased partner,[80] but cannot be specifically enforced. No one can become a partner without his consent, so the executor or other nominee may decline. As a precaution, his consent is sometimes obtained in advance. In this event, he is liable if he reneges, although he probably cannot be compelled to perform. The survivors can violate their contract becoming liable for damages. They cannot reject the substitute with impunity under

now been resolved in favor of taxability, at an amount appropriately reflecting contingencies and discount to present value. See Arthur H. Hull Estate, 38 T.C. 512 (1962), rev'd on other issue 325 F.2d 367 (3d Cir. 1963); Riegelman Estate v. Commissioner, 253 F.2d 315 (2d Cir. 1958). See also Int.Rev.Code of 1954, §§ 753, 736 and 691 (26 U.S.C.A.). Their combined effect is to give the recipient of the payments (which are also subject to income tax) an income tax deduction based on their estate tax value. Double taxation is partially eliminated in this way. See also Sec. 86(b)(3) above.

73. See, e. g., In re Streck's Estate, 35 Ill.App.2d 473, 183 N.E.2d 26 (1962) (reciprocal options to buy); Hagan v. Dundore, n. 89 below; Murphy v. Murphy, n. 67 above. But see Helms v. Duckworth, n. 69 above. Of course, the outgoing interest may prefer, and have, a damage action. See Dini v.

Dini, 188 Cal.App.2d 506, 10 Cal.Rptr. 570 (1961) (reciprocal obligations; damages measured by price fixed in agreement).

74. Wild v. Davenport, 48 N.J.L. 129, 7 A. 295, 300 (1886).

75. Compare the power of a partner in violation of the agreement to terminate the partnership at any time, U.P.A. § 31(2), Sec. 75(b) above.

76. Brew v. Hastings, 196 Pa. 222, 46 A. 257 (1900).

77. Shunk v. Commissioner, 173 F.2d 747, 751 (6th Cir. 1949).

78. U.P.A. § 7(4)(c); Sec. 18, above.

79. This is akin to the method described in Sec. 86(a)(4) above.

80. Phillips v. Blatchford, 137 Mass. 510 (1884); Wild v. Davenport, 48 N.J.L. 129, 7 A. 295 (1886).

the doctrine of delectus personae,[81] because they have already given their consent, in the agreement, either to the specific substitute or to anyone the outgoing partner may name. It may be assumed that the reason for allowing the deceased partner's interest to remain in the business was to a material degree his confidence in the participation in management as a partner of his nominee. If the latter declines to become a partner it would seem that there is a failure of the condition to postponement of settlement, and the survivors must immediately account for the decedent's interest unless they can secure an agreement with the representatives of the deceased partner for deferment.[82]

If the executor or other nominee of the decedent becomes a partner he is entitled to the rights and subject to the liabilities of a partner. If an executor, he may be entitled to exoneration out of the assets of the estate other than the interest in the partnership.[83] Therefore a court is reluctant to construe the articles as making the executor a partner.[84] Such a construction might be detrimental to the decedent's family in diverting a substantial part of the assets of the estate other than the interest in the partnership to the payment of claims of strangers. Solutions to this difficulty include creation by the decedent of a separate trust to hold the partnership interest, or provision in the partnership articles for conversion to a limited partnership (with the decedent's interest becoming a limited one).[85]

Legislation in many states authorizes probate courts to issue decrees enabling personal representatives to continue the business of the decedent for limited periods in order to conserve values. Some of these statutes permit continuance in partnership with others. An example of this sort of legislation is the Pennsylvania Fiduciaries Act of 1949.[86]

81. U.P.A. § 18(g), Sec. 5(c) above.

82. See Fuller, Partnership Agreements for Continuation of an Enterprise after the Death of a Partner, 50 Yale L.J. 202 (1940).

83. Phillips v. Blatchford, 137 Mass. 510 (1884); Stearns v. Brookline, 219 Mass. 238, 107 N.E. 57 (1914), a limited portion of general estate of deceased partner held in trust to be liable for future debts of continuing partners.

84. Stewart v. Robinson, 115 N.Y. 328, 22 N.E. 160 (1899); Wilcox v. Derickson, 168 Pa. 331, 31 A. 1080 (1895). See criticism of such construction, Fuller, Partnership Agreements for Continuation of an Enterprise after the Death of a Partner, 50 Yale.L.J. 202, 212 (1940).

85. See S.C.Code 1962, § 8–245 (corporate trustee holding partnership interest for minor beneficiaries not liable beyond trust assets). See Sec. 8A above.

86. "Continuance of Business. The court, aided by the report of a master if necessary, may authorize the personal representative to continue any business of the decedent for the benefit of the estate and in doing so the court, for cause shown, may disregard the provisions of the will, if any. The order may be with or without notice. If prior notice is not given to all parties in interest, it shall be given within five days after the order or within such extended time as the court, for cause shown, shall allow. Any party in interest may, at any time, petition the court to revoke or modify the order. The order may provide—

"(1) For the conduct of the business, by the personal representative alone

Such a statute has its limitations as applied to partnerships. The personal representative, if not a lawyer or other duly qualified member of a profession, could not become a member of a professional partnership. In the case of trading and other non-professional businesses the surviving partners should be allowed to make effective objection to taking in as partner one they might regard as incompetent or uncongenial. The personal representative, if a corporate fiduciary, would be incapable of becoming a partner, in some jurisdictions.

If neither articles nor will of deceased partner provide for the executor or administrator becoming a partner and continuing to risk the interest of the decedent's estate in the business, the personal representative cannot properly do so without order of court.[87] The surviving partner is responsible for the decedent estate's interest, with profits or legal interest. If loss to the estate results the personal representative may be subject to surcharge.

(e) Other Types of Dissolution

All the kinds of agreement for continuation after death can be drawn also to apply to other kinds of dissolution.[88] The dissolution of the firm, if it occurs, does not destroy the validity of the agreement, both because the partnership (along with the agreement) continues until winding up, and because the agreement (if properly drawn)

---

or jointly with others, or, unless restricted by the terms of the will, as a corporation to be formed;

"(2) The extent of the liability of the estate or any part thereof, or of the personal representative, for obligations incurred in the continuation of the business;

"(3) Whether liabilities incurred in the conduct of the business are to be chargeable solely to the part of the estate set aside for use in the business or to the estate as a whole;

"(4) The period of time the business may be conducted; and,

"(5) Such other regulations, including accountings, as the court shall deem advisable." 20 P.S. (Pa.) § 320–504.

This statute is somewhat similar to that recommended in Adelman, The Power to Carry on the Business of a Decedent, 36 Mich.L.Rev. 185. Other statutes are referred to in Bogert, Trusts and Trustees, § 572 (2d ed. 1960). It is there stated that the only statute to specifically authorize a decree for the continuance of a partnership is the Washington statute, Rem.Rev.Stat. § 1460, now RCWA 11.64.040. It also calls attention to McKinney's N.Y. Partnership Law, § 80.

87. Spivak v. Bronstein, 367 Pa. 70, 79 A.2d 205 (1951).

88. Lyon v. Sanger, 107 N.Y.S.2d 300 (Sup.Ct.1951) (any partner could be voted out at any time by the rest of the partners; they could buy his interest for his actual investment in the firm plus profits for the current half-year); Adams v. Jarvis, 23 Wis.2d 453, 127 N.W.2d 400 (1964) (partners remaining after withdrawal entitled to continue business and retain accounts receivable; payment of capital account and proportion of current year's profit to withdrawing partner); Devlin v. Rockey, 295 F.2d 266 (7th Cir. 1961) (Ill. law).

See also O'Donnell v. McLoughlin, 386 Pa. 187, 125 A.2d 370 (1956) (enforcing agreement that on any dissolution, partners should be free to compete and good will should not be sold).

is intended to cover just such a contingency.[89]   A continuation agreement may be made applicable to a partnership at will.[90]   But an agreement which merely gives one partner a right of first refusal on a co-partner's sale of his interest does not prevent the co-partner from dissolving and forcing liquidation.[91]

By skillful use of agreements, partnerships can be given virtually any desired degree of continuity.

DISSOLUTION OF LIMITED PARTNERSHIPS

§ 90B.   The causes and consequences of dissolution of limited partnerships resemble those of general partnerships.   General partners have essentially the same role, but limited partners can cause or obtain dissolution only by court decree.   Membership changes (in both general and limited partners) without dissolution are permitted more freely.   On distribution of assets, limited partners are prior to general partners but subordinate to firm creditors.

(a) Background

In the main, the principles of dissolution are alike for limited and general partnerships.   However, there are differences attributable to the wholly statutory and semi-public character of the limited partnership,[92] and the two-class structure of its participants.[93]   Since public filing, limited liability and passive investors are features common to limited partnerships and corporations, it is not surprising that in some aspects of continuity, limited partnerships resemble corporations more closely than they do general partnerships.

The analysis of dissolution in limited partnerships depends heavily on the U.P.A., which is applicable to limited partnerships except so far as it is not inconsistent with the U.L.P.A.[94]   The latter has few dissolution references, some of which *are* inconsistent.   The dissolution provisions of U.P.A. which are consistent would then appear to

---

89.   Hagan v. Dundore, 185 Md. 86, 43 A. 2d 181, 160 A.L.R. 517 (1945) (specific enforcement by buyer).   See Annot., Provision of partnership agreement giving one partner option to buy out the other, 160 A.L.R. 523, 530–32 (1946). However, a partner acting wrongfully may be barred from enforcing the agreement.   See id. 527–30.

90.   Devlin v. Rockey, n. 88 above.   Napoli v. Domnitch, 14 N.Y.2d 508, 248 N.Y.S.2d 228, 197 N.E.2d 623 (1964), affirming 18 App.Div.2d 707, 236 N. Y.S.2d 549 (1962) (partner had right to dissolve, subject to co-partner's right to buy his interest per agreement).

91.   Young v. Cooper, 30 Tenn.App. 55, 203 S.W.2d 376 (1947).   See also O'Donnell v. McLoughlin, 386 Pa. 187, 125 A.2d 370 (1956) (despite agreement for sale of interest of withdrawing partner, he was entitled to dissolution and liquidation where co-partner's conduct made it not reasonably practicable to carry on business with him, U. P.A. § 32(1) (d)).

92.   E. g., the requirement of public filing of a certificate, U.L.P.A. § 2(1) (b).

93.   Sec. 26 above.

94.   U.P.A. § 6(2).

be effective for limited firms.[95]   But many of them turn on some act of a "partner".   They become clouded because a limited partner is not a "partner" for most statutory purposes.   The U.L.P.A. includes both general and limited partners as "members," [96] thereby implying that limited partners are something less than "partners."   This is consistent with the restricted role permitted limited partners,[97] and was emphasized by the draftsmen *dehors*.[98]

(b) Causes of Dissolution

A limited partnership is dissolved by the expiration of its term or undertaking.[99]   It is probably dissolvable at the express will of any general partner when there is no definite term or undertaking,[1] or by all the general partners whose interests are not assigned or subject to charging orders.[2]   In neither case does it appear that limited partners have the right to dissolve, or need to give their consent to the general partners.[3]   However, dissolution by the general partners during a fixed term without consent of the limited partners is plainly a breach as to the latter.   The power to dissolve, when the right does not exist, appears to belong to general partners but not to limited ones.[4]

---

95. When U.P.A. is cited below for a proposition concerning limited partnerships, it is the author's conclusion that there is no inconsistent U.L.P.A. provision.

96. U.L.P.A. § 1. The term "partner" is almost never employed in U.L.P.A. without "general" or "limited" in front of it. An exception is § 2(1) (a) (XI). Elsewhere, "members" is used when both groups are meant, e. g., §§ 1, 14, 16, 25(1) (b).

97. Sec. 26 above. But see Executive Hotel Associates v. Elm Hotel Corp., n. 23 below.

98. "[T]he person who contributes the capital, though in accordance with custom called a limited partner, is not in any sense a partner. He is, however, a member of the association." Commissioners' Note, 8 Uniform Laws Ann. 4 (1922).

99. U.P.A. § 31(1) (a), sec. 74(a) above. Cheyenne Oil Corp. v. Oil and Gas Ventures, Inc., 204 A.2d 743 (Del.1964); Pierce v. DeRothermann, 82 N.Y.S.2d 837 (Sup.Ct.1948).

This Sec. 90B(b) is based on, but less comprehensive than, Bromberg, Partnership Dissolution—Causes, Consequences and Cures, 43 Texas L.Rev. 631, 640–44 (1965).

1. U.P.A. § 31(1) (b), Sec. 74(b) above. Most limited firms have fixed terms pursuant to the requirements for the certificates, U.L.P.A. § 2(1) (a) (V). However, there is no requirement for a definite term, and certificates are frequently drawn with terms that are either indefinite or measured by events of indefinite occurrence.

2. U.P.A. § 31(1) (c), Sec. 74(c) above.

3. See Sec. 90B(a) above.

4. U.P.A. § 31(2), Sec. 75 above; Sec. 90B(a) above. One of the usual reasons for conceding any partner the power to dissolve is the futility of specific enforcement of personal service by him. But only capital, not personal service is typically required of limited partners, so there is no basis for letting them dissolve without good cause; see below at n. 12. However, there is more convincing reason if the general partner is regarded as an agent; see Sec. 75 above. Even so, the limited partner, because of his limited liability, is not a true principal.

Illegality,[5] expulsion,[6] and bankruptcy [7] should operate similarly for general and limited partnerships. However, the bankruptcy of a limited partner ought not to dissolve, unless it precipitates a bankruptcy of the firm through his inability to pay sums for which he may be indebted to the firm.

Death of a general partner dissolves unless the agreement or certificate provides otherwise or all the members consent to continuation.[8] By implication, the death of a limited partner does not dissolve.[9]

The remaining statutory causes of dissolution,[10] those which require judicial action, are almost fully applicable to limited partnerships and may be invoked by general partners under their broad powers,[11] or by limited partners because of special statutory grant.[12] The question remains whether a limited partner is enough of a partner that his acts (for example, misconduct) would enable a court to decree dissolution at the request of a general partner or another limited parner. Because of the limited partner's narrow role, relatively few things he could do would seriously affect the firm,[13] but if he did (e. g.,

---

5. U.P.A. § 31(3), Sec. 76 above.

6. U.P.A. § 31(1)(d), Sec. 74(d) above.

7. U.P.A. § 31(5), Sec. 77 above. See also U.L.P.A. § 16(4) (b).

8. U.L.P.A. §§ 2(1) (a) (XIII), 20. At least one general partner must survive for § 20 to operate. A strict reading suggests that two may be necessary, but there is no good reason for this and it is refuted by § 2(1) (a) (XIII).

Only a few states expressly permit non-dissolution on death in general partnerships; see Sec. 73 above.

9. Death of a limited partner is treated in U.L.P.A. § 21, but there is no reference to dissolution. The conclusion is reinforced by the non-partner status of limited partners, Sec. 90B(a) above.

10. U.P.A. § 32(1), Sec. 78 above.

11. U.L.P.A. § 9.

12. U.L.P.A. § 10(1): "A limited partner shall have the same rights as a general partner to . . . (c) Have dissolution and winding up by decree of court." The judicial causes are captioned "Dissolution by decree of court," U.P.A. § 32.

Cases recognizing a limited partner's right to judicial dissolution include: Wallace v. Sinclair, 114 Cal.App.2d 220, 250 P.2d 154 (Dist.Ct.App.1953)

(numerous causes including losses, prejudicial conduct and breach) (no mention of U.L.P.A. which was enacted in the state after formation of the partnership but before the acts complained of); Copp v. Chestnutt, 23 Misc.2d 457, 196 N.Y.S.2d 752 (Sup. Ct.1960) (prejudicial conduct, breach, etc.); Cusano v. Cusano, 19 N.J.Super. 255, 88 A.2d 342 (1952) (dictum), certification denied 10 N.J. 310, 91 A.2d 228 (1952) (fraud, misconduct, breach).

See Novick v. Miller, 222 La. 469, 62 So. 2d 645 (1953) implying that a commendam partner, similar to a limited partner, can have dissolution for substantial causes as distinguished from the trifling ones alleged; Delong v. Marston, 308 Mich. 63, 13 N.W.2d 209 (1944) (receiver at petition of limited partner affirmed; merits of possible causes of dissolution not reached). See also SEC v. DuPont, Homsey & Co., 204 F.Supp. 944 (D.Mass.1962), appeal dismissed sub nom. Legate v. Maloney, 308 F.2d 228 (1st Cir. 1962), cert. denied 372 U.S. 912, 83 S.Ct. 726, 9 L.Ed.2d 720 (1963) (limited partner stated cause of action under U.P.A. § 39, Sec. 85 above, for rescission of partnership on ground of fraud in formation of firm).

13. See Skolny v. Richter, 139 App.Div. 534, 124 N.Y.S. 152 (1910) (limited partner's competition not ground for dissolution; general partner's would be).

by refusing to pay his capital contribution, or by interfering in management) it seems proper that a court should grant dissolution. In addition, a limited partner may dissolve when he rightfully, but unsuccessfully, demands the return of his contribution.[14]

The retirement of a general partner is a cause of dissolution unless the business is continued by general partners pursuant to the certificate or by consent of all the members.[15]

Like death, insanity of a general partner does not cause dissolution if the business is properly continued.[16] Nor, as noted above, is dissolution caused by the death or other acts of a limited partner, including the assignment of his interest.[17] Nor is it provoked by the admission of a new partner, whether general or limited.[18] In all these instances, the certificate must be amended to show the changes in membership.[19]

The agreement may specify causes of dissolution where the law is doubtful, e. g., by giving the general partners (or a majority of them) the right to dissolve.[20] Or it can effectively deny dissolution which might otherwise occur on death, retirement or insanity of a general partner.[21]

(c) Consequences of Dissolution

With few changes, the dissolution consequences of general partnerships carry over to limited firms. Thus, the firm continues past dissolution until winding up.[22] General partners have authority to wind up as in an ordinary firm.[23]. Their representatives, rather than

---

14. U.L.P.A. § 16(4) (a).

15. U.L.P.A. § 20; compare Sec. 73 above on retirement in a general partnership.

16. U.L.P.A. § 20.

17. U.L.P.A. § 19, by implication.

18. U.L.P.A. § 24(2) (c), (d), by implication.

19. U.L.P.A. § 20(2) (b)–(e).

20. See Wallace v. Sinclair, n. 12 above (agreement provided that partnership should dissolve on the happening of any event which is specified by law as a cause of dissolution for a general partnership).

21. Nn. 8, 15, 16 above.

22. U.P.A. § 30, Sec. 73 above. Engleman v. Malchow, 91 Cal.App.2d 341, 205 P.2d 413 (1949) (pre-U.L.P.A.) (since firm continues to exist, assignee

for creditors can sue limited partner for contribution).

If new business is undertaken, the limited partners may be treated as general partners. See Leventhal v. Atlantic Rainbow Painting Co., Ltd., 68 N.J. Super. 406, 172 A.2d 710 (1961) (as general partners, former limited partners in limited partnership *association* (Sec. 26A above) were not employees and could not claim workman's compensation). U.P.A. § 23 should be inapplicable because it is inconsistent with one of the essential purposes of U.L.P.A. if partners enjoy limited liability without a current certificate on file.

Meissel v. Finley, 198 Va. 577, 95 S.E. 2d 186 (1956) (limited partner's express non-competition covenant not terminated by dissolution or by cancellation of certificate).

23. U.L.P.A. § 9(1); U.P.A. § 37, Sec. 83.

A limited partner has been permitted to sign a petition in the firm name for

limited partners, succeed them. Limited partners have only the right to obtain winding up by court.[24]

Limited partners probably have the right to force liquidation after dissolution,[25] although this may not always be true.[26] If the general partners do continue the business, the limited partner presumably has the right to be paid the value of his interest at dissolution, plus an election of profits or interest on that value from dissolution until payment.[27]

The priorities in distribution of assets resemble those for general partnerships. Creditors, of course, are prior to partners, and limited partners naturally are prior to general partners.[28] For advancements other than capital contributions, the limited partner rates as a creditor.[29] However, without apparent reason, profits precede capital

rent due the firm, where the general partner has improperly assigned the firm's sole asset. Executive Hotel Associates v. Elm Hotel Corp., 41 Misc. 2d 354, 245 N.Y.S.2d 929 (Civ.Ct.1964) aff'd 43 Misc.2d 153, 250 N.Y.S.2d 351 (Sup.Ct.1964). The court viewed him as having the right to act as a general partner, if willing to sacrifice his limited liability. See discussion, Sec. 65(d) n. 59 above.

See also Klebanow v. New York Produce Exchange, 344 F.2d 294 (2d Cir. 1965) recognizing the capacity of limited partners to sue derivately on behalf of the firm for anti-trust triple damages, where the general partners allegedly surrendered all their powers to act for the firm. The Court analogizes limited partners to preferred shareholders. See Sec. 26(c) n. 52 above.

24. U.L.P.A. §§ 9, 10(1) (c); U.P.A. § 37. But see Klebanow v. New York Produce Exchange, n. 23 above, and Executive Hotel Associates v. Elm, n. 23 above. See also Sec. 26(c) n. 52 above.

25. U.L.P.A. § 16(4) (a) gives them the right to have firm affairs "wound up" (which presumably means "liquidated") whenever they rightfully but unsuccessfully demand the return of their contributions. This they can do at dissolution, U.L.P.A. § 16(2) (a), unless debts are unpaid, U.L.P.A. § 16(1) (a). In the latter instance, they have a separate right to obtain winding up, U.L.P.A. § 16(4) (b).

26. The rights discussed in the previous note are, by their terms, inoperative if the limited partners' contributions

are returned and the debts are paid. Miller v. Doyle, 5 Cal.Rptr. 254 (Dist. Ct.App.1960) holds that a liquidation decree obtained by a limited partner was not appealable. The court mentions the right to be paid in cash, and that liquidation is likely to be necessary for this firm since its debts exceed its cash. There is an intimation that the general partner might keep the physical assets if debts and limited partners' contributions could be satisfied without liquidation.

This latter view is consonant with Vanderplow v. Fredricks, 321 Mich. 483, 32 N.W.2d 718 (1948). The sole general partner in a beverage business continued operations after dissolution by agreement. He is ordered to pay the limited partners the value of their interests according to the books, plus their share of post-dissolution profits, plus their share of unrealized appreciation in real estate; otherwise, the real estate will be sold. He need not pay anything for good will of the business, which was largely due to his efforts, and he is permitted to continue the business.

27. U.P.A. § 42, Sec. 86(c) above.

28. U.L.P.A. § 23(1); U.P.A. § 40 Sec. 90 above. On creditor status for limited partners as lenders, see U.L.P.A. § 13(1), Sec. 93(e) below.

Inter se, limited partners share in proportion to their contributions and profit ratios. U.L.P.A. § 23(2).

29. U.L.P.A. § 23(1) (a), by implication. This was not true under former acts. White v. Hackett & Schenck, 20 N.Y.

contributions within the layer of payments to limited partners,[30] and within the layer for general partners.[31] This may reflect the importance of capital as an income-producing factor in the limited firm, but it hardly makes sense to exalt the income over the capital. Of course, if the firm is solvent, the results will be the same.[32] If a limited partner receives a return of his contribution before creditors are paid, he is liable to them to the extent of his distribution.[33] This is true even though the firm was solvent when the contribution was returned.[34] Just as in a general partnership, the internal priorities of distribution can be altered by agreement.[35]

178 (1859); Dunning's Appeal, 44 Pa. 150 (1863). But see Clapp v. Lacey, 35 Conn. 463 (1868).

30. U.L.P.A. § 23(1) (b), (c). Compare U.P.A. § 40(b) (III), (IV) (capital before profits).

31. U.L.P.A. § 23(1) (e), (f).

32. If the firm is insolvent, the contributions necessary to make it solvent can probably be enforced against the solvent general partners under U.P.A. § 40(a) (II), 40(d) and 18(a); see Sec. 90 above.

33. U.L.P.A. § 17(4). The implication is that he is not liable for profits distributed to him, unless by other laws such as fraudulent conveyances or bankruptcy. The implication assumes greater significance in connection with the precedence of profits over capital contributions, n. 30 above.

34. Kittredge v. Langley, 252 N.Y. 405, 169 N.E. 626, 67 A.L.R. 1087 (1930) interpreting U.L.P.A. §§ 16(1) (a), 17(4) and 23 as declaratory of the prior law applicable when the withdrawal occurred. Semble Neal v. U. S., 195 F. 2d 336 (5th Cir. 1952) (Texas law, pre-U.L.P.A.). See Annot., Liability of special partner who has withdrawn his capital, to creditors of the firms, 67 A.L.R. 1096 (1930).

35. Lanier v. Bowdoin, 282 N.Y. 32, 24 N.E.2d 732 (1930).

CHAPTER 9

DISSOLUTION AND WINDING UP OF INSOLVENT PARTNERSHIPS— BANKRUPTCY

Analysis

STATE LAW—DISSOLUTION AND DUAL PRIORITIES

§ 91. Bankruptcy of a partner or partnership dissolves the firm, with most of the usual consequences. In the critical competition for assets, partnership creditors have priority claims against partnership assets

522

and individual creditors against individual assets, **each with rights over if any surplus remains after satisfying the other.**

(a) Background

Bankruptcy is largely a matter of federal law, treated in the following sections. As a background, we note the effects of bankruptcy under state law. Many of these we have already considered. They take on new significance here because, by hypothesis, there aren't enough assets to go around. The competition among creditors and partners for the available funds and property is naturally intense.

Unless otherwise indicated, this section does not use bankruptcy in the federal sense of one adjudicated a bankrupt in a federal bankruptcy court. Rather, the word carries the meaning given by state law. The U.P.A. defines bankrupt to include "bankrupt . . . under any state insolvent act."[1] The generality of the quoted phrase, its non-exclusiveness, and the virtual pre-emption by federal law make the reference somewhat obscure. Interpretation of the phrase is scarce outside partnership law and apparently non-existent within it. Very likely the test of bankruptcy may be either of those recognized by various jurisdictions in diverse contexts: (1) whether total liabilities exceed total assets (balance sheet test) or (2) inability to meet obligations as they mature or, roughly, whether current liabilities exceed current assets (equity test). Because partners are jointly or jointly and severally liable on partnership obligations,[2] partnership bankruptcy normally means that all the partners are bankrupt. But the converse is not at all necessary, and is less likely to occur.

It is not clear whether one becomes "bankrupt" under the U.P.A. when he is in fact insolvent by the applicable test, or only when there is a court determination to this effect.

The reader will sense a vintage flavor in this chapter. Few of the cited cases come from the 20th century. He should not be misled into thinking partnership bankruptcy is a dead subject. True, the prosperity of recent decades has meant relatively fewer bankruptcies, but this can always change with the business cycle. Other reasons for the dearth of reported authority are the comparative clarity of the statute and the efficiency of the system of bankruptcy referees, whose decisions are not commonly published. The subject remains important and the old authorities are apparently still valid.

(b) Dual Priorities

The struggle for assets in bankruptcy stresses the significance of ranking or priority of creditors. The prevailing rule under the

---

1. U.P.A. § 2, Sec. 77(b) n. 24 above. It also includes bankrupt under federal law, which brings about dissolution. But the consequences are mainly academic because affairs are taken out of the partners' hands. See Secs. 91B–93 below.

2. U.P.A. § 15, Sec. 58 above.

U.P.A. and federal bankruptcy is one of dual priorities.[2A] Specifically, partnership creditors enjoy priority in partnership assets.[3] Creditors of individual partners have a corresponding priority in the respective individual assets.[4] Any shortage of partnership assets is to be made up by contributions of individual partners.[5] But this claim on their individual assets is deferred to claims of their individual creditors, which may mean that the partnership deficit is not made up. Any excess of partnership assets is distributed among the partners according to their claims for debt, capital and profits.[6] Each partner will then receive the value of his interest in the partnership, which becomes an individual asset available for his individual creditors. But partnership creditors have already been taken care of

Any shortage of a partner's individual assets leaves his individual creditors partially unpaid. Any excess after they are fully paid (or provided for) he may be called on to contribute to the partnership to satisfy its liabilities, or the excess may be reached more directly by a partnership creditor. Thus each group of creditors has prior claim on one class of assets with subordinate rights in any surplus of the other class.

Section 91A below considers the history of the dual priorities rule, its rationales, some criticisms which have been made of it, and its scope and possible exceptions.

2A. It is also known as the "jingle rule." For history of the epithet, see MacLachlan, Bankruptcy 424 (1956).

The rule and its ramifications in a non-U.P.A. state are discussed, Hutchison, Enforceability of Iowa Creditors' Judgments Against Partnership and Partners' Assets, 44 Iowa L.Rev. 643 (1959).

3. U.P.A. § 40(b), Sec. 90 above. See also U.P.A. § 40(h), applying the same rule if the assets are in the hands of a court for distribution. A partnership creditor's claim against partnership assets is superior to an individual creditor's, even though the latter obtained a charging order against the partner's interest before the partnership creditor levied on his claim. Shirk v. Caterbone, 201 Pa.Super. 544, 193 A.2d 664 (1963).

As a corollary of the dual priorities rule and of U.P.A. § 25(2) (c) (partner's right in partnership property not subject to execution except on claim against partnership), an individual creditor has no direct claim against partnership assets but must wait for partnership creditors to be satisfied and for any surplus to be distributed

to the debtor partner. See Stickney v. Kerry, 55 Wash.2d 535, 348 P.2d 655 (1960) (partner, claiming individually against co-partner, not entitled to be paid from partnership assets).

4. U.P.A. § 40(i), Sec. 90 above. Technically, this provision applies only to insolvent or bankrupt partners, but these are the only ones likely to matter. Others will have enough assets to pay all their creditors. See also U.P.A. § 40(h), discussed in n. 3 above, and U.P.A. § 36(4). The corollary here is that partnership creditors have no claim against individual assets until individual creditors are satisfied. For an example, see First and Peoples Bank v. Fielder, 323 S.W.2d 853 (Ky. 1959). The bank was held, on the facts, to be a creditor of a partnership rather than of an individual partner. It therefore failed to share in the partner's individual estate, whose assets were less than its liabilities. The partnership was also insolvent, presumably with a higher ratio of liabilities to assets.

5. U.P.A. §§ 18(a), 40(a)–(d), Secs. 65(a), 90 above.

6. U.P.A. § 40(b), Sec. 90 above.

(c) Other Consequences of Bankruptcy

Whichever of the bankruptcy tests described in (a) above is operative in the jurisdiction, the bankruptcy of a partner or of the partnership dissolves the firm.[7] The non-bankrupt partners have authority to wind up,[8] although it may be partially disrupted by creditors' foreclosures or executions on particular assets and it may be wholly superseded by receivership under state law or bankruptcy under federal. Bankrupt partners may, in fact, participate in the winding up if co-partners and creditors permit. Winding up partners generally lack authority to incur new obligations or undertake new business.[9] However, a non-bankrupt partner has apparent authority to bind the partnership in certain instances.[10] If he acts without knowledge or notice of another partner's bankruptcy, he is entitled to contribution from his co-partners.[11] In practice, the contribution right usually has value only against non-bankrupt partners. A bankrupt partner has no such apparent authority or right to contribution.[12]

If only one partner is bankrupt, it will often be possible for the others to preserve and continue the business by accounting to his estate or creditors for the value of his interest in the firm. Thus, his creditors, in the absence of agreement, proceed against his interest by a charging order, which the other partners may redeem before foreclosure.[13] Disputes are likely to center on valuation of the interest; in accordance with the dual priorities rule, it is computed after partnership liabilities, but there may be questions of what are partnership liabilities, and what is the value of its assets.

If the charged interest is not redeemed, a foreclosing creditor typically becomes its owner and acquires an express right to dissolution of the firm by court order, if the partnership is or has become one at will.[14] This right means little if bankruptcy has already caused dissolution. In such a case, although the U.P.A. fails to say so,[15] it seems that the creditor is entitled to force winding up of the partnership and settlement of the interest to which he has succeeded.

7. U.P.A. § 31(a) (5), Sec. 77(b) above.

8. U.P.A. § 37, Sec. 83(b) above.

9. U.P.A. § 33, Sec. 80 above.

10. U.P.A. § 35, Sec. 81 above.

11. U.P.A. § 34(b), Sec. 82 above.

12. U.P.A. § 35(3) (b), Sec. 81(b) above; U.P.A. § 34(b), Sec. 82 above.

13. U.P.A. § 28, Sec. 43 above.

14. U.P.A. § 32(2), Sec. 78(e) n. 80 above.

15. The liquidation right after dissolution is given explicitly only to partners. U.P.A. § 38(1), Sec. 83A at n. 42 above. The implication that it does not extend to persons claiming through partners is reinforced by the language of the section which expressly makes the liquidation right enforceable *against* persons claiming through a partner. Nonetheless, it seems better to recognize a liquidation right in a foreclosing creditor where dissolution has already occurred. Otherwise, he could be held at bay indefinitely by the co-partners. He does, however, have the federal bankruptcy threat; see Sec. 91B(b) below.

(d) Examples

Some illustrations may help. But bear in mind that things are rarely so tidy in the tangle that typically precedes bankruptcy. Assets may have been transferred back and forth between partners and partnership, thus obscuring their ownership. Some may be exempt from claims; others may have been secreted. There are likely to be valuation disputes. Partners may have assumed, paid or guaranteed partnership debts, or vice versa, thereby blurring their categorization as individual or partnership.[16] Partners or partnership creditors may contend that debts incurred by a partner are his personal obligations, not the firm's, e. g., because he acted without authority. Moreover, there may be confusion as to the status of claims of partners against the partnership (as to debts, capital or profits); they are all subordinate to those of outside creditors of the partnership, but can affect the relative amounts received by individual partners, and hence by the latters' creditors.

The following examples, for a 2-man firm (AB) assume away these complications, and assume that the assets are worth the value shown for them. Figures in parentheses are negative.

Example 1. Solvent Partnership, Insolvent Partner

AB Partnership Balance Sheet

Assets	$100	Liabilities to X (outsider)	$60
		Capital, Partner A	30
		Capital, Partner B	10
	$100		$100

A's Individual Balance Sheet

Interest in AB Partnership	$30	Liabilities to Y	$40
Other assets	50	Net worth	40
	$80		$80

B's Individual Balance Sheet

Interest in AB Partnership	$10	Liabilities to Z	$30
Other assets	15	Net worth	(5)
	$25		$25

The individual liabilities shown for A and B do not include their responsibility for partnership debts, since there are sufficient partnership assets to cover them.

---

16. See U.P.A. § 15(b), recognizing that a partner may separately obligate himself to perform a partnership contract. This includes a guarantee or endorsement of a partnership obligation; see Sec. 95(a) below.

If the firm were liquidated, $60 would be paid to creditor X (who has priority to this extent), $30 to Partner A and $10 to Partner B. B's $10, plus his other assets of $15 would be taken by his individual creditor (Z). The latter would have no further right to former partnership assets in the hands of A, since B's full economic interest in the firm has been put at his disposal. To say it differently, A (though solvent) has no responsibility for B's individual liabilities. He is responsible for partnership liabilities, but they have been taken care of.

If the firm were not voluntarily wound up, B's creditor could obtain a charging order. If foreclosed and the partnership dissolved, the creditor would receive B's share ($10) and would be in the same position as if the firm had been voluntarily liquidated.

In either case, B's creditor (Z) winds up $5 short; A's (Y) and the partnerships (X) are paid in full or provided for.

Example 2.   Insolvent Partnership, Insolvent Partners

AB Partnership Balance Sheet

Assets	$100	Liabilities to X (outsider)	$140
		Capital, Partner A	(30)
		Capital, Partner B	(10)
	$100		$100

A's Individual Balance Sheet

Interest in AB Partnership	($30)	Liabilities to Y	$40
Other assets	50	Net worth	(20)
	$20		$20

B's Individual Balance Sheet

Interest in AB Partnership	($10)	Liabilities to Z	$30
Other assets	15	Net worth	(25)
	$5		$5

Again, the individual liabilities shown for A and B do not include their responsibility for partnership obligations. These are reflected, in a sense, by the negative value given for their interests in the partnership. However, if their responsibility is the usual complete one, strict accuracy would require listing the full $40 deficit in partnership assets as a liability for each partner. The point is academic on these facts since there are insufficient individual assets left over after individual debts to pay even the pro rata part of the partnership shortage.

The partnership would have to be liquidated under these circumstances, although there would normally be nothing to prevent A and

B from continuing the business after the assets were applied to creditors (if it were economically feasible to do so). The entire $100 of assets would go to creditor X, who would be $40 short. A's $50 of gross assets would be paid, so far as necessary, to his creditor (Y), leaving $10 for the partnership creditor (X) pursuant to A's liability for partnership obligations. Thus X receives a total of $110 and is short $30.

B's $15 of gross assets would all be paid to his creditor (Z) who would still be $15 short. Nothing would be left to apply to partnership liability.

The results are rather different from what one would expect through the basic rule of partners' individual liability for firm debts. Because of the dual priorities system, partnership creditors do not get the full benefit of the personal liability when the partnership can't pay and the partners have heavy individual debts.

Recapitulating Example 2 in terms of creditors and their sources of payment:

Creditor	—Payment from— Partnership Assets	Individual Assets	Total Payment	Total Debt	Deficit	% of Debt Paid
X	$100	$10	$110	$140	$30	78.6%
Y	—	40	40	40	—	100.0
Z	—	15	15	30	15	50.0
	$100	$65	$165	$210	$45	78.6% Avg.

If the dual priorities rule were not controlling, it would be necessary to make some other adjustment between classes of creditors and assets. The possibilities include: (P) ignoring the partnership entity altogether, and letting partnership and individual creditors proceed free for all against partnership and individual assets, with no limitation other than 100% payment; (Q) maintaining the preference of partnership creditors in partnership assets but letting them share on parity with individual creditors in individual assets; (R) maintaining the preference of individual creditors in individual assets but letting them share on parity with partnership creditors in partnership assets. Choosing (Q) to illustrate, and assuming X is a creditor of partners A and B each for the full amount of the $40 deficit after exhaustion of partnership assets, the consequences would be:

Creditor	—Payment from— Partnership Assets	Individual Assets	Total Payment	Total Debt	Deficit	% of Debt Paid
X	$100.00	$33.57 *	$133.57	$140.00	$ 6.43	95.4%
Y	—	25.00 **	25.00	40.00	15.00	62.5
Z	—	6.43 ***	6.43	30.00	23.57	21.4
	$100.00	$65.00	$165.00	$210.00	$45.00	78.6% Avg.

* From A: 40/80 x $50 = $25; from B: 40/70 x $15 = $8.57
** 40/80 x $50
*** 30/70 x $15.

The partnership creditors would gain at the expense of the individual creditors.   Choosing pattern (R) would reverse the process. The results of pattern (P) would depend on the volume of assets and liabilities of partnership relative to partners, and of each partner relative to the others and to the firm.   Example 2 in a (P) distribution would look like this:

Creditor	—Payment from— Partnership Assets	Individual Assets	Total Payment	Total Debt	Deficit	% of Debt Paid
X	$ 66.67	$43.33	$110.00	$140.00	$30.00	78.6%
Y	19.05	12.38	31.43	40.00	8.57	78.6
Z	14.28	9.29	23.57	30.00	6.43	78.6
	$100.00	$65.00	$165.00	$210.00	$45.00	78.6%

Each creditor comes up with the same proportionate payment and deficit.   By coincidence, the partnership creditor is no better or worse off, but the creditor (Z) of the more heavily indebted partner (B) has improved his position relative to the creditor (Y) of the less heavily indebted partner (A), compared to either of the patterns we have tabulated.

(e) Shortcomings of State Law

The Uniform Partnership Act is far from complete as a bankruptcy statute, and was not designed as such.   It has no provision for (1) recovering assets transferred preferentially or in fraud of creditors, (2) enforcing the distribution of assets equitably among creditors, or (3) discharging the debtor if creditors are not paid in full.   Item (1) may be supplied by local law on fraudulent conveyances.   Local law takes care of some of Item (2), through equitable powers of the courts, particularly if a device like assignment for benefit of creditors is used by the debtor.   Item (3) is generally impossible under any state law because of federal pre-emption.

Sometimes a mutually satisfactory settlement, including release of the debtor, can be reached by agreement of debtor and creditors, but this will be rare.   Items (1) and (2) cause grief to creditors, Item (3) to debtors.   Since all three are remedied by federal law, it is easy to see why the latter tends to dominate the field.

(f) Limited Partnerships

The situation in a limited partnership resembles that in a general partnership, keeping in mind the restricted status of the limited partner.   Thus *his* bankruptcy will ordinarily not cause a dissolution, but a general partner's will.[17]   Winding up authority is in the non-bankrupt general partners, who distribute assets according to the usual priorities.[18]

---

17. Sec. 90B(b) at n. 7 above.   **18.** Sec. 90B(c) above.

The dual priorities rule is operative. However, a partnership creditor has rights over against a limited partner only to the extent that the latter has become liable as a general partner or is indebted to the firm.[19] A limited partner, unlike a general one, may be a creditor of the firm on a parity with outside creditors.[20]

DUAL PRIORITIES—HISTORY, CRITICISM AND SCOPE

§ 91A. The dual priorities rule is a venerable product of the equity courts and does rough justice. It has been criticized for frustrating partnership creditors in the pursuit of individual liability which they expect from partners.

(a) History and Rationale

The present form of the dual priorities rule has been stated in Sec. 91(b) above. We now look at its two components separately.

It has always been the rule in bankruptcy and in equity that partnership creditors are given priority in the distribution of the partnership estate. This rule can be rationalized quite readily under the theory that the partnership treated as a legal person should apply its property to the payment of its debts in priority to any distribution to its members or persons claiming under them, or in their rights. The rule, however, became settled long before the judicial recognition of the entity doctrine. It appears to have been considered an application, in equity, of the legal rule that the separate creditor cannot reach by execution anything more than his debtor's interest as partner in partnership property.[21] This explanation is suggested by the language of Lord Loughborough in Ex parte Elton: [22] "I was led to consider another thing: Is it possible to admit a separate creditor to take a dividend upon the joint estate rateably with the joint creditors? No case has gone to that; and it is impossible; for the separate creditor at law has no right to attach the partnership property. He can only attach the interest his debtor had in that property. If it stands as a rule of law, we must consider, what I have always understood to be settled by a vast variety of cases not only in bankruptcy but upon general equity, that the joint estate is applicable to partnership debts, the separate estate to the separate debts." The underlying reason for the rule of law is the partnership contract, and the nature of the rights of partners inter se in partnership property. "This exclusive liability of the partnership estate to the joint creditors is founded on no equity peculiar to themselves, but results from the nature of the contract of partnership, which requires the joint debts to be paid before the equity can be settled between the partners, each being individually liable till all is paid." [23] The priority of partnership creditors in partnership

---

19. See sec. 96A below.

20. Sec. 93(e) below.

21. See Sec. 43 above.

22. 3 Ves.Jr. 238, 30 Eng.Rep. 988 (1796).

23. Bell v. Newman, 5 Serg. & R. 78, 92 (Pa.1819). Case v. Beauregard, 99 U.S. 119, 25 L.Ed. 370 (1878) said: "The

estates has been universally followed and is incorporated into the Uniform Partnership Act [24] and the Bankruptcy Act.[25] It is so well established that it even operates against the United States as a creditor. "The Bankruptcy Act clearly recognizes the separate entity of the partnership for the purpose of applying the long-established rule as to the prior claim of partnership debts on partnership assets and of individual debts on individual assets, and 'establishes on a firm basis the respective equities of the individual and firm creditors.' " [26]

The other component of the dual priorities rule—the superior rights of individual creditors in individual assets—has an equally venerable but more troubled history.

Over two hundred years ago the rule of distribution in bankruptcy was stated by Lord Chancellor Cowper, in Ex parte Crowder: [27] "As the joint or partnership estate was in the first place to be applied to pay the joint or partnership debts; so in like manner the separate estate should be in the first place to pay all the separate debts; and as separate creditors are not to be let in upon the joint estate, until all the joint-debts are first paid; so likewise the creditors to the partnership shall not come in for any deficiency of the joint estate, upon the separate estate, until the separate debts are first paid." Except for a brief period this has remained the English rule.[28]

---

right of each partner extends only to the share of what may remain after payment of the debts of the firm and a settlement of its accounts. Growing out of the right, or rather included in it, is the right to have the partnership property applied to the payment of the partnership debts in preference to those of any individual partner. This is an equity that partners have between themselves, and in certain circumstances it inures to the benefit of the creditors of the firm. The latter are said to have the privilege or preference, sometimes loosely denominated a lien, to have the debts due them paid out of the assets of a firm in course of liquidation to the exclusion of the creditors of its several members. This equity is a derivative one. It is not held or enforceable in their own right. It is practically a subrogation to the equity of the individual partner, to be made effective only through him. Hence, if he is not in a condition to enforce it, the creditors of the firm cannot be. Rice v. Barnard, 20 Vt. 479, 50 Am.Dec. 54; York County Bank's Appeal, 32 Pa. 446. But so long as the equity of the partner remains in him, so long as he retains an interest in the firm assets, as a partner, a court of equity will allow the creditors of the firm to avail themselves of his equity, and enforce, through it, the application of those assets primarily to the payment of the debts due them, whenever the property comes under its administration."

24. Sec. 91 at n. 3 above.

25. Bankruptcy Act § 5g, 11 U.S.C.A. § 23(g).

26. U. S. v. Kaufman, 267 U.S. 408, 45 S.Ct. 322, 69 L.Ed. 685 (1925), holding that a claim for non-payment of federal income taxes due from a partner was not entitled to distribution from the estate of the bankrupt partnership until after payment of firm creditors. See U. S. v. Worley, 213 F.2d 509 (6th Cir. 1954), cert. denied 348 U.S. 918, 75 S.Ct. 302, 99 L.Ed. 720 (1955).

27. 2 Vern. 706, 23 Eng.Rep. 1064 (1715).

28. See historical reviews of the decisions and discussion of the merits of the question in In re Wilcox, 94 F. 84 (D.Mass.1899); Rodgers v. Meranda, 7 Ohio St. 179 (1857); Robinson v. Security Co., 87 Conn. 268, 87 A. 879, Ann.Cas.1915C, 1170 (1913).

Rodgers v. Meranda, supra, is the leading case in which the attempt is made to furnish a rational basis for the priority of separate creditors. "With what semblance of equity could one class of creditors, in preference to the rest, be exclusively entitled to the partnership fund, and concurrently with the rest, entitled to the separate estate of each partner? The joint creditors are no more meritorious than the separate creditors; and it frequently happens, that the separate debts are contracted to raise means to carry on the partnership business. Independently of this rule, the joint creditors have, as a general thing, a great advantage over the separate creditors. Besides being exclusively entitled to the partnership fund, they take their distributive share in the surplus of the separate estate of each of the several partners, after the payment of the separate creditors of each. It is a rule of equity, that where one creditor is in a situation to have two or more distinct securities of funds to rely on, the court will not allow him, neglecting his other funds, to attach himself to one of the funds to the prejudice of those who have a claim upon that, and no other to depend on. And besides the advantage, which the joint creditors have arising from the fact that the partnership fund is usually much the largest, as men of trade, in a great majority of cases, embark their all, or the chief part of their property in it; and besides their distributive rights in the surplus of the separate estate of the other partners, the joint creditors have a degree of security for their debts and facilities for recovering them, which the separate creditors have not; they can sell both the joint and the separate estate on an execution, while the separate creditors can sell only the separate property and the interest in the joint effects that may remain to the partners, after the accounts of the debts and effects of the firm are taken, as between the firm and its creditors, and also as between the partners themselves. With all these advantages in favor of the partnership creditors, it would be grossly inequitable to allow them the exclusive benefit of the joint fund, and then a concurrent right with individual creditors to an equal distribution in the separate estate of each partner. . . . The preference, therefore, of the individual creditors of a partner in the distribution of his separate estate, results, as a principle of equity, from the preference of partnership creditors in the partnership funds, and their advantages in having different funds to resort to, while the individual creditors have but the one."

In Robinson v. Security Company, supra, partnership creditors were allowed to share in the separate estate pari passu with separate creditors, after making allowance for dividends received from the joint estate. Commenting on the generally prevailing rule, the court said: "The underlying trouble with these reasons for the rule, and with the rule itself, including its exception, is that they entirely ignore the fundamental principle defining the nature of partnership obligations and the rights of partnership creditors. They forget the different positions which partnership creditors and the separate creditors of a partner occupy. . . . A creditor of a partnership can look to partnership property to satisfy his claim, or he can, at his option, enforce his judgment by direct levy upon the estate of any partner with an entire disregard of the partnership property. In equity his claim is a joint and several one. A creditor of a partner has no claim upon partnership property. The most that he can under any circumstances reach is the interest of the partner, which may be nothing at all if the firm liabilities make it such. A rule of distribution of assets in insolvency which overlooks these distinctions, whether heedlessly or in the search for equality as between the two classes of creditors, disregards an important factor in the situation."

The argument that joint creditors give primary credit to the partnership estate, and separate creditors to the separate estate, as a basis for the rule is thus answered in J. Parsons, Partnership, 191: "The theories which have been suggested to account for the course of distribution in equity do not go to the source of the change and explain the cause which brought about the departure from the common-law system. The notion of credit, that, as the joint creditors relied upon firm assets, the separate creditors looked to the separate estates for payment, is

No better justification can be found for the rule than that its balanced symmetry impresses one as being equitable. The predecessor of this work called it logically indefensible.[29] The present author feels less strongly and merely notes that the rule has been sharply criticized for destroying or diminishing the partnership creditor's rights against partners' separate property—which he has been led to expect by their joint or joint and several liability for firm debts—at the very time when he most needs them.[30] But the law has been settled long enough that creditors must be charged with knowledge of it and not permitted to complain of frustrated expectations. The critics have rarely suggested [30A] that individual creditors receive parity on partnership assets in return for giving up priority on individual assets. Therefore they must be assuming that partnership credit is socially or economically more important or productive than individual credit in order to enjoy priority in one arena and parity in the other. To the extent that partnership credit is business credit and individual credit is not, some such argument can be made. But it has not been proved. Moreover, it seems quite doubtful in the age of mass consumer credit (mostly individual) which looms so large in the American economy. On the whole, the rule seems to do rough justice. One would be hard put to improve, in the abstract, its approximate balance.

In any event, the priority of individual creditors in individual assets was accepted by the great majority of states at common law, was codified in the Uniform Act,[31] and was adopted in the Bankruptcy Act.[32] A few common law jurisdictions permit (or permitted) partnership creditors to share in individual assets in parity with individual

an assumption. It contradicts the experience which imputes to every man a knowledge of the law. The credit will depend upon the estate which the debtor had. The partners have joint and separate estates, which are both subject to firm debts. The credit would, of course, be given in reliance upon both estates. The partner has a resulting interest in the firm after all its debts are paid, and his separate estate, which is also subject to the firm debts. His creditor could expect nothing from the partner's share until the firm creditors had been satisfied, and he could only share the separate estate with them, unless insolvency supervened, which would give him a paramount title to the separate fund. The credit given to a debtor is not the cause of his estate, but a consequence of his possessing the means to pay the debt." See also Warren, Corporate Advantages Without Incorporation 56–65 (1929); Shroeder, Distribution of Assets of Bankrupt Partnerships and Partners, 18 Harv.L.Rev. 495 (1905); Crane, The Uniform Partnership Act— A Criticism, 28 Harv.L.Rev. 762, 784 (1915); Lewis, The Uniform Partnership Act—A Reply to Mr. Crane's Criticism, 29 Harv.L.Rev. 291, 306 (1916); Notes, 11 Colum.L.Rev. 569 (1911), 54 U.Pa.L.Rev. 210.

29. Crane, Partnership 514 (2d ed. 1952).

30. See, e. g., MacLachlan, Partnership Bankruptcy, 65 Com.L.J. 253 (1960).

30A. Richardson, Creditors' Rights and the Partnership, 40 Ky.L.J. 243, 260–61 (1951) does recommend complete commingling of assets and claims. He does not deal with the difficult problem of keeping the individual property of one partner from paying, in effect, the individual debts of another.

31. U.P.A. §§ 40(h), (i), 36(4).

32. Bankruptcy Act § 5g, 11 U.S.C.A. § 23(g).

creditors.[33] Almost all have since reversed themselves by adopting the Uniform Act.[34] One or two may have rejected the Act because of disagreement on this point.[34A] There has been strong, but so far unsuccessful, pressure to amend the Bankruptcy Act to permit partnership creditors parity against individual assets.[35]

Partnership creditors may avoid the disadvantage of the rule by insisting on individual as well as partnership obligations at the time they extend credit.[36] This will permit double proof of claims.[37]

(b) Scope and Exceptions

The priority of partnership creditors in partnership assets is a function of their furnishing credit to the partnership. It does not extend to joint creditors of the partners by reason of a non-partnership obligation,[38] nor to non-partnership property which the partners hap-

---

33. Robinson v. Security Co., supra n. 28; Blair v. Black, 31 S.C. 346, 9 S.E. 1033, 17 Am.St.Rep. 30 (1899); Webb v. Gregory, 49 Tex.Civ.App. 282, 108 S.W. 478 (1908); City Nat. Bank v. Greene, 279 S.W. 893 (Tex.Civ.App. 1926); Barton Nat. Bank v. Atkins, 72 Vt. 33, 45, 47 A. 176, 180 (1900).

The same result was reached by statute in Louisiana, Flower v. Their Creditors, 3 La.Ann. 189 (1848), and was the rule generally in civil law when surveyed by Brannon, The Separate Estates of Non-Bankrupt Partners, 20 Harv.L.Rev. 588, 592 (1907). More recent civil law approaches are described in MacLachlan, Partnership Bankruptcy, 65 Com.L.J. 253, 258–59 (1960). See also Miller v. New Orleans Acid & Fertilizer Co., 211 U.S. 496, 29 S.Ct. 176, 53 L.Ed. 300 (1909).

In pre-U.P.A. Kentucky, separate creditors shared the separate estate until their rate of dividend equalled that received by the partnership creditors from the partnership estate, after which both classes of creditors shared pari passu. Northern Bank v. Keizer, 63 Ky. (2 Duv.) 169 (1865); Hill v. Cornwall & Bro.'s Assignee, 95 Ky. 512, 26 S.W. 540 (1894). This rule is adopted by statute in Georgia. Johnson v. Gordon, 102 Ga. 350, 30 S.E. 507 (1897). It is presently found in Ga. Code Ann. § 75–311 (1964).

If there are no separate creditors, partnership creditors share in the separate estate, and the latter may be treated as part of the partnership estate to assure equality of distribution among the firm creditors. Fogg v. Tyler, 111 Me. 546, 90 A. 481, 7 A.L.R. 986 (1914).

34. Conn., Ky., S.C., Tex., Vt. On the North Carolina shifts, see Note, 36 N. C.L.Rev. 229 (1958).

34A. This was forecast by Crane, The Uniform Partnership Act—A Criticism, 28 Harv.L.Rev. 762, 785 (1915); cf. 29 Harv.L.Rev. 306 (1916).

35. See, e. g., MacLachlan, op. cit. supra n. 30; Kennedy, A New Deal for Partnership Bankruptcy, 60 Colum.L.Rev. 610, 630–32 (1960); Note, 48 Iowa L.J. 955 (1963). Other partnership bankruptcy proposed changes are considered, including a purely entity theory of partnership insolvency (excluding partners' individual surpluses from the computation) and new procedures concerning administration of a partner's property in a partnership bankruptcy.

36. See Sec. 91(d) at n. 16 above.

37. See Sec. 95(a) below.

38. Forsyth v. Woods, 11 Wall. 484, 20 L.Ed. 207 (1870); In re Nims, Fed.Cas. No.10,269, 16 Blatchf. 439 (1879); In re L. B. Weisenberg & Co., 131 F. 517 (D.Ky.1904); In re Nashville Laundry Co., 240 F. 795 (D.Tenn.1917); Whelan v. Shain, 115 Cal. 326, 47 P. 57 (1896); Dunnica v. Clinkscales, 73 Mo. 500 (1881); Huffman v. Bates, 348 S.W.2d 363 (Mo.App.1961); Second Nat. Bank v. Burt, 93 N.Y. 233 (1883).

The rule in England is otherwise. Hoare v. Oriental Bank, L.R. 2 App.Cas. 589 (1877).

pen to own in common. Whether an obligation is partnership or individual is a question of fact, dependent on the intentions of the parties to the transaction.[39] A similar inquiry is necessary to determine whether particular property is partnership or individual.[40]

The few English exceptions to the priority of separate creditors are mostly inoperative in the United States. (1) If there are no partnership assets available for the partnership creditors, it has been said that the reason for the priorities disappears, and both classes of creditors are permitted to share in the separate estate.[41] Neither the U.P.A. nor the Bankruptcy Act permits an exception of this sort.[42] (2) If a partner became indebted to the firm by reason of a separate trade or business (as opposed to personal) transactions, the partnership was allowed to prove and share with separate creditors.[43] This exception is no more cognizable than the first one under the Bankruptcy or Uniform Acts. (3) If a partner has fraudulently converted partnership property to the enrichment of his separate estate, the partnership creditors or estate have been allowed to share with separate creditors for purpose of restitution.[44] This or an equivalent result can often be worked out by the state or federal bankruptcy laws of fraudulent conveyances.[45] It may be thought of as a rough tracing process (of partnership property into individual property or its mutations) as well as an exception.

An offshoot of the dual priorities rule is a sometime requirement that each class of creditors exhaust its own fund before seeking re-

In New York, prior to the U.P.A., an execution by joint creditors levied on partnership property was preferred to a subsequent execution by partnership creditors. Saunders v. Reilly, 105 N.Y. 12, 12 N.E. 170, 59 Am.Rep. 472 (1887).

See also Steiner v. Peters Store Co., 119 Ala. 371, 24 So. 576 (1898).

39. In re Stevens, 104 F. 323 (D.Vt. 1900); Davis v. Turner, 120 F. 605 (4th Cir. 1903); In re Hurley Mercantile Co., 56 F.2d 1023 (5th Cir. 1932). Huffman v. Bates, n. 38 above.

An obligation signed in the names of all the partners may be shown to be a partnership obligation. Rouss v. Wallace, 10 Colo.App. 93, 50 P. 366 (1897).

40. See Sec. 37 above.

41. Ex parte Kensington, 14 Ves. 447 (1808).

See also Records v. McKim, 115 Md. 299, 80 A. 968, 43 L.R.A.,N.S., 197 (1911); Harris v. Peabody, 73 Me. 262 (1881); In re Robb's Estate, 5 Ohio Dec. 227 (1897); Curtis v. Woodward, 58 Wis.

499, 17 N.W. 328, 46 Am.Rep. 647 (1883).

A contrary view was held in Howe v. Lawrence, 9 Cush. 553, 57 Am.Dec. 68 (Mass.1852); In re Dauchy, 169 N.Y. 460, 62 N.E. 573 (1902).

42. Farmers' & Mechanics' Nat. Bank v. Ridge Ave. Bank, 240 U.S. 498, 36 S.Ct. 461, 60 L.Ed. 767 (1916). Some inferior federal courts had decided in favor of the exception under former bankruptcy acts. In re Lloyd, 22 F. 88 (D.Pa.1884); In re West, 39 F. 203 (S.D.N.Y.1889). Contra, In re Wilcox, 94 F. 84 (D.Mass.1899).

U.P.A. § 40(i) makes no provision for any exception.

43. Ex parte St. Barbe, 11 Ves. 413, 32 Eng.Rep. 1147 (1805). This exception reflects the supposed social superiority of trade credit over personal credit, discussed in (a) of this section.

44. Read v. Bailey, 3 App.Cas. 94 (1877).

45. McElroy v. Allfree, 131 Iowa 518, 108 N.W. 119 (1906).

course against the other. In particular, this would mean that partnership creditors could not move against individual assets as long as firm assets existed,[46] regardless whether individual creditors had been satisfied. In a bankruptcy or known insolvency where creditors are aware of the situation, and of the impossibility of reaching the other class of assets until the other class of creditors has had the first crack, this sorting process occurs more or less automatically. Creditors naturally proceed against their own class of assets while waiting to see if anything is left of the other. Consequently, the offshoot rule has little or no separate existence in bankruptcy and insolvency. It is argued more frequently when a partner (or ex-partner, or the estate of a dead partner) is resisting the claim of a partnership creditor by saying, in effect, go sue the firm first. Delaying or rejecting such a claim would considerably water down individual liability for partnership obligations. Courts have been unwilling to do this in the absence of claims from conflicting classes, and have generally permitted direct claims.[47]

FEDERAL BANKRUPTCY FOR PARTNERS AND PARTNERSHIPS—A PRÉCIS

§ 91B. Entity theory pervades the Bankruptcy Act, which treats partners and partnerships as distinct. Either may be the subject of a voluntary or involuntary petition and of an adjudication as bankrupt. Among the particular partnership problems are those of determining insolvency (which is done by considering as partnership assets the surplus of each partner's individual assets over liabilities, and by considering as individual property the value of a partner's interest in the firm) and of identifying acts of bankruptcy (which include any transfer of partnership property to a partner while the firm is insolvent).

(a) Basic Pattern

Under the U.S. Constitution, Congress has the power to establish "uniform laws on the subject of bankruptcies throughout the United States."[48] Congress has done so in a series of statutes collectively called the National Bankruptcy Act (abbreviated here as "B.A."), found in U.S. Code Annotated, Title 11. The principal partnership provisions are in B.A. § 5, 11 U.S.C.A. § 23, which is reproduced in Appendix IV.

Federal bankruptcy is often preferred by debtors and creditors alike, for it fills the three main gaps in state law.[49] It benefits creditors by giving them a representative empowered to recover property transferred in anticipation of bankruptcy in certain instances and to

---

46. Pahlman v. Graves, 26 Ill. 405 (1861) (partnership creditor must proceed against partnership assets in hands of partnership's assignee for benefit of creditors before claiming against partner's individual assets); Calhoun v. Bank of Greenwood, 42 S.C. 357, 20 S.E. 153 (1893).

47. E. g., Doggett v. Dill, 108 Ill. 560, 48 Am.Rep. 565 (1884), distinguishing Pahlman v. Graves, n. 46 above. See Sec. 58(d) above.

48. U.S.C.A.Const., Art. I, § 8, cl. 4.

49. Sec. 91(e) above.

distribute this and all other property ratably among claimants. It benefits debtors, if they have been honest, by releasing them from further liability after all their assets have been appropriated for creditors. This gives them a chance to start over, which would probably be barred if old liabilities dogged them. Federal bankruptcy offers comparative certainty and ease of administration.[50] When invoked, it supersedes all state proceedings, including those under the U.P.A.

Bankruptcy, in the remainder of this chapter, is used in the federal sense unless otherwise indicated.

Federal bankruptcy is an exceedingly complex field. Since a partnership is included in the definition of "person," [51] all the general provisions (which are framed as applicable to persons) operate on partnerships unless superseded by particular measures for partnerships.[52] This chapter explores only the more important partnership problems, and these in simplified form, sketching or skirting the central issues of non-partnership bankruptcy.[53]

Bankruptcy proceedings are initiated in federal court by a *petition:* voluntary (by the debtor) or involuntary (by creditors). There is an *adjudication* of bankruptcy. Then a trustee succeeds to and *administers* (i. e. assembles and sells) the debtor's *property* (other than that which is *exempt*). He uses the proceeds to pay the *claims* of creditors according to certain priorities. The debtor will be *discharged* in most instances.

The stressed words in the previous and subsequent paragraphs present special partnership problems which are considered below. For ease of comparison, some remarks appear in parallel columns: the left column pertains to a partnership, bankrupt with or without partners; the right column pertains to a partner who is bankrupt, with or without his partnership.

Partnership is not defined in the Bankruptcy Act. Federal courts look to state law for the existence of a partnership; it has been held, however, that estoppel does not create partnership for bankruptcy purposes.[54] Both general and limited partnerships may be bankrupt.[55]

---

50. This is not to say it is a flawless system, particularly for partnership. See Rifkind, Dilemma of Partnership Bankruptcy Administration under Present Section 5 of the Bankruptcy Act, 33 Ref.J. 108 (1959) and references in sec. 91A n. 35 above.

51. B.A. § 1(23), 11 U.S.C.A. § 1(23).

52. Accord B.A. § 5c, 11 U.S.C.A. § 23(c).

53. For general treatments, see MacLachlan, Bankruptcy (1956); Collier, Bankruptcy (14th ed. looseleaf). John-

son & Bateman, Bankruptcy of Partnerships, in State Bar of Texas, Creditors' Rights in Texas 546–84 (McKnight ed. 1963) is a good practical discussion focussed on one state but generally applicable wherever U.P.A. and U.L.P.A. are in force. See also Note, Bankruptcy—Partnerships —Partnerships in Bankruptcy, 31 N.C. L.Rev. 457 (1953).

54. Sec. 93(c) below.

55. See Sec. 96A below on limited partnerships.

(b) Petition

A voluntary petition may be filed:

For a partnership by any general partner, but must allege partnership *insolvency* if signed by less than all the partners.[56]	By any partner for himself individually, regardless of co-partners or partnership.

An involuntary petition may be filed:

By partnership creditors against a partnership, alleging a partnership *act of bankruptcy.*	By individual creditors against a partner, alleging an individual *act of bankruptcy.*

An involuntary petition requires signatures of three or more creditors with claims totalling $500 (if there are 12 or more creditors in all) or one or more with the same total (if there are less than 12).[57]

(c) Insolvency

A person is insolvent when his property "shall not at a fair valuation be sufficient in amount to pay his debts."[58]   Insolvency is determined:

By considering as partnership property the excess, if any, of each partner's individual property over his individual debts.[59] (In the case of a limited partner, the excess counted does not exceed his liability, if any, for partnership debts.)	By considering as individual property the partner's share in partnership surplus, i. e. his portion of the excess, if any, of partnership property over partnership debts.

This pattern accords with the dual priorities rule and with the obligation of partners to contribute toward partnership obligations.[60] However, it differs from conventional financial accounting [60A] which does not show the contribution right as a partnership asset.

(d) Act of Bankruptcy

"Acts of bankruptcy by a person shall consist of his having (1) concealed, removed, or permitted to be concealed or removed any part

---

56.   B.A. § 5b, 11 U.S.C.A. § 23(b).

57.   B.A. § 59b, 11 U.S.C.A. § 95(b).

58.   B.A. § 1(19), 11 U.S.C.A. § 1(19). See Sec. 95A n. 65 below.

59.   Francis v. McNeal, 228 U.S. 695, 33 S.Ct. 701, 57 L.Ed. 1029 (1913) (dictum); Kaufman-Brown Potato Co. v. Long, 182 F.2d 594, 601–02 (9th Cir. 1950); Tom v. Sampsell, 131 F.2d 799 (9th Cir. 1942); Vaccaro v. Security Bank, 103 F. 436 (6th Cir. 1900). With a single exception, the method of de-

termining partnership insolvency is implicit rather than explicit in the Bankruptcy Act. The exception is B. A. § 67d(1), 11 U.S.C.A. § 107(d) (1) which specifies essentially the same rule in connection with fraudulent conveyances. Partnership insolvency is analyzed in Kennedy, A New Deal for Partnership Bankruptcy, 60 Colum.L. Rev. 610, 612 (1960).

60.   Sec. 91 n. 5 above.

60A.   For examples, see Sec. 91(d) above.

of his property, with intent to hinder, delay, or defraud his creditors or any of them, or made or suffered a transfer of any of his property, *fraudulent* under the provisions of section 67 or 70 of this Act; or (2) made or suffered a *preferential* transfer, as defined in subdivision a of section 60 of this Act; or (3) suffered or permitted, while insolvent, any creditor to obtain a lien upon any of his property through legal proceedings or distraint and not having vacated or discharged such lien within thirty days from the date thereof or at least five days before the date set for any sale or other disposition of such property; or (4) made a general assignment for the benefit of his creditors; or (5) while insolvent or unable to pay his debts as they mature, procured, permitted, or suffered voluntarily or involuntarily the appointment of a receiver or trustee to take charge of his property; or (6) admitted in writing his inability to pay his debts and his willingness to be adjudged a bankrupt." [61]

An act of bankruptcy is essential to an involuntary petition, which may be filed up to four months after commission of the act, and in many instances still later.[62] The acts are designed to include most of the creditor-defeating moves a hard-pressed debtor may make.

Insolvency is material to all the acts, in one way or another. It is expressly mentioned in (3) and (5). It is inherent in the definition of preferential transfer in (2),[63] and typically present as a practical matter in (4) and (6). Finally, solvency is a defense to (1).[64]

Local law is used by the bankruptcy court to determine whether an act performed by a partner or agent is a partnership act. The usual criteria apply: authority, apparent authority, scope of the partnership business, etc.[65] Thus, without consent of his co-partners, a partner probably does not have authority to bind the partnership by an admission of insolvency and willingness to be adjudicated (6th act) [66] or by an assignment for benefit of creditors (4th act).[67]

---

61. B.A. § 3a, 11 U.S.C.A. § 21(a), emphasis added.

62. B.A. § 3b, 11 U.S.C.A. § 21(b).

63. See (e) below.

64. B.A. § 3c, 11 U.S.C.A. § 21(c).

65. See Ch. 5 above. For examples in the bankruptcy context, both involving the first act of bankruptcy, see Donadio v. Robetsky, 4 F.2d 51 (1st Cir. 1925) (conveyance of partnership property by partner with authority); In re Wellesley, 252 F. 854 (N.D.Cal.1917) (partner's withdrawal and concealment of funds from partnership bank account).

66. In re Wellesley, n. 65 above.
Steiner, Lobman & Frank v. T. S. Faulk & Co., 222 F. 61, 63 (5th Cir. 1915):

"The evidence tending to prove that the conduct of the business of the firm was left entirely with T. S. Faulk, and that the other partner had nothing to do with the management of the business, had no tendency to prove that T. S. Faulk was authorized to bind the partnership by his consent that it be adjudged bankrupt. The power which that evidence tended to prove was vested in T. S. Faulk was that of carrying on the firm business without consulting his associate, and did not include that of terminating the partnership by consenting that it be adjudged bankrupt."

67. Footnote 67 on page 540.

On the other hand, federal law classifies certain transactions regardless of state law, as discussed in the next two subsections. Local law is similarly used in deciding who owns a particular asset in question.[68]

Provision is made for trying the issues in an alleged act of bankruptcy (such as insolvency, ownership of property, and authority to act for the firm) if they are contested.[69]

(e) Preferential Transfers

"A preference is a transfer . . . of any of the property of a debtor to or for the benefit of a creditor for or on account of an antecedent debt, made or suffered by such debtor while insolvent and within four months before the filing by or against him of the petition initiating a proceeding under this Act, the effect of which transfer will be to enable such creditor to obtain a greater percentage of his debt than some other creditor of the same class."[70] In effect, any payment by an insolvent debtor to an existing creditor is a preference unless all creditors are simultaneously paid the same proportion of their claims.

A preferential transfer is not only an act of bankruptcy justifying an involuntary petition. The transferred property (or its value) is recoverable by the trustee (for the benefit of all creditors) if the transferee had reasonable cause to believe the debtor was insolvent at the time.[71]

The transfer of partnership property (1) to a partnership creditor can be a partnership preference but not an individual preference; (2) to an individual creditor can be a partnership preference and perhaps an individual preference.[72]

The transfer of individual property (1) to a partnership creditor can be an individual preference and perhaps a partnership preference; (2) to an individual creditor can be an individual preference but not a partnership preference.[72]

As already observed,[73] state law generally determines who has acted, whose property has been transferred, and which class a creditor falls in.

Cf. In re Kersten, 110 F. 929 (E.D.Wis. 1901) (partner's admission and consent effective; co-partner failed to object).

On the right of a partner under earlier law to petition the firm into bankruptcy, see Notes, 76 U.Pa.L.Rev. 85 (1927), 4 Texas L.Rev. 102 (1925). Present law is in (b) of this section.

U.P.A. § 9(3)(c) denies a partner's authority (without unanimous consent) to any act which will make it impossible to carry on the business.

This probably covers a bankruptcy admission and consent.

67. U.P.A. § 9(3) (a).

68. Secs. 37, 91A(b) n. 40 above.

69. B.A. §§ 18–19, 11 U.S.C.A. §§ 41–42.

70. B.A. § 60a(1), 11 U.S.C.A. § 96(a) (1).

71. B.A. § 60b, 11 U.S.C.A. § 96(b).

72. See Collier, Bankruptcy § 60.10 (14th ed. looseleaf).

73. Above at (d); see Sec. 91A(b) at nn. 39–40.

(f) Fraudulent Transfers

Fraudulent conveyances, which have been discussed earlier,[73A] include not only those made with actual intent to hinder, delay or defraud creditors,[74] but some made without fair consideration regardless of intent.[75] In particular, "Every transfer of partnership property and every partnership obligation incurred within one year . . . [of a bankruptcy petition] when the partnership is insolvent or will be thereby rendered insolvent, is fraudulent . . . without regard to actual intent if made or incurred (a) to a partner, whether with or without a promise by him to pay partnership debts, or (b) to a person not a partner without fair consideration to the partnership as distinguished from consideration to the individual partners."[76] Thus any distribution to, or withdrawal by a partner while the firm is insolvent is caught in the net.

A fraudulent transfer is not only an act of bankruptcy justifying an involuntary petition. The transferred property (or its value) is recoverable by the trustee (for the benefit of all creditors).

(g) Adjudication

" 'Adjudication' shall mean a determination whether by decree or by operation of law, that a person is bankrupt."[77] There may be an adjudication:

Of a partnership with or without adjudication of partners (and there must be adjudication of the partnership if all partners are adjudicated).[78] Partners may avoid partnership adjudication under an involuntary petition by successfully contesting the facts on which it is based (e. g., partnership insolvency, preference or fraudulent transfer). A partner not joining in a voluntary petition may treat it as involuntary.	Of a partner with or without adjudication of the partnership (but there must be an adjudication of the partnership if all partners are adjudicated).[79] A partner may avoid adjudication under an involuntary petition by successfully contesting the facts on which it is based (e. g., his insolvency, preference or fraudulent transfer).

A partnership composed of an adult and an infant may be adjudicated, although the infant is exempt from bankruptcy.[80] Insanity of

---

73A. Sec. 46 above.

74. B.A. § 67d(2) (d), 11 U.S.C.A. § 107 (d) (2) (d).

75. B.A. § 67d(2) (a)–(c), 11 U.S.C.A. § 107(d) (2) (a)–(c). See also B.A. § 67d (3), 11 U.S.C.A. § 107(d) (3). Any transfer void or fraudulent under state law is included by B.A. § 70e(1), 11 U.S.C.A. § 110(e) (1).

76. B.A. § 67d(4), 11 U.S.C.A. § 107(d) (4), based on the Uniform Fraudulent Conveyance Act, Sec. 46 above.

77. B.A. § 1(2), 11 U.S.C.A. § 1(2).

78. B.A. § 5a, i, 11 U.S.C.A. § 23(a), (i); see n. 85 below.

79. See n. 78 above.

80. In re Dunnigan, 95 F. 428 (D.Mass. 1899); In re Duguid, 100 F. 274 (E.D.

a partner does not prevent adjudication of the firm.[81]   Adjudication may occur after the death of a partner [82] or other event causing dissolution.[83]   That one or more partners are farmers or wage earners (hence personally exempt from involuntary proceedings) affords no defense to proceedings against the partnership.[84]

(h) The Prevalence of the Entity Theory

The entity theory pervades the bankruptcy treatment of partnerships.   The concept is central to the separateness of petitions against and adjudications of partnerships and partners.[85]   It is apparent in the determination of insolvency [86] and in the distinctions between firm and partners drawn in various acts of bankruptcy.[87]   It is equally

N.C.1900); Jennings v. William A. Stannus & Son, 191 F. 347 (9th Cir. 1911).

Cf. In re Dixon, 18 F.2d 961 (W.D.Mich. 1926). A petition was filed against a partnership alleged to be composed of a married woman, her husband, and another. Since Michigan law made her incapable of being a partner with her husband, and therefore not bound by partnership debts, her name was stricken from the adjudication decree.

81. In re L. Stein & Co., 127 F. 547 (7th Cir. 1904).

82. In re Wells, 298 F. 109 (S.D.Ohio 1924); Meek v. Beezer, 28 F.2d 343 (3d Cir. 1928).

83. B.A. § 5a, 11 U.S.C.A. § 23(a).

84. Dickas v. Barnes, 140 F. 849, 5 L.R. A.,N.S., 654 (6th Cir. 1905); In re Sugar Valley Gin Co., 292 F. 508 (N.D. Ga.1923).

Under prior law, a farming partnership was exempt from involuntary bankruptcy. H. D. Still's Sons v. American Nat. Bank, 209 F. 749 (4th Cir. 1913), cert. denied 232 U.S. 723, 34 S.Ct. 331, 58 L.Ed. 815 (1914). See Comment, 12 Mich.L.Rev. 483 (1914). The result is probably the same under present law, although changes in statutory language have created doubts not yet resolved. See Collier, Bankruptcy § 4.15 [5] (14th ed. looseleaf).

A partner, whose only business concern is a farming partnership, is exempt from involuntary bankruptcy though she does not reside on the farm and is comparatively inactive in its opera-

tion. In re Cox, 9 F.Supp. 244 (S.D. Ill.1935).

85. Above at (b) and (g). Meek v. Centre County Banking Co., 268 U.S. 426, 45 S.Ct. 560, 69 L.Ed. 1028 (1925): "There hence can be no doubt that a partnership may be adjudged bankrupt as a distinct legal entity." See also Liberty Nat. Bank v. Bear, 276 U.S. 215, 48 S.Ct. 252, 72 L.Ed. 536 (1928); In re Meyer, 98 F. 976 (2d Cir. 1899); In re Hurley Mercantile Co., 56 F.2d 1023 (5th Cir. 1932); C. J. Farley & Co. v. Stoll, 250 Mich. 495, 231 N.W. 71 (1930).

Schroder, Distribution of Assets of Bankrupt Partnerships and Partners, 18 Harv.L.Rev. 495, 498 (1905).

Adjudication of the partnership is not adjudication of individual partners. Liberty Nat. Bank v. Bear, supra; Hays v. Harris, 78 F.2d 66 (8th Cir. 1935). See above at nn. 78–79.

86. Above at (c). Entity theory under the B.A. was once considered to require so complete a separation of partnership and separate estates that a firm could be considered insolvent though one or more partners were individually solvent. See In re Bertenshaw, 157 F. 363, 17 L.R.A.,N.S., 886, 13 Ann.Cas. 986 (8th Cir. 1907); Hough, Some New Aspects of Partnership Bankruptcy under the Act of 1898, 8 Colum.L.Rev. 599 (1908). This view was effectually refuted by Holmes' opinion in Francis v. McNeal, 228 U.S. 695, 33 S.Ct. 701, 57 L.Ed. 1029 (1913), quoted in sec. 92 n. 96 below. See above at n. 59.

87. Above at (d)–(f).

manifest in the dual priorities rule [88] and the matters of administration and discharge considered in the remaining sections of this chapter.

ADMINISTRATION OF BANKRUPT ESTATES

§ 92. Upon adjudication, the property of a bankrupt passes to a trustee for administration. The trustee of a partnership may administer the separate estates of the partners, whether or not they are individually adjudicated. A partner's trustee does not administer partnership estate. The trustee has power to recover preferences and fraudulent conveyances.

Following adjudication of bankruptcy, a trustee of the debtor is appointed by the creditors.[89]

A trustee of a partnership administers property of the partnership and winds up the firm. He also administers property of adjudicated partners (unless creditors of the latter show cause why they should have a separate trustee) and property of unadjudicated partners to the extent necessary to settle partnership affairs.[90]

A trustee of a partner administers property of the individual partner but not (unless co-partners consent) partnership property.[91] Co-partners wind up the partnership and account to the partner's trustee for the partner's interest.

If two or more estates are administered by the same trustee, separate accounting is required.[92] In any event, it is necessary to distinguish property of the firm from that of individual partners.[93] Un-

---

88. See also Secs. 91, 91A above.

89. B.A. § 44a, 11 U.S.C.A. § 72(a) discussed with reference to limited partners, Sec. 93(e) n. 32 below.

90. B.A. § 5c. See below at n. 96.

In re Ira Haupt & Co., 240 F.Supp. 369 (S.D.N.Y.1965) contains a full discussion of the problem, and requires the unadjudicated partner to file schedules of assets and liabilities preparatory to the trustee's administration of his property.

The partnership trustee has no rights to the property of an unadjudicated limited partner. In re Tommie's Dine & Dance, 102 F.Supp. 627 (N.D.Tex. 1952). This result derives from the limited partner's lack of liability. To the extent a limited partner is responsible for partnership obligations, he would be treated as a general partner, B.A. § 5k, Sec. 96A below, and would be personally subject to administration by the firm's trustee.

On the uncertainties in procedures concerning unadjudicated partners, see Kennedy, A New Deal for Partnership Bankruptcy, 60 Colum.L.Rev. 610, 626–30 (1960).

91. Brandt & Brandt Printers, Inc. v. Klein, 220 F.2d 935 (2d Cir. 1955), requiring partnership assets in the hands of the bankrupt partner's trustee to be delivered to the other partner. Moreover the assets were not chargeable with fees for the trustee or his attorney since they were not subject to the trustee's administration. Id., 232 F.2d 151 (2d Cir. 1956), cert. denied Klein v. Brandt & Brandt Printers, Inc., 352 U.S. 835, 77 S.Ct. 53, 1 L.Ed.2d 54 (1956).

92. B.A. § 5e. Expenses are allocated by the court among the estates, id. § 5f.

93. See Secs. 37, 91A(b) at n. 40, 91B(d) at n. 68 above.

der the dual priorities rule, any surplus remaining after distribution of the individual estates to individual creditors is added to the partnership estate and used to pay partnership creditors.[94]   This implements their liability for partnership obligations and parallels the computation of insolvency for bankruptcy purposes.[95]   It is to produce this surplus, and for better, coordination, that a partnership trustee is permitted to administer the estates of partners even though they have not been adjudicated.[96]   Such administration is permitted though they are farmers or wage earners individually exempt from involuntary bankruptcy.[97]

The bankruptcy court may marshal the partnership and individual estates to prevent preferences and secure equitable distribution.[98] The trustee has power to recover for the bankrupt estate (and hence for creditors) property transferred in preferences and fraudulent conveyances.[99]   The complexities which may result are illustrated in Liberty Nat. Bank v. Bear.[1]   Partnership creditors obtained a judgment

---

94.   B.A. § 5f.

95.   Sec. 91B(c) above.

96.   Francis v. McNeal, 228 U.S. 695, 33 S.Ct. 701, 57 L.Ed. 1029, L.R.A.1915E, 706 (1913), "On the other hand, it would be an anomaly to allow proceedings in bankruptcy against joint debtors from some of whom, at any time before, pending, or after the proceedings, the debt could be collected in full.   If such proceedings were allowed, it would be a further anomaly not to distribute all the partnership assets.   Yet the individual estate, after paying private debts, is part of these assets, so far as needed.   Section 5f (11 U.S.C.A. § 23(f)).   Finally, it would be a third incongruity to grant a discharge in such a case from the debt considered as joint but to leave the same persons liable for it considered as several.   We say the same persons, for however much the difference between firm and member under the statute be dwelt upon, the firm remains at common law a group of men, and will be dealt with as such in the ordinary courts for use in which the discharge is granted.   If, as in the present case, the partnership and individual estates together are not enough to pay the partnership debts, the rational thing to do, and one certainly not forbidden by the act, is to administer both in bankruptcy.   If such a case is within section 5h (11 U.S.C.A. § 23(h)), it is enough that Francis has

never objected to the firm property being administered by the trustee."

See criticism of this case in 9 Ill.Law Rev. 52 (1914).

See also Notes, 13 Colum.L.Rev. 143 (1913); 22 Colum.L.Rev. 348 (1922); 29 Colum.L.Rev. 1134 (1929); 27 Harv. L.Rev. 175 (1913); 37 Harv.L.Rev. 614 (1924); 10 Mich.L.Rev. 215 (1912); 12 Mich.L.Rev. 483 (1914).

The trustee of the firm cannot arbitrarily take over the property of an alleged partner without affording him the right to be heard on the issue of whether he is a partner.   Tate v. Hoover, 345 Pa. 19, 26 A.2d 665 (1942), cert. denied 317 U.S. 677, 63 S.Ct. 159, 87 L.Ed. 543 (1942).   A trustee taking over the property of an unadjudicated partner takes it *cum onere* as of the date he takes over, hence subject to rights of third parties arising before that time though after filing of the bankruptcy petition.   Ibid.

97.   Dickas v. Barnes, 140 F. 849, 5 L.R. A.,N.S., 654 (6th Cir. 1905).

In re Sugar Valley Gin Co., 292 F. 508 (D.Ga.1923).

See Brannan, The Separate Estate of Non-Bankrupt Partners, 20 Harv.L. Rev. 589 (1907).

98.   B.A. § 5h, 11 U.S.C.A. § 23(h).

99.   Sec. 91B(e), (f) above.

1.   276 U.S. 215, 48 S.Ct. 252, 72 L.Ed. 536 (1928).

which operated (under Virginia law) as a lien on both partnership and separate real estate. Within four months the firm was adjudicated. The trustee resisted enforcement of the judgment liens on the separate property. He would have succeeded if they had been on partnership property. It was held that the liens were not voided by the bankruptcy of the firm, and that the trustee's "contention disregards entirely the principle established by the Bankruptcy Act that a partnership may be adjudged a bankrupt as a separate entity without reference to the bankruptcy of the partners as individuals." [2] The result would probably have been different if the non-lien creditors had been able to petition the partners individually into bankruptcy; apparently they made no effort to do so.

DISTRIBUTION OF PARTNERSHIP ESTATES

§ 93. By the dual priorities rule, partnership assets are first appropriated to the payment of partnership debts. Any surplus goes to the partners according to their interests and becomes subject to their individual creditors. Dormant partners are subject to the same rules. If there are no partners in fact but only partners by estoppel, there is no partnership estate and there are no partnership creditors entitled to priority. A partner's claim is generally subordinated and does not rate as a partnership creditor's. Contra for the claim (as a creditor) of a limited partner or of another partnership having a common partner. A partnership creditor holding security from a partner is not subject to the disadvantage he would face if he held security from the firm.

(a) Basic Pattern

The basic pattern for the distribution of partnership estates is priority for partnership creditors, with any surplus going to individual partners and their creditors. This has been discussed in connection with the dual priorities rule, of which it is a part.[3] The Bankruptcy Act is in accord.[4]

The intricate variations in possible partnership arrangements create a number of complications of the fundamentally simple rule. These are treated in the remainder of this Section.

(b) Dormant Partners

A dormant partner is liable on firm obligations to the same extent as more active or visible partners.[5] He may be brought involuntarily into a bankruptcy proceeding and his estate made available to partnership creditors like those of the conspicuous partners. Even after adjudication of the others, the petition may be amended to include him.[6]

---

2. Id. at 220–21, 48 S.Ct. at 253, 254. See Notes, 29 Colum.L.Rev. 1134 (1929); 23 Ill.L.Rev. 483 (1929); 41 Harv.L.Rev. 1044 (1928).

3. Secs. 91, 91A above.

4. B.A. § 5g, 11 U.S.C.A. § 23(g).

5. Sec. 24 above.

6. In re Fuller, 9 F.2d 553 (2d Cir. 1925), noted 25 Colum.L.Rev. 1077 (1925), 39 Harv.L.Rev. 1095 (1926). Compare In re Samuels, 215 F. 845 (2d Cir. 1914), holding that a dormant partner not made a party to the bankruptcy pro-

This is important since he may become known only in the course of the proceedings. He represents something of a windfall for the firm creditors.

Consider the ostensible sole trader whose dormant partner is discovered after credit has been granted. It may be questioned whether the trade creditors, who are unexpectedly found to be joint partnership creditors, are entitled to priority in the joint assets as against those who trusted to the apparent sole ownership of the active partner. The state courts have dealt with the problem in the situation of the disposition of property seized on execution and the proceeds of sales of such property. The dormant partner is estopped to object to the application of the joint property to the claims of joint creditors who have brought suit against the ostensible sole owner in ignorance of the existence of the partnership.[7] He is estopped also to object to its application to the claims of separate creditors of the apparent sole owner.[8] It seems that the dormant partner likewise should be estopped to object to the trustee in bankruptcy of the apparent sole owner distributing the joint property to joint and separate creditors of the bankrupt.[9] As between the partnership and separate creditors

ceedings, is not subject to orders for disclosure of his estate. It was suggested that a new adjudication might be necessary since, unless the dormant partner was insolvent, the partnership was not insolvent.

7. Callender & Co. v. Robinson, 96 Pa. 454 (1880).

The secret partner is estopped to deny the power of the apparent sole owner to mortgage the property for partnership purposes. Taylor v. Cummer Lumber Co., 59 Fla. 638, 52 So. 614 (1910).

As to the partnership creditors, no distinction is to be made as between those who bring suit against the apparent sole owner or those who bring suit against the partners. Lord v. Baldwin, 23 Mass. (6 Pick.) 348 (1828); Brown's Appeal, 17 Pa. 480 (1851).

As between the competing groups of creditors, priority to the partnership creditors has been allowed. Witter v. Richards, 10 Conn. 37 (1833).

8. Cammack v. Johnson, 2 N.J.Eq. 163 (1839); In re Flynn's Estate, 181 Wash. 254, 43 P.2d 8 (1935); How v. Kane, 2 Pin. 531, 54 Am.Dec. 152 (Wis.1850).
See contra, Posey v. Cocke, 263 Ky. 177, 92 S.W.2d 4 (1936).

In Braddock v. Gambill, 291 S.W. 306 (Tex.Civ.App.1927), suit was brought

against the two ostensible members of a partnership for partnership obligation, but discontinued as to one and judgment taken against the other. It was held that, this not being a form of judgment on which partnership property could be reached, a dormant partner could object to the garnishment of a claim due to the partnership.

A third person, sued by the ostensible sole owner of the business on a claim in fact belonging to the secret partnership, can set off a claim due from the plaintiff in its separate capacity. Dixon Livery Co. v. Bond, 117 Va. 656, 86 S.E. 106, L.R.A.1916A, 1211 (1915). Cf. Restatement, Second, Agency §§ 306, 307.

9. In White v. Farnham, 99 Me. 100, 58 A. 425, 105 Am.St.Rep. 261 (1904), it was held that the trustee in bankruptcy of the ostensible sole owner of a business was not subject to liability in trover to a third person claiming under a chattel mortgage executed by a dormant partner in the name of the partners. The third person knew that the property was apparently owned in its entirety by the ostensible sole owner.

In Hiller v. Olmstead, 54 F.2d 5 (6th Cir. 1931), a wife was apparently a de facto dormant partner with her husband in operating a store. Under the law

in a bankruptcy proceeding which turns out to be a partnership bankruptcy, the question is more difficult. It seems probable that the statutory rules of distribution would apply and that joint creditors would be awarded a priority in joint property and separate creditors in separate property, though neither group of creditors became such in the expectation that their rights would be different. But joint creditors who have dealt with a partner as ostensible sole proprietor of the business are entitled to prove as his creditors in bankruptcy, treating him as the agent of an undisclosed principal, and share in his separate estate.[10]

(c) Partners by Estoppel

Partners by estoppel are personally liable on contracts made with persons who rely upon their apparent membership in a firm.[11] But there is no provision in the Bankruptcy Act for adjudicating a partnership by estoppel [12] nor for adjudicating a partner by estoppel along with actual partners.[13] Since no partnership means no partnership property (in the usual sense), it appears impossible to award any priority in distribution of assets to those who dealt with a supposed but non-existent partnership. The majority of state courts, in administering insolvent estates, have given no priority in such cases.[14] In Eng-

of Michigan, where the business was carried on, a married woman lacked legal capacity to be a partner with her husband so as to be jointly liable on partnership obligations. [Farmers' Co-Operative Creamery Co. of Saranac v. Huhn, 241 Mich. 23, 216 N. W. 370 (1927)]. A fire insurance policy on the stock of merchandise was taken out in their joint names, and a fire loss occurred shortly before the husband was adjudicated bankrupt. It was held that the proceeds of the policy belonged to the trustee in bankruptcy and no share could be claimed by the wife. The court said: "The incapacity to contract partnership relations is solely that of the wife, and if property comes into her possession, directly or indirectly, under or by virtue of an attempt to enter into the prohibited relationship, she must in equity account for it to those who are ultimately interested and entitled, viz. the creditors." At the same time the court approved the allowance of a claim against the estate by the wife for advances to the business.

10. In Ex parte Reid, 2 Rose 84 (1814), the joint creditors were allowed to prove against the separate estate, leaving the joint estate undistributed. The separate creditors, who would have been paid in full had they alone proved against the separate estate, were allowed to share in the partner's share in the joint estate. Under the U.P.A. it seems that the surplus of the joint estate would go to the separate estate for distribution among those entitled to share in it as separate creditors.

11. U.P.A. § 16, Sec. 36 above.

12. In re Pinson & Co., 180 F. 787, 789 (N.D.Ala.1910): "The jurisdiction of the bankruptcy court to adjudicate and administer attached only upon a showing of an actually existing partnership, constituting a legal entity at the time of the filing of the petition." See also In re Kuntz, 33 F.2d 198 (M. D.Pa.1929); Tatum v. Acadian Production Corp., 35 F.Supp. 40 (E.D.La. 1940).

13. In re Kaplan, 234 F. 866 (7th Cir. 1916). See also In re Gibson, 191 F. 665 (D.S.D.1911).

14. "If the creditors of an actual partnership have no independent right to have the social assets subjected to the payment of their debts in preference to the creditors of the individual partners, but their right to such priority is a purely derivative one, by substitu-

land a contrary result was reached through a statute dealing with reputed ownership.[15] A leading American case, Thayer v. Humphrey,[16]
applied rules of estoppel to give personal creditors of a partner by estoppel, a priority over trade creditors in the distribution of his estate.
There has been some authority in accord.[17] The U.P.A. makes no provision for priority if there is no actual partnership, and is believed by
the draftman and commissioners to require adherence to the majority
rule, precluding priorities.[18]

tution to the rights of the partners as
between themselves, the creditors of
an ostensible partnership can only
have this right of priority by a like
substitution to the equities of the partners between themselves, unless the
creditors of an ostensible partnership
have rights superior to the rights of
the creditors of an actual partnership.
This of course cannot be so. Since, as
we have seen, there are no equities between the ostensible partners, there
being neither a partnership nor partnership property, there is nothing to
which its creditors can be substituted." Johnson v. Williams, 111 Va. 95,
68 S.E. 410, 411, 31 L.R.A.,N.S., 406,
Ann.Cas.1912A, 47 (1910).

Accord, Broadway Nat. Bank v. Wood,
165 Mass. 312, 43 N.E. 100 (1896);
Bremen Savings Bank v. Branch-
Crookes Saw Co., 104 Mo. 425, 16 S.W.
209 (1891); Taylor v. Wilson, 58 N.H.
465 (1878); Himmelreich v. Shaffer,
182 Pa. 201, 37 A. 1007, 61 Am.St.Rep.
698 (1897).

15. In re Rowland & Crankshaw, L.R. 1
Ch.App. 421 (1866); Ex parte Hayman, L.R. 8 Ch.Div. 11 (1878), basing
the result on the statutory rule of
reputed ownership embodied in the
English Bankruptcy Act, § 44. Ex
parte Hayman, said: "If the consequence that the stock in trade is to be
held to be joint property, where there
is an ostensible partnership, is merely
an offshoot of the doctrine of reputed
ownership, then I can well understand
that in such a case the rights of the
separate creditors should be barred,
and that they should not be entitled
to prove in competition with the joint
creditors. But if this result is supposed to flow from the doctrine of
ostensible partnership per se, then I
must say for myself that I cannot see
why in such a case the rights of the
separate creditors should be any less
than the rights of the joint creditors.

The law relating to ostensible partnership is founded upon the doctrine
of estoppel, and although the doctrine
of estoppel might be perfectly good as
between those who contract with the
joint creditors and the creditors themselves, I do not see why in the event
of bankruptcy that estoppel should apply to the separate creditors, whose
rights before bankruptcy stand very
much in the same position as those of
the joint creditors."

16. 91 Wis. 276, 64 N.W. 1007, 1011, 30
L.R.A. 549, 51 Am.St.Rep. 887 (1895),
the court saying that: "If a person allows another to carry on a business in
such a way as to amount to a holding
out to persons generally that he and
such other are partners, and credit is
given to both on the supposition that
they are partners in fact, the property
with which such business is carried
on, though in law that of such person,
in equity will be treated as the joint
property of such person and such other; and neither of them, nor the creditors of either, can prove in insolvency
in competition with the creditors who
have trusted the two as partners and
the business as that of the two."

It was also held that the creditors of
the ostensible partnership could not
share pari passu with the personal
creditors of the partner by estoppel.

17. Van Kleeck v. McCabe, 87 Mich. 599,
49 N.W. 872, 24 Am.St.Rep. 182 (1891);
Kelly v. Scott, 49 N.Y. 595 (1872).
See Note, 10 Harv.L.Rev. 49 (1896); 59
U.Pa.L.Rev. 183.

18. Commissioners' notes to U.P.A. § 16,
7 Unif.Laws Ann. 94, 95 (1949); Lewis,
The Uniform Partnership Act—A Reply to Mr. Crane's Criticism, 29 Harv.
L.Rev. 291, 300 (1916). Note, however,
that the Act is not very explicit on
this point and that "the law of estoppel shall apply under this act." U.P.

(d) Former Partners as Creditors

The obligation to an ex-partner for the retirement price of his interest or other obligation growing out of his former membership, is that of a creditor whose claim is provable, and prima facie entitled to parity with other creditors.[19] The situation is sometimes complicated by the existence of unpaid creditors of the former partnership, whose claims are (by operation of law or by assumption) obligations of the continuing firm.[20] As creditors of the ex-partner, they have grounds to object to his competing with his own creditors. The U.P.A. provides that any dividend credited to the ex-partner, or deceased partner's estate, shall be distributed to the unpaid creditors of the former firm.[21] This provision has been applied in bankruptcy.[22] Where, on dissolution of a 2-man firm, the continuing partner gives a note to the other for the value of his interest and later goes bankrupt, the retired partner cannot share in distribution until the old partnership creditors are paid.[23]

The objectives of such rules (and those in the next subsection) are two-fold. They hold a partner to his liability on firm obligations and prevent him from improving his status by deserting the sinking ship. And they avoid the circuity which would occur if he collected from the partnership or ongoing partner and then had to pay partnership creditors in satisfaction of his personal liability.

An existing or former partner who pays firm creditors has indemnification [24] or subrogation rights which permit him to claim against the partnership and other partners.[25]

A. § 4(2). See Crane, The Uniform Partnership Act—A Criticism, 28 Harv.L.Rev. 762, 780 (1915).

19. In re Lough, 182 F. 961 (2d Cir. 1910). See also In re Dillon, 100 F. 627 (D.Mass.1900) (retired partner, compelled to pay a firm debt after dissolution and assumption by the continuing partner, was entitled to prove and share for reimbursement in the latter's bankrupt estate).

If a purchase money obligation to a retiring partner for his interest is that of the individual partners rather than the partnership, it is, of course, not provable against the partnership. In re Rudy, 25 F.Supp. 912 (W.D.Ky. 1939).

20. Claims of the old creditors are claims against the partnership continuing the business under U.P.A. § 41.

21. U.P.A. § 41(8). The Act speaks in terms of priority, but the effect is stronger, as stated in the text; see Commissioners' Notes to U.P.A. § 41

(8), 7 Unif.Laws Ann. 232 (1949). Cf. U.P.A. § 42.

22. In re Hess, 1 F.2d 342 (W.D.Pa. 1923). See also In re Denning, 114 F. 219 (D.Mass.1902).

In Titus v. Maxwell, 281 F. 433 (6th Cir. 1922), the continuing partner gave the retiring partner a note for the value of his interest, secured by a chattel mortgage on the property. The retired partner was held to be a secured creditor, entitled to priority over both old and new creditors.

23. In re Jewett, Fed.Cas.No.7309 (N.D. Ill.1869). See also Stump v. Wilson, 100 W.Va. 227, 130 S.E. 463 (1925). But see Titus v. Maxwell, n. 22 above.

24. Cf. U.P.A. § 18(c), Sec. 65(b) above.

25. In re Dillon, n. 19 above; Matter of Hirth, 189 F. 926 (D.Minn.1911) (paying partner entitled to accounting in bankruptcy court and claim against bankrupt partner's estate for amount due).

(e) Partners as Creditors

A partner may be a creditor of the firm as well as a contributor of capital or owner of undistributed profits. But his liability for partnership obligations subordinates him to outside creditors,[26] whether he is claiming as a lender[27] or for profits or capital advances.[28] Otherwise, whatever he collected from the partnership would simply be taken away by the creditors. Strictly speaking, this distorts the dual priorities rule, since the value of his claim as a creditor of the partnership should be subject first to his individual creditors. The reason for the subordination, which appears not to have been scrutinized carefully in this respect, is perhaps that partners' claims against their firms are often not, in fact, neatly classified into debt, capital contributions and profits. And even if they were, the books might easily be juggled to convert one into another.[29]

The reasoning fails, and the rule reverses, in the case of a limited partner. He may be a creditor of the firm and share ratably with outside creditors.[30] Moreover, security in the form of a lien taken by him when the firm is solvent[31] is good in bankruptcy.[32] Of course, he remains subordinate to outside creditors in his claim for profits and capital contributions.[33]

A partnership may issue negotiable instruments to a partner on account of loans, distributions of profits, or capital. Such obligations in the hands of a third person, as holder in due course, are provable

---

26. U.P.A. § 40(b). The same is true in the extreme situation where he has been fraudulently induced to enter the partnership. Although given a right to rescind, his claim is subordinated to outside creditors. U.P.A. § 39, Sec. 85 above, esp. at n. 26.

27. In re Rice, 164 F. 509 (E.D.Pa.1908); In re Effinger, 184 F. 728 (D.Md.1911); Rodgers v. Meranda, 7 Ohio St. 179 (1857). See U.P.A. § 40(b).

Compare Husted v. Pogue, 249 Mich. 410, 228 N.W. 737 (1930) allowing partners (as depositors and as assignees of depositors) to share pari passu in the estate of an insolvent banking partnership.

28. Wallerstein v. Ervin, 112 F. 124 (3d Cir. 1901).

29. There is also a historical reluctance to isolate one claim from all those among partners and their firms; see sec. 70 above. Or the subordination may reflect a policy of preferring partnership creditors as to all assets in the firm not emanating from outside.

30. U.L.P.A. § 13(1); cf. id. § 23(1) (a).

31. In accordance with U.L.P.A. § 13(1) (b).

32. Hughes v. Dash, 309 F.2d 1 (5th Cir. 1962). A limited partner creditor is not the same as an outside creditor in all bankruptcy respects. He is too closely associated with management of the firm to vote in the election of a trustee, whose independence is an important safeguard for creditors. In the Matter of Ira Haupt & Co., 234 F. Supp. 167, 170–71 (S.D.N.Y.1964), two cases, 240 F.Supp. 10, 15–17 (S.D.N.Y. 1965), aff'd 343 F.2d 726 (2d Cir. 1965), cert. denied Klebanow v. Chase Manhattan Bank, 382 U.S. 890, 86 S.Ct. 182, 15 L.Ed.2d 148 (1965). The result is correct in terms of policy, but it involves a strained construction of the word "corporation" in B.A. § 1(8), 11 U.S.C.A. § 1(8) as it applies to voting eligibility in B.A. § 44c, 11 U.S.C.A. § 72(a).

33. U.L.P.A. § 23, Sec. 90B(c) above. He ranks above general partners but below outside creditors.

against the bankrupt or insolvent estate of the firm, and share in distribution on parity with partnership creditors generally.[34]   In the hands of a partner or his insolvent estate, they are postponed to the claims of third persons as partnership creditors,[35] as are obligations not represented by negotiable instruments.

Though the Bankruptcy Act permits proof of claims by the partnership estate against the separate estates of partners, and vice versa,[36] this does not affect the priorities of creditors in the distribution of the estates.

The holder of a non-negotiable chose in action assigned to him by a partner has been held to the same subordination as the partner.[37]

34. Miller's River Nat. Bank v. Jefferson, 138 Mass. 111 (1884); Buchanan v. Mechanics' Loan & Savings Institution, 84 Md. 430, 35 A. 1099 (1896); First Nat. Bank of Champlain v. Wood, 128 N.Y. 35, 27 N.E. 1020 (1891), transferee a donee while partnership was solvent.

Compare McCruden v. Jonas, 173 Pa. 507, 34 A. 224, 51 Am.St.Rep. 774 (1896), transferee with notice of condition of insolvency held to have no greater rights than transferor.

See also Cutting v. Daigneau, 151 Mass. 297, 23 N.E. 839 (1890), where a transfer after insolvency was held to give the transferee for the benefit of the transferor no better rights than the latter possessed.

35. McCruden v. Jonas, n. 34 above.

Negotiable notes and other instruments are often issued by joint-stock companies and business trusts. Hibbs v. Brown, 190 N.Y. 167, 82 N.E. 1108 (1907); Hamilton v. Young, 116 Kan. 128, 225 P. 1045, 35 A.L.R. 496 (1924); Gutelius v. Stanbon, 39 F.2d 621 (D. Mass.1929). Such obligations in the hands of third persons, though derived from members in ordinary course of negotiation, are doubtless enforceable on a parity with other claims. But in the hands of members who have taken them as a distribution of profits, or in redemption of shares, they should rate as preferred stock. See D'Ooge v. Leeds, 176 Mass. 558, 57 N.E. 1025 (1900). Compare the situation as to corporate securities, Stevens, Corporations § 60 (2d ed. 1949).

The Amoskeag Manufacturing Company, a business trust, was brought into the United States District Court, Massachusetts District, in proceedings for reorganization of a corporation under the Bankruptcy Act, § 77B, 11 U.S.C.A. § 207, in 1936 (No. 58,599). Some years previously preferred stock of the association had been redeemed by the issue of negotiable bonds. On liquidation of the association it was held that such bonds in the hands of members, to whom they had been issued, were subordinate to the claims of other creditors.

36. B.A. § 5h, 11 U.S.C.A. § 23(h).

37. McCruden v. Jonas, n. 34 above; Simrall v. O'Bannons, 7 B.Mon. (46 Ky.) 608 (1847).

But in Frank v. Anderson, 13 Lea (81 Tenn.) 695 (1884), an assignee of a partner, in good faith before insolvency proceedings, was allowed to share with other firm creditors.

In McCruden v. Jonas, supra, a firm of four became indebted in the course of a separate trade transaction, to a firm of three; all the latter were members of the debtor firm. It would seem that under the provisions of U.P.A. § 40(b), which classifies claims in their order of distribution as, "I. Those owing to creditors other than partner, II. Those owing to partners other than for capital and profits, III. Those owing to partners in respect to capital, and IV. Those owing to partners in respect of profits," such a claim should rate in the first class, the smaller firm not being a partner, as a unit, in the larger firm, unless "partners" in class II is construed so as to include a partnership composed of partners. The latter is far-fetched.

(f) Partnerships with Common Partners

There may be dealings between two partnerships having one or more common partners. The tendency of the law of contracts is to recognize the legal validity and enforceability of such transactions.[38] In such a situation, the creditor partnership is entitled to prove and share with other creditors of the bankrupt debtor partnership.[39] It has even been held that the same persons may form two or more partnerships with identical membership, and becoming insolvent, be adjudicated as several partnerships with proof of claims and distribution between the estates.[40] Mostly, however, the facts show only one partnership with branches operated, perhaps, under different names; thus there are both a single partnership estate and a single group of creditors.[41]

(g) Security Furnished by the Separate Estate

A partnership creditor may for his greater protection exact security when extending credits to the partnership. The security may be in the form of some asset of the individual partners, pledged to secure a partnership debt, or it may be the addition of a separate obligation of a partner collateral to the partnership obligation. On bankruptcy, the estates should be marshaled so as to place the burden so

---

38. Model [formerly Uniform] Inter-Party Agreement Act § 1: ". . . a conveyance, release or sale, may be made to, or by, two or more persons acting jointly, and one or more, but less than all of these persons, acting either for himself or themselves or with other persons, and a contract may be made between such parties."

See also Restatement, Contracts § 15, Comment b; Recent Case, 11 Harv. L.Rev.479 (1898); Sec. 70 above.

39. In re Buckhause, Fed.Cas. No. 2,086, 2 Lowell 331 (D.Mass.1874): "But Story at section 680 says: 'Courts of equity, in such cases, look behind the forms of the transactions to their substances, and treat the different firms for the purposes of substantial justice, exactly as if they were composed of strangers, or were in fact corporate companies.' It cannot be denied that, in substance, a debt from A and B to A and D, is a very different thing from a mere overdraft by A from the funds of A and B. To refuse to notice the distinction is to disregard the credit of D altogether. Whether there is a remedy in equity or not, while the firms remain solvent, it seems clear that there is a debt which equity can recognize, and which in bankruptcy

ought to be entitled to its share of dividends, in justice to the creditors of the creditor firm."

The same result has been reached under a statute permitting suits at law between firms having common members. In re Haines & Co.'s Assigned Estate, 176 Pa. 354, 35 A. 237 (1896).

40. In re Stanton, Fed.Cas. No. 13,295 (S.D.Miss.1845).

41. Gay v. Ray, 195 Mass. 8, 80 N.E. 693 (1907).

In re Vetterlein, 44 F. 57 (S.D.N.Y.1890) (one partnership with several branches). On the possibility of several firms with identical members, see Heinze v. Industrial Commission, 288 Ill. 342, 123 N.E. 598 (1919).

As to a partnership with branches separately operated, see Morristown Electrical Supply Co. v. State Dept. of Labor & Industry, 4 N.J.Super. 216, 66 A.2d 736 (1949) (unemployment compensation rating for firm as a whole was proper while it continued in business; on dissolution and division of the branches among the partners, each was to be treated as a new enterprise).

far as possible on the estate which is the primary debtor. If the creditor would receive a surplus through the concurrent or successive enforcement of all his remedies, the surplus should be remitted to the separate estate. This has been done in a case where the creditor foreclosed the security (real estate of a partner) and then was credited with a dividend from the partnership estate on the face value of the claim. The excess was turned over to the separate estate of the partner who had supplied the security.[42] The same result should follow, under the principles of marshaling, where the creditor holds a joint and several obligation, and dividends from the several estates exceed the amount of his claim.

Contrary to the early equity rule, the Bankruptcy Act requires a secured creditor of a bankrupt,[43] to surrender the security or else prove only for the difference between the original claim and the proceeds of the security.[44] A partnership creditor who holds security from the separate estate is not a secured creditor of the partnership, within the terms of the statute, and may both realize on the security and prove against the partnership estate for the face amount of the claim.[45]

---

42. In re Effinger, 184 F. 728 (D.Md. 1911). "The mere fact that the individual property in Virginia was disposed of before the partnership assets were finally distributed must not be allowed to make any difference in the rights of the parties. . . . Judge Wallace ruled that the matter should be adjusted in precisely the same way as it would have been had the creditor first proved his claim against the partnership estate and received his dividend therefrom, had then applied it upon his indebtedness, sold the individual securities, paid himself the balance remaining due to him out of their proceeds, and turned over all that remained to the individual estate. In re Foot, 9 Fed.Cas. 355 [No. 4,906]."

43. B.A. § 1(23), 11 U.S.C.A. § 1(23).

44. B.A. § 57h, 11 U.S.C.A. § 93(h). Many state courts have followed the English equity rule allowing secured creditors to prove for the full amount of their claims. Tebbets v. Rollins, 192 Mass. 169, 78 N.E. 299 (1906); People v. E. Remington & Sons, 121 N.Y. 328, 24 N.E. 793, 8 L.R.A. 458 (1890). See also Merrill v. National Bank, 173 U.S. 131, 19 S.Ct. 360, 43 L.Ed. 640 (1899).

45. In re Mertens, 144 F. 818 (2d Cir. 1906): "If the securities were not the property of the partnership when they were pledged to the bank as collateral for the payment of the indebtedness, the bank was entitled to have its claim against the partnership allowed, and allowed at its face without any deduction. If they were not part of the partnership assets, they were not part of the joint estate in bankruptcy, and as to that estate the bank was under no obligation to apply or realize their value in reduction of its claim. If they were the property of Jacob M. Mertens individually, and were pledged by him, the bank would have been at liberty upon selling them to apply the proceeds to the payment of his individual debt; and no application having been made at the time, the settled rule of equity and of the courts of bankruptcy required the application of the proceeds in exoneration of the individual estate." The case was affirmed, sub nom. Hiscock v. Varick Bank of New York, 206 U.S. 28, 27 S.Ct. 681, 51 L.Ed. 945 (1907). See in accord, Bank of Searcy v. Merchant's Grocer Co., 123 Ark. 403, 185 S.W. 806 (1916).

For the converse case, see Matter of Plummer, 1 Phil. 56 (1841).

DISTRIBUTION OF INDIVIDUAL ESTATES

§ 94.   By the dual priorities rule, individual assets are first appropriated to the payment of individual creditors.   Any surplus goes to partnership creditors or the partnership estate.

The basic pattern for the distribution of individual estates is the priority of individual creditors, with any surplus going to partnership creditors.   This has been discussed in connection with the dual priorities rule, of which it is the more controversial part.[46]   The Bankruptcy Act is in accord.[47]

If the partner is indebted to his partnership, it might appear that the firm would qualify as an individual creditor and share ratably with other individual creditors.   The opposite is, however, true.[48]

DOUBLE PROOF BY OUTSIDE CREDITORS;   CLAIMS BETWEEN PARTNERS' AND PARTNERSHIP ESTATES

§ 95.   If a partnership creditor has an individual claim against individual partners by operation of law or by express contract, he can share as a priority creditor in both partnership and individual estates.   Mere joint or joint and several liability will not suffice for this purpose.

The partnership estate is not entitled to share in the individual estate in payment of obligations owed by the partner to the partnership until individual creditors are paid.

A partner is allowed to share with other creditors in the individual estate of another partner on claims for contribution, according to the Bankruptcy Act, but is subordinated by the U.P.A.

(a) Double Proof by Outside Creditors

It is fundamental that a creditor of the partnership is a creditor of each partner because of the latter's responsibility for firm obligations.   However, consistency with the dual priorities rule requires treating the partnership creditor as less than an individual creditor, else the priority of individual creditors in individual assets would be lost.[49]   On the other hand, it is possible for a creditor to obtain by contract the *individual* obligation of one or more partners in addition to their obligations as members of the firm,[50] for example, by having the partners sign a partnership note as endorsers or co-makers, or guarantee the performance by the firm, or by a partner's assumption of a firm obligation (or vice versa).   Claims of this sort may be proved against both partnership and individual estates in state law [51] and in bank-

46. Secs. 91, 91A above.

47. B.A. § 5g, 11 U.S.C.A. § 23(g).

48. Sec. 95(b) below.

49. Sec. 91A(a) above notes the criticism of the dual priorities rule on this account.

50. U.P.A. § 15(b).

51. Fourth Nat. Bank v. Mead, 216 Mass. 521, 104 N.E. 377, 52 L.R.A., N.S., 225 (1914).

Simmons v. Simmons, 215 Iowa 654, 246 N.W. 597 (1933); In re Jamison & Co.'s Estate, 163 Pa. 143, 29 A. 1001 (1894).

ruptcy.[52] The creditor is permitted the benefit of his foresight in obtaining a double obligation, although he has circumvented the dual priorities rule and gotten the best of both worlds. Naturally, he may not obtain the equivalent of more than one full satisfaction.

Some decisions, mostly early ones, allowed double proof of all partnership claims where statutes made liability joint and several.[53] They concluded that the statutes also made it individual. This seems a misconception. For one thing, the joint liability replaced by the statutes was already individual in the sense that the entire amount could be recovered from one partner. For another, the statutes were mainly procedural, changing the requirement that all partners be sued together.[54] It does not seem that a statute intended to deal with procedure should affect the substantive right to priorities in distribution in the same manner as an express contract for dual liability.[55] Other states with like statutes have barred double proof where there is no more double obligation than that created by joint and several liability.[56] The U.P.A. contemplates this result when it is enacted with universal joint and several liability.[57] The essence of this argument is that several or joint and several liability for a firm obligation is not identical with individual liability for purposes of creditor priority, but is something less.

By the same reasoning, if a partnership note or other contract is, by its terms, only a joint and several promise, it may be doubted whether double proof is allowable. A joint judgment on a joint and several obligation of non-partner obligors has been said to operate as a merger, and to prevent a later judgment on the several obligation against one who is a party to the joint judgment.[58] Yet there are cases allowing double proof on a joint and several obligation of partners, which can be supported by personifying the partnership as a promisor, distinct from the partners who likewise promise by a superadded undertaking. "When the partners jointly agreed to pay (this

---

52. Mitchell v. Hampel, 276 U.S. 299, 48 S.Ct. 308, 72 L.Ed. 582 (1928). Bankruptcy cases are collected in 1 Collier, Bankruptcy 751–52 (14th ed. looseleaf).

53. McLain & Badgett v. Carson's Ex'r, 4 Ark. 164, 37 Am.Dec. 777 (1842); Virginia-Carolina Chemical Co. v. Walston, 187 N.C. 817, 123 S.E. 196 (1924), noted 19 Ill.L.Rev. 284 (1924); Ashby's Adm'r v. Porter, 26 Grat. (67 Va.) 455 (1875); Freeport Stone Co. v. Carey's Adm'r, 42 W.Va. 276, 26 S.E. 183 (1896).

54. See Sec. 58 above.

55. Accord, Note, 36 N.C.L.Rev. 229, 233 (1958) citing this treatise.

56. Smith v. Mallory's Ex'r, 24 Ala. 628 (1854); Ives v. Mahoney, 71 Minn. 155, 73 N.W. 720 (1898); Hundley v. Farris' Adm'r, 103 Mo. 78, 15 S.W. 312, 12 L.R.A. 254, 23 Am.St.Rep. 863 (1890).

57. States so enacting are listed in Sec. 58 n. 54 above. They retain U.P.A. § 40(i) which clearly subordinates partnership creditors to individual creditors, a provision which would be meaningless if all the former were really the latter.

58. Sessions v. Johnson, 95 U.S. 347, 24 L.Ed. 596 (1877); U. S. v. Ames, 99 U.S. 35, 25 L.Ed. 295 (1879).

See 1 Williston Contracts § 328 (3d ed. 1959); Restatement, Contracts § 119.

being a firm transaction), they bound the firm; and when they severally agreed to pay, they bound themselves as individuals. It is not apparent why this joint or firm obligation, and the several or individual obligations, should differ in principle or legal effect from that where the firm executes the obligation and the individual endorses it." [59]

(b) Partnership Estate's Rights in Individual Estate

The Bankruptcy Act, in providing for proof by one estate against the other [60] does not impair the priority of separate creditors in distribution. To allow the partnership estate, which is but the representative of the partnership creditors, to share with separate creditors, would annul the rule of priority of the latter. The partnership estate cannot prove and share in distribution on a claim for money loaned to the partner.[61] But where a partner has fraudulently diverted firm property to his separate estate without the knowledge or assent of his

---

[59]. Re W. S. Kuhn & Co., 241 F. 935 (W.D.Pa.1917), aff'd sub nom. Robinson v. Seaboard Nat. Bank, 247 F. 667 (3d Cir. 1918); Matter of Gray's Estate, 111 N.Y. 404, 18 N.E. 719 (1888). But see In re Mosier, 112 F. 138 (D. Vt.1901).

A partnership obligation signed in the names of the several partners has been treated as merely a joint obligation. Adams v. Deckers Valley Lumber Co., 202 F. 48 (4th Cir. 1912).

Although reducing a claim to judgment does not ordinarily change its character, it may be that a judgment against both firm and partners on a partnership debt would be entitled to double proof if obtained far enough in advance of bankruptcy so that it is not voided in the proceedings.

[60]. B.A. § 5h, 11 U.S.C.A. § 23(h).

[61]. In re Telfer, 184 F. 224 (6th Cir. 1910): "Proof, but not sharing, is mentioned in 5g. To permit sharing upon proof allowed under that paragraph is to ignore most important relations attending a partnership, where as here the partnership and its members are alike insolvent and adjudged bankrupts. Neither the bankrupt partnership nor its trustee can have any possible interest in the separate estate of any of the bankrupt partners, except only for the benefit of the partnership creditors. Whatever disability then can be predicated of the partnership creditors, respecting the separate estate and creditors of one of the partners ought to attach to the bankrupt partnership estate and its trustee."

In re Lane, Brett & Co., Fed.Cas.No. 8,044, 2 Lowell 333 (1874), "The first question is, whether the joint creditors of the firm can have recourse to the separate estate of Lane for money drawn out by him while the firm was solvent with the assent of his copartners. The general rule in bankruptcy is, that there can be no proof between the joint and separate estates of the partners, unless there is a surplus of the joint estate to be divided. This rule was adopted partly, as being, upon the whole, the most equitable, on the supposition that the joint creditors had given credit to the joint estate, and the separate creditors to the separate estates, respectively; and partly, I apprehend, upon the consideration that there is no such thing as a debt between the partners, or between a partner and his firm, in respect to partnership matters, excepting upon a winding up of all the affairs; and it was found to be very expensive and inconvenient to go into a general accounting in bankruptcy, and it was thought more expedient as well as more just, to take the estate as the parties left them: Story, Partn. § 390; Lindley, Partn. page 994; Harmon v. Clark, 13 Gray [Mass.] 114; Houseal's Appeal, 45 Pa. 484."

See also In re Wells, 298 F. 109 (S.D. Ohio 1924); Potts v. Schmucker, 84 Md. 535, 36 A. 592, 35 L.R.A. 392, 57 Am.St.Rep. 415 (1897).

co-partners, restitution should be made, and if it cannot be restored in specie, a pro rata dividend along with other creditors is allowed.[62]

(c) Partner's Proof and Sharing in Bankrupt Co-Partner's Estate

If one partner is a creditor of a co-partner in a non-partnership matter, there is no objection to his proving and sharing as a separate creditor. If the claim for which proof and distribution is sought is a partnership matter, such as the duty of the debtor partner to contribute to reimburse the creditor partner for his payment of partnership debts, it seems that the claim should be deferred, for it is a claim which is owing primarily to the partnership, for the purpose of settling the obligations of the partnership. The U.P.A. has consistently applied the conventional rules of priority in distribution in providing that the order of payment shall be: (I) Those owing to separate creditors; (II) those owing to partnership creditors; (III) those owing to partners by way of contribution.[63] Under the Bankruptcy Acts the solvent partner who has paid partnership creditors has been allowed to prove and share as a separate creditor in the distribution of the bankrupt partner's estate.[64]

EXEMPTIONS

§ 95A. State law exemptions are good in bankruptcy but ordinarily do not cover either partnership property or a partner's interest in the partnership.

The Bankruptcy Act permits debtors the same exemptions from creditors' claims that state laws give.[65] State exemptions are typical-

---

62. Read v. Bailey, L.R. 3 App.Cas. 94 (1877); McElroy v. Allfree, 131 Iowa 518, 108 N.W. 119 (1906). See also Ryan v. Cavanagh, 238 F. 604 (D.Iowa 1916).

63. U.P.A. § 40(i).

64. Ex parte Taylor, 2 Rose 175 (Ch. 1814); In re Dell, Fed.Cas.No.3,774, 5 Sawy. 344 (1878); In re Hirth, 189 F. 926 (D.Minn.1911); Olleman v. Reagan's Adm'r, 28 Ind. 109 (1867).

Since the estate of an insolvent should not compete with its own creditors, the estate of a bankrupt partner cannot share in the estate of a bankrupt copartner where there is a surplus for the payment of unpaid partnership creditors. Ex parte Topping, 4 De Gex, J. & S. 551 (1864).

A retired partner is not allowed to prove against the estate of his bankrupt partner who continued the business, in competition with unpaid creditors of the former partnership. In re Denning, 114 F. 219 (D.Mass.1902).

Compare U.P.A. § 42.

65. B.A. § 6, 11 U.S.C.A. § 24. Exempt property is not counted in measuring solvency for purposes of a fraudulent conveyance. B.A. § 67d(1) (a), 11 U.S. C.A. § 107(d) (1) (a). But it is (somewhat illogically) counted for purposes of other acts of bankruptcy, despite silence of the statute on this point. Cases are collected in 1 Collier, Bankruptcy 100–01 (14th ed. looseleaf). The special definition of partnership insolvency for fraudulent conveyances (B.A. § 67d(1) (d), 11 U.S.C.A. § 107 (d) (1) (d), discussed Sec. 91B(c) n. 59 above) says nothing about whether a partner's exempt property should be included in calculating the surplus, if any, which will be counted as partnership property. Logic and context argue for exclusion so that, for example, a partner's individually owned home-

ly for natural persons and thus, at best, run in favor of partners, not partnerships.[65A] The most prevalent state law, the Uniform Partnership Act, bars partners from claiming homestead or other exemptions in partnership property.[66] Such exemptions may attach to the individual property of a partner, including property withdrawn from the firm (if its withdrawal escapes the fraudulent conveyance provisions [67]). Exemption may be claimed for a partner's interest in the partnership [68] to the extent that applicable state law provides an exemption. Since the interest in the partnership is intangible personalty,[69] distinct from underlying partnership assets, it is not covered by any of the more common exemptions for homestead or tangible personalty (like tools of the trade, automobiles, clothing or household goods) or the more common exemptions for particular intangibles like life insurance. A partnership interest might be partly or wholly covered by a general exemption for property up to a certain dollar amount, but exemptions are rarely so broadly written. The usual result is no exemption for either partnership property or the interest in the partnership.

stead, exempt under local law, would not count toward his solvency or the firm's for fraudulent conveyances, although it would for other acts of bankruptcy.

Exemption cannot be claimed in property transferred or concealed by the bankrupt, B.A. § 6, 11 U.S.C.A. § 24, but property already exempt cannot be the subject of a fraudulent conveyance under B.A. § 67d, 11 U.S.C.A. § 107(d); see clause (1)(a) thereof and nn. 67, 70 below.

65A. See In re Lentz, 97 F. 486 (D.S.D. 1889), so construing the local exemption. There is an alternative holding or dictum that a partnership loses any right to exemption it may have because it ceases to exist on its dissolution by bankruptcy. This is doubtful under U.P.A. § 30, Sec. 73 above, which makes the firm continue after dissolution until it is wound up. In bankruptcy, the winding up is by the trustee but ordinarily is not completed until after the time exemptions are claimed.

See Sec. 44 above at n. 60; below at n. 70A.

66. U.P.A. § 25(2)(c), Sec. 44 above. In re Carroll & Sons Gravel Co., 95 F. Supp. 591 (D.Kan.1951). Earlier contrary cases are no longer controlling where U.P.A. has been adopted. In re Safady Bros., 228 F. 538 (W.D.Wis.

1915); Schefman v. DeGroot, 35 F.2d 950 (6th Cir. 1929), cert. denied 280 U.S. 562, 50 S.Ct. 19, 74 L.Ed. 616 (1929) (Mich. law). But most of the earlier cases rejected partners' exemptions claims in partnership property; see sec. 44 above and Annot., Right of individual partner to exemption in partnership property, 4 A.L.R. 300 (1919).

67. Sec. 91B(f) above. If the withdrawal is within a year of bankruptcy, the conveyance is fraudulent, the property is recoverable by the trustee, and no exemptions may be claimed. See In the Matter of Reese, 223 F.Supp. 626 (N.D.Cal.1963). A partner withdrew partnership funds and deposited them in individual credit union and savings and loan accounts within four months of bankruptcy. The withdrawal was held fraudulent and the funds were required to be turned over to the trustee. Any exemption for such accounts did not attach until funds were deposited. Hence, the funds were not exempt when withdrawn from the firm and were thus not excepted from the fraudulent conveyance provisions. Cf. n. 70 below.

See also B.A. § 6, 11 U.S.C.A. § 24, prohibiting exemptions in property transferred by a bankrupt.

68. U.P.A. § 28(3), Sec. 44 above.

69. U.P.A. § 26, Sec. 42 above.

However, in non-U.P.A. jurisdictions with a thorough-going aggregate view of the partnership, partners have been permitted to claim exemptions in partnership property.[70] While the U.P.A. bars partners from claiming exemptions in partnership property, it says nothing about the firm itself. This leaves open the possibility that some exemptions for kinds of property which partnerships often own—like life insurance [70A]—may be available to the partnership. If they are good by state law, they will be under the Bankruptcy Act also.

DISCHARGES IN BANKRUPTCY

§ 96. A partnership discharge does not relieve partners from their liability on partnership obligations. An individual discharge and proper scheduling of the liabilities are necessary for this purpose. Certain willful acts by a partner prevent his discharge and the firm's, but not discharge of innocent co-partners. Other willful acts which benefit the firm result in the creation of debts which are non-dischargeable as to the firm and all partners, even innocent ones.

From the debtor's viewpoint, the culmination of bankruptcy, and its chief attraction,[71] is the discharge from further liability on debts remaining unpaid after application of his non-exempt assets by the trustee.[72] Discharge is effective against claims under state and federal law and is available in voluntary and involuntary bankruptcies. Only a person who has been adjudicated a bankrupt may receive a discharge, and the discharge extends only to debts properly listed by the bankrupt in the schedule filed by him in the proceedings.[73]

---

70. See n. 66 above. Perhaps the most striking instance is Phillips v. C. Palomo & Sons, 270 F.2d 791 (5th Cir. 1959), involving Texas law prior to adoption of the U.P.A. Following Texas cases and the state's liberal attitude toward exemptions, the court permitted each of four partners to claim exemption in a truck-trailer, together worth $41,000, more than half the firm's total assets. Although appropriated to the individual partners only a week before bankruptcy, the court concluded that they already had sufficient property interest to sustain the exemption. Accordingly, the withdrawal from the firm consisted of exempt property and was not a fraudulent conveyance. The state statute under which the exemption was allowed specified two horses and a wagon; the modern equivalent was accepted. Finally, it was immaterial that the value of the truck-trailers considerably exceeded the capital accounts of several of the partners who drove them away.

70A. E. g., West's Ann.Cal.Code Civ. Proc. § 690.19 (exempting, generally, the amount of insurance which can be bought for a $500 annual premium). Much depends on how the exemption reads. Thus, a specific partial (but non-exclusive) life insurance exemption in B.A. § 70a, 11 U.S.C.A. § 110(a) is limited to "natural persons." For the variations, see Riesenfeld, Life Insurance and Creditors' Remedies in the United States, 4 U.C.L.A.L.Rev. 583 (1957). Cf. Cohen v. Gordon Ferguson, Inc., 56 N.D. 545, 218 N.W. 209 (1928).

See n. 65A above on the question whether the partnership exists long enough to claim an exemption.

71. Secs. 91(e), 91B(a) above.

72. B.A. § 17a, 11 U.S.C.A. § 35(a).

73. B.A. § 17a(3), 11 U.S.C.A. § 35(a) (3).

We have noted the particularization which generally permits partners to be adjudicated without partners and vice versa [74] and which may distinguish (1) partnership liability on partnership debts, (2) partners' individual liability on partnership debts, and (3) partners' individual liability on individual debts.[75] While this provides flexibility for creditors and employment for accountants, it can cause unfortunate complications for debtors in discharge.

Thus, without personal adjudication and discharge, a partner remains liable on partnership debts despite (A) adjudication and discharge of the partnership [76] or (B) adjudication and discharge of a co-partner from partnership debts.[77] Even though personally adjudicated and discharged, he will remain liable on partnership debts if he has not personally scheduled them.

There is some anomaly if a partner stays liable after the firm has been discharged on the joint or joint and several liability, and his property has been administered by the partnership trustee in aid of the proceedings.[78] But the burden on the partner is mainly to inform himself; he can obtain discharge from firm debts by relatively simple steps (i. e. a voluntary petition and proper scheduling), assuming he has committed no offense. He can simultaneously get discharge from his individual debts and from liabilities to his co-partners arising out of the firm affairs.[79] And he may obtain his discharge whether or not the partnership is adjudicated and discharged.[80]

The reverse anomaly of an undischarged partnership after all the partners have been discharged of their liability on partnership debts is a possibility, but only a slight one. If all the partners are adjudicated, the partnership must be.[81] If they are discharged, the partnership almost certainly will be too.

The discharge of a partner in an individual proceeding is no bar to a subsequent action against the partnership, which may be sued (under an appropriate statute) in its common name [82] or in the names of the non-bankrupt partners.[83]

---

74. Sec. 91B(g) above.

75. Secs. 91, 91A, 91B, 95(a) above.

76. B.A. § 5j, 11 U.S.C.A. § 23(j). See Note, 31 N.C.L.Rev. 457, 466–67 (1953).

77. B.A. § 16, 11 U.S.C.A. § 34.

78. B.A. § 5c, 11 U.S.C.A. § 23(c), Sec. 92 above.

79. Dycus v. Brown, 135 Ky. 140, 121 S.W. 1010, 28 L.R.A.,N.S., 190 (1909).

80. B.A. § 5j, 11 U.S.C.A. § 23(j). It may be in a separate or combined proceeding.

81. B.A. § 5i, 11 U.S.C.A. § 23(i), Sec. 91B(g) above.

82. Wagner Grocery Co. v. Dodd-Cooner Mercantile Co., 206 Ala. 627, 91 So. 487 (1921).

83. Mattix v. Leach, 16 Ind.App. 112, 43 N.E. 969 (1896); Lansing Liquidating Corp. v. Heinze, 184 App.Div. 129, 171 N.Y.S. 738 (1918).

Discharge is denied if the bankrupt has committed certain offenses.[84] The issue is determined in the bankruptcy proceeding on objections made by the creditors or the trustee. The main grounds for denial are certain affirmative, rather willful acts like fraudulent transfer or concealment of property, false statements of assets and liabilities in the bankruptcy proceeding, falsified or destroyed financial records, and false financial statements used to obtain credit. Such an act by a partner is sufficient to prevent his discharge.[85] If made in the general scope of his authority as a partner, it will be attributed to the partnership[86] and bar discharge of the firm. But it will ordinarily not be attributed to another partner who establishes his personal disengagement from and innocence in the transaction;[87] he is dischargeable. Other bases for denial of discharge are more generalized, such as failure to explain satisfactorily a loss or deficiency of assets. Here the duty seems to rest on all partners, not merely those most active in management.[88] Failure to keep adequate records produces the same no-discharge result.[89]

Even if discharge is granted, it does not cover certain kinds of debts, e. g., credit obtained by a false written financial statement, liability for willful and malicious injury to the property of another, and liability for misappropriation while acting in a fiduciary capacity.[90] These raise the same kinds of questions that we have just surveyed in connection with denial of discharge. They come up, not in the bankruptcy proceeding, but in later suits on the debts, often in state court. Perhaps because less is at stake (particular liabilities as opposed to all liabilities) and the plaintiff appears doubly wronged, the courts seem in this area more willing to hold one partner vicariously for the

---

84. B.A. § 14c, 11 U.S.C.A. § 32(c).

85. Weinstein v. Nussbaum, 302 F.2d 24 (2d Cir. 1962) (false financial statements, liabilities omitted); Chas. Edward & Associates v. England, 301 F. 2d 572 (2d Cir. 1962) (e. g., fraudulent transfers in the form of withdrawals by the partners); In re Richter, 57 F. 2d 159 (2d Cir. 1932); In re Perlmutter, 256 F. 862 (D.N.J.1919), aff'd sub nom. Perlmutter v. Hudspeth, 264 F. 957 (3d Cir. 1920); In re Singer, 251 F. 51 (2d Cir.1918) (incorporation of a department of the business and transfer of the shares to partners' relatives for nominal consideration).

86. See U.P.A. § 13.

87. In re Garrison, 149 F. 178 (2d Cir. 1906) (partner who lived a thousand miles away and had a small interest not barred by copartner's falsification of books; latter's intent not attributed to former); In re Livermore, 96 F.2d

93 (2d Cir. 1938) (partner abroad; practical impossibility of his knowing how books were kept in N. Y.); Matter of Harrell, 263 F. 954 (N.D.Ga. 1920) (partner ill); In re Schultz, 109 F. 264 (S.D.N.Y.1901).

88. In re Miller & Miller, 52 F.Supp. 526 (D.Fla.1943).

Cf. Rameson Bros. v. Goggin, 241 F.2d 271 (9th Cir. 1957) (discharge denied firm and both partners; one partner claimed ignorance, which the court does not discuss).

89. In re Herzog, 121 F.2d 581 (2d Cir. 1941), cert. denied Herzog v. Dorman, 315 U.S. 807, 62 S.Ct. 640, 86 L.Ed. 1206 (1942). However, after a partner sells his interest, the duty devolves on the buyers. In re Poff, 211 F.Supp. 495 (W.D.Va.1962).

90. B.A. § 17, 11 U.S.C.A. § 35.

acts of another by treating the debt as non-dischargeable.[91] An added reason in these cases is that the ill-gotten money or property typically went into the firm where each partner presumably had some benefit from it, so there is an element of unjust enrichment.

Additional questions of dischargeability surround claims of partners against each other, or of partnerships against their members. These usually concern improper withdrawals or other misappropriations of partnership property by individual partners. While a partner is a fiduciary in a general sense, it is well established that he is not within the Bankruptcy Act anti-discharge provision for fiduciary misappropriation, at least in the pre-dissolution phase of the firm.[92] However, such misappropriations are often held non-dischargeable as malicious injury to the property of another.[93]

LIMITED PARTNERSHIPS

§ 96A. Limited partnerships and their general partners are treated in bankruptcy much like ordinary partnerships and partners. A limited partner is aloof from the proceedings and may claim as an outside creditor for a debt owed him by the firm. But he is treated as a general partner to the extent of any liability he may have for the firm's debts.

Except for the special status of limited partners, limited partnerships are substantially the same as other partnerships in bankruptcy matters from petition to discharge. Because he is not liable for firm debts, a limited partner ordinarily cannot be drawn individually into the firm bankruptcy, nor would he benefit from a discharge if he did come in. His individual surplus of assets over liabilities is not counted as partnership property in determining partnership solvency, and his individual assets are not subject to administration by a partnership trustee.[94] He may be a creditor of the firm on a par with outside creditors [95] but may not vote as a creditor in the election of a trustee.[96]

Since 1938, he has been treated as a general partner to the extent of his liability for firm debts.[97] Such liability may arise if he has tak-

---

91. See Strang v. Bradner, 114 U.S. 555, 5 S.Ct. 1038, 29 L.Ed. 248 (1885) (no discharge of liability against one partner for debt fraudulently procured (under earlier version of statute) by co-partner within the latter's authority for the firm). McIntyre v. Kavanaugh, 242 U.S. 138, 37 S.Ct. 38, 61 L.Ed. 205 (1916). Crespi & Co. v. Giffen, 132 Cal.App. 526, 23 P.2d 47 (1933).

92. B.A. § 17a(4), 11 U.S.C.A. § 35(a) (4). Fooshe v. Sunshine, 96 Cal.App.2d 336, 215 P.2d 66 (1951). Cases are collected, Annot., Debt or liability arising from withdrawal or misappropriation of partnership funds by member of firm as dischargeable in bankrupt-

cy, 16 A.L.R.2d 1151 (1951). Fiduciary in this bankruptcy context is limited to express trusts or equivalents.

93. Lyon v. Prescott, 103 Vt. 442, 156 A. 679 (1931), noted 30 Mich.L.Rev. 807, 6 Temple L.Q. 412 (1932), and authorities in n. 92 above.

94. Sec. 92 n. 90 above.

95. Sec. 93(e) at nn. 30–33 above.

96. Sec. 93(e) n. 32 above.

97. B.A. § 5k, 11 U.S.C.A. § 23(k). Procedural and related questions are considered by Kennedy, A New Deal for Partnership Bankruptcy, 60 Colum.L. Rev. 610, 650–51 (1960). Apparently he

en part in the control of the partnership business,[98] or improperly in-cluded his name in the firm name.[99]   It may also occur if the firm has been defectively organized and he has not taken the necessary renun-ciatory steps on discovering the situation.[1]   In other circumstances, he becomes liable for an unpaid or withdrawn contribution.[2]   But this last appears to be a liability to the firm rather than for its debts, and thus should not subject his personal property to administration by a partnership trustee in bankruptcy.   Rather, he ought to be proceeded against like an outside debtor.

could not file a voluntary petition for the firm unless he were liable to some extent as a general partner.

[98].   U.L.P.A. § 7, Sec. 26 above.

[99].   U.L.P.A. § 5, Sec. 26 above.   Other holding out of him as a general part-ner may make him liable as such per U.P.A. § 16, Sec. 36 above.

[1].   U.L.P.A. § 11, Sec. 32 above.   Vid-ricksen v. Grover, 363 F.2d 372 (9th Cir. 1966).

[2].   U.L.P.A. § 17.

APPENDICES

CONTENTS

APPENDIX I

UNIFORM PARTNERSHIP ACT

[For places and dates of adoption, see Sec. 2, Table D above. Use Table of Statutory References to locate text discussion of particular Sections of the Act.]

Analysis

Part I—Preliminary Provisions
Sec.
1. Name of Act.
2. Definition of Terms.
3. Interpretation of Knowledge and Notice.
4. Rules of Construction.
5. Rules for Cases Not Provided for in This Act.

Part II—Nature of Partnership
6. Partnership Defined.
7. Rules for Determining the Existence of a Partnership.
8. Partnership Property.

Part III—Relations of Partners to Persons Dealing with the Partnership
9. Partner Agent of Partnership as to Partnership Business.
10. Conveyance of Real Property of the Partnership.
11. Partnership Bound by Admission of Partner.
12. Partnership Charged with Knowledge of or Notice to Partner.
13. Partnership Bound by Partner's Wrongful Act.
14. Partnership Bound by Partner's Breach of Trust.
15. Nature of Partner's Liability.
16. Partner by Estoppel.
17. Liability of Incoming Partner.

Part IV—Relations of Partners to One Another
18. Rules Determining Rights and Duties of Partners.
19. Partnership Books.
20. Duty of Partners to Render Information.

PART I

Preliminary Provisions

Section 1. [Name of Act.] This act may be cited as Uniform Partnership Act.

Section 2. [Definition of Terms.] In this act, "Court" includes every court and judge having jurisdiction in the case.

"Business" includes every trade, occupation, or profession.

"Person" includes individuals, partnerships, corporations, and other associations.

"Bankrupt" includes bankrupt under the Federal Bankruptcy Act or insolvent under any state insolvent act.

"Conveyance" includes every assignment, lease, mortgage, or encumbrance.

"Real property" includes land and any interest or estate in land.

Section 3.   [Interpretation of Knowledge and Notice.]   (1) A person has "knowledge" of a fact within the meaning of this act not only when he has actual knowledge thereof, but also when he has knowledge of such other facts as in the circumstances shows bad faith.

(2) A person has "notice" of a fact within the meaning of this act when the person who claims the benefit of the notice:

(a) States the fact to such person, or

(b) Delivers through the mail, or by other means of communication, a written statement of the fact to such person or to a proper person at his place of business or residence.

Section 4.   [Rules of Construction.]   (1) The rule that statutes in derogation of the common law are to be strictly construed shall have no application to this act.

(2) The law of estoppel shall apply under this act.

(3) The law of agency shall apply under this act.

(4) This act shall be so interpreted and construed as to effect its general purpose to make uniform the law of those states which enact it.

(5) This act shall not be construed so as to impair the obligations of any contract existing when the act goes into effect, nor to affect any action or proceedings begun or right accrued before this act takes effect.

Section 5.   [Rules for Cases Not Provided for in this Act.]   In any case not provided for in this act the rules of law and equity, including the law merchant, shall govern.

PART II

Nature of a Partnership

Section 6.   [Partnership Defined.]   (1) A partnership is an association of two or more persons to carry on as co-owners a business for profit.

(2) But any association formed under any other statute of this state, or any statute adopted by authority, other than the authority of this state, is not a partnership under this act, unless such association would have been a partnership in this state prior to the adoption of this act; but this act shall apply to limited partnerships except in so far as the statutes relating to such partnerships are inconsistent herewith.

Section 7.   [Rules for Determining the Existence of a Partnership.]   In determining whether a partnership exists, these rules shall apply:

(1) Except as provided by Section 16 persons who are not partners as to each other are not partners as to third persons.

(2) Joint tenancy, tenancy in common, tenancy by the entireties, joint property, common property, or part ownership does not of itself establish a partnership, whether such co-owners do or do not share any profits made by the use of the property.

(3) The sharing of gross returns does not of itself establish a partnership, whether or not the persons sharing them have a joint or common right or interest in any property from which the returns are derived.

(4) The receipt by a person of a share of the profits of a business is prima facie evidence that he is a partner in the business, but no such inference shall be drawn if such profits were received in payment:

(a) As a debt by installments or otherwise,

(b) As wages of an employee or rent to a landlord,

(c) As an annuity to a widow or representative of a deceased partner,

(d) As interest on a loan, though the amount of payment vary with the profits of the business,

(e) As the consideration for the sale of a good-will of a business or other property by installments or otherwise.

Section 8. [Partnership Property.] (1) All property originally brought into the partnership stock or subsequently acquired by purchase or otherwise, on account of the partnership, is partnership property.

(2) Unless the contrary intention appears, property acquired with partnership funds is partnership property.

(3) Any estate in real property may be acquired in the partnership name. Title so acquired can be conveyed only in the partnership name.

(4) A conveyance to a partnership in the partnership name, though without words of inheritance, passes the entire estate of the grantor unless a contrary intent appears.

PART III

Relations of Partners to Persons Dealing with the Partnership

Section 9. [Partner Agent of Partnership as to Partnership Business.] (1) Every partner is an agent of the partnership for the purpose of its business, and the act of every partner, including the execution in the partnership name of any instrument, for apparently carrying on in the usual way the business of the partnership of which he is a member binds the partnership, unless the partner so acting has in fact no authority to act for the partnership in the particular matter, and the person with whom he is dealing has knowledge of the fact that he has no such authority.

(2) An act of a partner which is not apparently for the carrying on of the business of the partnership in the usual way does not bind the partnership unless authorized by the other partners.

(3) Unless authorized by the other partners or unless they have abandoned the business, one or more but less than all the partners have no authority to:

(a) Assign the partnership property in trust for creditors or on the assignee's promise to pay the debts of the partnership,

(b) Dispose of the good-will of the business,

(c) Do any other act which would make it impossible to carry on the ordinary business of a partnership,

(d) Confess a judgment,

(e) Submit a partnership claim or liability to arbitration or reference.

(4) No act of a partner in contravention of a restriction on authority shall bind the partnership to persons having knowledge of the restriction.

Section 10. [**Conveyance of Real Property of the Partnership.**] (1) Where title to real property is in the partnership name, any partner may convey title to such property by a conveyance executed in the partnership name; but the partnership may recover such property unless the partner's act binds the partnership under the provisions of paragraph (1) of section 9 or unless such property has been conveyed by the grantee or a person claiming through such grantee to a holder for value without knowledge that the partner, in making the conveyance, has exceeded his authority.

(2) Where title to real property is in the name of the partnership, a conveyance executed by a partner, in his own name, passes the equitable interest of the partnership, provided the act is one within the authority of the partner under the provisions of paragraph (1) of section 9.

(3) Where title to real property is in the name of one or more but not all the partners, and the record does not disclose the right of the partnership, the partners in whose name the title stands may convey title to such property, but the partnership may recover such property if the partners' act does not bind the partnership under the provisions of paragraph (1) of section 9, unless the purchaser, or his assignee, is a holder for value, without knowledge.

(4) Where the title to real property is in the name of one or more or all the partners, or in a third person in trust for the partnership, a conveyance executed by a partner in the partnership name, or in his own name, passes the equitable interest of the partnership, provided the act is one within the authority of the partner under the provisions of paragraph (1) of section 9.

(5) Where the title to real property is in the names of all the partners a conveyance executed by all the partners passes all their rights in such property.

Section 11.   [Partnership Bound by Admission of Partner.]   An admission or representation made by any partner concerning partnership affairs within the scope of his authority as conferred by this act is evidence against the partnership.

Section 12.   [Partnership Charged with Knowledge of or Notice to Partner.]   Notice to any partner of any matter relating to partnership affairs, and the knowledge of the partner acting in the particular matter, acquired while a partner or then present to his mind, and the knowledge of any other partner who reasonably could and should have communicated it to the acting partner, operate as notice to or knowledge of the partnership, except in the case of a fraud on the partnership committed by or with the consent of that partner.

Section 13.   [Partnership Bound by Partner's Wrongful Act.]   Where, by any wrongful act or omission of any partner acting in the ordinary course of the business of the partnership or with the authority of his co-partners, loss or injury is caused to any person, not being a partner in the partnership, or any penalty is incurred, the partnership is liable therefor to the same extent as the partner so acting or omitting to act.

Section 14.   [Partnership Bound by Partner's Breach of Trust.]   The partnership is bound to make good the loss:

(a) Where one partner acting within the scope of his apparent authority receives money or property of a third person and misapplies it; and

(b) Where the partnership in the course of its business receives money or property of a third person and the money or property so received is misapplied by any partner while it is in the custody of the partnership.

Section 15.   [Nature of Partner's Liability.]   All partners are liable

(a) Jointly and severally for everything chargeable to the partnership under sections 13 and 14.

(b) Jointly for all other debts and obligations of the partnership; but any partner may enter into a separate obligation to perform a partnership contract.

Section 16.   [Partner by Estoppel.]   (1) When a person, by words spoken or written or by conduct, represents himself, or consents to another representing him to any one, as a partner in an existing partnership or with one or more persons not actual partners, he is liable to any such person to whom such representation has been made, who has, on the faith of such representation, given credit to the actual or apparent partnership, and if he has made such representation or consented to its being made in a public manner he is liable to such person, whether the representation has or has not been made or communicated to such person so giving credit by or with the knowledge of the apparent partner making the representation or consenting to its being made.

(a) When a partnership liability results, he is liable as though he were an actual member of the partnership.

(b) When no partnership liability results, he is liable jointly with the other persons, if any, so consenting to the contract or representation as to incur liability, otherwise separately.

(2) When a person has been thus represented to be a partner in an existing partnership, or with one or more persons not actual partners, he is an agent of the persons consenting to such representation to bind them to the same extent and in the same manner as though he were a partner in fact, with respect to persons who rely upon the representation. Where all the members of the existing partnership consent to the representation, a partnership act or obligation results; but in all other cases it is the joint act or obligation of the person acting and the persons consenting to the representation.

Section 17. [Liability of Incoming Partner.] A person admitted as a partner into an existing partnership is liable for all the obligations of the partnership arising before his admission as though he had been a partner when such obligations were incurred, except that this liability shall be satisfied only out of partnership property.

PART IV

Relations of Partners to One Another

Section 18. [Rules Determining Rights and Duties of Partners.] The rights and duties of the partners in relation to the partnership shall be determined, subject to any agreement between them, by the following rules:

(a) Each partner shall be repaid his contributions, whether by way of capital or advances to the partnership property and share equally in the profits and surplus remaining after all liabilities, including those to partners, are satisfied; and must contribute towards the losses, whether of capital or otherwise, sustained by the partnership according to his share in the profits.

(b) The partnership must indemnify every partner in respect of payments made and personal liabilities reasonably incurred by him in the ordinary and proper conduct of its business, or for the preservation of its business or property.

(c) A partner, who in aid of the partnership makes any payment or advance beyond the amount of capital which he agreed to contribute, shall be paid interest from the date of the payment or advance.

(d) A partner shall receive interest on the capital contributed by him only from the date when repayment should be made.

(e) All partners have equal rights in the management and conduct of the partnership business.

(f) No partner is entitled to remuneration for acting in the partnership business, except that a surviving partner is entitled to reasonable compensation for his services in winding up the partnership affairs.

(g) No person can become a member of a partnership without the consent of all the partners.

(h) Any difference arising as to ordinary matters connected with the partnership business may be decided by a majority of the partners; but no act in contravention of any agreement between the partners may be done rightfully without the consent of all the partners.

Section 19. **[Partnership Books.]** The partnership books shall be kept, subject to any agreement between the partners, at the principal place of business of the partnership, and every partner shall at all times have access to and may inspect and copy any of them.

Section 20. **[Duty of Partners to Render Information.]** Partners shall render on demand true and full information of all things affecting the partnership to any partner or the legal representative of any deceased partner or partner under legal disability.

Section 21. **[Partner Accountable as a Fiduciary.]** (1) Every partner must account to the partnership for any benefit, and hold as trustee for it any profits derived by him without the consent of the other partners from any transaction connected with the formation, conduct, or liquidation of the partnership or from any use by him of its property.

(2) This section applies also to the representatives of a deceased partner engaged in the liquidation of the affairs of the partnership as the personal representatives of the last surviving partner.

Section 22. **[Right to an Account.]** Any partner shall have the right to a formal account as to partnership affairs:

(a) If he is wrongfully excluded from the partnership business or possession of its property by his co-partners,

(b) If the right exists under the terms of any agreement,

(c) As provided by section 21,

(d) Whenever other circumstances render it just and reasonable.

Section 23. **[Continuation of Partnership Beyond Fixed Term.]** (1) When a partnership for a fixed term or particular undertaking is continued after the termination of such term or particular undertaking without any express agreement, the rights and duties of the partners remain the same as they were at such termination, so far as is consistent with a partnership at will.

(2) A continuation of the business by the partners or such of them as habitually acted therein during the term, without any settlement or liquidation of the partnership affairs, is prima facie evidence of a continuation of the partnership.

PART V

Property Rights of a Partner

Section 24. [Extent of Property Rights of a Partner.] The property rights of a partner are (1) his rights in specific partnership property, (2) his interest in the partnership, and (3) his right to participate in the management.

Section 25. [Nature of a Partner's Right in Specific Partnership Property.] (1) A partner is co-owner with his partners of specific partnership property holding as a tenant in partnership.

(2) The incidents of this tenancy are such that:

(a) A partner, subject to the provisions of this act and to any agreement between the partners, has an equal right with his partners to possess specific partnership property for partnership purposes; but he has no right to possess such property for any other purpose without the consent of his partners.

(b) A partner's right in specific partnership property is not assignable except in connection with the assignment of rights of all the the partners in the same property.

(c) A partner's right in specific partnership property is not subject to attachment or execution, except on a claim against the partnership. When partnership property is attached for a partnership debt the partners, or any of them, or the representatives of a deceased partner, cannot claim any right under the homestead or exemption laws.

(d) On the death of a partner his right in specific partnership property vests in the surviving partner or partners, except where the deceased was the last surviving partner, when his right in such property vests in his legal representative. Such surviving partner or partners, or the legal representative of the last surviving partner, has no right to possess the partnership property for any but a partnership purpose.

(e) A partner's right in specific partnership property is not subject to dower, curtesy, or allowances to widows, heirs, or next of kin.

Section 26. [Nature of Partner's Interest in the Partnership.] A partner's interest in the partnership is his share of the profits and surplus, and the same is personal property.

Section 27.   [Assignment of Partner's Interest.]   (1) A conveyance by a partner of his interest in the partnership does not of itself dissolve the partnership, nor, as against the other partners in the absence of agreement, entitle the assignee, during the continuance of the partnership, to interfere in the management or administration of the partnership business or affairs, or to require any information or account of partnership transactions, or to inspect the partnership books; but it merely entitles the assignee to receive in accordance with his contract the profits to which the assigning partner would otherwise be entitled.

(2) In case of a dissolution of the partnership, the assignee is entitled to receive his assignor's interest and may require an account from the date only of the last account agreed to by all the partners.

Section 28.   [Partner's Interest Subject to Charging Order.]   (1) On due application to a competent court by any judgment creditor of a partner, the court which entered the judgment, order, or decree, or any other court, may charge the interest of the debtor partner with payment of the unsatisfied amount of such judgment debt with interest thereon; and may then or later appoint a receiver of his share of the profits, and of any other money due or to fall due to him in respect of the partnership, and make all other orders, directions, accounts and inquiries which the debtor partner might have made, or which the circumstances of the case may require.

(2) The interest charged may be redeemed at any time before foreclosure, or in case of a sale being directed by the court may be purchased without thereby causing a dissolution:

(a) With separate property, by any one or more of the partners, or

(b) With partnership property, by any one or more of the partners with the consent of all the partners whose interests are not so charged or sold.

(3) Nothing in this act shall be held to deprive a partner of his right, if any, under the exemption laws, as regards his interest in the partnership.

PART VI

Dissolution and Winding Up

Section 29.   [Dissolution Defined.]   The dissolution of a partnership is the change in the relation of the partners caused by any partner ceasing to be associated in the carrying on as distinguished from the winding up of the business.

Section 30.   [Partnership Not Terminated by Dissolution.]   On dissolution the partnership is not terminated, but continues until the winding up of partnership affairs is completed.

Section 31. **[Causes of Dissolution.]** Dissolution is caused: (1) Without violation of the agreement between the partners,

(a) By the termination of the definite term or particular undertaking specified in the agreement,

(b) By the express will of any partner when no definite term or particular undertaking is specified,

(c) By the express will of all the partners who have not assigned their interests or suffered them to be charged for their separate debts, either before or after the termination of any specified term or particular undertaking,

(d) By the expulsion of any partner from the business bona fide in accordance with such a power conferred by the agreement between the partners;

(2) In contravention of the agreement between the partners, where the circumstances do not permit a dissolution under any other provision of this section, by the express will of any partner at any time;

(3) By any event which makes it unlawful for the business of the partnership to be carried on or for the members to carry it on in partnership;

(4) By the death of any partner;

(5) By the bankruptcy of any partner or the partnership;

(6) By decree of court under section 32.

Section 32. **[Dissolution by Decree of Court.]** (1) On application by or for a partner the court shall decree a dissolution whenever:

(a) A partner has been declared a lunatic in any judicial proceeding or is shown to be of unsound mind,

(b) A partner becomes in any other way incapable of performing his part of the partnership contract,

(c) A partner has been guilty of such conduct as tends to affect prejudicially the carrying on of the business,

(d) A partner wilfully or persistently commits a breach of the partnership agreement, or otherwise so conducts himself in matters relating to the partnership business that it is not reasonably practicable to carry on the business in partnership with him,

(e) The business of the partnership can only be carried on at a loss,

(f) Other circumstances render a dissolution equitable.

(2) On the application of the purchaser of a partner's interest under sections 28 or 29 [should read 27 or 28];

(a) After the termination of the specified term or particular undertaking,

(b) At any time if the partnership was a partnership at will when the interest was assigned or when the charging order was issued.

Section 33. [**General Effect of Dissolution on Authority of Partner.**] Except so far as may be necessary to wind up partnership affairs or to complete transactions begun but not then finished, dissolution terminates all authority of any partner to act for the partnership,

(1) With respect to the partners,

(a) When the dissolution is not by the act, bankruptcy or death of a partner; or

(b) When the dissolution is by such act, bankruptcy or death of a partner, in cases where section 34 so requires.

(2) With respect to persons not partners, as declared in section 35.

Section 34. [**Right of Partner to Contribution From Copartners After Dissolution.**] Where the dissolution is caused by the act, death or bankruptcy of a partner, each partner is liable to his copartners for his share of any liability created by any partner acting for the partnership as if the partnership had not been dissolved unless

(a) The dissolution being by act of any partner, the partner acting for the partnership had knowledge of the dissolution, or

(b) The dissolution being by the death or bankruptcy of a partner, the partner acting for the partnership had knowledge or notice of the death or bankruptcy.

Section 35. [**Power of Partner to Bind Partnership to Third Persons After Dissolution.**] (1) After dissolution a partner can bind the partnership except as provided in Paragraph (3)

(a) By any act appropriate for winding up partnership affairs or completing transactions unfinished at dissolution;

(b) By any transaction which would bind the partnership if dissolution had not taken place, provided the other party to the transaction

(I) Had extended credit to the partnership prior to dissolution and had no knowledge or notice of the dissolution; or

(II) Though he had not so extended credit, had nevertheless known of the partnership prior to dissolution, and, having no knowledge or notice of dissolution, the fact of dissolution had not been advertised in a newspaper of general circulation in the place (or in each place if more than one) at which the partnership business was regularly carried on.

(2) The liability of a partner under paragraph (1b) shall be satisfied out of partnership assets alone when such partner had been prior to dissolution

(a) Unknown as a partner to the person with whom the contract is made; and

(b) So far unknown and inactive in partnership affairs that the business reputation of the partnership could not be said to have been in any degree due to his connection with it.

(3) The partnership is in no case bound by any act of a partner after dissolution

(a) Where the partnership is dissolved because it is unlawful to carry on the business, unless the act is appropriate for winding up partnership affairs; or

(b) Where the partner has become bankrupt; or

(c) Where the partner has no authority to wind up partnership affairs; except by a transaction with one who

(I) Had extended credit to the partnership prior to dissolution and had no knowledge or notice of his want of authority; or

(II) Had not extended credit to the partnership prior to dissolution, and, having no knowledge or notice of his want of authority, the fact of his want of authority has not been advertised in the manner provided for advertising the fact of dissolution in paragraph (1bII).

(4) Nothing in this section shall affect the liability under section 16 of any person who after dissolution represents himself or consents to another representing him as a partner in a partnership engaged in carrying on business.

Section 36. [Effect of Dissolution on Partner's Existing Liability.] (1) The dissolution of the partnership does not of itself discharge the existing liability of any partner.

(2) A partner is discharged from any existing liability upon dissolution of the partnership by an agreement to that effect between himself, the partnership creditor and the person or partnership continuing the business; and such agreement may be inferred from the course of dealing between the creditor having knowledge of the dissolution and the person or partnership continuing the business.

(3) Where a person agrees to assume the existing obligations of a dissolved partnership, the partners whose obligations have been assumed shall be discharged from any liability to any creditor of the partnership who, knowing of the agreement, consents to a material alteration in the nature or time of payment of such obligations.

(4) The individual property of a deceased partner shall be liable for all obligations of the partnership incurred while he was a partner but subject to the prior payment of his separate debts.

Section 37. [Right to Wind Up.] Unless otherwise agreed the partners who have not wrongfully dissolved the partnership or the legal representative of the last surviving partner, not bankrupt, has the right to wind up the partnership affairs; provided, however, that any partner, his legal representative or his assignee, upon cause shown, may obtain winding up by the court.

Section 38. [**Rights of Partners to Application of Partnership Property.**] (1) When dissolution is caused in any way, except in contravention of the partnership agreement, each partner as against his co-partners and all persons claiming through them in respect of their interests in the partnership, unless otherwise agreed, may have the partnership property applied to discharge its liabilities, and the surplus applied to pay in cash the net amount owing to the respective partners. But if dissolution is caused by expulsion of a partner, bona fide under the partnership agreement and if the expelled partner is discharged from all partnership liabilities, either by payment or agreement under section 36 (2), he shall receive in cash only the net amount due him from the partnership.

(2) When dissolution is caused in contravention of the partnership agreement the rights of the partners shall be as follows:

(a) Each partner who has not caused dissolution wrongfully shall have,

(I) All the rights specified in paragraph (1) of this section, and

(II) The right, as against each partner who has caused the dissolution wrongfully, to damages for breach of the agreement.

(b) The partners who have not caused the dissolution wrongfully, if they all desire to continue the business in the same name, either by themselves or jointly with others, may do so, during the agreed term for the partnership and for that purpose may possess the partnership property, provided they secure the payment by bond approved by the court, or pay to any partner who has caused the dissolution wrongfully, the value of his interest in the partnership at the dissolution, less any damages recoverable under clause (2aII) of this section, and in like manner indemnify him against all present or future partnership liabilities.

(c) A partner who has caused the dissolution wrongfully shall have:

(I) If the business is not continued under the provisions of paragraph (2b) all the rights of a partner under paragraph (1), subject to clause (2aII), of this section,

(II) If the business is continued under paragraph (2b) of this section the right as against his co-partners and all claiming through them in respect of their interests in the partnership, to have the value of his interest in the partnership, less any damages caused to his co-partners by the dissolution, ascertained and paid to him in cash, or the payment secured by bond approved by the court, and to be released from all existing liabilities of the partnership; but in ascertaining the value of the partner's interest the value of the good-will of the business shall not be considered.

Section 39.   [Rights Where Partnership is Dissolved for Fraud or Misrepresentation.]   Where a partnership contract is rescinded on the ground of the fraud or misrepresentation of one of the parties thereto, the party entitled to rescind is, without prejudice to any other right, entitled,

(a) To a lien on, or right of retention of, the surplus of the partnership property after satisfying the partnership liabilities to third persons for any sum of money paid by him for the purchase of an interest in the partnership and for any capital or advances contributed by him; and

(b) To stand, after all liabilities to third persons have been satisfied, in the place of the creditors of the partnership for any payments made by him in respect of the partnership liabilities; and

(c) To be indemnified by the person guilty of the fraud or making the representation against all debts and liabilities of the partnership.

Section 40.   [Rules for Distribution.]   In settling accounts between the partners after dissolution, the following rules shall be observed, subject to any agreement to the contrary:

(a) The assets of the partnership are:

(I) The partnership property,

(II) The contributions of the partners necessary for the payment of all the liabilities specified in clause (b) of this paragraph.

(b) The liabilities of the partnership shall rank in order of payment, as follows:

(I) Those owing to creditors other than partners,

(II) Those owing to partners other than for capital and profits,

(III) Those owing to partners in respect of capital,

(IV) Those owing to partners in respect of profits.

(c) The assets shall be applied in the order of their declaration in clause (a) of this paragraph to the satisfaction of the liabilities.

(d) The partners shall contribute, as provided by section 18(a) the amount necessary to satisfy the liabilities; but if any, but not all, of the partners are insolvent, or, not being subject to process, refuse to contribute, the other parties shall contribute their share of the liabilities, and, in the relative proportions in which they share the profits, the additional amount necessary to pay the liabilities.

(e) An assignee for the benefit of creditors or any person appointed by the court shall have the right to enforce the contributions specified in clause (d) of this paragraph.

(f) Any partner or his legal representative shall have the right to enforce the contributions specified in clause (d) of this paragraph, to the extent of the amount which he has paid in excess of his share of the liability.

(g) The individual property of a deceased partner shall be liable for the contributions specified in clause (d) of this paragraph.

(h) When partnership property and the individual properties of the partners are in possession of a court for distribution, partnership creditors shall have priority on partnership property and separate creditors on individual property, saving the rights of lien or secured creditors as heretofore.

(i) Where a partner has become bankrupt or his estate is insolvent the claims against his separate property shall rank in the following order:

 (I) Those owing to separate creditors,

 (II) Those owing to partnership creditors,

 (III) Those owing to partners by way of contribution.

Section 41. [**Liability of Persons Continuing the Business in Certain Cases.**] (1) When any new partner is admitted into an existing partnership, or when any partner retires and assigns (or the representative of the deceased partner assigns) his rights in partnership property to two or more of the partners, or to one or more of the partners and one or more third persons, if the business is continued without liquidation of the partnership affairs, creditors of the first or dissolved partnership are also creditors of the partnership so continuing the business.

(2) When all but one partner retire and assign (or the representative of a deceased partner assigns) their rights in partnership property to the remaining partner, who continues the business without liquidation of partnership affairs, either alone or with others, creditors of the dissolved partnership are also creditors of the person or partnership so continuing the business.

(3) When any partner retires or dies and the business of the dissolved partnership is continued as set forth in paragraphs (1) and (2) of this section, with the consent of the retired partners or the representative of the deceased partner, but without any assignment of his right in partnership property, rights of creditors of the dissolved partnership and of the creditors of the person or partnership continuing the business shall be as if such assignment had been made.

(4) When all the partners or their representatives assign their rights in partnership property to one or more third persons who promise to pay the debts and who continue the business of the dissolved partnership, creditors of the dissolved partnership are also creditors of the person or partnership continuing the business.

(5) When any partner wrongfully causes a dissolution and the remaining partners continue the business under the provisions of section 38(2b), either alone or with others, and without liquidation of the partnership affairs, creditors of the dissolved partnership are also creditors of the person or partnership continuing the business.

(6) When a partner is expelled and the remaining partners continue the business either alone or with others, without liquidation of the partnership affairs, creditors of the dissolved partnership are also creditors of the person or partnership continuing the business.

(7) The liability of a third person becoming a partner in the partnership continuing the business, under this section, to the creditors of the dissolved partnership shall be satisfied out of partnership property only.

(8) When the business of a partnership after dissolution is continued under any conditions set forth in this section the creditors of the dissolved partnership, as against the separate creditors of the retiring or deceased partner or the representative of the deceased partner, have a prior right to any claim of the retired partner or the representative of the deceased partner against the person or partnership continuing the business, on account of the retired or deceased partner's interest in the dissolved partnership or on account of any consideration promised for such interest or for his right in partnership property.

(9) Nothing in this section shall be held to modify any right of creditors to set aside any assignment on the ground of fraud.

(10) The use by the person or partnership continuing the business of the partnership name, or the name of a deceased partner as part thereof, shall not of itself make the individual property of the deceased partner liable for any debts contracted by such person or partnership.

Section 42. **[Rights of Retiring or Estate of Deceased Partner When the Business is Continued.]** When any partner retires or dies, and the business is continued under any of the conditions set forth in section 41 (1, 2, 3, 5, 6), or section 38(2b), without any settlement of accounts as between him or his estate and the person or partnership continuing the business, unless otherwise agreed, he or his legal representative as against such persons or partnership may have the value of his interest at the date of dissolution ascertained, and shall receive as an ordinary creditor an amount equal to the value of his interest in the dissolved partnership with interest, or, at his option or at the option of his legal representative, in lieu of interest, the profits attributable to the use of his right in the property of the dissolved partnership; provided that the creditors of the dissolved partnership as against the separate creditors, or the representative of the retired or deceased partner, shall have priority on any claim arising under this section, as provided by section 41(8) of this act.

Section 43. [**Accrual of Actions.**] The right to an account of his interest shall accrue to any partner, or his legal representative, as against the winding up partners or the surviving partners or the person or partnership continuing the business, at the date of dissolution, in the absence of any agreement to the contrary.

PART VII

Miscellaneous Provisions

Section 44. [**When Act Takes Effect.**] This act shall take effect on the ——— day of ——— one thousand nine hundred and ———.

Section 45. [**Legislation Repealed.**] All acts or parts of acts inconsistent with this act are hereby repealed.

APPENDIX II

UNIFORM LIMITED PARTNERSHIP ACT

[For places and dates of adoption, see Sec. 2, Table D above. Use Tables of Statutory References to locate text discussion of particular Sections of the Act.]

Analysis

Section 1. [Limited Partnership Defined.] A limited partnership is a partnership formed by two or more persons under the provisions of Section 2, having as members one or more general partners and one or more limited partners. The limited partners as such shall not be bound by the obligations of the partnership.

Section 2. [Formation.] (1) Two or more persons desiring to form a limited partnership shall

(a) Sign and swear to a certificate, which shall state

I. The name of the partnership,

II. The character of the business,

III. The location of the principal place of business,

IV. The name and place of residence of each member; general and limited partners being respectively designated,

V. The term for which the partnership is to exist,

VI. The amount of cash and a description of and the agreed value of the other property contributed by each limited partner,

VII. The additional contributions, if any, agreed to be made by each limited partner and the times at which or events on the happening of which they shall be made,

VIII. The time, if agreed upon, when the contribution of each limited partner is to be returned,

IX. The share of the profits or the other compensation by way of income which each limited partner shall receive by reason of his contribution,

X. The right, if given, of a limited partner to substitute an assignee as contributor in his place, and the terms and conditions of the substitution,

XI. The right, if given, of the partners to admit additional limited partners,

XII. The right, if given, of one or more of the limited partners to priority over other limited partners, as to contributions or as to compensation by way of income, and the nature of such priority,

XIII. The right, if given, of the remaining general partner or partners to continue the business on the death, retirement or insanity of a general partner, and

XIV. The right, if given, of a limited partner to demand and receive property other than cash in return for his contribution.

(b) File for record the certificate in the office of [here designate the proper office].

(2) A limited partnership is formed if there has been substantial compliance in good faith with the requirements of paragraph (1).

Section 3. [Business Which May Be Carried On.] A limited partnership may carry on any business which a partnership without limited partners may carry on, except [here designate the business to be prohibited].

Section 4. [Character of Limited Partner's Contribution.] The contributions of a limited partner may be cash or other property, but not services.

Section 5. [A Name Not To Contain Surname of Limited Partner; Exceptions.] (1) The surname of a limited partner shall not appear in the partnership name, unless

(a) It is also the surname of a general partner, or

(b) Prior to the time when the limited partner became such the business had been carried on under a name in which his surname appeared.

(2) A limited partner whose name appears in a partnership name contrary to the provisions of paragraph (1) is liable as a general partner to partnership creditors who extend credit to the partnership without actual knowledge that he is not a general partner.

Section 6.   [Liability for False Statements in Certificate.] If the certificate contains a false statement, one who suffers loss by reliance on such statement may hold liable any party to the certificate who knew the statement to be false

(a) At the time he signed the certificate, or

(b) Subsequently, but within a sufficient time before the statement was relied upon to enable him to cancel or amend the certificate, or to file a petition for its cancellation or amendment as provided in Section 25(3).

Section 7.   [Limited Partner Not Liable to Creditors.] A limited partner shall not become liable as a general partner unless, in addition to the exercise of his rights and powers as a limited partner, he takes part in the control of the business.

Section 8.   [Admission of Additional Limited Partners.] After the formation of a limited partnership, additional limited partners may be admitted upon filing an amendment to the original certificate in accordance with the requirements of Section 25.

Section 9.   [Rights, Powers and Liabilities of a General Partner.] (1) A general partner shall have all the rights and powers and be subject to all the restrictions and liabilities of a partner in a partnership without limited partners, except that without the written consent or ratification of the specific act by all the limited partners, a general partner or all of the general partners have no authority to

(a) Do any act in contravention of the certificate,

(b) Do any act which would make it impossible to carry on the ordinary business of the partnership,

(c) Confess a judgment against the partnership,

(d) Possess partnership property, or assign their rights in specific partnership property, for other than a partnership purpose,

(e) Admit a person as a general partner,

(f) Admit a person as a limited partner, unless the right so to do is given in the certificate,

(g) Continue the business with partnership property on the death, retirement or insanity of a general partner, unless the right so to do is given in the certificate.

Section 10. **[Rights of a Limited Partner.]** (1) A limited partner shall have the same rights as a general partner to

(a) Have the partnership books kept at the principal place of business of the partnership, and at all times to inspect and copy any of them,

(b) Have on demand true and full information of all things affecting the partnership, and a formal account of partnership affairs, whenever circumstances render it just and reasonable, and

(c) Have dissolution and winding up by decree of court.

(2) A limited partner shall have the right to receive a share of the profits or other compensation by way of income, and to the return of his contribution as provided in Sections 15 and 16.

Section 11. **[Status of Person Erroneously Believing Himself a Limited Partner.]** A person who has contributed to the capital of a business conducted by a person or partnership erroneously believing that he has become a limited partner in a limited partnership, is not, by reason of his exercise of the rights of a limited partner, a general partner with the person or in the partnership carrying on the business, or bound by the obligations of such person or partnership; provided that on ascertaining the mistake he promptly renounces his interest in the profits of the business, or other compensation by way of income.

Section 12. **[One Person both General and Limited Partner.]** (1) A person may be a general partner and a limited partner in the same partnership at the same time.

(2) A person who is a general, and also at the same time a limited partner, shall have all the rights and powers and be subject to all the restrictions of a general partner; except that, in respect to his contribution, he shall have the rights against the other members which he would have had if he were not also a general partner.

Section 13. **[Loans and Other Business Transactions with Limited Partner.]** (1) A limited partner also may loan money to and transact other business with the partnership, and, unless he is also a general partner, receive on account of resulting claims against the partnership, with general creditors, a pro rata share of the assets. No limited partner shall in respect to any such claim

(a) Receive or hold as collateral security any partnership property, or

(b) Receive from a general partner or the partnership any payment, conveyance, or release from liability, if at the time the assets of the partnership are not sufficient to discharge partnership liabilities to persons not claiming as general or limited partners,

(2) The receiving of collateral security, or a payment, conveyance, or release in violation of the provisions of paragraph (1) is a fraud on the creditors of the partnership.

Section 14.   [Relation of Limited Partners Inter Se.]   Where there are several limited partners the members may agree that one or more of the limited partners shall have a priority over other limited partners as to the return of their contributions, as to their compensation by way of income, or as to any other matter. If such an agreement is made it shall be stated in the certificate, and in the absence of such a statement all the limited partners shall stand upon equal footing.

Section 15.   [Compensation of Limited Partner.]   A limited partner may receive from the partnership the share of the profits or the compensation by way of income stipulated for in the certificate; provided, that after such payment is made, whether from the property of the partnership or that of a general partner, the partnership assets are in excess of all liabilities of the partnership except liabilities to limited partners on account of their contributions and to general partners.

Section 16.   [Withdrawal or Reduction of Limited Partner's Contribution.]   (1) A limited partner shall not receive from a general partner or out of partnership property any part of his contribution until

(a) All liabilities of the partnership, except liabilities to general partners and to limited partners on account of their contributions, have been paid or there remains property of the partnership sufficient to pay them,

(b) The consent of all members is had, unless the return of the contribution may be rightfully demanded under the provisions of paragraph (2), and

(c) The certificate is cancelled or so amended as to set forth the withdrawal or reduction.

(2) Subject to the provisions of paragraph (1) a limited partner may rightfully demand the return of his contribution

(a) On the dissolution of a partnership, or

(b) When the date specified in the certificate for its return has arrived, or

(c) After he has given six months' notice in writing to all other members, if no time is specified in the certificate either for the return of the contribution or for the dissolution of the partnership.

(3) In the absence of any statement in the certificate to the contrary or the consent of all members, a limited partner, irrespective of the nature of his contribution, has only the right to demand and receive cash in return for his contribution.

(4) A limited partner may have the partnership dissolved and its affairs wound up when

(a) He rightfully but unsuccessfully demands the return of his contribution, or

(b) The other liabilities of the partnership have not been paid, or the partnership property is insufficient for their payment as required by paragraph (1a) and the limited partner would otherwise be entitled to the return of his contribution.

Section 17. **[Liability of Limited Partner to Partnership.]** (1) A limited partner is liable to the partnership

(a) For the difference between his contribution as actually made, and that stated in the certificate as having been made, and

(b) For any unpaid contribution which he agreed in the certificate to make in the future at the time and on the conditions stated in the certificate.

(2) A limited partner holds as trustee for the partnership

(a) Specific property stated in the certificate as contributed by him, but which was not contributed or which has been wrongfully returned, and

(b) Money or other property wrongfully paid or conveyed to him on account of his contribution.

(3) The liabilities of a limited partner as set forth in this section can be waived or compromised only by the consent of all members; but a waiver or compromise shall not affect the right of a creditor of a partnership, who extended credit or whose claim arose after the filing and before a cancellation or amendment of the certificate, to enforce such liabilities.

(4) When a contributor has rightfully received the return in whole or in part of the capital of his contribution, he is nevertheless liable to the partnership for any sum, not in excess of such return with interest, necessary to discharge its liabilities to all creditors who extended credit or whose claims arose before such return.

Section 18. **[Nature of Limited Partner's Interest in Partnership.]** A limited partner's interest in the partnership is personal property.

Section 19. **[Assignment of Limited Partner's Interest.]** (1) A limited partner's interest is assignable.

(2) A substituted limited partner is a person admitted to all the rights of a limited partner who has died or has assigned his interest in a partnership.

(3) An assignee, who does not become a substituted limited partner, has no right to require any information or account of the partnership transactions or to inspect the partnership books; he is only entitled to receive the share of the profits or other compensation by way of income, or the return of his contribution, to which his assignor would otherwise be entitled.

(4) An assignee shall have the right to become a substituted limited partner if all the members (except the assignor) consent thereto

or if the assignor, being thereunto empowered by the certificate, gives the assignee that right.

(5) An assignee becomes a substituted limited partner when the certificate is appropriately amended in accordance with Section 25.

(6) The substituted limited partner has all the rights and powers, and is subject to all the restrictions and liabilities of his assignor, except those liabilities of which he was ignorant at the time he became a limited partner and which could not be ascertained from the certificate.

(7) The substitution of the assignee as a limited partner does not release the assignor from liability to the partnership under Sections 6 and 17.

Section 20.   [Effect of Retirement, Death or Insanity of a General Partner.]   The retirement, death or insanity of a general partner dissolves the partnership, unless the business is continued by the remaining general partners

(a) Under a right so to do stated in the certificate, or

(b) With the consent of all members.

Section 21.   [Death of Limited Partner.]   (1) On the death of a limited partner his executor or administrator shall have all the rights of a limited partner for the purpose of settling his estate, and such power as the deceased had to constitute his assignee a substituted limited partner.

(2) The estate of a deceased limited partner shall be liable for all his liabilities as a limited partner.

Section 22.   [Rights of Creditors of Limited Partner.]   (1) On due application to a court of competent jurisdiction by any judgment creditor of a limited partner, the court may charge the interest of the indebted limited partner with payment of the unsatisfied amount of the judgment debt; and may appoint a receiver, and make all other orders, directions, and inquiries which the circumstances of the case may require.

> In those states where a creditor on beginning an action can attach debts due the defendant before he has obtained a judgment against the defendant it is recommended that paragraph (1) of this section read as follows:
> On due application to a court of competent jurisdiction by any creditor of a limited partner, the court may charge the interest of the indebted limited partner with payment of the unsatisfied amount of such claim; and may appoint a receiver, and make all other orders, directions, and inquiries which the circumstances of the case may require.

(2) The interest may be redeemed with the separate property of any general partner, but may not be redeemed with partnership property.

(3) The remedies conferred by paragraph (1) shall not be deemed exclusive of others which may exist.

(4) Nothing in this act shall be held to deprive a limited partner of his statutory exemption.

Section 23. [Distribution of Assets.] (1) In setting accounts after dissolution the liabilities of the partnership shall be entitled to payment in the following order:

(a) Those to creditors, in the order of priority as provided by law, except those to limited partners on account of their contributions, and to general partners,

(b) Those to limited partners in respect to their share of the profits and other compensation by way of income on their contributions,

(c) Those to limited partners in respect to the capital of their contributions,

(d) Those to general partners other than for capital and profits,

(e) Those to general partners in respect to profits,

(f) Those to general partners in respect to capital.

(2) Subject to any statement in the certificate or to subsequent agreement, limited partners share in the partnership assets in respect to their claims for capital, and in respect to their claims for profits or for compensation by way of income on their contributions respectively, in proportion to the respective amounts of such claims.

Section 24. [When Certificate Shall be Cancelled or Amended.] (1) The certificate shall be cancelled when the partnership is dissolved or all limited partners cease to be such.

(2) A certificate shall be amended when

(a) There is a change in the name of the partnership or in the amount or character of the contribution of any limited partner,

(b) A person is substituted as a limited partner,

(c) An additional limited partner is admitted,

(d) A person is admitted as a general partner,

(e) A general partner retires, dies or becomes insane, and the business is continued under Section 20.

(f) There is a change in the character of the business of the partnership,

(g) There is a false or erroneous statement in the certificate,

(h) There is a change in the time as stated in the certificate for the dissolution of the partnership or for the return of a contribution,

(i) A time is fixed for the dissolution of the partnership, or the return of a contribution, no time having been specified in the certificate, or

(j) The members desire to make a change in any other statement in the certificate in order that it shall accurately represent the agreement between them.

Section 25. [Requirements for Amendment and for Cancellation of Certificate.] (1) The writing to amend a certificate shall

(a) Conform to the requirements of Section 2(1a) as far as necessary to set forth clearly the change in the certificate which it is desired to make, and

(b) Be signed and sworn to by all members, and an amendment substituting a limited partner or adding a limited or general partner shall be signed also by the member to be substituted or added, and when a limited partner is to be substituted, the amendment shall also be signed by the assigning limited partner.

(2) The writing to cancel a certificate shall be signed by all members.

(3) A person desiring the cancellation or amendment of a certificate, if any person designated in paragraphs (1) and (2) as a person who must execute the writing refuses to do so, may petition the [here designate the proper court] to direct a cancellation or amendment thereof.

(4) If the court finds that the petitioner has a right to have the writing executed by a person who refuses to do so, it shall order the [here designate the responsible official in the office designated in Section 2] in the office where the certificate is recorded to record the cancellation or amendment of the certificate; and where the certificate is to be amended, the court shall also cause to be filed for record in said office a certified copy of its decree setting forth the amendment.

(5) A certificate is amended or cancelled when there is filed for record in the office [here designate the office designated in Section 2] where the certificate is recorded

(a) A writing in accordance with the provisions of paragraph (1), or (2) or

(b) A certified copy of the order of court in accordance with the provisions of paragraph (4).

(6) After the certificate is duly amended in accordance with this section, the amended certificate shall thereafter be for all purposes the certificate provided for by this act.

Section 26. [Parties to Actions.] A contributor, unless he is a general partner, is not a proper party to proceedings by or against a partnership, except where the object is to enforce a limited partner's right against or liability to the partnership.

Section 27. [Name of Act.] This act may be cited as The Uniform Limited Partnership Act.

Section 28. [Rules of Construction.] (1) The rule that statutes in derogation of the common law are to be strictly construed shall have no application to this act.

(2) This act shall be so interpreted and construed as to effect its general purpose to make uniform the law of those states which enact it.

(3) This act shall not be so construed as to impair the obligations of any contract existing when the act goes into effect, nor to affect any action on proceedings begun or right accrued before this act takes effect.

Section 29. [Rules for Cases not Provided for in this Act.] In any case not provided for in this act the rules of law and equity, including the law merchant, shall govern.

Section 30.[1] [Provisions for Existing Limited Partnerships.] (1) A limited partnership formed under any statute of this state prior to the adoption of this act, may become a limited partnership under this act by complying with the provisions of Section 2; provided the certificates sets forth

(a) The amount of the original contribution of each limited partner, and the time when the contribution was made, and

(b) That the property of the partnership exceeds the amount sufficient to discharge its liabilities to persons not claiming as general or limited partners by an amount greater than the sum of the contributions of its limited partners.

(2) A limited partnership formed under any statute of this state prior to the adoption of this act, until or unless it becomes a limited partnership under this act, shall continue to be governed by the provisions of [here insert proper reference to the existing limited partnership act or acts], except that such partnership shall not be renewed unless so provided in the original agreement.

Section 31.[1] [Act (Acts) Repealed.] Except as affecting existing limited partnerships to the extent set forth in Section 30, the act (acts) of [here designate the existing limited partnership act or acts] is (are) hereby repealed.

[1.] Sections 30, 31, will be omitted in any state which has not a limited partnership act.

APPENDIX III

UNIFORM FRAUDULENT CONVEYANCE ACT

[For adoption and discussion, see Sec. 46 above.]

The following sections concern partnerships:

Section 2. **[Insolvency.]** (2). In determining whether a partnership is insolvent there shall be added to the partnership property the present fair salable value of the separate assets of each general partner in excess of the amount probably sufficient to meet the claims of his separate creditors, and also the amount of any unpaid subscription to the partnership of each limited partner, provided the present fair salable value of the assets of such limited partner is probably sufficient to pay his debts, including such unpaid subscription.

Section 8. **[Conveyance of Partnership Property.]** Every conveyance of partnership property and every partnership obligation incurred when the partnership is or will be thereby rendered insolvent, is fraudulent as to partnership creditors, if the conveyance is made or obligation is incurred,

(a) To a partner, whether with or without a promise by him to pay partnership debts, or

(b) To a person not a partner without fair consideration to the partnership as distinguished from consideration to the individual partners.

APPENDIX IV

FEDERAL BANKRUPTCY ACT

[For discussion, see Secs. 91B–96A above.]

Section 5, 11 U.S.C.A. § 23. [Partners.]

a. A partnership, including a limited partnership containing one or more general partners, during the continuation of the partnership business or after its dissolution and before the final settlement thereof, may be adjudged a bankrupt either separately or jointly with one or more or all of its general partners.

b. A petition may be filed by one or more or all of the general partners in the separate behalf of a partnership or jointly in behalf of a partnership and of the general partner or partners filing the same: *Provided, however,* That where a petition is filed in behalf of a partnership by less than all of the general partners, the petition shall allege that the partnership is insolvent. A petition may be filed separately against a partnership or jointly against a partnership and one or more or all of its general partners.

c. The creditors of the bankrupt partnership shall appoint the trustee, who shall be the trustee of the individual estate of a general partner being administered in the proceeding: *Provided, however,* That the creditors of a general partner adjudged a bankrupt may, upon cause shown, be permitted to appoint their separate trustee for his estate. In other respects, so far as possible, the partnership estate shall be administered as herein provided for other estates.

d. The court of bankruptcy which has jurisdiction of one of the general partners may have jurisdiction of all the general partners and of the administration of the partnership and individual property.

e. The trustee or trustees shall keep separate accounts of the partnership property and of the property belonging to the individual general partners.

f. The expenses shall be paid from the partnership property and the individual property in such proportions as the court shall determine.

g. The net proceeds of the partnership property shall be appropriated to the payment of the partnership debts and the net proceeds of the individual estate of each general partner to the payment of his individual debts. Should any surplus remain of the property of any general partner after paying his individual debts, such surplus shall be added to the partnership assets and be applied to the payment of the partnership debts. Should any surplus of the partnership property remain after paying the partnership debts, such surplus shall be distributed among the individual partners, general or limited, or added to the estates of the general partners, as the case may be, in the proportion of their respective interests in the partnership and in the order of distribution provided by the laws of the State applicable thereto.

h. The court may permit the proof of the claim of the partnership estate against the individual estates, and vice versa, and may marshal the assets of the partnership estate and individual estates so as to prevent preferences and secure the equitable distribution of the property of the several estates.

i. Where all the general partners are adjudged bankrupt, the partnership shall also be adjudged bankrupt. In the event of one or more but not all of the general partners of a partnership being adjudged bankrupt, the partnership property shall not be administered in bankruptcy, unless by consent of the general partner or partners not adjudged bankrupt; but such general partner or partners not adjudged bankrupt shall settle the partnership business as expeditiously as its nature will permit and account for the interest of the general partner or partners adjudged bankrupt.

j. The discharge of a partnership shall not discharge the individual general partners thereof from the partnership debts. A general partner adjudged a bankrupt either in a joint or separate proceeding may, pursuant to the provisions of this title, obtain a discharge from both his partnership and individual debts.

k. If a limited partnership is adjudged bankrupt, any limited partner who is individually liable under the laws of the United States or of any State for any of the partnership debts shall be deemed a general partner as to such debts and, if he is insolvent, shall be subject to the provisions and entitled to the benefits of this title, as in the case of a general partner.

Section 67(d), 11 U.S.C.A. § 107(d). [Liens and Fraudulent Transfers.]

(1) For the purposes of, and exclusively applicable to this subdivision: . . . (d) a person is "insolvent" when the present fair salable value of his property is less than the amount required to pay his debts; and to determine whether a partnership is insolvent there shall be added to the partnership property the present fair salable value of the separate property of each general partner in excess of the amount required to pay his separate debts, and also the amount realizable on any unpaid subscription to the partnership of each limited partner; . . .

(4) Every transfer of partnership property and every partnership obligation incurred within one year prior to the filing of a petition in bankruptcy or of an original petition under this title by or against the partnership, when the partnership is insolvent or will be thereby rendered insolvent, is fraudulent as to partnership creditors existing at

the time of such transfer or obligation, without regard to actual intent if made or incurred (a) to a partner, whether with or without a promise by him to pay partnership debts, or (b) to a person not a partner without fair consideration to the partnership as distinguished from consideration to the individual partners.

APPENDIX V

A FORM OF GENERAL PARTNERSHIP AGREEMENT FOR USE UNDER THE UNIFORM PARTNERSHIP ACT

[Adapted from an article by Alan R. Bromberg and Joseph M. Stuhl, 24 Texas Bar Journal 933 (1961); used by permission.]

[Introductory Note. No particular form of agreement is prescribed for partnerships. Perhaps the most important characteristic of partnership is the freedom the partners have to devise their own arrangements. The form which follows is for a relatively simple mercantile business, and has a relatively simple provision for continuing the business by the partners remaining after death or retirement. It illustrates the range of problems a legal draftsman needs to consider.

Several Paragraphs repeat or paraphrase the U.P.A. They add nothing legally. But they may add something psychologically, and they certainly call things to the attention of the partners, who are unlikely to be familiar with the Act. On the other hand, certain portions of the Act which have daily importance have been omitted, Notable among these are the fiduciary rules of §§ 20–22, Secs. 67, 68, 72 above, whose inclusion might engender mistrust. Like most modern partnership agreements, this one is indebted to Mulder & Volz, The Drafting of Partnership Agreements (1955)

Although designed for use under the U.P.A., the agreement should work in non-U.P.A. jurisdictions too.

"Paragraph" references are to the agreement. "Section" references are to this treatise. "IRC" references are to Int.Rev.Code of 1954.]

Analysis

Art. 1—General
- 1.1   Parties.
- 1.2   Effective Date.
- 1.3   Name.
- 1.4   Purpose.
- 1.5   Place.
- 1.6   Term.

Art. 2—Capital, Income, Drawings
- 2.1   Initial Capital Contributions.
- 2.2   Subsequent Capital Contributions.
- 2.3   Capital Accounts.
- 2.4   Income Accounts.
- 2.5   Drawing Accounts.
- 2.6   Relation of Income Accounts to Capital Accounts.
- 2.7   Limitation on Withdrawals.
- 2.8   Closing of Accounts.

PARTNERSHIP AGREEMENT

Typhoon Marine Sales

The Parties agree to form a Partnership on the terms and conditions set forth in this Agreement.

ART. 1—GENERAL

1.1 Parties. The Parties (sometimes called the Partners) to this Agreement are Al Anchor (sometimes called "Anchor"), Bill Boat (sometimes called "Boat") and Charlie Cash (sometimes called "Cash").

1.2 Effective Date. The effective date of this Agreement shall be January 1, 19___.

1.3 Name. The Partnership name is TYPHOON MARINE SALES.

COMMENT. If the name differs from the Partners' names, the fictitious name statutes should be consulted. See Sec. 22 above. If it is intended that the same name may be used after the death or retirement of a Partner, specific provision should be made; see par. 6.6. Such use is permitted by U.P.A. § 41(10) without liability for the estate of a deceased Partner.

1.4 Purpose. The purpose of the Partnership is to engage in the sale, service, and repair of all types of outboard and inboard motor boats, outboard and inboard motors, and all character of marine equipment and accessories.

COMMENT. This paragraph serves to define the scope of the Partnership business, within which each Partner has authority (actual or apparent) to act for the Partnership, U.P.A. § 9(1), Secs. 48–50 above.

1.5 Place. The Partnership business shall be conducted at 12345 Tidal Avenue, Sunbay, Texas, and/or such other places as the Partners may determine.

1.6 Term. The Partnership shall continue until dissolved pursuant to par. 6.1.

1.6 Term (Alternate). The Partnership shall continue for two years unless dissolved by the occurrence of one of the events listed in par. 6.1(b) or 6.1(c). After the expiration of two years, the Partnership shall continue until dissolved pursuant to par. 6.1.

COMMENT. The first alternative gives an indefinite term; the second superimposes a minimum. A third alternative would be a fixed term without provision for continuation thereafter. In such a case, expiration of the term automatically dissolves the partnership, U.P.A. § 31(1) (a), Sec. 74(a) above, but any continuation of the business would be presumptively pursuant to the original agreement, U.P.A. § 23. The principal effect of a fixed term (alone or followed by an indefinite extension) is to subject a Partner to damages for breach of contract if he deliberately dissolves the partnership before the fixed term is over, and to let the other Partners continue the business if they choose. U.P.A. §§ 38(2), 31(2), Secs. 75, 83A above. With an indefinite term, any Partner may dissolve at will, U.P.A. § 31(1) (b), Sec. 74(b) above.

ART. 2—CAPITAL, INCOME, DRAWINGS

2.1 Initial Capital Contributions. The initial capital contributions of each Partner shall be as follows:

(a) Anchor: That certain tract of land locally known at 12345 Tidal Avenue, Sunbay, Texas, and all improvements thereon, consisting of a portable metal canopy covering an area 25′ x 50′, which property has a fair market value of $10,000 as of the effective date of this Agreement. This tract is more specifically described in Schedule A attached hereto.

(b) Boat: Those certain boats, motors and marine accessories described in Schedule B attached hereto, which have a fair market value of $10,000 as of the effective date of this Agreement.

(c) Cash: $10,000 in cash.

2.2 Subsequent Capital Contributions. The Partners, in proportion to their distributive shares (as defined in par. 3.3), shall make such subsequent capital contributions as are needed by the Partnership. If any Partner fails to make such contribution, the other Partners (as their option) may consider the sums thus advanced by them to be loans to the Partnership.

COMMENT. This provision could easily be omitted in favor of letting the Partners make this decision as circumstances develop. A distinction is suggested between a loan and a capital contribution in the event one partner defaults because loans have priority over capital contributions in distributions after dissolution, par. 6.9, U.P.A. §§ 40 (b), 18(a), Secs. 65(a), 90 above. U.P.A. § 18(c), Sec. 65(c) above, authorizes interest on advances. Cf. par. 3.4(a).

2.3 Capital Accounts. An individual Capital Account shall be maintained for each Partner. It shall be credited with his contributions and debited and credited in accordance with pars. 2.6 and 2.8.

COMMENT. The elaborate scheme of accounting prescribed by pars. 2.3–2.8 is convenient but not essential. It is designed so that the books of account will show, at a glance, all the different financial relations between Partners and Partnership. It could be replaced by a bare statement that books shall be kept in accordance with generally accepted accounting principles, but this leaves many questions unanswered.

Several alternative procedures might be specified:

(A) Capital account only. Capital contributions, income and withdrawals are all entered in it. This has the virtue of simplicity.

(B) Capital account and income account. Income and withdrawals are entered in the income account which is ultimately closed to the capital account.

(C) Capital account, accumulated income account and drawing account. This would be the same as in the Agreement, except that the capital account would be credited only with capital contributions and debited only with withdrawals of capital. Income would be entered in the accumulated income account which would be a balance sheet account (like earned surplus) to which drawings are closed. Such an arrangement would facilitate liquidation, in which capital contributions are repaid before profits, par. 6.9, U.P.A. § 40(b), Sec. 90 above, U.P.A. § 18(a), Sec. 65(a) above.

Wherever feasible, the Partnership accountant should be consulted before drafting provisions on accounting matters. This is particularly important where the Agreement concerns an existing partnership with established records.

2.4   Income Accounts.   An individual Income Account shall be maintained for each Partner.   It shall be credited with his Distributive Share of profits and debited with his Distributive Share of losses (subject to par. 2.6) as soon as practicable after the close of each fiscal year and at such times during the fiscal year as the Partners may determine.

2.5   Drawing Accounts.   An individual Drawing Account shall be maintained for each Partner.   It shall be debited with his withdrawals.

2.6   Relation of Income Accounts to Capital Accounts.   Any losses exceeding the credit balances in the Income Accounts shall be debited to the individual Capital Accounts.   If the Capital Account of a Partner is depleted by thus debiting losses, future profits of that Partner shall be credited to his Capital Account until such depletion has been made good.

2.7   Limitation on Withdrawals.   Except by unanimous agreement of the Partners, no Partner shall make a withdrawal which would:

(a) Reduce Partnership cash below $———, or

(b) Make the balance in his Drawing Account exceed the combined net credit balance of (i) his Capital Account, (ii) his Income Account and (iii) his Distributive Share of estimated profits or losses since the last entries in his Income Account.

Any excessive withdrawal shall be promptly restored.

COMMENT.   This provision is designed to discourage excessive withdrawals and can be made more stringent if desired.   The last sentence creates a duty to repay any excessive withdrawals; this provision can presumably be enforced without dissolving the Partnership.   Par. (a) is designed to keep a minimum working capital in the Partnership.   Par. (b) is intended to assure that no Partner is ever a net debtor to the Partnership.   See Sec. 41(a) above.

2.8   Closing of Accounts.   As soon as practicable after the closing of each fiscal year, the Income and Drawing Accounts shall be closed to the Capital Accounts.

ART. 3—OTHER FINANCIAL AND ACCOUNTING MATTERS

3.1   Method of Accounting.   The Partnership shall keep accounts on the accrual basis.   The accounts shall readily disclose items which the Partners take into account separately for income tax purposes.   As to matters of accounting not provided for in this agreement, generally accepted accounting principles shall govern.

COMMENT. The simpler cash method of accounting will be preferred in many instances. However, the accrual method is required in virtually all instances where inventories are maintained; Income Tax Regulations Sec. 1.446–1(b) (2) (i). Separately treated items are identified in IRC Sec. 702(a) (26 U.S.C.A.) and Regulations thereunder. Except in very unusual cases, the Partnership books should be kept in accordance with income tax requirements. See Sec. 66 above.

3.2 Fiscal Year. The fiscal year of the Partnership shall be the calendar year.

COMMENT. In most instances this is the only fiscal year a Partnership can have for tax purposes; see IRC 706(b) (26 U.S.C.A.).

3.3 Distributive Shares. The profits or losses of the Partnership shall be distributable or chargeable, as the case may be, in the following proportions (sometimes called Distributive Shares):

> Al Anchor $\frac{1}{3}$
> Bill Boat $\frac{1}{3}$
> Charlie Cash $\frac{1}{3}$

COMMENT. Sharing of profits equally and sharing losses in proportion to profits is provided by U.P.A. § 18(a), Sec. 65(a) above. Any variation shall be specified in the Partnership Agreement. The phrase "distributive share" is from IRC Sec. 704 (26 U.S.C.A.). The distributive share need not be the same for all items (e.g. gain v. loss, ordinary income v. capital gain) but variations must comply with IRC 704 (26 U.S.C.A.) and Income Tax Regulations Sec. 1.704–1(b) (2) to be effective for tax purposes. Non-partners may be compensated by a share of the profits; see U.P.A. § 7(4), Secs. 14A–20 above.

3.4 Other Compensation to Partners.

(a) No interest shall be paid on Capital Accounts.

(b) Anchor and Boat shall receive salaries of $75 per week. No increase in salaries shall be made without unanimous agreement. The payment of salaries to Partners shall be an obligation of the Partnership only to the extent that Partnership assets are available therefor, and shall not be an obligation of the Partners individually. Salaries shall, to this extent, be treated as an expense of the Partnership in determining profits or losses.

COMMENT. Unless the Agreement provides otherwise, interest is allowed on Capital Accounts from the date when repayment should be made (U.P.A. § 18(d), Sec. 65(c) above), and salaries are not allowed (U.P.A. § 18(f), Sec. 65(e) above). See par. 4.2 on rent.

3.5 Indemnification of Partners. The Partnership shall promptly indemnify each Partner in respect of payments reasonably made and personal liabilities reasonably incurred by him in the ordinary conduct of its business, or for the preservation of its business or property.

COMMENT. Since U.P.A. § 18(b), Sec. 65(b) above, so provides, this need not be repeated in the Agreement, although it is important that the Partners understand it.

ART. 4—PROPERTY

4.1 Partnership Property. The property described in par. 2.1 (Initial Capital Contributions) shall become partnership property. Other property may be contributed to the Partnership upon the same terms by unanimous agreement of the Partners. All Partnership property shall be so recorded in the Partnership accounts.

COMMENT. An enormous volume of litigation has resulted from failure to distinguish partnership property from property owned by the Partners individually but made available for Partnership use. Typical of the problems have been: (1) creditors' priorities, (2) partners' rights in property, (3) who shares gain or loss on disposition, and (4) who is entitled to the property on dissolution. The intent of the Partners has generally been held to govern. Pars. 4.1 and 4.2 are designed to make intent explicit and to require Partnership records to be kept accordingly. Capital contributions are credited to a Partner's capital account pursuant to par. 2.3. See Sec. 37 above.

A number of consequences flow from the characterization of property as partnership or individual. For example, partnership creditors have prior rights in partnership property and individual creditors in individual property. U.P.A. §§ 40(h), (i), Secs. 43, 91 above. The designation of partnership property is of vital significance because of the limited rights of an individual partner therein. These rights are itemized in U.P.A. § 25(2) and discussed in Secs. 40–45 above. They might well be paraphrased in the Agreement to avoid misunderstandings among the Partners. A Partner's interest in the partnership is legally distinct from his rights in specific partnership property. See Sec. 40 above.

4.2 Property Made Available for Partnership Use. Scedule C to this Agreement identifies certain property being made available for Partnership use. This property shall remain the property of the Partner presently owning it, but it shall not be withdrawn from partnership use prior to dissolution without unanimous consent of the Partners. (However, the tractor and trailer described in Item _____ of the Schedule is being made available to the Partnership by Cash for one year after the effective date of this Agreement; then Cash shall be free to withdraw the same.) No rental shall be paid by the Partnership for the use of such equipment, but all usual and customary operating expenses shall be treated as an expense of the Partnership in determining profits or losses. Such property shall not be recorded as Partnership assets in the Partnership accounts. Other property may be made available for Partnership use on such terms as the Partners may unanimously agree.

COMMENT. See Comment to par. 4.1.

4.3 Method of Holding Partnership Property. Partnership property (including real estate) may, by unanimous consent of the Partners, be acquired and conveyed in the name of any Partner or other person as nominee for the Partnership. Such property shall be recorded as Partnership property in the Partnership accounts.

COMMENT. Although all property, including real estate, can be held and conveyed in the partnership name (U.P.A. §§ 8(3), 10), it may be simpler to use a partner or someone else as nominee or trustee. It is important that the partnership accounts reflect the ownership; see Comment to Par. 4.1. See Sec. 38 above.

ART. 5—OPERATIONS

5.1 Management. All Partners shall have equal rights in the management of the Partnership business. Decisions shall be by majority vote (each Partner having one vote) except as provided in par. 5.2.

COMMENT. This restates U.P.A. § 18(e), (h), Secs. 65(d), (h) above.

5.2 Matters Requiring Unanimity. No Partner shall, without the consent of the other Partners (which consent shall not be unreasonably withheld), do any of the following:

(a) Assign the partnership property in trust for creditors or on the assignee's promise to pay the debts of the Partnership.

(b) Dispose of the good will of the business.

(c) Do any other act which would make it impossible to carry on the ordinary business of the Partnership.

(d) Confess a judgment.

(e) Submit a partnership claim or liability to arbitration or reference.

(f) Make, execute or deliver for the Partnership any bond, mortgage, deed of trust, guarantee, indemnity bond, surety bond or accommodation paper or accommodation endorsement.

(g) Borrow money in the partnership name or use Partnership property as collateral.

(h) Assign, transfer, pledge, compromise or release any claim of or debt owing to the Partnership except upon payment in full.

(i) Convey any Partnership real property.

(j) Pledge or transfer in any manner his interest in the Partnership except to another Partner.

(k) Any of the acts for which unanimity is required by other paragraphs of this Agreements, e.g. 2.7, 3.4, 4.1, 4.2, 4.3 and 6.1.

COMMENT. Limitations on a Partner's authority are generally not binding on third persons without knowledge. U.P.A. § 9(4), Secs. 53, 49 above. However, they are binding on the Partners; any breach might give rise to damages and might dissolve the partnership. Subpars. (a)–(e) of the Agreement restate U.P.A. § 9(3), Sec. 51 above, and are therefore presumably binding on third persons (by force of the Act) as well as upon Partners.

5.3 Time. Anchor and Boat shall each devote his entire time and attention to the business of the Partnership, except that each may devote reasonable time to civic, family, and personal affairs. Cash shall be free to devote his time and attention to other business matters.

COMMENT. This settles the legally uncertain extent of a Partner's duty to perform services. See Sec. 65(f) above. It also contains an implied non-competition agreement for Anchor and Boat, but not for Cash, which may be made explicit. Unless otherwise agreed, Partners are not free to compete with their firm. See Sec. 68 above.

5.4 Books. The Partnership books shall be kept at the principal place of business of the Partnership, and every Partner shall at all times have access to and may inspect and copy any of them.

COMMENT. Since U.P.A. § 19 so provides, this need not be repeated in the Agreement. See Sec. 66 above.

5.5 Bank Accounts. The Partnership shall maintain such bank accounts as the Partners shall determine. Checks shall be drawn for Partnership purposes only, and may be signed by any person or persons designated by the Partners. All moneys received by the Partnership shall be deposited in such account or accounts.

COMMENT. In establishing bank accounts, the bank's form of deposit agreement should be carefully scrutinized. It may modify the Partnership Agreement, e.g. as to borrowing authority.

ART. 6—DISSOLUTION

6.1 Causes of Dissolution. The Partnership shall be dissolved by the first of the following which happens:

(a) Retirement of a Partner,

(b) Death, disability or bankruptcy of a Partner,

(c) Unanimous agreement of the Partners to dissolve.

COMMENT. These are not the only causes of dissolution recognized by U.P.A. §§ 31, 32, Secs. 74–78 above. In particular, they do not deprive a Partner of the power to dissolve in violation of the Agreement, U.P.A. § 31(2), Sec. 75(a) above. They should, however, convert such a dissolution into a retirement, with consequent advantages to the remaining Partners, e.g., par. 6.6 and perhaps rights to damages if during a fixed term, U.P.A. § 38(2), Sec. 75(b) above. U.P.A. § 38(2)(b), Secs. 75(c), 83A above, allows a similar continuation of the business without express provision in the Agreement, but subject to rather more restrictive requirements. See also Comment to par. 1.6.

6.2 Manner of Retirement. Any Partner may retire upon 60 days prior written notice to the other Partners.

6.3 Definition of "Disability." Disability shall mean permanent physical or mental disability.

6.4 Notice of Dissolution. Actual notice of dissolution shall be given to all persons who have had dealings with the Partnership during the two years prior to dissolution.

COMMENT. U.P.A. §§ 35(1)(b) and 35(3)(c) encourage such notice by relieving the Partners from unauthorized post-dissolution liabilities if it is given. The agreement may well go further and call for notice of dissolution by newspaper advertisement which gives further protection under the sections cited.

6.5 Accounting on Dissolution. The Capital, Income and Drawing Accounts shall be posted as of the date of dissolution. Assets and liabilities shall be taken at book value, but no value shall be assigned to good will or firm name.

COMMENT. In some circumstances it will be desirable to have the assets appraised or to include value for good will or firm name. See Secs. 84, 90A above.

6.6 Right to Continue. If dissolution occurs under Par. 6.1(a) or (b), the remaining Partners shall have the right to continue the Partnership business under the same name, by themselves or with any other person or persons they may select. If the remaining Partners desire to continue the business, but not together, the Partnership shall be liquidated in accordance with Par. 6.9.

COMMENT. See Secs. 83A, 90A above. For continued use of the name, see Comment to par. 1.3.

6.7 Payment if Partnership Continued. If the remaining Partners continue the Partnership business under Par. 6.6, they shall pay to the other Partner or his legal representatives the value of his interest as of the date of dissolution, as determined under Par. 6.8 and no more. Payment shall be made at least one-half within six months of dissolution and the remainder within twelve months of dissolution.

COMMENT. See U.P.A. § 42, Sec. 86 above, for an alternative (foreclosed by this paragraph) allowing the retiring Partner or a deceased Partner's estate to leave property in the firm and receive a share of the profits.

6.8 Value of Interest. The value of a Partner's interest shall be:

(a) The sum of:

(1) His Capital Account,

(2) His Income Account,

(3) Any other amounts due and owing to him by the Partnership;

(b) Less the sum of:

(1) His Drawing Account,

(2) Any other amounts due and owing by him to the Partnership.

COMMENT. See Comment to Par. 6.5 concerning revaluation of the assets. In certain instances (e. g. professional or construction firms) it will be desirable to include the value of unrealized profits on uncompleted employments or projects. This method of valuation takes partnership liabilities into account; the continuing partnership remains responsible for them. U.P.A. § 41(1), Sec. 89 above.

6.9 Winding Up and Liquidation. Upon dissolution, if the Partnership business is not continued under par. 6.6, it shall be wound up and liquidated as rapidly as business circumstances will permit. The assets shall be applied to the following purposes in the following order:

(a) To pay or provide for all amounts owing by the Partnership to creditors other than Partners, and for expenses of winding up.

(b) To pay or provide for all amounts owing by the Partnership to Partners other than for capital and profits.

(c) To pay or provide for all amounts owing by the Partnership to Partners in respect of capital.

(d) To pay or provide for all amounts owing to the Partners in respect of profits.

COMMENT. Since U.P.A. § 40(b) generally so provides, this need not be repeated in the Agreement. A frequent alternative is to provide for the division among the partners in proportion to their capital accounts after payment or provision for loans to partners and other creditors. Depending on the method of computation of the capital accounts, this may well provide a different distribution from U.P.A. § 40(b). In particular, it impliedly relieves the partners from the obligations of U.P.A. §§ 40(d), 18(a), Secs. 65(a), 90 above, to make contributions sufficient to satisfy all the liabilities of the partnership, even those in respect of profits.

6.10 Authority to Wind Up. If dissolution occurs under par. 6.1 (a) or (b), the remaining Partners shall have the authority to wind up. If dissolution occurs under Par. 6.1(c), all Partners jointly shall have the authority to wind up.

COMMENT. U.P.A. § 37, Sec. 83 above, generally so provides. Implied authority and duty to convert assets into cash is supplied by Sec. 38(1).

6.11 Method of Distribution of Assets. To the extent feasible, all distributions in liquidation shall be made pro rata to the partners in kind.

COMMENT. This is a warning not to become entangled in IRC Sec. 751 (collapsible partnerships). Pro rata distributions are usually preferable for income tax purposes. See Comment to par. 6.10. If property contributed by a particular partner is to be returned to him, the Agreement should so state.

ART. 7—MISCELLANEOUS

7.1 Notice. Any notice to a partner required or permitted by this Agreement shall be in writing and shall be sufficient if sent by registered or certified mail to the last known address of the person to whom such notice is to be given. Any notice may be waived in writing by the person entitled to receive it.

7.2 Construction of Agreement. The captions used in this Agreement are for convenience only and shall not be construed in interpreting this Agreement. Whenever the context so requires, the masculine shall include the feminine and neuter, and the singular shall include the plural, and conversely. If any portion of this Agreement shall be held invalid or inoperative, then, so far as is reasonable and possible:

(a) The remainder of this Agreement shall be considered valid and operative, and

(b) Effect shall be given to the intent manifested by the portion held invalid or inoperative.

7.3 Binding Effect. This Agreement shall bind the partners, their heirs, personal representatives and assigns.

COMMENT. Consideration should be given to reciting that the wives of Partners are also bound, and having them sign the Agreement. This may be particularly important in a community property state. See Sec. 45(c) above. In any state it blunts a possible attack by a wife on continuation and payment provisions after a Partner's death. But making them signatories may require their consent to any amendment of the Agreement, unless provision is included for amendment by the Partners alone.

EXECUTED at Sunbay, Texas, in multiple copies December ———, 19——.

AL ANCHOR
BILL BOAT
CHARLIE CASH

COMMENT. See Comment to par. 7.3.

APPENDIX VI

HIGH CONTINUITY PROVISIONS FOR A GENERAL PARTNERSHIP AGREEMENT

[Adapted from Bromberg, Partnership Dissolution—Causes, Consequences, and Cures, 43 Texas L.Rev. 631, 663 (1965).]

[Introductory Note. These continuity provisions would replace par. 1.6 and Art. 6 in the preceding form, Appendix V. They are designed for a more prosperous firm with more members, who are tax conscious and want a high degree of continuity. As written, it would do for a service or professional firm. With appropriate changes in valuation (by appraisal provision or otherwise), it could be used for firms where asset values are relatively more important.

By these provisions, under any circumstances except liquidation, the firm pays an outgoing partner. This will usually be tax free because the partner's basis is about the same as the book value of his interest, which measures his payment. In addition, on retirement with proper notice, disability, or death, the outgoing partner's percentage in the firm's profits continues for the equivalent of three years, but is distributed over a period of eight years. These payments are ordinary income to the recipient and excludable by the other partners, who thus benefit by liquidating the interest with funds which are not taxed to them. See Sec. 86(b) (3) above.

A provision could be added for another payment at death, identified as being for good will (classed as additional partnership property). Although subject to estate tax, this increment would escape income tax because of the corresponding increase in basis at death. If the funds were furnished by life insurance proceeds, which are normally tax free, there would be no burden on the remaining partners.

In general, see Secs. 83A, 84, 86, 90A above.]

Analysis

Art. 1—General
    1.6 Term.

Art. 6—Dissolution
    6.1 Cause of Dissolution.
    6.2 Accounting on Dissolution.
    6.3 Winding Up and Liquidation.
    6.4 Method of Distribution of Assets.

Art. 7—Changes in Membership.
    7.1 No Dissolution on Admission or Withdrawal.
    7.2 Admission of New Partner.
    7.3 Retirement.
    7.4 Expulsion.
    7.5 Disability.
    7.6 Bankruptcy.

Art. 7—Changes in Membership—Continued

ART. 1.—GENERAL

. . .

1.6 TERM. The Partnership shall continue until dissolved pursuant to par. 6.1.

. . .

ART. 6.—DISSOLUTION

6.1 CAUSE OF DISSOLUTION. The Partnership shall be dissolved only by the vote of three-fourths of the Partners. Each Partner waives his right to dissolve or obtain dissolution in any other way.

6.2 ACCOUNTING ON DISSOLUTION. The Capital, Income and Drawing Accounts shall be posted as of the date of dissolution. Assets and liabilities shall be taken at book value, but no value shall be assigned to good will or Partnership name.

6.3 WINDING UP AND LIQUIDATION. Upon dissolution, the Partnership shall be wound up and liquidated as rapidly as business circumstances permit. The assets shall be applied to these purposes in this order:

(A) To pay or provide for all amounts owing by the Partnership to creditors other than Partners, and for expenses of winding up Partnership affairs.

(B) To pay or provide for all amounts owing by the Partnership to Partners other than in respect of capital and profits.

(C) To pay or provide for all amounts owing by the Partnership to Partners in respect of capital.

(D) To pay or provide for all amounts owing by the Partnership to the Partners in respect of profits (taking into account profits or losses after dissolution).

6.4 METHOD OF DISTRIBUTION OF ASSETS. To the extent feasible, all distributions in liquidation shall be made pro rata to the Partners in kind.

ART. 7.—CHANGES IN MEMBERSHIP

7.1 NO DISSOLUTION ON ADMISSION OR WITHDRAWAL. In particular, the Partnership shall not be dissolved by:

(A) The admission of a new Partner, or

(B) The withdrawal of a Partner (defined to mean expulsion, retirement, death, disability or bankruptcy of a Partner).

7.2 ADMISSION OF NEW PARTNER. By the vote of three-fourths of the Partners, any qualified person may be admitted as a new Partner at any time. The new Partner shall be subject to this Agreement as modified at the time of his admission. His admission shall be evidenced by an Addendum to this Agreement which shall be signed by the then Partners and the new Partner, and shall state:

(A) The date of execution of the Addendum;

(B) The effective date of this Agreement as to the new Partner;

(C) The Distributive Shares of the then Partners and the new Partner;

(D) The capital contribution of the New Partner, if any;

(E) Any amendments to this Agreement;

(F) Any other provisions that may be appropriate to integrate the new Partner into the scheme of this Agreement.

A new Partner shall be liable for all obligations of the Partnership arising before his admission (as though he had been a Partner when such obligations were incurred) except that his obligation shall be satisfied only out of Partnership property.

7.3 RETIREMENT. Any Partner may retire on three months prior notice to the other Partners. Any cessation of active participation in the Partnership affairs shall be deemed a retirement three months after it commences unless it is by virtue of expulsion, death, disability or bankruptcy. Failure to give notice shall not alter the character of the retirement.

7.4 EXPULSION. A Partner may at any time be expelled by the vote of three-fourths of the Partners for:

(A) Professional misconduct or disqualification.

(B) Willful or persistent breach of this Agreement, or

(C) Conduct which tends to affect prejudicially the carrying on of Partnership affairs.

A Partner may at any time be expelled, with or without cause, by unanimous vote of the other Partners.

7.5 DISABILITY. Disability shall mean physical or mental disability which has continued for six months and which the remaining Partners determine to be permanent. A Partner whose disability is under consideration shall submit to reasonable examinations by qualified physicians if requested by the other Partners.

7.6 BANKRUPTCY. Bankruptcy shall mean bankruptcy adjudicated under the National Bankruptcy Act or insolvency under the law of this state.

7.7 CONSEQUENCES OF WITHDRAWAL. Upon a withdrawal (as defined in par. 7.1(B)):

(A) The Partner involved shall immediately cease to be a partner;

(B) The good will of the Partnership (including the Partnership name, records, files (including clients' files)) and all other Partnership property shall belong to and remain solely vested in the Partnership;

(C) The Capital, Income and Drawing accounts shall be posted. (In so doing, assets and liabilities shall be taken at book value, but no value shall be assigned to good will (as defined above). In valuing the interest of a Partner at his death, insurance owned by the Partnership on his life shall be included only to the extent of its cash value at the last anniversary of the policy.);

(D) The remaining Partners shall review the situation and determine whether notice of the withdrawal should be given to third persons and, if so, to whom and in what manner.

7.8 VALUE OF INTEREST. The value of a Partner's interest shall be as follows, based on the books prepared in accordance with par. 7.7(C):

(A) The sum of—

(1) His Capital Account,

(2) His Income Account,

(3) His share (valued by the remaining Partners in accordance with past experience) of fees for services rendered but not yet reflected in his Income Account, and

(4) Any other amounts due and owing to him by the Partnership,

(B) Less the sum of

(1) His Drawing Account, and

(2) Any other amounts due and owing by him to the Partnership.

7.9 PAYMENT OF VALUE OF INTEREST ON WITHDRAWAL. On a withdrawal (as defined in par. 7.1(B)), the withdrawing Partner (or his estate or the person designated in his will in the event of death) shall be paid the value of his interest. Payment shall be made at least one-half within six months of the event and the remainder within eighteen months of the event. Payment shall be in cash unless the remaining Partners select some other medium. This payment is in satisfaction of all the Partner's property rights as a Partner, including his interest in the Partnership, all his rights in Partnership property and profits, and all rights against the Partnership and the Partners (except as otherwise provided in par. 7.10).

7.10 ADDITIONAL PAYMENT ON DEATH, RETIREMENT OR DISABILITY.

(A) If a Partner (1) dies while a Partner, (2) retires at or after age 60 on three months prior notice to the other Partners, or (3) is disabled (as defined in par. 7.5), then the Partnership shall pay him (or his estate or the person designated in his will in the event of death), in addition to the payment under par. 7.9:

(1) For the next four years, a percentage of the Partnership's net income for each of those years, equal to one-half the Partner's distributive share at the time of his death, retirement or disability, and

(2) For the four years after that, a percentage of the Partnership's net income for each of those years, equal to one-fourth the Partner's distributive share at the time of his death, retirement or disability.

(B) Payments shall be made as soon as possible after the close of each fiscal year of the Partnership; fractional periods shall be prorated on a reasonable basis.

(C) Payments shall cease and not resume if the Partner violates par. 7.12.

(D) The Partnership's net income shall be computed according to its regularly employed method of accounting, and shall not include proceeds of life insurance.

(E) The maximum amount payable in any one year to all retired or disabled Partners shall not exceed 15 per cent of the Partnership's net income. If necessary to effectuate this maximum, each such Partner's percentage for that year shall be reduced proportionately, and the number of years of payments to him shall be correspondingly increased.

7.11 TAX ELECTION AFTER PAYMENTS. During any year that payments are made under pars. 7.9 or 7.10, the Partners shall (if the election is not already in force) review the situation and determine whether to make an election under applicable income tax law to adjust the basis of remaining Partnership assets. Decision shall be by majority vote.

7.12 NON-COMPETITION COVENANT FOR RETIRING PARTNER. A Partner who retires from the Partnership shall not directly or indirectly compete with the Partnership in _____ County, _____, for a period of _____ years after his retirement.

7.13 ADJUSTMENT OF DISTRIBUTIVE SHARES AFTER WITHDRAWAL. After the withdrawal of a Partner (as defined in par. 7.1(B)), the Distributive Shares of each of the remaining Partners shall be increased by allocating among them the Distributive Share of the withdrawing Partner in proportion to their then existing Distributive Shares.

APPENDIX VII

A SIMPLE CERTIFICATE OF LIMITED PARTNERSHIP

[Introductory Note: The minimum formality required to form a limited partnership is the execution and filing of a certificate. See U.L.P.A. § 2. The certificate may contain any other provisions desired by the partners. The practice, however, is to make a separate, private agreement concerning any matters not required to be in the certificate; such an agreement resembles an ordinary partnership agreement. For an example, see Mulder & Volz, The Drafting of Partnership Agreements, 44–53 (1955) and comments thereto. The barest form of certificate might look like this.

In general, see Sec. 26 above.]

Analysis

1. Name.
2. Purpose.
3. Location.
4. Members and Designation.
5. Term.
6. Initial Contributions of Limited Partners.
7. Subsequent Contributions of Limited Partners.
8. Profit Shares of Limited Partners.

CERTIFICATE OF LIMITED PARTNERSHIP

The undersigned, desiring to form a limited partnership under the Uniform Limited Partnership Act of the State of Texas, make this certificate for that purpose.

1. NAME. The name of the partnership shall be "Sunnyside Dairy Company".

2. PURPOSE. The purpose of the partnership shall be to engage in the general dairy business, together with all other business necessary and related thereto, including the purchase, processing, manufacture, sale and distribution of milk, cream and other products which may conveniently be handled with such products.

3. LOCATION. The location of the partnership's principal place of business is Dallas County, Texas.

4. MEMBERS AND DESIGNATION. The names and places of residence of the members, and their designation as general or limited partners are:

John Smith	1000 Adams, Dallas, Texas	General Partner
Harold Jones	2000 Adams, Dallas, Texas	General Partner
Frank Brown	3000 Adams, Dallas, Texas	Limited Partner
George Green	4000 Adams, Dallas, Texas	Limited Partner

5. TERM. The term for which the partnership is to exist is indefinite.

6. INITIAL CONTRIBUTIONS OF LIMITED PARTNERS. The amount of cash and a description of the agreed value of the other property contributed by each limited partner are:

Frank Brown $10,000 cash
George Green $10,000 in the form of 200 shares of common stock
                            of General Motors Corp.

7. SUBSEQUENT CONTRIBUTIONS OF LIMITED PARTNERS. Each limited partner may (but shall not be obliged to) make such additional contributions to the capital of the partnership as may from time to time be agreed upon by the general partners.

8. PROFIT SHARES OF LIMITED PARTNERS. The share of the profits which each limited partner shall receive by reason of his contribution is:

Frank Brown   10%
George Green   10%

Signed January 2, 19——.

> JOHN SMITH
> HAROLD JONES
> FRANK BROWN
> GEORGE GREEN

Signed and sworn before me, the undersigned authority, this January 2, 19——.

> HOWARD HALE
> Notary Public
> Dallas County, Texas

TABLE OF CASES

References are to Pages

A

E

F

H

M

N

O

S

TABLE OF STATUTORY
ABBREVIATIONS

U.S.C.A.Const., Art., § —— _____United States Constitution
U.S.C.A. § —— _____United States Code Annotated
Ala.Code 1940, Tit. ——, § —— _____Alabama Code 1940
A.C.L.A.1949 (Alaska) § —— _____Alaska Compiled Laws Annotated
A.R.S. (Ariz.) § —— _____Arizona Revised Statutes
Ark.Stats. § —— _____Arkansas Statutes
West's Ann.Code (Cal.) § —— _____California Codes
C.R.S. '63 (Colo.) _____Colorado Revised Statutes 1963
C.G.S.A. (Conn.) § —— _____Connecticut General Statutes Annotated
—— Del.C.Ann. § —— _____Delaware Code Annotated
F.S.A. (Fla.) § —— _____Florida Statutes Annotated
Ga.Code, § —— _____Georgia Code
R.L.H.1955 (Haw.) § —— _____Revised Laws Hawaii 1955
I.C. (Idaho) § —— _____Idaho Code
Burns' Ann.St. (Ind.) § —— _____Indiana Statutes
Ill.Rev.Stat.1967, c. ——, § —— _____Illinois Revised Statutes
I.C.A. (Iowa) § —— _____Iowa Code Annotated
K.S.A. (Kan.) —— _____Kansas Statutes Annotated
L.S.A.—C.C. (La.) art. —— _____Louisiana Statutes Annotated—Civil Code
L.S.A.—C.C.P. (La.) art. —— ____Louisiana Statutes Annotated—Code Civ. Procedure
M.G.L.A. (Mass.) c. ——, § —— _____Massachusetts General Statutes Annotated
M.C.L.A. (Mich.) § —— _____Michigan Compiled Laws Annotated
M.S.A. (Minn.) § —— _____Minnesota Statutes Annotated
Miss.Code 1942, § —— _____Mississippi Code 1942
V.A.M.S. (Mo.) § —— _____Vernon's Annotated Missouri Statutes
R.C.M.1947 (Mont.), § —— _____Montana Revised Code 1947
R.R.S.1943 (Neb.), § —— _____Nebraska Revised Statutes 1943
N.R.S. (Nev.) —— _____Nevada Revised Statutes
RSA (N.H.) —— _____New Hampshire Revised Statutes Annotated
N.J.S.A. —— _____New Jersey Statutes Annotated
1953 Comp. (N.M.) § —— _____New Mexico 1953 Compiled Laws

New York Laws (McKinney's)

McKinney's N.Y. Business Corporation Law § —— _____
McKinney's CPLR (N.Y.) —— _____McKinney's Civil Practice Law and Rules
McKinney's N.Y. Debtor and Creditor Law § —— _____
McKinney's N.Y. Domestic Relations Law § —— _____
McKinney's N.Y. General Associations Law § —— _____
McKinney's N.Y. General Business Law § —— _____
McKinney's N.Y. General Obligations Law § —— _____
McKinney's N.Y. Partnership Law § —— _____
McKinney's N.Y. Penal Law § —— _____
McKinney's N.Y. Tax Law § —— _____

G.S. (No.Car.) § —— _____North Carolina General Statutes
NDCC —— _____North Dakota Century Code
R.C. (Ohio) § —— _____Ohio Revised Code
—— Okl.St.Ann. § —— _____Oklahoma Statutes Annotated
—— P.S. (Pa.) § —— _____Pennsylvania Statutes
Gen.Laws 1956 (R.I.) § —— _____Rhode Island General Laws 1956
Code 1962 (So.Car.) § —— _____South Carolina Code 1962
T.C.A. (Tenn.) § —— _____Tennessee Code Annotated
Vernon's Ann.Civ.St. (Tex.) art. —— _____Vernon's Annotated Tex. Civil Statutes

Vernon's Ann.P.C. (Tex.) art. —— _____Vernon's Annotated Texas Penal Code
V.A.T.S. Tax.-Gen. (Tex.) art. —— _____Vernon's Annotated Tex. Statutes—
Taxation—General
U.C.A.1953 (Utah) _____Utah Code Annotated 1953
—— V.S.A. (Vt.) § —— _____Vermont Statutes Annotated
Va.Code 1950, § —— _____Virginia Code 1950
RCWA (Wash.) —— _____Revised Code of Washington Annotated
W.Va.Code, —— _____West Virginia Code
W.S.A. (Wis.) —— _____Wisconsin Statutes Annotated
W.S.1957 (Wyo.) § —— _____Wyoming Statute 1957

TABLE OF STATUTORY REFERENCES

(See also Table of Court Rules)

UNITED STATES

UNITED STATES CONSTITUTION

U.S.C.A.
Const.

Art.	Page	Note
1, § 8, cl. 4	536	48
4, § 1	351	45
4, § 2	356	71
4, § 2, cl. 1	109	41

Amend.

	Page	Note
4	233	74
5	233	75

UNITED STATES CODE ANNOTATED

I U.S.C.A.—General Provisions

U.S.C.A.

Sec.	Page	Note
1	25	70

II U.S.C.A.—Bankruptcy

(Text of Sec. 23 and Sec. 107(d), p. 594)

	Page	Note
1(2)	541	77
1(8)	550	32
1(19)	538	58
1(23)	537	51
	553	43
21(a)	539	61
21(b)	539	62
21(c)	539	64
23	25	69
	536	
23(a)	541	78
	542	83
23(b)	538	56
23(c)	472	29
	537	52
	560	78
23(g)	531	25
	533	32
	545	4
	554	47
23(h)	544	98
	551	36
	556	60

UNITED STATES CODE ANNOTATED

II U.S.C.A.—Bankruptcy

(Text of Sec. 23 and Sec. 107(d), p. 594)

	Page	Note
23(i)	472	28
	541	78
	560	81
23(j)	560	76
	560	80
23(k)	562	97
24	557	65
	558	65
24	558	67
32(c)	561	84
34	560	77
35	561	90
35(a)	559	72
35(a) (3)	559	73
35(a) (4)	562	92
41–42	540	69
72(a)	543	89
	550	32
93(h)	553	44
95(b)	538	57
96(a) (1)	540	70
96(b)	540	71
107(d)	558	65
107(d) (1)	538	59
107(d) (1) (a)	557	65
107(d) (1) (d)	557	65
107(d) (2) (a)–(c)	541	75
107(d) (2) (d)	541	74
107(d) (3)	541	75
107(d) (4)	294	11
	541	76
110(a)	559	70A
110(c)	247	42
110(e) (1)	541	75
207	551	35

15 U.S.C.A.—Commerce and Trade

	Page	Note
32	233	76
77b(1)	140	10
	180	25
77b(2)	140	10
	180	25
77b(4)	140	10
77o	128	56
78c(a) (4)	108	38
78c(a) (5)	108	38
78c(a) (9)	108	38
78o(a) (1)	108	38
78(p) (b)	287	78
78t	128	56

NORTH DAKOTA
CENTURY CODE

NDCC Sec.	This Work Page	Note
32–30–01	350	40

OHIO
REVISED CODE

R.C. Sec.	This Work Page	Note
1775.07	223	25
1783.01–1783.12	152	68
1783.05	152	73
1779.04	491	41
2307.24	332	28
2325–21	350	40
2703.08	349	35
2703.25	344	5

OKLAHOMA
STATUTES ANNOTATED

Okl.Stat.Ann. Tit.	This Work Page	Note
12, § 178	344	6
54, § 231(4)	417	4
85, § 3(4)	315	33

PENNSYLVANIA
STATUTES

P.S. Tit.	This Work Page	Note
12, § 296	345	15
12, § 297	345	15
12 Appx.	344	3
14, § 197–15	186	63
14, § 197–17	186	68
18, § 4103	25	70
20, § 320–504	515	86
20, § 320.603	341	91
54, § 21	354	63
54, §§ 28.1–28.13	106	24A
59, § 97(1) (b) (II)	465	95
59, § 151	341	91
59, § 383	152	73

RHODE ISLAND
GENERAL LAWS 1956

Law Sec.	This Work Page	Note
7–12–1	511	66

SOUTH CAROLINA
CODE 1962

Code Sec.	This Work Page	Note
8–245	51	3
	514	85

TENNESSEE
CODE ANNOTATED

T.C.A. Sec.	This Work Page	Note
48–1802	172	82
48–1804(3)	172	82
61–105(3)	185	55
61–114	335	54

TEXAS

VERNON'S ANNOTATED STATUTES
VERNON'S ANNOTATED CIVIL STATUTES

V.A.T.S. Civ.Stats. Art.	This Work Page	Note
1302–2.02	162	35
	505	28
1986	347	24
2031b, § 1	357	76
2031b, § 3	357	76
2031b, § 4	355	64
2031b, § 5	357	79
2033	337	63
	349	35
2033(b)	353	54
2223	337	63
	346	18
	350	37
5547–83(b)	438	42
5924–5927	106	24A
6132b, § 6(3)	185	56
6132b, § 7(5)	154	83
6132b, § 15	335	54
6132b, § 18(2)	365	3
6132b, § 26	256	91
6132b, § 27(1)	240	4
6132b, § 27(1)	385	31
6132b, § 27(2)	500	3
6132b, § 28(1)	247	42
6132b, § 28–A(1)	259	4
6132b, § 28–A(2)	259	5
6132b, § 28–A(3)	259	4
6132b, § 28–B	259	8
6132b, § 28–B(1) (A)	259	6
6132b, § 31(4)	417	4
6132b, § 35(1) (b)	463	86
6132b, § 35(3) (c)	463	86
6133	181	27
6134	181	27
6137	179	19
	181	27
6138A	169	67

VERNON'S ANNOTATED PENAL CODE

V.A.P.C. Sec.	This Work Page	Note
1067–1070	106	24A

UNIFORM LIMITED PARTNERSHIP ACT
(Text, p. 583)

U.L.P.A. Sec.	This Work Page	Note
17(2)	263	26
17(4)	263	26
	521	33
	521	34
18	230	62
	256	91
19	149	51
	418	8
	418	9
	519	17
19(1)	239	95
19(3)	239	1
	239	3
19(4)	239	97
19(5)	239	97
19(6)	239	99
	239	1
	239	3
20	418	7
	437	37
	518	8
	519	15
	519	16
20(2) (b)–(e)	519	19
21	256	88
	418	9
	518	9
	246	39
	247	42
	247	43
	248	47
	249	55
22(2)	249	53
22(3)	249	57
22(4)	252	71
23	521	34
	550	33
23(1)	94	44
	520	28
23(1) (a)	520	29
	550	30
23(1) (b)	521	30
23(1) (C)	521	30
23(1) (e)	521	31
23(1) (f)	521	31
23(2)	520	28
24	146	31
	146	33
24(1)	421	30
24(2) (b)	239	97
	519	18
24(2) (c)	519	18
26	149	52
	328	7
28(1)	13	21
28(2)	13	22

UNIFORM PARTNERSHIP ACT
(Text, p. 565)

U.P.A. Sec.	This Work Page	Note
1	517	96
2	28	2
	54	20
	57	
	57	36
	290	95
	435	24
	523	1
3	290	92
	323	73
	463	88
	468	8
3(1)	304	71
3(2) (a)	463	89
4	273	2
4(1)	13	21
4(2)	197	19
	200	32
	548	18
4(3)	277	24
	317	38
	314	28
4(4)	13	22
5	28	3
6	39	38
	43	53
	44	59
	58	38
	59	48
	63	74
	70	23
	103	6
	166	55
6–7	32	1
6(1)	27	78
	31	
	37	25
	38	37
	44	
	48	77
	50	
	57	34
	58	
	59	48
	59	49
	63	73
6(2)	14	
	54	20
	150	54
	153	77
	246	39
	516	94
7	154	83
	166	55
	191	89
	273	2

UNIFORM PARTNERSHIP ACT
(Text, p. 565)

U.P.A. Sec.	This Work Page	Note
7(1)	37	30
	68	5
	165	52
7(2)	57	
	60	
	60	52
	69	16
	155	3
7(3)	69	13
	82	78
	87	6
	91	28
	155	4
7(4)	66	96A
	67	4
	76	
	79	
	80	72
	156	5
7(4) (a)	80	73
	82	76
	93	41
	150	61
7(4) (b)	69	15
	87	6
	91	28
7(4) (c)	92	34
	512	71
	513	78
7(4) (d)	93	41
	96	50
	150	61
7(4) (e)	93	36
	98	62
8	27	83
	223	25
	230	58A
8(1)	204	8
8(2)	202	
	204	
	207	25
	208	38
	208	40
8(3)	181	26
	221	
	223	25
	289	90
	290	93
8(4)	221	
	223	25
9	28	90
	66	96
	273	2
	277	24
	282	59
	283	59
	334	42

UNIFORM PARTNERSHIP ACT
(Text, p. 565)

U.P.A. Sec.	This Work Page	Note
9	353	54
	462	76
9–14	28	91
9(1)	274	9
	275	
	278	27
	281	46
	303	67
	354	62
	372	41
	467	3
9(2)	291	
9(3)	275	13
	296	
	343	2
	381	96
	383	9
9(3) (a)	297	25
	540	67
9(3) (b)	297	31
	478	66
9(3) (c)	288	84
	299	37
	540	66
9(3) (d)	300	46
9(3) (e)	301	56
9(4)	303	
	304	70
10	27	83
	273	2
	289	91
	290	95
10(1)	223	28
	224	29
	262	22
	290	92
10(2)	224	33
	239	98
	290	93
10(3)	222	23
	290	94
10(4)	290	94
10(5)	290	94
11	274	11
	320	
	334	43
12	310	97
	322	
	325	78
	326	81
	334	44
	353	54
13	273	3
	307	
	319	51
	317	42
	334	45

TABLE OF COURT RULES

INDEX

References are to Pages